Business Plans Handbook

Business Plans

A COMPILATION OF BUSINESS PLANS DEVELOPED BY INDIVIDUALS THROUGHOUT NORTH AMERICA

Handbook

VOLUME

31

Kristin B. Mallegg, Project Editor

 GALE
CENGAGE Learning·

Farmington Hills, Mich • San Francisco • New York • Waterville, Maine
Meriden, Conn • Mason, Ohio • Chicago

Business Plans Handbook, Volume 31

Project Editor: Kristin B. Mallegg

Content Developer: Michele P. LaMeau

Product Design: Jennifer Wahi

Composition and Electronic Prepress: Evi Seoud

Manufacturing: Rita Wimberley

Gale, a part of Cengage Learning
27500 Drake Rd.
Farmington Hills, MI 48331-3535

ISBN-13: 978-1-56995-842-1
1084-4473

Printed in Mexico
1 2 3 4 5 6 7 18 17 16 15 14

Contents

BUSINESS PLANS

CONTENTS

Highlights

Business Plans Handbook, Volume 31 (BPH-31) is a collection of business plans compiled by entrepreneurs seeking funding for small businesses throughout North America. For those looking for examples of how to approach, structure, and compose their own business plans, *BPH-31* presents 20 sample plans, including plans for the following businesses:

- 3-D Printing Service
- Beauty Salon
- Boat Cleaning Business
- Cafe
- Children's Party Planner
- Chimney Sweep
- Comic Book Publisher
- Crowdfunding Website
- Dental Laboratory
- Exotic Car Rental Service
- Fitness Center
- Home Organization Service
- Mobile Pet Grooming Business
- Painting Company
- Printing Business
- Scrap Yard
- Senior Concierge Service
- Smartphone and Tablet Screen Repair Service
- Tuxedo Rental Service
- Videographer

FEATURES AND BENEFITS

BPH-31 offers many features not provided by other business planning references including:

- Twenty business plans, each of which represent an attempt at clarifying (for themselves and others) the reasons that the business should exist or expand and why a lender should fund the enterprise.
- Two fictional plans that are used by business counselors at a prominent small business development organization as examples for their clients. (You will find these in the Business Plan Template Appendix.)

- A directory section that includes listings for venture capital and finance companies, which specialize in funding start-up and second-stage small business ventures, and a comprehensive listing of Service Corps of Retired Executives (SCORE) offices. In addition, the Appendix also contains updated listings of all Small Business Development Centers (SBDCs); associations of interest to entrepreneurs; Small Business Administration (SBA) Regional Offices; and consultants specializing in small business planning and advice. It is strongly advised that you consult supporting organizations while planning your business, as they can provide a wealth of useful information.

- A Small Business Term Glossary to help you decipher the sometimes confusing terminology used by lenders and others in the financial and small business communities.

- A cumulative index, outlining each plan profiled in the complete *Business Plans Handbook* series.

- A Business Plan Template which serves as a model to help you construct your own business plan. This generic outline lists all the essential elements of a complete business plan and their components, including the Summary, Business History and Industry Outlook, Market Examination, Competition, Marketing, Administration and Management, Financial Information, and other key sections. Use this guide as a starting point for compiling your plan.

- Extensive financial documentation required to solicit funding from small business lenders. You will find examples of Cash Flows, Balance Sheets, Income Projections, and other financial information included with the textual portions of the plan.

Introduction

Perhaps the most important aspect of business planning is simply doing it. More and more business owners are beginning to compile business plans even if they don't need a bank loan. Others discover the value of planning when they must provide a business plan for the bank. The sheer act of putting thoughts on paper seems to clarify priorities and provide focus. Sometimes business owners completely change strategies when compiling their plan, deciding on a different product mix or advertising scheme after finding that their assumptions were incorrect. This kind of healthy thinking and re-thinking via business planning is becoming the norm. The editors of *Business Plans Handbook, Volume 31* (*BPH-31*) sincerely hope that this latest addition to the series is a helpful tool in the successful completion of your business plan, no matter what the reason for creating it.

This thirty-first volume, like each volume in the series, offers business plans created by real people. *BPH-31* provides 20 business plans. The business and personal names and addresses and general locations have been changed to protect the privacy of the plan authors.

NEW BUSINESS OPPORTUNITIES

As in other volumes in the series, *BPH-31* finds entrepreneurs engaged in a wide variety of creative endeavors. Examples include a Home Organization Service, a Dental Laboratory, and a 3-D Printing Service. In addition, several other plans are provided, including a Senior Concierge Service, a Comic Book Publisher, and a Scrap Yard, among others.

Comprehensive financial documentation has become increasingly important as today's entrepreneurs compete for the finite resources of business lenders. Our plans illustrate the financial data generally required of loan applicants, including Income Statements, Financial Projections, Cash Flows, and Balance Sheets.

ENHANCED APPENDIXES

In an effort to provide the most relevant and valuable information for our readers, we have updated the coverage of small business resources. For instance, you will find a directory section, which includes listings of all of the Service Corps of Retired Executives (SCORE) offices; an informative glossary, which includes small business terms; and a cumulative index, outlining each plan profiled in the complete *Business Plans Handbook* series. In addition we have updated the list of Small Business Development Centers (SBDCs); Small Business Administration Regional Offices; venture capital and finance companies, which specialize in funding start-up and second-stage small business enterprises; associations of interest to entrepreneurs; and consultants, specializing in small business advice and planning. For your reference, we have also reprinted the business plan template, which provides a comprehensive overview of the essential components of a business plan and two fictional plans used by small business counselors.

SERIES INFORMATION

If you already have the first thirty volumes of *BPH*, with this thirty-first volume, you will now have a collection of over 600 business plans (not including the updated plans); contact information for hundreds of organizations and agencies offering business expertise; a helpful business plan template; more than 1,500 citations to valuable small business development material; and a comprehensive glossary of terms to help the business planner navigate the sometimes confusing language of entrepreneurship.

ACKNOWLEDGEMENTS

The Editors wish to sincerely thank the contributors to *BPH-31*, including:

- BizPlanDB.com
- Fran Fletcher
- Paul Greenland
- Zuzu Enterprises

COMMENTS WELCOME

Your comments on *Business Plans Handbook* are appreciated. Please direct all correspondence, suggestions for future volumes of *BPH*, and other recommendations to the following:

Managing Editor, Business Product
Business Plans Handbook
Gale, a part of Cengage Learning
27500 Drake Rd.
Farmington Hills, MI 48331-3535
Phone: (248)699-4253
Fax: (248)699-8052
Toll-Free: 800-347-GALE
E-mail: BusinessProducts@gale.com

3-D Printing Service

Dimensional Printing, Inc.

76667 W. 101 st St.
New York, NY 10051

BizPlanDB.com

The purpose of this business plan is to raise $100,000 for the development of a 3-D printing service while showcasing the expected financials and operations over the next three years. Dimensional Printing, Inc. ("the Company") is a New York-based corporation that will provide specialized model development and 3-D item printing (from sent files) to customers in its targeted market. The Company was founded by Peter Chu.

1.0 EXECUTIVE SUMMARY

The purpose of this business plan is to raise $100,000 for the development of a 3-D printing service while showcasing the expected financials and operations over the next three years. Dimensional Printing, Inc. ("the Company") is a New York-based corporation that will provide specialized model development and 3-D item printing (from sent files) to customers in its targeted market. The Company was founded by Peter Chu.

1.1 The Services

Dimensional Printing will provide services related to large scale component plastic mold printing, single item 3-D printing, and related services. The business intends to acquire state of the art of 3-D printers that will allow for most large scale plastic printing needs.

The business will earn ancillary fees for jobs that are extremely large or extremely complex in nature and require additional work.

The third section of the business plan will further describe the services offered by Dimensional Printing.

1.2 Financing

Mr. Chu is seeking to raise $100,000 from a bank loan. The interest rate and loan agreement are to be further discussed during negotiation. This business plan assumes that the business will receive a 10 year loan with a 9% fixed interest rate. The financing will be used for the following:

- Development of the Company's service location.
- Financing for the first six months of operation.
- Capital to purchase state of the art 3-D printers.

Mr. Chu will contribute $10,000 to the venture.

1.3 Mission Statement

Dimensional Printing's mission is to become the recognized leader in its targeted market for specialized plastic model printing services.

1

1.4 Management Team

The Company was founded by Peter Chu. Mr. Chu has more than 10 years of experience in the commercial design industry. Through his expertise, he will be able to bring the operations of the business to profitability within its first year of operations.

1.5 Sales Forecasts

Mr. Chu expects a strong rate of growth at the start of operations. Below are the expected financials over the next three years.

Proforma profit and loss (yearly)

Year	1	2	3
Sales	$567,378	$612,768	$661,790
Operating costs	$265,104	$275,932	$287,300
EBITDA	$174,721	$199,079	$225,711
Taxes, interest, and depreciation	$ 80,667	$ 86,227	$ 95,936
Net profit	$ 94,054	$112,852	$129,775

Sales, operating costs, and profit forecast

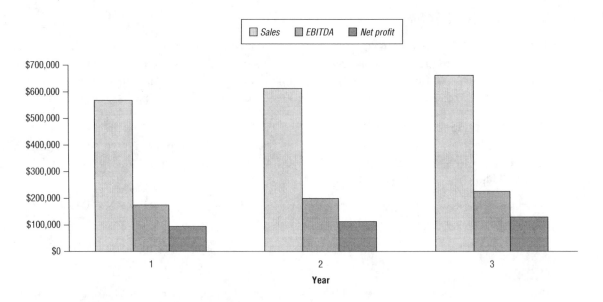

1.6 Expansion Plan

The Founder expects that the business will aggressively expand during the first three years of operation. Mr. Chu intends to implement marketing campaigns that will effectively target individuals and small businesses within the target market.

2.0 COMPANY AND FINANCING SUMMARY

2.1 Registered Name and Corporate Structure

The Company is registered as a corporation in the State of New York.

2.2 Required Funds

At this time, Dimensional Printing requires $100,000 of debt funds. Below is a breakdown of how these funds will be used:

Projected startup costs

Initial lease payments and deposits	$ 10,000
Working capital	$ 15,000
FF&E	$ 23,000
Leasehold improvements	$ 5,000
Security deposits	$ 5,000
Insurance	$ 2,500
3-D printing equipment	$ 37,000
Marketing budget	$ 7,500
Miscellaneous and unforeseen costs	$ 5,000
Total startup costs	**$110,000**

Use of funds

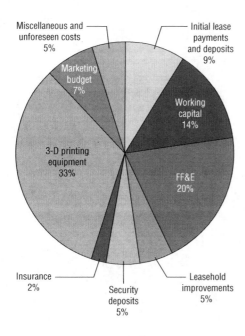

2.3 Investor Equity

Mr. Chu is not seeking an investment from a third party at this time.

2.4 Management Equity

Peter Chu owns 100% of the Dimensional Printing, Inc.

2.5 Exit Strategy

If the business is very successful, Mr. Chu may seek to sell the business to a third party for a significant earnings multiple. Most likely, the Company will hire a qualified business broker to sell the business on behalf of Dimensional Printing. Based on historical numbers, the business could fetch a sales premium of up to 4 times earnings.

3.0 PRODUCTS AND SERVICES

Below is a description of the services offered by Dimensional Printing.

3.1 Large 3-D Printing Services

The primary function of the business is to produce three dimensional plastic models produced from CAD files (primarily STL files) on behalf of individuals, small businesses, and large corporations. Through its state of art 3-D printers, the business will generally be able to produce 3-D models that are three cubic feet in size.

The company will also be able to provide mass scale 3-D printing for orders that exceed the Company's in-house printing capabilities. Mr. Chu is currently sourcing a number of other 3-D printing companies that will provide these services on behalf of the Company.

3.2 Small 3-D Printing Services

In addition to the Company's large scale printing capabilities, the business will also able to provide small single scale productions of 3-D models. This is an important part of the business because it provides a predictable stream of revenue from its high transaction volume. Some individuals that have produced a unique design want to have the item produced on a single item basis. As such, the business will be able to generate substantial business from the general public that design items on a hobby basis.

4.0 STRATEGIC AND MARKET ANALYSIS

4.1 Economic Outlook

This section of the analysis will detail the economic climate, the specialized printing industry, the customer profile, and the competition that the business will face as it progresses through its business operations.

Currently, the economic market condition in the United States is moderate. Unemployment rates have declined while asset prices have increased substantially. As such, it is an excellent time to launch Dimensional Printing. In times of economic difficulty, the business will be able to remain profitable and cash flow positive at all times due to its low operating costs.

4.2 Industry Analysis

In the United States there are approximately 800 businesses that provide specialized 3-D printing to both the individual and business general public. Each year, these businesses aggregate generate more than $900 million dollars of revenue and provide jobs for more than 5,000 people. Aggregate payrolls have reached $100 million dollars in each of the last four years.

The industry has undergone significant changes in the last five years as specialized printing technology has allowed smaller businesses to acquire 3-D printing equipment. Newer 3-D printer technology coupled with the increase in the number of technology manufacturers has significantly driven down the price of this type of service. However, the price of large scale 3-D printing equipment has remained high as small businesses and home based businesses do not have a regular need for this type of service.

4.3 Customer Profile

Common traits among clients will include:

- Is a small or medium sized that is in need of large scale 3-D printing and modeling services.

- Has a 3-D printing budget of $1,000 to $25,000.

- Is located within 200 miles of the Company's location.

- May place order via the Internet by sending STL (3-D printing) files with the intent to receive the items via mail.

4.4 Competition

The 3-D printing industry is nascent. Within the United States, there are only approximately 800 businesses that provide 3-D printing for businesses and the general public. The number of businesses within this industry is expected to increase substantially over the next five years as the technology improves. At the onset of operations, it will be imperative that the business provide discounts in order to generate large scale purchase orders from companies that have 3-D printing needs. Additionally, the business must have an online upload capacity so that 3-D products can be printed on a "just-in-time" production basis.

5.0 MARKETING PLAN

Dimensional Printing intends to maintain an extensive marketing campaign that will ensure maximum visibility for the business in its targeted market. Below is an overview of the marketing strategies and objectives of the Company.

5.1 Marketing Objectives

- Establish relationships with commercial printers that do not offer 3-D printing services within the targeted market.

- Develop relationships with hobbyists that want to have custom pieces 3-D printed on a regular basis.

- Develop relationships with promotional products companies that want to use the Company for the production of large orders of promotional products.

5.2 Marketing Strategies

Mr. Chu intends on using a number of marketing strategies that will allow Dimensional Printing to easily target individuals and businesses within the target market. These strategies include traditional print advertisements and ads placed on search engines on the internet.

Dimensional Printing will also use an internet based strategy. This is very important as many people seeking local services, such as outsourced 3-D printers, now use the internet to conduct their preliminary searches. Mr. Chu will register Dimensional Printing with online portals so that potential customers can easily reach the business. The Company will also develop its own online website. This website will allow individuals to upload individual 3-D printing files that the Company will use to produce items on behalf of individuals and corporate customers.

The Company will maintain a sizable amount of print and traditional advertising methods (primarily among trade journals) in order to generate revenues.

5.3 Pricing

The Company anticipates that each 3-D printed item will generate $5 of revenue for the business. The average purchase order for the business will be $750.

6.0 ORGANIZATIONAL PLAN AND PERSONNEL SUMMARY

6.1 Corporate Organization

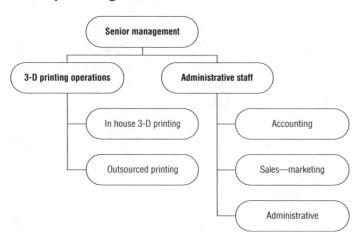

6.2 Organizational Budget

Personnel plan—yearly

Year	1	2	3
Owners	$ 30,000	$ 30,900	$ 31,827
Manager	$ 29,500	$ 30,385	$ 31,297
Employees	$ 57,000	$ 58,710	$ 60,471
Bookkeeper (P/T)	$ 12,500	$ 12,875	$ 13,261
Administrative	$ 25,000	$ 25,750	$ 26,523
Total	**$154,000**	**$158,620**	**$163,379**

Numbers of personnel

Owners	1	1	1
Manager	1	1	1
Employees	3	3	3
Bookkeeper (P/T)	1	1	1
Administrative	1	1	1
Totals	**7**	**7**	**7**

Personnel expense breakdown

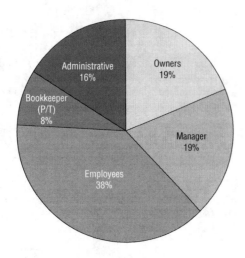

7.0 FINANCIAL PLAN

7.1 Underlying Assumptions

The Company has based its proforma financial statements on the following:

- Dimensional Printing will have an annual revenue growth rate of 8% per year.

- The Owner will acquire $100,000 of debt funds to develop the business.

- The loan will have a 10 year term with a 10% interest rate.

7.2 Sensitivity Analysis

In the event of an economic downturn, the business may have a decline in its revenues. However, small business and individuals will need 3-D printing services in any economic climate, and the high margins generated from print brokering services will ensure that the Company can remain profitable and cash flow positive at all times.

7.3 Source of Funds

Financing

Equity contributions

Management investment	$ 10,000.00
Total equity financing	**$ 10,000.00**
Banks and lenders	
Banks and lenders	$ 100,000.00
Total debt financing	**$100,000.00**
Total financing	**$110,000.00**

7.4 General Assumptions

General assumptions

Year	1	2	3
Short term interest rate	9.5%	9.5%	9.5%
Long term interest rate	10.0%	10.0%	10.0%
Federal tax rate	33.0%	33.0%	33.0%
State tax rate	5.0%	5.0%	5.0%
Personnel taxes	15.0%	15.0%	15.0%

7.5 Profit and Loss Statements

Proforma profit and loss (yearly)

Year	1	2	3
Sales	**$567,378**	**$612,768**	**$661,790**
Cost of goods sold	$127,553	$137,758	$148,778
Gross margin	77.52%	77.52%	77.52%
Operating income	**$439,825**	**$475,011**	**$513,011**
Expenses			
Payroll	$154,000	$158,620	$163,379
General and administrative	$ 10,000	$ 10,400	$ 10,816
Marketing expenses	$ 22,695	$ 24,511	$ 26,472
Professional fees and licensure	$ 3,500	$ 3,605	$ 3,713
Insurance costs	$ 12,000	$ 12,600	$ 13,230
Travel and vehicle costs	$ 8,000	$ 8,800	$ 9,680
Rent and utilities	$ 25,000	$ 26,250	$ 27,563
Miscellaneous costs	$ 6,809	$ 7,353	$ 7,941
Payroll taxes	$ 23,100	$ 23,793	$ 24,507
Total operating costs	**$265,104**	**$275,932**	**$287,300**
EBITDA	**$174,721**	**$199,079**	**$225,711**
Federal income tax	$ 57,658	$ 63,013	$ 72,020
State income tax	$ 8,736	$ 9,547	$ 10,912
Interest expense	$ 8,738	$ 8,131	$ 7,468
Depreciation expenses	$ 5,536	$ 5,536	$ 5,536
Net profit	**$ 94,054**	**$112,852**	**$129,775**
Profit margin	**16.58%**	**18.42%**	**19.61%**

Sales, operating costs, and profit forecast

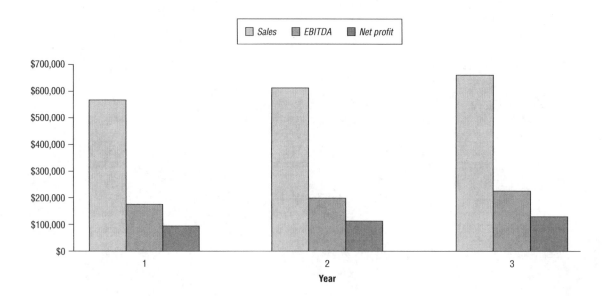

7.6 Cash Flow Analysis

Proforma cash flow analysis—yearly

Year	1	2	3
Cash from operations	$ 99,589	$118,387	$135,311
Cash from receivables	$ 0	$ 0	$ 0
Operating cash inflow	**$ 99,589**	**$118,387**	**$135,311**
Other cash inflows			
Equity investment	$ 10,000	$ 0	$ 0
Increased borrowings	$100,000	$ 0	$ 0
Sales of business assets	$ 0	$ 0	$ 0
A/P increases	$ 37,902	$ 43,587	$ 50,125
Total other cash inflows	**$147,902**	**$ 43,587**	**$ 50,125**
Total cash inflow	**$247,491**	**$161,975**	**$185,436**
Cash outflows			
Repayment of principal	$ 6,463	$ 7,070	$ 7,733
A/P decreases	$ 24,897	$ 29,876	$ 35,852
A/R increases	$ 0	$ 0	$ 0
Asset purchases	$ 77,500	$ 29,597	$ 33,828
Dividends	$ 69,712	$ 82,871	$ 94,718
Total cash outflows	**$178,573**	**$149,414**	**$172,130**
Net cash flow	**$ 68,918**	**$ 12,561**	**$ 13,306**
Cash balance	**$ 68,918**	**$ 81,479**	**$ 94,785**

Proforma cash flow (yearly)

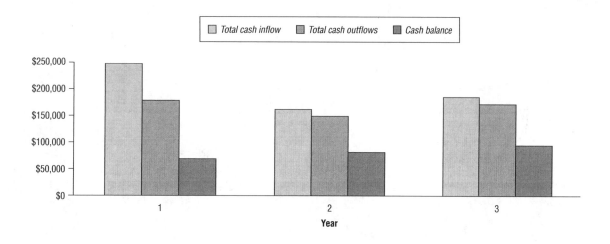

7.7 Balance Sheet

Proforma balance sheet—yearly

Year	1	2	3
Assets			
Cash	$ 68,918	$ 81,479	$ 94,785
Amortized development/expansion costs	$ 17,500	$ 20,460	$ 23,842
3D printing equipment	$ 37,000	$ 51,798	$ 68,712
FF&E	$ 23,000	$ 34,839	$ 48,370
Accumulated depreciation	($ 5,536)	($ 11,071)	($ 16,607)
Total assets	**$140,883**	**$177,504**	**$219,103**
Liabilities and equity			
Accounts payable	$ 13,005	$ 26,716	$ 40,990
Long term liabilities	$ 93,537	$ 86,467	$ 79,397
Other liabilities	$ 0	$ 0	$ 0
Total liabilities	**$106,542**	**$113,183**	**$120,387**
Net worth	**$ 34,341**	**$ 64,322**	**$ 98,716**
Total liabilities and equity	**$140,883**	**$177,504**	**$219,103**

Proforma balance sheet

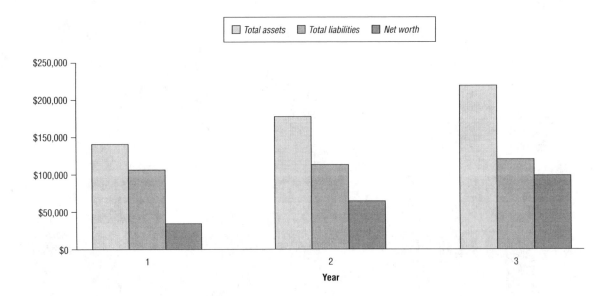

7.8 Breakeven Analysis

Monthly break even analysis

Year	1	2	3
Monthly revenue	$ 28,499	$ 29,663	$ 30,885
Yearly revenue	$341,986	$355,955	$370,620

Break even analysis

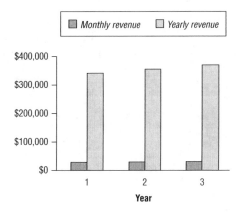

7.9 Business Ratios

Business ratios—yearly

Year	1	2	3
Sales			
Sales growth	0.0%	8.0%	8.0%
Gross margin	77.5%	77.5%	77.5%
Financials			
Profit margin	16.58%	18.42%	19.61%
Assets to liabilities	1.32	1.57	1.82
Equity to liabilities	0.32	0.57	0.82
Assets to equity	4.10	2.76	2.22
Liquidity			
Acid test	0.65	0.72	0.79
Cash to assets	0.49	0.46	0.43

7.10 Three Year Profit and Loss Statement

Profit and loss statement (first year)

Months	1	2	3	4	5	6	7
Sales	**$46,550**	**$46,683**	**$46,816**	**$46,949**	**$47,082**	**$47,215**	**$47,348**
Cost of goods sold	$10,465	$10,495	$10,525	$10,555	$10,585	$10,615	$10,644
Gross margin	77.5%	77.5%	77.5%	77.5%	77.5%	77.5%	77.5%
Operating income	**$36,085**	**$36,188**	**$36,291**	**$36,394**	**$36,497**	**$36,601**	**$36,704**
Expenses							
Payroll	$12,833	$12,833	$12,833	$12,833	$12,833	$12,833	$12,833
General and administrative	$ 833	$ 833	$ 833	$ 833	$ 833	$ 833	$ 833
Marketing expenses	$ 1,891	$ 1,891	$ 1,891	$ 1,891	$ 1,891	$ 1,891	$ 1,891
Professional fees and licensure	$ 292	$ 292	$ 292	$ 292	$ 292	$ 292	$ 292
Insurance costs	$ 1,000	$ 1,000	$ 1,000	$ 1,000	$ 1,000	$ 1,000	$ 1,000
Travel and vehicle costs	$ 667	$ 667	$ 667	$ 667	$ 667	$ 667	$ 667
Rent and utilities	$ 2,083	$ 2,083	$ 2,083	$ 2,083	$ 2,083	$ 2,083	$ 2,083
Miscellaneous costs	$ 567	$ 567	$ 567	$ 567	$ 567	$ 567	$ 567
Payroll taxes	$ 1,925	$ 1,925	$ 1,925	$ 1,925	$ 1,925	$ 1,925	$ 1,925
Total operating costs	**$22,092**	**$22,092**	**$22,092**	**$22,092**	**$22,092**	**$22,092**	**$22,092**
EBITDA	**$13,993**	**$14,096**	**$14,199**	**$14,302**	**$14,405**	**$14,509**	**$14,612**
Federal income tax	$ 4,730	$ 4,744	$ 4,758	$ 4,771	$ 4,785	$ 4,798	$ 4,812
State income tax	$ 717	$ 719	$ 721	$ 723	$ 725	$ 727	$ 729
Interest expense	$ 750	$ 746	$ 742	$ 738	$ 734	$ 730	$ 726
Depreciation expense	$ 461	$ 461	$ 461	$ 461	$ 461	$ 461	$ 461
Net profit	**$ 7,334**	**$ 7,426**	**$ 7,517**	**$ 7,609**	**$ 7,700**	**$ 7,792**	**$ 7,883**

Profit and loss statement (first year cont.)

Month	8	9	10	11	12	1
Sales	**$47,481**	**$47,614**	**$47,747**	**$47,880**	**$48,013**	**$567,378**
Cost of goods sold	$10,674	$10,704	$10,734	$10,764	$10,794	$127,553
Gross margin	77.5%	77.5%	77.5%	77.5%	77.5%	77.5%
Operating income	**$36,807**	**$36,910**	**$37,013**	**$37,116**	**$37,219**	**$439,825**
Expenses						
Payroll	$12,833	$12,833	$12,833	$12,833	$12,833	$154,000
General and administrative	$ 833	$ 833	$ 833	$ 833	$ 833	$ 10,000
Marketing expenses	$ 1,891	$ 1,891	$ 1,891	$ 1,891	$ 1,891	$ 22,695
Professional fees and licensure	$ 292	$ 292	$ 292	$ 292	$ 292	$ 3,500
Insurance costs	$ 1,000	$ 1,000	$ 1,000	$ 1,000	$ 1,000	$ 12,000
Travel and vehicle costs	$ 667	$ 667	$ 667	$ 667	$ 667	$ 8,000
Rent and utilities	$ 2,083	$ 2,083	$ 2,083	$ 2,083	$ 2,083	$ 25,000
Miscellaneous costs	$ 567	$ 567	$ 567	$ 567	$ 567	$ 6,809
Payroll taxes	$ 1,925	$ 1,925	$ 1,925	$ 1,925	$ 1,925	$ 23,100
Total operating costs	**$22,092**	**$22,092**	**$22,092**	**$22,092**	**$22,092**	**$265,104**
EBITDA	**$14,715**	**$14,818**	**$14,921**	**$15,024**	**$15,127**	**$174,721**
Federal income tax	$ 4,825	$ 4,839	$ 4,852	$ 4,866	$ 4,879	$ 57,658
State income tax	$ 731	$ 733	$ 735	$ 737	$ 739	$ 8,736
Interest expense	$ 722	$ 718	$ 714	$ 710	$ 706	$ 8,738
Depreciation expense	$ 461	$ 461	$ 461	$ 461	$ 461	$ 5,536
Net profit	**$ 7,975**	**$ 8,067**	**$ 8,158**	**$ 8,250**	**$ 8,342**	**$ 94,054**

Profit and loss statement (second year)

Quarter	Q1	2 Q2	Q3	Q4	2
Sales	$122,554	$153,192	$165,447	$171,575	$612,768
Cost of goods sold	$ 27,552	$ 34,439	$ 37,195	$ 38,572	$137,758
Gross margin	77.5%	77.5%	77.5%	77.5%	77.5%
Operating income	$ 95,002	$118,753	$128,253	$133,003	$475,011
Expenses					
Payroll	$ 31,724	$ 39,655	$ 42,827	$ 44,414	$158,620
General and administrative	$ 2,080	$ 2,600	$ 2,808	$ 2,912	$ 10,400
Marketing expenses	$ 4,902	$ 6,128	$ 6,618	$ 6,863	$ 24,511
Professional fees and licensure	$ 721	$ 901	$ 973	$ 1,009	$ 3,605
Insurance costs	$ 2,520	$ 3,150	$ 3,402	$ 3,528	$ 12,600
Travel and vehicle costs	$ 1,760	$ 2,200	$ 2,376	$ 2,464	$ 8,800
Rent and utilities	$ 5,250	$ 6,563	$ 7,088	$ 7,350	$ 26,250
Miscellaneous costs	$ 1,471	$ 1,838	$ 1,985	$ 2,059	$ 7,353
Payroll taxes	$ 4,759	$ 5,948	$ 6,424	$ 6,662	$ 23,793
Total operating costs	$ 55,186	$ 68,983	$ 74,502	$ 77,261	$275,932
EBITDA	$ 39,816	$ 49,770	$ 53,751	$ 55,742	$199,079
Federal income tax	$ 12,603	$ 15,753	$ 17,013	$ 17,644	$ 63,013
State income tax	$ 1,909	$ 2,387	$ 2,578	$ 2,673	$ 9,547
Interest expense	$ 2,092	$ 2,053	$ 2,013	$ 1,973	$ 8,131
Depreciation expense	$ 1,384	$ 1,384	$ 1,384	$ 1,384	$ 5,536
Net profit	$ 21,828	$ 28,193	$ 30,763	$ 32,068	$112,852

Profit and loss statement (third year)

Quarter	Q1	3 Q2	Q3	Q4	3
Sales	$132,358	$165,447	$178,683	$185,301	$661,790
Cost of goods sold	$ 29,756	$ 37,195	$ 40,170	$ 41,658	$148,778
Gross margin	77.5%	77.5%	77.5%	77.5%	77.5%
Operating income	$102,602	$128,253	$138,513	$143,643	$513,011
Expenses					
Payroll	$ 32,676	$ 40,845	$ 44,112	$ 45,746	$163,379
General and administrative	$ 2,163	$ 2,704	$ 2,920	$ 3,028	$ 10,816
Marketing expenses	$ 5,294	$ 6,618	$ 7,147	$ 7,412	$ 26,472
Professional fees and licensure	$ 743	$ 928	$ 1,003	$ 1,040	$ 3,713
Insurance costs	$ 2,646	$ 3,308	$ 3,572	$ 3,704	$ 13,230
Travel and vehicle costs	$ 1,936	$ 2,420	$ 2,614	$ 2,710	$ 9,680
Rent and utilities	$ 5,513	$ 6,891	$ 7,442	$ 7,718	$ 27,563
Miscellaneous costs	$ 1,588	$ 1,985	$ 2,144	$ 2,224	$ 7,941
Payroll taxes	$ 4,901	$ 6,127	$ 6,617	$ 6,862	$ 24,507
Total operating costs	$ 57,460	$ 71,825	$ 77,571	$ 80,444	$287,300
EBITDA	$ 45,142	$ 56,428	$ 60,942	$ 63,199	$225,711
Federal income tax	$ 14,404	$ 18,005	$ 19,445	$ 20,166	$ 72,020
State income tax	$ 2,182	$ 2,728	$ 2,946	$ 3,055	$ 10,912
Interest expense	$ 1,932	$ 1,889	$ 1,846	$ 1,802	$ 7,468
Depreciation expense	$ 1,384	$ 1,384	$ 1,384	$ 1,384	$ 5,536
Net profit	$ 25,240	$ 32,422	$ 35,321	$ 36,793	$129,775

7.11 Three Year Cash Flow Analysis

Cash flow analysis (first year)

Month	1	2	3	4	5	6	7
Cash from operations	$ 7,796	$ 7,887	$ 7,979	$ 8,070	$ 8,162	$ 8,253	$ 8,345
Cash from receivables	$ 0	$ 0	$ 0	$ 0	$ 0	$ 0	$ 0
Operating cash inflow	**$ 7,796**	**$ 7,887**	**$ 7,979**	**$ 8,070**	**$ 8,162**	**$ 8,253**	**$ 8,345**
Other cash inflows							
Equity investment	$ 10,000	$ 0	$ 0	$ 0	$ 0	$ 0	$ 0
Increased borrowings	$100,000	$ 0	$ 0	$ 0	$ 0	$ 0	$ 0
Sales of business assets	$ 0	$ 0	$ 0	$ 0	$ 0	$ 0	$ 0
A/P increases	$ 3,159	$ 3,159	$ 3,159	$ 3,159	$ 3,159	$ 3,159	$ 3,159
Total other cash inflows	**$113,159**	**$ 3,159**	**$ 3,159**	**$ 3,159**	**$ 3,159**	**$ 3,159**	**$ 3,159**
Total cash inflow	**$120,954**	**$11,046**	**$11,137**	**$11,229**	**$11,320**	**$11,412**	**$11,503**
Cash outflows							
Repayment of principal	$ 517	$ 521	$ 525	$ 528	$ 532	$ 536	$ 540
A/P decreases	$ 2,075	$ 2,075	$ 2,075	$ 2,075	$ 2,075	$ 2,075	$ 2,075
A/R increases	$ 0	$ 0	$ 0	$ 0	$ 0	$ 0	$ 0
Asset purchases	$ 77,500	$ 0	$ 0	$ 0	$ 0	$ 0	$ 0
Dividends	$ 0	$ 0	$ 0	$ 0	$ 0	$ 0	$ 0
Total cash outflows	**$ 80,092**	**$ 2,595**	**$ 2,599**	**$ 2,603**	**$ 2,607**	**$ 2,611**	**$ 2,615**
Net cash flow	**$ 40,863**	**$ 8,450**	**$ 8,538**	**$ 8,625**	**$ 8,713**	**$ 8,800**	**$ 8,888**
Cash balance	**$ 40,863**	**$49,313**	**$57,851**	**$66,476**	**$75,189**	**$83,990**	**$92,878**

Cash flow analysis (first year cont.)

Month	8	9	10	11	12	1
Cash from operations	$ 8,436	$ 8,528	$ 8,620	$ 8,711	$ 8,802	$ 99,589
Cash from receivables	$ 0	$ 0	$ 0	$ 0	$ 0	$ 0
Operating cash inflow	**$ 8,436**	**$ 8,528**	**$ 8,620**	**$ 8,711**	**$ 8,802**	**$ 99,589**
Other cash inflows						
Equity investment	$ 0	$ 0	$ 0	$ 0	$ 0	$ 10,000
Increased borrowings	$ 0	$ 0	$ 0	$ 0	$ 0	$100,000
Sales of business assets	$ 0	$ 0	$ 0	$ 0	$ 0	$ 0
A/P increases	$ 3,159	$ 3,159	$ 3,159	$ 3,159	$ 3,159	$ 37,902
Total other cash inflows	**$ 3,159**	**$ 3,159**	**$ 3,159**	**$ 3,159**	**$ 3,159**	**$147,902**
Total cash inflow	**$ 11,595**	**$ 11,686**	**$ 11,778**	**$ 11,870**	**$11,960**	**$247,491**
Cash outflows						
Repayment of principal	$ 545	$ 549	$ 553	$ 557	$ 561	$ 6,463
A/P decreases	$ 2,075	$ 2,075	$ 2,075	$ 2,075	$ 2,075	$ 24,897
A/R increases	$ 0	$ 0	$ 0	$ 0	$ 0	$ 0
Asset purchases	$ 0	$ 0	$ 0	$ 0	$ 0	$ 77,500
Dividends	$ 0	$ 0	$ 0	$ 0	$69,712	$ 69,712
Total cash outflows	**$ 2,619**	**$ 2,623**	**$ 2,627**	**$ 2,632**	**$72,348**	**$178,573**
Net cash flow	**$ 8,976**	**$ 9,063**	**$ 9,151**	**$ 9,238**	**−$60,387**	**$ 68,918**
Cash balance	**$101,853**	**$110,916**	**$120,067**	**$129,305**	**$68,918**	**$ 68,918**

Cash flow analysis (second year)

Quarter	Q1	2 Q2	Q3	Q4	2
Cash from operations	$23,677	$29,597	$31,965	$33,148	$118,387
Cash from receivables	$ 0	$ 0	$ 0	$ 0	$ 0
Operating cash inflow	**$23,677**	**$29,597**	**$31,965**	**$33,148**	**$118,387**
Other cash inflows					
Equity investment	$ 0	$ 0	$ 0	$ 0	$ 0
Increased borrowings	$ 0	$ 0	$ 0	$ 0	$ 0
Sales of business assets	$ 0	$ 0	$ 0	$ 0	$ 0
A/P increases	$ 8,717	$10,897	$11,769	$12,204	$ 43,587
Total other cash inflows	**$ 8,717**	**$10,897**	**$11,769**	**$12,204**	**$ 43,587**
Total cash inflow	**$32,395**	**$40,494**	**$43,733**	**$45,353**	**$161,975**
Cash outflows					
Repayment of principal	$ 1,708	$ 1,747	$ 1,787	$ 1,827	$ 7,070
A/P decreases	$ 5,975	$ 7,469	$ 8,067	$ 8,365	$ 29,876
A/R increases	$ 0	$ 0	$ 0	$ 0	$ 0
Asset purchases	$ 5,919	$ 7,399	$ 7,991	$ 8,287	$ 29,597
Dividends	$16,574	$20,718	$22,375	$23,204	$ 82,871
Total cash outflows	**$30,177**	**$37,333**	**$40,220**	**$41,684**	**$149,414**
Net cash flow	**$ 2,218**	**$ 3,160**	**$ 3,513**	**$ 3,669**	**$ 12,561**
Cash balance	**$71,136**	**$74,296**	**$77,810**	**$81,479**	**$ 81,479**

Cash flow analysis (third year)

Quarter	Q1	3 Q2	Q3	Q4	3
Cash from operations	$27,062	$33,828	$36,534	$37,887	$135,311
Cash from receivables	$ 0	$ 0	$ 0	$ 0	$ 0
Operating cash inflow	**$27,062**	**$33,828**	**$36,534**	**$37,887**	**$135,311**
Other cash inflows					
Equity investment	$ 0	$ 0	$ 0	$ 0	$ 0
Increased borrowings	$ 0	$ 0	$ 0	$ 0	$ 0
Sales of business assets	$ 0	$ 0	$ 0	$ 0	$ 0
A/P increases	$10,025	$12,531	$13,534	$14,035	$ 50,125
Total other cash inflows	**$10,025**	**$12,531**	**$13,534**	**$14,035**	**$ 50,125**
Total cash inflow	**$37,087**	**$46,359**	**$50,068**	**$51,922**	**$185,436**
Cash outflows					
Repayment of principal	$ 1,869	$ 1,911	$ 1,954	$ 1,999	$ 7,733
A/P decreases	$ 7,170	$ 8,963	$ 9,680	$10,038	$ 35,852
A/R increases	$ 0	$ 0	$ 0	$ 0	$ 0
Asset purchases	$ 6,766	$ 8,457	$ 9,133	$ 9,472	$ 33,828
Dividends	$18,944	$23,679	$25,574	$26,521	$ 94,718
Total cash outflows	**$34,748**	**$43,010**	**$46,342**	**$48,030**	**$172,130**
Net cash flow	**$ 2,339**	**$ 3,349**	**$ 3,726**	**$ 3,892**	**$ 13,306**
Cash balance	**$83,818**	**$87,167**	**$90,893**	**$94,785**	**$ 94,785**

Beauty Salon

Salon Flora

34 Destin St.
Naples, Florida 34102

Staff at BusinessandMarketingPlans.com

This business plan was created for two highly trained, veteran hair stylists with an established client base and lots of business savvy. They sought capital to open an upscale salon to further serve the styling needs of regional customers. This plan raised $77,000 for the company's owners.

This business plan appeared in a previous volume of Business Plans Handbook. *It has been updated for this edition.*

EXECUTIVE SUMMARY

Salon Flora is a beauty salon dedicated to providing customer satisfaction with excellent service, quality products, and an enjoyable atmosphere at an excellent price/value relationship.

Nature is not something you can hold onto, it is something we are borrowing from our children; we must do our part to keep the balance in life. We strive to keep balance in our clients' life by supplying services and products that enhance physical appearance and mental relaxation. We will maintain a friendly, fair, and creative work environment, which respects diversity, ideas, and hard work.

To achieve our objectives, Flora is seeking $77,000 in additional loan financing. This loan will be paid back from the cash flow of the business, will be collateralized by the assets of the company, and backed by the character, experience, and personal guarantees of the owners.

Financial highlights for the first three years of operations

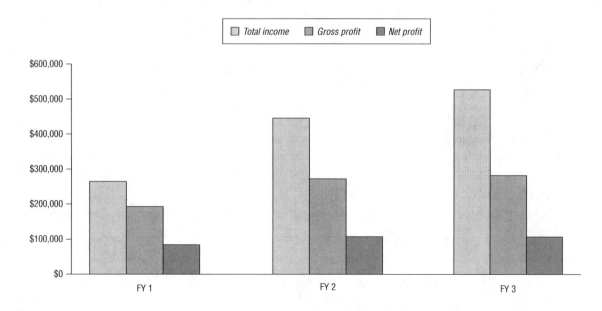

17

Keys to Success

The keys to success in our business are:

- **Location, Location, Location:** providing an easily accessible location for customers with plenty of off-street parking.

- **Environment:** providing an environment conducive to relaxation and professional service.

- **Convenience:** offering clients a variety of services in one setting as well as flexible business hours.

- **Reputation:** superior personal service reputation of the owners/managers and other "stylists."

BUSINESS OVERVIEW

Company Summary

Salon Flora is designed to enhance each client's image and outlook. We specialize in restoring balance to the body and mind, through the *HairFlux* philosophy of beauty, wellness, care for the environment and our passion for service and retail. We will provide a unique experience for our guests. We treat each client as if they were a guest in our home, offering a cup of *HairFlux's* comforting tea and a cozy robe to change into. Our outstanding stylists will benefit from ongoing *HairFlux* education classes both in the salon and at other choice locations.

Start-up summary

Start-up expenses

Legal	$ 1,500
Stationary	$ 150
Rent (deposit)	$ 7,400
Utilities	$ 250
Phone	$ 100
Total start-up expenses	**$ 9,400**

Start-up assets

Cash balance on starting date	$ 30,800
Total current assets	**$ 30,800**

Long-term assets

Leasehold improvements	$ 49,500
Equipment (chairs, mirrors, etc)	$ 20,900
Total long-term assets	**$ 70,400**
Total assets	**$101,200**

Owner's equity

Alan Wolvin	$ 20,000
Yvette DeVito	$ 20,000
Total owner's equity	**$ 40,000**
Total current liabilities	**$ 0**

Long-term liabilities

Loan	$ 77,000
Total long-term liabilities	**$ 77,000**
Loss at start-up	($ 15,800)
Total liabilities and owner's equity	**$101,200**

Products & Services

Salon Flora is considered an upscale beauty salon. We will offer a wide range of services that include:

- **Hair:** Precision cuts, relaxers, perms, colors, color correction, shampoo, conditioning, curling, re-constructing, weaving, waving, and a patented hair straightening system.

- **Skin Care:** European facials, body waxing, and massage.

- Provide added-value services to each of our guests, such as: a stress-relieving scalp treatment, stress-relieving hand massage, and make-up touch up after each service.

- Retail *HairFlux* products so that the client can reproduce their enhanced appearance.

Annual sales forecast

Sales	FY 1	FY 2	FY 3
Owners	$ 52,580	$ 53,680	$ 53,680
Stylist retail sales	$ 75,970	$171,800	$208,339
Treatment room rent	$ 11,880	$ 15,840	$ 19,008
Treatment rooms retail sales	$ 26,158	$ 59,532	$ 72,183
Station rental	$ 97,900	$145,200	$174,240
Total sales	**$264,488**	**$446,052**	**$527,450**
Cost of goods sold			
Owners	$ 24,384	$ 32,693	$ 39,436
Stylist retail sales	$ 35,234	$104,631	$153,055
Treatment room rent	N/A	N/A	N/A
Treatment rooms retail sales	$ 12,131	$ 36,257	$ 53,028
Station rental	N/A	N/A	N/A
Total cost of goods sold	**$ 71,749**	**$173,581**	**$245,519**

Competition

There are a number of salons in our area; however, none will be like Salon Flora. Salon Flora will set itself apart from other beauty salons. We will offer over twenty-five years of combined hair care experience, weekly education to our staff, added-value services and a full line of *HairFlux* products. Our business atmosphere is a relaxing one where clients can kick back and be pampered. Soft drinks, coffee, and tea will be offered to clients as they enter for service.

GROWTH STRATEGY

The major market for our products and services is singles, couples, and families within but not limited to a twenty mile radius. The owners/managers have clients that travel twenty to ninety miles, and many plan their business around their hair care needs. Salon Flora has easy access from a main highway with plenty of parking, a rarity in the downtown business district. Our service is for individuals but might be beneficial for companies and corporations through incentive programs such as business make over or other promotional services.

We will also promote bridal packages through local hotels and associated business and day-of-beauty packages complete with lunch and door-to-door limousine service, if desired. *HairFlux Corporation* will offer our services through their 800 phone number, website, and corporate store at the nearby Shady Oak Mall, along with our own Salon Flora website. We will concentrate on the Palma County area in southern Florida.

Marketing & Sales

Our marketing strategy is a simple one: satisfied clients are our best marketing tool. When a client leaves our business with a new look, he or she is broadcasting our name and quality to the public.

Most of our new clients are referrals from existing clients. We reward clients for referrals with free shampoo and/or conditioner. Distribution of coupons for a free gift with product purchases or services at the salon "grand opening" celebration will strengthen customer loyalty.

We will publish ads in local publications and magazines to promote our staff, services, and retail products. The publications we will work with are:

- *Best Images:* a full color, bimonthly advertising magazine with a 100,000 home circulation in the regional area. This full page, color ad will cost $4,500, and reach potential upper income clients.

- *All the News Magazine:* a trusted reference for business and shopping resources with a home circulation of 50,000 in the nearby coastal areas. These full page color ads cost $1,500 for an inside page, and $3,500 for front cover. These ads will reach potential clients with $60,000 to $175,000 incomes.

- We will also have our own Salon Flora—*HairFlux Institute* website. This website is always available for stylists and guests. Information on current promotions, upcoming events, education and links to the *HairFlux Corporation* are instantly available.

MANAGEMENT SUMMARY

Salon Flora is a *HairFlux* concept salon. The upscale brand recognition of *HairFlux* enhances the reputation of the salon. Salon Flora will be organized and managed in a creative and innovative fashion to generate very high levels of customer satisfaction, and to create a working climate conducive to a high degree of personal development and economic satisfaction for our staff.

Training classes to help improve employee product knowledge and skills will be conducted on a regular basis. As the business grows, the company will consider offering an employee benefit package to include health and vacation benefits for everyone.

Management Team

Yvette and Alan have both been independent contractors for a combined thirty-two years and have the experience, passion, and working knowledge to get the job done.

Alan F. Slinger

Owner/Manager/Artistic Director: Alan has been in the beauty industry for eighteen years and brings a large variety of experience to this venture; upon graduating from Monique Beauty College in 1996 he worked for one of New York's leading salons, helping with education and platform work for both *HairFlux* and *Matrix/Logics Corporations*. He was also a part-time Artistic Educator with *Matrix/Logics*, responsible for color and hair cutting classes in New York City. His previous experiences consist of commercial, retail stores, management, construction and manufacturing. Alan's retail management experience and general business knowledge grounds him in the realities of running a successful business. He loves dealing with people and has the drive, ambition, and discipline to manage the business and its employees. This career is his life, his calling.

Yvette Cruz

Owner/Manger: Yvette Cruz was born in Barcelona, Spain, forty years ago. She is the second child of nine. She began her career by mentoring her three cousins.

At age 21, she moved to the United States. After finishing her education at Monique Beauty College she went to work in her cousin's salon. Cruz is involved in various activities in the world of beauty. She is responsible for the designing and marketing of a specialty tool called the *Color–Wandz*, created to expedite the stylist time in color services. She has worked with the *HairFlux* product line for the past eleven years as an independent contractor, and also has been involved in many global events for *HairFlux*. She is a firm believer in donating her artistic talents for various events.

Personnel Plan

The personnel plan calls for a salon receptionist starting in the second year. The receptionist will answer the phone, book appointments, and receive payments for services and products. There will be eleven hair stylists, one artistic director/owner, one stylist/owner, two part-time assistant stylists, one esthetician and one massage therapist. Everyone but the salon receptionist and assistants will be independent contractors, and will pay a weekly fee for their station or treatment room.

Annual personnel plan

	FY 1	FY 2	FY 3
Receptionist	$0	$35,000	$40,000
Assistant	$0	$ 0	$ 0
Assistant	$0	$15,000	$15,000
Total payroll	**$0**	**$50,000**	**$55,000**

FINANCIAL ANALYSIS

Our goal is to be a profitable business beginning in the second month. The owners and stylists already have an existing client base.

The financials that are enclosed have a number of assumptions:

- Chair rental value is $275.00 per week x 11 chairs = $3,025.00 per week x 52 = $157,300 per year. This figure is not assumed until the end of the first year. Our projections are based on opening with three stylists. We will then add a stylist the second month, the third month, the fourth month, and the sixth month. Flora Salon will then add two more stylists in the eighth month and two more in the tenth month.

- Revenues will grow on chair rental each month and level off at the end of the first year with all chairs rented.

- Revenues will grow at an annual rate near 50% on retail sales in year one.

- Revenues are expected to increase in November and December due to holiday sales at this time of year. We anticipate this increase from gift certificates and increased product sales, and to stay steady throughout the following year to account for the normal flow of new clients coming into the salon and our aggressive marketing program.

- Estimates for sales revenue and growth are intentionally low, while anticipated expenses are exaggerated to illustrate a worst-case scenario.

We have included cost of goods sold in our calculation of net sales because we expect to do a high volume of retail through our salon. However, the majority of sales are coming from the services and rental income.

Product sales will be a major part of our business. We are projecting sales of $4,400 a month increasing each month thereafter as we add stylists to the salon. We expect each stylist to sell a minimum of $110.00 per day in retail. We also project the treatment rooms to generate a minimum of $190.00 per day in retail sales. We are certain that in time these services will be a large part of our revenue, but to err on the conservative side, we estimate revenues from these services to be only $4,021.00 a month for the first year.

To assure the initial capital fund lender that the owners are financially stable, personnel tax returns for both partners for the last three years are attached. Another source of collateral is Alan Slinger's home, valued at $550,000 with a payoff balance of $395,000.

Break-even analysis

Monthly units break-even	130
Monthly revenue break-even	$7,165
Average per-unit revenue	$60.00
Average per-unit variable cost	$12.57
Estimated monthly fixed cost	$5,676

General assumptions

	FY 1	FY 2	FY 3
Current interest rate	8.00%	8.00%	8.00%
Long-term interest rate	8.00%	8.00%	8.00%
Sales on credit	0.00%	0.00%	0.00%
Tax rate	33.00%	33.00%	33.00%

Projected Profit and Loss

We expect sales to hit nearly $265,000 at the end of the first year of business, and should increase to more than $527,450 by the third year as the reputation of the salon, its stylists, and services grow. Second year revenues also anticipate having a full staff.

Annual pro forma profit and loss

	FY 1	FY 2	FY 3
Total income	**$264,495**	**$446,050**	**$527,450**
Cost of goods sold	$ 71,748	$173,580	$245,520
Gross profit	**$192,748**	**$272,470**	**$281,930**
Gross profit %	80.16%	67.20%	58.80%
Expenses:			
Payroll	$ 0	$ 46,112	$ 50,512
Depreciation	$ 11,990	$ 11,990	$ 11,990
Rent	$ 29,568	$ 29,568	$ 29,568
Utilities	$ 6,600	$ 7,480	$ 7,700
Insurance	$ 1,320	$ 1,320	$ 1,320
Supplies	$ 13,090	$ 13,090	$ 13,090
Advertising	$ 4,620	$ 4,620	$ 4,620
Misc.	$ 924	$ 924	$ 924
Payroll taxes (17%)	$ 0	$ 6,917	$ 7,577
Total operating expenses	**$ 68,112**	**$122,021**	**$127,301**
Profit before interest and taxes	$124,636	$150,449	$154,629
Interest expense	$ 4,755	$ 3,254	$ 1,868
Taxes incurred	$ 35,965	$ 39,436	$ 45,828
Net profit	**$ 83,917**	**$107,759**	**$106,933**
Net profit/sales	34.90%	26.58%	22.30%

First year of operations monthly profits

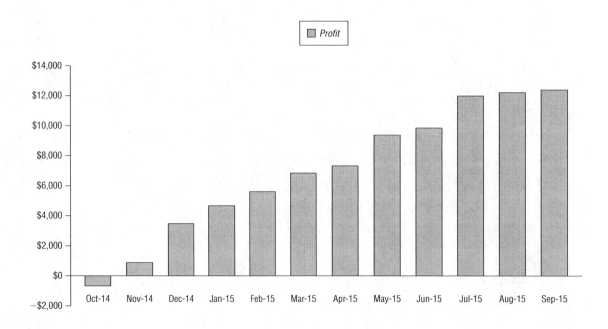

Second year of operations monthly profits

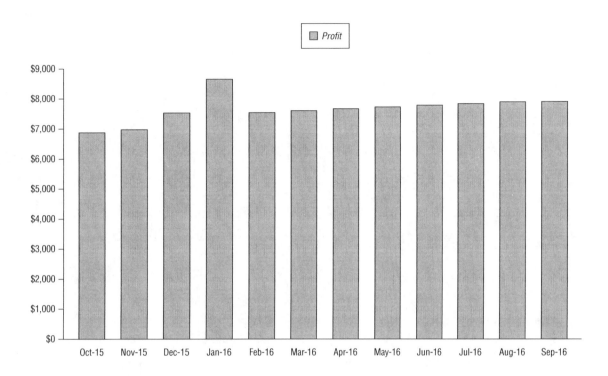

Annual pro forma cash flow

	FY 1	FY 2	FY 3
Cash received			
Cash from operations:			
Cash sales	$264,495	$446,050	$527,450
Cash from receivables	$ 0	$ 0	$ 0
Subtotal cash from operations	**$264,495**	**$446,050**	**$527,450**
Additional cash received			
Subtotal cash received	**$264,495**	**$446,050**	**$527,450**
Expenditures			
Expenditures from operations			
Cash spending	$ 0	$ 46,112	$ 50,512
Payments of accounts payable	$168,588	$280,189	$358,015
Subtotal spent on operations	**$168,588**	**$326,301**	**$408,527**
Additional cash spent			
Principle repayment of loan	$ 19,800	$ 19,800	$ 19,800
Change in inventory	$ 22,000	$ 22,000	$ 0
Subtotal cash spent	**$210,388**	**$368,101**	**$428,327**
Net cash flow	**$ 54,107**	**$ 77,949**	**$ 99,123**
Cash balance	**$ 84,940**	**$162,889**	**$262,012**

First year of operations monthly cash flow

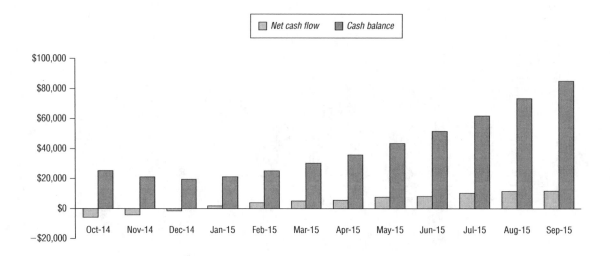

Pro forma balance sheet

Assets	FY 1	FY 2	FY 3
Current assets			
Cash	$ 84,940	$162,889	$262,012
Accounts receivable	$ 0	$ 0	$ 0
Inventory	$ 22,000	$ 44,000	$ 44,000
Total current assets	**$106,940**	**$206,889**	**$306,012**
Long-term assets			
Leasehold improvements	$ 49,500	$ 49,500	$ 49,500
Equipment	$ 20,900	$ 20,900	$ 20,900
Accumulated depreciation	$ 11,990	$ 23,980	$ 35,970
Total long-term assets	**$ 58,410**	**$ 46,420**	**$ 34,430**
Total assets	**$165,350**	**$253,309**	**$340,442**
Liabilities and owner's equity			
Current liabilities			
Accounts payable	$ 0	$ 0	$ 0
Total current liabilities	**$ 0**	**$ 0**	**$ 0**
Long-term liabilities			
Loan	$ 57,200	$ 37,400	$ 17,600
Total liabilities	**$ 57,200**	**$ 37,400**	**$ 17,600**
Paid-in capital	$ 33,000	$ 33,000	$ 33,000
Retained earnings	($ 8,767)	$ 75,150	$182,909
Earnings	$ 83,917	$107,759	$106,933
Total owner's equity	**$108,150**	**$215,909**	**$322,842**
Total liabilities and owner's equity	**$165,350**	**$253,309**	**$340,442**
Net worth	**$108,150**	**$215,909**	**$322,842**

Monthly sales forecast—fiscal year one

Monthly sales forecast	Oct-14	Nov-14	Dec-14	Jan-15	Feb-15	Mar-15
Sales						
Owners	$3,300	$4,400	$ 5,280	$ 4,400	$ 4,400	$ 4,400
Stylist retail sales	$ 0	$ 990	$ 4,950	$ 3,960	$ 4,950	$ 5,940
Treatment room rent	$ 0	$ 0	$ 0	$ 1,320	$ 1,320	$ 1,320
Treatment rooms retail sales	$ 0	$ 0	$ 0	$ 1,100	$ 2,200	$ 2,420
Station rental	$3,300	$4,400	$ 5,500	$ 6,600	$ 6,600	$ 7,700
Total sales	**$6,600**	**$9,790**	**$15,730**	**$17,380**	**$19,470**	**$21,780**
Cost of goods sold						
Owners	$1,530	$2,041	$ 2,449	$ 2,041	$ 2,041	$ 2,041
Stylist retail sales	$ 0	$ 459	$ 2,296	$ 1,836	$ 2,296	$ 2,754
Treatment room rent	N/A	N/A	N/A	N/A	N/A	N/A
Treatment rooms retail sales	$ 0	$ 0	$ 0	$ 510	$ 1,020	$ 1,122
Station rental	N/A	N/A	N/A	N/A	N/A	N/A
Total cost of goods sold	**$1,530**	**$2,499**	**$ 4,744**	**$ 4,387**	**$5,356**	**$ 5,917**

Monthly sales forecast	Apr-15	May-15	Jun-15	Jul-15	Aug-15	Sep-15
Sales						
Owners	$ 4,400	$ 4,400	$ 4,400	$ 4,400	$ 4,400	$ 4,400
Stylist retail sales	$ 7,150	$ 7,920	$ 8,910	$10,120	$10,362	$10,725
Treatment room rent	$ 1,320	$ 1,320	$ 1,320	$ 1,320	$ 1,320	$ 1,320
Treatment rooms retail sales	$ 2,475	$ 3,025	$ 3,300	$ 3,630	$ 3,960	$ 4,048
Station rental	$ 7,700	$ 9,900	$ 9,900	$12,100	$12,100	$12,100
Total sales	**$23,045**	**$26,565**	**$27,830**	**$31,570**	**$32,142**	**$32,593**
Cost of goods sold						
Owners	$ 2,041	$ 2,041	$ 2,041	$ 2,041	$ 2,041	$ 2,041
Stylist retail sales	$ 3,315	$ 3,673	$ 4,132	$ 4,693	$ 4,805	$ 4,973
Treatment room rent	N/A	N/A	N/A	N/A	N/A	N/A
Treatment rooms retail sales	$ 1,147	$ 1,403	$ 1,530	$ 1,683	$ 1,836	$ 1,878
Station rental	N/A	N/A	N/A	N/A	N/A	N/A
Total cost of goods sold	**$ 6,504**	**$ 7,116**	**$ 7,702**	**$ 8,417**	**$ 8,682**	**$ 8,891**

Monthly sales forecast—fiscal year two

Monthly sales forecast	Oct-15	Nov-15	Dec-15	Jan-16	Feb-16	Mar-16
Sales						
Owners	$ 4,400	$ 4,400	$ 4,400	$ 5,280	$ 4,400	$ 4,400
Stylist retail sales	$10,450	$11,000	$13,200	$15,840	$13,640	$14,080
Treatment room rent	$ 1,320	$ 1,320	$ 1,320	$ 1,320	$ 1,320	$ 1,320
Treatment rooms retail sales	$ 4,290	$ 4,400	$ 4,510	$ 5,412	$ 4,730	$ 4,840
Station rental	$12,100	$12,100	$12,100	$12,100	$12,100	$12,100
Total sales	**$32,560**	**$33,220**	**$35,530**	**$39,952**	**$36,190**	**$36,740**
Cost of goods sold						
Owners	$ 2,680	$ 2,680	$ 2,680	$ 3,215	$ 2,680	$ 2,680
Stylist retail sales	$ 6,365	$ 6,699	$ 8,039	$ 9,647	$ 8,307	$ 8,576
Treatment room rent	N/A	N/A	N/A	N/A	N/A	N/A
Treatment rooms retail sales	$ 2,613	$ 2,680	$ 2,747	$ 3,296	$ 2,881	$ 2,948
Station rental	N/A	N/A	N/A	N/A	N/A	N/A
Total cost of goods sold	**$11,657**	**$12,059**	**$13,466**	**$16,159**	**$13,868**	**$14,202**

Monthly sales forecast	Apr-16	May-16	Jun-16	Jul-16	Aug-16	Sep-16
Sales						
Owners	$ 4,400	$ 4,400	$ 4,400	$ 4,400	$ 4,400	$ 4,400
Stylist retail sales	$14,520	$14,960	$15,400	$15,840	$16,280	$16,588
Treatment room rent	$ 1,320	$ 1,320	$ 1,320	$ 1,320	$ 1,320	$ 1,320
Treatment rooms retail sales	$ 4,950	$ 5,060	$ 5,170	$ 5,280	$ 5,390	$ 5,500
Station rental	$12,100	$12,100	$12,100	$12,100	$12,100	$12,100
Total sales	**$37,290**	**$37,840**	**$38,390**	**$38,940**	**$39,490**	**$39,908**
Cost of goods sold						
Owners	$ 2,680	$ 2,680	$ 2,680	$ 2,680	$ 2,680	$ 2,680
Stylist retail sales	$ 8,843	$ 9,111	$ 9,379	$ 9,647	$ 9,915	$10,102
Treatment room rent	N/A	N/A	N/A	N/A	N/A	N/A
Treatment rooms retail sales	$ 3,015	$ 3,082	$ 3,148	$ 3,215	$ 3,282	$ 3,350
Station rental	N/A	N/A	N/A	N/A	N/A	N/A
Total cost of goods sold	**$14,538**	**$14,872**	**$15,208**	**$15,543**	**$15,877**	**$16,132**

Monthly profit and loss—fiscal year one

Monthly pro forma profit and loss	Oct-14	Nov-14	Dec-14	Jan-15	Feb-15	Mar-15
Total income	**$6,600**	**$9,790**	**$15,730**	**$17,380**	**$19,470**	**$21,780**
Cost of goods sold	$1,530	$2,499	$ 4,744	$ 4,387	$ 5,356	$ 5,917
Gross profit	**$5,070**	**$7,291**	**$10,986**	**$12,993**	**$14,114**	**$15,863**
Gross profit %	84.49%	81.92%	76.82%	82.24%	79.74%	80.11%
Expenses:						
Payroll	$ 0	$ 0	$ 0	$ 0	$ 0	$ 0
Depreciation	$ 999	$ 999	$ 999	$ 999	$ 999	$ 999
Rent	$2,464	$2,464	$ 2,464	$ 2,464	$ 2,464	$ 2,464
Utilities	$ 550	$ 550	$ 550	$ 550	$ 550	$ 550
Insurance	$ 110	$ 110	$ 110	$ 110	$ 110	$ 110
Supplies	$ 990	$ 990	$ 990	$ 1,320	$ 1,100	$ 1,100
Advertising	$ 385	$ 385	$ 385	$ 385	$ 385	$ 385
Misc.	$ 77	$ 77	$ 77	$ 77	$ 77	$ 77
Payroll taxes	$ 0	$ 0	$ 0	$ 0	$ 0	$ 0
Total operating expenses	**$5,575**	**$5,575**	**$ 5,575**	**$ 5,905**	**$ 5,685**	**$ 5,685**
Profit before interest and taxes	($ 506)	$1,715	$ 5,411	$ 7,088	$ 8,428	$10,177
Interest expense	$ 449	$ 440	$ 430	$ 420	$ 410	$ 402
Taxes incurred	($ 286)	$ 383	$ 1,494	$ 2,000	$ 2,406	$ 2,933
Net profit	**($ 669)**	**$ 893**	**$ 3,487**	**$ 4,667**	**$ 5,612**	**$ 6,843**
Net profit/sales	**−11.14%**	**10.03%**	**24.39%**	**29.54%**	**31.71%**	**34.56%**

Monthly pro forma profit and loss	Apr-15	May-15	Jun-15	Jul-15	Aug-15	Sep-15
Total income	**$23,045**	**$26,565**	**$27,830**	**$31,570**	**$32,142**	**$32,593**
Cost of goods sold	$ 6,504	$ 7,116	$ 7,702	$ 8,417	$ 8,682	$ 8,891
Gross profit	**$16,541**	**$19,449**	**$20,128**	**$23,153**	**$23,460**	**$23,702**
Gross profit %	78.96%	80.53%	79.55%	80.67%	80.29%	79.99%
Expenses:						
Payroll	$ 0	$ 0	$ 0	$ 0	$ 0	$ 0
Depreciation	$ 999	$ 999	$ 999	$ 999	$ 999	$ 999
Rent	$ 2,464	$ 2,464	$ 2,464	$ 2,464	$ 2,464	$ 2,464
Utilities	$ 550	$ 550	$ 550	$ 550	$ 550	$ 550
Insurance	$ 110	$ 110	$ 110	$ 110	$ 110	$ 110
Supplies	$ 1,100	$ 1,100	$ 1,100	$ 1,100	$ 1,100	$ 1,100
Advertising	$ 385	$ 385	$ 385	$ 385	$ 385	$ 385
Misc.	$ 77	$ 77	$ 77	$ 77	$ 77	$ 77
Payroll taxes	$ 0	$ 0	$ 0	$ 0	$ 0	$ 0
Total operating expenses	**$ 5,685**	**$ 5,685**	**$ 5,685**	**$ 5,685**	**$ 5,685**	**$ 5,685**
Profit before interest and taxes	$10,856	$13,763	$14,442	$17,468	$17,775	$18,017
Interest expense	$ 392	$ 382	$ 372	$ 363	$ 353	$ 343
Taxes incurred	$ 3,139	$ 4,015	$ 4,221	$ 5,132	$ 5,226	$ 5,302
Net profit	**$ 7,325**	**$ 9,368**	**$ 9,849**	**$11,974**	**$12,196**	**$12,372**
Net profit/sales	**34.97%**	**38.79%**	**38.93%**	**41.72%**	**41.73%**	**41.76%**

Monthly profit and loss—fiscal year two

Monthly pro forma profit and loss	Oct-15	Nov-15	Dec-15	Jan-16	Feb-16	Mar-16
Total income	**$32,560**	**$33,220**	**$35,530**	**$39,952**	**$36,190**	**$36,740**
Cost of goods sold	$11,657	$12,059	$13,466	$16,159	$13,868	$14,202
Gross profit	**$20,903**	**$21,161**	**$22,064**	**$23,793**	**$22,322**	**$22,538**
Gross profit %	70.62%	70.07%	68.31%	65.51%	67.85%	67.47%
Expenses:						
Payroll	$ 4,415	$ 4,503	$ 4,594	$ 4,686	$ 4,780	$ 4,875
Depreciation	$ 999	$ 999	$ 999	$ 999	$ 999	$ 999
Rent	$ 2,464	$ 2,464	$ 2,464	$ 2,464	$ 2,464	$ 2,464
Utilities	$ 550	$ 550	$ 550	$ 550	$ 550	$ 550
Insurance	$ 110	$ 110	$ 110	$ 110	$ 110	$ 110
Supplies	$ 1,091	$ 1,113	$ 1,135	$ 1,158	$ 1,181	$ 1,205
Advertising	$ 385	$ 385	$ 385	$ 385	$ 385	$ 385
Misc.	$ 77	$ 77	$ 77	$ 77	$ 77	$ 77
Payroll taxes	$ 662	$ 675	$ 689	$ 703	$ 717	$ 732
Total operating expenses	**$10,754**	**$10,877**	**$11,003**	**$11,131**	**$11,262**	**$11,396**
Profit before interest and taxes	$10,150	$10,284	$11,062	$12,662	$11,061	$11,142
Interest expense	$ 325	$ 315	$ 305	$ 295	$ 286	$ 276
Taxes incurred	$ 2,948	$ 2,991	$ 3,227	$ 3,710	$ 3,233	$ 3,259
Net profit	**$ 6,878**	**$ 6,978**	**$ 7,530**	**$ 8,657**	**$ 7,543**	**$ 7,607**
Net profit/sales	**23.23%**	**23.11%**	**23.31%**	**23.84%**	**22.92%**	**22.77%**

Monthly pro forma profit and loss	Apr-16	May-16	Jun-16	Jul-16	Aug-16	Sep-16
Total income	**$37,290**	**$37,840**	**$38,390**	**$38,940**	**$39,490**	**$39,908**
Cost of goods sold	$14,538	$14,872	$15,208	$15,543	$15,877	$16,132
Gross profit	**$22,752**	**$22,968**	**$23,183**	**$23,397**	**$23,613**	**$23,777**
Gross profit %	67.11%	66.77%	66.43%	66.10%	65.77%	65.54%
Expenses:						
Payroll	$ 4,972	$ 5,072	$ 5,173	$ 5,277	$ 5,382	$ 5,495
Depreciation	$ 999	$ 999	$ 999	$ 999	$ 999	$ 999
Rent	$ 2,464	$ 2,464	$ 2,464	$ 2,464	$ 2,464	$ 2,464
Utilities	$ 550	$ 550	$ 550	$ 550	$ 550	$ 550
Insurance	$ 110	$ 110	$ 110	$ 110	$ 110	$ 110
Supplies	$ 1,299	$ 1,253	$ 1,278	$ 1,305	$ 1,330	$ 1,356
Advertising	$ 385	$ 385	$ 385	$ 385	$ 385	$ 385
Misc.	$ 77	$ 77	$ 77	$ 77	$ 77	$ 77
Payroll taxes	$ 746	$ 761	$ 776	$ 791	$ 807	$ 826
Total operating expenses	**$11,532**	**$11,671**	**$11,813**	**$11,957**	**$12,104**	**$12,262**
Profit before interest and taxes	$11,221	$11,297	$11,370	$11,440	$11,508	$11,514
Interest expense	$ 266	$ 256	$ 248	$ 238	$ 228	$ 218
Taxes incurred	$ 3,287	$ 3,312	$ 3,337	$ 3,361	$ 3,384	$ 3,389
Net profit	**$ 7,668**	**$ 7,728**	**$ 7,786**	**$ 7,842**	**$ 7,896**	**$ 7,907**
Net profit/sales	**22.62%**	**22.46%**	**22.31%**	**22.15%**	**22.00%**	**21.79%**

Monthly cash flow—fiscal year one

Monthly pro forma cash flow	Oct-14	Nov-14	Dec-14	Jan-15	Feb-15	Mar-15
Cash received						
Cash from operations:						
cash sales	$ 6,600	$ 9,790	$15,730	$17,380	$19,470	$21,780
Cash from receivables	$ 0	$ 0	$ 0	$ 0	$ 0	$ 0
Subtotal cash from operations	**$ 6,600**	**$ 9,790**	**$15,730**	**$17,380**	**$19,470**	**$21,780**
Additional cash received						
Subtotal cash received	**$ 6,600**	**$ 9,790**	**$15,730**	**$17,380**	**$19,470**	**$21,780**
Expenditures						
Expenditures from operations						
Cash spending	$ 0	$ 0	$ 0	$ 0	$ 0	$ 0
Payments of accounts payable	$ 6,269	$ 7,898	$11,244	$11,714	$12,858	$13,937
Subtotal spent on operations	**$ 6,269**	**$ 7,898**	**$11,244**	**$11,714**	**$12,858**	**$13,937**
Additional cash spent						
Principle repayment of loan	$ 1,650	$ 1,650	$ 1,650	$ 1,650	$ 1,650	$ 1,650
Change in inventory	$ 4,400	$ 4,400	$ 4,400	$ 2,200	$ 1,100	$ 1,100
Subtotal cash spent	**$12,319**	**$13,948**	**$17,294**	**$15,564**	**$15,608**	**$16,687**
Net cash flow	**($ 5,719)**	**($ 4,158)**	**($ 1,564)**	**$ 1,816**	**$ 3,862**	**$ 5,093**
Cash balance	**$25,114**	**$20,956**	**$19,392**	**$21,208**	**$25,070**	**$30,163**

Monthly pro forma cash flow	Apr-15	May-15	Jun-15	Jul-15	Aug-15	Sep-15
Cash received						
Cash from operations:						
Cash sales	$23,045	$26,565	$27,830	$31,570	$32,142	$32,593
Cash from receivables	$ 0	$ 0	$ 0	$ 0	$ 0	$ 0
Subtotal cash from operations	**$23,045**	**$26,565**	**$27,830**	**$31,570**	**$32,142**	**$32,593**
Additional cash received						
Subtotal cash received	**$23,045**	**$26,565**	**$27,830**	**$31,570**	**$32,142**	**$32,593**
Expenditures						
Expenditures from operations						
Cash spending	$ 0	$ 0	$ 0	$ 0	$ 0	$ 0
Payments of accounts payable	$14,720	$16,199	$16,982	$18,597	$18,948	$19,223
Subtotal spent on operations	**$14,720**	**$16,199**	**$16,982**	**$18,597**	**$18,948**	**$19,223**
Additional cash spent						
Principle repayment of loan	$ 1,650	$ 1,650	$ 1,650	$ 1,650	$ 1,650	$ 1,650
Change in inventory	$ 1,100	$ 1,100	$ 1,100	$ 1,100	$ 0	$ 0
Subtotal cash spent	**$17,470**	**$18,949**	**$19,732**	**$21,347**	**$20,598**	**$20,873**
Net cash flow	**$ 5,575**	**$ 7,616**	**$ 8,098**	**$10,223**	**$11,545**	**$11,721**
Cash balance	**$35,737**	**$43,353**	**$51,451**	**$61,675**	**$73,219**	**$84,940**

Monthly balance sheet—fiscal year one

Pro forma balance sheet	Starting balances	Oct-14	Nov-14	Dec-14	Jan-15	Feb-15	Mar-15
Assets							
Current assets							
Cash	$ 30,833	$25,114	$20,956	$19,392	$ 21,208	$ 25,070	$ 30,163
Accounts receivable	$ 0	$ 0	$ 0	$ 0	$ 0	$ 0	$ 0
Inventory	$ 0	$ 4,400	$ 8,800	$13,200	$ 15,400	$ 16,500	$ 17,600
Total current assets	**$ 30,833**	**$29,514**	**$29,756**	**$32,592**	**$ 36,608**	**$ 41,570**	**$ 47,763**
Long-term assets							
Leasehold improvements	$ 49,500	$49,500	$49,500	$49,500	$ 49,500	$ 49,500	$ 49,500
Equipment	$ 20,900	$20,900	$20,900	$20,900	$ 20,900	$ 20,900	$ 20,900
Accumulated depreciation	$ 0	$ 999	$ 1,999	$ 2,998	$ 3,996	$ 4,996	$ 5,995
Total long-term assets	**$ 70,400**	**$69,401**	**$68,401**	**$67,403**	**$ 66,404**	**$ 65,404**	**$ 64,405**
Total assets	**$101,233**	**$98,914**	**$98,157**	**$99,994**	**$103,012**	**$106,974**	**$112,168**
Liabilities and owner's equity							
Current liabilities							
Accounts payable	$ 0	$ 0	$ 0	$ 0	$ 0	$ 0	$ 0
Total current liabilities	**$ 0**	**$ 0**	**$ 0**	**$ 0**	**$ 0**	**$ 0**	**$ 0**
Long-term liabilities							
Loan	$ 77,000	$75,350	$73,700	$72,050	$ 70,400	$ 68,750	$ 67,100
Total liabilities	**$ 77,000**	**$75,350**	**$73,700**	**$72,050**	**$ 70,400**	**$ 68,750**	**$ 67,100**
Paid-in capital	$ 33,000	$33,000	$33,000	$33,000	$ 33,000	$ 33,000	$ 33,000
Retained earnings	($ 8,767)	($ 8,767)	($ 8,767)	($ 8,767)	($ 8,767)	($ 8,767)	($ 8,767)
Earnings	$ 0	($ 669)	$ 224	$ 3,711	$ 8,379	$ 13,991	$ 20,835
Total owner's equity	**$ 24,233**	**$23,564**	**$24,457**	**$27,944**	**$ 32,612**	**$ 38,224**	**$ 45,068**
Total liabilities and owner's equity	**$101,233**	**$98,914**	**$98,157**	**$99,994**	**$103,012**	**$106,974**	**$112,168**
Net worth	**$ 24,233**	**$23,564**	**$24,457**	**$27,944**	**$ 32,612**	**$ 38,224**	**$ 45,068**

Pro forma balance sheet	Apr-15	May-15	Jun-15	Jul-15	Aug-15	Sep-15
Assets						
Current assets						
Cash	$ 35,737	$ 43,353	$ 51,451	$ 61,675	$ 73,219	$ 84,940
Accounts receivable	$ 0	$ 0	$ 0	$ 0	$ 0	$ 0
Inventory	$ 18,700	$ 19,800	$ 20,900	$ 22,000	$ 22,000	$ 22,000
Total current assets	**$ 54,437**	**$ 63,153**	**$ 72,351**	**$ 83,675**	**$ 95,219**	**$106,940**
Long-term assets						
Leasehold improvements	$ 49,500	$ 49,500	$ 49,500	$ 49,500	$ 49,500	$ 49,500
Equipment	$ 20,900	$ 20,900	$ 20,900	$ 20,900	$ 20,900	$ 20,900
Accumulated depreciation	$ 6,994	$ 7,994	$ 8,993	$ 9,991	$ 10,991	$ 11,990
Total long-term assets	**$ 63,406**	**$ 62,406**	**$ 61,408**	**$ 60,409**	**$ 59,409**	**$ 58,410**
Total assets	**$117,843**	**$125,561**	**$133,759**	**$144,084**	**$154,628**	**$165,350**
Liabilities and owner's equity						
Current liabilities						
Accounts payable	$ 0	$ 0	$ 0	$ 0	$ 0	$ 0
Total current liabilities	**$ 0**	**$ 0**	**$ 0**	**$ 0**	**$ 0**	**$ 0**
Long-term liabilities						
Loan	$ 65,450	$ 63,800	$ 62,150	$ 60,500	$ 58,850	$ 57,200
Total liabilities	**$ 65,450**	**$ 63,800**	**$ 62,150**	**$ 60,500**	**$ 58,850**	**$ 57,200**
Paid-in capital	$ 33,000	$ 33,000	$ 33,000	$ 33,000	$ 33,000	$ 33,000
Retained earnings	($ 8,767)	($ 8,767)	($ 8,767)	($ 8,767)	($ 8,767)	($ 8,767)
Earnings	$ 28,160	$ 37,528	$ 47,376	$ 59,351	$ 71,545	$ 83,917
Total owner's equity	**$ 52,393**	**$ 61,761**	**$ 71,609**	**$ 83,584**	**$ 95,778**	**$108,150**
Total liabilities and owner's equity	**$117,843**	**$125,561**	**$ 133,759**	**$144,084**	**$154,628**	**$165,350**
Net worth	**$ 52,393**	**$ 61,761**	**$ 71,609**	**$ 83,584**	**$ 95,778**	**$108,150**

Boat Cleaning Business

Triple B Boat Detailing Inc.

72 Retzer Ave.
Birchwood, WI 53000

Paul Greenland

Triple B Boat Detailing is a boat cleaning and storage business located in Birchwood, Wisconsin, near the shores of Lake Michigan.

EXECUTIVE SUMMARY

Business Overview

According to data from the National Marine Manufacturers Association (NMMA), 88 million people (37.8% of the U.S. adult population) participated in recreational boating at least once in 2012, up six percent from the previous year. This was the highest participation level since the association began collecting data in 1990. At that time, there were approximately 12.2 million registered boats in the United States.

Capitalizing on boating's popularity, brothers Sam, Alex, and Caleb Brown are establishing Triple B Boat Detailing in Birchwood, Wisconsin. Birchwood is located on the shores of Lake Michigan in Ozaukee County, which has 25 miles of shoreline and includes 900 square miles of Lake Michigan waters. The construction of several new marinas in the area has attracted more boaters to the area, resulting in the demand for services such as boat cleaning and storage. Each brother has specific skills that will help to ensure the success of the business.

MARKET ANALYSIS

Triple B Boat Detailing is based in Birchwood, Wisconsin, a community in Ozaukee County, which offers 25 miles of shoreline and includes 900 square miles of Lake Michigan waters. In 2013 the county was home to an estimated 87,072 people (34,567 households). The number of households is expected to grow more than 4 percent through 2018, reaching 37,000.

Based on an analysis of state registration data, estimated local boat ownership levels are nearly 30 percent, higher than the national average of 21 percent (as estimated by the NMMA). The number of boats registered in the county was 14,370 in 2013. The construction of several new marinas in Ozaukee County has attracted more boaters to Birchwood and the surrounding area, resulting in the demand for boating-related services, including cleaning, detailing, and storage.

Competition

A number of other businesses offer services similar to those provided by Triple B Boat Detailing. However, due to the aforementioned construction of new marinas, and corresponding demand for boating-related services, there is ample opportunity for new business in the Birchwood market.

INDUSTRY ANALYSIS

According to data from the NMMA, the U.S. recreational boating sector's economic value totaled $121.5 billion in 2013, supporting 964,000 direct, indirect, and induced jobs, as well as 338,526 direct jobs at approximately 35,000 businesses nationwide. Annual direct and indirect recreational boating-related spending totals approximately $83 billion. Despite challenging economic conditions, the association reported that retail sales of both sailboats and new powerboats reached 163,245 units in 2012, an increase of 10.7 percent from the previous year.

PERSONNEL

Triple B Boat Detailing is being established by brothers Sam, Alex, and Caleb Brown, who are all Birchwood natives. Each brother has specific skills that will help to ensure the success of the business. The Browns will draw modest salaries for the first three years to keep operational costs as low as possible.

Sam, the senior-most partner (51% ownership), formerly was the manager of Midtown Marina. In that role, which he held for nine years, Sam gained invaluable business skills and also established relationships with many area boaters. His main focus will be to oversee operations (finance, supply management, etc).

Alex (29% ownership), has operated a successful charter boat service for five years, and is seeking to expand his business interests in the Birchwood market. His role will be to focus on marketing and business development.

Caleb (20% ownership) is completing his final year as a student at Milwaukee Area Technical College, where he has attended the School of Business in preparation for a business ownership career. Caleb also is connected with many college students seeking seasonal employment, which will help Triple B Boat Detailing identify reliable temporary employees (a critical component of its business model). Initially, his focus will be to oversee contract labor and serve as work crew coordinator.

Professional & Advisory Support

Triple B Boat Detailing has established a business banking account with Birchwood Community Bank, including a merchant account for accepting credit card payments. Tax advisement is provided by Rockwell Partners LP. The Brown brothers utilized a popular online legal document service to establish their corporation.

GROWTH STRATEGY

The Brown brothers are anticipating steady growth for Triple B Boat Detailing during the business' first three years of operations. The following growth targets have been established:

Year One: Focus on generating awareness about Triple B Boat Detailing within the Birchwood boating community. Establish trust with boat owners, placing an emphasis on customer referrals. Generate gross revenues of $263,160.

Year Two: Continue to focus on building Triple B Boat Detailing's customer base. Increase gross revenues by 15 percent and generate net profits of approximately $7,500.

Year Three: Continue to focus on building Triple B Boat Detailing's customer base. Increase gross revenues by 15 percent and double net profits (approximately $14,000).

SERVICES

Service Packages & Pricing

Triple B Boat Detailing offers a full range of boat cleaning services. Typically, these services will be bundled into one of four packages. Pricing and results may vary depending on the condition of the boat being cleaned/detailed. Additional charges may apply to boats requiring extensive cleaning, or the use of special products. Triple B Boat Detailing provides services within its own facility, and also at a customer's location (weather permitting, during the regular boating season). However, cleaning is not available for boats that are in the water; customers requesting on-site service must have their vessel on a trailer or boat stands.

Typically, packages will be as follows:

1. *Sapphire ($7/foot):* The most basic package offered, the Sapphire includes a complete wash-down of the boat and waxing of the hull. All compartments and hatches will be cleaned. The inside and outside of the boat is chamois dried, including stainless steel components and windows.

2. *Emerald ($15/foot):* In addition to everything available in the Sapphire package, the Emerald includes conditioning vinyl, plastic, and leather, polishing all stainless steel surfaces, and rust stain removal.

3. *Ruby ($20/foot):* In addition to all services included in the Sapphire and Emerald packages, the Ruby includes buffing and waxing.

4. *Diamond ($25/foot):* This premium package includes everything offered at the Sapphire, Emerald, and Ruby levels, along with gelcoat enhancement. This entails the removal of previous wax coats and oxidation (the chalky white substance resulting from corrosion and sun) and a complete waxing of gelcoat surfaces with marine wax.

Monthly Boat Storage

Triple B Boat Detailing also will offer off-season indoor heated boat storage for approximately 30 vessels. Storage customers will receive a 15 percent discount on all cleaning services, which the Brown brothers will perform during the slow off-season months. Storage rates will be as follows:

Size	Rate
Up to 10'	$ 75/month
10' to 20'	$ 90/month
20' to 30'	$150/month
30' to 40'	$180/month
40' to 50'	$250/month
50' to 60'	$300/month

Size Ranges

The boats serviced by Triple B Boat Detailing will fall into a variety of size ranges. Following is an estimated breakdown by size:

Size	Percentage
Up to 10'	5%
10' to 20'	10%
20' to 30'	40%
30' to 40'	32%
40' to 50'	8%
50' to 60'	5%

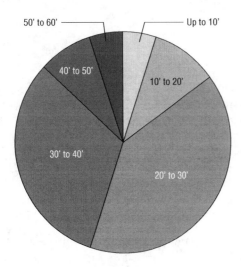

Boat Types

Triple B Boat Detailing will provide cleaning and detailing services for many different types of boats, including:

- Sailboats (e.g., sloops, cutters, catboats, and dinghies)

- Fishing Boats

- Ski Boats

- Runabouts (e.g., bowriders, deck boats, and cuddy cabins)

- Motor Yachts

MARKETING & SALES

Triple B Boat Detailing has developed a marketing plan that includes the following primary tactics:

1. A Web site describing the owners, available service packages, pricing, and service area. Dramatic "before" and "after" photographs of detailed boats will be included. Additionally, links to the business' social media sites (e.g., Facebook and LinkedIn) will be offered. A convenient online appointment request and contact form will enable customers to enter information about their vessel and receive an electronic estimate within 24 hours.

2. Several different promotional premium items (magnetic business cards, pens, floating keychains, and drink coolers) will be ordered to promote the business. These will be ideal for distribution at boating shows, special events, and to existing customers.

3. A high-quality, four-color flyer for distribution at boating shows, area marinas, and for use in seasonal direct mailings to registered boat owners within Triple B Boat Detailing's service area.

4. Membership in the Birchwood Chamber of Commerce.

5. Participation in regional boating, fishing, and outdoor shows.

6. A social media strategy involving Angie's List and Facebook, with a goal of generating new business and building/maintaining positive word-of-mouth.

7. A customer referral program, providing former clients with a 15 percent discount for referrals resulting in new business.

8. Regional print advertising in lifestyle publications and newspaper serving the Birchwood market.

OPERATIONS

Facility & Location

Triple B Boat Detailing will lease 15,000 square feet of former industrial/warehouse space at 72 Retzer Ave. in Birchwood, Wisconsin, which includes very large overhead door access, as well as enclosed space with ample lighting and access to electricity, water and, floor drains.

Equipment

The following equipment and supplies (total cost $8,500) will be needed before Triple B Boat Detailing can commence operations:

Equipment:
- Sponges
- Chamois
- Hoses
- Nozzles
- Pneumatic Air Polishers/Buffers
- Air Compressor
- Deck Brushes
- Telescoping Handles
- Stainless Steel Scrub Pads
- Commercial Power Washer
- Squeegees
- Mops
- Shop Vacuum
- Brooms
- Dustpan
- Scuff Eraser
- Tire Rim Cleaning Brush
- Enclosed 5 x 8 Trailer (for mobile service)

Supplies:
- Premium Boat Wax
- Marine Tallow

- Fiberglass and Non-Skid Deck Wax

- Aluminum Cleaner

- Marine Metal Polish/Restorer

- Corrosion Remover

- Heavy-Duty Oxidation Remover

- Microfiber Towels

- Fiberglass Reconditioner and Deoxidizer

- Speedcut Compound

- Marine Paste Compound

- Disposable Shop Towels

Hours of Operation

Triple B Boat Detailing typically will operate from 9 AM to 6 PM, Monday through Saturday, during the summer months, with limited off-season hours. Exceptions always will be made to accommodate customers' special needs. The business will offer expanded seasonal hours during the spring and fall, when customers prepare vessels for winter storage or summer operation.

LEGAL

Triple B Boat Detailing will maintain appropriate liability insurance policies. Coverage information will be available upon request, especially when performing services on-site at marinas and other businesses.

FINANCIAL ANALYSIS

After losing less than $1,000 during the business' first year of operations, Triple B Boat Detailing is projecting more than $13,000 in collective net profit by the end of year three. The Brown Brothers will provide the $50,000 in financial capital required to cover startup costs and cash flow, and expect to recoup their investment by the end of year four. Sam will invest $25,500 (51%), Alex will invest $14,500 (29%), and Caleb will invest $10,000 (20%).

Complete pro forma financial statements have been prepared for Triple B Boat Detailing and are available upon request. The following table provides an overview of key projections during the first three years of operations:

	2014	2015	2016
Sales			
Cleaning revenue	$243,180	$279,657	$321,606
Storage revenue	$ 19,980	$ 22,977	$ 26,424
Total revenue	**$263,160**	**$302,634**	**$348,030**
Expenses			
Marketing & advertising	$ 10,000	$ 12,000	$ 15,000
General/administrative	$ 500	$ 500	$ 500
Accounting/legal	$ 1,500	$ 1,500	$ 1,500
Office supplies	$ 625	$ 625	$ 625
Facility lease	$ 18,500	$ 18,500	$ 18,500
Equipment	$ 750	$ 750	$ 750
Supplies	$ 48,636	$ 55,931	$ 64,321
Business insurance	$ 2,025	$ 2,126	$ 2,232
Payroll	$ 80,000	$ 95,000	$115,000
Payroll taxes	$ 9,600	$ 11,400	$ 13,800
Contract labor	$ 79,872	$ 83,866	$ 88,059
Health insurance	$ 5,250	$ 5,500	$ 5,750
Postage	$ 1,850	$ 2,000	$ 2,150
Utilities	$ 2,000	$ 2,500	$ 3,000
Maintenance & repairs	$ 300	$ 400	$ 500
Telecommunications	$ 2,500	$ 2,500	$ 2,500
Total expenses	**$263,908**	**$295,098**	**$334,187**
Net income	**($ 748)**	**$ 7,536**	**$ 13,843**

Coffee Shop
Clockworks Coffee and Cafe

135 S. Main St.
Romeo, Michigan 48065

Zuzu Enterprises

Clockworks Coffee and Cafe is located in historic downtown Romeo, Michigan next to the town clock. It is an established business with a great reputation and is a perfect fit for new owners Jack and Linda Fredericks.

EXECUTIVE SUMMARY

Clockworks Coffee and Cafe is located in historic downtown Romeo, Michigan next to the town clock. The clock was donated by Gilbert Smith and erected in 1924 as a testimonial of his affection for his birthplace and has become a symbol of the city and its rich history. It is prominently displayed on the town website, the Chamber of Commerce website, local business directories, and the town library even has an annual coloring contest where kids of all ages color a cartoon version of the clock; the entries are displayed throughout town during the fall festival. This central location is perfect for a gathering place where people can come to eat, relax, study, and meet friends.

The cafe has been in operation since 2009 but was recently put on the market due to the unexpected death of the owner, "Mimi." New owners Jack and Linda Fredericks loved frequenting the place and are excited to continue the tradition of running this established business.

LOCATION

The Cafe is located in historic downtown Romeo, Michigan next to the town clock. The clock is a symbol for the town and receives a significant amount of publicity. It is also centrally located in the town and is convenient to other business, town offices, and the medical facility.

City

According to the 2010 census, the city of Romeo has a population of roughly 5,733 people. The city proper is only 2.7 square miles, but the small surrounding communities of Casco, Lenox, Columbus, Washington, and Romeo Townships greatly extend this area. There is a slow but steady population increase projected into the year 2040 and all types of households are experiencing population growth. A vast majority of people (91%) live in the same household as the same time last year.

Population and households	Census 2010	SEMCOG Dec 2013	SEMCOG 2040
Total population	**5,733**	**5,931**	**6,181**
Group quarters population	166	166	211
Household population	5,569	5,765	5,970
Housing units	2,478	2,479	—
Households (occupied units)	2,239	2,306	2,549
Residential vacancy rate	9.6%	7.0%	—
Average household size	2.49	2.50	2.34

Household types	Census 2000	Census 2010	Pct change 2000–2010
With seniors 65+	472	565	19.7%
Without seniors	1,504	1,674	11.3%
Two or more persons without children	747	906	21.3%
Live alone, 65+	218	225	3.2%
Live alone, under 65	331	365	10.3%
With children	680	743	9.3%
Total households	**1,976**	**2,239**	**13.3%**

Residence one year ago

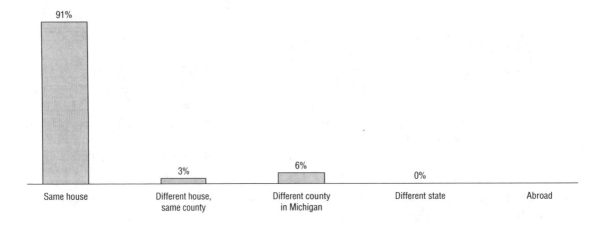

What this means to the cafe is that although the town itself it small, the surrounding areas contribute to the pool of potential customers. Romeo is at the center of these Townships and is seen as the hub and gathering place for businesses and services of all sorts. All of the areas are experiencing population growth, and, once here, people tend to stay. Potential customers become life-long customers.

Property Details

The property itself is a commercial property and consists of a 7,405 square foot lot with one structure. The building is two stories and features wood siding and a gable roof with asphalt shingles. The building was erected in 1947 but was refurbished in 2009, as was the roof. There are two bathrooms, a full basement, and forced air heating.

The property last sold in 2005 for $175,000 and an additional $30,000 worth of work was completed in 2009. The current assessed value is $57,000 with a market value of $195,000. When all appliances and furniture are factored into the value of the property, this number increases to $215,000. The property taxes on this equate to $3,152 per year. As market prices are slowly inching back up from the recent decline, this property is competitively priced with the potential to be worth significantly more in the next 10 years.

Atmosphere

The cafe has small-town charm and a warm, inviting atmosphere. The décor consists of an eclectic mixture of comfortable, overstuffed chairs, small one-to-two person tables, and a large gathering table with mismatched, yet coordinating seats. There is a gas fireplace in one corner that gets used often during the cold winter months. The colors are serene and the place has a laid-back vibe that encourages patrons to stay and relax.

COMPETITION

There is limited competition for the types of food and drinks we provide. Places that serve coffee nearby include:

Tim Horton's—Although close, Tim Horton's has long lines in morning and it is difficult to get out of parking lot on busy mornings due to traffic congestion. They do have a drive through window for convenience. Some people are turned off of this business because they do not participate in town activities or support local sports teams.

McDonalds—Coffee is known to be mediocre at best. It has a drive through window for convenience and inexpensive "senior" coffee.

Starbucks—The nearest Starbucks is approximately 30 minutes away. Although they do have a drive through, the distance from town does not make it a convenient option for most customers.

Panera—There is a Panera across the street from Starbucks. Again, this is approximately 30 minutes away from town and is therefore inconvenient. It does not have a drive through window.

HOURS OF OPERATION

The current hours of operation are Monday through Saturday from 8:00am until 9:00pm. Sunday hours are from 9:00am until 7:00pm. This is one area where we feel that change would be beneficial. We intend to open earlier to make it more convenient for people to get coffee on their way to work as well for parents who are dropping their kids off at the local schools. Our new hours will be Monday through Saturday from 6:30am until 9:00pm and Sunday from 7:00am until 7:00pm.

OPPORTUNITIES

We foresee many opportunities to expand our business and importance in the community. These opportunities are as follows:

- Our proximity to the Macomb Orchard Trail provides a unique opportunity to appeal to the cyclist crowd. We are exploring the possibility of sponsoring a race to be held on the trail and will appeal to the crowd by offering bike parking and tire repair tools to customers. We will explore the possibility of partnering with Hamilton Bikes for referral and additional services.

- The large, open upstairs room provides the opportunity to host private meetings for local organizations including PTA/PTO, Kiwanis, Masons, sports clubs/boards, and similar organizations.

- Offering free Wifi will appeal to younger customers as well as those with poor reception in the outlying rural areas.

- We will join the Chamber of Commerce and seek possible partnerships with local businesses and organizations. Possibilities include working with the local library to provide snacks and/or coffee for book clubs and other meetings and to serve foods made from ingredients sold at the local health foods store.

- The ample wall space throughout the facility provides a great place to display artwork and pottery as both decoration for the cafe as well as a display for local artisans looking to sell their work and local schools looking to display students' work.

- Cafe gift cards are a perfect gift for many occasions including appreciation days (teacher, secretary, etc.), holiday gifts, and contest prizes. Limited numbers of varying denominations will be provided to organizations and clubs seeking donations.

- Our location on the parade route is perfect for selling snacks and beverages for the fall festival.

- Drive through service would be relatively easy to accomplish using an existing window that can be retrofitted with a drive-through window. Some reconfiguration of the parking lot and landscaping will need to be done, but will not require a significant outlay of funds.

- "Senior" discounts may draw customers who are on a fixed income and who are used to frequenting other businesses that already offer the discount.

- A repeat customer rewards program would reward customers who routinely make purchases. Some kind of key tag with bar code/frequent buyer card would be utilized to track purchases and load rewards.

MENU

Drinks

Our drinks include a wide variety of hot and cold beverages. They consist of:

- Coffee
- Espresso
- Latte
- Caramel Latte
- Cappuccino
- Americano
- Red Eye
- Black Eye
- Cafe Mocha
- Hot cocoa
- Tea
- Iced coffee
- Iced tea
- Smoothies
- Frappe
- Soda pop
- Bottled water

Various flavorings, flavored creams, whipped cream, cream, half-n-half, soy milk, and almond milk are also options to add to the beverage choices to make each one unique and perfect for each individual customer.

Pastries

Our pastries are made in batches that try to anticipate and predict the daily need to ensure proper freshness.

- Bagels

- Scones

- Croissant

- Chocolate croissant

- Biscotti

- Muffins—blueberry crumble, lemon poppyseed, and pumpkin walnut.

- English muffins

Entrees

All entrees are available throughout the day. Breakfast sandwiches, salads, sandwiches, and paninis are made to order to ensure freshness and they are exactly what the customer wants. Limited quantities of the breakfast sandwich components (eggs and meat) are precooked and warmed in preparation for the busy morning rush to make sure those customers getting orders to go are served in a timely manner. Oatmeal and soups are made in batches and refreshed as necessary.

- Breakfast sandwiches—egg, cheese, and/or meat (sausage or bacon) on bagel, English muffin, or croissant

- Oatmeal

- Soup of the day

- Spinach and Strawberry Salad—Spinach, mozzarella, walnuts, strawberries, blueberries

- Michigan Salad—cherries, apples, goat cheese, pecans

- Antipasto Salad—Salami, turkey, ham, and cheese

- Sandwiches (various)

- Panini sandwiches (various)

Desserts

Desserts are made in batches that try to anticipate and predict the daily need to ensure proper freshness.

- Cheesecake

- Cookies—chocolate chip, No Bakes, oatmeal raisin, peanut butter

- Rice Krispie treats

- Shortbread

- Pound cake with fresh berries

- Brownies

- Lemon squares

REPUTATION

Clockworks Coffee and Cafe has an excellent reputation and a steady, established client base. Reviews on Facebook, Google, and Yelp are numerous and consistently glowing; the average rating is five out of five stars. While locals know about the Cafe, these reviews are great for encouraging new residents and those passing through for business or during one of the many recreational activities the town hosts. It is the intention of Jack and Linda Fredericks to uphold the level of service and quality of the wood and drinks to maintain this reputation.

FINANCIAL INFORMATION

Monthly Costs

Monthly fixed costs include such things as rent, taxes, and utilities and are detailed in the chart below.

Monthly fixed costs

Mortgage	$1,300
Taxes	$ 265
Phone/Wifi	$ 200
Utilities	$ 400
Insurance	$ 300
Salary	$2,000
Advertising	$ 100
Total	**$4,565**

Monthly variable costs include foodstuffs and hourly employee wages. These costs are broken down into an average per-transaction variable cost that is used to determine the break-even sales target as noted below.

Breakeven Analysis

Clockworks Coffee and Cafe will need to have roughly 28 transactions a day with an average sale of $8.00 per transaction. This equates to a daily sales goal of $224 to cover costs and break even. Additional sales would create profit.

Break even analysis

Break even analysis

Monthly transactions		830
Monthly sales	$	6,640
Assumptions		
Average per-transaction revenue	$	8.00
Average per-transaction variable cost	$	2.50
Estimated monthly fixed cost		$4,565.00

Current sales far exceed this goal. Opening earlier in the morning, providing the convenience of drive through service, and pursuing other opportunities as noted in this plan will only add to the bottom line and increase revenue.

Child Party Planning

PartyCentral Enterprises LLC

5789 Pinetree Pkwy.
Deerfield Springs, IL 50001

Paul Greenland

PartyCentral Enterprises specializes in planning birthday parties and other special celebrations for children.

EXECUTIVE SUMMARY

Business Overview

PartyCentral Enterprises specializes in planning birthday parties and other special celebrations for children. The business is being established as a part-time operation by Sarah Price. The mother of four children, Price worked as a wedding planner before leaving the field to be with her young children, now ages 7, 9, 13, and 17. Creative by nature, Price has gained a reputation for planning parties that are highly imaginative and fun for her children. She frequently is asked to assist with parties for friends and family members. Combined with her professional experience and love of children, this prompted her to establish her own children's party planning business.

PartyCentral Enterprises' main goal is to provide customers with the exact level of party planning support they need. In this regard, the business will offer two types of services: on-site party planning/ management and virtual/remote party planning. The full scope of services offered by the business will include (1) theme discovery and development, (2) pre-planning, and (3) party coordination and assistance, as outlined in the Services section of this plan.

MARKET ANALYSIS

PartyCentral Enterprises is located in the small community of Deerfield Springs, Illinois. Conveniently situated about 20 miles from Peoria, the business' primary service area will include both Deerfield Springs and Peoria. The target market for PartyCentral Enterprises' services will be children ages 14 and under, although teenage-oriented planning services will be offered for special birthdays and occasions (e.g., confirmations, graduations, 16th birthdays, etc.).

PartyCentral Enterprises' primary service area included approximately 47,740 households in 2013. This figure was expected to reach 48,911 by 2018. In 2013 nearly 20 percent of the population was under the age of 14. Individuals aged 0 to 4 accounted for 6.5 percent of the population, while those in the 5 to 14 age category accounted for 13 percent.

PartyCentral Enterprises will target its marketing initiatives toward households with income of $60,000 or more. In 2013, this represented about 41.2 percent of the market, broken down as follows:

- $60,000 and $74,999 (11%)

- $75,000—$99,999 (11.6%)

- $100,000—$124,999 (7.4%)

- $125,000—$149,999 (3.8%)

- More than $150,000 (7.4 %)

PERSONNEL

PartyCentral Enterprises is the brainchild of Sarah Price. The mother of four children, Price worked as a wedding planner before leaving the field to be with her young children, now ages 7, 9, 13, and 17. Creative by nature, Price has gained a reputation for planning parties that are highly imaginative and fun for her children. She frequently is asked to assist with parties for friends and family members. This, combined with her professional experience and love of children, prompted her to establish her own children's party planning business.

Sarah's teenage daughter, Maddie (a high school senior who plans to continue helping Sarah while attending a local community college), is available to serve as a helper (independent contractor) when necessary. In addition, Sarah's husband, Randy, is available to provide photography and videography services if desired.

Professional and Advisory Support

PartyCentral Enterprises will use a popular off-the-shelf accounting software application for bookkeeping purposes. Stanfield Accounting Inc., an accounting firm in Deerfield Springs, will provide assistance with quarterly/annual tax preparation. A commercial checking account has been established with Deerfield Springs Community Bank, which has agreed to provide the business with a merchant account so that credit card and debit card payments can be accepted. Legal services will be provided by Ken Kernberger, a local attorney who helped the business develop simple agreements to use with its customers.

BUSINESS STRATEGY

Sarah Price plans to achieve steady, measured growth for her new business and has identified the following targets for PartyCentral Enterprises' first three years of operations:

Year One: Establish PartyCentral Enterprises as a part-time operation. Build awareness about the business among parents in the local market. Begin by planning an average of four parties per month, generating gross revenues of $20,000.

Year Two: Transition to full-time operation. Emphasize virtual/remote planning services and growing the business via word-of-mouth advertising and referrals. Plan an average of 12 parties per month. Achieve gross revenues of $53,820.

Year Three: Use efficiencies gained from two years of operations experience to expand planning volume to an average of 18 parties per month (about two thirds of which will be virtual/remote in nature). Achieve revenues of $71,875.

Annual party volume

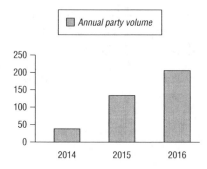

SERVICES

PartyCentral Enterprises' main goal is to provide customers with the exact level of party planning support they need. In this regard, the business will offer two types of services: on-site party planning/ management and virtual/remote party planning.

On-site services are limited to PartyCentral Enterprises' primary service area, as defined in the Market Analysis section of this plan.

Virtual/remote services are limited to plan development, and in some cases, ordering decorations from national suppliers. Customers using remote services are responsible for the actual execution and management of their child's party and making arrangements for any entertainment and/or rental equipment.

Some customers are in search of a planner who can coordinate and oversee every aspect of their child's party, from pre-planning to clean-up. In other cases, customers simply may want an outside opinion and/or assistance with specific aspects of their party. In any case, Sarah Price will utilize her planning skills, creativity, and relationships with suppliers, entertainers, and vendors to ensure an unforgettable party experience.

Service Packages

PartyCentral Enterprises will offer services at a rate of $50 per hour. However, by committing to a pre-bundled service package, customers can gain an additional hour of service at no charge. Sarah Price has developed the following three service packages:

1. The Party Starter ($200). This package will include five hours of service for the price of four.

2. The Prime Party ($300). This package will include seven hours of service for the price of six.

3. The Works ($500). This package will include 11 hours of service for the price of 10.

PROCESS

Following is a description of the party planning process that PartyCentral Enterprises follows with its customers (on-site services are not offered to virtual/remote customers).

1. Theme Discovery & Development

This initial phase involves identifying a specific theme for the party or celebration. Oftentimes, parents and their children know exactly what the theme will be. In other cases, they are in search of recommended possibilities. In either case, PartyCentral Enterprises will help families to identify a theme that everyone is excited about.

Thematic possibilities are endless, limited only by one's imagination. For example, Sarah Price was recently asked to assist a friend with a birthday party for a young boy who was fascinated by clocks. Although the theme was somewhat unusual, Sarah was able to create a fun experience by creating a "Party TIME " party, complete with a birthday cake that looked like the face of a clock, goody bags that included inexpensive wristwatches, "beat the clock" games, and more.

Potential birthday party themes include:

Themes
Transportation:

    Airplanes

    Boating

    Trains

    Trucks

    Rockets

    Racecars

    Tractors

Characters:

    Farmer/Barnyard

    Astronaut/Outer Space

    Robots

    Aliens

    Army Men

    Superheroes

    Cowboys

    Monsters

    Pirates

Fairytale:

    Knights

    Dragons

    Princess

    Butterfly Garden

    Neverland

    Tea Party

Sports:

    Bowling

    Sailing

    Golf

Camping

Swimming

Football

Baseball

Surfing

Soccer

Hockey

Basketball

Tennis

Volleyball

Objects:

Crayons

Kites

Jewelry

Candy

Entertainment:

Video Games

TV Shows

Cartoons

Movies

Creatures:

Dinosaurs

Dogs

Cats

Ducks

Bugs

Lions

Tigers

2. Pre-Planning

This phase preferably occurs at least 45—60 days prior to the party. PartyCentral Enterprises will maintain frequent communication with customers and develop a detailed plan with action items and target dates, discussing factors such as:

- Identifying desired attendees

- Choosing locations/making reservations

- Designing and sending invitations (including an RSVP date)

- Identifying/verifying availability of "VIP" guests (e.g., best friends)

- Booking entertainment and performing reference checks

- Arranging/coordinating photography and videography

- Identifying and planning fun games, crafts, and activities

- Renting/reserving attractions, equipment, and other amenities (e.g., cotton candy machines, popcorn machines, inflatable amusements, etc.)

- Choosing/ordering food, beverages, and supplies (e.g., napkins, plates, disposable silverware, etc.)

- Designing/ordering birthday cake

- Identifying/purchasing party favors

- Purchasing decorations

3. Party Coordination & Assistance

Finally, PartyCentral Enterprises provides much-needed assistance immediately before and the day of the big event. For on-site customers, Sarah Price will function as the event coordinator, ensuring that everything falls into place. This will begin with a prearranged visit to the party location one to three days before the big event to assist with arrangements. On the day of the party, Sarah will arrive one to three hours before guests (based on customer needs/expectations). Depending on the number of attendees, Sarah's teenage daughter, Maddie (a high school senior), is available to serve as a helper. In addition, her husband, Randy, is available to provide photography and videography services if desired. During this phase, PartyCentral Enterprises will:

- Assist with room/party space arrangement and configuration

- Arrange balloons and decorations

- Verify/coordinate the delivery of food and supplies

- Manage equipment vendors and entertainment

- Supervise games and activities

- Compile a gift list as presents are opened

- Help with cleanup activities if needed

- Develop, prepare and send thank-you cards

MARKETING & SALES

A marketing plan has been developed for PartyCentral Enterprises that includes these main tactics:

1. **Logo/Identity:** A local graphic designer has been hired to develop a unique logo for PartyCentral Enterprises.

2. **Web Site:** PartyCentral Enterprises has developed a basic Web site that lists information about Sarah Price and the services she offers. In addition to photos and video clips from successful parties, the site also will include details about prices, policies, contact information, and FAQs. An online calendar tool will allow customers to check Sarah's availability months in advance. The site will include links to social media outlets like Facebook, YouTube, and Pinterest. In order to keep costs low, Sarah Price has made a barter arrangement with a local Web designer, exchanging party planning services for two of the designer's children in exchange for initial site development.

3. **Social Media:** PartyCentral Enterprises will rely upon Pinterest, YouTube, and Facebook to visually show prospective customers examples of the party experiences Sarah Price helps to create. Release forms will be obtained from customers and the parents of party attendees any time pictures or

video clips are used on social media outlets. Sarah Price's daughter will provide assistance with setting up and monitoring social media accounts.

4. **Promotional Flier:** A four-color flier, targeted toward parents of young children, has been developed. This printed piece can be used for direct mailings, left behind, or posted at various public places. A local printer with a digital press can produce these in small quantities as needed, avoiding large print runs associated with a traditional offset press.

5. **Presentations:** Each quarter, Sarah Price will make at least one presentation to local parenting/ moms groups in the community, providing tips on successful party planning. She will leave behind flyers regarding PartyCentral Enterprises following her presentations. A schedule of planned presentations during the first year has been developed and is available upon request.

6. **Word-of-Mouth Marketing:** PartyCentral Enterprises will rely heavily upon word-of-mouth marketing to promote the business. To encourage referrals among family and friends, Sarah Price will offer a 15 percent discount off a customer's next booking if they make a successful referral. In addition, the discount will apply to the referred customer as well.

Sarah Price will evaluate the marketing plan for PartyCentral Enterprises on a semi-annual basis.

OPERATIONS

Hours

PartyCentral Enterprises will maintain variable hours in order to meet the needs of its owner and customers. Sarah Price will respond to all phone calls, e-mails, and Web site inquiries from customers within one business day.

Rates

PartyCentral Enterprises bases its fee on a rate of $50 per hour, but offers a slight discount to customers who buy a pre-defined service package, as outlined in the Services section of this plan.

Payment

A detailed estimate will be provided to all customers, who will be required to pay for 50 percent of the estimated balance in advance. Advance payment for all equipment rentals and entertainment services also will be required. In addition to cash, PartyCentral Enterprises will accept debit/credit card payments and money orders. Payments can be made via the business' Web site, by phone, or in person.

Facility and Location

PartyCentral Enterprises will operate as a home-based business at Sarah Price's residence. Sarah will utilize dedicated space within her home as office space. A home-office insurance rider will be obtained.

FINANCIAL ANALYSIS

Sarah Price is projecting that PartyCentral Enterprises will break even during its first year, generating a nominal profit of $375. The business is expected to generate collective net profits of nearly $10,500 by its third year of operation. Sarah will draw a nominal salary during the first year, in order to keep operating expenses low.

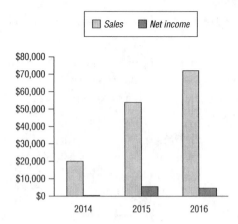

Complete pro forma financial statements have been prepared for PartyCentral Enterprises and are available upon request. The following table provides an overview of key projections during the first three years of operations:

	2014	2015	2016
Sales	**$20,000**	**$53,820**	**$71,875**
Expenses			
Marketing & advertising	$ 5,000	$ 5,000	$ 5,000
General/administrative	$ 500	$ 500	$ 500
Accounting/legal	$ 600	$ 600	$ 600
Office supplies	$ 475	$ 475	$ 475
Equipment	$ 750	$ 750	$ 750
Business insurance	$ 450	$ 450	$ 450
Payroll	$ 7,500	$30,000	$45,000
Payroll taxes	$ 900	$ 3,600	$ 5,400
Contract labor	$ 1,500	$ 4,000	$ 6,000
Postage	$ 1,000	$ 2,000	$ 2,150
Telecommunications	$ 950	$ 950	$ 950
Total expenses	**$19,625**	**$48,325**	**$67,275**
Net income	**$ 375**	**$ 5,495**	**$ 4,600**

Chimney Sweep

Chimneys By Charlie Inc.

14 Main St.
White Plains, NY 10600

Paul Greenland

Chimneys By Charlie is a "chimney sweep" business that provides chimney inspections and evaluations; chimney sweeping/fireplace cleaning; and chimney repair.

EXECUTIVE SUMMARY

Each year, there are roughly 25,000 residential fires attributed to fireplaces, chimneys, and solid fuel appliances. These result from the accumulation of creosote, a residue from wood-burning smoke. Chimney fires cause hundreds of millions of dollars in property damage. Annual chimney inspections prevent chimney fires, as well as the risk of carbon monoxide poisoning. Other chimney-related problems result from deterioration and/or structural flaws.

Chimneys By Charlie is a "chimney sweep" business that provides chimney inspections and evaluations; chimney sweeping/fireplace cleaning; and chimney repair. The business, located in White Plains, New York, is being established by Charlie Benson, a veteran who recently received an honorable discharge after eight years in the U.S. Army. Chimney and fireplace cleaning is a seasonal business, and Benson anticipates that 42 percent of business volume will occur during the winter. He is projecting gross revenues of $132,181 during the first year, and $163,187 by year three.

MARKET ANALYSIS

White Plains Housing Analysis

According to demographic data for the White Plains market, the community is comprised of approximately 24,500 housing units, 96 percent of which are occupied. Of these, 50 percent are owner-occupied properties. About 80 percent of area homes have a value of more than $200,000:

- $200,000-$249,999 (10.1%)

- $250,000-$299,999 (8.4%)

- $300,000-$399,999 (15.0%)

- $400,000-$499,999 (14.5%)

- $500,000-$749,999 (24.3%)

- $750,000-$999,999 (7.8%)

- $1,000,000+ (4.0%)

Competition

Chimneys By Charlie will face off against several established local competitors, including:

1. A-1 Chimney Sweep

2. Ballard Chimney Service

3. Longwood Chimney Maintenance

4. Gordon Brothers Chimney Co.

5. Rockwood Heating & Air Conditioning Inc.

Benson has conducted research regarding each potential competitor. Information was obtained by making phone calls to each business in order to learn about their rates, years in business, ownership, certifications/licenses, etc. Additionally, Benson requested references and also evaluated online sites such as Angie's List to gauge how satisfied local customers are with each business.

While conducting his research Benson learned that the Gordon family is planning to close Gordon Brothers Chimney Co. in the near future. Many customers have expressed dissatisfaction with the quality of work and customer service offered by Ballard Chimney Service. Additionally, Rockwood Heating & Air Conditioning offers chimney cleaning as a secondary service, focusing mainly on heating and air conditioning. Therefore, Benson's main competitors will be A-1 Chimney Sweep and Longwood Chimney Maintenance.

INDUSTRY ANALYSIS

According to a 2012 survey from the National Chimney Sweep Guild and the Chimney Safety Institute of America, there are approximately 5,000 companies in the industry, generating annual revenue of nearly $2.19 billion. Annual sales for industry businesses range between $182,000 and $521,000. The investment needed to start a chimney sweep business is low, and about 60 percent of industry players entered the field by establishing their own company. According to the survey, 31 percent of respondents had only one employee, 28 percent had two employees, 35 percent had between 2.5 and 10 employees, and 8 percent had more than 10 employees.

BUSINESS STRATEGY

Chimneys By Charlie is a seasonal business, with the majority of work occurring during the colder winter months. Based on prior experience and industry research, Benson expects that 42 percent of business volume will occur during the winter, followed by the fall (41%), spring (10%), and summer (7%).

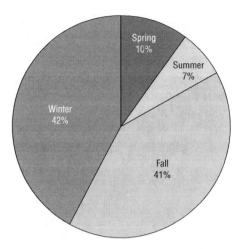

The following annual targets have been established for the first three years of operations:

2014: Focus on establishing Chimneys By Charlie in the White Plains market and developing relationships with new customers. Become a Better Business Bureau member. Purchase related education materials and prepare for the CSIA Certified Chimney Sweep exam. Achieve first-year revenue of $132,181 and net income of $27,411.

2015: Invest in high-tech fiber-optic camera and light technology, adding the capability to provide more comprehensive/advanced inspections. Earn the CSIA Certified Chimney Sweep credential from the Chimney Safety Institute of America. Increase revenue more than 10 percent (target of $146,868) and generate net income of $30,880.

2016: Hire a part-time seasonal (November-January) technician to accommodate increased volume. Increase revenue more than 10 percent (target of $163,187) and generate net income of $14,016. Utilize accumulated net income from the first three years of operations for potential expansion during years four and five (addition of a second service van and full-time technician to service a wider geographic market). Make preparations to begin selling and servicing gas fireplace logs to generate additional revenue.

PERSONNEL

Charlie Benson, Owner

Charlie Benson is a veteran who recently received an honorable discharge after eight years in the U.S. Army. A natural problem solver who enjoys working with people, Benson obtained some chimney maintenance-related experience in the military, but also worked as a part-time seasonal employee for a chimney sweep before he entered the service. Sensing a good opportunity, he is ready to apply these skills in the marketplace and build his own business from the ground up. Benson is seeking to establish a business that will allow him to spend time with his family during the warmer months, because his wife is a school teacher who does not work during the summertime.

Professional & Advisory Support

Chimneys By Charlie has established a business banking account with Central Community Bank, including a merchant account for accepting credit card payments. Tax advisement is provided by Weathers & Plank Accounting Inc. Benson worked with a local attorney to incorporate his business.

SERVICES

Overview

All customers are provided with an accurate time and cost estimate prior to any services being performed. Chimney inspections often require rooftop access, although cleaning typically is done from within the home. Chimneys By Charlie takes great effort to ensure that customer homes remain clean during and immediately after the chimney cleaning process. This involves the placement of tarps in the immediate cleaning area, and vacuuming/dusting as appropriate following cleanings.

When cleaning, Benson will use tools such as a high-powered vacuum, special lights, and rods of varying lengths, to which wire brushes and various attachments are affixed. For safety purposes he will wear protective clothing, use a respirator to protect his lungs, and wear goggles to protect his eyes. Heavy creosote buildup in chimneys often requires a chemical application and more than one visit to complete the cleaning.

When Chimneys By Charlie begins operations, the business will offer the following services:

I. Chimney Inspections & Evaluations (level I, II, or III depending on complexity)
Inspections will be billed at a rate of $75 per hour (one-hour minimum).

II. Chimney Sweeping/Fireplace Cleaning ($150; $75 2nd flue)
For cleaning a minimum fee will be charged (two-hour minimum).

III. Chimney Repairs ($75 per hour labor/plus material costs)
- Crown resurfacing/rebuilding
- Damper repair/replacement
- Custom and Standard Chimney Caps and Dampers
- Bird & Animal Guards
- Firebox Repairs
- Tuckpointing
- Chimney Waterproofing & Sealing
- Chimney Relining
- Dryer Vent and Furnace Flue Cleaning and Relining

Chimneys By Charlie plans to add gas fireplace log sales and service during the third year.

MARKETING & SALES

Chimneys By Charlie has developed a marketing plan that includes the following primary tactics:

1. A Web site with an extensive listing of services provided, a profile of Charlie Benson, and an online service request form that gives prospective customers the ability to submit a service request at any time. The site will include information about all certifications, insurance coverage, and licenses.

2. Magnetic business cards (e.g., refrigerator magnets) that can be left behind with customers, and also distributed at home shows and other events.

3. A color flyer with an extensive listing of services provided and details regarding all certifications, insurance coverage, and licenses. This can be used for distribution at home shows, special events, and also for promotional mailings.

4. Membership in the White Plains Chamber of Commerce.

5. Participation in home shows and other special events.

6. A social media strategy involving Angie's List and Facebook, with a goal of generating new business and building/maintaining positive word-of-mouth.

7. A customer referral program, providing existing clients with a 10 percent project discount for every referral.

8. Local radio advertising during the cold winter months.

9. Local print advertising during the cold winter months.

10. Participation in local safety fairs in coordination with the local fire department, EMS professionals, hospitals, and law enforcement.

11. Submission of seasonal press releases/guest columns to local media with chimney safety tips, helping to generate free exposure for the business.

12. A Yellow Page listing.

OPERATIONS

Location

Charlie Benson will operate Chimneys By Charlie from his home residence. He has allotted a small space to utilize as a home office, and will park his service van in his home garage. Benson's home office will include a dedicated business telephone line, as well as a personal computer, desk, and filing cabinet.

Fees

Chimneys By Charlie typically charges for services at a rate of $75 per hour.

Insurance

A liability insurance policy has been obtained to cover the scope of services provided.

Equipment

Chimneys By Charlie will require the following equipment at start-up, which Charlie Benson will cover from personal savings (with the exception of the van, for which a vehicle loan has been obtained):

- Rod and Brush Caddy $59.95

- Ash Vacuum $109.95

- Fireplace Cover $59.95

- Steel Rods $32.95

- Glaze Removal Chains $74.95

- Scraping Tool $49.95

- Curved Handle Wire Brush $4.95

- Poly Brushes (Metal Pipe Chimneys) & Wire Brushes (Masonry/Cement Chimneys)—8" Brush $24.95

- Poly Brushes (Metal Pipe Chimneys) & Wire Brushes (Masonry/Cement Chimneys)—12" Brush $29.95

- Poly Brushes (Metal Pipe Chimneys) & Wire Brushes (Masonry/Cement Chimneys)—16" Brush $34.95

- Ladder drop-down rack with lowering/raising mechanism $899

- Carhartt Flannel Lined Pants & Jacket $150

- 2008 Chevrolet Express Cargo Van $15,000

- Vehicle Graphic Panels $1,500

- Respirator $100

- Goggles $25

A Fiber-optic Inspection Camera will be purchased during the second year at a cost of $1,250.

Hours of Operation

Chimneys By Charlie will typically provide services Monday through Friday, from 7 AM to 6 PM. However, during periods of high seasonal activity, Benson will work Monday through Saturday, as determined by demand/customer requirements. The business will be closed on the following major holidays:

- Christmas Day

- Christmas Eve

- July 4

- Labor Day

- Memorial Day

- New Year's Day

- Thanksgiving Day

FINANCIAL ANALYSIS

The following table shows Chimneys by Charlie's projected monthly revenue for the first three years of operations (2014-2016):

Year	January	February	March	April	May	June
2014	$15,779	$ 8,496	$6,069	$3,641	$3,034	$3,034
2015	$17,532	$ 9,441	$6,743	$4,046	$3,372	$3,372
2016	$19,481	$10,490	$7,493	$4,496	$3,746	$3,746

Year	July	August	September	October	November	December
2014	$3,034	$3,034	$12,138	$18,207	$24,276	$31,437
2015	$3,372	$3,372	$13,487	$20,230	$26,973	$34,930
2016	$3,746	$3,746	$14,985	$22,478	$29,970	$38,811

Based on these monthly projections, steady annual revenue growth is anticipated for Chimneys By Charlie during the business' first three years. The owner anticipates that the business will be profitable during the first year. Although profits are projected to increase during the second year, they are expected to be slightly lower during year three due to the addition and training of a part-time employee, which is necessary to position the business for expansion during years four and five.

The following graph illustrates revenue and net income projections for 2014-2016:

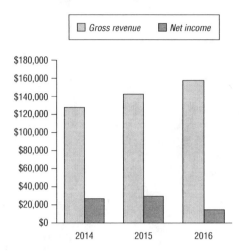

EVALUATION & ADJUSTMENT

This plan will be evaluated annually during the first three years of operations.

Comic Book Publisher

Perkins Publishing, Inc.

PO Box 12345
New York, NY 10012

BizPlanDB.com

The purpose of this business plan is to raise $250,000 for the development of a comic book publishing business while showcasing the expected financials and operations over the next three years. Perkins Publishing, Inc. ("the Company") is a New York-based corporation that will distribute produced and illustrated comic books, sourced from U.S.-based authors, on a nationwide basis. The Company was founded by Chris Perkins.

1.0 EXECUTIVE SUMMARY

The purpose of this business plan is to raise $250,000 for the development of a comic book publishing business while showcasing the expected financials and operations over the next three years. Perkins Publishing, Inc. ("the Company") is a New York-based corporation that will distribute produced and illustrated comic books, sourced from U.S.-based authors, on a nationwide basis. The Company was founded by Chris Perkins.

1.1 The Services

Perkins Publishing will specialize in sourcing manuscripts from up and coming comic book writers with the intent to sell them as hard copy comic books, soft copy comic books, e-books, and other forms of content distribution. The business will generate income from the wholesale distribution of items to booksellers as well as generating retail income from the direct sale of printed comic books/e-books to the general public.

The third section of the business plan will further describe the services offered by Perkins Publishing.

1.2 Financing

Mr. Perkins is seeking to raise $250,000 from a bank loan. The interest rate and loan agreement are to be further discussed during negotiation. This business plan assumes that the business will receive a 10 year loan with a 9% fixed interest rate. The financing will be used for the following:

- Development of the Company's office location.

- Financing for the first six months of operation.

- Capital for financing a marketing campaign to increase visibility of Perkins Publishing.

Mr. Perkins will contribute $50,000 to the venture.

1.3 Mission Statement

The mission of Perkins Publishing is to develop and distribute new comic books and visual novels (and related materials) that will captivate audiences.

1.4 Management Team

The Company was founded by Chris Perkins. Mr. Perkins has more than 10 years of experience in the publishing industry. Through his expertise, he will be able to bring the operations of the business to profitability within its first year of operations.

1.5 Sales Forecasts

Mr. Perkins expects a strong rate of growth at the start of operations. Below are the expected financials over the next three years.

Proforma profit and loss (yearly)

Year	1	2	3
Sales	$1,144,410	$1,373,292	$1,606,752
Operating costs	$ 743,671	$ 776,695	$ 810,643
EBITDA	$ 116,184	$ 255,130	$ 396,592
Taxes, interest, and depreciation	$ 83,851	$ 127,410	$ 180,138
Net profit	$ 32,332	$ 127,720	$ 216,454

Sales, operating costs, and profit forecast

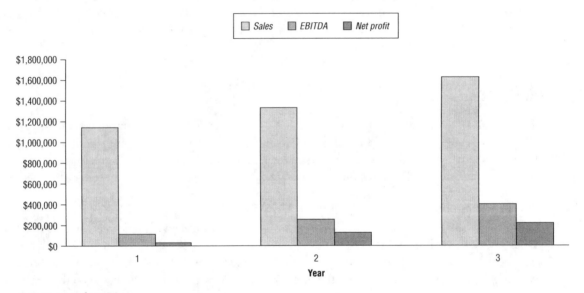

1.6 Expansion Plan

As time progresses, Perkins Publishing intends to continue to build its marketing reach by developing and expanding its presence on the Internet. The business will also acquire relationships with U.S.-based and international distributors that will purchase and distribute the Company's comic books to large scale metropolitan markets.

2.0 COMPANY AND FINANCING SUMMARY

2.1 Registered Name and Corporate Structure

The Company is registered as a corporation in the State of New York.

2.2 Required Funds

At this time, Perkins Publishing requires $250,000 of debt funds. Below is a breakdown of how these funds will be used:

Projected startup costs

Initial lease payments and deposits	$ 20,000
Working capital	$ 50,000
FF&E	$ 30,000
Leasehold improvements	$ 17,500
Security deposits	$ 15,000
Insurance	$ 12,500
Capital for running six comic books	$100,000
Marketing budget	$ 50,000
Miscellaneous and unforeseen costs	$ 5,000
Total startup costs	**$300,000**

Use of funds

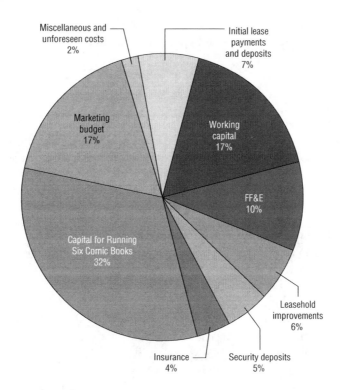

2.3 Investor Equity

Mr. Perkins is not seeking an investment from a third party at this time.

2.4 Management Equity

Chris Perkins owns 100% of Perkins Publishing, Inc.

2.5 Exit Strategy

If the business is very successful, Mr. Perkins may seek to sell the business to a third party for a significant earnings multiple. Most likely, the Company will hire a qualified business broker to sell the business on behalf of Perkins Publishing. Based on historical numbers, the business could fetch a sales premium of up to 7 times earnings.

3.0 PRODUCTS AND SERVICES

Below is a description of the content produced and distributed by Perkins Publishing, Inc.

3.1 Production of Comic Books

As stated in the executive summary, Perkins Publishing will actively solicit manuscripts from independent comic book writers, illustrators, as well as literary agents. Once reviewed and accepted, these books will be edited, printed, and distributed to major distribution platforms such as retail stores as well as through online retailers such as Amazon.com. The business will also sell directly to small comic book shops.

3.2 Online Content and Advertising Sales

In addition to maintaining extensive print operations for the comic books produced by the business, the business will also have an online platform, which will feature a number of articles, interviews, and reviews that are related to the comic books (and related characters) that have been published by the Company.

The Company's website will also feature a number of proprietary banner ad programs that Perkins Publishing will use to generate additional revenues for the business. These revenues are accumulated on a per 1000 visitor basis, and typically a website can expect to generate approximately $2 to $5 per advertising unit (1000 visitors).

4.0 STRATEGIC AND MARKET ANALYSIS

4.1 Economic Outlook

This section of the analysis will detail the economic climate, the general and comic book publishing industry, the customer profile, and the competition that the business will face as it progresses through its business operations.

Currently, the economic market condition in the United States is moderate. Unemployment rates have declined while asset prices (such as equities and real estate) have increased significantly. However, the low pricing points of the comic books sold by the business will ensure that the business is able to remain profitable and cash flow positive at all times.

4.2 Industry Analysis

There are approximately 2,900 book and magazine publishers in the United States. The last economic census indicates that the industry generates gross receipts in excess of $22 billion dollars a year. Publishers also employ more than 91,000 people, and provide average annual payrolls of $3.7 billion dollars. This trend is expected to increase as the number of writers that are opting to use self publishing services is increasing. The Internet has allowed many writers that would not normally have access to self-publishing businesses, the ability to print and sell copies of their work as they are ordered.

The industry has also changed significantly because of the Internet. There are now a number of magazines that operate solely through online media content. Perkins Publishing, Inc. intends to fully engage and embrace the Internet as an additional source of readership and advertising sales.

4.3 Customer Profile

As each new book published by the business is unique, it is difficult to develop an extensive demographic profile of people that will read publications produced by the business. This creates an immense demographic and potential market for readers. However, Management has developed a number of demographics of the expected target audience for the market:

• Has annual income in excess of $40,000 per year

• Is college educated or has some college education

- Lives within 50 miles of a major metropolitan statistical area

- Has an extreme interest in comic books and superheroes

- Spends $25 to $100 per month on comic book related items.

This broad set of demographics will allow Management to develop marketing campaigns for advertisers that are seeking to reach a specific demographic of readers. Once the business begins active publication of comic books, the business will begin an extensive data mining campaign which will further refine the demographics used by Perkins Publishing when determining which new pieces of literature are economically viable.

4.4 Competition

There are a number of major comic book publishers within the United States including Marvel Comics and DC Comics. However, among comic book and graphic novel enthusiasts, there is a tremendous demand for new comic books that feature new characters and story lines. As such, Perkins Publishing, with the correct marketing will be able to easily penetrate its market with its line of published books and graphic novels.

5.0 MARKETING PLAN

Perkins Publishing intends to maintain an extensive marketing campaign that will ensure maximum visibility for its publications in its targeted market. Below is an overview of the marketing strategies and objectives of the Company.

5.1 Marketing Objectives

- Frequently attend large scale comic conventions such as Comic Con and SXSW in order to promote content published by the Company.

- Establish relationships with advertising agencies and marketing firms that are seeking to target the demographics of the Company's readership.

5.2 Marketing Strategies

Management intends to use a number of marketing and sales strategies so that Perkins Publishing's operations can reach its intended audience. This campaign will include the use of traditional print and media advertising as well as the Internet. The business will also use several promotional strategies including large scale kick-off and comic book signing/launch events that will attract a significant amount of publicity.

Publicity activities will be designed to generate ongoing coverage about the Company and its associated writers and illustrators in targeted media by providing writers and editors with newsworthy releases, features, stories, briefs, and visual material for their columns. In depth coverage may also be obtained about the Company by hosting in-house interviews to be conducted by Mr. Perkins.

Timely coverage of Perkins Publishing (and its related publications) will be further directed through ongoing press relations and news releases.

5.3 Pricing

The cost of each comic book on a retail basis will be $2.50 to $5.00 depending on the size of the publication. On the Company's online website, the business will generate $2 to $5 per thousand impressions. Perkins Publishing, Inc. will generate aggregate gross margins of 75%.

6.0 ORGANIZATIONAL PLAN AND PERSONNEL SUMMARY

6.1 Corporate Organization

6.2 Organizational Budget

Personnel plan—yearly

Year	1	2	3
Senior management	$ 75,000	$ 77,250	$ 79,568
Editorial and writing staff	$225,000	$231,750	$238,703
Copywriters	$112,500	$115,875	$119,351
Accountant	$ 35,000	$ 36,050	$ 37,132
Administrative	$ 82,500	$ 84,975	$ 87,524
Total	**$530,000**	**$545,900**	**$562,277**

Numbers of personnel

Senior management	1	1	1
Editorial and writing staff	5	5	5
Copywriters	3	3	3
Accountant	1	1	1
Administrative	3	3	3
Totals	**13**	**13**	**13**

Personnel expense breakdown

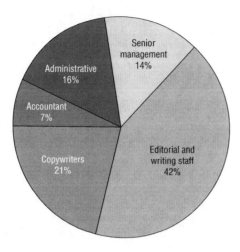

7.0 FINANCIAL PLAN

7.1 Underlying Assumptions

The Company has based its proforma financial statements on the following:

* Perkins Publishing will have an annual revenue growth rate of 16% per year.

* The Owner will acquire $250,000 of debt funds to develop the business.

* The loan will have a 10-year term with a 9% interest rate.

7.2 Sensitivity Analysis

Perkins Publishing's revenues are sensitive to the overall condition of the economic markets. Books are nonessential items, and in the event of economic recession, Management does expect that there will be a slight decline in gross revenues. However, the prices of media, magazine, books, videos, and related items has remained relatively price inelastic, and as such, the Company does not feel that it would have to significantly lower price in order to maintain sales levels.

7.3 Source of Funds

Financing

Equity contributions	
Management investment	$ 50,000.00
Total equity financing	**$ 50,000.00**
Banks and lenders	
Banks and lenders	$ 250,000.00
Total debt financing	**$250,000.00**
Total financing	**$300,000.00**

7.4 General Assumptions

General assumptions

Year	1	2	3
Short term interest rate	9.5%	9.5%	9.5%
Long term interest rate	10.0%	10.0%	10.0%
Federal tax rate	33.0%	33.0%	33.0%
State tax rate	5.0%	5.0%	5.0%
Personnel taxes	15.0%	15.0%	15.0%

7.5 Profit and Loss Statements

Proforma profit and loss (yearly)

Year	1	2	3
Sales	**$1,144,410**	**$1,373,292**	**$1,606,752**
Cost of goods sold	$ 284,556	$ 341,467	$ 399,517
Gross margin	75.14%	75.14%	75.14%
Operating income	**$ 859,854**	**$1,031,825**	**$1,207,235**
Expenses			
Payroll	$ 530,000	$ 545,900	$ 562,277
General and administrative	$ 25,200	$ 26,208	$ 27,256
Marketing and sales commission costs	$ 34,332	$ 41,199	$ 48,203
Professional fees and licensure	$ 15,000	$ 15,450	$ 15,914
Insurance costs	$ 12,500	$ 13,125	$ 13,781
Distribution costs	$ 17,166	$ 20,599	$ 24,101
Rent and utilities	$ 24,250	$ 25,463	$ 26,736
Miscellaneous costs	$ 5,722	$ 6,866	$ 8,034
Payroll taxes	$ 79,500	$ 81,885	$ 84,342
Total operating costs	**$ 743,671**	**$ 776,695**	**$ 810,643**
EBITDA	**$ 116,184**	**$ 255,130**	**$ 396,592**
Federal income tax	$ 38,341	$ 77,484	$ 124,714
State income tax	$ 5,809	$ 11,740	$ 18,896
Interest expense	$ 21,844	$ 20,328	$ 18,671
Depreciation expenses	$ 17,857	$ 17,857	$ 17,857
Net profit	**$ 32,332**	**$ 127,720**	**$ 216,454**
Profit margin	**2.83%**	**9.30%**	**13.47%**

Sales, operating costs, and profit forecast

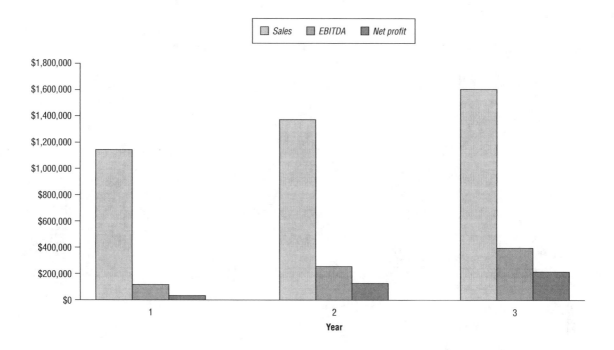

7.6 Cash Flow Analysis

Proforma cash flow analysis—yearly

Year	1	2	3
Cash from operations	$ 50,190	$145,577	$234,311
Cash from receivables	$ 0	$ 0	$ 0
Operating cash inflow	**$ 50,190**	**$145,577**	**$234,311**
Other cash inflows			
Equity investment	$ 50,000	$ 0	$ 0
Increased borrowings	$250,000	$ 0	$ 0
Sales of business assets	$ 0	$ 0	$ 0
A/P increases	$ 37,902	$ 43,587	$ 50,125
Total other cash inflows	**$337,902**	**$ 43,587**	**$ 50,125**
Total cash inflow	**$388,092**	**$189,164**	**$284,437**
Cash outflows			
Repayment of principal	$ 16,158	$ 17,674	$ 19,322
A/P decreases	$ 24,897	$ 29,876	$ 35,852
A/R increases	$ 0	$ 0	$ 0
Asset purchases	$250,000	$ 36,394	$ 58,578
Dividends	$ 35,133	$101,904	$164,018
Total cash outflows	**$326,188**	**$185,849**	**$277,780**
Net cash flow	**$ 61,903**	**$ 3,315**	**$ 6,657**
Cash balance	**$ 61,903**	**$ 65,219**	**$ 71,876**

Proforma cash flow (yearly)

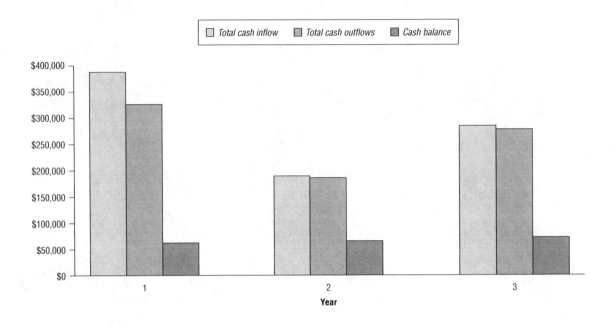

7.7 Balance Sheet

Proforma balance sheet—yearly

Year	1	2	3
Assets			
Cash	$ 61,908	$ 65,219	$ 71,876
Amortized development/expansion costs	$120,000	$123,639	$129,497
Intellectual property portfolio	$100,000	$118,197	$147,486
FF&E	$ 30,000	$ 44,558	$ 67,989
Accumulated depreciation	($ 17,857)	($ 35,714)	($ 53,571)
Total assets	**$294,046**	**$315,899**	**$363,277**
Liabilities and equity			
Accounts payable	$ 13,005	$ 26,716	$ 40,990
Long term liabilities	$233,842	$216,167	$198,493
Other liabilities	$ 0	$ 0	$ 0
Total liabilities	**$246,847**	**$242,883**	**$239,483**
Net worth	**$ 47,200**	**$ 73,016**	**$123,794**
Total liabilities and equity	**$294,046**	**$315,899**	**$363,277**

Proforma balance sheet

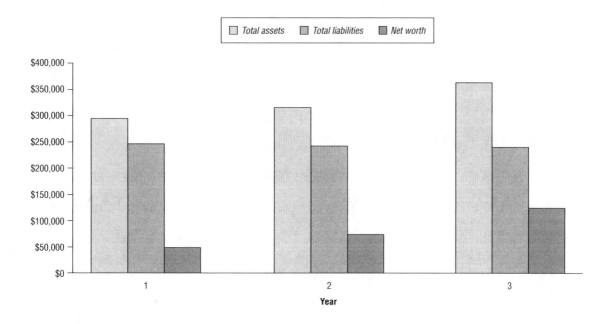

7.8 Breakeven Analysis

Monthly break even analysis

Year	1	2	3
Monthly revenue	$ 82,481	$ 86,144	$ 89,909
Yearly revenue	$989,777	$1,033,731	$1,078,913

Break even analysis

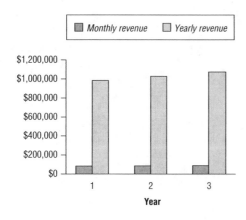

7.9 Business Ratios

Business ratios—yearly

Year	1	2	3
Sales			
Sales growth	0.0%	20.0%	17.0%
Gross margin	75.1%	75.1%	75.1%
Financials			
Profit margin	2.83%	9.30%	13.47%
Assets to liabilities	1.19	1.30	1.52
Equity to liabilities	0.19	0.30	0.52
Assets to equity	6.23	4.33	2.93
Liquidity			
Acid test	0.25	0.27	0.30
Cash to assets	0.21	0.21	0.20

7.10 Three Year Profit and Loss Statement

Profit and loss statement (first year)

Months	1	2	3	4	5	6	7
Sales	**$94,350**	**$94,535**	**$94,720**	**$94,905**	**$95,090**	**$95,275**	**$95,460**
Cost of goods sold	$23,460	$23,506	$23,552	$23,598	$23,644	$23,690	$23,736
Gross margin	75.1%	75.1%	75.1%	75.1%	75.1%	75.1%	75.1%
Operating income	**$70,890**	**$71,029**	**$71,168**	**$71,307**	**$71,446**	**$71,585**	**$71,724**
Expenses							
Payroll	$44,167	$44,167	$44,167	$44,167	$44,167	$44,167	$44,167
General and administrative	$ 2,100	$ 2,100	$ 2,100	$ 2,100	$ 2,100	$ 2,100	$ 2,100
Marketing and sales commission costs	$ 2,861	$ 2,861	$ 2,861	$ 2,861	$ 2,861	$ 2,861	$ 2,861
Professional fees and licensure	$ 1,250	$ 1,250	$ 1,250	$ 1,250	$ 1,250	$ 1,250	$ 1,250
Insurance costs	$ 1,042	$ 1,042	$ 1,042	$ 1,042	$ 1,042	$ 1,042	$ 1,042
Distribution costs	$ 1,431	$ 1,431	$ 1,431	$ 1,431	$ 1,431	$ 1,431	$ 1,431
Rent and utilities	$ 2,021	$ 2,021	$ 2,021	$ 2,021	$ 2,021	$ 2,021	$ 2,021
Miscellaneous costs	$ 477	$ 477	$ 477	$ 477	$ 477	$ 477	$ 477
Payroll taxes	$ 6,625	$ 6,625	$ 6,625	$ 6,625	$ 6,625	$ 6,625	$ 6,625
Total operating costs	**$61,973**	**$61,973**	**$61,973**	**$61,973**	**$61,973**	**$61,973**	**$61,973**
EBITDA	**$ 8,917**	**$ 9,056**	**$ 9,195**	**$ 9,334**	**$ 9,473**	**$ 9,612**	**$ 9,751**
Federal income tax	$ 3,161	$ 3,167	$ 3,173	$ 3,180	$ 3,186	$ 3,192	$ 3,198
State income tax	$ 479	$ 480	$ 481	$ 482	$ 483	$ 484	$ 485
Interest expense	$ 1,875	$ 1,865	$ 1,856	$ 1,846	$ 1,836	$ 1,826	$ 1,816
Depreciation expense	$ 1,488	$ 1,488	$ 1,488	$ 1,488	$ 1,488	$ 1,488	$ 1,488
Net profit	**$ 1,914**	**$ 2,056**	**$ 2,198**	**$ 2,339**	**$ 2,481**	**$ 2,623**	**$ 2,765**

Profit and loss statement (first year cont.)

Month	8	9	10	11	12	1
Sales	**$95,645**	**$95,830**	**$96,015**	**$96,200**	**$96,385**	**$1,144,410**
Cost of goods sold	$23,782	$23,828	$23,874	$23,920	$23,966	$ 284,556
Gross margin	75.1%	75.1%	75.1%	75.1%	75.1%	75.1%
Operating income	**$71,863**	**$72,002**	**$72,141**	**$72,280**	**$72,419**	**$ 859,854**
Expenses						
Payroll	$44,167	$44,167	$44,167	$44,167	$44,167	$ 530,000
General and administrative	$ 2,100	$ 2,100	$ 2,100	$ 2,100	$ 2,100	$ 25,200
Marketing and sales commission costs	$ 2,861	$ 2,861	$ 2,861	$ 2,861	$ 2,861	$ 34,332
Professional fees and licensure	$ 1,250	$ 1,250	$ 1,250	$ 1,250	$ 1,250	$ 15,000
Insurance costs	$ 1,042	$ 1,042	$ 1,042	$ 1,042	$ 1,042	$ 12,500
Distribution costs	$ 1,431	$ 1,431	$ 1,431	$ 1,431	$ 1,431	$ 17,166
Rent and utilities	$ 2,021	$ 2,021	$ 2,021	$ 2,021	$ 2,021	$ 24,250
Miscellaneous costs	$ 477	$ 477	$ 477	$ 477	$ 477	$ 5,722
Payroll taxes	$ 6,625	$ 6,625	$ 6,625	$ 6,625	$ 6,625	$ 79,500
Total operating costs	**$61,973**	**$61,973**	**$61,973**	**$61,973**	**$61,973**	**$ 743,671**
EBITDA	**$ 9,890**	**$10,029**	**$10,168**	**$10,307**	**$10,446**	**$ 116,184**
Federal income tax	$ 3,204	$ 3,211	$ 3,217	$ 3,223	$ 3,229	$ 38,341
State income tax	$ 486	$ 486	$ 487	$ 488	$ 489	$ 5,809
Interest expense	$ 1,806	$ 1,795	$ 1,785	$ 1,775	$ 1,764	$ 21,844
Depreciation expense	$ 1,488	$ 1,488	$ 1,488	$ 1,488	$ 1,488	$ 17,857
Net profit	**$ 2,907**	**$ 3,049**	**$ 3,191**	**$ 3,333**	**$ 3,476**	**$ 32,332**

Profit and loss statement (second year)

Quarter	Q1	2 Q2	Q3	Q4	2
Sales	**$274,658**	**$343,323**	**$370,789**	**$384,522**	**$1,373,292**
Cost of goods sold	$ 68,293	$ 85,367	$ 92,196	$ 95,611	$ 341,467
Gross margin	75.1%	75.1%	75.1%	75.1%	75.1%
Operating income	**$206,365**	**$257,956**	**$278,593**	**$288,911**	**$1,031,825**
Expenses					
Payroll	$109,180	$136,475	$147,393	$152,852	$ 545,900
General and administrative	$ 5,242	$ 6,552	$ 7,076	$ 7,338	$ 26,208
Marketing and sales commission costs	$ 8,240	$ 10,300	$ 11,124	$ 11,536	$ 41,199
Professional fees and licensure	$ 3,090	$ 3,863	$ 4,172	$ 4,326	$ 15,450
Insurance costs	$ 2,625	$ 3,281	$ 3,544	$ 3,675	$ 13,125
Distribution costs	$ 4,120	$ 5,150	$ 5,562	$ 5,768	$ 20,599
Rent and utilities	$ 5,093	$ 6,366	$ 6,875	$ 7,130	$ 25,463
Miscellaneous costs	$ 1,373	$ 1,717	$ 1,854	$ 1,923	$ 6,866
Payroll taxes	$ 16,377	$ 20,471	$ 22,109	$ 22,928	$ 81,885
Total operating costs	**$155,339**	**$194,174**	**$209,708**	**$217,475**	**$ 776,695**
EBITDA	**$ 51,026**	**$ 63,782**	**$ 68,885**	**$ 71,436**	**$ 255,130**
Federal income tax	$ 15,497	$ 19,371	$ 20,921	$ 21,696	$ 77,484
State income tax	$ 2,348	$ 2,935	$ 3,170	$ 3,287	$ 11,740
Interest expense	$ 5,230	$ 5,133	$ 5,034	$ 4,932	$ 20,328
Depreciation expense	$ 4,464	$ 4,464	$ 4,464	$ 4,464	$ 17,857
Net profit	**$ 23,487**	**$ 31,879**	**$ 35,296**	**$ 37,057**	**$ 127,720**

Profit and loss statement (third year)

Quarter	Q1	3 Q2	Q3	Q4	3
Sales	$321,350	$401,688	$433,823	$449,890	$1,606,752
Cost of goods sold	$ 79,903	$ 99,879	$107,869	$111,865	$ 399,517
Gross margin	75.1%	75.1%	75.1%	75.1%	75.1%
Operating income	$241,447	$301,809	$325,953	$338,026	$1,207,235
Expenses					
Payroll	$112,455	$140,569	$151,815	$157,438	$ 562,277
General and administrative	$ 5,451	$ 6,814	$ 7,359	$ 7,632	$ 27,256
Marketing and sales commission costs	$ 9,641	$ 12,051	$ 13,015	$ 13,497	$ 48,203
Professional fees and licensure	$ 3,183	$ 3,978	$ 4,297	$ 4,456	$ 15,914
Insurance costs	$ 2,756	$ 3,445	$ 3,721	$ 3,859	$ 13,781
Distribution costs	$ 4,820	$ 6,025	$ 6,507	$ 6,748	$ 24,101
Rent and utilities	$ 5,347	$ 6,684	$ 7,219	$ 7,486	$ 26,736
Miscellaneous costs	$ 1,607	$ 2,008	$ 2,169	$ 2,249	$ 8,034
Payroll taxes	$ 16,868	$ 21,085	$ 22,772	$ 23,616	$ 84,342
Total operating costs	$162,129	$202,661	$218,874	$226,980	$ 810,643
EBITDA	$ 79,318	$ 99,148	$107,080	$111,046	$ 396,592
Federal income tax	$ 24,943	$ 31,179	$ 33,673	$ 34,920	$ 124,714
State income tax	$ 3,779	$ 4,724	$ 5,102	$ 5,291	$ 18,896
Interest expense	$ 4,829	$ 4,723	$ 4,615	$ 4,504	$ 18,671
Depreciation expense	$ 4,464	$ 4,464	$ 4,464	$ 4,464	$ 17,857
Net profit	$ 41,303	$ 54,058	$ 59,226	$ 61,867	$ 216,454

7.11 Three Year Cash Flow Analysis

Cash flow analysis (first year)

Month	1	2	3	4	5	6	7
Cash from operations	$ 3,403	$ 3,544	$ 3,686	$ 3,827	$ 3,969	$ 4,111	$ 4,253
Cash from receivables	$ 0	$ 0	$ 0	$ 0	$ 0	$ 0	$ 0
Operating cash inflow	$ 3,403	$ 3,544	$ 3,686	$ 3,827	$ 3,969	$ 4,111	$ 4,253
Other cash inflows							
Equity investment	$ 50,000	$ 0	$ 0	$ 0	$ 0	$ 0	$ 0
Increased borrowings	$250,000	$ 0	$ 0	$ 0	$ 0	$ 0	$ 0
Sales of business assets	$ 0	$ 0	$ 0	$ 0	$ 0	$ 0	$ 0
A/P increases	$ 3,159	$ 3,159	$ 3,159	$ 3,159	$ 3,159	$ 3,159	$ 3,159
Total other cash inflows	$303,159	$ 3,159	$ 3,159	$ 3,159	$ 3,159	$ 3,159	$ 3,159
Total cash inflow	$306,561	$ 6,703	$ 6,844	$ 6,986	$ 7,128	$ 7,270	$ 7,411
Cash outflows							
Repayment of principal	$ 1,292	$ 1,302	$ 1,311	$ 1,321	$ 1,331	$ 1,341	$ 1,351
A/P decreases	$ 2,075	$ 2,075	$ 2,075	$ 2,075	$ 2,075	$ 2,075	$ 2,075
A/R increases	$ 0	$ 0	$ 0	$ 0	$ 0	$ 0	$ 0
Asset purchases	$250,000	$ 0	$ 0	$ 0	$ 0	$ 0	$ 0
Dividends	$ 0	$ 0	$ 0	$ 0	$ 0	$ 0	$ 0
Total cash outflows	$253,367	$ 3,376	$ 3,386	$ 3,396	$ 3,406	$ 3,416	$ 3,426
Net cash flow	$ 53,194	$ 3,326	$ 3,458	$ 3,590	$ 3,722	$ 3,854	$ 3,986
Cash balance	$ 53,194	$56,521	$59,979	$63,569	$67,291	$71,144	$75,130

Cash flow analysis (first year cont.)

Month	8	9	10	11	12	1
Cash from operations	$ 4,395	$ 4,537	$ 4,679	$ 4,821	$ 4,964	$ 50,190
Cash from receivables	$ 0	$ 0	$ 0	$ 0	$ 0	$ 0
Operating cash inflow	**$ 4,395**	**$ 4,537**	**$ 4,679**	**$ 4,821**	**$ 4,964**	**$ 50,190**
Other cash inflows						
Equity investment	$ 0	$ 0	$ 0	$ 0	$ 0	$ 50,000
Increased borrowings	$ 0	$ 0	$ 0	$ 0	$ 0	$250,000
Sales of business assets	$ 0	$ 0	$ 0	$ 0	$ 0	$ 0
A/P increases	$ 3,159	$ 3,159	$ 3,159	$ 3,159	$ 3,159	$ 37,902
Total other cash inflows	**$ 3,159**	**$ 3,159**	**$ 3,159**	**$ 3,159**	**$ 3,159**	**$337,902**
Total cash inflow	**$ 7,553**	**$ 7,696**	**$ 7,838**	**$ 7,980**	**$ 8,122**	**$388,092**
Cash outflows						
Repayment of principal	$ 1,361	$ 1,371	$ 1,382	$ 1,392	$ 1,403	$ 16,158
A/P decreases	$ 2,075	$ 2,075	$ 2,075	$ 2,075	$ 2,075	$ 24,897
A/R increases	$ 0	$ 0	$ 0	$ 0	$ 0	$ 0
Asset purchases	$ 0	$ 0	$ 0	$ 0	$ 0	$250,000
Dividends	$ 0	$ 0	$ 0	$ 0	$35,133	$ 35,133
Total cash outflows	**$ 3,436**	**$ 3,446**	**$ 3,457**	**$ 3,467**	**$38,610**	**$326,188**
Net cash flow	**$ 4,117**	**$ 4,249**	**$ 4,381**	**$ 4,513**	**-$30,488**	**$ 61,903**
Cash balance	**$79,248**	**$ 83,497**	**$ 87,878**	**$ 92,391**	**$61,903**	**$ 61,903**

Cash flow analysis (second year)

Quarter	Q1	2 Q2	Q3	Q4	2
Cash from operations	$29,115	$36,394	$39,306	$40,761	$145,577
Cash from receivables	$ 0	$ 0	$ 0	$ 0	$ 0
Operating cash inflow	**$29,115**	**$36,394**	**$39,306**	**$40,761**	**$145,577**
Other cash inflows					
Equity investment	$ 0	$ 0	$ 0	$ 0	$ 0
Increased borrowings	$ 0	$ 0	$ 0	$ 0	$ 0
Sales of business assets	$ 0	$ 0	$ 0	$ 0	$ 0
A/P increases	$ 8,717	$10,897	$11,769	$12,204	$ 43,587
Total other cash inflows	**$ 8,717**	**$10,897**	**$11,769**	**$12,204**	**$ 43,587**
Total cash inflow	**$37,833**	**$47,291**	**$51,074**	**$52,966**	**$189,164**
Cash outflows					
Repayment of principal	$ 4,271	$ 4,368	$ 4,467	$ 4,568	$ 17,674
A/P decreases	$ 5,975	$ 7,469	$ 8,067	$ 8,365	$ 29,876
A/R increases	$ 0	$ 0	$ 0	$ 0	$ 0
Asset purchases	$ 7,279	$ 9,099	$ 9,826	$10,190	$ 36,394
Dividends	$20,381	$25,476	$27,514	$28,533	$101,904
Total cash outflows	**$37,906**	**$46,412**	**$49,874**	**$51,657**	**$185,849**
Net cash flow	**–$ 73**	**$ 879**	**$ 1,200**	**$ 1,309**	**$ 3,315**
Cash balance	**$61,830**	**$62,710**	**$63,910**	**$65,219**	**$ 65,219**

Cash flow analysis (third year)

Quarter	Q1	3 Q2	Q3	Q4	3
Cash from operations	$46,862	$58,578	$63,264	$65,607	$234,311
Cash from receivables	$ 0	$ 0	$ 0	$ 0	$ 0
Operating cash inflow	**$46,862**	**$58,578**	**$63,264**	**$65,607**	**$234,311**
Other cash inflows					
Equity investment	$ 0	$ 0	$ 0	$ 0	$ 0
Increased borrowings	$ 0	$ 0	$ 0	$ 0	$ 0
Sales of business assets	$ 0	$ 0	$ 0	$ 0	$ 0
A/P increases	$10,025	$12,531	$13,534	$14,035	$ 50,125
Total other cash inflows	**$10,025**	**$12,531**	**$13,534**	**$14,035**	**$ 50,125**
Total cash inflow	**$56,887**	**$71,109**	**$76,798**	**$79,642**	**$284,437**
Cash outflows					
Repayment of principal	$ 4,672	$ 4,778	$ 4,886	$ 4,997	$ 19,332
A/P decreases	$ 7,170	$ 8,963	$ 9,680	$10,038	$ 35,852
A/R increases	$ 0	$ 0	$ 0	$ 0	$ 0
Asset purchases	$11,716	$14,644	$15,816	$16,402	$ 58,578
Dividends	$32,804	$41,005	$44,285	$45,925	$164,018
Total cash outflows	**$56,361**	**$69,390**	**$74,667**	**$77,362**	**$277,780**
Net cash flow	**$ 526**	**$ 1,720**	**$ 2,131**	**$ 2,280**	**$ 6,657**
Cash balance	**$65,745**	**$67,465**	**$69,596**	**$71,876**	**$ 71,876**

Crowdfunding Website

Impetus Crowdfunding

66989 5th Ave.
New York, NY 10012

BizPlanDB.com

The purpose of this business plan is to raise $150,000 for the development of a crowdfunding website that will provide a platform for businesses to raise capital for unique projects. The business will receive substantial fees from when a project is successfully funded coupled with upfront submission fees.

1.0 EXECUTIVE SUMMARY

The purpose of this business plan is to raise $150,000 for the development of a crowdfunding website that will provide a platform for businesses to raise capital for unique projects. The business will receive substantial fees when a project is successfully funded coupled with upfront submission fees. This business plan will also showcase the expected financials and operations over the next three years. Impetus Crowdfunding ("the Company") is a New York based corporation that will operate in a crowdfunding capacity for businesses and entrepreneurs that are seeking to raise capital via its online platform to users. The Company was founded by Cameron Smith.

1.1 The Site

As stated above, the primary revenue center for the business will come from ongoing success fees associated with a project that receives its funding (in full or in part). The business will take a 5% fee of the total amount of aggregate capital raised. Funds that have been raised via the website will be transferred via an automated clearing house transmission to the entrepreneur/company designated verified bank account.

The business will also earn revenues each time a new project is submitted to the website. For each project profile, the business will generate approximately $19.95 of revenue. This is an important secondary revenue center for the business as it will ensure that the Company will still earn revenue for projects that go unfunded.

1.2 Financing

Mr. Smith is seeking to raise $150,000 as a bank loan. The interest rate and loan agreement are to be further discussed during negotiation. This business plan assumes that the business will receive a 10-year loan with a 9% fixed interest rate. The financing will be used for the following:

- Development of the Company's crowdfunding website platform.

- Financing for the first six months of operation.

- Capital to purchase servers, computers, and related technology.

Mr. Smith will contribute $25,000 to the venture.

77

1.3 Mission Statement

Impetus Crowdfunding's mission is to become the recognized leader in its targeted market as a platform where businesses and startup entrepreneurs can raise capital for their projects.

1.4 Management Team

The Company was founded by Cameron Smith. Mr. Smith has more than 10 years of experience in the online and Internet industry. Through his expertise, he will be able to bring the operations of the business to profitability within its first year of operations.

1.5 Sales Forecasts

Mr. Smith expects a strong rate of growth at the start of operations. Below are the expected financials over the next three years.

Proforma profit and loss (yearly)

Year	1	2	3
Sales	$990,450	$1,436,153	$1,938,806
Operating costs	$429,373	$ 480,774	$ 536,571
EBITDA	$462,033	$ 811,763	$1,208,354
Taxes, interest, and depreciation	$197,607	$ 324,961	$ 475,048
Net profit	$264,425	$ 486,802	$ 733,305

Sales, operating costs, and profit forecast

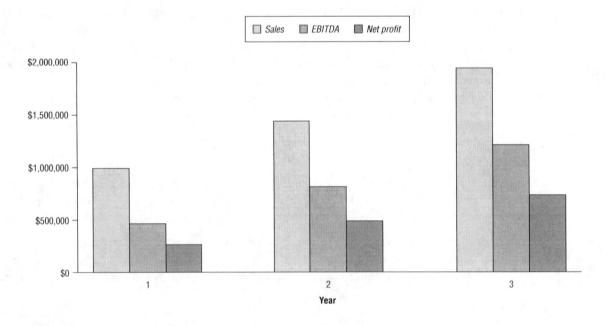

1.6 Expansion Plan

The Founder expects that the business will aggressively expand during the first three years of operation. Mr. Smith intends to implement marketing campaigns that will effectively target individuals and businesses that are seeking to start new businesses or develop new products within the Company's demographic.

2.0 COMPANY AND FINANCING SUMMARY

2.1 Registered Name and Corporate Structure

The Company is registered as a corporation in the State of New York.

2.2 Required Funds

At this time, Impetus Crowdfunding requires $150,000 of debt funds. Below is a breakdown of how these funds will be used:

Projected startup costs

Initial lease payments and deposits	$ 15,000
Working capital	$ 25,000
FF&E	$ 30,000
Website development	$ 42,500
Security deposits	$ 5,000
Insurance	$ 2,500
Servers and technology equipment	$ 25,000
Marketing budget	$ 25,000
Miscellaneous and unforeseen costs	$ 5,000
Total startup costs	**$175,000**

Use of funds

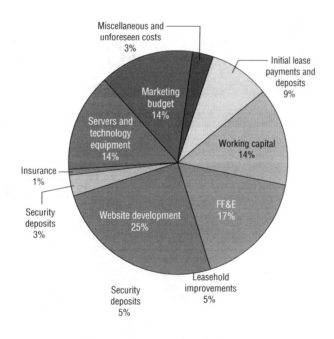

2.3 Investor Equity

Mr. Smith is not seeking an investment from a third party at this time.

2.4 Management Equity

Cameron Smith owns 100% of Impetus Crowdfunding.

2.5 Exit Strategy

If the business is very successful, Mr. Smith may seek to sell the business to a third party for a significant earnings multiple. Most likely, the Company will hire a qualified business broker to sell the business on behalf of Impetus Crowdfunding. Based on historical numbers, the business could fetch a sales premium of up to 10 times earnings.

3.0 PRODUCTS AND SERVICES

Below is a description of the operations of Impetus Crowdfunding:

3.1 Benefits of Impetus Crowdfunding

As stated in the executive summary, the primary revenue center for the business will come when a user successfully raises capital for their project, new product, or business. Impetus Crowdfunding, at the onset of operations, will only allow individuals and businesses to place requests for funding that provide an exchange of goods. No individual or company will be allowed to sell a stake in their business in exchange for capital. The primary benefit to the entrepreneur/company that is seeking to raise capital is the fact that they will be able to get the money they need to start their venture. For people contributing money to a venture, they will receive a product/service in exchange for their contribution.

The business will earn a fee equal to 5% of the total amount of capital raised per project.

However, and as will be discussed in the next section of the business plan—in the future (due to changing regulations from the Jobs Act of 2012)—the business may expand its platform to allow users to sell fractional ownership of their businesses in exchange for raised capital.

3.2 Profile Submission Revenues

The secondary stream of revenue for the business will come from submission fees for each entrepreneur/company that wants to upload a funding request profile to the website. The business will charge a fee of $19.95 per funding request profile. This will provide the business with a highly predictable stream of revenue for the business.

3.3 Future Revenue Center (Advertising)

In the future, the Company may develop its own internal advertising programs that will feature static advertisements within the website. These advertisements will be sold directly to advertisers rather than through a third party system, like Google AdSense. In the future, Impetus Crowdfunding will also seek to develop product affiliation and corporate sponsorship relationships which would further the Company's visibility and revenue streams.

4.0 STRATEGIC AND MARKET ANALYSIS

4.1 Economic Outlook

This section of the analysis will detail the economic climate, the crowdfunding industry, the customer profile, and the competition that the business will face as it progresses through its business operations.

Currently, the economic market condition in the United States is moderate. Unemployment rates have declined while asset prices have risen substantially. As such, starting a crowdfunding website in this economic environment is appropriate given that people have the extra capital available to contribute to unique and interesting products that are in development.

4.2 Industry Analysis

Crowdfunding websites are a relatively new industry within the United States. As many more people are looking to start their own businesses, the demand for capital has increased. As such, and as these websites have developed, millions of people from around the world are now using crowd funding websites in order to launch their business ventures. As of 2014, crowdfunding platforms have placed more than $6 billion of capital with small businesses. There are approximately 200 websites in operation that assist small businesses and entrepreneurs with raising capital for their businesses (in exchange for produced products and services). Each year, these websites have generated approximately $300 million in revenues. The year on year growth for this industry is 81%. This trend is expected to continue for at least five years.

In the future, the business may develop extensive operations as a platform for crowd funding capital (direct investment into companies) as outlined in the JOBS Act (Jumpstart Our Businesses Act) which was signed into law by President Obama in April of 2012. This new legislation provides for substantially greater access to private capital among small businesses that wish to engage in a public campaign to showcase their business operations and why they are a strong candidate for a small initial public offering. Once Impetus Crowdfunding is fully operational with the operations outlined in this business plan, the Company would be in an excellent position to continue to make investments into this business model that will allow US-based businesses to have readily accessible capital for startup and growth.

4.3 Customer Profile

Impetus Crowdfunding's average client will be an entrepreneur or established business that is seeking to raise capital for a new project or business venture. Common traits among these individuals will be:

- Seeking to raise $2,000 to $100,000.

- Is familiar with the idea of crowdfunding and how it works.

- Will be able to provide its developed product/service within six months of receiving capital.

- Is licensed to do business within their respective jurisdiction.

- Will actively promote their funding request via popular social media platforms.

4.4 Competition

Kickstarter.com is by far the largest competitor in the crowd funding marketplace. However, many other websites such as IndieGoGo.com, RocketHub.com, Peerbackers.com, SoMoLend.com, and several others have made strong headway into the market of crowdfunding. It is imperative that the Company develop a differentiating focus on the crowdfunding services it offers including linking to social media such as Twitter, FaceBook, and Instagram. The business will need to make continued and ongoing improvements to its operations in order to enter the market and remain competitive.

5.0 MARKETING PLAN

Impetus Crowdfunding intends to maintain an extensive marketing campaign that will ensure maximum visibility for the business in its targeted market. Below is an overview of the marketing strategies and objectives of Impetus Crowdfunding.

5.1 Marketing Objectives

- Develop an expansive online presence through the use of pay per click marketing and search engine optimization.

- Establish relationships with advertisers that are targeting a computer savvy younger demographic.

- Develop ongoing social media marketing campaigns that will target entrepreneurs and small businesses that are seeking to establish new companies and products.

5.2 Marketing Strategies

Mr. Smith intends to use a high impact marketing campaign that will generate a substantial amount of traffic to our site. These strategies include the use of search engine optimization and pay-per-click marketing.

The Company's web development firm will place large amounts of linking text on the website. For instance, when a person does a Google search for crowdfunding submission websites, the Company will appear on the first page of the search. This strategy is technically complicated, and Impetus Crowdfunding will use a search engine optimization firm to develop our visibility on a non-paid basis. Management expects that a SEO firm will place large amounts of linking data and text specific keywords into the business's website, which will allow the Company to appear more frequently among search engines. A majority of web portal and search engine companies use very complicated algorithms to determine a website's relevance in relation to a specific keyword. SEO firms place text and tags on the website to increase the rank of a specific website.

The Company will aggressively use social media websites such as Twitter, Instagram, and FaceBook in order to promote the launch. The business will hire a dedicated social media consultant that will appropriately market the Company's services to the general public.

5.3 Pricing

The Company will receive an aggregate fee of 5% of the total amount of capital raised by a startup project coupled with a flat fee of $19.95.

6.0 ORGANIZATIONAL PLAN AND PERSONNEL SUMMARY

6.1 Corporate Organization

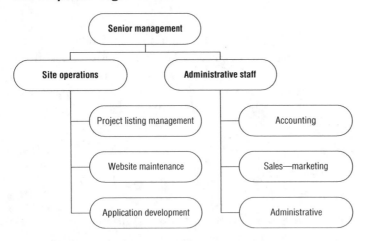

6.2 Organizational Budget

Personnel plan—yearly

Year	1	2	3
Owners	$ 80,000	$ 82,400	$ 84,872
Website manager	$ 35,000	$ 36,050	$ 37,132
Assistant	$ 32,500	$ 33,475	$ 34,479
Website marketing staff	$ 37,500	$ 51,500	$ 66,306
Administrative	$ 44,000	$ 45,320	$ 46,680
Total	**$229,000**	**$248,745**	**$269,469**

Numbers of personnel

Owners	2	2	2
Website manager	1	1	1
Assistant	1	1	1
Website marketing staff	3	4	5
Administrative	2	2	2
Totals	**9**	**10**	**11**

Personnel expense breakdown

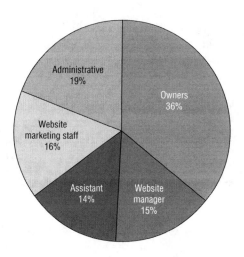

7.0 FINANCIAL PLAN

7.1 Underlying Assumptions

The Company has based its proforma financial statements on the following:

• Impetus Crowdfunding will have an annual revenue growth rate of 31% per year.

• The Owner will acquire $150,000 of debt funds to develop the business.

• The loan will have a 10-year term with a 9% interest rate.

7.2 Sensitivity Analysis

The demand for crowdfunding websites has increased significantly as the economy has improved. As such, Management feels that the low operating cost infrastructure of the business coupled with the high margin revenues generated by the Company will ensure that the business is able to remain profitable and cash flow positive at all times.

7.3 Source of Funds

Financing

Equity contributions	
Management investment	$ 25,000.00
Total equity financing	**$ 25,000.00**
Banks and lenders	
Banks and lenders	$150,000.00
Total debt financing	**$150,000.00**
Total financing	**$175,000.00**

7.4 General Assumptions

General assumptions

Year	1	2	3
Short term interest rate	9.5%	9.5%	9.5%
Long term interest rate	10.0%	10.0%	10.0%
Federal tax rate	33.0%	33.0%	33.0%
State tax rate	5.0%	5.0%	5.0%
Personnel taxes	15.0%	15.0%	15.0%

7.5 Profit and Loss Statements

Proforma profit and loss (yearly)

Year	1	2	3
Sales	**$990,450**	**$1,436,153**	**$1,938,806**
Cost of goods sold	$ 99,045	$ 143,615	$ 193,881
Gross margin	90.00%	90.00%	90.00%
Operating income	**$891,405**	**$1,292,537**	**$1,744,925**
Expenses			
Payroll	$229,000	$ 248,745	$ 269,469
General and administrative	$ 32,500	$ 33,800	$ 35,152
Marketing expenses	$ 39,618	$ 57,446	$ 77,552
Professional fees and licensure	$ 17,000	$ 17,510	$ 18,035
Insurance costs	$ 12,000	$ 12,600	$ 13,230
Server and technology costs	$ 25,000	$ 27,500	$ 30,250
Rent and utilities	$ 30,000	$ 31,500	$ 33,075
Miscellaneous costs	$ 9,905	$ 14,362	$ 19,388
Payroll taxes	$ 34,350	$ 37,312	$ 40,420
Total operating costs	**$429,373**	**$ 480,774**	**$ 536,571**
EBITDA	**$462,033**	**$ 811,763**	**$1,208,354**
Federal income tax	$152,471	$ 263,857	$ 395,060
State income tax	$ 23,102	$ 39,978	$ 59,858
Interest expense	$ 13,107	$ 12,197	$ 11,202
Depreciation expenses	$ 8,929	$ 8,929	$ 8,929
Net profit	**$264,425**	**$ 486,802**	**$ 733,305**
Profit margin	**26.70%**	**33.90%**	**37.82%**

Sales, operating costs, and profit forecast

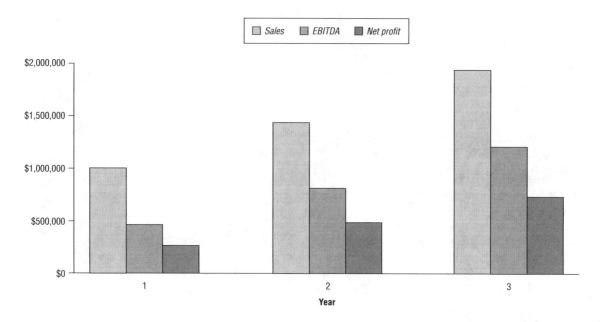

7.6 Cash Flow Analysis

Proforma cash flow analysis—yearly

Year	1	2	3
Cash from operations	$273,354	$495,731	$742,234
Cash from receivables	$ 0	$ 0	$ 0
Operating cash inflow	**$273,354**	**$495,731**	**$742,234**
Other cash inflows			
Equity investment	$ 25,000	$ 0	$ 0
Increased borrowings	$150,000	$ 0	$ 0
Sales of business assets	$ 0	$ 0	$ 0
A/P increases	$ 37,902	$ 43,587	$ 50,125
Total other cash inflows	**$212,902**	**$ 43,587**	**$ 50,125**
Total cash inflow	**$486,256**	**$539,318**	**$792,359**
Cash outflows			
Repayment of principal	$ 9,695	$ 10,605	$ 11,599
A/P decreases	$ 24,897	$ 29,876	$ 35,852
A/R increases	$ 0	$ 0	$ 0
Asset purchases	$125,000	$123,933	$185,558
Dividends	$191,348	$347,012	$519,564
Total cash outflows	**$350,940**	**$511,425**	**$752,573**
Net cash flow	**$135,316**	**$ 27,893**	**$ 39,786**
Cash balance	**$135,316**	**$163,209**	**$202,995**

Proforma cash flow (yearly)

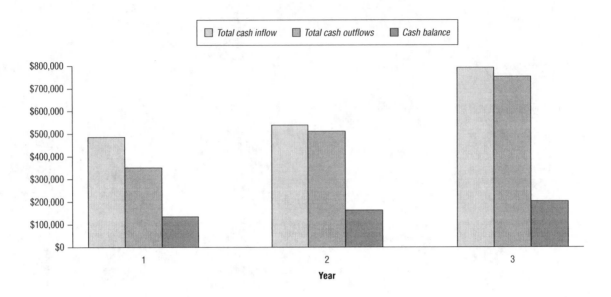

7.7 Balance Sheet

Proforma balance sheet—yearly

Year	1	2	3
Assets			
Cash	$135,316	$163,209	$202,995
Amortized development costs	$ 70,000	$ 82,393	$100,949
Servers and technology equipment	$ 25,000	$117,950	$257,118
FF&E	$ 30,000	$ 48,590	$ 76,424
Accumulated depreciation	($ 8,929)	($ 17,857)	($ 26,786)
Total assets	**$251,387**	**$394,284**	**$610,700**
Liabilities and equity			
Accounts payable	$ 13,005	$ 26,716	$ 40,990
Long term liabilities	$140,305	$129,700	$119,096
Other liabilities	$ 0	$ 0	$ 0
Total liabilities	**$153,310**	**$156,416**	**$160,085**
Net worth	**$ 98,078**	**$237,868**	**$450,615**
Total liabilities and equity	**$251,387**	**$394,284**	**$610,700**

Proforma balance sheet

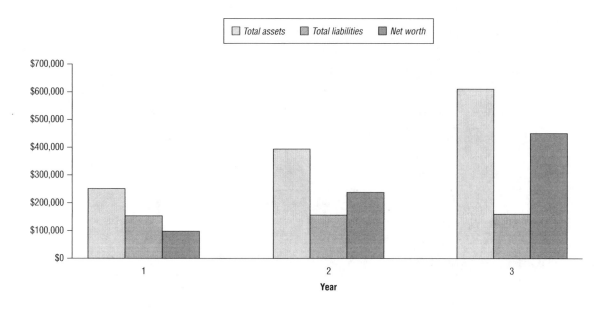

7.8 Breakeven Analysis

Monthly break even analysis

Year	1	2	3
Monthly revenue	$ 39,757	$ 44,516	$ 49,683
Yearly revenue	$477,081	$534,194	$596,191

Break even analysis

7.9 Business Ratios

Business ratios—yearly

Year	1	2	3
Sales			
Sales growth	0.0%	45.0%	35.0%
Gross margin	90.0%	90.0%	90.0%
Financials			
Profit margin	26.70%	33.90%	37.82%
Assets to liabilities	1.64	2.52	3.81
Equity to liabilities	0.64	1.52	2.81
Assets to equity	2.56	1.66	1.36
Liquidity			
Acid test	0.88	1.04	1.27
Cash to assets	0.54	0.41	0.33

7.10 Three Year Profit and Loss Statement

Profit and loss statement (first year)

Months	1	2	3	4	5	6	7
Sales	**$69,750**	**$72,075**	**$74,400**	**$76,725**	**$79,050**	**$81,375**	**$83,700**
Cost of goods sold	$ 6,975	$ 7,208	$ 7,440	$ 7,673	$ 7,905	$ 8,138	$ 8,370
Gross margin	90.0%	90.0%	90.0%	90.0%	90.0%	90.0%	90.0%
Operating income	**$62,775**	**$64,868**	**$66,960**	**$ 69,053**	**$71,145**	**$73,238**	**$75,330**
Expenses							
Payroll	$19,083	$19,083	$19,083	$19,083	$19,083	$19,083	$19,083
General and administrative	$ 2,708	$ 2,708	$ 2,708	$ 2,708	$ 2,708	$ 2,708	$ 2,708
Marketing expenses	$ 3,302	$ 3,302	$ 3,302	$ 3,302	$ 3,302	$ 3,302	$ 3,302
Professional fees and licensure	$ 1,417	$ 1,417	$ 1,417	$ 1,417	$ 1,417	$ 1,417	$ 1,417
Insurance costs	$ 1,000	$ 1,000	$ 1,000	$ 1,000	$ 1,000	$ 1,000	$ 1,000
Server and technology costs	$ 2,083	$ 2,083	$ 2,083	$ 2,083	$ 2,083	$ 2,083	$ 2,083
Rent and utilities	$ 2,500	$ 2,500	$ 2,500	$ 2,500	$ 2,500	$ 2,500	$ 2,500
Miscellaneous costs	$ 825	$ 825	$ 825	$ 825	$ 825	$ 825	$ 825
Payroll taxes	$ 2,863	$ 2,863	$ 2,863	$ 2,863	$ 2,863	$ 2,863	$ 2,863
Total operating costs	**$35,781**	**$35,781**	**$35,781**	**$35,781**	**$35,781**	**$35,781**	**$35,781**
EBITDA	**$26,994**	**$29,086**	**$31,179**	**$33,271**	**$35,364**	**$37,456**	**$39,549**
Federal income tax	$10,737	$11,095	$11,453	$11,811	$12,169	$12,527	$12,885
State income tax	$ 1,627	$ 1,681	$ 1,735	$ 1,790	$ 1,844	$ 1,898	$ 1,952
Interest expense	$ 1,125	$ 1,119	$ 1,113	$ 1,107	$ 1,101	$ 1,095	$ 1,089
Depreciation expense	$ 744	$ 744	$ 744	$ 744	$ 744	$ 744	$ 744
Net profit	**$12,761**	**$14,447**	**$16,133**	**$17,819**	**$19,506**	**$21,192**	**$22,878**

Profit and loss statement (first year cont.)

Month	8	9	10	11	12	1
Sales	**$86,025**	**$88,350**	**$90,675**	**$93,000**	**$95,325**	**$990,450**
Cost of goods sold	$ 8,603	$ 8,835	$ 9,068	$ 9,300	$ 9,533	$ 99,045
Gross margin	90.0%	90.0%	90.0%	90.0%	90.0%	90.0%
Operating income	**$77,423**	**$79,515**	**$81,608**	**$83,700**	**$85,793**	**$891,405**
Expenses						
Payroll	$19,083	$19,083	$19,083	$19,083	$19,083	$229,000
General and administrative	$ 2,708	$ 2,708	$ 2,708	$ 2,708	$ 2,708	$ 32,500
Marketing expenses	$ 3,302	$ 3,302	$ 3,302	$ 3,302	$ 3,302	$ 39,618
Professional fees and licensure	$ 1,417	$ 1,417	$ 1,417	$ 1,417	$ 1,417	$ 17,000
Insurance costs	$ 1,000	$ 1,000	$ 1,000	$ 1,000	$ 1,000	$ 12,000
Server and technology costs	$ 2,083	$ 2,083	$ 2,083	$ 2,083	$ 2,083	$ 25,000
Rent and utilities	$ 2,500	$ 2,500	$ 2,500	$ 2,500	$ 2,500	$ 30,000
Miscellaneous costs	$ 825	$ 825	$ 825	$ 825	$ 825	$ 9,905
Payroll taxes	$ 2,863	$ 2,863	$ 2,863	$ 2,863	$ 2,863	$ 34,350
Total operating costs	**$35,781**	**$35,781**	**$35,781**	**$35,781**	**$35,781**	**$429,373**
EBITDA	**$41,641**	**$43,734**	**$45,826**	**$47,919**	**$50,011**	**$462,033**
Federal income tax	$13,243	$13,601	$13,959	$14,317	$14,674	$152,471
State income tax	$ 2,006	$ 2,061	$ 2,115	$ 2,169	$ 2,223	$ 23,102
Interest expense	$ 1,083	$ 1,077	$ 1,071	$ 1,065	$ 1,059	$ 13,107
Depreciation expense	$ 744	$ 744	$ 744	$ 744	$ 744	$ 8,929
Net profit	**$24,565**	**$26,251**	**$27,938**	**$29,624**	**$31,311**	**$264,425**

Profit and loss statement (second year)

Quarter	Q1	2 Q2	Q3	Q4	2
Sales	**$287,231**	**$359,038**	**$387,761**	**$402,123**	**$1,436,153**
Cost of goods sold	$ 28,723	$ 35,904	$ 38,776	$ 40,212	$ 143,615
Gross margin	90.0%	90.0%	90.0%	90.0%	90.0%
Operating income	**$258,507**	**$323,134**	**$348,985**	**$361,910**	**$1,292,537**
Expenses					
Payroll	$ 49,749	$ 62,186	$ 67,161	$ 69,649	$ 248,745
General and administrative	$ 6,760	$ 8,450	$ 9,126	$ 9,464	$ 33,800
Marketing expenses	$ 11,489	$ 14,362	$ 15,510	$ 16,085	$ 57,446
Professional fees and licensure	$ 3,502	$ 4,378	$ 4,728	$ 4,903	$ 17,510
Insurance costs	$ 2,520	$ 3,150	$ 3,402	$ 3,528	$ 12,600
Server and technology costs	$ 5,500	$ 6,875	$ 7,425	$ 7,700	$ 27,500
Rent and utilities	$ 6,300	$ 7,875	$ 8,505	$ 8,820	$ 31,500
Miscellaneous costs	$ 2,872	$ 3,590	$ 3,878	$ 4,021	$ 14,362
Payroll taxes	$ 7,462	$ 9,328	$ 10,074	$ 10,447	$ 37,312
Total operating costs	**$ 96,155**	**$120,194**	**$129,809**	**$134,617**	**$ 480,774**
EBITDA	**$162,353**	**$202,941**	**$219,176**	**$227,294**	**$ 811,763**
Federal income tax	$ 52,771	$ 65,964	$ 71,241	$ 73,880	$ 263,857
State income tax	$ 7,996	$ 9,995	$ 10,794	$ 11,194	$ 39,978
Interest expense	$ 3,138	$ 3,080	$ 3,020	$ 2,959	$ 12,197
Depreciation expense	$ 2,232	$ 2,232	$ 2,232	$ 2,232	$ 8,929
Net profit	**$ 96,216**	**$121,670**	**$131,888**	**$137,028**	**$ 486,802**

Profit and loss statement (third year)

Quarter	Q1	3 Q2	Q3	Q4	3
Sales	$387,761	$484,701	$523,478	$542,866	$1,938,806
Cost of goods sold	$ 38,776	$ 48,470	$ 52,348	$ 54,287	$ 193,881
Gross margin	90.0%	90.0%	90.0%	90.0%	90.0%
Operating income	$348,985	$436,231	$471,130	$488,579	$1,744,925
Expenses					
Payroll	$ 53,894	$ 67,367	$ 72,757	$ 75,451	$ 269,469
General and administrative	$ 7,030	$ 8,788	$ 9,491	$ 9,843	$ 35,152
Marketing expenses	$ 15,510	$ 19,388	$ 20,939	$ 21,715	$ 77,552
Professional fees and licensure	$ 3,607	$ 4,509	$ 4,870	$ 5,050	$ 18,035
Insurance costs	$ 2,646	$ 3,308	$ 3,572	$ 3,704	$ 13,230
Server and technology costs	$ 6,050	$ 7,563	$ 8,168	$ 8,470	$ 30,250
Rent and utilities	$ 6,615	$ 8,269	$ 8,930	$ 9,261	$ 33,075
Miscellaneous costs	$ 3,878	$ 4,847	$ 5,235	$ 5,429	$ 19,388
Payroll taxes	$ 8,084	$ 10,105	$ 10,913	$ 11,318	$ 40,420
Total operating costs	$107,314	$134,143	$144,874	$150,240	$ 536,571
EBITDA	$241,671	$302,088	$326,256	$338,339	$1,208,354
Federal income tax	$ 79,012	$ 98,765	$106,666	$110,617	$ 395,060
State income tax	$ 11,972	$ 14,964	$ 16,162	$ 16,760	$ 59,858
Interest expense	$ 2,897	$ 2,834	$ 2,769	$ 2,702	$ 11,202
Depreciation expense	$ 2,232	$ 2,232	$ 2,232	$ 2,232	$ 8,929
Net profit	$145,558	$183,293	$198,427	$206,028	$ 733,305

7.11 Three Year Cash Flow Analysis

Cash flow analysis (first year)

Month	1	2	3	4	5	6	7
Cash from operations	$ 13,505	$15,191	$16,877	$ 18,563	$ 20,250	$ 21,936	$ 23,622
Cash from receivables	$ 0	$ 0	$ 0	$ 0	$ 0	$ 0	$ 0
Operating cash inflow	$ 13,505	$15,191	$16,877	$ 18,563	$ 20,250	$ 21,936	$ 23,622
Other cash inflows							
Equity investment	$ 25,000	$ 0	$ 0	$ 0	$ 0	$ 0	$ 0
Increased borrowings	$150,000	$ 0	$ 0	$ 0	$ 0	$ 0	$ 0
Sales of business assets	$ 0	$ 0	$ 0	$ 0	$ 0	$ 0	$ 0
A/P increases	$ 3,159	$ 3,159	$ 3,159	$ 3,159	$ 3,159	$ 3,159	$ 3,159
Total other cash inflows	$178,159	$ 3,159	$ 3,159	$ 3,159	$ 3,159	$ 3,159	$ 3,159
Total cash inflow	$191,663	$18,349	$20,036	$ 21,722	$ 23,408	$ 25,095	$ 26,781
Cash outflows							
Repayment of principal	$ 775	$ 781	$ 787	$ 793	$ 799	$ 805	$ 811
A/P decreases	$ 2,075	$ 2,075	$ 2,075	$ 2,075	$ 2,075	$ 2,075	$ 2,075
A/R increases	$ 0	$ 0	$ 0	$ 0	$ 0	$ 0	$ 0
Asset purchases	$125,000	$ 0	$ 0	$ 0	$ 0	$ 0	$ 0
Dividends	$ 0	$ 0	$ 0	$ 0	$ 0	$ 0	$ 0
Total cash outflows	$127,850	$ 2,856	$ 2,862	$ 2,867	$ 2,873	$ 2,879	$ 2,885
Net cash flow	$ 63,813	$15,494	$17,174	$ 18,854	$ 20,535	$ 22,215	$ 23,895
Cash balance	$ 63,813	$79,307	$96,481	$115,335	$135,870	$158,085	$181,981

Cash flow analysis (first year cont.)

Month	8	9	10	11	12	1
Cash from operations	$ 25,309	$ 26,995	$ 28,682	$ 30,368	$ 32,055	$273,354
Cash from receivables	$ 0	$ 0	$ 0	$ 0	$ 0	$ 0
Operating cash inflow	**$ 25,309**	**$ 26,995**	**$ 28,682**	**$ 30,368**	**$ 32,055**	**$273,354**
Other cash inflows						
Equity investment	$ 0	$ 0	$ 0	$ 0	$ 0	$ 25,000
Increased borrowings	$ 0	$ 0	$ 0	$ 0	$ 0	$150,000
Sales of business assets	$ 0	$ 0	$ 0	$ 0	$ 0	$ 0
A/P increases	$ 3,159	$ 3,159	$ 3,159	$ 3,159	$ 3,159	$ 37,902
Total other cash inflows	**$ 3,159**	**$ 3,159**	**$ 3,159**	**$ 3,159**	**$ 3,159**	**$212,902**
Total cash inflow	**$ 28,467**	**$ 30,154**	**$ 31,840**	**$ 33,527**	**$ 35,214**	**$486,256**
Cash outflows						
Repayment of principal	$ 817	$ 823	$ 829	$ 835	$ 842	$ 9,695
A/P decreases	$ 2,075	$ 2,075	$ 2,075	$ 2,075	$ 2,075	$ 24,897
A/R increases	$ 0	$ 0	$ 0	$ 0	$ 0	$ 0
Asset purchases	$ 0	$ 0	$ 0	$ 0	$ 0	$125,000
Dividends	$ 0	$ 0	$ 0	$ 0	$191,348	$191,348
Total cash outflows	**$ 2,892**	**$ 2,898**	**$ 2,904**	**$ 2,910**	**$194,264**	**$350,940**
Net cash flow	**$ 25,576**	**$ 27,256**	**$ 28,937**	**$ 30,617**	**−$159,051**	**$135,316**
Cash balance	**$207,557**	**$234,813**	**$263,749**	**$294,366**	**$135,316**	**$135,316**

Cash flow analysis (second year)

Quarter	Q1	2 Q2	Q3	Q4	2
Cash from operations	$ 99,146	$123,933	$133,847	$138,805	$495,731
Cash from receivables	$ 0	$ 0	$ 0	$ 0	$ 0
Operating cash inflow	**$ 99,146**	**$123,933**	**$133,847**	**$138,805**	**$495,731**
Other cash inflows					
Equity investment	$ 0	$ 0	$ 0	$ 0	$ 0
Increased borrowings	$ 0	$ 0	$ 0	$ 0	$ 0
Sales of business assets	$ 0	$ 0	$ 0	$ 0	$ 0
A/P increases	$ 8,717	$ 10,897	$ 11,769	$ 12,204	$ 43,587
Total other cash inflows	**$ 8,717**	**$ 10,897**	**$ 11,769**	**$ 12,204**	**$ 43,587**
Total cash inflow	**$107,864**	**$134,830**	**$145,616**	**$151,009**	**$539,318**
Cash outflows					
Repayment of principal	$ 2,563	$ 2,621	$ 2,680	$ 2,741	$ 10,605
A/P decreases	$ 5,975	$ 7,469	$ 8,067	$ 8,365	$ 29,876
A/R increases	$ 0	$ 0	$ 0	$ 0	$ 0
Asset purchases	$ 24,787	$ 30,983	$ 33,462	$ 34,701	$123,933
Dividends	$ 69,402	$ 86,753	$ 93,693	$ 97,163	$347,012
Total cash outflows	**$102,727**	**$127,826**	**$137,902**	**$142,971**	**$511,425**
Net cash flow	**$ 5,137**	**$ 7,004**	**$ 7,714**	**$ 8,038**	**$ 27,893**
Cash balance	**$140,453**	**$147,456**	**$155,171**	**$163,209**	**$163,209**

Cash flow analysis (third year)

Quarter	Q1	3 Q2	Q3	Q4	3
Cash from operations	$148,447	$185,558	$200,403	$207,826	$742,234
Cash from receivables	$ 0	$ 0	$ 0	$ 0	$ 0
Operating cash inflow	**$148,447**	**$185,558**	**$200,403**	**$207,826**	**$742,234**
Other cash inflows					
Equity investment	$ 0	$ 0	$ 0	$ 0	$ 0
Increased borrowings	$ 0	$ 0	$ 0	$ 0	$ 0
Sales of business assets	$ 0	$ 0	$ 0	$ 0	$ 0
A/P increases	$ 10,025	$ 12,531	$ 13,534	$ 14,035	$ 50,125
Total other cash inflows	**$ 10,025**	**$ 12,531**	**$ 13,534**	**$ 14,035**	**$ 50,125**
Total cash inflow	**$158,472**	**$198,090**	**$213,937**	**$221,861**	**$792,359**
Cash outflows					
Repayment of principal	$ 2,803	$ 2,867	$ 2,932	$ 2,998	$ 11,599
A/P decreases	$ 7,170	$ 8,963	$ 9,680	$ 10,038	$ 35,852
A/R increases	$ 0	$ 0	$ 0	$ 0	$ 0
Asset purchases	$ 37,112	$ 46,390	$ 50,101	$ 51,956	$185,558
Dividends	$103,913	$129,891	$140,282	$145,478	$519,564
Total cash outflows	**$150,998**	**$188,110**	**$202,995**	**$210,471**	**$752,573**
Net cash flow	**$ 7,474**	**$ 9,980**	**$ 10,942**	**$ 11,390**	**$ 39,786**
Cash balance	**$170,683**	**$180,663**	**$191,605**	**$202,995**	**$202,995**

Dental Laboratory

Graf Dental Products, Inc.

54446 3rd. St.
Staten Island, NY 10302

BizPlanDB.com

Graf Dental Products, Inc. ("the Company") is a New York-based corporation that will provide the production of dental appliances (as ordered by dental practitioners) in its targeted market. The Company was founded by Henry Graf.

1.0 EXECUTIVE SUMMARY

The purpose of this business plan is to raise $100,000 for the development of a dental laboratory while showcasing the expected financials and operations over the next three years. Graf Dental Products, Inc. ("the Company") is a New York based corporation that will provide the production of dental appliances (as ordered by dental practitioners) in its targeted market. The Company was founded by Henry Graf.

1.1 The Services

As stated above, Graf Dental Products will specialize in the outsourced production of crowns, moldings, dentures, retainers, and other dental appliances required for dental treatments. The Company anticipates that it will earn gross margins of 70% on each dollar of revenue generated through the sale of dental appliances.

Prior to the onset of operations, Mr. Graf intends to aggressively develop ongoing referral relationships with dentists, orthodontist, endodontists, and prosthodontists that require ongoing production of dental appliances. The marketing strategies that Graf Dental Products will use will be discussed in the fifth section of the business plan.

The third section of the business plan will further describe the services offered by Graf Dental Products.

1.2 Financing

Mr. Graf is seeking to raise $100,000 as a bank loan. The interest rate and loan agreement are to be further discussed during negotiation. This business plan assumes that the business will receive a 10 year loan with a 9% fixed interest rate. The financing will be used for the following:

- Development of the Company's location.
- Financing for the first six months of operation.
- Capital to purchase dental laboratory equipment.

Mr. Graf will contribute $10,000 to the venture.

1.3 Mission Statement

Mr. Graf's mission is to become recognized as an outstanding regional supplier of dental appliances to dental practitioners while complying with all laws regarding the production and distribution of dental products.

1.4 Management Team

The Company was founded by Henry Graf. Mr. Graf has more than 10 years of experience in the dental lab technician industry. Through his expertise, he will be able to bring the operations of the business to profitability within its first year of operations.

1.5 Sales Forecasts

Mr. Graf expects a strong rate of growth at the start of operations. Below are the expected financials over the next three years.

Proforma profit and loss (yearly)

Year	1	2	3
Sales	$667,260	$800,712	$936,833
Operating costs	$389,783	$439,834	$502,761
EBITDA	$ 46,969	$ 84,268	$110,439
Taxes, interest, and depreciation	$ 31,586	$ 42,063	$ 51,597
Net profit	$ 15,383	$ 42,205	$ 58,842

Sales, operating costs, and profit forecast

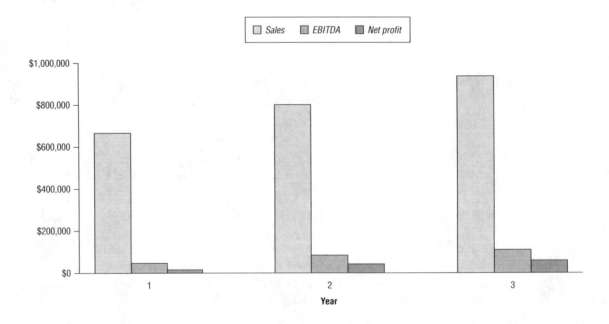

1.6 Expansion Plan

The Founder expects that the business will aggressively expand during the first three years of operation. Mr. Graf intends to implement marketing campaigns that will appeal to general dentists, endodontists, prosthodontists, and periodontists within the Company's targeted market.

2.0 COMPANY AND FINANCING SUMMARY

2.1 Registered Name and Corporate Structure

The Company is registered as a corporation in the State of New York.

2.2 Required Funds

At this time, Graf Dental Products requires $100,000 of debt funds. Below is a breakdown of how these funds will be used:

Projected startup costs

Initial lease payments	$ 10,000
Working capital	$ 35,000
FF&E	$ 10,000
Leasehold improvements	$ 5,000
Security deposits	$ 5,000
Insurance	$ 2,500
Laboratory Equipment	$ 30,000
Marketing budget	$ 7,500
Miscellaneous and unforeseen costs	$ 5,000
Total startup costs	**$110,000**

Use of funds

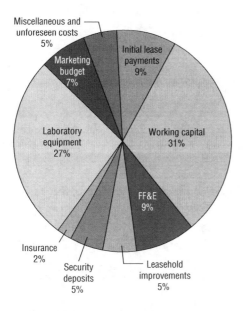

2.3 Investor Equity

Mr. Graf is not seeking an investment from a third party at this time.

2.4 Management Equity

Henry Graf owns 100% of Graf Dental Products, Inc.

2.5 Exit Strategy

If the business is very successful, Mr. Graf may seek to sell the business to a third party for a significant earnings multiple. Most likely, the Company will hire a qualified business broker to sell the business on behalf of Graf Dental Products. Based on historical numbers, the business could fetch a sales premium of up to 6 times earnings.

3.0 PRODUCTS AND SERVICES

Below is a description of the dental appliance production services offered by Graf Dental Products.

3.1 Production of Dental Appliances

As discussed in the executive summary, the Company will produce a number of customized dental appliances as ordered by dental practitioners that are clients of Graf Dental Products. These appliances include, but are not limited to:

- Dentures

- Retainers

- Crowns

- Moldings

- Dental Veneers

- Dental Implants

Mr. Graf expects that the business will earn gross margins of 70% of each dollar of revenue generated from the sale of these appliances to dental practitioners. An additional 10% of revenue will come from the distribution fees charged for shipping and handing of the manufactured dental products, on which the Company will earn contribute margins of 20%.

4.0 STRATEGIC AND MARKET ANALYSIS

4.1 Economic Outlook

This section of the analysis will detail the economic climate, the dental laboratory industry, the customer profile, and the competition that the business will face as it progresses through its business operations.

Dental laboratories operate with a strong degree of economic immunity for two reasons. First, people will continue to require quality dental care regardless of the state of the general economy. Secondly, a substantial number of people have dental insurance which covers the cost of dental appliances (i.e. very low out of pocket costs for dental appliances). As such, Graf Dental Products should have no issues with top line income despite the current downward economic trend.

4.2 Industry Analysis

Within the United States there are approximately 7,200 dental laboratories that produce dental appliances for dental practitioners. In each of the last five years, the industry has generated aggregate sales in excess of $3.3 billion while providing jobs to more than 50,000 people. Payrolls in each of the last five years have exceeded $1.5 billion.

The industry is expected to grow at a rate that is faster than that of the general economy as more people of the "Baby Boomer" generation will require specialized dental treatments as they enter their more mature years. Additionally, the demand for cosmetic dentistry has been on the rise over the last ten years as the wealth of the average American has grown. As such, Graf Dental Products is in a strong position to capitalize on this demand during the course of its business operations.

4.3 Customer Profile

The average client of Graf Dental Products will be a general dentist, cosmetic dentists, orthodontist, periodontist, or prosthodontist that is seeking to have an outsourced firm produce the dental appliances used in conjunction with their dental treatments. The field of dentistry is a wide and varied field with more than 135,000 practitioners in the United States. As such, it is hard to categorize the "average client" of the business. However, Management has outlined the following demographics that it will use when developing and implementing its marketing campaigns:

- Operates as a solo practitioner or small group practice

- Has annual billings exceeding $500,000 per year

- Has a continued need for dentures, implants, and other orthodontic/dental appliances for patients

- Will spend upwards of $10,000 with a dental laboratory firm

Within the Company's targeted market of the New York metropolitan area, there are approximately 5,000 dental practices that could become clients of Graf Dental Products.

4.4 Competition

As stated above, there are approximately 7,200 dental laboratories that operate within the United States. The internet has made it easier for companies that offer these services to enter the market as the business can solicit orders directly online from dental professionals. However, Management feels that by operating within the New York area the business will be able to do same day and next day delivery (via courier service). This will be a major competitive advantage for the Company as it progresses through its operations.

5.0 MARKETING PLAN

Graf Dental Products intends to maintain an extensive marketing campaign that will ensure maximum visibility for the business in its targeted market. Below is an overview of the marketing strategies and objectives.

5.1 Marketing Objectives

- Establish strong ongoing purchase order relationships on a regional basis with general dentists, prosthodontists, orthodontists, periodontists, and cosmetic dentists that will use the Company's dental lab services on a regular basis.

- Develop word of mouth referrals once the Company begins operations.

5.2 Marketing Strategies

Management intends on using a number of marketing strategies that will ensure that the business can develop ongoing relationships with dental professionals that will regularly call on Graf Dental Products for the production of dental appliances on behalf of their patients.

As discussed earlier, Mr. Graf intends to directly contact dentists and dental specialists to offer incentive discounts and better service arrangements so that the business can develop a roster of clients immediately. As Mr. Graf has been in the industry for some time, he will call on his list of current professional contacts to initially develop these client relationships.

The Company will also develop a website that showcases Graf Dental Products's operations, relevant contact information, and how a dentist/dental specialist can become a client of the business. To a limited extent, the website will also showcasing basic pricing of dental appliances produced by the business.

Graf Dental Products will also maintain print advertisements in state based and national level newsletters and periodicals targeted at the 135,000 practicing dentists and specialists within the United States.

5.3 Pricing

For each dental appliance produced by the Company, the business will generate $100 to $200 of revenue. The business will earn gross margins of approximately 70% on each dental appliance produced.

6.0 ORGANIZATIONAL PLAN AND PERSONNEL SUMMARY

6.1 Corporate Organization

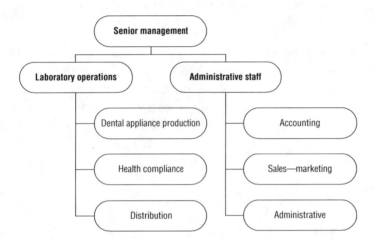

6.2 Organizational Budget

Personnel plan—yearly

Year	1	2	3
Owner	$ 45,000	$ 46,350	$ 47,741
Lab manager	$ 42,500	$ 43,775	$ 45,088
Lab technicians	$150,000	$154,500	$198,919
Administrative	$ 29,000	$ 59,740	$ 61,532
Accounting (P/T)	$ 22,000	$ 22,660	$ 23,340
Total	**$288,500**	**$327,025**	**$376,620**

Numbers of personnel

Owner	1	1	1
Lab manager	1	1	1
Lab technicians	4	4	5
Administrative	1	2	2
Accounting (P/T)	1	1	1
Totals	**8**	**9**	**10**

Personnel expense breakdown

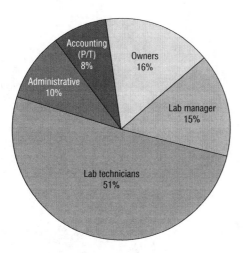

7.0 FINANCIAL PLAN

7.1 Underlying Assumptions

The Company has based its proforma financial statements on the following:

- Graf Dental Products will have an annual revenue growth rate of 16% per year.

- The Owner will acquire $100,000 of debt funds to develop the business.

- The loan will have a 10 year term with a 9% interest rate.

7.2 Sensitivity Analysis

In the event of an economic downturn, Management does not expect a decline it its revenues. People will continue to require specialized dental treatments regardless of the overall economic climate. Additionally, many dental insurance companies cover the cost of dental treatments that require dental appliances, and the out of pocket costs for a dental patient in regards to their dental appliance needs are minimal.

7.3 Source of Funds

Financing

Equity contributions	
Management investment	$ 10,000.00
Total equity financing	**$ 10,000.00**
Banks and lenders	
Banks and lenders	$ 100,000.00
Total debt financing	**$100,000.00**
Total financing	**$110,000.00**

7.4 General Assumptions

General assumptions

Year	1	2	3
Short term interest rate	9.5%	9.5%	9.5%
Long term interest rate	10.0%	10.0%	10.0%
Federal tax rate	33.0%	33.0%	33.0%
State tax rate	5.0%	5.0%	5.0%
Personnel taxes	15.0%	15.0%	15.0%

7.5 Profit and Loss Statements

Proforma profit and loss (yearly)

Year	1	2	3
Sales	**$667,260**	**$800,712**	**$936,833**
Cost of goods sold	$230,508	$276,610	$323,633
Gross margin	65.45%	65.45%	65.45%
Operating income	**$436,752**	**$524,102**	**$613,200**
Expenses			
Payroll	$ 288,500	$327,025	$376,620
General and administrative	$ 25,200	$ 26,208	$ 27,256
Marketing expenses	$ 3,336	$ 4,004	$ 4,684
Professional fees and licensure	$ 5,219	$ 5,376	$ 5,537
Insurance costs	$ 1,987	$ 2,086	$ 2,191
Laboratory expenses	$ 10,009	$ 12,011	$ 14,052
Rent and utilities	$ 4,250	$ 4,463	$ 4,686
Miscellaneous costs	$ 8,007	$ 9,609	$ 11,242
Payroll taxes	$ 43,275	$ 49,054	$ 56,493
Total operating costs	**$389,783**	**$439,834**	**$502,761**
EBITDA	**$ 46,969**	**$ 84,268**	**$110,439**
Federal income tax	$ 15,500	$ 25,125	$ 33,980
State income tax	$ 2,348	$ 3,807	$ 5,149
Interest expense	$ 8,738	$ 8,131	$ 7,468
Depreciation expenses	$ 5,000	$ 5,000	$ 5,000
Net profit	**$ 15,383**	**$ 42,205**	**$ 58,842**
Profit margin	**2.31%**	**5.27%**	**6.28%**

Sales, operating costs, and profit forecast

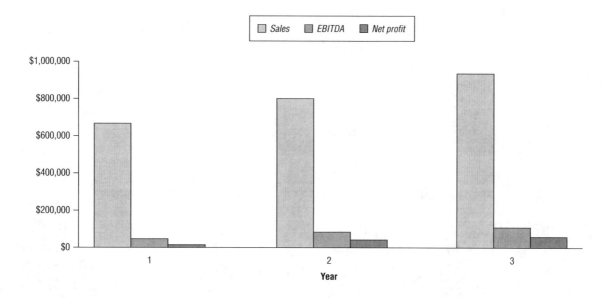

7.6 Cash Flow Analysis

Proforma cash flow analysis—yearly

Year	1	2	3
Cash from operations	$ 20,383	$47,205	$ 63,842
Cash from receivables	$ 0	$ 0	$ 0
Operating cash inflow	**$ 20,383**	**$47,205**	**$ 63,842**
Other cash inflows			
Equity investment	$ 10,000	$ 0	$ 0
Increased borrowings	$100,000	$ 0	$ 0
Sales of business assets	$ 0	$ 0	$ 0
A/P increases	$ 37,902	$43,587	$ 50,125
Total other cash inflows	**$147,902**	**$43,587**	**$ 50,125**
Total cash inflow	**$168,285**	**$90,792**	**$113,967**
Cash outflows			
Repayment of principal	$ 6,463	$ 7,070	$ 7,733
A/P decreases	$ 24,897	$29,876	$ 35,852
A/R increases	$ 0	$ 0	$ 0
Asset purchases	$ 67,500	$11,801	$ 15,961
Dividends	$ 14,268	$33,043	$ 44,689
Total cash outflows	**$113,128**	**$81,791**	**$104,235**
Net cash flow	**$ 55,156**	**$ 9,001**	**$ 9,733**
Cash balance	**$ 55,156**	**$64,158**	**$ 73,891**

Proforma cash flow (yearly)

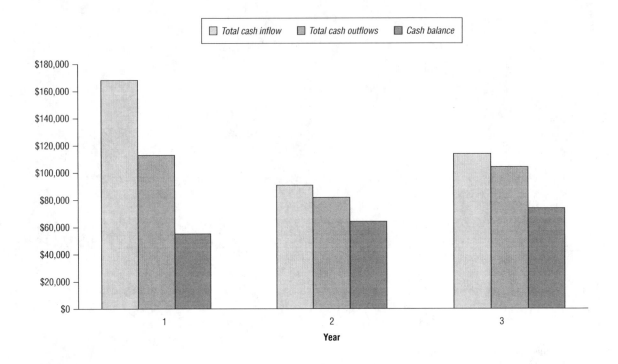

7.7 Balance Sheet

Proforma balance sheet—yearly

Year	1	2	3
Assets			
Cash	$ 55,156	$ 64,158	$ 73,891
Amortized expansion costs	$ 30,000	$ 31,180	$ 32,776
Dental equipment	$ 30,000	$ 38,851	$ 50,821
FF&E	$ 10,000	$ 11,770	$ 14,164
Accumulated depreciation	($ 5,000)	($ 10,000)	($ 15,000)
Total assets	**$120,156**	**$135,959**	**$156,653**
Liabilities and equity			
Accounts payable	$ 13,005	$ 26,716	$ 40,990
Long term liabilities	$ 93,537	$ 86,467	$ 79,397
Other liabilities	$ 0	$ 0	$ 0
Total liabilities	**$106,542**	**$113,183**	**$120,387**
Net worth	**$ 13,615**	**$ 22,776**	**$ 36,266**
Total liabilities and equity	**$120,156**	**$135,959**	**$156,653**

Proforma balance sheet

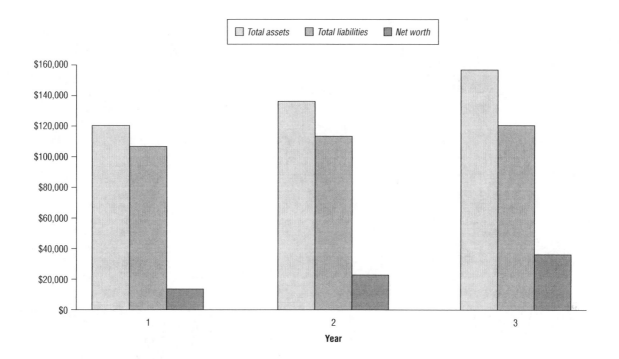

7.8 Breakeven Analysis

Monthly break even analysis

Year	1	2	3
Monthly revenue	$ 49,625	$ 55,997	$ 64,009
Yearly revenue	$595,502	$671,969	$768,106

Break even analysis

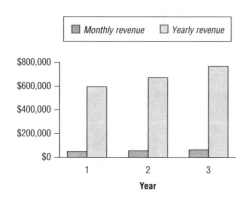

7.9 Business Ratios

Business ratios—yearly

Year	1	2	3
Sales			
Sales growth	0.0%	20.0%	17.0%
Gross margin	65.5%	65.5%	65.5%
Financials			
Profit margin	2.31%	5.27%	6.28%
Assets to liabilities	1.13	1.20	1.30
Equity to liabilities	0.13	0.20	0.30
Assets to equity	8.83	5.97	4.32
Liquidity			
Acid test	0.52	0.57	0.61
Cash to assets	0.46	0.47	0.47

7.10 Three Year Profit and Loss Statement

Profit and loss statement (first year)

Months	1	2	3	4	5	6	7
Sales	**$55,000**	**$55,110**	**$55,220**	**$55,330**	**$55,440**	**$55,550**	**$55,660**
Cost of goods sold	$19,000	$19,038	$19,076	$19,114	$19,152	$19,190	$19,228
Gross margin	65.5%	65.5%	65.5%	65.5%	65.5%	65.5%	65.5%
Operating income	**$36,000**	**$36,072**	**$36,144**	**$36,216**	**$36,288**	**$36,360**	**$36,432**
Expenses							
Payroll	$24,042	$24,042	$24,042	$24,042	$24,042	$24,042	$24,042
General and administrative	$ 2,100	$ 2,100	$ 2,100	$ 2,100	$ 2,100	$ 2,100	$ 2,100
Marketing expenses	$ 278	$ 278	$ 278	$ 278	$ 278	$ 278	$ 278
Professional fees and licensure	$ 435	$ 435	$ 435	$ 435	$ 435	$ 435	$ 435
Insurance costs	$ 166	$ 166	$ 166	$ 166	$ 166	$ 166	$ 166
Laboratory expenses	$ 834	$ 834	$ 834	$ 834	$ 834	$ 834	$ 834
Rent and utilities	$ 354	$ 354	$ 354	$ 354	$ 354	$ 354	$ 354
Miscellaneous costs	$ 667	$ 667	$ 667	$ 667	$ 667	$ 667	$ 667
Payroll taxes	$ 3,606	$ 3,606	$ 3,606	$ 3,606	$ 3,606	$ 3,606	$ 3,606
Total operating costs	**$32,482**	**$32,482**	**$32,482**	**$32,482**	**$32,482**	**$32,482**	**$32,482**
EBITDA	**$ 3,518**	**$ 3,590**	**$ 3,662**	**$ 3,734**	**$ 3,806**	**$ 3,878**	**$ 3,950**
Federal income tax	$ 1,278	$ 1,280	$ 1,283	$ 1,285	$ 1,288	$ 1,290	$ 1,293
State income tax	$ 194	$ 194	$ 194	$ 195	$ 195	$ 196	$ 196
Interest expense	$ 750	$ 746	$ 742	$ 738	$ 734	$ 730	$ 726
Depreciation expense	$ 417	$ 417	$ 417	$ 417	$ 417	$ 417	$ 417
Net profit	**$ 880**	**$ 953**	**$ 1,026**	**$ 1,099**	**$ 1,172**	**$ 1,245**	**$ 1,318**

Profit and loss statement (first year cont.)

Month	8	9	10	11	12	1
Sales	$55,770	$55,880	$55,990	$56,100	$56,210	$667,260
Cost of goods sold	$19,266	$19,304	$19,342	$19,380	$19,418	$230,508
Gross margin	65.5%	65.5%	65.5%	65.5%	65.5%	65.5%
Operating income	$36,504	$36,576	$36,648	$36,720	$36,792	$436,752
Expenses						
Payroll	$24,042	$24,042	$24,042	$24,042	$24,042	$288,500
General and administrative	$ 2,100	$ 2,100	$ 2,100	$ 2,100	$ 2,100	$ 25,200
Marketing expenses	$ 278	$ 278	$ 278	$ 278	$ 278	$ 3,336
Professional fees and licensure	$ 435	$ 435	$ 435	$ 435	$ 435	$ 5,219
Insurance costs	$ 166	$ 166	$ 166	$ 166	$ 166	$ 1,987
Laboratory expenses	$ 834	$ 834	$ 834	$ 834	$ 834	$ 10,009
Rent and utilities	$ 354	$ 354	$ 354	$ 354	$ 354	$ 4,250
Miscellaneous costs	$ 667	$ 667	$ 667	$ 667	$ 667	$ 8,007
Payroll taxes	$ 3,606	$ 3,606	$ 3,606	$ 3,606	$ 3,606	$ 43,275
Total operating costs	$32,482	$32,482	$32,482	$32,482	$32,482	$389,783
EBITDA	$ 4,022	$ 4,094	$ 4,166	$ 4,238	$ 4,310	$ 46,969
Federal income tax	$ 1,295	$ 1,298	$ 1,301	$ 1,303	$ 1,306	$ 15,500
State income tax	$ 196	$ 197	$ 197	$ 197	$ 198	$ 2,348
Interest expense	$ 722	$ 718	$ 714	$ 710	$ 706	$ 8,738
Depreciation expense	$ 417	$ 417	$ 417	$ 417	$ 417	$ 5,000
Net profit	$ 1,391	$ 1,465	$ 1,538	$ 1,611	$ 1,684	$ 15,383

Profit and loss statement (second year)

Quarter	Q1	2 Q2	Q3	Q4	2
Sales	$160,142	$200,178	$216,192	$224,199	$800,712
Cost of goods sold	$ 55,322	$ 69,152	$ 74,685	$ 77,451	$276,610
Gross margin	65.5%	65.5%	65.5%	65.5%	65.5%
Operating income	$104,820	$131,026	$141,508	$146,749	$524,102
Expenses					
Payroll	$ 65,405	$ 81,756	$ 88,297	$ 91,567	$327,025
General and administrative	$ 5,242	$ 6,552	$ 7,076	$ 7,338	$ 26,208
Marketing expenses	$ 801	$ 1,001	$ 1,081	$ 1,121	$ 4,004
Professional fees and licensure	$ 1,075	$ 1,344	$ 1,451	$ 1,505	$ 5,376
Insurance costs	$ 417	$ 522	$ 563	$ 584	$ 2,086
Laboratory expenses	$ 2,402	$ 3,003	$ 3,243	$ 3,363	$ 12,011
Rent and utilities	$ 893	$ 1,116	$ 1,205	$ 1,250	$ 4,463
Miscellaneous costs	$ 1,922	$ 2,402	$ 2,594	$ 2,690	$ 9,609
Payroll taxes	$ 9,811	$ 12,263	$ 13,245	$ 13,735	$ 49,054
Total operating costs	$ 87,967	$109,958	$118,755	$123,154	$439,834
EBITDA	$ 16,854	$ 21,067	$ 22,752	$ 23,595	$ 84,268
Federal income tax	$ 5,025	$ 6,281	$ 6,784	$ 7,035	$ 25,125
State income tax	$ 761	$ 952	$ 1,028	$ 1,066	$ 3,807
Interest expense	$ 2,092	$ 2,053	$ 2,013	$ 1,973	$ 8,131
Depreciation expense	$ 1,250	$ 1,250	$ 1,250	$ 1,250	$ 5,000
Net profit	$ 7,725	$ 10,531	$ 11,677	$ 12,271	$ 42,205

Profit and loss statement (third year)

Quarter	Q1	3 Q2	Q3	Q4	3
Sales	$187,367	$234,208	$252,945	$262,313	$936,833
Cost of goods sold	$ 64,727	$ 80,908	$ 87,381	$ 90,617	$323,633
Gross margin	65.5%	65.5%	65.5%	65.5%	65.5%
Operating income	$122,640	$153,300	$165,564	$171,696	$613,200
Expenses					
Payroll	$ 75,324	$ 94,155	$101,687	$105,453	$376,620
General and administrative	$ 5,451	$ 6,814	$ 7,359	$ 7,632	$ 27,256
Marketing expenses	$ 937	$ 1,171	$ 1,265	$ 1,312	$ 4,684
Professional fees and licensure	$ 1,107	$ 1,384	$ 1,495	$ 1,550	$ 5,537
Insurance costs	$ 438	$ 548	$ 591	$ 613	$ 2,191
Laboratory expenses	$ 2,810	$ 3,513	$ 3,794	$ 3,935	$ 14,052
Rent and utilities	$ 937	$ 1,171	$ 1,265	$ 1,312	$ 4,686
Miscellaneous costs	$ 2,248	$ 2,810	$ 3,035	$ 3,148	$ 11,242
Payroll taxes	$ 11,299	$ 14,123	$ 15,253	$ 15,818	$ 56,493
Total operating costs	$100,552	$125,690	$135,745	$140,773	$502,761
EBITDA	$ 22,088	$ 27,610	$ 29,819	$ 30,923	$110,439
Federal income tax	$ 6,796	$ 8,495	$ 9,175	$ 9,515	$ 33,980
State income tax	$ 1,030	$ 1,287	$ 1,390	$ 1,442	$ 5,149
Interest expense	$ 1,932	$ 1,889	$ 1,846	$ 1,802	$ 7,468
Depreciation expense	$ 1,250	$ 1,250	$ 1,250	$ 1,250	$ 5,000
Net profit	$ 11,080	$ 14,688	$ 16,158	$ 16,915	$ 58,842

7.11 Three Year Cash Flow Analysis

Cash flow analysis (first year)

Month	1	2	3	4	5	6	7
Cash from operations	$ 1,297	$ 1,370	$ 1,443	$ 1,516	$ 1,589	$ 1,662	$ 1,735
Cash from receivables	$ 0	$ 0	$ 0	$ 0	$ 0	$ 0	$ 0
Operating cash inflow	$ 1,297	$ 1,370	$ 1,443	$ 1,516	$ 1,589	$ 1,662	$ 1,735
Other cash inflows							
Equity investment	$ 10,000	$ 0	$ 0	$ 0	$ 0	$ 0	$ 0
Increased borrowings	$100,000	$ 0	$ 0	$ 0	$ 0	$ 0	$ 0
Sales of business assets	$ 0	$ 0	$ 0	$ 0	$ 0	$ 0	$ 0
A/P increases	$ 3,159	$ 3,159	$ 3,159	$ 3,159	$ 3,159	$ 3,159	$ 3,159
Total other cash inflows	$113,159	$ 3,159	$ 3,159	$ 3,159	$ 3,159	$ 3,159	$ 3,159
Total cash inflow	$114,455	$ 4,528	$ 4,601	$ 4,674	$ 4,747	$ 4,820	$ 4,893
Cash outflows							
Repayment of principal	$ 517	$ 521	$ 525	$ 528	$ 532	$ 536	$ 540
A/P decreases	$ 2,075	$ 2,075	$ 2,075	$ 2,075	$ 2,075	$ 2,075	$ 2,075
A/R increases	$ 0	$ 0	$ 0	$ 0	$ 0	$ 0	$ 0
Asset purchases	$ 67,500	$ 0	$ 0	$ 0	$ 0	$ 0	$ 0
Dividends	$ 0	$ 0	$ 0	$ 0	$ 0	$ 0	$ 0
Total cash outflows	$ 70,092	$ 2,595	$ 2,599	$ 2,603	$ 2,607	$ 2,611	$ 2,615
Net cash flow	$ 44,364	$ 1,933	$ 2,002	$ 2,071	$ 2,140	$ 2,209	$ 2,278
Cash balance	$ 44,364	$46,297	$48,299	$50,370	$52,510	$54,719	$56,997

Cash flow analysis (first year cont.)

Month	8	9	10	11	12	1
Cash from operations	$ 1,808	$ 1,881	$ 1,954	$ 2,028	$ 2,101	$ 20,383
Cash from receivables	$ 0	$ 0	$ 0	$ 0	$ 0	$ 0
Operating cash inflow	**$ 1,808**	**$ 1,881**	**$ 1,954**	**$ 2,028**	**$ 2,101**	**$ 20,383**
Other cash inflows						
Equity investment	$ 0	$ 0	$ 0	$ 0	$ 0	$ 10,000
Increased borrowings	$ 0	$ 0	$ 0	$ 0	$ 0	$100,000
Sales of business assets	$ 0	$ 0	$ 0	$ 0	$ 0	$ 0
A/P increases	$ 3,159	$ 3,159	$ 3,159	$ 3,159	$ 3,159	$ 37,902
Total other cash inflows	**$ 3,159**	**$ 3,159**	**$ 3,159**	**$ 3,159**	**$ 3,159**	**$147,902**
Total cash inflow	**$ 4,967**	**$ 5,040**	**$ 5,113**	**$ 5,186**	**$ 5,259**	**$168,285**
Cash outflows						
Repayment of principal	$ 545	$ 549	$ 553	$ 557	$ 561	$ 6,463
A/P decreases	$ 2,075	$ 2,075	$ 2,075	$ 2,075	$ 2,075	$ 24,897
A/R increases	$ 0	$ 0	$ 0	$ 0	$ 0	$ 0
Asset purchases	$ 0	$ 0	$ 0	$ 0	$ 0	$ 67,500
Dividends	$ 0	$ 0	$ 0	$ 0	$14,268	$ 14,268
Total cash outflows	**$ 2,619**	**$ 2,623**	**$ 2,627**	**$ 2,632**	**$16,904**	**$113,128**
Net cash flow	**$ 2,347**	**$ 2,416**	**$ 2,485**	**$ 2,554**	**−$11,644**	**$ 55,156**
Cash balance	**$59,345**	**$61,761**	**$64,246**	**$66,801**	**$55,156**	**$ 55,156**

Cash flow analysis (second year)

Quarter	Q1	2 Q2	Q3	Q4	2
Cash from operations	$ 9,441	$11,801	$12,745	$13,217	$47,205
Cash from receivables	$ 0	$ 0	$ 0	$ 0	$ 0
Operating cash inflow	**$ 9,441**	**$11,801**	**$12,745**	**$13,217**	**$47,205**
Other cash inflows					
Equity investment	$ 0	$ 0	$ 0	$ 0	$ 0
Increased borrowings	$ 0	$ 0	$ 0	$ 0	$ 0
Sales of business assets	$ 0	$ 0	$ 0	$ 0	$ 0
A/P increases	$ 8,717	$10,897	$11,769	$12,204	$43,587
Total other cash inflows	**$ 8,717**	**$10,897**	**$11,769**	**$12,204**	**$43,587**
Total cash inflow	**$18,158**	**$22,698**	**$24,514**	**$25,422**	**$90,792**
Cash outflows					
Repayment of principal	$ 1,708	$ 1,747	$ 1,787	$ 1,827	$ 7,070
A/P decreases	$ 5,975	$ 7,469	$ 8,067	$ 8,365	$29,876
A/R increases	$ 0	$ 0	$ 0	$ 0	$ 0
Asset purchases	$ 2,360	$ 2,950	$ 3,186	$ 3,304	$11,801
Dividends	$ 6,609	$ 8,261	$ 8,922	$ 9,252	$33,043
Total cash outflows	**$16,653**	**$20,427**	**$21,961**	**$22,749**	**$81,791**
Net cash flow	**$ 1,506**	**$ 2,271**	**$ 2,552**	**$ 2,673**	**$ 9,001**
Cash balance	**$56,662**	**$58,933**	**$61,485**	**$64,158**	**$64,158**

Cash flow analysis (third year)

Quarter	Q1	3 Q2	Q3	Q4	3
Cash from operations	$12,768	$15,961	$17,237	$17,876	$ 63,842
Cash from receivables	$ 0	$ 0	$ 0	$ 0	$ 0
Operating cash inflow	**$12,768**	**$15,961**	**$17,237**	**$17,876**	**$ 63,842**
Other cash inflows					
Equity investment	$ 0	$ 0	$ 0	$ 0	$ 0
Increased borrowings	$ 0	$ 0	$ 0	$ 0	$ 0
Sales of business assets	$ 0	$ 0	$ 0	$ 0	$ 0
A/P increases	$10,025	$12,531	$13,534	$14,035	$ 50,125
Total other cash inflows	**$10,025**	**$12,531**	**$13,534**	**$14,035**	**$ 50,125**
Total cash inflow	**$22,793**	**$28,492**	**$30,771**	**$31,911**	**$113,967**
Cash outflows					
Repayment of principal	$ 1,869	$ 1,911	$ 1,954	$ 1,999	$ 7,733
A/P decreases	$ 7,170	$ 8,963	$ 9,680	$10,038	$ 35,852
A/R increases	$ 0	$ 0	$ 0	$ 0	$ 0
Asset purchases	$ 3,192	$ 3,990	$ 4,309	$ 4,469	$ 15,961
Dividends	$ 8,938	$11,172	$12,066	$12,513	$ 44,689
Total cash outflows	**$21,169**	**$26,036**	**$28,010**	**$29,019**	**$104,235**
Net cash flow	**$ 1,624**	**$ 2,455**	**$ 2,761**	**$ 2,892**	**$ 9,733**
Cash balance	**$65,782**	**$68,238**	**$70,999**	**$73,891**	**$ 73,891**

Exotic Car Rental Service

New York Luxury Autos

PO Box 22901
New York, NY 10012

BizPlanDB.com

New York Luxury Autos ("the Company") is a New York-based corporation that will provide the rental of very high-end sports cars and luxury automobiles in its targeted market. The Company was founded by Les Roberts.

1.0 EXECUTIVE SUMMARY

The purpose of this business plan is to raise $300,000 for the development of a car rental agency that specializes in the rental of exotic cars while showcasing the expected financials and operations over the next three years. New York Luxury Autos ("the Company") is a New York-based corporation that will provide the rental of very high-end sports cars and luxury automobiles in its targeted market. The Company was founded by Les Roberts.

1.1 The Services

As mentioned above, New York Luxury Autos will be actively engaged in the rental of high-end vehicles within its targeted market. These vehicles will include brand name such as Rolls Royce, Porsche, Ferrari, Lamborghini, Lotus, Bentley, and related high-end vehicles. The bulk of the Company's revenues will come from the daily rental charges for vehicle usage. The business will also recognize revenues from the sale of insurance services and gasoline charges to customers.

At the onset of operations, the Company intends to have a fleet of 10 vehicles that will be acquired on a leased basis.

The third section of the business plan will further describe the services offered by New York Luxury Autos.

1.2 Financing

Mr. Roberts is seeking to raise $300,000 from a bank loan. The interest rate and loan agreement are to be further discussed during negotiation. This business plan assumes that the business will receive a 10-year loan with a 9% fixed interest rate. The financing will be used for the following:

- Development of the Company's location.

- Financing for the first six months of operation.

- Capital to lease 10 vehicles at the onset of operations.

Mr. Roberts will contribute $10,000 to the venture.

1.3 Mission Statement

It is the mission of New York Luxury Autos to become the recognized leader in its targeted market for renting high-end vehicles to the general public on a daily basis.

1.4 Management Team

The Company was founded by Les Roberts. Mr. Roberts has more than 10 years of experience in the automotive industry. Through his expertise, he will be able to bring the operations of the business to profitability within its first year of operations.

1.5 Sales Forecasts

Mr. Roberts expects a strong rate of growth at the start of operations. Below are the expected financials over the next three years.

Proforma profit and loss (yearly)

Year	1	2	3
Sales	$966,378	$1,159,654	$1,356,795
Operating costs	$476,488	$ 567,163	$ 600,012
EBITDA	$152,021	$ 187,048	$ 282,414
Taxes, interest, and depreciation	$103,088	$ 105,310	$ 140,315
Net profit	$ 48,933	$ 81,738	$ 142,099

Sales, operating costs, and profit forecast

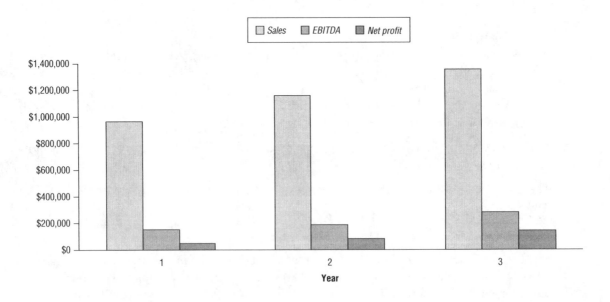

1.6 Expansion Plan

The Founder expects that the business will aggressively expand during the first three years of operation. Mr. Roberts intends to implement marketing campaigns that will effectively target individuals within the target market.

2.0 COMPANY AND FINANCING SUMMARY

2.1 Registered Name and Corporate Structure
The Company is registered as a corporation in the State of New York.

2.2 Required Funds
At this time, New York Luxury Autos requires $300,000 of debt funds. Below is a breakdown of how these funds will be used:

Projected startup costs

Initial lease payments and deposits	$ 10,000
Working capital	$ 35,000
FF&E	$ 10,000
Leasehold improvements	$ 75,000
Security deposits	$ 5,000
Insurance	$ 2,500
Deposits for exotic vehicle leases	$160,000
Marketing budget	$ 7,500
Miscellaneous and unforeseen costs	$ 5,000
Total startup costs	**$310,000**

Use of funds

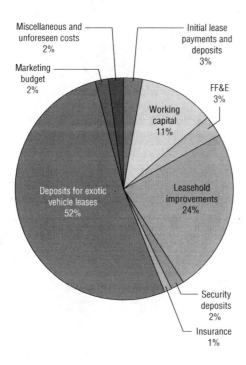

2.3 Investor Equity
Mr. Roberts is not seeking an investment from a third party at this time.

2.4 Management Equity
Les Roberts owns 100% of New York Luxury Autos, Inc.

2.5 Exit Strategy

If the business is very successful, Mr. Roberts may seek to sell the business to a third party for a significant earnings multiple. Most likely, the Company will hire a qualified business broker to sell the business on behalf of New York Luxury Autos. Based on historical numbers, the business could fetch a sales premium of up to 4 times earnings.

3.0 PRODUCTS AND SERVICES

Below is a description of the car rental services offered by New York Luxury Autos.

3.1 Daily Car Rentals

The primary source of revenue for the business will come from the direct daily rental of the Company's fleet of approximately 10 exotic vehicles. Management expects that 75% of all rentals will fall into the economy or standard class. Daily charges to clients will range from $500 to $750 per day depending on the type of vehicle they intend to rent.

The business will offer high-end services including the drop-off and pick up of vehicles for an additional fee. At all times, a customer will be able to reach the business in the event of an accident or emergency.

3.2 Insurance Fees and Ancillary Services

In addition to daily charges made to vehicle renters, the Company will earn secondary streams of revenue from the sale of additional insurance. This is an important secondary steam of revenue for the business as sales of additional car insurance will generate substantial gross margins for New York Luxury Autos. Additionally, the Company will charge substantial fees to customers that do not return the vehicles with full gas tanks. Approximately 25% of the Company's aggregate revenues will come from the sale of insurance and gas fees.

4.0 STRATEGIC AND MARKET ANALYSIS

4.1 Economic Outlook

This section of the analysis will detail the economic climate, the car rental industry, the customer profile, and the competition that the business will face as it progresses through its business operations.

Currently, the economic market condition in the United States is moderate. Unemployment rates have declined while asset prices have increased substantially. In the event of an economic recession, New York Luxury Autos may have a decline in its revenues as people pull back on luxury expenditures including the rental of high end cars.

4.2 Industry Analysis

Within the United States, there are more than 5,000 companies (that operate one or more locations) that provide daily car rental services to the general public. Each year, these businesses aggregately generate more than $20 billion dollars of revenue and provide jobs to more than 120,000 people. Aggregate payrolls in each of the last five years have exceeded $3.1 billion. Approximately 5% of all car rental agencies specialize specifically in the rental of exotic vehicles.

This is a mature industry, and the future expected growth rate is expected to equal that of the general economy. As mentioned above, despite the currently high gasoline prices, the industry will continue to remain profitable as business travelers will continue to require rented vehicles during their business trips.

4.3 Customer Profile

The Company's average client will be a middle to upper middle class individuals in the Company's target market. Common traits among clients will include:

- Annual household income exceeding $100,000.

- Will spend $400 to $700 per day with New York Luxury Autos.

- Lives or is within 50 miles of the Company's location.

Within the greater metropolitan area, there are approximately 200,000 individuals that fit the Company's demographic profile. As such, the business will seek to market to these affluent individuals that want to experience driving an exotic or high-end vehicle. The business will require that any individual that rents a car from the Company be at least 30 years of age.

4.4 Competition

In the Company's target market radius, there are five other car rental agencies that specialize in the daily rental of exotic and high-end cars to individuals. As such, the business (in order to remain competitive) must keep a fleet of new vehicles (that are in demand) that are popular among high-end car enthusiasts. The business will work closely with regional exotic vehicle dealers to ensure that the business can lease exotic vehicles with the intent to rent them to the general public at all times.

5.0 MARKETING PLAN

New York Luxury Autos intends to maintain an extensive marketing campaign that will ensure maximum visibility for the business in its targeted market. Below is an overview of the marketing strategies and objectives of New York Luxury Autos.

5.1 Marketing Objectives

- Establish relationships with airports and travel agents surrounding the target market.

- Develop relationships with car agencies that will provide referrals to the Company in regards to renting exotic and high-end cars.

- Maintain a large presence on the internet in order for individuals to reserve exotic vehicles to rent.

5.2 Marketing Strategies

Mr. Roberts intends on using a number of marketing strategies that will allow New York Luxury Autos to easily target tourists and residents living in target market. The business will primarily focus its marketing efforts towards affluent individuals as the daily charges related to renting an exotic vehicle are relatively high. The business will frequently advertise in regional lifestyle magazines that have a readership with a demographic profile similar to that discussed in the previous section of the business plan.

Mr. Roberts will register New York Luxury Autos with online portals so that potential customers can easily reach the business. The Company will also develop its own online website, which will include functionality for people to book and pay for vehicle rentals directly through the Company's online platform. This marketing feature is common to most companies that rent cars to the general public.

Mr. Roberts will also develop relationships with local travel agents that will make arrangements for rentals among people that are traveling through the target market and want to drive an exotic car while on vacation.

5.3 Pricing

The average daily fee for renting an exotic vehicle from the Company will be $500 per day.

6.0 ORGANIZATIONAL PLAN AND PERSONNEL SUMMARY

6.1 Corporate Organization

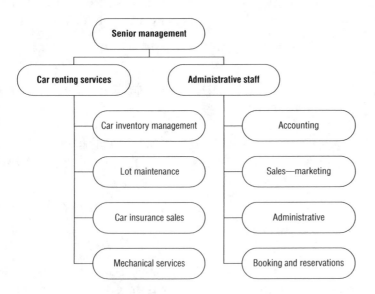

6.2 Organizational Budget

Personnel plan—yearly

Year	1	2	3
Owner	$ 50,000	$ 51,500	$ 53,045
General manager	$ 42,500	$ 43,775	$ 45,088
Agency employees	$110,000	$135,960	$140,039
Mechanic	$ 29,000	$ 59,740	$ 61,532
Administrative and accounting	$ 58,000	$ 59,740	$ 61,532
Total	**$289,500**	**$350,715**	**$361,236**

Numbers of personnel

Owner	1	1	1
General manager	1	1	1
Agency employees	5	6	6
Mechanic	1	2	2
Administrative and accounting	2	2	2
Totals	**10**	**12**	**12**

Personnel expense breakdown

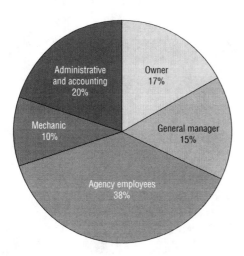

7.0 FINANCIAL PLAN

7.1 Underlying Assumptions

The Company has based its proforma financial statements on the following:

- New York Luxury Autos will have an annual revenue growth rate of 16% per year.

- The Owner will acquire $300,000 of debt funds to develop the business.

- The loan will have a 10-year term with a 9% interest rate.

7.2 Sensitivity Analysis

In the event of an economic downturn, the business may have a decline in its revenues. However, the high gross margins generated by the business will ensure that the business is able to remain profitable and cash flow positive at all times.

7.3 Source of Funds

Financing

Equity contributions	
Management investment	$ 10,000.00
Total equity financing	**$ 10,000.00**
Banks and lenders	
Banks and lenders	$ 100,000.00
Total debt financing	**$100,000.00**
Total financing	**$110,000.00**

7.4 General Assumptions

General assumptions

Year	1	2	3
Short term interest rate	9.5%	9.5%	9.5%
Long term interest rate	10.0%	10.0%	10.0%
Federal tax rate	33.0%	33.0%	33.0%
State tax rate	5.0%	5.0%	5.0%
Personnel taxes	15.0%	15.0%	15.0%

7.5 Profit and Loss Statement

Proforma profit and loss (yearly)

Year	1	2	3
Sales	**$966,378**	**$1,159,654**	**$1,356,795**
Cost of goods sold	$337,869	$ 405,443	$ 474,368
Gross margin	65.04%	65.04%	65.04%
Operating income	**$628,509**	**$ 754,211**	**$ 882,427**
Expenses			
Payroll	$289,500	$ 350,715	$ 361,236
General and administrative	$ 13,200	$ 13,728	$ 14,277
Marketing expenses	$ 28,991	$ 34,790	$ 40,704
Professional fees and licensure	$ 5,219	$ 5,376	$ 5,537
Insurance costs	$ 11,987	$ 12,586	$ 13,216
Vehicle maintenance costs	$ 48,319	$ 57,983	$ 67,840
Rent and utilities	$ 24,250	$ 25,463	$ 26,736
Miscellaneous costs	$ 11,597	$ 13,916	$ 16,282
Payroll taxes	$ 43,425	$ 52,607	$ 54,185
Total operating costs	**$476,488**	**$ 567,163**	**$ 600,012**
EBITDA	**$152,021**	**$ 187,048**	**$ 282,414**
Federal income tax	$ 50,167	$ 53,676	$ 85,803
State income tax	$ 7,601	$ 8,133	$ 13,000
Interest expense	$ 26,213	$ 24,394	$ 22,405
Depreciation expenses	$ 19,107	$ 19,107	$ 19,107
Net profit	**$ 48,933**	**$ 81,738**	**$ 142,099**
Profit margin	**5.06%**	**7.05%**	**10.47%**

Sales, operating costs, and profit forecast

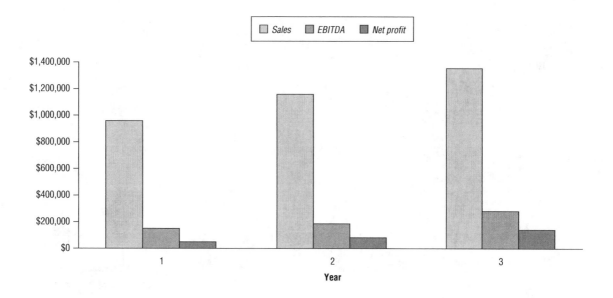

7.6 Cash Flow Analysis

Proforma cash flow analysis—yearly

Year	1	2	3
Cash from operations	$ 68,040	$100,845	$161,206
Cash from receivables	$ 0	$ 0	$ 0
Operating cash inflow	**$ 68,040**	**$100,845**	**$161,206**
Other cash inflows			
Equity investment	$ 10,000	$ 0	$ 0
Increased borrowings	$300,000	$ 0	$ 0
Sales of business assets	$ 0	$ 0	$ 0
A/P increases	$ 37,902	$ 43,587	$ 50,125
Total other cash inflows	**$347,902**	**$ 43,587**	**$ 50,125**
Total cash inflow	**$415,942**	**$144,433**	**$211,331**
Cash outflows			
Repayment of principal	$ 19,390	$ 21,209	$ 23,199
A/P decreases	$ 24,897	$ 29,876	$ 35,852
A/R increases	$ 0	$ 0	$ 0
Asset purchases	$267,500	$ 25,211	$ 40,302
Dividends	$ 40,824	$ 60,507	$ 96,724
Total cash outflows	**$352,611**	**$136,804**	**$196,075**
Net cash flow	**$ 63,331**	**$ 7,629**	**$ 15,256**
Cash balance	**$ 63,331**	**$ 70,959**	**$ 86,215**

Proforma cash flow (yearly)

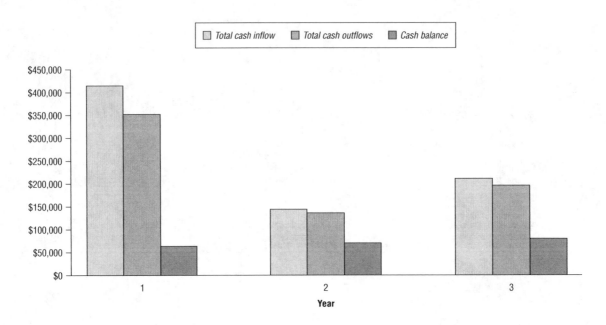

7.7 Balance Sheet

Proforma balance sheet—yearly

Year	1	2	3
Assets			
Cash	$ 63,331	$ 70,959	$ 86,215
Amortized expansion costs	$ 97,500	$100,021	$104,051
Vehicle deposits	$160,000	$178,909	$209,135
FF&E	$ 10,000	$ 13,782	$ 19,827
Accumulated depreciation	($ 19,107)	($ 38,214)	($ 57,321)
Total assets	**$311,724**	**$325,457**	**$361,907**
Liabilities and equity			
Accounts payable	$ 13,005	$ 26,716	$ 40,990
Long term liabilities	$280,610	$259,401	$238,192
Other liabilities	$ 0	$ 0	$ 0
Total liabilities	**$293,615**	**$286,117**	**$279,181**
Net worth	**$ 18,109**	**$ 39,340**	**$ 82,726**
Total liabilities and equity	**$311,724**	**$325,457**	**$361,907**

Proforma balance sheet

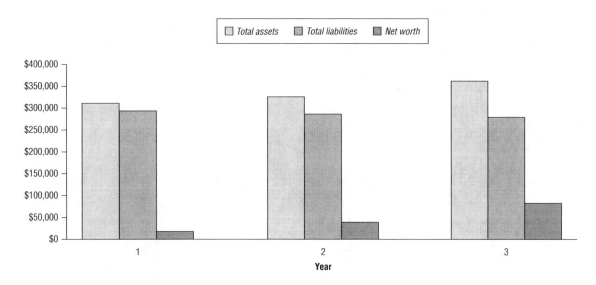

7.8 Breakeven Analysis

Monthly break even analysis

Year	1	2	3
Monthly revenue	$ 61,053	$ 72,671	$ 76,880
Yearly revenue	$732,634	$872,054	$922,562

Break even analysis

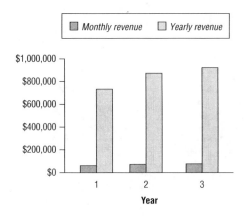

7.9 Business Ratios

Business ratios—yearly

Year	1	2	3
Sales			
Sales growth	0.0%	20.0%	17.0%
Gross margin	65.0%	65.0%	65.0%
Financials			
Profit margin	5.06%	7.05%	10.47%
Assets to liabilities	1.06	1.14	1.30
Equity to liabilities	0.06	0.14	0.30
Assets to equity	17.21	8.27	4.37
Liquidity			
Acid test	0.22	0.25	0.31
Cash to assets	0.20	0.22	0.24

7.10 Three Year Profit and Loss Statement

Profit and loss statement (first year)

Months	1	2	3	4	5	6	7
Sales	**$79,800**	**$79,933**	**$80,066**	**$80,199**	**$80,332**	**$80,465**	**$80,598**
Cost of goods sold	$27,900	$27,947	$27,993	$28,040	$28,086	$28,133	$28,179
Gross margin	65.0%	65.0%	65.0%	65.0%	65.0%	65.0%	65.0%
Operating income	**$51,900**	**$51,987**	**$52,073**	**$52,160**	**$52,246**	**$52,333**	**$52,419**
Expenses							
Payroll	$24,125	$24,125	$24,125	$24,125	$24,125	$24,125	$24,125
General and administrative	$ 1,100	$ 1,100	$ 1,100	$ 1,100	$ 1,100	$ 1,100	$ 1,100
Marketing expenses	$ 2,416	$ 2,416	$ 2,416	$ 2,416	$ 2,416	$ 2,416	$ 2,416
Professional fees and licensure	$ 435	$ 435	$ 435	$ 435	$ 435	$ 435	$ 435
Insurance costs	$ 999	$ 999	$ 999	$ 999	$ 999	$ 999	$ 999
Vehicle maintenance costs	$ 4,027	$ 4,027	$ 4,027	$ 4,027	$ 4,027	$ 4,027	$ 4,027
Rent and utilities	$ 2,021	$ 2,021	$ 2,021	$ 2,021	$ 2,021	$ 2,021	$ 2,021
Miscellaneous costs	$ 966	$ 966	$ 966	$ 966	$ 966	$ 966	$ 966
Payroll taxes	$ 3,619	$ 3,619	$ 3,619	$ 3,619	$ 3,619	$ 3,619	$ 3,619
Total operating costs	**$39,707**	**$39,707**	**$39,707**	**$39,707**	**$39,707**	**$39,707**	**$39,707**
EBITDA	**$12,193**	**$12,279**	**$12,366**	**$12,452**	**$12,539**	**$12,625**	**$12,712**
Federal income tax	$ 4,143	$ 4,150	$ 4,156	$ 4,163	$ 4,170	$ 4,177	$ 4,184
State income tax	$ 628	$ 629	$ 630	$ 631	$ 632	$ 633	$ 634
Interest expense	$ 2,250	$ 2,238	$ 2,227	$ 2,215	$ 2,203	$ 2,191	$ 2,179
Depreciation expense	$ 1,592	$ 1,592	$ 1,592	$ 1,592	$ 1,592	$ 1,592	$ 1,592
Net profit	**$ 3,580**	**$ 3,670**	**$ 3,761**	**$ 3,851**	**$ 3,941**	**$ 4,032**	**$ 4,123**

Profit and loss statement (first year cont.)

Month	8	9	10	11	12	1
Sales	**$80,731**	**$80,864**	**$80,997**	**$81,130**	**$81,263**	**$966,378**
Cost of goods sold	$28,226	$28,272	$28,319	$28,365	$28,412	$337,869
Gross margin	65.0%	65.0%	65.0%	65.0%	65.0%	65.0%
Operating income	**$52,506**	**$52,592**	**$52,679**	**$52,765**	**$52,852**	**$628,509**
Expenses						
Payroll	$24,125	$24,125	$24,125	$24,125	$24,125	$289,500
General and administrative	$ 1,100	$ 1,100	$ 1,100	$ 1,100	$ 1,100	$ 13,200
Marketing expenses	$ 2,416	$ 2,416	$ 2,416	$ 2,416	$ 2,416	$ 28,991
Professional fees and licensure	$ 435	$ 435	$ 435	$ 435	$ 435	$ 5,219
Insurance costs	$ 999	$ 999	$ 999	$ 999	$ 999	$ 11,987
Vehicle maintenance costs	$ 4,027	$ 4,027	$ 4,027	$ 4,027	$ 4,027	$ 48,319
Rent and utilities	$ 2,021	$ 2,021	$ 2,021	$ 2,021	$ 2,021	$ 24,250
Miscellaneous costs	$ 966	$ 966	$ 966	$ 966	$ 966	$ 11,597
Payroll taxes	$ 3,619	$ 3,619	$ 3,619	$ 3,619	$ 3,619	$ 43,425
Total operating costs	**$39,707**	**$39,707**	**$39,707**	**$39,707**	**$39,707**	**$476,488**
EBITDA	**$12,798**	**$12,885**	**$12,971**	**$13,058**	**$13,144**	**$152,021**
Federal income tax	$ 4,191	$ 4,198	$ 4,205	$ 4,212	$ 4,219	$ 50,167
State income tax	$ 635	$ 636	$ 637	$ 638	$ 639	$ 7,601
Interest expense	$ 2,167	$ 2,155	$ 2,142	$ 2,130	$ 2,117	$ 26,213
Depreciation expense	$ 1,592	$ 1,592	$ 1,592	$ 1,592	$ 1,592	$ 19,107
Net profit	**$ 4,213**	**$ 4,304**	**$ 4,395**	**$ 4,486**	**$ 4,577**	**$ 48,933**

Profit and loss statement (second year)

Quarter	Q1	2 Q2	Q3	Q4	2
Sales	**$231,931**	**$289,913**	**$313,106**	**$324,703**	**$1,159,654**
Cost of goods sold	$ 81,089	$101,361	$109,470	$113,524	$ 405,443
Gross margin	65.0%	65.0%	65.0%	65.0%	65.0%
Operating income	**$150,842**	**$188,553**	**$203,637**	**$211,179**	**$ 754,211**
Expenses					
Payroll	$ 70,143	$ 87,679	$ 94,693	$ 98,200	$ 350,715
General and administrative	$ 2,746	$ 3,432	$ 3,707	$ 3,844	$ 13,728
Marketing expenses	$ 6,958	$ 8,697	$ 9,393	$ 9,741	$ 34,790
Professional fees and licensure	$ 1,075	$ 1,344	$ 1,451	$ 1,505	$ 5,376
Insurance costs	$ 2,517	$ 3,147	$ 3,398	$ 3,524	$ 12,586
Vehicle maintenance costs	$ 11,597	$ 14,496	$ 15,655	$ 16,235	$ 57,983
Rent and utilities	$ 5,093	$ 6,366	$ 6,875	$ 7,130	$ 25,463
Miscellaneous costs	$ 2,783	$ 3,479	$ 3,757	$ 3,896	$ 13,916
Payroll taxes	$ 10,521	$ 13,152	$ 14,204	$ 14,730	$ 52,607
Total operating costs	**$113,433**	**$141,791**	**$153,134**	**$158,806**	**$ 567,163**
EBITDA	**$ 37,410**	**$ 46,762**	**$ 50,503**	**$ 52,373**	**$ 187,048**
Federal income tax	$ 10,735	$ 13,419	$ 14,492	$ 15,029	$ 53,676
State income tax	$ 1,627	$ 2,033	$ 2,196	$ 2,277	$ 8,133
Interest expense	$ 6,275	$ 6,159	$ 6,040	$ 5,919	$ 24,394
Depreciation expense	$ 4,777	$ 4,777	$ 4,777	$ 4,777	$ 19,107
Net profit	**$ 13,996**	**$ 20,374**	**$ 22,997**	**$ 24,371**	**$ 81,738**

Profit and loss statement (third year)

Quarter	Q1	3 Q2	Q3	Q4	3
Sales	**$271,359**	**$339,199**	**$366,335**	**$379,903**	**$1,356,795**
Cost of goods sold	$ 94,874	$118,592	$128,079	$132,823	$ 474,368
Gross margin	65.0%	65.0%	65.0%	65.0%	65.0%
Operating income	**$176,485**	**$220,607**	**$238,255**	**$247,079**	**$ 882,427**
Expenses					
Payroll	$ 72,247	$ 90,309	$ 97,534	$101,146	$ 361,236
General and administrative	$ 2,855	$ 3,569	$ 3,855	$ 3,998	$ 14,277
Marketing expenses	$ 8,141	$ 10,176	$ 10,990	$ 11,397	$ 40,704
Professional fees and licensure	$ 1,107	$ 1,384	$ 1,495	$ 1,550	$ 5,537
Insurance costs	$ 2,643	$ 3,304	$ 3,568	$ 3,700	$ 13,216
Vehicle maintenance costs	$ 13,568	$ 16,960	$ 18,317	$ 18,995	$ 67,840
Rent and utilities	$ 5,347	$ 6,684	$ 7,219	$ 7,486	$ 26,736
Miscellaneous costs	$ 3,256	$ 4,070	$ 4,396	$ 4,559	$ 16,282
Payroll taxes	$ 10,837	$ 13,546	$ 14,630	$ 15,172	$ 54,185
Total operating costs	**$120,002**	**$150,003**	**$162,003**	**$168,003**	**$ 600,012**
EBITDA	**$ 56,483**	**$ 70,604**	**$ 76,252**	**$ 79,076**	**$ 282,414**
Federal income tax	$ 17,161	$ 21,451	$ 23,167	$ 24,025	$ 85,803
State income tax	$ 2,600	$ 3,250	$ 3,510	$ 3,640	$ 13,000
Interest expense	$ 5,795	$ 5,668	$ 5,538	$ 5,405	$ 22,405
Depreciation expense	$ 4,777	$ 4,777	$ 4,777	$ 4,777	$ 19,107
Net profit	**$ 26,151**	**$ 35,458**	**$ 39,260**	**$ 41,229**	**$ 142,099**

7.11 Three Year Cash Flow Analysis

Cash flow analysis (first year)

Month	1	2	3	4	5	6	7
Cash from operations	$ 5,172	$ 5,263	$ 5,353	$ 5,443	$ 5,534	$ 5,624	$ 5,715
Cash from receivables	$ 0	$ 0	$ 0	$ 0	$ 0	$ 0	$ 0
Operating cash inflow	**$ 5,172**	**$ 5,263**	**$ 5,353**	**$ 5,443**	**$ 5,534**	**$ 5,624**	**$ 5,715**
Other cash inflows							
Equity investment	$ 10,000	$ 0	$ 0	$ 0	$ 0	$ 0	$ 0
Increased borrowings	$300,000	$ 0	$ 0	$ 0	$ 0	$ 0	$ 0
Sales of business assets	$ 0	$ 0	$ 0	$ 0	$ 0	$ 0	$ 0
A/P increases	$ 3,159	$ 3,159	$ 3,159	$ 3,159	$ 3,159	$ 3,159	$ 3,159
Total other cash inflows	**$313,159**	**$ 3,159**	**$ 3,159**	**$ 3,159**	**$ 3,159**	**$ 3,159**	**$ 3,159**
Total cash inflow	**$318,331**	**$ 8,421**	**$ 8,511**	**$ 8,602**	**$ 8,692**	**$ 8,783**	**$ 8,873**
Cash outflows							
Repayment of principal	$ 1,550	$ 1,562	$ 1,574	$ 1,585	$ 1,591	$ 1,609	$ 1,621
A/P decreases	$ 2,075	$ 2,075	$ 2,075	$ 2,075	$ 2,075	$ 2,075	$ 2,075
A/R increases	$ 0	$ 0	$ 0	$ 0	$ 0	$ 0	$ 0
Asset purchases	$267,500	$ 0	$ 0	$ 0	$ 0	$ 0	$ 0
Dividends	$ 0	$ 0	$ 0	$ 0	$ 0	$ 0	$ 0
Total cash outflows	**$271,125**	**$ 3,637**	**$ 3,648**	**$ 3,660**	**$ 3,672**	**$ 3,684**	**$ 3,696**
Net cash flow	**$ 47,206**	**$ 4,784**	**$ 4,863**	**$ 4,942**	**$ 5,020**	**$ 5,099**	**$ 5,177**
Cash balance	**$ 47,206**	**$51,990**	**$56,853**	**$61,795**	**$66,815**	**$71,914**	**$77,091**

Cash flow analysis (first year cont.)

Month	8	9	10	11	12	1
Cash from operations	$ 5,805	$ 5,896	$ 5,987	$ 6,078	$ 6,169	$ 68,040
Cash from receivables	$ 0	$ 0	$ 0	$ 0	$ 0	$ 0
Operating cash inflow	**$ 5,805**	**$ 5,896**	**$ 5,987**	**$ 6,078**	**$ 6,169**	**$ 68,040**
Other cash inflows						
Equity investment	$ 0	$ 0	$ 0	$ 0	$ 0	$ 10,000
Increased borrowings	$ 0	$ 0	$ 0	$ 0	$ 0	$300,000
Sales of business assets	$ 0	$ 0	$ 0	$ 0	$ 0	$ 0
A/P increases	$ 3,159	$ 3,159	$ 3,159	$ 3,159	$ 3,159	$ 37,902
Total other cash inflows	**$ 3,159**	**$ 3,159**	**$ 3,159**	**$ 3,159**	**$ 3,159**	**$347,902**
Total cash inflow	**$ 8,964**	**$ 9,055**	**$ 9,146**	**$ 9,237**	**$ 9,328**	**$415,942**
Cash outflows						
Repayment of principal	$ 1,634	$ 1,646	$ 1,658	$ 1,671	$ 1,683	$ 19,390
A/P decreases	$ 2,075	$ 2,075	$ 2,075	$ 2,075	$ 2,075	$ 24,897
A/R increases	$ 0	$ 0	$ 0	$ 0	$ 0	$ 0
Asset purchases	$ 0	$ 0	$ 0	$ 0	$ 0	$267,500
Dividends	$ 0	$ 0	$ 0	$ 0	$40,824	$ 40,824
Total cash outflows	**$ 3,708**	**$ 3,721**	**$ 3,733**	**$ 3,745**	**$44,582**	**$352,611**
Net cash flow	**$ 5,256**	**$ 5,334**	**$ 5,413**	**$ 5,491**	**−$35,254**	**$ 63,331**
Cash balance	**$82,346**	**$87,681**	**$93,094**	**$98,585**	**$63,331**	**$ 63,331**

Cash flow analysis (second year)

Quarter	Q1	2 Q2	Q3	Q4	2
Cash from operations	$20,169	$25,211	$27,228	$28,237	$100,845
Cash from receivables	$ 0	$ 0	$ 0	$ 0	$ 0
Operating cash inflow	**$20,169**	**$25,211**	**$27,228**	**$28,237**	**$100,845**
Other cash inflows					
Equity investment	$ 0	$ 0	$ 0	$ 0	$ 0
Increased borrowings	$ 0	$ 0	$ 0	$ 0	$ 0
Sales of business assets	$ 0	$ 0	$ 0	$ 0	$ 0
A/P increases	$ 8,717	$10,897	$11,769	$12,204	$ 43,587
Total other cash inflows	**$ 8,717**	**$10,897**	**$11,769**	**$12,204**	**$ 43,587**
Total cash inflow	**$28,887**	**$36,108**	**$38,997**	**$40,441**	**$144,433**
Cash outflows					
Repayment of principal	$ 5,125	$ 5,242	$ 5,360	$ 5,482	$ 21,209
A/P decreases	$ 5,975	$ 7,469	$ 8,067	$ 8,365	$ 29,876
A/R increases	$ 0	$ 0	$ 0	$ 0	$ 0
Asset purchases	$ 5,042	$ 6,303	$ 6,807	$ 7,059	$ 25,211
Dividends	$12,101	$15,127	$16,337	$16,942	$ 60,507
Total cash outflows	**$28,244**	**$34,140**	**$36,571**	**$37,848**	**$136,804**
Net cash flow	**$ 642**	**$ 1,968**	**$ 2,426**	**$ 2,593**	**$ 7,629**
Cash balance	**$63,973**	**$65,941**	**$68,367**	**$70,959**	**$ 70,959**

Cash flow analysis (third year)

Quarter	Q1	3 Q2	Q3	Q4	3
Cash from operations	$32,241	$40,302	$43,526	$45,138	$161,206
Cash from receivables	$ 0	$ 0	$ 0	$ 0	$ 0
Operating cash inflow	**$32,241**	**$40,302**	**$43,526**	**$45,138**	**$161,206**
Other cash inflows					
Equity investment	$ 0	$ 0	$ 0	$ 0	$ 0
Increased borrowings	$ 0	$ 0	$ 0	$ 0	$ 0
Sales of business assets	$ 0	$ 0	$ 0	$ 0	$ 0
A/P increases	$10,025	$12,531	$13,534	$14,035	$ 50,125
Total other cash inflows	**$10,025**	**$12,531**	**$13,534**	**$14,035**	**$ 50,125**
Total cash inflow	**$42,266**	**$52,833**	**$57,059**	**$59,173**	**$211,331**
Cash outflows					
Repayment of principal	$ 5,606	$ 5,733	$ 5,863	$ 5,996	$ 23,199
A/P decreases	$ 7,170	$ 8,963	$ 9,680	$10,038	$ 35,852
A/R increases	$ 0	$ 0	$ 0	$ 0	$ 0
Asset purchases	$ 8,060	$10,075	$10,881	$11,284	$ 40,302
Dividends	$19,345	$24,181	$26,115	$27,083	$ 96,724
Total cash outflows	**$40,182**	**$48,952**	**$52,540**	**$54,402**	**$196,075**
Net cash flow	**$ 2,085**	**$ 3,880**	**$ 4,520**	**$ 4,771**	**$ 15,256**
Cash balance	**$73,044**	**$76,925**	**$81,444**	**$86,215**	**$ 86,215**

Fitness Center

Superior Fitness Center

65123 Bridge St.
Bronx, NY 10453

BizPlanDB.com

Superior Fitness Center ("the Company") is a New York-based corporation that will provide fitness equipment usage and training services to customers in its targeted market. The Company was founded by Michael Carpenter.

1.0 EXECUTIVE SUMMARY

The purpose of this business plan is to raise $250,000 for the development of a fitness center while showcasing the expected financials and operations over the next three years. Superior Fitness Center ("the Company") is a New York-based corporation that will provide fitness equipment usage and training services to customers in its targeted market. The Company was founded by Michael Carpenter.

1.1 The Services

Management is seeking to develop a gym facility that will feature a number of standard fitness machines as well as services that compliment the needs of our customers. The business will primarily specialize in providing fitness services for people ranging from 14 to 80 years of age.

The Company's fitness and health services seek to develop the health of clients. Each of our fitness programs will be tailored to the needs of the individual based on their ability to handle certain fitness regimens and their personal goals for physical development.

The third section of the business plan will further describe the services offered by Superior Fitness Center.

1.2 Financing

Mr. Carpenter is seeking to raise $250,000 from a bank loan. The interest rate and loan agreement are to be further discussed during negotiation. This business plan assumes that the business will receive a 10 year loan with a 9% fixed interest rate. The financing will be used for the following:

- Development of the Company's Fitness Center location.

- Financing for the first six months of operation.

- Capital to purchase a company vehicle.

Mr. Carpenter will contribute $50,000 to the venture.

1.3 Mission Statement

Management's mission is to provide clients with a state of the art fitness center facility that they can use for maintaining their health and improving their appearance.

1.4 Management Team

The Company was founded by Michael Carpenter. Mr. Carpenter has more than 10 years of experience in the fitness and training industry. Through his expertise, he will be able to bring the operations of the business to profitability within its first year of operations.

1.5 Sales Forecasts

Mr. Carpenter expects a strong rate of growth at the start of operations. Below are the expected financials over the next three years.

Proforma profit and loss (yearly)

Year	1	2	3
Sales	$806,778	$968,134	$1,132,716
Operating costs	$341,317	$370,003	$ 400,056
EBITDA	$384,783	$501,317	$ 619,389
Taxes, interest, and depreciation	$185,026	$220,068	$ 263,908
Net profit	$199,757	$281,249	$ 355,481

Sales, operating costs, and profit forecast

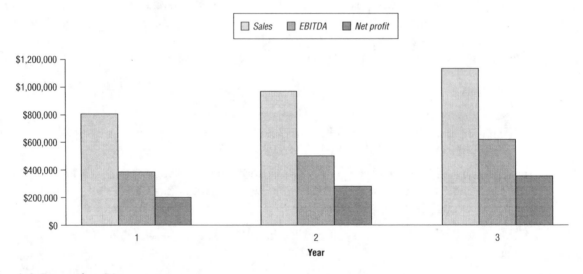

1.6 Expansion Plan

The Founder expects that the business will aggressively expand during the first three years of operation. Mr. Carpenter intends to implement marketing campaigns that will effectively target individuals within the target market.

2.0 COMPANY AND FINANCING SUMMARY

2.1 Registered Name and Corporate Structure

The Company is registered as a corporation in the State of New York.

2.2 Required Funds

At this time, Superior Fitness Center requires $250,000 of debt funds. Below is a breakdown of how these funds will be used:

Projected startup costs

Initial lease payments and deposits	$ 30,000
Working capital	$ 55,000
FF&E	$ 35,000
Leasehold improvements	$ 52,500
Security deposits	$ 5,000
Insurance	$ 10,000
Gym equipment	$100,000
Marketing budget	$ 7,500
Miscellaneous and unforeseen costs	$ 5,000
Total startup costs	**$300,000**

Use of funds

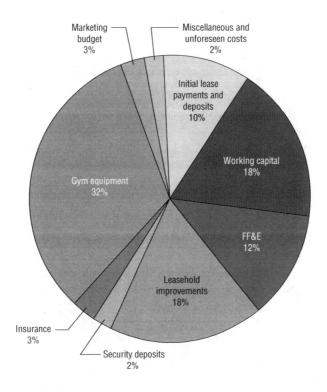

2.3 Investor Equity

Mr. Carpenter is not seeking an investment from a third party at this time.

2.4 Management Equity

Michael Carpenter owns 100% of Superior Fitness Center.

2.5 Exit Strategy

If the business is very successful, Mr. Carpenter may seek to sell the business to a third party for a significant earnings multiple. Most likely, the Company will hire a qualified business broker to sell the business on behalf of Superior Fitness Center. Based on historical numbers, the business could fetch a sales premium of up to 5 times earnings.

3.0 PRODUCTS AND SERVICES

Below is a description of the gym and training services offered by Superior Fitness Center.

3.1 Gym Membership

The Company will offer a full service gym, complete with state of the art fitness equipment, showers, towel service, and many other amenities offered by fitness facilities. While Superior Fitness Center will offer equipment for consumer use, our primary goal is to develop relationships with our clients so that we can provide them with ongoing support for their physical fitness development needs.

3.2 Training Services

Superior Fitness Center will offer an assortment of options to get and stay in shape for people and athletes interested in personal one on one sessions, or accessing their own online trainer and coach. They will receive a customized exercise program customized to their individual fitness level, implementing various components including strength training, weight management, cardiovascular training, flexibility training, and optional nutritional programs. Our program menu includes:

- General Training
- Sports Specific Training
- Medical Condition Training
- Special Population

4.0 STRATEGIC AND MARKET ANALYSIS

4.1 Economic Outlook

This section of the analysis will detail the economic climate, the fitness industry, the customer profile, and the competition that the business will face as it progresses through its business operations.

Currently, the economic market condition in the United States is moderate. The country has successfully rebounded from the great economic recession that lasted from 2008 until 2011. As of 2014, unemployment rates have declined substantially. However, it should be noted that fitness centers operate with great economic stability as people will continue to want to stay in shape and remain healthy despite deleterious changes in the general economy.

4.2 Industry Analysis

There are over 16,400 fitness establishments in the United States. These businesses produce over $7 billon dollars a year in gross receipts. Additionally, the business employs over 250,000 people, and generates payroll figures of $2.45 billion dollars a year. The industry has experienced a tremendous rate of growth over the last ten years. The fitness industry, over the past five years, experienced growth of more than 18% over the five year period. This industry is one of the fastest growing industries in the United States.

Additionally, the economic tastes of Americans have changed significantly over the last five years as the overall wealth of the country has grown. As Americans now have more access to capital and an increased borrowing capacity, their ability to spend money on brand name and luxury items has also increased. High-end physical fitness compliments the expanded purchasing capacity of Americans. More and more Americans are seeking to improve their physical fitness through non-medical means. However, the growth rate of this industry has slowed with the corresponding recession in the United States. More normalized growth (with more people signing up for gym memberships) is expected to resume towards the end of 2013.

4.3 Customer Profile

Superior Fitness Center's average client will be a middle to upper middle class man or woman living in the Company's target market. Common traits among clients will include:

- Annual household income exceeding $50,000.

- Lives or works no more than 15 miles from the Company's location.

- Will spend $50 to $100 per month at Superior Fitness Center.

4.4 Competition

Within the greater New York metropolitan area, there are more than 2,000 fitness centers that offer substantially similar services to that of Superior Fitness Center. The primary differentiating factor that the Company will use when marketing its operations is the fact that Superior Fitness Center will use state of the art equipment while hiring only the most qualified trainers to assist clients. This will be the central point in all advertising distributed by the business.

5.0 MARKETING PLAN

Superior Fitness Center intends to maintain an extensive marketing campaign that will ensure maximum visibility for the business in its targeted market. Below is an overview of the marketing strategies and objectives of Superior Fitness Center.

5.1 Marketing Objectives

- Develop relationships with concierge services among hotels that do not have gyms within their facilities.

- Work closely with real estate agents that will recommend Superior Fitness Center to people that are moving to the New York metropolitan area.

- Establish relationships with physical trainers within the targeted market.

5.2 Marketing Strategies

Mr. Carpenter intends on using a number of marketing strategies that will allow Superior Fitness Center to easily target men and women within the target market. Foremost, Management intends to work closely with independently contracted fitness trainers that will use the Company as their primary destination for working with their clients in regards to their training programs.

Superior Fitness Center will also develop an expansive online platform that showcases the state of art equipment that is available for use in the Company's facility. The website will also list the fitness trainers that are available at each location, their qualifications, and their hours of availability. The Company's website will feature functionality that allows individuals to enroll with Superior Fitness Center. The business will hire a search engine optimization firm in order to effectively manage the online advertising operations of the business.

Management will also take out several advertisements (prior to the location's launch and through continuation) in New York based magazines and newspapers that will frequently feature coupons and discounts for new membership enrollment.

5.3 Pricing

The business will charge $75 per month for membership fees to Superior Fitness Center. Per hour trainer fees will be approximately $60.

6.0 ORGANIZATIONAL PLAN AND PERSONNEL SUMMARY

6.1 Corporate Organization

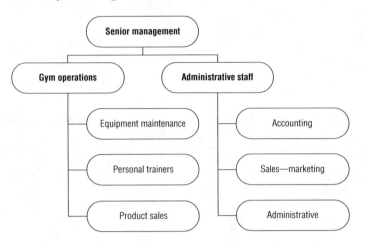

6.2 Organizational Budget

Personnel plan—yearly

Year	1	2	3
Owners	$ 80,000	$ 82,400	$ 84,872
Manager	$ 35,000	$ 36,050	$ 37,132
Assistant	$ 32,500	$ 33,475	$ 34,479
Personal trainers	$ 37,500	$ 51,500	$ 66,306
Receptionist	$ 44,000	$ 45,320	$ 46,680
Total	**$229,000**	**$248,745**	**$269,469**

Numbers of personnel

Owners	2	2	2
Manager	1	1	1
Assistant	1	1	1
Personal trainers	3	4	5
Receptionist	2	2	2
Totals	**9**	**10**	**11**

Personnel expense breakdown

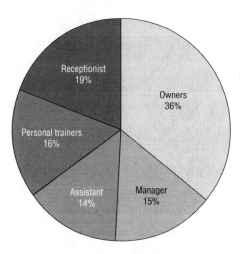

7.0 FINANCIAL PLAN

7.1 Underlying Assumptions

The Company has based its proforma financial statements on the following:

- Superior Fitness Center will have an annual revenue growth rate of 16% per year.

- The Owner will acquire $250,000 of debt funds to develop the business.

- The loan will have a 10 year term with a 9% interest rate.

7.2 Sensitivity Analysis

In the event of an economic downturn, the business may have a decline in its revenues. However, fitness services are demanded by individuals due to the simple fact that people want to remain healthy and in shape. As such, only a severe economic downturn would result in a decline in revenues.

7.3 Source of Funds

Financing

Equity contributions	
Management investment	$ 50,000.00
Total equity financing	**$ 50,000.00**
Banks and lenders	
Banks and lenders	$ 250,000.00
Total debt financing	**$250,000.00**
Total financing	**$300,000.00**

7.4 General Assumptions

General assumptions

Year	1	2	3
Short term interest rate	9.5%	9.5%	9.5%
Long term interest rate	10.0%	10.0%	10.0%
Federal tax rate	33.0%	33.0%	33.0%
State tax rate	5.0%	5.0%	5.0%
Personnel taxes	15.0%	15.0%	15.0%

7.5 Profit and Loss Statements

Proforma profit and loss (yearly)

Year	1	2	3
Sales	**$806,778**	**$968,134**	**$1,132,716**
Cost of goods sold	$ 80,678	$ 96,813	$ 113,272
Gross margin	90.00%	90.00%	90.00%
Operating income	**$726,100**	**$871,320**	**$1,019,445**
Expenses			
Payroll	$229,000	$248,745	$ 269,469
General and administrative	$ 25,200	$ 26,208	$ 27,256
Marketing expenses	$ 4,034	$ 4,841	$ 5,664
Professional fees and licensure	$ 5,219	$ 5,376	$ 5,537
Insurance costs	$ 1,987	$ 2,086	$ 2,191
Travel and vehicle costs	$ 7,596	$ 8,356	$ 9,191
Rent and utilities	$ 24,250	$ 25,463	$ 26,736
Miscellaneous costs	$ 9,681	$ 11,618	$ 13,593
Payroll taxes	$ 34,350	$ 37,312	$ 40,420
Total operating costs	**$341,317**	**$370,003**	**$ 400,056**
EBITDA	**$384,783**	**$501,317**	**$ 619,389**
Federal income tax	$126,978	$158,726	$ 198,237
State income tax	$ 19,239	$ 24,049	$ 30,036
Interest expense	$ 21,844	$ 20,328	$ 18,671
Depreciation expenses	$ 16,964	$ 16,964	$ 16,964
Net profit	**$199,757**	**$281,249**	**$ 355,481**
Profit margin	**24.76%**	**29.05%**	**31.38%**

Sales, operating costs, and profit forecast

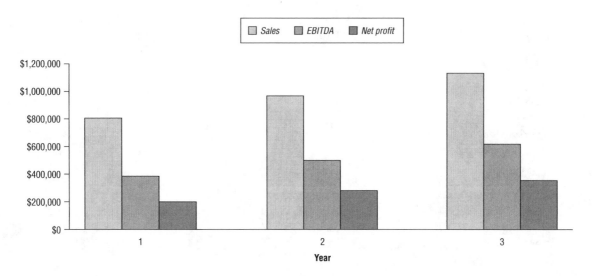

7.6 Cash Flow Analysis

Proforma cash flow analysis—yearly

Year	1	2	3
Cash from operations	$216,721	$298,213	$372,445
Cash from receivables	$ 0	$ 0	$ 0
Operating cash inflow	**$216,721**	**$298,213**	**$372,445**
Other cash inflows			
Equity investment	$ 50,000	$ 0	$ 0
Increased borrowings	$250,000	$ 0	$ 0
Sales of business assets	$ 0	$ 0	$ 0
A/P increases	$ 37,902	$ 43,587	$ 50,125
Total other cash inflows	**$337,902**	**$ 43,587**	**$ 50,125**
Total cash inflow	**$554,623**	**$341,800**	**$422,571**
Cash outflows			
Repayment of principal	$ 16,158	$ 17,674	$ 19,332
A/P decreases	$ 24,897	$ 29,876	$ 35,852
A/R increases	$ 0	$ 0	$ 0
Asset purchases	$237,500	$ 74,553	$ 93,111
Dividends	$151,705	$208,749	$260,712
Total cash outflows	**$430,260**	**$330,853**	**$409,007**
Net cash flow	**$124,363**	**$ 10,947**	**$ 13,564**
Cash balance	**$124,363**	**$135,310**	**$148,874**

Proforma cash flow (yearly)

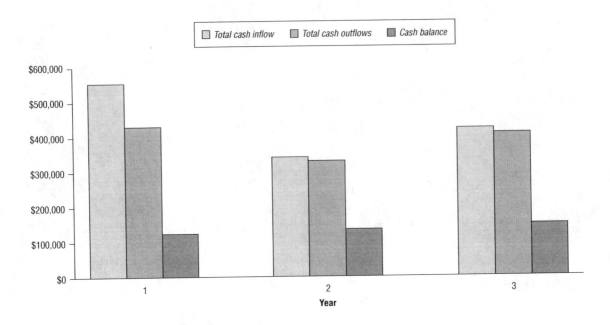

7.7 Balance Sheet

Proforma balance sheet—yearly

Year	1	2	3
Assets			
Cash	$124,363	$135,310	$148,874
Amortized development/expansion costs	$102,500	$109,955	$119,266
Gym equipment	$100,000	$155,915	$225,748
FF&E	$ 35,000	$ 46,183	$ 60,150
Accumulated depreciation	($ 16,964)	($ 33,929)	($ 50,893)
Total assets	**$344,899**	**$413,435**	**$503,146**
Liabilities and equity			
Accounts payable	$ 13,005	$ 26,716	$ 40,990
Long term liabilities	$233,842	$216,167	$198,493
Other liabilities	$ 0	$ 0	$ 0
Total liabilities	**$246,847**	**$242,883**	**$239,483**
Net worth	**$ 98,052**	**$170,552**	**$263,663**
Total liabilities and equity	**$344,899**	**$413,435**	**$503,146**

Proforma balance sheet

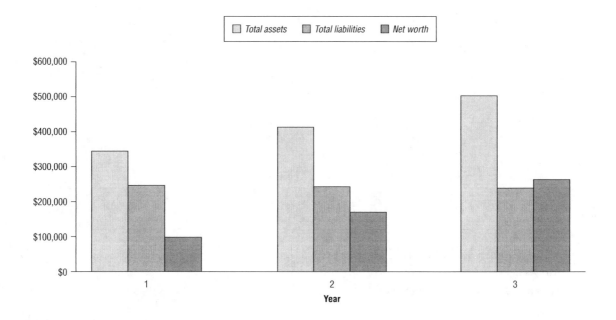

7.8 Breakeven Analysis

Monthly break even analysis

Year	1	2	3
Monthly revenue	$ 31,603	$ 34,260	$ 37,042
Yearly revenue	$379,241	$411,114	$444,506

Break even analysis

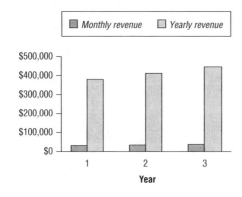

7.9 Business Ratios

Business ratios—yearly

Year	1	2	3
Sales			
Sales growth	0.0%	20.0%	17.0%
Gross margin	90.0%	90.0%	90.0%
Financials			
Profit margin	24.76%	29.05%	31.38%
Assets to liabilities	1.40	1.70	2.10
Equity to liabilities	0.40	0.70	1.10
Assets to equity	3.52	2.42	1.91
Liquidity			
Acid test	0.50	0.56	0.62
Cash to assets	0.36	0.33	0.30

7.10 Three Year Profit and Loss Statement

Profit and loss statement (first year)

Months	1	2	3	4	5	6	7
Sales	**$66,500**	**$66,633**	**$66,766**	**$66,899**	**$67,032**	**$67,165**	**$67,298**
Cost of goods sold	$ 6,650	$ 6,663	$ 6,677	$ 6,690	$ 6,703	$ 6,717	$ 6,730
Gross margin	90.0%	90.0%	90.0%	90.0%	90.0%	90.0%	90.0%
Operating income	**$59,850**	**$59,970**	**$60,089**	**$60,209**	**$60,329**	**$60,449**	**$60,568**
Expenses							
Payroll	$19,083	$19,083	$19,083	$19,083	$19,083	$19,083	$19,083
General and administrative	$ 2,100	$ 2,100	$ 2,100	$ 2,100	$ 2,100	$ 2,100	$ 2,100
Marketing expenses	$ 336	$ 336	$ 336	$ 336	$ 336	$ 336	$ 336
Professional fees and licensure	$ 435	$ 435	$ 435	$ 435	$ 435	$ 435	$ 435
Insurance costs	$ 166	$ 166	$ 166	$ 166	$ 166	$ 166	$ 166
Travel and vehicle costs	$ 633	$ 633	$ 633	$ 633	$ 633	$ 633	$ 633
Rent and utilities	$ 2,021	$ 2,021	$ 2,021	$ 2,021	$ 2,021	$ 2,021	$ 2,021
Miscellaneous costs	$ 807	$ 807	$ 807	$ 807	$ 807	$ 807	$ 807
Payroll taxes	$ 2,863	$ 2,863	$ 2,863	$ 2,863	$ 2,863	$ 2,863	$ 2,863
Total operating costs	**$28,443**	**$28,443**	**$28,443**	**$28,443**	**$28,443**	**$28,443**	**$28,443**
EBITDA	**$31,407**	**$31,527**	**$31,646**	**$31,766**	**$31,886**	**$32,005**	**$32,125**
Federal income tax	$10,466	$10,487	$10,508	$10,529	$10,550	$10,571	$10,592
State income tax	$ 1,586	$ 1,589	$ 1,592	$ 1,595	$ 1,599	$ 1,602	$ 1,605
Interest expense	$ 1,875	$ 1,865	$ 1,856	$ 1,846	$ 1,836	$ 1,826	$ 1,816
Depreciation expense	$ 1,414	$ 1,414	$ 1,414	$ 1,414	$ 1,414	$ 1,414	$ 1,414
Net profit	**$16,066**	**$16,171**	**$16,277**	**$16,382**	**$16,488**	**$16,593**	**$16,699**

Profit and loss statement (first year cont.)

Month	8	9	10	11	12	1
Sales	$67,431	$67,564	$67,697	$67,830	$67,963	$806,778
Cost of goods sold	$ 6,743	$ 6,756	$ 6,770	$ 6,783	$ 6,796	$ 80,678
Gross margin	90.0%	90.0%	90.0%	90.0%	90.0%	90.0%
Operating income	$60,688	$60,808	$60,927	$61,047	$61,167	$726,100
Expenses						
Payroll	$19,083	$19,083	$19,083	$19,083	$19,083	$229,000
General and administrative	$ 2,100	$ 2,100	$ 2,100	$ 2,100	$ 2,100	$ 25,200
Marketing expenses	$ 336	$ 336	$ 336	$ 336	$ 336	$ 4,034
Professional fees and licensure	$ 435	$ 435	$ 435	$ 435	$ 435	$ 5,219
Insurance costs	$ 166	$ 166	$ 166	$ 166	$ 166	$ 1,987
Travel and vehicle costs	$ 633	$ 633	$ 633	$ 633	$ 633	$ 7,596
Rent and utilities	$ 2,021	$ 2,021	$ 2,021	$ 2,021	$ 2,021	$ 24,250
Miscellaneous costs	$ 807	$ 807	$ 807	$ 807	$ 807	$ 9,681
Payroll taxes	$ 2,863	$ 2,863	$ 2,863	$ 2,863	$ 2,863	$ 34,350
Total operating costs	$28,443	$28,443	$28,443	$28,443	$28,443	$341,317
EBITDA	$32,245	$32,364	$32,484	$32,604	$32,724	$384,783
Federal income tax	$10,613	$10,634	$10,655	$10,676	$10,697	$126,978
State income tax	$ 1,608	$ 1,611	$ 1,614	$ 1,618	$ 1,621	$ 19,239
Interest expense	$ 1,806	$ 1,795	$ 1,785	$ 1,775	$ 1,764	$ 21,844
Depreciation expense	$ 1,414	$ 1,414	$ 1,414	$ 1,414	$ 1,414	$ 16,964
Net profit	$16,805	$16,910	$17,016	$17,122	$17,228	$199,757

Profit and loss statement (second year)

Quarter	Q1	2 Q2	Q3	Q4	2
Sales	$193,627	$242,033	$261,396	$271,077	$968,134
Cost of goods sold	$ 19,363	$ 24,203	$ 26,140	$ 27,108	$ 96,813
Gross margin	90.0%	90.0%	90.0%	90.0%	90.0%
Operating income	$174,264	$217,830	$235,256	$243,970	$871,320
Expenses					
Payroll	$ 49,749	$ 62,186	$ 67,161	$ 69,649	$248,745
General and administrative	$ 5,242	$ 6,552	$ 7,076	$ 7,338	$ 26,208
Marketing expenses	$ 968	$ 1,210	$ 1,307	$ 1,355	$ 4,841
Professional fees and licensure	$ 1,075	$ 1,344	$ 1,451	$ 1,505	$ 5,376
Insurance costs	$ 417	$ 522	$ 563	$ 584	$ 2,086
Travel and vehicle costs	$ 1,671	$ 2,089	$ 2,256	$ 2,340	$ 8,356
Rent and utilities	$ 5,093	$ 6,366	$ 6,875	$ 7,130	$ 25,463
Miscellaneous costs	$ 2,324	$ 2,904	$ 3,137	$ 3,253	$ 11,618
Payroll taxes	$ 7,462	$ 9,328	$ 10,074	$ 10,447	$ 37,312
Total operating costs	$ 74,001	$ 92,501	$ 99,901	$103,601	$370,003
EBITDA	$100,263	$125,329	$135,356	$140,369	$501,317
Federal income tax	$ 31,745	$ 39,682	$ 42,856	$ 44,443	$158,726
State income tax	$ 4,810	$ 6,012	$ 6,493	$ 6,734	$ 24,049
Interest expense	$ 5,230	$ 5,133	$ 5,034	$ 4,932	$ 20,328
Depreciation expense	$ 4,241	$ 4,241	$ 4,241	$ 4,241	$ 16,964
Net profit	$ 54,238	$ 70,262	$ 76,731	$ 80,018	$281,249

Profit and loss statement (third year)

Quarter	Q1	3 Q2	Q3	Q4	3
Sales	$226,543	$283,179	$305,833	$317,161	$1,132,716
Cost of goods sold	$ 22,654	$ 28,318	$ 30,583	$ 31,716	$ 113,272
Gross margin	90.0%	90.0%	90.0%	90.0%	90.0%
Operating income	**$203,889**	**$254,861**	**$275,250**	**$285,445**	**$1,019,445**
Expenses					
Payroll	$ 53,894	$ 67,367	$ 72,757	$ 75,451	$ 269,469
General and administrative	$ 5,451	$ 6,814	$ 7,359	$ 7,632	$ 27,256
Marketing expenses	$ 1,133	$ 1,416	$ 1,529	$ 1,586	$ 5,664
Professional fees and licensure	$ 1,107	$ 1,384	$ 1,495	$ 1,550	$ 5,537
Insurance costs	$ 438	$ 548	$ 591	$ 613	$ 2,191
Travel and vehicle costs	$ 1,838	$ 2,298	$ 2,482	$ 2,574	$ 9,191
Rent and utilities	$ 5,347	$ 6,684	$ 7,219	$ 7,486	$ 26,736
Miscellaneous costs	$ 2,719	$ 3,398	$ 3,670	$ 3,806	$ 13,593
Payroll taxes	$ 8,084	$ 10,105	$ 10,913	$ 11,318	$ 40,420
Total operating costs	**$ 80,011**	**$100,014**	**$108,015**	**$112,016**	**$ 400,056**
EBITDA	**$123,878**	**$154,847**	**$167,235**	**$173,429**	**$ 619,389**
Federal income tax	$ 39,647	$ 49,559	$ 53,524	$ 55,506	$ 198,237
State income tax	$ 6,007	$ 7,509	$ 8,110	$ 8,410	$ 30,036
Interest expense	$ 4,829	$ 4,723	$ 4,615	$ 4,504	$ 18,671
Depreciation expense	$ 4,241	$ 4,241	$ 4,241	$ 4,241	$ 16,964
Net profit	**$ 69,153**	**$ 88,815**	**$ 96,746**	**$100,767**	**$ 355,481**

7.11 Three Year Cash Flow Analysis

Cash flow analysis (first year)

Month	1	2	3	4	5	6	7
Cash from operations	$ 17,480	$17,585	$ 17,690	$ 17,796	$ 17,901	$ 18,007	$ 18,112
Cash from receivables	$ 0	$ 0	$ 0	$ 0	$ 0	$ 0	$ 0
Operating cash inflow	**$ 17,480**	**$17,585**	**$ 17,690**	**$ 17,796**	**$ 17,901**	**$ 18,007**	**$ 18,112**
Other cash inflows							
Equity investment	$ 50,000	$ 0	$ 0	$ 0	$ 0	$ 0	$ 0
Increased borrowings	$250,000	$ 0	$ 0	$ 0	$ 0	$ 0	$ 0
Sales of business assets	$ 0	$ 0	$ 0	$ 0	$ 0	$ 0	$ 0
A/P increases	$ 3,159	$ 3,159	$ 3,159	$ 3,159	$ 3,159	$ 3,159	$ 3,159
Total other cash inflows	**$303,159**	**$ 3,159**	**$ 3,159**	**$ 3,159**	**$ 3,159**	**$ 3,159**	**$ 3,159**
Total cash inflow	**$320,638**	**$20,743**	**$ 20,849**	**$ 20,954**	**$ 21,060**	**$ 21,165**	**$ 21,271**
Cash outflows							
Repayment of principal	$ 1,292	$ 1,302	$ 1,311	$ 1,321	$ 1,331	$ 1,341	$ 1,351
A/P decreases	$ 2,075	$ 2,075	$ 2,075	$ 2,075	$ 2,075	$ 2,075	$ 2,075
A/R increases	$ 0	$ 0	$ 0	$ 0	$ 0	$ 0	$ 0
Asset purchases	$237,500	$ 0	$ 0	$ 0	$ 0	$ 0	$ 0
Dividends	$ 0	$ 0	$ 0	$ 0	$ 0	$ 0	$ 0
Total cash outflows	**$240,867**	**$ 3,376**	**$ 3,386**	**$ 3,396**	**$ 3,406**	**$ 3,416**	**$ 3,426**
Net cash flow	**$ 79,772**	**$17,367**	**$ 17,463**	**$ 17,558**	**$ 17,654**	**$ 17,750**	**$ 17,845**
Cash balance	**$ 79,772**	**$97,139**	**$114,601**	**$132,160**	**$149,814**	**$167,563**	**$185,408**

Cash flow analysis (first year cont.)

Month	8	9	10	11	12	1
Cash from operations	$ 18,218	$ 18,324	$ 18,430	$ 18,536	$ 18,642	$216,721
Cash from receivables	$ 0	$ 0	$ 0	$ 0	$ 0	$ 0
Operating cash inflow	**$ 18,218**	**$ 18,324**	**$ 18,430**	**$ 18,536**	**$ 18,642**	**$216,721**
Other cash inflows						
Equity investment	$ 0	$ 0	$ 0	$ 0	$ 0	$ 50,000
Increased borrowings	$ 0	$ 0	$ 0	$ 0	$ 0	$250,000
Sales of business assets	$ 0	$ 0	$ 0	$ 0	$ 0	$0
A/P increases	$ 3,159	$ 3,159	$ 3,159	$ 3,159	$ 3,159	$ 37,902
Total other cash inflows	**$ 3,159**	**$ 3,159**	**$ 3,159**	**$ 3,159**	**$ 3,159**	**$337,902**
Total cash inflow	**$ 21,377**	**$ 21,483**	**$ 21,588**	**$ 21,694**	**$ 21,800**	**$554,623**
Cash outflows						
Repayment of principal	$ 1,361	$ 1,371	$ 1,382	$ 1,392	$ 1,403	$ 16,158
A/P decreases	$ 2,075	$ 2,075	$ 2,075	$ 2,075	$ 2,075	$ 24,897
A/R increases	$ 0	$ 0	$ 0	$ 0	$ 0	$ 0
Asset purchases	$ 0	$ 0	$ 0	$ 0	$ 0	$237,500
Dividends	$ 0	$ 0	$ 0	$ 0	$151,705	$151,705
Total cash outflows	**$ 3,436**	**$ 3,446**	**$ 3,457**	**$ 3,467**	**$155,182**	**$430,260**
Net cash flow	**$ 17,941**	**$ 18,036**	**$ 18,132**	**$ 18,227**	**−$133,382**	**$124,363**
Cash balance	**$203,349**	**$221,385**	**$239,517**	**$257,745**	**$124,363**	**$124,363**

Cash flow analysis (second year)

Quarter	Q1	2 Q2	Q3	Q4	2
Cash from operations	$ 59,643	$ 74,553	$ 80,518	$ 83,500	$298,213
Cash from receivables	$ 0	$ 0	$ 0	$ 0	$ 0
Operating cash inflow	**$ 59,643**	**$ 74,553**	**$ 80,518**	**$ 83,500**	**$298,213**
Other cash inflows					
Equity investment	$ 0	$ 0	$ 0	$ 0	$ 0
Increased borrowings	$ 0	$ 0	$ 0	$ 0	$ 0
Sales of business assets	$ 0	$ 0	$ 0	$ 0	$ 0
A/P increases	$ 8,717	$ 10,897	$ 11,769	$ 12,204	$ 43,587
Total other cash inflows	**$ 8,717**	**$ 10,897**	**$ 11,769**	**$ 12,204**	**$ 43,587**
Total cash inflow	**$ 68,360**	**$ 85,450**	**$ 92,286**	**$ 95,704**	**$341,800**
Cash outflows					
Repayment of principal	$ 4,271	$ 4,368	$ 4,467	$ 4,568	$ 17,674
A/P decreases	$ 5,975	$ 7,469	$ 8,067	$ 8,365	$ 29,876
A/R increases	$ 0	$ 0	$ 0	$ 0	$ 0
Asset purchases	$ 14,911	$ 18,638	$ 20,129	$ 20,875	$ 74,553
Dividends	$ 41,750	$ 52,187	$ 56,362	$ 58,450	$208,749
Total cash outflows	**$ 66,907**	**$ 82,663**	**$ 89,025**	**$ 92,258**	**$330,853**
Net cash flow	**$ 1,453**	**$ 2,787**	**$ 3,261**	**$ 3,446**	**$ 10,947**
Cash balance	**$125,816**	**$128,604**	**$131,864**	**$135,310**	**$135,310**

Cash flow analysis (third year)

Quarter	Q1	3 Q2	Q3	Q4	3
Cash from operations	$ 74,489	$ 93,111	$100,560	$104,285	$372,445
Cash from receivables	$ 0	$ 0	$ 0	$ 0	$ 0
Operating cash inflow	**$ 74,489**	**$ 93,111**	**$100,560**	**$104,285**	**$372,445**
Other cash inflows					
Equity investment	$ 0	$ 0	$ 0	$ 0	$ 0
Increased borrowings	$ 0	$ 0	$ 0	$ 0	$ 0
Sales of business assets	$ 0	$ 0	$ 0	$ 0	$ 0
A/P increases	$ 10,025	$ 12,531	$ 13,534	$ 14,035	$ 50,125
Total other cash inflows	**$ 10,025**	**$ 12,531**	**$ 13,534**	**$ 14,035**	**$ 50,125**
Total cash inflow	**$ 84,514**	**$105,643**	**$114,094**	**$118,320**	**$422,571**
Cash outflows					
Repayment of principal	$ 4,672	$ 4,778	$ 4,886	$ 4,997	$ 19,332
A/P decreases	$ 7,170	$ 8,963	$ 9,680	$ 10,038	$ 35,852
A/R increases	$ 0	$ 0	$ 0	$ 0	$ 0
Asset purchases	$ 18,622	$ 23,278	$ 25,140	$ 26,071	$ 93,111
Dividends	$ 52,142	$ 65,178	$ 70,392	$ 72,999	$260,712
Total cash outflows	**$ 82,607**	**$102,196**	**$110,098**	**$114,106**	**$409,007**
Net cash flow	**$ 1,907**	**$ 3,446**	**$ 3,996**	**$ 4,214**	**$ 13,564**
Cash balance	**$137,218**	**$140,664**	**$144,660**	**$148,874**	**$148,874**

Home Organization Service

Clutter Cutters, LLC

5252 Winders Way
Boston, Massachusetts 02204

Fran Fletcher

Clutter Cutters, LLC is a home organization company based in Boston, Massachusetts providing area residents with home and business organization services. Clutter Cutters is owned by Ansley Thomas and Cherie Mosely, best friends with a knack for organization.

BUSINESS OVERVIEW

Clutter Cutters, LLC is a home organization company based in Boston, Massachusetts providing area residents with home and business organization services.

Clutter Cutters is owned by Ansley Thomas and Cherie Mosely, best friends with a knack for organization. The idea for Clutter Cutters was born when Ms. Thomas and Ms. Mosely noticed numerous blogs about cleaning and getting organized. They realized that home organization does not come easily to all people and that there was a need for their expertise. Ms. Thomas and Ms. Mosely both have a wealth of knowledge in home organization that they can share with clients.

Clutter Cutters will be based out of Ms. Thomas's home office and they will travel to the client's home or business to evaluate their organizational issues. Clutter Cutters wants to take the drudgery out of organizing homes and offices and wants to help their clients live a productive, clutter free life.

Clutter Cutters will offer the following services:

- Unpacking/Organization
- Room-by-Room Organization
- Whole House Organization
- Office Organization
- Organization Plans
- Organization Seminars

There are a few competitors in Boston but currently no other businesses that offer unpacking services. The owners think this is a niche in the home organization business that they can cash in on.

Clutter Cutters's marketing plan includes being guests and giving household organizational tips on Boston TV during local interest segments. Clutter Cutters will also advertise through real estate agents and the Boston Welcome Center. Referrals are imperative in the service business, so the owners of

Clutter Cutters hope to quickly build clientele and make a name for themselves as experts in home organization.

Fortunately, Ms. Thomas and Ms. Mosely do not need to seek financing at this time. Start-up costs are only around $2,000 and each of them has a spouse who works. Using conservative estimates, Clutter Cutters will experience losses in the first three months, which the owners will absorb by decreasing their own wages. After three months, company profits should gradually increase and show an overall profit by the end of the first year.

COMPANY DESCRIPTION

Location
Clutter Cutters is located in Boston, Massachusetts. The owners will operate the business from Ms. Thomas's home office.

Hours of Operation
Monday—Friday, 9a.m. to 5p.m.

Personnel

Ansley Thomas (owner/consultant)
Ms. Thomas received a B.S. in Business from Northeastern University and has held various positions in the insurance industry.

Cherie Mosely (owner/consultant)
Ms. Mosely has worked in various office settings performing a myriad of administrative duties.

Business Services
Clutter Cutters will offer the following services:

- Unpacking and organizing after a move

- Room-by-Room organization

- Whole house organization

- Office organization

- Personalized organizational plans

- Organization seminars

MARKET ANALYSIS

Industry Overview
American households are at war with overwhelming clutter. Some surprising statistics include:

- Getting rid of clutter would eliminate 40% of housework in the average home (Cleaning Products Association)

- 25% of U.S. households with two-car garages do not park any cars in it and 32% only have room to park one car due to clutter (householdstatistics.com)

- Most people spend 55 minutes daily searching for things they know they own but can not find (householdstatistics.com)

- 80% of clutter is a result of disorganization, not lack of space (The National Detergent Association)

- The U.S. has 3% of the world's kid population, but 40% of the toys (Sloan Foundation)

Businesses are also experiencing problems with unorganized workspaces. Clutter Cutters will offer their services to companies that want to increase productivity and profits through better organization. Statistics include:

- The average executive wastes six weeks annually looking for important documents lost in clutter (*Wall Street Weekly*)

- 80% of filed documents are never looked at again (SBA)

Target Market

The primary target market for Clutter Cutters are families that have just moved to the area and are in need of unpacking services. Other target markets are households and businesses in Boston that need organization services.

Competition

There are only a few companies in the Boston area offering household organizational services. Clutter Cutters will set themselves apart from the competition by offering unpacking services. No other business in Boston currently offers this service. Other home organization businesses are:

Get Organized—16643-A Main St., Boston—home and business organization

Tidy Titans—5623 Harvard Highway, Suite 56, Boston—home organization

Charlyn's Cleaning Plus—8787 Industrial Blvd, Boston—cleaning services, home organization

GROWTH STRATEGY

The overall growth strategy of Clutter Cutters is to provide exceptional customer service when providing unpacking and home/office organizational services. The owners' primary strategy is making their company visible to clients who need organization services and to offer affordable prices that meet the needs of customers.

Referrals are imperative in the service industry. The primary focus of Clutter Cutters will be tailoring its services to the specific needs of each individual customer and controlling clutter as quickly and painlessly as possible.

Sales and Marketing

The owners have identified key tactics to support Clutter Cutters's growth strategy. They will make guest appearances during the local interest segments of Boston television stations where they will give tips on home organization.

Advertising/marketing for the primary target market will include:

- Advertising through local real estate agencies

- Advertising through the Boston Welcome Center

- Advertising on the Welcome to Boston website under service providers

- Mailing business brochures to industries who often have new workers from out of the area

Advertising/Marketing for the secondary target market includes:

- Advertising in the local newspapers

- Hosting seminars to individuals, groups, and businesses

FINANCIAL ANALYSIS

Start-up Costs

The majority of start-up related costs will be used for marketing purposes. Since all homes are unique, it will be difficult to stock organizational items and tools, so those will be purchased as needed.

Start-up costs

Business license	$ 250
Business cards	$ 150
Brochures	$ 300
Advertising	$ 500
Legal fees	$1,000
Total	**$2,200**

Financing

The owners are personally financing the start-up of Clutter Cutters.

Estimated Monthly Expenses

Clutter Cutters will operate as a limited liability corporation. Each employee will use her personal vehicle for work and will maintain a mileage/maintenance log as required by the Internal Revenue Service.

Monthly expenses

Phone/internet	$ 300
Advertising	$ 150
Liability insurance	$ 200
Transportation costs	$ 100
Wages for Ms. Mosely	$2,000
Wages for Ms. Thomas	$2,000
Total	**$4,750**

Estimated Monthly Income

The number of clients will determine estimated income. Project time will vary from one day to several weeks. The owners imagine that their time will be divided into the following sectors:

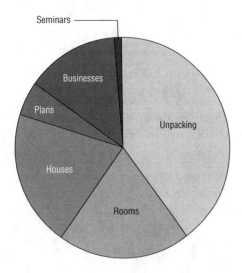

Price Schedule

Clutter Cutters imposes a $300 minimum for services. $50/hour for each consultant working on a project.

Service	Price
Unpacking/organizing	$50/per hour*
Room organization	$ 50/hour*
House organization (1 BR/loft)	$ 600/week
House organization (up to 1,200 sq feet)	$1,500/week
House organization (1,200–2,400 sq feet)	$2,000/week
House organization (2,400–3,600 sq feet)	$3,000/week
House organization (3,600–4,800 sq feet)	$4,200/week
House organization (over 4,800 sq feet)	TBD
Office organization	$ 50/hour*
Organization plans	$ 500
Seminars	$ 50/person

Profit/Loss

The owners of Clutter Cutters are using conservative estimates to determine monthly profit/loss. The chart below estimates how many of each service is expected each month. The company is conservatively estimating that unpacks will only take one day at the price of $300. The owners are using $1500 for its house organization estimate. Rooms and businesses are using the one-day price of $300. Seminars will be held quarterly and will be limited to 10 participants. Therefore, these conservative figures show Clutter Cutters with financial losses for the first three months. The owners have agreed to decrease their wages by the amount of the losses. The owners expect to see profits gradually increasing each month thereafter as they begin getting referrals.

Year 1 service estimates

	Month 1	Month 2	Month 3	Month 4	Month 5	Month 6	Month 7	Month 8	Month 9	Month 10	Month 11	Month 12
Unpack	2	3	3	3	4	4	4	5	5	5	6	6
House	1	1	1	2	2	2	2	2	2	3	3	3
Room	1	1	2	2	3	3	4	4	5	5	6	6
Business	0	1	1	1	1	1	2	2	2	2	2	2
Plan	0	0	0	1	1	1	2	2	2	2	2	2
Seminar	0	0	1	0	0	1	0	0	1	0	0	1

Monthly profit/loss

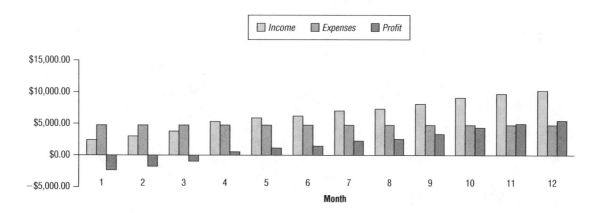

Profit Projections

Even with losses early on, Clutter Cutters is expected to end its first year with a nice profit of $21,000. The owners expect a 20% increase in income during the second year and will increase the wages of the owners from $2,000 per month to $3,000 per month. The owners expect another 20% increase of monthly income in the third year and will increase the wages of the owners from $3,000 per month to $4,000 per month. The chart indicates that profits are decreasing but the owners are giving themselves significant pay raises each year. At the end of the third year, it is estimated that the company will have secured $43,560 in profits. These profits will be used as a cushion during slower times.

Profit projections

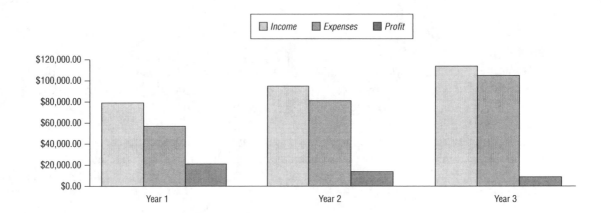

Mobile Pet Grooming Services

Pretty Paws Pet Salon, LLC

12675 Main St.
Colquitt, GA 39837

Fran Fletcher

Pretty Paws Pet Salon, LLC is a mobile pet grooming business owned by Kelly Schneider and based in Colquitt, Georgia. Pretty Paws Pet Salon will provide busy customers with a convenient way to have their furry family members groomed on a regular basis.

BUSINESS SUMMARY

Pretty Paws Pet Salon, LLC. is a mobile pet grooming business owned by Kelly Schneider and based in Colquitt, Georgia. Pretty Paws Pet Salon will provide busy customers with a convenient way to have their furry family members groomed on a regular basis.

The idea for a mobile grooming business was born while Kelly Schneider was working as a pet groomer at her home. Many customers would comment that they didn't have time to have their pets groomed on a regular basis, so Ms. Schneider had the idea of bringing grooming to the client.

Pet care is a billion-dollar industry and is expected to increase by 4% each year over the next several years. According to petdemographicsonline.com, the pet population in Pretty Paws Pet Salon's servicing area was 75,000 in 2010. An estimated 45,000 households in the region have pets. This large number of pet owners and the special treatment pets receive will provide a large customer base for the business. Pretty Paws Pet Salon has five local competitors including veterinarian offices, home grooming businesses, and a national chain; however, Pretty Paws Pet Salon is the only mobile pet grooming business in the area.

Pretty Paws Pet Salon will target busy individuals that work at local hospitals and factories and will have a set monthly schedule for its service areas. Ms. Schneider plans to set up her grooming bus at or near the workplaces of these clients. Pretty Paws Pet Salon's number one goal is to provide its furry clients with a nice comforting place to be groomed.

Marketing tactics include wrapping the mobile grooming bus with graphics and phone number, creating a moving billboard. Grand opening celebrations will be held at each potential service area. During this time, appointments will be scheduled and clients will be entered into a drawing to receive a free grooming package or pet product. In addition to the grand opening celebrations, Pretty Paws Pet Salon will advertise through local newspapers, radio, social media, and local veterinarian clinics.

Ms. Schneider is currently seeking financing for this venture in the form of a business loan or line of credit in the amount of $71,000 to cover start-up costs and three months of expenses. A mobile grooming bus will be the most expensive start-up purchase. Ms. Schneider has located a used bus that is fully equipped for pet grooming. Conservative projections show no profit the first month, then show an increase every month thereafter. If profits are made as planned, Ms. Schneider will be able to pay off the business loan by the end of the fifth year.

COMPANY DESCRIPTION

Location
Pretty Paws Pet Salon is a Colquitt, Georgia-based mobile pet salon. Colquitt is a small town but it is located near many other small towns that do not have pet grooming facilities. It is also located within 45 miles of three large hospitals and factories.

Hours of Operation
Pretty Paws Pet Salon will operate according to the following monthly schedule:

Hours will vary according to customer needs but will be approximately 8 a.m.—4 p.m.

	Monday	Tuesday	Wednesday	Thursday	Friday	Saturday
Week 1	Southeast AL hospital	Colquitt	Southwest GA hospital	Bainbridge School	Cats only Albany	
Week 2	Albany Mall	Blakely	Factory 1	Southwest GA hospital	Cats only Bainbridge Donalsonville	Open for Home Grooming
Week 3	Southwest GA hospital	Donalsonville	Bainbridge hospital	Southeast AL hospital	Cats only Blakely Colquitt	
Week 4	Factory 2	Southwest GA hospital	Arlington Vet	Albany Mall	Cats only Dothan	

Personnel

Kelly Schneider (owner/groomer)
Ms. Schneider is not new to pet grooming. She has groomed pets for the last five years at her home. Ms. Schneider will serve as head groomer and as the office manager.

Groomer(s)
A full time groomer or two part time groomers will be hired to assist with daily operations.

PRODUCTS AND SERVICES

Products
- Pet shampoo/conditioner
- Brushes/combs
- Hair accessories
- Pet jewelry
- Pet clothes
- Pet bandanas

Services

- Grooming
- Custom trims
- Fur dye
- Chalking
- Stenciling
- Nail trimming
- Nail polishing

MARKET ANALYSIS

Industry Overview

Mobile pet grooming falls under the animal care and service workers category. According to the Bureau of Labor Statistics, jobs in this field are expected to increase by 15% from 2012 to 2022. This increase is most likely due to the rise in pet ownership over the last ten years. According to the most recent pet survey, 82.5 million or 68% of American households are pet owners. Pet ownership is expected to increase especially in single-person and retiree households. Since there is an increasing trend in the humanization of pets, there is also increased demand for specialty products and services. The pet care industry is projected to grow 4% each year for the next five years.

According to petdemographicsonline.com, the pet population in Pretty Paws Pet Salon's servicing area was 75,000 in 2010. An estimated 45,000 households in the region have pets, which should supply an ample number of clients.

Target Market

Pretty Paws Pet Salon will target pet owners who treat their pets like family members but are busy and short on time. This type of pet owner will be willing to pay extra for the convenience of a mobile service.

Pretty Paws Pet Salon is going to target hospital and factory workers who work shifts, which makes it difficult to run errands. Ms. Schneider plans to set up her mobile unit in a convenient place for these workers. Ms. Schneider understands that their time away from work is very valuable and could cause grooming to be postponed or overlooked.

Pretty Paws will also travel to different small towns in the area where many residents do not want to travel to larger cities for service. Pretty Paws plans to park in centralized, but convenient, locations when offering mobile services. Grooming at the pet's home will also be offered for an additional fee.

Competition

There are currently no other mobile pet grooming businesses in the area. However, there are 3 other grooming businesses located within a veterinarian's office, 2 grooming businesses located at the owners' houses, and 1 chain store.

1. Paws and Claws—677 Brinson Rd., Colquitt, GA
2. Pet Mart—199976 South Circle, Dothan, AL - national chain
3. Jones Vet Clinic—2334 Old Airport Rd, Donalsonville, GA
4. South Georgia Vets—7886 N Slappey Blvd., Albany, GA

5. Peggy's Grooming—155 Winders Way, Bainbridge, GA

6. Carter's Vet Clinic—5443 Vet St., Bainbridge, GA

GROWTH STRATEGY

The overall growth strategy of Pretty Paws Pet Salon is to become the most sought after grooming service in southwest Georgia, with a six to eight week wait for appointments. Pretty Paws Pet Salon plans to achieve this growth by providing busy customers with top-notch, affordable pet grooming services.

Another strategy is to build a relationship with each of its furry clients so that Pretty Paws Pet Salon can provide grooming for the rest of the pet's life.

The company will offer many pet specialty products and services in order to fit the needs of its customers. Pretty Paws Pet Salon hopes to achieve financial independence during the first five years of operation. After funding is repaid and the owner has saved additional cash, she would consider buying a second grooming bus.

Sales and Marketing

Referrals are extremely important in any service industry, and pet grooming is no exception. The groomers at Pretty Paws Pet Salon will gain referrals by going the extra mile to make sure that clients and their owners get the best service possible.

The grooming bus will be wrapped with colorful graphics, including business name and phone number. It will serve as a moving billboard and will catch the attention of prospective clients.

The company will host a series of grand opening events. Events will be held at each hospital, factory, and community it will serve. During the celebrations, the groomers will schedule appointments and one new client will receive free grooming services, and another will receive a specialty pet product.

Advertising

In addition to grand opening events, Pretty Paws Pet Salon will utilize the following avenues:

• Advertising in the *Southwest Georgia Shopper*

• Advertising through local veterinarian clinics who do not offer onsite grooming

• Advertising through local pet stores, breeders, and shelters

• Company website

• Social media

• Sending out colorful appointment reminder cards

Keeping clients on a grooming schedule will be extremely important to the business's bottom line. It takes less time to groom an animal whose fur is maintained regularly and it will ensure steady income.

FINANCIAL ANALYSIS

Start-up Costs

The mobile grooming bus will be the largest start-up purchase. The owner plans to buy a used bus that is already equipped with everything needed, including tub, dryer, generator, grooming stations, and a pet holding area.

Estimated start-up costs

Legal fees	$ 5,000
Grooming bus	$40,000
Business license	$ 250
Website	$ 50
Initial advertising	$ 500
Supplies	$ 2,000
Insurance	$ 500
Total	**$48,300**

Estimated Monthly Expenses

With the exception of advertising, monthly expenses are expected to increase each year.

Monthly expenses

	Year 1	Year 2	Year 3	Year 4	Year 5
Gas	$ 800	$ 900	$1,000	$1,100	$ 1,200
Phone/internet	$ 150	$ 150	$ 150	$ 150	$ 150
Advertising	$ 100	$ 50	$ 50	$ 50	$ 50
Loan repayment	$ 350	$ 400	$ 450	$ 500	$ 550
Insurance	$ 100	$ 125	$ 150	$ 175	$ 200
Wages owner	$3,000	$3,500	$3,750	$4,000	$ 4,200
Wages assistant groomer	$2,000	$2,800	$3,200	$3,500	$ 3,750
Inventory	$ 400	$ 450	$ 500	$ 500	$ 500
Total	**$6,900**	**$8,375**	**$9,250**	**$9,975**	**$10,600**

Estimated Monthly Income

Pretty Paws conservatively estimates that it will groom five dogs a day during the first month of operation while they are trying to become established. In order to estimate monthly income, the company is using the $75 full grooming service for medium dogs. The company plans to groom three cats on "cats only" days and uses $75 for that estimate as well. The company projects monthly sales to start at $6,900 per month for the first month, and then expects to add on an additional two pets per day each month as the business becomes established in the community.

Prices for services

Dogs

Full groom small	$ 50
Full groom medium	$ 75
Full groom large	$100
Wash/dry	$ 35
Flea treatment	$ 10
De-matting	$ 12
Nail trimming	$ 15

Cats

Full groom	$ 75
Wash/dry	$ 50
Nail trimming	$ 25
Flea treatment	$ 20

Misc

Mobile fee	$ 20

Profit/Loss

According to estimated expenses and income data, Pretty Paws Pet Salon will break even the first month. Ms. Schneider is prepared to personally absorb any profit losses that may occur in the first months of operation by reducing her salary. In Month 2, a small profit is made and steadily increases until Month 6 when Pretty Paws Pet Salon hopes to have a full schedule of 15 clients per day. Estimates show profits remaining steady for the next six months. The estimated profits are shown in the "Annual Profit/Loss" chart.

Monthly profit/loss

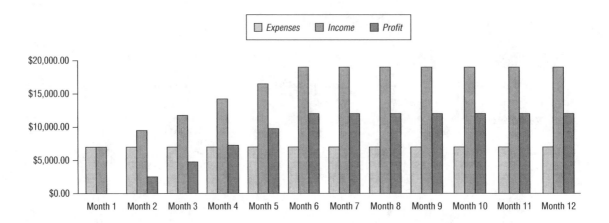

Annual profit/loss

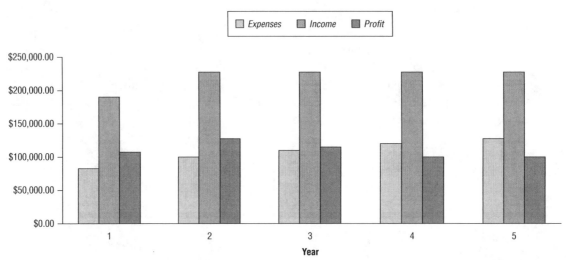

Financing

Pretty Paws Pet Salon is currently seeking financing for start-up expenses in the amount of $71,000. This will cover the cost of the grooming bus, additional start-up costs and expenses for three months.

Repayment Plan

Ms. Schneider has placed the loan payment in her monthly expenses and is confident that she will be able to repay this loan within five years as illustrated in the "Repayment Plan" chart. At the end of each year, the company will take 10% of its profit and pay a lump sum on the business loan. This will enable repayment of the loan before the end of the fifth year.

Repayment plan

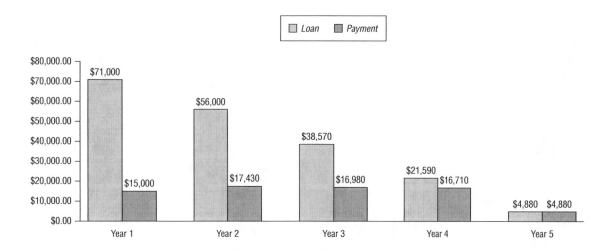

Painting Company
Ko-Bas Painting Company

1700 West State Street
Hartland, Michigan 48353

The focus of Ko-Bas Painting Company is to provide high-quality surface preparation, finished painting, and refinishing services to residential, commercial, municipal building, and facilities clients primarily in the most-populated area within the tri-county communities defined as Wayne, Oakland, and Washtenaw counties.

*This business planned appeared in a previous edition of **Business Plans Handbook**. It has been updated for this edition.*

INTRODUCTION

Ko-Bas Painting Company was formed to meet the growing demand and ongoing need for professional-grade painting and refinishing services in Southeastern Michigan.

The focus of Ko-Bas Painting Company is to provide high-quality surface preparation, finished painting and refinishing services to residential, commercial, municipal building and facilities clients primarily in the most-populated area within the tri-county communities defined as Wayne, Oakland and Washtenaw counties.

MISSION & PRINCIPLES

Ko-Bas Painting will be known for providing a high-quality service product. We will become known as a premium provider of custom and commercial painting and finishing services, operating at multiple levels within our prospective and existing client community.

To achieve our mission, Ko-Bas Painting will have to succeed at doing the following:

- Provide unique, practical, and professional services to our clients on a timely basis, applying and leveraging time-tested and state-of-the-art techniques and practices. To succeed at meeting our goals, our first responsibility is to our customers.

- Maintain a strong financial environment to allow us to establish ourselves as a multi-faceted service provider in the regional market we serve.

- Behave with the philosophy that our customers are entitled to a professional service performed to above-expectation satisfaction, in a reasonable, agreed-to amount of time and at a competitive, attractive price.

- Treat our partners, employees and customers with fairness and consideration.

- Bring value to our business operations community and client community.

We expect that through the effective application of these philosophies and principles we will succeed in achieving our mission.

GROWTH, MARKET AND CLIENTS WE SERVE

Market factors have indicated a current trend of moderately increasing income and commercial budgets with a pent-up demand for convenience and beautification services. The ailing economy had prevented many from beautifying their homes and facilities for the past several years, but the current upswing in the market has encouraged business owners and homeowners to proceed with the deferred projects. It will not be unreasonable for the number of potential residential and commercial customers to increase 10—20% each year.

Market and Prospect Client Base

Who: Ko-Bas painting company serves a marketplace made up of commercial and residential clients. Our ongoing focus is to develop and serve the correct blend of work to ensure ongoing revenue requirements. Our market focus is typically made up of an even split of residential and commercial clients. Our commercial clients are made up of municipal buildings, school buildings, and private businesses , both manufacturing and/or retail.

Where & Why: We choose our clients in this market to ensure that we do not extend our operations beyond reasonable areas of service and to manage and moderate costs in drive time, customer follow-up servicing, quoting and inspections.

SERVICE DELIVERY EXPECTATIONS

In order for Ko-Bas to attain its business objective, the following goals must be achieved:

- Acquire proper number of prospective clients for manageable growth

- Complete service at or below the price forecasted in the client financial quote

- Complete above-expectation service for the home or commercial client on or before the agreed-to deadline

- Leverage the customer as a reference for the next potential customer

- Utilize the recognition of the quality work to develop a demand for continued revenue growth

ABOUT THE COMPANY

Ko-Bas Painting Company was founded in 2009, by Karen and Ken Ko-Bas. The Ko-Bas Company sprang out of an idea that "we should make a go of this on our own!" Five years later, Ko-Bas is a highly successful, growing concern with all the unique business challenges faced by a locally-owned, expanding business.

The founders of Ko-Bas Painting Company, Ken and Karen Ko-Bas, have served the Southeast Michigan business and residential community for a combined total of more than 18 years. Their experience and dedication to the service industry has provided a positive force on multiple levels.

Ken Ko-Bas has brought value to customers as a paint and surface-coating consultant at the retail management level as well as commercial coatings applications sales management. Karen has achieved multiple certifications in custom and commercial finishing and designer coating applications. She also provides operational expertise and leadership to the company.

Ko-Bas Painting Company manages a focused team of highly experienced, professional painters and coating specialists to execute on any level of service required by a client. We select and manage our team to satisfy our ultimate goal—to treat each project as if it was our own. We pride ourselves on our legacy and service provided and intend to ensure ongoing satisfaction through quality service, operational management, and relationships with our employees, partners, and clients. We will continue to develop and leave behind a reputation nothing short of first class.

BUSINESS OBJECTIVE

Grow the company to a targeted achievement of 10-20% operating margin year-to-year.

We've maintained an objective view and take a conservative approach to developing and attempting to achieve our business goals. The financial data and business model provided is based on a year-to-year running operational and growth plan that is developed on an as-needed basis, typically by quarterly review. Thus, the numbers provided are based on a blend of real and approximated costs using the most conservative expense expectations available and are based on our considerable experience.

BUSINESS CHALLENGES AND ECONOMIC RISKS

The basic risks that Ko-Bas faces on a day-to-day basis are not unique to the average small business owner. However, when considering local economic pressures we may need to change our mix of business to "flex" to market demands and fill market needs.

The following list outlines many of our ongoing tactical and strategic concerns.

- Maintaining client base to sustain growth.

- Significant changes in the market demand for high-quality, premium services.

- Ongoing ability to attract and retain qualified, dependable employees.

- Significant unforeseen insurance event beyond reasonable expectations for on-the-job related injury.

COMPETITION AND MARKET POSITION

The competitive environment and the upswing of local and national economies put us in an enviable position for the last year in terms of the demand for convenience services and client custom/commercial coatings requirements. This created a positive competitive environment, as there were not enough service providers to satisfy the body of available work.

It is our position that by adapting our mix of business, competitive client pursuit and pricing practices we have been able to remain competitive and, most importantly, growing. Ko-Bas competes on service and price. We gather market-based information on an ongoing basis and develop our pricing and cost strategies based on market norms specific to our client profile and geographic considerations.

Our competitors range from the small independent 1-2 man painting service for residential and light commercial work to the medium-size 10-20 man commercial-only shops. To find out who to beat and who's getting the work, we need to look no further than the local online directory and by having those tough discussions with our client prospects that select another provider and asking them "why weren't we chosen?"

We have found that dealing with reality and modifying our tactics with reality has helped us keep an edge when it comes to beating the competition.

On any given day in our particular market segment, we have to keep an eye out for an average of 10-15 competitors in our market, particularly in the commercial and municipal service sector.

MARKETING STRATEGY

Our marketing strategy is simple—use the available channels appropriately to impact growth. We need to gain considerable name recognition through word-of-mouth advertising. Contracting for painting and finishing services in our commercial and municipal markets is not an impulse decision, so the primary thrust of the marketing strategy is to inform our prospective clients of reference work similar to the services they require.

In rank order, we have identified where our priorities lie in developing market presence to acquire clients.

1. Word-of-mouth

2. Client testimonials

3. Local business associations

4. Traditional print media, internet and social media advertising, and miscellaneous promotion techniques

Market Perception and Positioning Strategy

Our marketing, advertising and promotion strategy is to differentiate Ko-Bas Painting as a premium provider. The Ko-Bas Company's marketing strategy incorporates plans to educate and recruit potential homeowners and commercial prospects through several proven channels:

- Newspaper advertising will target specific local buyers

- Direct reference channels from satisfied current and previous clients

- Direct sales contact with property management and municipal property portfolio managers

- Small business network community

KEY PARTNERS

We view our partners and network of business contacts as a reflection of how we get business done. Without the partners and business contacts, we could not operate as an operationally-lean company and, most importantly, leverage this network for continued sales and business growth. The following list provides a window into the depth and breadth of engagement required to make our business go.

- Paint product and supply manufacturers

- Commercial/retail suppliers at large

- Financial institutions

- Community-Based Business Network

- Business Associations

- Better Business Bureau

- Michigan Economic Development Corporation (MEDC)

LEGAL CONSIDERATIONS

Ko-Bas Painting is a Michigan company based in Hartland, Michigan. Ko-Bas retains and maintains relationships with legal representation experienced in contracting and building service provider industries. Our company is organized to minimize risk to our operations while providing for maximum safety and security to our employees, their families, and client community.

CONCLUSION

The future looks bright for Ko-bas Painting Co. and we fully expect to be recognized in the market place. We will be able to achieve growth and sustain profitable operations through reputation and adherence to our most basic operating philosophies for maximum competitive advantage.

Printing Business
Superior Graphics and Printing

34221 South Park Blvd.
Lake Orion, Michigan 48360

Zuzu Enterprises

Superior Graphics and Printing is owned and operated by Hank Bergen. Hank purchased the existing business from his predecessor in September, 2013 with plans to expand and improve sales by increasing service and product offerings.

EXECUTIVE SUMMARY

Superior Graphics and Printing is owned and operated by Hank Bergen. Hank purchased the existing business from his predecessor in September, 2013 with plans to expand and improve sales by increasing service and product offerings. The store has been around and successful since 1982 and has offered the traditional products of a local print shop, including business cards, letterhead, stamps, and the like. Mr. Bergen plans to continue this tradition while also adding services to help businesses fulfill all of their advertising and marketing needs.

Businesses today need to focus on their core activities to remain competitive and lean. They don't have the time or staff to dedicate to marketing and advertising but when these areas are neglected, business suffers. Superior Graphics offers the services and expertise to tailor marketing and advertising pieces to each individual business and their own, unique situation. Our graphic designer and sales associates meet with business owners with a specific checklist and questions so that they get all of the information they need to design custom, successful solutions. The partnership with the client continues until the final products are delivered and found to be exceptional.

SERVICES

Superior Graphics and Printing will offer the following service lines:

- Printing and copying
- Traditional products, including business cards, envelopes, etc.
- Signs, posters, banners, and photos
- Promotional Products
- Creative Services
- Mailing Services

- Direct marketing

- Trade shows

- Other Services, including laminating and binding

Printing/Copying

Printing and copying are the most common services we provide. From walk-in service to large-scale print jobs, we have the machines to get any job done quickly and cost effectively. Our printing and copying services include:

- High speed black and white copying

- Color copying

- Offset printing

- Digital printing

- Book printing

- Direct-to-plate printing

- Large format and wide format printing

- One-to-one printing

- Variable printing

Traditional Products

A wide variety of traditional products are offered at Superior Graphics and Printing. Clients can choose from a standard set of pre-designed samples or we will design a custom product to meet their individual needs and tastes. All items are customizable with corporate logos, photos, or other unique design features.

The traditional products we offer include:

- Business cards

- Envelopes

- Letterhead

- Holiday cards

- Brochures

- Flyers

- Invitations

- Postcards

- Rack cards

- Return address labels

- Postcards

- Engineering prints

- Name badges

- Business forms

- Checks

- Custom stamps

- Announcements

- Stationery

Signs, Banners, and Other Graphics

In addition to the traditional products offered by a print shop, Superior Graphics and Printing now offers a wide variety of signs and banners of all different sizes and types. Some of our offerings include:

- Corrugated plastic signs

- Vinyl banners

- Vehicle magnets

- Bumper stickers

- Dry erase boards

- Photo enlargements

- Photo standees

- Canvas prints

- Floor graphics

- Car graphics

- Wall graphics

- Calendars

These signs and other products are useful for a number of different businesses and organizations from retail stores and restaurants to corporations, educational institutions, and community groups. Politicians and real estate agents make up a significant portion of this market as well. Another use for these types of products is trade shows. Signs, banners and other booth displays support the brand message and can draw attention to your presence, setting you apart from the crowd.

Promotional Products

Promotional products are a relatively new offering that it proving to be very popular and in-demand. Politicians, community groups, and all types of businesses want potential clients to remember them. Businesses want to cultivate their brand. What better way than by handing out promotional items that are used time and time again? Promotional products include:

- Pens, pencils

- Bags/backpacks

- T-shirts, aprons, hats, and other clothing

- Toys (such as frisbees, yo-yos, etc.)

- Water bottles, coffee mugs, thermal mugs

- Keychains

- Luggage tags

- Magnets

- Mouse pads

These items can serve as give-aways to potential or current clients, and they can be used by staff both in the office and at home to encourage a sense of pride and community. Clients consider using promotional products for such various reasons as:

- Customer goodwill and retention
- Trade shows
- Employee relations and events
- Brand awareness
- Public relations
- New customer/account generation
- Employee service awards
- Not-for-profit programs
- Internal promotions
- New product/service introductions

Creative Services

Superior Graphics and Printing also offers a variety of creative services to our clients. From graphic design to copyediting, clients can count on us to develop all of their print and electronic messages. Our full line of creative services includes:

- Graphic design
- Logo design
- Copywriting
- Brochures
- Direct mail print ads
- Outdoor advertising
- Newsletters
- Press releases
- Website design

Mailing Services

Mailing services are another offering of Superior Graphics and Printing. These services include:

- Envelope supply
- Folding
- Inserting and hand assembly
- Tab sealing
- Shrink wrapping
- Kitting
- Addressing
- Labeling
- Metering

- Live stamps

- Bar coding

- Automation processing

- Presorting

- Non-profit mailings

Direct Marketing

Research shows that sending personalized messages to a targeted audience increases response rates up to 15 times. At Superior Graphics and Printing, we can now create, print, and send unique, targeted marketing pieces including direct mail postcards, brochures, fliers, and newsletters. We can also procure personalized URLs and establish email and social media components to your direct marketing campaign.

Specifically, our direct marketing services include:

- Direct mail design, production and response tracking

- One-to-one marketing (personalized marketing)

- Email marketing

- Integrated direct marketing using personalized URLs and website landing pages

- Variable data printed materials

- Personal web pages

- Trackable 800 numbers

- Business reply cards

Trade Shows

Trade shows present a distinct set of challenges for even the most self-sufficient businesses. Superior Graphics and Printing can help with all aspects of the trade show, including:

- Pre- and post-show direct mail and email campaigns

- Signs, banners and posters to support your brand message

- Assistance with obtaining booth displays

- Promotional products for booth giveaways

- Effective follow-up programs to keep your company in mind after the show

Other Services

Other services offered by Superior Graphics and Printing include such things as laminating and binding. In the near future, we plan to purchase a 3-D printing machine so that we can begin to offer 3-D printing services as well.

EQUIPMENT

All of these services require equipment. As an existing business, Superior Graphics and Printing already owns the following equipment:

- Printers—Including color printer, large format printer, digital printer, and offset printer

- Copiers—Including color copier, high-speed copier, large format copier, and basic copier model for walk-in customer use

- Scanner

- Fax machine

- Paper cutter

- Folding machine

- Binding machine

- Paper shredder

- Paper jogger

- Pressure sealer

- Laminating machine

- Computers with design software and accounting software

As mentioned above, the purchase of a 3-D printer is planned in the next six months. Other machines will be evaluated on a case-by-case basis to determine if they need to be replaced or upgraded.

PERSONNEL

Superior Graphics and Printing is a relatively small operation, employing only four persons in addition to the owner/operator, Hank Bergen. The staff includes:

- One graphic designer

- One machine operator

- Two customer service representatives

Both the graphic designer and the machine operator have been employed at Superior for a number of years. They are exceptional at what they do and know the business inside and out. They are employed full-time.

The two customer service representatives are part-time employees and have been here for 2 and 1 years, respectively. Both are college students pursuing degrees at a local university.

Hank Bergen is able to fill in on all aspects of the business as well as handles large-volume sales to corporations, organizations, and municipalities. He is heavily involved in the Lake Orion Chamber of Commerce and is active on the Economic Development Corporation.

HOURS

Superior Graphics and Printing is open six days a week, Monday through Saturday. Hours are 9 am to 5pm all days. Last minute or rush jobs that require additional time will be billed accordingly.

WEBSITE

The website of Superior Graphics and Printing includes a full listing of our products and services, as well as pricing information and contact information. In addition, the website offers potential and established clients the convenience of uploading and managing their print orders from the convenience of their office. We find this is incredibly useful when ordering reprints of existing orders of business cards, pamphlets, and the like.

CONCLUSION

Superior Graphics and Printing is an established business in a thriving community. Several new products and services expanded our offerings and make us even more valuable to the businesses, organizations, and individuals we serve. We are poised to deal with every advertising and marketing need of our clients and have the experienced staff and equipment to make it successful. The new business ventures will add revenue to the business that will allow for the purchase of a 3-D printing machine in the next six months.

Scrap Yard
Ridgewood Recycling

12433 Jefferson Ave.
Ridgewood, NY 11385

BizPlanDB.com

Ridgewood Recycling ("the Company") is a New York-based corporation that will acquire recyclable scrap metal with the intent to sort, smelt, and resell bulk inventories of metal to distributors in its targeted market. The Company was founded by Parker Empson.

1.0 EXECUTIVE SUMMARY

The purpose of this business plan is to raise $500,000 for the development of a scrap yard while showcasing the expected financials and operations over the next three years. Ridgewood Recycling ("the Company") is a New York-based based corporation that will acquire recyclable scrap metal with the intent to sort, smelt, and resell bulk inventories of metal to distributors in its targeted market. The Company was founded by Parker Empson.

1.1 The Services

The primary revenue streams for the business will come from the sale of bulk metal that will be sold to manufacturers and wholesalers throughout the target market. The Company will acquire these inventories by acting as a scrap yard where individuals, general contractors, and subcontractors can drop off their waste recyclable metals. Within its facility, Ridgewood Recycling will have all of the necessary equipment to process and repackage waste scrap metal into saleable inventories.

The third section of the business plan will further describe the services offered by Ridgewood Recycling.

1.2 Financing

Mr. Empson is seeking to raise $500,000 as a bank loan. The interest rate and loan agreement are to be further discussed during negotiation. This business plan assumes that the business will receive a 10 year loan with a 9% fixed interest rate. The financing will be used for the following:

- Development of the Company's location.

- Financing for the first six months of operation.

- Capital to purchase FF and E and recycling equipment.

Mr. Empson will contribute $100,000 to the venture.

1.3 Mission Statement

Ridgewood Recycling's mission is to provide the local market with an expansive amount of scrap metal that can be reused within manufacturing and construction processes.

1.4 Management Team

The Company was founded by Parker Empson. Mr. Empson has more than 10 years of experience in the waste management industry. Through his expertise, he will be able to bring the operations of the business to profitability within its first year of operations.

1.5 Sales Forecasts

Mr. Empson expects a strong rate of growth at the start of operations. Below are the expected financials over the next three years.

Proforma profit and loss (yearly)

Year	1	2	3
Sales	$1,806,600	$1,987,260	$2,185,986
Operating costs	$ 427,778	$ 444,235	$ 461,478
EBITDA	$ 385,192	$ 450,032	$ 522,216
Taxes, interest, and depreciation	$ 225,597	$ 231,755	$ 257,129
Net profit	$ 159,595	$ 218,277	$ 265,087

Sales, operating costs, and profit forecast

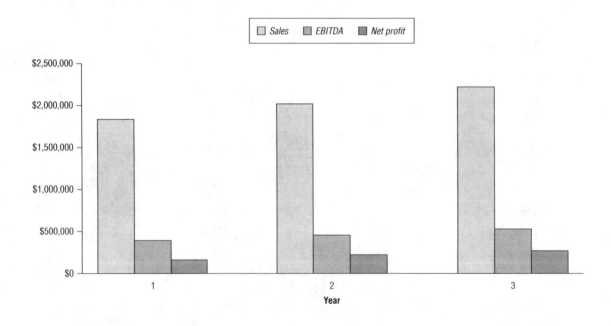

1.6 Expansion Plan

The Founder expects that the business will aggressively expand during the first three years of operation. Mr. Empson intends to implement marketing campaigns that will effectively target contractors, and wholesale buyers of recyclable scrap metals within the target market.

2.0 COMPANY AND FINANCING SUMMARY

2.1 Registered Name and Corporate Structure
The Company is registered as a corporation in the State of New York.

2.2 Required Funds
At this time, Ridgewood Recycling requires $500,000 of debt funds. Below is a breakdown of how these funds will be used:

Projected startup costs

Initial lease payments and deposits	$ 32,500
Working capital	$ 85,000
FF&E	$100,000
Leasehold improvements	$ 50,000
Security deposits	$ 25,000
Insurance	$ 35,000
Recycling equipment	$250,000
Marketing budget	$ 17,500
Miscellaneous and unforeseen costs	$ 5,000
Total startup costs	**$600,000**

Use of funds

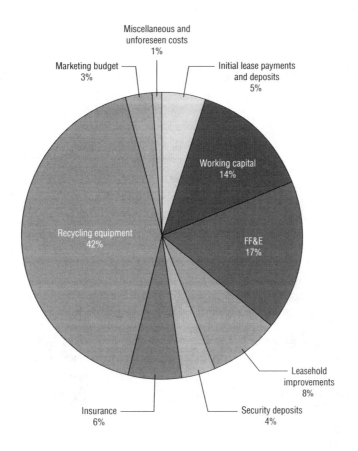

2.3 Investor Equity

Mr. Empson is not seeking an investment from a third party at this time.

2.4 Management Equity

Parker Empson owns 100% of Ridgewood Recycling.

2.5 Exit Strategy

If the business is very successful, Mr. Empson may seek to sell the business to a third party for a significant earnings multiple. Most likely, the Company will hire a qualified business broker to sell the business on behalf of Ridgewood Recycling. Based on historical numbers, the business could fetch a sales premium of up to 5 to 7 times earnings.

3.0 METAL OPERATIONS

Once the business receives its capital infusion, the Company will actively begin sorting, packaging, and reselling recyclable scrap metals to the open market. There is a large host of manufacturers, wholesalers, and recyclable metal product dealers that are seeking to acquire large inventories (typically on a per ton basis). Their primary intent is to either reuse the materials in their business processes or sell them to other third parties. Once the private scrap yard facility is operational, the business will have the ability to generate substantial income from the ongoing sale of scrap metal and related materials that will primarily consist of steel.

Please note that the expected per ton pricing for the Company's scrap metal inventories can be found in the fifth section of the business plan.

4.0 STRATEGIC AND MARKET ANALYSIS

4.1 Economic Outlook

The economic market condition in the United States is moderate. Unemployment rates have fallen while overall asset prices have increased. Although some economists feel that there is still a slight risk of a double dip recession. However, as people will continue to recycle their used materials (metal), the business will be able to continually smelt and repackage these metals for sale on the open market. This will ensure that Ridgewood Recycling can remain profitable and cash flow positive at all times.

4.2 Industry Analysis

Within the United States, there are approximately 8,000 businesses that provide waste management, private recycling, scrap metal dealing, and removal for non-hazardous recyclable waste from construction sites. These companies aggregately generate more than $26 billion dollars per year and provide jobs for more than 160,000 people.

The industry is a mature, and the expected future growth rate is anticipated to equal that of the general growth of the US economy. These businesses' revenues are directly tied to the housing market, which has been strong in recent years. However, severe increases in the general interest rate may slow the growth of new constructions, additions, and other work that allows the Company to generate revenue. In this event, Ridgewood Recycling may experience a slight decline in revenues.

4.3 Customer Profile

The Company anticipates that its average client will be a general construction or specialty subcontractor that operates within the target market. Since this demographic is extremely large, the exact demographics of each client will vary greatly, but they will all have the common need to have repackaged scrap metal that can be acquired at a reasonable price.

4.4 Competition

Within the greater New York metropolitan area, there are approximately 300 locations that operate in a scrap yard capacity. The primary differentiating factor that the business will use as it progresses through operations is that the business will accept any form of recyclable material as well as scrap metals. This will allow contractors that are removing refuse to use Ridgewood Recycling as a one stop shop. Only a handful of scrap yards operate within this capacity, and it will provide the Company with a strong competitive advantage at the onset of operations.

5.0 MARKETING PLAN

Ridgewood Recycling intends to maintain an extensive marketing campaign that will ensure maximum visibility for the business in its targeted market. Below is an overview of the marketing strategies and objectives of the Company.

5.1 Marketing Objectives

- Develop ongoing relationships with general and subcontractors that need a venue to discard recyclable waste materials.

- Establish relationships with companies that purchase wholesale and bulk inventories of repackaged scrap metal and bulk scrap metal.

5.2 Marketing Strategies

The business will use a multitude of marketing strategies to promote and expand the visibility of Ridgewood Recycling so that construction and manufacturing businesses use the site to drop off their recyclable waste scrap metals. The Company will maintain its listing in the Yellow pages, create marketing campaigns within local newspapers, and promote the business through word of mouth advertising.

Additionally, Management intends to continue to develop a number of referral and contractual relationships with area general and subcontractors. This will allow the Company to continually expand its inventories of recyclable scrap metals.

Finally, the business will develop ongoing purchase order relationships with bulk purchasers of scrap metals including third party distribution companies and manufacturing businesses that will use recycled materials in their production processes.

5.3 Pricing

For each ton of scrap steel, the business will generate approximately $830 of revenue. For per-ton aluminum, the business will generate $300 of revenue. Copper wiring, copper tubing, and smelted copper will be sold at a market rate price. As of 2014, the average cost of a ton of copper is $3,000 per ton.

6.0 ORGANIZATIONAL PLAN AND PERSONNEL SUMMARY

6.1 Corporate Organization

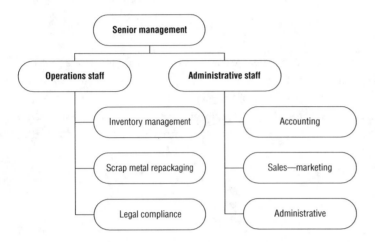

6.2 Organizational Budget

Personnel plan—yearly

Year	1	2	3
Owner	$ 40,000	$ 41,200	$ 42,436
Site manager	$ 35,000	$ 36,050	$ 37,132
Sorting and distribution staff	$130,000	$133,900	$137,917
Accountant (P/T)	$ 12,500	$ 12,875	$ 13,261
Administrative	$ 50,000	$ 51,500	$ 53,045
Total	**$267,500**	**$275,525**	**$283,791**

Numbers of personnel

Owner	1	1	1
Site manager	1	1	1
Sorting and distribution staff	4	4	4
Accountant (P/T)	1	1	1
Administrative	2	2	2
Totals	**9**	**9**	**9**

Personnel expense breakdown

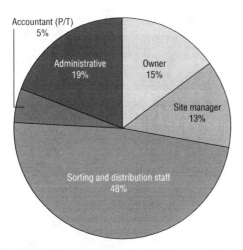

7.0 FINANCIAL PLAN

7.1 Underlying Assumptions

The Company has based its proforma financial statements on the following:

- Ridgewood Recycling will have an annual revenue growth rate of 10% per year.

- The Owner will acquire $500,000 of debt funds to develop the business.

- The loan will have a 10 year term with a 9% interest rate.

7.2 Sensitivity Analysis

The Company's revenues are sensitive to a number of external environmental factors including changes in the bulk price of metal as well changes in the price of oil. However, the Company will develop strict selling protocols that ensure that the pricing inputs for the Company's scrap metal distribution operations are well known for each transaction. As such, the business is only modestly sensitive to pricing shocks or unexpected pricing changes.

7.3 Source of Funds
Financing

Equity contributions	
Management investment	$ 100,000.00
Total equity financing	**$100,000.00**
Banks and lenders	
Banks and lenders	$ 500,000.00
Total debt financing	**$500,000.00**
Total financing	**$600,000.00**

7.4 General Assumptions

General assumptions

Year	1	2	3
Short term interest rate	9.5%	9.5%	9.5%
Long term interest rate	10.0%	10.0%	10.0%
Federal tax rate	33.0%	33.0%	33.0%
State tax rate	5.0%	5.0%	5.0%
Personnel taxes	15.0%	15.0%	15.0%

7.5 Profit and Loss Statements

Proforma profit and loss (yearly)

Year	1	2	3
Sales	**$1,806,600**	**$1,987,260**	**$2,185,986**
Cost of goods sold	$ 993,630	$1,092,993	$1,202,292
Gross margin	45.00%	45.00%	45.00%
Operating income	**$ 812,970**	**$ 894,267**	**$ 983,694**
Expenses			
Payroll	$ 267,500	$ 275,525	$ 283,791
General and administrative	$ 25,200	$ 26,208	$ 27,256
Marketing expenses	$ 9,033	$ 9,936	$ 10,930
Professional fees and licensure	$ 7,500	$ 7,725	$ 7,957
Insurance costs	$ 15,000	$ 15,750	$ 16,538
Travel and vehicle costs	$ 18,000	$ 19,800	$ 21,780
Rent and utilities	$ 40,000	$ 42,000	$ 44,100
Miscellaneous costs	$ 5,420	$ 5,962	$ 6,558
Payroll taxes	$ 40,125	$ 41,329	$ 42,569
Total operating costs	**$ 427,778**	**$ 444,235**	**$ 461,478**
EBITDA	**$ 385,192**	**$ 450,032**	**$ 522,216**
Federal income tax	$ 127,113	$ 135,094	$ 160,009
State income tax	$ 19,260	$ 20,469	$ 24,244
Interest expense	$ 43,689	$ 40,657	$ 37,341
Depreciation expenses	$ 35,536	$ 35,536	$ 35,536
Net profit	**$ 159,595**	**$ 218,277**	**$ 265,087**
Profit margin	**8.83%**	**10.98%**	**12.13%**

Sales, operating costs, and profit forecast

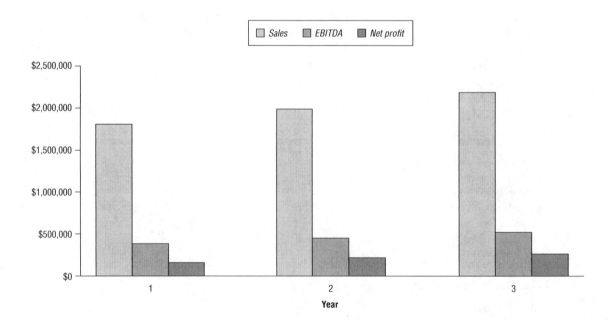

7.6 Cash Flow Analysis

Proforma cash flow analysis—yearly

Year	1	2	3
Cash from operations	$195,131	$253,813	$300,622
Cash from receivables	$ 0	$ 0	$ 0
Operating cash inflow	**$195,131**	**$253,813**	**$300,622**
Other cash inflows			
Equity investment	$100,000	$ 0	$ 0
Increased borrowings	$500,000	$ 0	$ 0
Sales of business assets	$ 0	$ 0	$ 0
A/P increases	$ 37,902	$ 43,587	$ 50,125
Total other cash inflows	**$637,902**	**$ 43,587**	**$ 50,125**
Total cash inflow	**$833,033**	**$297,400**	**$350,748**
Cash outflows			
Repayment of principal	$ 32,317	$ 35,349	$ 38,664
A/P decreases	$ 24,897	$ 29,876	$ 35,852
A/R increases	$ 0	$ 0	$ 0
Asset purchases	$497,500	$ 63,453	$ 75,156
Dividends	$136,591	$152,288	$180,373
Total cash outflows	**$691,305**	**$280,966**	**$330,045**
Net cash flow	**$141,727**	**$ 16,434**	**$ 20,703**
Cash balance	**$141,727**	**$158,162**	**$178,864**

Proforma cash flow (yearly)

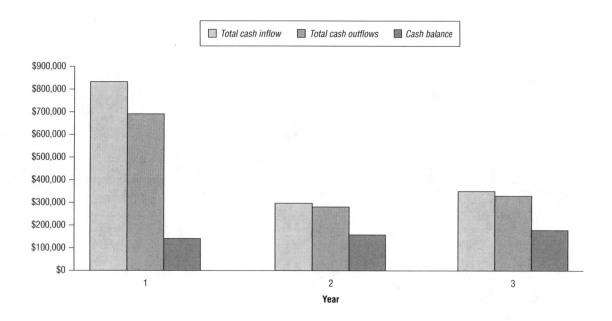

7.7 Balance Sheet

Proforma balance sheet—yearly

Year	1	2	3
Assets			
Cash	$141,727	$158,162	$178,864
Amortized development/expansion costs	$147,500	$153,845	$161,361
Equipment	$250,000	$281,727	$319,304
FF&E	$100,000	$125,381	$155,444
Accumulated depreciation	($ 35,536)	($ 71,071)	($106,607)
Total assets	**$603,692**	**$648,043**	**$708,366**
Liabilities and equity			
Accounts payable	$ 13,005	$ 26,716	$ 40,990
Long term liabilities	$467,683	$432,335	$396,986
Other liabilities	$ 0	$ 0	$ 0
Total liabilities	**$480,688**	**$459,050**	**$437,976**
Net worth	**$123,003**	**$188,993**	**$270,390**
Total liabilities and equity	**$603,692**	**$648,043**	**$708,366**

Proforma balance sheet

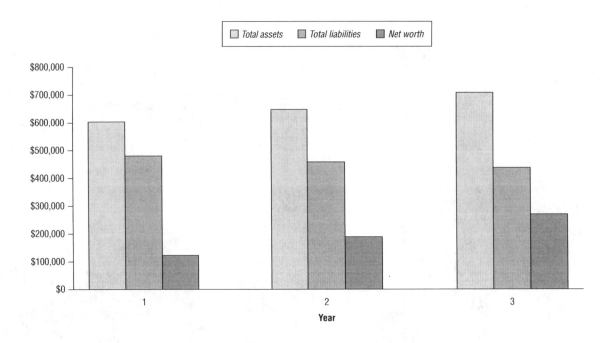

7.8 Breakeven Analysis

Monthly break even analysis

Year	1	2	3
Monthly revenue	$ 79,218	$ 82,266	$ 85,459
Yearly revenue	$950,617	$987,189	$1,025,506

Break even analysis

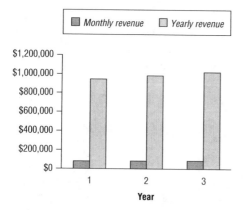

7.9 Business Ratios

Business ratios—yearly

Year	1	2	3
Sales			
Sales growth	0.0%	10.0%	10.0%
Gross margin	45.0%	45.0%	45.0%
Financials			
Profit margin	8.83%	10.98%	12.13%
Assets to liabilities	1.26	1.41	1.62
Equity to liabilities	0.26	0.41	0.62
Assets to equity	4.91	3.43	2.62
Liquidity			
Acid test	0.29	0.34	0.41
Cash to assets	0.23	0.24	0.25

7.10 Three Year Profit and Loss Statement

Profit and loss statement (first year)

Months	1	2	3	4	5	6	7
Sales	**$150,000**	**$150,100**	**$150,200**	**$150,300**	**$150,400**	**$150,500**	**$150,600**
Cost of goods sold	$ 82,500	$ 82,555	$ 82,610	$ 82,665	$ 82,720	$ 82,775	$ 82,830
Gross margin	45.0%	45.0%	45.0%	45.0%	45.0%	45.0%	45.0%
Operating income	**$ 67,500**	**$ 67,545**	**$ 67,590**	**$ 67,635**	**$ 67,680**	**$ 67,725**	**$ 67,770**
Expenses							
Payroll	$ 22,292	$ 22,292	$ 22,292	$ 22,292	$ 22,292	$ 22,292	$ 22,292
General and administrative	$ 2,100	$ 2,100	$ 2,100	$ 2,100	$ 2,100	$ 2,100	$ 2,100
Marketing expenses	$ 753	$ 753	$ 753	$ 753	$ 753	$ 753	$ 753
Professional fees and licensure	$ 625	$ 625	$ 625	$ 625	$ 625	$ 625	$ 625
Insurance costs	$ 1,250	$ 1,250	$ 1,250	$ 1,250	$ 1,250	$ 1,250	$ 1,250
Travel and vehicle costs	$ 1,500	$ 1,500	$ 1,500	$ 1,500	$ 1,500	$ 1,500	$ 1,500
Rent and utilities	$ 3,333	$ 3,333	$ 3,333	$ 3,333	$ 3,333	$ 3,333	$ 3,333
Miscellaneous costs	$ 452	$ 452	$ 452	$ 452	$ 452	$ 452	$ 452
Payroll taxes	$ 3,344	$ 3,344	$ 3,344	$ 3,344	$ 3,344	$ 3,344	$ 3,344
Total operating costs	**$ 35,648**	**$ 35,648**	**$ 35,648**	**$ 35,648**	**$ 35,648**	**$ 35,648**	**$ 35,648**
EBITDA	**$ 31,852**	**$ 31,897**	**$ 31,942**	**$ 31,987**	**$ 32,032**	**$ 32,077**	**$ 32,122**
Federal income tax	$ 10,554	$ 10,561	$ 10,568	$ 10,575	$ 10,582	$ 10,589	$ 10,596
State income tax	$ 1,599	$ 1,600	$ 1,601	$ 1,602	$ 1,603	$ 1,604	$ 1,606
Interest expense	$ 3,750	$ 3,731	$ 3,711	$ 3,691	$ 3,672	$ 3,652	$ 3,632
Depreciation expense	$ 2,961	$ 2,961	$ 2,961	$ 2,961	$ 2,961	$ 2,961	$ 2,961
Net profit	**$ 12,987**	**$ 13,044**	**$ 13,100**	**$ 13,157**	**$ 13,213**	**$ 13,270**	**$ 13,327**

Profit and loss statement (first year cont.)

Month	8	9	10	11	12	1
Sales	$150,700	$150,800	$150,900	$151,000	$151,100	$1,806,600
Cost of goods sold	$ 82,885	$ 82,940	$ 82,995	$ 83,050	$ 83,105	$ 993,630
Gross margin	45.0%	45.0%	45.0%	45.0%	45.0%	45.0%
Operating income	$ 67,815	$ 67,860	$ 67,905	$ 67,950	$ 67,995	$ 812,970
Expenses						
Payroll	$ 22,292	$ 22,292	$ 22,292	$ 22,292	$ 22,292	$ 267,500
General and administrative	$ 2,100	$ 2,100	$ 2,100	$ 2,100	$ 2,100	$ 25,200
Marketing expenses	$ 753	$ 753	$ 753	$ 753	$ 753	$ 9,033
Professional fees and licensure	$ 625	$ 625	$ 625	$ 625	$ 625	$ 7,500
Insurance costs	$ 1,250	$ 1,250	$ 1,250	$ 1,250	$ 1,250	$ 15,000
Travel and vehicle costs	$ 1,500	$ 1,500	$ 1,500	$ 1,500	$ 1,500	$ 18,000
Rent and utilities	$ 3,333	$ 3,333	$ 3,333	$ 3,333	$ 3,333	$ 40,000
Miscellaneous costs	$ 452	$ 452	$ 452	$ 452	$ 452	$ 5,420
Payroll taxes	$ 3,344	$ 3,344	$ 3,344	$ 3,344	$ 3,344	$ 40,125
Total operating costs	$ 35,648	$ 35,648	$ 35,648	$ 35,648	$ 35,648	$ 427,778
EBITDA	$ 32,167	$ 32,212	$ 32,257	$ 32,302	$ 32,347	$ 385,192
Federal income tax	$ 10,603	$ 10,610	$ 10,617	$ 10,624	$ 10,631	$ 127,113
State income tax	$ 1,607	$ 1,608	$ 1,609	$ 1,610	$ 1,611	$ 19,260
Interest expense	$ 3,611	$ 3,591	$ 3,570	$ 3,550	$ 3,529	$ 43,689
Depreciation expense	$ 2,961	$ 2,961	$ 2,961	$ 2,961	$ 2,961	$ 35,536
Net profit	$ 13,384	$ 13,442	$ 13,499	$ 13,557	$ 13,615	$ 159,595

Profit and loss statement (second year)

Quarter	Q1	2 Q2	Q3	Q4	2
Sales	$397,452	$496,815	$536,560	$556,433	$1,987,260
Cost of goods sold	$218,599	$273,248	$295,108	$306,038	$1,092,993
Gross margin	45.0%	45.0%	45.0%	45.0%	45.0%
Operating income	$178,853	$223,567	$241,452	$250,395	$ 894,267
Expenses					
Payroll	$ 55,105	$ 68,881	$ 74,392	$ 77,147	$ 275,525
General and administrative	$ 5,242	$ 6,552	$ 7,076	$ 7,338	$ 26,208
Marketing expenses	$ 1,987	$ 2,484	$ 2,683	$ 2,782	$ 9,936
Professional fees and licensure	$ 1,545	$ 1,931	$ 2,086	$ 2,163	$ 7,725
Insurance costs	$ 3,150	$ 3,938	$ 4,253	$ 4,410	$ 15,750
Travel and vehicle costs	$ 3,960	$ 4,950	$ 5,346	$ 5,544	$ 19,800
Rent and utilities	$ 8,400	$ 10,500	$ 11,340	$ 11,760	$ 42,000
Miscellaneous costs	$ 1,192	$ 1,490	$ 1,610	$ 1,669	$ 5,962
Payroll taxes	$ 8,266	$ 10,332	$ 11,159	$ 11,572	$ 41,329
Total operating costs	$ 88,847	$111,059	$119,943	$124,386	$ 444,235
EBITDA	$ 90,006	$112,508	$121,509	$126,009	$ 450,032
Federal income tax	$ 27,019	$ 33,773	$ 36,475	$ 37,826	$ 135,094
State income tax	$ 4,094	$ 5,117	$ 5,527	$ 5,731	$ 20,469
Interest expense	$ 10,459	$ 10,265	$ 10,067	$ 9,865	$ 40,657
Depreciation expense	$ 8,884	$ 8,884	$ 8,884	$ 8,884	$ 35,536
Net profit	$ 39,551	$ 54,468	$ 60,555	$ 63,703	$ 218,277

Profit and loss statement (third year)

Quarter	Q1	Q2	Q3	Q4	3
		3			
Sales	**$437,197**	**$546,497**	**$590,216**	**$612,076**	**$2,185,986**
Cost of goods sold	$240,458	$300,573	$324,619	$336,642	$1,202,292
Gross margin	45.0%	45.0%	45.0%	45.0%	45.0%
Operating income	**$196,739**	**$245,923**	**$265,597**	**$275,434**	**$ 983,694**
Expenses					
Payroll	$ 56,758	$ 70,948	$ 76,624	$ 79,461	$ 283,791
General and administrative	$ 5,451	$ 6,814	$ 7,359	$ 7,632	$ 27,256
Marketing expenses	$ 2,186	$ 2,732	$ 2,951	$ 3,060	$ 10,930
Professional fees and licensure	$ 1,591	$ 1,989	$ 2,148	$ 2,228	$ 7,957
Insurance costs	$ 3,308	$ 4,134	$ 4,465	$ 4,631	$ 16,538
Travel and vehicle costs	$ 4,356	$ 5,445	$ 5,881	$ 6,098	$ 21,780
Rent and utilities	$ 8,820	$ 11,025	$ 11,907	$ 12,348	$ 44,100
Miscellaneous costs	$ 1,312	$ 1,639	$ 1,771	$ 1,836	$ 6,558
Payroll taxes	$ 8,514	$ 10,642	$ 11,494	$ 11,919	$ 42,569
Total operating costs	**$ 92,296**	**$115,369**	**$124,599**	**$129,214**	**$ 461,478**
EBITDA	**$104,443**	**$130,554**	**$140,998**	**$146,220**	**$ 522,216**
Federal income tax	$ 32,002	$ 40,002	$ 43,202	$ 44,802	$ 160,009
State income tax	$ 4,849	$ 6,061	$ 6,546	$ 6,788	$ 24,244
Interest expense	$ 9,658	$ 9,446	$ 9,229	$ 9,008	$ 37,341
Depreciation expense	$ 8,884	$ 8,884	$ 8,884	$ 8,884	$ 35,536
Net profit	**$ 49,051**	**$ 66,161**	**$ 73,137**	**$ 76,738**	**$ 265,087**

7.11 Three Year Cash Flow Analysis

Cash flow analysis (first year)

Month	1	2	3	4	5	6	7
Cash from operations	$ 15,949	$ 16,005	$ 16,061	$ 16,118	$ 16,175	$ 16,232	$ 16,289
Cash from receivables	$ 0	$ 0	$ 0	$ 0	$ 0	$ 0	$ 0
Operating cash inflow	**$ 15,949**	**$ 16,005**	**$ 16,061**	**$ 16,118**	**$ 16,175**	**$ 16,232**	**$ 16,289**
Other cash inflows							
Equity investment	$100,000	$ 0	$ 0	$ 0	$ 0	$ 0	$ 0
Increased borrowings	$500,000	$ 0	$ 0	$ 0	$ 0	$ 0	$ 0
Sales of business assets	$ 0	$ 0	$ 0	$ 0	$ 0	$ 0	$ 0
A/P increases	$ 3,159	$ 3,159	$ 3,159	$ 3,159	$ 3,159	$ 3,159	$ 3,159
Total other cash inflows	**$603,159**	**$ 3,159**	**$ 3,159**	**$ 3,159**	**$ 3,159**	**$ 3,159**	**$ 3,159**
Total cash inflow	**$619,107**	**$ 19,163**	**$ 19,220**	**$ 19,276**	**$ 19,333**	**$ 19,390**	**$ 19,447**
Cash outflows							
Repayment of principal	$ 2,584	$ 2,603	$ 2,623	$ 2,642	$ 2,662	$ 2,682	$ 2,702
A/P decreases	$ 2,075	$ 2,075	$ 2,075	$ 2,075	$ 2,075	$ 2,075	$ 2,075
A/R increases	$ 0	$ 0	$ 0	$ 0	$ 0	$ 0	$ 0
Asset purchases	$497,500	$ 0	$ 0	$ 0	$ 0	$ 0	$ 0
Dividends	$ 0	$ 0	$ 0	$ 0	$ 0	$ 0	$ 0
Total cash outflows	**$502,159**	**$ 4,678**	**$ 4,697**	**$ 4,717**	**$ 4,737**	**$ 4,757**	**$ 4,777**
Net cash flow	**$116,949**	**$ 14,486**	**$ 14,522**	**$ 14,559**	**$ 14,596**	**$ 14,633**	**$ 14,670**
Cash balance	**$116,949**	**$131,434**	**$145,957**	**$160,516**	**$175,112**	**$189,745**	**$204,415**

SCRAP YARD

Cash flow analysis (first year cont.)

Month	8	9	10	11	12	1
Cash from operations	$ 16,346	$ 16,403	$ 16,460	$ 16,518	$ 16,576	$195,131
Cash from receivables	$ 0	$ 0	$ 0	$ 0	$ 0	$ 0
Operating cash inflow	**$ 16,346**	**$ 16,403**	**$ 16,460**	**$ 16,518**	**$ 16,576**	**$195,131**
Other cash inflows						
Equity investment	$ 0	$ 0	$ 0	$ 0	$ 0	$100,000
Increased borrowings	$ 0	$ 0	$ 0	$ 0	$ 0	$500,000
Sales of business assets	$ 0	$ 0	$ 0	$ 0	$ 0	$ 0
A/P increases	$ 3,159	$ 3,159	$ 3,159	$ 3,159	$ 3,159	$ 37,902
Total other cash inflows	**$ 3,159**	**$ 3,159**	**$ 3,159**	**$ 3,159**	**$ 3,159**	**$637,902**
Total cash inflow	**$ 19,504**	**$ 19,562**	**$ 19,619**	**$ 19,677**	**$ 19,734**	**$833,033**
Cash outflows						
Repayment of principal	$ 2,723	$ 2,743	$ 2,764	$ 2,784	$ 2,805	$ 32,317
A/P decreases	$ 2,075	$ 2,075	$ 2,075	$ 2,075	$ 2,075	$ 24,897
A/R increases	$ 0	$ 0	$ 0	$ 0	$ 0	$ 0
Asset purchases	$ 0	$ 0	$ 0	$ 0	$ 0	$497,500
Dividends	$ 0	$ 0	$ 0	$ 0	$136,591	$136,591
Total cash outflows	**$ 4,797**	**$ 4,818**	**$ 4,838**	**$ 4,859**	**$141,471**	**$691,305**
Net cash flow	**$ 14,707**	**$ 14,744**	**$ 14,781**	**$ 14,818**	**−$121,737**	**$141,727**
Cash balance	**$219,122**	**$233,866**	**$248,647**	**$263,464**	**$141,728**	**$141,727**

Cash flow analysis (second year)

Quarter	Q1	2 Q2	Q3	Q4	2
Cash from operations	$ 50,763	$ 63,453	$ 68,529	$ 71,068	$253,813
Cash from receivables	$ 0	$ 0	$ 0	$ 0	$ 0
Operating cash inflow	**$ 50,763**	**$ 63,453**	**$ 68,529**	**$ 71,068**	**$253,813**
Other cash inflows					
Equity investment	$ 0	$ 0	$ 0	$ 0	$ 0
Increased borrowings	$ 0	$ 0	$ 0	$ 0	$ 0
Sales of business assets	$ 0	$ 0	$ 0	$ 0	$ 0
A/P increases	$ 8,717	$ 10,897	$ 11,769	$ 12,204	$ 43,587
Total other cash inflows	**$ 8,717**	**$ 10,897**	**$ 11,769**	**$ 12,204**	**$ 43,587**
Total cash inflow	**$ 59,480**	**$ 74,350**	**$ 80,298**	**$ 83,272**	**$297,400**
Cash outflows					
Repayment of principal	$ 8,542	$ 8,736	$ 8,934	$ 9,136	$ 35,349
A/P decreases	$ 5,975	$ 7,469	$ 8,067	$ 8,365	$ 29,876
A/R increases	$ 0	$ 0	$ 0	$ 0	$ 0
Asset purchases	$ 12,691	$ 15,863	$ 17,132	$ 17,767	$ 63,453
Dividends	$ 30,458	$ 38,072	$ 41,118	$ 42,641	$152,288
Total cash outflows	**$ 57,666**	**$ 70,140**	**$ 75,251**	**$ 77,909**	**$280,966**
Net cash flow	**$ 1,814**	**$ 4,210**	**$ 5,047**	**$ 5,363**	**$ 16,434**
Cash balance	**$143,542**	**$147,751**	**$152,799**	**$158,162**	**$158,162**

Cash flow analysis (third year)

Quarter	Q1	3 Q2	Q3	Q4	3
Cash from operations	$ 60,124	$ 75,156	$ 81,168	$ 84,174	$300,622
Cash from receivables	$ 0	$ 0	$ 0	$ 0	$ 0
Operating cash inflow	**$ 60,124**	**$ 75,156**	**$ 81,168**	**$ 84,174**	**$300,622**
Other cash inflows					
Equity investment	$ 0	$ 0	$ 0	$ 0	$ 0
Increased borrowings	$ 0	$ 0	$ 0	$ 0	$ 0
Sales of business assets	$ 0	$ 0	$ 0	$ 0	$ 0
A/P increases	$ 10,025	$ 12,531	$ 13,534	$ 14,035	$ 50,125
Total other cash inflows	**$ 10,025**	**$ 12,531**	**$ 13,534**	**$ 14,035**	**$ 50,125**
Total cash inflow	**$ 70,150**	**$ 87,687**	**$ 94,702**	**$ 98,209**	**$350,748**
Cash outflows					
Repayment of principal	$ 9,344	$ 9,555	$ 9,772	$ 9,994	$ 38,664
A/P decreases	$ 7,170	$ 8,963	$ 9,680	$ 10,038	$ 35,852
A/R increases	$ 0	$ 0	$ 0	$ 0	$ 0
Asset purchases	$ 15,031	$ 18,789	$ 20,292	$ 21,044	$ 75,156
Dividends	$ 36,075	$ 45,093	$ 48,701	$ 50,505	$180,373
Total cash outflows	**$ 67,620**	**$ 82,401**	**$ 88,445**	**$ 91,580**	**$330,045**
Net cash flow	**$ 2,530**	**$ 5,286**	**$ 6,257**	**$ 6,629**	**$ 20,703**
Cash balance	**$160,691**	**$165,978**	**$172,235**	**$178,864**	**$178,864**

Senior Concierge Services

Hampton SeniorServ Inc.

45667 Ridgeway Dr.
Hampton Center, IL 60678

Paul Greenland

Hampton SeniorServ Inc. is a concierge service specializing in the senior citizen market.

EXECUTIVE SUMMARY

Business Overview

Hampton SeniorServ LLC is a concierge service specializing in the senior citizen market. The business coordinates and oversees a wide range of services for its clients, mainly in the home services, personal services, and errand categories. Examples of the services coordinated by Hampton SeniorServ include shopping (business, personal, grocery, etc.); home care (snow removal, lawn maintenance, landscaping, repairs, etc.); research (product, travel, etc.); and making reservations (travel, entertainment, etc.).

Hampton SeniorServ focuses on making its clients' lives as worry- and hassle-free as possible. The business serves as a liaison between senior consumers and a wide range of trusted, reputable service providers, ensuring that work meets acceptable quality standards. Hampton SeniorServ is an especially attractive option for "snow birds" who spend part of the year out-of-state and need someone to watch over their home, and senior citizens who simply need some extra assistance with the business of everyday life.

According to figures from the Administration on Aging, about 13 percent of the U.S. population was over the age of 65 in 2009 (39.6 million people). By 2030 this age group will account for 19 percent of the population (72.1 million people). As the senior citizen community grows in size, all communities will face a growing demand for a variety of services.

Established by entrepreneur Mary Rodgers, Hampton SeniorServ is located in the village of Hampton Center, Illinois, 25 miles west of Chicago in DuPage County. The village's population is older and more affluent than the national average.

MARKET ANALYSIS

The population of Hampton Center, Illinois, included 51,168 people in 2013. Individuals over the age of 55 accounted for 29 percent of the population (higher than the national average of 25.4 percent). By 2018 the population is projected to reach 56,286 people, at which time individuals over 55 will account for 36 percent of the population (compared to 27.3 percent nationally). The following tables provide detailed actual and projected breakdowns of the over-55 population:

I. 2013 Actual Population

Age	Percentage	Population
55–64	15%	7,675
65–74	7%	3,582
75–84	4%	2,047
85+	3%	1,535
Total	**29%**	**14,839**

II. 2018 Population Projection

Age	Percentage	Population
55–64	17%	9,569
65–74	10%	5,629
75–84	5%	2,814
85+	4%	2,251
Total	**36%**	**20,263**

In 2013, the average household income for Hampton Center, Illinois, was $230,006. Household incomes of $150,000 and more represented 49.4 percent of the population, followed by household income between $125,000 and $149,999 (7.2%); $100,000 and $124,999 (8.6%); and $75,000 and $99,999 (6.4%). That year, 94 percent of the community's housing units were owner occupied. Average household expenditures totaled $67,797. Annual expenditures on maintenance and repair services alone averaged $1,734.

Competitive Analysis

In early 2014 there were no concierge services focusing exclusively on the senior market in Hampton Center. A1 Concierge and Chicago Specialty Concierge were two general concierge services. However, the services focused mainly on the Metropolitan Chicago market and the Near West and Northwest suburbs. Because of its specialized business model and geographic focus, Hampton SeniorServ will have an advantage in the local Hampton Center market. However, due to the aging of the population and significant opportunity, there is a strong likelihood that new competitors will enter the marketplace within three to five years.

INDUSTRY ANALYSIS

According to figures from the Administration on Aging, the portion of the U.S. population over the age of 65 will increase from 39.6 million people in 2009 to 72.1 million people by 2030. As the senior citizen community grows in size, all communities will face a growing demand for a variety of supporting services. Businesses like Hampton SeniorServ, which improve the quality of life for older citizens, are projected to achieve healthy growth for the foreseeable future.

According to the United States Department of Labor, Bureau of Labor Statistics, concierges are utilized in a variety of settings. Many provide personal service assistance to patrons of office buildings, hotels, and apartments. In May of 2012, there were approximately 25,880 concierges employed nationwide.

PERSONNEL

Mary Rodgers (President)

Entrepreneur Mary Rodgers has been a successful businesswoman for more than 15 years. In 1999 she established her own wine retailing business, after taking courses about wine and studying extensively in Napa Valley, California. After starting on a small scale, her business achieved strong growth and a loyal following from customers throughout the Midwest. In 2011 Mary was recognized as one of the nation's leading independent wine retailers. The following year she sold her business to spend more time supporting her aging parents. This experience, coupled with her entrepreneurial spirit, prompted her to establish Hampton SeniorServ. Mary will concentrate her efforts on operations and new business development.

Staff

During Hampton SeniorServ's first year of operations, Mary will be supported by one full-time service coordinator who functions as the principal liaison between the business and its customers. The coordinator will oversee two part-time associate employees, who will concentrate on service delivery. Job descriptions for the president, service coordinator, and associate positions are available upon request.

Additional service coordinators and associates will be added as the business grows. Projected workforce growth is summarized in the Growth Strategy section of this plan. Projected salary expenses are summarized in the following table.

Position	2014	2015	2016
Owner	$ 50,000	$ 60,000	$ 70,000
Service coordinators	$ 31,200	$ 62,400	$ 93,600
Associates	$ 22,880	$ 68,640	$ 91,520
	$104,080	**$191,040**	**$255,120**

Professional & Advisory Support

Hampton SeniorServ has established a business banking account with Hampton Center Community Bank, including a merchant account for accepting credit card payments. Tax advisement is provided by Rex Gabay & Associates LLC. In addition, legal services are provided by the Law offices of Worth & Myers LP.

GROWTH STRATEGY

Strong revenue growth is projected for Hampton SeniorServ during its first three years of operations. Although a small net loss is projected during the first year, profitability is expected during the second year. The company has outlined the following growth strategy:

Year One: Bill 5,200 service hours. Achieve revenues of $182,000. In addition to the owner, begin operations with one full-time service coordinator and two part-time associate employees. Focus on building trust with area seniors and becoming a good community partner.

Year Two: Bill 11,440 service hours. Earn net income of $101,806 on revenues of $400,400. Become profitable during the early part of the year, recouping the net loss sustained during year one. In addition to the owner, employ two full-time service coordinators and six part-time associate employees.

Year Three: Bill 15,600 service hours. Earn net income of $167,872 on revenues of $546,000. In addition to the owner, employ three full-time service coordinators and eight part-time associate employees. Begin developing a strategy to expand into the neighboring village of Hinsdale in year four (utilizing net income earned during years two and three).

The following table provides a snapshot of Hampton SeniorServ's projected billable service hours for 2014-2016:

Billable hours

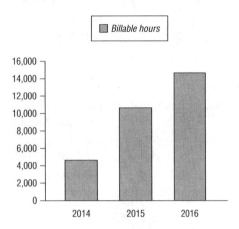

SERVICES

Hampton SeniorServ coordinates and oversees a wide range of services for its clients, mainly in the home coordination, personal services, and errand categories. The business focuses on making its clients' lives as worry- and hassle-free as possible. While some services (e.g., errands, research, etc.) are provided directly by Hampton SeniorServ employees, in other cases Hampton SeniorServ serves as a liaison between senior consumers and a wide range of trusted, reputable service providers, ensuring that work meets acceptable quality standards. The business' services include, but are not limited to:

Home Coordination
- Computer/technology set up assistance
- Furniture delivery
- Gutter cleaning
- Landscaping
- Lawn maintenance
- Locksmith
- Plant care
- Repairs
- Snow plowing
- Window washing

Personal Services
- Balloons and flowers
- Car rental
- Car wash/detail
- Clothing alterations
- Dry cleaning/laundry
- Eyeglass repair

- Film developing

- Gift buying

- Gift wrapping

- Holiday-related projects

- Hospitality

- License plate renewal

- Making reservations (airline, event, restaurant, travel)

- Packaging/shipping

- Personal shopping

- Photocopying

- Purchasing city stickers

- Research (product, travel, accountant, attorney, physician, etc.)

- Shoe repair

- Ticket ordering

- Travel planning

Errand Services

- Automotive maintenance coordination (oil changes, etc.)

- Exchanging/returning merchandise

- Gift/flower delivery

- Grocery shopping

- Home/property surveillance

- Item pick-up/drop-off

- Newspaper cancellation/start-up

- Pet care

- Picking up mail

Pricing

Hampton SeniorServ bills services at an hourly rate of $35. Additional fees will apply to services provided outside of normal business hours (20%), on weekends (35%), and on holidays (75%).

Hampton SeniorServ will consider its service territory to be a 10-mile radius around the community of Hampton Center, Illinois. An additional 20 percent fee will apply to services requiring Hampton SeniorServ staff to travel outside the company's normal service territory.

Customers are required to pay for services in advance, via check, cash, or credit card. Hampton SeniorServ also provides customers in need of regular or ongoing assistance with a special retainer program called PayAhead. By paying for services in advance, we will offer customers a 10 percent discount off of our regular base rate fees (excluding surcharges).

MARKETING & SALES

Hampton SeniorServ has developed a marketing plan that includes the following primary tactics:

1. A glossy color brochure, with a graphic design that appeals to the upscale senior citizen demographic. In addition to the description of the business and services provided, the brochure also will feature the Better Business Bureau logo, a profile of owner Mary Rodgers and Hampton SeniorServ's service coordinators. The brochure will emphasize that the business is both locally owned and fully bonded and insured, in order to build confidence and trust with prospective customers. Brochures will be used in Hampton SeniorServ's direct marketing campaigns, and when customers request information about the business.

2. Regular direct mailings to households with residents over the age of 55 and reported household income of at least $150,000. A Chicago-area mail house has been identified to assist with mailings to key prospects four times per year. In addition to preparing the actual mailings, the mail house also will provide targeted mailing lists for each campaign.

3. A Web site with complete details about Hampton SeniorServ and the services it provides.

4. Membership in the local Chamber of Commerce, Better Business Bureau, as well as service clubs (e.g., Kiwanis and Rotary) to establish a position of trust and build awareness with key community stakeholders.

5. Participation in events targeted toward older citizens (e.g., health fairs, senior expos, etc.).

6. Placemat advertising at local family restaurants frequented by retired consumers.

7. Refrigerator magnets, which can be distributed at events and also included in direct marketing initiatives.

8. Promotional graphics for all company vehicles, providing mobile marketing exposure.

9. A Facebook page to connect with prospective customers and, in some cases, their adult children.

10. Submission of periodic "success stories" featuring Hampton SeniorServ and its customers to local TV network affiliates (e.g., ABC, CBS, NBC, and FOX) and newspapers.

This marketing plan will be adjusted/expanded annually as the business grows and faces rising competition.

OPERATIONS

Facility & Location

Hampton SeniorServ has secured a three-year lease for office space in the Pinnacle Building, located in downtown Hampton Center at 45667 Ridgeway Dr. The facility includes a 12 x 12 waiting area, six 15 x 15 offices, a 25 x 25 conference room (shared with other building tenants), access to bathroom facilities and a small kitchenette. The offices are wired for high-speed Internet service.

Vehicles

Hampton SeniorServ will lease two fuel-efficient service vehicles during its first year of operation for a maximum annual cost of $10,000. An additional vehicle will be leased during year two, increasing costs to $15,000, followed by a third vehicle in year three, increasing total vehicle leasing costs to $20,000 annually.

Equipment

Furnishings will be purchased at a cost of $15,000. An additional $5,500 will be used to purchase two PCs, four tablet computers, customer relationship management software, a color laser printer, and GPS Navigation Systems for two company vehicles.

Hours of Operation

Hampton SeniorServ will provide services at normal rates between the hours of 8 AM and 5 PM, Monday through Friday. Services are available outside of normal business hours, including holidays, but premium rates will be charged.

LEGAL

Hampton SeniorServ will maintain appropriate liability and automotive insurance policies (available upon request). In addition, criminal background checks, drug and alcohol testing, and CPR/first aid certification will be required for all employees.

FINANCIAL ANALYSIS

Hampton SeniorServ is anticipating a net loss of approximately $14,036 during its first year of operation. The business is expected to break even during its second year, generating a net profit of $101,806. By the end of year three, Hampton SeniorServ should have more than $250,000 available for expansion into nearby geographic markets.

Net income

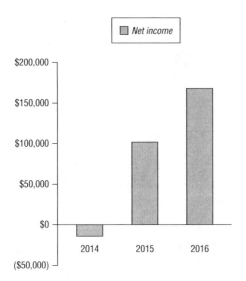

Mary Rodgers will provide the financial capital required to cover all initial start-up costs associated with Hampton SeniorServ. She is seeking a $50,000 business loan, payable within three years, for operations purposes.

A complete set of pro forma financial statements has been prepared for Hampton SeniorServ. These are available from our accountants upon request. The following table provides an overview of key projections during the first three years of operations:

	2014	2015	2016
Sales	**$182,000**	**$400,400**	**$546,000**
Expenses			
Salaries	$104,080	$191,040	$255,120
Payroll tax	$ 5,204	$ 9,552	$ 12,756
Business loan	$ 18,252	$ 18,252	$ 18,252
Facility lease	$ 8,200	$ 8,200	$ 8,200
Utilities	$ 1,350	$ 1,500	$ 1,650
Marketing & advertising	$ 40,000	$ 45,000	$ 50,000
Vehicle leases	$ 10,000	$ 15,000	$ 20,000
General/administrative	$ 700	$ 800	$ 900
Accounting/legal	$ 1,500	$ 1,000	$ 1,000
Office supplies	$ 750	$ 750	$ 750
Insurance	$ 1,000	$ 1,250	$ 1,500
Postage	$ 2,000	$ 2,250	$ 3,000
Telecommunications	$ 3,000	$ 4,000	$ 5,000
Total expenses	**$196,036**	**$298,594**	**$378,128**
Net income	**($ 14,036)**	**$101,806**	**$167,872**

Smartphone and Tablet Screen Repair

Scratched

Flint River Mall
Kiosk 452C
Albany, GA 31704

Fran Fletcher

Scratched is a smartphone/tablet screen repair business located in Albany, Georgia. It is owned and operated by Trent Roberts. Scratched will provide screen repair services to clients on all brands of smartphones and tablets, including the latest versions of iPhone and iPad.

EXECUTIVE SUMMARY

Scratched is a smartphone/tablet screen repair business located in Albany, Georgia. It is owned and operated by Trent Roberts. Scratched will provide screen repair services to clients on all brands of smartphones and tablets, including the latest versions of iPhone and iPad.

Mr. Roberts has 3 years of experience in the electronics repair business, and sees a need in the community for a fast, convenient, and affordable smartphone/tablet screen repair provider. The nearest eStore repair facility is 200 miles away and is not convenient for most people in the area. Scratched will be located in a kiosk in the Flint River Mall and will offer one-hour screen repairs. Thousands of customers shop at the mall each week and the kiosk will be located in a highly traveled area near the food court.

According to recent statistics, 56% of the population own a smartphone and 48% own a tablet. Assuming the same is true in Albany, Scratched will have approximately 59,000 potential customers.

The only businesses in the area offering similar services are mobile phone retail stores. Mr. Roberts is confident that Scratched will stand out from its competitors by:

- Repairing phones/tablets within one hour.

- Offering customers a convenient location and extended hours of operation.

- Carrying replacement screens for all types of smartphones.

Scratched will initially advertise through newspaper and radio ads. Referrals are crucial in the electronics repair business, and Mr. Roberts will work hard to gain the respect of clients by providing fast, friendly, and affordable service.

Conservative estimates reveal that Scratched will generate a small profit the first month. Profits will increase in subsequent months and then should plateau and remain steady.

Mr. Roberts is seeking a business line of credit in the amount of $45,000 to finance this venture. Financing will cover start-up fees and three months expenses. Mr. Roberts plans to repay the line of credit within three years.

COMPANY DESCRIPTION

Location

Scratched is located in the Flint River Mall in Albany, Georgia. Scratched will service mall customers from a kiosk conveniently located near the main entrance and food court.

Hours of Operations

Monday—Friday 12 PM—9 PM

Saturday 10 AM—9 PM

Sunday 2 PM—6 PM

Personnel

Trent Roberts (Owner)

Mr. Roberts will provide smartphone/tablet screen repairs. He has 3 years of experience repairing small electronics and has been replacing phone/tablet screens for his friends and family at home for more than a year. Mr. Roberts will also perform all accounting duties associated with the business.

Repair Assistant

A part time assistant will be hired to help provide service on the weekends. An additional assistant may be hired as profits grow and as business volume dictates.

PRODUCTS AND SERVICES

Products

- Screen protectors
- Cases
- Covers
- Chargers

Services

- Repair of smartphone and tablet screens
- Installation of screen protectors

MARKET ANALYSIS

Industry Overview

According to the Bureau of Labor Statistics, jobs in the electronics repair industry are expected to remain unchanged from 2010 to 2020. Mr. Roberts believes he has found a service niche in which there is a great need in the community. According to *Entrepreneur Daily Magazine*, carts and kiosks are a $10 billion dollar industry and should work great as a place for this business.

Mobile growth statistics show that 56% percent of the population own a smartphone. The average age of first time cell phone ownership is 13. Forty-eight percent of U.S. households currently own a tablet, and this number is only expected to increase.

According to demographic data, the population of Albany was 77,615 in 2010, with approximately 70% being between the ages of 13 and 75. This means that there are over 59,000 potential clients in the Albany metro area. Albany is also the largest city in southwest Georgia and therefore sees a great number of out of town shoppers. These shoppers will serve as an important addition to Scratched's potential client base.

Target Market

The target market for Scratched will be smartphone and tablet owners in the southwest Georgia area who do not want to be without their device for any length of time and desire a convenient location for getting their cracked screens repaired.

Competition

There are currently no similar services being offered in Albany at this time. The nearest iPhone store is located in Atlanta, which is approximately 200 miles away. Scratched is the only business in the area offering 1- hour repairs on all models of smartphones and tablets. Smartphone owners with insurance plans are granted approximately two repairs per year; however, having phones repaired at local mobile phone stores is not very convenient since it may take hours for repairs to be completed. Local mobile phone stores in the area are:

1. Horizon Wireless, 41006 Petit St., offers repair with insurance plan on models currently sold

2. ET&T Wireless, 24400 Pinewood Way, offers repair with insurance plan on models currently carried in the store

GROWTH STRATEGY

The overall growth strategy of the company is to gain a reputation for fast, convenient repairs of smartphone/tablet screens. The company will stock a wide selection of replacement screens for every model that customers might bring. Scratched wishes to achieve strong financial growth during the first year of operation. Mr. Roberts wants to become well established while he is the only one in the area providing this service. Mr. Roberts plans to hire additional staff to help with weekend customers.

Sales and Marketing

According to the Small Business Development Center, referrals serve as the main advertising method for electronics repair facilities. Referrals will be extremely important in Mr. Roberts's marketing strategy. In addition to referrals, Mr. Roberts thinks that it is very important to let people know about his business through advertising. Mr. Roberts has identified key advertising avenues and tactics to bring in customers while building a reputation for quality.

Scratched will market the following:

- Repairs completed in one hour

- On-site service

- Discount with valid student I.D.

Advertising

Initial advertising will include:

- Placing fliers at local universities

- Placing an ad in the Albany newspaper (which has many subscribers in the region outside of the Albany metro area)

- Placing ads on the food court tables

Ongoing advertising will include:

- Advertising in the mall's food court

- Social media

- Local newspaper

- Local radio station

- Local universities

FINANCIAL ANALYSIS

Start-up costs

Estimated start-up costs

Kiosk	$ 1,500
Parts inventory	$10,500
Business license	$ 250
Initial advertising	$ 500
Total	**$12,750**

Prices for Services

Service	Price
Smartphone repair	$150
Tablet repair	$150

Prices for Goods

Scratched will offer a wide variety of unique phone/tablet accessories. Prices will be marked up 100% of cost for most items.

Estimated Monthly Expenses

Loan payment	$ 400
Phone/internet	$ 100
Advertising	$ 100
Insurance	$ 100
Wages for Mr. Roberts (est.)	$ 4,000
Wages for employee (est.)	$ 1,500
Parts	$ 7,000
Mall rent*	$ 2,000
Total	**$15,200**

The base rent will be $2,000 per month. The mall also requires 5% of the kiosk's profit.

Profit/Loss

Mr. Roberts conservatively estimates that in the first month of operation, he will repair three phone/tablet screens per day on weekdays and six screens per day on weekends. Accessories are not expected to bring notable profit and therefore are not included in the profit/loss estimates.

Mr. Roberts takes a conservative approach and estimates $16,200 income in the first month, and a 5% increase each subsequent month during the first six months, with income remaining constant for the next six months.

Mr. Roberts expects monthly expenses to be around $16,000 the first month and to increase 3% each month thereafter. Expenses will fluctuate depending on income and inventory maintenance.

Mr. Roberts expects to make minimal profit the first month, but he expects the profits to steadily increase each month.

Estimated profits months 1–6

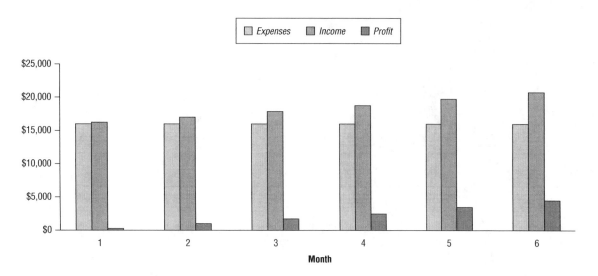

Estimated profits months 7–12

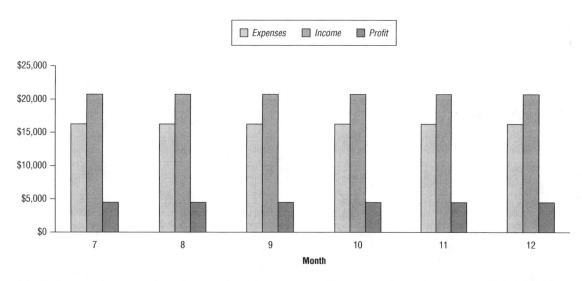

Mr. Roberts conservatively estimates that his expenses will increase about 3% a year and that his income will increase about 5% a year.

Financing

Mr. Roberts would like to obtain a business line of credit for $45,000, the amount needed to cover the start-up costs and three months' expenses. Mr. Roberts will use his home as collateral for the line of credit and plans to repay the line of credit in the third year of operation. He has budgeted $400 per month for loan repayment, but will pay a lump sum on the loan (approximately 25% of annual profit) at the end of each year. If profit projections are met, Mr. Roberts will be able to pay off the line of credit at the end of the third year.

Repayment plan

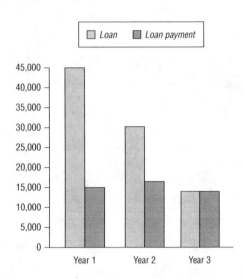

Tuxedo Rental Service

Modern Formal Wear

45612 E. Barkley St.
Elizabeth, NJ 07207

BozPlanDB.com

Modern Formal Wear ("the Company") is a New Jersey-based corporation that will provide rental of tuxedos (and occasional sales of tuxedos) to customers in its targeted market. The Company was founded by John Pringle.

1.0 EXECUTIVE SUMMARY

The purpose of this business plan is to raise $75,000 for the development of a tuxedo rental business while showcasing the expected financials and operations over the next three years. Modern Formal Wear ("the Company") is a New Jersey-based corporation that will provide rental of tuxedos (and occasional sales of tuxedos) to customers in its targeted market. The Company was founded by John Pringle.

1.1 The Services

Modern Formal Wear will generate extremely high gross margins from the ongoing rental of tuxedos to the general public. The business, as a secondary revenue center, will also generate substantial gross incomes from the sale of tuxedos.

The business will develop ongoing relationships with local event planners, schools (for prom tuxedo rentals), and wedding planners so that Modern Formal Wear can receive a constant stream of referrals.

The third section of the business plan will further describe the services offered by the Modern Formal Wear.

1.2 Financing

Mr. Pringle is seeking to raise $75,000 via a bank loan for the development of the business. The terms, interest rate, and loan covenants are to be determined at the time of negotiation. However, this business plan assumes that the Company will receive a 10 year loan with a 9% interest rate due on the outstanding principal balance. This loan financing will be used for the following:

- Development of the Company's Modern Formal Wear location.

- Financing for the first six months of operation.

- Capital to purchase tuxedo inventories.

The second section of the business plan will further document the usage of funds.

1.3 Mission Statement

Modern Formal Wear's mission is to develop an expansive facility that will provide an expansive array of tuxedos for all types of special events.

1.4 Management Team

Mr. Pringle is an experienced business person that will be able to effectively manage the day to day operations of Modern Formal Wear. His biography is available upon request.

1.5 Sales Forecasts

Mr. Pringle expects a strong rate of growth at the start of operations. Below are the expected financials over the next three years.

Proforma profit and loss (yearly)

Year	1	2	3
Sales	$244,030	$292,836	$342,618
Operating costs	$172,585	$179,040	$185,725
EBITDA	$ 40,676	$ 76,873	$113,693
Taxes, interest, and depreciation	$ 26,117	$ 37,100	$ 50,783
Net profit	$ 14,558	$ 39,773	$ 62,910

Sales, operating costs, and profit forecast

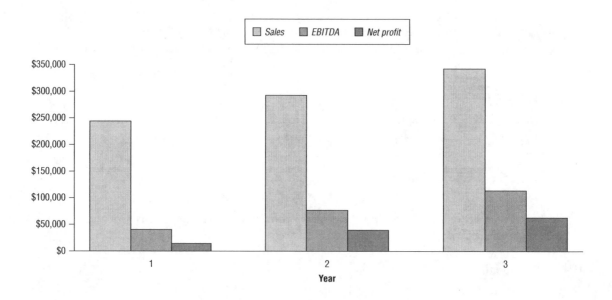

1.6 Expansion Plan

The Founder expects that the business will aggressively expand during the first three years of operation. Mr. Pringle intends to implement marketing campaigns that will effectively target individuals and local event planners within the target market.

2.0 COMPANY AND FINANCING SUMMARY

2.1 Registered Name and Corporate Structure

The Company is registered as a corporation in the State of New Jersey.

2.2 Required Funds

At this time, Modern Formal Wear requires $75,000 of debt funds. Below is a breakdown of how these funds will be used:

Projected startup costs

Working capital	$15,000
FF&E	$ 7,500
Leasehold improvements	$ 5,000
Security deposits	$ 2,500
Insurance	$ 2,500
Inventory	$ 5,000
Marketing budget	$ 2,500
Tuxedo inventory	$30,000
Misc. development costs	$ 5,000
Total startup costs	**$75,000**

Use of funds

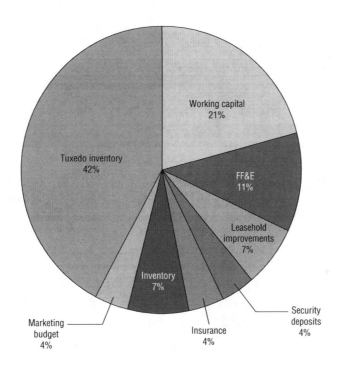

2.3 Investor Equity

Mr. Pringle is not seeking an investment from a third party at this time.

2.4 Management Equity

John Pringle owns 100% of Modern Formal Wear.

2.5 Exit Strategy

If the business is very successful, Mr. Pringle may seek to sell the business to a third party for a significant earnings multiple. Most likely, the Company will hire a qualified business broker to sell the business on behalf of Modern Formal Wear. Based on historical numbers, the business could fetch a sales premium of up to 3 times earnings.

3.0 TUXEDO RENTAL AND SALES

As stated in the executive summary, the Company's primary revenue stream will come from the continued rental of tuxedos to the general public for special events such as proms, weddings, Bar/Bat mitzvahs, and other events that require black tie attire. The Company will charge approximately $100 for a nightly rental of a tuxedo, which will provide Modern Formal Wear will a substantial return on clothing purchase investments.

The Company's secondary revenue center will come from the occasional sale of tuxedos to people that wish to purchase a black tie suit rather than needing to continuously rent one. Additionally, in the event where a customer loses their rented tuxedo, they will be required to pay for its replacement. This segment of the Company's operations will account for approximately 25% of the Company's revenues.

4.0 STRATEGIC AND MARKET ANALYSIS

4.1 Economic Outlook

This section of the analysis will detail the economic climate, the tuxedo rental industry, the customer profile, and the competition that the business will face as it progresses through its business operations.

Currently, the economic market condition in the United States is moderate. The country's economy has rebounded successfully from the major recession that started six years ago and ended three years ago. As such, Modern Formal Wear will be able to remain profitable and cash flow positive due to the fact that people have resumed normal spending as it relates to large scale events. Additionally, major events (such as proms) occur on a yearly basis despite any negative changes in the economy. This will further ensure that the business is moderately immune from negative changes in the economy.

4.2 Industry Analysis

Within the United States, there are approximately 2,700 companies that specialize in the rental of tuxedos to the general public. Many of these businesses operate more than one retail location. In each of the last five years, these businesses have aggregate generated more than $920 million of revenue while providing jobs to more than 20,000 people. Annual payrolls in each of the last five years have exceeded $250 million.

The growth rate of these businesses has been in step with that of the general growth of the economy.

4.3 Customer Profile

Modern Formal Wear's average client will be a middle to upper middle class man living in the Company's target market. Common traits among clients will include:

• Annual household income exceeding $50,000

• Lives or works no more than 15 miles from the Company's location.

• Will spend $100 to $200 on the rental of a tuxedo.

Within the Company's target market of the New Jersey metropolitan area, there are more than 9 million residents. Among these residents, median household income exceeds $60,000 per year. Each year, there are approximately 300,000 residents that attend a prom (among high school aged students).

4.4 Competition

Directly within the New Jersey metropolitan area, there are approximately 125 locations that offer tuxedo rental services to the general public. The way that Modern Formal Wear will be able to be effective in entering this market is by maintaining a number of different styles of tuxedo in order to draw a large number of people to its location. Additionally, for large parties (such as wedding parties), the business will provide drop off and pick up of tuxedos that have been rented by the Company.

5.0 MARKETING PLAN

Modern Formal Wear intends to maintain an extensive marketing campaign that will ensure maximum visibility for the business in its targeted market. Below is an overview of the marketing strategies and objectives of the Company.

5.1 Marketing Objectives

- Establish relationships with schools, event planners, and wedding planners.

- Develop an online website that allows individuals to place orders for rental of tuxedos.

- Implement a local campaign with the Company's targeted market via the use of flyers, local newspaper advertisements, and word of mouth advertising.

5.2 Marketing Strategies

Mr. Pringle intends on using a number of marketing strategies that will allow Modern Formal Wear to easily target the general public, wedding planners, and event planners within the target market. These strategies include traditional print advertisements and ads placed on search engines on the Internet. Below is a description of how the business intends to market its services to the general public.

The Company will also use an internet based strategy. This is very important as many people seeking local services, such as tuxedo rental services, now use the Internet to conduct their preliminary searches. The business' website will feature functionality that will allow an individual to place a tuxedo on hold (by entering their relevant size). This is a feature that is not commonly used among other tuxedo rental services within the New Jersey metropolitan area.

Modern Formal Wear will also develop ongoing referral relationships with wedding planners, event planners, and schools that will send their clients to the Company's retail location for black tie attire for planned events.

5.3 Pricing

For a tuxedo rental, the business will generate $100 to $300 of revenue. For drop off and pick up services, Modern Formal Wear will generate $50 to $100 of revenue.

6.0 ORGANIZATIONAL PLAN AND PERSONNEL SUMMARY

6.1 Corporate Organization

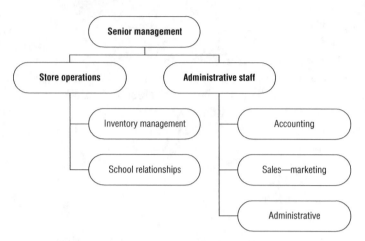

6.2 Organizational Budget

Personnel plan—yearly

Year	1	2	3
Owner	$ 25,000	$ 25,750	$ 26,523
Store manager	$ 27,500	$ 28,325	$ 29,175
Store employees	$ 47,000	$ 48,410	$ 49,862
Bookkeeper (P/T)	$ 7,500	$ 7,725	$ 7,957
Administrative (P/T)	$ 12,500	$ 12,875	$ 13,261
Total	**$119,500**	**$123,085**	**$126,778**

Numbers of personnel

Owner	1	1	1
Store manager	1	1	1
Store employees	2	2	2
Bookkeeper (P/T)	1	1	1
Administrative (P/T)	1	1	1
Totals	**6**	**6**	**6**

Personnel expense breakdown

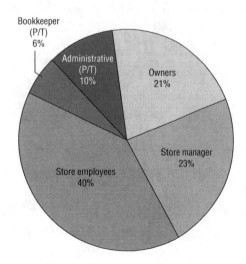

7.0 FINANCIAL PLAN

7.1 Underlying Assumptions

The Company has based its proforma financial statements on the following:

- Modern Formal Wear will have an annual revenue growth rate of 16% per year.

- The Owner will acquire $75,000 of debt to develop the business.

- Management will settle most short term payables on a monthly basis.

7.2 Sensitivity Analysis

In the event of an economic downturn, the business may have a decline in its revenues. However, rental of tuxedos are always in demand among individuals. As such, only a continued severe economic downturn would result in a decline in revenues.

7.3 Source of Funds

Financing

Equity contributions	
Owner investment	$10,000.00
Total equity financing	**$10,000.00**
Banks and lenders	
Bank loan	$75,000.00
Total debt financing	**$75,000.00**
Total financing	**$85,000.00**

7.4 General Assumptions

General assumptions

Year	1	2	3
Short term interest rate	9.5%	9.5%	9.5%
Long term interest rate	10.0%	10.0%	10.0%
Federal tax rate	33.0%	33.0%	33.0%
State tax rate	5.0%	5.0%	5.0%
Personnel taxes	15.0%	15.0%	15.0%

7.5 Profit and Loss Statements

Proforma profit and loss (yearly)

Year	1	2	3
Sales	**$244,030**	**$292,836**	**$342,618**
Cost of goods sold	$ 30,769	$ 36,923	$ 43,200
Gross margin	87.39%	87.39%	87.39%
Operating income	**$213,261**	**$255,913**	**$299,418**
Expenses			
Payroll	$119,500	$123,085	$126,778
General and administrative	$ 10,000	$ 10,400	$ 10,816
Marketing expenses	$ 2,440	$ 2,928	$ 3,426
Professional fees and licensure	$ 2,500	$ 2,575	$ 2,652
Insurance costs	$ 3,000	$ 3,150	$ 3,308
Travel and vehicle costs	$ 3,500	$ 3,850	$ 4,235
Rent and utilities	$ 12,500	$ 13,125	$ 13,781
Miscellaneous costs	$ 1,220	$ 1,464	$ 1,713
Payroll taxes	$ 17,925	$ 18,463	$ 19,017
Total operating costs	**$172,585**	**$179,040**	**$185,725**
EBITDA	**$ 40,676**	**$ 76,873**	**$113,693**
Federal income tax	$ 13,423	$ 23,356	$ 35,670
State income tax	$ 2,034	$ 3,539	$ 5,405
Interest expense	$ 6,553	$ 6,099	$ 5,601
Depreciation expenses	$ 4,107	$ 4,107	$ 4,107
Net profit	**$ 14,558**	**$ 39,773**	**$ 62,910**
Profit margin	**5.97%**	**13.58%**	**18.36%**

Sales, operating costs, and profit forecast

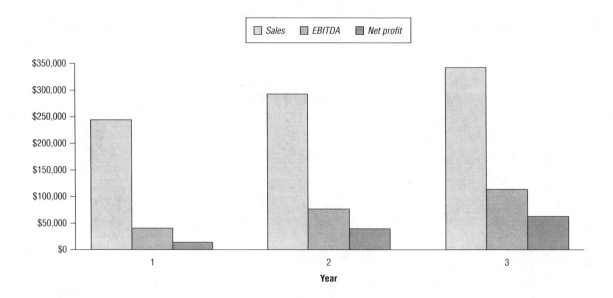

7.6 Cash Flow Analysis

Proforma cash flow analysis—yearly

Year	1	2	3
Cash from operations	$ 18,666	$43,880	$67,017
Cash from receivables	$ 0	$ 0	$ 0
Operating cash inflow	**$ 18,666**	**$43,880**	**$67,017**
Other cash inflows			
Equity investment	$ 10,000	$ 0	$ 0
Increased borrowings	$ 75,000	$ 0	$ 0
Sales of business assets	$ 0	$ 0	$ 0
A/P increases	$ 2,000	$ 2,300	$ 2,645
Total other cash inflows	**$ 87,000**	**$ 2,300**	**$ 2,645**
Total cash inflow	**$105,666**	**$46,180**	**$69,662**
Cash outflows			
Repayment of principal	$ 4,848	$ 5,302	$ 5,800
A/P decreases	$ 1,000	$ 1,200	$ 1,440
A/R increases	$ 0	$ 0	$ 0
Asset purchases	$ 57,500	$10,970	$16,754
Dividends	$ 13,066	$26,328	$40,210
Total cash outflows	**$ 76,413**	**$43,800**	**$64,204**
Net cash flow	**$ 29,252**	**$ 2,380**	**$ 5,458**
Cash balance	**$ 29,252**	**$31,632**	**$37,090**

Proforma cash flow (yearly)

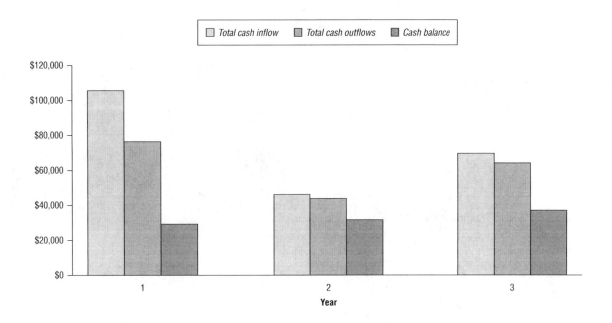

7.7 Balance Sheet

Proforma balance sheet—yearly

Year	1	2	3
Assets			
Cash	$29,252	$31,632	$ 37,090
Amortized expansion costs	$15,000	$16,097	$ 17,772
G&A assets	$ 5,000	$ 6,097	$ 7,772
FF&E	$ 7,500	$ 8,049	$ 8,886
Tuxedo inventory	$30,000	$38,228	$ 50,793
Accumulated depreciation	($ 4,107)	($ 8,214)	($ 12,321)
Total assets	**$82,645**	**$91,888**	**$109,993**
Liabilities and equity			
Accounts payable	$ 1,000	$ 2,100	$ 3,305
Long term liabilities	$70,152	$64,850	$ 59,548
Other liabilities	$ 0	$ 0	$ 0
Total liabilities	**$71,152**	**$66,950**	**$ 62,853**
Net worth	**$11,493**	**$24,937**	**$ 47,140**
Total liabilities and equity	**$82,645**	**$91,888**	**$109,993**

Proforma balance sheet

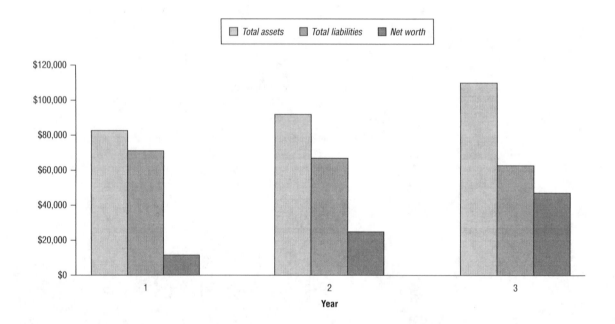

7.8 Breakeven Analysis

Monthly break even analysis

Year	1	2	3
Monthly revenue	$ 16,457	$ 17,073	$ 17,710
Yearly revenue	$197,486	$204,872	$212,522

Break even analysis

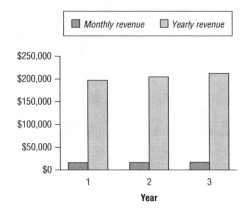

7.9 Business Ratios

Business ratios—yearly

Year	1	2	3
Sales			
Sales growth	0.0%	20.0%	17.0%
Gross margin	87.4%	87.4%	87.4%
Financials			
Profit margin	5.97%	13.58%	18.36%
Assets to liabilities	1.16	1.37	1.75
Equity to liabilities	0.16	0.37	0.75
Assets to equity	7.19	3.68	2.33
Liquidity			
Acid test	0.41	0.47	0.59
Cash to assets	0.35	0.34	0.34

7.10 Three Year Profit and Loss Statement

Profit and loss statement (first year)

Months	1	2	3	4	5	6	7
Sales	$17,250	$17,365	$17,480	$17,595	$34,500	$34,615	$17,250
Cost of goods sold	$ 2,175	$ 2,190	$ 2,204	$ 2,219	$ 4,350	$ 4,365	$ 2,175
Gross margin	87.4%	87.4%	87.4%	87.4%	87.4%	87.4%	87.4%
Operating income	$15,075	$15,176	$15,276	$15,377	$30,150	$30,251	$15,075
Expenses							
Payroll	$ 9,958	$ 9,958	$ 9,958	$ 9,958	$ 9,958	$ 9,958	$ 9,958
General and administrative	$ 833	$ 833	$ 833	$ 833	$ 833	$ 833	$ 833
Marketing expenses	$ 203	$ 203	$ 203	$ 203	$ 203	$ 203	$ 203
Professional fees and licensure	$ 208	$ 208	$ 208	$ 208	$ 208	$ 208	$ 208
Insurance costs	$ 250	$ 250	$ 250	$ 250	$ 250	$ 250	$ 250
Travel and vehicle costs	$ 292	$ 292	$ 292	$ 292	$ 292	$ 292	$ 292
Rent and utilities	$ 1,042	$ 1,042	$ 1,042	$ 1,042	$ 1,042	$ 1,042	$ 1,042
Miscellaneous costs	$ 102	$ 102	$ 102	$ 102	$ 102	$ 102	$ 102
Payroll taxes	$ 1,494	$ 1,494	$ 1,494	$ 1,494	$ 1,494	$ 1,494	$ 1,494
Total operating costs	$14,382	$14,382	$14,382	$14,382	$14,382	$14,382	$14,382
EBITDA	$ 693	$ 793	$ 894	$ 994	$15,768	$15,868	$ 693
Federal income tax	$ 949	$ 955	$ 961	$ 968	$ 1,898	$ 1,904	$ 949
State income tax	$ 144	$ 145	$ 146	$ 147	$ 288	$ 288	$ 144
Interest expense	$ 563	$ 560	$ 557	$ 554	$ 551	$ 548	$ 545
Depreciation expense	$ 342	$ 342	$ 342	$ 342	$ 342	$ 342	$ 342
Net profit	−$ 1,304	−$ 1,208	−$ 1,112	−$ 1,016	$12,690	$12,786	−$ 1,287

Profit and loss statement (first year cont.)

Month	8	9	10	11	12	1
Sales	$17,365	$17,480	$17,595	$17,710	$17,825	$244,030
Cost of goods sold	$ 2,190	$ 2,204	$ 2,219	$ 2,233	$ 2,248	$ 30,769
Gross margin	87.4%	87.4%	87.4%	87.4%	87.4%	87.4%
Operating income	$15,176	$15,276	$15,377	$15,477	$15,578	$213,261
Expenses						
Payroll	$ 9,958	$ 9,958	$ 9,958	$ 9,958	$ 9,958	$119,500
General and administrative	$ 833	$ 833	$ 833	$ 833	$ 833	$ 10,000
Marketing expenses	$ 203	$ 203	$ 203	$ 203	$ 203	$ 2,440
Professional fees and licensure	$ 208	$ 208	$ 208	$ 208	$ 208	$ 2,500
Insurance costs	$ 250	$ 250	$ 250	$ 250	$ 250	$ 3,000
Travel and vehicle costs	$ 292	$ 292	$ 292	$ 292	$ 292	$ 3,500
Rent and utilities	$ 1,042	$ 1,042	$ 1,042	$ 1,042	$ 1,042	$ 12,500
Miscellaneous costs	$ 102	$ 102	$ 102	$ 102	$ 102	$ 1,220
Payroll taxes	$ 1,494	$ 1,494	$ 1,494	$ 1,494	$ 1,494	$ 17,925
Total operating costs	$14,382	$14,382	$14,382	$14,382	$14,382	$172,585
EBITDA	$ 793	$ 894	$ 994	$ 1,095	$ 1,195	$ 40,676
Federal income tax	$ 955	$ 961	$ 968	$ 974	$ 980	$ 13,423
State income tax	$ 145	$ 146	$ 147	$ 148	$ 149	$ 2,034
Interest expense	$ 542	$ 539	$ 536	$ 532	$ 529	$ 6,553
Depreciation expense	$ 342	$ 342	$ 342	$ 342	$ 342	$ 4,107
Net profit	−$ 1,190	−$ 1,094	−$ 998	−$ 902	−$ 805	$ 14,558

Profit and loss statement (second year)

Quarter	Q1	2 Q2	Q3	Q4	2
Sales	$58,567	$73,209	$79,066	$81,994	$292,836
Cost of goods sold	$ 7,385	$ 9,231	$ 9,969	$10,338	$ 36,923
Gross margin	87.4%	87.4%	87.4%	87.4%	87.4%
Operating income	$51,183	$63,978	$69,097	$71,656	$255,913
Expenses					
Payroll	$24,617	$30,771	$33,233	$34,464	$123,085
General and administrative	$ 2,080	$ 2,600	$ 2,808	$ 2,912	$ 10,400
Marketing expenses	$ 586	$ 732	$ 791	$ 820	$ 2,928
Professional fees and licensure	$ 515	$ 644	$ 695	$ 721	$ 2,575
Insurance costs	$ 630	$ 788	$ 851	$ 882	$ 3,150
Travel and vehicle costs	$ 770	$ 963	$ 1,040	$ 1,078	$ 3,850
Rent and utilities	$ 2,625	$ 3,281	$ 3,544	$ 3,675	$ 13,125
Miscellaneous costs	$ 293	$ 366	$ 395	$ 410	$ 1,464
Payroll taxes	$ 3,693	$ 4,616	$ 4,985	$ 5,170	$ 18,463
Total operating costs	$35,808	$44,760	$48,341	$50,131	$179,040
EBITDA	$15,375	$19,218	$20,756	$21,524	$ 76,873
Federal income tax	$ 4,671	$ 5,839	$ 6,306	$ 6,540	$ 23,356
State income tax	$ 708	$ 885	$ 955	$ 991	$ 3,539
Interest expense	$ 1,569	$ 1,540	$ 1,510	$ 1,480	$ 6,099
Depreciation expense	$ 1,027	$ 1,027	$ 1,027	$ 1,027	$ 4,107
Net profit	$ 7,400	$ 9,928	$10,957	$11,487	$ 39,773

Profit and loss statement (third year)

Quarter	Q1	3 Q2	Q3	Q4	3
Sales	$68,524	$85,655	$92,507	$95,933	$342,618
Cost of goods sold	$ 8,640	$10,800	$11,664	$12,096	$ 43,200
Gross margin	0.0%	0.0%	0.0%	0.0%	0.0%
Operating income	$59,884	$74,855	$80,843	$83,837	$299,418
Expenses					
Payroll	$25,356	$31,694	$34,230	$35,498	$126,778
General and administrative	$ 2,163	$ 2,704	$ 2,920	$ 3,028	$ 10,816
Marketing expenses	$ 685	$ 857	$ 925	$ 959	$ 3,426
Professional fees and licensure	$ 530	$ 663	$ 716	$ 743	$ 2,652
Insurance costs	$ 662	$ 827	$ 893	$ 926	$ 3,308
Travel and vehicle costs	$ 847	$ 1,059	$ 1,143	$ 1,186	$ 4,235
Rent and utilities	$ 2,756	$ 3,445	$ 3,721	$ 3,859	$ 13,781
Miscellaneous costs	$ 343	$ 428	$ 463	$ 480	$ 1,713
Payroll taxes	$ 3,803	$ 4,754	$ 5,134	$ 5,325	$ 19,017
Total operating costs	$37,145	$46,431	$50,146	$52,003	$185,725
EBITDA	$22,739	$28,423	$30,697	$31,834	$113,693
Federal income tax	$ 7,134	$ 8,918	$ 9,631	$ 9,988	$ 35,670
State income tax	$ 1,081	$ 1,351	$ 1,459	$ 1,513	$ 5,405
Interest expense	$ 1,449	$ 1,417	$ 1,384	$ 1,351	$ 5,601
Depreciation expense	$ 1,027	$ 1,027	$ 1,027	$ 1,027	$ 4,107
Net profit	$12,048	$15,711	$17,196	$17,955	$ 62,910

7.11 Three Year Cash Flow Analysis

Cash flow analysis (first year)

Month	1	2	3	4	5	6	7
Cash from operations	−$ 962	−$ 866	−$ 770	−$ 674	$13,032	$13,128	−$ 944
Cash from receivables	$ 0	$ 0	$ 0	$ 0	$ 0	$ 0	$ 0
Operating cash inflow	**−$ 962**	**−$ 866**	**−$ 770**	**−$ 674**	**$13,032**	**$13,128**	**−$ 944**
Other cash inflows							
Equity investment	$10,000	$ 0	$ 0	$ 0	$ 0	$ 0	$ 0
Increased borrowings	$75,000	$ 0	$ 0	$ 0	$ 0	$ 0	$ 0
Sales of business assets	$ 0	$ 0	$ 0	$ 0	$ 0	$ 0	$ 0
A/P increases	$ 167	$ 167	$ 167	$ 167	$ 167	$ 167	$ 167
Total other cash inflows	**$85,167**	**$ 167**	**$ 167**	**$ 167**	**$ 167**	**$ 167**	**$ 167**
Total cash inflow	**$84,204**	**−$ 699**	**−$ 603**	**−$ 507**	**$13,199**	**$13,295**	**−$ 778**
Cash outflows							
Repayment of principal	$ 388	$ 390	$ 393	$ 396	$ 399	$ 402	$ 405
A/P decreases	$ 83	$ 83	$ 83	$ 83	$ 83	$ 83	$ 83
A/R increases	$ 0	$ 0	$ 0	$ 0	$ 0	$ 0	$ 0
Asset purchases	$57,500	$ 0	$ 0	$ 0	$ 0	$ 0	$ 0
Dividends	$ 0	$ 0	$ 0	$ 0	$ 0	$ 0	$ 0
Total cash outflows	**$57,971**	**$ 474**	**$ 477**	**$ 480**	**$ 483**	**$ 486**	**$ 489**
Net cash flow	**$26,234**	**−$ 1,173**	**−$ 1,080**	**−$ 987**	**$12,716**	**$12,809**	**−$ 1,266**
Cash balance	**$26,234**	**$25,060**	**$23,980**	**$22,993**	**$35,709**	**$48,519**	**$47,252**

Cash flow analysis (first year cont.)

Month	8	9	10	11	12	1
Cash from operations	−$ 848	−$ 752	−$ 656	−$ 559	−$ 463	$ 18,666
Cash from receivables	$ 0	$ 0	$ 0	$ 0	$ 0	$ 0
Operating cash inflow	**−$ 848**	**−$ 752**	**−$ 656**	**−$ 559**	**−$ 463**	**$ 18,666**
Other cash inflows						
Equity investment	$ 0	$ 0	$ 0	$ 0	$ 0	$ 10,000
Increased borrowings	$ 0	$ 0	$ 0	$ 0	$ 0	$ 75,000
Sales of business assets	$ 0	$ 0	$ 0	$ 0	$ 0	$ 0
A/P increases	$ 167	$ 167	$ 167	$ 167	$ 167	$ 2,000
Total other cash inflows	**$ 167**	**$ 167**	**$ 167**	**$ 167**	**$ 167**	**$ 87,000**
Total cash inflow	**−$ 682**	**−$ 585**	**−$ 489**	**−$ 393**	**−$ 296**	**$105,666**
Cash outflows						
Repayment of principal	$ 408	$ 411	$ 415	$ 418	$ 421	$ 4,848
A/P decreases	$ 83	$ 83	$ 83	$ 83	$ 83	$ 1,000
A/R increases	$ 0	$ 0	$ 0	$ 0	$ 0	$ 0
Asset purchases	$ 0	$ 0	$ 0	$ 0	$ 0	$ 57,500
Dividends	$ 0	$ 0	$ 0	$ 0	$13,066	$ 13,066
Total cash outflows	**$ 492**	**$ 495**	**$ 498**	**$ 501**	**$13,570**	**$ 76,413**
Net cash flow	**−$ 1,173**	**−$ 1,080**	**−$ 987**	**−$ 894**	**−$13,866**	**$ 29,252**
Cash balance	**$46,079**	**$44,999**	**$44,012**	**$43,118**	**$29,252**	**$ 29,252**

Cash flow analysis (second year)

Quarter	Q1	2 Q2	Q3	Q4	2
Cash from operations	$ 8,776	$10,970	$11,848	$12,286	$43,880
Cash from receivables	$ 0	$ 0	$ 0	$ 0	$ 0
Operating cash inflow	**$ 8,776**	**$10,970**	**$11,848**	**$12,286**	**$43,880**
Other cash inflows					
Equity investment	$ 0	$ 0	$ 0	$ 0	$ 0
Increased borrowings	$ 0	$ 0	$ 0	$ 0	$ 0
Sales of business assets	$ 0	$ 0	$ 0	$ 0	$ 0
A/P increases	$ 460	$ 575	$ 621	$ 644	$ 2,300
Total other cash inflows	**$ 460**	**$ 575**	**$ 621**	**$ 644**	**$ 2,300**
Total cash inflow	**$ 9,236**	**$11,545**	**$12,469**	**$12,930**	**$46,180**
Cash outflows					
Repayment of principal	$ 1,281	$ 1,310	$ 1,340	$ 1,370	$ 5,302
A/P decreases	$ 240	$ 300	$ 324	$ 336	$ 1,200
A/R increases	$ 0	$ 0	$ 0	$ 0	$ 0
Asset purchases	$ 2,194	$ 2,743	$ 2,962	$ 3,072	$10,970
Dividends	$ 5,266	$ 6,582	$ 7,109	$ 7,372	$26,328
Total cash outflows	**$ 8,981**	**$10,935**	**$11,735**	**$12,150**	**$43,800**
Net cash flow	**$ 255**	**$ 610**	**$ 734**	**$ 780**	**$ 2,380**
Cash balance	**$29,507**	**$30,117**	**$30,851**	**$31,632**	**$31,632**

Cash flow analysis (third year)

Quarter	Q1	3 Q2	Q3	Q4	3
Cash from operations	$13,403	$16,754	$18,095	$18,765	$67,017
Cash from receivables	$ 0	$ 0	$ 0	$ 0	$ 0
Operating cash inflow	**$13,403**	**$16,754**	**$18,095**	**$18,765**	**$67,017**
Other cash inflows					
Equity investment	$ 0	$ 0	$ 0	$ 0	$ 0
Increased borrowings	$ 0	$ 0	$ 0	$ 0	$ 0
Sales of business assets	$ 0	$ 0	$ 0	$ 0	$ 0
A/P increases	$ 529	$ 661	$ 714	$ 741	$ 2,645
Total other cash inflows	**$ 529**	**$ 661**	**$ 714**	**$ 741**	**$ 2,645**
Total cash inflow	**$13,932**	**$17,415**	**$18,809**	**$19,505**	**$69,662**
Cash outflows					
Repayment of principal	$ 1,402	$ 1,433	$ 1,466	$ 1,499	$ 5,800
A/P decreases	$ 288	$ 360	$ 389	$ 403	$ 1,440
A/R increases	$ 0	$ 0	$ 0	$ 0	$ 0
Asset purchases	$ 3,351	$ 4,189	$ 4,524	$ 4,691	$16,754
Dividends	$ 8,042	$10,053	$10,857	$11,259	$40,210
Total cash outflows	**$13,082**	**$16,034**	**$17,235**	**$17,852**	**$64,204**
Net cash flow	**$ 850**	**$ 1,381**	**$ 1,574**	**$ 1,653**	**$ 5,458**
Cash balance	**$32,482**	**$33,863**	**$35,437**	**$37,090**	**$37,090**

Videographer

Precious Moments Videography

765 Bayou Avenue
New Orleans, Louisiana 70139

Fran Fletcher

Precious Moments Videography is owned and operated by Lesa Harrison. The New Orleans-based business specializes in providing videography for all of life's special occasions. Its motto is "Capturing life's precious moments through video."

EXECUTIVE SUMMARY

Ms. Harrison has five years of experience videoing special occasions for herself, friends, and family. The idea for a videography business surfaced after she was not pleased with video taken at her own wedding, and after getting tired of always videoing and not being able to enjoy her children's birthday parties.

Precious Moments Videography will capture those special events. No special occasion is too big or too small, including:

- Weddings
- Birthday Parties
- Anniversary Parties
- Baby Showers
- Bridal Showers
- Baptisms/Christenings/Baby Dedications
- Baby Deliveries (where allowed)
- Recitals
- Plays
- Beauty Pageants
- Parades
- Funerals
- Honors Day Programs

Videography has become standard practice at weddings and other events along with photography. New Orleans' mild climate and tourist attractions make it a popular place for nuptials.

Brides in the area who want more than just a standard wedding video will serve as the target market for Precious Moments Videography. New Orleans is home to 177,000 single adults, and these residents will provide a large potential customer base for the business.

There are other videography businesses in the area, but Ms. Harrison's knack for creative and personalized video editing will make her stand out in the crowd. Precious Moments Videography will obtain clients predominantly through referrals. Additionally, Ms. Harrison will list her services with bridal boutiques, party supply stores, and through local wedding planners.

Ms. Harrison is seeking a business line of credit in the amount of $20,000 to finance her venture. Financing will cover start-up fees and personal expenses for three months. This will provide a cushion while the business is building its client base. Ms. Harrison expects her appointment schedule to reach maximum capacity within six months. She expects a pre-tax profit of $44,000 the first year, and expects subsequent years to be comparable. Ms. Harrison plans to repay the line of credit within three years.

COMPANY DESCRIPTION

Location
Precious Moments Videography is located in New Orleans, Louisiana. Ms. Harrison plans to work out of her home since services will be provided on-site at the client's event.

Hours of Operations
Videography services will be available as dictated by customer need. Many parties, weddings, and other special events occur on the weekends and Precious Moments Videography will be available to capture these moments for its clients.

Personnel

Lesa Harrison (Owner)
Ms. Harrison will provide all videography services. She is experienced with a video camera and editing software and has videoed parties and weddings for family and friends for the past five years.

PRODUCTS AND SERVICES

Services
Precious Moments Videography will capture memories at:

- Weddings
- Birthday Parties
- Anniversary Parties
- Baby Showers
- Bridal Showers
- Baptisms/Christenings/Baby Dedications
- Baby Deliveries (where allowed)
- Recitals
- Plays

- Beauty Pageants
- Parades
- Funerals
- Honors Day Programs

MARKET ANALYSIS

Industry Overview

According to the Bureau of Labor Statistics, videography jobs are expected to remain constant from 2010 to 2020. Videography is becoming more popular and professionals with software skills will be considered more valuable.

New Orleans is home to more than 385,000 residents. According to census data, 46% of adults are not married which should provide a large customer base of 177,000 for wedding videography. Fifteen percent of the population are children aged 0 to 11, which will provide a customer base of nearly 58,000 for party videography.

Target Market

Precious Moments Videography will market its services to residents of New Orleans who are in need of a videographer for their life events. Precious Moments Videography will target brides in the area who wish to have all aspects of their wedding documented, including the engagement party, bachelorette party, bridesmaids' luncheon, rehearsal dinner, rehearsal, wedding, and reception.

The owner will also target parents who want to sit back, relax, and enjoy their child's party instead of having to video everything.

Competition

There are currently three other businesses offering videography in the New Orleans area.

1. Videos by Vanessa, 2413 Alligator Alley—wedding videos only
2. Time to Remember, 383 St. Charles Place—offers photography and videography
3. Jernigan's Videography, 640 Parish Ave.—miscellaneous videography services

GROWTH STRATEGY

The growth strategy of the company is to make a name for itself as the best videography business in the area. Ms. Harrison will achieve this growth one client at a time with her deep commitment to preserving memories and special occasions and creativity in video editing. As the sole proprietor, Ms. Harrison hopes to build personal relationships with her clients, and be asked to capture all future precious moments.

Sales and Marketing

Referrals will be the backbone of the company's marketing strategy. While she is building clientele and a great reputation, Ms. Harrison has identified avenues for bringing clients to her business.

Precious Moments Videography will market the following:

- Reasonable hourly rates
- Timely video editing (10-day turnaround)

Advertising

Initial advertising will include:

- Social media

- Local newspaper

- Bridal stores

- Party stores

- Funeral homes

- Dance studios

FINANCIAL ANALYSIS

Start-up costs

Estimated start-up costs

Video equipment	$5,000
Video editing software	$ 900
Advertising	$ 100
Business cards/flyers	$ 100
Total	**$6,100**

Estimated Monthly Income

Monthly income will be determined by number of clients and hours worked.

Prices for Services

Precious Moments Videography will charge $100 per hour with a 2-hour minimum. This price includes video editing and 2 DVDs.

The following chart details the wedding packages that are available.

Package	Platinum	Gold	Silver	Bronze
Price	**$3,000**	**$2,000**	**$1,000**	**$500**
Events filmed	Engagement party Bridal shower Rehearsal Wedding Reception 2 additional events (12 hours)	Engagement party Bridal shower Rehearsal Wedding Reception (8 hours)	Rehearsal Wedding Reception (4 hours)	Wedding Reception (2.5 hours)

Estimated Monthly Expenses

Expenses will be kept to a minimum. Ms. Harrison would like to earn $3,200 monthly. However, the number of clients and scheduled services will determine her salary.

Monthly expenses

Loan payment	$ 300
Phone/internet	$ 100
Gas	$ 400
Insurance	$ 200
Wages for Ms. Harrison (est.)	$3,200
Advertising	$ 100
Total	**$4,300**

Profit/Loss

At first, Ms. Harrison expects to receive overflow business from videographers who are more established while she is building her customer base.

Ms. Harrison expects an increase in wedding videography from the months of April through September. This increase is expected because more couples get married during those months, New Orleans has a moderate climate, and because it is a vacation destination. Since realistically only one wedding can be videoed per weekend, she will only book Platinum Wedding Packages during these peak months, ensuring that she makes maximum profits to help carry her through less busy seasons.

Ms. Harrison is conservatively estimating that from October through March, her income will consist of two silver and two bronze wedding packages, four parties, and one miscellaneous event. This results in a loss of $300 a month during these months. However, the profits during the other half of the year are more than enough to make up for the loss.

Ms. Harrison does not expect her expenses to increase unless she needs to buy new equipment. Precious Moments Videography should realize a pre-tax profit of approximately $44,400 each year for the first three years. This profit will be used to carry the business during less busy times.

Estimated profits (April–September)

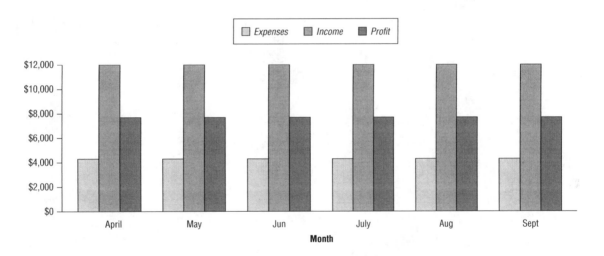

Estimated profits (October–March)

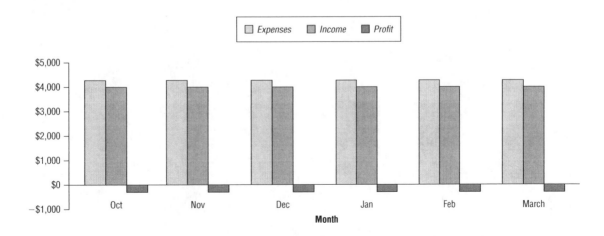

Estimated profits years 1–3

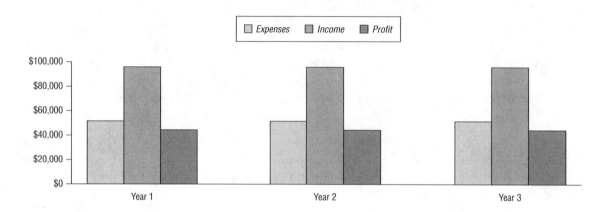

Financing

Ms. Harrison will obtain a business line of credit for $20,000, the amount needed to cover the start-up costs and three months' expenses. Ms. Harrison will use her home as collateral.

Repayment Plan

Ms. Harrison plans to repay the line of credit in the third year of operation. She has budgeted $300 per month for loan repayment, but intends to use 10% of the annual profit to pay additional principal.

Repayment plan

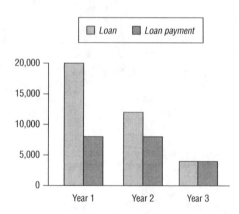

BUSINESS PLAN TEMPLATE

USING THIS TEMPLATE

A business plan carefully spells out a company's projected course of action over a period of time, usually the first two to three years after the start-up. In addition, banks, lenders, and other investors examine the information and financial documentation before deciding whether or not to finance a new business venture. Therefore, a business plan is an essential tool in obtaining financing and should describe the business itself in detail as well as all important factors influencing the company, including the market, industry, competition, operations and management policies, problem solving strategies, financial resources and needs, and other vital information. The plan enables the business owner to anticipate costs, plan for difficulties, and take advantage of opportunities, as well as design and implement strategies that keep the company running as smoothly as possible.

This template has been provided as a model to help you construct your own business plan. Please keep in mind that there is no single acceptable format for a business plan, and that this template is in no way comprehensive, but serves as an example.

The business plans provided in this section are fictional and have been used by small business agencies as models for clients to use in compiling their own business plans.

GENERIC BUSINESS PLAN

Main headings included below are topics that should be covered in a comprehensive business plan. They include:

Business Summary

Purpose
Provides a brief overview of your business, succinctly highlighting the main ideas of your plan.

Includes

- Name and Type of Business
- Description of Product/Service
- Business History and Development
- Location
- Market
- Competition
- Management
- Financial Information
- Business Strengths and Weaknesses
- Business Growth

Table of Contents

Purpose
Organized in an Outline Format, the Table of Contents illustrates the selection and arrangement of information contained in your plan.

Includes

- Topic Headings and Subheadings
- Page Number References

Business History and Industry Outlook

Purpose

Examines the conception and subsequent development of your business within an industry specific context.

Includes

- Start-up Information
- Owner/Key Personnel Experience
- Location
- Development Problems and Solutions
- Investment/Funding Information
- Future Plans and Goals
- Market Trends and Statistics
- Major Competitors
- Product/Service Advantages
- National, Regional, and Local Economic Impact

Product/Service

Purpose

Introduces, defines, and details the product and/or service that inspired the information of your business.

Includes

- Unique Features
- Niche Served
- Market Comparison
- Stage of Product/Service Development
- Production
- Facilities, Equipment, and Labor
- Financial Requirements
- Product/Service Life Cycle
- Future Growth

Market Examination

Purpose

Assessment of product/service applications in relation to consumer buying cycles.

Includes

- Target Market
- Consumer Buying Habits
- Product/Service Applications
- Consumer Reactions
- Market Factors and Trends
- Penetration of the Market
- Market Share
- Research and Studies
- Cost
- Sales Volume and Goals

Competition

Purpose

Analysis of Competitors in the Marketplace.

Includes

- Competitor Information
- Product/Service Comparison
- Market Niche
- Product/Service Strengths and Weaknesses
- Future Product/Service Development

Marketing

Purpose

Identifies promotion and sales strategies for your product/service.

Includes

- Product/Service Sales Appeal
- Special and Unique Features
- Identification of Customers
- Sales and Marketing Staff
- Sales Cycles
- Type of Advertising/Promotion
- Pricing
- Competition
- Customer Services

Operations

Purpose

Traces product/service development from production/inception to the market environment.

Includes

- Cost Effective Production Methods
- Facility
- Location
- Equipment
- Labor
- Future Expansion

Administration and Management

Purpose

Offers a statement of your management philosophy with an in-depth focus on processes and procedures.

Includes

- Management Philosophy
- Structure of Organization
- Reporting System
- Methods of Communication
- Employee Skills and Training
- Employee Needs and Compensation
- Work Environment
- Management Policies and Procedures
- Roles and Responsibilities

Key Personnel

Purpose

Describes the unique backgrounds of principle employees involved in business.

Includes

- Owner(s)/Employee Education and Experience
- Positions and Roles
- Benefits and Salary
- Duties and Responsibilities
- Objectives and Goals

Potential Problems and Solutions

Purpose

Discussion of problem solving strategies that change issues into opportunities.

Includes

- Risks
- Litigation
- Future Competition
- Economic Impact
- Problem Solving Skills

Financial Information

Purpose

Secures needed funding and assistance through worksheets and projections detailing financial plans, methods of repayment, and future growth opportunities.

Includes

- Financial Statements
- Bank Loans
- Methods of Repayment
- Tax Returns
- Start-up Costs
- Projected Income (3 years)
- Projected Cash Flow (3 Years)
- Projected Balance Statements (3 years)

Appendices

Purpose

Supporting documents used to enhance your business proposal.

Includes

- Photographs of product, equipment, facilities, etc.
- Copyright/Trademark Documents
- Legal Agreements
- Marketing Materials
- Research and or Studies
- Operation Schedules
- Organizational Charts
- Job Descriptions
- Resumes
- Additional Financial Documentation

Fictional Food Distributor

Commercial Foods, Inc.

3003 Avondale Ave.
Knoxville, TN 37920

This plan demonstrates how a partnership can have a positive impact on a new business. It demonstrates how two individuals can carve a niche in the specialty foods market by offering gourmet foods to upscale restaurants and fine hotels. This plan is fictional and has not been used to gain funding from a bank or other lending institution.

STATEMENT OF PURPOSE

Commercial Foods, Inc. seeks a loan of $75,000 to establish a new business. This sum, together with $5,000 equity investment by the principals, will be used as follows:

- Merchandise inventory $25,000
- Office fixture/equipment $12,000
- Warehouse equipment $14,000
- One delivery truck $10,000
- Working capital $39,000
- Total $100,000

DESCRIPTION OF THE BUSINESS

Commercial Foods, Inc. will be a distributor of specialty food service products to hotels and upscale restaurants in the geographical area of a 50 mile radius of Knoxville. Richard Roberts will direct the sales effort and John Williams will manage the warehouse operation and the office. One delivery truck will be used initially with a second truck added in the third year. We expect to begin operation of the business within 30 days after securing the requested financing.

MANAGEMENT

A. Richard Roberts is a native of Memphis, Tennessee. He is a graduate of Memphis State University with a Bachelor's degree from the School of Business. After graduation, he worked for a major manufacturer of specialty food service products as a detail sales person for five years, and, for the past three years, he has served as a product sales manager for this firm.

B. John Williams is a native of Nashville, Tennessee. He holds a B.S. Degree in Food Technology from the University of Tennessee. His career includes five years as a product development chemist in gourmet food products and five years as operations manager for a food service distributor.

Both men are healthy and energetic. Their backgrounds complement each other, which will ensure the success of Commercial Foods, Inc. They will set policies together and personnel decisions will be made jointly. Initial salaries for the owners will be $1,000 per month for the first few years. The spouses of both principals are successful in the business world and earn enough to support the families.

They have engaged the services of Foster Jones, CPA, and William Hale, Attorney, to assist them in an advisory capacity.

PERSONNEL

The firm will employ one delivery truck driver at a wage of $8.00 per hour. One office worker will be employed at $7.50 per hour. One part-time employee will be used in the office at $5.00 per hour. The driver will load and unload his own trucks. Mr. Williams will assist in the warehouse operation as needed to assist one stock person at $7.00 per hour. An additional delivery truck and driver will be added the third year.

LOCATION

The firm will lease a 20,000 square foot building at 3003 Avondale Ave., in Knoxville, which contains warehouse and office areas equipped with two-door truck docks. The annual rental is $9,000. The building was previously used as a food service warehouse and very little modification to the building will be required.

PRODUCTS AND SERVICES

The firm will offer specialty food service products such as soup bases, dessert mixes, sauce bases, pastry mixes, spices, and flavors, normally used by upscale restaurants and nice hotels. We are going after a niche in the market with high quality gourmet products. There is much less competition in this market than in standard run of the mill food service products. Through their work experiences, the principals have contacts with supply sources and with local chefs.

THE MARKET

We know from our market survey that there are over 200 hotels and upscale restaurants in the area we plan to serve. Customers will be attracted by a direct sales approach. We will offer samples of our products and product application data on use of our products in the finished prepared foods. We will cultivate the chefs in these establishments. The technical background of John Williams will be especially useful here.

COMPETITION

We find that we will be only distributor in the area offering a full line of gourmet food service products. Other foodservice distributors offer only a few such items in conjunction with their standard product line. Our survey shows that many of the chefs are ordering products from Atlanta and Memphis because of a lack of adequate local supply.

SUMMARY

Commercial Foods, Inc. will be established as a foodservice distributor of specialty food in Knoxville. The principals, with excellent experience in the industry, are seeking a $75,000 loan to establish the business. The principals are investing $25,000 as equity capital.

The business will be set up as an S Corporation with each principal owning 50% of the common stock in the corporation.

FICTIONAL HARDWARE STORE
OSHKOSH HARDWARE, INC.

123 Main St.
Oshkosh, WI 54901

The following plan outlines how a small hardware store can survive competition from large discount chains by offering products and providing expert advice in the use of any product it sells. This plan is fictional and has not been used to gain funding from a bank or other lending institution.

EXECUTIVE SUMMARY

Oshkosh Hardware, Inc. is a new corporation that is going to establish a retail hardware store in a strip mall in Oshkosh, Wisconsin. The store will sell hardware of all kinds, quality tools, paint, and housewares. The business will make revenue and a profit by servicing its customers not only with needed hardware but also with expert advice in the use of any product it sells.

Oshkosh Hardware, Inc. will be operated by its sole shareholder, James Smith. The company will have a total of four employees. It will sell its products in the local market. Customers will buy our products because we will provide free advice on the use of all of our products and will also furnish a full refund warranty.

Oshkosh Hardware, Inc. will sell its products in the Oshkosh store staffed by three sales representatives. No additional employees will be needed to achieve its short and long range goals. The primary short range goal is to open the store by October 1, 1994. In order to achieve this goal a lease must be signed by July 1, 1994 and the complete inventory ordered by August 1, 1994.

Mr. James Smith will invest $30,000 in the business. In addition, the company will have to borrow $150,000 during the first year to cover the investment in inventory, accounts receivable, and furniture and equipment. The company will be profitable after six months of operation and should be able to start repayment of the loan in the second year.

THE BUSINESS

The business will sell hardware of all kinds, quality tools, paint, and housewares. We will purchase our products from three large wholesale buying groups.

In general our customers are homeowners who do their own repair and maintenance, hobbyists, and housewives. Our business is unique in that we will have a complete line of all hardware items and will be able to get special orders by overnight delivery. The business makes revenue and profits by servicing our customers not only with needed hardware but also with expert advice in the use of any product we sell. Our major costs for bringing our products to market are cost of merchandise of 36%, salaries of $45,000, and occupancy costs of $60,000.

229

Oshkosh Hardware, Inc.'s retail outlet will be located at 1524 Frontage Road, which is in a newly developed retail center of Oshkosh. Our location helps facilitate accessibility from all parts of town and reduces our delivery costs. The store will occupy 7500 square feet of space. The major equipment involved in our business is counters and shelving, a computer, a paint mixing machine, and a truck.

THE MARKET

Oshkosh Hardware, Inc. will operate in the local market. There are 15,000 potential customers in this market area. We have three competitors who control approximately 98% of the market at present. We feel we can capture 25% of the market within the next four years. Our major reason for believing this is that our staff is technically competent to advise our customers in the correct use of all products we sell.

After a careful market analysis, we have determined that approximately 60% of our customers are men and 40% are women. The percentage of customers that fall into the following age categories are:

Under 16: 0%
17-21: 5%
22-30: 30%
31-40: 30%
41-50: 20%
51-60: 10%
61-70: 5%
Over 70: 0%

The reasons our customers prefer our products is our complete knowledge of their use and our full refund warranty.

We get our information about what products our customers want by talking to existing customers. There seems to be an increasing demand for our product. The demand for our product is increasing in size based on the change in population characteristics.

SALES

At Oshkosh Hardware, Inc. we will employ three sales people and will not need any additional personnel to achieve our sales goals. These salespeople will need several years experience in home repair and power tool usage. We expect to attract 30% of our customers from newspaper ads, 5% of our customers from local directories, 5% of our customers from the yellow pages, 10% of our customers from family and friends, and 50% of our customers from current customers. The most cost effect source will be current customers. In general our industry is growing.

MANAGEMENT

We would evaluate the quality of our management staff as being excellent. Our manager is experienced and very motivated to achieve the various sales and quality assurance objectives we have set. We will use a management information system that produces key inventory, quality assurance, and sales data on a weekly basis. All data is compared to previously established goals for that week, and deviations are the primary focus of the management staff.

GOALS IMPLEMENTATION

The short term goals of our business are:

1. Open the store by October 1, 1994
2. Reach our breakeven point in two months
3. Have sales of $100,000 in the first six months

In order to achieve our first short term goal we must:

1. Sign the lease by July 1, 1994
2. Order a complete inventory by August 1, 1994

In order to achieve our second short term goal we must:

1. Advertise extensively in Sept. and Oct.
2. Keep expenses to a minimum

In order to achieve our third short term goal we must:

1. Promote power tool sales for the Christmas season
2. Keep good customer traffic in Jan. and Feb.

The long term goals for our business are:

1. Obtain sales volume of $600,000 in three years
2. Become the largest hardware dealer in the city
3. Open a second store in Fond du Lac

The most important thing we must do in order to achieve the long term goals for our business is to develop a highly profitable business with excellent cash flow.

FINANCE

Oshkosh Hardware, Inc. Faces some potential threats or risks to our business. They are discount house competition. We believe we can avoid or compensate for this by providing quality products complimented by quality advice on the use of every product we sell. The financial projections we have prepared are located at the end of this document.

JOB DESCRIPTION-GENERAL MANAGER

The General Manager of the business of the corporation will be the president of the corporation. He will be responsible for the complete operation of the retail hardware store which is owned by the corporation. A detailed description of his duties and responsibilities is as follows.

Sales

Train and supervise the three sales people. Develop programs to motivate and compensate these employees. Coordinate advertising and sales promotion effects to achieve sales totals as outlined in budget. Oversee purchasing function and inventory control procedures to insure adequate merchandise at all times at a reasonable cost.

Finance

Prepare monthly and annual budgets. Secure adequate line of credit from local banks. Supervise office personnel to insure timely preparation of records, statements, all government reports, control of receivables and payables, and monthly financial statements.

Administration

Perform duties as required in the areas of personnel, building leasing and maintenance, licenses and permits, and public relations.

Organizations, Agencies, & Consultants

A listing of Associations and Consultants of interest to entrepreneurs, followed by the ten Small Business Administration Regional Offices, Small Business Development Centers, Service Corps of Retired Executives offices, and Venture Capital and Finance Companies.

Associations

This section contains a listing of associations and other agencies of interest to the small business owner. Entries are listed alphabetically by organization name.

American Business Women's Association
9100 Ward Pkwy.
PO Box 8728
Kansas City, MO 64114-0728
(800)228-0007
E-mail: abwa@abwa.org
Website: http://www.abwa.org
Jeanne Banks, National President

American Franchisee Association
53 W Jackson Blvd., Ste. 1157
Chicago, IL 60604
(312)431-0545
E-mail: info@franchisee.org
Website: http://www.franchisee.org
Susan P. Kezios, President

American Independent Business Alliance
222 S Black Ave.
Bozeman, MT 59715
(406)582-1255
E-mail: info@amiba.net
Website: http://www.amiba.net
Jennifer Rockne, Director

American Small Businesses Association
206 E College St., Ste. 201
Grapevine, TX 76051
800-942-2722
E-mail: info@asbaonline.org
Website: http://www.asbaonline.org/
Bill Hill, Sr., Pres

Association for Enterprise Opportunity
1601 N Kent St., Ste. 1101
Arlington, VA 22209
(703)841-7760
Fax: (703)841-7748
E-mail: aeo@assoceo.org
Website: http://www.microenterpriseworks.org
Connie Evans, Pres./CEO

Association of Small Business Development Centers
c/o Tee Rowe
8990 Burke Lake Rd.
Burke, VA 22015
(703)764-9850
Fax: (703)764-1234
E-mail: info@asbdc-us.org
Website: http://www.asbdc-us.org
Charles E. Rowe, Pres./CEO

BEST Employers Association
2505 McCabe Way
Irvine, CA 92614
(949)253-4080
800-433-0088
Fax: (714)553-0883
E-mail: info@bestlife.com
Website: http://www.beassoc.org

Coalition for Government Procurement
1990 M St. NW, Ste. 400
Washington, DC 20036
(202)331-0975
E-mail: info@thecgp.org
Website: http://thecgp.org/
Roger Waldron, Pres.

Employers of America
PO Box 1874
Mason City, IA 50402-1874
(641)424-3187
800-728-3187
Fax: (641)424-1673
E-mail: employer@employerhelp.org
Website: http://www.employerhelp.org
Jim Collison, Pres.

Family Firm Institute
200 Lincoln St., Ste. 201
Boston, MA 02111
(617)482-3045
Fax: (617)482-3049
E-mail: ffi@ffi.org
Website: http://www.ffi.org
Judy L. Green, Ph.D., Exec.Dir.

Independent Visually Impaired Enterprisers
500 S 3rd St., Apt. H
Burbank, CA 91502
(818)238-9321
E-mail: abazyn@bazyncommunications.com
http://www.ivie-acb.org
Carla Hayes, Pres.

International Council for Small Business
The George Washington University School of Business and Public Management
2115 G St. NW, Ste. 403
Washington, DC 20052
(202)994-0704
Fax: (202)994-4930
E-mail: icsb@gwu.edu
Website: http://www.icsb.org
Ki-Chan Kim, Pres.-Elect

Kauffman Foundation
4801 Rockhill Rd.
Kansas City, MO 64110-2046
(816)932-1000
E-mail: info@kauffman.org
Website: http://www.kauffman.org

National Association for the Self-Employed
PO Box 612067
DFW Airport
Dallas, TX 75261-2067
(800)232-6273
E-mail: mpetron@nase.org
Website: http://www.nase.org

National Business Association
PO Box 700728
5151 Beltline Rd., Ste. 1150
Dallas, TX 75370
(972)458-0900
800-456-0440
Fax: (972)960-9149
E-mail: info@nationalbusiness.org
Website: http://
www.nationalbusiness.org

National Business Owners Association
1400 I St., NW, Ste. 850
Washington, DC 20005
(202)407-7140
Fax: (202)354-4944
E-mail: membershipservices@nboa.org
Website: http://www.nboa.org
Jeffrey Shields, Pres.

National Family Business Council
1640 W. Kennedy Rd.
Lake Forest, IL 60045
(847)295-1040
Fax: (847)295-1898
E-mail: lmsnfbc@email.msn.com
Jogn E. Messervey, Pres.

National Federation of Independent Business
53 Century Blvd., Ste. 250
Nashville, TN 37214
(615)872-5800
800-NFIBNOW
Fax: (615)872-5353
Website: http://www.nfib.org
Jack Faris, Pres. and CEO

National Small Business Association
1156 15th St. NW, Ste. 1100
Washington, DC 20005
(202)293-8830
800-345-6728
Fax: (202)872-8543
E-mail: press@nsba.biz
Website: http://www.nsba.biz
Todd McCracken, Pres.

Sales Professionals USA
1400 W. 122nd Ave., 101
Westminster, CO 80234
(303)534-4937

888-736-7767
E-mail: salespro@salesprofessionals-usa.com
Website: http://www.salesprofessionals-usa.com

Score Association - Service Corps of Retired Executives
409 3rd St. SW, 6th Fl.
Washington, DC 20024
(202)205-6762
800-634-0245
Fax: (202)205-7636
E-mail: media@score.org
Website: http://www.score.org
W. Kenneth Yancey, Jr., CEO

Small Business and Entrepreneurship Council
1920 L St. NW, Ste. 200
Washington, DC 20036
(202)785-0238
Fax: (202)822-8118
E-mail: membership@sbec.org
Website: http://www.sbecouncil.org
Karen Kerrigan, Pres./CEO

Small Business Investor Alliance
1100 H Street, NW, Ste 610
Washington, DC 20005
(202)628-5055
E-mail: info@sbia.org
Website: http://www.sbia.org

Small Business Legislative Council
1010 Massachusetts Ave. NW, Ste. 540
Washington, DC 20005
(202)639-8500
Fax: (202)296-5333
E-mail: email@sblc.org
Website: http://www.sblc.org
Paula Calimafde, Pres.

Small Business Service Bureau
554 Main St.
PO Box 15014
Worcester, MA 01615-0014
(508)756-3513
800-343-0939
Fax: (508)770-0528
E-mail: info@sbsb.com
Website: http://www.sbsb.com
Francis R. Carroll, Pres.

Structured Employment Economic Development Corporation
22 Cortlandt St., 33rd Fl.
New York, NY 10007
(212)473-0255
Fax: (212)473-0357
E-mail: info@seedco.org

Website: http://www.seedco.org
Barbara Dwyer Gunn, CEO

Support Services Alliance
107 Prospect St.
Schoharie, NY 12157
800-836-4772
E-mail: info@ssamembers.com
Website: http://www.ssainfo.com
Steve COle, Pres.

United States Association for Small Business and Entrepreneurship
975 University Ave., No. 3260
Madison, WI 53706
(608)262-9982
Fax: (608)
263-0818
E-mail: jgillman@wisc.edu
Website: http://www.ususbe.org
Joan Gillman, Exec. Dir.

Consultants

This section contains a listing of consultants specializing in small business development. It is arranged alphabetically by country, then by state or province, then by city, then by firm name.

Canada

Alberta

Common Sense Solutions
3405 16A Ave.
Edmonton, AB, Canada
(403)465-7330
Fax: (403)465-7380
E-mail: gcoulson@comsensesolutions.com
Website: http://www.comsensesolutions.com

Varsity Consulting Group
School of Business
University of Alberta
Edmonton, AB, Canada T6G 2R6
(780)492-2994
Fax: (780)492-5400
Website: http://www.bus.ualberta.ca/vcg

Viro Hospital Consulting
42 Commonwealth Bldg., 9912-106 St. NW
Edmonton, AB, Canada T5K 1C5
(403)425-3871
Fax: (403)425-3871
E-mail: rpb@freenet.edmonton.ab.ca

British Columbia

SRI Strategic Resources Inc.
4330 Kingsway, Ste. 1600
Burnaby, BC, Canada V5H 4G7
(604)435-0627
Fax: (604)435-2782
E-mail: inquiry@sri.bc.ca
Website: http://www.sri.com

Andrew R. De Boda Consulting
1523 Milford Ave.
Coquitlam, BC, Canada V3J 2V9
(604)936-4527
Fax: (604)936-4527
E-mail: deboda@intergate.bc.ca
Website: http://www.ourworld
.compuserve.com/homepages/deboda

The Sage Group Ltd.
980 - 355 Burrard St.
744 W Haistings, Ste. 410
Vancouver, BC, Canada V6C 1A5
(604)669-9269
Fax: (604)669-6622

Tikkanen-Bradley
1345 Nelson St., Ste. 202
Vancouver, BC, Canada V6E 1J8
(604)669-0583
E-mail:
webmaster@tikkanenbradley.com
Website: http://
www.tikkanenbradley.com

Ontario

The Cynton Co.
17 Massey St.
Brampton, ON, Canada L6S 2V6
(905)792-7769
Fax: (905)792-8116
E-mail: cynton@home.com
Website: http://www.cynton.com

Begley & Associates
RR 6
Cambridge, ON, Canada N1R 5S7
(519)740-3629
Fax: (519)740-3629
E-mail: begley@in.on.ca
Website: http://www.in.on.ca/~begley/
index.htm

CRO Engineering Ltd.
1895 William Hodgins Ln.
Carp, ON, Canada K0A 1L0
(613)839-1108
Fax: (613)839-1406
E-mail: J.Grefford@ieee.ca

Website: http://www.geocities.com/
WallStreet/District/7401/

Task Enterprises
Box 69, RR 2 Hamilton
Flamborough, ON, Canada L8N 2Z7
(905)659-0153
Fax: (905)659-0861

HST Group Ltd.
430 Gilmour St.
Ottawa, ON, Canada K2P 0R8
(613)236-7303
Fax: (613)236-9893

Harrison Associates
BCE Pl.
181 Bay St., Ste. 3740
PO Box 798
Toronto, ON, Canada M5J 2T3
(416)364-5441
Fax: (416)364-2875

**TCI Convergence Ltd. Management
Consultants**
99 Crown's Ln.
Toronto, ON, Canada M5R 3P4
(416)515-4146
Fax: (416)515-2097
E-mail: tci@inforamp.net
Website: http://tciconverge.com/
index.1.html

Ken Wyman & Associates Inc.
64B Shuter St., Ste. 200
Toronto, ON, Canada M5B 1B1
(416)362-2926
Fax: (416)362-3039
E-mail: kenwyman@compuserve.com

JPL Business Consultants
82705 Metter Rd.
Wellandport, ON, Canada L0R 2J0
(905)386-7450
Fax: (905)386-7450
E-mail: plamarch@freenet.npiec.on.ca

Quebec

The Zimmar Consulting Partnership Inc.
Westmount
PO Box 98
Montreal, QC, Canada H3Z 2T1
(514)484-1459
Fax: (514)484-3063

Saskatchewan

Trimension Group
No. 104-110 Research Dr.
Innovation Place, SK, Canada S7N 3R3

(306)668-2560
Fax: (306)975-1156
E-mail: trimension@trimension.ca
Website: http://www.trimension.ca

Corporate Management Consultants
40 Government Road - PO Box 185
Prud Homme, SK, Canada, S0K 3K0
(306)654-4569
Fax: (650)618-2742
E-mail:
cmccorporatemanagement@shaw.ca
Website: http://www.Corporate
managementconsultants.com
Gerald Rekve

United states

Alabama

Business Planning Inc.
300 Office Park Dr.
Birmingham, AL 35223-2474
(205)870-7090
Fax: (205)870-7103

Tradebank of Eastern Alabama
546 Broad St., Ste. 3
Gadsden, AL 35901
(205)547-8700
Fax: (205)547-8718
E-mail: mansion@webex.com
Website: http://www.webex.com/~tea

Alaska

AK Business Development Center
3335 Arctic Blvd., Ste. 203
Anchorage, AK 99503
(907)562-0335
Free: 800-478-3474
Fax: (907)562-6988
E-mail: abdc@gci.net
Website: http://www.abdc.org

Business Matters
PO Box 287
Fairbanks, AK 99707
(907)452-5650

Arizona

Carefree Direct Marketing Corp.
8001 E Serene St.
PO Box 3737
Carefree, AZ 85377-3737
(480)488-4227
Fax: (480)488-2841

Trans Energy Corp.
1739 W 7th Ave.
Mesa, AZ 85202
(480)827-7915
Fax: (480)967-6601
E-mail: aha@clean-air.org
Website: http://www.clean-air.org

CMAS
5125 N 16th St.
Phoenix, AZ 85016
(602)395-1001
Fax: (602)604-8180

Comgate Telemanagement Ltd.
706 E Bell Rd., Ste. 105
Phoenix, AZ 85022
(602)485-5708
Fax: (602)485-5709
E-mail: comgate@netzone.com
Website: http://www.comgate.com

Moneysoft Inc.
1 E Camelback Rd. #550
Phoenix, AZ 85012
Free: 800-966-7797
E-mail: mbray@moneysoft.com

Harvey C. Skoog
PO Box 26439
Prescott Valley, AZ 86312
(520)772-1714
Fax: (520)772-2814

LMC Services
8711 E Pinnacle Peak Rd., No. 340
Scottsdale, AZ 85255-3555
(602)585-7177
Fax: (602)585-5880
E-mail: louws@earthlink.com

**Sauerbrun Technology
Group Ltd.**
7979 E Princess Dr., Ste. 5
Scottsdale, AZ 85255-5878
(602)502-4950
Fax: (602)502-4292
E-mail: info@sauerbrun.com
Website: http://www.sauerbrun.com

Gary L. McLeod
PO Box 230
Sonoita, AZ 85637
Fax: (602)455-5661

Van Cleve Associates
6932 E 2nd St.
Tucson, AZ 85710
(520)296-2587
Fax: (520)296-3358

California

Acumen Group Inc.
(650)949-9349
Fax: (650)949-4845
E-mail: acumen-g@ix.netcom.com
Website: http://pw2.netcom.com/
~janed/acumen.html

**On-line Career and Management
Consulting**
420 Central Ave., No. 314
Alameda, CA 94501
(510)864-0336
Fax: (510)864-0336
E-mail: career@dnai.com
Website: http://www.dnai.com/~career

**Career Paths-Thomas E. Church
& Associates Inc.**
PO Box 2439
Aptos, CA 95001
(408)662-7950
Fax: (408)662-7955
E-mail: church@ix.netcom.com
Website: http://www.careerpaths-
tom.com

Keck & Co. Business Consultants
410 Walsh Rd.
Atherton, CA 94027
(650)854-9588
Fax: (650)854-7240
E-mail: info@keckco.com
Website: http://www.keckco.com

**Ben W. Laverty III, PhD,
REA, CEI**
4909 Stockdale Hwy., Ste. 132
Bakersfield, CA 93309
(661)283-8300
Free: 800-833-0373
Fax: (661)283-8313
E-mail: cstc@cstcsafety.com
Website: http://www.cstcsafety.com/cstc

**Lindquist Consultants-Venture
Planning**
225 Arlington Ave.
Berkeley, CA 94707
(510)524-6685
Fax: (510)527-6604

Larson Associates
PO Box 9005
Brea, CA 92822
(714)529-4121
Fax: (714)572-3606
E-mail: ray@consultlarson.com
Website: http://www.consultlarson.com

Kremer Management Consulting
PO Box 500
Carmel, CA 93921
(408)626-8311
Fax: (408)624-2663
E-mail: ddkremer@aol.com

W and J PARTNERSHIP
PO Box 2499
18876 Edwin Markham Dr.
Castro Valley, CA 94546
(510)583-7751
Fax: (510)583-7645
E-mail: wamorgan@wjpartnership.com
Website: http://www.wjpartnership.com

JB Associates
21118 Gardena Dr.
Cupertino, CA 95014
(408)257-0214
Fax: (408)257-0216
E-mail: semarang@sirius.com

House Agricultural Consultants
PO Box 1615
Davis, CA 95617-1615
(916)753-3361
Fax: (916)753-0464
E-mail: infoag@houseag.com
Website: http://www.houseag.com/

3C Systems Co.
16161 Ventura Blvd., Ste. 815
Encino, CA 91436
(818)907-1302
Fax: (818)907-1357
E-mail: mark@3CSysCo.com
Website: http://www.3CSysCo.com

Technical Management Consultants
3624 Westfall Dr.
Encino, CA 91436-4154
(818)784-0626
Fax: (818)501-5575
E-mail: tmcrs@aol.com

**RAINWATER-GISH & Associates,
Business Finance & Development**
317 3rd St., Ste. 3
Eureka, CA 95501
(707)443-0030
Fax: (707)443-5683

Global Tradelinks
451 Pebble Beach Pl.
Fullerton, CA 92835
(714)441-2280
Fax: (714)441-2281
E-mail: info@globaltradelinks.com
Website: http://
www.globaltradelinks.com

Strategic Business Group
800 Cienaga Dr.
Fullerton, CA 92835-1248
(714)449-1040
Fax: (714)525-1631

Burnes Consulting
20537 Wolf Creek Rd.
Grass Valley, CA 95949
(530)346-8188
Free: 800-949-9021
Fax: (530)346-7704
E-mail: kent@burnesconsulting.com
Website: http://www.burnesconsulting.com

Pioneer Business Consultants
9042 Garfield Ave., Ste. 312
Huntington Beach, CA 92646
(714)964-7600

Beblie, Brandt & Jacobs Inc.
16 Technology, Ste. 164
Irvine, CA 92618
(714)450-8790
Fax: (714)450-8799
E-mail: darcy@bbjinc.com
Website: http://198.147.90.26

Fluor Daniel Inc.
3353 Michelson Dr.
Irvine, CA 92612-0650
(949)975-2000
Fax: (949)975-5271
E-mail: sales.consulting@fluordaniel.com
Website: http://www.fluordaniel
consulting.com

MCS Associates
18300 Von Karman, Ste. 710
Irvine, CA 92612
(949)263-8700
Fax: (949)263-0770
E-mail: info@mcsassociates.com
Website: http://www.mcs
associates.com

Inspired Arts Inc.
4225 Executive Sq., Ste. 1160
La Jolla, CA 92037
(619)623-3525
Free: 800-851-4394
Fax: (619)623-3534
E-mail: info@inspiredarts.com
Website: http://www.inspiredarts.com

The Laresis Companies
PO Box 3284
La Jolla, CA 92038
(619)452-2720
Fax: (619)452-8744

RCL & Co.
PO Box 1143
737 Pearl St., Ste. 201
La Jolla, CA 92038
(619)454-8883
Fax: (619)454-8880

Comprehensive Business Services
3201 Lucas Cir.
Lafayette, CA 94549
(925)283-8272
Fax: (925)283-8272

The Ribble Group
27601 Forbes Rd., Ste. 52
Laguna Niguel, CA 92677
(714)582-1085
Fax: (714)582-6420
E-mail: ribble@deltanet.com

Norris Bernstein, CMC
9309 Marina Pacifica Dr. N
Long Beach, CA 90803
(562)493-5458
Fax: (562)493-5459
E-mail: norris@ctecomputer.com
Website: http://foodconsultants.com/
bernstein/

Horizon Consulting Services
1315 Garthwick Dr.
Los Altos, CA 94024
(415)967-0906
Fax: (415)967-0906

Brincko Associates Inc.
1801 Avenue of the Stars, Ste. 1054
Los Angeles, CA 90067
(310)553-4523
Fax: (310)553-6782

**Rubenstein/Justman Management
Consultants**
2049 Century Park E, 24th Fl.
Los Angeles, CA 90067
(310)282-0800
Fax: (310)282-0400
E-mail: info@rjmc.net
Website: http://www.rjmc.net

F.J. Schroeder & Associates
1926 Westholme Ave.
Los Angeles, CA 90025
(310)470-2655
Fax: (310)470-6378
E-mail: fjsacons@aol.com
Website: http://www.mcninet.com/
GlobalLook/Fjschroe.html

Western Management Associates
5959 W Century Blvd., Ste. 565
Los Angeles, CA 90045-6506

(310)645-1091
Free: (888)788-6534
Fax: (310)645-1092
E-mail: gene@cfoforrent.com
Website: http://www.cfoforrent.com

Darrell Sell and Associates
Los Gatos, CA 95030
(408)354-7794
E-mail: darrell@netcom.com

Leslie J. Zambo
3355 Michael Dr.
Marina, CA 93933
(408)384-7086
Fax: (408)647-4199
E-mail: 104776.1552@compuserve.com

Marketing Services Management
PO Box 1377
Martinez, CA 94553
(510)370-8527
Fax: (510)370-8527
E-mail: markserve@biotechnet.com

William M. Shine Consulting Service
PO Box 127
Moraga, CA 94556-0127
(510)376-6516

Palo Alto Management Group Inc.
2672 Bayshore Pky., Ste. 701
Mountain View, CA 94043
(415)968-4374
Fax: (415)968-4245
E-mail: mburwen@pamg.com

BizplanSource
1048 Irvine Ave., Ste. 621
Newport Beach, CA 92660
Free: 888-253-0974
Fax: 800-859-8254
E-mail: info@bizplansource.com
Website: http://www.bizplansource.com
Adam Greengrass, President

The Market Connection
4020 Birch St., Ste. 203
Newport Beach, CA 92660
(714)731-6273
Fax: (714)833-0253

Muller Associates
PO Box 7264
Newport Beach, CA 92658
(714)646-1169
Fax: (714)646-1169

International Health Resources
PO Box 329
North San Juan, CA 95960-0329

(530)292-1266
Fax: (530)292-1243
Website: http://
www.futureofhealthcare.com

NEXUS - Consultants to Management
PO Box 1531
Novato, CA 94948
(415)897-4400
Fax: (415)898-2252
E-mail: jimnexus@aol.com

Aerospcace.Org
PO Box 28831
Oakland, CA 94604-8831
(510)530-9169
Fax: (510)530-3411
Website: http://www.aerospace.org

Intelequest Corp.
722 Gailen Ave.
Palo Alto, CA 94303
(415)968-3443
Fax: (415)493-6954
E-mail: frits@iqix.com

McLaughlin & Associates
66 San Marino Cir.
Rancho Mirage, CA 92270
(760)321-2932
Fax: (760)328-2474
E-mail: jackmcla@msn.com

Carrera Consulting Group, a division of Maximus
2110 21st St., Ste. 400
Sacramento, CA 95818
(916)456-3300
Fax: (916)456-3306
E-mail: central@carreraconsulting.com
Website: http://
www.carreraconsulting.com

Bay Area Tax Consultants and Bayhill Financial Consultants
1150 Bayhill Dr., Ste. 1150
San Bruno, CA 94066-3004
(415)952-8786
Fax: (415)588-4524
E-mail: baytax@compuserve.com
Website: http://www.baytax.com/

AdCon Services, LLC
8871 Hillery Dr.
Dan Diego, CA 92126
(858)433-1411
E-mail: adam@adconservices.com
Website: http://www.adconservices.com
Adam Greengrass

California Business Incubation Network
101 W Broadway, No. 480
San Diego, CA 92101
(619)237-0559
Fax: (619)237-0521

G.R. Gordetsky Consultants Inc.
11414 Windy Summit Pl.
San Diego, CA 92127
(619)487-4939
Fax: (619)487-5587
E-mail: gordet@pacbell.net

Freeman, Sullivan & Co.
131 Steuart St., Ste. 500
San Francisco, CA 94105
(415)777-0707
Free: 800-777-0737
Fax: (415)777-2420
Website: http://www.fsc-research.com

Ideas Unlimited
2151 California St., Ste. 7
San Francisco, CA 94115
(415)931-0641
Fax: (415)931-0880

Russell Miller Inc.
300 Montgomery St., Ste. 900
San Francisco, CA 94104
(415)956-7474
Fax: (415)398-0620
E-mail: rmi@pacbell.net
Website: http://www.rmisf.com

PKF Consulting
425 California St., Ste. 1650
San Francisco, CA 94104
(415)421-5378
Fax: (415)956-7708
E-mail: callahan@pkfc.com
Website: http://www.pkfonline.com

Welling & Woodard Inc.
1067 Broadway
San Francisco, CA 94133
(415)776-4500
Fax: (415)776-5067

Highland Associates
16174 Highland Dr.
San Jose, CA 95127
(408)272-7008
Fax: (408)272-4040

ORDIS Inc.
6815 Trinidad Dr.
San Jose, CA 95120-2056
(408)268-3321
Free: 800-446-7347

Fax: (408)268-3582
E-mail: ordis@ordis.com
Website: http://www.ordis.com

Stanford Resources Inc.
20 Great Oaks Blvd., Ste. 200
San Jose, CA 95119
(408)360-8400
Fax: (408)360-8410
E-mail: sales@stanfordsources.com
Website: http://
www.stanfordresources.com

Technology Properties Ltd. Inc.
PO Box 20250
San Jose, CA 95160
(408)243-9898
Fax: (408)296-6637
E-mail: sanjose@tplnet.com

Helfert Associates
1777 Borel Pl., Ste. 508
San Mateo, CA 94402-3514
(650)377-0540
Fax: (650)377-0472

Mykytyn Consulting Group Inc.
185 N Redwood Dr., Ste. 200
San Rafael, CA 94903
(415)491-1770
Fax: (415)491-1251
E-mail: info@mcgi.com
Website: http://www.mcgi.com

Omega Management Systems Inc.
3 Mount Darwin Ct.
San Rafael, CA 94903-1109
(415)499-1300
Fax: (415)492-9490
E-mail: omegamgt@ix.netcom.com

The Information Group Inc.
4675 Stevens Creek Blvd., Ste. 100
Santa Clara, CA 95051
(408)985-7877
Fax: (408)985-2945
E-mail: dvincent@tig-usa.com
Website: http://www.tig-usa.com

Cast Management Consultants
1620 26th St., Ste. 2040N
Santa Monica, CA 90404
(310)828-7511
Fax: (310)453-6831

Cuma Consulting Management
Box 724
Santa Rosa, CA 95402
(707)785-2477
Fax: (707)785-2478

The E-Myth Academy
131B Stony Cir., Ste. 2000
Santa Rosa, CA 95401
(707)569-5600
Free: 800-221-0266
Fax: (707)569-5700
E-mail: info@e-myth.com
Website: http://www.e-myth.com

Reilly, Connors & Ray
1743 Canyon Rd.
Spring Valley, CA 91977
(619)698-4808
Fax: (619)460-3892
E-mail: davidray@adnc.com

Management Consultants
Sunnyvale, CA 94087-4700
(408)773-0321

RJR Associates
1639 Lewiston Dr.
Sunnyvale, CA 94087
(408)737-7720
E-mail: bobroy@rjrassoc.com
Website: http://www.rjrassoc.com

Schwafel Associates
333 Cobalt Way, Ste. 21
Sunnyvale, CA 94085
(408)720-0649
Fax: (408)720-1796
E-mail: schwafel@ricochet.net
Website: http://www.patca.org

Staubs Business Services
23320 S Vermont Ave.
Torrance, CA 90502-2940
(310)830-9128
Fax: (310)830-9128
E-mail: Harry_L_Staubs@Lamg.com

Out of Your Mind...and Into the Marketplace
13381 White Sands Dr.
Tustin, CA 92780-4565
(714)544-0248
Free: 800-419-1513
Fax: (714)730-1414
E-mail: lpinson@aol.com
Website: http://www.business-plan.com

Independent Research Services
PO Box 2426
Van Nuys, CA 91404-2426
(818)993-3622

Ingman Company Inc.
7949 Woodley Ave., Ste. 120
Van Nuys, CA 91406-1232
(818)375-5027
Fax: (818)894-5001

Innovative Technology Associates
3639 E Harbor Blvd., Ste. 203E
Ventura, CA 93001
(805)650-9353

Grid Technology Associates
20404 Tufts Cir.
Walnut, CA 91789
(909)444-0922
Fax: (909)444-0922
E-mail: grid_technology@msn.com

Ridge Consultants Inc.
100 Pringle Ave., Ste. 580
Walnut Creek, CA 94596
(925)274-1990
Fax: (510)274-1956
E-mail: info@ridgecon.com
Website: http://www.ridgecon.com

Bell Springs Publishing
PO Box 1240
Willits, CA 95490
(707)459-6372
E-mail: bellsprings@sabernet
Website: http://www.bellsprings.com

Hutchinson Consulting and Appraisal
23245 Sylvan St., Ste. 103
Woodland Hills, CA 91367
(818)888-8175
Free: 800-977-7548
Fax: (818)888-8220
E-mail: r.f.hutchinson-cpa@worldnet.att.net

Colorado

Sam Boyer & Associates
4255 S Buckley Rd., No. 136
Aurora, CO 80013
Free: 800-785-0485
Fax: (303)766-8740
E-mail: samboyer@samboyer.com
Website: http://www.samboyer.com/

Ameriwest Business Consultants Inc.
PO Box 26266
Colorado Springs, CO 80936
(719)380-7096
Fax: (719)380-7096
E-mail: email@abchelp.com
Website: http://www.abchelp.com

GVNW Consulting Inc.
2270 La Montana Way
Colorado Springs, CO 80936
(719)594-5800
Fax: (719)594-5803
Website: http://www.gvnw.com

M-Squared Inc.
755 San Gabriel Pl.
Colorado Springs, CO 80906
(719)576-2554
Fax: (719)576-2554

Thornton Financial FNIC
1024 Centre Ave., Bldg. E
Fort Collins, CO 80526-1849
(970)221-2089
Fax: (970)484-5206

TenEyck Associates
1760 Cherryville Rd.
Greenwood Village, CO 80121-1503
(303)758-6129
Fax: (303)761-8286

Associated Enterprises Ltd.
13050 W Ceder Dr., Unit 11
Lakewood, CO 80228
(303)988-6695
Fax: (303)988-6739
E-mail: ael1@classic.msn.com

The Vincent Company Inc.
200 Union Blvd., Ste. 210
Lakewood, CO 80228
(303)989-7271
Free: 800-274-0733
Fax: (303)989-7570
E-mail: vincent@vincentco.com
Website: http://www.vincentco.com

Johnson & West Management Consultants Inc.
7612 S Logan Dr.
Littleton, CO 80122
(303)730-2810
Fax: (303)730-3219

Western Capital Holdings Inc.
10050 E Applwood Dr.
Parker, CO 80138
(303)841-1022
Fax: (303)770-1945

Connecticut

Stratman Group Inc.
40 Tower Ln.
Avon, CT 06001-4222
(860)677-2898
Free: 800-551-0499
Fax: (860)677-8210

Cowherd Consulting Group Inc.
106 Stephen Mather Rd.
Darien, CT 06820
(203)655-2150
Fax: (203)655-6427

Greenwich Associates
8 Greenwich Office Park
Greenwich, CT 06831-5149
(203)629-1200
Fax: (203)629-1229
E-mail: lisa@greenwich.com
Website: http://www.greenwich.com

Follow-up News
185 Pine St., Ste. 818
Manchester, CT 06040
(860)647-7542
Free: 800-708-0696
Fax: (860)646-6544
E-mail: Followupnews@aol.com

Lovins & Associates Consulting
309 Edwards St.
New Haven, CT 06511
(203)787-3367
Fax: (203)624-7599
E-mail: Alovinsphd@aol.com
Website: http://www.lovinsgroup.com

JC Ventures Inc.
4 Arnold St.
Old Greenwich, CT 06870-1203
(203)698-1990
Free: 800-698-1997
Fax: (203)698-2638

Charles L. Hornung Associates
52 Ned's Mountain Rd.
Ridgefield, CT 06877
(203)431-0297

Manus
100 Prospect St., S Tower
Stamford, CT 06901
(203)326-3880
Free: 800-445-0942
Fax: (203)326-3890
E-mail: manus1@aol.com
Website: http://www.RightManus.com

RealBusinessPlans.com
156 Westport Rd.
Wilton, CT 06897
(914)837-2886
E-mail: ct@realbusinessplans.com
Website: http://www.RealBusinessPlans.com
Tony Tecce

Delaware

Focus Marketing
61-7 Habor Dr.
Claymont, DE 19703
(302)793-3064

Daedalus Ventures Ltd.
PO Box 1474
Hockessin, DE 19707
(302)239-6758
Fax: (302)239-9991
E-mail: daedalus@mail.del.net

The Formula Group
PO Box 866
Hockessin, DE 19707
(302)456-0952
Fax: (302)456-1354
E-mail: formula@netaxs.com

Selden Enterprises Inc.
2502 Silverside Rd., Ste. 1
Wilmington, DE 19810-3740
(302)529-7113
Fax: (302)529-7442
E-mail: selden2@bellatlantic.net
Website: http://www.selden
enterprises.com

District of Columbia

Bruce W. McGee and Associates
7826 Eastern Ave. NW, Ste. 30
Washington, DC 20012
(202)726-7272
Fax: (202)726-2946

McManis Associates Inc.
1900 K St. NW, Ste. 700
Washington, DC 20006
(202)466-7680
Fax: (202)872-1898
Website: http://www.mcmanis-mmi.com

Smith, Dawson & Andrews Inc.
1000 Connecticut Ave., Ste. 302
Washington, DC 20036
(202)835-0740
Fax: (202)775-8526
E-mail: webmaster@sda-inc.com
Website: http://www.sda-inc.com

Florida

BackBone, Inc.
20404 Hacienda Court
Boca Raton, FL 33498
(561)470-0965
Fax: 516-908-4038
E-mail: BPlans@backboneinc.com
Website: http://www.backboneinc.com
Charles Epstein, President

Whalen & Associates Inc.
4255 Northwest 26 Ct.
Boca Raton, FL 33434
(561)241-5950

Fax: (561)241-7414
E-mail: drwhalen@ix.netcom.com

E.N. Rysso & Associates
180 Bermuda Petrel Ct.
Daytona Beach, FL 32119
(386)760-3028
E-mail: erysso@aol.com

Virtual Technocrats LLC
560 Lavers Circle, #146
Delray Beach, FL 33444
(561)265-3509
E-mail: josh@virtualtechnocrats.com;
info@virtualtechnocrats.com
Website: http://www.virtual
technocrats.com
Josh Eikov, Managing Director

Eric Sands Consulting Services
6193 Rock Island Rd., Ste. 412
Fort Lauderdale, FL 33319
(954)721-4767
Fax: (954)720-2815
E-mail: easands@aol.com
Website: http://www.ericsand
sconsultig.com

Professional Planning Associates, Inc.
1975 E. Sunrise Blvd. Suite 607
Fort Lauderdale, FL 33304
(954)764-5204
Fax: 954-463-4172
E-mail: Mgoldstein@proplana.com
Website: http://proplana.com
Michael Goldstein, President

Host Media Corp.
3948 S 3rd St., Ste. 191
Jacksonville Beach, FL 32250
(904)285-3239
Fax: (904)285-5618
E-mail: msconsulting@compuserve.com
Website: http://www.mediaservices
group.com

William V. Hall
1925 Brickell, Ste. D-701
Miami, FL 33129
(305)856-9622
Fax: (305)856-4113
E-mail: williamvhall@compuserve.com

F.A. McGee Inc.
800 Claughton Island Dr., Ste. 401
Miami, FL 33131
(305)377-9123

Taxplan Inc.
Mirasol International Ctr.
2699 Collins Ave.

Miami Beach, FL 33140
(305)538-3303

T.C. Brown & Associates
8415 Excalibur Cir., Apt. B1
Naples, FL 34108
(941)594-1949
Fax: (941)594-0611
E-mail: tcater@naples.net.com

RLA International Consulting
713 Lagoon Dr.
North Palm Beach, FL 33408
(407)626-4258
Fax: (407)626-5772

Comprehensive Franchising Inc.
2465 Ridgecrest Ave.
Orange Park, FL 32065
(904)272-6567
Free: 800-321-6567
Fax: (904)272-6750
E-mail: theimp@cris.com
Website: http://www.franchise411.com

Hunter G. Jackson Jr. - Consulting Environmental Physicist
PO Box 618272
Orlando, FL 32861-8272
(407)295-4188
E-mail: hunterjackson@juno.com

F. Newton Parks
210 El Brillo Way
Palm Beach, FL 33480
(561)833-1727
Fax: (561)833-4541

Avery Business Development Services
2506 St. Michel Ct.
Ponte Vedra Beach, FL 32082
(904)285-6033
Fax: (904)285-6033

Strategic Business Planning Co.
PO Box 821006
South Florida, FL 33082-1006
(954)704-9100
Fax: (954)438-7333
E-mail: info@bizplan.com
Website: http://www.bizplan.com

Dufresne Consulting Group Inc.
10014 N Dale Mabry, Ste. 101
Tampa, FL 33618-4426
(813)264-4775
Fax: (813)264-9300
Website: http://www.dcg
consult.com

Agrippa Enterprises Inc.
PO Box 175
Venice, FL 34284-0175
(941)355-7876
E-mail: webservices@agrippa.com
Website: http://www.agrippa.com

Center for Simplified Strategic Planning Inc.
PO Box 3324
Vero Beach, FL 32964-3324
(561)231-3636
Fax: (561)231-1099
Website: http://www.cssp.com

Georgia

Marketing Spectrum Inc.
115 Perimeter Pl., Ste. 440
Atlanta, GA 30346
(770)395-7244
Fax: (770)393-4071

Business Ventures Corp.
1650 Oakbrook Dr., Ste. 405
Norcross, GA 30093
(770)729-8000
Fax: (770)729-8028

Informed Decisions Inc.
100 Falling Cheek
Sautee Nacoochee, GA 30571
(706)878-1905
Fax: (706)878-1802
E-mail: skylake@compuserve.com

Tom C. Davis & Associates, P.C.
3189 Perimeter Rd.
Valdosta, GA 31602
(912)247-9801
Fax: (912)244-7704
E-mail: mail@tcdcpa.com
Website: http://www.tcdcpa.com/

Illinois

TWD and Associates
431 S Patton
Arlington Heights, IL 60005
(847)398-6410
Fax: (847)255-5095
E-mail: tdoo@aol.com

Management Planning Associates Inc.
2275 Half Day Rd., Ste. 350
Bannockburn, IL 60015-1277
(847)945-2421
Fax: (847)945-2425

Phil Faris Associates
86 Old Mill Ct.
Barrington, IL 60010
(847)382-4888
Fax: (847)382-4890
E-mail: pfaris@meginsnet.net

Seven Continents Technology
787 Stonebridge
Buffalo Grove, IL 60089
(708)577-9653
Fax: (708)870-1220

Grubb & Blue Inc.
2404 Windsor Pl.
Champaign, IL 61820
(217)366-0052
Fax: (217)356-0117

ACE Accounting Service Inc.
3128 N Bernard St.
Chicago, IL 60618
(773)463-7854
Fax: (773)463-7854

AON Consulting Worldwide
200 E Randolph St., 10th Fl.
Chicago, IL 60601
(312)381-4800
Free: 800-438-6487
Fax: (312)381-0240
Website: http://www.aon.com

FMS Consultants
5801 N Sheridan Rd., Ste. 3D
Chicago, IL 60660
(773)561-7362
Fax: (773)561-6274

Grant Thornton
800 1 Prudential Plz.
130 E Randolph St.
Chicago, IL 60601
(312)856-0001
Fax: (312)861-1340
E-mail: gtinfo@gt.com
Website: http://www.grantthornton.com

Kingsbury International Ltd.
5341 N Glenwood Ave.
Chicago, IL 60640
(773)271-3030
Fax: (773)728-7080
E-mail: jetlag@mcs.com
Website: http://www.kingbiz.com

MacDougall & Blake Inc.
1414 N Wells St., Ste. 311
Chicago, IL 60610-1306
(312)587-3330
Fax: (312)587-3699
E-mail: jblake@compuserve.com

James C. Osburn Ltd.
6445 N. Western Ave., Ste. 304
Chicago, IL 60645
(773)262-4428
Fax: (773)262-6755
E-mail: osburnltd@aol.com

Tarifero & Tazewell Inc.
211 S Clark
Chicago, IL 60690
(312)665-9714
Fax: (312)665-9716

Human Energy Design Systems
620 Roosevelt Dr.
Edwardsville, IL 62025
(618)692-0258
Fax: (618)692-0819

China Business Consultants Group
931 Dakota Cir.
Naperville, IL 60563
(630)778-7992
Fax: (630)778-7915
E-mail: cbcq@aol.com

Center for Workforce Effectiveness
500 Skokie Blvd., Ste. 222
Northbrook, IL 60062
(847)559-8777
Fax: (847)559-8778
E-mail: office@cwelink.com
Website: http://www.cwelink.com

Smith Associates
1320 White Mountain Dr.
Northbrook, IL 60062
(847)480-7200
Fax: (847)480-9828

Francorp Inc.
20200 Governors Dr.
Olympia Fields, IL 60461
(708)481-2900
Free: 800-372-6244
Fax: (708)481-5885
E-mail: francorp@aol.com
Website: http://www.francorpinc.com

Camber Business Strategy Consultants
1010 S Plum Tree Ct
Palatine, IL 60078-0986
(847)202-0101
Fax: (847)705-7510
E-mail: camber@ameritech.net

Partec Enterprise Group
5202 Keith Dr.
Richton Park, IL 60471
(708)503-4047
Fax: (708)503-9468

Rockford Consulting Group Ltd.
Century Plz., Ste. 206
7210 E State St.
Rockford, IL 61108
(815)229-2900
Free: 800-667-7495
Fax: (815)229-2612
E-mail: rligus@RockfordConsulting.com
Website: http://www.Rockford
Consulting.com

RSM McGladrey Inc.
1699 E Woodfield Rd., Ste. 300
Schaumburg, IL 60173-4969
(847)413-6900
Fax: (847)517-7067
Website: http://www.rsmmcgladrey.com

A.D. Star Consulting
320 Euclid
Winnetka, IL 60093
(847)446-7827
Fax: (847)446-7827
E-mail: startwo@worldnet.att.net

Indiana

Modular Consultants Inc.
3109 Crabtree Ln.
Elkhart, IN 46514
(219)264-5761
Fax: (219)264-5761
E-mail: sasabo5313@aol.com

Midwest Marketing Research
PO Box 1077
Goshen, IN 46527
(219)533-0548
Fax: (219)533-0540
E-mail: 103365.654@compuserve

Ketchum Consulting Group
8021 Knue Rd., Ste. 112
Indianapolis, IN 46250
(317)845-5411
Fax: (317)842-9941

MDI Management Consulting
1519 Park Dr.
Munster, IN 46321
(219)838-7909
Fax: (219)838-7909

Iowa

McCord Consulting Group Inc.
4533 Pine View Dr. NE
PO Box 11024
Cedar Rapids, IA 52410
(319)378-0077
Fax: (319)378-1577

E-mail: smmccord@hom.com
Website: http://www.mccordgroup.com

Management Solutions L.C.
3815 Lincoln Pl. Dr.
Des Moines, IA 50312
(515)277-6408
Fax: (515)277-3506
E-mail: wasunimers@uswest.net

Grandview Marketing
15 Red Bridge Dr.
Sioux City, IA 51104
(712)239-3122
Fax: (712)258-7578
E-mail: eandrews@pionet.net

Kansas

Assessments in Action
513A N Mur-Len
Olathe, KS 66062
(913)764-6270
Free: (888)548-1504
Fax: (913)764-6495
E-mail: lowdene@qni.com
Website: http://www.assessments-in-
action.com

Maine

Edgemont Enterprises
PO Box 8354
Portland, ME 04104
(207)871-8964
Fax: (207)871-8964

Pan Atlantic Consultants
5 Milk St.
Portland, ME 04101
(207)871-8622
Fax: (207)772-4842
E-mail: pmurphy@maine.rr.com
Website: http://www.panatlantic.net

Maryland

Clemons & Associates Inc.
5024-R Campbell Blvd.
Baltimore, MD 21236
(410)931-8100
Fax: (410)931-8111
E-mail: info@clemonsmgmt.com
Website: http://www.clemonsmgmt.com

Imperial Group Ltd.
305 Washington Ave., Ste. 204
Baltimore, MD 21204-6009
(410)337-8500
Fax: (410)337-7641

Leadership Institute

3831 Yolando Rd.

Baltimore, MD 21218

(410)366-9111

Fax: (410)243-8478

E-mail: behconsult@aol.com

Burdeshaw Associates Ltd.

4701 Sangamore Rd.

Bethesda, MD 20816-2508

(301)229-5800

Fax: (301)229-5045

E-mail: jstacy@burdeshaw.com

Website: http://www.burdeshaw.com

Michael E. Cohen

5225 Pooks Hill Rd., Ste. 1119 S

Bethesda, MD 20814

(301)530-5738

Fax: (301)530-2988

E-mail: mecohen@crosslink.net

World Development Group Inc.

5272 River Rd., Ste. 650

Bethesda, MD 20816-1405

(301)652-1818

Fax: (301)652-1250

E-mail: wdg@has.com

Website: http://www.worlddg.com

Swartz Consulting

PO Box 4301

Crofton, MD 21114-4301

(301)262-6728

Software Solutions International Inc.

9633 Duffer Way

Gaithersburg, MD 20886

(301)330-4136

Fax: (301)330-4136

Strategies Inc.

8 Park Center Ct., Ste. 200

Owings Mills, MD 21117

(410)363-6669

Fax: (410)363-1231

E-mail: strategies@strat1.com

Website: http://www.strat1.com

Hammer Marketing Resources

179 Inverness Rd.

Severna Park, MD 21146

(410)544-9191

Fax: (305)675-3277

E-mail: info@gohammer.com

Website: http://www.gohammer.com

Andrew Sussman & Associates

13731 Kretsinger

Smithsburg, MD 21783

(301)824-2943

Fax: (301)824-2943

Massachusetts

Geibel Marketing and Public Relations

PO Box 611

Belmont, MA 02478-0005

(617)484-8285

Fax: (617)489-3567

E-mail: jgeibel@geibelpr.com

Website: http://www.geibelpr.com

Bain & Co.

2 Copley Pl.

Boston, MA 02116

(617)572-2000

Fax: (617)572-2427

E-mail: corporate.inquiries@bain.com

Website: http://www.bain.com

Mehr & Co.

62 Kinnaird St.

Cambridge, MA 02139

(617)876-3311

Fax: (617)876-3023

E-mail: mehrco@aol.com

Monitor Company Inc.

2 Canal Park

Cambridge, MA 02141

(617)252-2000

Fax: (617)252-2100

Website: http://www.monitor.com

Information & Research Associates

PO Box 3121

Framingham, MA 01701

(508)788-0784

Walden Consultants Ltd.

252 Pond St.

Hopkinton, MA 01748

(508)435-4882

Fax: (508)435-3971

Website: http://www.walden
consultants.com

Jeffrey D. Marshall

102 Mitchell Rd.

Ipswich, MA 01938-1219

(508)356-1113

Fax: (508)356-2989

Consulting Resources Corp.

6 Northbrook Park

Lexington, MA 02420

(781)863-1222

Fax: (781)863-1441

E-mail: res@consultingresources.net

Website: http://
www.consultingresources.net

Planning Technologies Group L.L.C.

92 Hayden Ave.

Lexington, MA 02421

(781)778-4678

Fax: (781)861-1099

E-mail: ptg@plantech.com

Website: http://www.plantech.com

Kalba International Inc.

23 Sandy Pond Rd.

Lincoln, MA 01773

(781)259-9589

Fax: (781)259-1460

E-mail: info@kalbainternational.com

Website: http://www.kalba
international.com

VMB Associates Inc.

115 Ashland St.

Melrose, MA 02176

(781)665-0623

Fax: (425)732-7142

E-mail: vmbinc@aol.com

The Company Doctor

14 Pudding Stone Ln.

Mendon, MA 01756

(508)478-1747

Fax: (508)478-0520

Data and Strategies Group Inc.

190 N Main St.

Natick, MA 01760

(508)653-9990

Fax: (508)653-7799

E-mail: dsginc@dsggroup.com

Website: http://www.dsggroup.com

The Enterprise Group

73 Parker Rd.

Needham, MA 02494

(617)444-6631

Fax: (617)433-9991

E-mail: lsacco@world.std.com

Website: http://www.enterprise-
group.com

PSMJ Resources Inc.

10 Midland Ave.

Newton, MA 02458

(617)965-0055

Free: 800-537-7765

Fax: (617)965-5152

E-mail: psmj@tiac.net

Website: http://www.psmj.com

**Scheur Management
Group Inc.**

255 Washington St., Ste. 100

Newton, MA 02458-1611

(617)969-7500

Fax: (617)969-7508
E-mail: smgnow@scheur.com
Website: http://www.scheur.com

I.E.E.E., Boston Section
240 Bear Hill Rd., 202B
Waltham, MA 02451-1017
(781)890-5294
Fax: (781)890-5290

Business Planning and Consulting Services
20 Beechwood Ter.
Wellesley, MA 02482
(617)237-9151
Fax: (617)237-9151

Michigan

Walter Frederick Consulting
1719 South Blvd.
Ann Arbor, MI 48104
(313)662-4336
Fax: (313)769-7505

Fox Enterprises
6220 W Freeland Rd.
Freeland, MI 48623
(517)695-9170
Fax: (517)695-9174
E-mail: foxjw@concentric.net
Website: http://www.cris.com/~foxjw

G.G.W. and Associates
1213 Hampton
Jackson, MI 49203
(517)782-2255
Fax: (517)782-2255

Altamar Group Ltd.
6810 S Cedar, Ste. 2-B
Lansing, MI 48911
(517)694-0910
Free: 800-443-2627
Fax: (517)694-1377

Sheffieck Consultants Inc.
23610 Greening Dr.
Novi, MI 48375-3130
(248)347-3545
Fax: (248)347-3530
E-mail: cfsheff@concentric.net

Rehmann, Robson PC
5800 Gratiot
Saginaw, MI 48605
(517)799-9580
Fax: (517)799-0227
Website: http://www.rrpc.com

Francis & Co.
17200 W 10 Mile Rd., Ste. 207
Southfield, MI 48075
(248)559-7600
Fax: (248)559-5249

Private Ventures Inc.
16000 W 9 Mile Rd., Ste. 504
Southfield, MI 48075
(248)569-1977
Free: 800-448-7614
Fax: (248)569-1838
E-mail: pventuresi@aol.com

JGK Associates
14464 Kerner Dr.
Sterling Heights, MI 48313
(810)247-9055
Fax: (248)822-4977
E-mail: kozlowski@home.com

Minnesota

Health Fitness Corp.
3500 W 80th St., Ste. 130
Bloomington, MN 55431
(612)831-6830
Fax: (612)831-7264

Consatech Inc.
PO Box 1047
Burnsville, MN 55337
(612)953-1088
Fax: (612)435-2966

Robert F. Knotek
14960 Ironwood Ct.
Eden Prairie, MN 55346
(612)949-2875

DRI Consulting
7715 Stonewood Ct.
Edina, MN 55439
(612)941-9656
Fax: (612)941-2693
E-mail: dric@dric.com
Website: http://www.dric.com

Markin Consulting
12072 87th Pl. N
Maple Grove, MN 55369
(612)493-3568
Fax: (612)493-5744
E-mail: markin@markinconsulting.com
Website: http://www.markin
consulting.com

Minnesota Cooperation Office for Small Business & Job Creation Inc.
5001 W 80th St., Ste. 825
Minneapolis, MN 55437

(612)830-1230
Fax: (612)830-1232
E-mail: mncoop@msn.com
Website: http://www.mnco.org

Enterprise Consulting Inc.
PO Box 1111
Minnetonka, MN 55345
(612)949-5909
Fax: (612)906-3965

Amdahl International
724 1st Ave. SW
Rochester, MN 55902
(507)252-0402
Fax: (507)252-0402
E-mail: amdahl@best-service.com
Website: http://www.wp.com/
amdahl_int

Power Systems Research
1365 Corporate Center Curve, 2nd Fl.
St. Paul, MN 55121
(612)905-8400
Free: (888)625-8612
Fax: (612)454-0760
E-mail: Barb@Powersys.com
Website: http://www.powersys.com

Missouri

Business Planning and Development Corp.
4030 Charlotte St.
Kansas City, MO 64110
(816)753-0495
E-mail: humph@bpdev.demon.co.uk
Website: http://www.bpdev.
demon.co.uk

CFO Service
10336 Donoho
St. Louis, MO 63131
(314)750-2940
E-mail: jskae@cfoservice.com
Website: http://www.cfoservice.com

Nebraska

International Management Consulting Group Inc.
1309 Harlan Dr., Ste. 205
Bellevue, NE 68005
(402)291-4545
Free: 800-665-IMCG
Fax: (402)291-4343
E-mail: imcg@neonramp.com
Website: http://www.mgt
consulting.com

Heartland Management Consulting Group
1904 Barrington Pky.
Papillion, NE 68046
(402)339-2387
Fax: (402)339-1319

Nevada

The DuBois Group
865 Tahoe Blvd., Ste. 108
Incline Village, NV 89451
(775)832-0550
Free: 800-375-2935
Fax: (775)832-0556
E-mail: DuBoisGrp@aol.com

New Hampshire

Wolff Consultants
10 Buck Rd.
Hanover, NH 03755
(603)643-6015

BPT Consulting Associates Ltd.
12 Parmenter Rd., Ste. B-6
Londonderry, NH 03053
(603)437-8484
Free: (888)278-0030
Fax: (603)434-5388
E-mail: bptcons@tiac.net
Website: http://www.bptconsulting.com

New Jersey

Bedminster Group Inc.
1170 Rte. 22 E
Bridgewater, NJ 08807
(908)500-4155
Fax: (908)766-0780
E-mail: info@bedminstergroup.com
Website: http://
www.bedminstergroup.com
Fax: (202)806-1777
Terry Strong, Acting Regional Dir.

Delta Planning Inc.
PO Box 425
Denville, NJ 07834
(913)625-1742
Free: 800-672-0762
Fax: (973)625-3531
E-mail: DeltaP@worldnet.att.net
Website: http://deltaplanning.com

Kumar Associates Inc.
1004 Cumbermeade Rd.
Fort Lee, NJ 07024
(201)224-9480
Fax: (201)585-2343

E-mail: mail@kumarassociates.com
Website: http://kumarassociates.com

John Hall & Company Inc.
PO Box 187
Glen Ridge, NJ 07028
(973)680-4449
Fax: (973)680-4581
E-mail: jhcompany@aol.com

Market Focus
PO Box 402
Maplewood, NJ 07040
(973)378-2470
Fax: (973)378-2470
E-mail: mcss66@marketfocus.com

Vanguard Communications Corp.
100 American Rd.
Morris Plains, NJ 07950
(973)605-8000
Fax: (973)605-8329
Website: http://www.vanguard.net/

ConMar International Ltd.
1901 US Hwy. 130
North Brunswick, NJ 08902
(732)940-8347
Fax: (732)274-1199

KLW New Products
156 Cedar Dr.
Old Tappan, NJ 07675
(201)358-1300
Fax: (201)664-2594
E-mail: lrlarsen@usa.net
Website: http://www.klwnew
products.com

PA Consulting Group
315A Enterprise Dr.
Plainsboro, NJ 08536
(609)936-8300
Fax: (609)936-8811
E-mail: info@paconsulting.com
Website: http://www.pa-consulting.com

Aurora Marketing Management Inc.
66 Witherspoon St., Ste. 600
Princeton, NJ 08542
(908)904-1125
Fax: (908)359-1108
E-mail: aurora2@voicenet.com
Website: http://
www.auroramarketing.net

Smart Business Supersite
88 Orchard Rd., CN-5219
Princeton, NJ 08543
(908)321-1924

Fax: (908)321-5156
E-mail: irv@smartbiz.com
Website: http://www.smartbiz.com

Tracelin Associates
1171 Main St., Ste. 6K
Rahway, NJ 07065
(732)381-3288

Schkeeper Inc.
130-6 Bodman Pl.
Red Bank, NJ 07701
(732)219-1965
Fax: (732)530-3703

Henry Branch Associates
2502 Harmon Cove Twr.
Secaucus, NJ 07094
(201)866-2008
Fax: (201)601-0101
E-mail: hbranch161@home.com

Robert Gibbons & Company Inc.
46 Knoll Rd.
Tenafly, NJ 07670-1050
(201)871-3933
Fax: (201)871-2173
E-mail: crisisbob@aol.com

PMC Management Consultants Inc.
6 Thistle Ln.
Three Bridges, NJ 08887-0332
(908)788-1014
Free: 800-PMC-0250
Fax: (908)806-7287
E-mail: int@pmc-management.com
Website: http://www.pmc-management.com

R.W. Bankart & Associates
20 Valley Ave., Ste. D-2
Westwood, NJ 07675-3607
(201)664-7672

New Mexico

Vondle & Associates Inc.
4926 Calle de Tierra, NE
Albuquerque, NM 87111
(505)292-8961
Fax: (505)296-2790
E-mail: vondle@aol.com

InfoNewMexico
2207 Black Hills Rd., NE
Rio Rancho, NM 87124
(505)891-2462
Fax: (505)896-8971

New York

**Powers Research and
Training Institute**
PO Box 78
Bayville, NY 11709
(516)628-2250
Fax: (516)628-2252
E-mail: powercocch@compuserve.com
Website: http://www.nancypowers.com

Consortium House
296 Wittenberg Rd.
Bearsville, NY 12409
(845)679-8867
Fax: (845)679-9248
E-mail: eugenegs@aol.com
Website: http://www.chpub.com

Progressive Finance Corp.
3549 Tiemann Ave.
Bronx, NY 10469
(718)405-9029
Free: 800-225-8381
Fax: (718)405-1170

Wave Hill Associates Inc.
2621 Palisade Ave., Ste. 15-C
Bronx, NY 10463
(718)549-7368
Fax: (718)601-9670
E-mail: pepper@compuserve.com

Management Insight
96 Arlington Rd.
Buffalo, NY 14221
(716)631-3319
Fax: (716)631-0203
E-mail:
michalski@foodserviceinsight.com
Website: http://www.food
serviceinsight.com

**Samani International Enterprises,
Marions Panyaught Consultancy**
2028 Parsons
Flushing, NY 11357-3436
(917)287-8087
Fax: 800-873-8939
E-mail: vjp2@biostrategist.com
Website: http://www.biostrategist.com

Marketing Resources Group
71-58 Austin St.
Forest Hills, NY 11375
(718)261-8882

**Mangabay Business Plans &
Development**
Subsidiary of Innis Asset Allocation
125-10 Queens Blvd., Ste. 2202

Kew Gardens, NY 11415
 (905)527-1947
Fax: 509-472-1935
E-mail: mangabay@mangabay.com
Website: http://www.mangabay.com
Lee Toh, Managing Partner

ComputerEase Co.
1301 Monmouth Ave.
Lakewood, NY 08701
(212)406-9464
Fax: (914)277-5317
E-mail: crawfordc@juno.com

Boice Dunham Group
30 W 13th St.
New York, NY 10011
(212)924-2200
Fax: (212)924-1108

Elizabeth Capen
27 E 95th St.
New York, NY 10128
(212)427-7654
Fax: (212)876-3190

Haver Analytics
60 E 42nd St., Ste. 2424
New York, NY 10017

(212)986-9300
Fax: (212)986-5857
E-mail: data@haver.com
Website: http://www.haver.com

The Jordan, Edmiston Group Inc.
150 E 52nd Ave., 18th Fl.
New York, NY 10022
(212)754-0710
Fax: (212)754-0337

KPMG International
345 Park Ave.
New York, NY 10154-0102
(212)758-9700
Fax: (212)758-9819
Website: http://www.kpmg.com

Mahoney Cohen Consulting Corp.
111 W 40th St., 12th Fl.
New York, NY 10018
(212)490-8000
Fax: (212)790-5913

Management Practice Inc.
342 Madison Ave.
New York, NY 10173-1230
(212)867-7948
Fax: (212)972-5188
Website: http://www.mpiweb.com

Moseley Associates Inc.
342 Madison Ave., Ste. 1414
New York, NY 10016
(212)213-6673
Fax: (212)687-1520

Practice Development Counsel
60 Sutton Pl. S
New York, NY 10022
(212)593-1549
Fax: (212)980-7940
E-mail: pwhaserot@pdcounsel.com
Website: http://www.pdcounsel.com

Unique Value International Inc.
575 Madison Ave., 10th Fl.
New York, NY 10022-1304
(212)605-0590
Fax: (212)605-0589

The Van Tulleken Co.
126 E 56th St.
New York, NY 10022
(212)355-1390
Fax: (212)755-3061
E-mail: newyork@vantulleken.com

Vencon Management Inc.
301 W 53rd St.
New York, NY 10019
(212)581-8787
Fax: (212)397-4126
Website: http://www.venconinc.com

Werner International Inc.
55 E 52nd, 29th Fl.
New York, NY 10055
(212)909-1260
Fax: (212)909-1273
E-mail: richard.downing@rgh.com
Website: http://www.wernertex.com

Zimmerman Business Consulting Inc.
44 E 92nd St., Ste. 5-B
New York, NY 10128
(212)860-3107
Fax: (212)860-7730
E-mail: ljzzbci@aol.com
Website: http://www.zbcinc.com

Overton Financial
7 Allen Rd.
Peekskill, NY 10566
(914)737-4649
Fax: (914)737-4696

Stromberg Consulting
2500 Westchester Ave.
Purchase, NY 10577
(914)251-1515
Fax: (914)251-1562

E-mail: strategy@stromberg
_consulting.com
Website: http://www.stromberg
_consulting.com

**Innovation Management
Consulting Inc.**
209 Dewitt Rd.
Syracuse, NY 13214-2006
(315)425-5144
Fax: (315)445-8989
E-mail: missonneb@axess.net

M. Clifford Agress
891 Fulton St.
Valley Stream, NY 11580
(516)825-8955
Fax: (516)825-8955

Destiny Kinal Marketing Consultancy
105 Chemung St.
Waverly, NY 14892
(607)565-8317
Fax: (607)565-4083

Valutis Consulting Inc.
5350 Main St., Ste. 7
Williamsville, NY 14221-5338
(716)634-2553
Fax: (716)634-2554
E-mail: valutis@localnet.com
Website: http://www.valutis
consulting.com

North Carolina

Best Practices L.L.C.
6320 Quadrangle Dr., Ste. 200
Chapel Hill, NC 27514
(919)403-0251
Fax: (919)403-0144
E-mail: best@best:in/class
Website: http://www.best-in-class.com

Norelli & Co.
Bank of America Corporate Ctr.
100 N Tyron St., Ste. 5160
Charlotte, NC 28202-4000
(704)376-5484
Fax: (704)376-5485
E-mail: consult@norelli.com
Website: http://www.norelli.com

North Dakota

Center for Innovation
4300 Dartmouth Dr.
PO Box 8372
Grand Forks, ND 58202
(701)777-3132
Fax: (701)777-2339

E-mail: bruce@innovators.net
Website: http://www.innovators.net

Ohio

Transportation Technology Services
208 Harmon Rd.
Aurora, OH 44202
(330)562-3596

Empro Systems Inc.
4777 Red Bank Expy., Ste. 1
Cincinnati, OH 45227-1542
(513)271-2042
Fax: (513)271-2042

Alliance Management International Ltd.
1440 Windrow Ln.
Cleveland, OH 44147-3200
(440)838-1922
Fax: (440)838-0979
E-mail: bgruss@amiltd.com
Website: http://www.amiltd.com

Bozell Kamstra Public Relations
1301 E 9th St., Ste. 3400
Cleveland, OH 44114
(216)623-1511
Fax: (216)623-1501
E-mail:
jfeniger@cleveland.bozellkamstra.com
Website: http://www.bozellkamstra.com

Cory Dillon Associates
111 Schreyer Pl. E
Columbus, OH 43214
(614)262-8211
Fax: (614)262-3806

Holcomb Gallagher Adams
300 Marconi, Ste. 303
Columbus, OH 43215
(614)221-3343
Fax: (614)221-3367
E-mail: riadams@acme.freenet.oh.us

Young & Associates
PO Box 711
Kent, OH 44240
(330)678-0524
Free: 800-525-9775
Fax: (330)678-6219
E-mail: online@younginc.com
Website: http://www.younginc.com

Robert A. Westman & Associates
8981 Inversary Dr. SE
Warren, OH 44484-2551
(330)856-4149
Fax: (330)856-2564

Oklahoma

Innovative Partners L.L.C.
4900 Richmond Sq., Ste. 100
Oklahoma City, OK 73118
(405)840-0033
Fax: (405)843-8359
E-mail: ipartners@juno.com

Oregon

**INTERCON - The International
Converting Institute**
5200 Badger Rd.
Crooked River Ranch, OR 97760
(541)548-1447
Fax: (541)548-1618
E-mail:
johnbowler@crookedriverranch.com

Talbott ARM
HC 60, Box 5620
Lakeview, OR 97630
(541)635-8587
Fax: (503)947-3482

Management Technology Associates Ltd.
2768 SW Sherwood Dr, Ste. 105
Portland, OR 97201-2251
(503)224-5220
Fax: (503)224-5334
E-mail: lcuster@mta-ltd.com
Website: http://www.mgmt-tech.com

Pennsylvania

Healthscope Inc.
400 Lancaster Ave.
Devon, PA 19333
(610)687-6199
Fax: (610)687-6376
E-mail: health@voicenet.com
Website: http://www.healthscope.net/

Elayne Howard & Associates Inc.
3501 Masons Mill Rd., Ste. 501
Huntingdon Valley, PA 19006-3509
(215)657-9550

GRA Inc.
115 West Ave., Ste. 201
Jenkintown, PA 19046
(215)884-7500
Fax: (215)884-1385
E-mail: gramail@gra-inc.com
Website: http://www.gra-inc.com

**Mifflin County Industrial Development
Corp.**
Mifflin County Industrial Plz.
6395 SR 103 N

Bldg. 50
Lewistown, PA 17044
(717)242-0393
Fax: (717)242-1842
E-mail: mcide@acsworld.net

Autech Products
1289 Revere Rd.
Morrisville, PA 19067
(215)493-3759
Fax: (215)493-9791
E-mail: autech4@yahoo.com

Advantage Associates
434 Avon Dr.
Pittsburgh, PA 15228
(412)343-1558
Fax: (412)362-1684
E-mail: ecocba1@aol.com

Regis J. Sheehan & Associates
Pittsburgh, PA 15220
(412)279-1207

James W. Davidson Company Inc.
23 Forest View Rd.
Wallingford, PA 19086
(610)566-1462

Puerto Rico

Diego Chevere & Co.
Metro Parque 7, Ste. 204
Metro Office
Caparra Heights, PR 00920
(787)774-9595
Fax: (787)774-9566
E-mail: dcco@coqui.net

Manuel L. Porrata and Associates
898 Munoz Rivera Ave., Ste. 201
San Juan, PR 00927
(787)765-2140
Fax: (787)754-3285
E-mail: m_porrata@manuelporrata.com
Website: http://manualporrata.com

South Carolina

Aquafood Business Associates
PO Box 13267
Charleston, SC 29422
(843)795-9506
Fax: (843)795-9477
E-mail: rraba@aol.com

Profit Associates Inc.
PO Box 38026
Charleston, SC 29414
(803)763-5718
Fax: (803)763-5719

E-mail: bobrog@awod.com
Website: http://www.awod.com/gallery/business/proasc

Strategic Innovations International
12 Executive Ct.
Lake Wylie, SC 29710
(803)831-1225
Fax: (803)831-1177
E-mail: stratinnov@aol.com
Website: http://www.strategic innovations.com

Minus Stage
Box 4436
Rock Hill, SC 29731
(803)328-0705
Fax: (803)329-9948

Tennessee

Daniel Petchers & Associates
8820 Fernwood CV
Germantown, TN 38138
(901)755-9896

Business Choices
1114 Forest Harbor, Ste. 300
Hendersonville, TN 37075-9646
(615)822-8692
Free: 800-737-8382
Fax: (615)822-8692
E-mail: bz-ch@juno.com

RCFA Healthcare Management Services L.L.C.
9648 Kingston Pke., Ste. 8
Knoxville, TN 37922
(865)531-0176
Free: 800-635-4040
Fax: (865)531-0722
E-mail: info@rcfa.com
Website: http://www.rcfa.com

Growth Consultants of America
3917 Trimble Rd.
Nashville, TN 37215
(615)383-0550
Fax: (615)269-8940
E-mail: 70244.451@compuserve.com

Texas

Integrated Cost Management Systems Inc.
2261 Brookhollow Plz. Dr., Ste. 104
Arlington, TX 76006
(817)633-2873
Fax: (817)633-3781
E-mail: abm@icms.net
Website: http://www.icms.net

Lori Williams
1000 Leslie Ct.
Arlington, TX 76012
(817)459-3934
Fax: (817)459-3934

Business Resource Software Inc.
2013 Wells Branch Pky., Ste. 305
Austin, TX 78728
Free: 800-423-1228
Fax: (512)251-4401
E-mail: info@brs-inc.com
Website: http://www.brs-inc.com

Erisa Adminstrative Services Inc.
12325 Hymeadow Dr., Bldg. 4
Austin, TX 78750-1847
(512)250-9020
Fax: (512)250-9487
Website: http://www.cserisa.com

R. Miller Hicks & Co.
1011 W 11th St.
Austin, TX 78703
(512)477-7000
Fax: (512)477-9697
E-mail: millerhicks@rmhicks.com
Website: http://www.rmhicks.com

Pragmatic Tactics Inc.
3303 Westchester Ave.
College Station, TX 77845
(409)696-5294
Free: 800-570-5294
Fax: (409)696-4994
E-mail: ptactics@aol.com
Website: http://www.ptatics.com

Perot Systems
12404 Park Central Dr.
Dallas, TX 75251
(972)340-5000
Free: 800-688-4333
Fax: (972)455-4100
E-mail: corp.comm@ps.net
Website: http://www.perotsystems.com

ReGENERATION Partners
3838 Oak Lawn Ave.
Dallas, TX 75219
(214)559-3999
Free: 800-406-1112
E-mail: info@regeneration-partner.com
Website: http://www.regeneration-partners.com

High Technology Associates - Division of Global Technologies Inc.
1775 St. James Pl., Ste. 105
Houston, TX 77056
(713)963-9300

Fax: (713)963-8341
E-mail: hta@infohwy.com

MasterCOM
103 Thunder Rd.
Kerrville, TX 78028
(830)895-7990
Fax: (830)443-3428
E-mail:
jmstubblefield@mastertraining.com
Website: http://www.mastertraining.com

PROTEC
4607 Linden Pl.
Pearland, TX 77584
(281)997-9872
Fax: (281)997-9895
E-mail: p.oman@ix.netcom.com

Alpha Quadrant Inc.
10618 Auldine
San Antonio, TX 78230
(210)344-3330
Fax: (210)344-8151
E-mail: mbussone@sbcglobal.net
Website:http://www.a-quadrant.com
Michele Bussone

Bastian Public Relations
614 San Dizier
San Antonio, TX 78232
(210)404-1839
E-mail: lisa@bastianpr.com
Website: http://www.bastianpr.com
Lisa Bastian CBC

**Business Strategy Development
Consultants**
PO Box 690365
San Antonio, TX 78269
(210)696-8000
Free: 800-927-BSDC
Fax: (210)696-8000

Tom Welch, CPC
6900 San Pedro Ave., Ste. 147
San Antonio, TX 78216-6207
(210)737-7022
Fax: (210)737-7022
E-mail: bplan@iamerica.net
Website: http://www.moneywords.com

Utah

Business Management Resource
PO Box 521125
Salt Lake City, UT 84152-1125
(801)272-4668
Fax: (801)277-3290
E-mail: pingfong@worldnet.att.net

Virginia

Tindell Associates
209 Oxford Ave.
Alexandria, VA 22301
(703)683-0109
Fax: 703-783-0219
E-mail: scott@tindell.net
Website: http://www.tindell.net
Scott Lockett, President

Elliott B. Jaffa
2530-B S Walter Reed Dr.
Arlington, VA 22206
(703)931-0040
E-mail: thetrainingdoctor@excite.com
Website: http://www.tregistry.com/
jaffa.htm

Koach Enterprises - USA
5529 N 18th St.
Arlington, VA 22205
(703)241-8361
Fax: (703)241-8623

Federal Market Development
5650 Chapel Run Ct.
Centreville, VA 20120-3601
(703)502-8930
Free: 800-821-5003
Fax: (703)502-8929

Huff, Stuart & Carlton
2107 Graves Mills Rd., Ste. C
Forest, VA 24551
(804)316-9356
Free: (888)316-9356
Fax: (804)316-9357
Website: http://www.wealthmgt.net

AMX International Inc.
1420 Spring Hill Rd. , Ste. 600
McLean, VA 22102-3006
(703)690-4100
Fax: (703)643-1279
E-mail: amxmail@amxi.com
Website: http://www.amxi.com

Charles Scott Pugh (Investor)
4101 Pittaway Dr.
Richmond, VA 23235-1022
(804)560-0979
Fax: (804)560-4670

John C. Randall and Associates Inc.
PO Box 15127
Richmond, VA 23227
(804)746-4450
Fax: (804)730-8933
E-mail: randalljcx@aol.com
Website: http://www.johncrandall.com

McLeod & Co.
410 1st St.
Roanoke, VA 24011
(540)342-6911
Fax: (540)344-6367
Website: http://www.mcleodco.com/

Salzinger & Company Inc.
8000 Towers Crescent Dr., Ste. 1350
Vienna, VA 22182
(703)442-5200
Fax: (703)442-5205
E-mail: info@salzinger.com
Website: http://www.salzinger.com

The Small Business Counselor
12423 Hedges Run Dr., Ste. 153
Woodbridge, VA 22192
(703)490-6755
Fax: (703)490-1356

Washington

Burlington Consultants
10900 NE 8th St., Ste. 900
Bellevue, WA 98004
(425)688-3060
Fax: (425)454-4383
E-mail:
partners@burlingtonconsultants.com
Website: http://www.burlington
consultants.com

Perry L. Smith Consulting
800 Bellevue Way NE, Ste. 400
Bellevue, WA 98004-4208
(425)462-2072
Fax: (425)462-5638

St. Charles Consulting Group
1420 NW Gilman Blvd.
Issaquah, WA 98027
(425)557-8708
Fax: (425)557-8731
E-mail: info@stcharlesconsulting.com
Website: http://www.stcharles
consulting.com

**Independent Automotive Training
Services**
PO Box 334
Kirkland, WA 98083
(425)822-5715
E-mail: ltunney@autosvccon.com
Website: http://www.autosvccon.com

Kahle Associate Inc.
6203 204th Dr. NE
Redmond, WA 98053
(425)836-8763
Fax: (425)868-3770

E-mail: randykahle@kahleassociates.com
Website: http://www.kahleassociates.com

Dan Collin
3419 Wallingord Ave N, No. 2
Seattle, WA 98103
(206)634-9469
E-mail: dc@dancollin.com
Website: http://members.home.net/
dcollin/

**ECG Management
Consultants Inc.**
1111 3rd Ave., Ste. 2700
Seattle, WA 98101-3201
(206)689-2200
Fax: (206)689-2209
E-mail: ecg@ecgmc.com
Website: http://www.ecgmc.com

**Northwest Trade Adjustment
Assistance Center**
900 4th Ave., Ste. 2430
Seattle, WA 98164-1001
(206)622-2730
Free: 800-667-8087
Fax: (206)622-1105
E-mail: matchingfunds@nwtaac.org
Website: http://www.taacenters.org

Business Planning Consultants
S 3510 Ridgeview Dr.
Spokane, WA 99206
(509)928-0332
Fax: (509)921-0842
E-mail: bpci@nextdim.com

West Virginia

**Stanley & Associates Inc./
BusinessandMarketingPlans.com**
1687 Robert C. Byrd Dr.
Beckley, WV 25801
(304)252-0324
Free: 888-752-6720
Fax: (304)252-0470
E-mail: cclay@charterinternet.com
Website: http://www.Businessand
MarketingPlans.com
Christopher Clay

Wisconsin

White & Associates Inc.
5349 Somerset Ln. S
Greenfield, WI 53221
(414)281-7373
Fax: (414)281-7006
E-mail: wnaconsult@aol.com

Small business administration regional offices

This section contains a listing of Small Business Administration offices arranged numerically by region. Service areas are provided. Contact the appropriate office for a referral to the nearest field office, or visit the Small Business Administration online at www.sba.gov.

Region 1

U.S. Small Business Administration
Region I Office
10 Causeway St., Ste. 812
Boston, MA 02222-1093
Phone: (617)565-8415
Fax: (617)565-8420
Serves Connecticut, Maine, Massachusetts, New Hampshire, Rhode Island, and Vermont.

Region 2

U.S. Small Business Administration
Region II Office
26 Federal Plaza, Ste. 3108
New York, NY 10278
Phone: (212)264-1450
Fax: (212)264-0038
Serves New Jersey, New York, Puerto Rico, and the Virgin Islands.

Region 3

U.S. Small Business Administration
Region III Office
Robert N C Nix Sr. Federal Building
900 Market St., 5th Fl.
Philadelphia, PA 19107
(215)580-2807
Serves Delaware, the District of Columbia, Maryland, Pennsylvania, Virginia, and West Virginia.

Region 4

U.S. Small Business Administration
Region IV Office
233 Peachtree St. NE
Harris Tower 1800
Atlanta, GA 30303
Phone: (404)331-4999
Fax: (404)331-2354
Serves Alabama, Florida, Georgia, Kentucky, Mississippi, North Carolina, South Carolina, and Tennessee.

Region 5

U.S. Small Business Administration
Region V Office
500 W. Madison St.
Citicorp Center, Ste. 1240
Chicago, IL 60661-2511
Phone: (312)353-0357
Fax: (312)353-3426
Serves Illinois, Indiana, Michigan, Minnesota, Ohio, and Wisconsin.

Region 6

U.S. Small Business Administration
Region VI Office
4300 Amon Carter Blvd., Ste. 108
Fort Worth, TX 76155
Phone: (817)684-5581
Fax: (817)684-5588
Serves Arkansas, Louisiana, New Mexico, Oklahoma, and Texas.

Region 7

U.S. Small Business Administration
Region VII Office
323 W. 8th St., Ste. 307
Kansas City, MO 64105-1500
Phone: (816)374-6380
Fax: (816)374-6339
Serves Iowa, Kansas, Missouri, and Nebraska.

Region 8

U.S. Small Business Administration
Region VIII Office
721 19th St., Ste. 400
Denver, CO 80202
Phone: (303)844-0500
Fax: (303)844-0506
Serves Colorado, Montana, North Dakota, South Dakota, Utah, and Wyoming.

Region 9

U.S. Small Business Administration
Region IX Office
330 N Brand Blvd., Ste. 1270
Glendale, CA 91203-2304
Phone: (818)552-3434
Fax: (818)552-3440
Serves American Samoa, Arizona, California, Guam, Hawaii, Nevada, and the Trust Territory of the Pacific Islands.

Region 10

U.S. Small Business Administration
Region X Office
2401 Fourth Ave., Ste. 400
Seattle, WA 98121
Phone: (206)553-5676
Fax: (206)553-4155
Serves Alaska, Idaho, Oregon, and
Washington.

Small business development centers

This section contains a listing of all Small Business Development Centers, organized alphabetically by state/U.S. territory, then by city, then by agency name.

Alabama

Alabama SBDC
UNIVERSITY OF ALABAMA
2800 Milan Court Suite 124
Birmingham, AL 35211-6908
Phone: 205-943-6750
Fax: 205-943-6752
E-Mail: wcampbell@provost.uab.edu
Website: http://www.asbdc.org
Mr. William Campbell Jr,
State Director

Alaska

Alaska SBDC
UNIVERSITY OF ALASKA - ANCHORAGE
430 West Seventh Avenue, Suite 110
Anchorage, AK 99501
Phone: 907-274 -7232
Fax: 907-274-9524
E-Mail: anerw@uaa.alaska.edu
Website: http://www.aksbdc.org
Ms. Jean R. Wall, State Director

American Samoa

American Samoa SBDC
AMERICAN SAMOA COMMUNITY COLLEGE
P.O. Box 2609
Pago Pago, American Samoa 96799
Phone: 011-684-699-4830
Fax: 011-684-699-6132
E-Mail: htalex@att.net
Mr. Herbert Thweatt, Director

Arizona

Arizona SBDC
MARICOPA COUNTY COMMUNITY COLLEGE
2411 West 14th Street, Suite 132
Tempe, AZ 85281
Phone: 480-731-8720
Fax: 480-731-8729
E-Mail:
mike.york@domail.maricopa.edu
Website: http://www.dist.maricopa
.edu.sbdc
Mr. Michael York, State Director

Arkansas

Arkansas SBDC
UNIVERSITY OF ARKANSAS
2801 South University Avenue
Little Rock, AR 72204
Phone: 501-324-9043
Fax: 501-324-9049
E-Mail: jmroderick@ualr.edu
Website: http://asbdc.ualr.edu
Ms. Janet M. Roderick, State Director

California

California - San Francisco SBDC
Northern California SBDC Lead Center
HUMBOLDT STATE UNIVERSITY
Office of Economic Development
1 Harpst Street 2006A, Siemens Hall
Arcata, CA, 95521
Phone: 707-826-3922
Fax: 707-826-3206
E-Mail: gainer@humboldt.edu
Ms. Margaret A. Gainer, Regional
Director

California - Sacramento SBDC
CALIFORNIA STATE UNIVERSITY - CHICO
Chico, CA 95929-0765
Phone: 530-898-4598
Fax: 530-898-4734
E-Mail: dripke@csuchico.edu
Website: http://gsbdc.csuchico.edu
Mr. Dan Ripke, Interim Regional
Director

California - San Diego SBDC
SOUTHWESTERN COMMUNITY COLLEGE DISTRICT
900 Otey Lakes Road
Chula Vista, CA 91910
Phone: 619-482-6388
Fax: 619-482-6402

E-Mail: dtrujillo@swc.cc.ca.us
Website: http://www.sbditc.org
Ms. Debbie P. Trujillo, Regional Director

California - Fresno SBDC
UC Merced Lead Center
UNIVERSITY OF CALIFORNIA - MERCED
550 East Shaw, Suite 105A
Fresno, CA 93710
Phone: 559-241-6590
Fax: 559-241-7422
E-Mail: crosander@ucmerced.edu
Website: http://sbdc.ucmerced.edu
Mr. Chris Rosander, State Director

California - Santa Ana SBDC
Tri-County Lead SBDC
CALIFORNIA STATE UNIVERSITY - FULLERTON
800 North State College Boulevard,
LH640
Fullerton, CA 92834
Phone: 714-278-2719
Fax: 714-278-7858
E-Mail: vpham@fullerton.edu
Website: http://www.leadsbdc.org
Ms. Vi Pham, Lead Center Director

California - Los Angeles Region SBDC
LONG BEACH COMMUNITY COLLEGE DISTRICT
3950 Paramount Boulevard, Ste 101
Lakewood, CA 90712
Phone: 562-938-5004
Fax: 562-938-5030
E-Mail: ssloan@lbcc.edu
Ms. Sheneui Sloan, Interim Lead Center
Director

Colorado

Colorado SBDC
OFFICE OF ECONOMIC DEVELOPMENT
1625 Broadway, Suite 170
Denver, CO 80202
Phone: 303-892-3864
Fax: 303-892-3848
E-Mail: Kelly.Manning@state.co.us
Website: http://www.state.co.us/oed/sbdc
Ms. Kelly Manning, State Director

Connecticut

Connecticut SBDC
UNIVERSITY OF CONNECTICUT
1376 Storrs Road, Unit 4094
Storrs, CT 06269-1094
Phone: 860-870-6370

Organizations, Agencies, & Consultants

Fax: 860-870-6374
E-Mail: richard.cheney@uconn.edu
Website: http://www.sbdc.uconn.edu
Mr. Richard Cheney, Interim State
Director

Delaware

Delaware SBDC
DELAWARE TECHNOLOGY PARK
1 Innovation Way, Suite 301
Newark, DE 19711
Phone: 302-831-2747
Fax: 302-831-1423
E-Mail: Clinton.tymes@mvs.udel.edu
Website: http://www.delawaresbdc.org
Mr. Clinton Tymes, State Director

District of Columbia

District of Columbia SBDC
HOWARD UNIVERSITY
2600 6th Street, NW Room 128
Washington, DC 20059
Phone: 202-806-1550
Fax: 202-806-1777
E-Mail: hturner@howard.edu
Website: http://www.dcsbdc.com/
Mr. Henry Turner, Executive Director

Florida

Florida SBDC
UNIVERSITY OF WEST FLORIDA
401 East Chase Street, Suite 100
Pensacola, FL 32502
Phone: 850-473-7800
Fax: 850-473-7813
E-Mail: jcartwri@uwf.edu
Website: http://www.floridasbdc.com
Mr. Jerry Cartwright, State Director

Georgia

Georgia SBDC
UNIVERSITY OF GEORGIA
1180 East Broad Street
Athens, GA 30602
Phone: 706-542-6762
Fax: 706-542-6776
E-mail: aadams@sbdc.uga.edu
Website: http://www.sbdc.uga.edu
Mr. Allan Adams, Interim State Director

Guam

Guam Small Business Development Center
UNIVERSITY OF GUAM
Pacific Islands SBDC

P.O. Box 5014 - U.O.G. Station
Mangilao, GU 96923
Phone: 671-735-2590
Fax: 671-734-2002
E-mail: casey@pacificsbdc.com
Website: http://www.uog.edu/sbdc
Mr. Casey Jeszenka, Director

Hawaii

Hawaii SBDC
UNIVERSITY OF HAWAII - HILO
308 Kamehameha Avenue, Suite 201
Hilo, HI 96720
Phone: 808-974-7515
Fax: 808-974-7683
E-Mail: darrylm@interpac.net
Website: http://www.hawaii-sbdc.org
Mr. Darryl Mleynek, State Director

Idaho

Idaho SBDC
BOISE STATE UNIVERSITY
1910 University Drive
Boise, ID 83725
Phone: 208-426-3799
Fax: 208-426-3877
E-mail: jhogge@boisestate.edu
Website: http://www.idahosbdc.org
Mr. Jim Hogge, State Director

Illinois

Illinois SBDC
DEPARTMENT OF COMMERCE AND ECONOMIC OPPORTUNITY
620 E. Adams, S-4
Springfield, IL 62701
Phone: 217-524-5700
Fax: 217-524-0171
E-mail: mpatrilli@ildceo.net
Website: http://www.ilsbdc.biz
Mr. Mark Petrilli, State Director

Indiana

Indiana SBDC
INDIANA ECONOMIC DEVELOPMENT CORPORATION
One North Capitol, Suite 900
Indianapolis, IN 46204
Phone: 317-234-8872
Fax: 317-232-8874
E-mail: dtrocha@isbdc.org
Website: http://www.isbdc.org
Ms. Debbie Bishop Trocha, State Director

Iowa

Iowa SBDC
IOWA STATE UNIVERSITY
340 Gerdin Business Bldg.
Ames, IA 50011-1350
Phone: 515-294-2037
Fax: 515-294-6522
E-Mail: jonryan@iastate.edu
Website: http://www.iabusnet.org
Mr. Jon Ryan, State Director

Kansas

Kansas SBDC
FORT HAYS STATE UNIVERSITY
214 SW Sixth Street, Suite 301
Topeka, KS 66603
Phone: 785-296-6514
Fax: 785-291-3261
E-mail: ksbdc.wkearns@fhsu.edu
Website: http://www.fhsu.edu/ksbdc
Mr. Wally Kearns, State Director

Kentucky

Kentucky SBDC
UNIVERSITY OF KENTUCKY
225 Gatton College of Business
Economics Building
Lexington, KY 40506-0034
Phone: 859-257-7668
Fax: 859-323-1907
E-mail: lrnaug0@pop.uky.edu
Website: http://www.ksbdc.org
Ms. Becky Naugle, State Director

Louisiana

Louisiana SBDC
UNIVERSITY OF LOUISIANA - MONROE
College of Business Administration
700 University Avenue
Monroe, LA 71209
Phone: 318-342-5506
Fax: 318-342-5510
E-mail: wilkerson@ulm.edu
Website: http://www.lsbdc.org
Ms. Mary Lynn Wilkerson, State Director

Maine

Maine SBDC
UNIVERSITY OF SOUTHERN MAINE
96 Falmouth Street P.O. Box 9300
Portland, ME 04103
Phone: 207-780-4420
Fax: 207-780-4810

E-mail: jrmassaua@maine.edu
Website: http://www.mainesbdc.org
Mr. John Massaua, State Director

Maryland

Maryland SBDC
UNIVERSITY OF MARYLAND
7100 Baltimore Avenue, Suite 401
College Park, MD 20742
Phone: 301-403-8300
Fax: 301-403-8303
E-mail: rsprow@mdsbdc.umd.edu
Website: http://www.mdsbdc.umd.edu
Ms. Renee Sprow, State Director

Massachusetts

Massachusetts SBDC
UNIVERSITY OF MASSACHUSETTS
School of Management, Room 205
Amherst, MA 01003-4935
Phone: 413-545-6301
Fax: 413-545-1273
E-mail: gep@msbdc.umass.edu
Website: http://msbdc.som.umass.edu
Ms. Georgianna Parkin, State Director

Michigan

Michigan SBTDC
GRAND VALLEY STATE UNIVERSITY
510 West Fulton Avenue
Grand Rapids, MI 49504
Phone: 616-331-7485
Fax: 616-331-7389
E-mail: lopuckic@gvsu.edu
Website: http://www.misbtdc.org
Ms. Carol Lopucki, State Director

Minnesota

Minnesota SBDC
MINNESOTA SMALL BUSINESS DEVELOPMENT CENTER
1st National Bank Building
332 Minnesota Street, Suite E200
St. Paul, MN 55101-1351
Phone: 651-297-5773
Fax: 651-296-5287
E-mail: michael.myhre@state.mn.us
Website: http://www.mnsbdc.com
Mr. Michael Myhre, State Director

Mississippi

Mississippi SBDC
UNIVERSITY OF MISSISSIPPI
B-19 Jeanette Phillips Drive
P.O. Box 1848

University, MS 38677
Phone: 662-915-5001
Fax: 662-915-5650
E-mail: wgurley@olemiss.edu
Website: http://www.olemiss.edu/depts/mssbdc
Mr. Doug Gurley, Jr., State Director

Missouri

Missouri SBDC
UNIVERSITY OF MISSOURI
1205 University Avenue, Suite 300
Columbia, MO 65211
Phone: 573-882-1348
Fax: 573-884-4297
E-mail: summersm@missouri.edu
Website: http://www.mo-sbdc.org/index.shtml
Mr. Max Summers, State Director

Montana

Montana SBDC
DEPARTMENT OF COMMERCE
301 South Park Avenue, Room 114 / P.O. Box 200505
Helena, MT 59620
Phone: 406-841-2746
Fax: 406-444-1872
E-mail: adesch@state.mt.us
Website: http://commerce.state.mt.us/brd/BRD_SBDC.html
Ms. Ann Desch, State Director

Nebraska

Nebraska SBDC
UNIVERSITY OF NEBRASKA - OMAHA
60th & Dodge Street, CBA Room 407
Omaha, NE 68182
Phone: 402-554-2521
Fax: 402-554-3473
E-mail: rbernier@unomaha.edu
Website: http://nbdc.unomaha.edu
Mr. Robert Bernier, State Director

Nevada

Nevada SBDC
UNIVERSITY OF NEVADA - RENO
Reno College of Business
Administration, Room 411
Reno, NV 89557-0100
Phone: 775-784-1717
Fax: 775-784-4337
E-mail: males@unr.edu
Website: http://www.nsbdc.org
Mr. Sam Males, State Director

New Hampshire

New Hampshire SBDC
UNIVERSITY OF NEW HAMPSHIRE
108 McConnell Hall
Durham, NH 03824-3593
Phone: 603-862-4879
Fax: 603-862-4876
E-mail: Mary.Collins@unh.edu
Website: http://www.nhsbdc.org
Ms. Mary Collins, State Director

New Jersey

New Jersey SBDC
RUTGERS UNIVERSITY
49 Bleeker Street
Newark, NJ 07102-1993
Phone: 973-353-5950
Fax: 973-353-1110
E-mail: bhopper@njsbdc.com
Website: http://www.njsbdc.com/home
Ms. Brenda Hopper, State Director

New Mexico

New Mexico SBDC
SANTA FE COMMUNITY COLLEGE
6401 Richards Avenue
Santa Fe, NM 87505
Phone: 505-428-1362
Fax: 505-471-9469
E-mail: rmiller@santa-fe.cc.nm.us
Website: http://www.nmsbdc.org
Mr. Roy Miller, State Director

New York

New York SBDC
STATE UNIVERSITY OF NEW YORK
SUNY Plaza, S-523
Albany, NY 12246
Phone: 518-443-5398
Fax: 518-443-5275
E-mail: j.king@nyssbdc.org
Website: http://www.nyssbdc.org
Mr. Jim King, State Director

North Carolina

North Carolina SBDTC
UNIVERSITY OF NORTH CAROLINA
5 West Hargett Street, Suite 600
Raleigh, NC 27601
Phone: 919-715-7272
Fax: 919-715-7777
E-mail: sdaugherty@sbtdc.org
Website: http://www.sbtdc.org
Mr. Scott Daugherty, State Director

North Dakota

North Dakota SBDC
UNIVERSITY OF NORTH DAKOTA
1600 E. Century Avenue, Suite 2
Bismarck, ND 58503
Phone: 701-328-5375
Fax: 701-328-5320
E-mail:
christine.martin@und.nodak.edu
Website: http://www.ndsbdc.org
Ms. Christine Martin-Goldman, State
Director

Ohio

Ohio SBDC
**OHIO DEPARTMENT OF
DEVELOPMENT**
77 South High Street
Columbus, OH 43216
Phone: 614-466-5102
Fax: 614-466-0829
E-mail: mabraham@odod.state.oh.us
Website: http://www.ohiosbdc.org
Ms. Michele Abraham, State Director

Oklahoma

Oklahoma SBDC
**SOUTHEAST OKLAHOMA STATE
UNIVERSITY**
517 University, Box 2584, Station A
Durant, OK 74701
Phone: 580-745-7577
Fax: 580-745-7471
E-mail: gpennington@sosu.edu
Website: http://www.osbdc.org
Mr. Grady Pennington, State Director

Oregon

Oregon SBDC
LANE COMMUNITY COLLEGE
99 West Tenth Avenue, Suite 390
Eugene, OR 97401-3021
Phone: 541-463-5250
Fax: 541-345-6006
E-mail: carterb@lanecc.edu
Website: http://www.bizcenter.org
Mr. William Carter, State Director

Pennsylvania

Pennsylvania SBDC
UNIVERSITY OF PENNSYLVANIA
The Wharton School
3733 Spruce Street
Philadelphia, PA 19104-6374

Phone: 215-898-1219
Fax: 215-573-2135
E-mail: ghiggins@wharton.upenn.edu
Website: http://pasbdc.org
Mr. Gregory Higgins, State Director

Puerto Rico

Puerto Rico SBDC
**INTER-AMERICAN UNIVERSITY OF
PUERTO RICO**
416 Ponce de Leon Avenue, Union Plaza,
Seventh Floor
Hato Rey, PR 00918
Phone: 787-763-6811
Fax: 787-763-4629
E-mail: cmarti@prsbdc.org
Website: http://www.prsbdc.org
Ms. Carmen Marti, Executive Director

Rhode Island

Rhode Island SBDC
BRYANT UNIVERSITY
1150 Douglas Pike
Smithfield, RI 02917
Phone: 401-232-6923
Fax: 401-232-6933
E-mail: adawson@bryant.edu
Website: http://www.risbdc.org
Ms. Diane Fournaris, Interim State
Director

South Carolina

South Carolina SBDC
UNIVERSITY OF SOUTH CAROLINA
College of Business Administration
1710 College Street
Columbia, SC 29208
Phone: 803-777-4907
Fax: 803-777-4403
E-mail: lenti@moore.sc.edu
Website: http://scsbdc.moore.sc.edu
Mr. John Lenti, State Director

South Dakota

South Dakota SBDC
UNIVERSITY OF SOUTH DAKOTA
414 East Clark Street, Patterson Hall
Vermillion, SD 57069
Phone: 605-677-6256
Fax: 605-677-5427
E-mail: jshemmin@usd.edu
Website: http://www.sdsbdc.org
Mr. John S. Hemmingstad, State
Director

Tennessee

Tennessee SBDC
**TENNESSEE BOARD OF
REGENTS**
1415 Murfressboro Road, Suite 540
Nashville, TN 37217-2833
Phone: 615-898-2745
Fax: 615-893-7089
E-mail: pgeho@mail.tsbdc.org
Website: http://www.tsbdc.org
Mr. Patrick Geho, State Director

Texas

Texas-North SBDC
**DALLAS COUNTY COMMUNITY
COLLEGE**
1402 Corinth Street
Dallas, TX 75215
Phone: 214-860-5835
Fax: 214-860-5813
E-mail: emk9402@dcccd.edu
Website: http://www.ntsbdc.org
Ms. Liz Klimback, Region Director

Texas-Houston SBDC
UNIVERSITY OF HOUSTON
2302 Fannin, Suite 200
Houston, TX 77002
Phone: 713-752-8425
Fax: 713-756-1500
E-mail: fyoung@uh.edu
Website: http://sbdcnetwork.uh.edu
Mr. Mike Young, Executive Director

Texas-NW SBDC
TEXAS TECH UNIVERSITY
2579 South Loop 289, Suite 114
Lubbock, TX 79423
Phone: 806-745-3973
Fax: 806-745-6207
E-mail: c.bean@nwtsbdc.org
Website: http://www.nwtsbdc.org
Mr. Craig Bean, Executive Director

**Texas-South-West Texas Border
Region SBDC**
**UNIVERSITY OF TEXAS - SAN
ANTONIO**
501 West Durango Boulevard
San Antonio, TX 78207-4415
Phone: 210-458-2742
Fax: 210-458-2464
E-mail: albert.salgado@utsa.edu
Website: http://www.iedtexas.org
Mr. Alberto Salgado, Region
Director

Utah

Utah SBDC
SALT LAKE COMMUNITY COLLEGE
9750 South 300 West
Sandy, UT 84070
Phone: 801-957-3493
Fax: 801-957-3488
E-mail: Greg.Panichello@slcc.edu
Website:http://www.slcc.edu/sbdc
Mr. Greg Panichello, State Director

Vermont

Vermont SBDC
VERMONT TECHNICAL COLLEGE
PO Box 188, 1 Main Street
Randolph Center, VT 05061-0188
Phone: 802-728-9101
Fax: 802-728-3026
E-mail: lquillen@vtc.edu
Website: http://www.vtsbdc.org
Ms. Lenae Quillen-Blume, State Director

Virgin Islands

Virgin Islands SBDC
UNIVERSITY OF THE VIRGIN ISLANDS
8000 Nisky Center, Suite 720
St. Thomas, VI 00802-5804
Phone: 340-776-3206
Fax: 340-775-3756
E-mail: wbush@webmail.uvi.edu
Website: http://rps.uvi.edu/SBDC
Mr. Warren Bush, State Director

Virginia

Virginia SBDC
GEORGE MASON UNIVERSITY
4031 University Drive, Suite 200
Fairfax, VA 22030-3409
Phone: 703-277-7727
Fax: 703-352-8515
E-mail: jkeenan@gmu.edu
Website: http://www.virginiasbdc.org
Ms. Jody Keenan, Director

Washington

Washington SBDC
WASHINGTON STATE UNIVERSITY
534 E. Trent Avenue
P.O. Box 1495
Spokane, WA 99210-1495
Phone: 509-358-7765
Fax: 509-358-7764
E-mail: barogers@wsu.edu
Website: http://www.wsbdc.org
Mr. Brett Rogers, State Director

West Virginia

West Virginia SBDC
WEST VIRGINIA DEVELOPMENT OFFICE
Capital Complex, Building 6, Room 652
Charleston, WV 25301
Phone: 304-558-2960
Fax: 304-558-0127
E-mail: csalyer@wvsbdc.org
Website: http://www.wvsbdc.org
Mr. Conley Salyor, State Director

Wisconsin

Wisconsin SBDC
UNIVERSITY OF WISCONSIN
432 North Lake Street, Room 423
Madison, WI 53706
Phone: 608-263-7794
Fax: 608-263-7830
E-mail: erica.kauten@uwex.edu
Website: http://www.wisconsinsbdc.org
Ms. Erica Kauten, State Director

Wyoming

Wyoming SBDC
UNIVERSITY OF WYOMING
P.O. Box 3922
Laramie, WY 82071-3922
Phone: 307-766-3505
Fax: 307-766-3406
E-mail: DDW@uwyo.edu
Website: http://www.uwyo.edu/sbdc
Ms. Debbie Popp, Acting State Director

Service corps of retired executives (score) offices

This section contains a listing of all SCORE offices organized alphabetically by state/U.S. territory, then by city, then by agency name.

Alabama

SCORE Office (Northeast Alabama)
1330 Quintard Ave.
Anniston, AL 36202
(256)237-3536

SCORE Office (North Alabama)
901 South 15th St, Rm. 201
Birmingham, AL 35294-2060
(205)934-6868
Fax: (205)934-0538

SCORE Office (Baldwin County)
29750 Larry Dee Cawyer Dr.
Daphne, AL 36526
(334)928-5838

SCORE Office (Shoals)
612 S. COurt
Florence, AL 35630
(256)764-4661
Fax: (256)766-9017
E-mail: shoals@shoalschamber.com

SCORE Office (Mobile)
600 S Court St.
Mobile, AL 36104
(334)240-6868
Fax: (334)240-6869

SCORE Office (Alabama Capitol City)
600 S. Court St.
Montgomery, AL 36104
(334)240-6868
Fax: (334)240-6869

SCORE Office (East Alabama)
601 Ave. A
Opelika, AL 36801
(334)745-4861
E-mail: score636@hotmail.com
Website: http://www.angelfire.com/sc/score636/

SCORE Office (Tuscaloosa)
2200 University Blvd.
Tuscaloosa, AL 35402
(205)758-7588

Alaska

SCORE Office (Anchorage)
510 L St., Ste. 310
Anchorage, AK 99501
(907)271-4022
Fax: (907)271-4545

Arizona

SCORE Office (Lake Havasu)
10 S. Acoma Blvd.
Lake Havasu City, AZ 86403
(520)453-5951
E-mail: SCORE@ctaz.com
Website: http://www.scorearizona.org/lake_havasu/

SCORE Office (East Valley)
Federal Bldg., Rm. 104
26 N. MacDonald St.
Mesa, AZ 85201
(602)379-3100
Fax: (602)379-3143

Organizations, Agencies, & Consultants

E-mail: 402@aol.com
Website: http://www.scorearizona.org/
mesa/

SCORE Office (Phoenix)
2828 N. Central Ave., Ste. 800
Central & One Thomas
Phoenix, AZ 85004
(602)640-2329
Fax: (602)640-2360
E-mail: e-mail@SCORE-phoenix.org
Website: http://www.score-phoenix.org/

SCORE Office (Prescott Arizona)
1228 Willow Creek Rd., Ste. 2
Prescott, AZ 86301
(520)778-7438
Fax: (520)778-0812
E-mail: score@northlink.com
Website: http://www.scorearizona.org/
prescott/

SCORE Office (Tucson)
110 E. Pennington St.
Tucson, AZ 85702
(520)670-5008
Fax: (520)670-5011
E-mail: score@azstarnet.com
Website: http://www.scorearizona.org/
tucson/

SCORE Office (Yuma)
281 W. 24th St., Ste. 116
Yuma, AZ 85364
(520)314-0480
E-mail: score@C2i2.com
Website: http://www.scorearizona.org/
yuma

Arkansas

SCORE Office (South Central)
201 N. Jackson Ave.
El Dorado, AR 71730-5803
(870)863-6113
Fax: (870)863-6115

SCORE Office (Ozark)
Fayetteville, AR 72701
(501)442-7619

SCORE Office (Northwest Arkansas)
Glenn Haven Dr., No. 4
Ft. Smith, AR 72901
(501)783-3556

SCORE Office (Garland County)
Grand & Ouachita
PO Box 6012
Hot Springs Village, AR 71902
(501)321-1700

SCORE Office (Little Rock)
2120 Riverfront Dr., Rm. 100
Little Rock, AR 72202-1747
(501)324-5893
Fax: (501)324-5199

SCORE Office (Southeast Arkansas)
121 W. 6th
Pine Bluff, AR 71601
(870)535-7189
Fax: (870)535-1643

California

SCORE Office (Golden Empire)
1706 Chester Ave., No. 200
Bakersfield, CA 93301
(805)322-5881
Fax: (805)322-5663

SCORE Office (Greater Chico Area)
1324 Mangrove St., Ste. 114
Chico, CA 95926
(916)342-8932
Fax: (916)342-8932

SCORE Office (Concord)
2151-A Salvio St., Ste. B
Concord, CA 94520
(510)685-1181
Fax: (510)685-5623

SCORE Office (Covina)
935 W. Badillo St.
Covina, CA 91723
(818)967-4191
Fax: (818)966-9660

**SCORE Office
(Rancho Cucamonga)**
8280 Utica, Ste. 160
Cucamonga, CA 91730
(909)987-1012
Fax: (909)987-5917

SCORE Office (Culver City)
PO Box 707
Culver City, CA 90232-0707
(310)287-3850
Fax: (310)287-1350

SCORE Office (Danville)
380 Diablo Rd., Ste. 103
Danville, CA 94526
(510)837-4400

SCORE Office (Downey)
11131 Brookshire Ave.
Downey, CA 90241
(310)923-2191
Fax: (310)864-0461

SCORE Office (El Cajon)
109 Rea Ave.
El Cajon, CA 92020
(619)444-1327
Fax: (619)440-6164

SCORE Office (El Centro)
1100 Main St.
El Centro, CA 92243
(619)352-3681
Fax: (619)352-3246

SCORE Office (Escondido)
720 N. Broadway
Escondido, CA 92025
(619)745-2125
Fax: (619)745-1183

SCORE Office (Fairfield)
1111 Webster St.
Fairfield, CA 94533
(707)425-4625
Fax: (707)425-0826

SCORE Office (Fontana)
17009 Valley Blvd., Ste. B
Fontana, CA 92335
(909)822-4433
Fax: (909)822-6238

SCORE Office (Foster City)
1125 E. Hillsdale Blvd.
Foster City, CA 94404
(415)573-7600
Fax: (415)573-5201

SCORE Office (Fremont)
2201 Walnut Ave., Ste. 110
Fremont, CA 94538
(510)795-2244
Fax: (510)795-2240

SCORE Office (Central California)
2719 N. Air Fresno Dr., Ste. 200
Fresno, CA 93727-1547
(559)487-5605
Fax: (559)487-5636

SCORE Office (Gardena)
1204 W. Gardena Blvd.
Gardena, CA 90247
(310)532-9905
Fax: (310)515-4893

SCORE Office (Lompoc)
330 N. Brand Blvd., Ste. 190
Glendale, CA 91203-2304
(818)552-3206
Fax: (818)552-3323

SCORE Office (Los Angeles)
330 N. Brand Blvd., Ste. 190

Glendale, CA 91203-2304
(818)552-3206
Fax: (818)552-3323

SCORE Office (Glendora)
131 E. Foothill Blvd.
Glendora, CA 91740
(818)963-4128
Fax: (818)914-4822

SCORE Office (Grover Beach)
177 S. 8th St.
Grover Beach, CA 93433
(805)489-9091
Fax: (805)489-9091

SCORE Office (Hawthorne)
12477 Hawthorne Blvd.
Hawthorne, CA 90250
(310)676-1163
Fax: (310)676-7661

SCORE Office (Hayward)
22300 Foothill Blvd., Ste. 303
Hayward, CA 94541
(510)537-2424

SCORE Office (Hemet)
1700 E. Florida Ave.
Hemet, CA 92544-4679
(909)652-4390
Fax: (909)929-8543

SCORE Office (Hesperia)
16367 Main St.
PO Box 403656
Hesperia, CA 92340
(619)244-2135

SCORE Office (Holloster)
321 San Felipe Rd., No. 11
Hollister, CA 95023

SCORE Office (Hollywood)
7018 Hollywood Blvd.
Hollywood, CA 90028
(213)469-8311
Fax: (213)469-2805

SCORE Office (Indio)
82503 Hwy. 111
PO Drawer TTT
Indio, CA 92202
(619)347-0676

SCORE Office (Inglewood)
330 Queen St.
Inglewood, CA 90301
(818)552-3206

SCORE Office (La Puente)
218 N. Grendanda St. D.

La Puente, CA 91744
(818)330-3216
Fax: (818)330-9524

SCORE Office (La Verne)
2078 Bonita Ave.
La Verne, CA 91750
(909)593-5265
Fax: (714)929-8475

**SCORE Office
(Lake Elsinore)**
132 W. Graham Ave.
Lake Elsinore, CA 92530
(909)674-2577

SCORE Office (Lakeport)
PO Box 295
Lakeport, CA 95453
(707)263-5092

SCORE Office (Lakewood)
5445 E. Del Amo Blvd., Ste. 2
Lakewood, CA 90714
(213)920-7737

SCORE Office (Long Beach)
1 World Trade Center
Long Beach, CA 90831

SCORE Office (Los Alamitos)
901 W. Civic Center Dr., Ste. 160
Los Alamitos, CA 90720

SCORE Office (Los Altos)
321 University Ave.
Los Altos, CA 94022
(415)948-1455

SCORE Office (Manhattan Beach)
PO Box 3007
Manhattan Beach, CA 90266
(310)545-5313
Fax: (310)545-7203

SCORE Office (Merced)
1632 N. St.
Merced, CA 95340
(209)725-3800
Fax: (209)383-4959

SCORE Office (Milpitas)
75 S. Milpitas Blvd., Ste. 205
Milpitas, CA 95035
(408)262-2613
Fax: (408)262-2823

SCORE Office (Yosemite)
1012 11th St., Ste. 300
Modesto, CA 95354
(209)521-9333

SCORE Office (Montclair)
5220 Benito Ave.
Montclair, CA 91763

SCORE Office (Monterey Bay)
380 Alvarado St.
PO Box 1770
Monterey, CA 93940-1770
(408)649-1770

SCORE Office (Moreno Valley)
25480 Alessandro
Moreno Valley, CA 92553

SCORE Office (Morgan Hill)
25 W. 1st St.
PO Box 786
Morgan Hill, CA 95038
(408)779-9444
Fax: (408)778-1786

SCORE Office (Morro Bay)
880 Main St.
Morro Bay, CA 93442
(805)772-4467

SCORE Office (Mountain View)
580 Castro St.
Mountain View, CA 94041
(415)968-8378
Fax: (415)968-5668

SCORE Office (Napa)
1556 1st St.
Napa, CA 94559
(707)226-7455
Fax: (707)226-1171

SCORE Office (North Hollywood)
5019 Lankershim Blvd.
North Hollywood, CA 91601
(818)552-3206

SCORE Office (Northridge)
8801 Reseda Blvd.
Northridge, CA 91324
(818)349-5676

SCORE Office (Novato)
807 De Long Ave.
Novato, CA 94945
(415)897-1164
Fax: (415)898-9097

SCORE Office (East Bay)
519 17th St.
Oakland, CA 94612
(510)273-6611
Fax: (510)273-6015
E-mail: webmaster@eastbayscore.org
Website: http://www.eastbayscore.org

SCORE Office (Oceanside)
928 N. Coast Hwy.
Oceanside, CA 92054
(619)722-1534

SCORE Office (Ontario)
121 West B. St.
Ontario, CA 91762
Fax: (714)984-6439

SCORE Office (Oxnard)
PO Box 867
Oxnard, CA 93032
(805)385-8860
Fax: (805)487-1763

SCORE Office (Pacifica)
450 Dundee Way, Ste. 2
Pacifica, CA 94044
(415)355-4122

SCORE Office (Palm Desert)
72990 Hwy. 111
Palm Desert, CA 92260
(619)346-6111
Fax: (619)346-3463

SCORE Office (Palm Springs)
650 E. Tahquitz Canyon
Way Ste. D
Palm Springs, CA 92262-6706
(760)320-6682
Fax: (760)323-9426

SCORE Office (Lakeside)
2150 Low Tree
Palmdale, CA 93551
(805)948-4518
Fax: (805)949-1212

SCORE Office (Palo Alto)
325 Forest Ave.
Palo Alto, CA 94301
(415)324-3121
Fax: (415)324-1215

SCORE Office (Pasadena)
117 E. Colorado Blvd., Ste. 100
Pasadena, CA 91105
(818)795-3355
Fax: (818)795-5663

SCORE Office (Paso Robles)
1225 Park St.
Paso Robles, CA 93446-2234
(805)238-0506
Fax: (805)238-0527

SCORE Office (Petaluma)
799 Baywood Dr., Ste. 3
Petaluma, CA 94954
(707)762-2785
Fax: (707)762-4721

SCORE Office (Pico Rivera)
9122 E. Washington Blvd.
Pico Rivera, CA 90660

SCORE Office (Pittsburg)
2700 E. Leland Rd.
Pittsburg, CA 94565
(510)439-2181
Fax: (510)427-1599

SCORE Office (Pleasanton)
777 Peters Ave.
Pleasanton, CA 94566
(510)846-9697

SCORE Office (Monterey Park)
485 N. Garey
Pomona, CA 91769

SCORE Office (Pomona)
485 N. Garey Ave.
Pomona, CA 91766
(909)622-1256

SCORE Office (Antelope Valley)
4511 West Ave. M-4
Quartz Hill, CA 93536
(805)272-0087
E-mail: avscore@ptw.com
Website: http://www.score.av.org/

SCORE Office (Shasta)
737 Auditorium Dr.
Redding, CA 96099
(916)225-2770

SCORE Office (Redwood City)
1675 Broadway
Redwood City, CA 94063
(415)364-1722
Fax: (415)364-1729

SCORE Office (Richmond)
3925 MacDonald Ave.
Richmond, CA 94805

SCORE Office (Ridgecrest)
PO Box 771
Ridgecrest, CA 93555
(619)375-8331
Fax: (619)375-0365

SCORE Office (Riverside)
3685 Main St., Ste. 350
Riverside, CA 92501
(909)683-7100

SCORE Office (Sacramento)
9845 Horn Rd., 260-B
Sacramento, CA 95827

(916)361-2322
Fax: (916)361-2164
E-mail: sacchapter@directcon.net

SCORE Office (Salinas)
PO Box 1170
Salinas, CA 93902
(408)424-7611
Fax: (408)424-8639

SCORE Office (Inland Empire)
777 E. Rialto Ave.
Purchasing
San Bernardino, CA 92415-0760
(909)386-8278

SCORE Office (San Carlos)
San Carlos Chamber of Commerce
PO Box 1086
San Carlos, CA 94070
(415)593-1068
Fax: (415)593-9108

SCORE Office (Encinitas)
550 W. C St., Ste. 550
San Diego, CA 92101-3540
(619)557-7272
Fax: (619)557-5894

SCORE Office (San Diego)
550 West C. St., Ste. 550
San Diego, CA 92101-3540
(619)557-7272
Fax: (619)557-5894
Website: http://www.score-sandiego.org

SCORE Office (Menlo Park)
1100 Merrill St.
San Francisco, CA 94105
(415)325-2818
Fax: (415)325-0920

SCORE Office (San Francisco)
455 Market St., 6th Fl.
San Francisco, CA 94105
(415)744-6827
Fax: (415)744-6750
E-mail: sfscore@sfscore.
Website: http://www.sfscore.com

SCORE Office (San Gabriel)
401 W. Las Tunas Dr.
San Gabriel, CA 91776
(818)576-2525
Fax: (818)289-2901

SCORE Office (San Jose)
Deanza College
208 S. 1st. St., Ste. 137
San Jose, CA 95113

(408)288-8479
Fax: (408)535-5541

SCORE Office (Silicon Valley)
84 W. Santa Clara St., Ste. 100
San Jose, CA 95113
(408)288-8479
Fax: (408)535-5541
E-mail: info@svscore.org
Website: http://www.svscore.org

SCORE Office (San Luis Obispo)
3566 S. Hiquera, No. 104
San Luis Obispo, CA 93401
(805)547-0779

SCORE Office (San Mateo)
1021 S. El Camino, 2nd Fl.
San Mateo, CA 94402
(415)341-5679

SCORE Office (San Pedro)
390 W. 7th St.
San Pedro, CA 90731
(310)832-7272

SCORE Office (Orange County)
200 W. Santa Anna Blvd., Ste. 700
Santa Ana, CA 92701
(714)550-7369
Fax: (714)550-0191
Website: http://www.score114.org

SCORE Office (Santa Barbara)
3227 State St.
Santa Barbara, CA 93130
(805)563-0084

SCORE Office (Central Coast)
509 W. Morrison Ave.
Santa Maria, CA 93454
(805)347-7755

SCORE Office (Santa Maria)
614 S. Broadway
Santa Maria, CA 93454-5111
(805)925-2403
Fax: (805)928-7559

SCORE Office (Santa Monica)
501 Colorado, Ste. 150
Santa Monica, CA 90401
(310)393-9825
Fax: (310)394-1868

SCORE Office (Santa Rosa)
777 Sonoma Ave., Rm. 115E
Santa Rosa, CA 95404
(707)571-8342
Fax: (707)541-0331
Website: http://www.pressdemo.com/
community/score/score.html

SCORE Office (Scotts Valley)
4 Camp Evers Ln.
Scotts Valley, CA 95066
(408)438-1010
Fax: (408)438-6544

SCORE Office (Simi Valley)
40 W. Cochran St., Ste. 100
Simi Valley, CA 93065
(805)526-3900
Fax: (805)526-6234

SCORE Office (Sonoma)
453 1st St. E
Sonoma, CA 95476
(707)996-1033

SCORE Office (Los Banos)
222 S. Shepard St.
Sonora, CA 95370
(209)532-4212

SCORE Office (Tuolumne County)
39 North Washington St.
Sonora, CA 95370
(209)588-0128
E-mail: score@mlode.com

SCORE Office (South San Francisco)
445 Market St., Ste. 6th Fl.
South San Francisco, CA 94105
(415)744-6827
Fax: (415)744-6812

SCORE Office (Stockton)
401 N. San Joaquin St., Rm. 215
Stockton, CA 95202
(209)946-6293

SCORE Office (Taft)
314 4th St.
Taft, CA 93268
(805)765-2165
Fax: (805)765-6639

SCORE Office (Conejo Valley)
625 W. Hillcrest Dr.
Thousand Oaks, CA 91360
(805)499-1993
Fax: (805)498-7264

SCORE Office (Torrance)
3400 Torrance Blvd., Ste. 100
Torrance, CA 90503
(310)540-5858
Fax: (310)540-7662

SCORE Office (Truckee)
PO Box 2757
Truckee, CA 96160
(916)587-2757
Fax: (916)587-2439

SCORE Office (Visalia)
113 S. M St,
Tulare, CA 93274
(209)627-0766
Fax: (209)627-8149

SCORE Office (Upland)
433 N. 2nd Ave.
Upland, CA 91786
(909)931-4108

SCORE Office (Vallejo)
2 Florida St.
Vallejo, CA 94590
(707)644-5551
Fax: (707)644-5590

SCORE Office (Van Nuys)
14540 Victory Blvd.
Van Nuys, CA 91411
(818)989-0300
Fax: (818)989-3836

SCORE Office (Ventura)
5700 Ralston St., Ste. 310
Ventura, CA 93001
(805)658-2688
Fax: (805)658-2252
E-mail: scoreven@jps.net
Website: http://www.jps.net/scoreven

SCORE Office (Vista)
201 E. Washington St.
Vista, CA 92084
(619)726-1122
Fax: (619)226-8654

SCORE Office (Watsonville)
PO Box 1748
Watsonville, CA 95077
(408)724-3849
Fax: (408)728-5300

SCORE Office (West Covina)
811 S. Sunset Ave.
West Covina, CA 91790
(818)338-8496
Fax: (818)960-0511

SCORE Office (Westlake)
30893 Thousand Oaks Blvd.
Westlake Village, CA 91362
(805)496-5630
Fax: (818)991-1754

Colorado

SCORE Office (Colorado Springs)
2 N. Cascade Ave., Ste. 110
Colorado Springs, CO 80903
(719)636-3074

Website: http://www.cscc.org/score02/
index.html

SCORE Office (Denver)
US Custom's House, 4th Fl.
721 19th St.
Denver, CO 80201-0660
(303)844-3985
Fax: (303)844-6490
E-mail: score62@csn.net
Website: http://www.sni.net/score62

SCORE Office (Tri-River)
1102 Grand Ave.
Glenwood Springs, CO 81601
(970)945-6589

SCORE Office (Grand Junction)
2591 B & 3/4 Rd.
Grand Junction, CO 81503
(970)243-5242

SCORE Office (Gunnison)
608 N. 11th
Gunnison, CO 81230
(303)641-4422

SCORE Office (Montrose)
1214 Peppertree Dr.
Montrose, CO 81401
(970)249-6080

SCORE Office (Pagosa Springs)
PO Box 4381
Pagosa Springs, CO 81157
(970)731-4890

SCORE Office (Rifle)
0854 W. Battlement Pky., Apt. C106
Parachute, CO 81635
(970)285-9390

SCORE Office (Pueblo)
302 N. Santa Fe
Pueblo, CO 81003
(719)542-1704
Fax: (719)542-1624
E-mail: mackey@iex.net
Website: http://www.pueblo.org/score

SCORE Office (Ridgway)
143 Poplar Pl.
Ridgway, CO 81432

SCORE Office (Silverton)
PO Box 480
Silverton, CO 81433
(303)387-5430

SCORE Office (Minturn)
PO Box 2066
Vail, CO 81658
(970)476-1224

Connecticut

SCORE Office (Greater Bridgeport)
230 Park Ave.
Bridgeport, CT 06601-0999
(203)576-4369
Fax: (203)576-4388

SCORE Office (Bristol)
10 Main St. 1st. Fl.
Bristol, CT 06010
(203)584-4718
Fax: (203)584-4722

SCORE office (Greater Danbury)
246 Federal Rd.
Unit LL2, Ste. 7
Brookfield, CT 06804
(203)775-1151

SCORE Office (Greater Danbury)
246 Federal Rd., Unit LL2, Ste. 7
Brookfield, CT 06804
(203)775-1151

SCORE Office (Eastern Connecticut)
Administration Bldg., Rm. 313
PO 625
61 Main St. (Chapter 579)
Groton, CT 06475
(203)388-9508

SCORE Office (Greater Hartford County)
330 Main St.
Hartford, CT 06106
(860)548-1749
Fax: (860)240-4659
Website: http://www.score56.org

SCORE Office (Manchester)
20 Hartford Rd.
Manchester, CT 06040
(203)646-2223
Fax: (203)646-5871

SCORE Office (New Britain)
185 Main St., Ste. 431
New Britain, CT 06051
(203)827-4492
Fax: (203)827-4480

SCORE Office (New Haven)
25 Science Pk., Bldg. 25, Rm. 366
New Haven, CT 06511
(203)865-7645

SCORE Office (Fairfield County)
24 Beldon Ave., 5th Fl.
Norwalk, CT 06850
(203)847-7348
Fax: (203)849-9308

SCORE Office (Old Saybrook)
146 Main St.
Old Saybrook, CT 06475
(860)388-9508

SCORE Office (Simsbury)
Box 244
Simsbury, CT 06070
(203)651-7307
Fax: (203)651-1933

SCORE Office (Torrington)
23 North Rd.
Torrington, CT 06791
(203)482-6586

Delaware

SCORE Office (Dover)
Treadway Towers
PO Box 576
Dover, DE 19903
(302)678-0892
Fax: (302)678-0189

SCORE Office (Lewes)
PO Box 1
Lewes, DE 19958
(302)645-8073
Fax: (302)645-8412

SCORE Office (Milford)
204 NE Front St.
Milford, DE 19963
(302)422-3301

SCORE Office (Wilmington)
824 Market St., Ste. 610
Wilmington, DE 19801
(302)573-6652
Fax: (302)573-6092
Website: http://www.scoredelaware.com

District of Columbia

SCORE Office (George Mason University)
409 3rd St. SW, 4th Fl.
Washington, DC 20024
800-634-0245

SCORE Office (Washington DC)
1110 Vermont Ave. NW, 9th Fl.
Washington, DC 20043
(202)606-4000
Fax: (202)606-4225
E-mail: dcscore@hotmail.com
Website: http://www.scoredc.org/

Florida

SCORE Office (Desota County Chamber of Commerce)
16 South Velucia Ave.
Arcadia, FL 34266
(941)494-4033

SCORE Office (Suncoast/Pinellas)
Airport Business Ctr.
4707 - 140th Ave. N, No. 311
Clearwater, FL 33755
(813)532-6800
Fax: (813)532-6800

SCORE Office (DeLand)
336 N. Woodland Blvd.
DeLand, FL 32720
(904)734-4331
Fax: (904)734-4333

SCORE Office (South Palm Beach)
1050 S. Federal Hwy., Ste. 132
Delray Beach, FL 33483
(561)278-7752
Fax: (561)278-0288

SCORE Office (Ft. Lauderdale)
Federal Bldg., Ste. 123
299 E. Broward Blvd.
Ft. Lauderdale, FL 33301
(954)356-7263
Fax: (954)356-7145

SCORE Office (Southwest Florida)
The Renaissance
8695 College Pky., Ste. 345 & 346
Ft. Myers, FL 33919
(941)489-2935
Fax: (941)489-1170

SCORE Office (Treasure Coast)
Professional Center, Ste. 2
3220 S. US, No. 1
Ft. Pierce, FL 34982
(561)489-0548

SCORE Office (Gainesville)
101 SE 2nd Pl., Ste. 104
Gainesville, FL 32601
(904)375-8278

SCORE Office (Hialeah Dade Chamber)
59 W. 5th St.
Hialeah, FL 33010
(305)887-1515
Fax: (305)887-2453

SCORE Office (Daytona Beach)
921 Nova Rd., Ste. A
Holly Hills, FL 32117

(904)255-6889
Fax: (904)255-0229
E-mail: score87@dbeach.com

SCORE Office (South Broward)
3475 Sheridian St., Ste. 203
Hollywood, FL 33021
(305)966-8415

SCORE Office (Citrus County)
5 Poplar Ct.
Homosassa, FL 34446
(352)382-1037

SCORE Office (Jacksonville)
7825 Baymeadows Way, Ste. 100-B
Jacksonville, FL 32256
(904)443-1911
Fax: (904)443-1980
E-mail: scorejax@juno.com
Website: http://www.scorejax.org/

SCORE Office (Jacksonville Satellite)
3 Independent Dr.
Jacksonville, FL 32256
(904)366-6600
Fax: (904)632-0617

SCORE Office (Central Florida)
5410 S. Florida Ave., No. 3
Lakeland, FL 33801
(941)687-5783
Fax: (941)687-6225

SCORE Office (Lakeland)
100 Lake Morton Dr.
Lakeland, FL 33801
(941)686-2168

SCORE Office (St. Petersburg)
800 W. Bay Dr., Ste. 505
Largo, FL 33712
(813)585-4571

SCORE Office (Leesburg)
9501 US Hwy. 441
Leesburg, FL 34788-8751
(352)365-3556
Fax: (352)365-3501

SCORE Office (Cocoa)
1600 Farno Rd., Unit 205
Melbourne, FL 32935
(407)254-2288

SCORE Office (Melbourne)
Melbourne Professional Complex
1600 Sarno, Ste. 205
Melbourne, FL 32935
(407)254-2288
Fax: (407)245-2288

SCORE Office (Merritt Island)
1600 Sarno Rd., Ste. 205
Melbourne, FL 32935
(407)254-2288
Fax: (407)254-2288

SCORE Office (Space Coast)
Melbourn Professional Complex
1600 Sarno, Ste. 205
Melbourne, FL 32935
(407)254-2288
Fax: (407)254-2288

SCORE Office (Dade)
49 NW 5th St.
Miami, FL 33128
(305)371-6889
Fax: (305)374-1882
E-mail: score@netrox.net
Website: http://www.netrox.net/~score/

SCORE Office (Naples of Collier)
International College
2654 Tamiami Trl. E
Naples, FL 34112
(941)417-1280
Fax: (941)417-1281
E-mail: score@naples.net
Website: http://www.naples.net/clubs/
score/index.htm

SCORE Office (Pasco County)
6014 US Hwy. 19, Ste. 302
New Port Richey, FL 34652
(813)842-4638

SCORE Office (Southeast Volusia)
115 Canal St.
New Smyrna Beach, FL 32168
(904)428-2449
Fax: (904)423-3512

SCORE Office (Ocala)
110 E. Silver Springs Blvd.
Ocala, FL 34470
(352)629-5959

Clay County SCORE Office
Clay County Chamber of Commerce
1734 Kingsdey Ave.
PO Box 1441
Orange Park, FL 32073
(904)264-2651
Fax: (904)269-0363

SCORE Office (Orlando)
80 N. Hughey Ave.
Rm. 445 Federal Bldg.
Orlando, FL 32801
(407)648-6476
Fax: (407)648-6425

SCORE Office (Emerald Coast)
19 W. Garden St., No. 325
Pensacola, FL 32501
(904)444-2060
Fax: (904)444-2070

SCORE Office (Charlotte County)
201 W. Marion Ave., Ste. 211
Punta Gorda, FL 33950
(941)575-1818
E-mail: score@gls3c.com
Website: http://www.charlotte-
florida.com/business/scorepg01.htm

SCORE Office (St. Augustine)
1 Riberia St.
St. Augustine, FL 32084
(904)829-5681
Fax: (904)829-6477

SCORE Office (Bradenton)
2801 Fruitville, Ste. 280
Sarasota, FL 34237
(813)955-1029

SCORE Office (Manasota)
2801 Fruitville Rd., Ste. 280
Sarasota, FL 34237
(941)955-1029
Fax: (941)955-5581
E-mail: score116@gte.net
Website: http://www.score-suncoast.org/

SCORE Office (Tallahassee)
200 W. Park Ave.
Tallahassee, FL 32302
(850)487-2665

SCORE Office (Hillsborough)
4732 Dale Mabry Hwy. N, Ste. 400
Tampa, FL 33614-6509
(813)870-0125

SCORE Office (Lake Sumter)
122 E. Main St.
Tavares, FL 32778-3810
(352)365-3556

SCORE Office (Titusville)
2000 S. Washington Ave.
Titusville, FL 32780
(407)267-3036
Fax: (407)264-0127

SCORE Office (Venice)
257 N. Tamiami Trl.
Venice, FL 34285
(941)488-2236
Fax: (941)484-5903

SCORE Office (Palm Beach)
500 Australian Ave. S, Ste. 100

West Palm Beach, FL 33401
(561)833-1672
Fax: (561)833-1712

SCORE Office (Wildwood)
103 N. Webster St.
Wildwood, FL 34785

Georgia

SCORE Office (Atlanta)
Harris Tower, Suite 1900
233 Peachtree Rd., NE
Atlanta, GA 30309
(404)347-2442
Fax: (404)347-1227

SCORE Office (Augusta)
3126 Oxford Rd.
Augusta, GA 30909
(706)869-9100

SCORE Office (Columbus)
School Bldg.
PO Box 40
Columbus, GA 31901
(706)327-3654

SCORE Office (Dalton-Whitfield)
305 S. Thorton Ave.
Dalton, GA 30720
(706)279-3383

SCORE Office (Gainesville)
PO Box 374
Gainesville, GA 30503
(770)532-6206
Fax: (770)535-8419

SCORE Office (Macon)
711 Grand Bldg.
Macon, GA 31201
(912)751-6160

SCORE Office (Brunswick)
4 Glen Ave.
St. Simons Island, GA 31520
(912)265-0620
Fax: (912)265-0629

SCORE Office (Savannah)
111 E. Liberty St., Ste. 103
Savannah, GA 31401
(912)652-4335
Fax: (912)652-4184
E-mail: info@scoresav.org
Website: http://www.coastal
empire.com/score/index.htm

Guam

SCORE Office (Guam)
Pacific News Bldg., Rm. 103
238 Archbishop Flores St.
Agana, GU 96910-5100
(671)472-7308

Hawaii

SCORE Office (Hawaii, Inc.)
1111 Bishop St., Ste. 204
PO Box 50207
Honolulu, HI 96813
(808)522-8132
Fax: (808)522-8135
E-mail: hnlscore@juno.com

SCORE Office (Kahului)
250 Alamaha, Unit N16A
Kahului, HI 96732
(808)871-7711

SCORE Office (Maui, Inc.)
590 E. Lipoa Pkwy., Ste. 227
Kihei, HI 96753
(808)875-2380

Idaho

SCORE Office (Treasure Valley)
1020 Main St., No. 290
Boise, ID 83702
(208)334-1696
Fax: (208)334-9353

SCORE Office (Eastern Idaho)
2300 N. Yellowstone, Ste. 119
Idaho Falls, ID 83401
(208)523-1022
Fax: (208)528-7127

Illinois

SCORE Office (Fox Valley)
40 W. Downer Pl.
PO Box 277
Aurora, IL 60506
(630)897-9214
Fax: (630)897-7002

SCORE Office (Greater Belvidere)
419 S. State St.
Belvidere, IL 61008
(815)544-4357
Fax: (815)547-7654

SCORE Office (Bensenville)
1050 Busse Hwy. Suite 100
Bensenville, IL 60106

(708)350-2944
Fax: (708)350-2979

SCORE Office (Central Illinois)
402 N. Hershey Rd.
Bloomington, IL 61704
(309)644-0549
Fax: (309)663-8270
E-mail: webmaster@central-illinois-score.org
Website: http://www.central-illinois-score.org/

SCORE Office
(Southern Illinois)
150 E. Pleasant Hill Rd.
Box 1
Carbondale, IL 62901
(618)453-6654
Fax: (618)453-5040

SCORE Office (Chicago)
Northwest Atrium Ctr.
500 W. Madison St., No. 1250
Chicago, IL 60661
(312)353-7724
Fax: (312)886-5688
Website: http://www.mcs.net/~bic/

SCORE Office (Chicago–Oliver Harvey College)
Pullman Bldg.
1000 E. 11th St., 7th Fl.
Chicago, IL 60628
Fax: (312)468-8086

SCORE Office (Danville)
28 W. N. Street
Danville, IL 61832
(217)442-7232
Fax: (217)442-6228

SCORE Office (Decatur)
Milliken University
1184 W. Main St.
Decatur, IL 62522
(217)424-6297
Fax: (217)424-3993
E-mail: charding@mail.millikin.edu
Website: http://www.millikin.edu/academics/Tabor/score.html

SCORE Office (Downers Grove)
925 Curtis
Downers Grove, IL 60515
(708)968-4050
Fax: (708)968-8368

SCORE Office (Elgin)
24 E. Chicago, 3rd Fl.
PO Box 648

Elgin, IL 60120
(847)741-5660
Fax: (847)741-5677

SCORE Office (Freeport Area)
26 S. Galena Ave.
Freeport, IL 61032
(815)233-1350
Fax: (815)235-4038

SCORE Office (Galesburg)
292 E. Simmons St.
PO Box 749
Galesburg, IL 61401
(309)343-1194
Fax: (309)343-1195

SCORE Office (Glen Ellyn)
500 Pennsylvania
Glen Ellyn, IL 60137
(708)469-0907
Fax: (708)469-0426

SCORE Office (Greater Alton)
Alden Hall
5800 Godfrey Rd.
Godfrey, IL 62035-2466
(618)467-2280
Fax: (618)466-8289
Website: http://www.altonweb.com/score/

SCORE Office (Grayslake)
19351 W. Washington St.
Grayslake, IL 60030
(708)223-3633
Fax: (708)223-9371

SCORE Office (Harrisburg)
303 S. Commercial
Harrisburg, IL 62946-1528
(618)252-8528
Fax: (618)252-0210

SCORE Office (Joliet)
100 N. Chicago
Joliet, IL 60432
(815)727-5371
Fax: (815)727-5374

SCORE Office (Kankakee)
101 S. Schuyler Ave.
Kankakee, IL 60901
(815)933-0376
Fax: (815)933-0380

SCORE Office (Macomb)
216 Seal Hall, Rm. 214
Macomb, IL 61455
(309)298-1128
Fax: (309)298-2520

SCORE Office (Matteson)
210 Lincoln Mall
Matteson, IL 60443
(708)709-3750
Fax: (708)503-9322

SCORE Office (Mattoon)
1701 Wabash Ave.
Mattoon, IL 61938
(217)235-5661
Fax: (217)234-6544

SCORE Office (Quad Cities)
622 19th St.
Moline, IL 61265
(309)797-0082
Fax: (309)757-5435
E-mail: score@qconline.com
Website: http://www.qconline.com/business/score/

SCORE Office (Naperville)
131 W. Jefferson Ave.
Naperville, IL 60540
(708)355-4141
Fax: (708)355-8355

SCORE Office (Northbrook)
2002 Walters Ave.
Northbrook, IL 60062
(847)498-5555
Fax: (847)498-5510

SCORE Office (Palos Hills)
10900 S. 88th Ave.
Palos Hills, IL 60465
(847)974-5468
Fax: (847)974-0078

SCORE Office (Peoria)
124 SW Adams, Ste. 300
Peoria, IL 61602
(309)676-0755
Fax: (309)676-7534

SCORE Office (Prospect Heights)
1375 Wolf Rd.
Prospect Heights, IL 60070
(847)537-8660
Fax: (847)537-7138

SCORE Office (Quincy Tri-State)
300 Civic Center Plz., Ste. 245
Quincy, IL 62301
(217)222-8093
Fax: (217)222-3033

SCORE Office (River Grove)
2000 5th Ave.
River Grove, IL 60171

(708)456-0300
Fax: (708)583-3121

SCORE Office (Northern Illinois)
515 N. Court St.
Rockford, IL 61103
(815)962-0122
Fax: (815)962-0122

SCORE Office (St. Charles)
103 N. 1st Ave.
St. Charles, IL 60174-1982
(847)584-8384
Fax: (847)584-6065

SCORE Office (Springfield)
511 W. Capitol Ave., Ste. 302
Springfield, IL 62704
(217)492-4416
Fax: (217)492-4867

SCORE Office (Sycamore)
112 Somunak St.
Sycamore, IL 60178
(815)895-3456
Fax: (815)895-0125

SCORE Office (University)
Hwy. 50 & Stuenkel Rd.
Ste. C3305
University Park, IL 60466
(708)534-5000
Fax: (708)534-8457

Indiana

SCORE Office (Anderson)
205 W. 11th St.
Anderson, IN 46015
(317)642-0264

SCORE Office (Bloomington)
Star Center
216 W. Allen
Bloomington, IN 47403
(812)335-7334
E-mail: wtfische@indiana.edu
Website: http://
www.brainfreezemedia.com/score527/

SCORE Office (South East Indiana)
500 Franklin St.
Box 29
Columbus, IN 47201
(812)379-4457

SCORE Office (Corydon)
310 N. Elm St.
Corydon, IN 47112
(812)738-2137
Fax: (812)738-6438

SCORE Office (Crown Point)
Old Courthouse Sq. Ste. 206
PO Box 43
Crown Point, IN 46307
(219)663-1800

SCORE Office (Elkhart)
418 S. Main St.
Elkhart, IN 46515
(219)293-1531
Fax: (219)294-1859

SCORE Office (Evansville)
1100 W. Lloyd Expy., Ste. 105
Evansville, IN 47708
(812)426-6144

SCORE Office (Fort Wayne)
1300 S. Harrison St.
Ft. Wayne, IN 46802
(219)422-2601
Fax: (219)422-2601

SCORE Office (Gary)
973 W. 6th Ave., Rm. 326
Gary, IN 46402
(219)882-3918

SCORE Office (Hammond)
7034 Indianapolis Blvd.
Hammond, IN 46324
(219)931-1000
Fax: (219)845-9548

SCORE Office (Indianapolis)
429 N. Pennsylvania St., Ste. 100
Indianapolis, IN 46204-1873
(317)226-7264
Fax: (317)226-7259
E-mail: inscore@indy.net
Website: http://www.score-indianapolis.org/

SCORE Office (Jasper)
PO Box 307
Jasper, IN 47547-0307
(812)482-6866

SCORE Office (Kokomo/Howard Counties)
106 N. Washington St.
Kokomo, IN 46901
(765)457-5301
Fax: (765)452-4564

SCORE Office (Logansport)
300 E. Broadway, Ste. 103
Logansport, IN 46947
(219)753-6388

SCORE Office (Madison)
301 E. Main St.
Madison, IN 47250

(812)265-3135
Fax: (812)265-2923

SCORE Office (Marengo)
Rt. 1 Box 224D
Marengo, IN 47140
Fax: (812)365-2793

SCORE Office (Marion/Grant Counties)
215 S. Adams
Marion, IN 46952
(765)664-5107

SCORE Office (Merrillville)
255 W. 80th Pl.
Merrillville, IN 46410
(219)769-8180
Fax: (219)736-6223

SCORE Office (Michigan City)
200 E. Michigan Blvd.
Michigan City, IN 46360
(219)874-6221
Fax: (219)873-1204

SCORE Office (South Central Indiana)
4100 Charleston Rd.
New Albany, IN 47150-9538
(812)945-0066

SCORE Office (Rensselaer)
104 W. Washington
Rensselaer, IN 47978

SCORE Office (Salem)
210 N. Main St.
Salem, IN 47167
(812)883-4303
Fax: (812)883-1467

SCORE Office (South Bend)
300 N. Michigan St.
South Bend, IN 46601
(219)282-4350
E-mail: chair@southbend-score.org
Website: http://www.southbend-score.org/

SCORE Office (Valparaiso)
150 Lincolnway
Valparaiso, IN 46383
(219)462-1105
Fax: (219)469-5710

SCORE Office (Vincennes)
27 N. 3rd
PO Box 553
Vincennes, IN 47591
(812)882-6440
Fax: (812)882-6441

SCORE Office (Wabash)
PO Box 371

Wabash, IN 46992
(219)563-1168
Fax: (219)563-6920

Iowa

SCORE Office (Burlington)
Federal Bldg.
300 N. Main St.
Burlington, IA 52601
(319)752-2967

SCORE Office (Cedar Rapids)
2750 1st Ave. NE, Ste 350
Cedar Rapids, IA 52401-1806
(319)362-6405
Fax: (319)362-7861
E:mail: score@scorecr.org
Website: http://www.scorecr.org

SCORE Office (Illowa)
333 4th Ave. S
Clinton, IA 52732
(319)242-5702

SCORE Office (Council Bluffs)
7 N. 6th St.
Council Bluffs, IA 51502
(712)325-1000

SCORE Office (Northeast Iowa)
3404 285th St.
Cresco, IA 52136
(319)547-3377

SCORE Office (Des Moines)
Federal Bldg., Rm. 749
210 Walnut St.
Des Moines, IA 50309-2186
(515)284-4760

SCORE Office (Ft. Dodge)
Federal Bldg., Rm. 436
205 S. 8th St.
Ft. Dodge, IA 50501
(515)955-2622

SCORE Office (Independence)
110 1st. St. east
Independence, IA 50644
(319)334-7178
Fax: (319)334-7179

SCORE Office (Iowa City)
210 Federal Bldg.
PO Box 1853
Iowa City, IA 52240-1853
(319)338-1662

SCORE Office (Keokuk)
401 Main St.
Pierce Bldg., No. 1

Keokuk, IA 52632
(319)524-5055

SCORE Office (Central Iowa)
Fisher Community College
709 S. Center
Marshalltown, IA 50158
(515)753-6645

SCORE Office (River City)
15 West State St.
Mason City, IA 50401
(515)423-5724

SCORE Office (South Central)
SBDC, Indian Hills Community College
525 Grandview Ave.
Ottumwa, IA 52501
(515)683-5127
Fax: (515)683-5263

SCORE Office (Dubuque)
10250 Sundown Rd.
Peosta, IA 52068
(319)556-5110

SCORE Office (Southwest Iowa)
614 W. Sheridan
Shenandoah, IA 51601
(712)246-3260

SCORE Office (Sioux City)
Federal Bldg.
320 6th St.
Sioux City, IA 51101
(712)277-2324
Fax: (712)277-2325

SCORE Office (Iowa Lakes)
122 W. 5th St.
Spencer, IA 51301
(712)262-3059

SCORE Office (Vista)
119 W. 6th St.
Storm Lake, IA 50588
(712)732-3780

SCORE Office (Waterloo)
215 E. 4th
Waterloo, IA 50703
(319)233-8431

Kansas

SCORE Office (Southwest Kansas)
501 W. Spruce
Dodge City, KS 67801
(316)227-3119

SCORE Office (Emporia)
811 Homewood

Emporia, KS 66801
(316)342-1600

SCORE Office (Golden Belt)
1307 Williams
Great Bend, KS 67530
(316)792-2401

SCORE Office (Hays)
PO Box 400
Hays, KS 67601
(913)625-6595

SCORE Office (Hutchinson)
1 E. 9th St.
Hutchinson, KS 67501
(316)665-8468
Fax: (316)665-7619

SCORE Office (Southeast Kansas)
404 Westminster Pl.
PO Box 886
Independence, KS 67301
(316)331-4741

SCORE Office (McPherson)
306 N. Main
PO Box 616
McPherson, KS 67460
(316)241-3303

SCORE Office (Salina)
120 Ash St.
Salina, KS 67401
(785)243-4290
Fax: (785)243-1833

SCORE Office (Topeka)
1700 College
Topeka, KS 66621
(785)231-1010

SCORE Office (Wichita)
100 E. English, Ste. 510
Wichita, KS 67202
(316)269-6273
Fax: (316)269-6499

SCORE Office (Ark Valley)
205 E. 9th St.
Winfield, KS 67156
(316)221-1617

Kentucky

SCORE Office (Ashland)
PO Box 830
Ashland, KY 41105
(606)329-8011
Fax: (606)325-4607

SCORE Office (Bowling Green)
812 State St.
PO Box 51
Bowling Green, KY 42101
(502)781-3200
Fax: (502)843-0458

SCORE Office (Tri-Lakes)
508 Barbee Way
Danville, KY 40422-1548
(606)231-9902

SCORE Office (Glasgow)
301 W. Main St.
Glasgow, KY 42141
(502)651-3161
Fax: (502)651-3122

SCORE Office (Hazard)
B & I Technical Center
100 Airport Gardens Rd.
Hazard, KY 41701
(606)439-5856
Fax: (606)439-1808

SCORE Office (Lexington)
410 W. Vine St., Ste. 290, Civic C
Lexington, KY 40507
(606)231-9902
Fax: (606)253-3190
E-mail: scorelex@uky.campus.mci.net

SCORE Office (Louisville)
188 Federal Office Bldg.
600 Dr. Martin L. King Jr. Pl.
Louisville, KY 40202
(502)582-5976

SCORE Office (Madisonville)
257 N. Main
Madisonville, KY 42431
(502)825-1399
Fax: (502)825-1396

SCORE Office (Paducah)
Federal Office Bldg.
501 Broadway, Rm. B-36
Paducah, KY 42001
(502)442-5685

Louisiana

SCORE Office (Central Louisiana)
802 3rd St.
Alexandria, LA 71309
(318)442-6671

SCORE Office (Baton Rouge)
564 Laurel St.
PO Box 3217
Baton Rouge, LA 70801

(504)381-7130
Fax: (504)336-4306

SCORE Office (North Shore)
2 W. Thomas
Hammond, LA 70401
(504)345-4457
Fax: (504)345-4749

SCORE Office (Lafayette)
804 St. Mary Blvd.
Lafayette, LA 70505-1307
(318)233-2705
Fax: (318)234-8671
E-mail: score302@aol.com

SCORE Office (Lake Charles)
120 W. Pujo St.
Lake Charles, LA 70601
(318)433-3632

SCORE Office (New Orleans)
365 Canal St., Ste. 3100
New Orleans, LA 70130
(504)589-2356
Fax: (504)589-2339

SCORE Office (Shreveport)
400 Edwards St.
Shreveport, LA 71101
(318)677-2536
Fax: (318)677-2541

Maine

SCORE Office (Augusta)
40 Western Ave.
Augusta, ME 04330
(207)622-8509

SCORE Office (Bangor)
Peabody Hall, Rm. 229
One College Cir.
Bangor, ME 04401
(207)941-9707

SCORE Office (Central & Northern Arroostock)
111 High St.
Caribou, ME 04736
(207)492-8010
Fax: (207)492-8010

SCORE Office (Penquis)
South St.
Dover Foxcroft, ME 04426
(207)564-7021

SCORE Office (Maine Coastal)
Mill Mall
Box 1105
Ellsworth, ME 04605-1105

(207)667-5800
E-mail: score@arcadia.net

SCORE Office (Lewiston-Auburn)
BIC of Maine-Bates Mill Complex
35 Canal St.
Lewiston, ME 04240-7764
(207)782-3708
Fax: (207)783-7745

SCORE Office (Portland)
66 Pearl St., Rm. 210
Portland, ME 04101
(207)772-1147
Fax: (207)772-5581
E-mail: Score53@score.maine.org
Website: http://www.score.maine.org/
chapter53/

SCORE Office (Western Mountains)
255 River St.
PO Box 252
Rumford, ME 04257-0252
(207)369-9976

SCORE Office (Oxford Hills)
166 Main St.
South Paris, ME 04281
(207)743-0499

Maryland

SCORE Office (Southern Maryland)
2525 Riva Rd., Ste. 110
Annapolis, MD 21401
(410)266-9553
Fax: (410)573-0981
E-mail: score390@aol.com
Website: http://members.aol.com/
score390/index.htm

SCORE Office (Baltimore)
The City Crescent Bldg., 6th Fl.
10 S. Howard St.
Baltimore, MD 21201
(410)962-2233
Fax: (410)962-1805

SCORE Office (Bel Air)
108 S. Bond St.
Bel Air, MD 21014
(410)838-2020
Fax: (410)893-4715

SCORE Office (Bethesda)
7910 Woodmont Ave., Ste. 1204
Bethesda, MD 20814
(301)652-4900
Fax: (301)657-1973

SCORE Office (Bowie)
6670 Race Track Rd.
Bowie, MD 20715
(301)262-0920
Fax: (301)262-0921

SCORE Office (Dorchester County)
203 Sunburst Hwy.
Cambridge, MD 21613
(410)228-3575

SCORE Office (Upper Shore)
210 Marlboro Ave.
Easton, MD 21601
(410)822-4606
Fax: (410)822-7922

SCORE Office (Frederick County)
43A S. Market St.
Frederick, MD 21701
(301)662-8723
Fax: (301)846-4427

SCORE Office (Gaithersburg)
9 Park Ave.
Gaithersburg, MD 20877
(301)840-1400
Fax: (301)963-3918

SCORE Office (Glen Burnie)
103 Crain Hwy. SE
Glen Burnie, MD 21061
(410)766-8282
Fax: (410)766-9722

SCORE Office (Hagerstown)
111 W. Washington St.
Hagerstown, MD 21740
(301)739-2015
Fax: (301)739-1278

SCORE Office (Laurel)
7901 Sandy Spring Rd. Ste. 501
Laurel, MD 20707
(301)725-4000
Fax: (301)725-0776

SCORE Office (Salisbury)
300 E. Main St.
Salisbury, MD 21801
(410)749-0185
Fax: (410)860-9925

Massachusetts

SCORE Office (NE Massachusetts)
100 Cummings Ctr., Ste. 101 K
Beverly, MA 01923
(978)922-9441
Website: http://www1.shore.net/~score/

SCORE Office (Boston)
10 Causeway St., Rm. 265
Boston, MA 02222-1093
(617)565-5591
Fax: (617)565-5598
E-mail: boston-score-
20@worldnet.att.net
Website: http://www.scoreboston.org/

SCORE office (Bristol/Plymouth County)
53 N. 6th St., Federal Bldg.
Bristol, MA 02740
(508)994-5093

SCORE Office (SE Massachusetts)
60 School St.
Brockton, MA 02401
(508)587-2673
Fax: (508)587-1340
Website: http://
www.metrosouthchamber.com/
score.html

SCORE Office (North Adams)
820 N. State Rd.
Cheshire, MA 01225
(413)743-5100

SCORE Office (Clinton Satellite)
1 Green St.
Clinton, MA 01510
Fax: (508)368-7689

SCORE Office (Greenfield)
PO Box 898
Greenfield, MA 01302
(413)773-5463
Fax: (413)773-7008

SCORE Office (Haverhill)
87 Winter St.
Haverhill, MA 01830
(508)373-5663
Fax: (508)373-8060

SCORE Office (Hudson Satellite)
PO Box 578
Hudson, MA 01749
(508)568-0360
Fax: (508)568-0360

SCORE Office (Cape Cod)
Independence Pk., Ste. 5B
270 Communications Way
Hyannis, MA 02601
(508)775-4884
Fax: (508)790-2540

SCORE Office (Lawrence)
264 Essex St.
Lawrence, MA 01840
(508)686-0900
Fax: (508)794-9953

SCORE Office (Leominster Satellite)
110 Erdman Way
Leominster, MA 01453
(508)840-4300
Fax: (508)840-4896

SCORE Office (Bristol/Plymouth Counties)
53 N. 6th St., Federal Bldg.
New Bedford, MA 02740
(508)994-5093

SCORE Office (Newburyport)
29 State St.
Newburyport, MA 01950
(617)462-6680

SCORE Office (Pittsfield)
66 West St.
Pittsfield, MA 01201
(413)499-2485

SCORE Office (Haverhill-Salem)
32 Derby Sq.
Salem, MA 01970
(508)745-0330
Fax: (508)745-3855

SCORE Office (Springfield)
1350 Main St.
Federal Bldg.
Springfield, MA 01103
(413)785-0314

SCORE Office (Carver)
12 Taunton Green, Ste. 201
Taunton, MA 02780
(508)824-4068
Fax: (508)824-4069

SCORE Office (Worcester)
33 Waldo St.
Worcester, MA 01608
(508)753-2929
Fax: (508)754-8560

Michigan

SCORE Office (Allegan)
PO Box 338
Allegan, MI 49010
(616)673-2479

SCORE Office (Ann Arbor)
425 S. Main St., Ste. 103
Ann Arbor, MI 48104
(313)665-4433

SCORE Office (Battle Creek)
34 W. Jackson Ste. 4A
Battle Creek, MI 49017-3505
(616)962-4076
Fax: (616)962-6309

SCORE Office (Cadillac)
222 Lake St.
Cadillac, MI 49601
(616)775-9776
Fax: (616)768-4255

SCORE Office (Detroit)
477 Michigan Ave., Rm. 515
Detroit, MI 48226
(313)226-7947
Fax: (313)226-3448

SCORE Office (Flint)
708 Root Rd., Rm. 308
Flint, MI 48503
(810)233-6846

SCORE Office (Grand Rapids)
111 Pearl St. NW
Grand Rapids, MI 49503-2831
(616)771-0305
Fax: (616)771-0328
E-mail: scoreone@iserv.net
Website: http://www.iserv.net/~scoreone/

SCORE Office (Holland)
480 State St.
Holland, MI 49423
(616)396-9472

SCORE Office (Jackson)
209 East Washington
PO Box 80
Jackson, MI 49204
(517)782-8221
Fax: (517)782-0061

SCORE Office (Kalamazoo)
345 W. Michigan Ave.
Kalamazoo, MI 49007
(616)381-5382
Fax: (616)384-0096
E-mail: score@nucleus.net

SCORE Office (Lansing)
117 E. Allegan
PO Box 14030
Lansing, MI 48901
(517)487-6340
Fax: (517)484-6910

SCORE Office (Livonia)
15401 Farmington Rd.
Livonia, MI 48154
(313)427-2122
Fax: (313)427-6055

SCORE Office (Madison Heights)
26345 John R
Madison Heights, MI 48071
(810)542-5010
Fax: (810)542-6821

SCORE Office (Monroe)
111 E. 1st
Monroe, MI 48161
(313)242-3366
Fax: (313)242-7253

SCORE Office (Mt. Clemens)
58 S/B Gratiot
Mt. Clemens, MI 48043
(810)463-1528
Fax: (810)463-6541

SCORE Office (Muskegon)
PO Box 1087
230 Terrace Plz.
Muskegon, MI 49443
(616)722-3751
Fax: (616)728-7251

SCORE Office (Petoskey)
401 E. Mitchell St.
Petoskey, MI 49770
(616)347-4150

SCORE Office (Pontiac)
Executive Office Bldg.
1200 N. Telegraph Rd.
Pontiac, MI 48341
(810)975-9555

SCORE Office (Pontiac)
PO Box 430025
Pontiac, MI 48343
(810)335-9600

SCORE Office (Port Huron)
920 Pinegrove Ave.
Port Huron, MI 48060
(810)985-7101

SCORE Office (Rochester)
71 Walnut Ste. 110
Rochester, MI 48307
(810)651-6700
Fax: (810)651-5270

SCORE Office (Saginaw)
901 S. Washington Ave.
Saginaw, MI 48601
(517)752-7161
Fax: (517)752-9055

SCORE Office (Upper Peninsula)
2581 I-75 Business Spur
Sault Ste. Marie, MI 49783
(906)632-3301

SCORE Office (Southfield)
21000 W. 10 Mile Rd.
Southfield, MI 48075
(810)204-3050
Fax: (810)204-3099

SCORE Office (Traverse City)
202 E. Grandview Pkwy.
PO Box 387
Traverse City, MI 49685
(616)947-5075
Fax: (616)946-2565

SCORE Office (Warren)
30500 Van Dyke, Ste. 118
Warren, MI 48093
(810)751-3939

Minnesota

SCORE Office (Aitkin)
Aitkin, MN 56431
(218)741-3906

SCORE Office (Albert Lea)
202 N. Broadway Ave.
Albert Lea, MN 56007
(507)373-7487

SCORE Office (Austin)
PO Box 864
Austin, MN 55912
(507)437-4561
Fax: (507)437-4869

SCORE Office (South Metro)
Ames Business Ctr.
2500 W. County Rd., No. 42
Burnsville, MN 55337
(612)898-5645
Fax: (612)435-6972
E-mail: southmetro@scoreminn.org
Website: http://www.scoreminn.org/
southmetro/

SCORE Office (Duluth)
1717 Minnesota Ave.
Duluth, MN 55802
(218)727-8286
Fax: (218)727-3113
E-mail: duluth@scoreminn.org
Website: http://www.scoreminn.org

SCORE Office (Fairmont)
PO Box 826
Fairmont, MN 56031
(507)235-5547
Fax: (507)235-8411

SCORE Office (Southwest Minnesota)
112 Riverfront St.

Box 999
Mankato, MN 56001
(507)345-4519
Fax: (507)345-4451
Website: http://www.scoreminn.org/

SCORE Office (Minneapolis)
North Plaza Bldg., Ste. 51
5217 Wayzata Blvd.
Minneapolis, MN 55416
(612)591-0539
Fax: (612)544-0436
Website: http://www.scoreminn.org/

SCORE Office (Owatonna)
PO Box 331
Owatonna, MN 55060
(507)451-7970
Fax: (507)451-7972

SCORE Office (Red Wing)
2000 W. Main St., Ste. 324
Red Wing, MN 55066
(612)388-4079

SCORE Office (Southeastern Minnesota)
220 S. Broadway, Ste. 100
Rochester, MN 55901
(507)288-1122
Fax: (507)282-8960
Website: http://www.scoreminn.org/

SCORE Office (Brainerd)
St. Cloud, MN 56301

SCORE Office (Central Area)
1527 Northway Dr.
St. Cloud, MN 56301
(320)240-1332
Fax: (320)255-9050
Website: http://www.scoreminn.org/

SCORE Office (St. Paul)
350 St. Peter St., No. 295
Lowry Professional Bldg.
St. Paul, MN 55102
(651)223-5010
Fax: (651)223-5048
Website: http://www.scoreminn.org/

SCORE Office (Winona)
Box 870
Winona, MN 55987
(507)452-2272
Fax: (507)454-8814

SCORE Office (Worthington)
1121 3rd Ave.
Worthington, MN 56187
(507)372-2919
Fax: (507)372-2827

Mississippi

SCORE Office (Delta)
915 Washington Ave.
PO Box 933
Greenville, MS 38701
(601)378-3141

SCORE Office (Gulfcoast)
1 Government Plaza
2909 13th St., Ste. 203
Gulfport, MS 39501
(228)863-0054

SCORE Office (Jackson)
1st Jackson Center, Ste. 400
101 W. Capitol St.
Jackson, MS 39201
(601)965-5533

SCORE Office (Meridian)
5220 16th Ave.
Meridian, MS 39305
(601)482-4412

Missouri

SCORE Office (Lake of the Ozark)
University Extension
113 Kansas St.
PO Box 1405
Camdenton, MO 65020
(573)346-2644
Fax: (573)346-2694
E-mail: score@cdoc.net
Website: http://sites.cdoc.net/score/

Chamber of Commerce (Cape Girardeau)
PO Box 98
Cape Girardeau, MO 63702-0098
(314)335-3312

SCORE Office (Mid-Missouri)
1705 Halstead Ct.
Columbia, MO 65203
(573)874-1132

SCORE Office (Ozark-Gateway)
1486 Glassy Rd.
Cuba, MO 65453-1640
(573)885-4954

SCORE Office (Kansas City)
323 W. 8th St., Ste. 104
Kansas City, MO 64105
(816)374-6675
Fax: (816)374-6692
E-mail: SCOREBIC@AOL.COM
Website: http://www.crn.org/score/

SCORE Office (Sedalia)
Lucas Place
323 W. 8th St., Ste.104
Kansas City, MO 64105
(816)374-6675

SCORE office (Tri-Lakes)
PO Box 1148
Kimberling, MO 65686
(417)739-3041

SCORE Office (Tri-Lakes)
HCRI Box 85
Lampe, MO 65681
(417)858-6798

SCORE Office (Mexico)
111 N. Washington St.
Mexico, MO 65265
(314)581-2765

SCORE Office (Southeast Missouri)
Rte. 1, Box 280
Neelyville, MO 63954
(573)989-3577

SCORE office (Poplar Bluff Area)
806 Emma St.
Poplar Bluff, MO 63901
(573)686-8892

SCORE Office (St. Joseph)
3003 Frederick Ave.
St. Joseph, MO 64506
(816)232-4461

SCORE Office (St. Louis)
815 Olive St., Rm. 242
St. Louis, MO 63101-1569
(314)539-6970
Fax: (314)539-3785
E-mail: info@stlscore.org
Website: http://www.stlscore.org/

SCORE Office (Lewis & Clark)
425 Spencer Rd.
St. Peters, MO 63376
(314)928-2900
Fax: (314)928-2900
E-mail: score01@mail.win.org

SCORE Office (Springfield)
620 S. Glenstone, Ste. 110
Springfield, MO 65802-3200
(417)864-7670
Fax: (417)864-4108

SCORE office (Southeast Kansas)
1206 W. First St.
Webb City, MO 64870
(417)673-3984

Montana

SCORE Office (Billings)
815 S. 27th St.
Billings, MT 59101
(406)245-4111

SCORE Office (Bozeman)
1205 E. Main St.
Bozeman, MT 59715
(406)586-5421

SCORE Office (Butte)
1000 George St.
Butte, MT 59701
(406)723-3177

SCORE Office (Great Falls)
710 First Ave. N
Great Falls, MT 59401
(406)761-4434
E-mail: scoregtf@in.tch.com

SCORE Office (Havre, Montana)
518 First St.
Havre, MT 59501
(406)265-4383

SCORE Office (Helena)
Federal Bldg.
301 S. Park
Helena, MT 59626-0054
(406)441-1081

SCORE Office (Kalispell)
2 Main St.
Kalispell, MT 59901
(406)756-5271
Fax: (406)752-6665

SCORE Office (Missoula)
723 Ronan
Missoula, MT 59806
(406)327-8806
E-mail: score@safeshop.com
Website: http://missoula.bigsky.net/score/

Nebraska

SCORE Office (Columbus)
Columbus, NE 68601
(402)564-2769

SCORE Office (Fremont)
92 W. 5th St.
Fremont, NE 68025
(402)721-2641

SCORE Office (Hastings)
Hastings, NE 68901
(402)463-3447

SCORE Office (Lincoln)
8800 O St.
Lincoln, NE 68520
(402)437-2409

SCORE Office (Panhandle)
150549 CR 30
Minatare, NE 69356
(308)632-2133
Website: http://www.tandt.com/SCORE

SCORE Office (Norfolk)
3209 S. 48th Ave.
Norfolk, NE 68106
(402)564-2769

SCORE Office (North Platte)
3301 W. 2nd St.
North Platte, NE 69101
(308)532-4466

SCORE Office (Omaha)
11145 Mill Valley Rd.
Omaha, NE 68154
(402)221-3606
Fax: (402)221-3680
E-mail: infoctr@ne.uswest.net
Website: http://www.tandt.com/score/

Nevada

SCORE Office (Incline Village)
969 Tahoe Blvd.
Incline Village, NV 89451
(702)831-7327
Fax: (702)832-1605

SCORE Office (Carson City)
301 E. Stewart
PO Box 7527
Las Vegas, NV 89125
(702)388-6104

SCORE Office (Las Vegas)
300 Las Vegas Blvd. S, Ste. 1100
Las Vegas, NV 89101
(702)388-6104

SCORE Office (Northern Nevada)
SBDC, College of Business
Administration
Univ. of Nevada
Reno, NV 89557-0100
(702)784-4436
Fax: (702)784-4337

New Hampshire

SCORE Office (North Country)
PO Box 34
Berlin, NH 03570
(603)752-1090

SCORE Office (Concord)
143 N. Main St., Rm. 202A
PO Box 1258
Concord, NH 03301
(603)225-1400
Fax: (603)225-1409

SCORE Office (Dover)
299 Central Ave.
Dover, NH 03820
(603)742-2218
Fax: (603)749-6317

SCORE Office (Monadnock)
34 Mechanic St.
Keene, NH 03431-3421
(603)352-0320

SCORE Office (Lakes Region)
67 Water St., Ste. 105
Laconia, NH 03246
(603)524-9168

SCORE Office (Upper Valley)
Citizens Bank Bldg., Rm. 310
20 W. Park St.
Lebanon, NH 03766
(603)448-3491
Fax: (603)448-1908
E-mail: billt@valley.net
Website: http://www.valley.net/~score/

SCORE Office (Merrimack Valley)
275 Chestnut St., Rm. 618
Manchester, NH 03103
(603)666-7561
Fax: (603)666-7925

SCORE Office (Mt. Washington Valley)
PO Box 1066
North Conway, NH 03818
(603)383-0800

SCORE Office (Seacoast)
195 Commerce Way, Unit-A
Portsmouth, NH 03801-3251
(603)433-0575

New Jersey

SCORE Office (Somerset)
Paritan Valley Community College, Rte. 28
Branchburg, NJ 08807
(908)218-8874
E-mail: nj-score@grizbiz.com.
Website: http://www.nj-score.org/

SCORE Office (Chester)
5 Old Mill Rd.
Chester, NJ 07930
(908)879-7080

SCORE Office (Greater Princeton)
4 A George Washington Dr.
Cranbury, NJ 08512
(609)520-1776

SCORE Office (Freehold)
36 W. Main St.
Freehold, NJ 07728
(908)462-3030
Fax: (908)462-2123

SCORE Office (North West)
Picantinny Innovation Ctr.
3159 Schrader Rd.
Hamburg, NJ 07419
(973)209-8525
Fax: (973)209-7252
E-mail: nj-score@grizbiz.com
Website: http://www.nj-score.org/

SCORE Office (Monmouth)
765 Newman Springs Rd.
Lincroft, NJ 07738
(908)224-2573
E-mail: nj-score@grizbiz.com
Website: http://www.nj-score.org/

SCORE Office (Manalapan)
125 Symmes Dr.
Manalapan, NJ 07726
(908)431-7220

SCORE Office (Jersey City)
2 Gateway Ctr., 4th Fl.
Newark, NJ 07102
(973)645-3982
Fax: (973)645-2375

SCORE Office (Newark)
2 Gateway Center, 15th Fl.
Newark, NJ 07102-5553
(973)645-3982
Fax: (973)645-2375
E-mail: nj-score@grizbiz.com
Website: http://www.nj-score.org

SCORE Office (Bergen County)
327 E. Ridgewood Ave.
Paramus, NJ 07652
(201)599-6090
E-mail: nj-score@grizbiz.com
Website: http://www.nj-score.org/

SCORE Office (Pennsauken)
4900 Rte. 70
Pennsauken, NJ 08109
(609)486-3421

**SCORE Office
(Southern New Jersey)**
4900 Rte. 70

Pennsauken, NJ 08109
(609)486-3421
E-mail: nj-score@grizbiz.com
Website: http://www.nj-score.org/

**SCORE Office (Greater
Princeton)**
216 Rockingham Row
Princeton Forrestal Village
Princeton, NJ 08540
(609)520-1776
Fax: (609)520-9107
E-mail: nj-score@grizbiz.com
Website: http://www.nj-score.org/

SCORE Office (Shrewsbury)
Hwy. 35
Shrewsbury, NJ 07702
(908)842-5995
Fax: (908)219-6140

SCORE Office (Ocean County)
33 Washington St.
Toms River, NJ 08754
(732)505-6033
E-mail: nj-score@grizbiz.com
Website: http://www.nj-score.org/

SCORE Office (Wall)
2700 Allaire Rd.
Wall, NJ 07719
(908)449-8877

SCORE Office (Wayne)
2055 Hamburg Tpke.
Wayne, NJ 07470
(201)831-7788
Fax: (201)831-9112

New Mexico

SCORE Office (Albuquerque)
525 Buena Vista, SE
Albuquerque, NM 87106
(505)272-7999
Fax: (505)272-7963

SCORE Office (Las Cruces)
Loretto Towne Center
505 S. Main St., Ste. 125
Las Cruces, NM 88001
(505)523-5627
Fax: (505)524-2101
E-mail: score.397@zianet.com

SCORE Office (Roswell)
Federal Bldg., Rm. 237
Roswell, NM 88201
(505)625-2112
Fax: (505)623-2545

SCORE Office (Santa Fe)
Montoya Federal Bldg.
120 Federal Place, Rm. 307
Santa Fe, NM 87501
(505)988-6302
Fax: (505)988-6300

New York

SCORE Office (Northeast)
1 Computer Dr. S
Albany, NY 12205
(518)446-1118
Fax: (518)446-1228

SCORE Office (Auburn)
30 South St.
PO Box 675
Auburn, NY 13021
(315)252-7291

**SCORE Office (South Tier
Binghamton)**
Metro Center, 2nd Fl.
49 Court St.
PO Box 995
Binghamton, NY 13902
(607)772-8860

**SCORE Office
(Queens County City)**
12055 Queens Blvd., Rm. 333
Borough Hall, NY 11424
(718)263-8961

SCORE Office (Buffalo)
Federal Bldg., Rm. 1311
111 W. Huron St.
Buffalo, NY 14202
(716)551-4301
Website: http://www2.pcom.net/score/
buf45.html

SCORE Office (Canandaigua)
Chamber of Commerce Bldg.
113 S. Main St.
Canandaigua, NY 14424
(716)394-4400
Fax: (716)394-4546

SCORE Office (Chemung)
333 E. Water St., 4th Fl.
Elmira, NY 14901
(607)734-3358

SCORE Office (Geneva)
Chamber of Commerce Bldg.
PO Box 587
Geneva, NY 14456
(315)789-1776
Fax: (315)789-3993

SCORE Office (Glens Falls)
84 Broad St.
Glens Falls, NY 12801
(518)798-8463
Fax: (518)745-1433

SCORE Office (Orange County)
40 Matthews St.
Goshen, NY 10924
(914)294-8080
Fax: (914)294-6121

SCORE Office (Huntington Area)
151 W. Carver St.
Huntington, NY 11743
(516)423-6100

SCORE Office (Tompkins County)
904 E. Shore Dr.
Ithaca, NY 14850
(607)273-7080

SCORE Office (Long Island City)
120-55 Queens Blvd.
Jamaica, NY 11424
(718)263-8961
Fax: (718)263-9032

SCORE Office (Chatauqua)
101 W. 5th St.
Jamestown, NY 14701
(716)484-1103

SCORE Office (Westchester)
2 Caradon Ln.
Katonah, NY 10536
(914)948-3907
Fax: (914)948-4645
E-mail: score@w-w-w.com
Website: http://w-w-w.com/score/

SCORE Office (Queens County)
Queens Borough Hall
120-55 Queens Blvd. Rm. 333
Kew Gardens, NY 11424
(718)263-8961
Fax: (718)263-9032

SCORE Office (Brookhaven)
3233 Rte. 112
Medford, NY 11763
(516)451-6563
Fax: (516)451-6925

SCORE Office (Melville)
35 Pinelawn Rd., Rm. 207-W
Melville, NY 11747
(516)454-0771

SCORE Office (Nassau County)
400 County Seat Dr., No. 140
Mineola, NY 11501

(516)571-3303
E-mail: Counse1998@aol.com
Website: http://members.aol.com/
Counse1998/Default.htm

SCORE Office (Mt. Vernon)
4 N. 7th Ave.
Mt. Vernon, NY 10550
(914)667-7500

SCORE Office (New York)
26 Federal Plz., Rm. 3100
New York, NY 10278
(212)264-4507
Fax: (212)264-4963
E-mail: score1000@erols.com
Website: http://users.erols.com/
score-nyc/

SCORE Office (Newburgh)
47 Grand St.
Newburgh, NY 12550
(914)562-5100

SCORE Office (Owego)
188 Front St.
Owego, NY 13827
(607)687-2020

SCORE Office (Peekskill)
1 S. Division St.
Peekskill, NY 10566
(914)737-3600
Fax: (914)737-0541

SCORE Office (Penn Yan)
2375 Rte. 14A
Penn Yan, NY 14527
(315)536-3111

SCORE Office (Dutchess)
110 Main St.
Poughkeepsie, NY 12601
(914)454-1700

SCORE Office (Rochester)
601 Keating Federal Bldg., Rm. 410
100 State St.
Rochester, NY 14614
(716)263-6473
Fax: (716)263-3146
Website: http://www.ggw.org/score/

SCORE Office (Saranac Lake)
30 Main St.
Saranac Lake, NY 12983
(315)448-0415

SCORE Office (Suffolk)
286 Main St.
Setauket, NY 11733
(516)751-3886

SCORE Office (Staten Island)
130 Bay St.
Staten Island, NY 10301
(718)727-1221

SCORE Office (Ulster)
Clinton Bldg., Rm. 107
Stone Ridge, NY 12484
(914)687-5035
Fax: (914)687-5015
Website: http://www.scoreulster.org/

SCORE Office (Syracuse)
401 S. Salina, 5th Fl.
Syracuse, NY 13202
(315)471-9393

SCORE Office (Utica)
SUNY Institute of Technology, Route 12
Utica, NY 13504-3050
(315)792-7553

SCORE Office (Watertown)
518 Davidson St.
Watertown, NY 13601
(315)788-1200
Fax: (315)788-8251

North Carolina

SCORE office (Asheboro)
317 E. Dixie Dr.
Asheboro, NC 27203
(336)626-2626
Fax: (336)626-7077

SCORE Office (Asheville)
Federal Bldg., Rm. 259
151 Patton
Asheville, NC 28801-5770
(828)271-4786
Fax: (828)271-4009

SCORE Office (Chapel Hill)
104 S. Estes Dr.
PO Box 2897
Chapel Hill, NC 27514
(919)967-7075

SCORE Office (Coastal Plains)
PO Box 2897
Chapel Hill, NC 27515
(919)967-7075
Fax: (919)968-6874

SCORE Office (Charlotte)
200 N. College St., Ste. A-2015
Charlotte, NC 28202
(704)344-6576
Fax: (704)344-6769
E-mail: CharlotteSCORE47@AOL.com

Website: http://www.charweb.org/
business/score/

SCORE Office (Durham)
411 W. Chapel Hill St.
Durham, NC 27707
(919)541-2171

SCORE Office (Gastonia)
PO Box 2168
Gastonia, NC 28053
(704)864-2621
Fax: (704)854-8723

SCORE Office (Greensboro)
400 W. Market St., Ste. 103
Greensboro, NC 27401-2241
(910)333-5399

SCORE Office (Henderson)
PO Box 917
Henderson, NC 27536
(919)492-2061
Fax: (919)430-0460

SCORE Office (Hendersonville)
Federal Bldg., Rm. 108
W. 4th Ave. & Church St.
Hendersonville, NC 28792
(828)693-8702
E-mail: score@circle.net
Website: http://www.wncguide.com/
score/Welcome.html

SCORE Office (Unifour)
PO Box 1828
Hickory, NC 28603
(704)328-6111

SCORE Office (High Point)
1101 N. Main St.
High Point, NC 27262
(336)882-8625
Fax: (336)889-9499

SCORE Office (Outer Banks)
Collington Rd. and Mustain
Kill Devil Hills, NC 27948
(252)441-8144

SCORE Office (Down East)
312 S. Front St., Ste. 6
New Bern, NC 28560
(252)633-6688
Fax: (252)633-9608

SCORE Office (Kinston)
PO Box 95
New Bern, NC 28561
(919)633-6688

SCORE Office (Raleigh)
Century Post Office Bldg., Ste. 306
300 Federal St. Mall
Raleigh, NC 27601
(919)856-4739
E-mail: jendres@ibm.net
Website: http://www.intrex.net/score96/
score96.htm

SCORE Office (Sanford)
1801 Nash St.
Sanford, NC 27330
(919)774-6442
Fax: (919)776-8739

SCORE Office (Sandhills Area)
1480 Hwy. 15-501
PO Box 458
Southern Pines, NC 28387
(910)692-3926

SCORE Office (Wilmington)
Corps of Engineers Bldg.
96 Darlington Ave., Ste. 207
Wilmington, NC 28403
(910)815-4576
Fax: (910)815-4658

North Dakota

SCORE Office (Bismarck-Mandan)
700 E. Main Ave., 2nd Fl.
PO Box 5509
Bismarck, ND 58506-5509
(701)250-4303

SCORE Office (Fargo)
657 2nd Ave., Rm. 225
Fargo, ND 58108-3083
(701)239-5677

SCORE Office (Upper Red River)
4275 Technology Dr., Rm. 156
Grand Forks, ND 58202-8372
(701)777-3051

SCORE Office (Minot)
100 1st St. SW
Minot, ND 58701-3846
(701)852-6883
Fax: (701)852-6905

Ohio

SCORE Office (Akron)
1 Cascade Plz., 7th Fl.
Akron, OH 44308
(330)379-3163
Fax: (330)379-3164

SCORE Office (Ashland)
Gill Center
47 W. Main St.
Ashland, OH 44805
(419)281-4584

SCORE Office (Canton)
116 Cleveland Ave. NW, Ste. 601
Canton, OH 44702-1720
(330)453-6047

SCORE Office (Chillicothe)
165 S. Paint St.
Chillicothe, OH 45601
(614)772-4530

SCORE Office (Cincinnati)
Ameritrust Bldg., Rm. 850
525 Vine St.
Cincinnati, OH 45202
(513)684-2812
Fax: (513)684-3251
Website: http://
www.score.chapter34.org/

SCORE Office (Cleveland)
Eaton Center, Ste. 620
1100 Superior Ave.
Cleveland, OH 44114-2507
(216)522-4194
Fax: (216)522-4844

SCORE Office (Columbus)
2 Nationwide Plz., Ste. 1400
Columbus, OH 43215-2542
(614)469-2357
Fax: (614)469-2391
E-mail: info@scorecolumbus.org
Website: http://www.score
columbus.org/

SCORE Office (Dayton)
Dayton Federal Bldg., Rm. 505
200 W. Second St.
Dayton, OH 45402-1430
(513)225-2887
Fax: (513)225-7667

SCORE Office (Defiance)
615 W. 3rd St.
PO Box 130
Defiance, OH 43512
(419)782-7946

SCORE Office (Findlay)
123 E. Main Cross St.
PO Box 923
Findlay, OH 45840
(419)422-3314

SCORE Office (Lima)
147 N. Main St.
Lima, OH 45801
(419)222-6045
Fax: (419)229-0266

SCORE Office (Mansfield)
55 N. Mulberry St.
Mansfield, OH 44902
(419)522-3211

SCORE Office (Marietta)
Thomas Hall
Marietta, OH 45750
(614)373-0268

SCORE Office (Medina)
County Administrative Bldg.
144 N. Broadway
Medina, OH 44256
(216)764-8650

SCORE Office (Licking County)
50 W. Locust St.
Newark, OH 43055
(614)345-7458

SCORE Office (Salem)
2491 State Rte. 45 S
Salem, OH 44460
(216)332-0361

SCORE Office (Tiffin)
62 S. Washington St.
Tiffin, OH 44883
(419)447-4141
Fax: (419)447-5141

SCORE Office (Toledo)
608 Madison Ave, Ste. 910
Toledo, OH 43624
(419)259-7598
Fax: (419)259-6460

SCORE Office (Heart of Ohio)
377 W. Liberty St.
Wooster, OH 44691
(330)262-5735
Fax: (330)262-5745

SCORE Office (Youngstown)
306 Williamson Hall
Youngstown, OH 44555
(330)746-2687

Oklahoma

SCORE Office (Anadarko)
PO Box 366
Anadarko, OK 73005
(405)247-6651

SCORE Office (Ardmore)
410 W. Main
Ardmore, OK 73401
(580)226-2620

SCORE Office (Northeast Oklahoma)
210 S. Main
Grove, OK 74344
(918)787-2796
Fax: (918)787-2796
E-mail: Score595@greencis.net

SCORE Office (Lawton)
4500 W. Lee Blvd., Bldg. 100, Ste. 107
Lawton, OK 73505
(580)353-8727
Fax: (580)250-5677

SCORE Office (Oklahoma City)
210 Park Ave., No. 1300
Oklahoma City, OK 73102
(405)231-5163
Fax: (405)231-4876
E-mail: score212@usa.net

SCORE Office (Stillwater)
439 S. Main
Stillwater, OK 74074
(405)372-5573
Fax: (405)372-4316

SCORE Office (Tulsa)
616 S. Boston, Ste. 406
Tulsa, OK 74119
(918)581-7462
Fax: (918)581-6908
Website: http://www.ionet.net/~tulscore/

Oregon

SCORE Office (Bend)
63085 N. Hwy. 97
Bend, OR 97701
(541)923-2849
Fax: (541)330-6900

SCORE Office (Willamette)
1401 Willamette St.
PO Box 1107
Eugene, OR 97401-4003
(541)465-6600
Fax: (541)484-4942

SCORE Office (Florence)
3149 Oak St.
Florence, OR 97439
(503)997-8444
Fax: (503)997-8448

SCORE Office (Southern Oregon)
33 N. Central Ave., Ste. 216
Medford, OR 97501

(541)776-4220
E-mail: pgr134f@prodigy.com

SCORE Office (Portland)
1515 SW 5th Ave., Ste. 1050
Portland, OR 97201
(503)326-3441
Fax: (503)326-2808
E-mail: gr134@prodigy.com

SCORE Office (Salem)
416 State St. (corner of Liberty)
Salem, OR 97301
(503)370-2896

Pennsylvania

SCORE Office (Altoona-Blair)
1212 12th Ave.
Altoona, PA 16601-3493
(814)943-8151

SCORE Office (Lehigh Valley)
Rauch Bldg. 37
Lehigh University
621 Taylor St.
Bethlehem, PA 18015
(610)758-4496
Fax: (610)758-5205

SCORE Office (Butler County)
100 N. Main St.
PO Box 1082
Butler, PA 16003
(412)283-2222
Fax: (412)283-0224

SCORE Office (Harrisburg)
4211 Trindle Rd.
Camp Hill, PA 17011
(717)761-4304
Fax: (717)761-4315

SCORE Office (Cumberland Valley)
75 S. 2nd St.
Chambersburg, PA 17201
(717)264-2935

SCORE Office (Monroe County-Stroudsburg)
556 Main St.
East Stroudsburg, PA 18301
(717)421-4433

SCORE Office (Erie)
120 W. 9th St.
Erie, PA 16501
(814)871-5650
Fax: (814)871-7530

SCORE Office (Bucks County)
409 Hood Blvd.
Fairless Hills, PA 19030
(215)943-8850
Fax: (215)943-7404

SCORE Office (Hanover)
146 Broadway
Hanover, PA 17331
(717)637-6130
Fax: (717)637-9127

SCORE Office (Harrisburg)
100 Chestnut, Ste. 309
Harrisburg, PA 17101
(717)782-3874

SCORE Office (East Montgomery County)
Baederwood Shopping Center
1653 The Fairways, Ste. 204
Jenkintown, PA 19046
(215)885-3027

SCORE Office (Kittanning)
2 Butler Rd.
Kittanning, PA 16201
(412)543-1305
Fax: (412)543-6206

SCORE Office (Lancaster)
118 W. Chestnut St.
Lancaster, PA 17603
(717)397-3092

SCORE Office (Westmoreland County)
300 Fraser Purchase Rd.
Latrobe, PA 15650-2690
(412)539-7505
Fax: (412)539-1850

SCORE Office (Lebanon)
252 N. 8th St.
PO Box 899
Lebanon, PA 17042-0899
(717)273-3727
Fax: (717)273-7940

SCORE Office (Lewistown)
3 W. Monument Sq., Ste. 204
Lewistown, PA 17044
(717)248-6713
Fax: (717)248-6714

SCORE Office (Delaware County)
602 E. Baltimore Pike
Media, PA 19063
(610)565-3677
Fax: (610)565-1606

SCORE Office (Milton Area)
112 S. Front St.
Milton, PA 17847

(717)742-7341
Fax: (717)792-2008

SCORE Office (Mon-Valley)
435 Donner Ave.
Monessen, PA 15062
(412)684-4277
Fax: (412)684-7688

SCORE Office (Monroeville)
William Penn Plaza
2790 Mosside Blvd., Ste. 295
Monroeville, PA 15146
(412)856-0622
Fax: (412)856-1030

SCORE Office (Airport Area)
986 Brodhead Rd.
Moon Township, PA 15108-2398
(412)264-6270
Fax: (412)264-1575

SCORE Office (Northeast)
8601 E. Roosevelt Blvd.
Philadelphia, PA 19152
(215)332-3400
Fax: (215)332-6050

SCORE Office (Philadelphia)
1315 Walnut St., Ste. 500
Philadelphia, PA 19107
(215)790-5050
Fax: (215)790-5057
E-mail: score46@bellatlantic.net
Website: http://www.pgweb.net/
score46/

SCORE Office (Pittsburgh)
1000 Liberty Ave., Rm. 1122
Pittsburgh, PA 15222
(412)395-6560
Fax: (412)395-6562

SCORE Office (Tri-County)
801 N. Charlotte St.
Pottstown, PA 19464
(610)327-2673

SCORE Office (Reading)
601 Penn St.
Reading, PA 19601
(610)376-3497

SCORE Office (Scranton)
Oppenheim Bldg.
116 N. Washington Ave., Ste. 650
Scranton, PA 18503
(717)347-4611
Fax: (717)347-4611

SCORE Office (Central Pennsylvania)
200 Innovation Blvd., Ste. 242-B
State College, PA 16803
(814)234-9415
Fax: (814)238-9686
Website: http://countrystore.org/
business/score.htm

SCORE Office (Monroe-Stroudsburg)
556 Main St.
Stroudsburg, PA 18360
(717)421-4433

SCORE Office (Uniontown)
Federal Bldg.
Pittsburg St.
PO Box 2065 DTS
Uniontown, PA 15401
(412)437-4222
E-mail: uniontownscore@lcsys.net

SCORE Office (Warren County)
315 2nd Ave.
Warren, PA 16365
(814)723-9017

SCORE Office (Waynesboro)
323 E. Main St.
Waynesboro, PA 17268
(717)762-7123
Fax: (717)962-7124

SCORE Office (Chester County)
Government Service Center, Ste. 281
601 Westtown Rd.
West Chester, PA 19382-4538
(610)344-6910
Fax: (610)344-6919
E-mail: score@locke.ccil.org

SCORE Office (Wilkes-Barre)
7 N. Wilkes-Barre Blvd.
Wilkes Barre, PA 18702-5241
(717)826-6502
Fax: (717)826-6287

SCORE Office (North Central Pennsylvania)
240 W. 3rd St., Rm. 227
PO Box 725
Williamsport, PA 17703
(717)322-3720
Fax: (717)322-1607
E-mail: score234@mail.csrlink.net
Website: http://www.lycoming.org/
score/

SCORE Office (York)
Cyber Center
2101 Pennsylvania Ave.
York, PA 17404

(717)845-8830
Fax: (717)854-9333

Puerto Rico

SCORE Office (Puerto Rico & Virgin Islands)
PO Box 12383-96
San Juan, PR 00914-0383
(787)726-8040
Fax: (787)726-8135

Rhode Island

SCORE Office (Barrington)
281 County Rd.
Barrington, RI 02806
(401)247-1920
Fax: (401)247-3763

SCORE Office (Woonsocket)
640 Washington Hwy.
Lincoln, RI 02865
(401)334-1000
Fax: (401)334-1009

SCORE Office (Wickford)
8045 Post Rd.
North Kingstown, RI 02852
(401)295-5566
Fax: (401)295-8987

SCORE Office (J.G.E. Knight)
380 Westminster St.
Providence, RI 02903
(401)528-4571
Fax: (401)528-4539
Website: http://www.riscore.org

SCORE Office (Warwick)
3288 Post Rd.
Warwick, RI 02886
(401)732-1100
Fax: (401)732-1101

SCORE Office (Westerly)
74 Post Rd.
Westerly, RI 02891
(401)596-7761
800-732-7636
Fax: (401)596-2190

South Carolina

SCORE Office (Aiken)
PO Box 892
Aiken, SC 29802
(803)641-1111
800-542-4536
Fax: (803)641-4174

SCORE Office (Anderson)
Anderson Mall
3130 N. Main St.
Anderson, SC 29621
(864)224-0453

SCORE Office (Coastal)
284 King St.
Charleston, SC 29401
(803)727-4778
Fax: (803)853-2529

SCORE Office (Midlands)
Strom Thurmond Bldg., Rm. 358
1835 Assembly St., Rm 358
Columbia, SC 29201
(803)765-5131
Fax: (803)765-5962
Website: http://www.score
midlands.org/

SCORE Office (Piedmont)
Federal Bldg., Rm. B-02
300 E. Washington St.
Greenville, SC 29601
(864)271-3638

SCORE Office (Greenwood)
PO Drawer 1467
Greenwood, SC 29648
(864)223-8357

SCORE Office (Hilton Head Island)
52 Savannah Trail
Hilton Head, SC 29926
(803)785-7107
Fax: (803)785-7110

SCORE Office (Grand Strand)
937 Broadway
Myrtle Beach, SC 29577
(803)918-1079
Fax: (803)918-1083
E-mail: score381@aol.com

SCORE Office (Spartanburg)
PO Box 1636
Spartanburg, SC 29304
(864)594-5000
Fax: (864)594-5055

South Dakota

SCORE Office (West River)
Rushmore Plz. Civic Ctr.
444 Mount Rushmore Rd., No. 209
Rapid City, SD 57701
(605)394-5311
E-mail: score@gwtc.net

SCORE Office (Sioux Falls)
First Financial Center
110 S. Phillips Ave., Ste. 200
Sioux Falls, SD 57104-6727
(605)330-4231
Fax: (605)330-4231

Tennessee

SCORE Office (Chattanooga)
Federal Bldg., Rm. 26
900 Georgia Ave.
Chattanooga, TN 37402
(423)752-5190
Fax: (423)752-5335

SCORE Office (Cleveland)
PO Box 2275
Cleveland, TN 37320
(423)472-6587
Fax: (423)472-2019

SCORE Office (Upper Cumberland Center)
1225 S. Willow Ave.
Cookeville, TN 38501
(615)432-4111
Fax: (615)432-6010

SCORE Office (Unicoi County)
PO Box 713
Erwin, TN 37650
(423)743-3000
Fax: (423)743-0942

SCORE Office (Greeneville)
115 Academy St.
Greeneville, TN 37743
(423)638-4111
Fax: (423)638-5345

SCORE Office (Jackson)
194 Auditorium St.
Jackson, TN 38301
(901)423-2200

SCORE Office (Northeast Tennessee)
1st Tennessee Bank Bldg.
2710 S. Roan St., Ste. 584
Johnson City, TN 37601
(423)929-7686
Fax: (423)461-8052

SCORE Office (Kingsport)
151 E. Main St.
Kingsport, TN 37662
(423)392-8805

SCORE Office (Greater Knoxville)
Farragot Bldg., Ste. 224
530 S. Gay St.

Knoxville, TN 37902
(423)545-4203
E-mail: scoreknox@ntown.com
Website: http://www.scoreknox.org/

SCORE Office (Maryville)
201 S. Washington St.
Maryville, TN 37804-5728
(423)983-2241
800-525-6834
Fax: (423)984-1386

SCORE Office (Memphis)
Federal Bldg., Ste. 390
167 N. Main St.
Memphis, TN 38103
(901)544-3588

SCORE Office (Nashville)
50 Vantage Way, Ste. 201
Nashville, TN 37228-1500
(615)736-7621

Texas

SCORE Office (Abilene)
2106 Federal Post Office and Court Bldg.
Abilene, TX 79601
(915)677-1857

SCORE Office (Austin)
2501 S. Congress
Austin, TX 78701
(512)442-7235
Fax: (512)442-7528

SCORE Office (Golden Triangle)
450 Boyd St.
Beaumont, TX 77704
(409)838-6581
Fax: (409)833-6718

SCORE Office (Brownsville)
3505 Boca Chica Blvd., Ste. 305
Brownsville, TX 78521
(210)541-4508

SCORE Office (Brazos Valley)
3000 Briarcrest, Ste. 302
Bryan, TX 77802
(409)776-8876
E-mail: 102633.2612@compuserve.com

SCORE Office (Cleburne)
Watergarden Pl., 9th Fl., Ste. 400
Cleburne, TX 76031
(817)871-6002

SCORE Office (Corpus Christi)
651 Upper North Broadway, Ste. 654
Corpus Christi, TX 78477

(512)888-4322
Fax: (512)888-3418

SCORE Office (Dallas)
6260 E. Mockingbird
Dallas, TX 75214-2619
(214)828-2471
Fax: (214)821-8033

SCORE Office (El Paso)
10 Civic Center Plaza
El Paso, TX 79901
(915)534-0541
Fax: (915)534-0513

SCORE Office (Bedford)
100 E. 15th St., Ste. 400
Ft. Worth, TX 76102
(817)871-6002

SCORE Office (Ft. Worth)
100 E. 15th St., No. 24
Ft. Worth, TX 76102
(817)871-6002
Fax: (817)871-6031
E-mail: fwbac@onramp.net

SCORE Office (Garland)
2734 W. Kingsley Rd.
Garland, TX 75041
(214)271-9224

SCORE Office (Granbury Chamber of Commerce)
416 S. Morgan
Granbury, TX 76048
(817)573-1622
Fax: (817)573-0805

SCORE Office (Lower Rio Grande Valley)
222 E. Van Buren, Ste. 500
Harlingen, TX 78550
(956)427-8533
Fax: (956)427-8537

SCORE Office (Houston)
9301 Southwest Fwy., Ste. 550
Houston, TX 77074
(713)773-6565
Fax: (713)773-6550

SCORE Office (Irving)
3333 N. MacArthur Blvd., Ste. 100
Irving, TX 75062
(214)252-8484
Fax: (214)252-6710

SCORE Office (Lubbock)
1205 Texas Ave., Rm. 411D
Lubbock, TX 79401
(806)472-7462
Fax: (806)472-7487

SCORE Office (Midland)
Post Office Annex
200 E. Wall St., Rm. P121
Midland, TX 79701
(915)687-2649

SCORE Office (Orange)
1012 Green Ave.
Orange, TX 77630-5620
(409)883-3536
800-528-4906
Fax: (409)886-3247

SCORE Office (Plano)
1200 E. 15th St.
PO Drawer 940287
Plano, TX 75094-0287
(214)424-7547
Fax: (214)422-5182

SCORE Office (Port Arthur)
4749 Twin City Hwy., Ste. 300
Port Arthur, TX 77642
(409)963-1107
Fax: (409)963-3322

SCORE Office (Richardson)
411 Belle Grove
Richardson, TX 75080
(214)234-4141
800-777-8001
Fax: (214)680-9103

SCORE Office (San Antonio)
Federal Bldg., Rm. A527
727 E. Durango
San Antonio, TX 78206
(210)472-5931
Fax: (210)472-5935

SCORE Office (Texarkana State College)
819 State Line Ave.
Texarkana, TX 75501
(903)792-7191
Fax: (903)793-4304

SCORE Office (East Texas)
RTDC
1530 SSW Loop 323, Ste. 100
Tyler, TX 75701
(903)510-2975
Fax: (903)510-2978

SCORE Office (Waco)
401 Franklin Ave.
Waco, TX 76701
(817)754-8898
Fax: (817)756-0776
Website: http://www.brc-waco.com/

SCORE Office (Wichita Falls)
Hamilton Bldg.
900 8th St.
Wichita Falls, TX 76307
(940)723-2741
Fax: (940)723-8773

Utah

SCORE Office (Northern Utah)
160 N. Main
Logan, UT 84321
(435)746-2269

SCORE Office (Ogden)
1701 E. Windsor Dr.
Ogden, UT 84604
(801)629-8613
E-mail: score158@netscape.net

SCORE Office (Central Utah)
1071 E. Windsor Dr.
Provo, UT 84604
(801)373-8660

SCORE Office (Southern Utah)
225 South 700 East
St. George, UT 84770
(435)652-7751

SCORE Office (Salt Lake)
310 S Main St.
Salt Lake City, UT 84101
(801)746-2269
Fax: (801)746-2273

Vermont

SCORE Office (Champlain Valley)
Winston Prouty Federal Bldg.
11 Lincoln St., Rm. 106
Essex Junction, VT 05452
(802)951-6762

SCORE Office (Montpelier)
87 State St., Rm. 205
PO Box 605
Montpelier, VT 05601
(802)828-4422
Fax: (802)828-4485

SCORE Office (Marble Valley)
256 N. Main St.
Rutland, VT 05701-2413
(802)773-9147

SCORE Office (Northeast Kingdom)
20 Main St.
PO Box 904
St. Johnsbury, VT 05819
(802)748-5101

Virgin Islands

SCORE Office (St. Croix)
United Plaza Shopping Center
PO Box 4010, Christiansted
St. Croix, VI 00822
(809)778-5380

SCORE Office (St. Thomas-St. John)
Federal Bldg., Rm. 21
Veterans Dr.
St. Thomas, VI 00801
(809)774-8530

Virginia

SCORE Office (Arlington)
2009 N. 14th St., Ste. 111
Arlington, VA 22201
(703)525-2400

SCORE Office (Blacksburg)
141 Jackson St.
Blacksburg, VA 24060
(540)552-4061

SCORE Office (Bristol)
20 Volunteer Pkwy.
Bristol, VA 24203
(540)989-4850

SCORE Office (Central Virginia)
1001 E. Market St., Ste. 101
Charlottesville, VA 22902
(804)295-6712
Fax: (804)295-7066

SCORE Office (Alleghany Satellite)
241 W. Main St.
Covington, VA 24426
(540)962-2178
Fax: (540)962-2179

SCORE Office (Central Fairfax)
3975 University Dr., Ste. 350
Fairfax, VA 22030
(703)591-2450

SCORE Office (Falls Church)
PO Box 491
Falls Church, VA 22040
(703)532-1050
Fax: (703)237-7904

SCORE Office (Glenns)
Glenns Campus
Box 287
Glenns, VA 23149
(804)693-9650

SCORE Office (Peninsula)
6 Manhattan Sq.
PO Box 7269
Hampton, VA 23666
(757)766-2000
Fax: (757)865-0339
E-mail: score100@seva.net

SCORE Office (Tri-Cities)
108 N. Main St.
Hopewell, VA 23860
(804)458-5536

SCORE Office (Lynchburg)
Federal Bldg.
1100 Main St.
Lynchburg, VA 24504-1714
(804)846-3235

SCORE Office (Greater Prince William)
8963 Center St
Manassas, VA 20110
(703)368-4813
Fax: (703)368-4733

SCORE Office (Martinsvile)
115 Broad St.
Martinsville, VA 24112-0709
(540)632-6401
Fax: (540)632-5059

SCORE Office (Hampton Roads)
Federal Bldg., Rm. 737
200 Grandby St.
Norfolk, VA 23510
(757)441-3733
Fax: (757)441-3733
E-mail: scorehr60@juno.com

SCORE Office (Norfolk)
Federal Bldg., Rm. 737
200 Granby St.
Norfolk, VA 23510
(757)441-3733
Fax: (757)441-3733

SCORE Office (Virginia Beach)
Chamber of Commerce
200 Grandby St., Rm 737
Norfolk, VA 23510
(804)441-3733

SCORE Office (Radford)
1126 Norwood St.
Radford, VA 24141
(540)639-2202

SCORE Office (Richmond)
Federal Bldg.
400 N. 8th St., Ste. 1150
PO Box 10126
Richmond, VA 23240-0126
(804)771-2400
Fax: (804)771-8018
E-mail: scorechapter12@yahoo.com
Website: http://www.cvco.org/score/

SCORE Office (Roanoke)
Federal Bldg., Rm. 716
250 Franklin Rd.
Roanoke, VA 24011
(540)857-2834
Fax: (540)857-2043
E-mail: scorerva@juno.com
Website: http://hometown.aol.com/
scorerv/Index.html

SCORE Office (Fairfax)
8391 Old Courthouse Rd., Ste. 300
Vienna, VA 22182
(703)749-0400

SCORE Office (Greater Vienna)
513 Maple Ave. West
Vienna, VA 22180
(703)281-1333
Fax: (703)242-1482

**SCORE Office (Shenandoah
Valley)**
301 W. Main St.
Waynesboro, VA 22980
(540)949-8203
Fax: (540)949-7740
E-mail: score427@intelos.net

SCORE Office (Williamsburg)
201 Penniman Rd.
Williamsburg, VA 23185
(757)229-6511
E-mail: wacc@williamsburgcc.com

SCORE Office (Northern Virginia)
1360 S. Pleasant Valley Rd.
Winchester, VA 22601
(540)662-4118

Washington

SCORE Office (Gray's Harbor)
506 Duffy St.
Aberdeen, WA 98520
(360)532-1924
Fax: (360)533-7945

SCORE Office (Bellingham)
101 E. Holly St.

Bellingham, WA 98225
(360)676-3307

SCORE Office (Everett)
2702 Hoyt Ave.
Everett, WA 98201-3556
(206)259-8000

SCORE Office (Gig Harbor)
3125 Judson St.
Gig Harbor, WA 98335
(206)851-6865

SCORE Office (Kennewick)
PO Box 6986
Kennewick, WA 99336
(509)736-0510

SCORE Office (Puyallup)
322 2nd St. SW
PO Box 1298
Puyallup, WA 98371
(206)845-6755
Fax: (206)848-6164

SCORE Office (Seattle)
1200 6th Ave., Ste. 1700
Seattle, WA 98101
(206)553-7320
Fax: (206)553-7044
E-mail: score55@aol.com
Website: http://www.scn.org/civic/score-
online/index55.html

SCORE Office (Spokane)
801 W. Riverside Ave., No. 240
Spokane, WA 99201
(509)353-2820
Fax: (509)353-2600
E-mail: score@dmi.net
Website: http://www.dmi.net/score/

SCORE Office (Clover Park)
PO Box 1933
Tacoma, WA 98401-1933
(206)627-2175

SCORE Office (Tacoma)
1101 Pacific Ave.
Tacoma, WA 98402
(253)274-1288
Fax: (253)274-1289

SCORE Office (Fort Vancouver)
1701 Broadway, S-1
Vancouver, WA 98663
(360)699-1079

SCORE Office (Walla Walla)
500 Tausick Way
Walla Walla, WA 99362
(509)527-4681

SCORE Office (Mid-Columbia)
1113 S. 14th Ave.
Yakima, WA 98907
(509)574-4944
Fax: (509)574-2943
Website: http://www.ellensburg.com/
~score/

West Virginia

SCORE Office (Charleston)
1116 Smith St.
Charleston, WV 25301
(304)347-5463
E-mail: score256@juno.com

SCORE Office (Virginia Street)
1116 Smith St., Ste. 302
Charleston, WV 25301
(304)347-5463

SCORE Office (Marion County)
PO Box 208
Fairmont, WV 26555-0208
(304)363-0486

**SCORE Office (Upper Monongahela
Valley)**
1000 Technology Dr., Ste. 1111
Fairmont, WV 26555
(304)363-0486
E-mail: score537@hotmail.com

SCORE Office (Huntington)
1101 6th Ave., Ste. 220
Huntington, WV 25701-2309
(304)523-4092

SCORE Office (Wheeling)
1310 Market St.
Wheeling, WV 26003
(304)233-2575
Fax: (304)233-1320

Wisconsin

SCORE Office (Fox Cities)
227 S. Walnut St.
Appleton, WI 54913
(920)734-7101
Fax: (920)734-7161

SCORE Office (Beloit)
136 W. Grand Ave., Ste. 100
PO Box 717
Beloit, WI 53511
(608)365-8835
Fax: (608)365-9170

SCORE Office (Eau Claire)
Federal Bldg., Rm. B11

510 S. Barstow St.
Eau Claire, WI 54701
(715)834-1573
E-mail: score@ecol.net
Website: http://www.ecol.net/~score/

SCORE Office (Fond du Lac)
207 N. Main St.
Fond du Lac, WI 54935
(414)921-9500
Fax: (414)921-9559

SCORE Office (Green Bay)
835 Potts Ave.
Green Bay, WI 54304
(414)496-8930
Fax: (414)496-6009

SCORE Office (Janesville)
20 S. Main St., Ste. 11
PO Box 8008
Janesville, WI 53547
(608)757-3160
Fax: (608)757-3170

SCORE Office (La Crosse)
712 Main St.
La Crosse, WI 54602-0219
(608)784-4880

SCORE Office (Madison)
505 S. Rosa Rd.
Madison, WI 53719
(608)441-2820

SCORE Office (Manitowoc)
1515 Memorial Dr.
PO Box 903
Manitowoc, WI 54221-0903
(414)684-5575
Fax: (414)684-1915

SCORE Office (Milwaukee)
310 W. Wisconsin Ave., Ste. 425
Milwaukee, WI 53203
(414)297-3942
Fax: (414)297-1377

SCORE Office (Central Wisconsin)
1224 Lindbergh Ave.
Stevens Point, WI 54481
(715)344-7729

SCORE Office (Superior)
Superior Business Center Inc.
1423 N. 8th St.
Superior, WI 54880
(715)394-7388
Fax: (715)393-7414

SCORE Office (Waukesha)
223 Wisconsin Ave.

Waukesha, WI 53186-4926
(414)542-4249

SCORE Office (Wausau)
300 3rd St., Ste. 200
Wausau, WI 54402-6190
(715)845-6231

SCORE Office (Wisconsin Rapids)
2240 Kingston Rd.
Wisconsin Rapids, WI 54494
(715)423-1830

Wyoming

SCORE Office (Casper)
Federal Bldg., No. 2215
100 East B St.
Casper, WY 82602
(307)261-6529
Fax: (307)261-6530

Venture capital & financing companies

This section contains a listing of financing and loan companies in the United States and Canada. These listing are arranged alphabetically by country, then by state or province, then by city, then by organization name.

Canada

Alberta

Launchworks Inc.
1902J 11th St., S.E.
Calgary, AB, Canada T2G 3G2
(403)269-1119
Fax: (403)269-1141
Website: http://www.launchworks.com

Native Venture Capital Company, Inc.
21 Artist View Point, Box 7
Site 25, RR 12
Calgary, AB, Canada T3E 6W3
(903)208-5380

Miralta Capital Inc.
4445 Calgary Trail South
888 Terrace Plaza Alberta
Edmonton, AB, Canada T6H 5R7
(780)438-3535
Fax: (780)438-3129

Vencap Equities Alberta Ltd.
10180-101st St., Ste. 1980
Edmonton, AB, Canada T5J 3S4
(403)420-1171
Fax: (403)429-2541

British Columbia

Discovery Capital
5th Fl., 1199 West Hastings
Vancouver, BC, Canada V6E 3T5
(604)683-3000
Fax: (604)662-3457
E-mail: info@discoverycapital.com
Website: http://www.discovery
capital.com

Greenstone Venture Partners
1177 West Hastings St.
Ste. 400
Vancouver, BC, Canada V6E 2K3
(604)717-1977
Fax: (604)717-1976
Website: http://www.greenstonevc.com

Growthworks Capital
2600-1055 West Georgia St.
Box 11170 Royal Centre
Vancouver, BC, Canada V6E 3R5
(604)895-7259
Fax: (604)669-7605
Website: http://www.wofund.com

MDS Discovery Venture Management, Inc.
555 W. Eighth Ave., Ste. 305
Vancouver, BC, Canada V5Z 1C6
(604)872-8464
Fax: (604)872-2977
E-mail: info@mds-ventures.com

Ventures West Management Inc.
1285 W. Pender St., Ste. 280
Vancouver, BC, Canada V6E 4B1
(604)688-9495
Fax: (604)687-2145
Website: http://www.ventureswest.com

Nova Scotia

ACF Equity Atlantic Inc.
Purdy's Wharf Tower II
Ste. 2106
Halifax, NS, Canada B3J 3R7
(902)421-1965
Fax: (902)421-1808

Montgomerie, Huck & Co.
146 Bluenose Dr.
PO Box 538
Lunenburg, NS, Canada B0J 2C0
(902)634-7125
Fax: (902)634-7130

Ontario

IPS Industrial Promotion Services Ltd.
60 Columbia Way, Ste. 720
Markham, ON, Canada L3R 0C9
(905)475-9400
Fax: (905)475-5003

Betwin Investments Inc.
Box 23110
Sault Ste. Marie, ON, Canada P6A 6W6
(705)253-0744
Fax: (705)253-0744

Bailey & Company, Inc.
594 Spadina Ave.
Toronto, ON, Canada M5S 2H4
(416)921-6930
Fax: (416)925-4670

BCE Capital
200 Bay St.
South Tower, Ste. 3120
Toronto, ON, Canada M5J 2J2
(416)815-0078
Fax: (416)941-1073
Website: http://www.bcecapital.com

Castlehill Ventures
55 University Ave., Ste. 500
Toronto, ON, Canada M5J 2H7
(416)862-8574
Fax: (416)862-8875

CCFL Mezzanine Partners of Canada
70 University Ave.
Ste. 1450
Toronto, ON, Canada M5J 2M4
(416)977-1450
Fax: (416)977-6764
E-mail: info@ccfl.com
Website: http://www.ccfl.com

Celtic House International
100 Simcoe St., Ste. 100
Toronto, ON, Canada M5H 3G2
(416)542-2436
Fax: (416)542-2435
Website: http://www.celtic-house.com

Clairvest Group Inc.
22 St. Clair Ave. East
Ste. 1700
Toronto, ON, Canada M4T 2S3
(416)925-9270
Fax: (416)925-5753

Crosbie & Co., Inc.
One First Canadian Place
9th Fl.
PO Box 116

Toronto, ON, Canada M5X 1A4
(416)362-7726
Fax: (416)362-3447
E-mail: info@crosbieco.com
Website: http://www.crosbieco.com

Drug Royalty Corp.
Eight King St. East
Ste. 202
Toronto, ON, Canada M5C 1B5
(416)863-1865
Fax: (416)863-5161

Grieve, Horner, Brown & Asculai
8 King St. E, Ste. 1704
Toronto, ON, Canada M5C 1B5
(416)362-7668
Fax: (416)362-7660

Jefferson Partners
77 King St. West
Ste. 4010
PO Box 136
Toronto, ON, Canada M5K 1H1
(416)367-1533
Fax: (416)367-5827
Website: http://www.jefferson.com

J.L. Albright Venture Partners
Canada Trust Tower, 161 Bay St.
Ste. 4440
PO Box 215
Toronto, ON, Canada M5J 2S1
(416)367-2440
Fax: (416)367-4604
Website: http://www.jlaventures.com

McLean Watson Capital Inc.
One First Canadian Place
Ste. 1410
PO Box 129
Toronto, ON, Canada M5X 1A4
(416)363-2000
Fax: (416)363-2010
Website: http://www.mcleanwatson.com

Middlefield Capital Fund
One First Canadian Place
85th Fl.
PO Box 192
Toronto, ON, Canada M5X 1A6
(416)362-0714
Fax: (416)362-7925
Website: http://www.middlefield.com

Mosaic Venture Partners
24 Duncan St.
Ste. 300
Toronto, ON, Canada M5V 3M6
(416)597-8889
Fax: (416)597-2345

Onex Corp.
161 Bay St.
PO Box 700
Toronto, ON, Canada M5J 2S1
(416)362-7711
Fax: (416)362-5765

Penfund Partners Inc.
145 King St. West
Ste. 1920
Toronto, ON, Canada M5H 1J8
(416)865-0300
Fax: (416)364-6912
Website: http://www.penfund.com

Primaxis Technology Ventures Inc.
1 Richmond St. West, 8th Fl.
Toronto, ON, Canada M5H 3W4
(416)313-5210
Fax: (416)313-5218
Website: http://www.primaxis.com

Priveq Capital Funds
240 Duncan Mill Rd., Ste. 602
Toronto, ON, Canada M3B 3P1
(416)447-3330
Fax: (416)447-3331
E-mail: priveq@sympatico.ca

Roynat Ventures
40 King St. West, 26th Fl.
Toronto, ON, Canada M5H 1H1
(416)933-2667
Fax: (416)933-2783
Website: http://www.roynatcapital.com

Tera Capital Corp.
366 Adelaide St. East, Ste. 337
Toronto, ON, Canada M5A 3X9
(416)368-1024
Fax: (416)368-1427

Working Ventures Canadian Fund Inc.
250 Bloor St. East, Ste. 1600
Toronto, ON, Canada M4W 1E6
(416)934-7718
Fax: (416)929-0901
Website: http://www.workingventures.ca

Quebec

Altamira Capital Corp.
202 University
Niveau de Maisoneuve, Bur. 201
Montreal, QC, Canada H3A 2A5
(514)499-1656
Fax: (514)499-9570

Federal Business Development Bank
Venture Capital Division
Five Place Ville Marie, Ste. 600

Montreal, QC, Canada H3B 5E7
(514)283-1896
Fax: (514)283-5455

Hydro-Quebec Capitech Inc.
75 Boul, Rene Levesque Quest
Montreal, QC, Canada H2Z 1A4
(514)289-4783
Fax: (514)289-5420
Website: http://www.hqcapitech.com

Investissement Desjardins
2 complexe Desjardins
C.P. 760
Montreal, QC, Canada H5B 1B8
(514)281-7131
Fax: (514)281-7808
Website: http://www.desjardins.com/id

Marleau Lemire Inc.
One Place Ville-Marie, Ste. 3601
Montreal, QC, Canada H3B 3P2
(514)877-3800
Fax: (514)875-6415

Speirs Consultants Inc.
365 Stanstead
Montreal, QC, Canada H3R 1X5
(514)342-3858
Fax: (514)342-1977

Tecnocap Inc.
4028 Marlowe
Montreal, QC, Canada H4A 3M2
(514)483-6009
Fax: (514)483-6045
Website: http://www.technocap.com

Telsoft Ventures
1000, Rue de la Gauchetiere
Quest, 25eme Etage
Montreal, QC, Canada H3B 4W5
(514)397-8450
Fax: (514)397-8451

Saskatchewan

Saskatchewan Government Growth Fund
1801 Hamilton St., Ste. 1210
Canada Trust Tower
Regina, SK, Canada S4P 4B4
(306)787-2994
Fax: (306)787-2086

United states

Alabama

FHL Capital Corp.
600 20th Street North
Suite 350

Birmingham, AL 35203
(205)328-3098
Fax: (205)323-0001

Harbert Management Corp.
One Riverchase Pkwy. South
Birmingham, AL 35244
(205)987-5500
Fax: (205)987-5707
Website: http://www.harbert.net

Jefferson Capital Fund
PO Box 13129
Birmingham, AL 35213
(205)324-7709

Private Capital Corp.
100 Brookwood Pl., 4th Fl.
Birmingham, AL 35209
(205)879-2722
Fax: (205)879-5121

21st Century Health Ventures
One Health South Pkwy.
Birmingham, AL 35243
(256)268-6250
Fax: (256)970-8928

FJC Growth Capital Corp.
200 W. Side Sq., Ste. 340
Huntsville, AL 35801
(256)922-2918
Fax: (256)922-2909

Hickory Venture Capital Corp.
301 Washington St. NW
Suite 301
Huntsville, AL 35801
(256)539-1931
Fax: (256)539-5130
E-mail: hvcc@hvcc.com
Website: http://www.hvcc.com

Southeastern Technology Fund
7910 South Memorial Pkwy., Ste. F
Huntsville, AL 35802
(256)883-8711
Fax: (256)883-8558

Cordova Ventures
4121 Carmichael Rd., Ste. 301
Montgomery, AL 36106
(334)271-6011
Fax: (334)260-0120
Website: http://
www.cordovaventures.com

**Small Business Clinic of Alabama/AG
Bartholomew & Associates**
PO Box 231074
Montgomery, AL 36123-1074
(334)284-3640

Arizona

Miller Capital Corp.
4909 E. McDowell Rd.
Phoenix, AZ 85008
(602)225-0504
Fax: (602)225-9024
Website: http://www.themillergroup.com

The Columbine Venture Funds
9449 North 90th St., Ste. 200
Scottsdale, AZ 85258
(602)661-9222
Fax: (602)661-6262

Koch Ventures
17767 N. Perimeter Dr., Ste. 101
Scottsdale, AZ 85255
(480)419-3600
Fax: (480)419-3606
Website: http://www.kochventures.com

McKee & Co.
7702 E. Doubletree Ranch Rd.
Suite 230
Scottsdale, AZ 85258
(480)368-0333
Fax: (480)607-7446

Merita Capital Ltd.
7350 E. Stetson Dr., Ste. 108-A
Scottsdale, AZ 85251
(480)947-8700
Fax: (480)947-8766

**Valley Ventures / Arizona Growth
Partners L.P.**
6720 N. Scottsdale Rd., Ste. 208
Scottsdale, AZ 85253
(480)661-6600
Fax: (480)661-6262

Estreetcapital.com
660 South Mill Ave., Ste. 315
Tempe, AZ 85281
(480)968-8400
Fax: (480)968-8480
Website: http://www.estreetcapital.com

Coronado Venture Fund
PO Box 65420
Tucson, AZ 85728-5420
(520)577-3764
Fax: (520)299-8491

Arkansas

Arkansas Capital Corp.
225 South Pulaski St.
Little Rock, AR 72201
(501)374-9247

Fax: (501)374-9425
Website: http://www.arcapital.com

California

Sundance Venture Partners, L.P.
100 Clocktower Place, Ste. 130
Carmel, CA 93923
(831)625-6500
Fax: (831)625-6590

Westar Capital (Costa Mesa)
949 South Coast Dr., Ste. 650
Costa Mesa, CA 92626
(714)481-5160
Fax: (714)481-5166
E-mail: mailbox@westarcapital.com
Website: http://www.westarcapital.com

Alpine Technology Ventures
20300 Stevens Creek Boulevard, Ste. 495
Cupertino, CA 95014
(408)725-1810
Fax: (408)725-1207
Website: http://www.alpineventures.com

Bay Partners
10600 N. De Anza Blvd.
Cupertino, CA 95014-2031
(408)725-2444
Fax: (408)446-4502
Website: http://www.baypartners.com

Novus Ventures
20111 Stevens Creek Blvd., Ste. 130
Cupertino, CA 95014
(408)252-3900
Fax: (408)252-1713
Website: http://www.novusventures.com

Triune Capital
19925 Stevens Creek Blvd., Ste. 200
Cupertino, CA 95014
(310)284-6800
Fax: (310)284-3290

Acorn Ventures
268 Bush St., Ste. 2829
Daly City, CA 94014
(650)994-7801
Fax: (650)994-3305
Website: http://www.acornventures.com

Digital Media Campus
2221 Park Place
El Segundo, CA 90245
(310)426-8000
Fax: (310)426-8010
E-mail: info@thecampus.com
Website: http://www.digitalmedia
campus.com

BankAmerica Ventures / BA Venture Partners
950 Tower Ln., Ste. 700
Foster City, CA 94404
(650)378-6000
Fax: (650)378-6040
Website: http://
www.baventurepartners.com

Starting Point Partners
666 Portofino Lane
Foster City, CA 94404
(650)722-1035
Website: http://www.startingpoint
partners.com

Opportunity Capital Partners
2201 Walnut Ave., Ste. 210
Fremont, CA 94538
(510)795-7000
Fax: (510)494-5439
Website: http://www.ocpcapital.com

Imperial Ventures Inc.
9920 S. La Cienega Boulevar, 14th Fl.
Inglewood, CA 90301
(310)417-5409
Fax: (310)338-6115

Ventana Global (Irvine)
18881 Von Karman Ave., Ste. 1150
Irvine, CA 92612
(949)476-2204
Fax: (949)752-0223
Website: http://www.ventanaglobal.com

Integrated Consortium Inc.
50 Ridgecrest Rd.
Kentfield, CA 94904
(415)925-0386
Fax: (415)461-2726

Enterprise Partners
979 Ivanhoe Ave., Ste. 550
La Jolla, CA 92037
(858)454-8833
Fax: (858)454-2489
Website: http://www.epvc.com

Domain Associates
28202 Cabot Rd., Ste. 200
Laguna Niguel, CA 92677
(949)347-2446
Fax: (949)347-9720
Website: http://www.domainvc.com

Cascade Communications Ventures
60 E. Sir Francis Drake Blvd., Ste. 300
Larkspur, CA 94939
(415)925-6500
Fax: (415)925-6501

Allegis Capital
One First St., Ste. Two
Los Altos, CA 94022
(650)917-5900
Fax: (650)917-5901
Website: http://www.allegiscapital.com

Aspen Ventures
1000 Fremont Ave., Ste. 200
Los Altos, CA 94024
(650)917-5670
Fax: (650)917-5677
Website: http://www.aspenventures.com

AVI Capital L.P.
1 First St., Ste. 2
Los Altos, CA 94022
(650)949-9862
Fax: (650)949-8510
Website: http://www.avicapital.com

Bastion Capital Corp.
1999 Avenue of the Stars, Ste. 2960
Los Angeles, CA 90067
(310)788-5700
Fax: (310)277-7582
E-mail: ga@bastioncapital.com
Website: http://www.bastioncapital.com

Davis Group
PO Box 69953
Los Angeles, CA 90069-0953
(310)659-6327
Fax: (310)659-6337

Developers Equity Corp.
1880 Century Park East, Ste. 211
Los Angeles, CA 90067
(213)277-0300

Far East Capital Corp.
350 S. Grand Ave., Ste. 4100
Los Angeles, CA 90071
(213)687-1361
Fax: (213)617-7939
E-mail: free@fareastnationalbank.com

Kline Hawkes & Co.
11726 San Vicente Blvd., Ste. 300
Los Angeles, CA 90049
(310)442-4700
Fax: (310)442-4707
Website: http://www.klinehawkes.com

Lawrence Financial Group
701 Teakwood
PO Box 491773
Los Angeles, CA 90049
(310)471-4060
Fax: (310)472-3155

Riordan Lewis & Haden
300 S. Grand Ave., 29th Fl.
Los Angeles, CA 90071
(213)229-8500
Fax: (213)229-8597

Union Venture Corp.
445 S. Figueroa St., 9th Fl.
Los Angeles, CA 90071
(213)236-4092
Fax: (213)236-6329

Wedbush Capital Partners
1000 Wilshire Blvd.
Los Angeles, CA 90017
(213)688-4545
Fax: (213)688-6642
Website: http://www.wedbush.com

Advent International Corp.
2180 Sand Hill Rd., Ste. 420
Menlo Park, CA 94025
(650)233-7500
Fax: (650)233-7515
Website: http://www.advent
international.com

Altos Ventures
2882 Sand Hill Rd., Ste. 100
Menlo Park, CA 94025
(650)234-9771
Fax: (650)233-9821
Website: http://www.altosvc.com

Applied Technology
1010 El Camino Real, Ste. 300
Menlo Park, CA 94025
(415)326-8622
Fax: (415)326-8163

APV Technology Partners
535 Middlefield, Ste. 150
Menlo Park, CA 94025
(650)327-7871
Fax: (650)327-7631
Website: http://www.apvtp.com

**August Capital
Management**
2480 Sand Hill Rd., Ste. 101
Menlo Park, CA 94025
(650)234-9900
Fax: (650)234-9910
Website: http://www.augustcap.com

Baccharis Capital Inc.
2420 Sand Hill Rd., Ste. 100
Menlo Park, CA 94025
(650)324-6844
Fax: (650)854-3025

Benchmark Capital
2480 Sand Hill Rd., Ste. 200
Menlo Park, CA 94025
(650)854-8180
Fax: (650)854-8183
E-mail: info@benchmark.com
Website: http://www.bench
mark.com

**Bessemer Venture Partners
(Menlo Park)**
535 Middlefield Rd., Ste. 245
Menlo Park, CA 94025
(650)853-7000
Fax: (650)853-7001
Website: http://www.bvp.com

The Cambria Group
1600 El Camino Real Rd., Ste. 155
Menlo Park, CA 94025
(650)329-8600
Fax: (650)329-8601
Website: http://www.cambria
group.com

Canaan Partners
2884 Sand Hill Rd., Ste. 115
Menlo Park, CA 94025
(650)854-8092
Fax: (650)854-8127
Website: http://www.canaan.com

Capstone Ventures
3000 Sand Hill Rd., Bldg. One, Ste. 290
Menlo Park, CA 94025
(650)854-2523
Fax: (650)854-9010
Website: http://www.capstonevc.com

**Comdisco Venture Group
(Silicon Valley)**
3000 Sand Hill Rd., Bldg. 1, Ste. 155
Menlo Park, CA 94025
(650)854-9484
Fax: (650)854-4026

Commtech International
535 Middlefield Rd., Ste. 200
Menlo Park, CA 94025
(650)328-0190
Fax: (650)328-6442

**Compass Technology
Partners**
1550 El Camino Real, Ste. 275
Menlo Park, CA 94025-4111
(650)322-7595
Fax: (650)322-0588
Website: http://www.compasstech
partners.com

Convergence Partners
3000 Sand Hill Rd., Ste. 235
Menlo Park, CA 94025
(650)854-3010
Fax: (650)854-3015
Website: http://www.convergence
partners.com

The Dakota Group
PO Box 1025
Menlo Park, CA 94025
(650)853-0600
Fax: (650)851-4899
E-mail: info@dakota.com

Delphi Ventures
3000 Sand Hill Rd.
Bldg. One, Ste. 135
Menlo Park, CA 94025
(650)854-9650
Fax: (650)854-2961
Website: http://www.delphi
ventures.com

El Dorado Ventures
2884 Sand Hill Rd., Ste. 121
Menlo Park, CA 94025
(650)854-1200
Fax: (650)854-1202
Website: http://
www.eldoradoventures.com

Glynn Ventures
3000 Sand Hill Rd., Bldg. 4, Ste. 235
Menlo Park, CA 94025
(650)854-2215

Indosuez Ventures
2180 Sand Hill Rd., Ste. 450
Menlo Park, CA 94025
(650)854-0587
Fax: (650)323-5561
Website: http://www.indosuez
ventures.com

**Institutional Venture
Partners**
3000 Sand Hill Rd., Bldg. 2, Ste. 290
Menlo Park, CA 94025
(650)854-0132
Fax: (650)854-5762
Website: http://www.ivp.com

**Interwest Partners (Menlo
Park)**
3000 Sand Hill Rd., Bldg. 3, Ste. 255
Menlo Park, CA 94025-7112
(650)854-8585
Fax: (650)854-4706
Website: http://www.interwest.com

Kleiner Perkins Caufield & Byers (Menlo Park)
2750 Sand Hill Rd.
Menlo Park, CA 94025
(650)233-2750
Fax: (650)233-0300
Website: http://www.kpcb.com

Magic Venture Capital LLC
1010 El Camino Real, Ste. 300
Menlo Park, CA 94025
(650)325-4149

Matrix Partners
2500 Sand Hill Rd., Ste. 113
Menlo Park, CA 94025
(650)854-3131
Fax: (650)854-3296
Website: http://www.matrixpartners.com

Mayfield Fund
2800 Sand Hill Rd.
Menlo Park, CA 94025
(650)854-5560
Fax: (650)854-5712
Website: http://www.mayfield.com

McCown De Leeuw and Co. (Menlo Park)
3000 Sand Hill Rd., Bldg. 3, Ste. 290
Menlo Park, CA 94025-7111
(650)854-6000
Fax: (650)854-0853
Website: http://www.mdcpartners.com

Menlo Ventures
3000 Sand Hill Rd., Bldg. 4, Ste. 100
Menlo Park, CA 94025
(650)854-8540
Fax: (650)854-7059
Website: http://www.menloventures.com

Merrill Pickard Anderson & Eyre
2480 Sand Hill Rd., Ste. 200
Menlo Park, CA 94025
(650)854-8600
Fax: (650)854-0345

New Enterprise Associates (Menlo Park)
2490 Sand Hill Rd.
Menlo Park, CA 94025
(650)854-9499
Fax: (650)854-9397
Website: http://www.nea.com

Onset Ventures
2400 Sand Hill Rd., Ste. 150
Menlo Park, CA 94025
(650)529-0700
Fax: (650)529-0777
Website: http://www.onset.com

Paragon Venture Partners
3000 Sand Hill Rd., Bldg. 1, Ste. 275
Menlo Park, CA 94025
(650)854-8000
Fax: (650)854-7260

Pathfinder Venture Capital Funds (Menlo Park)
3000 Sand Hill Rd., Bldg. 3, Ste. 255
Menlo Park, CA 94025
(650)854-0650
Fax: (650)854-4706

Rocket Ventures
3000 Sandhill Rd., Bldg. 1, Ste. 170
Menlo Park, CA 94025
(650)561-9100
Fax: (650)561-9183
Website: http://www.rocketventures.com

Sequoia Capital
3000 Sand Hill Rd., Bldg. 4, Ste. 280
Menlo Park, CA 94025
(650)854-3927
Fax: (650)854-2977
E-mail: sequoia@sequioacap.com
Website: http://www.sequoiacap.com

Sierra Ventures
3000 Sand Hill Rd., Bldg. 4, Ste. 210
Menlo Park, CA 94025
(650)854-1000
Fax: (650)854-5593
Website: http://www.sierraventures.com

Sigma Partners
2884 Sand Hill Rd., Ste. 121
Menlo Park, CA 94025-7022
(650)853-1700
Fax: (650)853-1717
E-mail: info@sigmapartners.com
Website: http://www.sigmapartners.com

Sprout Group (Menlo Park)
3000 Sand Hill Rd.
Bldg. 3, Ste. 170
Menlo Park, CA 94025
(650)234-2700
Fax: (650)234-2779
Website: http://www.sproutgroup.com

TA Associates (Menlo Park)
70 Willow Rd., Ste. 100
Menlo Park, CA 94025
(650)328-1210
Fax: (650)326-4933
Website: http://www.ta.com

Thompson Clive & Partners Ltd.
3000 Sand Hill Rd., Bldg. 1, Ste. 185
Menlo Park, CA 94025-7102

(650)854-0314
Fax: (650)854-0670
E-mail: mail@tcvc.com
Website: http://www.tcvc.com

Trinity Ventures Ltd.
3000 Sand Hill Rd., Bldg. 1, Ste. 240
Menlo Park, CA 94025
(650)854-9500
Fax: (650)854-9501
Website: http://www.trinityventures.com

U.S. Venture Partners
2180 Sand Hill Rd., Ste. 300
Menlo Park, CA 94025
(650)854-9080
Fax: (650)854-3018
Website: http://www.usvp.com

USVP-Schlein Marketing Fund
2180 Sand Hill Rd., Ste. 300
Menlo Park, CA 94025
(415)854-9080
Fax: (415)854-3018
Website: http://www.usvp.com

Venrock Associates
2494 Sand Hill Rd., Ste. 200
Menlo Park, CA 94025
(650)561-9580
Fax: (650)561-9180
Website: http://www.venrock.com

Brad Peery Capital Inc.
145 Chapel Pkwy.
Mill Valley, CA 94941
(415)389-0625
Fax: (415)389-1336

Dot Edu Ventures
650 Castro St., Ste. 270
Mountain View, CA 94041
(650)575-5638
Fax: (650)325-5247
Website: http://www.dotedu
ventures.com

Forrest, Binkley & Brown
840 Newport Ctr. Dr., Ste. 480
Newport Beach, CA 92660
(949)729-3222
Fax: (949)729-3226
Website: http://www.fbbvc.com

Marwit Capital LLC
180 Newport Center Dr., Ste. 200
Newport Beach, CA 92660
(949)640-6234
Fax: (949)720-8077
Website: http://www.marwit.com

Kaiser Permanente / National Venture Development
1800 Harrison St., 22nd Fl.
Oakland, CA 94612
(510)267-4010
Fax: (510)267-4036
Website: http://www.kpventures.com

Nu Capital Access Group, Ltd.
7677 Oakport St., Ste. 105
Oakland, CA 94621
(510)635-7345
Fax: (510)635-7068

Inman and Bowman
4 Orinda Way, Bldg. D, Ste. 150
Orinda, CA 94563
(510)253-1611
Fax: (510)253-9037

Accel Partners (San Francisco)
428 University Ave.
Palo Alto, CA 94301
(650)614-4800
Fax: (650)614-4880
Website: http://www.accel.com

Advanced Technology Ventures
485 Ramona St., Ste. 200
Palo Alto, CA 94301
(650)321-8601
Fax: (650)321-0934
Website: http://www.atvcapital.com

Anila Fund
400 Channing Ave.
Palo Alto, CA 94301
(650)833-5790
Fax: (650)833-0590
Website: http://www.anila.com

Asset Management Company Venture Capital
2275 E. Bayshore, Ste. 150
Palo Alto, CA 94303
(650)494-7400
Fax: (650)856-1826
E-mail: postmaster@assetman.com
Website: http://www.assetman.com

BancBoston Capital / BancBoston Ventures
435 Tasso St., Ste. 250
Palo Alto, CA 94305
(650)470-4100
Fax: (650)853-1425
Website: http://
www.bancbostoncapital.com

Charter Ventures
525 University Ave., Ste. 1400
Palo Alto, CA 94301

(650)325-6953
Fax: (650)325-4762
Website: http://
www.charterventures.com

Communications Ventures
505 Hamilton Avenue, Ste. 305
Palo Alto, CA 94301
(650)325-9600
Fax: (650)325-9608
Website: http://www.comven.com

HMS Group
2468 Embarcadero Way
Palo Alto, CA 94303-3313
(650)856-9862
Fax: (650)856-9864

Jafco America Ventures, Inc.
505 Hamilton Ste. 310
Palto Alto, CA 94301
(650)463-8800
Fax: (650)463-8801
Website: http://www.jafco.com

New Vista Capital
540 Cowper St., Ste. 200
Palo Alto, CA 94301
(650)329-9333
Fax: (650)328-9434
E-mail: fgreene@nvcap.com
Website: http://www.nvcap.com

Norwest Equity Partners (Palo Alto)
245 Lytton Ave., Ste. 250
Palo Alto, CA 94301-1426
(650)321-8000
Fax: (650)321-8010
Website: http://www.norwestvp.com

Oak Investment Partners
525 University Ave., Ste. 1300
Palo Alto, CA 94301
(650)614-3700
Fax: (650)328-6345
Website: http://www.oakinv.com

**Patricof & Co. Ventures, Inc.
(Palo Alto)**
2100 Geng Rd., Ste. 150
Palo Alto, CA 94303
(650)494-9944
Fax: (650)494-6751
Website: http://www.patricof.com

RWI Group
835 Page Mill Rd.
Palo Alto, CA 94304
(650)251-1800
Fax: (650)213-8660
Website: http://www.rwigroup.com

Summit Partners (Palo Alto)
499 Hamilton Ave., Ste. 200
Palo Alto, CA 94301
(650)321-1166
Fax: (650)321-1188
Website: http://
www.summitpartners.com

Sutter Hill Ventures
755 Page Mill Rd., Ste. A-200
Palo Alto, CA 94304
(650)493-5600
Fax: (650)858-1854
E-mail: shv@shv.com

Vanguard Venture Partners
525 University Ave., Ste. 600
Palo Alto, CA 94301
(650)321-2900
Fax: (650)321-2902
Website: http://www.vanguard
ventures.com

Venture Growth Associates
2479 East Bayshore St., Ste. 710
Palo Alto, CA 94303
(650)855-9100
Fax: (650)855-9104

Worldview Technology Partners
435 Tasso St., Ste. 120
Palo Alto, CA 94301
(650)322-3800
Fax: (650)322-3880
Website: http://www.worldview.com

Draper, Fisher, Jurvetson / Draper Associates
400 Seaport Ct., Ste.250
Redwood City, CA 94063
(415)599-9000
Fax: (415)599-9726
Website: http://www.dfj.com

Gabriel Venture Partners
350 Marine Pkwy., Ste. 200
Redwood Shores, CA 94065
(650)551-5000
Fax: (650)551-5001
Website: http://www.gabrielvp.com

Hallador Venture Partners, L.L.C.
740 University Ave., Ste. 110
Sacramento, CA 95825-6710
(916)920-0191
Fax: (916)920-5188
E-mail: chris@hallador.com

Emerald Venture Group
12396 World Trade Dr., Ste. 116
San Diego, CA 92128

(858)451-1001
Fax: (858)451-1003
Website: http://www.emerald
venture.com

Forward Ventures
9255 Towne Centre Dr.
San Diego, CA 92121
(858)677-6077
Fax: (858)452-8799
E-mail: info@forwardventure.com
Website: http://www.forward
venture.com

Idanta Partners Ltd.
4660 La Jolla Village Dr., Ste. 850
San Diego, CA 92122
(619)452-9690
Fax: (619)452-2013
Website: http://www.idanta.com

Kingsbury Associates
3655 Nobel Dr., Ste. 490
San Diego, CA 92122
(858)677-0600
Fax: (858)677-0800

Kyocera International Inc.
Corporate Development
8611 Balboa Ave.
San Diego, CA 92123
(858)576-2600
Fax: (858)492-1456

Sorrento Associates, Inc.
4370 LaJolla Village Dr., Ste. 1040
San Diego, CA 92122
(619)452-3100
Fax: (619)452-7607
Website: http://www.sorrento
ventures.com

Western States Investment Group
9191 Towne Ctr. Dr., Ste. 310
San Diego, CA 92122
(619)678-0800
Fax: (619)678-0900

Aberdare Ventures
One Embarcadero Center, Ste. 4000
San Francisco, CA 94111
(415)392-7442
Fax: (415)392-4264
Website: http://www.aberdare.com

Acacia Venture Partners
101 California St., Ste. 3160
San Francisco, CA 94111
(415)433-4200
Fax: (415)433-4250
Website: http://www.acaciavp.com

Access Venture Partners
319 Laidley St.
San Francisco, CA 94131
(415)586-0132
Fax: (415)392-6310
Website: http://
www.accessventurepartners.com

Alta Partners
One Embarcadero Center, Ste. 4050
San Francisco, CA 94111
(415)362-4022
Fax: (415)362-6178
E-mail: alta@altapartners.com
Website: http://www.altapartners.com

Bangert Dawes Reade Davis & Thom
220 Montgomery St., Ste. 424
San Francisco, CA 94104
(415)954-9900
Fax: (415)954-9901
E-mail: bdrdt@pacbell.net

**Berkeley International
Capital Corp.**
650 California St., Ste. 2800
San Francisco, CA 94108-2609
(415)249-0450
Fax: (415)392-3929
Website: http://www.berkeleyvc.com

Blueprint Ventures LLC
456 Montgomery St., 22nd Fl.
San Francisco, CA 94104
(415)901-4000
Fax: (415)901-4035
Website: http://www.blueprint
ventures.com

Blumberg Capital Ventures
580 Howard St., Ste. 401
San Francisco, CA 94105
(415)905-5007
Fax: (415)357-5027
Website: http://www.blumberg-
capital.com

**Burr, Egan, Deleage, and Co.
(San Francisco)**
1 Embarcadero Center, Ste. 4050
San Francisco, CA 94111
(415)362-4022
Fax: (415)362-6178

Burrill & Company
120 Montgomery St., Ste. 1370
San Francisco, CA 94104
(415)743-3160
Fax: (415)743-3161
Website: http://www.burrillandco.com

CMEA Ventures
235 Montgomery St., Ste. 920
San Francisco, CA 94401
(415)352-1520
Fax: (415)352-1524
Website: http://www.cmeaventures.com

Crocker Capital
1 Post St., Ste. 2500
San Francisco, CA 94101
(415)956-5250
Fax: (415)959-5710

Dominion Ventures, Inc.
44 Montgomery St., Ste. 4200
San Francisco, CA 94104
(415)362-4890
Fax: (415)394-9245

Dorset Capital
Pier 1
Bay 2
San Francisco, CA 94111
(415)398-7101
Fax: (415)398-7141
Website: http://www.dorsetcapital.com

Gatx Capital
Four Embarcadero Center, Ste. 2200
San Francisco, CA 94904
(415)955-3200
Fax: (415)955-3449

IMinds
135 Main St., Ste. 1350
San Francisco, CA 94105
(415)547-0000
Fax: (415)227-0300
Website: http://www.iminds.com

LF International Inc.
360 Post St., Ste. 705
San Francisco, CA 94108
(415)399-0110
Fax: (415)399-9222
Website: http://www.lfvc.com

Newbury Ventures
535 Pacific Ave., 2nd Fl.
San Francisco, CA 94133
(415)296-7408
Fax: (415)296-7416
Website: http://www.newburyven.com

**Quest Ventures (San
Francisco)**
333 Bush St., Ste. 1750
San Francisco, CA 94104
(415)782-1414
Fax: (415)782-1415

Robertson-Stephens Co.
555 California St., Ste. 2600
San Francisco, CA 94104
(415)781-9700
Fax: (415)781-2556
Website: http://
www.omegaadventures.com

Rosewood Capital, L.P.
One Maritime Plaza, Ste. 1330
San Francisco, CA 94111-3503
(415)362-5526
Fax: (415)362-1192
Website: http://www.rosewoodvc.com

Ticonderoga Capital Inc.
555 California St., No. 4950
San Francisco, CA 94104
(415)296-7900
Fax: (415)296-8956

**21st Century Internet
Venture Partners**
Two South Park
2nd Floor
San Francisco, CA 94107
(415)512-1221
Fax: (415)512-2650
Website: http://www.21vc.com

VK Ventures
600 California St., Ste.1700
San Francisco, CA 94111
(415)391-5600
Fax: (415)397-2744

**Walden Group of Venture Capital
Funds**
750 Battery St., Seventh Floor
San Francisco, CA 94111
(415)391-7225
Fax: (415)391-7262

Acer Technology Ventures
2641 Orchard Pkwy.
San Jose, CA 95134
(408)433-4945
Fax: (408)433-5230

Authosis
226 Airport Pkwy., Ste. 405
San Jose, CA 95110
(650)814-3603
Website: http://www.authosis.com

Western Technology Investment
2010 N. First St., Ste. 310
San Jose, CA 95131
(408)436-8577
Fax: (408)436-8625
E-mail: mktg@westerntech.com

Drysdale Enterprises
177 Bovet Rd., Ste. 600
San Mateo, CA 94402
(650)341-6336
Fax: (650)341-1329
E-mail: drysdale@aol.com

Greylock
2929 Campus Dr., Ste. 400
San Mateo, CA 94401
(650)493-5525
Fax: (650)493-5575
Website: http://www.greylock.com

Technology Funding
2000 Alameda de las Pulgas, Ste. 250
San Mateo, CA 94403
(415)345-2200
Fax: (415)345-1797

2M Invest Inc.
1875 S. Grant St.
Suite 750
San Mateo, CA 94402
(650)655-3765
Fax: (650)372-9107
E-mail: 2minfo@2minvest.com
Website: http://www.2minvest.com

Phoenix Growth Capital Corp.
2401 Kerner Blvd.
San Rafael, CA 94901
(415)485-4569
Fax: (415)485-4663

NextGen Partners LLC
1705 East Valley Rd.
Santa Barbara, CA 93108
(805)969-8540
Fax: (805)969-8542
Website: http://
www.nextgenpartners.com

Denali Venture Capital
1925 Woodland Ave.
Santa Clara, CA 95050
(408)690-4838
Fax: (408)247-6979
E-mail: wael@denaliventure
capital.com
Website: http://www.denaliventure
capital.com

Dotcom Ventures LP
3945 Freedom Circle, Ste. 740
Santa Clara, CA 95045
(408)919-9855
Fax: (408)919-9857
Website: http://www.dotcom
venturesatl.com

Silicon Valley Bank
3003 Tasman
Santa Clara, CA 95054
(408)654-7400
Fax: (408)727-8728

Al Shugart International
920 41st Ave.
Santa Cruz, CA 95062
(831)479-7852
Fax: (831)479-7852
Website: http://www.alshugart.com

Leonard Mautner Associates
1434 Sixth St.
Santa Monica, CA 90401
(213)393-9788
Fax: (310)459-9918

Palomar Ventures
100 Wilshire Blvd., Ste. 450
Santa Monica, CA 90401
(310)260-6050
Fax: (310)656-4150
Website: http://www.palomarventures.com

Medicus Venture Partners
12930 Saratoga Ave., Ste. D8
Saratoga, CA 95070
(408)447-8600
Fax: (408)447-8599
Website: http://www.medicusvc.com

Redleaf Venture Management
14395 Saratoga Ave., Ste. 130
Saratoga, CA 95070
(408)868-0800
Fax: (408)868-0810
E-mail: nancy@redleaf.com
Website: http://www.redleaf.com

Artemis Ventures
207 Second St., Ste. E
3rd Fl.
Sausalito, CA 94965
(415)289-2500
Fax: (415)289-1789
Website: http://www.artemis
ventures.com

Deucalion Venture Partners
19501 Brooklime
Sonoma, CA 95476
(707)938-4974
Fax: (707)938-8921

Windward Ventures
PO Box 7688
Thousand Oaks, CA 91359-7688
(805)497-3332
Fax: (805)497-9331

National Investment Management, Inc.
2601 Airport Dr., Ste.210
Torrance, CA 90505
(310)784-7600
Fax: (310)784-7605

Southern California Ventures
406 Amapola Ave. Ste. 125
Torrance, CA 90501
(310)787-4381
Fax: (310)787-4382

Sandton Financial Group
21550 Oxnard St., Ste. 300
Woodland Hills, CA 91367
(818)702-9283

Woodside Fund
850 Woodside Dr.
Woodside, CA 94062
(650)368-5545
Fax: (650)368-2416
Website: http://www.woodsidefund.com

Colorado

Colorado Venture Management
Ste. 300
Boulder, CO 80301
(303)440-4055
Fax: (303)440-4636

Dean & Associates
4362 Apple Way
Boulder, CO 80301
Fax: (303)473-9900

Roser Ventures LLC
1105 Spruce St.
Boulder, CO 80302
(303)443-6436
Fax: (303)443-1885
Website: http://www.roserventures.com

Sequel Venture Partners
4430 Arapahoe Ave., Ste. 220
Boulder, CO 80303
(303)546-0400
Fax: (303)546-9728
E-mail: tom@sequelvc.com
Website: http://www.sequelvc.com

New Venture Resources
445C E. Cheyenne Mtn. Blvd.
Colorado Springs, CO 80906-4570
(719)598-9272
Fax: (719)598-9272

The Centennial Funds
1428 15th St.
Denver, CO 80202-1318

(303)405-7500
Fax: (303)405-7575
Website: http://www.centennial.com

Rocky Mountain Capital Partners
1125 17th St., Ste. 2260
Denver, CO 80202
(303)291-5200
Fax: (303)291-5327

Sandlot Capital LLC
600 South Cherry St., Ste. 525
Denver, CO 80246
(303)893-3400
Fax: (303)893-3403
Website: http://www.sandlotcapital.com

Wolf Ventures
50 South Steele St., Ste. 777
Denver, CO 80209
(303)321-4800
Fax: (303)321-4848
E-mail: businessplan@wolf ventures.com
Website: http://www.wolf ventures.com

The Columbine Venture Funds
5460 S. Quebec St., Ste. 270
Englewood, CO 80111
(303)694-3222
Fax: (303)694-9007

Investment Securities of Colorado, Inc.
4605 Denice Dr.
Englewood, CO 80111
(303)796-9192

Kinship Partners
6300 S. Syracuse Way, Ste. 484
Englewood, CO 80111
(303)694-0268
Fax: (303)694-1707
E-mail: block@vailsys.com

Boranco Management, L.L.C.
1528 Hillside Dr.
Fort Collins, CO 80524-1969
(970)221-2297
Fax: (970)221-4787

Aweida Ventures
890 West Cherry St., Ste. 220
Louisville, CO 80027
(303)664-9520
Fax: (303)664-9530
Website: http://www.aweida.com

Access Venture Partners
8787 Turnpike Dr., Ste. 260
Westminster, CO 80030
(303)426-8899
Fax: (303)426-8828

Medmax Ventures LP
1 Northwestern Dr., Ste. 203
Bloomfield, CT 06002
(860)286-2960
Fax: (860)286-9960

James B. Kobak & Co.
Four Mansfield Place
Darien, CT 06820
(203)656-3471
Fax: (203)655-2905

Orien Ventures
1 Post Rd.
Fairfield, CT 06430
(203)259-9933
Fax: (203)259-5288

ABP Acquisition Corporation
115 Maple Ave.
Greenwich, CT 06830
(203)625-8287
Fax: (203)447-6187

Catterton Partners
9 Greenwich Office Park
Greenwich, CT 06830
(203)629-4901
Fax: (203)629-4903
Website: http://www.cpequity.com

Consumer Venture Partners
3 Pickwick Plz.
Greenwich, CT 06830
(203)629-8800
Fax: (203)629-2019

Insurance Venture Partners
31 Brookside Dr., Ste. 211
Greenwich, CT 06830
(203)861-0030
Fax: (203)861-2745

The NTC Group
Three Pickwick Plaza
Ste. 200
Greenwich, CT 06830
(203)862-2800
Fax: (203)622-6538

Regulus International Capital Co., Inc.
140 Greenwich Ave.
Greenwich, CT 06830
(203)625-9700
Fax: (203)625-9706

Axiom Venture Partners
City Place II
185 Asylum St., 17th Fl.
Hartford, CT 06103
(860)548-7799
Fax: (860)548-7797
Website: http://www.axiom
ventures.com

Conning Capital Partners
City Place II
185 Asylum St.
Hartford, CT 06103-4105
(860)520-1289
Fax: (860)520-1299
E-mail: pe@conning.com
Website: http://www.conning.com

First New England Capital L.P.
100 Pearl St.
Hartford, CT 06103
(860)293-3333
Fax: (860)293-3338
E-mail: info@firstnewengland
capital.com
Website: http://www.firstnewengland
capital.com

Northeast Ventures
One State St., Ste. 1720
Hartford, CT 06103
(860)547-1414
Fax: (860)246-8755

Windward Holdings
38 Sylvan Rd.
Madison, CT 06443
(203)245-6870
Fax: (203)245-6865

Advanced Materials Partners, Inc.
45 Pine St.
PO Box 1022
New Canaan, CT 06840
(203)966-6415
Fax: (203)966-8448
E-mail: wkb@amplink.com

RFE Investment Partners
36 Grove St.
New Canaan, CT 06840
(203)966-2800
Fax: (203)966-3109
Website: http://www.rfeip.com

Connecticut Innovations, Inc.
999 West St.
Rocky Hill, CT 06067
(860)563-5851
Fax: (860)563-4877

E-mail:
pamela.hartley@ctinnovations.com
Website: http://www.ctinnovations.com

Canaan Partners
105 Rowayton Ave.
Rowayton, CT 06853
(203)855-0400
Fax: (203)854-9117
Website: http://www.canaan.com

Landmark Partners, Inc.
10 Mill Pond Ln.
Simsbury, CT 06070
(860)651-9760
Fax: (860)651-8890
Website: http://www.landmark
partners.com

Sweeney & Company
PO Box 567
Southport, CT 06490
(203)255-0220
Fax: (203)255-0220
E-mail: sweeney@connix.com

Baxter Associates, Inc.
PO Box 1333
Stamford, CT 06904
(203)323-3143
Fax: (203)348-0622

Beacon Partners Inc.
6 Landmark Sq., 4th Fl.
Stamford, CT 06901-2792
(203)359-5776
Fax: (203)359-5876

Collinson, Howe, and Lennox, LLC
1055 Washington Blvd., 5th Fl.
Stamford, CT 06901
(203)324-7700
Fax: (203)324-3636
E-mail: info@chlmedical.com
Website: http://www.chlmedical.com

Prime Capital Management Co.
550 West Ave.
Stamford, CT 06902
(203)964-0642
Fax: (203)964-0862

Saugatuck Capital Co.
1 Canterbury Green
Stamford, CT 06901
(203)348-6669
Fax: (203)324-6995
Website: http://www.saugatuck
capital.com

Soundview Financial Group Inc.
22 Gatehouse Rd.
Stamford, CT 06902
(203)462-7200
Fax: (203)462-7350
Website: http://www.sndv.com

TSG Ventures, L.L.C.
177 Broad St., 12th Fl.
Stamford, CT 06901
(203)406-1500
Fax: (203)406-1590

Whitney & Company
177 Broad St.
Stamford, CT 06901
(203)973-1400
Fax: (203)973-1422
Website: http://www.jhwhitney.com

Cullinane & Donnelly Venture Partners L.P.
970 Farmington Ave.
West Hartford, CT 06107
(860)521-7811

The Crestview Investment and Financial Group
431 Post Rd. E, Ste. 1
Westport, CT 06880-4403
(203)222-0333
Fax: (203)222-0000

Marketcorp Venture Associates, L.P. (MCV)
274 Riverside Ave.
Westport, CT 06880
(203)222-3030
Fax: (203)222-3033

Oak Investment Partners (Westport)
1 Gorham Island
Westport, CT 06880
(203)226-8346
Fax: (203)227-0372
Website: http://www.oakinv.com

Oxford Bioscience Partners
315 Post Rd. W
Westport, CT 06880-5200
(203)341-3300
Fax: (203)341-3309
Website: http://www.oxbio.com

Prince Ventures (Westport)
25 Ford Rd.
Westport, CT 06880
(203)227-8332
Fax: (203)226-5302

LTI Venture Leasing Corp.
221 Danbury Rd.
Wilton, CT 06897
(203)563-1100
Fax: (203)563-1111
Website: http://www.ltileasing.com

Delaware

Blue Rock Capital
5803 Kennett Pike, Ste. A
Wilmington, DE 19807
(302)426-0981
Fax: (302)426-0982
Website: http://www.bluerock capital.com

District of Columbia

Allied Capital Corp.
1919 Pennsylvania Ave. NW
Washington, DC 20006-3434
(202)331-2444
Fax: (202)659-2053
Website: http://www.alliedcapital.com

Atlantic Coastal Ventures, L.P.
3101 South St. NW
Washington, DC 20007
(202)293-1166
Fax: (202)293-1181
Website: http://www.atlanticcv.com

Columbia Capital Group, Inc.
1660 L St. NW, Ste. 308
Washington, DC 20036
(202)775-8815
Fax: (202)223-0544

Core Capital Partners
901 15th St., NW
9th Fl.
Washington, DC 20005
(202)589-0090
Fax: (202)589-0091
Website: http://www.core-capital.com

Next Point Partners
701 Pennsylvania Ave. NW, Ste. 900
Washington, DC 20004
(202)661-8703
Fax: (202)434-7400
E-mail: mf@nextpoint.vc
Website: http://www.nextpointvc.com

Telecommunications Development Fund
2020 K. St. NW
Ste. 375
Washington, DC 20006
(202)293-8840
Fax: (202)293-8850
Website: http://www.tdfund.com

Wachtel & Co., Inc.
1101 4th St. NW
Washington, DC 20005-5680
(202)898-1144

Winslow Partners LLC
1300 Connecticut Ave. NW
Washington, DC 20036-1703
(202)530-5000
Fax: (202)530-5010
E-mail: winslow@winslowpartners.com

Women's Growth Capital Fund
1054 31st St., NW
Ste. 110
Washington, DC 20007
(202)342-1431
Fax: (202)341-1203
Website: http://www.wgcf.com

Sigma Capital Corp.
22668 Caravelle Circle
Boca Raton, FL 33433
(561)368-9783

North American Business Development Co., L.L.C.
111 East Las Olas Blvd.
Ft. Lauderdale, FL 33301
(305)463-0681
Fax: (305)527-0904
Website: http://www.northamerican fund.com

Chartwell Capital Management Co. Inc.
1 Independent Dr., Ste. 3120
Jacksonville, FL 32202
(904)355-3519
Fax: (904)353-5833
E-mail: info@chartwellcap.com

CEO Advisors
1061 Maitland Center Commons
Ste. 209
Maitland, FL 32751
(407)660-9327
Fax: (407)660-2109

Henry & Co.
8201 Peters Rd., Ste. 1000
Plantation, FL 33324
(954)797-7400

Avery Business Development Services
2506 St. Michel Ct.
Ponte Vedra, FL 32082
(904)285-6033

New South Ventures
5053 Ocean Blvd.
Sarasota, FL 34242

(941)358-6000
Fax: (941)358-6078
Website: http:// www.newsouthventures.com

Venture Capital Management Corp.
PO Box 2626
Satellite Beach, FL 32937
(407)777-1969

Florida Capital Venture Ltd.
325 Florida Bank Plaza
100 W. Kennedy Blvd.
Tampa, FL 33602
(813)229-2294
Fax: (813)229-2028

Quantum Capital Partners
339 South Plant Ave.
Tampa, FL 33606
(813)250-1999
Fax: (813)250-1998
Website: http:// www.quantumcapitalpartners.com

South Atlantic Venture Fund
614 W. Bay St.
Tampa, FL 33606-2704
(813)253-2500
Fax: (813)253-2360
E-mail: venture@southatlantic.com
Website: http://www.southatlantic.com

LM Capital Corp.
120 S. Olive, Ste. 400
West Palm Beach, FL 33401
(561)833-9700
Fax: (561)655-6587
Website: http://www.lmcapital securities.com

Georgia

Venture First Associates
4811 Thornwood Dr.
Acworth, GA 30102
(770)928-3733
Fax: (770)928-6455

Alliance Technology Ventures
8995 Westside Pkwy., Ste. 200
Alpharetta, GA 30004
(678)336-2000
Fax: (678)336-2001
E-mail: info@atv.com
Website: http://www.atv.com

Cordova Ventures
2500 North Winds Pkwy., Ste. 475
Alpharetta, GA 30004

(678)942-0300
Fax: (678)942-0301
Website: http://
www.cordovaventures.com

Advanced Technology Development Fund
1000 Abernathy, Ste. 1420
Atlanta, GA 30328-5614
(404)668-2333
Fax: (404)668-2333

CGW Southeast Partners
12 Piedmont Center, Ste. 210
Atlanta, GA 30305
(404)816-3255
Fax: (404)816-3258
Website: http://www.cgwlp.com

Cyberstarts
1900 Emery St., NW
3rd Fl.
Atlanta, GA 30318
(404)267-5000
Fax: (404)267-5200
Website: http://www.cyberstarts.com

EGL Holdings, Inc.
10 Piedmont Center, Ste. 412
Atlanta, GA 30305
(404)949-8300
Fax: (404)949-8311

Equity South
1790 The Lenox Bldg.
3399 Peachtree Rd. NE
Atlanta, GA 30326
(404)237-6222
Fax: (404)261-1578

Five Paces
3400 Peachtree Rd., Ste. 200
Atlanta, GA 30326
(404)439-8300
Fax: (404)439-8301
Website: http://www.fivepaces.com

Frontline Capital, Inc.
3475 Lenox Rd., Ste. 400
Atlanta, GA 30326
(404)240-7280
Fax: (404)240-7281

Fuqua Ventures LLC
1201 W. Peachtree St. NW, Ste. 5000
Atlanta, GA 30309
(404)815-4500
Fax: (404)815-4528
Website: http://www.fuquaventures.com

Noro-Moseley Partners
4200 Northside Pkwy., Bldg. 9
Atlanta, GA 30327
(404)233-1966
Fax: (404)239-9280
Website: http://www.noro-moseley.com

Renaissance Capital Corp.
34 Peachtree St. NW, Ste. 2230
Atlanta, GA 30303
(404)658-9061
Fax: (404)658-9064

River Capital, Inc.
Two Midtown Plaza
1360 Peachtree St. NE, Ste. 1430
Atlanta, GA 30309
(404)873-2166
Fax: (404)873-2158

State Street Bank & Trust Co.
3414 Peachtree Rd. NE, Ste. 1010
Atlanta, GA 30326
(404)364-9500
Fax: (404)261-4469

UPS Strategic Enterprise Fund
55 Glenlake Pkwy. NE
Atlanta, GA 30328
(404)828-8814
Fax: (404)828-8088
E-mail: jcacyce@ups.com
Website: http://www.ups.com/sef/sef_home

Wachovia
191 Peachtree St. NE, 26th Fl.
Atlanta, GA 30303
(404)332-1000
Fax: (404)332-1392
Website: http://www.wachovia.com/wca

Brainworks Ventures
4243 Dunwoody Club Dr.
Chamblee, GA 30341
(770)239-7447

First Growth Capital Inc.
Best Western Plaza, Ste. 105
PO Box 815
Forsyth, GA 31029
(912)781-7131

Financial Capital Resources, Inc.
21 Eastbrook Bend, Ste. 116
Peachtree City, GA 30269
(404)487-6650

Hawaii

HMS Hawaii Management Partners
Davies Pacific Center

841 Bishop St., Ste. 860
Honolulu, HI 96813
(808)545-3755
Fax: (808)531-2611

Idaho

Sun Valley Ventures
160 Second St.
Ketchum, ID 83340
(208)726-5005
Fax: (208)726-5094

Illinois

Open Prairie Ventures
115 N. Neil St., Ste. 209
Champaign, IL 61820
(217)351-7000
Fax: (217)351-7051
E-mail: inquire@openprairie.com
Website: http://www.openprairie.com

ABN AMRO Private Equity
208 S. La Salle St., 10th Fl.
Chicago, IL 60604
(312)855-7079
Fax: (312)553-6648
Website: http://www.abnequity.com

Alpha Capital Partners, Ltd.
122 S. Michigan Ave., Ste. 1700
Chicago, IL 60603
(312)322-9800
Fax: (312)322-9808
E-mail: acp@alphacapital.com

Ameritech Development Corp.
30 S. Wacker Dr., 37th Fl.
Chicago, IL 60606
(312)750-5083
Fax: (312)609-0244

Apex Investment Partners
225 W. Washington, Ste. 1450
Chicago, IL 60606
(312)857-2800
Fax: (312)857-1800
E-mail: apex@apexvc.com
Website: http://www.apexvc.com

Arch Venture Partners
8725 W. Higgins Rd., Ste. 290
Chicago, IL 60631
(773)380-6600
Fax: (773)380-6606
Website: http://www.archventure.com

The Bank Funds
208 South LaSalle St., Ste. 1680
Chicago, IL 60604

(312)855-6020
Fax: (312)855-8910

Batterson Venture Partners
303 W. Madison St., Ste. 1110
Chicago, IL 60606-3309
(312)269-0300
Fax: (312)269-0021
Website: http://www.battersonvp.com

William Blair Capital Partners, L.L.C.
222 W. Adams St., Ste. 1300
Chicago, IL 60606
(312)364-8250
Fax: (312)236-1042
E-mail: privateequity@wmblair.com
Website: http://www.wmblair.com

Bluestar Ventures
208 South LaSalle St., Ste. 1020
Chicago, IL 60604
(312)384-5000
Fax: (312)384-5005
Website: http://www.bluestar
ventures.com

The Capital Strategy Management Co.
233 S. Wacker Dr.
Box 06334
Chicago, IL 60606
(312)444-1170

DN Partners
77 West Wacker Dr., Ste. 4550
Chicago, IL 60601
(312)332-7960
Fax: (312)332-7979

Dresner Capital Inc.
29 South LaSalle St., Ste. 310
Chicago, IL 60603
(312)726-3600
Fax: (312)726-7448

Eblast Ventures LLC
11 South LaSalle St., 5th Fl.
Chicago, IL 60603
(312)372-2600
Fax: (312)372-5621
Website: http://www.eblastventures.com

Essex Woodlands Health Ventures, L.P.
190 S. LaSalle St., Ste. 2800
Chicago, IL 60603
(312)444-6040
Fax: (312)444-6034
Website: http://
www.essexwoodlands.com

First Analysis Venture Capital
233 S. Wacker Dr., Ste. 9500
Chicago, IL 60606

(312)258-1400
Fax: (312)258-0334
Website: http://www.firstanalysis.com

Frontenac Co.
135 S. LaSalle St., Ste.3800
Chicago, IL 60603
(312)368-0044
Fax: (312)368-9520
Website: http://www.frontenac.com

GTCR Golder Rauner, LLC
6100 Sears Tower
Chicago, IL 60606
(312)382-2200
Fax: (312)382-2201
Website: http://www.gtcr.com

High Street Capital LLC
311 South Wacker Dr., Ste. 4550
Chicago, IL 60606
(312)697-4990
Fax: (312)697-4994
Website: http://www.highstr.com

IEG Venture Management, Inc.
70 West Madison
Chicago, IL 60602
(312)644-0890
Fax: (312)454-0369
Website: http://www.iegventure.com

JK&B Capital
180 North Stetson, Ste. 4500
Chicago, IL 60601
(312)946-1200
Fax: (312)946-1103
E-mail: gspencer@jkbcapital.com
Website: http://www.jkbcapital.com

Kettle Partners L.P.
350 W. Hubbard, Ste. 350
Chicago, IL 60610
(312)329-9300
Fax: (312)527-4519
Website: http://www.kettlevc.com

Lake Shore Capital Partners
20 N. Wacker Dr., Ste. 2807
Chicago, IL 60606
(312)803-3536
Fax: (312)803-3534

LaSalle Capital Group Inc.
70 W. Madison St., Ste. 5710
Chicago, IL 60602
(312)236-7041
Fax: (312)236-0720

Linc Capital, Inc.
303 E. Wacker Pkwy., Ste. 1000

Chicago, IL 60601
(312)946-2670
Fax: (312)938-4290
E-mail: bdemars@linccap.com

Madison Dearborn Partners, Inc.
3 First National Plz., Ste. 3800
Chicago, IL 60602
(312)895-1000
Fax: (312)895-1001
E-mail: invest@mdcp.com
Website: http://www.mdcp.com

Mesirow Private Equity Investments Inc.
350 N. Clark St.
Chicago, IL 60610
(312)595-6950
Fax: (312)595-6211
Website: http://
www.meisrowfinancial.com

Mosaix Ventures LLC
1822 North Mohawk
Chicago, IL 60614
(312)274-0988
Fax: (312)274-0989
Website: http://
www.mosaixventures.com

Nesbitt Burns
111 West Monroe St.
Chicago, IL 60603
(312)416-3855
Fax: (312)765-8000
Website: http://www.harrisbank.com

Polestar Capital, Inc.
180 N. Michigan Ave., Ste. 1905
Chicago, IL 60601
(312)984-9090
Fax: (312)984-9877
E-mail: wl@polestarvc.com
Website: http://www.polestarvc.com

Prince Ventures (Chicago)
10 S. Wacker Dr., Ste. 2575
Chicago, IL 60606-7407
(312)454-1408
Fax: (312)454-9125

Prism Capital
444 N. Michigan Ave.
Chicago, IL 60611
(312)464-7900
Fax: (312)464-7915
Website: http://www.prismfund.com

Third Coast Capital
900 N. Franklin St., Ste. 700
Chicago, IL 60610
(312)337-3303

Fax: (312)337-2567
E-mail: manic@earthlink.com
Website: http://
www.thirdcoastcapital.com

Thoma Cressey Equity Partners
4460 Sears Tower, 92nd Fl.
233 S. Wacker Dr.
Chicago, IL 60606
(312)777-4444
Fax: (312)777-4445
Website: http://www.thomacressey.com

Tribune Ventures
435 N. Michigan Ave., Ste. 600
Chicago, IL 60611
(312)527-8797
Fax: (312)222-5993
Website: http://www.tribune
ventures.com

Wind Point Partners (Chicago)
676 N. Michigan Ave., Ste. 330
Chicago, IL 60611
(312)649-4000
Website: http://www.wppartners.com

Marquette Venture Partners
520 Lake Cook Rd., Ste. 450
Deerfield, IL 60015
(847)940-1700
Fax: (847)940-1724
Website: http://www.marquette
ventures.com

Duchossois Investments Limited, LLC
845 Larch Ave.
Elmhurst, IL 60126
(630)530-6105
Fax: (630)993-8644
Website: http://www.duchtec.com

Evanston Business Investment Corp.
1840 Oak Ave.
Evanston, IL 60201
(847)866-1840
Fax: (847)866-1808
E-mail: t-parkinson@nwu.com
Website: http://www.ebic.com

Inroads Capital Partners L.P.
1603 Orrington Ave., Ste. 2050
Evanston, IL 60201-3841
(847)864-2000
Fax: (847)864-9692

The Cerulean Fund/WGC Enterprises
1701 E. Lake Ave., Ste. 170
Glenview, IL 60025
(847)657-8002
Fax: (847)657-8168

Ventana Financial Resources, Inc.
249 Market Sq.
Lake Forest, IL 60045
(847)234-3434

Beecken, Petty & Co.
901 Warrenville Rd., Ste. 205
Lisle, IL 60532
(630)435-0300
Fax: (630)435-0370
E-mail: hep@bpcompany.com
Website: http://www.bpcompany.com

Allstate Private Equity
3075 Sanders Rd., Ste. G5D
Northbrook, IL 60062-7127
(847)402-8247
Fax: (847)402-0880

KB Partners
1101 Skokie Blvd., Ste. 260
Northbrook, IL 60062-2856
(847)714-0444
Fax: (847)714-0445
E-mail: keith@kbpartners.com
Website: http://www.kbpartners.com

Transcap Associates Inc.
900 Skokie Blvd., Ste. 210
Northbrook, IL 60062
(847)753-9600
Fax: (847)753-9090

**Graystone Venture Partners, L.L.C. /
Portage Venture Partners**
One Northfield Plaza, Ste. 530
Northfield, IL 60093
(847)446-9460
Fax: (847)446-9470
Website: http://www.portage
ventures.com

Motorola Inc.
1303 E. Algonquin Rd.
Schaumburg, IL 60196-1065
(847)576-4929
Fax: (847)538-2250
Website: http://www.mot.com/mne

Indiana

Irwin Ventures LLC
500 Washington St.
Columbus, IN 47202
(812)373-1434
Fax: (812)376-1709
Website: http://www.irwinventures.com

**Cambridge Venture
Partners**
4181 East 96th St., Ste. 200
Indianapolis, IN 46240

(317)814-6192
Fax: (317)944-9815

CID Equity Partners
One American Square, Ste. 2850
Box 82074
Indianapolis, IN 46282
(317)269-2350
Fax: (317)269-2355
Website: http://www.cidequity.com

Gazelle Techventures
6325 Digital Way, Ste. 460
Indianapolis, IN 46278
(317)275-6800
Fax: (317)275-1101
Website: http://www.gazellevc.com

Monument Advisors Inc.
Bank One Center/Circle
111 Monument Circle, Ste. 600
Indianapolis, IN 46204-5172
(317)656-5065
Fax: (317)656-5060
Website: http://www.monumentadv.com

MWV Capital Partners
201 N. Illinois St., Ste. 300
Indianapolis, IN 46204
(317)237-2323
Fax: (317)237-2325
Website: http://www.mwvcapital.com

First Source Capital Corp.
100 North Michigan St.
PO Box 1602
South Bend, IN 46601
(219)235-2180
Fax: (219)235-2227

Iowa

Allsop Venture Partners
118 Third Ave. SE, Ste. 837
Cedar Rapids, IA 52401
(319)368-6675
Fax: (319)363-9515

**InvestAmerica Investment
Advisors, Inc.**
101 2nd St. SE, Ste. 800
Cedar Rapids, IA 52401
(319)363-8249
Fax: (319)363-9683

Pappajohn Capital Resources
2116 Financial Center
Des Moines, IA 50309
(515)244-5746
Fax: (515)244-2346
Website: http://www.pappajohn.com

Berthel Fisher & Company Planning Inc.
701 Tama St.
PO Box 609
Marion, IA 52302
(319)497-5700
Fax: (319)497-4244

Kansas

Enterprise Merchant Bank
7400 West 110th St., Ste. 560
Overland Park, KS 66210
(913)327-8500
Fax: (913)327-8505

Kansas Venture Capital, Inc. (Overland Park)
6700 Antioch Plz., Ste. 460
Overland Park, KS 66204
(913)262-7117
Fax: (913)262-3509
E-mail: jdalton@kvci.com

Child Health Investment Corp.
6803 W. 64th St., Ste. 208
Shawnee Mission, KS 66202
(913)262-1436
Fax: (913)262-1575
Website: http://www.chca.com

Kansas Technology Enterprise Corp.
214 SW 6th, 1st Fl.
Topeka, KS 66603-3719
(785)296-5272
Fax: (785)296-1160
E-mail: ktec@ktec.com
Website: http://www.ktec.com

Kentucky

Kentucky Highlands Investment Corp.
362 Old Whitley Rd.
London, KY 40741
(606)864-5175
Fax: (606)864-5194
Website: http://www.khic.org

Chrysalis Ventures, L.L.C.
1850 National City Tower
Louisville, KY 40202
(502)583-7644
Fax: (502)583-7648
E-mail: bobsany@chrysalisventures.com
Website: http://
www.chrysalisventures.com

Humana Venture Capital
500 West Main St.
Louisville, KY 40202
(502)580-3922
Fax: (502)580-2051

E-mail: gemont@humana.com
George Emont, Director

Summit Capital Group, Inc.
6510 Glenridge Park Pl., Ste. 8
Louisville, KY 40222
(502)332-2700

Louisiana

Bank One Equity Investors, Inc.
451 Florida St.
Baton Rouge, LA 70801
(504)332-4421
Fax: (504)332-7377

Advantage Capital Partners
LLE Tower
909 Poydras St., Ste. 2230
New Orleans, LA 70112
(504)522-4850
Fax: (504)522-4950
Website: http://www.advantagecap.com

Maine

CEI Ventures / Coastal Ventures LP
2 Portland Fish Pier, Ste. 201
Portland, ME 04101
(207)772-5356
Fax: (207)772-5503
Website: http://www.ceiventures.com

Commwealth Bioventures, Inc.
4 Milk St.
Portland, ME 04101
(207)780-0904
Fax: (207)780-0913

Maryland

Annapolis Ventures LLC
151 West St., Ste. 302
Annapolis, MD 21401
(443)482-9555
Fax: (443)482-9565
Website: http://
www.annapolisventures.com

Delmag Ventures
220 Wardour Dr.
Annapolis, MD 21401
(410)267-8196
Fax: (410)267-8017
Website: http://
www.delmagventures.com

Abell Venture Fund
111 S. Calvert St., Ste. 2300
Baltimore, MD 21202
(410)547-1300

Fax: (410)539-6579
Website: http://www.abell.org

ABS Ventures (Baltimore)
1 South St., Ste. 2150
Baltimore, MD 21202
(410)895-3895
Fax: (410)895-3899
Website: http://www.absventures.com

Anthem Capital, L.P.
16 S. Calvert St., Ste. 800
Baltimore, MD 21202-1305
(410)625-1510
Fax: (410)625-1735
Website: http://www.anthemcapital.com

Catalyst Ventures
1119 St. Paul St.
Baltimore, MD 21202
(410)244-0123
Fax: (410)752-7721

Maryland Venture Capital Trust
217 E. Redwood St., Ste. 2200
Baltimore, MD 21202
(410)767-6361
Fax: (410)333-6931

New Enterprise Associates (Baltimore)
1119 St. Paul St.
Baltimore, MD 21202
(410)244-0115
Fax: (410)752-7721
Website: http://www.nea.com

T. Rowe Price Threshold Partnerships
100 E. Pratt St., 8th Fl.
Baltimore, MD 21202
(410)345-2000
Fax: (410)345-2800

Spring Capital Partners
16 W. Madison St.
Baltimore, MD 21201
(410)685-8000
Fax: (410)727-1436
E-mail: mailbox@springcap.com

Arete Corporation
3 Bethesda Metro Ctr., Ste. 770
Bethesda, MD 20814
(301)657-6268
Fax: (301)657-6254
Website: http://www.arete-microgen.com

Embryon Capital
7903 Sleaford Place
Bethesda, MD 20814

(301)656-6837
Fax: (301)656-8056

Potomac Ventures
7920 Norfolk Ave., Ste. 1100
Bethesda, MD 20814
(301)215-9240
Website: http://www.potomacventures.com

Toucan Capital Corp.
3 Bethesda Metro Center, Ste. 700
Bethesda, MD 20814
(301)961-1970
Fax: (301)961-1969
Website: http://www.toucancapital.com

Kinetic Ventures LLC
2 Wisconsin Cir., Ste. 620
Chevy Chase, MD 20815
(301)652-8066
Fax: (301)652-8310
Website: http://www.kineticventures.com

Boulder Ventures Ltd.
4750 Owings Mills Blvd.
Owings Mills, MD 21117
(410)998-3114
Fax: (410)356-5492
Website: http://
www.boulderventures.com

Grotech Capital Group
9690 Deereco Rd., Ste. 800
Timonium, MD 21093
(410)560-2000
Fax: (410)560-1910
Website: http://www.grotech.com

Massachusetts

Adams, Harkness & Hill, Inc.
60 State St.
Boston, MA 02109
(617)371-3900

Advent International
75 State St., 29th Fl.
Boston, MA 02109
(617)951-9400
Fax: (617)951-0566
Website: http://www.adventiner
national.com

American Research and Development
30 Federal St.
Boston, MA 02110-2508
(617)423-7500
Fax: (617)423-9655

Ascent Venture Partners
255 State St., 5th Fl.

Boston, MA 02109
(617)270-9400
Fax: (617)270-9401
E-mail: info@ascentvp.com
Website: http://www.ascentvp.com

Atlas Venture
222 Berkeley St.
Boston, MA 02116
(617)488-2200
Fax: (617)859-9292
Website: http://www.atlasventure.com

Axxon Capital
28 State St., 37th Fl.
Boston, MA 02109
(617)722-0980
Fax: (617)557-6014
Website: http://www.axxoncapital.com

BancBoston Capital/BancBoston Ventures
175 Federal St., 10th Fl.
Boston, MA 02110
(617)434-2509
Fax: (617)434-6175
Website: http://www.bancboston
capital.com

Boston Capital Ventures
Old City Hall
45 School St.
Boston, MA 02108
(617)227-6550
Fax: (617)227-3847
E-mail: info@bcv.com
Website: http://www.bcv.com

Boston Financial & Equity Corp.
20 Overland St.
PO Box 15071
Boston, MA 02215
(617)267-2900
Fax: (617)437-7601
E-mail: debbie@bfec.com

Boston Millennia Partners
30 Rowes Wharf
Boston, MA 02110
(617)428-5150
Fax: (617)428-5160
Website: http://www.millennia
partners.com

Bristol Investment Trust
842A Beacon St.
Boston, MA 02215-3199
(617)566-5212
Fax: (617)267-0932

Brook Venture Management LLC
50 Federal St., 5th Fl.
Boston, MA 02110
(617)451-8989
Fax: (617)451-2369
Website: http://www.brookventure.com

Burr, Egan, Deleage, and Co. (Boston)
200 Clarendon St., Ste. 3800
Boston, MA 02116
(617)262-7770
Fax: (617)262-9779

Cambridge/Samsung Partners
One Exeter Plaza
Ninth Fl.
Boston, MA 02116
(617)262-4440
Fax: (617)262-5562

Chestnut Street Partners, Inc.
75 State St., Ste. 2500
Boston, MA 02109
(617)345-7220
Fax: (617)345-7201
E-mail: chestnut@chestnutp.com

Claflin Capital Management, Inc.
10 Liberty Sq., Ste. 300
Boston, MA 02109
(617)426-6505
Fax: (617)482-0016
Website: http://www.claflincapital.com

Copley Venture Partners
99 Summer St., Ste. 1720
Boston, MA 02110
(617)737-1253
Fax: (617)439-0699

Corning Capital / Corning Technology Ventures
121 High Street, Ste. 400
Boston, MA 02110
(617)338-2656
Fax: (617)261-3864
Website: http://www.corning
ventures.com

Downer & Co.
211 Congress St.
Boston, MA 02110
(617)482-6200
Fax: (617)482-6201
E-mail: cdowner@downer.com
Website: http://www.downer.com

Fidelity Ventures
82 Devonshire St.
Boston, MA 02109
(617)563-6370

Fax: (617)476-9023
Website: http://www.fidelity
ventures.com

**Greylock Management Corp.
(Boston)**
1 Federal St.
Boston, MA 02110-2065
(617)423-5525
Fax: (617)482-0059

Gryphon Ventures
222 Berkeley St., Ste.1600
Boston, MA 02116
(617)267-9191
Fax: (617)267-4293
E-mail: all@gryphoninc.com

Halpern, Denny & Co.
500 Boylston St.
Boston, MA 02116
(617)536-6602
Fax: (617)536-8535

Harbourvest Partners, LLC
1 Financial Center, 44th Fl.
Boston, MA 02111
(617)348-3707
Fax: (617)350-0305
Website: http://www.hvpllc.com

Highland Capital Partners
2 International Pl.
Boston, MA 02110
(617)981-1500
Fax: (617)531-1550
E-mail: info@hcp.com
Website: http://www.hcp.com

Lee Munder Venture Partners
John Hancock Tower T-53
200 Clarendon St.
Boston, MA 02103
(617)380-5600
Fax: (617)380-5601
Website: http://www.leemunder.com

M/C Venture Partners
75 State St., Ste. 2500
Boston, MA 02109
(617)345-7200
Fax: (617)345-7201
Website: http://
www.mcventurepartners.com

Massachusetts Capital Resources Co.
420 Boylston St.
Boston, MA 02116
(617)536-3900
Fax: (617)536-7930

**Massachusetts Technology
Development Corp. (MTDC)**
148 State St.
Boston, MA 02109
(617)723-4920
Fax: (617)723-5983
E-mail: jhodgman@mtdc.com
Website: http://www.mtdc.com

New England Partners
One Boston Place, Ste. 2100
Boston, MA 02108
(617)624-8400
Fax: (617)624-8999
Website: http://www.nepartners.com

North Hill Ventures
Ten Post Office Square
11th Fl.
Boston, MA 02109
(617)788-2112
Fax: (617)788-2152
Website: http://
www.northhillventures.com

OneLiberty Ventures
150 Cambridge Park Dr.
Boston, MA 02140
(617)492-7280
Fax: (617)492-7290
Website: http://www.oneliberty.com

Schroder Ventures
Life Sciences
60 State St., Ste. 3650
Boston, MA 02109
(617)367-8100
Fax: (617)367-1590
Website: http://
www.shroderventures.com

**Shawmut Capital
Partners**
75 Federal St., 18th Fl.
Boston, MA 02110
(617)368-4900
Fax: (617)368-4910
Website: http://www.shawmut
capital.com

Solstice Capital LLC
15 Broad St., 3rd Fl.
Boston, MA 02109
(617)523-7733
Fax: (617)523-5827
E-mail: solticecapital@solcap.com

Spectrum Equity Investors
One International Pl., 29th Fl.
Boston, MA 02110
(617)464-4600

Fax: (617)464-4601
Website: http://
www.spectrumequity.com

Spray Venture Partners
One Walnut St.
Boston, MA 02108
(617)305-4140
Fax: (617)305-4144
Website: http://www.sprayventure.com

The Still River Fund
100 Federal St., 29th Fl.
Boston, MA 02110
(617)348-2327
Fax: (617)348-2371
Website: http://www.stillriverfund.com

Summit Partners
600 Atlantic Ave., Ste. 2800
Boston, MA 02210-2227
(617)824-1000
Fax: (617)824-1159
Website: http://
www.summitpartners.com

TA Associates, Inc. (Boston)
High Street Tower
125 High St., Ste. 2500
Boston, MA 02110
(617)574-6700
Fax: (617)574-6728
Website: http://www.ta.com

**TVM Techno Venture
Management**
101 Arch St., Ste. 1950
Boston, MA 02110
(617)345-9320
Fax: (617)345-9377
E-mail: info@tvmvc.com
Website: http://www.tvmvc.com

UNC Ventures
64 Burough St.
Boston, MA 02130-4017
(617)482-7070
Fax: (617)522-2176

**Venture Investment Management
Company (VIMAC)**
177 Milk St.
Boston, MA 02190-3410
(617)292-3300
Fax: (617)292-7979
E-mail: bzeisig@vimac.com
Website: http://www.vimac.com

MDT Advisers, Inc.
125 Cambridge Park Dr.
Cambridge, MA 02140-2314

(617)234-2200
Fax: (617)234-2210
Website: http://www.mdtai.com

TTC Ventures
One Main St., 6th Fl.
Cambridge, MA 02142
(617)528-3137
Fax: (617)577-1715
E-mail: info@ttcventures.com

Zero Stage Capital Co. Inc.
101 Main St., 17th Fl.
Cambridge, MA 02142
(617)876-5355
Fax: (617)876-1248
Website: http://www.zerostage.com

Atlantic Capital
164 Cushing Hwy.
Cohasset, MA 02025
(617)383-9449
Fax: (617)383-6040
E-mail: info@atlanticcap.com
Website: http://www.atlanticcap.com

Seacoast Capital Partners
55 Ferncroft Rd.
Danvers, MA 01923
(978)750-1300
Fax: (978)750-1301
E-mail: gdeli@seacoastcapital.com
Website: http://www.seacoastcapital.com

Sage Management Group
44 South Street
PO Box 2026
East Dennis, MA 02641
(508)385-7172
Fax: (508)385-7272
E-mail: sagemgt@capecod.net

Applied Technology
1 Cranberry Hill
Lexington, MA 02421-7397
(617)862-8622
Fax: (617)862-8367

Royalty Capital Management
5 Downing Rd.
Lexington, MA 02421-6918
(781)861-8490

Argo Global Capital
210 Broadway, Ste. 101
Lynnfield, MA 01940
(781)592-5250
Fax: (781)592-5230
Website: http://www.gsmcapital.com

Industry Ventures
6 Bayne Lane
Newburyport, MA 01950
(978)499-7606
Fax: (978)499-0686
Website: http://www.industry ventures.com

Softbank Capital Partners
10 Langley Rd., Ste. 202
Newton Center, MA 02459
(617)928-9300
Fax: (617)928-9305
E-mail: clax@bvc.com

Advanced Technology Ventures (Boston)
281 Winter St., Ste. 350
Waltham, MA 02451
(781)290-0707
Fax: (781)684-0045
E-mail: info@atvcapital.com
Website: http://www.atvcapital.com

Castile Ventures
890 Winter St., Ste. 140
Waltham, MA 02451
(781)890-0060
Fax: (781)890-0065
Website: http://www.castileventures.com

Charles River Ventures
1000 Winter St., Ste. 3300
Waltham, MA 02451
(781)487-7060
Fax: (781)487-7065
Website: http://www.crv.com

Comdisco Venture Group (Waltham)
Totton Pond Office Center
400-1 Totten Pond Rd.
Waltham, MA 02451
(617)672-0250
Fax: (617)398-8099

Marconi Ventures
890 Winter St., Ste. 310
Waltham, MA 02451
(781)839-7177
Fax: (781)522-7477
Website: http://www.marconi.com

Matrix Partners
Bay Colony Corporate Center
1000 Winter St., Ste.4500
Waltham, MA 02451
(781)890-2244
Fax: (781)890-2288
Website: http://www.matrixpartners.com

North Bridge Venture Partners
950 Winter St. Ste. 4600
Waltham, MA 02451
(781)290-0004
Fax: (781)290-0999
E-mail: eta@nbvp.com

Polaris Venture Partners
Bay Colony Corporate Ctr.
1000 Winter St., Ste. 3500
Waltham, MA 02451
(781)290-0770
Fax: (781)290-0880
E-mail: partners@polarisventures.com
Website: http:// www.polarisventures.com

Seaflower Ventures
Bay Colony Corporate Ctr.
1000 Winter St. Ste. 1000
Waltham, MA 02451
(781)466-9552
Fax: (781)466-9553
E-mail: moot@seaflower.com
Website: http://www.seaflower.com

Ampersand Ventures
55 William St., Ste. 240
Wellesley, MA 02481
(617)239-0700
Fax: (617)239-0824
E-mail: info@ampersandventures.com
Website: http://www.ampers andventures.com

Battery Ventures (Boston)
20 William St., Ste. 200
Wellesley, MA 02481
(781)577-1000
Fax: (781)577-1001
Website: http://www.battery.com

Commonwealth Capital Ventures, L.P.
20 William St., Ste.225
Wellesley, MA 02481
(781)237-7373
Fax: (781)235-8627
Website: http://www.ccvlp.com

Fowler, Anthony & Company
20 Walnut St.
Wellesley, MA 02481
(781)237-4201
Fax: (781)237-7718

Gemini Investors
20 William St.
Wellesley, MA 02481
(781)237-7001
Fax: (781)237-7233

Grove Street Advisors Inc.
20 William St., Ste. 230
Wellesley, MA 02481
(781)263-6100
Fax: (781)263-6101
Website: http://
www.grovestreetadvisors.com

Mees Pierson Investeringsmaat B.V.
20 William St., Ste. 210
Wellesley, MA 02482
(781)239-7600
Fax: (781)239-0377

Norwest Equity Partners
40 William St., Ste. 305
Wellesley, MA 02481-3902
(781)237-5870
Fax: (781)237-6270
Website: http://www.norwestvp.com

**Bessemer Venture Partners
(Wellesley Hills)**
83 Walnut St.
Wellesley Hills, MA 02481
(781)237-6050
Fax: (781)235-7576
E-mail: travis@bvpny.com
Website: http://www.bvp.com

Venture Capital Fund of New England
20 Walnut St., Ste. 120
Wellesley Hills, MA 02481-2175
(781)239-8262
Fax: (781)239-8263

Prism Venture Partners
100 Lowder Brook Dr., Ste. 2500
Westwood, MA 02090
(781)302-4000
Fax: (781)302-4040
E-mail: dwbaum@prismventure.com

Palmer Partners LP
200 Unicorn Park Dr.
Woburn, MA 01801
(781)933-5445
Fax: (781)933-0698

Michigan

Arbor Partners, L.L.C.
130 South First St.
Ann Arbor, MI 48104
(734)668-9000
Fax: (734)669-4195
Website: http://www.arborpartners.com

EDF Ventures
425 N. Main St.
Ann Arbor, MI 48104
(734)663-3213

Fax: (734)663-7358
E-mail: edf@edfvc.com
Website: http://www.edfvc.com

White Pines Management, L.L.C.
2401 Plymouth Rd., Ste. B
Ann Arbor, MI 48105
(734)747-9401
Fax: (734)747-9704
E-mail: ibund@whitepines.com
Website: http://www.whitepines.com

Wellmax, Inc.
3541 Bendway Blvd., Ste. 100
Bloomfield Hills, MI 48301
(248)646-3554
Fax: (248)646-6220

Venture Funding, Ltd.
Fisher Bldg.
3011 West Grand Blvd., Ste. 321
Detroit, MI 48202
(313)871-3606
Fax: (313)873-4935

Investcare Partners L.P. / GMA Capital LLC
32330 W. Twelve Mile Rd.
Farmington Hills, MI 48334
(248)489-9000
Fax: (248)489-8819
E-mail: gma@gmacapital.com
Website: http://www.gmacapital.com

Liberty Bidco Investment Corp.
30833 Northwestern Highway, Ste. 211
Farmington Hills, MI 48334
(248)626-6070
Fax: (248)626-6072

Seaflower Ventures
5170 Nicholson Rd.
PO Box 474
Fowlerville, MI 48836
(517)223-3335
Fax: (517)223-3337
E-mail: gibbons@seaflower.com
Website: http://www.seaflower.com

Ralph Wilson Equity Fund LLC
15400 E. Jefferson Ave.
Gross Pointe Park, MI 48230
(313)821-9122
Fax: (313)821-9101
Website: http://
www.RalphWilsonEquityFund.com
J. Skip Simms, President

Minnesota

Development Corp. of Austin
1900 Eighth Ave., NW
Austin, MN 55912

(507)433-0346
Fax: (507)433-0361
E-mail: dca@smig.net
Website: http://www.spamtownusa.com

Northeast Ventures Corp.
802 Alworth Bldg.
Duluth, MN 55802
(218)722-9915
Fax: (218)722-9871

Medical Innovation Partners, Inc.
6450 City West Pkwy.
Eden Prairie, MN 55344-3245
(612)828-9616
Fax: (612)828-9596

St. Paul Venture Capital, Inc.
10400 Vicking Dr., Ste. 550
Eden Prairie, MN 55344
(612)995-7474
Fax: (612)995-7475
Website: http://www.stpaulvc.com

Cherry Tree Investments, Inc.
7601 France Ave. S, Ste. 150
Edina, MN 55435
(612)893-9012
Fax: (612)893-9036
Website: http://www.cherrytree.com

Shared Ventures, Inc.
6550 York Ave. S
Edina, MN 55435
(612)925-3411

Sherpa Partners LLC
5050 Lincoln Dr., Ste. 490
Edina, MN 55436
(952)942-1070
Fax: (952)942-1071
Website: http://www.sherpapartners.com

Affinity Capital Management
901 Marquette Ave., Ste. 1810
Minneapolis, MN 55402
(612)252-9900
Fax: (612)252-9911
Website: http://www.affinitycapital.com

Artesian Capital
1700 Foshay Tower
821 Marquette Ave.
Minneapolis, MN 55402
(612)334-5600
Fax: (612)334-5601
E-mail: artesian@artesian.com

Coral Ventures
60 S. 6th St., Ste. 3510
Minneapolis, MN 55402

(612)335-8666
Fax: (612)335-8668
Website: http://www.coralventures.com

Crescendo Venture Management, L.L.C.
800 LaSalle Ave., Ste. 2250
Minneapolis, MN 55402
(612)607-2800
Fax: (612)607-2801
Website: http://www.crescendoventures.com

Gideon Hixon Venture
1900 Foshay Tower
821 Marquette Ave.
Minneapolis, MN 55402
(612)904-2314
Fax: (612)204-0913

Norwest Equity Partners
3600 IDS Center
80 S. 8th St.
Minneapolis, MN 55402
(612)215-1600
Fax: (612)215-1601
Website: http://www.norwestvp.com

Oak Investment Partners (Minneapolis)
4550 Norwest Center
90 S. 7th St.
Minneapolis, MN 55402
(612)339-9322
Fax: (612)337-8017
Website: http://www.oakinv.com

Pathfinder Venture Capital Funds (Minneapolis)
7300 Metro Blvd., Ste. 585
Minneapolis, MN 55439
(612)835-1121
Fax: (612)835-8389
E-mail: jahrens620@aol.com

U.S. Bancorp Piper Jaffray Ventures, Inc.
800 Nicollet Mall, Ste. 800
Minneapolis, MN 55402
(612)303-5686
Fax: (612)303-1350
Website: http://www.paperjaffreyventures.com

The Food Fund, Ltd. Partnership
5720 Smatana Dr., Ste. 300
Minnetonka, MN 55343
(612)939-3950
Fax: (612)939-8106

Mayo Medical Ventures
200 First St. SW
Rochester, MN 55905
(507)266-4586

Fax: (507)284-5410
Website: http://www.mayo.edu

Missouri

Bankers Capital Corp.
3100 Gillham Rd.
Kansas City, MO 64109
(816)531-1600
Fax: (816)531-1334

Capital for Business, Inc. (Kansas City)
1000 Walnut St., 18th Fl.
Kansas City, MO 64106
(816)234-2357
Fax: (816)234-2952
Website: http://www.capitalforbusiness.com

De Vries & Co. Inc.
800 West 47th St.
Kansas City, MO 64112
(816)756-0055
Fax: (816)756-0061

InvestAmerica Venture Group Inc. (Kansas City)
Commerce Tower
911 Main St., Ste. 2424
Kansas City, MO 64105
(816)842-0114
Fax: (816)471-7339

Kansas City Equity Partners
233 W. 47th St.
Kansas City, MO 64112
(816)960-1771
Fax: (816)960-1777
Website: http://www.kcep.com

Bome Investors, Inc.
8000 Maryland Ave., Ste. 1190
St. Louis, MO 63105
(314)721-5707
Fax: (314)721-5135
Website: http://www.gatewayventures.com

Capital for Business, Inc. (St. Louis)
11 S. Meramac St., Ste. 1430
St. Louis, MO 63105
(314)746-7427
Fax: (314)746-8739
Website: http://www.capitalforbusiness.com

Crown Capital Corp.
540 Maryville Centre Dr., Ste. 120
Saint Louis, MO 63141
(314)576-1201

Fax: (314)576-1525
Website: http://www.crown-cap.com

Gateway Associates L.P.
8000 Maryland Ave., Ste. 1190
St. Louis, MO 63105
(314)721-5707
Fax: (314)721-5135

Harbison Corp.
8112 Maryland Ave., Ste. 250
Saint Louis, MO 63105
(314)727-8200
Fax: (314)727-0249

Heartland Capital Fund, Ltd.
PO Box 642117
Omaha, NE 68154
(402)778-5124
Fax: (402)445-2370
Website: http://www.heartlandcapitalfund.com

Odin Capital Group
1625 Farnam St., Ste. 700
Omaha, NE 68102
(402)346-6200
Fax: (402)342-9311
Website: http://www.odincapital.com

Nevada

Edge Capital Investment Co. LLC
1350 E. Flamingo Rd., Ste. 3000
Las Vegas, NV 89119
(702)438-3343
E-mail: info@edgecapital.net
Website: http://www.edgecapital.net

The Benefit Capital Companies Inc.
PO Box 542
Logandale, NV 89021
(702)398-3222
Fax: (702)398-3700

Millennium Three Venture Group LLC
6880 South McCarran Blvd., Ste. A-11
Reno, NV 89509
(775)954-2020
Fax: (775)954-2023
Website: http://www.m3vg.com

New Jersey

Alan I. Goldman & Associates
497 Ridgewood Ave.
Glen Ridge, NJ 07028
(973)857-5680
Fax: (973)509-8856

CS Capital Partners LLC
328 Second St., Ste. 200

Lakewood, NJ 08701
(732)901-1111
Fax: (212)202-5071
Website: http://www.cs-capital.com

Edison Venture Fund
1009 Lenox Dr., Ste. 4
Lawrenceville, NJ 08648
(609)896-1900
Fax: (609)896-0066
E-mail: info@edisonventure.com
Website: http://www.edisonventure.com

Tappan Zee Capital Corp. (New Jersey)
201 Lower Notch Rd.
PO Box 416
Little Falls, NJ 07424
(973)256-8280
Fax: (973)256-2841

The CIT Group/Venture Capital, Inc.
650 CIT Dr.
Livingston, NJ 07039
(973)740-5429
Fax: (973)740-5555
Website: http://www.cit.com

Capital Express, L.L.C.
1100 Valleybrook Ave.
Lyndhurst, NJ 07071
(201)438-8228
Fax: (201)438-5131
E-mail: niles@capitalexpress.com
Website: http://www.capitalexpress.com

Westford Technology Ventures, L.P.
17 Academy St.
Newark, NJ 07102
(973)624-2131
Fax: (973)624-2008

Accel Partners
1 Palmer Sq.
Princeton, NJ 08542
(609)683-4500
Fax: (609)683-4880
Website: http://www.accel.com

Cardinal Partners
221 Nassau St.
Princeton, NJ 08542
(609)924-6452
Fax: (609)683-0174
Website: http://
www.cardinalhealthpartners.com

Domain Associates L.L.C.
One Palmer Sq., Ste. 515
Princeton, NJ 08542
(609)683-5656
Fax: (609)683-9789
Website: http://www.domainvc.com

Johnston Associates, Inc.
181 Cherry Valley Rd.
Princeton, NJ 08540
(609)924-3131
Fax: (609)683-7524
E-mail: jaincorp@aol.com

Kemper Ventures
Princeton Forrestal Village
155 Village Blvd.
Princeton, NJ 08540
(609)936-3035
Fax: (609)936-3051

Penny Lane Parnters
One Palmer Sq., Ste. 309
Princeton, NJ 08542
(609)497-4646
Fax: (609)497-0611

Early Stage Enterprises L.P.
995 Route 518
Skillman, NJ 08558
(609)921-8896
Fax: (609)921-8703
Website: http://www.esevc.com

MBW Management Inc.
1 Springfield Ave.
Summit, NJ 07901
(908)273-4060
Fax: (908)273-4430

BCI Advisors, Inc.
Glenpointe Center W.
Teaneck, NJ 07666
(201)836-3900
Fax: (201)836-6368
E-mail: info@bciadvisors.com
Website: http://www.bcipartners.com

Demuth, Folger & Wetherill / DFW Capital Partners
Glenpointe Center E., 5th Fl.
300 Frank W. Burr Blvd.
Teaneck, NJ 07666
(201)836-2233
Fax: (201)836-5666
Website: http://www.dfwcapital.com

First Princeton Capital Corp.
189 Berdan Ave., No. 131
Wayne, NJ 07470-3233
(973)278-3233
Fax: (973)278-4290
Website: http://www.lytellcatt.net

Edelson Technology Partners
300 Tice Blvd.
Woodcliff Lake, NJ 07675
(201)930-9898

Fax: (201)930-8899
Website: http://www.edelsontech.com

New Mexico

Bruce F. Glaspell & Associates
10400 Academy Rd. NE, Ste. 313
Albuquerque, NM 87111
(505)292-4505
Fax: (505)292-4258

High Desert Ventures, Inc.
6101 Imparata St. NE, Ste. 1721
Albuquerque, NM 87111
(505)797-3330
Fax: (505)338-5147

New Business Capital Fund, Ltd.
5805 Torreon NE
Albuquerque, NM 87109
(505)822-8445

SBC Ventures
10400 Academy Rd. NE, Ste. 313
Albuquerque, NM 87111
(505)292-4505
Fax: (505)292-4528

Technology Ventures Corp.
1155 University Blvd. SE
Albuquerque, NM 87106
(505)246-2882
Fax: (505)246-2891

New York

New York State Science & Technology Foundation
Small Business Technology Investment Fund
99 Washington Ave., Ste. 1731
Albany, NY 12210
(518)473-9741
Fax: (518)473-6876

Rand Capital Corp.
2200 Rand Bldg.
Buffalo, NY 14203
(716)853-0802
Fax: (716)854-8480
Website: http://www.randcapital.com

Seed Capital Partners
620 Main St.
Buffalo, NY 14202
(716)845-7520
Fax: (716)845-7539
Website: http://www.seedcp.com

Coleman Venture Group
5909 Northern Blvd.
PO Box 224

East Norwich, NY 11732
(516)626-3642
Fax: (516)626-9722

Vega Capital Corp.
45 Knollwood Rd.
Elmsford, NY 10523
(914)345-9500
Fax: (914)345-9505

Herbert Young Securities, Inc.
98 Cuttermill Rd.
Great Neck, NY 11021
(516)487-8300
Fax: (516)487-8319

Sterling/Carl Marks Capital, Inc.
175 Great Neck Rd., Ste. 408
Great Neck, NY 11021
(516)482-7374
Fax: (516)487-0781
E-mail: stercrlmar@aol.com
Website: http://www.serlingcarl
marks.com

Impex Venture Management Co.
PO Box 1570
Green Island, NY 12183
(518)271-8008
Fax: (518)271-9101

Corporate Venture Partners L.P.
200 Sunset Park
Ithaca, NY 14850
(607)257-6323
Fax: (607)257-6128

Arthur P. Gould & Co.
One Wilshire Dr.
Lake Success, NY 11020
(516)773-3000
Fax: (516)773-3289

Dauphin Capital Partners
108 Forest Ave.
Locust Valley, NY 11560
(516)759-3339
Fax: (516)759-3322
Website: http://www.dauphincapital.com

550 Digital Media Ventures
555 Madison Ave., 10th Fl.
New York, NY 10022
Website: http://www.550dmv.com

Aberlyn Capital Management Co., Inc.
500 Fifth Ave.
New York, NY 10110
(212)391-7750
Fax: (212)391-7762

Adler & Company
342 Madison Ave., Ste. 807
New York, NY 10173
(212)599-2535
Fax: (212)599-2526

Alimansky Capital Group, Inc.
605 Madison Ave., Ste. 300
New York, NY 10022-1901
(212)832-7300
Fax: (212)832-7338

Allegra Partners
515 Madison Ave., 29th Fl.
New York, NY 10022
(212)826-9080
Fax: (212)759-2561

The Argentum Group
The Chyrsler Bldg.
405 Lexington Ave.
New York, NY 10174
(212)949-6262
Fax: (212)949-8294
Website: http://www.argentum
group.com

Axavision Inc.
14 Wall St., 26th Fl.
New York, NY 10005
(212)619-4000
Fax: (212)619-7202

Bedford Capital Corp.
18 East 48th St., Ste. 1800
New York, NY 10017
(212)688-5700
Fax: (212)754-4699
E-mail: info@bedfordnyc.com
Website: http://www.bedfordnyc.com

Bloom & Co.
950 Third Ave.
New York, NY 10022
(212)838-1858
Fax: (212)838-1843

Bristol Capital Management
300 Park Ave., 17th Fl.
New York, NY 10022
(212)572-6306
Fax: (212)705-4292

Citicorp Venture Capital Ltd. (New York City)
399 Park Ave., 14th Fl.
Zone 4
New York, NY 10043
(212)559-1127
Fax: (212)888-2940

CM Equity Partners
135 E. 57th St.
New York, NY 10022
(212)909-8428
Fax: (212)980-2630

Cohen & Co., L.L.C.
800 Third Ave.
New York, NY 10022
(212)317-2250
Fax: (212)317-2255
E-mail: nlcohen@aol.com

Cornerstone Equity Investors, L.L.C.
717 5th Ave., Ste. 1100
New York, NY 10022
(212)753-0901
Fax: (212)826-6798
Website: http://www.cornerstone-equity.com

CW Group, Inc.
1041 3rd Ave., 2nd fl.
New York, NY 10021
(212)308-5266
Fax: (212)644-0354
Website: http://www.cwventures.com

DH Blair Investment Banking Corp.
44 Wall St., 2nd Fl.
New York, NY 10005
(212)495-5000
Fax: (212)269-1438

Dresdner Kleinwort Capital
75 Wall St.
New York, NY 10005
(212)429-3131
Fax: (212)429-3139
Website: http://www.dresdnerkb.com

East River Ventures, L.P.
645 Madison Ave., 22nd Fl.
New York, NY 10022
(212)644-2322
Fax: (212)644-5498

Easton Hunt Capital Partners
641 Lexington Ave., 21st Fl.
New York, NY 10017
(212)702-0950
Fax: (212)702-0952
Website: http://www.eastoncapital.com

Elk Associates Funding Corp.
747 3rd Ave., Ste. 4C
New York, NY 10017
(212)355-2449
Fax: (212)759-3338

EOS Partners, L.P.
320 Park Ave., 22nd Fl.
New York, NY 10022
(212)832-5800
Fax: (212)832-5815
E-mail: mfirst@eospartners.com
Website: http://www.eospartners.com

Euclid Partners
45 Rockefeller Plaza, Ste. 3240
New York, NY 10111
(212)218-6880
Fax: (212)218-6877
E-mail: graham@euclidpartners.com
Website: http://www.euclidpartners.com

Evergreen Capital Partners, Inc.
150 East 58th St.
New York, NY 10155
(212)813-0758
Fax: (212)813-0754

Exeter Capital L.P.
10 E. 53rd St.
New York, NY 10022
(212)872-1172
Fax: (212)872-1198
E-mail: exeter@usa.net

Financial Technology Research Corp.
518 Broadway
Penthouse
New York, NY 10012
(212)625-9100
Fax: (212)431-0300
E-mail: fintek@financier.com

4C Ventures
237 Park Ave., Ste. 801
New York, NY 10017
(212)692-3680
Fax: (212)692-3685
Website: http://www.4cventures.com

Fusient Ventures
99 Park Ave., 20th Fl.
New York, NY 10016
(212)972-8999
Fax: (212)972-9876
E-mail: info@fusient.com
Website: http://www.fusient.com

Generation Capital Partners
551 Fifth Ave., Ste. 3100
New York, NY 10176
(212)450-8507
Fax: (212)450-8550
Website: http://www.genpartners.com

Golub Associates, Inc.
555 Madison Ave.
New York, NY 10022
(212)750-6060
Fax: (212)750-5505

Hambro America Biosciences Inc.
650 Madison Ave., 21st Floor
New York, NY 10022
(212)223-7400
Fax: (212)223-0305

Hanover Capital Corp.
505 Park Ave., 15th Fl.
New York, NY 10022
(212)755-1222
Fax: (212)935-1787

Harvest Partners, Inc.
280 Park Ave, 33rd Fl.
New York, NY 10017
(212)559-6300
Fax: (212)812-0100
Website: http://www.harvpart.com

Holding Capital Group, Inc.
10 E. 53rd St., 30th Fl.
New York, NY 10022
(212)486-6670
Fax: (212)486-0843

Hudson Venture Partners
660 Madison Ave., 14th Fl.
New York, NY 10021-8405
(212)644-9797
Fax: (212)644-7430
Website: http://www.hudsonptr.com

IBJS Capital Corp.
1 State St., 9th Fl.
New York, NY 10004
(212)858-2018
Fax: (212)858-2768

InterEquity Capital Partners, L.P.
220 5th Ave.
New York, NY 10001
(212)779-2022
Fax: (212)779-2103
Website: http://www.interequity-capital.com

The Jordan Edmiston Group Inc.
150 East 52nd St., 18th Fl.
New York, NY 10022
(212)754-0710
Fax: (212)754-0337

Josephberg, Grosz and Co., Inc.
633 3rd Ave., 13th Fl.
New York, NY 10017

(212)974-9926
Fax: (212)397-5832

J.P. Morgan Capital Corp.
60 Wall St.
New York, NY 10260-0060
(212)648-9000
Fax: (212)648-5002
Website: http://www.jpmorgan.com

The Lambda Funds
380 Lexington Ave., 54th Fl.
New York, NY 10168
(212)682-3454
Fax: (212)682-9231

Lepercq Capital Management Inc.
1675 Broadway
New York, NY 10019
(212)698-0795
Fax: (212)262-0155

Loeb Partners Corp.
61 Broadway, Ste. 2400
New York, NY 10006
(212)483-7000
Fax: (212)574-2001

Madison Investment Partners
660 Madison Ave.
New York, NY 10021
(212)223-2600
Fax: (212)223-8208

MC Capital Inc.
520 Madison Ave., 16th Fl.
New York, NY 10022
(212)644-0841
Fax: (212)644-2926

McCown, De Leeuw and Co. (New York)
65 E. 55th St., 36th Fl.
New York, NY 10022
(212)355-5500
Fax: (212)355-6283
Website: http://www.mdcpartners.com

Morgan Stanley Venture Partners
1221 Avenue of the Americas, 33rd Fl.
New York, NY 10020
(212)762-7900
Fax: (212)762-8424
E-mail: msventures@ms.com
Website: http://www.msvp.com

Nazem and Co.
645 Madison Ave., 12th Fl.
New York, NY 10022
(212)371-7900
Fax: (212)371-2150

Needham Capital Management, L.L.C.
445 Park Ave.
New York, NY 10022
(212)371-8300
Fax: (212)705-0299
Website: http://www.needhamco.com

Norwood Venture Corp.
1430 Broadway, Ste. 1607
New York, NY 10018
(212)869-5075
Fax: (212)869-5331
E-mail: nvc@mail.idt.net
Website: http://www.norven.com

Noveltek Venture Corp.
521 Fifth Ave., Ste. 1700
New York, NY 10175
(212)286-1963

Paribas Principal, Inc.
787 7th Ave.
New York, NY 10019
(212)841-2005
Fax: (212)841-3558

Patricof & Co. Ventures, Inc. (New York)
445 Park Ave.
New York, NY 10022
(212)753-6300
Fax: (212)319-6155
Website: http://www.patricof.com

The Platinum Group, Inc.
350 Fifth Ave, Ste. 7113
New York, NY 10118
(212)736-4300
Fax: (212)736-6086
Website: http://
www.platinumgroup.com

Pomona Capital
780 Third Ave., 28th Fl.
New York, NY 10017
(212)593-3639
Fax: (212)593-3987
Website: http://www.pomonacapital.com

Prospect Street Ventures
10 East 40th St., 44th Fl.
New York, NY 10016
(212)448-0702
Fax: (212)448-9652
E-mail: wkohler@prospectstreet.com
Website: http://www.prospectstreet.com

Regent Capital Management
505 Park Ave., Ste. 1700
New York, NY 10022
(212)735-9900
Fax: (212)735-9908

Rothschild Ventures, Inc.
1251 Avenue of the Americas, 51st Fl.
New York, NY 10020
(212)403-3500
Fax: (212)403-3652
Website: http://www.nmrothschild.com

Sandler Capital Management
767 Fifth Ave., 45th Fl.
New York, NY 10153
(212)754-8100
Fax: (212)826-0280

Siguler Guff & Company
630 Fifth Ave., 16th Fl.
New York, NY 10111
(212)332-5100
Fax: (212)332-5120

Spencer Trask Ventures Inc.
535 Madison Ave.
New York, NY 10022
(212)355-5565
Fax: (212)751-3362
Website: http://www.spencertrask.com

Sprout Group (New York City)
277 Park Ave.
New York, NY 10172
(212)892-3600
Fax: (212)892-3444
E-mail: info@sproutgroup.com
Website: http://www.sproutgroup.com

US Trust Private Equity
114 W.47th St.
New York, NY 10036
(212)852-3949
Fax: (212)852-3759
Website: http://www.ustrust.com/
privateequity

Vencon Management Inc.
301 West 53rd St., Ste. 10F
New York, NY 10019
(212)581-8787
Fax: (212)397-4126
Website: http://www.venconinc.com

Venrock Associates
30 Rockefeller Plaza, Ste. 5508
New York, NY 10112
(212)649-5600
Fax: (212)649-5788
Website: http://www.venrock.com

Venture Capital Fund of America, Inc.
509 Madison Ave., Ste. 812
New York, NY 10022
(212)838-5577
Fax: (212)838-7614

E-mail: mail@vcfa.com
Website: http://www.vcfa.com

Venture Opportunities Corp.
150 E. 58th St.
New York, NY 10155
(212)832-3737
Fax: (212)980-6603

Warburg Pincus Ventures, Inc.
466 Lexington Ave., 11th Fl.
New York, NY 10017
(212)878-9309
Fax: (212)878-9200
Website: http://www.warburgpincus.com

Wasserstein, Perella & Co. Inc.
31 W. 52nd St., 27th Fl.
New York, NY 10019
(212)702-5691
Fax: (212)969-7879

Welsh, Carson, Anderson, & Stowe
320 Park Ave., Ste. 2500
New York, NY 10022-6815
(212)893-9500
Fax: (212)893-9575

Whitney and Co. (New York)
630 Fifth Ave. Ste. 3225
New York, NY 10111
(212)332-2400
Fax: (212)332-2422
Website: http://www.jhwitney.com

Winthrop Ventures
74 Trinity Place, Ste. 600
New York, NY 10006
(212)422-0100

The Pittsford Group
8 Lodge Pole Rd.
Pittsford, NY 14534
(716)223-3523

Genesee Funding
70 Linden Oaks, 3rd Fl.
Rochester, NY 14625
(716)383-5550
Fax: (716)383-5305

Gabelli Multimedia Partners
One Corporate Center
Rye, NY 10580
(914)921-5395
Fax: (914)921-5031

Stamford Financial
108 Main St.
Stamford, NY 12167

(607)652-3311
Fax: (607)652-6301
Website: http://
www.stamfordfinancial.com

Northwood Ventures LLC
485 Underhill Blvd., Ste. 205
Syosset, NY 11791
(516)364-5544
Fax: (516)364-0879
E-mail: northwood@northwood.com
Website: http://
www.northwoodventures.com

Exponential Business Development Co.
216 Walton St.
Syracuse, NY 13202-1227
(315)474-4500
Fax: (315)474-4682
E-mail: dirksonn@aol.com
Website: http://www.exponential-ny.com

Onondaga Venture Capital Fund Inc.
714 State Tower Bldg.
Syracuse, NY 13202
(315)478-0157
Fax: (315)478-0158

Bessemer Venture Partners (Westbury)
1400 Old Country Rd., Ste. 109
Westbury, NY 11590
(516)997-2300
Fax: (516)997-2371
E-mail: bob@bvpny.com
Website: http://www.bvp.com

Ovation Capital Partners
120 Bloomingdale Rd., 4th Fl.
White Plains, NY 10605
(914)258-0011
Fax: (914)684-0848
Website: http://www.ovationcapital.com

North Carolina

Carolinas Capital Investment Corp.
1408 Biltmore Dr.
Charlotte, NC 28207
(704)375-3888
Fax: (704)375-6226

First Union Capital Partners
1st Union Center, 12th Fl.
301 S. College St.
Charlotte, NC 28288-0732
(704)383-0000
Fax: (704)374-6711
Website: http://www.fucp.com

Frontier Capital LLC
525 North Tryon St., Ste. 1700
Charlotte, NC 28202
(704)414-2880
Fax: (704)414-2881
Website: http://www.frontierfunds.com

Kitty Hawk Capital
2700 Coltsgate Rd., Ste. 202
Charlotte, NC 28211
(704)362-3909
Fax: (704)362-2774
Website: http://
www.kittyhawkcapital.com

Piedmont Venture Partners
One Morrocroft Centre
6805 Morisson Blvd., Ste. 380
Charlotte, NC 28211
(704)731-5200
Fax: (704)365-9733
Website: http://www.piedmontvp.com

Ruddick Investment Co.
1800 Two First Union Center
Charlotte, NC 28282
(704)372-5404
Fax: (704)372-6409

The Shelton Companies Inc.
3600 One First Union Center
301 S. College St.
Charlotte, NC 28202
(704)348-2200
Fax: (704)348-2260

Wakefield Group
1110 E. Morehead St.
PO Box 36329
Charlotte, NC 28236
(704)372-0355
Fax: (704)372-8216
Website: http://
www.wakefieldgroup.com

Aurora Funds, Inc.
2525 Meridian Pkwy., Ste. 220
Durham, NC 27713
(919)484-0400
Fax: (919)484-0444
Website: http://www.aurorafunds.com

Intersouth Partners
3211 Shannon Rd., Ste. 610
Durham, NC 27707
(919)493-6640
Fax: (919)493-6649
E-mail: info@intersouth.com
Website: http://www.intersouth.com

Geneva Merchant Banking Partners
PO Box 21962
Greensboro, NC 27420
(336)275-7002
Fax: (336)275-9155
Website: http://www.genevamerchant bank.com

The North Carolina Enterprise Fund, L.P.
3600 Glenwood Ave., Ste. 107
Raleigh, NC 27612
(919)781-2691
Fax: (919)783-9195
Website: http://www.ncef.com

Ohio

Senmend Medical Ventures
4445 Lake Forest Dr., Ste. 600
Cincinnati, OH 45242
(513)563-3264
Fax: (513)563-3261

The Walnut Group
312 Walnut St., Ste. 1151
Cincinnati, OH 45202
(513)651-3300
Fax: (513)929-4441
Website: http://www.thewalnutgroup.com

Brantley Venture Partners
20600 Chagrin Blvd., Ste. 1150
Cleveland, OH 44122
(216)283-4800
Fax: (216)283-5324

Clarion Capital Corp.
1801 E. 9th St., Ste. 1120
Cleveland, OH 44114
(216)687-1096
Fax: (216)694-3545

Crystal Internet Venture Fund, L.P.
1120 Chester Ave., Ste. 418
Cleveland, OH 44114
(216)263-5515
Fax: (216)263-5518
E-mail: jf@crystalventure.com
Website: http://www.crystalventure.com

Key Equity Capital Corp.
127 Public Sq., 28th Fl.
Cleveland, OH 44114
(216)689-3000
Fax: (216)689-3204
Website: http://www.keybank.com

Morgenthaler Ventures
Terminal Tower
50 Public Square, Ste. 2700
Cleveland, OH 44113
(216)416-7500

Fax: (216)416-7501
Website: http://www.morgenthaler.com

National City Equity Partners Inc.
1965 E. 6th St.
Cleveland, OH 44114
(216)575-2491
Fax: (216)575-9965
E-mail: nccap@aol.com
Website: http://www.nccapital.com

Primus Venture Partners, Inc.
5900 LanderBrook Dr., Ste. 2000
Cleveland, OH 44124-4020
(440)684-7300
Fax: (440)684-7342
E-mail: info@primusventure.com
Website: http://www.primusventure.com

Banc One Capital Partners (Columbus)
150 East Gay St., 24th Fl.
Columbus, OH 43215
(614)217-1100
Fax: (614)217-1217

Battelle Venture Partners
505 King Ave.
Columbus, OH 43201
(614)424-7005
Fax: (614)424-4874

Ohio Partners
62 E. Board St., 3rd Fl.
Columbus, OH 43215
(614)621-1210
Fax: (614)621-1240

Capital Technology Group, L.L.C.
400 Metro Place North, Ste. 300
Dublin, OH 43017
(614)792-6066
Fax: (614)792-6036
E-mail: info@capitaltech.com
Website: http://www.capitaltech.com

Northwest Ohio Venture Fund
4159 Holland-Sylvania R., Ste. 202
Toledo, OH 43623
(419)824-8144
Fax: (419)882-2035
E-mail: bwalsh@novf.com

Oklahoma

Moore & Associates
1000 W. Wilshire Blvd., Ste. 370
Oklahoma City, OK 73116
(405)842-3660
Fax: (405)842-3763

Chisholm Private Capital Partners
100 West 5th St., Ste. 805

Tulsa, OK 74103
(918)584-0440
Fax: (918)584-0441
Website: http://www.chisholmvc.com

Davis, Tuttle Venture Partners (Tulsa)
320 S. Boston, Ste. 1000
Tulsa, OK 74103-3703
(918)584-7272
Fax: (918)582-3404
Website: http://www.davistuttle.com

RBC Ventures
2627 E. 21st St.
Tulsa, OK 74114
(918)744-5607
Fax: (918)743-8630

Oregon

Utah Ventures II LP
10700 SW Beaverton-Hillsdale Hwy., Ste. 548
Beaverton, OR 97005
(503)574-4125
E-mail: adishlip@uven.com
Website: http://www.uven.com

Orien Ventures
14523 SW Westlake Dr.
Lake Oswego, OR 97035
(503)699-1680
Fax: (503)699-1681

OVP Venture Partners (Lake Oswego)
340 Oswego Pointe Dr., Ste. 200
Lake Oswego, OR 97034
(503)697-8766
Fax: (503)697-8863
E-mail: info@ovp.com
Website: http://www.ovp.com

Oregon Resource and Technology Development Fund
4370 NE Halsey St., Ste. 233
Portland, OR 97213-1566
(503)282-4462
Fax: (503)282-2976

Shaw Venture Partners
400 SW 6th Ave., Ste. 1100
Portland, OR 97204-1636
(503)228-4884
Fax: (503)227-2471
Website: http://www.shawventures.com

Pennsylvania

Mid-Atlantic Venture Funds
125 Goodman Dr.
Bethlehem, PA 18015

(610)865-6550
Fax: (610)865-6427
Website: http://www.mavf.com

Newspring Ventures
100 W. Elm St., Ste. 101
Conshohocken, PA 19428
(610)567-2380
Fax: (610)567-2388
Website: http://www.newsprintventures.com

Patricof & Co. Ventures, Inc.
455 S. Gulph Rd., Ste. 410
King of Prussia, PA 19406
(610)265-0286
Fax: (610)265-4959
Website: http://www.patricof.com

Loyalhanna Venture Fund
527 Cedar Way, Ste. 104
Oakmont, PA 15139
(412)820-7035
Fax: (412)820-7036

Innovest Group Inc.
2000 Market St., Ste. 1400
Philadelphia, PA 19103
(215)564-3960
Fax: (215)569-3272

Keystone Venture Capital Management Co.
1601 Market St., Ste. 2500
Philadelphia, PA 19103
(215)241-1200
Fax: (215)241-1211
Website: http://www.keystonevc.com

Liberty Venture Partners
2005 Market St., Ste. 200
Philadelphia, PA 19103
(215)282-4484
Fax: (215)282-4485
E-mail: info@libertyvp.com
Website: http://www.libertyvp.com

Penn Janney Fund, Inc.
1801 Market St., 11th Fl.
Philadelphia, PA 19103
(215)665-4447
Fax: (215)557-0820

Philadelphia Ventures, Inc.
The Bellevue
200 S. Broad St.
Philadelphia, PA 19102
(215)732-4445
Fax: (215)732-4644

Birchmere Ventures Inc.
2000 Technology Dr.
Pittsburgh, PA 15219-3109
(412)803-8000
Fax: (412)687-8139
Website: http://www.birchmerevc.com

CEO Venture Fund
2000 Technology Dr., Ste. 160
Pittsburgh, PA 15219-3109
(412)687-3451
Fax: (412)687-8139
E-mail: ceofund@aol.com
Website: http://www.ceoventure
fund.com

Innovation Works Inc.
2000 Technology Dr., Ste. 250
Pittsburgh, PA 15219
(412)681-1520
Fax: (412)681-2625
Website: http://www.innovation
works.org

**Keystone Minority Capital
Fund L.P.**
1801 Centre Ave., Ste. 201
Williams Sq.
Pittsburgh, PA 15219
(412)338-2230
Fax: (412)338-2224

Mellon Ventures, Inc.
One Mellon Bank Ctr., Rm. 3500
Pittsburgh, PA 15258
(412)236-3594
Fax: (412)236-3593
Website: http://www.mellon
ventures.com

**Pennsylvania Growth
Fund**
5850 Ellsworth Ave., Ste. 303
Pittsburgh, PA 15232
(412)661-1000
Fax: (412)361-0676

**Point Venture
Partners**
The Century Bldg.
130 Seventh St., 7th Fl.
Pittsburgh, PA 15222
(412)261-1966
Fax: (412)261-1718

Cross Atlantic Capital Partners
5 Radnor Corporate Center, Ste. 555
Radnor, PA 19087
(610)995-2650
Fax: (610)971-2062
Website: http://www.xacp.com

**Meridian Venture Partners
(Radnor)**
The Radnor Court Bldg., Ste. 140
259 Radnor-Chester Rd.
Radnor, PA 19087
(610)254-2999
Fax: (610)254-2996
E-mail: mvpart@ix.netcom.com

TDH
919 Conestoga Rd., Bldg. 1, Ste. 301
Rosemont, PA 19010
(610)526-9970
Fax: (610)526-9971

Adams Capital Management
500 Blackburn Ave.
Sewickley, PA 15143
(412)749-9454
Fax: (412)749-9459
Website: http://www.acm.com

S.R. One, Ltd.
Four Tower Bridge
200 Barr Harbor Dr., Ste. 250
W. Conshohocken, PA 19428
(610)567-1000
Fax: (610)567-1039

**Greater Philadelphia Venture Capital
Corp.**
351 East Conestoga Rd.
Wayne, PA 19087
(610)688-6829
Fax: (610)254-8958

PA Early Stage
435 Devon Park Dr., Bldg. 500, Ste. 510
Wayne, PA 19087
(610)293-4075
Fax: (610)254-4240
Website: http://www.paearly
stage.com

The Sandhurst Venture Fund, L.P.
351 E. Constoga Rd.
Wayne, PA 19087
(610)254-8900
Fax: (610)254-8958

TL Ventures
700 Bldg.
435 Devon Park Dr.
Wayne, PA 19087-1990
(610)975-3765
Fax: (610)254-4210
Website: http://www.tl
ventures.com

Rockhill Ventures, Inc.
100 Front St., Ste. 1350
West Conshohocken, PA 19428

(610)940-0300
Fax: (610)940-0301

Puerto Rico

Advent-Morro Equity Partners
Banco Popular Bldg.
206 Tetuan St., Ste. 903
San Juan, PR 00902
(787)725-5285
Fax: (787)721-1735

North America Investment Corp.
Mercantil Plaza, Ste. 813
PO Box 191831
San Juan, PR 00919
(787)754-6178
Fax: (787)754-6181

Rhode Island

Manchester Humphreys, Inc.
40 Westminster St., Ste. 900
Providence, RI 02903
(401)454-0400
Fax: (401)454-0403

Navis Partners
50 Kennedy Plaza, 12th Fl.
Providence, RI 02903
(401)278-6770
Fax: (401)278-6387
Website: http://www.navis
partners.com

South Carolina

Capital Insights, L.L.C.
PO Box 27162
Greenville, SC 29616-2162
(864)242-6832
Fax: (864)242-6755
E-mail: jwarner@capitalinsights.com
Website: http://www.capitalinsights.com

**Transamerica Mezzanine
Financing**
7 N. Laurens St., Ste. 603
Greenville, SC 29601
(864)232-6198
Fax: (864)241-4444

Tennessee

Valley Capital Corp.
Krystal Bldg.
100 W. Martin Luther King Blvd., Ste. 212
Chattanooga, TN 37402
(423)265-1557
Fax: (423)265-1588

Coleman Swenson Booth Inc.
237 2nd Ave. S
Franklin, TN 37064-2649
(615)791-9462
Fax: (615)791-9636
Website: http://www.colemans
wenson.com

Capital Services & Resources, Inc.
5159 Wheelis Dr., Ste. 106
Memphis, TN 38117
(901)761-2156
Fax: (907)767-0060

Paradigm Capital Partners LLC
6410 Poplar Ave., Ste. 395
Memphis, TN 38119
(901)682-6060
Fax: (901)328-3061

SSM Ventures
845 Crossover Ln., Ste. 140
Memphis, TN 38117
(901)767-1131
Fax: (901)767-1135
Website: http://www.ssm
ventures.com

Capital Across America L.P.
501 Union St., Ste. 201
Nashville, TN 37219
(615)254-1414
Fax: (615)254-1856
Website: http://www.capitalacross
america.com

Equitas L.P.
2000 Glen Echo Rd., Ste. 101
PO Box 158838
Nashville, TN 37215-8838
(615)383-8673
Fax: (615)383-8693

Massey Burch Capital Corp.
One Burton Hills Blvd., Ste. 350
Nashville, TN 37215
(615)665-3221
Fax: (615)665-3240
E-mail: tcalton@masseyburch.com
Website: http://www.masseyburch.com

Nelson Capital Corp.
3401 West End Ave., Ste. 300
Nashville, TN 37203
(615)292-8787
Fax: (615)385-3150

Texas

Phillips-Smith Specialty Retail Group
5080 Spectrum Dr., Ste. 805 W
Addison, TX 75001
(972)387-0725
Fax: (972)458-2560
E-mail: pssrg@aol.com
Website: http://www.phillips-smith.com

Austin Ventures, L.P.
701 Brazos St., Ste. 1400
Austin, TX 78701
(512)485-1900
Fax: (512)476-3952
E-mail: info@ausven.com
Website: http://www.austin
ventures.com

The Capital Network
3925 West Braker Lane, Ste. 406
Austin, TX 78759-5321
(512)305-0826
Fax: (512)305-0836

Techxas Ventures LLC
5000 Plaza on the Lake
Austin, TX 78746
(512)343-0118
Fax: (512)343-1879
E-mail: bruce@techxas.com
Website: http://www.techxas.com

Alliance Financial of Houston
218 Heather Ln.
Conroe, TX 77385-9013
(936)447-3300
Fax: (936)447-4222

Amerimark Capital Corp.
1111 W. Mockingbird, Ste. 1111
Dallas, TX 75247
(214)638-7878
Fax: (214)638-7612
E-mail: amerimark@amcapital.com
Website: http://www.amcapital.com

AMT Venture Partners / AMT Capital Ltd.
5220 Spring Valley Rd., Ste. 600
Dallas, TX 75240
(214)905-9757
Fax: (214)905-9761
Website: http://www.amtcapital.com

Arkoma Venture Partners
5950 Berkshire Lane, Ste. 1400
Dallas, TX 75225
(214)739-3515
Fax: (214)739-3572
E-mail: joelf@arkomavp.com

Capital Southwest Corp.
12900 Preston Rd., Ste. 700
Dallas, TX 75230
(972)233-8242
Fax: (972)233-7362
Website: http://
www.capitalsouthwest.com

Dali, Hook Partners
One Lincoln Center, Ste. 1550
5400 LBJ Freeway
Dallas, TX 75240
(972)991-5457
Fax: (972)991-5458
E-mail: dhook@hookpartners.com
Website: http://www.hookpartners.com

HO2 Partners
Two Galleria Tower
13455 Noel Rd., Ste. 1670
Dallas, TX 75240
(972)702-1144
Fax: (972)702-8234
Website: http://www.ho2.com

Interwest Partners (Dallas)
2 Galleria Tower
13455 Noel Rd., Ste. 1670
Dallas, TX 75240
(972)392-7279
Fax: (972)490-6348
Website: http://www.interwest.com

Kahala Investments, Inc.
8214 Westchester Dr., Ste. 715
Dallas, TX 75225
(214)987-0077
Fax: (214)987-2332

MESBIC Ventures Holding Co.
2435 North Central Expressway, Ste. 200
Dallas, TX 75080
(972)991-1597
Fax: (972)991-4770
Website: http://www.mvhc.com

North Texas MESBIC, Inc.
9500 Forest Lane, Ste. 430
Dallas, TX 75243
(214)221-3565
Fax: (214)221-3566

Richard Jaffe & Company, Inc,
7318 Royal Cir.
Dallas, TX 75230
(214)265-9397
Fax: (214)739-1845

Sevin Rosen Management Co.
13455 Noel Rd., Ste. 1670
Dallas, TX 75240

(972)702-1100
Fax: (972)702-1103
E-mail: info@srfunds.com
Website: http://www.srfunds.com

Stratford Capital Partners, L.P.
300 Crescent Ct., Ste. 500
Dallas, TX 75201
(214)740-7377
Fax: (214)720-7393
E-mail: stratcap@hmtf.com

Sunwestern Investment Group
12221 Merit Dr., Ste. 935
Dallas, TX 75251
(972)239-5650
Fax: (972)701-0024

Wingate Partners
750 N. St. Paul St., Ste. 1200
Dallas, TX 75201
(214)720-1313
Fax: (214)871-8799

Buena Venture Associates
201 Main St., 32nd Fl.
Fort Worth, TX 76102
(817)339-7400
Fax: (817)390-8408
Website: http://www.buenaventure.com

The Catalyst Group
3 Riverway, Ste. 770
Houston, TX 77056
(713)623-8133
Fax: (713)623-0473
E-mail: herman@thecatalystgroup.net
Website: http://www.thecatalystgroup.net

Cureton & Co., Inc.
1100 Louisiana, Ste. 3250
Houston, TX 77002
(713)658-9806
Fax: (713)658-0476

Davis, Tuttle Venture Partners (Dallas)
8 Greenway Plaza, Ste. 1020
Houston, TX 77046
(713)993-0440
Fax: (713)621-2297
Website: http://www.davistuttle.com

Houston Partners
401 Louisiana, 8th Fl.
Houston, TX 77002
(713)222-8600
Fax: (713)222-8932

Southwest Venture Group
10878 Westheimer, Ste. 178
Houston, TX 77042

(713)827-8947
(713)461-1470

AM Fund
4600 Post Oak Place, Ste. 100
Houston, TX 77027
(713)627-9111
Fax: (713)627-9119

Ventex Management, Inc.
3417 Milam St.
Houston, TX 77002-9531
(713)659-7870
Fax: (713)659-7855

MBA Venture Group
1004 Olde Town Rd., Ste. 102
Irving, TX 75061
(972)986-6703

First Capital Group Management Co.
750 East Mulberry St., Ste. 305
PO Box 15616
San Antonio, TX 78212
(210)736-4233
Fax: (210)736-5449

The Southwest Venture Partnerships
16414 San Pedro, Ste. 345
San Antonio, TX 78232
(210)402-1200
Fax: (210)402-1221
E-mail: swvp@aol.com

Medtech International Inc.
1742 Carriageway
Sugarland, TX 77478
(713)980-8474
Fax: (713)980-6343

Utah

First Security Business Investment Corp.
15 East 100 South, Ste. 100
Salt Lake City, UT 84111
(801)246-5737
Fax: (801)246-5740

Utah Ventures II, L.P.
423 Wakara Way, Ste. 206
Salt Lake City, UT 84108
(801)583-5922
Fax: (801)583-4105
Website: http://www.uven.com

Wasatch Venture Corp.
1 S. Main St., Ste. 1400
Salt Lake City, UT 84133
(801)524-8939
Fax: (801)524-8941
E-mail: mail@wasatchvc.com

Vermont

North Atlantic Capital Corp.
76 Saint Paul St., Ste. 600
Burlington, VT 05401
(802)658-7820
Fax: (802)658-5757
Website: http://
www.northatlanticcapital.com

Green Mountain Advisors Inc.
PO Box 1230
Quechee, VT 05059
(802)296-7800
Fax: (802)296-6012
Website: http://www.gmtcap.com

Virginia

Oxford Financial Services Corp.
Alexandria, VA 22314
(703)519-4900
Fax: (703)519-4910
E-mail: oxford133@aol.com

Continental SBIC
4141 N. Henderson Rd.
Arlington, VA 22203
(703)527-5200
Fax: (703)527-3700

Novak Biddle Venture Partners
1750 Tysons Blvd., Ste. 1190
McLean, VA 22102
(703)847-3770
Fax: (703)847-3771
E-mail: roger@novakbiddle.com
Website: http://www.novakbiddle.com

Spacevest
11911 Freedom Dr., Ste. 500
Reston, VA 20190
(703)904-9800
Fax: (703)904-0571
E-mail: spacevest@spacevest.com
Website: http://www.spacevest.com

Virginia Capital
1801 Libbie Ave., Ste. 201
Richmond, VA 23226
(804)648-4802
Fax: (804)648-4809
E-mail: webmaster@vacapital.com
Website: http://www.vacapital.com

Calvert Social Venture Partners
402 Maple Ave. W
Vienna, VA 22180
(703)255-4930
Fax: (703)255-4931
E-mail: calven2000@aol.com

Fairfax Partners
8000 Towers Crescent Dr., Ste. 940
Vienna, VA 22182
(703)847-9486
Fax: (703)847-0911

Global Internet Ventures
8150 Leesburg Pike, Ste. 1210
Vienna, VA 22182
(703)442-3300
Fax: (703)442-3388
Website: http://www.givinc.com

Walnut Capital Corp. (Vienna)
8000 Towers Crescent Dr., Ste. 1070
Vienna, VA 22182
(703)448-3771
Fax: (703)448-7751

Washington

Encompass Ventures
777 108th Ave. NE, Ste. 2300
Bellevue, WA 98004
(425)486-3900
Fax: (425)486-3901
E-mail: info@evpartners.com
Website: http://www.encompass
ventures.com

Fluke Venture Partners
11400 SE Sixth St., Ste. 230
Bellevue, WA 98004
(425)453-4590
Fax: (425)453-4675
E-mail: gabelein@flukeventures.com
Website: http://www.flukeventures.com

Pacific Northwest Partners SBIC, L.P.
15352 SE 53rd St.
Bellevue, WA 98006
(425)455-9967
Fax: (425)455-9404

Materia Venture Associates, L.P.
3435 Carillon Pointe
Kirkland, WA 98033-7354
(425)822-4100
Fax: (425)827-4086

OVP Venture Partners (Kirkland)
2420 Carillon Pt.
Kirkland, WA 98033
(425)889-9192
Fax: (425)889-0152
E-mail: info@ovp.com
Website: http://www.ovp.com

Digital Partners
999 3rd Ave., Ste. 1610
Seattle, WA 98104
(206)405-3607
Fax: (206)405-3617
Website: http://www.digitalpartners.com

Frazier & Company
601 Union St., Ste. 3300
Seattle, WA 98101
(206)621-7200
Fax: (206)621-1848
E-mail: jon@frazierco.com

Kirlan Venture Capital, Inc.
221 First Ave. W, Ste. 108
Seattle, WA 98119-4223
(206)281-8610
Fax: (206)285-3451
Website: http://www.kirlanventure.com

Phoenix Partners
1000 2nd Ave., Ste. 3600
Seattle, WA 98104
(206)624-8968
Fax: (206)624-1907

Voyager Capital
800 5th St., Ste. 4100
Seattle, WA 98103
(206)470-1180
Fax: (206)470-1185
E-mail: info@voyagercap.com
Website: http://www.
voyagercap.com

Northwest Venture Associates
221 N. Wall St., Ste. 628
Spokane, WA 99201

(509)747-0728
Fax: (509)747-0758
Website: http://www.nwva.com

Wisconsin

Venture Investors Management, L.L.C.
University Research Park
505 S. Rosa Rd.
Madison, WI 53719
(608)441-2700
Fax: (608)441-2727
E-mail: roger@venture
investors.com
Website: http://www.venture
investers.com

Capital Investments, Inc.
1009 West Glen Oaks Lane,
Ste. 103
Mequon, WI 53092
(414)241-0303
Fax: (414)241-8451
Website: http://www.capital
investmentsinc.com

Future Value Venture, Inc.
2745 N. Martin Luther King Dr.,
Ste. 204
Milwaukee, WI 53212-2300
(414)264-2252
Fax: (414)264-2253
E-mail: fvventures@aol.com
William Beckett, President

Lubar and Co., Inc.
700 N. Water St., Ste. 1200
Milwaukee, WI 53202
(414)291-9000
Fax: (414)291-9061

GCI
20875 Crossroads Cir., Ste. 100
Waukesha, WI 53186
(262)798-5080
Fax: (262)798-5087

Glossary of Small Business Terms

Absolute liability
Liability that is incurred due to product defects or negligent actions. Manufacturers or retail establishments are held responsible, even though the defect or action may not have been intentional or negligent.

ACE
See Active Corps of Executives

Accident and health benefits
Benefits offered to employees and their families in order to offset the costs associated with accidental death, accidental injury, or sickness.

Account statement
A record of transactions, including payments, new debt, and deposits, incurred during a defined period of time.

Accounting system
System capturing the costs of all employees and/or machinery included in business expenses.

Accounts payable
See Trade credit

Accounts receivable
Unpaid accounts which arise from unsettled claims and transactions from the sale of a company's products or services to its customers.

Active Corps of Executives (ACE)
A group of volunteers for a management assistance program of the U.S. Small Business Administration; volunteers provide one-on-one counseling and teach workshops and seminars for small firms.

ADA
See Americans with Disabilities Act

Adaptation
The process whereby an invention is modified to meet the needs of users.

Adaptive engineering
The process whereby an invention is modified to meet the manufacturing and commercial requirements of a targeted market.

Adverse selection
The tendency for higher-risk individuals to purchase health care and more comprehensive plans, resulting in increased costs.

Advertising
A marketing tool used to capture public attention and influence purchasing decisions for a product or service. Utilizes various forms of media to generate consumer response, such as flyers, magazines, newspapers, radio, and television.

Age discrimination
The denial of the rights and privileges of employment based solely on the age of an individual.

Agency costs
Costs incurred to insure that the lender or investor maintains control over assets while allowing the borrower or entrepreneur to use them. Monitoring and information costs are the two major types of agency costs.

Agribusiness
The production and sale of commodities and products from the commercial farming industry.

America Online
An online service which is accessible by computer modem. The service features Internet access, bulletin boards, online periodicals, electronic mail, and other services for subscribers.

Americans with Disabilities Act (ADA)
Law designed to ensure equal access and opportunity to handicapped persons.

Annual report

Yearly financial report prepared by a business that adheres to the requirements set forth by the Securities and Exchange Commission (SEC).

Antitrust immunity

Exemption from prosecution under antitrust laws. In the transportation industry, firms with antitrust immunity are permitted under certain conditions to set schedules and sometimes prices for the public benefit.

Applied research

Scientific study targeted for use in a product or process.

Asians

A minority category used by the U.S. Bureau of the Census to represent a diverse group that includes Aleuts, Eskimos, American Indians, Asian Indians, Chinese, Japanese, Koreans, Vietnamese, Filipinos, Hawaiians, and other Pacific Islanders.

Assets

Anything of value owned by a company.

Audit

The verification of accounting records and business procedures conducted by an outside accounting service.

Average cost

Total production costs divided by the quantity produced.

Balance Sheet

A financial statement listing the total assets and liabilities of a company at a given time.

Bankruptcy

The condition in which a business cannot meet its debt obligations and petitions a federal district court either for reorganization of its debts (Chapter 11) or for liquidation of its assets (Chapter 7).

Basic research

Theoretical scientific exploration not targeted to application.

Basket clause

A provision specifying the amount of public pension funds that may be placed in investments not included on a state's legal list (see separate citation).

BBS

See Bulletin Board Service

BDC

See Business development corporation

Benefit

Various services, such as health care, flextime, day care, insurance, and vacation, offered to employees as part of a hiring package. Typically subsidized in whole or in part by the business.

BIDCO

See Business and industrial development company

Billing cycle

A system designed to evenly distribute customer billing throughout the month, preventing clerical backlogs.

Birth

See Business birth

Blue chip security

A low-risk, low-yield security representing an interest in a very stable company.

Blue sky laws

A general term that denotes various states' laws regulating securities.

Bond

A written instrument executed by a bidder or contractor (the principal) and a second party (the surety or sureties) to assure fulfillment of the principal's obligations to a third party (the obligee or government) identified in the bond. If the principal's obligations are not met, the bond assures payment to the extent stipulated of any loss sustained by the obligee.

Bonding requirements

Terms contained in a bond (see separate citation).

Bonus

An amount of money paid to an employee as a reward for achieving certain business goals or objectives.

Brainstorming

A group session where employees contribute their ideas for solving a problem or meeting a company objective without fear of retribution or ridicule.

Brand name
The part of a brand, trademark, or service mark that can be spoken. It can be a word, letter, or group of words or letters.

Bridge financing
A short-term loan made in expectation of intermediateterm or long-term financing. Can be used when a company plans to go public in the near future.

Broker
One who matches resources available for innovation with those who need them.

Budget
An estimate of the spending necessary to complete a project or offer a service in comparison to cash-on-hand and expected earnings for the coming year, with an emphasis on cost control.

Bulletin Board Service (BBS)
An online service enabling users to communicate with each other about specific topics.

Business and industrial development company (BIDCO)
A private, for-profit financing corporation chartered by the state to provide both equity and long-term debt capital to small business owners (see separate citations for equity and debt capital).

Business birth
The formation of a new establishment or enterprise. The appearance of a new establishment or enterprise in the Small Business Data Base (see separate citation).

Business conditions
Outside factors that can affect the financial performance of a business.

Business contractions
The number of establishments that have decreased in employment during a specified time.

Business cycle
A period of economic recession and recovery. These cycles vary in duration.

Business death
The voluntary or involuntary closure of a firm or establishment. The disappearance of an establishment or enterprise from the Small Business Data Base (see separate citation).

Business development corporation (BDC)
A business financing agency, usually composed of the financial institutions in an area or state, organized to assist in financing businesses unable to obtain assistance through normal channels; the risk is spread among various members of the business development corporation, and interest rates may vary somewhat from those charged by member institutions. A venture capital firm in which shares of ownership are publicly held and to which the Investment Act of 1940 applies.

Business dissolution
For enumeration purposes, the absence of a business that was present in the prior time period from any current record.

Business entry
See Business birth

Business ethics
Moral values and principles espoused by members of the business community as a guide to fair and honest business practices.

Business exit
See Business death

Business expansions
The number of establishments that added employees during a specified time.

Business failure
Closure of a business causing a loss to at least one creditor.

Business format franchising
The purchase of the name, trademark, and an ongoing business plan of the parent corporation or franchisor by the franchisee.

Business license
A legal authorization issued by municipal and state governments and required for business operations.

Business name
Enterprises must register their business names with local governments usually on a "doing business as" (DBA) form. (This name is sometimes referred to as a

"fictional name.") The procedure is part of the business licensing process and prevents any other business from using that same name for a similar business in the same locality.

Business norms
See Financial ratios

Business permit
See Business license

Business plan
A document that spells out a company's expected course of action for a specified period, usually including a detailed listing and analysis of risks and uncertainties. For the small business, it should examine the proposed products, the market, the industry, the management policies, the marketing policies, production needs, and financial needs. Frequently, it is used as a prospectus for potential investors and lenders.

Business proposal
See Business plan

Business service firm
An establishment primarily engaged in rendering services to other business organizations on a fee or contract basis.

Business start
For enumeration purposes, a business with a name or similar designation that did not exist in a prior time period.

Cafeteria plan
See Flexible benefit plan

Capacity
Level of a firm's, industry's, or nation's output corresponding to full practical utilization of available resources.

Capital
Assets less liabilities, representing the ownership interest in a business. A stock of accumulated goods, especially at a specified time and in contrast to income received during a specified time period. Accumulated goods devoted to production. Accumulated possessions calculated to bring income.

Capital expenditure
Expenses incurred by a business for improvements that will depreciate over time.

Capital gain
The monetary difference between the purchase price and the selling price of capital. Capital gains are taxed at a rate of 28% by the federal government.

Capital intensity
The relative importance of capital in the production process, usually expressed as the ratio of capital to labor but also sometimes as the ratio of capital to output.

Capital resource
The equipment, facilities and labor used to create products and services.

Caribbean Basin Initiative
An interdisciplinary program to support commerce among the businesses in the nations of the Caribbean Basin and the United States. Agencies involved include: the Agency for International Development, the U.S. Small Business Administration, the International Trade Administration of the U.S. Department of Commerce, and various private sector groups.

Catastrophic care
Medical and other services for acute and long-term illnesses that cost more than insurance coverage limits or that cost the amount most families may be expected to pay with their own resources.

CDC
See Certified development corporation

CD-ROM
Compact disc with read-only memory used to store large amounts of digitized data.

Certified development corporation (CDC)
A local area or statewide corporation or authority (for profit or nonprofit) that packages U.S. Small Business Administration (SBA), bank, state, and/or private money into financial assistance for existing business capital improvements. The SBA holds the second lien on its maximum share of 40 percent involvement. Each state has at least one certified development corporation. This program is called the SBA 504 Program.

Certified lenders
Banks that participate in the SBA guaranteed loan program (see separate citation). Such banks must have a good track record with the U.S. Small Business Administration (SBA) and must agree to certain conditions set forth by the agency. In return, the SBA agrees to process any guaranteed loan application within three business days.

Champion
An advocate for the development of an innovation.

Channel of distribution
The means used to transport merchandise from the manufacturer to the consumer.

Chapter 7 of the 1978 Bankruptcy Act
Provides for a court-appointed trustee who is responsible for liquidating a company's assets in order to settle outstanding debts.

Chapter 11 of the 1978 Bankruptcy Act
Allows the business owners to retain control of the company while working with their creditors to reorganize their finances and establish better business practices to prevent liquidation of assets.

Closely held corporation
A corporation in which the shares are held by a few persons, usually officers, employees, or others close to the management; these shares are rarely offered to the public.

Code of Federal Regulations
Codification of general and permanent rules of the federal government published in the Federal Register.

Code sharing
See Computer code sharing

Coinsurance
Upon meeting the deductible payment, health insurance participants may be required to make additional health care cost-sharing payments. Coinsurance is a payment of a fixed percentage of the cost of each service; copayment is usually a fixed amount to be paid with each service.

Collateral
Securities, evidence of deposit, or other property pledged by a borrower to secure repayment of a loan.

Collective ratemaking
The establishment of uniform charges for services by a group of businesses in the same industry.

Commercial insurance plan
See Underwriting

Commercial loans
Short-term renewable loans used to finance specific capital needs of a business.

Commercialization
The final stage of the innovation process, including production and distribution.

Common stock
The most frequently used instrument for purchasing ownership in private or public companies. Common stock generally carries the right to vote on certain corporate actions and may pay dividends, although it rarely does in venture investments. In liquidation, common stockholders are the last to share in the proceeds from the sale of a corporation's assets; bondholders and preferred shareholders have priority. Common stock is often used in firstround start-up financing.

Community development corporation
A corporation established to develop economic programs for a community and, in most cases, to provide financial support for such development.

Competitor
A business whose product or service is marketed for the same purpose/use and to the same consumer group as the product or service of another.

Computer code sharing
An arrangement whereby flights of a regional airline are identified by the two-letter code of a major carrier in the computer reservation system to help direct passengers to new regional carriers.

Consignment
A merchandising agreement, usually referring to secondhand shops, where the dealer pays the owner of an item a percentage of the profit when the item is sold.

Consortium
A coalition of organizations such as banks and corporations for ventures requiring large capital resources.

Consultant
An individual that is paid by a business to provide advice and expertise in a particular area.

Consumer price index
A measure of the fluctuation in prices between two points in time.

Consumer research
Research conducted by a business to obtain information about existing or potential consumer markets.

Continuation coverage
Health coverage offered for a specified period of time to employees who leave their jobs and to their widows, divorced spouses, or dependents.

Contractions
See Business contractions

Convertible preferred stock
A class of stock that pays a reasonable dividend and is convertible into common stock (see separate citation). Generally the convertible feature may only be exercised after being held for a stated period of time. This arrangement is usually considered second-round financing when a company needs equity to maintain its cash flow.

Convertible securities
A feature of certain bonds, debentures, or preferred stocks that allows them to be exchanged by the owner for another class of securities at a future date and in accordance with any other terms of the issue.

Copayment
See Coinsurance

Copyright
A legal form of protection available to creators and authors to safeguard their works from unlawful use or claim of ownership by others. Copyrights may be acquired for works of art, sculpture, music, and published or unpublished manuscripts. All copyrights should be registered at the Copyright Office of the Library of Congress.

Corporate financial ratios
The relationship between key figures found in a company's financial statement expressed as a numeric value. Used to evaluate risk and company performance. Also known as Financial averages, Operating ratios, and Business ratios.

Corporation
A legal entity, chartered by a state or the federal government, recognized as a separate entity having its own rights, privileges, and liabilities distinct from those of its members.

Cost containment
Actions taken by employers and insurers to curtail rising health care costs; for example, increasing employee cost sharing (see separate citation), requiring second opinions, or preadmission screening.

Cost sharing
The requirement that health care consumers contribute to their own medical care costs through deductibles and coinsurance (see separate citations). Cost sharing does not include the amounts paid in premiums. It is used to control utilization of services; for example, requiring a fixed amount to be paid with each health care service.

Cottage industry
Businesses based in the home in which the family members are the labor force and family-owned equipment is used to process the goods.

Credit Rating
A letter or number calculated by an organization (such as Dun & Bradstreet) to represent the ability and disposition of a business to meet its financial obligations.

Customer service
Various techniques used to ensure the satisfaction of a customer.

Cyclical peak
The upper turning point in a business cycle.

Cyclical trough
The lower turning point in a business cycle.

DBA
See Business name

Death
See Business death

Debenture

A certificate given as acknowledgment of a debt (see separate citation) secured by the general credit of the issuing corporation. A bond, usually without security, issued by a corporation and sometimes convertible to common stock.

Debt

Something owed by one person to another. Financing in which a company receives capital that must be repaid; no ownership is transferred.

Debt capital

Business financing that normally requires periodic interest payments and repayment of the principal within a specified time.

Debt financing

See Debt capital

Debt securities

Loans such as bonds and notes that provide a specified rate of return for a specified period of time.

Deductible

A set amount that an individual must pay before any benefits are received.

Demand shock absorbers

A term used to describe the role that some small firms play by expanding their output levels to accommodate a transient surge in demand.

Demographics

Statistics on various markets, including age, income, and education, used to target specific products or services to appropriate consumer groups.

Demonstration

Showing that a product or process has been modified sufficiently to meet the needs of users.

Deregulation

The lifting of government restrictions; for example, the lifting of government restrictions on the entry of new businesses, the expansion of services, and the setting of prices in particular industries.

Desktop Publishing

Using personal computers and specialized software to produce camera-ready copy for publications.

Disaster loans

Various types of physical and economic assistance available to individuals and businesses through the U.S. Small Business Administration (SBA). This is the only SBA loan program available for residential purposes.

Discrimination

The denial of the rights and privileges of employment based on factors such as age, race, religion, or gender.

Diseconomies of scale

The condition in which the costs of production increase faster than the volume of production.

Dissolution

See Business dissolution

Distribution

Delivering a product or process to the user.

Distributor

One who delivers merchandise to the user.

Diversified company

A company whose products and services are used by several different markets.

Doing business as (DBA)

See Business name

Dow Jones

An information services company that publishes the Wall Street Journal and other sources of financial information.

Dow Jones Industrial Average

An indicator of stock market performance.

Earned income

A tax term that refers to wages and salaries earned by the recipient, as opposed to monies earned through interest and dividends.

Economic efficiency

The use of productive resources to the fullest practical extent in the provision of the set of goods and services that is most preferred by purchasers in the economy.

Economic indicators

Statistics used to express the state of the economy. These include the length of the average work week, the rate of unemployment, and stock prices.

Economically disadvantaged
See Socially and economically disadvantaged

Economies of scale
See Scale economies

EEOC
See Equal Employment Opportunity Commission

8(a) Program
A program authorized by the Small Business Act that directs federal contracts to small businesses owned and operated by socially and economically disadvantaged individuals.

Electronic mail (e-mail)
The electronic transmission of mail via phone lines.

E-mail
See Electronic mail

Employee leasing
A contract by which employers arrange to have their workers hired by a leasing company and then leased back to them for a management fee. The leasing company typically assumes the administrative burden of payroll and provides a benefit package to the workers.

Employee tenure
The length of time an employee works for a particular employer.

Employer identification number
The business equivalent of a social security number. Assigned by the U.S. Internal Revenue Service.

Enterprise
An aggregation of all establishments owned by a parent company. An enterprise may consist of a single, independent establishment or include subsidiaries and other branches under the same ownership and control.

Enterprise zone
A designated area, usually found in inner cities and other areas with significant unemployment, where businesses receive tax credits and other incentives to entice them to establish operations there.

Entrepreneur
A person who takes the risk of organizing and operating a new business venture.

Entry
See Business entry

Equal Employment Opportunity Commission (EEOC)
A federal agency that ensures nondiscrimination in the hiring and firing practices of a business.

Equal opportunity employer
An employer who adheres to the standards set by the Equal Employment Opportunity Commission (see separate citation).

Equity
The ownership interest. Financing in which partial or total ownership of a company is surrendered in exchange for capital. An investor's financial return comes from dividend payments and from growth in the net worth of the business.

Equity capital
See Equity; Equity midrisk venture capital

Equity financing
See Equity; Equity midrisk venture capital

Equity midrisk venture capital
An unsecured investment in a company. Usually a purchase of ownership interest in a company that occurs in the later stages of a company's development.

Equity partnership
A limited partnership arrangement for providing start-up and seed capital to businesses.

Equity securities
See Equity

Equity-type
Debt financing subordinated to conventional debt.

Establishment
A single-location business unit that may be independent (a single-establishment enterprise) or owned by a parent enterprise.

Establishment and Enterprise Microdata File
See U.S. Establishment and Enterprise Microdata File

Establishment birth
See Business birth

Establishment Longitudinal Microdata File
See U.S. Establishment Longitudinal Microdata File

Ethics
See Business ethics

Evaluation
Determining the potential success of translating an invention into a product or process.

Exit
See Business exit

Experience rating
See Underwriting

Export
A product sold outside of the country.

Export license
A general or specific license granted by the U.S. Department of Commerce required of anyone wishing to export goods. Some restricted articles need approval from the U.S. Departments of State, Defense, or Energy.

Failure
See Business failure

Fair share agreement
An agreement reached between a franchisor and a minority business organization to extend business ownership to minorities by either reducing the amount of capital required or by setting aside certain marketing areas for minority business owners.

Feasibility study
A study to determine the likelihood that a proposed product or development will fulfill the objectives of a particular investor.

Federal Trade Commission (FTC)
Federal agency that promotes free enterprise and competition within the U.S.

Federal Trade Mark Act of 1946
See Lanham Act

Fictional name
See Business name

Fiduciary
An individual or group that hold assets in trust for a beneficiary.

Financial analysis
The techniques used to determine money needs in a business. Techniques include ratio analysis, calculation

of return on investment, guides for measuring profitability, and break-even analysis to determine ultimate success.

Financial intermediary
A financial institution that acts as the intermediary between borrowers and lenders. Banks, savings and loan associations, finance companies, and venture capital companies are major financial intermediaries in the United States.

Financial ratios
See Corporate financial ratios; Industry financial ratios

Financial statement
A written record of business finances, including balance sheets and profit and loss statements.

Financing
See First-stage financing; Second-stage financing; Thirdstage financing

First-stage financing
Financing provided to companies that have expended their initial capital, and require funds to start full-scale manufacturing and sales. Also known as First-round financing.

Fiscal year
Any twelve-month period used by businesses for accounting purposes.

504 Program
See Certified development corporation

Flexible benefit plan
A plan that offers a choice among cash and/or qualified benefits such as group term life insurance, accident and health insurance, group legal services, dependent care assistance, and vacations.

FOB
See Free on board

Format franchising
See Business format franchising; Franchising

401(k) plan
A financial plan where employees contribute a percentage of their earnings to a fund that is invested in stocks, bonds, or money markets for the purpose of saving money for retirement.

Four Ps
Marketing terms referring to Product, Price, Place, and Promotion.

Franchising
A form of licensing by which the owner-the franchisor- distributes or markets a product, method, or service through affiliated dealers called franchisees. The product, method, or service being marketed is identified by a brand name, and the franchisor maintains control over the marketing methods employed. The franchisee is often given exclusive access to a defined geographic area.

Free on board (FOB)
A pricing term indicating that the quoted price includes the cost of loading goods into transport vessels at a specified place.

Frictional unemployment
See Unemployment

FTC
See Federal Trade Commission

Fulfillment
The systems necessary for accurate delivery of an ordered item, including subscriptions and direct marketing.

Full-time workers
Generally, those who work a regular schedule of more than 35 hours per week.

Garment registration number
A number that must appear on every garment sold in the U.S. to indicate the manufacturer of the garment, which may or may not be the same as the label under which the garment is sold. The U.S. Federal Trade Commission assigns and regulates garment registration numbers.

Gatekeeper
A key contact point for entry into a network.

GDP
See Gross domestic product

General obligation bond
A municipal bond secured by the taxing power of the municipality. The Tax Reform Act of 1986 limits the purposes for which such bonds may be issued and establishes volume limits on the extent of their issuance.

GNP
See Gross national product

Good Housekeeping Seal
Seal appearing on products that signifies the fulfillment of the standards set by the Good Housekeeping Institute to protect consumer interests.

Goods sector
All businesses producing tangible goods, including agriculture, mining, construction, and manufacturing businesses.

GPO
See Gross product originating

Gross domestic product (GDP)
The part of the nation's gross national product (see separate citation) generated by private business using resources from within the country.

Gross national product (GNP)
The most comprehensive single measure of aggregate economic output. Represents the market value of the total output of goods and services produced by a nation's economy.

Gross product originating (GPO)
A measure of business output estimated from the income or production side using employee compensation, profit income, net interest, capital consumption, and indirect business taxes.

HAL
See Handicapped assistance loan program

Handicapped assistance loan program (HAL)
Low-interest direct loan program through the U.S. Small Business Administration (SBA) for handicapped persons. The SBA requires that these persons demonstrate that their disability is such that it is impossible for them to secure employment, thus making it necessary to go into their own business to make a living.

Health maintenance organization (HMO)
Organization of physicians and other health care professionals that provides health services to subscribers and their dependents on a prepaid basis.

Health provider

An individual or institution that gives medical care. Under Medicare, an institutional provider is a hospital, skilled nursing facility, home health agency, or provider of certain physical therapy services.

Hispanic

A person of Cuban, Mexican, Puerto Rican, Latin American (Central or South American), European Spanish, or other Spanish-speaking origin or ancestry.

HMO

See Health maintenance organization

Home-based business

A business with an operating address that is also a residential address (usually the residential address of the proprietor).

Hub-and-spoke system

A system in which flights of an airline from many different cities (the spokes) converge at a single airport (the hub). After allowing passengers sufficient time to make connections, planes then depart for different cities.

Human Resources Management

A business program designed to oversee recruiting, pay, benefits, and other issues related to the company's work force, including planning to determine the optimal use of labor to increase production, thereby increasing profit.

Idea

An original concept for a new product or process.

Import

Products produced outside the country in which they are consumed.

Income

Money or its equivalent, earned or accrued, resulting from the sale of goods and services.

Income statement

A financial statement that lists the profits and losses of a company at a given time.

Incorporation

The filing of a certificate of incorporation with a state's secretary of state, thereby limiting the business owner's liability.

Incubator

A facility designed to encourage entrepreneurship and minimize obstacles to new business formation and growth, particularly for high-technology firms, by housing a number of fledgling enterprises that share an array of services, such as meeting areas, secretarial services, accounting, research library, on-site financial and management counseling, and word processing facilities.

Independent contractor

An individual considered self-employed (see separate citation) and responsible for paying Social Security taxes and income taxes on earnings.

Indirect health coverage

Health insurance obtained through another individual's health care plan; for example, a spouse's employersponsored plan.

Industrial development authority

The financial arm of a state or other political subdivision established for the purpose of financing economic development in an area, usually through loans to nonprofit organizations, which in turn provide facilities for manufacturing and other industrial operations.

Industry financial ratios

Corporate financial ratios averaged for a specified industry. These are used for comparison purposes and reveal industry trends and identify differences between the performance of a specific company and the performance of its industry. Also known as Industrial averages, Industry ratios, Financial averages, and Business or Industrial norms.

Inflation

Increases in volume of currency and credit, generally resulting in a sharp and continuing rise in price levels.

Informal capital

Financing from informal, unorganized sources; includes informal debt capital such as trade credit or loans from friends and relatives and equity capital from informal investors.

Initial public offering (IPO)

A corporation's first offering of stock to the public.

Innovation
The introduction of a new idea into the marketplace in the form of a new product or service or an improvement in organization or process.

Intellectual property
Any idea or work that can be considered proprietary in nature and is thus protected from infringement by others.

Internal capital
Debt or equity financing obtained from the owner or through retained business earnings.

Internet
A government-designed computer network that contains large amounts of information and is accessible through various vendors for a fee.

Intrapreneurship
The state of employing entrepreneurial principles to nonentrepreneurial situations.

Invention
The tangible form of a technological idea, which could include a laboratory prototype, drawings, formulas, etc.

IPO
See Initial public offering

Job description
The duties and responsibilities required in a particular position.

Job tenure
A period of time during which an individual is continuously employed in the same job.

Joint marketing agreements
Agreements between regional and major airlines, often involving the coordination of flight schedules, fares, and baggage transfer. These agreements help regional carriers operate at lower cost.

Joint venture
Venture in which two or more people combine efforts in a particular business enterprise, usually a single transaction or a limited activity, and agree to share the profits and losses jointly or in proportion to their contributions.

Keogh plan
Designed for self-employed persons and unincorporated businesses as a tax-deferred pension account.

Labor force
Civilians considered eligible for employment who are also willing and able to work.

Labor force participation rate
The civilian labor force as a percentage of the civilian population.

Labor intensity
The relative importance of labor in the production process, usually measured as the capital-labor ratio; i.e., the ratio of units of capital (typically, dollars of tangible assets) to the number of employees. The higher the capital-labor ratio exhibited by a firm or industry, the lower the capital intensity of that firm or industry is said to be.

Labor surplus area
An area in which there exists a high unemployment rate. In procurement (see separate citation), extra points are given to firms in counties that are designated a labor surplus area; this information is requested on procurement bid sheets.

Labor union
An organization of similarly-skilled workers who collectively bargain with management over the conditions of employment.

Laboratory prototype
See Prototype

LAN
See Local Area Network

Lanham Act
Refers to the Federal Trade Mark Act of 1946. Protects registered trademarks, trade names, and other service marks used in commerce.

Large business-dominated industry
Industry in which a minimum of 60 percent of employment or sales is in firms with more than 500 workers.

LBO
See Leveraged buy-out

Leader pricing
A reduction in the price of a good or service in order to generate more sales of that good or service.

Legal list
A list of securities selected by a state in which certain institutions and fiduciaries (such as pension funds, insurance companies, and banks) may invest. Securities not on the list are not eligible for investment. Legal lists typically restrict investments to high quality securities meeting certain specifications. Generally, investment is limited to U.S. securities and investment-grade blue chip securities (see separate citation).

Leveraged buy-out (LBO)
The purchase of a business or a division of a corporation through a highly leveraged financing package.

Liability
An obligation or duty to perform a service or an act. Also defined as money owed.

License
A legal agreement granting to another the right to use a technological innovation.

Limited partnerships
See Venture capital limited partnerships

Liquidity
The ability to convert a security into cash promptly.

Loans
See Commercial loans; Disaster loans; SBA direct loans; SBA guaranteed loans; SBA special lending institution categories Local Area Network (LAN) Computer networks contained within a single building or small area; used to facilitate the sharing of information.

Local development corporation
An organization, usually made up of local citizens of a community, designed to improve the economy of the area by inducing business and industry to locate and expand there. A local development corporation establishes a capability to finance local growth.

Long-haul rates
Rates charged by a transporter in which the distance traveled is more than 800 miles.

Long-term debt
An obligation that matures in a period that exceeds five years.

Low-grade bond
A corporate bond that is rated below investment grade by the major rating agencies (Standard and Poor's, Moody's).

Macro-efficiency
Efficiency as it pertains to the operation of markets and market systems.

Managed care
A cost-effective health care program initiated by employers whereby low-cost health care is made available to the employees in return for exclusive patronage to program doctors.

Management Assistance Programs
See SBA Management Assistance Programs

Management and technical assistance
A term used by many programs to mean business (as opposed to technological) assistance.

Mandated benefits
Specific treatments, providers, or individuals required by law to be included in commercial health plans.

Market evaluation
The use of market information to determine the sales potential of a specific product or process.

Market failure
The situation in which the workings of a competitive market do not produce the best results from the point of view of the entire society.

Market information
Data of any type that can be used for market evaluation, which could include demographic data, technology forecasting, regulatory changes, etc.

Market research
A systematic collection, analysis, and reporting of data about the market and its preferences, opinions, trends, and plans; used for corporate decision-making.

Market share
In a particular market, the percentage of sales of a specific product.

Marketing
Promotion of goods or services through various media.

Master Establishment List (MEL)
A list of firms in the United States developed by the U.S. Small Business Administration; firms can be selected by industry, region, state, standard metropolitan statistical area (see separate citation), county, and zip code.

Maturity
The date upon which the principal or stated value of a bond or other indebtedness becomes due and payable.

Medicaid (Title XIX)
A federally aided, state-operated and administered program that provides medical benefits for certain low income persons in need of health and medical care who are eligible for one of the government's welfare cash payment programs, including the aged, the blind, the disabled, and members of families with dependent children where one parent is absent, incapacitated, or unemployed.

Medicare (Title XVIII)
A nationwide health insurance program for disabled and aged persons. Health insurance is available to insured persons without regard to income. Monies from payroll taxes cover hospital insurance and monies from general revenues and beneficiary premiums pay for supplementary medical insurance.

MEL
See Master Establishment List

MESBIC
See Minority enterprise small business investment corporation

MET
See Multiple employer trust

Metropolitan statistical area (MSA)
A means used by the government to define large population centers that may transverse different governmental jurisdictions. For example, the Washington, D.C. MSA includes the District of Columbia and contiguous parts of Maryland and Virginia because all of these geopolitical areas comprise one population and economic operating unit.

Mezzanine financing
See Third-stage financing

Micro-efficiency
Efficiency as it pertains to the operation of individual firms.

Microdata
Information on the characteristics of an individual business firm.

Mid-term debt
An obligation that matures within one to five years.

Midrisk venture capital
See Equity midrisk venture capital

Minimum premium plan
A combination approach to funding an insurance plan aimed primarily at premium tax savings. The employer self-funds a fixed percentage of estimated monthly claims and the insurance company insures the excess.

Minimum wage
The lowest hourly wage allowed by the federal government.

Minority Business Development Agency
Contracts with private firms throughout the nation to sponsor Minority Business Development Centers which provide minority firms with advice and technical assistance on a fee basis.

Minority Enterprise Small Business Investment Corporation (MESBIC)
A federally funded private venture capital firm licensed by the U.S. Small Business Administration to provide capital to minority-owned businesses (see separate citation).

Minority-owned business
Businesses owned by those who are socially or economically disadvantaged (see separate citation).

Mom and Pop business
A small store or enterprise having limited capital, principally employing family members.

Moonlighter
A wage-and-salary worker with a side business.

MSA
See Metropolitan statistical area

Multi-employer plan
A health plan to which more than one employer is required to contribute and that may be maintained through a collective bargaining agreement and required to meet standards prescribed by the U.S. Department of Labor.

Multi-level marketing
A system of selling in which you sign up other people to assist you and they, in turn, recruit others to help them. Some entrepreneurs have built successful companies on this concept because the main focus of their activities is their product and product sales.

Multimedia
The use of several types of media to promote a product or service. Also, refers to the use of several different types of media (sight, sound, pictures, text) in a CD-ROM (see separate citation) product.

Multiple employer trust (MET)
A self-funded benefit plan generally geared toward small employers sharing a common interest.

NAFTA
See North American Free Trade Agreement

NASDAQ
See National Association of Securities Dealers Automated Quotations

National Association of Securities Dealers Automated Quotations
Provides price quotes on over-the-counter securities as well as securities listed on the New York Stock Exchange.

National income
Aggregate earnings of labor and property arising from the production of goods and services in a nation's economy.

Net assets
See Net worth

Net income
The amount remaining from earnings and profits after all expenses and costs have been met or deducted. Also known as Net earnings.

Net profit
Money earned after production and overhead expenses (see separate citations) have been deducted.

Net worth
The difference between a company's total assets and its total liabilities.

Network
A chain of interconnected individuals or organizations sharing information and/or services.

New York Stock Exchange (NYSE)
The oldest stock exchange in the U.S. Allows for trading in stocks, bonds, warrants, options, and rights that meet listing requirements.

Niche
A career or business for which a person is well-suited. Also, a product which fulfills one need of a particular market segment, often with little or no competition.

Nodes
One workstation in a network, either local area or wide area (see separate citations).

Nonbank bank
A bank that either accepts deposits or makes loans, but not both. Used to create many new branch banks.

Noncompetitive awards
A method of contracting whereby the federal government negotiates with only one contractor to supply a product or service.

Nonmember bank
A state-regulated bank that does not belong to the federal bank system.

Nonprofit
An organization that has no shareholders, does not distribute profits, and is without federal and state tax liabilities.

Norms
See Financial ratios

North American Free Trade Agreement (NAFTA)
Passed in 1993, NAFTA eliminates trade barriers among businesses in the U.S., Canada, and Mexico.

NYSE
See New York Stock Exchange

Occupational Safety & Health Administration (OSHA)
Federal agency that regulates health and safety standards within the workplace.

Optimal firm size
The business size at which the production cost per unit of output (average cost) is, in the long run, at its minimum.

Organizational chart
A hierarchical chart tracking the chain of command within an organization.

OSHA
See Occupational Safety & Health Administration

Overhead
Expenses, such as employee benefits and building utilities, incurred by a business that are unrelated to the actual product or service sold.

Owner's capital
Debt or equity funds provided by the owner(s) of a business; sources of owner's capital are personal savings, sales of assets, or loans from financial institutions.

P & L
See Profit and loss statement

Part-time workers
Normally, those who work less than 35 hours per week. The Tax Reform Act indicated that part-time workers who work less than 17.5 hours per week may be excluded from health plans for purposes of complying with federal nondiscrimination rules.

Part-year workers
Those who work less than 50 weeks per year.

Partnership
Two or more parties who enter into a legal relationship to conduct business for profit. Defined by the U.S. Internal Revenue Code as joint ventures, syndicates, groups, pools, and other associations of two or more persons organized for profit that are not specifically classified in the IRS code as corporations or proprietorships.

Patent
A grant made by the government assuring an inventor the sole right to make, use, and sell an invention for a period of 17 years.

PC
See Professional corporation

Peak
See Cyclical peak

Pension
A series of payments made monthly, semiannually, annually, or at other specified intervals during the lifetime of the pensioner for distribution upon retirement. The term is sometimes used to denote the portion of the retirement allowance financed by the employer's contributions.

Pension fund
A fund established to provide for the payment of pension benefits; the collective contributions made by all of the parties to the pension plan.

Performance appraisal
An established set of objective criteria, based on job description and requirements, that is used to evaluate the performance of an employee in a specific job.

Permit
See Business license

Plan
See Business plan

Pooling
An arrangement for employers to achieve efficiencies and lower health costs by joining together to purchase group health insurance or self-insurance.

PPO
See Preferred provider organization

Preferred lenders program
See SBA special lending institution categories

Preferred provider organization (PPO)
A contractual arrangement with a health care services organization that agrees to discount its health care rates in return for faster payment and/or a patient base.

Premiums
The amount of money paid to an insurer for health insurance under a policy. The premium is generally paid periodically (e.g., monthly), and often is split between the employer and the employee. Unlike deductibles and coinsurance or copayments,

premiums are paid for coverage whether or not benefits are actually used.

Prime-age workers
Employees 25 to 54 years of age.

Prime contract
A contract awarded directly by the U.S. Federal Government.

Private company
See Closely held corporation

Private placement
A method of raising capital by offering for sale an investment or business to a small group of investors (generally avoiding registration with the Securities and Exchange Commission or state securities registration agencies). Also known as Private financing or Private offering.

Pro forma
The use of hypothetical figures in financial statements to represent future expenditures, debts, and other potential financial expenses.

Proactive
Taking the initiative to solve problems and anticipate future events before they happen, instead of reacting to an already existing problem or waiting for a difficult situation to occur.

Procurement
A contract from an agency of the federal government for goods or services from a small business.

Prodigy
An online service which is accessible by computer modem. The service features Internet access, bulletin boards, online periodicals, electronic mail, and other services for subscribers.

Product development
The stage of the innovation process where research is translated into a product or process through evaluation, adaptation, and demonstration.

Product franchising
An arrangement for a franchisee to use the name and to produce the product line of the franchisor or parent corporation.

Production
The manufacture of a product.

Production prototype
See Prototype

Productivity
A measurement of the number of goods produced during a specific amount of time.

Professional corporation (PC)
Organized by members of a profession such as medicine, dentistry, or law for the purpose of conducting their professional activities as a corporation. Liability of a member or shareholder is limited in the same manner as in a business corporation.

Profit and loss statement (P & L)
The summary of the incomes (total revenues) and costs of a company's operation during a specific period of time. Also known as Income and expense statement.

Proposal
See Business plan

Proprietorship
The most common legal form of business ownership; about 85 percent of all small businesses are proprietorships. The liability of the owner is unlimited in this form of ownership.

Prospective payment system
A cost-containment measure included in the Social Security Amendments of 1983 whereby Medicare payments to hospitals are based on established prices, rather than on cost reimbursement.

Prototype
A model that demonstrates the validity of the concept of an invention (laboratory prototype); a model that meets the needs of the manufacturing process and the user (production prototype).

Prudent investor rule or standard
A legal doctrine that requires fiduciaries to make investments using the prudence, diligence, and intelligence that would be used by a prudent person in making similar investments. Because fiduciaries make investments on behalf of third-party beneficiaries, the

standard results in very conservative investments. Until recently, most state regulations required the fiduciary to apply this standard to each investment. Newer, more progressive regulations permit fiduciaries to apply this standard to the portfolio taken as a whole, thereby allowing a fiduciary to balance a portfolio with higher-yield, higher-risk investments. In states with more progressive regulations, practically every type of security is eligible for inclusion in the portfolio of investments made by a fiduciary, provided that the portfolio investments, in their totality, are those of a prudent person.

Public equity markets
Organized markets for trading in equity shares such as common stocks, preferred stocks, and warrants. Includes markets for both regularly traded and nonregularly traded securities.

Public offering
General solicitation for participation in an investment opportunity. Interstate public offerings are supervised by the U.S. Securities and Exchange Commission (see separate citation).

Quality control
The process by which a product is checked and tested to ensure consistent standards of high quality.

Rate of return
The yield obtained on a security or other investment based on its purchase price or its current market price. The total rate of return is current income plus or minus capital appreciation or depreciation.

Real property
Includes the land and all that is contained on it.

Realignment
See Resource realignment

Recession
Contraction of economic activity occurring between the peak and trough (see separate citations) of a business cycle.

Regulated market
A market in which the government controls the forces of supply and demand, such as who may enter and what price may be charged.

Regulation D
A vehicle by which small businesses make small offerings and private placements of securities with limited disclosure requirements. It was designed to ease the burdens imposed on small businesses utilizing this method of capital formation.

Regulatory Flexibility Act
An act requiring federal agencies to evaluate the impact of their regulations on small businesses before the regulations are issued and to consider less burdensome alternatives.

Research
The initial stage of the innovation process, which includes idea generation and invention.

Research and development financing
A tax-advantaged partnership set up to finance product development for start-ups as well as more mature companies.

Resource mobility
The ease with which labor and capital move from firm to firm or from industry to industry.

Resource realignment
The adjustment of productive resources to interindustry changes in demand.

Resources
The sources of support or help in the innovation process, including sources of financing, technical evaluation, market evaluation, management and business assistance, etc.

Retained business earnings
Business profits that are retained by the business rather than being distributed to the shareholders as dividends.

Revolving credit
An agreement with a lending institution for an amount of money, which cannot exceed a set maximum, over a specified period of time. Each time the borrower repays a portion of the loan, the amount of the repayment may be borrowed yet again.

Risk capital
See Venture capital

Risk management
The act of identifying potential sources of financial loss and taking action to minimize their negative impact.

Routing
The sequence of steps necessary to complete a product during production.

S corporations
See Sub chapter S corporations

SBA
See Small Business Administration

SBA direct loans
Loans made directly by the U.S. Small Business Administration (SBA); monies come from funds appropriated specifically for this purpose. In general, SBA direct loans carry interest rates slightly lower than those in the private financial markets and are available only to applicants unable to secure private financing or an SBA guaranteed loan.

SBA 504 Program
See Certified development corporation

SBA guaranteed loans
Loans made by lending institutions in which the U.S. Small Business Administration (SBA) will pay a prior agreed-upon percentage of the outstanding principal in the event the borrower of the loan defaults. The terms of the loan and the interest rate are negotiated between theborrower and the lending institution, within set parameters.

SBA loans
See Disaster loans; SBA direct loans; SBA guaranteed loans; SBA special lending institution categories

SBA Management Assistance Programs
Classes, workshops, counseling, and publications offered by the U.S. Small Business Administration.

SBA special lending institution categories
U.S. Small Business Administration (SBA) loan program in which the SBA promises certified banks a 72-hour turnaround period in giving its approval for a loan, and in which preferred lenders in a pilot program are allowed to write SBA loans without seeking prior SBA approval.

SBDB
See Small Business Data Base

SBDC
See Small business development centers

SBI
See Small business institutes program

SBIC
See Small business investment corporation

SBIR Program
See Small Business Innovation Development Act of 1982

Scale economies
The decline of the production cost per unit of output (average cost) as the volume of output increases.

Scale efficiency
The reduction in unit cost available to a firm when producing at a higher output volume.

SCORE
See Service Corps of Retired Executives

SEC
See Securities and Exchange Commission

SECA
See Self-Employment Contributions Act

Second-stage financing
Working capital for the initial expansion of a company that is producing, shipping, and has growing accounts receivable and inventories. Also known as Second-round financing.

Secondary market
A market established for the purchase and sale of outstanding securities following their initial distribution.

Secondary worker
Any worker in a family other than the person who is the primary source of income for the family.

Secondhand capital
Previously used and subsequently resold capital equipment (e.g., buildings and machinery).

Securities and Exchange Commission (SEC)
Federal agency charged with regulating the trade of securities to prevent unethical practices in the investor market.

Securitized debt
A marketing technique that converts long-term loans to marketable securities.

Seed capital
Venture financing provided in the early stages of the innovation process, usually during product development.

Self-employed person
One who works for a profit or fees in his or her own business, profession, or trade, or who operates a farm.

Self-Employment Contributions Act (SECA)
Federal law that governs the self-employment tax (see separate citation).

Self-employment income
Income covered by Social Security if a business earns a net income of at least $400.00 during the year. Taxes are paid on earnings that exceed $400.00.

Self-employment retirement plan
See Keogh plan

Self-employment tax
Required tax imposed on self-employed individuals for the provision of Social Security and Medicare. The tax must be paid quarterly with estimated income tax statements.

Self-funding
A health benefit plan in which a firm uses its own funds to pay claims, rather than transferring the financial risks of paying claims to an outside insurer in exchange for premium payments.

Service Corps of Retired Executives (SCORE)
Volunteers for the SBA Management Assistance Program who provide one-on-one counseling and teach workshops and seminars for small firms.

Service firm
See Business service firm

Service sector
Broadly defined, all U.S. industries that produce intangibles, including the five major industry divisions of transportation, communications, and utilities; wholesale trade; retail trade; finance, insurance, and real estate; and services.

Set asides
See Small business set asides

Short-haul service
A type of transportation service in which the transporter supplies service between cities where the maximum distance is no more than 200 miles.

Short-term debt
An obligation that matures in one year.

SIC codes
See Standard Industrial Classification codes

Single-establishment enterprise
See Establishment

Small business
An enterprise that is independently owned and operated, is not dominant in its field, and employs fewer than 500 people. For SBA purposes, the U.S. Small Business Administration (SBA) considers various other factors (such as gross annual sales) in determining size of a business.

Small Business Administration (SBA)
An independent federal agency that provides assistance with loans, management, and advocating interests before other federal agencies.

Small Business Data Base
A collection of microdata (see separate citation) files on individual firms developed and maintained by the U.S. Small Business Administration.

Small business development centers (SBDC)
Centers that provide support services to small businesses, such as individual counseling, SBA advice, seminars and conferences, and other learning center activities. Most services are free of charge, or available at minimal cost.

Small business development corporation
See Certified development corporation

Small business-dominated industry
Industry in which a minimum of 60 percent of employment or sales is in firms with fewer than 500 employees.

Small Business Innovation Development Act of 1982
Federal statute requiring federal agencies with large extramural research and development budgets to

allocate a certain percentage of these funds to small research and development firms. The program, called the Small Business Innovation Research (SBIR) Program, is designed to stimulate technological innovation and make greater use of small businesses in meeting national innovation needs.

Small business institutes (SBI) program
Cooperative arrangements made by U.S. Small Business Administration district offices and local colleges and universities to provide small business firms with graduate students to counsel them without charge.

Small business investment corporation (SBIC)
A privately owned company licensed and funded through the U.S. Small Business Administration and private sector sources to provide equity or debt capital to small businesses.

Small business set asides
Procurement (see separate citation) opportunities required by law to be on all contracts under $10,000 or a certain percentage of an agency's total procurement expenditure.

Smaller firms
For U.S. Department of Commerce purposes, those firms not included in the Fortune 1000.

SMSA
See Metropolitan statistical area

Socially and economically disadvantaged
Individuals who have been subjected to racial or ethnic prejudice or cultural bias without regard to their qualities as individuals, and whose abilities to compete are impaired because of diminished opportunities to obtain capital and credit.

Sole proprietorship
An unincorporated, one-owner business, farm, or professional practice.

Special lending institution categories
See SBA special lending institution categories

Standard Industrial Classification (SIC) codes
Four-digit codes established by the U.S. Federal Government to categorize businesses by type of economic activity; the first two digits correspond to major groups such as construction and manufacturing, while the last two digits correspond to subgroups such as home construction or highway construction.

Standard metropolitan statistical area (SMSA)
See Metropolitan statistical area

Start-up
A new business, at the earliest stages of development and financing.

Start-up costs
Costs incurred before a business can commence operations.

Start-up financing
Financing provided to companies that have either completed product development and initial marketing or have been in business for less than one year but have not yet sold their product commercially.

Stock
A certificate of equity ownership in a business.

Stop-loss coverage
Insurance for a self-insured plan that reimburses the company for any losses it might incur in its health claims beyond a specified amount.

Strategic planning
Projected growth and development of a business to establish a guiding direction for the future. Also used to determine which market segments to explore for optimal sales of products or services.

Structural unemployment
See Unemployment

Sub chapter S corporations
Corporations that are considered noncorporate for tax purposes but legally remain corporations.

Subcontract
A contract between a prime contractor and a subcontractor, or between subcontractors, to furnish supplies or services for performance of a prime contract (see separate citation) or a subcontract.

Surety bonds
Bonds providing reimbursement to an individual, company, or the government if a firm fails to complete

a contract. The U.S. Small Business Administration guarantees surety bonds in a program much like the SBA guaranteed loan program (see separate citation).

Swing loan
See Bridge financing

Target market
The clients or customers sought for a business' product or service.

Targeted Jobs Tax Credit
Federal legislation enacted in 1978 that provides a tax credit to an employer who hires structurally unemployed individuals.

Tax number
A number assigned to a business by a state revenue department that enables the business to buy goods without paying sales tax.

Taxable bonds
An interest-bearing certificate of public or private indebtedness. Bonds are issued by public agencies to finance economic development.

Technical assistance
See Management and technical assistance

Technical evaluation
Assessment of technological feasibility.

Technology
The method in which a firm combines and utilizes labor and capital resources to produce goods or services; the application of science for commercial or industrial purposes.

Technology transfer
The movement of information about a technology or intellectual property from one party to another for use.

Tenure
See Employee tenure

Term
The length of time for which a loan is made.

Terms of a note
The conditions or limits of a note; includes the interest rate per annum, the due date, and transferability and convertibility features, if any.

Third-party administrator
An outside company responsible for handling claims and performing administrative tasks associated with health insurance plan maintenance.

Third-stage financing
Financing provided for the major expansion of a company whose sales volume is increasing and that is breaking even or profitable. These funds are used for further plant expansion, marketing, working capital, or development of an improved product. Also known as Third-round or Mezzanine financing.

Time deposit
A bank deposit that cannot be withdrawn before a specified future time.

Time management
Skills and scheduling techniques used to maximize productivity.

Trade credit
Credit extended by suppliers of raw materials or finished products. In an accounting statement, trade credit is referred to as "accounts payable."

Trade name
The name under which a company conducts business, or by which its business, goods, or services are identified. It may or may not be registered as a trademark.

Trade periodical
A publication with a specific focus on one or more aspects of business and industry.

Trade secret
Competitive advantage gained by a business through the use of a unique manufacturing process or formula.

Trade show
An exhibition of goods or services used in a particular industry. Typically held in exhibition centers where exhibitors rent space to display their merchandise.

Trademark
A graphic symbol, device, or slogan that identifies a business. A business has property rights to its trademark from the inception of its use, but it is still prudent to register all trademarks with the Trademark Office of the U.S. Department of Commerce.

Translation
See Product development

Treasury bills
Investment tender issued by the Federal Reserve Bank in amounts of $10,000 that mature in 91 to 182 days.

Treasury bonds
Long-term notes with maturity dates of not less than seven and not more than twenty-five years.

Treasury notes
Short-term notes maturing in less than seven years.

Trend
A statistical measurement used to track changes that occur over time.

Trough
See Cyclical trough

UCC
See Uniform Commercial Code

UL
See Underwriters Laboratories

Underwriters Laboratories (UL)
One of several private firms that tests products and processes to determine their safety. Although various firms can provide this kind of testing service, many local and insurance codes specify UL certification.

Underwriting
A process by which an insurer determines whether or not and on what basis it will accept an application for insurance. In an experience-rated plan, premiums are based on a firm's or group's past claims; factors other than prior claims are used for community-rated or manually rated plans.

Unfair competition
Refers to business practices, usually unethical, such as using unlicensed products, pirating merchandise, or misleading the public through false advertising, which give the offending business an unequitable advantage over others.

Unfunded accrued liability
The excess of total liabilities, both present and prospective, over present and prospective assets.

Unemployment
The joblessness of individuals who are willing to work, who are legally and physically able to work, and who are seeking work. Unemployment may represent the temporary joblessness of a worker between jobs (frictional unemployment) or the joblessness of a worker whose skills are not suitable for jobs available in the labor market (structural unemployment).

Uniform Commercial Code (UCC)
A code of laws governing commercial transactions across the U.S., except Louisiana. Their purpose is to bring uniformity to financial transactions.

Uniform product code (UPC symbol)
A computer-readable label comprised of ten digits and stripes that encodes what a product is and how much it costs. The first five digits are assigned by the Uniform Product Code Council, and the last five digits by the individual manufacturer.

Unit cost
See Average cost

UPC symbol
See Uniform product code

U.S. Establishment and Enterprise Microdata (USEEM) File
A cross-sectional database containing information on employment, sales, and location for individual enterprises and establishments with employees that have a Dun & Bradstreet credit rating.

U.S. Establishment Longitudinal Microdata (USELM) File
A database containing longitudinally linked sample microdata on establishments drawn from the U.S. Establishment and Enterprise Microdata file (see separate citation).

U.S. Small Business Administration 504 Program
See Certified development corporation

USEEM
See U.S. Establishment and Enterprise Microdata File

USELM
See U.S. Establishment Longitudinal Microdata File

VCN
See Venture capital network

Venture capital
Money used to support new or unusual business ventures that exhibit above-average growth rates, significant potential for market expansion, and are in need of additional financing to sustain growth or further research and development; equity or equity-type financing traditionally provided at the commercialization stage, increasingly available prior to commercialization.

Venture capital company
A company organized to provide seed capital to a business in its formation stage, or in its first or second stage of expansion. Funding is obtained through public or private pension funds, commercial banks and bank holding companies, small business investment corporations licensed by the U.S. Small Business Administration, private venture capital firms, insurance companies, investment management companies, bank trust departments, industrial companies seeking to diversify their investment, and investment bankers acting as intermediaries for other investors or directly investing on their own behalf.

Venture capital limited partnerships
Designed for business development, these partnerships are an institutional mechanism for providing capital for young, technology-oriented businesses. The investors' money is pooled and invested in money market assets until venture investments have been selected. The general partners are experienced investment managers who select and invest the equity and debt securities of firms with high growth potential and the ability to go public in the near future.

Venture capital network (VCN)
A computer database that matches investors with entrepreneurs.

WAN
See Wide Area Network

Wide Area Network (WAN)
Computer networks linking systems throughout a state or around the world in order to facilitate the sharing of information.

Withholding
Federal, state, social security, and unemployment taxes withheld by the employer from employees' wages; employers are liable for these taxes and the corporate umbrella and bankruptcy will not exonerate an employer from paying back payroll withholding. Employers should escrow these funds in a separate account and disperse them quarterly to withholding authorities.

Workers' compensation
A state-mandated form of insurance covering workers injured in job-related accidents. In some states, the state is the insurer; in other states, insurance must be acquired from commercial insurance firms. Insurance rates are based on a number of factors, including salaries, firm history, and risk of occupation.

Working capital
Refers to a firm's short-term investment of current assets, including cash, short-term securities, accounts receivable, and inventories.

Yield
The rate of income returned on an investment, expressed as a percentage. Income yield is obtained by dividing the current dollar income by the current market price of the security. Net yield or yield to maturity is the current income yield minus any premium above par or plus any discount from par in purchase price, with the adjustment spread over the period from the date of purchase to the date of maturity.

Index

Index

Business
Plans
Handbook

Business Plans

A COMPILATION OF BUSINESS PLANS DEVELOPED BY INDIVIDUALS THROUGHOUT NORTH AMERICA

Handbook

VOLUME

18

**Lynn M. Pearce,
Project Editor**

GALE
CENGAGE Learning™

Detroit • New York • San Francisco • New Haven, Conn • Waterville, Maine • London

Business Plans Handbook, Volume 18

Project Editor: Lynn M. Pearce

Product Manager: Jenai Drouillard

Product Design: Jennifer Wahi

Composition and Electronic Prepress: Evi Seoud

Manufacturing: Rita Wimberley

Gale, a part of Cengage Learning
27500 Drake Rd.
Farmington Hills, MI 48331-3535

ISBN-13: 978-14144-5823-6
1084-4473

Printed in the United States of America
1 2 3 4 5 6 7 12 11 10

Contents

Highlights

Business Plans Handbook, Volume 18 (BPH-18) is a collection of business plans compiled by entrepreneurs seeking funding for small businesses throughout North America. For those looking for examples of how to approach, structure, and compose their own business plans, *BPH-18* presents 20 sample plans, including plans for the following businesses:

- Automobile Advertising
- Bookstore
- Car Service
- Children's Catering Business
- Combination Coffeehouse/Play Spot
- Custom Denim Retailer
- Daycare/Preschool
- Family Entertainment Center
- Grant Writer
- Green/Sustainability Consulting Firm
- Jewelry Designer
- Media Conversion Company
- Party Planning
- Pizza & Pasta Restaurant
- Private Investigation Service
- Resale Clothing Store
- Self–Defense/Anti–Bullying Training Company
- Tea Shop
- Tutoring Service
- Vegetarian Fast Food Restaurant

FEATURES AND BENEFITS

BPH-18 offers many features not provided by other business planning references including:

- Twenty business plans, each of which represent an attempt at clarifying (for themselves and others) the reasons that the business should exist or expand and why a lender should fund the enterprise.
- Two fictional plans that are used by business counselors at a prominent small business development organization as examples for their clients. (You will find these in the Business Plan Template Appendix.)
- A directory section that includes: listings for venture capital and finance companies, which specialize in funding start-up and second-stage small business ventures, and a comprehensive

listing of Service Corps of Retired Executives (SCORE) offices. In addition, the Appendix also contains updated listings of all Small Business Development Centers (SBDCs); associations of interest to entrepreneurs; Small Business Administration (SBA) Regional Offices; and consultants specializing in small business planning and advice. It is strongly advised that you consult supporting organizations while planning your business, as they can provide a wealth of useful information.

- A Small Business Term Glossary to help you decipher the sometimes confusing terminology used by lenders and others in the financial and small business communities.

- A cumulative index, outlining each plan profiled in the complete *Business Plans Handbook* series.

- A Business Plan Template which serves as a model to help you construct your own business plan. This generic outline lists all the essential elements of a complete business plan and their components, including the Summary, Business History and Industry Outlook, Market Examination, Competition, Marketing, Administration and Management, Financial Information, and other key sections. Use this guide as a starting point for compiling your plan.

- Extensive financial documentation required to solicit funding from small business lenders. You will find examples of: Cash Flows, Balance Sheets, Income Projections, and other financial information included with the textual portions of the plan.

Introduction

Perhaps the most important aspect of business planning is simply doing it. More and more business owners are beginning to compile business plans even if they don't need a bank loan. Others discover the value of planning when they must provide a business plan for the bank. The sheer act of putting thoughts on paper seems to clarify priorities and provide focus. Sometimes business owners completely change strategies when compiling their plan, deciding on a different product mix or advertising scheme after finding that their assumptions were incorrect. This kind of healthy thinking and re-thinking via business planning is becoming the norm. The editors of *Business Plans Handbook, Volume 18 (BPH-18)* sincerely hope that this latest addition to the series is a helpful tool in the successful completion of your business plan, no matter what the reason for creating it.

This eighteenth volume, like each volume in the series, offers business plans used and created by real people. *BPH-18* provides 20 business plans. The business and personal names and addresses and general locations have been changed to protect the privacy of the plan authors.

NEW BUSINESS OPPORTUNITIES

As in other volumes in the series, *BPH-18* finds entrepreneurs engaged in a wide variety of creative endeavors. Examples include a proposal for car service, a daycare/preschool, and a private investigator service. In addition, several other plans are provided, including a green consulting firm, a grant writer, a reseal clothing store, and two restaurants, among others.

Comprehensive financial documentation has become increasingly important as today's entrepreneurs compete for the finite resources of business lenders. Our plans illustrate the financial data generally required of loan applicants, including Income Statements, Financial Projections, Cash Flows, and Balance Sheets.

ENHANCED APPENDIXES

In an effort to provide the most relevant and valuable information for our readers, we have updated the coverage of small business resources. For instance, you will find: a directory section, which includes listings of all of the Service Corps of Retired Executives (SCORE) offices; an informative glossary, which includes small business terms; and a cumulative index, outlining each plan profiled in the complete Business Plans Handbook series. In addition we have updated the list of Small Business Development Centers (SBDCs); Small Business Administration Regional Offices; venture capital and finance companies, which specialize in funding start-up and second-stage small business enterprises; associations of interest to entrepreneurs; and consultants, specializing in small business advice and planning. For your reference, we have also reprinted the business plan template, which provides a comprehensive overview of the essential components of a business plan and two fictional plans used by small business counselors.

SERIES INFORMATION

If you already have the first seventeen volumes of *BPH*, with this eighteenth volume, you will now have a collection of over 380 business plans (not including the one updated plan in the second volume, whose original appeared in the first, or the two fictional plans in the Business Plan Template Appendix section of the second, third, fourth, fifth, sixth, and seventh volumes); contact information for hundreds of organizations and agencies offering business expertise; a helpful business plan template; more than 1,500 citations to valuable small business development material; and a comprehensive glossary of terms to help the business planner navigate the sometimes confusing language of entrepreneurship.

ACKNOWLEDGEMENTS

The Editors wish to sincerely thank the contributors to *BPH-18*, including:

- Michael Cisar
- Heidi Denler
- Paul Greenland
- Cullen Hayes
- Kari Lucke
- Joyce McCauley
- Morgan McRae
- Gerald Rekve and Elisha Violet Rekve, Corporate Management Consultants
- Jintong Tang, St. Louis University
- Mariana Valdesuso

COMMENTS WELCOME

Your comments on *Business Plans Handbook* are appreciated. Please direct all correspondence, suggestions for future volumes of *BPH*, and other recommendations to the following:

Managing Editor, Business Product
Business Plans Handbook
Gale, a part of Cengage Learning
27500 Drake Rd.
Farmington Hills, MI 48331-3535
Phone: (248)699-4253
Fax: (248)699-8052
Toll-Free: 800-347-GALE
E-mail: BusinessProducts@gale.com

Automobile Advertising

Carvertising STL

667 Washington Ave.
St. Louis, MO 63116

Cullen Hayes, Joyce McCauley, and Morgan McRae

Carvertising STL is the region's first company that can say, "It pays to drive." We are a liaison between private drivers and local businesses. Carvertising STL pays private drivers in the St. Louis area to put advertisements on their vehicles. Everybody wins. Drivers get paid for what they already do on a constant basis: drive. Businesses, on the other hand, benefit from our innovative new form of marketing that is bound to turn heads.

1.0 EXECUTIVE SUMMARY

Think about how much time you spend in your car each day. It takes you everywhere you want to go. You commute to and from work. You drop off and pick up the kids from soccer practice. You swing by the grocery store to get some food. You may even catch the latest blockbuster at your nearest theatre. Finally, you're off to the mall to wrap up that holiday shopping.

Now think about how often you find yourself sitting in traffic. The St. Louis region's infrastructure is often filled with traffic jams and irritated commuters. You spend a majority of the time bumper to bumper rather than enjoying the company of friends and family, watching the Monday night football game, or catching up on some much needed sleep. It drives us all crazy.

Wouldn't it be nice if the hours we spent on the road were actually worth it?

Carvertising STL is the region's first company that can say, "It pays to drive." We are a liaison between private drivers and local businesses. Carvertising STL pays private drivers in the St. Louis area to put advertisements on their vehicles. Everybody wins. Drivers get paid for what they already do on a constant basis: drive. Businesses on the other hand, benefit from our innovative new form of marketing that is bound to turn heads.

Carvertising STL will initially target St. Louis–based advertising agencies. Once the relationship is established, advertising agencies use Carvertising STL's services to promote their clients. Our customers benefit from a highly effective and unique medium. By pairing with agencies, we are able to focus on our own service, opposed to generating new accounts with independent businesses. Finding individual customers can be timely and costly.

Carvertising STL's underlying passion is to aid in the growth of local business. Our efforts are focused on providing small businesses with a competitively priced, yet cost–effective method for reaching the public eye. We will continuously assist with the future development of the small business community. Our ultimate dream is to contribute to the expansion of the local economy and businesses. With the use of Carvertising STL's services, both consumers and organizations will experience the benefits.

1

Consumers will earn money while running errands, going to work, or picking up their children from school. Businesses select a predetermined (and guaranteed) number of cars for their advertising fleet. Carvertisements are less costly than the standard stationary billboard, yet more effective because they can capture public attention at eye–level. Carvertising STL provides a win–win situation for everyone in the St. Louis area. When we pay drivers on a monthly basis, this money is then put directly back into the very businesses that Carvertise. This helps the region's commerce.

Next time you are traveling, take a moment to recognize the potential. While sitting in traffic, notice the cars in front of you at the stoplight. Glance at that SUV in the brand new passing lane of I–64. Check out that sedan in the Galleria parking lot. Think about the limitless potential of this form of marketing. Each vehicle is a blank canvas with an array of marketing possibilities. Each can benefit local businesses. Each driver can gain some positive cash flow from the use of that space.

Partner with Carvertising STL and your business can take advantage of countless possibilities. Our medium can help you grow and develop because it is innovative, effective, and unique.

Please enjoy our business plan. Take note of our new idea and accompanying business model. We are confident that Carvertising STL will outperform local competition in the marketing industry by proving that "it pays to drive."

1.1 Objectives
The objectives of Carvertising STL are to:

- Form strategic partnerships with local St. Louis advertising agencies who will extend our benefits to their clients

- Reward local drivers with regularly recurring cash inflows for an activity they already engage in

- Assist with the economical development of the St. Louis region

- Grow into surrounding metropolitan locations by our fifth year

1.2 Vision and Mission
"Carvertising STL seeks to provide a cutting–edge advertising medium for customers."

We are motivated by our vision of building St. Louis. There are few cost–effective advertising options available for small businesses. We will become the go–to resource for growing and developing organizations. Carvertising STL will provide businesses with an increase in clients, sales, and overall publicity. We are focused on creating that win–win situation for everyone involved.

We ensure that our customers will receive top-quality products and customer service. We seek to simultaneously develop long–term relationships with clients and drivers and to assist with the economic expansion of the local community for years to come.

Our mission is to be among the preferred advertising methods for St. Louis small businesses that are seeking low–cost, effective options for success and longevity.

1.3 Success Factors
Carvertising STL will attain success by:

- Evaluating mediums currently available and providing an alternative for each.

- Initiating head–turning advertising campaigns throughout St. Louis to create larger customer bases

- Producing effective service packages that satisfy and ensure recurring sales

- Achieving brand awareness in the St. Louis marketplace to gain credibility

2.0 COMPANY SUMMARY

Carvertising STL provides a new advertising medium and serves as a liaison between businesses and drivers. Driving takes up a large portion of the average working American's day. According to the U.S. Census Bureau, the average commute to or from work is 25.3 minutes. In 2000, the average travel time on the road for St. Louis workers over age 16 was 24 minutes. The down time that occurs during commutes accounts for a significant percentage of one's day. Thus, Carvertising STL recognizes and takes advantage of this opportunity.

Our plan takes the market share that was once dominated by radio commercials. Radio used to be the ideal medium to target consumers on the road. They promote goods and services to people who are unoccupied or bored during daily commutes. Catchy jingles were once forced upon individuals who had no other listening options. Due to technology advancements like the iPod and satellite radio, drivers now avoid these advertisements.

Carvertising STL recognizes the inefficiency of radio commercials and the opportunity for our company. We capture this available place in the market and keep individuals entertained during their daily commutes. We host business advertisements on fleets with a minimum of five cars. Rather than promoting blasts of information to large areas at once, Carvertising STL will specifically target a niche region that aligns with the advertising campaigns of our clients.

Carvertising STL will gradually enter the industry and gain credibility with trial run versions. Two trial run versions will take place. The first includes Carvertisements posted on vehicles that promote Carvertising STL. These Carvertisements, paired with our number, 1–877–STL–PAYS, encourage drivers to call and find out why, "it pays to drive."

The second trial run will be conducted alongside local area businesses. They will benefit from a complimentary three–month Carvertising promotion. The purpose of this trial run is to determine if their business improves as a result of our campaign. Business owners will be asked to compensate Carvertising STL at the end of the campaign according to how effective they deem our services. These testimonials will then be used for pitching to advertising agencies.

From conversations with St. Louis–based advertising agencies, Carvertising STL will recognize the most popular markets that businesses wish to target. Carvertising STL will then gather drivers in that area and deploy the fleets throughout St. Louis.

Compared to traditional advertising options, Carvertising STL is the ideal choice. While driving a typical daily commute to work, drivers often depart and arrive at the same times consistently. Think about the cars you recognize during your recurring routes. More often than not, you travel with the same group of vehicles for the duration of your drive. On the other hand, you only pass a billboard once and the impression lasts for a mere two seconds. You may glance at the product or service right before it leaves the mind as quickly as it entered.

However, Carvertising STL drivers drive with the public and thus, potential customers. The Carvertisement is a moving billboard that is with these individuals from anywhere between 5 and 60 minutes. We provide moving advertisements that may be next to targeted consumers for extended periods of time as they sit in traffic or wait at the drive–through.

Carvertising STL has established a strategic partnership with Craftsmen Industries. According to the company website and on–site visits, Craftsmen Industries has been in business for over 25 years. Today, they have more than 200 employees at their 129,000 square foot location in St. Charles, Missouri.

Craftsmen Industries is a certified 3M Scotchprint graphics manufacturer and installer. The company specializes in vehicle graphics design, printing, manufacturing, installation and removal, distribution, and painting.

Carvertising STL's partnership with Craftsmen Industries allows us to print our advertisements at a low cost. The partnership is ideal because of their qualifications and extensive knowledge of the marketing industry. Not only do they have a reputable foothold in the market, but they also have served as a mentor during Carvertising STL's first months of business.

As a 3M Certified Company, Craftsmen Industries can provide us with quality printing services. If unforeseen problems with the product arise, (for example, installation or removal issues) Craftsmen Industries' team of knowledgeable and professional employees will be able to assist.

Craftsmen Industries has been the recipient of many awards which highlight their dedication and quality of service: two Exawards, one Gold Award for Vehicle Design at this year's Experiential Marketing Summit, and the Editors Choice for the FleetOwner Awards in 2008. In addition, CEO Joe Helmsing was the recipient of the Circle of Champions Award in 2004 and the Small Businessperson of the Year for the state of Missouri in 2003.

Carvertising STL believes that St. Louis, Missouri is the ideal region to initially target.

According to the U.S. Census Bureau, the population of St. Louis County in July 2008 was 991,830.

Transit advertising on private vehicles is an untapped market with great potential that Carvertising STL will realize in the St. Louis, Missouri region.

3.0 PRODUCT AND SERVICE

Carvertising STL utilizes certified 3M products to provide our one-of-a-kind service. We have based our decision on primary research conducted with both potential drivers and potential clients.

All advertisements for Carvertising STL use 3M's Controltac Graphic Film with Comply v2 Adhesive. According to 3M, "[The films] have slideable, repositionable, pressure–activated adhesive, and non–visible Comply adhesive air release channels for fast and easy, bubble–free graphic installations." The recommended uses of this product are for indoor and outdoor graphic signs, commercial vehicle and fleet graphics, emblems or striping, and bus graphics. The material can last for 3 years on a vehicle before leaving residual substance behind.

The 3M ControltacTM Graphic Film with ComplyTM v2 Adhesive is the ideal product for Carvertising STL. This material performs best on vehicles and cannot be tampered with or easily removed. Thus, the Carvertisements will last for the intended duration.

If for some reason the material cannot be successfully removed, or an excessive amount of adhesive residue remains on surface, because of our partnership with 3M certified Craftsmen Industries, 3M will reimburse the extra removal costs.

3.1 Production
All Carvertisements are printed at Craftsmen Industries located in St. Charles, Missouri.

3.2 Operations
The process for Carvertising STL occurs in the following stages:

1. Acquisition of drivers in select areas based upon recommendations from the advertising agencies.

2. Interested drivers fill out the registration form found on our website. All information provided to Carvertising STL remains confidential. The purpose of the information is to determine the qualifications and eligibility of each driver, prior to the selection for a Carvertising campaign. Information entered into the form includes:

Demographic information

- Name

- Gender

- Date of Birth

- Marital status

- Race

- Phone number

- Email address

Vehicle information

- Picture of vehicle

- Copy of car insurance

- Copy of drivers license

- Vehicle registration

- Parking location of vehicle

Driver behavior

- Daily driving route

- Availability during the week and weekends

- Intended duration for living in the St. Louis area for the next two years

- Frequency of long-distance travel

- Driving days per week

- Hours driven per day

- Referrals for other individuals that might be interested in learning why, "It pays to drive."

3. Information from qualified drivers is entered into a database. This database serves as an internal resource for Carvertising STL. When creating the fleets, the database ensures that our clients' needs are met. The database may be used for any of the following:

- To ensure that the physical appearances and attitudes of drivers displaying Carvertisements align with the brand of the client and their product or service.

- To select drivers within a specific region

- To select drivers based on their daily mileages

- To select drivers based on their vehicle and the image it portrays

4. Once the database is filled with a minimum of 300 qualified drivers, Carvertising STL focuses on the acquisition of clients.

5. Once the small business is sold on the concept of Carvertising STL, the ideal Carvertising campaign is selected for that particular company. The options when forming a Carvertising campaign include the following:

Fleet size

- Clients select from a quantity of 5, 10, 15, 30, 50, 75, 100, 125, or 150 vehicles.

Driving route or region

- The driving route or region of the driver may be of significance to the client. If this is the case, Carvertising STL will define the target market and select drivers for the fleet based on their driving route or frequent locations they visit. Since these cars are in the desired neighborhoods, they will be ideal for promoting the businesses we help.

Driving mileage

- Some clients may prefer to have drivers operate their vehicles for a minimum number of miles. If this is the case, this information helps us to determine who drives farther or for longer durations.

Driver appearance

- Based on primary research conducted, some St. Louis business owners believe that the appearance of the driver is an important factor for the Carvertising campaign. 50% of those surveyed stated that the physical appearance is important.

- With a picture on file of the qualified drivers, we can easily determine whether or not a particular individual aligns with the client's requests (if applicable).

Vehicle appearance

- The vehicle appearance is important to some small business owners. According to business owners surveyed, the make and model of a vehicle were more important than the quality or the color.

Duration

- The client determines the length of time for the campaign. Carvertising campaigns last for 3, 6, 9, 12, 15, 18, 21, or 24 months.

- The maximum duration is two years because of the limitations of the 3M material. We also believe that few small businesses will desire to run the same campaign for longer than two years.

Carvertisement design

- A Carvertisement design, ideally designed by the client, must be selected for the campaign. If the client requires further assistance, Carvertising STL will outsource the job to Craftsmen Industries' graphic design department.

Carvertisement placement

- Each client decides how he wishes to decorate the cars in his fleet. For example, he can choose the number of side panels per car, if the fleet should have back window advertisements, and whether or not a hood advertisement should be included, etc.

- Carvertising STL provides our customers with the option to use either standard square Carvertisements or optional i–cut graphics in their campaigns. Although i–cut graphics tend to be more expensive, Carvertising STL wishes to provide this provision at no extra cost to the client. The i–cut graphics appear professional and modern.

- Thus, the campaign is catered to the client and his preferences for the Carvertisement. Often, the advertising industry causes those with lower budgets to choose cheap and ineffective marketing options. We do not want the client's campaign decisions to be hindered solely by his budget. Rather, we want the client to benefit from the unique features available, regardless of startup price.

- The numbers have been arranged in our financials to ensure that the client will receive the optimal Carvertising campaign. The price per month remains constant, depending upon the size of the fleet. The only price that differs is the setup fee.

- Each client signs a waiver in which he agrees to the terms of Carvertising STL. We provide to the client the space on the vehicles that are rented for our Carvertisements. Their signature states that they understand Carvertising STL is not liable for the driver.

6. Once information is finalized with the client, Carvertising STL sends the graphics to Craftsmen Industries for printing.

7. Fleet drivers selected for a particular campaign are notified. They are then required to provide Carvertising STL with a driving history background from their insurance provider. Once Carvertising STL receives the driving history background, the driver is assigned an application appointment location and time. Appointments are scheduled on select days and the times that align with the drivers' schedule.

Within the next month Carvertising STL plans to establish mutually beneficial partnerships with carwashes throughout the St. Louis metropolitan region. Carvertising STL will apply, remove, and inspect our Carvertisements at these locations. The use of a carwash site is a mutually beneficial relationship because most drivers will be required to wash their car prior to the Carvertisement's application. We guarantee that the carwashes will experience a regular inflow of customers in exchange for the use of a small portion of their property. In the future, when more capital is available, Carvertising STL may choose to purchase property that spans the geography of St. Louis for this purpose.

Our initial partnership will be with Waterway Gas & Wash Company. Waterway spans the local St. Louis community from 1–170 all the way to the Spirit of St. Louis Airport to the West.

8. Once printing is completed (an estimated two to three days), a member of the Carvertising STL team picks up the completed Carvertisements.

9. With an efficient application process, Carvertisements can be applied virtually anywhere—including the lots of local carwashes. The application process of the 3M Controltac Graphic Film with Comply v2 Adhesive is simple. The largest Carvertisement is 4 feet by 2 feet. Thus, the 3M material can be applied to any vehicle with only one worker and a squeegee. A typical Carvertisement takes approximately 5 minutes to apply.

Prior to the application, the driver signs a waiver in which he agrees to monthly maintenance checks, that he will not tamper with the Carvertisement, and will refrain from road rage and aggressive or destructive driving behavior. Carvertising STL reserves the right to terminate drivers for any reason we deem necessary.

10. The driver will receive his first payment after a month of driving and if he passes the monthly inspection. Rather than requiring an initial payment, this serves as the down payment. If, after the first month of driving, the driver does not pass the inspection, he will not receive his money. Carvertising STL understands that individuals who sign up most likely have low amounts of discretionary income and are unwilling to provide a down payment. Failure to comply with our terms will affect their monthly cash payment. This process ensures that they still have skin in the game, but are not required to take anything out of their pocket.

If for some reason a Carvertisement has been tampered with, the driver must notify Carvertising STL within 24 hours of the occurrence. Failure to notify Carvertising STL of the incident could result in loss of compensation for that particular month.

If the Carvertisement has clearly been tampered with at the point of the monthly inspection and Carvertising STL has not been notified, the driver will not be compensated for that month.

If the driver fails to appear for his monthly inspection he will not receive his compensation for that month.

The 3M material can only be applied once. This allows Carvertising STL to effectively control the Carvertising campaigns. If the Carvertisement is tampered with, the driver will not be able to reapply the product unnoticeably.

During the monthly Carvertisement inspection, the mileage for each vehicle is checked as well. In some cases, mileage is monitored to ensure that the vehicle has been driven and that the particular Carvertisement has left impressions on people in the region.

11. Carvertising STL clients are billed at the beginning of the campaign. Each bill is divided based on duration and the size of the fleet. Thus, the net terms for each campaign will differ.

12. At the end of the campaign, the vehicle is checked for the final inspection and the removal process occurs. The 3M Controltac Graphic Film with Comply v2 Adhesive is removable with heat and/or chemicals. According to Craftsmen Industries' CEO, Joe Helmsing, the material can easily be removed with heat.

3.3 Costs

Costs incurred for Carvertising STL include the printing setup and fees for basic materials and window graphics, the fleet drivers' pay, and the shipping of our Carvertisements.

3.4 Pricing

Based on the industry, Carvertising STL provides clients with an effective service that is reasonably and competitively priced. We charge businesses a one–time per campaign setup fee plus a monthly cost.

The setup fee is determined by the quantity of Carvertisements per vehicle (based on square footage) and the types of Carvertisements selected. The setup fee covers the printing costs incurred at no extra markup. Carvertising STL does not specialize in the printing industry and does not intend to compete with Craftsmen Industries. Thus, we will not markup the initial cost.

The number of vehicles selected for the fleet determines the monthly cost, which accounts for the drivers' payment. Carvertising STL applies a 60% markup to the $100 driver payment.

The following charts depict the different fleet sizes available, the costs incurred with each, and the price clients are charged.

Fleet: 5 Cars

	BW	H	2SS	2RS	2FS	BW+H	BW+2SS	BW+2RS
Cars	5	5	5	5	5	5	5	5
Startup COST	210	345	195	345	555	480	330	480
Monthly COGS	500	500	500	500	500	500	500	500
Markup %	60%	60%	60%	60%	60%	60%	60%	60%
Markup $	300	300	300	300	300	300	300	300
Monthly price	800	800	800	800	800	800	800	800

	BW+2FS	H+2SS	H+2RS	H+2FS	H+BW+2SS	H+BW+RS	H+BW+2FS
Cars	5	5	5	5	5	5	5
Startup COST	690	465	615	825	600	750	960
Monthly COGS	500	500	500	500	500	500	500
Markup %	60%	60%	60%	60%	60%	60%	60%
Markup $	300	300	300	300	300	300	300
Monthly price	800	800	800	800	800	800	800

Fleet: 10 Cars

	BW	H	2SS	2RS	2FS	BW+H	BW+2SS	BW+2RS
Cars	10	10	10	10	10	10	10	10
Startup COST	345	615	315	615	1,035	885	585	885
Monthly COGS	1,000	1,000	1,000	1,000	1,000	1,000	1,000	1,000
Markup %	58%	58%	58%	58%	58%	58%	58%	58%
Markup $	580	580	580	580	580	580	580	580
Monthly price	1,580	1,580	1,580	1,580	1,580	1,580	1,580	1,580

	BW+2FS	H+2SS	H+2RS	H+2FS	H+BW+2SS	H+BW+RS	H+BW+2FS
Cars	10	10	10	10	10	10	10
Startup COST	1,305	855	1,155	1,575	1,125	1,425	1,845
Monthly COGS	1,000	1,000	1,000	1,000	1,000	1,000	1,000
Markup %	58%	58%	58%	58%	58%	58%	58%
Markup $	580	580	580	580	580	580	580
Monthly price	1,580	1,580	1,580	1,580	1,580	1,580	1,580

Fleet: 15 Cars

	BW	H	2SS	2RS	2FS	BW+H	BW+2SS	BW+2RS
Cars	15	15	15	15	15	15	15	15
Startup COST	480	885	435	885	1,515	1,290	840	1,290
Monthly COGS	1,500	1,500	1,500	1,500	1,500	1,500	1,500	1,500
Markup %	56%	56%	56%	56%	56%	56%	56%	56%
Markup $	840	840	840	840	840	840	840	840
Monthly price	2,340	2,340	2,340	2,340	2,340	2,340	2,340	2,340

	BW+2FS	H+2SS	H+2RS	H+2FS	H+BW+2SS	H+BW+RS	H+BW+2FS
Cars	15	15	15	15	15	15	15
Startup COST	1,920	1,245	1,695	2,325	1,650	2,100	2,730
Monthly COGS	1,500	1,500	1,500	1,500	1,500	1,500	1,500
Markup %	56%	56%	56%	56%	56%	56%	56%
Markup $	840	840	840	840	840	840	840
Monthly price	2,340	2,340	2,340	2,340	2,340	2,340	2,340

Fleet: 30 Cars

	BW	H	2SS	2RS	2FS	BW+H	BW+2SS	BW+2RS
Cars	30	30	30	30	30	30	30	30
Startup COST	885	1,695	795	1,695	2,955	2,505	1,605	2,505
Monthly COGS	3,000	3,000	3,000	3,000	3,000	3,000	3,000	3,000
Markup %	52%	52%	52%	52%	52%	52%	52%	52%
Markup $	1,560	1,560	1,560	1,560	1,560	1,560	1,560	1,560
Monthly price	4,560	4,560	4,560	4,560	4,560	4,560	4,560	4,560

	BW+2FS	H+2SS	H+2RS	H+2FS	H+BW+2SS	H+BW+RS	H+BW+2FS
Cars	30	30	30	30	30	30	30
Startup COST	3,765	2,415	3,315	4,575	3,225	4,125	5,385
Monthly COGS	3,000	3,000	3,000	3,000	3,000	3,000	3,000
Markup %	52%	52%	52%	52%	52%	52%	52%
Markup $	1,560	1,560	1,560	1,560	1,560	1,560	1,560
Monthly price	4,560	4,560	4,560	4,560	4,560	4,560	4,560

Fleet: 50 Cars

	BW	H	2SS	2RS	2FS	BW+H	BW+2SS	BW+2RS
Cars	50	50	50	50	50	50	50	50
Startup COST	1,425	2,775	1,275	2,775	4,875	4,125	2,625	4,125
Monthly COGS	5,000	5,000	5,000	5,000	5,000	5,000	5,000	5,000
Markup %	45%	45%	45%	45%	45%	45%	45%	45%
Markup $	2,250	2,250	2,250	2,250	2,250	2,250	2,250	2,250
Monthly price	7,250	7,250	7,250	7,250	7,250	7,250	7,250	7,250

	BW+2FS	H+2SS	H+2RS	H+2FS	H+BW+2SS	H+BW+RS	H+BW+2FS
Cars	50	50	50	50	50	50	50
Startup COST	6,225	3,975	5,475	7,575	5,325	6,825	8,925
Monthly COGS	5,000	5,000	5,000	5,000	5,000	5,000	5,000
Markup %	45%	45%	45%	45%	45%	45%	45%
Markup $	2,250	2,250	2,250	2,250	2,250	2,250	2,250
Monthly price	7,250	7,250	7,250	7,250	7,250	7,250	7,250

Fleet: 75 Cars

	BW	H	2SS	2RS	2FS	BW+H	BW+2SS	BW+2RS
Cars	75	75	75	75	75	75	75	75
Startup COST	2,100	4,125	1,875	4,125	7,275	6,150	3,900	6,150
Monthly COGS	7,500	7,500	7,500	7,500	7,500	7,500	7,500	7,500
Markup %	40%	40%	40%	40%	40%	40%	40%	40%
Markup $	3,000	3,000	3,000	3,000	3,000	3,000	3,000	3,000
Monthly price	10,500	10,500	10,500	10,500	10,500	10,500	10,500	10,500

	BW+2FS	H+2SS	H+2RS	H+2FS	H+BW+2SS	H+BW+RS	H+BW+2FS
Cars	75	75	75	75	75	75	75
Startup COST	9,300	5,925	8,175	11,325	7,950	10,200	13,350
Monthly COGS	7,500	7,500	7,500	7,500	7,500	7,500	7,500
Markup %	40%	40%	40%	40%	40%	40%	40%
Markup $	3,000	3,000	3,000	3,000	3,000	3,000	3,000
Monthly price	10,500	10,500	10,500	10,500	10,500	10,500	10,500

Fleet: 100 Cars

	BW	H	2SS	2RS	2FS	BW+H	BW+2SS	BW+2RS
Cars	100	100	100	100	100	100	100	100
Startup COST	2,775	5,475	2,475	5,475	9,675	8,175	5,175	8,175
Monthly COGS	10,000	10,000	10,000	10,000	10,000	10,000	10,000	10,000
Markup %	35%	35%	35%	35%	35%	35%	35%	35%
Markup $	3,500	3,500	3,500	3,500	3,500	3,500	3,500	3,500
Monthly price	13,500	13,500	13,500	13,500	13,500	13,500	13,500	13,500

	BW+2FS	H+2SS	H+2RS	H+2FS	H+BW+2SS	H+BW+RS	H+BW+2FS
Cars	100	100	100	100	100	100	100
Startup COST	12,375	7,875	10,875	15,075	10,575	13,575	17,775
Monthly COGS	10,000	10,000	10,000	10,000	10,000	10,000	10,000
Markup %	35%	35%	35%	35%	35%	35%	35%
Markup $	3,500	3,500	3,500	3,500	3,500	3,500	3,500
Monthly price	13,500	13,500	13,500	13,500	13,500	13,500	13,500

Fleet: 150 Cars

	BW	H	2SS	2RS	2FS	BW+H	BW+2SS	BW+2RS
Cars	150	150	150	150	150	150	150	150
Startup COST	4,125	8,175	3,675	8,175	14,475	12,225	7,725	12,225
Monthly COGS	15,000	15,000	15,000	15,000	15,000	15,000	15,000	15,000
Markup %	25%	25%	25%	25%	25%	25%	25%	25%
Markup $	3,750	3,750	3,750	3,750	3,750	3,750	3,750	3,750
Monthly price	18,750	18,750	18,750	18,750	18,750	18,750	18,750	18,750

	BW+2FS	H+2SS	H+2RS	H+2FS	H+BW+2SS	H+BW+RS	H+BW+2FS
Cars	150	150	150	150	150	150	150
Startup COST	18,525	11,775	16,275	22,575	15,825	20,325	26,625
Monthly COGS	15,000	15,000	15,000	15,000	15,000	15,000	15,000
Markup %	25%	25%	25%	25%	25%	25%	25%
Markup $	3,750	3,750	3,750	3,750	3,750	3,750	3,750
Monthly price	18,750	18,750	18,750	18,750	18,750	18,750	18,750

4.0 MARKET AND DEMOGRAPHIC ANALYSIS

According to the *St. Louis Business Journal*, the greater St. Louis area ranks 18th in the nation for its population size. This ranking is due to a .4 percent increase in the metropolitan area over the course of a year. The population is now estimated at 2,816,710. These numbers make St. Louis an ideal market. With over 2 million individuals, we have a large sample size for potential consumers for the Carvertising businesses.

The U.S. Department of Transportation's Federal Highway Administration states that in 2000, the state of Missouri had a total of 4,579,629 registered vehicles and of that, 3,856,271 were licensed drivers. According to the St. Louis Fed, "[in July 2004], the total number of registered vehicles in St. Louis City, St. Louis County and St. Clair County [was] about 1.4 million." The U.S. Department of Transportation estimates that the typical driver commutes about 17,396 miles per year.

If Carvertising STL is able to capture a mere fraction of these registered vehicles, one Carvertisement could capture as many as 2,816,710 eyes. One Carvertisement has the potential to travel over 17,000 miles during the course of a twelve–month campaign. This provides far more exposure than any stationary advertisement.

Transit advertising on private vehicles is an untapped area with great potential. Carvertising STL seeks to capture this opportunity in the St. Louis region throughout the coming years.

Based on information obtained from City–Data.com, the estimated median household income in 2007 for St. Louis residents was $34,191, up from $27,156 in 2000. When compared across time, income is not as high as it could be. This means that there are more people willing to put advertisements on their cars in return for steady income. As mentioned before, St. Louis is ranked number 18 in the nation for population size. This provides Carvertising STL with a large group of potential drivers who could use the extra income.

In recent years, greater St. Louis has earned national recognition as having a favorable business climate with a competitive cost of doing business and a highly skilled work force. In fact, St. Louis has recently been recognized in many publications for its business environment.

St. Louis provides a positive environment for startups that could benefit from our services. Listed below is evidence from the St. Louis Regional Chamber and Growth Association (RCGA):

- St. Louis ranks as the 7th most cost–competitive location to do business among 20 U.S. metros with populations exceeding 2 million. This information is based on the Competitive Alternatives study done by KPMG LLP, released March 27, 2008. The study measured the combined impact of location–sensitive business–operating costs, such as labor, facility, transportation and utility costs, as well as income taxes. Carvertising STL would only be adding to this positive environment by providing low–cost advertising mediums.

- *Forbes* magazine ranked St. Louis number 76 in its ranking of "Best Places for Business and Careers" for lowest cost of doing business among 200 of the largest metro areas in March 2009. St. Louis ranked ahead of cities like Tampa, Milwaukee, and even Denver, Colorado. For this reason, there are many businesses that purposely incorporate themselves within our region. This is especially the case among smaller startups that would appreciate our service.

- The *Dow Jones Market Watch* named the St. Louis metro area the 19th "Best City for Business" for 2007. The list was compiled after ranking the nations 50 biggest cities by number of started, grown, and retained businesses and after interviewing business leaders from each of the cities.

- St. Louis was named as a "Five–Star Logistics Metro" by *Expansion Management* magazine, October 2007. The region placed in the 99th percentile, which is the highest possible rating. *Expansion Management* also ranked St. Louis as having the 5th "Best Interstate Highway Connectivity."

- St. Louis ranks number 19 in the country on *MarketWatch's* Top 50 "Best U.S. Cities for Business," published in 2007. Populations of 1 million or more were ranked according to per–capita lists, small businesses, unemployment, population growth, and job growth.

64% of St. Louis metro workers live and work in the same county. The remaining 36% travel outside of their county of residence to get to work. The second group is better for Carvertising STL's purposes, because they would guarantee that Carvertisements would be on the road for longer periods of time on a daily basis.

4.1 St. Louis Infrastructure

The St. Louis metropolitan area and surrounding region have the major benefit of an extensive highway system. Four different interstate highways, I–44, I–55, I–64, and I–70, intersect the St. Louis vicinity. In addition to these, four other interstate linkages, I–255, I–170, I–270, and I–370, provide further connections and accessibility for St. Louis motorists. In certain cities, the working class will avoid obtaining jobs that may cause them to travel long distances on a daily basis because of a lack of infrastructure. St. Louis has an extensive network of interlocking highway systems, so a larger percentage of the population commutes to work on a daily basis. This has positive implications for Carvertising STL, because it means more cars are regularly on the road traveling to and from destinations.

The city itself is comprised of 79 different neighborhoods. Each one bears a different demographic, history and development plan. As previously mentioned, Carvertising STL will converse with advertising agencies to determine local areas in the greater St. Louis region that businesses wish to target. Specifically, we look for neighborhoods with a good mixture of residential and commercial establishments. This mixture includes businesses that can use our service, and drivers who are guaranteed to be moving throughout the area.

Based on the marketing strategy to acquire drivers, we believe this process to be fairly simple. The campaign is dependent upon the drivers, rather than the drivers being dependent upon the campaign. Because of this reasoning, the acquisition of drivers comes after defining target markets.

Targeting specific neighborhoods makes it relatively easy for Carvertising STL to collect drivers with desirable daily commutes. For example, if a company wants to advertise in midtown, we would select drivers whose commutes begin on one side of midtown and end on the other. This way, we can ensure that the advertisement is circulating through the desired area. This is essentially the method we would use to select all of our drivers, unless of course a company's advertising campaign seeks to cover a much wider geographic area. Until now, there has not been a company with an efficient means of specifically targeting areas in this way.

4.2 Targeting and Segmentation—Clients

Carvertising STL is not an advertising agency. However, we plan to target advertising agencies because we are a marketing medium. Therefore, we have decided to initially leave the job of finding clients to the agencies. We act as a tool or medium for advertising agencies to employ our services for the benefit of their customers: St. Louis businesses.

Specifically, we will target Rodgers Townsend, Geile Leon Marketing Communications, Media Cross Marketing Powerhouse, Schupp, Global Spectrum, and Group 360. Additionally, there are organizations such as the American Association of Advertising Agencies that can help us to gain recognition across the board.

4.3 Targeting and Segmentation—Drivers

Carvertising STL must also market to our potential drivers. Initially, we plan to target three specific groups of individuals to drive. The three groups are working mothers, college students, and factory commuters.

Working mothers

Working mothers are constantly on the go. While at work, their children attend day–care or school on a daily basis. These women constantly shuffle around the city. Although they are employed, chances are they spend a large amount of money on gas, their children, and household expenses. The idea of getting monthly pay for what they already do will appeal to this targeted group of individuals. They are always on the road, have relatively constant driving routes, and are often in traffic. The graph shown below shows the rise of women in the workplace since 1955.

Labor force participation rate

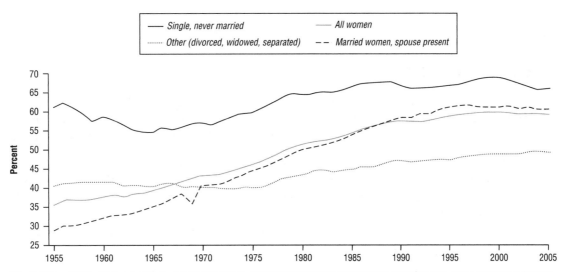

Note: Data from 1955 to 1975 come from the U.S. Census Bureau, *Statistical Abstract of the United States, 2003*, Data from 1976 to 2005 come from the Bureau of Labor Statistics.

In addition, these mothers may also recommend the option to get paid while you drive to their teenage sons and daughters, coworkers, or friends and family. Working mothers communicate frequently with individuals of various demographics. By targeting a working mother, Carvertising STL also targets her children, co–workers, husband, close friends, and extended family members. Carvertising STL will benefit from this word of mouth marketing.

College students

College students, more specifically commuters, are a great resource in the St. Louis area. Commuters drive to class daily. Often times, college students drive to an internship or work. They often frequent highly–populated destinations in the city at all hours of the day and night.

The St. Louis area is comprised of a variety of universities such as Saint Louis University, Washington University, Fontbonne, and more, that are easily accessible and in the midtown St. Louis area. These institutions have a large number of students who might listen to our message.

For example, the University of Missouri, St. Louis in 2009 had an enrollment of 15,543 students. Many colleges, at least 30 more, are located in the greater St. Louis area and have similar populations. If we entice even a small percentage of these students to drive, we will be well on our way to an established database.

As a side note, high school students may account for a large amount of drivers for our company. However, they may be more apt to drive erratically and reflect poorly upon the businesses, which their Carvertisements represent. When qualifying high school students, Carvertising STL will use more caution to determine their maturity level and driving habits.

Factory commuters

Factory commuters the ideal target driver to acquire for Carvertising STL. The idea behind this targeted segment is that they typically drive long distances on a daily basis to and from work. Specifically, we will target businesses that lie on the outskirts of St. Louis City.

The typical factory worker, as opposed to a downtown business executive, may be more inclined to post a Carvertisement on his vehicle, because of lower amounts of discretionary income. The idea of getting paid to go to work each day may appeal to them.

Businesses currently being considered for this segment include World Wide Technology located in Westport, MO and Edwardsville, IL; Metro Industrial Supply located in Chesterfield, MO, and the Machinery Specialty, in St. Charles, MO.

5.0 INDUSTRY ANALYSIS

Carvertising STL is involved in the billboard and outdoor display industry. This industry includes outdoor display advertising services, billboard displays, advertising services, and transit advertising services. Within this industry, businesses use techniques such as bus, subway, and taxicab card marketing.

Currently, the billboard and outdoor display advertising industry is operating in a highly competitive environment with constantly increasing competition. That being said, the economy is currently recovering from recession. Declining revenue paired with an increase in competitive new mediums like digital billboards and Internet ads has largely impacted companies within the industry. In addition, clients have decreased the amount of their budgets allocated to advertising. This decreases potential revenue earned by companies within Carvertising STL's industry.

Since 2006, total media expenditures by businesses have continuously decreased every year. In 2008, total advertising expenditures were at $221.2 billion, a 5.23% decrease from 2007's numbers. Presently (2009), total media expenditures are still on the decline; IBIS World predicts total media spending to reach $207.6 billion, another 6.15% decrease from 2008. However, there are positive projections in the near future. Even in the current economy where businesses have turned toward frugal spending habits, IBIS World foresees an upturn in large expenditures where businesses feel that costly outlays are justified.

Projections during this revival suggest an increase in total media expenditures of 1.01% ($209.7 billion) in 2010 and 4.01% ($218.1 billion) in 2011, with growth continuing every year up to 2014 ($245.3 billion). The graph depicts past figures as well as future projections for total media expenditures.

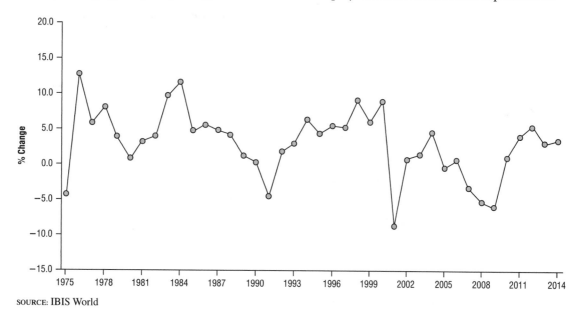

SOURCE: IBIS World

In spite of a real increase in disposable income during the third quarter of 2009, personal consumption outlay has declined by 4.3%. This reduction in consumption spending has resulted from consumer fear about future income levels and job security. Consumer fear during the current economic climate has created a risk–averse environment, which results in increased household savings. Less spending translates into less revenue flowing toward businesses. This deficiency in revenue inflow suggests to businesses that their advertising expenses are not worth it over the long run.

However, according to our primary research, many small businesses have advertising budgets that allow them to spend $5,000 to $49,999 per year. If this is the case on a countrywide scale, Carvertising STL has the perfect opportunity to appeal to these small businesses. We have the ability to maximize impressions at a comparatively small price. Businesses will quickly observe the effectiveness of advertising through our company.

Carvertising STL understands the current economic climate. By penetrating the industry now, we will take advantage of the cautious advertising expenditures of local St. Louis businesses. In shaping prudent advertising budgets, Carvertising STL will be viewed as a fresh, cost–effective alternative to more expensive mediums. Additionally, by entering the market at this point in time, Carvertising STL will create relationships with businesses that could potentially have larger advertising budgets in the future. This will convert their cautious budgets into increasing sales for Carvertising STL in the years to come.

5.1 Industry Trends

Midway through the 1990's, large U.S. outdoor advertisers took on a more significant role within the global market for billboard and outdoor displays. This was a result of major acquisitions and mergers within the industry. The ideology of globalization seeks to fulfill the need to expand revenue and profit when the U.S. markets have increased competition. In addition, many large clients preferred to have one company operating their promotional and advertising activities on a global level rather than having to rely on two separate companies.

The 2000 United States Census determined that audiences are increasing their active lifestyles, keeping them away from their living rooms. Therefore, cheaper methods of advertising are being employed because they are now rendered more efficient and cost effective. In other words, it does not cost as much comparatively to reach today's target audiences in their diverse demographics and active lifestyles.

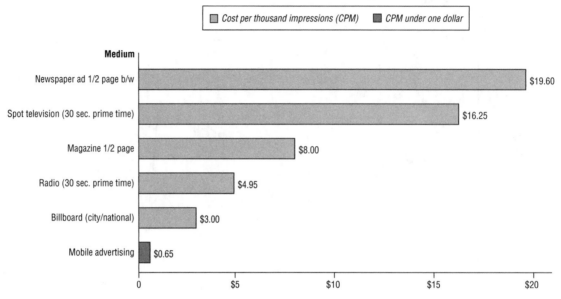

SOURCE: http://www.busads.com/yellow_mediakit.pdf

The graph above provided by Yellow Fleet Advertising, shows that mobile advertising is the least expensive method in effectively receiving impressions from a wide audience. In the graph, mobile advertising's CPM (Cost per Thousand Impressions), is a mere 65 cents. According to another study by Arbitron Corporation, Americans are more mobile than ever. Arbitron reported that Americans are traveling an average of 302 miles in their vehicles during a typical seven–day period. The average round trip commute lasts around 54 minutes.

The latest study from Arbitron shows that outdoor media has roughly the same effect as television and radio during a given week. This fact is portrayed in the following graph.

Outdoor, television and radio advertising reach practically the total U.S. adult population per week

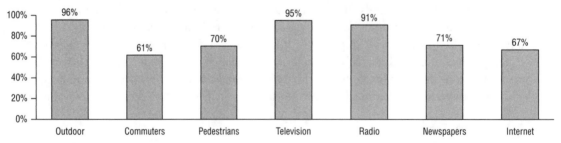

Explanation of media reach (in the past week)

Outdoor: traveled in a vehicle.
Commuters: spent time commuting to work one way.
Pedestrians: walked in a town/city.
Television: watched network or cable TV.
Radio: listened to AM/FM radio.
Newspapers: read a print newspaper.
Internet: accessed the Internet.

SOURCE: Scarborough USA+2008 release 2.12 months. Base: United States residents aged 18 or older.

Therefore, advertising with Carvertising STL can reach just as much of an audience as any other available advertising medium. Why not advertise with a cheaper alternative like our own.

The American Trucking Association (courtesy of SmartDollarAds) also alludes to the fact that mobile advertising is an effective marketing tool.

- 91% of the people surveyed reported that they do notice words and pictures on mobile advertising vehicles

- 75% reported that they developed a positive impression of the company when graphics were used

- 29% said they would base a buying decision on these impressions

Matrix Media2 asserts:

- Outdoor advertising is the second fastest growing marketing sector after internet advertising

- Over the past 10 years, spending on outdoor ads has increased 97%

US Coachways, Inc. advocates, "Mobile advertising is the fastest growing form of advertising. [There was] over $1.3 billion spent last year on outdoor advertising alone." An Arbitron, Inc. study shows that more than 95% of Americans travel by car each week, which creates a massive audience for our medium. They also claim that advertising on one vehicle produces up to 70,000 impressions per day. If a business uses Carvertising STL, each strategically picked vehicle involved in a campaign fleet could generate up to this amount every day.

6.0 COMPETITION

Our direct competition consists of all mobile marketing forms. Many companies that specialize in vehicle services employ the extra space on their fleets of vehicles. For example, bus, taxi, and public transportation services traditionally include external advertisements to generate extra revenue since their cars will be on the road anyway.

Mobile advertising potentially appears to be the least costly method for receiving impressions from a targeted audience. Mobile advertising in direct competition with Carvertising STL includes the following:

Buses

Regardless of location, buses always have advertisements on their sides. They are employed due to the large amount of space, which would otherwise be wasted. An important distinction between bus companies and Carvertising STL is that bus companies use their own fleet. They allow other companies to advertise on their unused space to incur additional revenue. Bus companies are usually nationwide and have different divisions for their mix of metropolitan regions.

The major benefit of bus advertising is the large amount of space that acts as a blank canvas for advertisements. This is especially the case if the advertisement includes window coverage. This makes bus advertising very appealing to certain companies. However, with buses, you can only advertise on a small quantity of actual vehicles, and it can become quite costly.

While buses make their daily rounds in the city, they display their advertisement to huge audiences no matter where they are. Bus ads cannot be turned off like a radio or television promotion. In other words, they are difficult to ignore.

Mobile Advertising

Mobile Advertising is the most direct competition to Carvertising STL. In fact, many companies exist with plans similar to our own. Often times, they include full–car wraps and do not attempt to swarm the public with large fleets of Carvertisements. This form of mobile advertising is more commonly found in Europe. However, there are a few companies doing similar things in the United States. Fortunately, none have broken into the St. Louis metropolitan market yet, so we have a window of opportunity within the next year to get started.

Freecarindex.com is a model in which the driver pays an upfront cost to become a member of the program. Members have access to a database of companies that offer free cars, or that will pay people to drive with ads on their private vehicles. They also provide drivers with tips on how to improve their chances of being selected. Unlike this service, Carvertising STL eliminates any work on the potential driver's part. We select drivers to be a part of the process based on their qualifications. They do not even have to change their driving habits.

AdsOnWheels.com is a similar service. Although they specialize in vehicle and bus wraps, they do not produce a database of drivers and businesses. If they created a new division that specialized in linking businesses with private drivers, they would become direct competitors of our company. Since they only wrap cars, their profit margin comes from the production of advertisements, not from exploiting private vehicle space. They do not serve as a liaison between companies and drivers like Carvertising STL.

FreeCarMedia.com may be our closest and most direct competitor. They do not charge their drivers an upfront fee to be entered into the database, and drivers can be paid up to $900 a month. However, the businesses or clients select the drivers from the database. Carvertising STL is unique because it assumes the responsibility of matching a fleet of valuable resources with the companies that wish to utilize this form of advertising. We make it easier for businesses to get started.

Some companies in Europe also include wheel advertising, a practice that could eventually branch out in the United States. Carvertising STL may employ this unique form of advertising in the future to gain extra competitive edge within the marketplace.

Media Max is a company in Europe that employs this form of advertising. If Media Max enters the United States' market, we may partner in the future to obtain this extra flair, increase the products we offer, and help Media Max gain a foothold in the American market. With their help, we could expand our service to include wheel ads on top of our traditional window and side ads.

At Carvertising STL, we must also take into consideration our indirect competitors. Indirect advertising includes all traditional forms of advertising that have dominated the marketing industry in the past. Even though each of these well–established forms has its benefits, each has downfalls that provide our company with opportunities to steal some market share.

Radio

Radio advertisements have many different advantages and are the biggest indirect competitor of Carvertising STL. These ads reach individuals when they are in their cars, at home, on the Internet, or even in public.

However, recent advances in music technology are hurting radio's ability to effectively advertise to wide audiences. When people are in their homes, they use an mp3 player, or quickly streaming Internet services like Pandora.com to hear music. This practice is even gaining ground in the car. People are listening to their mp3 players and smart phones while driving. They only hear music they like, and are able to avoid radio commercials. Since the invention of the mp3 player, sales in radio promotion have gone down. It is simply not as effective a form of advertising anymore. Carvertising STL seeks to steal market share from the radio's old spot.

Since people currently listen to their radios less, something needs to be able to promote while on the road. Carvertising STL fills in these gaps. With our service, advertisements become impossible to miss. One cannot change the channel and make traffic suddenly disappear!

Billboards

Billboards come in two different forms. There are print billboards and new ones that utilize electricity. Although billboards are large, some companies host advertisements on a rotating schedule and lose the benefit. They do this so that specific advertisements can circulate throughout a given area. The theory is that if they move billboards around a city, different sets of eyes will see them over time, causing more impressions. In other words, these companies recognize the fact that a moving billboard is better than a stationary one. This is exactly what Carvertising STL provides; only we can guarantee dozens of them at a time.

A disadvantage of billboards is that when a person drives by, they have only two or three seconds to look at it. They give it a passing glance and quickly forget it. With Carvertising STL's medium, you may actually drive for several minutes alongside a particular advertisement on your way to work. It's much harder to forget the advertisement that followed you throughout traffic for ten miles than the billboard you sped by.

Another problem arises alongside electronic billboards. They may be eye–catching, (in fact, they have more of an effect than regular billboards) but they are far less energy efficient. In fact, electronic billboards are not green at all. Carvertisements are attached to vehicles already on the road. In other words, our medium does not contribute poorly to the environment.

Direct mailings

Direct mailings are one of the oldest advertising mediums. Often times, individuals know the majority of envelopes in their mailboxes are junk. They do not even spend the time or effort to open them. Therefore, direct mailings may not be very effective at all. This form can be regarded as blast marketing. It is not a long–term solution, or a high quality service.

Direct mailing does have some benefits. Companies are able to acquire lists of individuals listed by demographics. This is what Carvertising STL will seek to do with its positioning and selection of drivers. Instead of relying on the fact that potential viewers will open an envelope, they will simply be unable to avoid looking at us. When someone is bored in traffic, their eyes wander. Carvertising STL will be there to grab their attention.

Television

Television marketing is a highly effective form of advertising and can be pinpointed toward certain demographics. It is able to target people based on the types of shows they're watching. Also, television reaches very large audiences at one time. Usually, this audience is much larger than those available for newspaper ads and other forms. Since there are fewer television stations than radio stations in a given area, each TV audience is divided into much larger segments. This enables companies to reach a larger, yet more diverse audience.

Television has the ability to convey the message with sight, sound and motion. It can give a product or service instant validity and prominence. Businesses can easily reach targeted audiences. Even children can be targeted during cartoon programming. Housewives can be targeted during their afternoon soap operas and insomniacs after midnight.

However, television does have some disadvantages that Carvertising STL does not. Just like the radio, modern advancements in technology are making the television a less effective tool. People who own Tivo and other programs can simply skip commercials. Many people change the channel or watch movies to avoid commercials. TV ads are also in direct competition with the viewer's environment. Viewers can distract themselves at home with anything in the room. This is not the case when these same people are on the road or stuck in traffic.

The standard television spot is quite short (generally 30 seconds), and does not always provide adequate exposure to get a company's point across. There is also the plain fact that people are spending less time in front of the TV than they used to. Modern people are out and about in the world, and often times, in traffic.

Internet and Social Media

The Internet and social media are also indirect competitors of Carvertising STL. However, they share the television's problem of reaching too broad an audience. With Google Adsense for example, it is hard to target specific individuals in geographical locations. Think about, for example, people living in smaller neighborhoods who have seen a local restaurant's Carvertisement. There is no way that the same restaurant could look to the Internet in order to reach these people. They would reach too broad an audience and it wouldn't be worth the money they had spent for the effect it created.

Think about how many times you get online to look things up in your neighborhood. Chances are, you use a search engine to find information on businesses outside of the vicinity because you want to learn more about them. If you buy keywords for "Soulard" or "Central West End," the viewing audience will not be your target clients, but rather, individuals from out of the area. These people are less likely to come into your business.

With Carvertising STL, there is more of a chance that people in the right location will randomly stumble upon your advertisement and be enticed to find out more (through the Internet or a walk–in visit). Using our medium, companies can direct people at street level to their website for more information. You could ask them to call a number, visit the store, or become a fan of the business on Facebook.

We encourage our clients to use social media and the Internet as a means to share information, current promotions, and be perceived as a leader in the industry. However, these methods should not be a business' only advertising. Facebook (among other social media outlets) are declining in effectiveness. As you can see from the graph below, the advertisement's effectiveness has already begun to decline.

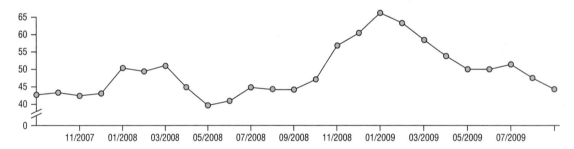

Thus, social media tools are not openly social, and often charge advertisers based on their CPM rather than on a pay–per–click basis. This ends up becoming more expensive for those who purchase this type of advertisement. Advertisers on social media can go to the Nielson ratings to determine how customers feel about their marketing. They cannot find out if the ads will be successful, only what people think about them.

7.0 SWOT ANALYSIS

A SWOT analysis was conducted to define Carvertising STL's strengths, weakness, opportunities and threats.

7.1 Strengths

Carvertising STL is able to pinpoint specific places, and allow for specified durations of advertising campaigns based on market location and the general point of the promotion. We can offer fully customizable options for our customers. They can pick from a variety of fleet sizes, number of advertisements and durations to pin down a perfect combination for their marketing efforts.

Our database is a major asset to the company. Carvertising STL's database includes a comprehensive list of potential drivers and their qualities and characteristics. This information includes basic elements like vehicle details, a map of the driver's routes, and information about the driver. This will help us to find the perfect drivers and routes for our businesses. With the database, we fully satisfy the needs of our clients.

We can beat out our competitors in overall effectiveness. The aforementioned section describes how we have significant competitive advantages over virtually all other forms of advertising. The main reason is that the general public has become desensitized to traditional marketing endeavors. Carvertising STL will be different and able to break through the filter that consumers have created. In other words, there will be no way to avoid our ads!

Carvertisement sightings can be a unique, rare, and exciting encounter. Drivers may see a creative one and instantly become intrigued. Rather than the information being blasted at the customer, our advertisements will interest the customer or drive away. These individuals will be enticed to actively seek out additional information to fulfill the curiosity we create.

Businesses will employ our services since we provide an advertising option guaranteed to turn heads at street level. Our technique quietly encourages the public to converse about the companies we advertise. Potential drivers on the other hand, will actively seek out our company so they too can be paid to drive. Remember, our drivers are not even required to change their established driving routes and habits.

7.2 Weaknesses

Carvertising STL is a newly formed startup in the billboard and outdoor advertising industry. We will experience difficulty breaking the current barriers that other mediums have put up. Initially, attaining customers will be a difficult task, because some potential clients may view our service as frivolous and ineffective. To some, the costs may appear to outweigh the benefits.

For this reason, we need to obtain information and statistics based on test markets. By displaying ads for Carvertising STL itself on our own private vehicles, we will have an easy way to track the effectiveness of this medium. With that data, we will have relevant information to use when pitching the idea to potential clients.

Some businesses may be content with their current means and will not be searching for additional or alternative methods with which to reach their target market.

7.3 Opportunities

There are many opportunities available now to help us break into the St. Louis market. Our business model is simple and does not require the acquisition of land or real estate. It is a relatively easy business to get off the ground. We have the opportunity to engage in trial runs to gain market information. Through our partnership with Craftsmen Industries, we are able to get our printing done quickly and at a low cost.

Programs like Build STL will also help our company. Build STL describes itself as a network of united businesses in favor of independent and local development. We will involve ourselves with this network to gain support and potential clients for our company.

The recent opening of I–64 means that traffic will be circulating more than it has in the past two years. People will be on the road and ready to display Carvertisements on their vehicles. Of course, these benefits will extend on to the businesses that are using our service.

7.4 Threats

The recession creates additional problems for Carvertising STL. People have not been paying as much for advertising as they have in the past. This could affect our company negatively, especially since we are a startup. People may not have the confidence in Carvertising STL that they have in more traditional forms of advertising. Since businesses need to ensure that their marketing dollar goes as far as possible, they may overlook our service and choose traditional means instead. However, the recession does help us in our search for drivers who need extra spending cash.

7.5 Competitive Edge

The obstacles Carvertising STL faces are entering the advertising industry, capturing the attention of businesses that might hire us for our services, and providing an effective and competitive marketing medium. Carvertising STL's competitive edge is our ability to take advantage of a market that has not been tapped into: private vehicles. The utilization of private vehicles is what sets our client's campaigns apart from their competition that utilize already saturated markets such as television, radio, internet, or billboards.

Unlike stationary billboards or radio commercials that are blasted to a variety of people at once, Carvertising STL clients can cater a Carvertising campaign to areas that will benefit their company the most. As previously mentioned, they can customize their fleet based on quantity, location driven, driver appearance, vehicle appearance, and duration.

Our ultimate goal is to help these businesses succeed. This goal is displayed in the relationships we form with our clients and in the variety of options they can select from. As seen in our financials, the monthly cost to the clients remains constant based on the fleet size. The only additional costs clients will incur are different set–up costs dependent upon the quantity and sizes of Carvertisements selected.

Carvertising STL is on the client's side. Rather than taking the client's money, posting an advertisement on a billboard, and hoping it helps their business, we will strive to constantly provide the client with the best possible campaign and results. The value we provide and the unique edge is that we tap into an upcoming market, provide an effective option for businesses, and develop a strong relationship with the client.

8.0 MARKETING STRATEGIES

Carvertising STL has developed two distinct marketing strategies for the businesses, (our clients) and for the individuals that will drive while displaying Carvertisements.

8.1 Marketing to the clients

Initially, Carvertising STL will target advertising agencies with well–established customer bases. In developing these partnerships, we benefit from their client base, and they gain access to our medium. We essentially offer a new alternative to other methods of advertising. In forming these strategic partnerships, Carvertising STL needs to ensure that agencies will not add extra markup to our prices. This will be specified in the original agreement. They will benefit from the added value of our product, which extends into their own business. If we allow advertising agencies to tack on an additional markup, our service will be less accessible.

We will gain the attention of advertising agencies through the use of the following mediums:

- Social media – When used properly, social media often produces positive results. Carvertising STL attracts advertising agencies through programs like Twitter, Facebook, and LinkedIn. Better yet, it's completely free and a great way to draw positive attention to Carvertising STL. These sites are ideal for increasing brand awareness and recognition, networking, and establishing legitimacy in the business world. For example, Carvertising STL gained immediate response when posting the status: "Looking for small business owners for new advertising promotion."

- Cold calls (in person visits and emails) – These may be the best way to initiate relationships with advertising agencies and business leaders. Some agencies may not be convinced about the service until they speak with a representative from our company in person. The in–person visits also give representatives of Carvertising STL a firsthand look at the culture, current problems in the industry, or opportunities for growth.

- Public relations releases are somewhat easy to do in the St. Louis region through its variety of newspapers, community newsletters, and news stations. We plan to send releases to these outlets: *St. Louis Business Journal,* STLToday.com, KMOV 4, KSDK 5, and KTVI Fox 2 News. PR releases will focus on Carvertising STL's service and our advertising medium's added benefit. By making the public aware of our service, they will know the brand connected with our advertisements that start to pop up around the city.

- Carvertising STL is the cheapest form of advertising we can use. What better way to promote our company than through our own service? Carvertising STL will post promotional Carvertisements on vehicles of management, family and friends who voluntary provide us with space on their private vehicles. In the future, we may launch wide scale marketing campaigns and pay drivers.

8.2 Marketing to the Drivers

Carvertising STL is unique in that, we do not market only to our potential clients. Rather, we also have the added task of marketing toward our inventory: drivers. As mentioned earlier we plan to target three types of people specifically to drive for us. These include working mothers, college students, and factory commuters. To reach these different people, Carvertising STL will need to use different strategies.

Working mothers

Many working mothers attend school–sponsored events such as fundraisers, plays, or athletic games. Carvertising STL will take advantage of this opportunity and post information regarding our promotions in flyers, pamphlets, and other literature that is bound to be seen by these mothers.

We will also take advantage of the Internet. Many schools and daycares use a personal webpage on the Internet as a means to communicate with parents.

We will also employ various social media methods to entice the working mothers that have currently turned to Facebook, Twitter and Linked In.

Carvertising STL also plans to target the mothers at their work environment through word of mouth, or authorized flyers posted around the firm.

College students

College students living on or off campus, attend class each day. Carvertising STL can take advantage of a variety of school sponsored marketing options such as weekly emails, classroom verbal announcements, classroom flyers, handbills, raffles, word of mouth, university newspaper advertisements, and university radio commercials. Social media, especially Facebook, can also be utilized for this segment. Carvertising STL can take advantage of Facebook fan pages, advertisements on the sides, and Facebook events to increase the popularity and brand awareness of our company.

Factory commuters

When marketing to these individuals, Carvertising STL will employ its own medium and frequent daily commutes in areas with a high concentration of workers.

If permitted, Carvertising STL will also post flyers in the breakout areas of the facilities and other authorized locations.

When targeting the businesses that employ potential drivers, we must examine the type of business and estimate the average employee's income level. We plan to market to businesses that we suspect have lower overall income levels. This will ensure that our marketing efforts will be more fruitful in the end. If we target high–income businesses, we are less likely to secure any drivers, since these workers will not desire the extra cash inflows we provide.

Other possible means

Because the business model of Carvertising STL is so flexible, we may also employ various gorilla techniques to target the general population.

One such technique is strategic placement of flyers in locations accessible to individuals that have a car, such as car washes, gas stations, or auto repair shops. This ensures that those reading the flyer have a car, are able to drive, and most likely have incurred some type of cost that needs to be paid. We can use options such as this to grow our database to an extensive and helpful resource.

9.0 SALES STRATEGY

Several steps exist when securing sales in the open market. In order to gain a customer base, we will provide complimentary trial runs for companies. The purpose of the trial runs is to determine the effectiveness of the campaigns and accumulate testimonials. Companies will compensate Carvertising STL for how much they feel the service is worth.

With testimonials and new credibility, Carvertising STL will then reach out to advertising agencies. We will discover the markets that businesses are currently trying to capture. We will then find drivers, based on the aforementioned marketing strategy. The drivers will be located in the respective areas and thus provide the agencies with the most possible benefits from advertising through us.

At this point, we are able to attain specific advertising campaigns on a given number of cars in geographically pinpointed areas. After several campaigns have run their course, we will have also acquired information on our effectiveness. We will continue to ask for testimonials from the leaders in our industry and individual business owners. This will only help to solidify our image in the industry and make us more credible.

In the first months, we will target large agencies with extensive customer bases. This will get the word out there, and cause smaller businesses to come to us. Of course, Carvertising STL will be happy to extend our services to these independent businesses.

Once Carvertising STL is viewed as an efficient and effective medium, (ideally at the 6–month mark), independent small businesses without advertising agencies will actively seek our service. In this case, we will offer our services on a much smaller scale. We may never directly advertise to these small businesses.

We do not actually ever make a sale to the drivers. Rather, our efforts are considered a success if owners agree to host ads on their vehicle.

10.0 MILESTONES

- Carvertising STL plans to breakeven in year one.
- Initially, Carvertising STL will target only advertising agencies. With time, other businesses will actively seek our service.

- By year five, Carvertising STL will expand and establish itself in at least one other metropolitan location.

- If necessary, Carvertising STL will form a design department to specialize in the graphics for the Carvertisements.

11.0 MANAGEMENT AND PERSONNEL SUMMARY

When Carvertising STL initially enters the marketplace, the management team will oversee all operations between them. As business picks up throughout the first year, the team will be able to expand and hire on employees to oversee the various departments. As the team stands now, each member brings something important and unique to the company. The team members all possess an equal share of ownership in the company. Their various positions are as follows:

Morgan McRae, CEO has spent four years at the John Cook School of Business at Saint Louis University working toward a degree in Entrepreneurship and Music Studies. For Carvertising STL's operations, Morgan helped in organizing the overall business plan alongside his partners. Once operations are up and running, Morgan will oversee efficiency of operations in all line positions throughout the company and pitch to potential clients.

Cullen Hayes, CFO is also a JCSB student working toward degrees in both Finance and Entrepreneurship. He is perfect for overseeing financial projections and general feasibility of operations. Cullen has played a huge part in organizing the initial three–year projections. Once incorporated, he will monitor daily cash flows and financial stability for the short and long term.

Joyce McCauley, CMO is also a JCSB student working toward her degree in Entrepreneurship. She will receive a minor in marketing and certificates for Spanish. Her background in both marketing and entrepreneurship make her a great resource on the team. Joyce came up with the original idea for Carvertising STL, and has created our marketing plan for advertising agencies and drivers.

As Carvertising STL progresses as a business, each team member will gradually step backward to oversee the broader scope of operations. In doing so, various new employees will be hired on to manage the specific operations in each department. Additional line positions may eventually need to be hired on for designing and IT management. These areas have not presented much of a problem in the startup, but may need to be addressed in the following years.

Carvertising STL includes two separate categories of human resources. Our primary workers are the aforementioned CEO, CFO, and CMO. These line position employees will eventually hire on more staff positions for application and removal procedures. Our third group of human resources includes the drivers themselves. These people are the greatest asset to our business. They actually act as our inventory in a way. However, we must work alongside these resources and ensure that the company maintains good relationships with each and every one.

12.0 THE INVESTMENT

In order to get our operations off the ground, we are requesting an initial investment of $5,000. The team wishes to acquire this investment through debt financing so that all three members can retain total ownership of Carvertising STL between three people. This investment allows us to purchase the necessary equipment that we need to get started, pay for transportation expenses, and have cash on hand for unexpected events. We are also asking for this amount to cover our initial market research. In order to be seen as a credible advertising medium, we need to present some real world market data proving our effectiveness. This can only be done by running some tests with Carvertisements.

Please review our financial assumptions for further information regarding our anticipated cash flow and investment required to move forward.

13.0 FINANCIAL ASSUMPTIONS

One of our main costs comes from printing of materials. According to Craftsmen Industries, the cost of printing is based on a one–time setup fee, and the materials needed for production of ads. The setup fee is $75. Additionally, the 3M material attached to the cars costs $4 per square foot. Graphics attached to windows must still permit visibility and are thus composed of a different material. This material costs about $6 per square foot.

The second major cost we incur is payment to our drivers. Carvertising STL pays the drivers $100 every month for their service. Printing fees and driver pay are the only costs of goods sold included in our product. A setup fee that we will pass on to clients during the first month of their campaign will cover the printing cost. Carvertising STL will not add extra markup to this cost since we are not in the business of printing. Rather, we will only charge a markup on driver pay since this is the major benefit of doing business through us. Hence, our profit margin which comes only from a markup on driver pay, which will be covered during monthly payments.

We will also incur costs associated with shipping, application and removal of the comply material from cars. However, these costs are not included in our marked up variable costs. We consider these expenses of doing business, and they will appear on our income statement. In marking up our driver pay, we need to ensure a large enough profit margin to cover these expenses and still have extra money to reinvest in Carvertising STL.

In the future, we may extend additional benefits to our customers and as a result, gain more revenue. We may extend our service to include a graphic design department. The department will be helpful for smaller businesses without an advertising agency or marketing department. For this service, we may include an additional $10–$15 in additional setup fees since we assume that this work will take about an hour to complete. Prices may be higher for additional time spent in the design department.

General Assumptions
- Our fiscal year begins in January and ends in December
- Income Statements are released on a regular monthly basis
- Our Balance Sheet and Cash Flow Statements are presented on a cumulative basis
- General operations will start in the third month after incorporation
- For the first year, Carvertising STL will work from satellite locations at the three owners' homes

Revenue Assumptions
- Campaign durations are in multiples of three months
- Campaign contract revenue is Carvertising STL's main source of income
- Revenue comes from profit margin based on driver pay
- Contracts received are founded on specific company campaigns based on duration, square footage of advertising, and number of cars in a fleet

- Total revenue throughout the first year is projected at $812,055

- Total revenue throughout the third year is projected at $5,094,270

- Breakeven occurs in the 3rd month after incorporation since all costs are covered in the initial payment.

- Jobs requiring special design or other provisions will include added fees for the setup pricing

- We will simultaneously work multiple jobs during normal operations

- Our billings are set up so that we receive a large enough portion of campaign payment to cover the initial startup fees, and first month's driver pay before the campaign begins.

- Subsequent payments cover the rest of the campaign at half of the campaign's life.

- For each job, we assume a 60% markup on driver pay.

Cost Assumptions

- Employees in application and removal are paid based on an hourly wage

- Costs account for a higher percentage of revenue alongside campaigns with larger fleet sizes

- Material costs are considered a separate cost of goods sold that are paid for apart from the monthly campaign rate

- Monthly salary rate for all three employees combined is an expense set at $2,760

- All additional employees hired onto the staff in line positions start at the same salary rate.

- We intend to offer health care and other benefits to our office employees and owners.

- After year three, we intend to raise office employee salaries by 2% each year

Funding

- Our startup funding of $5,000 will be entirely debt funding, which will be paid back within the first 2 years after incorporation.

- In the first year after incorporation, we will acquire a line of credit through US Bank

- We do not anticipate having to use our line of credit frequently after the first year once we have enough cash on hand to pay the initial printing and driver costs.

Carvertising STL

Income statement

Year 1 ended December 31

Revenues	Jan.	Feb.	Mar.	Apr.	May	Jun.	Jul.
Sales	—	—	22,695	39,390	35,295	56,115	61,320
Total revenue	**—**	**—**	**22,695**	**39,390**	**35,295**	**56,115**	**61,320**
Cost of goods sold							
Printing & setup cost	—	—	3,945	6,465	4,545	6,165	6,570
Total cost of goods sold	**—**	**—**	**3,945**	**6,465**	**4,545**	**6,165**	**6,570**
Gross profit	**—**	**—**	**18,750**	**32,925**	**30,750**	**49,950**	**54,750**
Operating expenses							
Salary	—	—	2,760	2,760	2,760	2,760	2,760
Rent expense	—	—	6,995	15,790	18,595	23,715	16,500
Reserve fund	—	—	252	252	252	252	252
Telephone	90	90	90	90	90	90	90
Transportation	50	50	171	234	221	245	253
Insurance	250	250	250	250	250	250	250
Legal & accounting	450	—	—	—	—	—	–
Office supplies	20	20	20	20	20	20	20
Wage expense	—	—	—	2,000	2,000	5,000	5,000
Benefits expense	—	—	1,380	2,380	2,380	3,880	3,880
Total payroll tax	—	—	239	412	412	671	671
Marketing expense	50	50	50	—	—	—	50
Website expense	14	14	468	802	720	1,136	1,241
Total operating expenses	**924**	**474**	**12,675**	**24,990**	**27,700**	**38,020**	**30,967**
Net income (loss) before taxes	**(924)**	**(474)**	**6,075**	**7,935**	**3,050**	**11,930**	**23,783**
Provision (benefit) for income taxes	(139)	(71)	911	1,190	458	1,790	3,567
Net income (loss)	**(786)**	**(403)**	**5,164**	**6,745**	**2,593**	**10,141**	**20,216**

Revenues	Aug.	Sep.	Oct.	Nov.	Dec.	Total
Sales	79,740	97,350	105,765	145,380	169,005	
Total revenue	**79,740**	**97,350**	**105,765**	**145,380**	**169,005**	**812,055**
Cost of goods sold						
Printing & setup cost	8,190	9,000	10,215	11,430	13,455	
Total cost of goods sold	**8,190**	**9,000**	**10,215**	**11,430**	**13,455**	**79,980**
Gross profit	**71,550**	**88,350**	**95,550**	**133,950**	**155,550**	**732,075**
Operating expenses						
Salary	2,760	2,760	2,760	2,760	2,760	
Rent expense	33,240	41,050	50,765	59,980	72,005	
Reserve fund	252	252	252	252	252	
Telephone	90	90	90	90	90	
Transportation	247	261	243	245	248	
Insurance	250	250	250	250	250	
Legal & accounting	—	—	—	—	—	
Office supplies	20	20	20	20	20	
Wage expense	5,000	5,000	6,000	7,000	10,000	
Benefits expense	3,880	3,880	4,380	4,880	6,380	
Total payroll tax	671	671	758	844	1,104	
Marketing expense	50	50	—	—	—	
Website expense	1,609	1,961	2,129	2,922	3,394	
Total operating expenses	**48,069**	**56,245**	**67,647**	**79,243**	**96,503**	**483,457**
Net income (loss) before taxes	**23,481**	**32,105**	**27,903**	**54,707**	**59,047**	
Provision (benefit) for income taxes	3,522	4,816	4,185	8,206	8,857	
Net income (loss)	**19,959**	**27,289**	**23,717**	**46,501**	**50,190**	**211,325**

Carvertising STL

Balance sheet

Year 1 ended Dec. 31

	Balance	Jan.	Feb.	Mar.	Apr.	May	Jun.	Jul.
Assets								
Current assets								
Cash	5,000	—	—	—	—	—	—	—
Accounts receivable	—	—	—	22,695	39,390	35,295	56,115	61,320
Total current assets	**5,000**	**—**		**22,695**	**39,390**	**35,295**	**56,115**	**61,320**
Property & equipment								
Land & building								
Machinery & equipment								
Less: Accumulated depreciation								
Net book value	**—**	**—**	**—**	**—**	**—**	**—**		**—**
Other assets								
Total other assets	**—**	**—**	**—**	**—**	**—**	**—**	**—**	**—**
Total assets	**—**	**5,000**	**—**	**22,695**	**39,390**	**35,295**	**56,115**	**61,320**
Liabilities & owner's equity								
Current liabilities								
Accounts payable		924	474	16,620	31,455	32,245	44,185	37,537
Short-term debt								
Interest on short term debt								
Interest on long-term debt								
Total current liabilities								
Current portion of long-term debt								
Total current liabilities		**924**	**474**	**16,620**	**31,455**	**32,245**	**44,185**	**37,537**
Long-term liabilities								
Long-term debt								
Total long-term liabilities		**—**	**—**	**—**	**—**	**—**	**—**	**—**
Owner's equity								
Investment by owner		5,000	—	—				
Retained earnings		(924)	(474)	6,075	7,935	3,050	11,930	23,783
Total owner's equity		**4,076**	**(474)**	**6,075**	**7,935**	**3,050**	**11,930**	**23,783**
Total liabilities and equity	**—**	**5,000**	**—**	**22,695**	**39,390**	**35,295**	**56,115**	**61,320**

continued

Carvertising STL [CONTINUED]

Balance sheet

Year 1 ended Dec. 31

	Aug.	Sep.	Oct.	Nov.	Dec.	Year 1 total	Overall total
Assets							
Current assets							
Cash	—	—	—	—	—	—	
Accounts receivable	79,740	97,350	105,765	145,380	169,005	812,055	
Total current assets	**79,740**	**97,350**	**105,765**	**145,380**	**169,005**	**817,055**	
Property & equipment							
Land & building							
Machinery & equipment							
Less: Accumulated depreciation							
Net book value	—	—	—	—	—	—	
Other assets							
Total other assets	—	—	—	—	—	—	
Total assets	**79,740**	**97,350**	**105,765**	**145,380**	**169,005**	**817,055**	**817,055**
Liabilities & owner's equity							
Current liabilities							
Accounts payable	56,259	65,245	77,862	90,673	109,958	563,437	
Short-term debt							
Interest on short term debt							
Interest on long-term debt							
Total current liabilities							
Current portion of long-term debt							
Total current liabilities	**56,259**	**65,245**	**77,862**	**90,673**	**109,958**	**563,437**	
Long-term liabilities							
Long-term debt							
Total long-term liabilities	—	—	—	—	—	—	
Owner's equity							
Investment by owner	—	—	—	—	—	—	
Retained earnings	23,481	32,105	27,903	54,707	59,047	248,618	
Total owner's equity	**23,481**	**32,105**	**27,903**	**54,707**	**59,047**	**253,618**	
Total liabilities and equity	**79,740**	**97,350**	**105,765**	**145,380**	**169,005**	**817,055**	**817,055**

Carvertising STL

Cash flow statement

Year 1 ended Dec. 31

	Jan.	Feb.	Mar.	Apr.	May	Jun.
Cash flow from operations						
Receipts						
Cash sales	—	—	—	—	—	—
Accts. receivable collections	—	—	9,095	21,790	27,295	34,515
Total cash received	—	—	**9,095**	**21,790**	**27,295**	**34,515**
Disbursements						
Operating expenses	924	474	12,675	24,990	27,700	38,020
Interest on loans	—	—	—	—	—	—
Total cash used	**924**	**474**	**12,675**	**24,990**	**27,700**	**38,020**
Net cash flow from operations	**(924)**	**(474)**	**(3,580)**	**(3,200)**	**(405)**	**(3,505)**
Cash flow from investing activities						
Purchase of land	—	—	—	—	—	—
Purchase of building/equipment	—	—	—	—	—	—
Total cash used	—	—	—	—	—	—
Net cash flow from investing	—	—	—	—	—	—
Cash flow from financing activities						
Equity						
Investment by owners	5,000	—	—	—	—	—
Debt						
Long-term loan additions (payments)	—	—	—	—	—	—
Net cash flow from financing	**5,000**	—	—	—	—	—
Net increase (decrease) in cash	4,076	(474)	(3,580)	(3,200)	(405)	(3,505)
Short-term loan increase (decrease)	—	—	—	—	—	—
Beginning cash	—	4,076	3,602	22	(3,178)	(3,583)
Ending cash	4,076	3,602	22	(3,178)	(3,583)	(7,087)

	Jul.	Aug.	Sep.	Oct.	Nov.	Dec.
Cash flow from operations						
Receipts						
Cash sales	—	—	—	—	—	—
Accts. receivable collections	36,520	48,540	60,550	75,365	89,380	107,405
Total cash received	**36,520**	**48,540**	**60,550**	**75,365**	**89,380**	**107,405**
Disbursements						
Operating expenses	30,967	48,069	56,245	67,647	79,243	96,503
Interest on loans	—	—	—	—	—	—
Total cash used	**30,967**	**48,069**	**56,245**	**67,647**	**79,243**	**96,503**
Net cash flow from operations	**5,553**	**771**	**4,305**	**7,718**	**10,137**	**10,902**
Cash flow from investing activities						
Purchase of land	—	—	—	—	—	—
Purchase of building/equipment	—	—	—	—	—	—
Total cash used	—	—	—	—	—	—
Net cash flow from investing	—	—	—	—	—	—
Cash flow from financing activities						
Equity						
Investment by owners	—	—	—	—	—	—
Debt						
Long-term loan additions (payments)	—	—	—	—	—	—
Net cash flow from financing	—	—	—	—	—	—
Net increase (decrease) in cash	5,553	471	4,305	7,718	10,137	10,902
Short-term loan increase (decrease)	—	—	—	—	—	—
Beginning cash	(7,087)	(1,534)	(1,063)	3,241	10,959	21,096
Ending cash	(1,534)	(1,063)	3,241	10,959	21,096	31,998

Carvertising STL

Income statement

Year 2 ended December 31

Revenues	Jan.	Feb.	Mar.	Apr.	May	Jun.	Jul.
Sales	140,985	227,670	184,185	185,400	235,425	145,440	234,240
Total revenue	**140,985**	**227,670**	**184,185**	**185,400**	**235,425**	**145,440**	**234,240**
Cost of goods sold							
Printing & setup cost	11,835	17,145	11,835	13,050	15,075	16,740	16,290
Total cost of goods sold	**11,835**	**17,145**	**11,835**	**13,050**	**15,075**	**16,740**	**16,290**
Gross profit	**129,150**	**210,525**	**172,350**	**172,350**	**220,350**	**128,700**	**217,950**
Operating expenses							
Salary	10,000	10,000	10,000	10,000	10,000	10,000	10,000
Rent expense	76,385	94,970	94,885	102,600	110,125	114,840	120,340
Reserve fund	252	252	252	252	252	252	252
Telephone	90	90	90	90	90	90	90
Transportation	253	260	261	254	267	251	243
Insurance	250	250	250	250	250	250	250
Legal & accounting	300	—	—	—	—	—	—
Office supplies	20	20	20	20	20	20	20
Wage expense	15,000	15,000	15,000	15,000	18,000	18,000	20,000
Benefits expense	12,500	12,500	12,500	12,500	14,000	14,000	15,000
Total payroll tax	2,163	2,163	2,163	2,163	2,422	2,422	2,595
Marketing expense	50	50	50	—	—	—	50
Website expense	2,834	4,568	3,698	3,722	4,723	2,923	4,699
Total operating expenses	**120,096**	**140,122**	**139,168**	**146,851**	**160,149**	**163,048**	**173,539**
Net Income (loss) before taxes	**9,054**	**70,403**	**33,182**	**25,499**	**60,201**	**(34,348)**	**44,411**
Provision (benefit) for income taxes	1,358	17,601	4,977	3,825	9,030	(5,152)	6,662
Net income (loss)	**7,696**	**52,802**	**28,204**	**21,674**	**51,171**	**(29,196)**	**37,749**

Revenues	Aug.	Sep.	Oct.	Nov.	Dec.	Total
Sales	254,625	223,050	288,690	260,700	291,930	
Total revenue	**254,625**	**223,050**	**288,690**	**260,700**	**291,930**	**2,672,340**
Cost of goods sold						
Printing & setup cost	15,075	17,100	20,340	21,150	23,580	
Total cost of goods sold	**15,075**	**17,100**	**20,340**	**21,150**	**23,580**	**199,215**
Gross profit	**239,550**	**205,950**	**268,350**	**239,550**	**268,350**	**2,473,125**
Operating expenses						
Salary	10,000	10,000	10,000	10,000	10,000	
Rent expense	114,625	118,150	134,890	150,200	171,130	
Reserve fund	252	252	252	252	252	
Telephone	90	90	90	90	90	
Transportation	239	247	245	250	259	
Insurance	250	250	250	250	250	
Legal & accounting	—	—	—	—	—	
Office supplies	20	20	20	20	20	
Wage expense	21,000	21,000	21,000	21,000	22,000	
Benefits expense	15,500	15,500	15,500	15,500	16,000	
Total payroll tax	2,682	2,682	2,682	2,682	2,768	
Marketing expense	50	50	—	—	—	
Website expense	5,107	4,475	5,788	5,228	5,853	
Total operating expenses	**169,814**	**172,716**	**190,716**	**205,472**	**228,622**	**2,010,313**
Net Income (loss) before taxes	**69,736**	**33,234**	**77,634**	**34,078**	**39,728**	
Provision (benefit) for income taxes	17,434	4,985	19,408	5,112	5,959	
Net income (loss)	**52,302**	**28,249**	**58,225**	**28,967**	**33,769**	**371,613**

Carvertising STL

Balance sheet

Year 1 ended Dec. 31

	Balance	Jan.	Feb.	Mar.	Apr.	May	Jun.	Jul.
Assets								
Current assets								
Cash		—	—	—	—	—	—	—
Accounts receivable		140,985	227,670	184,185	185,400	235,425	145,440	234,240
Total current assets		**140,985**	**227,670**	**184,185**	**185,400**	**235,425**	**145,440**	**234,240**
Property & equipment								
Land & building								
Machinery & equipment								
Less: accumulated depreciation								
Net book value		—	—	—	—	—	—	—
Other assets								
Total other assets		—	—	—	—	—	—	—
Total assets	**817,055**	**140,985**	**227,670**	**184,185**	**185,400**	**235,425**	**145,440**	**234,240**
Liabilities & owner's equity								
Current liabilities								
Accounts payable		131,931	157,267	151,003	159,901	175,224	179,788	189,829
Short-term debt								
Interest on short term debt								
Interest on long-term debt								
Total current liabilities								
Current portion of long-term debt								
Total current liabilities		**131,931**	**157,267**	**151,003**	**159,901**	**175,224**	**179,788**	**189,829**
Long-term liabilities								
Long-term debt								
Total long-term liabilities		—	—	—	—	—	—	—
Owner's equity								
Investment by owner		—	—	—	—	—	—	—
Retained earnings		9,054	70,403	33,182	25,499	60,201	(34,348)	44,411
Total owner's equity		**9,054**	**70,403**	**33,182**	**25,499**	**60,201**	**(34,348)**	**44,411**
Total liabilities and equity	**817,055**	**140,985**	**227,670**	**184,185**	**185,400**	**235,425**	**145,440**	**234,240**

continued

Carvertising STL [CONTINUED]

Balance sheet

Year 2 ended Dec. 31

	Aug.	Sep.	Oct.	Nov.	Dec.	Year 1 total	Overall total
Assets							
Current assets							
Cash	—	—	—	—	—	—	
Accounts receivable	254,625	223,050	288,690	260,700	291,930	2,672,340	
Total current assets	**254,625**	**223,050**	**288,690**	**260,700**	**291,930**	**2,672,340**	
Property & equipment							
Land & building							
Machinery & equipment							
Less: Accumulated depreciation							
Net book value	—	—	—	—	—		
Other assets							
Total other assets	—	—	—	—	—		
Total assets	**254,625**	**223,050**	**288,690**	**260,700**	**291,930**	**2,672,340**	**3,489,395**
Liabilities & owner's equity							
Current liabilities							
Accounts payable	184,889	189,816	211,056	226,622	252,202	2,209,528	
Short-term debt							
Interest on short term debt							
Interest on long-term debt							
Total current liabilities							
Current portion of long-term debt							
Total current liabilities	**184,889**	**189,816**	**211,056**	**226,622**	**252,202**	**2,209,528**	
Long-term liabilities							
Long-term debt							
Total long-term liabilities	—	—	—	—	—		
Owner's equity							
Investment by owner	—	—	—	—	—		
Retained earnings	69,736	33,234	77,634	34,078	39,728	462,812	
Total owner's equity	**69,736**	**33,234**	**77,634**	**34,078**	**39,728**	**462,812**	
Total liabilities and equity	**254,625**	**223,050**	**288,690**	**260,700**	**291,930**	**2,672,340**	**3,489,395**

Carvertising STL

Cash flow statement

Year 2 ended Dec. 31

Cash flow from operations	Jan.	Feb.	Mar.	Apr.	May	Jun.
Receipts						
Cash sales	—	—	—	—	—	—
Accts. receivable collections	115,385	142,070	144,985	156,600	167,425	174,240
Total cash received	**115,385**	**142,070**	**144,985**	**156,600**	**167,425**	**174,240**
Disbursements						
Operating expenses	120,096	140,122	139,168	146,851	160,149	163,048
Interest on loans	—	—	—			
Total cash used	**120,096**	**140,122**	**139,168**	**146,851**	**160,149**	**163,048**
Net cash flow from operations	**(4,711)**	**1,948**	**5,817**	**9,749**	**7,276**	**11,192**
Cash flow from investing activities						
Purchase of land	—	—	—	—	—	—
Purchase of building/equip.	—	—	—	—	—	—
Total cash used	**—**	**—**	**—**	**—**	**—**	**—**
Net cash flow from investing	**—**	**—**	**—**	**—**	**—**	**—**
Cash flow from financing activities						
Equity						
Investment by owners	—	—	—	—	—	—
Debt						
Long-term loan additions (payments)	—	—	—	—	—	—
Net cash flow from financing	**—**	**—**	**—**	**—**	**—**	**—**
Net increase (decrease) in cash	(4,711)	1,948	5,817	9,749	7,276	11,192
Short-term loan increase (decrease)	—	—	—	—	—	—
Beginning cash	31,998	27,287	29,235	35,051	44,801	52,077
Ending cash	27,287	29,235	35,051	44,801	52,077	63,269

Cash flow from operations	Jul.	Aug.	Sep.	Oct.	Nov.	Dec.
Receipts						
Cash sales	—	—	—	—	—	—
Accts. receivable collections	183,040	174,625	179,050	203,890	227,900	259,930
Total cash received	**183,040**	**174,625**	**179,050**	**203,890**	**227,900**	**259,930**
Disbursements						
Operating expenses	173,539	169,814	172,716	190,716	205,472	228,622
Interest on loans	—	—	—	—	—	—
Total cash used	**173,539**	**169,814**	**172,716**	**190,716**	**205,472**	**228,622**
Net cash flow from operations	**9,501**	**4,811**	**6,334**	**13,174**	**22,428**	**31,308**
Cash flow from investing activities						
Purchase of land	—	—	—	—	—	—
Purchase of building/equip.	—	—	—	—	—	—
Total cash used	**—**	**—**	**—**	**—**	**—**	**—**
Net cash flow from investing	**—**	**—**	**—**	**—**	**—**	**—**
Cash flow from financing activities						
Equity						
Investment by owners	—	—	—	—	—	—
Debt						
Long-term loan additions (payments)	—	—	—	—	—	—
Net cash flow from financing	**—**	**—**	**—**	**—**	**—**	**—**
Net increase (decrease) in cash	9,501	4,811	6,334	13,174	22,428	31,308
Short-term loan increase (decrease)	—	—	—	—	—	—
Beginning cash	63,269	72,770	77,581	83,915	97,089	119,517
Ending cash	72,770	77,581	83,915	97,089	119,517	150,825

Carvertising STL

Income statement

Year 3 ended December 31

Revenues	Jan.	Feb.	Mar.	Apr.	May	Jun.	Jul.
Sales	439,515	527,010	464,730	626,775	410,310	399,960	410,715
Total revenue	**439,515**	**527,010**	**464,730**	**626,775**	**410,310**	**399,960**	**410,715**
Cost of goods sold							
Printing & setup cost	22,365	28,485	23,580	27,225	21,960	26,010	22,365
Total cost of goods sold	**22,365**	**28,485**	**23,580**	**27,225**	**21,960**	**26,010**	**22,365**
Gross profit	**417,150**	**498,525**	**441,150**	**599,550**	**388,350**	**373,950**	**388,350**
Operating expenses							
Salary	25,000	25,000	25,000	25,000	25,000	25,000	25,000
Rent expense	178,915	208,310	208,130	225,275	213,010	220,060	216,415
Reserve fund	252	252	252	252	252	252	252
Telephone	90	90	90	90	90	90	90
Transportation	252	263	275	256	248	271	273
Insurance	250	250	250	250	250	250	250
Legal & accounting	300	—	—	—	—	—	—
Office supplies	20	20	20	20	20	20	20
Wage expense	31,000	36,000	36,000	37,000	37,000	35,000	35,000
Benefits expense	28,000	30,500	30,500	31,000	31,000	30,000	30,000
Total payroll tax	4,844	5,277	5,277	5,363	5,363	5,190	5,190
Marketing expense	50	50	50	—	—	—	50
Website expense	8,804	10,554	9,309	12,550	8,220	8,013	8,228
Total operating expenses	**277,777**	**316,566**	**315,152**	**337,056**	**320,453**	**324,146**	**320,768**
Net income (loss) before taxes	**139,373**	**181,959**	**125,998**	**262,494**	**67,897**	**49,804**	**67,582**
Provision (benefit) for income taxes	54,355	70,964	49,139	102,373	16,974	7,471	16,895
Net income (loss)	**85,017**	**110,995**	**76,859**	**160,122**	**50,922**	**42,333**	**50,686**

Revenues	Aug.	Sep.	Oct.	Nov.	Dec.	Total
Sales	324,315	344,730	351,495	413,955	380,760	
Total revenue	**324,315**	**344,730**	**351,495**	**413,955**	**380,760**	**5,094,270**
Cost of goods sold						
Printing & setup cost	22,365	23,580	20,745	25,605	26,010	
Total cost of goods sold	**22,365**	**23,580**	**20,745**	**25,605**	**26,010**	**290,295**
Gross profit	**301,950**	**321,150**	**330,750**	**388,350**	**354,750**	**4,803,975**
Operating expenses						
Salary	25,000	25,000	25,000	25,000	25,000	
Rent expense	223,915	238,130	244,795	267,155	269,560	
Reserve fund	252	252	252	252	252	
Telephone	90	90	90	90	90	
Transportation	267	257	256	264	261	
Insurance	250	250	250	250	250	
Legal & accounting	—	—	—	—	—	
Office supplies	20	20	20	20	20	
Wage expense	34,000	32,000	32,000	32,000	30,000	
Benefits expense	29,500	28,500	28,500	28,500	27,500	
Total payroll tax	5,104	4,931	4,931	4,931	4,758	
Marketing expense	50	50	—	—	—	
Website expense	6,500	6,909	7,044	8,293	7,629	
Total operating expenses	**324,948**	**336,388**	**343,138**	**366,755**	**365,320**	**3,948,468**
Net income (loss) before taxes	**(22,998)**	**(15,238)**	**(12,388)**	**21,595**	**(10,570)**	
Provision (benefit) for income taxes	(3,450)	(2,286)	(1,858)	3,239	(1,585)	
Net income (loss)	**(19,548)**	**(12,953)**	**(10,529)**	**18,356**	**(8,984)**	**543,276**

Carvertising STL

Balance sheet

Year 3 ended Dec. 31

	Balance	Jan.	Feb.	Mar.	Apr.	May	Jun.	Jul.
Assets								
Current assets								
Cash		—	—	—	—	—	—	—
Accounts receivable		439,515	527,010	464,730	626,775	410,310	399,960	410,715
Total current assets		**439,515**	**527,010**	**464,730**	**626,775**	**410,310**	**399,960**	**410,715**
Property & equipment								
Land & building								
Machinery & equipment								
Less: Accumulated depreciation								
Net book value		—	—	—	—	—	—	—
Other assets								
Total other assets		—	—	—	—	—	—	—
Total assets	**3,489,395**	**439,515**	**527,010**	**464,730**	**626,775**	**410,310**	**399,960**	**410,715**
Liabilities & owner's equity								
Current liabilities								
Accounts payable		300,142	345,051	338,732	364,281	342,413	350,156	343,133
Short-term debt								
Interest on short term debt								
Interest on long-term debt								
Total current liabilities								
Current portion of long-term debt								
Total current liabilities		**300,142**	**345,051**	**338,732**	**364,281**	**342,413**	**350,156**	**343,133**
Long-term liabilities								
Long-term debt								
Total long-term liabilities		—	—	—	—	—	—	—
Owner's equity								
Investment by owner		—	—	—	—	—	—	—
Retained earnings		139,373	181,959	125,998	262,494	67,897	49,804	67,582
Total owner's equity		**139,373**	**181,959**	**125,998**	**262,494**	**67,897**	**49,804**	**67,582**
Total liabilities and equity	**3,489,395**	**439,515**	**527,010**	**464,730**	**626,775**	**410,310**	**399,960**	**410,715**

continued

Carvertising STL [CONTINUED]

Balance sheet

Year 3 ended Dec. 31

	Aug.	Sep.	Oct.	Nov.	Dec.	Year 3 total	Overall total
Assets							
Current assets							
Cash	—	—	—	—	—		
Accounts receivable	324,315	344,730	351,495	413,955	380,760	5,094,270	
Total current assets	**324,315**	**344,730**	**351,495**	**413,955**	**380,760**	**5,094,270**	
Property & equipment							
Land & building							
Machinery & equipment							
Less: Accumulated depreciation							
Net book value	—	—	—	—	—		
Other assets							
Total other assets	—	—	—	—	—		
Total assets	**324,315**	**344,730**	**351,495**	**413,955**	**380,760**	**5,094,270**	**8,583,665**
Liabilities & owner's equity							
Current liabilities							
Accounts payable	347,313	359,968	363,883	392,360	391,330	4,238,763	
Short-term debt							
Interest on short term debt							
Interest on long-term debt							
Total current liabilities							
Current portion of long-term debt							
Total current liabilities	**347,313**	**359,968**	**363,883**	**392,360**	**391,330**	**4,238,763**	
Long-term liabilities							
Long-term debt							
Total long-term liabilities	—	—	—	—	—		
Owner's equity							
Investment by owner	—	—	—	—	—		
Retained earnings	(22,998)	(15,238)	(12,388)	21,595	(10,570)	855,507	
Total owner's equity	**(22,998)**	**(15,238)**	**(12,388)**	**21,595**	**(10,570)**	**855,507**	
Total liabilities and equity	**324,315**	**344,730**	**351,495**	**413,955**	**380,760**	**5,094,270**	**8,583,665**

Carvertising STL

Cash flow statement

Year 3 ended Dec. 31

	Jan.	Feb.	Mar.	Apr.	May	Jun.
Cash flow from operations						
Receipts						
Cash sales	—	—	—	—	—	—
Accts. receivable collections	273,115	316,610	319,130	344,375	327,910	336,760
Total cash received	**273,115**	**316,610**	**319,130**	**344,375**	**327,910**	**336,760**
Disbursements						
Operating expenses	277,777	316,566	315,152	337,056	320,453	324,146
Interest on loans	—	—	—	—	—	—
Total cash used	**277,777**	**316,566**	**315,152**	**337,056**	**320,453**	**324,146**
Net cash flow from operations	**(4,662)**	**44**	**3,978**	**7,319**	**7,457**	**12,614**
Cash flow from investing activities						
Purchase of land	—	—	—	—	—	—
Purchase of building/equip.	—	—	—	—	—	—
Total cash used	—	—	—	—	—	—
Net cash flow from investing	—	—	—	—	—	—
Cash flow from financing activities						
Equity						
Investment by owners	—	—	—	—	—	—
Debt						
Long-term loan additions (payments)	—	—	—	—	—	—
Net cash flow from financing	—	—	—	—	—	—
Net increase (decrease) in cash	(4,662)	44	3,978	7,319	7,457	12,614
Short-term loan increase (decrease)	—	—	—	—	—	—
Beginning cash	150,825	146,163	146,207	150,185	157,504	164,961
Ending cash	146,163	146,207	150,185	157,504	164,961	177,574

	Jul.	Aug.	Sep.	Oct.	Nov.	Dec.
Cash flow from operations						
Receipts						
Cash sales	—	—	—	—	—	—
Accts. receivable collections	333,115	345,115	367,130	379,495	412,355	415,960
Total cash received	**333,115**	**345,115**	**367,130**	**379,495**	**412,355**	**415,960**
Disbursements						
Operating expenses	320,768	324,948	336,388	343,138	366,755	365,320
Interest on loans	—	—	—	—	—	—
Total cash used	**320,768**	**324,948**	**336,388**	**343,138**	**366,755**	**365,320**
Net cash flow from operations	**12,347**	**20,167**	**30,742**	**36,357**	**45,600**	**50,640**
Cash flow from investing activities						
Purchase of land	—	—	—	—	—	—
Purchase of building/equip.	—	—	—	—	—	—
Total cash used	—	—	—	—	—	—
Net cash flow from investing	—	—	—	—	—	—
Cash flow from financing activities						
Equity						
Investment by owners	—	—	—	—	—	—
Debt						
Long-term loan additions (payments)	—	—	—	—	—	—
Net cash flow from financing	—	—	—	—	—	—
Net increase (decrease) in cash	12,347	20,167	30,742	36,357	45,600	50,640
Short-term loan increase (decrease)	—	—	—	—	—	—
Beginning cash	177,574	189,921	210,088	240,830	277,187	322,787
Ending cash	189,921	210,088	240,830	277,187	322,787	373,427

Bookstore

Betty's Books

729 Main St.
Miami, Florida 33109

Gerald Rekve

Betty's Books is a start–up used bookstore in Miami, Florida. It is the target of the company's management to acquire local market share in the used bookstore industry through low price, a sthe osition are olid inventory of books, a variety of services including a new and used books, hard-to-find and antiquarian books, plus a relaxing, friendly environment that encourages browsing and reading. New to book stores will be a place for people to sit and read while enjoying a nice brewed coffee from a list of fine coffee makers.

EXECUTIVE SUMMARY

Introduction

Betty's Books is a start–up used bookstore in Miami, Florida. It is the target of the company's management to acquire local market share in the used bookstore industry through low price, a solid inventory of books, a variety of services including a new and used books, hard-to-find and antiquarian books, plus a relaxing, friendly environment that encourages browsing and reading. New to book stores will be a place for people to sit and read while enjoying a nice brewed coffee from a list of fine coffee makers.

Company

Betty's store will be set up in a strip mall in an upper-end section of town. The company will be jointly owned by Mr. Bob Brown, a former head librarian of the Florida City Library, and his wife Betty.

Mr. Brown is establishing this firm as a growth–oriented endeavor in order to supplement his retirement, continue meeting people with similar interests, and to leave a viable business to his children.

Betty's Books will be establishing its store in one of the busiest sections of Miami. This area is well know for its upscale residents and high–quality establishments. Our facility is a former 8,000 square foot furniture store which allows the company to stock a large amount of inventory.

Products/Services

Betty's Books will offer a wide range of new books, magazines, and music selections. This includes just about every conceivable category including fiction, non–fiction, business, science, children's, hobbies, collecting, and other types of books. Our music selection will concentrate on CDs as these are the most popular and take up the least amount of floor space. In addition, we will be offering a competitive buy and trade service to assist in lowering our inventory acquisition costs and making our store more attractive to

41

our customers. We will also offer a search and order service for customers seeking to find hard-to-get items. Betty's Books will have a relaxed "reading room" type atmosphere that we will encourage through the placement of chairs, couches, etc.

Market

Our market has faced a decline in growth over the past two years. This is attributed to the overall weak economy. Book store industry sales rose only 3.6% for 2002 whereas overall U.S. retail sales grew by 4.1%. However, management believes that this may be an advantage to the used bookstore industry. As customers cut back on purchasing, used bookstores will look more attractive to customers who still wish to purchase books. Therefore, management believes this may be a good time to get into the industry and gain market share.

The bookstore industry as a whole is going through a large consolidation. Previously, the market was dominated by local, small stores and regional chains. With the advent of the "superstore" as created by Chapters, the largest players in the market have been able to gather significant market share and drive many independent booksellers out of the market.

Where independent booksellers can still create a viable position for themselves within the market is in the used books segment. This segment generally does not attract big companies since the superstore concept is much more difficult to replicate in a market with such low profit margins. This tends to favor the local independent bookseller in the used book market segment as long as they can acquire a sufficiently large enough facility to house an attractive inventory and compete with the national chains.

Financial Considerations

Our start-up expenses come to $157,820, which are single-time fees associated with opening the store. These costs are financed by both private investors and SBA loans. Please note that we expect to be operating at a loss for the first couple of months before advertising begins to take effect and draw in customers.

Funding will cover operating expenses during the first two years as it strives toward sustainable profitability. Funding has been arranged through lending institutions and private investors already. We do not anticipate any cash flow problems during the next three years.

These are the goals for the next three years for Betty's Books:

- Achieve profitability by July 2009

- Earn approximately $200,000 in sales by 2010

- Start paying dividends by 2009

Mission

Betty's Book's mission is to provide used quality literature of all types at the lowest possible prices in the Miami, Florida area. The company additionally seeks to provide a comfortable atmosphere for its clients that promotes browsing, relaxation, and an enjoyable environment to spend extend time in. Betty's attraction to its customers will be our large selection of books, magazines, used CDs and our purchasing/buyback option, which lower our book acquisition costs and allows our customers to discard unwanted books/CDs in exchange for cash or credit for future store purchases.

Keys to Success

Building a business, Betty's Books must keep the following issues in mind:

- Have solid group of books, with inventory books that are the best

- Gain large group of solid clients

- We must attain a high level of visibility through the media, billboards, and other advertising.

- We must establish rigid procedures for cost control and incentives for maintaining tight control in order to become the low–cost leader in used books.

- In order to continually attract customers, we must be able to keep the maximum amount of inventory available and achieve a high level of customer service.

COMPANY SUMMARY

Betty's will be a limited liability corporation registered in the state of Florida. The company will be jointly owned by Mr. Bob Brown, a former head librarian of the Florida City Library, and his wife, Betty.

Betty's Books will be establishing its store in one of the busiest sections of Miami, Florida. This area is well know for its upscale residents and high–quality establishments. Our facility is a former 8,000 square foot furniture store which allows the company to stock a large amount of inventory.

Company Ownership

Betty's will be a limited liability corporation registered in the state of Florida. The company will be jointly owned by Mr. Bob Brown a former head librarian of the Florida City Library, and his wife Betty Due to high start–up costs, the income and dividends to the principals will be limited for at least the first three years of operation.

The company plans to be leveraged through private investment and a limited number of loans. Mr. Brown is establishing this firm as a growth–oriented endeavor in order to supplement his retirement, continue meeting people with similar interests, and to leave a viable business to his children. Betty's Books will be established one of the busiest sections of Miami, Florida. This area is well know for its upscale residents and high–quality establishments. Our facility is a former 8,000 square foot furniture store which allows the company to stock a large amount of inventory. This facility is located in the front of the Town Square strip mall. This is an excellent location since it is across the street from the Twin Towers shopping mall.

Start–up Summary

Our start–up expenses come to $157,820, which are largely single time fees associated with opening the store. These costs are financed by both private investment and short– and long-term SBA guaranteed loans.

Start–up Requirements

Start–up Expenses

Legal—$2,400

Pre–sale advertising/marketing—$4,000

Land location and finders fee—$20,000

Insurance—$2,000

Rent—$6,500

Expensed Equipment—$15,000

Initial store facilities—$54,400

Other—$3,700

Total Start–up Expenses—$108,000

Start–up Assets Needed

Cash Balance on Starting Date—$33,820

Start–up Inventory—$16,000

Other Current Assets—$8,000

Total Current Assets—$57,820

Long–term Assets—$8,000

Total Assets—$63,820

Total Requirements—$157,820

Funding

Mr. Bob Brown—$55,000

Mrs. Betty Brown—$22,000

Total Investment—$77,000

Current Liabilities

Accounts Payable—$8,000

Current Borrowing—$15,000

Other Current Liabilities—$10,000

Current Liabilities—$33,000

Long–term Liabilities—$75,000

Total Liabilities—$108,000

PRODUCTS

Betty's Books will offer a wide range of book, magazine, and music selections. This includes just about every conceivable category including fiction, non–fiction, business, science, children's, hobbies, collecting, and other types of books.

Our music selection will concentrate on CDs as these are the most popular and take up the least amount of floor space. In addition, we will be offering a competitive buy and trade service to assist in lowering our inventory acquisition costs and making our store more attractive to our customers. We also offer a search and order service for customer seeking hard to find items. Another less obvious service to our customers will be the relaxed "reading room" type atmosphere that we will encourage through the placement of chairs, couches, and etc.

We strongly encourage our customers to spend as long as they like reading through our book selection and enjoying a quiet, relaxing environment. Our store hours will be 9:30 a.m. to 9:00 p.m. Monday— Friday and 10:00 a.m. to 6:00 p.m. Saturday and Sunday. Once profitability becomes stable, we may extend these hours.

MARKET ANALYSIS SUMMARY

Our market is facing a decline in growth over the past two years. This is attributed to the overall weak economy. Book store industry sales rose only 3.6% for 2009 whereas overall U.S. retail sales grew by 4.3%. Management believes that the economic slump may be an advantage to the used bookstore industry. As customers cut back on purchasing, used bookstores will look more attractive to customers who still wish to purchase books. Therefore, management believes this may be a good time to get into the industry and gain market share.

Used bookstores serve the entire purchasing population of its geographical area but focuses on the customer who desire to purchase books/music at a discount price and, with regards to books, often do not see a long–term attachment to the product.

Our main competitors are: Chapters (which holds approximately 22% nationwide market share), Borders (which holds approximately 15%), and other local new and used bookstores.

Market Segmentation

The company anticipates serving the needs of all the potential customers within a 10- to 30-mile radius in which the approximate population is 150,000 (based on census information).

The majority of the residents in this area are Caucasian (78.8%) Black (13.6%) and Hispanic (9%) with occupations classified as professional, homemaker, or retired. The majority of household incomes range from $50,000—$100,000 (50.3%).

The median income in this area is $49,980, compared to the whole Miami area which is $32,100. The typical head of household age is 25–34 (22.4%) or age 34–44 (23.1%) with a median age of 42.4 years old and an average age of 34 years old.

Target market segments

Used bookstores serve the entire purchasing population of its geographical area but focuses on customers who desire to purchase books/music at discount prices because they are seen either as near commodity items or, in the case of books, are not considered to be a long–term investment (i.e. they will trade them back).

Because of this relatively low value placed upon our merchandise by potential customers, Betty's Books can still flourish in an upscale environment like Miami. This is especially true with people seeking to cut costs with the bad economy. Even though we service the entire book reading population in Miami and the surrounding area, we can divide our customers based on purchasing habits.

- *Casual Shoppers*: These are customers who go to the bookstore with no set idea of what they want to purchase. They seek to spend a fair amount of time browsing the store and often are considered impulse buyers. Often they leave the store with small purchases or without buying anything. These customers are attracted to bookstores with low prices and large inventory.

- *Hard-to-Find Shoppers*: These are customers with very specific needs. They are looking for a difficult to obtain item, usually a book that is out of print. If we can satisfy this customer, then we are able to build significant customer loyalty. These clients are generally price insensitive and are also drawn to stores that have large inventory.

- *Specific Category Shoppers*: These customers are those types that generally buy books or music of one category, such as fiction or romance. These customers generally have a good idea of what they want to purchase and have the greatest buyback/trade potential. These customers represent the highest volume purchaser, often leaving the store having spent $44–$56.

Industry Analysis

Our market is facing a decline in growth over the past two years. This is attributed to the overall weak economy. Book store industry sales rose only 3.6% for 2009 whereas overall U.S. retail sales grew by 4.6%.

However, management believes that this may be an advantage to the used bookstore industry. According to interviews made by Mr. Brown with bookstore owners and managers, the used book industry has typically done better than other retailers during economic downturns. As customers cut back on purchasing, used bookstores will look more attractive to purchase books. Therefore, management believes this may be a good time to get into the industry and gain market share. As the weak economy continues, we expect growth to be initially quite high but overall volume sales to be low, and then seeing this taper off to industry norms.

The bookstore industry as a whole is going through a large consolidation. Previously, the market was dominated by local, small stores and regional chains. With the advent of the superstore as created by Chapters, the largest players in the market have been able to gather significant market share and drive a lot of independent booksellers out of the market.

Where independent booksellers can still create a viable position for themselves is within the used books segment. This segment generally does not attract big companies since the superstore concept is much more difficult to replicate in a market with such low profit margins. Dominant selection, both in used and new books is the key to bringing in new customers and the only way to do that is to operate at a low–price leader. These two factors tend to favor the local independent bookseller in the used book market segment as long as they can acquire a sufficiently large enough facility to house an attractive inventory and locally compete with the national chains.

Competition and Buying Patterns

Our main competitors are: Chapters (which holds approximately 22% nationwide market share), Borders (which holds approximately 15%), and other local new and used bookstores. The used bookstore that most closely rivals our own is Chapters Books which is located approximately 13 miles away from our store. It is estimated that they hold 9% of the local market share.

Management feels it must be clearly stated that we do not intend to directly compete with the Chapters superstores. Superstores are large and carry approximately 50,000 titles per location. Over the years, these large companies has successfully leveraged their resources to engineer customer experience to a degree that consistently differentiates otherwise commodity–like products and services. This differentiation provides these companies strategic competitive advantage. Resources such as distribution technology, strategic alliances, process research and development, and brand name combine into value–added services that provide the customer with proximity, dominant selection, discounts, and store ambiance.

This is simply beyond our capacity and we will be fulfilling a sufficiently different need for our customers. However, we believe that we can successfully duplicate the differentiated experience for our customer without the overall costs.

STRATEGY AND IMPLEMENTATION SUMMARY

Betty's competitive edge will be the lower prices we will charge our customers and the dominant selection above what our used bookstore rivals can offer. This is based on management's industry knowledge, greater capitalization, and excellent location. One of the most critical element of Betty's success will be its marketing and advertising.

In order to capture attention and sales our company will use prominent signs at the store locations, billboards, media bites on local news, and radio advertisements to capture customers. We expect an average 2.5% increase in sales during the first few years as we establish ourselves in the community.

After that we assume a much higher average growth of between 12%–14% growth over the next five years with growth then tapering off to the industry average of 2.5% from year to year. These figures may seem very high, but considering the level of initial sales and the growth possibilities, management actually considers this to be conservative.

Competitive Edge

The company's competitive edge will be the lower prices we will charge our customers and the larger selection we can offer: through our large store, buyback/trade program, and leveraging management's excellent supplier contacts. As stated before, in the bookstore industry, low cost and dominate selection are the two success criteria. We plan to create these advantages in a new, comforting environment that will retain customers.

Marketing Strategy

One of the most critical elements of Betty's Book's success will be its marketing and advertising. In order to capture attention and sales, our company will use prominent signs at the store locations, billboards, media bites on local news, and radio advertisements to capture customers. Also we will be focused on internet advertising and newspaper advertising.

Sales Strategy

Since our store will be a stand-alone facility, there is little in the way to directly influence how we close the sale other than to have an attractive storefront with our low prices and excellent selection. We believe this in itself is its own seller. One critical procedure we will be establishing is to insure top customer service and reliability and that our store always has enough inventory of all our products. We will be using industry data on inventory for bookstore chains to assist us.

MANAGEMENT SUMMARY

As stated earlier, Betty's Books will be an sole proprietor company owned by Mr. Bob Brown and his wife, Betty. Mrs. Brown is expected to assist Mr. Brown in various ways and to act as the company's bookkeeper.

The owner's son, Ben, is currently a business major at Florida State University and is expected to graduate in 2009. He has expressed an interest in eventually taking over the management of the company and will be working as a part–time manager with this goal in mind. The company also plans to hire various part–time salespeople as needed. Additional personnel will be added if necessary.

Personnel Plan

Initially the company will have a small staff including upper management and sales personnel. We expect to expand our personnel and extended hours once we begin to make a profit.

FINANCIAL PLAN

Please note that we expect to be operating at a loss for the first couple of months before advertising begins to take effect and draw in customers.

Car Service

The Personal Touch Car Service

123 Main St.
Plymouth, MI 48170

Heidi Denler

The Personal Touch Car Service seeks to offer residents of the western suburbs of Detroit an elegant option to get from point A to point B for any occasion from weddings and proms to funerals to rides to the airport.

COMPANY SUMMARY

The Personal Touch Car Service seeks to offer residents of the western suburbs of Detroit an elegant option to get from point A to point B for any occasion from weddings and proms to funerals to rides to the airport. Even a trip as simple as getting Grandma to her doctor's appointment will be handled with dignity and caring. Jason Mandel, Kevin Lincoln, and Carl Smith will form an equal partnership that will be the basis for Personal Touch.

MANAGEMENT SUMMARY

Jason Mandel has been a charter bus and limousine driver for the past 12 years, the last five of which were combined with management of 10 drivers and their limos. Kevin Lincoln has had office management experience in the area transit authority main office, where he has been employed for almost 15 years, learning not only management skills, but also gaining an understanding of the needs and wants of area residents in regard to transportation. Carl Smith has been a successful entrepreneur since he started a video recording business in when he was in high school. He has continued to create niche businesses based on keen observation of those around him. As a result, he put himself through college and received his MBA from the Wharton School with no debt. That experience will be put to use guiding Jason and Kevin as they start Personal Touch. The trio is confident that they will show a profit almost immediately.

Legal matters will be handled initially by Carl's company attorney, who is well-versed in corporate law and has been with Carl since the start. Financial concerns will be managed by an outside CPA that is an associate of Carl's.

MISSION STATEMENT

The Personal Touch will provide the ultimate premium ride for any event in a person's life, whether it is as special as bringing home a new baby or as mundane as a ride to the doctor's office.

VISION STATEMENT

The customer base of The Personal Touch will grow through personal references; affiliation with event planners, high schools, and colleges; and understated advertising.

VALUES STATEMENT

The partners are committed to providing quality service with a certain elegance, giving clients individual attention and consummate consideration.

BUSINESS PHILOSOPHY

Personal Touch Car Service will provide just what its name implies—a personal touch. Any client who engages the company will be treated royally, with great attention paid to detail.

ORGANIZATION STRUCTURE

The three owners will work together in one office attached to garage space where they will store and maintain their vehicles. They plan to begin operations with three vehicles: two stretch sedans and a party bus. All three owners have the required state licensing to drive the three vehicles, and they will hire a part-time driver who will be on-call to allow at least one owner to remain in the office during peak hours.

ADVERTISING AND PROMOTION

The target market for Personal Touch will be weddings/proms/night on the town, sightseeing, and transportation of the elderly and non-driving community. Airport transportation and corporate accounts will be offered, but are not expected to be primary sources of revenue.

Direct marketing efforts will be made to event planners, hotel concierge services, B&Bs, and assisted living communities, who offer the company contacts with their target audience. Tri-fold color brochures with photos of the car fleet and photos representative of Personal Touch's offerings will be printed to place in racks at B&Bs and hotels, as well as at the airport. These would especially point to the sightseeing and special outing (casino, night on the town, concert) aspect of the business. A second brochure will be created to address the specific needs of event planners.

Business cards and magnets will be ordered from Allegra Printing in the Renaissance Center, which provides quality results in a timely manner.

Brochures, business cards, and magnets will be available in the cars as well, for customers to take with them at the end of their trip.

A web site is being developed to help build a customer base for out of town visitors to the area. Ads will be placed in local newspapers and in local telephone books, as well as magazines, such as *Hour Detroit*.

Press releases announcing Personal Touch will be sent to all local print, radio, and television venues. Personal phone and e-mail follow-up will be made to build a relationship with area media personalities, which is expected to result in free positive marketing and promotion.

CUSTOMER BASE

Hotel guests, event planners, and transportation for the growing senior non-driving population form a significant segment of the company's customer base. These customers are less susceptible to price concerns and are seeking reliable, quality service. Satisfied customers will be encouraged to provide feedback to their hotel concierge or event planner, which will encourage future business and foster a good working relationship with those sources.

The owners and future staff of Personal Touch will offer the diverse clientele reliable, time-saving service at a competitive price.

PRODUCTS AND SERVICES

Personal Touch Car Service will offer reliable transportation service to its neighbors along the I-275 corridor, which is lined with hotels. B&Bs are within a 15-mile radius, and the company will be close to Detroit Metro Airport, as well as being within a short drive to either the renowned University of Michigan Hospital and the Detroit Medical Center. The area is rebounding with sporting events and is a major stop for performers on concert tours. Group trips to the three Detroit casinos will also be offered.

Three vehicles will be in service at the beginning of operations. The two stretch sedans will be used for local transportation and sightseeing, while the party bus will be available for rental for a night on the town, family reunion transportation/sightseeing for groups up to 15, and airport transportation, although that will not be the primary focus for the company's services.

PERSONNEL REQUIREMENTS

The owners will be the primary drivers for the first two years. They will hire a knowledgeable mechanic, who will also be able to fill in as a driver as needed to provide a respite for the owners.

LOCATION

The partners have found a property in Plymouth, Michigan, that has 2,400 square feet total space, including 450 square feet of office space. The property has two 12 foot by 14 foot garage doors that would provide the necessary garage storage for the company's vehicles. Currently, the lease for the property would be $1,600 a month, which includes taxes, trash, and snow removal. The median age of area residents is 39, and they have an average income of $72,283 per year.

STORE DESIGN & EQUIPMENT

The base of operations for Personal Touch will be an office attached to a garage that will house the company's sedan, stretch sedan, and a limo coach.

The office will house a desk for each partner, along with filing cabinets, and shelving to store brochures and office supplies. The partners' laptops will be linked, and they will have a multi-line phone on each desk so anyone in the office can answer customer calls.

Two-meter shortwaves will be in all cars and at the office, along with cell phones and an Onstar/Sync form of hands-free communication, will keep the drivers and office in constant contact.

The garage will be stocked with equipment and supplies for minor repairs that are not covered under the company's leases. The staff mechanic will detail each car when it returns from an assignment so it is ready for the next client.

FINANCIAL

Start up costs will include lease payments on the three vehicles, rent for the office and garage, and the purchase of office and garage equipment and supplies. In addition, the company will pay the fees for standard security deposits and licensing by state and local governmental agencies. Other start up costs will include any fees for registration of the name and the business with all government authorities. In addition, the owners will have typical overhead costs of rent/mortgage payments, taxes, payroll, payroll taxes, key man insurance, property insurance, liability insurance, inventory, telephone and utilities, an alarm system, and advertising.

Personal Touch will also incur expenses for car washes (at least five per week at $10 each), advertising, gas, oil changes (done on site by the in-house mechanic), dues and subscriptions (for professional organizations and newspapers for customers), registrations and transfer fees for the vehicles, telephone and other utilities, credit card user fees, etc.

Expenses per hour for the sedans are projected to be approximately $18 per hour, including insurance and the driver, as well as fuel and oil. The company plans to charge $40 per hour with a two-hour minimum for typical limousine services. However, the minimum will be waived for driving the elderly to a medical appointment, and the rate will be reduced to $20 per hour.

Expenses per hour for the limo coach are expected to be around $28 per hour, and the company will charge $55 per hour with a three-hour minimum. Up to 15 people can travel in the limo coach comfortably, making a trip to the casino or a concert safe, reliable, and comfortable—and a special occasion.

PROFESSIONAL & ADVISORY SUPPORT

Personal Touch will use Carl Smith's corporate attorney for all legal matters. They will work with Smith's financial planners for life, health, dental, and key man insurance, as well as for retirement savings, property-casualty insurance, and liability insurance.

Personal Touch is seeking a line of credit to cover start-up costs and any losses for the first year of business, at which time the partners expect to be showing a strong profit margin.

BUSINESS AND GROWTH STRATEGY

Slow, steady growth is anticipated. The owners do not want to get caught in a trap of expanding too quickly, which would overextend their physical and personal resources.

As profits provide for additional cars to be leased, the company will expand its driving team. At the end of five years, the owners will only be driving occasionally. This will allow them to maintain a feel for customer needs and wants beyond the profit/loss statement, making adjustments to services offered.

Fleet vehicles will be maintained in the passenger area as well as under the hood, and will be replaced as deemed necessary to provide optimum, quality surroundings for customer comfort.

Telephone and web site contacts will be responded to promptly, recognizing that the customer's needs are a priority for the company. Repeat business will be important to the company, as will customer referral. To that end, courtesy, reliability, and customer comfort will be a priority.

COMPETITION

The transportation segment in Metropolitan Detroit is fairly competitive. However, there is no competition in the city of Plymouth. Personal Touch will target the wedding/prom/night on the town, sightseeing, and transportation of the elderly, non-driving segment of the community.

WEB SITE

Personal Touch plans an online presence for prospective customers to inquire about services and plan their outings. Return customers will be able to use the interactive web site to reserve the company's services.

CONCLUSION

Within 12 months, Jason, Kevin, and Carl expect that Personal Touch will be making enough of a profit to reinvest some of that money into a fourth vehicle, which will be a white limo, suitable for weddings. They have experience on their side, and are determined to fill a niche in their community that will enable them to be successful.

Children's Catering Business

Katering2Kidz Inc.

70 Main St.
Chestnut Grove, MS 38777

Paul Greenland

Katering2Kidz is a catering business focused on the children's market.

EXECUTIVE SUMMARY

Business Overview

Catering is often associated with weddings, fancy parties, and corporate events. A Mississippi corporation, Katering2Kidz Inc. will differentiate itself by focusing exclusively on the children's market. Specifically, we will provide catering services to daycares and private kindergarten programs, as well as to individual consumers who need assistance with birthday parties, picnics, and other kid–focused celebrations. In addition to providing everything from snacks and beverages to complete meal solutions, we also provide decorations for events and celebrations and recommend entertainment options known to us through affiliations with local and regional children's entertainers.

To further differentiate our business in the marketplace, we have established an agreement with Mack's, a locally–owned restaurant chain that serves high–quality fast food and is popular with both children and parents alike.

MARKET ANALYSIS

According to U.S. Census Bureau data, the state of Mississippi had an estimated population of 2.94 million people in 2008. That year, 7.5 percent of the population was under five years of age, compared to a national average of 6.9 percent.

The community of Chestnut Grove (population 17,862) is located within 25 miles of the larger city of Jacksonburg, Mississippi, which had an estimated population of 176,614 people in 2008. Roughly 8.3 percent of the population was under the age of five, compared to 7.5 percent statewide and will 6.9 percent nationally.

In 2010 Chestnut Grove was home to five daycare centers. Another ten centers were located in the smaller neighboring communities of Watertown and Greenhills. Of these daycare centers, three offer all–day kindergarten programs. For planning purposes, we will consider the communities of Chestnut Grove, Watertown, and Greenhills to be our primary service area (PSA).

Considerable opportunity exists within the larger Jacksonburg market, which was home to 65 daycare centers in 2010, 15 of which offered all–day kindergarten programs. Our business will consider Jacksonburg to be our secondary service area (SSA), where we will focus on expanding after establishing a strong foothold in our PSA.

Before deciding to move forward with our business, we conducted an informal survey of daycare centers in both our PSA and SSA, in order to gauge potential demand for our services. The survey was conducted via direct mail. In order to ensure a high response rate, recipients were provided with a postage paid return envelope. Additionally, follow–up phone calls were made to each center two weeks after the mailing. Our survey yielded the following results:

- 55 percent of respondents currently prepare both meals and snacks in–house.

- 30 percent currently rely on an outside source for both meal and snack preparation.

- 15 percent have parents pack meals and snacks

- Of the centers that currently prepare both meals and snacks in–house, 35 percent indicated a potential interest in outsourcing this service within the next 24 months, if that service offered food of a comparable quality at a lower price.

Based on the results of this survey, we feel that we have excellent growth prospects in our PSA and SSA.

INDUSTRY ANALYSIS

According to data from the firm Research and Markets, the catering industry included more than 10,000 companies during the late 2000s, generating a collective $5 billion in annual revenues. With the largest 50 firms generating less than 15 percent of revenues, our industry is very fragmented. The catering industry also is very labor–intensive. Off–premises caterers constitute 40 percent of the industry, while on–premises caterers represent 40 percent of the industry.

In early 2010, the publication *Food Service Director* released the results of its "2009 Catering Study," drawn from the responses of large food service operators. According to the research, 91 percent of respondents offered continental breakfast, followed by lunches with deli meats, salads, and buffets (89%). A like percentage offered break service (pastries and cookies), 86 percent provided hot and cold buffets, 83 percent served both box and plated meals, and 56 percent provided service for cocktail receptions. The same *Food Service Director* study found that mid–day meals constituted the majority of business (41%) for large food service operators. Breakfast was the next largest category at 26 percent, followed by dinner (24%) and special events (9%).

According to the Bureau of Labor Statistics' *Occupational Outlook Handbook, 2010–11 Edition*, employment of non–restaurant food servers totaled 189,800 in 2008, and was projected to reach 209,100 in 2018, an increase of 10 percent.

PERSONNEL

Katering2Kidz is owned and operated by Brian and Sandy Rogers, who have 25 years of combined experience in the food service industry. Before getting married, the Rogers met while working at a restaurant in Lexington, Kentucky. When family circumstances prompted them to return to Chestnut Grove, Brian and Sandy decided to pursue a long–time dream: owning their own business.

With two teenage children, the Rogers had plenty of experience planning birthday parties and special celebrations for both children and adolescents. Realizing that Chestnut Grove was home to a disproportionately large number of families with children, they decided to take advantage of an untapped market niche that made use of their party planning knowledge and food service industry experience.

The Rogers are responsible for the day–to–day operation of the business. The owners are joined by two part–time staff members who assist with food preparation and delivery. In addition, when help is needed with larger parties or functions, they will contract with a small team of reliable independent contractors.

Professional & Advisory Support

Katering2Kidz has established a business banking account with Central Community Bank, including a merchant account for credit card payments. Tax advisement is provided by Chestnut Grove Tax Advisors LLC. In addition, legal services are provided by the Law offices of Robert M. Smith.

GROWTH STRATEGY

Our catering business plans to spend its first year of operations developing a reputation within the local market and building a base of core customers comprised of daycare centers and private kindergarten programs. It is our belief that customers such as these are the most "recession proof," compared to individuals hosting parties and special events, which are more dependent upon discretionary income. After our core customer base has been established, we will begin to focus more on the party and celebration market (e.g., likely during our second year of operations). In addition, we also will focus on new markets such as museums and conservation centers, which frequently host large groups of children on field trips.

The local church that leases the facility in which our kitchen is located (a former restaurant) has plans to relocate to a new building in 24 months. At that time, the building owner has given us an option to lease the remainder of the facility, or purchase the property from him. Assuming that our growth projections are accurate, during our third year of operations we have tentative plans to purchase the facility and use it for children's (ages 12 and under) birthday parties and related functions. Our plan is to initially add play equipment (e.g., climbing towers and ball pits, etc.) on the second story, and use the existing multipurpose space on the first story for food service and entertainment.

Longer–term (potentially in five to seven years), our vision is to take advantage of the facility's large lot and add mini putting and batting cages on the premises, as well as a service counter selling ice cream, soft drinks, and other refreshments. The local market is currently lacking an entertainment destination such as this.

SERVICES

From snacktime to lunchtime, we offer daycare centers and private kindergarten programs comprehensive, turnkey food and beverage solutions. In addition to meeting daycare operators' daily needs in these areas, we also provide services for special events, such as holiday parties, open houses, fun fairs, field trips, school picnics, and more.

Katering2Kidz ownership is the primary contact with our clients. The Rogers meet with daycare operators and individuals to discuss their goals. They then work through the planning process and develop custom catering solutions based on their customers' unique needs. All meals are prepared off–premises and delivered to the customer.

Although there is a certain degree of flexibility to the food and beverage selections we are able to offer, the following is a list of core items that comprise the majority of our menu:

Beverages

- Low–Fat Chocolate Milk
- 2% Milk
- Whole Milk
- Skim Milk
- Cherry Juice
- Orange Juice
- Apple–Grape Juice
- Strawberry Juice

Breakfast Selections

- Flavored Oatmeal
- Cereal (Chex, Cheerios, Kix, Froot Loops, Frosted Flakes, Golden Grahams)
- Muffins (Blueberry, Apple/Cinnamon, Banana)
- Jelly Toast
- Cinnamon Rolls
- Pancakes
- Apple Wedges
- Bananas
- Bagels
- Fresh Fruit

Morning Snack Selections

- Banana Bread
- Animal Crackers
- Hard Boiled Eggs
- Bread Dough Inch Worms
- Ritz Crackers with Cheese Spread
- Granola Bars
- String Cheese
- Apple Cubes
- Donut Holes
- Raw Veggies
- Cottage Cheese
- Raisins

Lunch

- Peanut Butter & Jelly Sandwiches
- Turkey and Cheese Sandwiches
- Ham and Cheese Sandwiches
- Beef Tacos
- Tomato Soup
- Chicken Noodle Soup
- Raw Veggies
- Mixed Vegetables
- Pears
- Nectarines
- Hotdogs
- Chicken Fingers
- Macaroni & Cheese
- Fish Sticks
- Assorted Fruits

Afternoon Snack

- Graham Crackers
- Pretzels
- Fruit Snacks
- Cheese Crackers
- Strawberries
- Bananas
- Cheese Cubes
- Ritz Crackers

To further differentiate our business in the marketplace, we have established an agreement with Mack's, a locally–owned restaurant chain that serves high–quality fast food and is popular with both children and parents alike. Mack's does not have the resources to provide catering services directly. However, we have made arrangements to occasionally provide a number of their popular menu selections to our customers in exchange for a share of the profits.

MARKETING & SALES

Katering2Kidz has developed a marketing plan that focuses on the following target markets:

Primary Target Markets:

- Daycare Centers
- Private Kindergarten Programs

Secondary Target Markets:

- Museums
- Conservation Centers
- Children's Birthday Parties
- Special Events
- Picnics

Our marketing plan involves the following primary tactics:

- A color flier describing our business.
- Periodic direct mailings to prospective customers.
- A Web site with complete details about our business and the services we offer.
- "Drop–ins" to prospective customers, which will provide us with an opportunity to develop a face–to–face connection with key decision–makers.
- "Bonus Days," where we will provide prospective customers with one meal (breakfast or lunch) and one snack for their school at cost, in order for them to experience how we work and our customer service.
- A referral program, whereby we will give existing customers a 15 percent discount off their monthly bill for each customer they refer to us.

OPERATIONS

Customers

Our business has established contracts with five daycare centers (four in our PSA, and one in our SSA), and will begin providing services in June 2010. Our customers include:

1. Small Smiles Daycare—This church–based daycare program has 20 students, to whom we will provide breakfast, lunch, and two snacks.

2. Happy Beginnings Daycare—Based at local community center, this daycare program has 25 students, as well as 20 students in an all–day kindergarten program, to whom we will provide breakfast, lunch, and two snacks.

3. PlayWorld Daycare—This daycare program, which includes 22 students, is sponsored by a local manufacturing company, mainly for its employees. We will provide breakfast, lunch, and two snacks.

4. Rainbow Connection Daycare—This home–based daycare program has six students, to whom we will provide lunch and one snack only.

5. Miss Patty's Daycare—This home–based daycare program has eight students, to whom we will provide lunch and one snack only.

Facility & Location

Katering2Kidz operates from a former family restaurant that closed its doors during the economic recession of the late 2000s. We made arrangements to lease the fully equipped commercial kitchen for our business. The building owner has included all utilities in our lease. Although no telephone service is provided, we have purchased a cellular phone contract, which enables customers to reach us anywhere, at any time.

The owner of the building has converted the former dining room area into a multipurpose room. This space is currently utilized by a new church for Wednesday evening and Sunday worship services. One unique aspect of the former restaurant is that it is a two–story facility, with elevator service and additional dining space upstairs. The church currently leases this space as well, for storage and meeting purposes.

As mentioned in the Growth Strategy section of this plan, the building owner has given us an option to lease the remainder of the facility, or purchase the property from him, once the church's lease expires in two years. This facility will allow us to expand our business in a number of different ways.

Vehicles

Our business has purchased a used catering truck (2000 Ford F–350), equipped with a refrigerated compartment that operates on the road, or via a standard electrical outlet. The truck includes an oven in the rear, as well as various storage compartments. The purchase price for the truck is $7,450. In addition, we also have purchased a used support trailer ($6,500), which includes storage compartments, a refrigeration unit, a generator, and a warming compartment. We have financed these vehicles for three years (10% interest).

Equipment

A number of equipment items are needed for ongoing operations. These include table setting items (dinner plates, silverware, and cups) and serving equipment (water pitchers, bus tubs, serving trays, serving utensils, etc.). We also will need to purchase a variety of disposable items (disposable silverware, cups, table cloths, plastic wrap, tinfoil, hand sanitizer, garbage bags, cleaning rags, paper towels, etc.) on an ongoing basis.

Suppliers

Katering2Kidz has negotiated supplier agreements with several regional and national food–service wholesalers:

- Brandenburg Foods

- Bountiful Harvest Bread Co.

- Reynolds Produce

- Lexington Food Products Corp.

LEGAL

Katering2Kidz adheres to all local, state, and federal regulations pertaining to food handling and safety. Specifically, we adhere to the Mississippi Food Code, which follows national standards for food safety issued by the U.S. Food and Drug Administration. As required, we have secured a food permit from the Mississippi Department of Public Health, and comply with all regulations established by our county health department.

Even when following recommended practices, food poisoning is always a potential risk for businesses in the food industry. For example, food poisoning may result due to negligence on the part of a food distributor, wholesaler, or supplier. Our business has secured appropriate insurance coverage pertaining to personal liability, equipment, and vehicles.

FINANCIAL ANALYSIS

Following is Katering2Kidz's projected balance sheet for its first year of operations (fiscal year beginning June 1, 2010), based upon the contracts we have established with our new customers, as well as estimated revenue from parties and special events.

In addition to covering initial kitchen equipment costs of $12,000, the owners are contributing $25,000 from savings toward daily business operations. Additionally, lines of credit have been established with the aforementioned food wholesalers.

Sales

Small Smiles Daycare	$ 30,600
Happy Beginnings Daycare	$ 68,850
Play World Daycare	$ 33,660
Rainbow Connection Daycare	$ 8,545
Miss Pat's Daycare	$ 10,254
Parties & special functions	$ 12,540
Total sales	**$164,449**

Expenses

Advertising & marketing	$ 1,000
General/administrative	$ 500
Legal	$ 2,250
Accounting	$ 2,000
Office supplies	$ 668
Computers/peripherals	$ 1,000
Business insurance	$ 2,500
Payroll	$ 85,000
Payroll taxes	$ 12,750
Facility lease	$ 4,800
Postage	$ 500
Telecommunications	$ 1,250
Kitchen equipment/supplies	$ 1,000
Vehicle loan	$ 5,400
Mileage	$ 6,000
Wholesale food	$ 83,200
Total expenses	**$209,818**
Net income	**($ 45,369)**

Although our business will declare a net loss during its first year of operations, we expect to turn a profit during our second year. Our projections are based on the addition of two to three clients per year, as well as growth in our parties and special functions business. In particular, we expect this portion of our business to begin growing during our third year, at which time we plan to purchase the facility in which we are currently leasing the kitchen only. Beyond the wholesale cost of food, our projections include major expense increases in the areas of payroll, mileage, and a commercial mortgage loan payment that includes the addition of commercial grade play equipment on the second level of the facility.

Net Income Projections

	2010	2011	2012
Sales	$164,449	$265,996	$335,521
Expenses	$209,818	$259,425	$316,775
Net income	($ 45,369)	$ 6,571	$ 18,746

Combination Coffeehouse/Play Spot

JavaJumpz LLC

2133 Swanson Ave., Store #146B
Richfield Park, IL 61116

Paul Greenland

JavaJumpz LLC is a new combination coffeehouse/play spot located in Richfield Park, Illinois. It is a relaxing place where parents can enjoy gourmet coffee, delicious sandwiches, desserts and adult conversation while their children have fun in an adjacent play area under the supervision of trained staff.

EXECUTIVE SUMMARY

Business Overview

JavaJumpz LLC is a new combination coffeehouse/play spot located in Richfield Park, Illinois. It is a relaxing place where parents can enjoy gourmet coffee, delicious sandwiches, desserts and adult conversation while their children have fun in an adjacent play area under the supervision of trained staff.

At JavaJumpz, we are committed to doing the right thing and setting a good example for the next generation. As much as possible, we purchase locally grown, organic food products from area growers and farmers. In addition, we serve fair trade coffee, in order to promote economic stability and self–sufficiency in developing countries.

In addition to utilizing the coffeehouse, at JavaJumpz parents have the option of shopping within the larger mall while their children play. A pager system is utilized to contact parents in the event of a problem. For security purposes, parents and children are provided with matching bracelets upon check–in.

History

JavaJumpz was established when two potential new business owners happened to be in the right place at the right time. Tracey Park was meeting with the owner of a coffeehouse that was for sale in the Richfield Park Mall. At the same time Michelle Upton, who had plans to open a business that provided supervised play for children while their parents shopped, was meeting with mall officials to discuss the vacant storefront next to the coffeehouse. After briefly discussing their respective plans, Upton and Park quickly discovered that their business ideas were complementary in a number of ways. Several meetings followed, resulting in the concept for JavaJumpz—a relaxing place where parents can enjoy coffee, food, and adult conversation while their children have fun in an engaging, supervised environment.

Business Philosophy

JavaJumpz is the destination of choice for busy parents who need a little time for themselves.

MARKET ANALYSIS

The growing community of Richfield Park is located in northern Illinois. In 2009 the area was home to 47,863 residents (18,743 households). According to a recent economic development study, the population is expected to grow through 2014, reaching 50,978 people (22,483 households). Median household income in 2009 was $62,883, compared to a national median of $53,684. In terms of race and ethnicity, 92.4 percent of the residents were white, followed by black (4.3%), Hispanic (2.8%), and Asian/Pacific Islander (0.5%). Richfield Park was home to 1,928 business establishments in 2009. White–collar employees accounted for 59.3 percent of the workforce, while blue–collar employees accounted for the remaining 40.7 percent.

The Richfield Park Mall, where our business will be based, is a destination not only for local residents, but also numerous households in smaller, neighboring communities.

Because our business concept is unique in the local marketplace, we have no pure competitors. The Richfield Park Mall does not currently offer any other type of daycare or supervised play business. Our main competition comes from other food and beverage retailers within the mall, especially those in the coffee and juice segment. Principal competitors include Starbucks, Joey's Java, Orange Julius, and Jamba Juice.

Market Segmentation

Based on a statistically significant independent survey of prospective mall customers, which the owners conducted with the assistance of students in a graduate statistics class at Richfield Park College, we anticipate our customer base will be segmented as follows:

- Two–Parent Households (60%)
- Single–Parent Households (20%)
- Grandparents (10%)
- Small Groups (10%)

INDUSTRY ANALYSIS

Due to the uniqueness of our business model, JavaJumpz is not included in one specific industry segment. According to research conducted by the owners, similar businesses have been established in other parts of North America, including the eastern United States and western Canada.

Food and beverage sales are a significant part of our operation. According to data from the National Restaurant Association (NRA), the restaurant industry had sales of $580 billion in 2010. According to the association's *2010 Restaurant Industry Overview*, the industry is a leading private–sector employer, providing jobs for approximately 12.7 million people who work at about 945,000 locations. Our establishment is part of the Eating Places segment of the industry, which generated sales of $388.5 billion in 2010.

PERSONNEL

Management

Tracey Park

A graduate of Northern State University, where she earned an undergraduate degree in business administration, Tracey Park's love affair with coffee began at an early age. During high school she worked as a waitress in a local hospital coffee shop that purchased its beans from a local roaster. In addition to being an avid coffee drinker herself, this job allowed her to learn about the business first-hand. In college, Park worked in a campus coffeehouse for four years, eventually rising to the position of assistant manager. Following graduation, Park secured a business development position for regional restaurant chain, which provided additional first-hand exposure to the food and beverage industry—especially the steps involved in establishing new locations. An entrepreneur at heart, she dreamed of the day and she could establish her own coffeehouse.

Michelle Upton

A graduate of Richfield Park College, Michelle Upton knows all about the needs of busy parents. A mother of three children who are close in age, she took a temporary break from professional life to concentrate as much time as possible on her young ones. Even so, she realized that a busy mom needs time for herself, and with her spouse. Now that her children are in junior and senior high school, Upton is ready to put her business skills back to work. Her professional background includes experience managing a temporary staffing service, where she was responsible for managing budgets, business development, and customer relationship management. She also has unique insight into the staffing challenges faced by businesses in a wide range of industries.

Staffing

In addition to the owners, JavaJumpz will employ 13 part-time staff, including:

- 2 kitchen staff
- 3 counter staff
- 6 play area staff
- 2 baby room staff

Kitchen staff will provide coverage in four-hour shifts (10:30 AM—2:30 PM and 3:30 PM—7:30 PM, Monday through Saturday; 10:30 AM—2:30 PM on Sunday).

Counter staff will work six-hour shifts Monday through Saturday (9:30 AM—3:30 PM and 3:30 PM—9:30 PM) and eight-hour shifts on Sundays (10:30 AM—6:30 PM).

Play area and baby room staff will work six-hour shifts Monday through Saturday (9:30 AM—3:30 PM and 3:30 PM—9:30 PM) and eight-hour shifts on Sundays (10:30 AM—6:30 PM).

Generally speaking, one counter person will be on duty at all times, with the exception of peak hours (11 AM—1 PM, and 5 PM—7 PM), when the assistance of an additional counter person (or one of the owners) will be needed. Typically, two play area staff will be on duty at all times, except during peak hours, when three staff members will be on duty. One staff member will be dedicated to the baby area at all times.

Professional and Advisory Support

JavaJumpz has retained the local accounting firm of Blake & Associates to assist us with bookkeeping and tax responsibilities. Commercial checking accounts have been established with Richfield Park Bank, a local bank that also is providing us with partial financing. Additionally, Richfield Park Bank has assisted us with the establishment of merchant accounts, so that we are able to accept credit card and debit card payments.

BUSINESS STRATEGY

JavaJumpz's business strategy is simple. First, we are dedicated to providing busy parents with a little time for themselves. Our business not only allows adults to make the most of their leisure time, it creates leisure time.

Second, our business is committed to our customers' good health. According to data from the American Restaurant Association, compared to only two years ago 73 percent of adults are trying to eat healthier while at eating establishments. Along these same lines, ARA data suggest that more than half of adults are more likely to visit establishments offering food that is either organically grown or grown in an environmentally–friendly manner. With this information in mind, we will always provide a selection of wholesome drinks, desserts, and sandwiches for health–conscious eaters, incorporating organic and/or locally grown ingredients whenever possible. For those parents who are trying to set a good example for their children, we also will offer a wide range of healthy snacks and items for children to eat while they are with their parents.

Finally, JavaJumpz will place a high premium on customer trust and loyalty. We realize that parents must feel good about the environment in which their children are playing, as well as the staff that is caring for them, so that they can truly relax. In addition to focusing on these things, we will treat our regular customers well by providing a loyalty program that offers discounts during their next visit. The strategy is in tandem with studies conducted by the ARA, which indicate that approximately 52 percent of adults choose to patronize establishments that offer a reward program.

Looking ahead, JavaJumpz will consider its first three years of operation as a "pilot phase," during which time the owners will consider the possibility of establishing additional locations in other communities. Potential expansion opportunities exist in the cities of Groverton (to the north) and Stanton (to the south). These communities are approximately 60 miles away from Richfield Park, within easy driving distance for the owners, and both have shopping malls.

PRODUCTS & SERVICES

JavaJumpz will offer the following menu items:

Beverages

All Natural Fruit Smoothies
- Banana
- Mango
- Peach
- Strawberry
- Wild Berry
- Strawberry Banana

Coffee & Tea Drinks (Single/Double sizes)
- Coffee
- Shot of Espresso
- Americano
- Breve
- Cafe Latte
- Chai Latte
- Cappuccino
- Mocha

- White Mocha

- Snickers

- Steamer

- White Chocolate Raz

- Hot Chocolate

- Green Tea

- Chai Tea

Special flavored coffees are offered daily (e.g, Hazelnut, Jamaican Me Crazy, etc.). Flavor and Varietal Coffees also sold by the half– and full–pound.

Sandwiches

- Turkey

- Ham

- Chicken Salad

White, Rye, Sourdough, or Wheat bread; Cheddar, American, or Swiss cheese.

Specialty Sandwiches
- Char Grilled Tuna Steak on Peasant Bread

- Fresh mozzarella, Tomato & Olives on Tuscan Bread with basil pesto

- Vegan Wrap—grilled tofu with summer vegetables wrapped in a fresh tortilla

Salads

- Caesar

- Garden

- Chicken Salad

- Fruit 'N Nut

Sides
- Potato Salad

- Pasta Salad

- Grapes

- Macaroni Salad

- Chips

There is one side free with sandwich purchase.

Desserts
- Pastries

- Muffins

- Croissants

- Scones

- Danishes

Kids Menu

Sandwiches
- Cheese

- Ham

- Turkey

- PB&J

Snacks
- Pretzels

- Fruit Snacks

- Apple Wedges

- Crackers

- Cookies

Beverages
- Fruit Juices

- Milk

- Water

MARKETING & SALES

A comprehensive marketing plan has been developed for JavaJumpz. The plan includes both short–term and ongoing tactics.

Short–Term Tactics

In the short–term, a number of promotions and activities are planned around launch of the business in the summer of 2010. Specifically, we will host three "You Deserve a Break" days, where we'll give away a free bottomless cup of coffee and one hour of complimentary supervised playtime for 20 lucky winners. We will publicize this promotion via radio advertising, as well as countertop displays and posters in the shopping mall. In addition, during our first year of operations we will pass out a limited number of coupons for a free cup of coffee to prospective customers (e.g., those with small children) walking around the mall.

Long–term Tactics

- *Coupons and Specials*—Each day, we'll offer special discounts on various food and beverage items. We will promote these on a special sign in front of our location, for easy viewing by passersby.

- *Loyalty Program*—We will develop a database of loyal customers, to whom we will send member–only coupons. In addition, for our loyalty club members, every fifth cup of coffee is free, and every fifth hour of playtime also is on–the–house.

- *Online Advertising*—JavaJumpz will advertise regularly on popular social media sites, such as Facebook. Compared to traditional print advertising, this is a cost effective tactic that will allow us to reach prospects in a highly targeted way (e.g., based on criteria such as age, gender, geography, etc.).

- *Web Site*—JavaJumpz will develop a simple Web site, which will provide basic information about our business, online sign–up for our loyalty club, our menu, pricing information, a JavaJumpz blog, as well as links to our presence on the aforementioned social media channels.

- *Radio Advertising*—During our first six months of operation, and during the busy holiday shopping season, our business will advertise on local country and soft rock stations, which have the highest concentrations of female listeners under the age of 40.

OPERATIONS

Suppliers

JavaJumpz has negotiated supplier agreements with several local food–service wholesalers and coffee wholesalers in the Richfield Park area that have a reputation for quality and reliability:

- Mean Beans Coffee Roasters

- Richfield Park Meats

- Healthy Harvest Bread Co.

- Forsberg's Bakery

- Sally's Organics

In the event that one of the aforementioned specialty suppliers cannot meet our needs, the following national suppliers can both provide all of the food–service products that we require. In addition, these wholesalers will supply us with general cooking and restaurant supplies:

- Lexington Food Products Corp.

- Croteau Food Supply Inc.

Hours

JavaJumpz will be open Monday through Saturday from 10 AM to 9:00 PM, and on Sunday from 11:00 AM to 6:00 PM.

Facility and Location

JavaJumpz is located within the Richfield Park Mall.

The footprint for our business consists of two adjacent storefronts. In addition to an existing coffee-house business, which has been in operation for five years, the new owners have purchased an adjoining retail space that will be converted into a supervised play area.

Separate entrances are available for the play area (for customers who choose to drop off their children and go shopping), as well as our coffeehouse (for customers who choose to relax and enjoy food and beverages). A four–sided counter allows staff to interact with and answer questions from passersby in the larger mall, check children in to the play area, and also interact with play area staff.

Specifically, 1,000 square feet of our operations is dedicated to the coffeehouse, while 1,500 square feet is devoted to our supervised play business. Separating both businesses is a multi–purpose area with a stage that children can use for puppet shows or dress–up activities. This space also can be utilized for special events, meetings, presentations, and entertainment.

Also located between the coffeehouse and the larger play area is Baby Land, an area dedicated specifically for infants (maximum capacity of six). This space is enclosed by four glass walls, allowing open viewing of the space from either the coffeehouse, the larger play area, or the multipurpose room.

Finally, the larger play area features padded rubber safety flooring (to prevent injuries) and several large play stations (e.g., with towers, slides, and ball pits). In addition, there are dedicated areas for arts and crafts/activities, as well as toys and game playing. Storage cubbies are provided for our guests to store their shoes, coats, and other belongings. A small space is available for the storage of collapsible baby strollers. Large windows allow mall patrons to watch children at play and see our business in action. The maximum capacity for our play area is 35 children. However, our policy is to limit capacity to 30 children at any one time. For security purposes, parents and children are provided with matching bracelets upon check–in.

Equipment

The coffeehouse portion of our business includes all necessary equipment and furnishings, because it is an existing operation. The supervised play portion of our operations will require a number of capital purchases, including:

- 1 Large Funhouse Climbing Station. Includes two towers, two slides, and a ball pit—$7,286

- 1 Medium Play Station. Includes one multi–platform cube and two slides—$5,456

- 2 Table–and–Chair Sets for Eight—$1,416

- 1 Balancing Bridge—$683

- Play Area Safety Surfacing (floor padding for 1,500 square feet)—$4,100

- 2 Dress–up Carousels—$500

- 3 Eight–bin Storage Units with Casters—$568

- 2 Wooden Storage Units (includes 12 plastic storage bins each)—$450

- 2 Storage Cubbies—$450

- 2 Wooden Book Display Units—$350

- 3 Shallow Arts & Craft Storage Tray Units—$1,000

- Wall Shelving—$500

- Wooden Changing Cabinet with Clear Trays—$550

- 2 Wooden Art Stations (each unit includes two easels, as well as plastic storage bins)—$725

- Assorted Toys, Games, Costumes, and Art Supplies—$3,000

FINANCIAL ANALYSIS

Following is a projected three–year income statement for our business. During the first three years of operation, we are projecting that supervised play revenues will increase at a compound annual rate of 2 percent, and food and beverage revenues will increase at a compound annual rate of 5 percent.

	2010	2011	2012
Sales			
Supervised play	$342,576	$ 349,428	$356,416
Food & beverage	$144,000	$ 151,200	$158,760
Total sales	**$486,576**	**$500,628**	**$515,176**
Expenses			
Advertising & marketing	$ 2,500	$ 2,500	$ 2,500
General/administrative	$ 1,500	$ 1,500	$ 1,500
Legal	$ 1,500	$ 750	$ 750
Accounting	$ 4,500	$ 3,750	$ 4,000
Office supplies	$ 1,500	$ 1,000	$ 1,250
Computers/peripherals	$ 12,500	$ 5,000	$ 5,000
Business insurance	$ 6,500	$ 7,000	$ 7,500
Payroll	$282,676	$296,810	$311,650
Payroll taxes	$ 42,014	$ 44,522	$ 46,748
Facility lease	$ 28,800	$ 30,240	$ 31,752
Postage	$ 500	$ 500	$ 500
Utilities	$ 12,600	$ 13,230	$ 13,892
Telecommunications	$ 1,800	$ 1,890	$ 1,985
Startup loan	$ 24,336	$ 24,336	$ 24,336
Play equipment	$ 25,584	$ 4,500	$ 4,500
Coffee distributor	$ 1,000	$ 1,050	$ 1,103
Food wholesalers	$ 1,675	$ 1,759	$ 1,846
Bakery	$ 850	$ 893	$ 937
Total expenses	**$452,335**	**$441,230**	**$461,749**
Net income	**$ 34,241**	**$ 59,398**	**$ 53,427**

Financing for JavaJumpz will consist of a $100,000 commercial loan (terms of five years, 8% interest) from Richfield Park Bank, which also has agreed to supply us with a $15,000 line of credit. In addition, each owner will contribute $40,000 of her own income from personal savings. We anticipate profits will increase considerably in 2015, following the payoff of the commercial loan.

Custom Denim Retailer

Patch Denim Company

Delmar Loop
University City, MO 63130

Michael Cisar and Mariana Valdesuso

Patch Denim Company is a custom denim retailer inspired by the raw nature of the Vans Warped Tour concert series which is in its 18th year of operation and sells over 1,000,000 tickets each year. It is an atmosphere where one can't help but get caught up in the music and let their inner–rocker come to life.

EXECUTIVE SUMMARY

There is nothing like the rush of a killer guitar solo played on a hot July afternoon in front of 20,000 screaming fans. When the guitars are plugged in to 10,000 watts of power, you feel every stroke as they sizzle on your skin. When the drummer pounds his thunderous double–bass pedal, your heart skips a beat. When the crowd can't stand the anticipation of their favorite band to take the stage, time stands still.

I don't know if you have ever experienced a rock concert where these sensations were a regular feeling, but until you do, you haven't experienced today's rock music. Music was never intended to be confined to your car's stock speakers. It was meant to be enjoyed in a live atmosphere where people live and breathe the lyrics, and wear clothing that mimics the lifestyle.

There is a subculture that exists in this country—a subculture that understands the power of a great song and an even better performance. This subculture is prevalent during the summer months and has come together with force over the past two decades. They call themselves punk rockers, and gather together on a regular basis every summer to celebrate rock music the way it was intended under the name: The Vans Warped Tour.

Patch Denim Company is a custom denim retailer inspired by the raw nature of the Vans Warped Tour concert series which is in its 18th year of operation and sells over 1,000,000 tickets each year. It is an atmosphere where one can't help but get caught up in the music and let their inner–rocker come to life.

Patch Denim will enter the market by acquiring a booth at the Vans Warped Tour. This booth will offer our products to fans and will be a great fit with the flea market atmosphere that compliments the acts on stage.

Most of the people that attend this series fall within the 16–24 demographic. These kids come with excitement and an expectation to get their hands on the next best trend in music, be it fashion, album releases, etc. This subculture is obsessed with being the first to discover something new. We plan to take a new idea and make it an essential element to the culture.

With our booth at the Vans Warped Tour, fans will be able to experience a slimmed–down version (compared to a future storefront) of what our artists can do, and what our products will look like. It will allow us to get our foot in the door of a very tough retail market, and it will attach our brand image to the atmosphere.

It is our passion at Patch Denim to offer a product that is truly unique. Fashion should not be mass–produced. It should be experienced in a raw, on–the–spot, creative way that transforms inspiration into lifestyle.

OBJECTIVES

1. Provide fans with a pair of jeans that no one else in the world has.

2. Become profitable after 2 years of business.

3. Open a storefront in Delmar Loop in third year of operation.

4. Build a polarizing brand image.

VISION AND MISSION

To combine creativity and attitude in a way that personality is tangibly expressed.

Patch Denim is in business to make a stand against mediocrity. We are tired of people having to settle for what's popular. We want to create options. We want those who want more out of life to get more. We want to help people make a statement about themselves through their jeans. We want people to wear a pair of jeans that can start a conversation.

We are dedicated to a higher moral standard than the government has given us. We are taking a stand. We are doing the right thing when no one is looking, and we are engaging people that are willing to listen. Denim may be our product, but we are in the business of changing lives.

COMPANY SUMMARY

Patch Denim Company (PDC) is a self–proclaimed retail–hybrid that combines the customization of Build–A–Bear Workshop with the quality standards of Abercrombie & Fitch, and the attitude and culture of today's alternative rock music. PDC will attach itself to the energy and excitement of the Vans Warped Tour (which is a nationwide, summer–long alternative rock concert series in its 18th year of business put on annually by Vans) with hopes of establishing a retail storefront on the Delmar Loop shopping district of University City, Missouri by September of its third year.

The focus of PDC is marketing and selling customized denim to alternative rock fans across the country. We have limited ourselves to this specific group of people, because our style of customization is already extremely popular within that subculture. We will hire fashion students to help ensure our customer's ideas are properly executed. The first two years of operation will focus on featuring our product at a major concert series across the country. The third year (and beyond) will continue the concert series as well as implement a plan to execute a storefront to compliment the established brand.

We believe that splitting up the launch into a two–step plan will allow us to take full advantage of the market without substantial risk in the early stages of development. The Vans Warped Tour allows us to test–run our products in many different cities across the country. We will be able to gather sales information that will help us determine which city is most receptive to what we have to offer. Furthermore, the up–front investment is significantly reduced by using this market penetration strategy.

During our first year of business we plan to establish a working relationship with a manufacturer; develop a product line; build a relationship with the Vans Warped Tour; and make all necessary transactions to ensure a smooth month of sales in July. We will hit only 20 stops during the month of July in an effort to test the market on a relatively low budget. We believe that in order to properly build a brand image and market our product as laid out in the plan, we will need to acquire a small business loan. This loan will be enough to cover all expenses and asset acquisitions for the first year of business. Our second year will consist of a full tour, and will build on the success of the first year.

We plan to launch our storefront in the third year of business. This storefront will require an additional investment in order to be properly constructed. It will also cover all expenses and asset acquisitions, as well as provide necessary cash to cover any unprofitable sales months.

PRODUCTS

Patch Denim Company puts fashion in the hands of the customer. The product line will be kept simple, but the possibilities for what each customer can walk away with are endless. After an extensive search, we have decided to contract with Weihai Kinzer Apparel Company, Ltd. They are a relatively new manufacturer, but come with high credibility. Their operation is small enough that they value new customers, but big enough to provide the products we need at a price we can work with. It is our goal to visit China for an extensive plant tour in August 2010. We will then settle on a product line and begin production in order to have the necessary items shipped to St. Louis, Missouri in time to sell at the Vans Warped Tour 2011.

Below is a breakdown of each aspect of PDC (Vans Warped Tour and Delmar Location) that will help describe the process in detail as it pertains to each, respectively.

Vans Warped Tour

The Process:
Select a Canvas

Canvas choices consist of three basic styles with sizes ranging from 29 to 38 for guys and 0 to 12 for girls. Customers are welcome to try on any canvas in our fitting rooms to help decide which one best brings out their inner rocker. The size range has been selected based on our survey responses and personal interaction with fans at the tour.

Choose Your Package

Packages consist of customization options that customers can choose from. "The Opener" (Package 1) is the cheapest package available. It comes with 10 minutes of studio time (or design time with the artist) and allows the customer to apply bleach and cutting/fraying. "The Headliner" (Package 2) is the recommended best value package. It comes with 20 minutes of studio time and allows the customer to apply bleach, 1 solo (a free–handed sketch as per request of the customer that is applied with a permanent fabric pen), and cutting/fraying. "The Encore" (Package 3) is the premium package. It comes with 25 minutes of studio time and allows the customer to apply bleach, 2 solos, and cutting/fraying. Based on survey results and expected contribution margins, we believe these three customizing options will be the most popular and provide the best profitability. Studio time will be limited due to the expected high volume and limited workspace.

Create Design

Once a canvas and package are chosen, the customer will be paired with an artist to develop a blueprint. The blueprint features a front and back view of the canvas, and space on the back for the artist to develop a solo. Blueprints allow the artist and customer to develop a design that the customer wants and the artist can produce. Depending on the package purchased, the artist and customer will have only a few minutes of studio time to reach an agreement. Extra studio time can be purchased by the customer if they so choose.

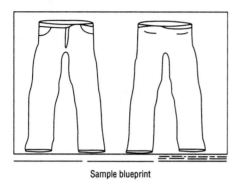

Sample blueprint

Sign Blueprint

Once the design is perfected, both the customer and the artist will sign the blueprint. This is a binding contract that states PDC will produce the product by the end of the day as per the design on the blueprint. Should PDC fail to provide the canvas as agreed upon, the money will be refunded.

Pay and Receive Pick–up Ticket

The actual production does not require any more time from the customer. However, production will not be started until payment has been received. Once paid for, the blueprint and corresponding canvas will be assigned a number that has also been given to the customer. This is to ensure proper delivery at the end of the day.

Backstage Pass (What we do while the customer enjoys the rest of the day)

PDC offers three simple customizing options each with their own required time of application. An artist's solo is a tedious effort that requires the most attention by our artists, and is therefore the most expensive option due to its opportunity cost. Although bleaching requires the canvas to be washed and dried immediately after application, multiple canvases can be washed and dried simultaneously. Furthermore, washing and drying will not require any artistic ability, and can be the responsibility of the part–time help. Cutting and fraying will be a quick process.

The Costs:
The Canvas

We are currently working on contract terms for a purchase order with Kinzer Apparel. Some basic information about denim purchasing is as follows:

- Custom labeling is available

- Minimum order quantity is 300 pieces per style

- Price per piece ranges from $6 to $10 (tax and shipping not included)

The Elements—Each element has been broken down into per unit costs:

- *Studio Time*—We pay our artists $100 per day, plus a $20 meal allowance per day, plus $40 to cover the price of admission. The concert is an 11–hour event; our artists will get two 30–minute breaks for meals; and will be expected to help set–up and tear–down at the start/end of each day. The total hours of work per day is expected to be 11 hours: 11–hour event plus 1 hour of breaks and 1 hour of set–up/tear–down. Total cost per day, per artist is $160. Therefore, it costs PDC $.25 a minute per artist.

- *Bleach*—Bleach is purchased in bulk powder form. On a per–unit basis, bleach will cost approximately $1 per canvas (wash and dry time included).

- *Cutting/Fraying*—Cutting/fraying costs are derived from the time it takes to produce the desired holes. This process is expected to take anywhere from 5–10 minutes (depending on the number of holes) resulting in an expected average cost of $2.

- *Artist Solos*—Solo costs are derived from the time it takes to produce the free–handed design, which is dependent on the intricacy of the solo. The average time spent on a solo is expected to be 15–25 minutes resulting in an expected artist cost of $3.75–$6.25. Also, the cost of the fabric pen per canvas is expected to be $0.50.

- *Blueprint*—Each blueprint will cost a total of $.05 (paper and printing)

The Packages—Based on the per unit element costs, the packages have been broken down into expected total costs:

"The Opener"

Studio time	$ 2.50 (10 minutes)
Bleach	$ 1.00
Cutting/fraying	$ 2.00
Canvas	$15.00
Blueprint	$ 0.05
Total package cost	**$20.55**

"The Headliner"

Studio time	$ 5.00 (20 minutes)
Bleach	$ 1.00
Cutting/fraying	$ 2.00
Artist solo	$ 5.00 (1 solo)
Canvas	$15.00
Blueprint	$ 0.05
Total package cost	**$28.05**

"The Encore"

Studio time	$ 6.25 (25 minutes)
Bleach	$ 1.00
Cutting/fraying	$ 2.00
Artist solo	$10.00 (2 solos)
Canvas	$15.00
Blueprint	$ 0.05
Total package cost	**$34.30**

The Pricing:

Based on survey results, current competitor prices, and personal experience, we believe the market will bear the following pricing scheme:

The Canvas—Canvas pricing will be one flat price for any style for both guys and girls. PDC expects that the market will support a base price of $25 per canvas, resulting in an expected per–item profit of $10 after shipping costs and taxes are applied.

The Packages—A package is a group of customizing options and are as follows:

"The Opener"

Basic package

Studio time	$10.00 ($1.00 per minute)
Bleach	$ 4.00
Cutting/fraying	$ 5.00
Canvas	$25.00
Blueprint	$ 0.00
Total package price	**$44.00 ($23.45 CM)**

"The Headliner"

Best value

Studio time	$15.00 ($0.75 per minute)
Bleach	$ 4.00
Cutting/fraying	$ 5.00
Artist solo	$10.00
Canvas	$25.00
Blueprint	$ 0.00
Total package price	**$59.00 ($30.95 CM)**

"The Encore"

Premium package

Studio time	$18.00 ($0.72 per minute)
Bleach	$ 4.00
Cutting/fraying	$ 5.00
Artist solo	$15.00 (2 solos)
Canvas	$25.00
Blueprint	$ 0.00
Total package price	**$67.00 ($32.70 CM)**

Extra Studio Time—In the event that a customer wants more time with our artist than allotted by his/ her package, they can choose to purchase extra studio time at the following rates:

10 minutes	$10	($1.00 per minute)
15 minutes	$12	($0.80 per minute)
20 minutes	$17	($0.85 per minute)

Delmar Loop Storefront

The Process:

Select a Canvas

Canvas choices in the storefront will be expanded to five denim styles as well as a basic 100% cotton T–shirt available in a variety of colors that can be customized. Customers are welcome to try on any canvas in our fitting rooms to help decide which one best brings out the inner rocker.

Choose Your Package

Packages consist of customization options that customers can choose from. "The Opener" (Package 1) is the cheapest package available. It comes with 15 minutes of studio time(design time with the artist) and allows the customer to apply any 2 verses (basic customizing options). "The Headliner" (Package 2) is the recommended best value package. It comes with 25 minutes of studio time and allows the customer to apply any 2 verses and 1 solo(a free–handed sketch as per request of the customer that is applied with a permanent fabric pen). "The Encore" (Package 3) is the premium package. It comes with 30 minutes of studio time and allows the customer to apply any 3 verses and 2 solos. Please note: although the studio time is limited, customers will be allowed to spend as much time in the store as they need to determine what they want. This luxury comes from the fact that the storefront will have much more room than the booth on tour. We will still charge for the time with our artists, but with an expanded array of customizing options, we understand the difficulty of making a decision.

Below is a detailed breakdown of the available verses.

The Set List (menu):

1. *Bleaching*—basic option that allows the customer to apply bleach to the canvas. It is generally a random, artistic application. This option will be applied after all other options have been applied, and requires washing and drying.

2. *Cutting/Fraying*—basic option that requires an artist's attention in full. With our tools, it is not a time–intense activity, however, messing this option up could mean having to start over.

3. *Patching*—basic option that allows the customer to apply a patch from their favorite band. We will have featured artists of the month and market them with CD releases and popular tour dates.

4. *Paint Splatter*—(add $4)—this option allows the customer to apply non–washable paint to their canvas in a splatter pattern. It is generally a random, artistic application.

5. *Stencil*—(add $7)—this option allows the customer to apply paint with a bit more structure. We will have a vinyl cutter that will cut out any picture in the form of a stencil.

6. *Screen print*—(add $10)—this option allows the customer to take any picture they want (assuming they have legal permission) and screen print it onto their canvas.

7. *Remix*—(add $20)—this option comes with an extra 15 minutes of studio time allows the customer to use their imagination and apply any of our options in a new way. It will generally be time–intense for our artists, but the freedom leads to new innovations.

Please note: solos can be traded for an extra verse, and extra verses can be purchased for an additional $3 each.

Create Design

Once a canvas and package are chosen, the customer will be paired with an artist to develop a blueprint. The blueprint features a front and back view of the canvas on a piece of paper that will allow the artist and customer to develop a design that the customer wants and the artist can produce. Depending on the package purchased, the artist and customer will have only a few minutes of studio time to reach an agreement. Extra studio time can be purchased.

Sign Blueprint

Once the design is perfected, both the customer and the artist will sign the blueprint. This is a binding contract that states PDC will produce the product by the end of the day as per the design on the blueprint.

Pay and Receive Pick–up Ticket

The actual production does not require any more time from the customer. However, production will not be started until payment has been received. Once paid for, the blueprint and corresponding canvas will be assigned a number that has also been given to the customer. This is to ensure proper delivery at the end of the day. Should PDC fail to provide the canvas as agreed upon, the money will be refunded.

The Costs:

The Canvas

We are currently working on contract terms for a purchase order with Kinzer Apparel. Some basic information about denim purchasing is as follows:

• Custom labeling is available

• Minimum order quantity is 300 pieces per style

• Price per piece ranges from $6 to $10 (for jeans) and $2–$5 (for tops)

The Verses—Each verse has been broken down into per unit costs:

• *Studio Time*—Each artist has a fixed cost of $0.15 per minute, and is paid 7.5% of the total selling price of each pair they work on.

- *Bleaching*—Bleach is purchased in bulk powder form. On a per–unit basis, bleach will cost approximately $1 per canvas (wash and dry time included).

- *Cutting/Fraying*—Cutting/fraying costs are derived from the time it takes to produce the desired holes. This process is expected to take anywhere from 5–10 minutes (depending on the number of holes) resulting in an expected cost of $2 per canvas.

- *Patching*—Patching is an inexpensive verse. The cost per patch varies depending on size and band, but we expect that the average price per patch will be $0.05 each due to bulk purchasing. The major costs incurred are a result of sewing the patch on. This process is expected to take 5–10 minutes resulting in artist time costs of $0.75–$1.50.

- *Artist Solos*—Solo costs are derived from the time it takes to produce the free–handed design, which is dependent on the intricacy of the solo. The average time spent on a solo is expected to be 15–25 minutes resulting in an expected artist cost of $2.25–$3.75. Also, the cost of the fabric pen per canvas is expected to be $0.50.

- *Paint Splatter*—Splattering paint is a quick process; however, the dry time is lengthy. The cost of paint is expected to be $0.75 per ounce. Artist time costs are expected to be $1.50–$2.25.

- *Stenciling*—Stenciling is a time–intense verse that requires detailed artist attention. Artist time costs are expected to be $2.25. Vinyl and paint costs are expected to be $2 per pair.

- *Screen Printing*—is an expensive option that requires artist time and special machinery. Machine costs are high due to per–item use. Expected artist time costs $4.50. Expected machine–use costs $3.

- *The Remix*—This option allows the customer to take our verses to the next level. It is often time–intense, uses a lot of equipment, and requires a lot of attention to detail by our artists; but the results are groundbreaking. Nothing parallels new imagination.

- *Blueprint*—Each blueprint will cost a total of $.05 (paper and printing)

The Packages—Based on the per unit element costs, the packages have been broken down into expected total costs. Please note: for Tops, use canvas cost $5. All verse costs will remain the same.

"The Opener"

Studio time	$ 1.50 (10 minutes)
2 basic verses	$ 5.00 (average cost)
Artist's cut	$ 3.53 (assuming sale price $47.00)
Canvas	$10.00
Blueprint	$ 0.05
Total package cost	**$20.08**

"The Headliner"

Studio time	$ 3.00 (20 minutes)
2 basic verses	$ 5.00 (average cost)
Artist solo	$ 3.00 (1 solo)
Artist's cut	$ 4.50 (assuming sale price $60.00)
Canvas	$10.00
Blueprint	$ 0.05
Total package cost	**$25.55**

"The Encore"

Studio time	$ 3.75 (25 minutes)
3 basic verses	$ 7.50 (average cost)
Artist solo	$ 6.00 (2 solos)
Artist's cut	$ 5.63 (assuming sale price $75.00)
Canvas	$10.00
Blueprint	$ 0.05
Total package cost	**$32.93**

The Pricing:

Based on survey results, current competitor prices, and personal experience, we believe the market will bear the following pricing scheme:

The Canvas—Canvas pricing will be one flat price for any style for both guys and girls. PDC expects that the market will support a base price of $25 per denim canvas and $10 per top canvas; resulting in an expected per–denim profit of $10 and per–top profit of $5 after shipping costs and taxes are applied.

The Packages—A package is a group of customizing options and are as follows:

"The Opener"

Basic package

Studio time	$10.00 ($1.00 per minute)
2 basic verses	$12.00
Canvas	$25.00
Blueprint	$ 0.00
Total package price	**$47.00 ($26.93 CM)**

"The Headliner"

Best value

Studio time	$15.00 ($0.75 per minute)
2 basic verses	$10.00
Artist solo	$10.00
Canvas	$25.00
Blueprint	$ 0.00
Total package price	**$60.00 ($34.45 CM)**

"The Encore"

Premium package

Studio time	$17.50 ($0.70 per minute)
3 basic verses	$15.00
Artist solo	$17.50 (2 solos)
Canvas	$25.00
Blueprint	$ 0.00
Total package price	**$75.00 ($42.08 CM)**

Extra Studio Time—In the event that a customer wants more time with our artist than allotted by his/her package, they can choose to purchase extra studio time at the following rates:

10 minutes	$10	($1.00 per minute)
15 minutes	$12	($0.80 per minute)
20 minutes	$15	($0.75 per minute)

MARKET AND DEMOGRAPHICS ANALYSIS

Vans Warped Tour

The Vans Warped Tour is an all–day rock concert that sweeps the country—visiting the top 50 rock cities every summer. The concert usually starts around 11:00am and finishes around 9:00pm (give or take a few minutes depending on encores). It is a summer event that starts at the end of June and it will go until the middle of August. Last year the tour estimated anywhere from 16,000 to 20,000 in attendance per stop, and sold over a million tickets during its entirety. This number has been increasing each year, making it the perfect storm for our market penetration strategy.

The average age group that attends these concerts falls between 16 to 25 years old. This age group is notorious for casual denim wear and self–expression. The tour is all about celebrating music, social movements, and making a statement. It is our goal to harness the excitement in the Vans Warped Tour atmosphere and use it to promote Patch Denim Sales.

Warped Tour fans know what to expect from this nationwide event. They will oftentimes bring loads of spending cash in expectation of the flea–market atmosphere full of band booths selling merchandise, street vendors selling random trinkets and food, and sponsors (such as Coca–Cola and Toyota) marketing their new products.

Our target market consists of those who have expendable cash and are willing to spend it on an unforgettable day. We are fully prepared to help our customers find that one item that will help them remember this day forever.

Our jeans will be competitively priced (as compared to Aeropostale, Hollister Co., Abercrombie & Fitch, Hot Topic, and The Buckle) with prices ranging from $19.99 up to $178.00. Understand that this is no ordinary pair of jeans. In fact, PDC jeans are the only jeans worth wearing to a concert. Your pair will be the only one like it in the world... completely unique to your personality, and one that even the rockers on stage will envy you for.

Delmar Loop Storefront

University City, Missouri is famous for its eclectic shopping strip known as the Delmar Loop. The Loop is an entertainment, cultural and restaurant district that is expanding eastward into the City of St. Louis proper. In 2007, the American Planning Association named the Delmar Loop one of the 10 best streets in America.

Most of the attractions are located along Delmar Boulevard, a major east–west thoroughfare that continues east to downtown St. Louis. A MetroLink station and parking garage are on the east side of the area. There are plans to build a 2.2 mile trolley from the Loop to Forest Park.

Major establishments in the Loop include: the Community Music School, the Craft Alliance, Vintage Vinyl, The Pageant Concert Nightclub, Tivoli Theater, Cicero's Italian Eatery and Entertainment Complex, Star Clipper, Blueberry Hill.

The Loop attracts an eclectic clientele and wide variety of street life, due in part to its proximity to Washington University. Although Delmar Loop is the closest thing to a college town retail area next to the university, few of the shops and restaurants have an exclusively college–student clientele. The Loop attracts young professionals and local teens as well as students from the nearby dorms.

Below is a breakdown of pertinent demographic information regarding the Loop and the surrounding Saint Louis Metropolitan area. These are estimates from 2008.

Area	Population	Target market	Avg. household income
Saint Louis metropolitan	2,820,816	33.70%	$43,000
Saint Louis County	995,118	23.50%	$51,000
Saint Charles County	343,952	37.20%	$57,000

INDUSTRY ANALYSIS

Our industry is commonly referred to as the Family Clothing Industry. The competitors offer a wide range of clothing styles and colors ranging from purple socks to upscale–casual wear. Sales are generally made to customers without further product development. Some of the main expenditures include: customer service, product merchandising, advertising, inventory control, and cash handling.

Patch Denim will be a new twist on an old trick. We will be one of the very, very few on–site clothing customization shops in the country, and therefore believe we will have a distinct competitive advantage over the competition. Some of those competitors include: Abercrombie & Fitch, Hollister Co., Aeropostale, Pacific Sunwear, Hot Topic, American Eagle, etc. In order to separate ourselves from the pack, we will not be found in malls with the rest of these clothing giants. In fact, we will only be found in the eclectic shopping districts of major metropolitan areas such as Delmar Loop in University City, Missouri.

The industry segmentation suggests that women's wear is the most profitable piece of the pie. Women's purchases make up 50% of the sales each year, while men's purchases make up 37%, and children's purchases make up 13%. Those numbers are expected to shift. Men's clothing purchases are expected to drop while the other two categories see a benefit. One major explanation is the fact that with less expendable income, men are choosing to buy for their families first, and spend what's left on themselves.

The recession has had an immediate negative impact on the family clothing industry. Less disposable income has led to a decrease in sales. Decreasing sales has caused retailers to make aggressive discounts. Those discounts have negatively affected the contribution margins. The industry is expected to undergo a reconstruction as companies refocus to a more concentrated approach. Many companies are planning to cut some of the styles and focus much more intently on offering only the most popular styles. Growth is not expected again until the second quarter of 2010. Any market growth and gains can be credited to the ventures of new stores, and not the sales of existing establishments.

The industry has steady, moderate barriers to entry: there are high costs to creating and managing a brand image; merchandise prices are at an all–time low to keep a competitive advantage; and the expertise required to predict future fashion trends takes years of experience.

The cost structure for a typical clothing retail store breaks down into six categories: purchases (69%), wages (10%), rent (5%), depreciation (1%), advertising (1%), other (10%). Profits generally come out to about 4% of the revenues generated for the month.

KEYS TO SUCCESS

Some key success factors for a typical clothing retail store include: having a clear market position, ability to control stock on hand, superior debt and financial management, production of currently favored goods, establishment of a brand name, attractive product presentation, and an experienced workforce. We want to briefly address each of the issues listed above as they pertain to the success of Patch Denim Company.

Having a clear market position: We feel there is a specific niche market that will appreciate our services. It is hard to put into words the adrenaline rush that comes from being caught in a mob of 2,000 screaming rock 'n' roll fans at a Coheed & Cambria concert, so we think it's best to let the denim do the talking. We know that we will not appeal to everyone, and we don't want to. Exclusivity is a powerful feeling.

Ability to control stock on hand: We are following the examples set forth by our competition in order to have the best guesstimate possible. We will implore the wisdom passed on by our mentors and our own past experiences as stock managers to help predict what's best for our situation from month to month.

Superior debt and financial management: Our finances will be handled by a third party accountant. We will rely on the advice from mentors and data collected from financial statements to help make informed decisions.

Production of currently favored goods: The most difficult part of this aspect of a successful retail store is figuring out the most–popular fits. We will also need our artists to be continually reading up on new looks and styles so they are familiar with the hottest new trends and have a grasp on any new fashion lingo. As of late, the popular fits for denim has been the revolutionary low–rise boot cut and family.

Establishment of a brand name: We believe that our brand name is catchy by nature, and we will do just about anything to get the attention of our target audience. During the few months prior to opening our first storefront location, our employees will spend much of their training out on Delmar Loop in their new Patch Denim jeans to interact with potential customers. We will hit the market hard and in a way that cannot be ignored.

Attractive product presentation: Our store will feature our artists' artwork more than the actual pieces of clothing. We plan to use the entire wall behind the cash register as a giant menu with all of the different articles of clothing on display with product specifications and prices. Should customers want to feel, touch, and try on our products, they simply need to ask an artist who will be happy to pull a size from the back.

Experienced workforce: Our workforce will be highly trained in the purest definition of sales—helping people find what they want or need. We will take a no–pressure approach from an expertise standpoint. We will assume that everyone who steps foot in our store already knows what they want, they just need help figuring out how to get it. Our artists will be trained fashion and fine arts majors that have a true passion for their work. Our managers will be business majors that have had experience in other retail stores. We will be the place that retail people want to work.

COMPETITION

Our main competitors include Abercrombie & Fitch, Hollister Company, Pacific Sunwear, Aeropostale, The Buckle, Hot Topic, and American Eagle Outfitters. All of these companies sell jeans to the same market demographic as Patch Denim. Aeropostale reported the cheapest price ($20) and The Buckle reported the most expensive ($178).

Abercrombie & Fitch is an American fashion retailer headed by chairman and CEO Michael S. Jeffries. The A&F brand focuses on casual wear for a target consumer ages of 18 through 22. With over 300 locations in the United States, the brand has embarked on international expansion throughout various world markets.

Hollister Co. is an American lifestyle brand by Abercrombie & Fitch. The concept is designed to attract consumers aged 14–18 through its So–Cal inspired image and casual wear. Goods are available in–store and through the company's online store. Despite the age target, the appeal of the HCO brand is universal like its parent brand and was ranked as the second most preferred teen clothing brand in 2008 by US Bancorp Piper Jaffray.

Pacific Sunwear of California Inc. is a US–based retail clothing company rooted in the youth culture and fashion vibe of Southern California. The company sells casual apparel with a limited selection of accessories and footwear designed to meet the needs of teens and young adults. As of May 2, 2009, the company operated 927 stores in 50 states and Puerto Rico. PacSun is headquartered in Anaheim, California and operates a distribution center in Olathe, Kansas. The company's regional directors, district managers and store positions are located throughout the United States.

Aeropostale, Inc. is an American clothing retailer that sells casual clothing with over 900 stores in the United States, Canada, Puerto Rico, and the United Arab Emirates. Their stores are located in shopping malls. Aeropostale sells fashion apparel including shirts, jeans, hoodies, accessories, etc. Their clothing is targeted at teenagers and young adults. Building on the success of the Aeropostale teen brand the company has now launched a new brand, P.S. from Aeropostale, that sells tween clothing.

The Buckle markets a wide variety of brand name and private label casual apparel including other casual bottoms, fashion tops, sportswear, outerwear, accessories and footwear. Some of the more popular brands they carry include: Lucky Brand Jeans, O'Neil, Fossil, Ed Hardy, and Diesel. The company emphasizes personalized attention to its guests (customers) and provides individual customer services such as free alterations, free gift wrapping, layaways and a frequent shopper program. Most stores are located in upscale malls across the country and have an online store at buckle.com.

Hot Topic is an American retail chain specializing in music and pop culture–related clothing and accessories, including licensed music recordings. As of April, 2008, Hot Topic had 688 locations in the United States and six stores in Puerto Rico, the majority of which are located in regional shopping malls. The first Hot Topic store was opened in 1988 by Orv Madden, who retired as CEO in 2000 and was replaced by Betsey McLaughlin. The company went public and began trading on NASDAQ in 1996. In 2006, Hot Topic was named number 53 on Fortune 500s Top Companies To Work For list.

American Eagle Outfitters is an American clothing and accessories retailer based in Pittsburgh, PA. It was founded in 1977 by Mark and Jerry Silverman as a subsidiary of Retail Ventures, Inc., a company which also owned and operated Silverman's Menswear. The Silvermans sold their ownership interests in 1991. American Eagle targets teens and young adults. Some of the best–selling products of American Eagle Outfitters are Low–rise jeans, Polo shirts, graphic T–shirts, and swimwear.

SWOT ANALYSIS

Vans Warped Tour

Strengths:

- Exposes our product to an environment where everyone fits our target market.

- Relatively cost efficient—allows for bootstrapping.

- Traveling with the tour allows us to target more people.

Weaknesses:

- High risk of poorly trained help.

- More prone to inventory issues.

- Lack of brand recognition.

- Highly seasonal.

- Operations are weather permitting only.

Opportunities:

- Potential to reach a significantly bigger target market.

- Potential to establish a recognizable brand in multiple cities.

- Potential to establish a good relationship with popular bands to help with promotional efforts in the future.

Threats:

- Vans Warped Tour could be canceled.

- Attendance may take a plunge due to economy.

- People may spend more money on food and water than extras.

- New competition may enter Warped Tour Market.

Delmar Loop Storefront

Strengths:

- Exposes our product/service in an atmosphere that embraces new ideas pertaining to self–expression.

- Legitimizes the brand.

- Allows our staff to focus much more on customer service in a more laid–back environment.

- Decreases per unit cost.

- High foot traffic due to similar market stores in the area.

Weaknesses:

- Sizable initial investment.

- Limited to one location until profitable enough to expand.

Opportunities:

- Potential to expand brand image to new markets.

- Potential to explore new options for customers.

- Potential to develop good relationships with other store owners for promotions.

Threats:

- Delmar Loop may change its market strategy to appeal to different people.

- Customers may not respond well to Patch Denim.

- Bad economy may lead to insufficient sales.

- Competitors may enter the market.

MARKETING STRATEGY

Vans Warped Tour

Patch Denim Company will work to establish a recognizable brand within the rock 'n' roll community created by the Vans Warped Tour. We have chosen this venue as our point of entry for the simple fact that we will have direct access to a very defined target market in an exciting, once–a–year atmosphere. It is our goal to attach our brand name to the success of the tour and develop a solid repeat customer base. We plan to achieve this goal through various marketing tactics including: band promotions, word–of–mouth, effective signage, personal use, and product promotions. Please note: these promotions will be used to build brand recognition during the first two years on the Vans Warped Tour prior to opening the storefront. Once the storefront is opened, these campaigns will be evaluated; at which point the unprofitable campaigns will be removed to make room for the storefront marketing budget.

Band Promotions—The bands are the only reason 20,000 fans swarm to a venue on a hot July day. We understand the success of these bands depends on their ability to promote their music. We want to put a pair of Patch Denim jeans on the legs of every major performer at the concert. We will provide the jeans free of charge to the band members, and in return they will grant us the rights to apply their band name and lyrics to our jeans. We believe this basic partnership will benefit both parties due to the mutual promotion interests.

Word–of–Mouth—The best form of advertising is a good recommendation from a friend. It's free and leads to higher sales than any other form of advertising. At Patch Denim, we want to create a loyal fan base that is passionate about our products. We believe the best way to achieve this is to offer an incentive for people to talk about their jeans. New customers will be asked if they would like to join our Groupies club. Membership is free, and puts you on a mailing list that is full of information pertaining to the music scene, PDC discounts, concert details, and more. Plus, members are encouraged to promote new sales by talking to their friends about their new jeans. Any denim sale resulting from their efforts results in a 15% off coupon for both the new customer and the referring groupie. We estimate this will have an impact on 10% of sales.

Effective Signage—The Vans Warped Tour is notorious for its out–of–control flea market environment. The aisles are overcrowded, and the energy is high. We plan to gain the attention of patrons by placing fliers around the venue, and having a custom tent with our artists' artwork on it. To do so will cost nothing, and it will make a huge statement about our style. The tent, itself, will cost $300. 250 fliers will cost $12.50 per stop, and will include a coupon for a 10% discount. We estimate this will have an impact on 5% of sales.

Personal Use—Our employees will be granted 3 free pairs of jeans each that they are welcome to customize how they wish. These jeans will be worn on a daily basis and will be walking advertisements for our brand throughout each day.

Product Promotions—The energy drink market is a huge part of the Warped Tour culture. As such, we feel it will be necessary and beneficial to have a steady supply of XS Energy to be handed out with each purchase (while supplies last). This will not only satisfy a thirst on a hot summer day, but also create another point of reference for our brand. Share the drink, share our story. To keep a steady supply of cold XS available will cost us $145 for the cooler, and $120 per stop.

Delmar Loop Storefront

In our third year of operation, Patch Denim Company plans to open a storefront that will help solidify the brand image. The location will bring the Vans Warped Tour atmosphere to the Delmar Loop. We plan to build a buzz around the grand opening of the store that will create enough revenues to help us seize a position as a major element in the area from day one. We plan to expand from that location to many other eclectic shopping districts around the country, but it all starts with the success of one store. In order to achieve these aspirations, we will execute a marketing plan that includes the following marketing tactics: personal use, word–of–mouth, candid concerts, and effective signage.

Personal Use—Our employees will be granted 3 free pairs of jeans each that they are welcome to customize how they wish. These jeans will be worn on a daily basis and will be walking advertisements for our brand throughout each day.

Word–of–Mouth—The best form of advertising is a good recommendation from a friend. It's free and leads to higher sales than any other form of advertising. At Patch Denim, we want to create a loyal fan base that is passionate about our products. We believe the best way to achieve this is to offer an incentive for people to talk about their jeans. New customers will be asked if they would like to join our Groupies club. Membership is free, and puts you on a mailing list that is full of information pertaining to the music scene, PDC discounts, concert details, and more. Plus, members are encouraged to promote new sales by talking to their friends about their new jeans. Any denim sale resulting from their efforts results in a 15% off coupon for both the new customer and the referring groupie. We estimate this will have an impact on 5% of sales.

Candid Concerts—One popular aspect of Delmar Loop is the way the music is intertwined with the street. We plan to utilize that dimension and host our own candid concerts free of charge to the public. We will host popular local bands, and other nationally–recognized acts when feasible. These concerts will only be announced to Groupies club members. Everyone else will find out via word of mouth, or by stumbling across it during their day of shopping on the Loop. This program will be a great way to keep customers/fans on their toes, as well as help build a brand image that is unpredictable and exciting. Bands will be paid 5% of the sales for that day on top of their expenses (within reason).

Effective Signage—Delmar will be flooded with Patch Denim fliers the month leading up to the grand opening event. Our store front will be engaging to the customer as they walk by, and the sidewalks will be covered in Patch Denim logos. The fliers will have a 10% discount coupon printed on them, and the sidewalk will be tagged by our artists with sidewalk chalk. We estimate this will have an impact on 5% of sales.

OPERATIONS AND FACILITIES

Vans Warped Tour

Patch Denim company will secure a 10'x20' booth at the Vans Warped Tour by reserving it as early as September 2011. This space will be occupied by a team of 5 artists, 3 sorority girls, and the owners. It will also house a check–in table, inventory closet, 2 dressing rooms, a design studio, a cashier's table, and a manufacturing line. Renting the booth will cost $500 per stop. Below is a sketch of how the space will be utilized:

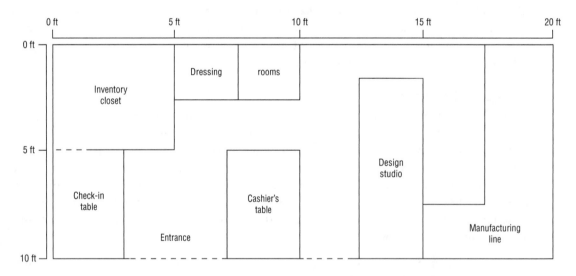

Check–In Table—The purpose of this table is to greet guests as they enter the tent. We will hire 3 sorority girls from a local university to run this table. The girls will be hired on a part–time basis, and their labor will be donated in return for a contribution to their philanthropy. The contribution will be 10% of the day's profits. Their job will be to explain the process, help the customer determine the right canvas and package, and act as liaison for the customer to the artist. They will also be in charge of storing the completed canvases and make sure they are delivered to the right people during pick–up. This area will need a standard folding table ($70), 2 folding chairs ($20 each), and various inventory control supplies.

Inventory Closet—The inventory closet will house enough denim to supply the day's demand. It will be a 5'x5' area made up of inventory storage boxes and 4 black wardrobes from Upper Furniture. They will cost $153 each and their dimensions are H60" x L30"x W21". It will also house the finished products for easy pick–up. This area will be restricted to employee access only.

Dressing Rooms—The dressing rooms provide the luxury of privacy for our customers while they determine their favorite canvas. The dressing room dimensions are L36" x W36" x H72". We will purchase 2 from markertek.com for $24.95 each.

Design Studio—The design studio will host the interaction between the artists and the customers. It will feature 2 folding tables that have all the necessary items for the design process including the Patch Blueprints, pencils, and samples of the artist's work. This area will also require 4 folding chairs.

Cashier's Table—The cashier's table will generally be run by the owners. This is where the sales are finalized and the money will be handled. Customers will receive a ticket that corresponds to their canvas, and will be informed as to what time to pick–up. Also, as per our product promotion, they will be given a free XS Energy drink as a parting gift. This area will require a folding table, 2 folding chairs, a Royal Consumer cash register ($93), a Sentry safe ($87), an XS Energy Cooler ($145), and various inventory control supplies.

Manufacturing Line—This area will be accessed by only our employees. It will house all the necessary supplies and equipment for our artists to produce the desired pair of jeans including bleach ($119), cutting/fraying tools, a water trough from agrisupply.com ($22) for hand washing the denim, and a General Electric energy–efficient mobile dryer ($737).

As a customer, you can expect personalized service and quality artwork. The process is simple, and has been laid out below:

1. Enter the tent.

2. Be instantly greeted by our lovely sorority girls.

3. Pick out your favorite canvas.

4. Pick out your favorite package.

5. Work with artist to design a pair of jeans that is truly unique.

6. Sign Blueprint.

7. Pay and receive pick–up ticket.

8. Enjoy the rest of the concert.

9. Pick up new jeans before leaving the venue.

Expected Output Capacities

Based on survey results and product demonstrations, we have determined the following plausible output capacities.

Maximum Capacity

- 5 artists
- 10 hours
- 20 canvases per hour
- 200 canvases per day

Expected Capacity

- 5 artists
- 10 hours

- 10 canvases per hour

- 100 canvases per day

Minimum Capacity

- 5 artists

- 10 hours

- 5 canvases per hour

- 50 canvases per day

In order to get from stop to stop, we will rent an RV and a Penske truck to move our core group of artists and inventory/equipment. RV rental will be $3,500 for year one, and $10,000 for years two and three. Truck rental will be $1,600 for year one, and $4,900 for years two and three. We believe this alternative is cost–effective compared to hotel reservations.

We estimate that off–season months will require massive networking with bands and venues in order to build our band promotions. This effort will require free labor from the owners, and an estimated $50 per month in various office supplies, and $200 a month for phones.

Delmar Loop Storefront

As of right now, we have not determined what our storefront is going to look like in detail. However, we do know the atmosphere that we want our location to portray. We feel its much better to leave the details to a licensed architect that we trust to help us determine how our building can help build brand image. Based on current listings, rent is expected to be $1,200 per month for 1,200 sq/ft. According to the best estimate provided by Metropolitan Design and Building, construction/renovation on the property will be approximately $100 sq/ft. Although the structure will change, the process will remain relatively the same. The main difference will be the variety in the selection. We will offer more canvases and more verses.

In order to produce the options available at the storefront, additional equipment will be purchased. The following chart shows what will be purchased.

Equipment (purchased)	Quantity	Price
GE washing machines	2	$ 379
GE dryers	4	$ 737
Graphtec vinyl cutters	2	$ 289
HP computers	6	$ 684
Folding chairs	20	$ 20
Total		**$8,788**

The transition from a seasonal business into a year–round storefront business will mean increases in monthly phone/internet bills (from $200 to $325), insurance (from $200 to $400), and office supplies (from $50 to $75).

INVESTMENT OPPORTUNITY

As a business we hope to thrive, make a difference, and make money. It is our goal to implement this business plan as early as September 2011. In order to do so, we are currently looking for a co–signer to help us secure a $70,000 small business loan at a low interest rate. This money will cover all asset acquisitions and expenses during our first year of business, and will leave a $5,000 cushion for any unforeseen expenses. Ending cash for year one is expected to be $102,000 and will be enough for us to operate in year two.

Year three will require $120,000 for construction on the storefront. We are asking for a $120,000 investment to cover this project in order to protect the normal operations of the business. To help alleviate some of the investment, each owner/operator will commit to invest $1,000 each month (excluding tour months) into the business from month one until the storefront is open. This will result in a total of $42,000 that will help cover expenses during the off–season of the first three years. We are currently seeking accredited investors for $120,000 to operate in year three. After this stage of development, we estimate that Patch Denim Company will be properly funded and will be able to operate and expand using income from operations. Ending cash is expected to be $150,000.

The following table displays a yearly breakdown of costs to cover, and is the basis of our asking amounts for the first three years of operation.

Costs to cover	Year 1	Year 2	Year 3
Inventory	$37,500	$ 60,000	$ 90,000
Equipment	$ 3,416	$ 0	$ 8,788
Rentals and fees	$15,244	$ 40,733	$ 52,733
Wages	$ 9,570	$ 38,280	$ 60,450
Construction, etc.	$ 0	$ 0	$120,000
Total	**$65,730**	**$139,013**	**$331,971**

FINANCIAL ASSUMPTIONS

Vans Warped Tour

Monthly Canvas Sales

- Operations will take place at every stop.

- 20 stops in 2011

- 50 stops in 2012–13

- 100 canvases sold per stop in 2011

- 105 canvases sold per stop in 2012

- 110 canvases sold per stop in 2013

Monthly Package Sales

- Every canvas is sold with a package

- "The Opener" will make up 40% of package sales in 2011, and 30% in 2012–13

- "The Headliner" will make up 40% of package sales in 2011, and 50% in 2012–13

- "The Encore" will make up 20% of package sales in all 3 years

Product Cost vs. Price

- Expected costs are accurately represented

- Primary data collected is representative of target market

- Competitor pricing remains consistent

Equipment Costs

- Expected costs are accurately represented

- Useful life on purchased equipment is 3 years

Salaries

- Owners are free labor

- Artists are willing to work for $160 per day

- Sororities will supply labor for 5% of the profit

Delmar Loop Storefront

Monthly Canvas Sales

- Store sales trends follow St. Louis average for similar stores

Monthly Package Sales

- Every canvas is sold with a package

- Customers will favor cheaper packages

Product Cost vs. Price

- Expected costs are accurately represented

- Economies of scale will reduce COGS

Equipment Costs

- Expected costs are accurately represented

- Useful equipment life is 4 years

Salaries

- Employees will work for proposed wages

- Owners will draw income from retained earnings

FINANCIAL SUMMARY

Sales Assumptions

	Year 1	Year 2	Year 3
Warped Tour sales (units)	2,000	5,250	5,500
Storefront sales (units)	0	0	4,686
Total units sold	2,000	5,250	10,186
Total sales ($)	109,200	294,525	512,068
COGS ($)	52,348	141,188	238,708
Gross profit ($)	56,852	153,337	273,360

Income statement for the fiscal year ending March 31, 2010

	Year 1	Year 2	Year 3
Total sales	109,200	294,525	512,068
COGS	52,348	141,188	238,708
Gross profit	56,852	153,337	273,360
Direct expenses	38,797	111,006	238,298
Operating margin	18,055	42,331	35,062
Total G&A	6,660	13,799	23,880
EBIT	11,395	28,532	11,182
Income tax	712	1,783	699
Net income	10,683	26,749	10,483

Balance sheet

For the fiscal year ending March 31, 20XX

	Year 1	Year 2	Year 3
Assets			
Cash	102,855	147,070	150,429
Inventory	0	0	15,970
Fixed assets	2,790	2,106	8,930
Total assets	**105,645**	**149,177**	**175,328**
Liabilities			
Long-term loan	75,000	75,000	75,000
Loan interest	250	250	16,220
Total liabilities	**75,250**	**75,250**	**91,220**
Owner equity			
Owner investment	22,000	40,000	162,000
Retained earnings	8,395	33,927	−77,892
Net equity	30,395	73,927	84,108
Total liab. & owners	**105,645**	**149,177**	**175,328**

Statement of retained earnings

	Year 1	Year 2	Year 3
Beginning R/E	0	10,683	37,431
Net income	10,683	26,749	10,483
Dividends	0	0	0
Retained earnings	10,683	37,431	47,914

Survey results

Total number of participants	186
Average age of participants	19
Males	38%
Females	62%
Average price paid for new jeans	$57
Average time people are willing to spend on process	45 minutes
People that attend Warped Tour	17%

Daycare/Preschool

Little Lambs Daycare and Preschool

1500 S. Winding Trails Road
Columbia, MO 65202

Kari Lucke

Little Lambs Daycare and Preschool aims to help children learn academic and social skills through play and a structured curriculum while building their self–confidence and character.

1.0. INTRODUCTION

1.1. Mission Statement

Little Lambs Daycare and Preschool aims to help children learn academic and social skills through play and a structured curriculum while building their self–confidence and character.

1.2. Executive Summary

Little Lambs Daycare and Preschool is designed as both a childcare facility and an academic facility for preschoolers. Children ages 3 to 5 who have not yet started kindergarten will be accepted for enrollment. Children will follow a structured curriculum in the mornings and have naptime and playtime in the afternoon.

There are three types of child care facilities licensed by the state of Missouri: group home, childcare center, and family home. Because Little Lambs will enroll 10 or fewer children and be located in Rachel Voss's home, it is classified as a family home.

1.3. Business Overview

According to the U.S. Census Bureau, 51 percent of mothers in the United States return to work within four months of having their first child. Other figures show that 55 percent of mothers with small children work outside the home. In Missouri, 66 percent of children under the age of 6 live with two working parents (U.S. Department of Health). These statistics illustrate the increased need for quality childcare. Preschool training is also becoming more important. Whereas it used to be children went to kindergarten to learn their letters and numbers, write their name, and so on, now they are expected to be able to perform these basic academic functions by the time they start school.

Preschool is beneficial for children in many ways. According to the U.S. Center for the Childcare Workforce, children who attend high–quality preschools experience the following (from http://www.ccw.org):

- better higher–order thinking and attention skills

- better reading, writing, and mathematical abilities

- better social skills

- less grade retention

- higher graduation rates

- fewer special education placements

- fewer behavioral problems

- less societal disengagement later in life

- more economic productivity later in life

- less dependency on welfare later in life

- higher sense of social stability later in life

1.4. Goals and Objectives

The goals of Little Lambs are to:

- reach full enrollment capacity within the first three months of business.

- realize a profit in the first year of business.

2.0. INDUSTRY AND MARKET

2.1. Industry Analysis

Due to the large numbers of working parents in the United States, the need for childcare is increasing. In addition, as competition for the best schools increases and the expectations for even the youngest students rise, people are seeing the value of sending their children to preschool and giving them a head start on their schooling. The demand in both of these areas—childcare and early education—is expected to continue to increase throughout the next decade.

2.2. Market Analysis

The market area for Little Lambs is Columbia, Missouri. Columbia has grown significantly in the past decade, with its population increasing from 62,000 in 1980 to over 100,000 by 2009, and it is expected to see continued growth. With this growth comes an increased need for quality childcare services.

Columbia is consistently rated one of the best places to live in America by such well–known entities as *Forbes*, *Money* magazine, and Kiplinger.com due to its excellent educational systems, access to health care, and quality of life. For example, in 2007 *Forbes* ranked Columbia "Third Best Metro for Business and Careers" in its study that factored in the cost of doing business, job growth, and educational attainment.

Due to these factors of demographics and growth trends as well as others, we see significant potential for a daycare/preschool in this location. Unlike many small towns in Missouri, which are losing population, Columbia's population is growing.

2.3. Competition

Competition will come in the forms of other home–based preschools and daycares. Larger daycare centers, such as Apple Schools and Kindercare, are in a separate category and are not considered direct competition for Little Lambs. There are several advantages of home–based child care as opposed to large centers, such as more personalized attention, homier atmosphere, and less bureaucracy, and usually parents who are looking for home–based care already understand these differences and are focused on finding a home–based facility.

Location is an important factor to parents looking for childcare. Because Little Lambs will be located in the northwestern part of Columbia, home–based centers that are accepting children in this part of town are considered the main source of competition for Little Lambs. Due to the large demand for childcare for this age group in Columbia, many of the home–based daycare centers are already full, and some even have waiting lists. As of early 2010, preschool/child care centers that are accepting new children include the following:

- Let's Learn Preschool and Daycare, 1600 N. Church Road

- Angie's Preschool, 805 Applewood Drive

- Wee Care, 4500 Richards Drive

3.0. PERSONNEL

3.1. Management
Rachel Voss is the sole owner and proprietor of Little Lambs Daycare and Preschool. Rachel has a Bachelor of Arts degree in early childhood education from Truman State University and has worked as a preschool teacher for two different facilities (Oak River Preschool and Country Hill Nursery School) for the past 10 years. Rachel has a deep and true compassion for children, and she shows in every interaction she has with them, from helping one recover from a skinned knee to patiently guiding a young hand while learning letters. With her educational background and experience in preschool teaching, Rachel is perfectly suited to operate a preschool and daycare center.

Other attributes necessary to a home–based preschool teacher include patience in dealing with children, diplomacy and level–headedness in dealing with sometimes anxious and overworked parents, and a seemingly unending reserve of energy. Rachel has all of these characteristics and more. In addition, Rachel fulfills the state requirement of knowledge of child CPR.

3.2. Staffing
The only other staff member will be on call for when Rachel is sick or experiences emergency situations in which she cannot care for the children. This person is Rachel's mother, Helen Georges. Helen was an elementary school teacher for 30 years before retiring at the age of 60 in 2009. Helen is an ideal substitute for Rachel because she can fill in at a moment's notice, she has years of experience caring for and teaching children, and she has the good health and high level of energy necessary for the demanding job of preschool teacher. Helen will be paid a flat rate of $50 a day for substituting.

3.3. Professional and Advisory Support
Rachel is a member of the National Association of Child Care Providers and the National Education Association. Both of these organizations provide up–to–date information about the industry and resources for preschool teachers and child care workers.

Other outside support will be provided by George Smith, attorney, and Dennis Naught, insurance agent.

4.0. BUSINESS STRATEGY

The aim of Little Lambs Daycare and Preschool is to ready young children for school and other social and academic situations. This is best done through use of a regular, formal curriculum integrated with free play and more informal instruction. Little Lambs will use the ABC Home Preschool Curriculum, which includes all of the necessary components for the academics of a home–based preschool, including worksheets, downloads, and software.

The business goal of Little Lambs will be to keep enrollment at capacity as much as possible. Although there will naturally be turnover of children, as they age out of the program, Little Lambs will continue to supply the highest quality child care, academic stimulation, and caring environment possible in order to encourage positive word–of–mouth promotion and an ongoing flow of children through the program.

5.0. PRODUCTS AND SERVICES

5.1. Description

Little Lambs Daycare and Preschool will provide child care and academic instruction for children ages 3 to 5. A typical day will be structured as follows:

7:00–8:30—Arrival time and free play, including drawing/coloring, blocks and other manipulatives, dress–up, reading or listening to books

8:30–9:00—Welcome group time. Attendance, daily prayer, welcome song, calendar

9:00–9:30—Language arts instruction

9:30–10:00—Math instruction

10:00 –10:15—Snack time

10:15–10:45—Recess—outdoors if possible; otherwise, free play inside

10:45–11:15—Art

11:15–11:45—Music

11:45–12:00—Restroom and washing hands

12:00 –12:30—Lunch

12:30–1:00—Storytime

1:00–2:00—Rest/nap time

2:00–3:00—Extended recess—outdoors if possible; otherwise, free play inside

3:00 –3:15—Restroom and washing hands

3:15–3:30—Snack time

3:30–5:00—Free play

5:00–6:00—Parent pick–up

5.2. Pricing

Prices for Little Lambs Daycare and Preschool will be based on the going rates for such services in the Columbia area. Half–day preschool (8:30 a.m. to 12:00 noon) will be offered Monday, Wednesday, and Friday for $80 a week. Full–day daycare and preschool will be offered Monday through Friday (8:00 a.m. to 6:00 p.m.) for $150 a week. Rates may be adjusted based on parents' specific needs.

6.0. MARKETING AND SALES

6.1. Advertising and Promotion

Initially the main forms of advertising will be flyers posted on bulletin boards at churches, schools, grocery stores, and other public places in the northwest part of Columbia, a classified ad in the

Columbia Daily Tribune, and a web page. Rachel will also utilize such free services as Craigslist.com to get the word out that she is accepting children at Little Lambs. Later, as parents use Rachel's services and have positive experiences, word–of–mouth is expected to be a significant and free form of advertising.

6.2. Cost

Initial cost of advertising is expected to be minimal and will include about $100 for printing flyers and $200 for the classified newspaper ad.

7.0. OPERATIONS

7.1. Customers

Our market consists of children ages 3 to 5 years old in Columbia, Missouri. Columbia is a town of approximately 94,000, and statistics show that almost 7 percent of the population is under 5 years old. This is similar to the national average. The median household income in Columbia is $42,163, with a race distribution of 83 percent White, 9 percent Black, and 8 percent other. Estimates show that about 28 percent of the households in the city are middle– and upper–income families with children. In addition, research shows that well–educated parents are particularly invested in making sure their children receive a good education, which can begin at the preschool age. Statistics show that more than 50 percent of Columbia residents have a bachelor's degree and more than 25 percent have graduate degrees, making it thirteenth most highly educated city in the United States.

7.2. Equipment

Some of the items needed to equip Little Lambs Daycare and Preschool for operation include the following:

- Child–size table and chairs (three sets of table/four chairs)

- Large rug for group time

- Container system (bins) for children's belongings

- Container systems for toys and games

- Nap cots (10)

- Sand table

- Selection of books, toys, puzzles, and other items

- Computer stations, including computers and monitors

7.3. Hours

Little Lambs Daycare and Preschool will be open from 7:00 a.m. to 6:00 p.m. Monday through Friday year–round, with no school the week between Christmas and New Years and during one week in the summer.

7.4. Facility and Location

Little Lambs Daycare and Preschool will be located at Rachel Voss's 3,200–square–foot home at 1500 S. Winding Trails Road, Columbia, Missouri. The home is located on the northwest edge of the city on a one–half acre lot in the neighborhood known as Oak View. The location is easily accessible and is only two blocks from the main road that runs through the subdivision.

The entire downstairs portion of the house, constituting about 1,600 square feet, will be dedicated to Little Lambs. According to state regulations, there must be at least 35 square feet of useable space per child in licensed daycare centers, so this size space is more than enough to accommodate 10 children. The walkout basement includes a large open area where the children will spend most of their time during the day. The area will be divided into stations, with each station hosting a particular activity (e.g., blocks, dress–up, books, computers, work/lunch/snack tables, coats and cubbies, etc.). The group time area, designated by a large rug with marked spots for the children to sit, will be in the center of the room.

The basement of the house includes a bathroom and two bedrooms, as well as a kitchenette, making it convenient for Rachel to fix lunch and snacks. The bathroom will be remodeled for use by children (e.g., child–size toilet and lowered vanity/sink). The bedrooms will house the nap cots, with younger children in one room and older children in the other.

There is a walkout door in the basement, which provides easy access to the fenced backyard, where the children will spend their recess time if weather permits. The playground, which at this point consists of a large wooden swing set and climbing structure with a slide, will be enhanced with additional, state–approved equipment.

The facility will meet all state expectations regarding safety, as specified by the Missouri Division 30: Chapter 61 Licensing Rules for Family Day Care Homes (5–2002). Because the home is relatively new (built in 2007), there are no concerns with deteriorating structures, lead paint, and so on.

7.5. Legal Environment

Daycare centers and preschools in Missouri must follow strict and detailed rules as designated by the state department of health. According to these guidelines, one preschool teacher/daycare provider can care for 10 children ages 3 to 5. In addition, Rachel must undergo a background criminal and child abuse check, be proficient in CPR techniques, and receive 12 hours of childcare training a year from an approved training organization. Rachel and Helen will both undergo physical exams by their primary care physician in order to fulfill the health information requirement.

Little Lambs will be licensed by the state department of health and will undergo all necessary inspections regarding health issues, fire safety, and sanitation prior to opening its doors. Also, Rachel will require from each child information including a medical report (describing the child's current state of health), emergency contact details, and proof of vaccinations. Although being licensed is not a requirement in Missouri for daycare centers operated out of a home, licensing will increase the center's credibility as well as provide parents with peace of mind and confidence that their child will be safe and well–tended while at Little Lambs.

Another legal aspect of starting the center relates to the parent contract. This document, which will be signed by both Rachel and the parents of the enrolled child, will include all details on Little Lambs' policies and procedures, what is expected of parents, what will happen in case of an emergency, what the parent will be charged and when and how that fee will be collected, hours and days of operation, and so on. This document will be reviewed by attorney George Smith before it is utilized, to be sure that all legal aspects of the relationship between parent and center are covered adequately.

8.0. FINANCIAL ANALYSIS

Initial start–up costs are as follows:

- Child–size tables and chairs—$900

- Other furnishings (rugs, soft chairs)—$250

- Personal belongings container system (cubbies)—$300
- Container system for toys—$300
- Nap cots and bedding—$1,000
- Sand table—$100
- Books, toys, games, puzzles—$500
- Bathroom remodel—$750
- Computer stations—$1,000
- Playground equipment—$500
- Miscellaneous items—$200
- Advertising—$300
- Insurance—$200
- Business License —$100
- Total Start–up Expenses—$5,400

Funding for start–up costs will be provided by money from a personal savings account.

Ongoing expenses will be minimal and will consist mainly of the cost of food.

Monthly Expenses
- Food (lunch, two snacks a day) —$1,000
- Estimated substitute teacher salary—$150
- Insurance—$50
- Other—$100
- Total Monthly Expenses, Year 1—$1,300

Monthly Income
- Four children at half–day—$1,280
- Six children at full day—$3,600
- Total Gross Monthly Income, Year 1 (at full capacity) —$4,880

There may be lag times when children leave the center and the spot is open until filled. We allow six weeks of zero income on two full–day children to account for this scenario. In that case, the first year's financials would approximate the following:

- $4,800/month x 12 = $57,600/year income minus $9,000 lag time allowance = $48,600/year
- Minus monthly expenses ($1300 x 12 = $15,600) = $33,0000 gross income/year

Family Entertainment Center

FunXplosion LLC

23344 Milton St.
Fargo, ND 58102

Paul Greenland

FunXplosion is an indoor family entertainment center that offers a range of enjoyable leisure activities to consumers.

EXECUTIVE SUMMARY

Business Overview

Located in Fargo, North Dakota, FunXplosion LLC is an indoor family entertainment center (FEC). Our business offers a range of enjoyable leisure activities to consumers, regardless of how cold it is outside. We are strategically located in North Dakota's largest city, with convenient access to the nearby city of Grand Forks (the state's third-largest city).

FunXplosion offers the following activities to customers:

- Video Arcade
- Laser Tag/Lazer Maze
- Bounce Play/Inflatable Area
- Indoor Miniature Golf
- Room Rentals
- Food/Concession Area

FunXplosion is owned by real estate developer John Chu, general contractor Mike Robinson, and attorney Peter Wagner. Well-established businessmen in Fargo, the owners have an excellent long-term working relationship and have made a number of joint investments in land and real estate development projects throughout North Dakota.

Business Philosophy

Good times are always on at FunXplosion.

MARKET ANALYSIS

North Dakota is the nation's second-coldest state, with a mean annual temperature of 40.43 degrees (second to Alaska, which has a mean annual temperature of 32.13 degrees). Especially during the cold winter months, area residents of all ages need entertainment options. FunXplosion has something to offer for everyone, regardless of age. However, our primary markets are young families, adolescents, and organizations (e.g., schools, churches, youth programs, civic organizations, Boy Scout and Girl Scout programs, employers, etc.).

The demographic breakdown of FunXplosion's primary (Fargo) and secondary (Grand Forks) markets is very favorable. Fargo is North Dakota's largest city. According to DemographicsNow, Fargo had about 97,650 residents in 2009. By 2014 the population is projected to increase 10.6 percent, reaching 107,961.

In 2009 those aged 25 to 34 represented the most predominant age group (19.5% of the population), followed by 35 to 44 (12.5%); 20 to 24 (12.1%); and 45 to 54 (11.7%). Although those aged 5 to 14 accounted for 11.3 percent of the population in 2009, this segment was expected to increase 22.5 percent by 2014. In addition, the segment of the population under the age of four is expected to increase 19.5 percent between 2009 and 2014.

DemographicsNow further indicates that 19.3 percent of the population had a household income between $50,000 and $74,999 in 2009. A close second were those with a household income between $35,000 and $49,999 (16.6%). In addition, 54.3 percent of Fargo residents have access to more than two vehicles, while 37.8 percent have access to at least one vehicle.

Our business also is accessible to the residents of nearby Grand Forks, which is North Dakota's third-largest city. According to DemographicsNow, Grand Forks had about 53,330 residents in 2009. By 2014 the population is projected to increase 10.8 percent, reaching 59,112. Grand Forks is expecting a baby boom during the early 2010s. The segment of the population under age four is expected to increase 51.1 percent between 2009 and 2014. Household income in this market is very similar to that of Fargo. In addition, the majority of the population has access to at least one vehicle (37.2% have one vehicle and 54.8% have at least two vehicles), making our destination easily accessible to this neighboring city, which is about 80 minutes away.

INDUSTRY ANALYSIS

Family entertainment centers like ours are part of the amusement park industry, which generated estimated revenues of $12 billion in 2007 according to the International Association of Amusement Parks and Attractions (IAAPA). On average, family entertainment centers host approximately 381,000 guests each year. Larger facilities may serve 622,000 guests. The IAAPA reports that patrons of family entertainment centers visit more than three times each season.

In 2010 family entertainment centers operated in a dire economic climate. Even during the worst of times, businesses like ours tend to fare well because we provide families with affordable entertainment options. Although no industry is truly recession-proof, the family entertainment industry is somewhat recession-resistant.

Miniature golf is the main attraction at FunXplosion. This form of entertainment truly has stood the test of time. According to the Miniature Golf Association, the game originated in 1919, on the private North Carolina estate of James Barber. During the 1920s miniature golf emerged as a popular rooftop game in New York City. By the Great Depression the nation was home to between 25,000 and 50,000 miniature golf courses. These mainly small, independently owned operations provided an escape from difficult times.

It was during the 1970s and 1980s that miniature golf was added to smaller amusement parks, along with arcades and go-kart tracks. Miniature golf's popularity continued during the early 2010s. By that time 18-hole courses were being designed with wheelchair accessibility, making the activity available to a wider range of consumers. Beyond actual courses, enthusiasts were able to enjoy games like Mini Golf 99 Holes Theme Park, an application for the popular Apple iPhone and Apple iPod touch developed by a company named Digital Chocolate.

PERSONNEL

FunXplosion is owned by real estate developer John Chu, general contractor Mike Robinson, and attorney Peter Wagner. Well-established and successful Fargo businessmen, the owners have an excellent long-term working relationship and have made a number of joint investments in land and real estate development projects throughout North Dakota. Chu and Wagner each have 25 percent stakes in the business, while Robinson (who owns the facility in which the business is located) has a 50 percent stake. In addition to the owners, FunXplosion will employ one full-time manager, one full-time assistant manager, and 10 part-time employees.

Professional and Advisory Support

FunXplosion has retained Fargo Tax Advisory Inc., a local accounting firm, to assist us with book-keeping and tax responsibilities. Commercial checking accounts have been established with Bennington Bank, which has agreed to provide merchant accounts so that we are able to accept credit card and debit card payments. Legal services will be provided by co-owner and attorney Peter Wagner.

BUSINESS STRATEGY

Following our grand opening in June of 2010, FunXplosion will devote its first year of operations to becoming the recreation destination of choice in the local marketplace. Our marketing efforts will concentrate on both the Fargo area, as well as the nearby Grand Forks community.

We realize that a successful family entertainment center continuously introduces new attractions. With this in mind, we will make it a point to introduce new videogames within our arcade each year. Because we are working with a third party to provide games, this should be relatively easy to do. Furthermore, every three years, we will evaluate the feasibility of changing the thematics of our miniature golf courses.

In addition to refreshing existing features, we plan to introduce new ones based upon business volume and customer interest. These include outdoor attractions that will draw large volumes of people to our facility during the summer months, including:

• Baseball diamonds

• Soccer fields

• Outdoor miniature golf

• A jogging course/walking path

The possibility of adding features such as these is very feasible, thanks to 10 undeveloped acres of land (owned by co-owner and real estate developer John Chu) which are located behind FunXplosion.

SERVICES

Our business offers the following leisure activities:

Video Arcade—Videogames are essential to the success of a family entertainment center. Our arcade offers a generous selection of the latest/most popular video games, as well as classics (appreciated by parents who grew up during the 1980s) such as Pac-Man, Galga, Dig Dug, and Spy Hunter. Games are operated by tokens, which customers pre-purchase upon entering the facility. Based on performance, games issue tickets which can be redeemed for prizes in our PrizeDepot redemption area. The arcade also includes table games such as pool, bumper pool, and air hockey.

LaserZone—This area includes two separate attractions that are fun for children and adults alike: laser tag and a laser maze. Although laser tag is well known, our timed laser maze involves the use of black lights and mirrors to produce intertwining laser beams, which participants must navigate through without touching.

PlayWorld—An essential for our youngest customers, our bounce/inflatable play area includes a large inflatable slide, several climbing towers, and a ball pit for fun that is both unlimited and safe.

Indoor Miniature Golf—The main attraction at FunXplosion is miniature golf. We offer two themed (outer space and beneath the sea) 18-hole courses, both of which are wheelchair accessible. Both courses, which include original props consistent with each theme, come complete with features such as sand traps, rough areas, water hazards, and risers. Each uses black lights and fluorescent paint to create an otherworldly experience.

Room Rentals—We offers six party rooms, which are available as part of celebration packages that include a pre-determined number of tokens. Customers are allowed to bring in their own food and cake, or obtain these items through our food/concession area.

Food/Concession Area—Our food/concession area offers all of the yummy food that kids want, from hot dogs and hamburgers to chicken nuggets and pizza. In addition, we offer a wide selection of soft drinks and cool treats like ice cream sandwiches.

FunXplosion Birthday Party Package—We offer a turn-key birthday package for families (four-guest minimum) that includes the following:

- 30 Game Tokens per Child
- 10 bonus tokens for the birthday child
- 180-minute party room reservation
- Choice of child-sized hamburger or hot dog
- Unlimited French fry baskets
- Unlimited soft drinks
- Balloons and streamers (party room decorations)
- Tablecloth and plateware
- Special sticker for birthday child

MARKETING & SALES

A marketing plan has been developed for FunXplosion that includes these main tactics:

Web Site—FunXplosion has developed a Web site that lists information about our attractions, party packages, prices, and hours. In addition, the site includes information about special deals, as well as directions to our facility.

Brochure—A tri-fold, four-color brochure, targeted toward parents of young children and organizations interested in group outings, has been developed. This printed piece provides many of the same details included on our Web site.

Advertising—A regular advertising presence will be established in INFORUM, a leading online news resource in North Dakota that reaches more than 350,000 unique visitors per month. In addition, we will take out print advertisements in the West Fargo Pioneer, a weekly community newspaper, as well as a weekly shopper named The Midweek.

Sales Promotion—Each month, our manager will make four to six presentations to local groups and organizations promoting FunXplosion. He or she will provide passes for complementary rounds of miniature golf, as an incentive for decision-makers to visit and evaluate our facility as a destination for their group.

Grand Opening Celebration Campaign—FunXplosion will commence operations with a grand opening celebration in the summer of 2010. To generate awareness and build excitement surrounding our grand opening in June, we will place billboard advertisements throughout Fargo in the month of May. Simultaneously, we will run aggressive radio and print media campaigns during the second half of the month.

We will evaluate our marketing plan on a quarterly basis during our first year of operations, and semi-annually thereafter.

OPERATIONS

Hours

- Monday through Thursday—3 PM to 9 PM
- Friday—3 PM to 10 PM
- Saturday—Noon to 10 PM
- Sunday—Noon to 8 PM

*We offer expanded offers on school holidays and over winter and holiday breaks by opening our doors at 1 PM.

Rates

Miniature Golf

- Adults: $7
- Children (12 and under): $5

LaserZone

- Adults: $5
- Children (12 and under): $3

PlayWorld

- Children (12 and under): $3

Game Tokens

- $1 = 4 tokens
- $5 = 25 tokens
- $10 = 50 tokens

FunXplosion Birthday Party Package—$10 per child

Facility and Location

FunXplosion is located in a 40,000-square-foot facility. A former warehouse, the building is owned by co-owner Mike Robinson, who had previously used the building to store equipment and materials for his construction business. Converting the structure into a family entertainment center (which Robinson was largely able to do at cost) was relatively simple, given that the facility already was an open, multipurpose space.

The main level of FunXplosion, which spans about 30,000 square feet, is divided into several main zones. Upon entering the facility, visitors find a circular customer service center desk, where they are able to purchase tokens, rounds of miniature golf, tickets to other attractions, and receive instructions related to room reservations. Our private party rooms are located to the left of the customer service desk. Play-World, our bounce/inflatable play area, is located on the right-hand side of the customer service desk.

Moving deeper into the facility, customers find our food/concession area, which includes an open space with tables and chairs where families can spread out and relax. PlayWorld borders the food/concession area, so that parents can watch their small children play while enjoying a beverage or something to eat. To the left of the food/concession area is the LaserZone. Laser attractions are provided in partnership with a third-party, from whom we lease equipment via a profit-sharing arrangement.

Finally, our two miniature golf courses are located in the rear of the facility, occupying a total of 10,000 square feet. We have purchased modular miniature golf courses from a recognized national vendor, ensuring quality and the very best player experience.

In the food/concession area, customers find a wide, open staircase, as well as an elevator for guests with special needs, which provide access to a 10,000-square-foot loft located above the miniature golf courses. This level contains our arcade, as well as a redemption center where guests can redeem tickets for prizes. Arcade games and redemptions are provided in partnership with a third-party, from whom we lease equipment via a profit-sharing arrangement.

In addition to the arcade area, the loft includes a small business office for facility management, equipped with a two-way mirror from which activity below can be viewed, as well as video cameras that provide additional views of the main level (including night vision cameras within the miniature golf courses).

Our facility has ample parking and an overhang that provides protection from the elements for guests who are being dropped off at the main entrance.

LEGAL

Our business is in full compliance with all legal and regulatory requirements pertaining to the operation of our business. Specifically, we adhere to the requirements set forth in the North Dakota Century Code, pertaining to the licensing of amusement games. We also meet requirements of the Americans with Disabilities Act. In addition, we have obtained appropriate business and liability insurance.

FINANCIAL ANALYSIS

Start-up Costs

The main startup costs for FunXplosion are as follows:

- Modular Golf Course Construction—$300,000

- Facility Remodeling—$100,000

- Play Equipment—$20,000

- Total—$420,000

Co-owners John Chu, Mike Robinson, and Peter Wagner will provide working capital, as well as funding to cover start-up costs. Based upon projected net income, the owners will recoup their investment and begin generating profits from the business during the fourth year of operations.

Grant Writer

Whitfield Resources LLC

8609 John St.
Fullerton, CA 92834

Paul Greenland

Whitfield Resources writes grant proposals, helps organizations identify potential funding sources, and provides proposal evaluation/review services (e.g., assessing, proofreading, editing, and rewriting existing proposals).

EXECUTIVE SUMMARY

Business Overview

Nonprofit organizations depend on a steady stream of funding to maintain operations and carry out their respective missions. While some of this funding comes in the form of donations, grants are another very important source. Grant writing is the practice of securing funding from foundations, government agencies, individuals, or corporations. Whitfield Resources provides clients with a variety of services related to grant writing. In addition to writing grant proposals, we also help organizations identify potential funding sources and provide proposal evaluation/review services (e.g., assessing, proofreading, editing, and rewriting existing proposals).

Whitfield Resources is owned by Carl Whitfield. After a 10-year career in the corporate communications field, where his responsibilities included proposal writing for a large packaged goods company, Whitfield decided to put his research, writing, and human relations skills to work in the nonprofit sector.

MARKET ANALYSIS

Whitfield Resources is based in Fullerton, California. Located 22 miles southeast of Los Angeles, the city is one of the largest in Orange County and is characterized by a solid commercial, industrial, residential, and educational base.

According to U.S. Census data, in 2006 the city of Fullerton had 132,918 residents, up from 126,003 in 2000. White individuals represented 61.9 percent of the population, followed by persons of Hispanic or Latino origin (30.2%). The home ownership rate in 2000 was 53.9 percent, compared to 56.9 percent for California as a whole. Individuals living below the poverty line totaled approximately 11.4 percent, a figure that was lower than the state level of 14.2 percent.

Orange County was home to 3.01 million individuals in 2008, an increase of 5.8 percent from 2000. At 78.4 percent, White individuals were the largest demographic group, followed by persons of Hispanic or

Latino origin (33.8%). Persons with disabilities (over age 5) totaled approximately 434,000 during the early 2000s. The homeownership rate of 61.4 percent was slightly higher than the state as a whole (56.9%). County-wide, 8.9 percent of the population lived below the poverty line in 2007, compared to 12.4 percent for California as a whole. In 2008, federal spending for Orange County totaled approximately $17.7 million.

As is the case nationwide, the nonprofit sector plays a central role in ensuring the quality of life in Orange County. However, by 2009 the national economic crisis was having a significant impact on foundations throughout the local market. According to a study conducted by The Orange County Funders Roundtable, a coalition of local foundations, although 66 percent of nonprofit organizations reported increased demand for services, 58 percent indicated their revenues had declined. This situation was exacerbated by a budget crisis at the state level that impacted the availability of many that services. Nonprofit agencies have addressed these challenges in a number of ways, including cutbacks, increasing efficiency, and stepping up efforts to secure donations.

INDUSTRY

According to data from the U.S. Bureau of Labor Statistics' *2010-11 Career Guide to Industries*, the advocacy, grantmaking, and civic organizations sector employed 1.3 million salaried individuals in 2008. In terms of establishments, the industry was comprised of four main categories. Business, professional, labor, political, and similar organizations constituted 50.4 percent of establishments, followed by civic and social organizations (23.9%), social advocacy organizations (14.9%), and grant-making and giving services (10.8%).

Nonprofit organizations help to provide funding beyond the scope of government agencies in areas such as education, science, literature, religion, and charity. According to a 2009 report from the firm Research and Markets, there were more than 1 million nonprofit organizations in the United States, with collective annual revenues exceeding $1 trillion. More than 80 percent of the sector's annual revenue was generated by only 6 percent of organizations (those with assets exceeding $10 million). Examples of these large organizations include the Bill & Melinda Gates Foundation, as well as Goodwill Industries and the National Cancer Institute. Federal, state, and local governments also are major sources of funding.

During the late 2000s, nonprofit organizations were contending with the effects of a struggling economy. According to a study conducted by Bridgespan, which began in late 2008 and was updated in May 2009, among approximately 100 leading nonprofit organizations, 92 percent indicated that they had been impacted by the struggling economy. Specifically, 49 percent indicated that their financial situation had declined between late 2008 and mid-2009. Furthermore, those experiencing funding cuts increased from 52 percent to 69 percent. As a result of these difficulties, 41 percent reported that they were laying off staff.

Even though funding sources are dealing with declining donation levels, individuals and organizations continue to seek grant funding. As competition for more limited resources increases, so do opportunities for successful, proven grant writers.

PERSONNEL

Carl Whitfield is the sole employee of Whitfield Resources. His writing skills were apparent at an early age, when he served as editor of his school newspaper in both junior and senior high school. He began writing successful proposals in college, pitching article ideas to newspapers and magazines. Eventually,

Whitfield authored several of his own non-fiction books and, after writing effective book proposals, placed them with established publishers.

Whitfield later pursued a career in the corporate communications field, where his responsibilities included proposal writing for a large packaged goods company. After working in this capacity for 10 years, he decided to put his research, writing, and human relation skills to work in the nonprofit sector. Whitfield began acquiring grant-writing experience by working with local nonprofit agencies on a volunteer basis. From 2005 to 2007, he gained experience helping these organizations secure grants from local foundations, as well as from the state of California. Whitfield began charging fees for his services in 2008, when he began working as a freelance grant writer. With two years of paid experience, he is ready to begin working in this capacity exclusively in 2010.

Whitfield has established a business banking account with Orange County Community Bank, as well as a merchant account for accepting credit card payments. Legal services are provided by the law offices of Fox, Holloway & Johnson, and tax advisory services are provided by Bottom Line Accounting LLC.

GROWTH STRATEGY

As previously mentioned, Carl Whitfield has already been working as a freelance grant writer for two years. Based on his knowledge of the local market, Whitfield projects that he will be able to increase his project volume at a steady base over the course of his first three years as a full-time grant writer. Following are three-year projections for Whitfield Resources' billable hours.

Billable hours	2010	2011	2012
Grant writing	500	600	700
Consulting	240	300	360

Based upon these figures, Whitfield still has ample time in his schedule to perform administrative tasks related to the business and take advantage of other revenue-generating and/or promotional opportunities, such as writing "expert" articles for industry and trade publications and serving as a guest speaker.

SERVICES

Whitfield Resources provides clients with a variety of services related to grant writing, including:

- Writing grant proposals
- Helping organizations identify potential funding sources
- Providing proposal evaluation/review services (e.g., assessing, proofreading, editing, and rewriting existing proposals)

Examples of the organizations that we provide services to include:

- Hospitals
- Colleges & Universities
- Schools
- Symphonies
- Museums

- Homeless Shelters

- Daycare Centers

- Advocacy Groups

- Conservation/Natural Resource Organizations

- Scientific Researchers

- Churches & Religious Organizations

- Neighborhood Associations

In order to identify grant opportunities for our clients, our business will secure a professional-level subscription to the Foundation Center's Foundation Directory Online, which provides profiles of approximately 100,000 grantmakers (trustees, donors, officers, etc.), as well as more than 1.8 million grants. The database is searchable by county, ZIP code, congressional district, city, state, metropolitan area, and more. Among its many features is the ability to export search results into an Excel spreadsheet, and exclude grantmakers that don't accept unsolicited applications.

MARKETING & SALES

Although Whitfield Resources is a new business enterprise, Carl Whitfield already has established a reputation for success in the local marketplace. After writing several successful grant applications, his name began to circulate quickly throughout the nonprofit community. Although Whitfield estimates that there is plenty of opportunity in the local market, he plans to promote his services in a number of ways:

- A Web site with complete details about Whitfield Resources. This will include details about the services we provide, as well as a fact-gathering/intake form for potential new clients.

- A Yellow Page listing.

- Membership in the local chamber of commerce.

- Regular phone calls to the directors of local nonprofit organizations, in order to stay informed of their challenges and objectives and discuss potential funding opportunities.

- A semiannual newsletter to local nonprofit agencies, in order to keep them informed of trends related to grants/funding, share some of our success stories, and maintain visibility.

OPERATIONS

Facility & Location

Carl Whitfield will operate Whitfield Resources as a home-based business. He has devoted space within his home for business purposes. In addition, Whitfield has installed a dedicated telephone line for the business, and has established a small home office equipped with a computer, multi-functional peripheral device (e.g., copy, fax, scanner), and file storage area. Whitfield also has purchased a smart phone, which will allow him to be accessible via voice, text message, and e-mail at all times.

Payment & Fees

To some degree, Whitfield Resources' fees are negotiable. Typically, our business estimates work on a per-project basis. This flat fee is based on a detailed assessment of the project, and an hourly rate of approximately $75 per hour. We do not work on commission (e.g., based upon successful reception of the grant).

FINANCIAL ANALYSIS

Following are three-year financial projections for Whitfield Resources, based on Carl Whitfield's knowledge of the local market. This plan will be revised in year four (2013).

	2010	2011	2012
Revenue			
Grant writing	$37,500	$45,000	$52,500
Consulting	$18,000	$22,500	$27,000
Other	$ 1,500	$ 2,250	$ 3,875
Total revenue	**$57,000**	**$69,750**	**$83,375**
Expenses			
Advertising & marketing	$ 500	$ 500	$ 500
Miscellaneous items	$ 250	$ 300	$ 350
Legal	$ 250	$ 250	$ 250
Accounting	$ 500	$ 500	$ 500
Office supplies	$ 250	$ 250	$ 250
Computers/peripherals	$ 1,500	$ 0	$ 0
Business insurance	$ 500	$ 500	$ 500
Salaries	$45,000	$55,000	$65,000
Postage	$ 350	$ 350	$ 350
Telecommunications	$ 500	$ 500	$ 500
Travel	$ 500	$ 600	$ 750
Subscriptions	$ 1,750	$ 2,250	$ 2,500
Total expenses	**$51,850**	**$61,000**	**$71,450**
Net income	**$ 5,150**	**$ 8,750**	**$11,925**

Green/Sustainability Consulting Firm

Ward & O'Neil LLC

2701 Forest View Rd.
Pikesburg, OH 43042

Paul Greenland

Ward & O'Neil LLC is a green/sustainability consulting firm serving both consumer and commercial markets.

EXECUTIVE SUMMARY

Business Overview

More than ever before, environmental sustainability is a high priority for consumers and businesses alike. "Going green" is more than just a passing fad. In fact, for many it has become a way of life. According to *Sustainability: The Rise of Consumer Responsibility*, a 2009 study conducted by the Hartman Group, 88 percent of consumers indicated that they were engaged in sustainable behaviors during the late 2000s.

In order to benefit the environment and take advantage of tax incentives and credits from energy companies, consumers and businesses were actively seeking opportunities to engage in environmentally sustainable behavior. From insulating homes and harvesting rainwater for reuse to installing wind power turbines and engaging in environmentally responsible land development, those interested in going green had a seemingly endless (and sometimes confusing) list of options to choose from.

Established in 2008, Ward & O'Neil LLC is a green/sustainability consulting firm serving both consumer and commercial markets. Our business works with individuals, as well as small and medium-sized companies, to help them identify opportunities for incorporating environmental sustainability into their everyday lives and business practices. Education is a large component of what we do.

Organizational Structure

Ward & O'Neil is a limited liability corporation based in the state of Ohio. Our business structure offers the liability protection of a corporation, along with the advantage of being treated as a partnership. Our firm is owned by John Ward, a former home inspector and commercial construction firm manager, and mechanical engineer Sharon O'Neil.

MARKET ANALYSIS

Covering 65 square miles, the city of Pikesburg, Ohio, was home to 167,438 residents and 69,378 households in 2009, according to a community study conducted by the City of Pikesburg. Median household income was $55,023. The city was home to 8,754 businesses, including a once-strong manufacturing base that has been negatively impacted by off–shoring, outsourcing, and the general economic downturn.

Numerous opportunities for green consulting services exist in our local market. Although new construction activity is currently limited due to the economy, many local service and manufacturing operations stand to benefit from modifying their operations to incorporate simple energy– and cost–saving strategies. In addition, some businesses have expressed an interest in retrofitting their existing facilities to become more energy efficient.

On a different level, opportunities exist to consult with companies about new business opportunities in the green industry. Green technology, such as solar cells, wind turbines, solar panels, and other components, depend upon assemblers, installers, welders, machinists, and so on. Manufacturers who have seen their traditional business decline may be able to take advantage of opportunities related to green technology. One unique attribute of our community is the Pikesburg Green Chamber of Commerce. Separate from our traditional Metropolitan Chamber of Commerce, the organization was established two years ago to encourage policy change at the government level and bring green industry jobs to our city.

Pikesburg's consumer market also offers ample opportunities. According to the aforementioned survey, more than 50 percent of the homes in our community are older (including many built shortly after World War II). This translates into considerable opportunity for our firm, in terms of teaching area homeowners how to maximize the energy efficiency of their homes. Contrary to popular belief, going green does not have to be expensive. In many cases, we can provide simple, commonsense tips to help homeowners conserve energy and save money. Sometimes this is as simple as sealing doorframes, adding weather stripping, tuning up their furnace, or installing an electronic thermostat.

INDUSTRY ANALYSIS

The green industry is much broader than many people realize. Numerous new job opportunities exist pertaining to wind and solar technology, construction management, climate change, and sustainability. Opportunities exist for positions ranging from architectural designers to executive directors. Nationwide, the leading cities for green jobs include Washington, DC; San Francisco; Chicago; Boston; Seattle; New York; Portland, Oregon; and Burlington, Vermont. According to a report from the Pew Charitable Trusts, clean energy–related jobs grew 9.1 percent nationally between 1998 and 2007, compared to a growth rate of 3.7 percent for traditional jobs.

Recent industry trends include so–called eco–construction, especially in the retail and hospitality industries. The London 2012 Olympics has a formal sustainable development strategy, overseen by a head of sustainability. In addition, by late 2009 there were nearly 250 insurers, brokers, insurance organizations, and reinsurers offering a wide range of eco–friendly products. Examples include special policies for certified "green" homes and buildings, premium discounts for hybrid vehicle owners, pay–as–you–drive insurance programs that benefit those who drive fewer miles, and policies covering lost income (due to power outages) for those who generate their own wind, solar, or geothermal energy and sell surplus back to the local power grid.

There is strong evidence of the industry's growth. According to the U.S. Green Building Council, the green building products and services market was projected to reach $60 billion by 2010, up from $12 billion in 2007. According to a report prepared by the Lawrence Berkeley National Laboratory for the U.S. Department of Energy, the United States had the world's fastest–growing wind power market in 2008. That year, wind power capacity additions grew at a rate of 60 percent, fueled by investments of $16 million. In addition, wind power represented 42 percent of the nation's new electric–generating capacity.

One of the leading trade associations in our industry is the U.S. Green Building Council. Based in Washington, D.C., the non–profit USGBC is "committed to a prosperous and sustainable future for our nation through cost–efficient and energy–saving green buildings." During the late 2000s, the association had more than 20,000 member companies or organizations and approximately 100,000 LEED Accredited Professionals. In addition, the USGBC operated the LEED Green Building Rating System, which rated green buildings in the areas of design, construction, and operation. As the association explains, "by using less energy, LEED–certified buildings save money for families, businesses and taxpayers; reduce greenhouse gas emissions; and contribute to a healthier environment for residents, workers and the larger community."

PERSONNEL

Ward & O'Neil is owned and operated by John Ward, a former home inspector and commercial construction firm manager, and mechanical engineer Sharon O'Neil. Both have pursued specialized education and training specific to the operation of this consulting firm. For example, they have completed continuing education courses specific to:

- Solar Electricity
- Solar Hot Water Systems
- Wind Generators
- Pollution Prevention Planning
- Erosion and Sediment Control
- Sustainable Business Practices
- Building Energy Evaluation
- Green Design
- Green Construction Technology
- Sustainable Lifestyles

John Ward

John Ward began his career as a carpenter, working in residential and light commercial construction. In time, he was promoted to foreman and earned an associate's degree in construction engineering technology from City College. After earning an undergraduate degree in Construction Management from the State University of Upper Ohio, Ward began working as a project engineer, where his responsibilities included estimating, scheduling, and planning. Prior to co–founding Ward & O'Neil, Ward served as the construction manager of a large construction firm in Massachusetts, where he was involved in numerous commercial and residential projects. Ward is a member of the Project Management Institute, as well as the Construction Management Association of America.

Sharon O'Neil, LEED A.P.

After earning an undergraduate degree in mechanical engineering from Virginia Commonwealth University, followed by a graduate degree from Northern City College, O'Neil worked for a large engineering firm in Toledo, Ohio. There, her responsibilities included planning, designing, and directing a variety of projects. In addition to possessing good people and teamwork skills, O'Neil is knowledgeable about U.S. structural and building codes. In addition, she also is proficient at interpreting architectural drawings, as well as using software applications such as Auto CAD. O'Neil has earned the LEED AP credential from the Green Building Institute, signifying her expertise in green building.

In addition to the owners, Ward & O'Neil also employs Sharon Menke, a full–time administrative assistant who is responsible for managing our schedules, facilitating communications with clients and subcontractors, performing basic bookkeeping, ordering office supplies and other items, managing inbound and outgoing U.S. mail and overnight packages, and performing a wide range of other duties.

Professional & Advisory Support

Due to the sometimes complex nature of our work, we have formed a professional relationship with Johnson & Smith, a law firm specializing in the area of environmental and construction law. Additionally, our firm has established a business banking account with Pikesburg Community Bank, including a merchant account for credit card payments. Tax advisement is provided by A–1 Accounting Inc.

GROWTH STRATEGY

Ward & O'Neil's initial two years of operation have been extremely successful, despite a difficult economic climate. Established with $20,000 of capital, with equal amounts provided by each owner, we achieved remarkable growth during our second year. Elsewhere in the United States, we are aware of similar consulting firms that have achieved annual growth of 400 to 700 percent. In our local market, we anticipate that there will be ample opportunities to support compound annual growth of 35 percent for five to seven years. Long–term, our strategy will be to add additional staff (with construction and engineering expertise) starting in 2013, which will be needed to prepare for regional expansion.

SERVICES

Generally speaking, the services provided by our firm fall into several broad areas, including education, consulting, and project management.

In the area of education, we provide courses and seminars for both consumers and businesses at Pikesburg Community Center, where we lease classroom space for a nominal fee. These include:

Consumers
- Sustainable Lifestyle Development
- Introduction to Alternative Energy
- Introduction to Green Home Design/Retrofitting
- Advanced Green Home Design/Retrofitting

Businesses
- Sustainable Business Strategies
- Introduction to Building Energy Evaluation
- Advanced Building Energy Evaluation
- Introduction to Green Building Design/Retrofitting
- Advanced Green Building Design/Retrofitting

The consulting services we offer are based on the specific needs of the client, but generally pertain to all of the areas named above. In this capacity, we work with individuals and businesses to help them identify opportunities for incorporating environmental sustainability into their everyday lives and business practices. This may involve everything from helping companies learn about new business opportunities in the green industry to choosing green cleaning products for their maintenance staff to conducting audits of a home or commercial facility to identify opportunities for better energy efficiency.

Project management may range from overseeing the implementation of some simple energy–saving tactics in a consumer's home to helping manage construction of a new green building. Upon request, we hire the appropriate installers and contractors on behalf of our clients. Examples of projects we have overseen include:

- Home Insulation
- Rainwater Harvesting
- Wind Power Turbine Installation
- Solar Hot Water System Installation
- Green Building Retrofitting and Construction

MARKETING & SALES

We have developed a marketing plan that involves the following primary tactics:

1. Printed collateral describing our business.

2. Distribution of information about our firm to participants in all of the workshops and classes we teach at the local community center.

3. Advertisements in several print and online industry and professional directories.

4. A Web site with complete details about our business and the services we offer.

5. Two monthly e–mail newsletters (one for consumers and one for businesses), which provide case studies of successful project completions, as well as tips.

6. A public relations campaign that involves the submission of successful case studies (in the form of press releases) to appropriate national business and trade magazines, as well as our local newspaper and a regional business magazine. Specifically, case studies illustrate how we helped a client to lower energy costs, save money, and benefit the environment.

7. Membership and active participation in the Pikesburg Green Chamber of Commerce.

8. Tradeshow/exhibition marketing. Specifically, we will present at regional home repair and improvement shows, as well as local, regional, and state business expos.

OPERATIONS

Appropriately, our offices are located in the Pikesburg Professional Center, a green office building that we helped bring to the community with the help of our local Green Chamber of Commerce and city officials. This energy–efficient building, located in the heart of downtown Pikesburg, is also home to the Green Chamber of Commerce, several architects, attorneys, non–profit agencies, and a local advertising firm. The facility serves as a tangible example of our work when meet with clients.

Fees

Fees for the courses we teach through the Pikesburg Community Center range from $20–$50 per person for consumer courses, and $750–$2,500 for business–oriented courses. Basic consultations with consumers are offered at a rate of $50 per hour, while business consulting services are generally provided at a rate of $85 per hour. Project management generally is provided at a rate of $75 per hour. For large projects, we typically request 1/3 of our fees in advance, with the remainder due upon completion. Through an arrangement with a local finance company, we are able to provide qualified customers with financing for certain projects. In addition to cash and checks, we also accept credit card payments.

Hours of Operation

Our firm is typically open from 8:00 a.m. to 5:00 p.m., Monday through Friday. Meetings are offered by appointment only. When working on construction projects, clients and subcontractors are provided with our cell phone numbers, so that we are available at any time should an urgent situation arise.

LEGAL

Our firm has secured all necessary licenses to work in our field. We are bonded and insured, and adhere to all local, state, and federal building codes and construction laws. When providing oversight on specific construction projects, we ensure that the proper permits are obtained from the local building department, and we work with building inspectors to obtain all necessary approvals.

FINANCIAL ANALYSIS

Following is Ward & O'Neil's balance sheet for 2009, followed by two-year projections that take into account compound annual growth of 35 percent. Additional professional staff will be needed to sustain this growth rate in 2013 and beyond.

2009 Balance sheet

Revenue

Education	$ 66,500
Consulting	$101,250
Project management	$ 27,500
Total revenue	**$195,250**

Expenses

Salaries	$135,000
Utilities	$ 2,894
Rent	$ 12,500
Insurance	$ 7,982
Office supplies	$ 1,560
Equipment	$ 6,200
Marketing & advertising	$ 6,789
Telecommunications & internet	$ 3,872
Professional development	$ 12,567
Travel & entertainment	$ 1,509
Subscriptions & dues	$ 865
Taxes & fees	$ 2,587
Total expenses	**$194,325**

Two-Year Projections

Projections	2010	2012
Revenue	$263,588	$355,843
Net income	$ 33,330	$ 64,060

Jewelry Designer

Oswipi Custom Costume Jewelry Designs

77890 Washington Ave.
Cleveland, OH 44104

Heidi Denler

Oswipi Custom Costume Jewelry Designs offers discerning customers elegant costume necklaces, bracelets, and earrings created from Swarovski crystals and pearls. A second line features inexpensive children's and teen jewelry created from fun, hip beads and semi-precious stones. The company will primarily serve the online community and will be based at the owner's home.

COMPANY SUMMARY

Oswipi Custom Costume Jewelry Designs offers discerning customers elegant costume necklaces, bracelets, and earrings created from Swarovski crystals and pearls. A second line features inexpensive children's and teen jewelry created from fun, hip beads and semi-precious stones. The company will primarily serve the online community and will be based at the owner's home.

MANAGEMENT SUMMARY

Following an impulse six years ago, Maggie Mulcahy signed up for a beginner's jewelry making class. Before long, she was creating more jewelry than she could wear, and her friends could all expect gifts of her jewelry, no matter what the occasion. They encouraged her to start selling her work, which she did, starting with craft shows. As she became known, her work began to sell out. However, craft shows demand a huge investment of time. For that reason, Maggie decided to create an online presence with a web site of her own.

Mulcahy holds a BA in art history from Wayne State University. As a small child, she preferred being creative to playing sports or following many other childhood pursuits. She has designed needlepoint for sale at juried craft shows and enjoys making knitting and crocheting patterns her own by making changes to the patterns. She currently has a small studio in her basement where she crafts the jewelry that she has been selling at area juried art shows for the last several years.

She has hired an attorney familiar with start up companies, who is also well-versed in online businesses. Her husband, Jim Smith, is a CPA, and he will handle the books.

MISSION STATEMENT

Oswipi Costume Jewelry Designs will offer unique, custom-made costume jewelry to a discriminating clientele via online sales.

VISION STATEMENT

The future of Oswipi Costume Jewelry Designs is dependent on the owner, Maggie Mulcahy, following fashion trends and responding to them with cutting edge designs in colors and styles in keeping with the current fashion.

VALUES STATEMENT

Maggie Mulcahy is determined to provide quality work, using quality materials, with reliable delivery of the finished product to the customer.

BUSINESS PHILOSOPHY

Simplicity. Elegance. Custom-designs. Competitive pricing. This is what will set Oswipi Custom Costume Jewelry Designs apart from the other online jewelry sales.

OBJECTIVES

Recognizing that sitting for hours behind tables at craft shows is counterproductive, Mulcahy has set the creation of unique costume jewelry for a discriminating clientele online as her main objective. She will also offer a standard line of bracelets, necklaces, and earrings. A secondary objective is to place her jewelry in galleries. Mulcahy plans to increase the number of designs in her standard line 10 percent in the first year of operations. Within that time, she projects that she will be operating at a profit.

ORGANIZATION STRUCTURE

Owner Maggie Mulcahy will operate Oswipi Custom Costume Jewelry Designs as a sole proprietorship. She will handle designs, orders, customer conferencing, and shipping. Outside help will be required for legal and financial matters, leaving Mulcahy free to work on what she really loves—designing and creating fabulous jewelry.

ADVERTISING AND PROMOTION

Mulcahy will work with a web site design company to ensure that her company will be at or near the top of every search engine list. As profits grow, she will investigate becoming a paid sponsor of at least one search engine, such as GoodSearch or Bing.

Although web-based, Mulcahy will send press releases announcing the launch of her web site to local print, radio, and television media. Personal phone and e-mail follow-up will be made to build a relationship with area media personalities, which is expected to result in additional free positive marketing and promotion.

CUSTOMER BASE

The customer base for Oswipi Custom Costume Jewelry Designs will be the discerning online shopper, who seeks a competitive price range for quality design and workmanship. Reliability, quality of product, quality of service, and an ability to work with the client will be key factors in Mulcahy's online presence, as will competitive pricing.

Her secondary objective of placing her standard jewelry line in galleries will put her in contact with gallery and high-end gift shop owners/managers.

Each customer base is expected to result in long-term relationships with clients worldwide.

Galleries will purchase Oswipi's designs on a wholesale basis, and Mulcahy understands that the profit margin will be lower than on sales made directly online. Mulcahy expects Oswipi's online customers to provide "word-of-mouth" advertising to friends in person and online. She is considering a page on FaceBook to send more viewers to her site.

Until the web site is profitable, Mulcahy will continue to do a select number of juried shows. She will take advantage of the one-on-one interaction with new and repeat customers to direct them to her new web site.

PRODUCTS AND SERVICES

Maggie Mulcahy has created hundreds of custom designs for juried art shows in Ohio. In addition to necklaces, bracelets, and earrings that she has created for these shows, she has worked with individuals to design jewelry based on customer specifications. She works easily with clients to put their ideas for jewelry on paper for their approval before creating the actual piece. Using a digital camera and a scanner, she has worked with out-of-town clients over the last two years to create jewelry based on individual choices made by those clients.

Mulcahy attends gem and jewelry shows in the Midwest and shops the Internet to get the highest quality crystals, stones, and finding at the best prices. Swarovski crystals, pearls, and sterling silver comprise the basic components for her jewelry.

Mulcahy guarantees her work and will repair any item that requires it, ensuring high quality work. Since she has begun marketing her jewelry, no pieces have been returned for repair of any kind.

Oswipi will have a competitive advantage from her several years of successful design experience and lifelong artistic bent. Each piece of jewelry will be a work of wearable art.

PERSONNEL REQUIREMENTS

As sole proprietor Mulcahy will generate all designs and purchases of supplies for the company. She will consider training a long-time friend and neighbor who took that first jewelry-making class with her to implement her designs. However, the actual design of all jewelry will remain in the capable hands of Ms. Mulcahy. After six months of operation, Mulcahy will assess the need to hire someone part-time to handles packing and shipping.

LOCATION

As a web-based enterprise, Oswipi Custom Costume Jewelry Designs will not require actual rental office space. Instead, Mulcahy plans to expand the studio she currently uses in her basement to accommodate additional inventory and business. The cost for this expansion will be minimal.

COMPANY DESIGN & EQUIPMENT

In addition to a desk dedicated to designing jewelry, a large work table will be the centerpiece of the studio. A second desk will be available for the business end of the enterprise, with a filing cabinet; separate laptop for maintaining business records and inventory, ordering components, and communicating with clients; and typical office supplies. A landline phone with two lines, a fax machine, and a desktop computer for graphic design of jewelry will be housed at a second desk. The work table in the center of the room will be covered in felt and will have a shelf under it to store covered bead boards for work in progress. Ott lights will be at each work station to provide optimal light for design and work.

Several hundred clear plastic boxes of varying sizes, holding components, will be stocked on shelving units. Components will include Swarovski crystals, semi-precious stones, a wide variety of sterling silver beads, sterling silver crimp beads, sterling silver closures (i.e., toggles, lobster claws, etc.), beading wires in various sizes, and sterling silver wire to create individual closures and pendants. Tools needed include pliers (bent-nose, cutting, round nose, wire wrapping, flat nose, crimping, and split ring), measuring tools, reamers, safety glasses, and needles. Non-bead and non-crystal supplies will include anti-tarnish strips, polishing cloths, charts, and design software for the computer.

Display stands will be needed for bracelets, necklaces, and earrings. Sales supplies will include price tags and bags and jewelry boxes in various sizes with the company name imprinted on them. These supplies will be stored on the previously mentioned shelving units.

While Mulcahy has some of the requisite tools and supplies, she will need additional for the staff she plans to hire. Sales supplies are in constant need of replenishment.

FINANCIAL

Start-up costs will include any fees for registration of the company name and the business with all government authorities. In addition, the owner will have typical overhead costs of a percentage of the mortgage on her home, taxes, payroll, property insurance, liability insurance, inventory, telephone and a portion of her home's utilities, an alarm system, DSL Internet connection, and advertising/sponsorship for search engines. Of prime importance will be the amount invested in the creation and design of the web site.

Mulcahy will finance the startup with a business credit card she has secured from Visa. She expects to pay off those expenses in between six and twelve months. After one year, Mulcahy expects Oswipi Designs to be profitable. She projects that she will be able to make a living from profits within three years of beginning operations.

PROFESSIONAL & ADVISORY SUPPORT

Mulcahy has retained a local attorney who is well-known for working with start-up companies. She met Angie Dawson at an SBA conference she attended to learn more about starting a company based on her much-loved hobby. Dawson has 10 years of experience in working with online businesses and is well-versed with the intricacies of securing domain names and other issues that pertain to an Internet-based business.

She will hire her husband, a CPA, to handle tax matters for the business. She will handle simple bookkeeping tasks on her own for the first year, after which she will work with her husband to determine if she should turn over the business aspects of the company to him on a full-time basis.

BUSINESS AND GROWTH STRATEGY

Mulcahy expects to build the customer base for Oswipi Custom Costume Jewelry Designs slowly and steadily. She knows it is important to keep her private life separate from her business operation. Mulcahy will set specific hours for updating her web site and working with clients on their orders, as well as completing those orders. She will also set specific times for ordering supplies online each week. She plans to attend gem and jewelry shows at least quarterly.

Time will be set aside for increasing the number of original designs she will offer to galleries. As profits increase, Mulcahy plans to hire someone to work as a sales representative to allow her to devote her time to her real love—creating unique wearable artwork. The sales representative will visit local galleries to show jewelry specifically related to the type of artwork on display at each gallery. Once Oswipi's jewelry designs are successfully placed in these local galleries, the sales representative will widen the area he/she visits to place Oswipi jewelry in galleries increasingly farther from Mulcahy's home base. Eventually jewelry designs will be featured in a catalog to send to galleries around the country.

Mulcahy is constantly working to build inventory in preparation for shows, a process that will not alter for the first few months. Once the web site is launched, Mulcahy expects to make sales almost immediately.

COMPETITION

There is no limit to the competition in handmade jewelry in the early 21st century. By specializing in Swarovski crystal and pearl creations, Oswipi Custom Costume Jewelry Designs will serve a more elegant niche market. She will also offer semi-precious stone creations for those customers demanding a modern look.

Mulcahy will be looking to serve a market composed of discerning clients who seek affordable, stylish, elegant jewelry that truly is wearable art, especially when she begins marketing her creations to galleries. She hopes to fill a niche for those customers wishing to find unique pieces that will not be seen on others.

Oswipi Custom Costume Jewelry Designs will offer artistic, trendy jewelry for customers buying gifts, as well as those buying for themselves, especially those making impulsive purchases online. The jewelry will be marketed as fashionable accessories for those who are looking for cutting edge fashion or for traditional pieces. Creative, unique designs made in conjunction with customer input. Each custom piece will be unique to the customer's wants and needs, making a distinctive accessory.

WEB SITE

With an online business, the design of the web site is of prime importance. For this reason, even though Mulcahy is proficient at computer work and has designed a web page for her needlework, she will turn to Sunside Designs to build the web site for Oswipi Custom Costume Jewelry Designs. Visitors to the web site will be greeted by an opening page that will have buttons to navigate through the site. The site will have separate pages for necklaces, bracelets, and earrings, as well as for sets. Available pieces will be displayed for viewing after having been photographed by Mulcahy and uploaded to the site. Swarovski crystal and pearl pieces will be separate from the semi-precious pieces because they are aimed at two different target audiences.

Web site visitors will have the option of clicking on a button beneath the photo to get pricing information and order that piece directly or clicking on a second button beneath the photo to contact Mulcahy to work on a custom piece based on the photo. One page will be dedicated to custom order inquiries, which Mulcahy will respond to within 24 hours. In the instances when she is out-of-town at gem and jewelry shows, she will leave a notice on the web site that she is away and that there will be a delay in response time. However, by traveling with a laptop, she will be able to connect to her web site to monitor inquiries and contact those customers directly as she travels.

CONCLUSION

Oswipi Custom Costume Jewelry Designs will provide customers with a unique opportunity to purchase a piece of distinctive wearable art. The company will realize the creative dream of its owner while growing to include gallery sales along with start-up online sales. As such, profitability will be inherent in the time invested by the owner, and in time, the sales representative she hires. Working in her home studio, Mulcahy will be able to work on custom and standard pieces when creativity strikes.

Media Conversion Company

The Memory Keeper

66324 Hayes
Utica, MI 48316

Heidi Denler

Because photographs, slides, movies, and videotapes (magnetic films) have a relatively short shelf life, transfer to DVD, which has unlimited shelf life, is the best technology to save the memories captured on those formats. Customers will be encouraged to transfer those images sooner rather than later with the help of The Memory Keeper.

COMPANY SUMMARY

The Memory Keeper began operations as a photography shop and studio. Customers would drop off film that would be processed on-site. They would often hang around the shop to chat while they looked at the latest in photographic equipment. As technology moved to the digital age, owner Todd Denton had a choice to make. He could close up shop and try to find work as a photographer, or he could move his shop and studio into digital technology. He chose the latter, and his shop evolved to help his faithful customers as well as new ones as they embraced the new technology together. Denton recognized that selling digital cameras and processing digital photographs was not going to pay the bills and began to research related photographic services. He quickly discovered that people were interested in preserving their traditional photographs and movies. Denton's plan is to expand his current business to help his customers and friends keep their memories alive in modern formats.

Because photographs, slides, movies, and videotapes (magnetic films) have a relatively short shelf life, transfer to DVD, which has unlimited shelf life, is the best technology to save the memories captured on those formats. Customers will be encouraged to transfer those images sooner rather than later. The Memory Keeper will work with the customer to create bookmarked chapters that will make DVDs easy to watch using an on-screen menu. The DVD format is relatively inexpensive, making it easy to share memories of weddings, parties, kids' sports, and vacations.

MANAGEMENT SUMMARY

Todd Denton has 27 years of experience owning his own business and working with customers. He purchased his original photography shop and studio from his employer of eight years, who was retiring. Denton has made a practice of hiring co-op students from the local high school to work after school and on weekends. He has an office manager who has been with him for 10 years, handling inventory and the books. Either Denton or the office manager are on the premises, and more often than not, both of them are there. During busy seasons Denton's wife, Trish, assists with the transfer process to keep orders filled in a timely fashion.

The owner's experience, coupled with the careful hiring of staff that will be carefully mentored to learn the business, will provide customers with assistance to choose the right end product for the job. Quality, attention to detail, reliability, and customer service will be of prime importance to all employees of The Memory Keeper.

Denton's long-time friend and attorney will continue to handle all legal matters, while the office manager will continue to work with the shop's accountant to handle all financial business, including taxes and insurance.

MISSION STATEMENT

The Memory Keeper will enable customers to preserve family photographic and movie memories that are captured on old-fashioned film by transferring them to digital technology in a timely fashion. Customer service is the core of the family business dedicated to the preservation of memories on film.

VISION STATEMENT

The Memory Keeper will grow through offering quality products to customers and providing only the best in customer service.

VALUES STATEMENT

Todd Denton is dedicated to provide his customers—who have become his friends—with quality service and quality products at reasonable prices.

BUSINESS PHILOSOPHY

Friendly service and customer satisfaction, together with a quality product, will bring customers back to The Memory Keeper time and time again for all their photographic and video needs.

GOALS AND OBJECTIVES

Todd Denton has built a customer base that has grown over the years as he became friends with fellow photographers. He plans to expand the business to include amateur videographers who have captured family birthdays and holidays.

Denton plans a "Grand Re-opening" of his "new" shop during which he will advertise special offers for discounted and two-for-one services. A new graphic logo will be unveiled at an open house for current customers and their friends and family. That logo will be the focal point of new ads for local papers and Yellow Pages advertisements. He will also include it on ads in local free publications found in the lobbies of many establishments in Metro Detroit.

During slow months between peak holiday busy seasons, Denton will offer additional specials for his services on a rotating basis.

As the business grows, Denton plans to hire additional staff to take the burden off himself as he prepares to retire in about 10 years. He hopes to find an employee he can mentor, much like he was mentored, and who will eventually buy the business.

Because Denton is embracing technology for his reinvented business, he will launch a Web site that will allow him to provide his services for customers outside the Metro Detroit area. They will be able to send him their photos and movies that he will transfer to DVD format and return to the customers along with their original data formats.

ORGANIZATION STRUCTURE

The Memory Keeper will shift from a sole proprietorship to a partnership as Todd Denton brings his wife into the equation as a full partner. This will ease the transition later when the Dentons will sell the business. Particular attention will have to be paid to keeping the Dentons personal property and investments separated from the business, so additional legal fees will be incurred.

ADVERTISING AND PROMOTION

Invitations will be sent to current customers for the "Grand Re-opening," which will feature samples of the products that the new business will offer. The event will take place on a Sunday evening, with wine, soft drinks, and hearty hors d'oeuvres being served.

During the week following the invitation-only party, customers will be offered complimentary coffee and cookies as they work with Denton to choose the services best suited to their photos and/or videos as well as to the intended use of the new DVD being created by The Memory Keeper staff.

Flyers will be distributed to homes in the immediate neighborhood (within a 5 mile radius of the shop). They will also be included in the local weekly newspaper.

Ads will be placed announcing the Grand Re-opening, and press releases announcing the re-opening will be sent to the local in an effort to have articles written for free advertising. The ads will include a coupon for 10 percent off a customer's initial purchase over $50. Personal phone calls and e-mail follow-up will be made to build a relationship with area media in an effort to garner free promotions and marketing.

CUSTOMER BASE

The primary customer base for The Memory Keeper will be a demographic of those over the age of 30 who have a substantial collection of family photographs and movies/videos in traditional formats of 35mm photographs, 8mm, 16mm, VHS, or even Betamax. Family memories of bridal and baby showers, weddings and rehearsal dinners, bachelor and bachelorette parties, graduations from elementary, middle, and high school or college, and children's sports and birthday parties can be transferred to DBD format to be shared and passed on to future generations.

Sports teams and athletic departments will be able to take advantage of The Memory Keeper's services to create montages of team highlights for playback at awards banquets and for use as a video yearbook.

Denton plans to expand his customer base by word of mouth referrals as well as from one-on-one meetings with event planners, athletic directors, and the like. He will also take advantage of free and paid publicity in the form of ads and press releases.

The customer base will extend to the Internet with the launch of The Memory Keeper's Web site, which will allow Denton to move beyond the Metro Detroit area for his customer base.

PRODUCTS AND SERVICES

Hours for The Memory Keeper's brick-and-mortar shop will be set to accommodate the customers. The shop will be open from 11 AM to 8 PM Monday through Thursday and from 10 AM to 5 PM Friday and Saturday. Sunday hours might be added in the future, as business demands and additional staff is hired.

The web site will be checked daily and updated as necessary to reflect specials, sales, etc. The e-mail and orders generated by web site traffic will be checked at least once every morning and every afternoon to ensure prompt attention to Internet customers orders and inquiries.

Customers who continue to use traditional 35mm cameras and film will still be able to have their cameras serviced and film developed at The Memory Keeper. Enlargements and specialty items made from favorite photographs and slides will also be offered as in the past.

Photo restoration will also continue to be available. Digital technology will enable The Memory Keeper to "repair" cracks and tears as well as remove stains and eliminate faded images.

In addition to traditional film and camera service, The Memory Keeper will offer film transfer for 8mm, Super 8, and 16 mm movies, as well as video tape transfers, including VHS, Betamax, Digital 8, and others.

All transfers will be made carefully and fully, frame by frame in the case of 8mm, Super 8, and 16mm, onto DVDs that can be played on a standard home DVD player. Because of the age of those images, The Memory Keeper will examine the film, and make necessary repairs to the film and to the sprockets on the reels prior to transferring the images to a DVD. In addition, slides, negatives, and old photos can be transferred by The Memory Keeper.

Originals will be returned with the new DVD(s). Customers will not see color, light, or speed being compromised in the transferred images.

Optional enhancement and blow-up services will also be available at prices competitive with FedEx/ Kinkos, Staples, etc.

Photo montages for weddings, anniversaries, birthdays, graduations, funerals, and wakes will be another option for customers who want to preserve memories. Montages will include titles and can include music of the customer's choice. Photos will be cropped electronically to highlight the picture's subject, and borders will be available at an added charge.

DVDs will all come with visual bookmarks and menus to enable customers to go directly to the image(s) they want to view. Each bookmark will be identified with a title decided by the customer for easier searching and identification of memorable events.

DVDs will be professionally labeled, not just a name scribbled on the DVD with a Sharpie.

LOCATION

The Memory Keeper will remain in its current location in Utica, Michigan, although it will expand to incorporate the neighboring storefront when it becomes available. That lease will be available in approximately 9 months, which gives Denton about three months to prepare the space and update according to his needs in order to announce the expansion at the one-year anniversary of The Memory Keeper. Customers are familiar with the location and it is on a main road in a popular strip mall that also features a Kroger store, a Walgreens, a Dollar Store, and a dry cleaner in an upper middle class suburb.

Denton currently pays $1,024 a month for his leased retail space. He is working with his landlord to work out an arrangement that will double his square footage without doubling his lease payment. Currently his lease includes taxes, utilities, trash removal, and snow removal. Denton would be interested in purchasing the properties, and his attorney is in discussion with the landlord.

STORE DESIGN AND EQUIPMENT

Denton plans minor renovations to the current photography shop and studio. A large flat screen plasma TV will be mounted on the wall behind the main service counter. Two desks with two chairs for customer seating opposite the tech representative will be on either side of the room for consultation purposes.

A computer at the main service counter will serve to track sales, monitor inventory, and track purchasing trends. That computer will be connected with a computer in the office that will track payroll, employee benefits, taxes, and standard operating expenses, including utilities, rent, insurance, and all banking transactions.

The majority of the studio will be for the actual work being done. A computer will be at each work station. The dedicated lab will house scanners and 3CCD cameras for transfer (with three chips to capture colors rather than just one chip in the 1CCD cameras).

Film processing equipment will remain in house for work on traditional cameras and photo processing for long-time customers who have not yet embraced the latest in digital photography. Equipment in the lab will be serviced routinely for the best possible transfer of the customers' images.

FINANCIAL

Denton will continue to work with his current financial manager, who has been with him for the last 15 years. They have established an excellent working relationship, and when the manager is away, his partner handles Denton's business and personal finances.

Other start up costs will include any fees for registration of the name and the business with all government authorities. In addition, the owners will have typical overhead costs of rent/mortgage payments, taxes, payroll, payroll taxes, key man insurance, property insurance, liability insurance, inventory, telephone and utilities, an alarm system, and advertising.

PROFESSIONAL AND ADVISORY SUPPORT

As with managing the financial aspect of The Memory Keeper, Denton will continue to work with the attorney he has retained for 10 years. He is well versed in small business law in Michigan.

Denton will also continue to work with the insurance agency he has worked with for 20 years to provide life, health, and dental insurance, as well as property-casualty coverage for the store, its inventory, technology, and customer's photos.

Denton will work with TCF Bank to finance the purchase of equipment needed to open The Memory Keeper and for renovations when he acquires the lease on the neighboring store. Denton will be able to access his line of credit to help him finance the initial days of his reinvented shop and services.

BUSINESS AND GROWTH STRATEGY

Staying on the cutting edge of technology will be of prime importance to continue providing a quality product. Only professional equipment will be used, unlike some competitors, who use amateur equipment that can be purchased from the local appliance and computer store. The Memory Keeper will maintain a dedicated lab environment for all transfer work. Images from slides, negatives, and photos will be scanned and converted to JPEG files that will then be saved in DVD format that can be used on either a computer or DVD player. The images can be sent electronically via e-mail to friends and family, or used to create an electronic scrapbook. All scanning will be done on-site, giving customers peace of mind that original photo memories are not in danger of being lost in transit. Nothing will be outsourced. Costs will remain competitive, and turnaround for completion of a job will be within a week's time or less. Customer service will be primary importance, so one-on-one consulting will enable each customer to ask questions before an order is placed, while an order is being completed, and after the job is finished.

Options that will be available will be adding music to a video montage, conversion of old home movies for a family movie DVD, picture transition timed to music, depending on customer feedback and inquiries.

Staying in tune with technology and evolving to meet the needs of today's customer while saving yesterday's memories will allow The Memory Keeper to continue to serve a growing customer base.

COMPETITION

While several shops offer to transfer images to DVD technology, The Memory Keeper will set itself apart with quality - in equipment, customer service, product, and reliability. Denton's business will cater to a changing world, blending the best of traditional photography and movies with the latest in technology.

Prices will remain competitive. Specials will be offered, including volume discounts.

WEB SITE

Denton plans an online presence with a store web site that will provide the usual contact information, hours, and a map to the store location. The web site will also provide an interactive chat room for customers to consult over the Internet with on-site staff. Customers from outside Metro Detroit will be able to access price lists, online specials, and an annotated list of transfer services offered by The Memory Keeper. Denton will have the web site built by professionals in keeping with the professional image he plans to present and maintain for a growing customer base.

CONCLUSION

The reinvention of Todd Denton's photography shop as The Memory Keeper will bridge his current customer base of traditional photographers with new technology to save precious images and memories on traditional film on DVDs. Within a year, the size of the shop will double, with three quarters of the expanded square footage being devoted to dedicated equipment and technology to continue to build the profitable business.

Party Planning

Perfect Party

567 Oak St.
Shelby Township, MI 48316

Heidi Denler

Perfect Parties will offer clients everything from assistance in planning parties to full-scale party and event planning. Perfect Party will be the number one resource for party and event planning in the area.

COMPANY SUMMARY

Traditional values will partner with attention to detail that will produce quality results for hosts and hostesses. Perfect Parties will offer clients everything from assistance in planning parties to full-scale party and event planning. The client will be able to sit back, relax, and enjoy his or her event instead of worrying about the details. Interactive, cutting-edge party planning software will be a key factor in Perfect Parties event kits, called Perfect Party Pax, which will enable clients to plan and host an event, covering everything from invitations to menus to entertainment to clean-up. Perfect Party will be the number one resource for party and event planning in the area.

EXECUTIVE SUMMARY

Nancy Dawson has been an executive assistant and second in command at a prestigious event planning company in New York. When her husband was transferred to Metro Detroit for his job, she left the company with the blessings of the owner, who promised to offer full support to Dawson to open her own event planning business.

MISSION STATEMENT

Perfect Party will provide casual or elegant experiences and everything in between for personal celebrations of any event in a client's life.

VISION STATEMENT

Perfect Party will grow in the immediate community of the northeast suburbs of Detroit. At least 25 percent of the profits will be put back into the company for expansion purposes. Within a year, Perfect Party will offer party planning services beyond a 25-mile radius, expanding not only office space, but also personnel to staff increasing number of events.

VALUES STATEMENT

Ms. Dawson's priorities for Perfect Party are to establish a clientele that will return for repeat business; expand through advertising in local media, as well as by word-of-mouth; and offer discounts to encourage new business from referrals as well as return business.

BUSINESS PHILOSOPHY

Perfect Party will remove the stress for clients as they focus on the reason for the event rather than the details involved in planning the event. Reasonable, competitive pricing will join with professionalism to make every party perfect.

Vendors and employees will also be treated with professionalism in their contracts and working environments.

A third priority is to allow the owner to make a profit that will allow her to put some money back into Perfect Parties while allowing her family to live comfortably in the area she serves.

By keeping up to date with the latest local and national industry trends, Perfect Party will offer every client individual attention to detail to plan the perfect party.

GOALS AND OBJECTIVES

Perfect Party will offer assistance in planning any event from a child's birthday party to a to a family reunion to a wake. With over 20 years of experience in event planning and contacts across the United States, as well as technological expertise, even video conference set-up will be available to include those unable to travel an opportunity to participate in life-changing events.

ORGANIZATION STRUCTURE

Initially, Perfect Party will be a sole proprietorship, with owner Nancy Dawson will plan events and contract with vendors, including venues, caterers, decorators, DJs, and bands to create perfect parties. In addition to a paralegal on staff to finalize contracts with the vendors, Ms. Dawson will employ an office manager who will handle finances and two event managers who will work the events with her to coordinate activities at the parties.

Ms. Dawson will look at her staff to bring an especially talented employee onboard as a partner within the first year of doing business. When hiring staff, she will look for detail-oriented, dedicated, energetic individuals who demonstrate creative ability to "think outside the box" and who express interest in development of skills to grow within the company.

ADVERTISING AND PROMOTION

Initially, advertising and promotion will include advertisements in local newspapers and Detroit-specific magazines, such as *Hour Detroit*, as well as brochures placed in vendor offices and event sites. Client e-mail addresses will be used to send advance notice for special events and birthday/anniversary and holiday greetings throughout the year. This will serve to keep Perfect Party's name in their minds when it is time for them to host their next events.

Press releases announcing the opening of the store and ensuing promotional events, such as high teas and tea tastings, will be sent to all local print, radio, and television. Personal phone and e-mail follow-up will be made to build a relationship with area media personalities, which is expected to result in free positive marketing and promotion.

CUSTOMER BASE

Perfect Party will serve a diverse customer base, including private organizations, businesses, community governments, schools, and individuals. Ms. Dawson will serve private organizations and businesses with uncompromising planning and execution for any size event, but will specialize in large scale holiday events for this sector. Assistance will be provided to local governments as they plan and coordinate community celebrations and charity events. Schools will benefit from Ms. Dawson's services because they will be able to concentrate on attending rather than planning activities that draw the learning community together toward a single goal. Individuals will be able to hire Ms. Dawson or simply be guided by her should they choose to take advantage of her Perfect Party Pax.

There is no age limit for Perfect Party's customer base, but Ms. Dawson expects that the middle to upper class family will generate a significant portion of revenues for the company. This target audience is most likely to look for assistance when planning celebrations of life-changing events, including birthdays, weddings, graduations, and funerals. The burden of planning a celebration will fall on Perfect Party, rather than on overwhelmed family members or overtaxed employees.

PRODUCTS AND SERVICES

Ms. Dawson initially will work from a home office, but within six months plans to have a storefront location to allow for growth. She plans regular hours Wednesday through Sunday from 12 to 8. Dawson and the staff will also be available to consult by appointment outside of those hours.

Care-free events that go off without a hitch are key concepts for Perfect Party. Planning will be conducted in concert with the host/hostess to ensure that any event of any size and within any budget will be perfect.

Following the event, clients will be encouraged to offer feedback via forms included with the final accounting package. Ms. Dawson and her staff will send thank you letters to the host/hostess and the vendors to generate goodwill and future business and create a good working relationship.

When clients purchase a customized Perfect Party Pax, they will have a complete kit to create any party. Perfect Party Pax will include everything a host will need, including invitations, decorations, tableware (plates, cups, napkins, cutlery), theme music CDs, tablecloths, and recipes for punch and snacks. Pax will also include a step-by-step guide for planning and hosting as well as suggestions for theme lighting. Eventually, this will be available for sale on the company web site.

Perfect Party clients will be able to hire the company to plan business retreats and training sessions, conferences and workshops, and company picnics, banquets, and awards dinners; birthday, anniversary, and graduation parties; holiday parties; wedding and baby showers; and weddings.

SUPPLIERS

Ms. Dawson is in the process of compiling a resource manual that will contain lists of approved caterers, decorators, DJs, bands, and venues, based on input from other event planners in the area, as well as from her own personal research.

LOCATION

The Shelby Township area is one of great growth in Metro Detroit. The median income in 2009 was $70,069, and the median age was 37. New subdivisions and strip malls are opening and many businesses are relocating or opening in the area. This growth offers great potential for a need for event planning.

At first, Perfect Party will be a home-based business, with client meetings held at the client's home, proposed outside venues, etc. Within six months, Ms. Dawson expects to have turned enough of a profit to invest in a rental business property. Within a year, Dawson will investigate opening a branch in the booming I-275 corridor in Livonia or Canton.

MEETING SPACE AND EQUIPMENT

Ms. Dawson will purchase two computers that will have high-speed Internet access, an all-in-one printer/scanner/copier for light duty. She will rent a color photocopy machine to do in-house printing of invitations, menus, etc., for events.

Event equipment will include walkie-talkies and headsets, cell phones, portable fax machines, and a laptop computer.

After moving her operation out of her home office and into rented office space, prospective clients will be greeted by a receptionist/office manager in a small "meet and greet" area as they walk in the door. A sample table set-up will be changed every couple of weeks, reflecting the season and current trends.

There will be office space for an office manager and three to four part-time employees. Ms. Dawson will share the office space, but her office will be set apart with glass dividers. A small conference room will be used for client meetings. That room will be set up with a white board and a document camera for presentations.

A small lunchroom will be available for employees with a microwave, toaster oven, refrigerator, two square tables, and eight chairs.

There will also be a storage/prep room that will be used to store paper goods, tablecloths, cups, glasses, chafing dishes, and other items required to host a Perfect Party, including a small supply of tables and chairs.

Most tables and chairs and tents will be rented for the first year. Ms. Dawson will begin purchasing inventory of these items as her profit line increases.

FINANCIAL

There will be little be minimal overhead at the start up of Perfect Party (see Appendix). These costs will include licensing by state and local health boards and governmental agencies that oversee small businesses. Initial purchases will be two computers, one of which will be a laptop that can be used at events, an A-I-O printer/scanner/copier, fax machine, 2 sets of walkie-talkies and headsets, and cell phones for each employee. Ms. Dawson will lease a color photocopier. Paper for invitations, brochures, menus, etc., will be purchased as needed from the local big box office supply store, where basic office supplies (copier paper, pens, pencils, binders, file cabinets, printer ink cartridges, etc.) will also be purchased. A portable white board and a document camera will be purchased for presentation purposes.

Costs that will be incurred after six months of operations, when Dawson plans to expand office space from her home office to actual office space, will include additional desks and chairs for employees, and outfitting the lunchroom (microwave, toaster oven, refrigerator, two square tables, and eight chairs), and a stock of paper goods, tablecloths, cups, glasses, chafing dishes, and a small supply of tables and chairs for events at clients' homes.

Other start up costs will include fees for registering the Perfect Party name and the business with the SBA and other government authorities. Dawson plans to cover the payment of taxes, payroll, payroll taxes, key man insurance, property insurance, liability insurance, inventory, telephone and utilities, an alarm system, and advertising by setting of break-even/profit goal of 20 events per month during the first six months.

By beginning as a home-based business, costs will be minimal. Vendors will provide most of the materials and supplies required for events. Staff can be hired on an as-needed basis until a move is made to official office space. Debt will be minimal, and will be assumed by the owner.

A move to a rental commercial property will add significantly to Dawson's overhead. As of early 2010, office space in Shelby Township runs between $1,200 and $1,500 a month for 1,400 to 1,500 square feet. Dawson will investigate carefully before making a move from her home office, given the high rental rate.

PROFESSIONAL AND ADVISORY SUPPORT

Dawson will work with a local attorney with SBA expertise to set up her sole proprietorship, handle any interim legal issues, review contracts with clients and vendors, and help with expansion six months after start up.

The partners will work with J. Kotts and the Ledder Agency to provide optimal coverage for life, health, and dental insurance and retirement savings. Mr. Kotts will work with a local property-casualty agency to cover insurance on the store and its inventory. Any staff hired will be offered low cost benefits at their own expense.

Dawson will use personal assets as collateral to establish a credit card account and a line of credit with Chase Bank to cover the costs of initial purchases. The event-planning business is essentially self-sustaining, with client down payments covering necessary down payments for securing vendors for their events.

BUSINESS AND GROWTH STRATEGY

Ms. Dawson will draw on her 20 years of experience of party and event planning in New York to create a successful event planning company in Shelby Township. She has taken business classes at NYU to strengthen her background and enable her to handle the business end of the company as well as the event planning operations. However, she will hire a local CPA to handle the books for the first year, after which she will hire an in-house office manager who will assume that responsibility.

COMPETITION

While other event planners in Southeast Michigan are established concerns, Perfect Party will offer traditional values, experience, and personal involvement in creating a "Perfect Party." Dawson will give back to her new community by hiring local collegians to work events for everything from valet parking to serving to cleanup. Her keen eye, developed over the past 20 years, will enable her to select from among those part-time employees for office staff and event personnel when she expands her business.

The main competition will be from other local event planners because there are few hotels and conference centers that offer complete planning services for such a wide variety of events. The unique

Perfect Party Pax will give clients who could not otherwise afford an event planner to benefit from the expertise of Dawson's 20 years experience without paying full price. This will also free Dawson to serve clients who can afford the complete package.

WEB SITE

Perfect Party will begin operations with a strong online presence. Prospective clients will be able to view photos of events. Current clients will be able to use a personal code to access details about their upcoming event and to communicate with Ms. Dawson and her staff regarding questions and plans, as well as make secure payments.

CONCLUSION

Success for Perfect Party will lie in the hands of the competent, professional, highly-experienced owner, Nancy Dawson. Clients will experience consistent planning and execution at competitive pricing based on the client's budget, while still allowing a significant profit. The future will bring expansion, with new offices having an office manager who will report directly to Ms. Dawson, two to three full-time event site managers.

As a home-based business, Perfect Party will show a profit from the very start, and that profit will continue to grow as the company grows.

APPENDIX

Start up expenses

Legal	$ 800
Stationery, business cards	$ 150
Logo design	$ 200
Brochures	$ 200
Consultants (legal, financial)	$ 500
Insurance	$1,000
Rent	$ 150
Office equipment	$4,000
Office supplies	$ 200
Total start-up expenses	**$7,200**

Start up funding

Expenses to fund	$7,200

Assets

Non-cash assets	$ 0
Cash balance expected on opening date	$2,500
Total assets	**$2,500**
Liabilities	$ 0

Pizza & Pasta Restaurant

Geno's Pizza & Pasta Restaurant

999 Alligator Way
Miami, FL 33109

Gerald Rekve

This business plan for Geno's Pizza & Pasta Restaurant—Miami reflects the opportunity to purchase the assets and leasehold improvements of the restaurant currently operating as Anthony's. The current owner is interested in selling the operations, as the store is not doing the volume he thought it would and he would like to get out of this location and the debt service he has incurred. My goal is to submit this business plan to his bank in the event he is unable to make loan or rent payments and defaults on the loan. We will be in a position to take over the SBA loan, and with additional funds added, convert this location to a profitable Geno's Pizza & Pasta Co. franchise restaurant.

1.0 EXECUTIVE SUMMARY

This business plan for Geno's Pizza & Pasta Restaurant—Miami reflects the opportunity to purchase the assets and leasehold improvements of the restaurant currently operating as Anthony's. The current owner is interested in selling the operations, as the store is not doing the volume he thought it would and he would like to get out of this location and the debt service he has incurred. My goal is to submit this business plan to his bank in the event he is unable to make loan or rent payments and defaults on the loan. We will be in a position to take over the SBA loan, and with additional funds added, convert this location to a profitable Geno's Pizza & Pasta Restaurant Co. franchise restaurant.

The location is only 1/4 of a mile away from the largest land moving project to put in a major shopping complex in the state of Florida. The rent is half what it would be for other retail shops in Miami, yet the location offers the same opportunity for sales. The recently completed Highway 123 offers access to hundreds of thousands of local residents, shoppers from outside the area, and travelers that use this new highway. Despite this high concentration of customers, there are no Italian restaurants in the area and therefore there is a tremendous need for an upscale family restaurant that offers items for both children and adults.

This restaurant will seat 150 customers and is the perfect size for a family operation. With the current leasehold improvements and quality kitchen equipment it would take very little to renovate this location to the legendary winning formula. The growth in numbers of middle to high income families in the Miami area is projected at over 30%. There is a need for a fine dining, family restaurant in the Miami area. It would be the perfect neighborhood restaurant in the perfect neighborhood.

Geno's Pizza & Pasta Restaurant in Miami will be the second location for Geno Brown who has operated a successful franchise unit in Miami, Florida for 20 years. Geno's Pizza & Pasta Restaurant is based out of Miami, and now has over 3 successful company and franchise locations in the United States.

Geno's will have a prime location, great food, a proven concept, super franchise support, no competition, a senior management and crew, a fantastic neighborhood marketing program, a huge catering base to build on, personalized service in a warm Italian imported grocery store atmosphere, and the support of the community resulting in a highly profitable restaurant.

1.1 Objectives

The goal is to purchase the current assets and leasehold improvements of Anthony's and convert the existing restaurant to a profitable and successful Geno's Pizza & Pasta Restaurant Co. franchise unit. I plan to duplicate the successful formula used at Geno's Pizza & Pasta Restaurant, Adam Crescent location, which I have owned and operated for over 20 years. Using the same strategies and having an in–depth management crew to back me up will ensure outstanding results at this new fast–growing location. My objectives are as follows:

- Provide the highest quality Geno's Pizza & Pasta Restaurant food and service that the community has been receiving for over 20 years at the Adam Crescent location.

- Create an atmosphere where each person can work as a team member, with clear goals and high standards that profit everyone.

- Combine the corporate marketing strategies with my own to build volume quickly.

- First year sales to hit between $1.7 and $2.4 million with 11% growth in first few years.

- Gross margin of 71% with a net profit of 5% of total sales.

- Maintain food and labor costs consistently.

- Maintain and expand my outstanding reputation.

- Remain a neighborhood family restaurant.

- Be the first fine dining Italian Restaurant in the fastest growing community in Florida.

1.2 Mission

Geno's mission is to be a full service, family Italian restaurant offering affordable, high-quality Italian cuisine inspired by authentic family recipes. Our goal is to provide our customers with an entire dining experience that exceeds their expectations on every visit. We do this by recommending add–on items that will enhance their dining experience. Our restaurant is clean and the quality is always high.

We value the people who work for us. Quality employees make quality food, keep the restaurant cleaner, give better service, and stay employed longer because they like working at Geno's Pizza & Pasta Restaurant. We have found that friendly managers hire friendly crew people and friendly crew people attract customers.

1.3 Keys to Success

- Geno's Pizza & Pasta Restaurant's name and reputation is well known in the area.

- The products we serve are of the highest quality. We combine this quality with great service and atmosphere. We then add menu items that appeal to all ages of the family as well as single adults.

- Current management staff and crew have a great deal of experience.

- Location, Location, Location! Some people have named the intersection of Hwy 22 and 55 Street, "the open road." Miami is the fastest growing community in the entire state of Florida!

- This shopping center location is three years old. Every spot in the center is filled and the main anchor is a Denny Gas & Confectionary store, the highest-quality service station chain in the area.

- This location offers private rooms on a reservation basis. I have developed the bulk food and catering large parties' concept at my other location and plan to promote it with the party rooms.

- A frequent diner program and birthday club will be available to promote repeat customers as well as a tool to track sales.

- Management that treats every employee equally. We create an atmosphere where employees love coming to work and can earn good money.

- Great employees make for a great restaurant.

2.0 COMPANY SUMMARY

Geno's Pizza & Pasta Restaurant in Adam Crescent has been very successfully serving the Adam Crescent area for 20 years. We have sponsored 25 Little League baseball teams, donated to thousands of events, worked with schools and churches to better the community, catered thousands of events in the area, and hired and worked with hundreds of young people, adults, and their families. Topic "5.3.1, Sales Forecast" shows our tremendous yearly sales growth rate over the last 20 years. This year is on track to be another record year.

Our "Frequent Diner Program" is in place at Adam Crescent with over 4,000 customers who frequent the restaurant. This loyalty program rewards customers with a $45.00 Gift Certificate when they spend $150.00, as well as a Birthday and Anniversary cards to celebrate a meal with us. The program has been a huge success for the past three years, rewarding customers and insuring future repeat business. Ask anyone who lives in Miami and you will find we have developed quite a reputation in the community.

Geno's Pizza & Pasta Restaurant was founded in 1994, and they have built it to 4 locations in USA.

The Miami restaurant will reflect the intimate charm of an Italian Grocery Store with framed Italian prints and Italian American pop art. Both the menu and ambiance will appeal to an upscale customer as well as the entire family.

2.1 Start–up Summary

The Geno's facility would come with all equipment, food, liquor, leasehold improvements, employees, and management staff.

We would assume the current SBA loan of $125,000, and start–up expense of $250,000. With cash input from investors of $55,000 the loan balance using an SBA secured loan would be $500,000 at 9.5% interest over a 15-year term.

A starting bank account of $90,000 will be used, only if needed, for unexpected costs associated with the start up.

Start–up equipment list would include the following items: (quality used equipment will be purchased whenever possible to control costs, and then, only if equipment is in like–new condition)

- Fifty quart Hobart mixer

- Three Steam kettle

- Refrigerated 4 drawer system

- Freezer 2 drawer system

- Pizza box refrigerated stand alone box

- Dessert display case

- Eight–burner commercial gas stove

- Commercial Parmesan cheese grinder

- Meat slicer

- Flip top refrigerated 6–foot saute box

- Stand up Freezer

- Kitchen and dining room small wares

- Less trade–in or sale of used equipment not needed in the current operations

3.0 PRODUCTS

Geno's Pizza & Pasta Restaurant's menu offers large pasta varieties and nine specialty chicken, veal, and seafood entries, along with an assortment of appetizers, sandwiches and salads, including the famous "special salad" served in unlimited refills. It serves an interesting variety of wines, cocktails, and desserts to complement each meal.

Working with the freshest ingredients, imported pasta, and top quality cuts of meat, Geno's Pizza & Pasta Restaurant owes a great deal of its successful menu to its purveyors.

The menu also offers several items that provide the same generous portions and quality flavors as the regular menu, but with low–fat, low–calorie, and low–cholesterol benefits.

A fun children's menu for ages 13 and under features a friendly character who suggests favorites like spaghetti and meatball pizza and toasted ravioli in portions just right for smaller appetites.

In an effort to provide dining patrons with new tastes in Italian cuisine, Geno's Pizza & Pasta Restaurant works on an ongoing basis to improve existing dishes and to develop new menu items that appeal to today's increasing number of consumers who insist on consistently high–quality, good tasting Italian fare with authentic "old country" flavor.

As a full service fine dining menu, we offer a full array of mixed drinks, beers and wines. With a full bar area Geno's Pizza & Pasta Restaurant offers a place where young adults, families, and singles to enjoy a drink while waiting for a to–go, waiting for a table, or a friendly place to meet and talk before dinner. We are a family array business and have never been known as a "Bar." There will be no "Late–night Drinking Crowd" as this is not part of our customer base.

4.0 MARKET ANALYSIS SUMMARY

The part of the city where we will operate our store area has 38 restaurants which include:

- 3 Fast Food/Pizza/Sub Restaurants

- 2 Sports bars/Up Scale Burger Restaurants

- 4 Barbecue Restaurants

- 3 Chinese Restaurants

- 4 Banquet/Catering Operations

- 4 Breakfast/Lunch Restaurants

- 2 Upscale Full–Service Restaurants

The marketing plan is to provide a fine dining, full service, family restaurant, where the entire family can enjoy a great meal at a reasonable price. Geno's Pizza & Pasta Restaurant is the perfect neighborhood restaurant where adults and children can always find their favorite dish, receive consistent quality food, and get great customer service.

With the addition of the new shopping complex less than 1/4 of a mile away, this addition will bring more customers and families from all over to shop and eat in the area. The market customers for Geno's Pizza & Pasta Restaurant would develop from:

- Local Neighborhood Marketing Program
- Customer Frequent Diner Loyalty Program
- Suggestive Selling Program to increase average check
- Birthday and Anniversary marketing mailings
- Market saturation and community outreach programs
- High shopping in the area
- Tremendous growth in upper level family income

4.1 Market Segmentation
Market analysis shows that within a three mile radius of the restaurant, 98% are families. This is the customer base which we cater to.

4.2 Target Market Segment Strategy
Our focus is the middle- to upper-income level families living and shopping in the area. Geno's Pizza & Pasta Restaurant will focus on the income level of at least $40,000 and above, and the families living and shopping in the area.

We focus on these specific groups because these are the types of people who frequent Geno's Pizza & Pasta Restaurant. They are the ones that are willing to spend their money on good dining and service at a value price.

4.3 Industry Analysis
The competition for the upper-level income business has been intense. National chains that were not here 10 years ago have poured into the area. The number of new restaurants has increased dramatically over the last several years and should continue to expand, all with the intent of capturing a portion of the upper-level market.

5.0 STRATEGY AND IMPLEMENTATION SUMMARY

Every customer who has eaten at a Geno's Pizza & Pasta Restaurant is a potential customer. The better we run this Geno's Pizza & Pasta Restaurant location, the more business we will do. Customers will know that they can get better quality food at this location. They will know that the service is better, and the people are better. The look of the new location will be fresh and clean. The area needs a fine dining family restaurant. The area needs a big name, local operation with a home–grown name like Geno's Pizza & Pasta Restaurant.

5.1 Competitive Edge
This is what gives us the competitive edge to insure a profitable home–grown expansion:

- Proven Geno's Pizza & Pasta Restaurant Co. concept since 1999
- Proven track record of Adam Crescent serving the area for over 20 years
- Best home–grown training in the industry

- Senior Adam Crescent management and crew to open with

- Local marketing in all age ranges

- Known costs with purchase of an turnkey restaurant

- Current staff and management

- Close and strong support of President and Senior Management

- Strong food and supply vendors with very high quality products

- On–going support from Corporation

5.2 Marketing Strategy

We at Geno's Pizza & Pasta Restaurant, including all management, crew personnel, supervisors, vendors, design people, family and friends, and new hires will put forth 100% effort to insure a profitable opening and on–going operations.

5.3 Sales Strategy

The sales strategy is to sign up as many frequent diner customers as possible at the new location. Using the Frequent Diner Program in place at Adam Crescent for three years, we plan to further cement the loyal customers in the area. We will honor 3,000 club members with points at both locations.

We plan on taking advantage of Geno's Pizza & Pasta Restaurant market saturation. We will build and expand on that customer base by exceeding customers' expectations. This will bring back old customers and bring in new customers to the new location.

We plan on up–selling customers with our current suggestive selling program. From the hostess to the waiters and waitress our staff has successfully increased the average check for add–on sales from 5% of the average check three years ago to over 13%. This insures an increase in profit without having to depend on an increase in customer counts or price increases.

5.3.1 Sales Forecast

A sales forecast of 5.0% increase in volume over the current Adam Crescent location is based on the following:

- Increased visibility and known area of Geno's Pizza.

- Increased traffic flow with the intersection, with over double the traffic in the area.

- Increased customers staying in the area to shop. Two major shopping centers compared to a 20 year old strip center.

- Increased retail employee business.

- 26% larger space inside, with 30% more customer seating.

- Outside seating area during the spring through fall seasons increases the seating by 60%.

- Brand new look inside.

- Private rooms available to cater private parties.

- Closer to the eight hotels in the area.

5.4 Milestones

I have full confidence in all of the managers, designers, and people who will make this a huge success.

Geno Brown
- SBA loan and Business Plan

- Bank Account

- Franchise Purchase

- Legal and review of Lease

- Equipment Purchase

- Sign Purchases and install

- Software POS system install

- Corporation set up, Insurance, Deposits, Liquor License

- Design Work with Joe Fresta of Geno's Pizza Pasta Restaurant

- Oversee entire transformation and operations of the group

Ben Brown

- Crew and manager hiring and training

- New equipment installed

- Food & liquor purchases delivery and stocking

- Crew and manager scheduling

- Maintenance and repairs

- Advertising

Betty Brown

- Design work walls and floors design with Bill Brown of PHC

- Shelving and displays in place

- Design of dining room look

- Record keeping of purchases and budget

- Permits, liquor licenses, start up requirements paperwork

Joe Fresta, Vice President of Geno's Pizza & Pasta Restaurant

- Design work and construction work

- Oversee display of dining room

- Oversee kitchen equipment purchase and layout

- Advise owner when needed

6.0 WEB PLAN SUMMARY

Our site will include information about our local franchise units. We also plan to expand the marketing of using a website by customers and the crew.

In this age of communication more and more customers look to a website for information and assistance in purchasing products. We will be part of that great communication tool used by everyone everyday.

6.1 Website Marketing Strategy

Marketing in an Internet retail business depends on recognition for expertise. It starts with our existing store front customer base, informing them of our Internet presence and encouraging their word–of–mouth recommendations.

We will develop and maintain a database of our 6,000 loyalty Frequent Diner customers. From there the website will serve the following needs of our customer base.

- Provide local information about our locations to the local community

- New customers can sign up for our frequent diner/birthday programs

- Customers can check their Frequent Diner points online

- Catering information and contacts provided

- Provide references and pictures of successful catering jobs

- With a special password, crew can check their schedule on a moment's notice

- Purchase Gift Certificates from our stores

- Purchase the new Gift Cards

- Purchase retail items online and have them shipped as gifts

- Gift Basket information

- Employment information online

- Company-wide promotions and new store openings

- Promotional coupons online

- Provide new food items in the restaurant

- General information on other events in the area

6.2 Development Requirements

Because corporate has a website, I plan on working very closely with their Web designer. Each year the best websites are posted. Using this source will enable me to enhance our website to a simple but very effective tool to increase sales at the retail level. Development of the site will change based on our customers needs now and in the future as new ideas come forward for using this communication tool.

7.0 MANAGEMENT SUMMARY

The management team to run the day–to–day operations and shifts at the new location will include Geno Brown, Terry Tantardini, Karen Tantardini, an additional dining room manager, and a kitchen manager, both to be named closer to the opening date. The Adam Crescent managers will include Geno Brown, Janet Boxx, two new managers and a kitchen manager to be named later.

People are the single most important element in our operations.

We value the managers and staff as the single most important element in running a quality operation; the managers need to be all on the same page of operations. We have found that friendly strong managers make friendly strong crew people. From that crew comes the next generation of managers and a quality operation. The customers can see it in the quality of the food, how clean the store is and how friendly and fast they are served. In the past 19 years we have had eight crew people go on to become managers at other Geno's Pizza & Pasta Restaurant locations and other restaurants. We also have a deep bench to select our management team from. The current Geno's store also has managers that I have been told are doing a fine job. We will consider them as manager candidates and make decisions based on the best interests of the restaurant. Below is our management game plan:

Miami Management Staff

Geno Brown, Owner–Operator/President
- Owner Operator of Geno's Pizza & Pasta Restaurant franchise located in Adam Crescent since 1983.

- *Duties:* strategic development, back–office administration, financial analysis, internal control, taxes and accounting records, payroll, daily operations, quality control, advertising, food costs, labor costs, liquor cost, oversee management controls, maintenance and repairs, and building the business profits.

Terry Tantardini, General Manager
- General Manager of Geno's Pizza & Pasta Restaurant Adam Crescent for 15 years. Before that Terry worked as a waiter at several Geno's Pizza Pasta Restaurant locations.

- *Duties:* daily operations, new management development, scheduling, ordering, food, labor, and liquor controls, quality controls, maintenance/repairs, crew training, employment, crew's hourly wages, pay increases, and overall store operations.

Karen Tantardini, Dining Room/Kitchen Manager
- Kitchen Manager of Geno's Pizza & Pasta Restaurant Adam Crescent for 4 years. Karen has recently completed training, been promoted to Dining Room manager and has been running shifts for the past year. Karen has a real talent for dealing with all aspects of the business.

- *Duties:* daily operations, ordering, inventory, quality controls, kitchen procedures, labor and food controls, scheduling, new hires, crew moral, and overall kitchen operations. Karen will use her experience to train and oversee the new kitchen manager coming on board.

Adam Crescent Management Staff

Geno Brown, Owner–Operator/President
- Geno will work 2–3 shifts per week as the manager on duty at Adam Crescent until management staff can be trained and cover the shifts.

Ed Galonzoksy, General Manager
- Kitchen crew person, kitchen manager, Dining Room manager, and general manager for Geno's Pizza & Pasta Restaurant for 13 years. Ed has done a fine job at Adam Crescent as a manager for the past eight years. One of Ed's strengths is his ability to deal with people. Because of Ed and his people skills, we have lost very few crew people to other locations.

- *Duties:* daily operations, scheduling, ordering, food, labor, and liquor controls, quality controls, crew training, employment, and overall store operations.

Private Investigation Service

Ferguson Investigation LLC

15869 San Mateo Blvd.
San Bernardino, CA 92401

Paul Greenland

Ferguson Investigation is a private investigation firm serving attorneys, insurance companies, businesses, and individuals.

EXECUTIVE SUMMARY

Business Overview

Ferguson Investigation is a private investigation firm serving attorneys, insurance companies, businesses, and individuals. We help clients uncover information pertaining to many different personal, legal, business, and financial situations. Generally speaking, our services involve:

- Investigating crimes

- Determining the identity, business, occupation, or character of an individual (e.g. background checks)

- Finding lost individuals or stolen property

- Performing investigations regarding accidents, loss, injury, or damage

- Securing witnesses and/or evidence for court cases

Our services are not always related to criminal or malicious behavior. For example, law firms occasionally hire private investigators to find their own clients (e.g., during the course of lengthy liability insurance cases), who may have relocated to another area. Private investigators also are hired by families and businesses to locate missing individuals.

Ferguson Investigation gathers information via different tactics, including computer research, records analysis, interviews, and surveillance. In addition to gathering information, our firm provides the necessary analysis and interpretation our clients need to make sound decisions.

Company History

Ferguson Investigation was established by Brian Ferguson, a retired law enforcement officer from Colorado. Following a 25-year career with the Rocky Ridge Police Department, where he retired as lead investigator at age 50, Ferguson decided to relocate to California. After assisting a local private investigator for several years, Ferguson has decided to go into business for himself and establish his own private investigation firm.

MARKET ANALYSIS

Situated in the heart of Southern California, the historic city of San Bernardino is located adjacent to the I-215 and I-10 Freeways, the Ontario International Airport, and is in close proximity to mountain resorts such as Big Bear and Lake Arrowhead.

The larger San Bernardino County area included an estimated 2.02 million residents in 2008, residing in the communities of:

- Adelanto
- Apple Valley
- Barstow
- Big Bear Lake
- Chino
- Chino Hills
- Colton
- Crestline - Lake Gregory
- Edwards AFB
- Fontana
- Fort Irwin
- Hesperia
- Highland
- Lake Havasu
- Loma Linda
- Lucerne Valley
- Montclair
- Newberry Springs
- Nipton
- Ontario
- Rancho Cucamonga
- Redlands
- Rialto
- San Bernardino
- Twentynine Palms
- Upland
- Victorville
- Yucaipa
- Yucca Valley

According to U.S. Census Bureau data, the region included 687,352 housing units and 528,594 households. In terms of demographics, 47.5 percent of residents were of Hispanic or Latino origin, while white persons not of Hispanic origin totaled 35.7 percent, and black persons accounted for 9.4 percent of residents. Median household income in 2007 was $55,995.

San Bernardino County has a thriving business community. In 2007 the area included approximately 114,798 firms. During the early 2000s retail sales totaled roughly $16 billion, while wholesale trade sales totaled $21.2 billion and manufacturers' shipments totaled $14.3 billion.

The County of San Bernardino breaks down its business market as follows:

- Services (22.7%)

- Retail Trade (20.2%)

- Government (19.6%)

- Manufacturing (12.6%)

- Construction (9.3%)

- Transportation & Public Utilities (4.7%)

- Finance, Insurance & Real Estate (4.1%)

- Wholesale Trade (3.8%)

- Agriculture (3.1%)

Although San Bernardino is known as "the friendly city," illegal and dishonest acts occur in our market, as they do in any community. Based on data from the California Department of Justice, our community was impacted by a number of unfortunate offenses in 2007 (the most recent data available). These included 10,238 violent crimes; 40,220 property crimes; 33,756 cases of larceny-theft; and 517 cases of arson.

Competition

There is significant competition among private investigators within the San Bernardino market. In fact, California is home to the largest number of private investigators of any state (5,420), according to the Bureau of Labor Statistics. California also is one of the highest-paying states for our occupation (along with Virginia, New Jersey, Alaska, and New York), and the Riverside-San Bernardino-Ontario, California market is the best-paying nationwide, with a mean hourly wage of $38.52 and an annual mean wage of $80,130. According to the BLS, there were 360 private investigators in the Riverside-San Bernardino-Ontario market in 2008.

INDUSTRY

BLS reports indicate that 45,500 private detectives and investigators were employed throughout the United States in 2008. This figure is expected to grow 22 percent by 2018, reaching 55,500. The BLS attributes this faster-than-average projected growth to several factors, including increased litigation, rising criminal activity on the Internet, copyright infringement, and the protection of property and confidential information. Approximately 21 percent of individuals within our industry are self-employed. Among those employed by others, the majority are employed by investigation and security services or state governments.

Our industry includes several leading professional organizations. Established in 1967, the National Association of Legal Investigators (NALI) included approximately 500 members during the late 2000s. According to the association, its "primary focus is to educate and advance the art and science of legal investigation, and to ensure the highest standard of professional ethics."

The NALI offers a Certified Legal Investigator program, which "certifies that qualified investigators possess superior knowledge in the field of legal investigation." There are numerous requirements for certification, including a primary focus on negligence investigations for the plaintiff and/or criminal defense, as well as state licensure (if required) and a certain amount of work experience/education.

Another leading organization is ASIS International. Established in 1955, ASIS is "dedicated to increasing the effectiveness and productivity of security professionals by developing educational programs and materials that address broad security interests." As of 2009, the organization included more than 200 chapters and 37,000 members throughout the world. In addition, it offered number of certifications, including Professional Certified Investigator (PCI).

PERSONNEL

Brian Ferguson earned an undergraduate Criminal Justice degree from Central State College. In addition, he has attended the FBI National Academy for Police Officers and earned a Computer Forensics Certificate from the Community College of Colorado. After beginning his career as a patrol officer in Denver, Colorado, Ferguson rose through the ranks, and was eventually promoted to detective. He ended his law enforcement career as lead investigator with the Rocky Ridge Police Department. He has earned Professional Certified Investigator status through ASIS International.

Ferguson has established a business banking account with Blackhawk Community Bank, as well as a merchant account for accepting credit card payments. Legal services are provided by the law offices of Burton, Moore, Smith & Provenza, and tax advisory services are provided by Accurate Financial Services LLC.

BUSINESS STRATEGY

For the first five years of operations, Brian Ferguson will concentrate on establishing his firm's reputation in the local market. During this time he will be the sole employee of Ferguson Investigation. In years six and seven, tentative plans exist to add a total of two additional investigators.

Ferguson will maintain an informal affiliation with Chuck Webster, the private investigator with whom he worked after relocating to California. Webster's firm currently consists of three investigators, and has been in business for about 10 years. In addition to occasionally assisting each other, the two investigators have tentatively discussed merging their firms at some point in the future, which would create one of the largest private investigation firms in our local market.

SERVICES

Generally speaking, the services provided by our firm include:

- Investigating crimes
- Determining the identity, business, occupation, or character of an individual (e.g. background checks)
- Finding lost individuals or stolen property
- Performing investigations regarding accidents, loss, injury or damage
- Securing witnesses and/or evidence for court cases

Personal investigations often pertain to:

- Adoption
- Child Custody

- Divorce/Infidelity
- Premarital
- Record Searches
- Runaways/Missing Persons

Workplace investigations focus mainly on:

- Computer Crimes
- Covert Surveillance
- Fraud & Embezzlement/White Collar Crime
- Loss Prevention/Internal Theft
- Personal Injury Fraud
- Sexual Harassment
- Workplace Violence

During the course of our work, Ferguson may perform a wide range of different tasks, including records searches and video surveillance. Investigations may involve relying upon one or more of the following types of information:

- Addresses
- Bankruptcy Information
- Corporate Records
- Criminal and Civil Records
- Driving Records
- E-mail Addresses
- Governmental Watch Lists
- Motor Vehicles
- Phone Numbers
- Real Property
- Relatives and Associates
- Warrants and Arrest Records

MARKETING & SALES

Ferguson Investigation has developed a marketing plan that involves the following primary tactics:

- A Web site with complete details about our business and the services we offer.
- A Yellow Page listing under the Private Investigators category.
- Cold calls to local law firms, insurance companies, and businesses promoting our services.
- Regular direct mailings to local law firms, insurance companies, and businesses promoting our services.

OPERATIONS

Facility & Location

Brian Ferguson has dedicated a small portion of his private residence to be used exclusively for the administrative and research functions of Ferguson Investigation. He has installed a dedicated telephone line for the business, and has established a small home office equipped with a computer, multi-functional peripheral device (e.g., copy, fax, scanner), and file storage area. Beyond research activities, the majority of Ferguson Investigation's services are provided in the field (e.g., surveillance activities, etc.), or within the offices and/or facilities of our clients.

Payment & Fees

Ferguson Investigation's fees range from $65 to $85 per hour. Based on a specific client's needs and the length/nature of the assignment, the hourly fee is negotiable. We normally require a retainer prior to beginning work for a client. Generally speaking, Ferguson Investigation requires clients to purchase four hours of service in advance—especially when surveillance services are required. In addition to our hourly fee, clients are billed for expenses incurred during the investigation (e.g., mileage, telecommunication charges, etc.). Whenever possible, expenses are discussed with the client beforehand.

LEGAL

Brian Ferguson meets all requirements established by the California Bureau of Security and Investigative Services related to licensure as a private investigator. Specifically, to meet these requirements one must:

- Be at least 18 years of age.

- Pass criminal background check performed by the California Department of Justice and the Federal Bureau of Investigation.

- Meet stringent work and/or education requirements including: "three years (2,000 hours each year, totaling 6,000 hours) of compensated experience in investigative work; or a law or police science degree plus two years (4,000 hours) of experience; or an AA degree in police science, criminal law, or justice and 2 and a half years (5,000 hours) of experience."

- Successfully pass a multiple–choice exam covering evidence handling, undercover investigations and surveillance, terminology, laws and regulations, and civil/criminal liability.

- Pay a $175 licensing fee.

Brian Ferguson has received a firearm permit from the California Department of Consumer Affairs, which requires completion of courses in:

- The Power to Arrest (three hours)

- Carrying and Use of Firearms (14 hours)

Ferguson also has completed the Department of Consumer Affairs-approved training required to receive a Tear Gas Permit.

Finally, per state requirements, Ferguson has secured insurance coverage in the amount of $1 million ($500,000 for one loss due to injury or destruction of property and $500,000 for one loss due to bodily injury).

Additional information regarding licensure is available from the Bureau of Security and Investigative Services by calling (800) 952-5210, or accessing www.bsis.ca.gov.

FINANCIAL ANALYSIS

Following are five-year financial projections for Ferguson Investigation, based on Brian Ferguson's knowledge of the local market and law enforcement experience.

As mentioned in the Business Strategy section of this plan, Ferguson Investigation will concentrate on establishing its reputation in the local market during the initial years of operation. This especially will be the case during years one through three. In year four, Brian Ferguson anticipates that his firm will begin growing at a compound annual rate of approximately 12 percent.

This plan will be revised in year five (2014), when short- and long-term expansion plans are more clearly defined.

	2010	2011	2012	2013	2014
Revenue					
Fees	$65,335	$76,785	$85,135	$95,351	$106,793
Total revenue	**$65,335**	**$76,785**	**$85,135**	**$95,351**	**$106,793**
Expenses					
Salaries	$35,000	$40,000	$45,000	$50,000	$ 55,000
Insurance	$ 3,000	$ 3,000	$ 3,500	$ 3,500	$ 3,750
Office supplies	$ 350	$ 350	$ 350	$ 350	$ 350
Computers & office equipment	$ 1,250	$ 350	$ 350	$ 350	$ 1,500
Marketing & advertising	$ 500	$ 500	$ 500	$ 500	$ 500
Telecommunications & internet	$ 1,000	$ 1,000	$ 1,000	$ 1,000	$ 1,000
Firearms & equipment	$ 3,000	$ 2,500	$ 1,500	$ 1,500	$ 4,500
Database subscriptions	$ 500	$ 500	$ 500	$ 500	$ 500
Professional development	$ 1,000	$ 1,000	$ 1,000	$ 1,000	$ 1,000
Travel & entertainment	$ 500	$ 500	$ 500	$ 500	$ 500
Subscriptions & dues	$ 350	$ 350	$ 350	$ 350	$ 350
Taxes & fees	$ 1,345	$ 1,439	$ 1,540	$ 1,648	$ 1,763
Total expenses	**$47,795**	**$51,489**	**$56,090**	**$61,198**	**$ 70,713**
Net income	**$17,540**	**$25,296**	**$29,045**	**$34,153**	**$ 36,080**

Resale Clothing Store

New to You Resale Clothing Store

3400 E. Broadway
Columbia, MO 65201

Kari Lucke

New to You is a resale clothing store that will offer only the highest quality name–brand clothing items for men, women, and children.

1.0. INTRODUCTION

1.1. Mission Statement

New to You is a resale clothing store that will offer only the highest quality name–brand clothing items for men, women, and children.

1.2. Executive Summary

As owner and manager of New to You, Cynthia Miller will offer a variety of used clothing at a reasonable price, including casual and business wear, special–event clothing, and children's wear. The target audience includes the young adult population (ages 21 to 35) of Columbia, Missouri. Customers will include college students, young businesspeople, and parents of young children (ages 0–8). Due to the down economy, people are looking for ways to save money, yet they do not want to decrease their standard of living if possible. New to You helps these people maintain their upscale wardrobes by offering the same clothing at a fraction of department and mall store prices.

1.3. Business Overview

The resale clothing business is based on the idea that people can buy the same quality and brand of clothes as they can at retail stores for a lot less. The only difference is the clothes are not brand new. The best resale clothing stores carry only items that are in top condition and barely used. They also offer these items for very reasonable prices, and they offer the same type of customer service and shopping environment as retail stores.

1.4. Business Philosophy

The philosophy at New to You is that shopping at a resale clothing store can resemble shopping at a retail store. There are three factors that New to You will address in its store that are often neglected at resale clothing stores: setting/atmosphere, quality of selection, and organization.

1.5. Goals and Objectives

The long–term goal of New to You is to become the most popular resale clothing store in Columbia, building on the idea that the clothes are reasonably priced and in good condition, the location is convenient, the store atmosphere is pleasing, the customer service is excellent, and the desired clothing items are easy to locate within the store.

Financially, owner Cynthia Miller aims to make a small profit by the second year of operation. By the third year, the goal is to gain an annual profit near $10,000.

2.0. INDUSTRY AND MARKET

2.1. Industry Analysis

According to the National Association of Resale and Thrift Shop (NARTS), the world's largest resale trade association, the future of resale is bright, partly due to the dim U.S. economy. In an October 22, 2009, press release, NARTS stated, "The resale industry is one of the few recession–proof segments of retailing. Not only does it survive during economic downturns but it grows and thrives… The appeal is twofold: consumers are attracted to buying quality merchandise at a fraction of the original cost, and there is a financial incentive to sell, consign, or donate their unused or unwanted items" (www.narts.org).

In a recent survey conducted by NARTS, almost 70 percent of members surveyed experienced an increase in sales in the third quarter of 2009 as compared to the same period of 2008. New to You is in a prime position to capitalize on these trends.

2.2. Market Analysis

The market for New to You consists of residents of Columbia, Missouri, the population of which is around 100,000. The market also includes the student population of around 30,000. Columbia is home to two private four–year colleges (Columbia College and Stephens College) as well as the flagship state university, the University of Missouri.

The median household income of Columbia residents is $42,163, with a race distribution of 83 percent White, 9 percent Black, and 8 percent other. Columbia has a relatively young population, with 27 percent between the ages of 18 and 24 and 29 percent ages 25 to 44. The median age of the population is 27 years. About 26 percent of households include children under the age of 18. These demographics are all positive signs for a business like New to You that focuses on young adults and families with children.

Columbia has seen significant growth since the early 2000s and is expected to see continued growth. It is consistently rated one of the "Best Places to Live in America" by such well–known entities as *Forbes*, *Money* magazine, and Kiplinger.com due to its excellent educational systems, access to health care, and quality of life. For example, in 2007 *Forbes* ranked Columbia "Third Best Metro for Business and Careers" in its study that factored in the cost of doing business, job growth, and educational attainment.

Although there may be some stigma against shopping at a resale store, New to You plans to alleviate any misgivings on the customers' part from the moment they enter the store. The store's downtown location, bright and open floor plan, and quality service and merchandise will help dispel misconceptions about a resale store being shady, low–class, or otherwise undesirable.

2.3. Competition

There are three other resale clothing stores in Columbia: Hello Again, Back in the Day, and Kids' Place. Hello Again is an established store in downtown Columbia that has been selling consignment clothing for several years. However, New to You will have several advantages over New Beginnings. New Beginnings is located in the basement of an office building and thus does not have the advantage of natural light. The inventory overflows the space, so there is little room to maneuver, and clothes are jammed onto racks and are often in disarray. One of New to You's most significant advantages is its location in a street–level storefront that allows natural light and easier access. In addition, the layout of New to You will afford wider aisles and easy–to–see items.

Back in the Day specializes in vintage clothing and thus is not seen as a direct competitor to New to You, which will focus on newer styles and clothing. Kids' Place carries children's clothing, toys, and accessories, so it could be considered a competitor in the area of children's wear. However, Kids' Place is also located on the far south end of town, so New to You will have a distinct location advantage with its convenient downtown setting.

Another advantage New to You will have over these stores is atmosphere. Many resale clothing stores tend to have a very musty smell, which can be distracting and unpleasant for customers. New to You strives to eliminate odors through thorough cleaning of all items before stocking as well as the use of air fresheners, candles, potpourri, and other ambiance–enhancing features.

3.0. PERSONNEL

3.1. Management

Owner Cynthia Miller will run the store on a daily basis. She holds a bachelor's degree in business, so is adept at handling the financial and administrative aspects of operating a store. In addition, she worked part–time in a consignment clothing store, Upscale Resale, while attending college at the University of Missouri–Kansas City. This experience granted her extensive knowledge of the ins and outs of a resale business and in fact is what made her decide she would like to own and manage her own store. Having seen some of the mistakes and successes at the store where she worked, Cynthia can launch her own business with a grounded knowledge in the best way to operate a resale business.

3.2. Staffing

Although Cynthia Miller will be on–site a majority of the time, she will need back–up for times when she has to be away from the store, and this will be provided by her daughter Denise. Denise is a college student at the University of Missouri–Columbia and is available to help in the store as needed. Through a personal arrangement, Denise will not earn a salary for working at the store. Cynthia's husband, Doug, who is a local contractor in the area, will also be available for emergency or extra assistance if needed. If further help is needed later on, or when Denise is no longer available, Cynthia will hire a part–time employee. This person will help in all aspects of on–site activity, such as assisting customers, handling transactions, stocking, inspecting inventory, working on store displays, and so on. Because it is expected that Denise will be available to work at the store for at least the next three years, an additional employee is not factored into the business plan at this time.

3.3. Professional and Advisory Support

As the sole owner and operator of New to You, Cynthia Miller is the only member of the board of directors. Outside support will be provided by State Farm Insurance agent Bill Jolson and attorney George Smith. Cynthia is also a member of the trade organization NARTS (National Association of Resale and Thrift Stores), which offers up–do–date information about the industry on its website and via meetings, an annual conference, and various publications. As a member of NARTS, Cynthia is able to stay current on trends as well as receive support and advice from seasoned resale professionals.

4.0. BUSINESS STRATEGIES

New to You's business strategy is simple and straightforward. Rather than accepting clothing on a consign-ment basis—a situation in which a resale owner must keep very detailed records, maintain client contracts, and possibly deal with issues of disagreement, out–of–date contact information, and so on—Cynthia will pay for items for the store's inventory up front. Although this will require more of an investment, the initial cost will more than pay off in terms of ease of managing the business.

5.0. PRODUCTS AND SERVICES

5.1. Description

New to You will include the following categories of used clothing:

Women's

- Jeans and Pants
- Shirts and Blouses
- Sweaters
- Suits
- Coats and Jackets
- Shoes
- Skirts
- Dresses

Men's

- Jeans and Pants
- Shirts (dress and casual)
- Sweaters
- Suits
- Coats and Jackets
- Shoes

Special Occasion

- Wedding and Bridesmaid Dresses
- Prom Dresses
- Tuxedos

Maternity

Children's

In the interest of maintaining a clean and organized feel to the store, New to You will not sell purses or other similar accessories. It may include some miscellaneous items such as scarves. Due to hygiene issues, New to You will also not sell lingerie, sleepwear, or swimwear.

5.2. Unique Features/Niche

The key to New to You's success will be the reputation it earns with its clients. Unlike some other resale stores, every item of clothing in the store will be like new. No substandard items will be accepted for inventory, and that fact will be advertised and emphasized. In some cases, this approach may cause the loss of customers whose standards are not high, but in time that will become another unique feature of this store.

In addition, unlike many resale stores, the items will be categorized and departmentalized so that they are very easy to find. New to You does not intend to be an oversized garage sale. Items will be marked clearly with computerized labels and placed on racks with plenty of room in between. Racks will be placed far enough apart that customers can browse comfortably. Each category of clothing will have its own area of the store, marked with clear and professional signage.

Lastly, New to You will look, sound, smell, and feel like a retail store. The store displays, lighting, layout, customer service counter, and other aspects of the store's appearance will be similar to that one would find in a department or mall store. Appropriate music will play over a quality stereo system, and every detail of a customer's senses will receive attention. That is not something one usually finds in a resale store.

5.3. Product/Service Life Cycle

Inventory will need to be seasonal and updated often. If an item has not sold within a specific period of time, it will be moved to a clearance rack, and from there it will be donated to an appropriate charity.

5.4. Pricing

New to You will purchase name–brand, good quality used clothing based on a price sheet composed by Cynthia. For example, long–sleeved women's t–shirts from stores like Hollister, American Eagle, and Abercrombie will be worth $2, assuming they are in excellent condition and a current style. Cynthia will then sell the t–shirts for $5, which will result in a profit margin of 60 percent.

Purchases by customers can be made by cash, check, or credit/debit card. In keeping with the industry standard, all items will be nonreturnable.

6.0. MARKETING AND SALES

6.1. Advertising and Promotion

New to You will use three types of advertising at the start: flyers, a website, and a newspaper ad. Before the store opens, flyers will be printed and distributed around town in such places as grocery stores, beauty salons, convenience stores, and other places that allow free posting of fliers and that receive heavy traffic from women. The flyer will include promotional text as well as the location of and date that the store will open and the URL of the website. The website will offer details about the store's policies, including what types of clothing the store buys and sells. It will also include a photo of the front of the store (so that people will recognize it) and pictures of sample items, as well as a weekly blog by Cynthia, links to fashion advice, and other relevant information. Testimonials will be used later on as Cynthia gains satisfied customers. Lastly, a eighth–page ad for New to You will appear in the local newspaper, the *Columbia Daily Tribune*. Word–of–mouth will be an important, free form of advertising once the business gets underway.

6.2. Cost

Start–up advertising costs are estimated to be $500 as follows:

- Flyers: 200 x $0.50 each = $100

- Website: $100 for domain

- Newspaper ad: $100 x 3 weeks = $300

The website will provide ongoing advertising. More newspaper ads may be used in the future to advertise special events/sales.

6.3. Image

Image is important at New to You, especially considering that resale stores do not automatically lend themselves to an automatic positive impression. This impression must be earned. According to Adele Meyer, director of the National Association of Resale and Thrift Shops (NARTS), the appearance of a resale store is vital to its success. Says Meyers, "If people start coming in, and racks are too full or clothes are not displayed properly, people will never come back and tell their friends don't bother coming in" (online.wsj.com, July 18, 2005). Thus one of the focuses of the store will be on attractive displays, wide aisles, and organized, easy–to–find inventory. As mentioned previously, New to You will also sell only the best used clothing in terms of name brands and quality. The goal is to present an image of a resale store that is upscale and provides a pleasant shopping experience.

7.0. OPERATIONS

7.1. Customers

New to You customers will be mainly women, ages 18 to 40. These will include college students, young professional women, and mothers of young children. According to demographic figures from the Census Bureau, 27 percent of Columbia's population is between 18 and 24 and 29 percent is between 25 and 44. Fifty–one percent of the total population is female. The median age of the population is 27 years. About 26 percent of households include children under the age of 18.

7.2. Suppliers

The public will supply the majority of inventory at New to You. Part of the promotional campaign will include information on selling clothing to the store. Flyers advertising the fact that New to You is buying clothing will be put out three months prior to the store's opening in order to gain a basic inventory by the store's opening date. Other sources of inventory will include garage sales, from which Cynthia will choose appropriate items, and friends and family. The goal is to have three–quarters of the capacity of the store filled by the time of opening, leaving room for additional items that come in after customers visit the store and become aware of how easy it is to bring in items for sale.

7.3. Equipment

Equipment for the store includes clothing racks and shelves, customer service counter, computer hardware, and furniture. Much of this equipment will be purchased used in order to save on costs.

7.4. Hours

New to You will be open Monday through Saturday from 10 a.m. to 5 p.m. The store will be closed on Sunday.

7.5. Facility and Location

New to You will be located at 3400 E. Broadway, Columbia, Missouri. This location is part of a historical building in downtown Columbia that houses other businesses, including a coffee shop, jewelry store, and attorney's office. The facility was previously used as a real estate office, so some remodeling will be necessary. Remodeling costs, including the installation of dressing rooms, new paint, and some furniture, are estimated at $2,000.

Metered parking is readily available in front of the store, and the store is located within walking distance of the University of Missouri campus.

Rent on the 1,000–square–foot space is $800 a month, plus water, electricity, and phone/Internet service, which is estimated at $300 a month.

8.0. FINANCIAL ANALYSIS

Start-up costs

Initial inventory	$ 5,000
Fixtures, furniture, equipment	$ 2,000
Computer and software	$ 1,000
Cash register	$ 300
Advertising	$ 500
Rent and deposit	$ 2,000
Business license/LLC	$ 500
Price tags, office supplies, bags	$ 200
Storefront sign	$ 300
Total	**$11,800**

Start–up costs will be financed by a small business loan from Landmark National Bank.

Profit and loss statement*

	Year 1	Year 2	Year 3
Net sales	30,000	40,000	50,000
Cost of sales	12,000	16,000	20,000
Gross profit margin ($)	18,000	24,000	30,000
Gross profit margin (%)	60%	60%	60%
Operating expenses			
Rent	9,600	9,888	10,185
Utilities and phone	3,600	3,710	3,820
Insurance	1,200	1,240	1,280
Advertising	1,000	1,030	1,060
Supplies	1,200	1,240	1,280
Business loan payment	3,600	3,600	3,600
Total expenses	**20,200**	**20,708**	**21,225**
Pretax profit	**$ 2,200**	**$ 3,292**	**$ 8,775**

Most expenses are expected to increase at an approximate rate of 3 percent per year. Figures are rounded.

Self–Defense/Anti–Bullying Training Company

Safe Zone Personal Defense LLC

7821 Cherry St.
Storybook Grove, WI 66205

Paul Greenland

Safe Zone Personal Defense is a provider of basic self–defense and anti–bullying programs for individuals, schools, businesses, and other organizations.

EXECUTIVE SUMMARY

Mission Statement

Safe Zone Personal Defense is dedicated to the preservation of life and personal safety. We are committed to providing individuals of every age with the essential skills for physical self defense, as well as social and emotional intelligence.

Business Overview

Every day, human beings face a wide variety of potential threats. Sometimes these threats are verbal or social in nature. Examples include being subject to "bullying" behavior such as name–calling, exclusion from group activities, intimidation, and teasing. Threats also come in the form of physical violence, such as slapping, hitting, kicking, pushing, shoving, attempted rape, and other forms of serious physical assault. Self–defense is the act of resisting these aforementioned threats. It is every individual's legal right.

Safe Zone Personal Defense provides the instruction and training that people need to ensure their personal safety. We offer ongoing basic self–defense classes, as well as one–time seminars and workshops for groups, schools, businesses, and other organizations. In addition, our business also provides anti–bullying seminars and workshops for individual schools, school districts, and organizations. Contrary to popular belief, bullying is not only a widespread problem in schools; it also is common in the workplace.

Company History

Our company was formed in 2007, when high school guidance counselor and football coach Buck Taylor (a third degree black belt and former U.S. Marine) partnered with family therapist and certified self–defense instructor Julie Taman to fulfill what they perceived as an unmet need in their community. In response to a variety of situations at Central High School in 2006, Taylor and Taman began hosting informal self–defense and anti–bullying classes and seminars for teachers and students.

When their classes and seminars were well received, Taylor and Taman decided to establish a part–time business, develop formal programs, and offer them to other schools within the district.

Continued success prompted expansion to other school districts throughout the region in 2008. The following year, the partners began offering programs tailored to the needs of other types of groups and organizations.

MARKET ANALYSIS

Storybook Grove, Wisconsin, is located near the border with Illinois. The community has a strong industrial base, consisting of several hundred small and medium–sized businesses devoted to fabrication and manufacturing. In addition, our community is home to several large corporations that have based their manufacturing operations here. These include a major confectionery operation, an automotive manufacturing plant, as well as a wire and cable manufacturer. According to recent population data, the city had an estimated 176,333 residents in 2008. This marked a 6 percent increase from 2000.

Beyond individuals, our target markets include schools, school districts, churches, colleges, community centers, retirement centers, businesses, and other organizations.

In addition to a large community college, as well as a private four–year college, two school districts serve our local market. The Storybook Grove School District consists of 14 elementary schools, eight middle schools, and six high schools. The Lichfield Consolidated School District includes an additional nine elementary schools, as well as one middle school and one high school. Collectively, these schools are home to hundreds of teachers and thousands of students.

Statistics

Based on arrest reports from the Storybook Grove Police Department, area residents were impacted by a number of unfortunate offenses in 2008:

- Forcible Rape (78)

- Robbery (160)

- Aggravated Assault (498)

- Simple Assault (3,237)

- Intimidation (237)

- Extortion/Blackmail (5)

- Purse–Snatching (18)

In addition to these offenses, bullying is a widespread problem. In 2007, researchers at the Stanford University School of Medicine and Lucile Packard Children's Hospital released the results of a preliminary study which found that nine of every 10 elementary students had been bullied by their peers. In addition, six of every 10 students indicated they had participated in some form of bullying activity themselves.

In late 2009 the U.S. Health Resources and Services Administration (USHRSA) presented the results of a study based on surveys of 10,000 anonymous middle school students. According to the research, approximately 43 percent of students revealed that they had been physically bullied within the last month. A larger number of students (66%) indicated they had been bullied in more than one way (e.g., not just physical bullying). Contrary to popular belief, bullying is not mainly limited to playgrounds. The USHRSA revealed that a significant share of bullying activity happens in the classroom, school hallways, and lunchroom, as opposed to playgrounds and out–of–the–way locations.

Beyond schools, bullying activity also is a significant workplace issue. According to a 2007 survey from the Workplace Bullying Institute, compared to other types of harassment bullying is four times more prevalent. Not surprisingly, bosses constitute 72 percent of workplace bullies. In 57 percent of bullying cases, women were the target. However, among these cases, 71 percent were bullied by other women.

Due to the significance of workplace bullying, by late 2009 anti–bullying legislation had been implemented by 13 states, including California, Hawaii, and Connecticut.

Competition

Although several local martial arts studios provide self–defense classes, we are fortunate that no one else is providing the unique blend of services that we are currently offering. Specifically, no other local organization provides anti–bullying training in our community.

PERSONNEL

Buck Taylor and Julie Taman are the sole employees of Safe Zone Personal Defense. In addition, the co–owners have secured professional and advisory support in a number of key areas. For example, they have established a business banking account with Storybook Community Bank, as well as a merchant account for accepting credit card payments. Legal services are provided by the law offices of John Cacciatore & Associates, and tax advisory services are provided by Dun–Rite Tax Service Inc.

GROWTH STRATEGY

Buck Taylor and Julie Taman operate Safe Zone Personal Defense as a part–time business. The partners have achieved steady growth from 2007 to 2009. Taylor plans to retire from his job as a school counselor and football coach in 2010 and devote more time to the business (especially the self–defense component).

However, Safe Zone's real growth potential seems to rest with its anti–bullying programs. Because the local and regional programs offered by Safe Zone have been so successful, in 2010 Taylor and Taman plan to conduct basic research and document objective outcomes in both workplace and school settings. A graduate statistics class in the education program at a local college has agreed to perform this research at no cost.

With statistically significant data in–hand, the partners hope to produce a series of training videos (available on DVD and online) and printed materials that can be used as part of a national program roll–out. If this approach proves to be successful, Taman plans to join Safe Zone full–time and focus her efforts on business development.

The co–owners have identified low–cost ways to produce program materials needed for national expansion, taking advantage of a local DVD production source, as well as digital printing technology that allows the production of attractive four–color materials as needed (as opposed to offset printing that requires the production of larger quantities).

SERVICES

Safe Zone Personal Defense provides services in two main categories: self–defense training and anti–bullying programs. Sometimes, we offer blended programs that address both areas, based on the needs of the individual or organization.

Self–Defense Training

All of our self–defense classes begin with instruction about basic awareness. We teach individuals to be mindful of their surroundings, and to avoid potentially dangerous situations. For example, remembering to lock car doors is one simple strategy to staying safe when traveling in an automobile. Other common sense techniques include parking in well–lit areas and safeguarding one's home against burglaries.

When physical self–defense is needed, we train people in the basic techniques they need to defend themselves. Simplicity is a major theme in all of our training, because individuals need to recall defense strategies quickly when they are in a threatening situation. Projecting confidence and employing verbal strategies are other major themes, because they are very effective in fending off potential attackers and avoiding physical entanglements. Compared to traditional martial arts, our training is more akin to basic streetfighting.

In terms of actual techniques, we teach a variety of methods, including:

- Palm–Thrusts (to break an attacker's nose)
- Elbow Strikes
- Knee–to–Groin Strikes
- Eye Jabs

We teach people how to get out of specific situations, including:

- Chokeholds
- Bearhugs
- Headlocks
- Wrist Grabs
- Hair Grabs

The objective of our training is not to necessarily incapacitate an attacker, but to allow someone to free herself from a situation and get away safely.

In addition to ongoing self–defense classes, for which participants pay a flat monthly fee, we offer an eight–hour basic self–defense class, as well as a more in–depth self–defense class that lasts a total of 25 hours.

Anti–Bullying Programs

Individuals of all ages are subject to potential forms of bullying behavior. These include, but are not limited to:

- Name–Calling
- Exclusion from Group Activities
- Intimidation
- Teasing
- Physical Violence
- Cyber Bullying

Our anti–bullying programs are concentrated on several key areas, including the promotion of:

- Policy Development
- Attitude Change

- Heightened Awareness
- Parental Support (in schools)
- Prevention Strategies
- Appropriate Responses

Programs are offered for three key audiences:

1. Individuals

2. Employers (employees and management)

3. Schools (teachers, students, counselors, monitors, coaches, administrators, etc.)

In addition to regular instruction, we offer an in–depth "train–the–trainer" program, which allows an individual to host an anti–bullying training program at their own organization. As mentioned in the Growth Strategy section of this plan, this will likely serve as the basis for Safe Zone's future expansion.

MARKETING & SALES

We have developed a marketing plan that involves the following primary tactics:

1. A four–color flier describing our business.

2. A Web site with complete details about our business and the services we offer.

3. Presentations at local chamber of commerce to generate awareness of our services among the business community.

4. Newspaper advertisements in the chamber of commerce's monthly member newspaper.

5. Direct mailings to area businesses, churches, community groups, and other organizations.

6. A public relations campaign that involves the submission of periodic human interest and/or "success" stories to both national education publications and area newspapers and news media, illustrating the effectiveness of our services.

7. Presentations to school administrators, principals, teachers, counselors, and union representatives.

OPERATIONS

Facility & Location

Buck Taylor has dedicated a small portion of his private residence to be used exclusively for the administrative functions related to Safe Zone Personal Defense. He has installed a dedicated telephone line for the business, and has established a small home office equipped with a computer, multi–functional peripheral device (e.g., copy, fax, scanner), and file storage area.

Most services are provided directly on the premises of other organizations. However, in the case of our ongoing self–defense classes, we rent space from Storybook Gymnastics Academy at an affordable rate.

Payment & Fees

Self–Defense Training

Safe Zone Personal Defense charges $50 per month for ongoing self–defense classes (one class per week).

We charge $50 per person (limit 20 per class) for one–day self–defense workshops.

Our advanced self–defense workshop costs $150 per person.

Anti–Bullying Programs

Our typical 8–hour educational workshop is offered at a cost of $50 per person (limit 20 per class)

"Train–the–Trainer" courses are offered at a cost of $150 per person (class size limited to 10 individuals)

FINANCIAL ANALYSIS

As previously mentioned, Safe Zone has been a part–time business during its initial three years of operations. Buck Taylor plans to devote more time to the business in 2010, after retiring from his job as a guidance counselor and football coach. A national roll–out of Safe Zone's anti–bullying program is tentatively planned for 2011. The following financial data takes these factors into consideration.

	2007	2008	2009	2010	2011
Revenue					
Self-defense training	$20,000	$25,000	$27,000	$30,000	$32,000
Anti-bullying programs	$ 5,000	$ 8,500	$15,000	$20,500	$68,000
Total revenue	**$25,000**	**$33,500**	**$42,000**	**$50,500**	**$98,500**
Expenses					
Advertising & marketing	$ 350	$ 750	$ 1,250	$ 2,150	$ 5,000
Miscellaneous items	$ 250	$ 250	$ 400	$ 400	$ 1,000
Legal	$ 1,250	$ 1,250	$ 1,250	$ 1,250	$ 1,250
Accounting	$ 800	$ 800	$ 800	$ 1,000	$ 1,350
Office supplies	$ 150	$ 250	$ 350	$ 350	$ 850
Computers/peripherals	$ 1,250	$ 0	$ 0	$ 0	$ 1,550
Liability insurance	$ 2,500	$ 2,500	$ 2,500	$ 2,500	$ 2,500
Salaries	$15,000	$17,500	$20,000	$35,000	$65,000
Postage	$ 0	$ 350	$ 450	$ 550	$ 1,200
Telecommunications	$ 0	$ 500	$ 500	$ 500	$ 500
Travel	$ 0	$ 500	$ 750	$ 1,000	$ 4,500
Training material production	$ 150	$ 450	$ 450	$ 725	$ 5,000
Facility lease	$ 1,500	$ 1,500	$ 1,500	$ 2,000	$ 2,000
Total expenses	**$23,200**	**$26,600**	**$30,200**	**$47,425**	**$91,700**
Net income	**$ 1,800**	**$ 6,900**	**$11,800**	**$ 3,075**	**$ 6,800**

Tea Shop

Cuppa!

12345 12 Gratiot Rd.
Roseville, MI 48066

Heidi Denler

Cuppa! will be located in Roseville, Michigan, a middle class suburb of Detroit. The intent of Cuppa! is to offer a quiet location to sip of cup of tea or glass of freshly brewed iced tea, prepared from a wide variety of loose teas or bagged teas.

COMPANY SUMMARY

Cuppa! will be located in Roseville, Michigan, a middle class suburb of Detroit. The area has an abundance of chain coffee shops and one or two independent coffee shops, none of which offers a wide variety of tea. In fact, the coffee shops offer only bagged teas along with one or two "teas" made from high-calorie, highly sugared mixes. The intent of Cuppa! is to offer a quiet location to sip of cup of tea or glass of freshly brewed iced tea, prepared from a wide variety of loose teas or bagged teas.

In the caffeine-drenched age of people moving at a frenetic pace, Cuppa! will provide an oasis of calm where patrons can sit with friends to chat, yet feel comfortable enough to come in alone and finish a chapter in a favorite books or even work on a knitting project.

MANAGEMENT SUMMARY

Heather MacDonald, who was born and raised in England, brings her childhood tea time experience to Cuppa!. She shared her memories of stealing a quiet hour with her grandmother and mother, and later her friends, while sipping tea and eating scones, with her daughter Jane. When Jane MacDonald lost her job as the manager of a coffee shop franchise, she and her mother decided to use their savings to create similar memories for friends and neighbors.

Legal matters will be handled initially by the family's personal attorney, who is a general practice attorney and is familiar with the legalities of small businesses. A local CPA will manage financial matters.

MISSION STATEMENT

Cuppa! A quiet place to meet a friend for conversation or to simply sit and read a book, write, or even knit, all while enjoying a quality cup of tea in a warm, friendly setting.

VISION STATEMENT

Growth in customer base and everything to make the experience of going out for tea enjoyable so that customers become friends and return often.

VALUES STATEMENT

The owners of Cuppa! are dedicated to delivering quality products in comfortable, friendly surroundings to encourage repeat business. Customer service is number one.

BUSINESS PHILOSOPHY

Cuppa! will provide customer satisfaction by offering friendly service, customer education, and quality teas and tea service.

GOALS AND OBJECTIVES

Heather and Jane MacDonald plan to build their customer base through friendly, high-quality service. Promotion and advertising will be low-key at the beginning, including flyers placed on cars in local parking lots and advertising in local free and paid publications.

The mother-daughter pair will offer weekly tea tastings to educate their customers about new teas and encourage repeat business to try new and exciting teas. High tea service will be available to groups and on Sunday afternoons by reservation.

Food service will be available, including scones, crumpets, cookies, and a small selection of traditional tea sandwiches, all baked on the premises.

Initially, Heather and Jane will staff the shop, along with Jim MacDonald, Heather's husband and Jane's father. High school co-op students will be hired to work part-time in the shop, allowing the owners to devote time to customer relations. A baker will also be on the payroll, since neither owner is an accomplished baker.

ORGANIZATION STRUCTURE

Cuppa! will be run as a partnership between Heather and Jane MacDonald. They will share equally in the responsibility and profits of Cuppa!, with the understanding that profits will not be immediately forthcoming. For that reason, the partners are seeking a line of credit from their bank and the Small Business Association.

ADVERTISING AND PROMOTION

Initially, advertising and promotion will be flyers placed on cars in local parking lots and hand-delivered door-to-door. A Web site is under development to build a strong customer base. Ads will be placed in local newspapers. Patrons will be asked to provide their e-mail addresses to receive advance notice for special events and coupons at Cuppa!

Press releases announcing the opening of the store and ensuing promotional events, such as high teas and tea tastings, will be sent to all local print, radio, and television. Personal phone and e-mail follow-up will be made to build a relationship with area media personalities, which is expected to result in free positive marketing and promotion.

CUSTOMER BASE

The main customer base for Cuppa! will be local residents and workers of all ages who are looking for a respite from the frenzy that has come to define the early 21st century. Customers will be able to purchase tea-related products and baked goods to take the experience home.

The partners expect to broaden the customer base by word of mouth referrals from friends and neighboring businesses, as well as through flyers, advertising, and e-mail contact.

Seniors will be offered a 10 percent discount on all purchases every afternoon between 1PM and 3 PM. A frequent buyer card will be available for both tea and bakery purchases to encourage repeat business.

PRODUCTS AND SERVICES

Cuppa! will be open from 11AM to 9PM Tuesday through Friday. Saturday hours will be from 9AM to 10PM. High tea will be served by reservation only on Sundays at 2 PM. The store will be closed on Mondays except for private parties.

Fair trade and organic teas will be available as well as such familiar brands as Tazo and Stash. Standard Earl Grey and English Breakfast teas will share the menu with licorice and mango pomegranate flavored black, green, and white teas.

Customers will be able to purchase teapots, tea cozies, tea bags, loose teas, baked goods—anything that can bring the experience home. Items for sale will be placed on antique buffets, tables, and curio cabinets placed around the shop, creating a warm and inviting ambience for each seating area.

The shop will be divided into cozy areas. Some will have soft lighting and overstuffed chairs and loveseats for intimate conversations. Some will have lighting conducive to reading needlework patterns and working on a favorite project. Some will have larger tables that will allow small groups, such as PTOs or committees to meet. A separate room will be available for such larger groups as book clubs to meet and for private parties, such as high teas and children's tea parties.

Sunday afternoons will be reserved for high tea and themed parties, including "Mad Hatter" and tea tastings. Tea tastings will be scheduled weekly to encourage new and old customers to try new teas and to learn the art of brewing tea.

LOCATION

Unofficial market research in the fall of 2009 narrowed the search for a location to Roseville, Michigan. Research included talking to friends, shoppers in the area, customers of coffee shops, and shop owners, as well as real estate analysis. The average age of Roseville residents is 39, and the average income is $69,900. Recognizing that coffee is not everyone's "cup of tea," Cuppa! will fill a niche by providing an alternative to coffee shops.

Heather and Jane MacDonald's choice of location was also based on a desire to serve their hometown. They are working with a real estate agent to find retail space that they can rent at first, with an option to buy. The pair is committed to serving the community.

STORE DESIGN AND EQUIPMENT

The tea room will be at the front of the store, with the kitchen taking up the back quarter to third. The cash register will be camouflaged in an armoire, so as not to detract from the relaxing atmosphere desired by the owners. A small office will be housed in the basement storage area, near the stairway. By having storage and office space in the basement, maximum floor space will be available where it counts—in the customer area.

There will be a large open area with several tables and chairs as the main part of the tea room. In addition, there will be a few areas that will be sectioned off by placement of decorative screens and furniture to create cozy areas for quiet conversation or even sitting alone to reflect and relax. There will be one large private room, decorated to resemble a cozy sitting room in one's home. Private tea parties will be held in that room. A second private room will hold an oversized dining table and 14 to 20 dining chairs. That room will be the location for tea tastings.

Closer to the register, cabinets and antique shelf units will house displays of tea pots, tea cozies, and a variety of teas that will be offered for sale. Scones and tea cookies made on the premises will be displayed in a glass cabinet/display case near the armoire with the register. The cash register will actually be a computer with software to track sales, inventory, and trends that will be connected on a LAN with the computer in the office that will have a password-protected program to keep track of payroll, employee benefits, taxes, and such business expenses as utility bills, mortgage and banking, and insurance.

The food prep area of the kitchen will have one restaurant quality stove and two restaurant quality ovens, with possible expansion as Cuppa!'s customer base grows. It will also have a dishwasher, sink, and storage for items needed for food prep, bakeware, tea cups/saucers, silverware, and cleaning of silver. The kitchen will be outfitted with high-quality kettles for boiling water for the tea.

FINANCIAL

The MacDonalds are working with a commercial real estate agent and have found a potential location. It is currently operating as a sandwich shop and would offer the quickest and least expensive turn-around for reinvention as a tea shop.

Start up costs will include standard security deposits and licensing by state and local health boards. Family antique tables, cabinets, and hutches will be used initially. As the shop becomes profitable, the MacDonalds will replace personal belongings with items purchased at area antique stores and estate sales. Tea pots, tea cups, mugs, plates, and silverware will be purchased new, but with an eye to an antique look.

Some interior work will need to be done to the building to suit the purposes of Cuppa!, including moving and removing dividing walls to create cozy corners and one private room. The current owner has an office established in the rear of the store. A unisex lavatory facility will require updated fixtures. The entire shop will require painting and placement of prints and pictures to complete the ambience sought by the owners.

The kitchen will be converted to allow for optimal boiling of water and preparation of baked goods that will be offered to the customers.

The office area will require two linked computers, one in the shop to serve as a cash register and inventory control, and the other in the office for payroll, taxes, and other company business. The MacDonalds will not offer Wi-fi in Cuppa! to keep the atmosphere one of relaxation and conversation.

Other start up costs will include any fees for registration of the name and the business with all government authorities. In addition, the owners will have typical overhead costs of rent/mortgage payments, taxes, payroll, payroll taxes, key man insurance, property insurance, liability insurance, inventory, telephone and utilities, an alarm system, and advertising.

PROFESSIONAL AND ADVISORY SUPPORT

The MacDonald family attorney is a general practice attorney who is well-versed in small business practices and law in the state of Michigan. He will work on a sliding scale basis, charging minimal fees until the tea room is showing a profit.

The partners will work with J. Denler and Seymour Gill Agency to provide optimal coverage for life, health, and dental insurance and retirement savings. Mr. Denler will work with a local property-casualty agency to cover insurance on the store and its inventory. Any staff hired will be offered low cost benefits at their own expense.

The owners have an established relationship with Flagstar Bank, and has secured financing for 50 percent of the start-up costs, as well as a line of credit to see Cuppa! through its first six months.

BUSINESS AND GROWTH STRATEGY

Strengths of the owners of Cuppa! include knowledge of teas, tea service, and creating a cozy environment for customers to relax. While the neither of the owners holds a business degree, they have taken classes at the local community college to learn about operating a small business. They plan to hire a local, independent CPA to handle the financial aspect of the business.

Expansion will include adding services, depending on customer feedback. They will attend tea conventions to stay on top of the latest trends in the industry and bring them back to introduce them slowly to Cuppa!. Heather and Jane MacDonald have already attended several weeklong seminars on teas, and consider themselves to be well-prepared to open their shop.

COMPETITION

The nearest tea shop is about 35 miles away to the south, while the next closest is 50 miles away to the north. Cuppa! is proposed as a way to fill the need for a quiet place to get away from the hustle and bustle of a caffeine-based world.

WEB SITE

Cuppa! plans an online presence with a store web site that will provide contact information, hours, and a map to the store location. The web site will also provide a list of teas and a menu for customers to preview. In addition, online visitors will be able to access a calendar of upcoming special events and make reservations for them.

CONCLUSION

Within two years, Heather and Jane MacDonald propose that Cuppa! will break even in the first month or two. As shoppers discover the tea shop and paid, as well as word of mouth, advertising begins to have an impact, the MacDonald mother and daughter team expect Cuppa! to become increasingly profitable. They have solid backing from their local bank, and their family background will add to Jane's experience as a barista will bode well for the shop.

Tutoring Service

Ellen's English Tutoring Service

761 Pine Ave.
Columbia, MO 65203

Kari Lucke

Ellen's English Tutoring Service will provide reading and writing tutoring services to middle and junior high school students in the Columbia, Missouri, area, enabling them both achieve better grades and establish a base of knowledge and skills that will help them do well academically as they enter the high school years.

1.0. INTRODUCTION

1.1. Mission Statement

Ellen's English Tutoring Service will provide reading and writing tutoring services to middle and junior high school students in the Columbia, Missouri, area, enabling them both achieve better grades and establish a base of knowledge and skills that will help them do well academically as they enter the high school years.

1.2. Executive Summary

As owner and operator of Ellen's English Tutoring Service, Ellen Bowers will offer tutoring in the areas of English / language arts, focusing on helping students read, write, and communicate more effectively. Students will become more proficient in these areas, will experience an increase in self–confidence regarding their abilities in these areas, and will show tangible improvement in the form of better grades in their related classes at school.

1.3. Business Philosophy

At Ellen's English Tutoring Service, the student comes first. Although grades are often a focus, and many parents gauge whether the tutoring is worth the money based on this concrete measurement, building students' self–confidence and a belief in themselves is another important aspect of tutoring, according to Ellen Bowers.

1.4. Goals and Objectives

The short–term goals of Ellen's English Tutoring Service are as follows:

- Build a client base of at least 10 students, on average, by the end of the first year of business

- Gain a reputation as an effective, caring, and affordable option for tutoring in the Columbia area

- Realize a profit by the end of the first year of business

2.0. INDUSTRY AND MARKET

2.1. Industry Analysis

Tutoring is a growing industry. According to a study published in *The Economist*, 22 percent of parents surveyed had engaged tutoring services for their 11– to 16–year–old children in the past year. This shows an increase from 18 percent four years ago. One reason cited for the rise in demand for tutoring is the increasing competition to get into the country's top universities. According to the report in *The Economist* (September 12, 2009), "Even in the era of university top–up fees it is the taxpayer, not the student, who pays most of the cost of a degree. To limit its liability the government caps student numbers." The article goes on to say that due to the resulting limited number of spots to fill, some universities "approach admissions as an exercise in finding reasons to say no."

In this climate of intense competition, high school grades become vitally important. Even parents paying for private schooling for their children at the middle, junior, and high school level may consider tutoring a "near–compulsory insurance policy" in order to ensure that their students are in the running when it comes time to apply for college admission. Such a situation, although unfortunate in some ways to students and parents, is ideal for a person who has the skills, knowledge, and passion to offer these highly sought–after services.

2.2. Market Analysis

The market for Ellen's English Tutoring Services consists of children ages 11 to 16 and their parents in Columbia and the surrounding areas. Columbia's population is around 94,000, and it is home to three public middle schools (grades 6 and 7) and three public junior high schools (grades 8 and 9), as well as four smaller private schools that include these grades. The population of Boone County, which includes the towns of Ashland, Centralia, and Hallsville, is around 146,000. Each of these towns has one public middle/junior high school. As of 2010, enrollment in public middle schools in Columbia totaled 2,477, and enrollment in public junior high schools in the city was 2,450. Enrollment figures for the private schools are not available.

Demographic factors that affect the demand for tutoring services in the area is ethnicity and first language other than English. Columbia is a very diverse community. As home to the state's largest university, the University of Missouri, Columbia draws academics from many different backgrounds and ethnicities, and the racial diversity extends into the schools. For example, approximately 6 percent and 5 percent, respectively, of all junior high and middle school students in Columbia are Asian. About 4 percent of all junior high students and 6 percent of all middle school students are Hispanic. These children present a unique audience for tutoring services, as many of them need extra help in mastering and making the most effective use of the English language.

Of course the demand for tutoring services also comes from those classified as Caucasian and Black, which represents 83 percent and 9 percent, respectively, of the total Columbia population.

2.3. Competition

Competition for Ellen's English Tutoring Service comes in the form of franchise–type tutoring organizations, such as Sylvan Learning, and other individual, at–home tutoring services.

Despite the vast amount of advertising done by franchise organizations like Sylvan, such centers do not always have a good reputation. Indeed, the negative side of having such a large public presence is that the organization opens itself up to the possibility and accessibility of public criticism. For example, anyone surfing the Internet about Sylvan is just as likely to come across negative reviews as they are happy customers. Such issues as quality control, employee turnover, and bureaucratic hang–ups deter these organizations from providing the best possible service to their customers. In addition, they are usually more expensive than private tutors.

Indirect competition comes from online tutoring, which has grown in popularity over the past several years. Students can sign up and log on to receive help with any subject. The benefits are that they do not have to leave home and can do it anytime. However, the drawbacks of an increased need for self–motivation and the lack of one–on–one interaction, among other obstacles, often outweigh the advantages for many students.

Other individuals who provide tutoring, on the other hand, pose a more direct source of competition for Ellen's English Tutoring Service. However, Ellen's will have several unique features that other similar services do not have. For example, Ellen has a separate room in her home designed only for tutoring. This room, which has the feel of a spacious home office, includes a study table, a computer, bookshelves, and resources for the student. Although there are no windows (to minimize distraction), the room is well lighted and painted in cool, reflective colors. The goal of the design is to appear inviting but not playful, homey but purposeful. Although the cost of setting up and maintaining such a room is minimal, the availability of a special place for Ellen to work with her students will enhance Ellen's professional image, impress parents, and make students feel focused and positive. Needless to say, this set–up, as compared to someone's dining room table in the midst of the family's everyday life, is preferable and will be seen as more professional to students and parents.

The service itself, of course, is the most important aspect of the business. Ellen's friendly, outgoing nature, professional and positive attitude, and genuine desire to help students is the business's best–selling feature.

3.0. PERSONNEL

3.1. Management

As the sole proprietor, Ellen Bowers will provide all services offered by the business. She will also handle all paperwork, invoicing, and scheduling. Ellen received her master's degree in education from the University of Missouri in 1985 and is a certified schoolteacher in the state of Missouri. Ellen is also certified as a Master Tutor by the National Tutoring Association. Ellen taught English and language arts for 20 years, with positions in two different middle schools and one junior high school. From 2005 to 2009 she worked as an English tutor for Horizons Learning Center in Columbia, where she taught and interacted with a variety of students, including many whose first language was not English. Ellen's experience and background provide her with the skills and knowledge she needs to be an effective private English tutor.

3.2. Professional and Advisory Support

Ellen receives professional advice and support from her membership in the National Tutoring Association, a trade organization founded in 1992 that had more than 16,000 members by 2010. Benefits of membership include access to an annual conference, training, articles and other resources about the industry, and an online community of professionals.

Other outside support is provided by Accounting and More, which prepares the business's tax returns; State Farm insurance agent Dennis Nash, who provides related liability insurance coverage and support regarding insurance issues; and attorney George Smith, who provides legal advice and assists with the design of client contracts and other relevant paperwork.

4.0. BUSINESS STRATEGY

Ellen's English Tutoring Service will use materials from Ellen's library, which she has built up over the past 20 years of teaching, as well as the Internet and new resources as needed. Part of the strategy of helping students improve their reading and writing skills is a "learn by" doing philosophy. In other words, Ellen will work with students as they complete their assignments. For writing assignments, for example, Ellen may read the student's first draft and make suggestions for where the writing can be improved and where the writing shows strengths. The student would then make revisions and present a second draft, and so on. As Ellen reviews each draft in the student's presence, she can explain rules and tips that can help the student improve his or her skills in particular areas. Other methods that have been proven effective will also be used to help students improve their reading and writing skills.

5.0. PRODUCTS AND SERVICES

5.1. Description

Every student who engages in Ellen's English Tutoring Service receives a tutoring plan specifically formulated to address his or her needs, goals, and special circumstances. This plan is formed after Ellen meets with the parents and the student and is signed by all parties after agreement on its content. The plan includes information on the methods and resources that will be used to tutor the student, dates and times for the tutoring sessions, what goals will be reached at certain points along the timeline agreed upon by parents and Ellen, and other information necessary for a comprehensive and effective plan. The rights and responsibilities of each of the parties (student, tutor, parents) will also be detailed in the plan.

Ellen's English Tutoring Service will specialize in instructing students on reading and writing in the English language. The methods and resources used will depend on the individual student's needs and skills but could include having the student read aloud, having the student write answers to questions about a reading, helping the student complete a reading or writing assignment from school, reviewing the student's schoolwork and helping him or her find the strengths and weaknesses of the work, and so on. Additional resources used may include relevant Internet sites and DVDs. Ellen's positive and encouraging approach will increase students' self-confidence as well as their skills in—and thus their enjoyment of—reading and writing.

5.2. Pricing

As of 2010, the average rate in the Columbia area for private tutors was between $20 and $50 an hour. Because Ellen is interested in gaining a good base of customers initially, and because price is a factor to people looking for tutors, Ellen's services will start in the lower range, at $25 an hour. Clients will be expected to pay per session or set up a payment plan in which they pay weekly or monthly. Ellen will provide a simple payment contract if clients choose the latter.

6.0. MARKETING AND SALES

6.1. Advertising and Promotion

Because advertising funds are limited until Ellen gains some clients and resulting cash flow, the main forms of advertising will be low cost and consist of a web site, flyers, and business cards. The flyers will include information on the business as well as some simple promotional text and will be posted on bulletin boards at places families—particularly mothers, who are most often the ones involved in securing the children's education—frequent, including grocery stores, hair salons, recreation centers, and so on. Business cards will be distributed to middle and junior high school counselors and teachers, so that these people can give them out to parents who ask for a tutor recommendation. Finally, Ellen will maintain a web site that provides information about her services as well as links to sites that emphasize the value and advantages of hiring a private tutor.

As the business grows, word of mouth will become a very important form of advertising. As clients use Ellen's service and are happy with it, they will pass her name on to friends and family. This kind of advertising is particularly important in this line of work, where people want to be sure they are going to get their money's worth. Families do not want to invest in a tutor who is not going to do their child any good, and there are those in the market who do not have the skills or knowledge to do an adequate job of tutoring middle and junior high school children. Often the only way to know if a tutor is "good" is to hear from someone else who has used him or her.

6.2. Cost

Cost of start–up advertising will be minimal and will consist of the cost of printing flyers and business cards, estimated at $300.

6.3. Image

Ellen's English Tutoring Service will strive to include three main characteristics in its public image: professional, caring, and effective.

Because Ellen has taught English at the middle and junior high school level, has an advanced degree in education, is certified by the National Tutoring Association, and has experience as a paid tutor, it will not be difficult to portray herself as a professional in the field. This professional image is also carried over into her general demeanor, appearance, and interactions with clients. For example, Ellen's dress code is business casual; she does not wear jeans when meeting with clients. Although this is not a necessary component in the tutoring business, it does promote a good first impression and projects a more professional and trustworthy image.

Ellen cares about her students—and not just their success in school. She is interested in being a positive influence in her students' lives by helping them increase their self–confidence, develop an optimistic attitude, and become constructive participants in their families and schools.

Finally, effectiveness is perhaps the most important component of the business's image. No parent wants to spend money on a tutor that is not effective; in other words, students must show improvement in their reading and writing while utilizing Ellen's services. Ellen's effectiveness comes from her experience as a teacher and tutor as well as various training programs and resources provided by the National Tutoring Association regarding successful methods and philosophies. For example, Ellen has completed the Tutoring Foundations course, which covers every aspect of tutoring, from how students learn, to how to individualize tutoring services to specific learning styles and personalities, to working with parents and teachers. Ellen uses tutoring strategies that have been proven to be effective by the National Tutoring Association and professionals in the field.

7.0. OPERATIONS

7.1. Customers

The market for this business consists of the parents of the approximately 5,000 middle and junior high school children attending public school in Columbia, as well as other children ages 11 to 16 that attend private school or are home–schooled. Parents of these children are generally middle to upper class and well educated. Generally, parents who are well educated are interested in raising children who are the same. In addition, because tutoring costs are an extra expense that many lower–income families cannot afford, the targeted market includes those who have the discretionary income to afford the services.

7.2. Equipment

Basically the only equipment required for the business is a computer and a printer. As mentioned earlier, Ellen will have a separate room in her home in which to conduct the tutoring, and it will be outfitted with a large table, chairs, and bookshelves.

7.3. Hours

Hours of business will depend on students' schedules and needs. Ellen will be available for tutoring sessions anywhere between 7 a.m. and 9 p.m. Monday through Saturday and 12 noon and 9 p.m. on Sundays.

7.4. Facility and Location

The business will be operated out of Ellen's home at 3500 Foxboro Lane in Columbia, Missouri. When/ if necessary, Ellen will meet with students in their home or at another location such as the library.

8.0. FINANCIAL ANALYSIS

Because tutoring requires very little investment, Ellen's English Tutoring Service should experience profits within the first year of business. The only restrictions on profit will be the number of clients that can be attracted. The profit figures given below are conservative and may very well exceed these estimates.

One session is considered one hour, although some sessions may be a half hour depending on students' needs and schedules. Students may be tutored every day, several times a week, or even once a week. For the purposes of making estimates, we have figured one 1–hour tutoring session a week per student, at a rate of $25 per hour. Also, because this type of service has a constant turnover (students "graduate" and new students are taken on), these estimates are based on average students per year (10 in Year 1; 15 in Year 2; 20 in Year 3) and 50 working weeks per year. Expenses are estimated to increase 3 percent per year. Figures are rounded.

	Year 1	Year 2	Year 3
Income	$12,500	$18,750	$25,000
Expenses			
Insurance	1,200	1,240	1,280
Supplies	500	515	530
Advertising	300	310	320
Other	200	210	220
Total	**$ 2,200**	**$ 2,275**	**$ 2,350**
Pre-tax profit	$10,300	$16,475	$22,650

Vegetarian Fast Food Restaurant

Benny & Dell's

4 Bradford Avenue
Madison, WI 53710

Paul Greenland

Benny & Dell's is a vegetarian fast–food restaurant featuring both dine–in and drive–through service.

EXECUTIVE SUMMARY

Business Overview

Benny & Dell's is a vegetarian fast–food restaurant featuring both dine–in and drive–through service. At first glance, one might assume that there is a limited market for vegetarian fast food. However, this is far from the case. By the 21st century's second decade a growing number of Americans were making healthier food choices. While a few became vegetarians, many simply reduced their meat consumption. These so–called "flexitarians" are an especially lucrative market segment. In addition, our business will benefit from the fact that Madison, Wisconsin, is home to a larger–than–average vegetarian population. In fact, the city was included in GoVeg.com's "America's Best Vegetarian–Friendly Small Cities" ranking.

History

Benny and Adelaide (Dell) Harrison never dreamed of owning their own business when they began their careers. However, life circumstances would change all of that. In 2003 a good friend of the Harrisons—a busy, on–the–go businessman—had a heart attack at the age of 38. A hospital dietitian, Dell came to the rescue by teaching their friend how to make healthy (mostly vegetarian) food choices, which along with exercise and stress management, was just what the doctor ordered. After this experience the Harrisons quickly realized that there was a real market for healthy fast food. Both vegetarians, this situation inspired them to establish a vegetarian fast–food restaurant.

Business Philosophy

Benny & Dell's makes healthy eating easy.

MARKET ANALYSIS

At first glance, one might assume that there is a limited market for vegetarian fast food. However, this is far from the case. Beyond the relatively small portion of the population that is truly vegetarian, by the 21st century's second decade a growing number of Americans were simply reducing their meat consumption and making healthier food choices. In 2010 the American Restaurant Association reported that that 73 percent of adults were trying to eat healthier at restaurants than they did in 2008.

Target Markets

Benny & Dell's will serve two primary market segments: flexitarians and vegetarians.

Flexitarians

In 2007 the Baltimore, Maryland–based Vegetarian Resource Group reported that between 30 percent and 50 percent of U.S. adults were eating between two and three meatless meals weekly. Several years earlier, a 2005 survey conducted by Opinion Research found that about 25 percent of Americans were looking to reduce their meat consumption. The same research revealed that 14 percent of Americans consumed meat occasionally, but considered themselves to be mainly vegetarian (a population sometimes referred to as "flexitarian").

The rising popularity of vegetarian cuisine can be seen by the growing number of restaurants that offer meat–free meals. In mid–2007 the publication *Nation's Restaurant News* reported that, in a survey of more than 1,000 American Culinary Federation members, 59 percent indicated that vegetarian entrees and meatless meals were "hot." In addition to restaurants, supermarkets continue to expand their range of related items. Examples include everything from soy milks and cheeses to meatless burgers and sausages.

Vegetarians

While a large portion of our customers will be those simply looking to reduce meat consumption and grab something healthy to eat while they're pressed for time, true vegetarians obviously are an important market for our restaurant. According to research conducted in 2009 by Harris Interactive, on behalf of the Vegetarian Resource Group, 8 percent of U.S. adults do not eat meat. Three percent (classified in the study as vegetarians) do not consume meat, poultry, or fish/seafood. Among vegetarians, approximately one–third to one–fourth of individuals do not consume eggs, dairy, or honey.

Community Overview

According to the U.S. Census Bureau, Madison, Wisconsin, was home to an estimated 223,389 people in 2006. Based on the aforementioned data from The Vegetarian Resource Group, one can assume that at least 18,000 people in Madison do not consume meat, and another 2,200 are true vegetarians. However, it's very likely that these numbers are much higher in our market, because Madison is home to a larger–than–average vegetarian population. For example, in 2010 GoVeg.com ranked Madison eighth on its list of America's Best Vegetarian–Friendly Small Cities.

Wisconsin's capital city, Madison is home to the University of Wisconsin–Madison, which was home to more than 42,000 students during the early 2010s. Not surprisingly, Madison is home to a highly educated population. In fact, 48.2 percent of the population over age 25 had a bachelor's degree or higher, compared to the Wisconsin state average of 22.4 percent.

Madison has a reputation for residents who are receptive to and supportive of alternative lifestyles. It is a vibrant city, and has been recognized by a number of national publications. For example, in 2004 *Forbes* named Madison as the "Best City in the Nation for Business and Careers." That same year, *Men's Journal* dubbed Madison as the "Best Small City to Live."

Competitors

Madison, Wisconsin–area residents have a number of options available to them for vegetarian dining. In addition to many restaurants that are "vegetarian friendly" but still offer meat–based meals, a number of locations are exclusively vegetarian. Because some of these restaurants focus on a particular type of cuisine or food, we do not consider them to be primary competitors. With this in mind, we have categorized the competition as follows:

Primary Competitors:

Dandelion—an all–vegetarian lunch cart in the downtown area. This is a seasonal competitor, as the business does not operate during the winter months. Dandelion offers selections such as sweet potato wraps, stuffed poblano peppers, salads, chips, and vegan peanut butter cups.

Blue Plate Diner—offers a wide range of vegetarian food choices, including vegan barbecued pork, meatless meatloaf, and vegetarian chili.

Elizabeth Waters Dining Hall (University of Wisconsin–Madison campus)—primarily limited to the university community, this dining hall offers a wide range of vegetarian selections, including a salad bar and selections such as jerk tofu and mango rundown tofu.

Secondary Competitors:

- King of Falafel

- India Darbar Restaurant (Indian cuisine)

- Mother Fool's Coffeehouse (Cookies, Pastries, Scones, and Muffins)

INDUSTRY ANALYSIS

According to the American Restaurant Association (ARA), restaurant industry sales were expected to reach $580 billion in 2010. Of this amount, eating places accounted for $388.5 billion in sales. The ARA reports that single–unit operations like Benny & Dell's represent about 70 percent of all eating and drinking places. On average, quick–serve restaurants like ours generated approximately $717,000 per location in 2007.

PERSONNEL

Management

Benny Harrison

Although he has never owned a restaurant before, Benny Harrison is no stranger to the business. For more than 15 years, he has worked as a salesman for Preston Food Supply Inc., a major U.S. food supply company. A graduate of the University of Wisconsin–Madison, where he earned a under-graduate business degree, Benny knows what it takes to run a successful food services operation. He has served clients in retail, wholesale, and institutional settings. Specifically, his experience includes:

- Developing new accounts

- Performing research related to prospecting and qualifying

- Account management/relations

- Merchandising activities

- Involvement with marketing/branding initiatives

In 2007 Benny was named as Preston Food Supply's salesman of the year.

Adelaide (Dell) Harrison

A licensed dietitian and University of Idaho graduate, Dell Harrison spent the early years of her career working for several nursing homes in the Madison, Wisconsin area. Next, she went to work for Madison General Hospital. In that role she provided nutrition counseling to a wide range of patients, helping them to develop customized meal plans based on their lifestyles and health situations. Specifically, Dell counseled patients with:

- Cancer

- Cardiovascular disease/hypertension

- Diabetes and pre–diabetes

- Digestive disorders

- Eating disorders

- Pregnancy

- Obesity

- Osteoporosis

During the final three years of her 15–year career at Madison General, Dell served as manager of the Nutrition Services department, where her responsibilities included overseeing a staff of five dietitians, conducting performance appraisals, and managing the department budget. Dell has resigned from her position at Madison General Hospital in order to be involved with the daily management and operation of Benny & Dell's.

Staffing

In addition to the owners, Benny & Dell's will employ 10 staff members, including:

- 3 full–time kitchen staff

- 4 part–time counter/drive–through staff

- 3 part–time delivery staff

Professional and Advisory Support

Benny & Dell has retained Mad City Financial, a local accounting firm, to assist us with bookkeeping and tax responsibilities. Commercial checking accounts have been established with AMCORE Financial, which has agreed to provide merchant accounts so that we are able to accept credit card and debit card payments.

BUSINESS STRATEGY

Along with profitability, Benny & Dell's main focus is to provide people, no matter how busy they are, with access to food choices that are both healthy and delicious. Because the Madison area is home to an educated consumer base with many dining options, as well as a larger–than–average vegetarian population, our first focus as a new enterprise will be to develop a reputation for quality and excellent customer service.

We are establishing our new business during one of the most challenging economic climates in American history. With this in mind, we also realize the importance of value. Because vegetable–based products typically are more affordable than meat, poultry, and fish, we feel that our vegetarian concept will work to our advantage in this regard. Organic products are admittedly more expensive, but we will work with local producers to secure organic ingredients at the best price, whenever possible.

Assuming that our first location is a success, we eventually will look to establish a second restaurant in the nearby city of Chicago, which also is home to a vibrant vegetarian and health–conscious population. The larger Chicagoland market includes a number of affluent suburbs that would be ideal for continued expansion. After establishing a location in downtown Chicago, the area surrounding Woodfield Mall in Schaumburg, Illinois, would be ideal for a second location.

PRODUCTS & SERVICES

Following is a listing of Benny & Dell's main menu items. Periodically, we will offer seasonal and/or special selections. In addition, we will offer catering services on a limited basis. Many of our menu items are made using soy–based meat substitutes and soy cheese. These items are marked with an asterisk.

Salads & Wraps
- House Salad
- *Chick/Bacon Ranch Salad
- Peanut Noodle Salad
- Greek Salad
- Taco Salad
- Grilled Tempeh (soybean cake) Salad

Dressings: Bleu Cheese, Ranch, Oil & Vinegar, Caesar, and Honey Mustard

Soups & Stews
- Black Eyed Peas Soup
- Refried Beans Soup
- Vegan Roasted Red Pepper Soup
- Veggie Stew
- Vegetarian Chili

Sandwiches
- *Grilled Chick Caesar Club
- Tempeh Ruben
- *Chick Cordon Bleu
- *Italian Hero
- Cheese Melt
- *Sausage & Peppers Hero

Hotdogs & Burgers
- *Burger
- *Quarter–Pound Burger
- *Cheeseburger
- *Buffalo Burger
- *Hot Dog
- *Chili Dog
- *Corndog

Sides
- Seasoned Potato Wedges (baked)
- Spicy Potato Wedges (baked)
- Mixed Fruit
- Reduced Fat Potato Chips
- Salsa
- Pasta Salad

Drinks
- Organic Soda (Orange, Cola, Grape, Black Cherry, and Root Beer)
- Freshly Squeezed Organic Lemonade
- Freshly Squeezed Organic Orange Juice
- Bottled Water
- Soy Milk (plain, vanilla, chocolate)
- Fair Trade Coffee
- Chai Tea
- Green Tea

Desserts
Benny & Dell's will offer a number of different vegan (e.g., containing no dairy products) desserts. Selections will vary weekly.

MARKETING & SALES

A comprehensive marketing plan, which includes both short–term and long–term tactics, has been developed for Benny & Dell's.

Short–Term Tactics

Benny & Dell's will commence operations on July 1, 2010, beginning with a grand opening celebration. During our first week of business we will conduct heavy radio advertising, including give–aways via contests on popular stations. In addition, each day we will provide specials (e.g., half–price lunch selections, buy–one–get–one–free, free appetizers, etc.).

During the summer and autumn months, we will put a heavy emphasis on building our customer base. Because we're confident that once people taste our food, they're sure to come back for more, we will offer a limited number of our menu selections at several big events throughout Madison, where we also will offer free samples.

Examples of the events we will exhibit at include:
- The Dane County Fair, July 14–18
- Willy Street Fair (late summer)
- 12th Annual Food for Thought Festival, September 24–25

Long–Term Tactics

- Web Site: Benny & Dell's will develop a Web site that lists our menu, hours, and details about our customer loyalty program.

- Coupons and Specials: Each day, we'll offer special discounts on various food and beverage items. We will promote these on a special sign in front of our restaurant, and will push out limited–time offers to Madison's tech–savvy population via social media channels such as Twitter.

- Customer Loyalty Program: Benny & Dell's will reward repeat customers with special coupons, as well as a punch card entitling them to their 10th meal free.

- Online Advertising: We will advertise regularly on popular social media sites, such as Facebook. Compared to traditional print advertising, this is a cost–effective tactic that will allow us to reach prospects in a highly targeted way (e.g., based on criteria such as age, gender, geography, etc.).

- Fliers: On a periodic basis, we will circulate promotional fliers that contain coupons throughout downtown Madison and the University of Wisconsin–Madison campus.

- Event Marketing: Benny & Dell's will have a presence at many of Madison's most popular festival and events.

Evaluation & Adjustment

We will evaluate our marketing plan on a quarterly basis during our first year of operations, and semi–annually thereafter.

OPERATIONS

Suppliers

Benny & Dell's will buy produce and other ingredients locally whenever possible. ARA research indicates that 70 percent of adults will be more likely to visit a restaurant that provides locally grown food. In addition, we will attempt to purchase organic ingredients when it is financially feasible to do so. In addition to ensuring that our ingredients are as fresh and healthful as possible, we are convinced that this will help to attract customers to our restaurant. Our position is supported by ARA research indicating that 56 percent of adults are more likely to frequent a restaurant offering food that is either organic or grown in an environmentally–responsible manner.

Benny & Dell's has negotiated supplier agreements with several local food–service wholesalers and coffee wholesalers in the Madison, Wisconsin, area that have a reputation for quality and reliability:

- Zion Coffee Roasting Co.

- Golden Grains Bread Co.

- Flavorful Fruit

- Fantastic Organics

- Gemini Produce Inc.

In the event that one of the aforementioned specialty suppliers cannot meet our needs, the following national suppliers can both provide all of the food–service products that we require. In addition, these wholesalers will supply us with general cooking and restaurant supplies:

- Smithfield Products Corp.

- Brooks Foods LLC

- Preston Food Supply Inc.

Hours

Benny & Dell's will keep the following hours:

- Monday–Saturday: 11:00 a.m.–9:00 p.m.

- Sunday: 11:00 a.m.–7:00 p.m.

Facility and Location

Benny & Dell's will operate in a former Taco Bell restaurant, which has been vacated since the fast–food chain constructed a new–format restaurant several blocks away. Located within walking and/or biking distance of the University of Wisconsin–Madison campus, more than 30,000 cars pass by this location every day. The restaurant is equipped with all necessary fixtures, equipment, and furniture. Leased for a reasonable monthly fee, this restaurant is equipped with a drive–through and a light pole sign.

LEGAL

Our business has obtained all necessary permits from the State of Wisconsin, License, Permit, and Registration Services. We are in full compliance with all necessary public health rules and regulations, including HFS 196, the Wisconsin Administrative Code for Restaurants.

FUNDING

Financing for Benny & Dell's will consist of a $100,000 commercial loan (terms of five years, 8% interest), as well as a $150,000 investment from the owners.

Business Plan Template

USING THIS TEMPLATE

A business plan carefully spells out a company's projected course of action over a period of time, usually the first two to three years after the start-up. In addition, banks, lenders, and other investors examine the information and financial documentation before deciding whether or not to finance a new business venture. Therefore, a business plan is an essential tool in obtaining financing and should describe the business itself in detail as well as all important factors influencing the company, including the market, industry, competition, operations and management policies, problem solving strategies, financial resources and needs, and other vital information. The plan enables the business owner to anticipate costs, plan for difficulties, and take advantage of opportunities, as well as design and implement strategies that keep the company running as smoothly as possible.

This template has been provided as a model to help you construct your own business plan. Please keep in mind that there is no single acceptable format for a business plan, and that this template is in no way comprehensive, but serves as an example.

The business plans provided in this section are fictional and have been used by small business agencies as models for clients to use in compiling their own business plans.

GENERIC BUSINESS PLAN

Main headings included below are topics that should be covered in a comprehensive business plan. They include:

Business Summary

Purpose
Provides a brief overview of your business, succinctly highlighting the main ideas of your plan.

Includes

- Name and Type of Business
- Description of Product/Service
- Business History and Development
- Location
- Market
- Competition
- Management
- Financial Information
- Business Strengths and Weaknesses
- Business Growth

Table of Contents

Purpose
Organized in an Outline Format, the Table of Contents illustrates the selection and arrangement of information contained in your plan.

Includes

- Topic Headings and Subheadings
- Page Number References

Business History and Industry Outlook

Purpose

Examines the conception and subsequent development of your business within an industry specific context.

Includes

- Start-up Information
- Owner/Key Personnel Experience
- Location
- Development Problems and Solutions
- Investment/Funding Information
- Future Plans and Goals
- Market Trends and Statistics
- Major Competitors
- Product/Service Advantages
- National, Regional, and Local Economic Impact

Product/Service

Purpose

Introduces, defines, and details the product and/or service that inspired the information of your business.

Includes

- Unique Features
- Niche Served
- Market Comparison
- Stage of Product/Service Development
- Production
- Facilities, Equipment, and Labor
- Financial Requirements
- Product/Service Life Cycle
- Future Growth

Market Examination

Purpose

Assessment of product/service applications in relation to consumer buying cycles.

Includes

- Target Market
- Consumer Buying Habits
- Product/Service Applications
- Consumer Reactions
- Market Factors and Trends
- Penetration of the Market
- Market Share
- Research and Studies
- Cost
- Sales Volume and Goals

Competition

Purpose

Analysis of Competitors in the Marketplace.

Includes

- Competitor Information
- Product/Service Comparison
- Market Niche
- Product/Service Strengths and Weaknesses
- Future Product/Service Development

Marketing

Purpose

Identifies promotion and sales strategies for your product/service.

Includes

- Product/Service Sales Appeal
- Special and Unique Features
- Identification of Customers
- Sales and Marketing Staff
- Sales Cycles

- Type of Advertising/ Promotion
- Pricing
- Competition
- Customer Services

Operations

Purpose

Traces product/service development from production/inception to the market environment.

Includes

- Cost Effective Production Methods
- Facility
- Location

- Equipment
- Labor
- Future Expansion

Administration and Management

Purpose

Offers a statement of your management philosophy with an in-depth focus on processes and procedures.

Includes

- Management Philosophy
- Structure of Organization
- Reporting System
- Methods of Communication
- Employee Skills and Training

- Employee Needs and Compensation
- Work Environment
- Management Policies and Procedures
- Roles and Responsibilities

Key Personnel

Purpose

Describes the unique backgrounds of principle employees involved in business.

Includes

- Owner(s)/Employee Education and Experience
- Positions and Roles

- Benefits and Salary
- Duties and Responsibilities
- Objectives and Goals

Potential Problems and Solutions

Purpose

Discussion of problem solving strategies that change issues into opportunities.

Includes

- Risks
- Litigation
- Future Competition

- Economic Impact
- Problem Solving Skills

Financial Information

Purpose

Secures needed funding and assistance through worksheets and projections detailing financial plans, methods of repayment, and future growth opportunities.

Includes

- Financial Statements
- Bank Loans
- Methods of Repayment
- Tax Returns
- Start-up Costs
- Projected Income (3 years)
- Projected Cash Flow (3 Years)
- Projected Balance Statements (3 years)

Appendices

Purpose

Supporting documents used to enhance your business proposal.

Includes

- Photographs of product, equipment, facilities, etc.
- Copyright/Trademark Documents
- Legal Agreements
- Marketing Materials
- Research and or Studies
- Operation Schedules
- Organizational Charts
- Job Descriptions
- Resumes
- Additional Financial Documentation

Fictional Food Distributor

Commercial Foods, Inc.

3003 Avondale Ave.
Knoxville, TN 37920

This plan demonstrates how a partnership can have a positive impact on a new business. It demonstrates how two individuals can carve a niche in the specialty foods market by offering gourmet foods to upscale restaurants and fine hotels. This plan is fictional and has not been used to gain funding from a bank or other lending institution.

STATEMENT OF PURPOSE

Commercial Foods, Inc. seeks a loan of $75,000 to establish a new business. This sum, together with $5,000 equity investment by the principals, will be used as follows:

- Merchandise inventory $25,000

- Office fixture/equipment $12,000

- Warehouse equipment $14,000

- One delivery truck $10,000

- Working capital $39,000

- Total $100,000

DESCRIPTION OF THE BUSINESS

Commercial Foods, Inc. will be a distributor of specialty food service products to hotels and upscale restaurants in the geographical area of a 50 mile radius of Knoxville. Richard Roberts will direct the sales effort and John Williams will manage the warehouse operation and the office. One delivery truck will be used initially with a second truck added in the third year. We expect to begin operation of the business within 30 days after securing the requested financing.

MANAGEMENT

A. Richard Roberts is a native of Memphis, Tennessee. He is a graduate of Memphis State University with a Bachelor's degree from the School of Business. After graduation, he worked for a major manufacturer of specialty food service products as a detail sales person for five years, and, for the past three years, he has served as a product sales manager for this firm.

B. John Williams is a native of Nashville, Tennessee. He holds a B.S. Degree in Food Technology from the University of Tennessee. His career includes five years as a product development chemist in gourmet food products and five years as operations manager for a food service distributor.

Both men are healthy and energetic. Their backgrounds complement each other, which will ensure the success of Commercial Foods, Inc. They will set policies together and personnel decisions will be made jointly. Initial salaries for the owners will be $1,000 per month for the first few years. The spouses of both principals are successful in the business world and earn enough to support the families.

They have engaged the services of Foster Jones, CPA, and William Hale, Attorney, to assist them in an advisory capacity.

PERSONNEL

The firm will employ one delivery truck driver at a wage of $8.00 per hour. One office worker will be employed at $7.50 per hour. One part-time employee will be used in the office at $5.00 per hour. The driver will load and unload his own trucks. Mr. Williams will assist in the warehouse operation as needed to assist one stock person at $7.00 per hour. An additional delivery truck and driver will be added the third year.

LOCATION

The firm will lease a 20,000 square foot building at 3003 Avondale Ave., in Knoxville, which contains warehouse and office areas equipped with two-door truck docks. The annual rental is $9,000. The building was previously used as a food service warehouse and very little modification to the building will be required.

PRODUCTS AND SERVICES

The firm will offer specialty food service products such as soup bases, dessert mixes, sauce bases, pastry mixes, spices, and flavors, normally used by upscale restaurants and nice hotels. We are going after a niche in the market with high quality gourmet products. There is much less competition in this market than in standard run of the mill food service products. Through their work experiences, the principals have contacts with supply sources and with local chefs.

THE MARKET

We know from our market survey that there are over 200 hotels and upscale restaurants in the area we plan to serve. Customers will be attracted by a direct sales approach. We will offer samples of our products and product application data on use of our products in the finished prepared foods. We will cultivate the chefs in these establishments. The technical background of John Williams will be especially useful here.

COMPETITION

We find that we will be only distributor in the area offering a full line of gourmet food service products. Other foodservice distributors offer only a few such items in conjunction with their standard product line. Our survey shows that many of the chefs are ordering products from Atlanta and Memphis because of a lack of adequate local supply.

SUMMARY

Commercial Foods, Inc. will be established as a foodservice distributor of specialty food in Knoxville. The principals, with excellent experience in the industry, are seeking a $75,000 loan to establish the business. The principals are investing $25,000 as equity capital.

The business will be set up as an S Corporation with each principal owning 50% of the common stock in the corporation.

Fictional Hardware Store

Oshkosh Hardware, Inc.

123 Main St.
Oshkosh, WI 54901

The following plan outlines how a small hardware store can survive competition from large discount chains by offering products and providing expert advice in the use of any product it sells. This plan is fictional and has not been used to gain funding from a bank or other lending institution.

EXECUTIVE SUMMARY

Oshkosh Hardware, Inc. is a new corporation that is going to establish a retail hardware store in a strip mall in Oshkosh, Wisconsin. The store will sell hardware of all kinds, quality tools, paint, and housewares. The business will make revenue and a profit by servicing its customers not only with needed hardware but also with expert advice in the use of any product it sells.

Oshkosh Hardware, Inc. will be operated by its sole shareholder, James Smith. The company will have a total of four employees. It will sell its products in the local market. Customers will buy our products because we will provide free advice on the use of all of our products and will also furnish a full refund warranty.

Oshkosh Hardware, Inc. will sell its products in the Oshkosh store staffed by three sales representatives. No additional employees will be needed to achieve its short and long range goals. The primary short range goal is to open the store by October 1, 1994. In order to achieve this goal a lease must be signed by July 1, 1994 and the complete inventory ordered by August 1, 1994.

Mr. James Smith will invest $30,000 in the business. In addition, the company will have to borrow $150,000 during the first year to cover the investment in inventory, accounts receivable, and furniture and equipment. The company will be profitable after six months of operation and should be able to start repayment of the loan in the second year.

THE BUSINESS

The business will sell hardware of all kinds, quality tools, paint, and housewares. We will purchase our products from three large wholesale buying groups.

In general our customers are homeowners who do their own repair and maintenance, hobbyists, and housewives. Our business is unique in that we will have a complete line of all hardware items and will be able to get special orders by overnight delivery. The business makes revenue and profits by servicing our customers not only with needed hardware but also with expert advice in the use of any product we sell. Our major costs for bringing our products to market are cost of merchandise of 36%, salaries of $45,000, and occupancy costs of $60,000.

Oshkosh Hardware, Inc.'s retail outlet will be located at 1524 Frontage Road, which is in a newly developed retail center of Oshkosh. Our location helps facilitate accessibility from all parts of town and reduces our delivery costs. The store will occupy 7500 square feet of space. The major equipment involved in our business is counters and shelving, a computer, a paint mixing machine, and a truck.

THE MARKET

Oshkosh Hardware, Inc. will operate in the local market. There are 15,000 potential customers in this market area. We have three competitors who control approximately 98% of the market at present. We feel we can capture 25% of the market within the next four years. Our major reason for believing this is that our staff is technically competent to advise our customers in the correct use of all products we sell.

After a careful market analysis, we have determined that approximately 60% of our customers are men and 40% are women. The percentage of customers that fall into the following age categories are:

Under 16: 0%
17-21: 5%
22-30: 30%
31-40: 30%
41-50: 20%
51-60: 10%
61-70: 5%
Over 70: 0%

The reasons our customers prefer our products is our complete knowledge of their use and our full refund warranty.

We get our information about what products our customers want by talking to existing customers. There seems to be an increasing demand for our product. The demand for our product is increasing in size based on the change in population characteristics.

SALES

At Oshkosh Hardware, Inc. we will employ three sales people and will not need any additional personnel to achieve our sales goals. These salespeople will need several years experience in home repair and power tool usage. We expect to attract 30% of our customers from newspaper ads, 5% of our customers from local directories, 5% of our customers from the yellow pages, 10% of our customers from family and friends, and 50% of our customers from current customers. The most cost effect source will be current customers. In general our industry is growing.

MANAGEMENT

We would evaluate the quality of our management staff as being excellent. Our manager is experienced and very motivated to achieve the various sales and quality assurance objectives we have set. We will use a management information system that produces key inventory, quality assurance, and sales data on a weekly basis. All data is compared to previously established goals for that week, and deviations are the primary focus of the management staff.

GOALS IMPLEMENTATION

The short term goals of our business are:

1. Open the store by October 1, 1994
2. Reach our breakeven point in two months
3. Have sales of $100,000 in the first six months

In order to achieve our first short term goal we must:

1. Sign the lease by July 1, 1994
2. Order a complete inventory by August 1, 1994

In order to achieve our second short term goal we must:

1. Advertise extensively in Sept. and Oct.
2. Keep expenses to a minimum

In order to achieve our third short term goal we must:

1. Promote power tool sales for the Christmas season
2. Keep good customer traffic in Jan. and Feb.

The long term goals for our business are:

1. Obtain sales volume of $600,000 in three years
2. Become the largest hardware dealer in the city
3. Open a second store in Fond du Lac

The most important thing we must do in order to achieve the long term goals for our business is to develop a highly profitable business with excellent cash flow.

FINANCE

Oshkosh Hardware, Inc. Faces some potential threats or risks to our business. They are discount house competition. We believe we can avoid or compensate for this by providing quality products complimented by quality advice on the use of every product we sell. The financial projections we have prepared are located at the end of this document.

JOB DESCRIPTION-GENERAL MANAGER

The General Manager of the business of the corporation will be the president of the corporation. He will be responsible for the complete operation of the retail hardware store which is owned by the corporation. A detailed description of his duties and responsibilities is as follows.

Sales

Train and supervise the three sales people. Develop programs to motivate and compensate these employees. Coordinate advertising and sales promotion effects to achieve sales totals as outlined in budget. Oversee purchasing function and inventory control procedures to insure adequate merchandise at all times at a reasonable cost.

Finance

Prepare monthly and annual budgets. Secure adequate line of credit from local banks. Supervise office personnel to insure timely preparation of records, statements, all government reports, control of receivables and payables, and monthly financial statements.

Administration

Perform duties as required in the areas of personnel, building leasing and maintenance, licenses and permits, and public relations.

Organizations, Agencies, & Consultants

A listing of Associations and Consultants of interest to entrepreneurs, followed by the ten Small Business Administration Regional Offices, Small Business Development Centers, Service Corps of Retired Executives offices, and Venture Capital and Finance Companies.

Associations

This section contains a listing of associations and other agencies of interest to the small business owner. Entries are listed alphabetically by organization name.

American Business Women's Association
9100 Ward Pkwy.
PO Box 8728
Kansas City, MO 64114-0728
(800)228-0007
E-mail: abwa@abwa.org
Website: http://www.abwa.org
Jeanne Banks, National President

American Franchisee Association
53 W Jackson Blvd., Ste. 1157
Chicago, IL 60604
(312)431-0545
E-mail: info@franchisee.org
Website: http://www.franchisee.org
Susan P. Kezios, President

American Independent Business Alliance
222 S Black Ave.
Bozeman, MT 59715
(406)582-1255
E-mail: info@amiba.net
Website: http://www.amiba.net
Jennifer Rockne, Director

American Small Businesses Association
206 E College St., Ste. 201
Grapevine, TX 76051
800-942-2722
E-mail: info@asbaonline.org
Website: http://www.asbaonline.org/

American Women's Economic Development Corporation
216 East 45th St., 10th Floor
New York, NY 10017
(917)368-6100

Fax: (212)986-7114
E-mail: info@awed.org
Website: http://www.awed.org
Roseanne Antonucci, Exec. Dir.

Association for Enterprise Opportunity
1601 N Kent St., Ste. 1101
Arlington, VA 22209
(703)841-7760
Fax: (703)841-7748
E-mail: aeo@assoceo.org
Website: http://www.micro enterpriseworks.org
Bill Edwards, Exec.Dir.

Association of Small Business Development Centers
c/o Don Wilson
8990 Burke Lake Rd.
Burke, VA 22015
(703)764-9850
Fax: (703)764-1234
E-mail: info@asbdc-us.org
Website: http://www.asbdc-us.org
Don Wilson, Pres./CEO

BEST Employers Association
2505 McCabe Way
Irvine, CA 92614
(949)253-4080
800-433-0088
Fax: (714)553-0883
E-mail: info@bestlife.com
Website: http://www.bestlife.com
Donald R. Lawrenz, CEO

Center for Family Business
PO Box 24219
Cleveland, OH 44124
(440)460-5409
E-mail: grummi@aol.com
Dr. Leon A. Danco, Chm.

Coalition for Government Procurement
1990 M St. NW, Ste. 400
Washington, DC 20036
(202)331-0975
E-mail: info@thecgp.org
Website: http://www.coalgovpro.org
Paul Caggiano, Pres.

Employers of America
PO Box 1874
Mason City, IA 50402-1874
(641)424-3187
800-728-3187
Fax: (641)424-1673
E-mail: employer@employerhelp.org
Website: http://www.employerhelp.org
Jim Collison, Pres.

Family Firm Institute
200 Lincoln St., Ste. 201
Boston, MA 02111
(617)482-3045
Fax: (617)482-3049
E-mail: ffi@ffi.org
Website: http://www.ffi.org
Judy L. Green, Ph.D., Exec.Dir.

Independent Visually Impaired Enterprisers
500 S 3rd St., Apt. H
Burbank, CA 91502
(818)238-9321
E-mail: abazyn@bazyn communications.com
http://www.acb.org/affiliates
Adris Bazyn, Pres.

International Association for Business Organizations
3 Woodthorn Ct., Ste. 12
Owings Mills, MD 21117
(410)581-1373
E-mail: nahbb@msn.com
Rudolph Lewis, Exec. Officer

International Council for Small Business
The George Washington University
School of Business and Public
Management
2115 G St. NW, Ste. 403
Washington, DC 20052
(202)994-0704
Fax: (202)994-4930
E-mail: icsb@gwu.edu
Website: http://www.icsb.org
Susan G. Duffy. Admin.

International Small Business Consortium
3309 Windjammer St.
Norman, OK 73072
E-mail: sb@isbc.com
Website: http://www.isbc.com

Kauffman Center for Entrepreneurial Leadership
4801 Rockhill Rd.
Kansas City, MO 64110-2046
(816)932-1000
E-mail: info@kauffman.org
Website: http://www.entreworld.org

National Alliance for Fair Competition
3 Bethesda Metro Center, Ste. 1100
Bethesda, MD 20814
(410)235-7116
Fax: (410)235-7116
E-mail: ampesq@aol.com
Tony Ponticelli, Exec.Dir.

National Association for the Self-Employed
PO Box 612067
DFW Airport
Dallas, TX 75261-2067
(800)232-6273
E-mail: mpetron@nase.org
Website: http://www.nase.org
Robert Hughes, Pres.

National Association of Business Leaders
4132 Shoreline Dr., Ste. J & H
Earth City, MO 63045
Fax: (314)298-9110
E-mail: nabl@nabl.com
Website: http://www.nabl.com/
Gene Blumenthal, Contact

National Association of Private Enterprise
PO Box 15550
Long Beach, CA 90815
888-224-0953

Fax: (714)844-4942
Website: http://www.napeonline.net
Laura Squiers, Exec.Dir.

National Association of Small Business Investment Companies
666 11th St. NW, Ste. 750
Washington, DC 20001
(202)628-5055
Fax: (202)628-5080
E-mail: nasbic@nasbic.org
Website: http://www.nasbic.org
Lee W. Mercer, Pres.

National Business Association
PO Box 700728
5151 Beltline Rd., Ste. 1150
Dallas, TX 75370
(972)458-0900
800-456-0440
Fax: (972)960-9149
E-mail: info@nationalbusiness.org
Website: http://www.national
business.org
Raj Nisankarao, Pres.

National Business Owners Association
PO Box 111
Stuart, VA 24171
(276)251-7500
(866)251-7505
Fax: (276)251-2217
E-mail: membershipservices@nboa.org
Website: http://www.rvmdb.com.nboa
Paul LaBarr, Pres.

National Center for Fair Competition
PO Box 220
Annandale, VA 22003
(703)280-4622
Fax: (703)280-0942
E-mail: kentonp1@aol.com
Kenton Pattie, Pres.

National Family Business Council
1640 W. Kennedy Rd.
Lake Forest, IL 60045
(847)295-1040
Fax: (847)295-1898
E-mail: lmsnfbc@email.msn.com
Jogn E. Messervey, Pres.

National Federation of Independent Business
53 Century Blvd., Ste. 250
Nashville, TN 37214
(615)872-5800
800-NFIBNOW
Fax: (615)872-5353
Website: http://www.nfib.org
Jack Faris, Pres. and CEO

National Small Business Association
1156 15th St. NW, Ste. 1100
Washington, DC 20005
(202)293-8830
800-345-6728
Fax: (202)872-8543
E-mail: press@nsba.biz
Website: http://www.nsba.biz
Rob Yunich, Dir. of Communications

PUSH Commercial Division
930 E 50th St.
Chicago, IL 60615-2702
(773)373-3366
Fax: (773)373-3571
E-mail: info@rainbowpush.org
Website: http://www.rainbowpush.org
Rev. Willie T. Barrow, Co-Chm.

Research Institute for Small and Emerging Business
722 12th St. NW
Washington, DC 20005
(202)628-8382
Fax: (202)628-8392
E-mail: info@riseb.org
Website: http://www.riseb.org
Allan Neece, Jr., Chm.

Sales Professionals USA
PO Box 149
Arvada, CO 80001
(303)534-4937
888-736-7767
E-mail: salespro@salesprofessionals-
usa.com
Website: http://www.salesprofessionals-
usa.com
Sharon Herbert, Natl. Pres.

Score Association - Service Corps of Retired Executives
409 3rd St. SW, 6th Fl.
Washington, DC 20024
(202)205-6762
800-634-0245
Fax: (202)205-7636
E-mail: media@score.org
Website: http://www.score.org
W. Kenneth Yancey, Jr., CEO

Small Business and Entrepreneurship Council
1920 L St. NW, Ste. 200
Washington, DC 20036
(202)785-0238
Fax: (202)822-8118
E-mail: membership@sbec.org
Website: http://www.sbecouncil.org
Karen Kerrigan, Pres./CEO

Small Business in Telecommunications
1331 H St. NW, Ste. 500
Washington, DC 20005
(202)347-4511
Fax: (202)347-8607
E-mail: sbt@sbthome.org
Website: http://www.sbthome.org
Lonnie Danchik, Chm.

Small Business Legislative Council
1010 Massachusetts Ave. NW, Ste. 540
Washington, DC 20005
(202)639-8500
Fax: (202)296-5333
E-mail: email@sblc.org
Website: http://www.sblc.org
John Satagaj, Pres.

Small Business Service Bureau
554 Main St.
PO Box 15014
Worcester, MA 01615-0014
(508)756-3513
800-343-0939
Fax: (508)770-0528
E-mail: membership@sbsb.com
Website: http://www.sbsb.com
Francis R. Carroll, Pres.

Small Publishers Association of North America
1618 W COlorado Ave.
Colorado Springs, CO 80904
(719)475-1726
Fax: (719)471-2182
E-mail: span@spannet.org
Website: http://www.spannet.org
Scott Flora, Exec. Dir.

SOHO America
PO Box 941
Hurst, TX 76053-0941
800-495-SOHO
E-mail: soho@1sas.com
Website: http://www.soho.org

Structured Employment Economic Development Corporation
915 Broadway, 17th Fl.
New York, NY 10010
(212)473-0255
Fax: (212)473-0357
E-mail: info@seedco.org
Website: http://www.seedco.org
William Grinker, CEO

Support Services Alliance
107 Prospect St.
Schoharie, NY 12157
800-836-4772

E-mail: info@ssamembers.com
Website: http://www.ssainfo.com
Steve COle, Pres.

United States Association for Small Business and Entrepreneurship
975 University Ave., No. 3260
Madison, WI 53706
(608)262-9982
Fax: (608)263-0818
E-mail: jgillman@wisc.edu
Website: http://www.ususbe.org
Joan Gillman, Exec. Dir.

Consultants

This section contains a listing of consultants specializing in small business development. It is arranged alphabetically by country, then by state or province, then by city, then by firm name.

Canada

Alberta

Common Sense Solutions
3405 16A Ave.
Edmonton, AB, Canada
(403)465-7330
Fax: (403)465-7380
E-mail: gcoulson@comsense solutions.com
Website: http://www.comsense solutions.com

Varsity Consulting Group
School of Business
University of Alberta
Edmonton, AB, Canada T6G 2R6
(780)492-2994
Fax: (780)492-5400
Website: http://www.bus.ualberta.ca/vcg

Viro Hospital Consulting
42 Commonwealth Bldg., 9912 - 106 St. NW
Edmonton, AB, Canada T5K 1C5
(403)425-3871
Fax: (403)425-3871
E-mail: rpb@freenet.edmonton.ab.ca

British Columbia

SRI Strategic Resources Inc.
4330 Kingsway, Ste. 1600
Burnaby, BC, Canada V5H 4G7
(604)435-0627
Fax: (604)435-2782

E-mail: inquiry@sri.bc.ca
Website: http://www.sri.com

Andrew R. De Boda Consulting
1523 Milford Ave.
Coquitlam, BC, Canada V3J 2V9
(604)936-4527
Fax: (604)936-4527
E-mail: deboda@intergate.bc.ca
Website: http://www.ourworld. compuserve.com/homepages/deboda

The Sage Group Ltd.
980 - 355 Burrard St.
744 W Haistings, Ste. 410
Vancouver, BC, Canada V6C 1A5
(604)669-9269
Fax: (604)669-6622

Tikkanen-Bradley
1345 Nelson St., Ste. 202
Vancouver, BC, Canada V6E 1J8
(604)669-0583
E-mail: webmaster@tikkanen bradley.com
Website: http://www.tikkanenbradley.com

Ontario

The Cynton Co.
17 Massey St.
Brampton, ON, Canada L6S 2V6
(905)792-7769
Fax: (905)792-8116
E-mail: cynton@home.com
Website: http://www.cynton.com

Begley & Associates
RR 6
Cambridge, ON, Canada N1R 5S7
(519)740-3629
Fax: (519)740-3629
E-mail: begley@in.on.ca
Website: http://www.in.on.ca/~begley/index.htm

CRO Engineering Ltd.
1895 William Hodgins Ln.
Carp, ON, Canada K0A 1L0
(613)839-1108
Fax: (613)839-1406
E-mail: J.Grefford@ieee.ca
Website: http://www.geocities.com/WallStreet/District/7401/

Task Enterprises
Box 69, RR 2 Hamilton
Flamborough, ON, Canada L8N 2Z7
(905)659-0153
Fax: (905)659-0861

HST Group Ltd.
430 Gilmour St.
Ottawa, ON, Canada K2P 0R8
(613)236-7303
Fax: (613)236-9893

Harrison Associates
BCE Pl.
181 Bay St., Ste. 3740
PO Box 798
Toronto, ON, Canada M5J 2T3
(416)364-5441
Fax: (416)364-2875

TCI Convergence Ltd. Management Consultants
99 Crown's Ln.
Toronto, ON, Canada M5R 3P4
(416)515-4146
Fax: (416)515-2097
E-mail: tci@inforamp.net
Website: http://tciconverge.com/index.1.html

Ken Wyman & Associates Inc.
64B Shuter St., Ste. 200
Toronto, ON, Canada M5B 1B1
(416)362-2926
Fax: (416)362-3039
E-mail: kenwyman@compuserve.com

JPL Business Consultants
82705 Metter Rd.
Wellandport, ON, Canada L0R 2J0
(905)386-7450
Fax: (905)386-7450
E-mail: plamarch@freenet.npiec.on.ca

Quebec

The Zimmar Consulting Partnership Inc.
Westmount
PO Box 98
Montreal, QC, Canada H3Z 2T1
(514)484-1459
Fax: (514)484-3063

Saskatchewan

Trimension Group
No. 104-110 Research Dr.
Innovation Place, SK, Canada S7N 3R3
(306)668-2560
Fax: (306)975-1156
E-mail: trimension@trimension.ca
Website: http://www.trimension.ca

Corporate Management Consultants
40 Government Road - PO Box 185
Prud Homme, SK, Canada, S0K 3K0
(306)654-4569
Fax: (650)618-2742

E-mail: cmccorporatemanagement@shaw.ca
Website: http://www.Corporate managementconsultants.com
Gerald Rekve

United States

Alabama

Business Planning Inc.
300 Office Park Dr.
Birmingham, AL 35223-2474
(205)870-7090
Fax: (205)870-7103

Tradebank of Eastern Alabama
546 Broad St., Ste. 3
Gadsden, AL 35901
(205)547-8700
Fax: (205)547-8718
E-mail: mansion@webex.com
Website: http://www.webex.com/~tea

Alaska

AK Business Development Center
3335 Arctic Blvd., Ste. 203
Anchorage, AK 99503
(907)562-0335
Free: 800-478-3474
Fax: (907)562-6988
E-mail: abdc@gci.net
Website: http://www.abdc.org

Business Matters
PO Box 287
Fairbanks, AK 99707
(907)452-5650

Arizona

Carefree Direct Marketing Corp.
8001 E Serene St.
PO Box 3737
Carefree, AZ 85377-3737
(480)488-4227
Fax: (480)488-2841

Trans Energy Corp.
1739 W 7th Ave.
Mesa, AZ 85202
(480)827-7915
Fax: (480)967-6601
E-mail: aha@clean-air.org
Website: http://www.clean-air.org

CMAS
5125 N 16th St.
Phoenix, AZ 85016

(602)395-1001
Fax: (602)604-8180

Comgate Telemanagement Ltd.
706 E Bell Rd., Ste. 105
Phoenix, AZ 85022
(602)485-5708
Fax: (602)485-5709
E-mail: comgate@netzone.com
Website: http://www.comgate.com

Moneysoft Inc.
1 E Camelback Rd. #550
Phoenix, AZ 85012
Free: 800-966-7797
E-mail: mbray@moneysoft.com

Harvey C. Skoog
PO Box 26439
Prescott Valley, AZ 86312
(520)772-1714
Fax: (520)772-2814

LMC Services
8711 E Pinnacle Peak Rd., No. 340
Scottsdale, AZ 85255-3555
(602)585-7177
Fax: (602)585-5880
E-mail: louws@earthlink.com

Sauerbrun Technology Group Ltd.
7979 E Princess Dr., Ste. 5
Scottsdale, AZ 85255-5878
(602)502-4950
Fax: (602)502-4292
E-mail: info@sauerbrun.com
Website: http://www.sauerbrun.com

Gary L. McLeod
PO Box 230
Sonoita, AZ 85637
Fax: (602)455-5661

Van Cleve Associates
6932 E 2nd St.
Tucson, AZ 85710
(520)296-2587
Fax: (520)296-3358

California

Acumen Group Inc.
(650)949-9349
Fax: (650)949-4845
E-mail: acumen-g@ix.netcom.com
Website: http://pw2.netcom.com/~janed/acumen.html

On-line Career and Management Consulting
420 Central Ave., No. 314
Alameda, CA 94501

(510)864-0336
Fax: (510)864-0336
E-mail: career@dnai.com
Website: http://www.dnai.com/~career

Career Paths-Thomas E. Church & Associates Inc.
PO Box 2439
Aptos, CA 95001
(408)662-7950
Fax: (408)662-7955
E-mail: church@ix.netcom.com
Website: http://www.careerpaths-tom.com

Keck & Co. Business Consultants
410 Walsh Rd.
Atherton, CA 94027
(650)854-9588
Fax: (650)854-7240
E-mail: info@keckco.com
Website: http://www.keckco.com

Ben W. Laverty III, PhD, REA, CEI
4909 Stockdale Hwy., Ste. 132
Bakersfield, CA 93309
(661)283-8300
Free: 800-833-0373
Fax: (661)283-8313
E-mail: cstc@cstcsafety.com
Website: http://www.cstcsafety.com/cstc

Lindquist Consultants-Venture Planning
225 Arlington Ave.
Berkeley, CA 94707
(510)524-6685
Fax: (510)527-6604

Larson Associates
PO Box 9005
Brea, CA 92822
(714)529-4121
Fax: (714)572-3606
E-mail: ray@consultlarson.com
Website: http://www.consultlarson.com

Kremer Management Consulting
PO Box 500
Carmel, CA 93921
(408)626-8311
Fax: (408)624-2663
E-mail: ddkremer@aol.com

W and J PARTNERSHIP
PO Box 2499
18876 Edwin Markham Dr.
Castro Valley, CA 94546
(510)583-7751
Fax: (510)583-7645
E-mail: wamorgan@wjpartnership.com
Website: http://www.wjpartnership.com

JB Associates
21118 Gardena Dr.
Cupertino, CA 95014
(408)257-0214
Fax: (408)257-0216
E-mail: semarang@sirius.com

House Agricultural Consultants
PO Box 1615
Davis, CA 95617-1615
(916)753-3361
Fax: (916)753-0464
E-mail: infoag@houseag.com
Website: http://www.houseag.com/

3C Systems Co.
16161 Ventura Blvd., Ste. 815
Encino, CA 91436
(818)907-1302
Fax: (818)907-1357
E-mail: mark@3CSysCo.com
Website: http://www.3CSysCo.com

Technical Management Consultants
3624 Westfall Dr.
Encino, CA 91436-4154
(818)784-0626
Fax: (818)501-5575
E-mail: tmcrs@aol.com

RAINWATER-GISH & Associates, Business Finance & Development
317 3rd St., Ste. 3
Eureka, CA 95501
(707)443-0030
Fax: (707)443-5683

Global Tradelinks
451 Pebble Beach Pl.
Fullerton, CA 92835
(714)441-2280
Fax: (714)441-2281
E-mail: info@globaltradelinks.com
Website: http://www.globaltradelinks.com

Strategic Business Group
800 Cienaga Dr.
Fullerton, CA 92835-1248
(714)449-1040
Fax: (714)525-1631

Burnes Consulting
20537 Wolf Creek Rd.
Grass Valley, CA 95949
(530)346-8188
Free: 800-949-9021
Fax: (530)346-7704
E-mail: kent@burnesconsulting.com
Website: http://www.burnesconsulting.com

Pioneer Business Consultants
9042 Garfield Ave., Ste. 312
Huntington Beach, CA 92646
(714)964-7600

Beblie, Brandt & Jacobs Inc.
16 Technology, Ste. 164
Irvine, CA 92618
(714)450-8790
Fax: (714)450-8799
E-mail: darcy@bbjinc.com
Website: http://198.147.90.26

Fluor Daniel Inc.
3353 Michelson Dr.
Irvine, CA 92612-0650
(949)975-2000
Fax: (949)975-5271
E-mail: sales.consulting@fluordaniel.com
Website: http://www.fluordaniel consulting.com

MCS Associates
18300 Von Karman, Ste. 710
Irvine, CA 92612
(949)263-8700
Fax: (949)263-0770
E-mail: info@mcsassociates.com
Website: http://www.mcsassociates.com

Inspired Arts Inc.
4225 Executive Sq., Ste. 1160
La Jolla, CA 92037
(619)623-3525
Free: 800-851-4394
Fax: (619)623-3534
E-mail: info@inspiredarts.com
Website: http://www.inspiredarts.com

The Laresis Companies
PO Box 3284
La Jolla, CA 92038
(619)452-2720
Fax: (619)452-8744

RCL & Co.
PO Box 1143
737 Pearl St., Ste. 201
La Jolla, CA 92038
(619)454-8883
Fax: (619)454-8880

Comprehensive Business Services
3201 Lucas Cir.
Lafayette, CA 94549
(925)283-8272
Fax: (925)283-8272

The Ribble Group
27601 Forbes Rd., Ste. 52
Laguna Niguel, CA 92677

(714)582-1085
Fax: (714)582-6420
E-mail: ribble@deltanet.com

Norris Bernstein, CMC
9309 Marina Pacifica Dr. N
Long Beach, CA 90803
(562)493-5458
Fax: (562)493-5459
E-mail: norris@ctecomputer.com
Website: http://foodconsultants.com/
bernstein/

Horizon Consulting Services
1315 Garthwick Dr.
Los Altos, CA 94024
(415)967-0906
Fax: (415)967-0906

Brincko Associates Inc.
1801 Avenue of the Stars, Ste. 1054
Los Angeles, CA 90067
(310)553-4523
Fax: (310)553-6782

Rubenstein/Justman Management Consultants
2049 Century Park E, 24th Fl.
Los Angeles, CA 90067
(310)282-0800
Fax: (310)282-0400
E-mail: info@rjmc.net
Website: http://www.rjmc.net

F.J. Schroeder & Associates
1926 Westholme Ave.
Los Angeles, CA 90025
(310)470-2655
Fax: (310)470-6378
E-mail: fjsacons@aol.com
Website: http://www.mcninet.com/
GlobalLook/Fjschroe.html

Western Management Associates
5959 W Century Blvd., Ste. 565
Los Angeles, CA 90045-6506
(310)645-1091
Free: (888)788-6534
Fax: (310)645-1092
E-mail: gene@cfoforrent.com
Website: http://www.cfoforrent.com

Darrell Sell and Associates
Los Gatos, CA 95030
(408)354-7794
E-mail: darrell@netcom.com

Leslie J. Zambo
3355 Michael Dr.
Marina, CA 93933
(408)384-7086

Fax: (408)647-4199
E-mail: 104776.1552@compuserve.com

Marketing Services Management
PO Box 1377
Martinez, CA 94553
(510)370-8527
Fax: (510)370-8527
E-mail: markserve@biotechnet.com

William M. Shine Consulting Service
PO Box 127
Moraga, CA 94556-0127
(510)376-6516

Palo Alto Management Group Inc.
2672 Bayshore Pky., Ste. 701
Mountain View, CA 94043
(415)968-4374
Fax: (415)968-4245
E-mail: mburwen@pamg.com

BizplanSource
1048 Irvine Ave., Ste. 621
Newport Beach, CA 92660
Free: 888-253-0974
Fax: 800-859-8254
E-mail: info@bizplansource.com
Website: http://www.bizplansource.com
Adam Greengrass, President

The Market Connection
4020 Birch St., Ste. 203
Newport Beach, CA 92660
(714)731-6273
Fax: (714)833-0253

Muller Associates
PO Box 7264
Newport Beach, CA 92658
(714)646-1169
Fax: (714)646-1169

International Health Resources
PO Box 329
North San Juan, CA 95960-0329
(530)292-1266
Fax: (530)292-1243
Website: http://www.futureof
healthcare.com

NEXUS - Consultants to Management
PO Box 1531
Novato, CA 94948
(415)897-4400
Fax: (415)898-2252
E-mail: jimnexus@aol.com

Aerospcace.Org
PO Box 28831
Oakland, CA 94604-8831

(510)530-9169
Fax: (510)530-3411
Website: http://www.aerospace.org

Intelequest Corp.
722 Gailen Ave.
Palo Alto, CA 94303
(415)968-3443
Fax: (415)493-6954
E-mail: frits@iqix.com

McLaughlin & Associates
66 San Marino Cir.
Rancho Mirage, CA 92270
(760)321-2932
Fax: (760)328-2474
E-mail: jackmcla@msn.com

Carrera Consulting Group, a division of Maximus
2110 21st St., Ste. 400
Sacramento, CA 95818
(916)456-3300
Fax: (916)456-3306
E-mail: central@carreraconsulting.com
Website: http://www.carreraconsulting.com

Bay Area Tax Consultants and Bayhill Financial Consultants
1150 Bayhill Dr., Ste. 1150
San Bruno, CA 94066-3004
(415)952-8786
Fax: (415)588-4524
E-mail: baytax@compuserve.com
Website: http://www.baytax.com/

AdCon Services, LLC
8871 Hillery Dr.
Dan Diego, CA 92126
(858)433-1411
E-mail: adam@adconservices.com
Website: http://www.adconservices.com
Adam Greengrass

California Business Incubation Network
101 W Broadway, No. 480
San Diego, CA 92101
(619)237-0559
Fax: (619)237-0521

G.R. Gordetsky Consultants Inc.
11414 Windy Summit Pl.
San Diego, CA 92127
(619)487-4939
Fax: (619)487-5587
E-mail: gordet@pacbell.net

Freeman, Sullivan & Co.
131 Steuart St., Ste. 500
San Francisco, CA 94105
(415)777-0707

Free: 800-777-0737
Fax: (415)777-2420
Website: http://www.fsc-research.com

Ideas Unlimited
2151 California St., Ste. 7
San Francisco, CA 94115
(415)931-0641
Fax: (415)931-0880

Russell Miller Inc.
300 Montgomery St., Ste. 900
San Francisco, CA 94104
(415)956-7474
Fax: (415)398-0620
E-mail: rmi@pacbell.net
Website: http://www.rmisf.com

PKF Consulting
425 California St., Ste. 1650
San Francisco, CA 94104
(415)421-5378
Fax: (415)956-7708
E-mail: callahan@pkfc.com
Website: http://www.pkfonline.com

Welling & Woodard Inc.
1067 Broadway
San Francisco, CA 94133
(415)776-4500
Fax: (415)776-5067

Highland Associates
16174 Highland Dr.
San Jose, CA 95127
(408)272-7008
Fax: (408)272-4040

ORDIS Inc.
6815 Trinidad Dr.
San Jose, CA 95120-2056
(408)268-3321
Free: 800-446-7347
Fax: (408)268-3582
E-mail: ordis@ordis.com
Website: http://www.ordis.com

Stanford Resources Inc.
20 Great Oaks Blvd., Ste. 200
San Jose, CA 95119
(408)360-8400
Fax: (408)360-8410
E-mail: sales@stanfordsources.com
Website: http://www.stanfordresources.com

Technology Properties Ltd. Inc.
PO Box 20250
San Jose, CA 95160
(408)243-9898
Fax: (408)296-6637
E-mail: sanjose@tplnet.com

Helfert Associates
1777 Borel Pl., Ste. 508
San Mateo, CA 94402-3514
(650)377-0540
Fax: (650)377-0472

Mykytyn Consulting Group Inc.
185 N Redwood Dr., Ste. 200
San Rafael, CA 94903
(415)491-1770
Fax: (415)491-1251
E-mail: info@mcgi.com
Website: http://www.mcgi.com

Omega Management Systems Inc.
3 Mount Darwin Ct.
San Rafael, CA 94903-1109
(415)499-1300
Fax: (415)492-9490
E-mail: omegamgt@ix.netcom.com

The Information Group Inc.
4675 Stevens Creek Blvd., Ste. 100
Santa Clara, CA 95051
(408)985-7877
Fax: (408)985-2945
E-mail: dvincent@tig-usa.com
Website: http://www.tig-usa.com

Cast Management Consultants
1620 26th St., Ste. 2040N
Santa Monica, CA 90404
(310)828-7511
Fax: (310)453-6831

Cuma Consulting Management
Box 724
Santa Rosa, CA 95402
(707)785-2477
Fax: (707)785-2478

The E-Myth Academy
131B Stony Cir., Ste. 2000
Santa Rosa, CA 95401
(707)569-5600
Free: 800-221-0266
Fax: (707)569-5700
E-mail: info@e-myth.com
Website: http://www.e-myth.com

Reilly, Connors & Ray
1743 Canyon Rd.
Spring Valley, CA 91977
(619)698-4808
Fax: (619)460-3892
E-mail: davidray@adnc.com

Management Consultants
Sunnyvale, CA 94087-4700
(408)773-0321

RJR Associates
1639 Lewiston Dr.
Sunnyvale, CA 94087
(408)737-7720
E-mail: bobroy@rjrassoc.com
Website: http://www.rjrassoc.com

Schwafel Associates
333 Cobalt Way, Ste. 21
Sunnyvale, CA 94085
(408)720-0649
Fax: (408)720-1796
E-mail: schwafel@ricochet.net
Website: http://www.patca.org

Staubs Business Services
23320 S Vermont Ave.
Torrance, CA 90502-2940
(310)830-9128
Fax: (310)830-9128
E-mail: Harry_L_Staubs@Lamg.com

Out of Your Mind...and Into the Marketplace
13381 White Sands Dr.
Tustin, CA 92780-4565
(714)544-0248
Free: 800-419-1513
Fax: (714)730-1414
E-mail: lpinson@aol.com
Website: http://www.business-plan.com

Independent Research Services
PO Box 2426
Van Nuys, CA 91404-2426
(818)993-3622

Ingman Company Inc.
7949 Woodley Ave., Ste. 120
Van Nuys, CA 91406-1232
(818)375-5027
Fax: (818)894-5001

Innovative Technology Associates
3639 E Harbor Blvd., Ste. 203E
Ventura, CA 93001
(805)650-9353

Grid Technology Associates
20404 Tufts Cir.
Walnut, CA 91789
(909)444-0922
Fax: (909)444-0922
E-mail: grid_technology@msn.com

Ridge Consultants Inc.
100 Pringle Ave., Ste. 580
Walnut Creek, CA 94596
(925)274-1990
Fax: (510)274-1956
E-mail: info@ridgecon.com
Website: http://www.ridgecon.com

Bell Springs Publishing
PO Box 1240
Willits, CA 95490
(707)459-6372
E-mail: bellsprings@sabernet
Website: http://www.bellsprings.com

Hutchinson Consulting and Appraisal
23245 Sylvan St., Ste. 103
Woodland Hills, CA 91367
(818)888-8175
Free: 800-977-7548
Fax: (818)888-8220
E-mail: r.f.hutchinson-cpa@worldnet.
att.net

Colorado

Sam Boyer & Associates
4255 S Buckley Rd., No. 136
Aurora, CO 80013
Free: 800-785-0485
Fax: (303)766-8740
E-mail: samboyer@samboyer.com
Website: http://www.samboyer.com/

Ameriwest Business Consultants Inc.
PO Box 26266
Colorado Springs, CO 80936
(719)380-7096
Fax: (719)380-7096
E-mail: email@abchelp.com
Website: http://www.abchelp.com

GVNW Consulting Inc.
2270 La Montana Way
Colorado Springs, CO 80936
(719)594-5800
Fax: (719)594-5803
Website: http://www.gvnw.com

M-Squared Inc.
755 San Gabriel Pl.
Colorado Springs, CO 80906
(719)576-2554
Fax: (719)576-2554

Thornton Financial FNIC
1024 Centre Ave., Bldg. E
Fort Collins, CO 80526-1849
(970)221-2089
Fax: (970)484-5206

TenEyck Associates
1760 Cherryville Rd.
Greenwood Village, CO 80121-1503
(303)758-6129
Fax: (303)761-8286

Associated Enterprises Ltd.
13050 W Ceder Dr., Unit 11
Lakewood, CO 80228

(303)988-6695
Fax: (303)988-6739
E-mail: ael1@classic.msn.com

The Vincent Company Inc.
200 Union Blvd., Ste. 210
Lakewood, CO 80228
(303)989-7271
Free: 800-274-0733
Fax: (303)989-7570
E-mail: vincent@vincentco.com
Website: http://www.vincentco.com

**Johnson & West Management
Consultants Inc.**
7612 S Logan Dr.
Littleton, CO 80122
(303)730-2810
Fax: (303)730-3219

Western Capital Holdings Inc.
10050 E Applwood Dr.
Parker, CO 80138
(303)841-1022
Fax: (303)770-1945

Connecticut

Stratman Group Inc.
40 Tower Ln.
Avon, CT 06001-4222
(860)677-2898
Free: 800-551-0499
Fax: (860)677-8210

Cowherd Consulting Group Inc.
106 Stephen Mather Rd.
Darien, CT 06820
(203)655-2150
Fax: (203)655-6427

Greenwich Associates
8 Greenwich Office Park
Greenwich, CT 06831-5149
(203)629-1200
Fax: (203)629-1229
E-mail: lisa@greenwich.com
Website: http://www.greenwich.com

Follow-up News
185 Pine St., Ste. 818
Manchester, CT 06040
(860)647-7542
Free: 800-708-0696
Fax: (860)646-6544
E-mail: Followupnews@aol.com

Lovins & Associates Consulting
309 Edwards St.
New Haven, CT 06511
(203)787-3367

Fax: (203)624-7599
E-mail: Alovinsphd@aol.com
Website: http://www.lovinsgroup.com

JC Ventures Inc.
4 Arnold St.
Old Greenwich, CT 06870-1203
(203)698-1990
Free: 800-698-1997
Fax: (203)698-2638

Charles L. Hornung Associates
52 Ned's Mountain Rd.
Ridgefield, CT 06877
(203)431-0297

Manus
100 Prospect St., S Tower
Stamford, CT 06901
(203)326-3880
Free: 800-445-0942
Fax: (203)326-3890
E-mail: manus1@aol.com
Website: http://www.RightManus.com

RealBusinessPlans.com
156 Westport Rd.
Wilton, CT 06897
(914)837-2886
E-mail: ct@realbusinessplans.com
Website: http://www.RealBusinessPlans.com
Tony Tecce

Delaware

Focus Marketing
61-7 Habor Dr.
Claymont, DE 19703
(302)793-3064

Daedalus Ventures Ltd.
PO Box 1474
Hockessin, DE 19707
(302)239-6758
Fax: (302)239-9991
E-mail: daedalus@mail.del.net

The Formula Group
PO Box 866
Hockessin, DE 19707
(302)456-0952
Fax: (302)456-1354
E-mail: formula@netaxs.com

Selden Enterprises Inc.
2502 Silverside Rd., Ste. 1
Wilmington, DE 19810-3740
(302)529-7113
Fax: (302)529-7442
E-mail: selden2@bellatlantic.net
Website: http://www.seldenenterprises.com

District of Columbia

Bruce W. McGee and Associates

7826 Eastern Ave. NW, Ste. 30
Washington, DC 20012
(202)726-7272
Fax: (202)726-2946

McManis Associates Inc.

1900 K St. NW, Ste. 700
Washington, DC 20006
(202)466-7680
Fax: (202)872-1898
Website: http://www.mcmanis-mmi.com

Smith, Dawson & Andrews Inc.

1000 Connecticut Ave., Ste. 302
Washington, DC 20036
(202)835-0740
Fax: (202)775-8526
E-mail: webmaster@sda-inc.com
Website: http://www.sda-inc.com

Florida

BackBone, Inc.

20404 Hacienda Court
Boca Raton, FL 33498
(561)470-0965
Fax: 516-908-4038
E-mail: BPlans@backboneinc.com
Website: http://www.backboneinc.com
Charles Epstein, President

Whalen & Associates Inc.

4255 Northwest 26 Ct.
Boca Raton, FL 33434
(561)241-5950
Fax: (561)241-7414
E-mail: drwhalen@ix.netcom.com

E.N. Rysso & Associates

180 Bermuda Petrel Ct.
Daytona Beach, FL 32119
(386)760-3028
E-mail: erysso@aol.com

Virtual Technocrats LLC

560 Lavers Circle, #146
Delray Beach, FL 33444
(561)265-3509
E-mail: josh@virtualtechnocrats.com;
info@virtualtechnocrats.com
Website: http://www.virtualtechno
crats.com
Josh Eikov, Managing Director

Eric Sands Consulting Services

6193 Rock Island Rd., Ste. 412
Fort Lauderdale, FL 33319
(954)721-4767

Fax: (954)720-2815
E-mail: easands@aol.com
Website: http://www.ericsandsconsultig.com

Professional Planning Associates, Inc.

1975 E. Sunrise Blvd. Suite 607
Fort Lauderdale, FL 33304
(954)764-5204
Fax: 954-463-4172
E-mail: Mgoldstein@proplana.com
Website: http://proplana.com
Michael Goldstein, President

Host Media Corp.

3948 S 3rd St., Ste. 191
Jacksonville Beach, FL 32250
(904)285-3239
Fax: (904)285-5618
E-mail: msconsulting@compuserve.com
Website: http://www.media
servicesgroup.com

William V. Hall

1925 Brickell, Ste. D-701
Miami, FL 33129
(305)856-9622
Fax: (305)856-4113
E-mail: williamvhall@compuserve.com

F.A. McGee Inc.

800 Claughton Island Dr., Ste. 401
Miami, FL 33131
(305)377-9123

Taxplan Inc.

Mirasol International Ctr.
2699 Collins Ave.
Miami Beach, FL 33140
(305)538-3303

T.C. Brown & Associates

8415 Excalibur Cir., Apt. B1
Naples, FL 34108
(941)594-1949
Fax: (941)594-0611
E-mail: tcater@naples.net.com

RLA International Consulting

713 Lagoon Dr.
North Palm Beach, FL 33408
(407)626-4258
Fax: (407)626-5772

Comprehensive Franchising Inc.

2465 Ridgecrest Ave.
Orange Park, FL 32065
(904)272-6567
Free: 800-321-6567
Fax: (904)272-6750
E-mail: theimp@cris.com
Website: http://www.franchise411.com

Hunter G. Jackson Jr. - Consulting Environmental Physicist

PO Box 618272
Orlando, FL 32861-8272
(407)295-4188
E-mail: hunterjackson@juno.com

F. Newton Parks

210 El Brillo Way
Palm Beach, FL 33480
(561)833-1727
Fax: (561)833-4541

Avery Business Development Services

2506 St. Michel Ct.
Ponte Vedra Beach, FL 32082
(904)285-6033
Fax: (904)285-6033

Strategic Business Planning Co.

PO Box 821006
South Florida, FL 33082-1006
(954)704-9100
Fax: (954)438-7333
E-mail: info@bizplan.com
Website: http://www.bizplan.com

Dufresne Consulting Group Inc.

10014 N Dale Mabry, Ste. 101
Tampa, FL 33618-4426
(813)264-4775
Fax: (813)264-9300
Website: http://www.dcgconsult.com

Agrippa Enterprises Inc.

PO Box 175
Venice, FL 34284-0175
(941)355-7876
E-mail: webservices@agrippa.com
Website: http://www.agrippa.com

Center for Simplified Strategic Planning Inc.

PO Box 3324
Vero Beach, FL 32964-3324
(561)231-3636
Fax: (561)231-1099
Website: http://www.cssp.com

Georgia

Marketing Spectrum Inc.

115 Perimeter Pl., Ste. 440
Atlanta, GA 30346
(770)395-7244
Fax: (770)393-4071

Business Ventures Corp.

1650 Oakbrook Dr., Ste. 405
Norcross, GA 30093
(770)729-8000
Fax: (770)729-8028

Informed Decisions Inc.
100 Falling Cheek
Sautee Nacoochee, GA 30571
(706)878-1905
Fax: (706)878-1802
E-mail: skylake@compuserve.com

Tom C. Davis & Associates, P.C.
3189 Perimeter Rd.
Valdosta, GA 31602
(912)247-9801
Fax: (912)244-7704
E-mail: mail@tcdcpa.com
Website: http://www.tcdcpa.com/

Illinois

TWD and Associates
431 S Patton
Arlington Heights, IL 60005
(847)398-6410
Fax: (847)255-5095
E-mail: tdoo@aol.com

Management Planning Associates Inc.
2275 Half Day Rd., Ste. 350
Bannockburn, IL 60015-1277
(847)945-2421
Fax: (847)945-2425

Phil Faris Associates
86 Old Mill Ct.
Barrington, IL 60010
(847)382-4888
Fax: (847)382-4890
E-mail: pfaris@meginsnet.net

Seven Continents Technology
787 Stonebridge
Buffalo Grove, IL 60089
(708)577-9653
Fax: (708)870-1220

Grubb & Blue Inc.
2404 Windsor Pl.
Champaign, IL 61820
(217)366-0052
Fax: (217)356-0117

ACE Accounting Service Inc.
3128 N Bernard St.
Chicago, IL 60618
(773)463-7854
Fax: (773)463-7854

AON Consulting Worldwide
200 E Randolph St., 10th Fl.
Chicago, IL 60601
(312)381-4800
Free: 800-438-6487
Fax: (312)381-0240
Website: http://www.aon.com

FMS Consultants
5801 N Sheridan Rd., Ste. 3D
Chicago, IL 60660
(773)561-7362
Fax: (773)561-6274

Grant Thornton
800 1 Prudential Plz.
130 E Randolph St.
Chicago, IL 60601
(312)856-0001
Fax: (312)861-1340
E-mail: gtinfo@gt.com
Website: http://www.grantthornton.com

Kingsbury International Ltd.
5341 N Glenwood Ave.
Chicago, IL 60640
(773)271-3030
Fax: (773)728-7080
E-mail: jetlag@mcs.com
Website: http://www.kingbiz.com

MacDougall & Blake Inc.
1414 N Wells St., Ste. 311
Chicago, IL 60610-1306
(312)587-3330
Fax: (312)587-3699
E-mail: jblake@compuserve.com

James C. Osburn Ltd.
6445 N. Western Ave., Ste. 304
Chicago, IL 60645
(773)262-4428
Fax: (773)262-6755
E-mail: osburnltd@aol.com

Tarifero & Tazewell Inc.
211 S Clark
Chicago, IL 60690
(312)665-9714
Fax: (312)665-9716

Human Energy Design Systems
620 Roosevelt Dr.
Edwardsville, IL 62025
(618)692-0258
Fax: (618)692-0819

China Business Consultants Group
931 Dakota Cir.
Naperville, IL 60563
(630)778-7992
Fax: (630)778-7915
E-mail: cbcq@aol.com

Center for Workforce Effectiveness
500 Skokie Blvd., Ste. 222
Northbrook, IL 60062
(847)559-8777
Fax: (847)559-8778

E-mail: office@cwelink.com
Website: http://www.cwelink.com

Smith Associates
1320 White Mountain Dr.
Northbrook, IL 60062
(847)480-7200
Fax: (847)480-9828

Francorp Inc.
20200 Governors Dr.
Olympia Fields, IL 60461
(708)481-2900
Free: 800-372-6244
Fax: (708)481-5885
E-mail: francorp@aol.com
Website: http://www.francorpinc.com

Camber Business Strategy Consultants
1010 S Plum Tree Ct
Palatine, IL 60078-0986
(847)202-0101
Fax: (847)705-7510
E-mail: camber@ameritech.net

Partec Enterprise Group
5202 Keith Dr.
Richton Park, IL 60471
(708)503-4047
Fax: (708)503-9468

Rockford Consulting Group Ltd.
Century Plz., Ste. 206
7210 E State St.
Rockford, IL 61108
(815)229-2900
Free: 800-667-7495
Fax: (815)229-2612
E-mail: rligus@RockfordConsulting.com
Website: http://www.Rockford
Consulting.com

RSM McGladrey Inc.
1699 E Woodfield Rd., Ste. 300
Schaumburg, IL 60173-4969
(847)413-6900
Fax: (847)517-7067
Website: http://www.rsmmcgladrey.com

A.D. Star Consulting
320 Euclid
Winnetka, IL 60093
(847)446-7827
Fax: (847)446-7827
E-mail: startwo@worldnet.att.net

Indiana

Modular Consultants Inc.
3109 Crabtree Ln.
Elkhart, IN 46514

(219)264-5761
Fax: (219)264-5761
E-mail: sasabo5313@aol.com

Midwest Marketing Research
PO Box 1077
Goshen, IN 46527
(219)533-0548
Fax: (219)533-0540
E-mail: 103365.654@compuserve

Ketchum Consulting Group
8021 Knue Rd., Ste. 112
Indianapolis, IN 46250
(317)845-5411
Fax: (317)842-9941

MDI Management Consulting
1519 Park Dr.
Munster, IN 46321
(219)838-7909
Fax: (219)838-7909

Iowa

McCord Consulting Group Inc.
4533 Pine View Dr. NE
PO Box 11024
Cedar Rapids, IA 52410
(319)378-0077
Fax: (319)378-1577
E-mail: smmccord@hom.com
Website: http://www.mccordgroup.com

Management Solutions L.C.
3815 Lincoln Pl. Dr.
Des Moines, IA 50312
(515)277-6408
Fax: (515)277-3506
E-mail: wasunimers@uswest.net

Grandview Marketing
15 Red Bridge Dr.
Sioux City, IA 51104
(712)239-3122
Fax: (712)258-7578
E-mail: eandrews@pionet.net

Kansas

Assessments in Action
513A N Mur-Len
Olathe, KS 66062
(913)764-6270
Free: (888)548-1504
Fax: (913)764-6495
E-mail: lowdene@qni.com
Website: http://www.assessments-in-action.com

Maine

Edgemont Enterprises
PO Box 8354
Portland, ME 04104
(207)871-8964
Fax: (207)871-8964

Pan Atlantic Consultants
5 Milk St.
Portland, ME 04101
(207)871-8622
Fax: (207)772-4842
E-mail: pmurphy@maine.rr.com
Website: http://www.panatlantic.net

Maryland

Clemons & Associates Inc.
5024-R Campbell Blvd.
Baltimore, MD 21236
(410)931-8100
Fax: (410)931-8111
E-mail: info@clemonsmgmt.com
Website: http://www.clemonsmgmt.com

Imperial Group Ltd.
305 Washington Ave., Ste. 204
Baltimore, MD 21204-6009
(410)337-8500
Fax: (410)337-7641

Leadership Institute
3831 Yolando Rd.
Baltimore, MD 21218
(410)366-9111
Fax: (410)243-8478
E-mail: behconsult@aol.com

Burdeshaw Associates Ltd.
4701 Sangamore Rd.
Bethesda, MD 20816-2508
(301)229-5800
Fax: (301)229-5045
E-mail: jstacy@burdeshaw.com
Website: http://www.burdeshaw.com

Michael E. Cohen
5225 Pooks Hill Rd., Ste. 1119 S
Bethesda, MD 20814
(301)530-5738
Fax: (301)530-2988
E-mail: mecohen@crosslink.net

World Development Group Inc.
5272 River Rd., Ste. 650
Bethesda, MD 20816-1405
(301)652-1818
Fax: (301)652-1250
E-mail: wdg@has.com
Website: http://www.worlddg.com

Swartz Consulting
PO Box 4301
Crofton, MD 21114-4301
(301)262-6728

Software Solutions International Inc.
9633 Duffer Way
Gaithersburg, MD 20886
(301)330-4136
Fax: (301)330-4136

Strategies Inc.
8 Park Center Ct., Ste. 200
Owings Mills, MD 21117
(410)363-6669
Fax: (410)363-1231
E-mail: strategies@strat1.com
Website: http://www.strat1.com

Hammer Marketing Resources
179 Inverness Rd.
Severna Park, MD 21146
(410)544-9191
Fax: (305)675-3277
E-mail: info@gohammer.com
Website: http://www.gohammer.com

Andrew Sussman & Associates
13731 Kretsinger
Smithsburg, MD 21783
(301)824-2943
Fax: (301)824-2943

Massachusetts

Geibel Marketing and Public Relations
PO Box 611
Belmont, MA 02478-0005
(617)484-8285
Fax: (617)489-3567
E-mail: jgeibel@geibelpr.com
Website: http://www.geibelpr.com

Bain & Co.
2 Copley Pl.
Boston, MA 02116
(617)572-2000
Fax: (617)572-2427
E-mail: corporate.inquiries@bain.com
Website: http://www.bain.com

Mehr & Co.
62 Kinnaird St.
Cambridge, MA 02139
(617)876-3311
Fax: (617)876-3023
E-mail: mehrco@aol.com

Monitor Company Inc.
2 Canal Park
Cambridge, MA 02141

(617)252-2000
Fax: (617)252-2100
Website: http://www.monitor.com

Information & Research Associates
PO Box 3121
Framingham, MA 01701
(508)788-0784

Walden Consultants Ltd.
252 Pond St.
Hopkinton, MA 01748
(508)435-4882
Fax: (508)435-3971
Website: http://www.waldencon
sultants.com

Jeffrey D. Marshall
102 Mitchell Rd.
Ipswich, MA 01938-1219
(508)356-1113
Fax: (508)356-2989

Consulting Resources Corp.
6 Northbrook Park
Lexington, MA 02420
(781)863-1222
Fax: (781)863-1441
E-mail: res@consultingresources.net
Website: http://www.consulting
resources.net

Planning Technologies Group L.L.C.
92 Hayden Ave.
Lexington, MA 02421
(781)778-4678
Fax: (781)861-1099
E-mail: ptg@plantech.com
Website: http://www.plantech.com

Kalba International Inc.
23 Sandy Pond Rd.
Lincoln, MA 01773
(781)259-9589
Fax: (781)259-1460
E-mail: info@kalbainternational.com
Website: http://www.kalbainter
national.com

VMB Associates Inc.
115 Ashland St.
Melrose, MA 02176
(781)665-0623
Fax: (425)732-7142
E-mail: vmbinc@aol.com

The Company Doctor
14 Pudding Stone Ln.
Mendon, MA 01756
(508)478-1747
Fax: (508)478-0520

Data and Strategies Group Inc.
190 N Main St.
Natick, MA 01760
(508)653-9990
Fax: (508)653-7799
E-mail: dsginc@dsggroup.com
Website: http://www.dsggroup.com

The Enterprise Group
73 Parker Rd.
Needham, MA 02494
(617)444-6631
Fax: (617)433-9991
E-mail: lsacco@world.std.com
Website: http://www.enterprise-group.com

PSMJ Resources Inc.
10 Midland Ave.
Newton, MA 02458
(617)965-0055
Free: 800-537-7765
Fax: (617)965-5152
E-mail: psmj@tiac.net
Website: http://www.psmj.com

Scheur Management Group Inc.
255 Washington St., Ste. 100
Newton, MA 02458-1611
(617)969-7500
Fax: (617)969-7508
E-mail: smgnow@scheur.com
Website: http://www.scheur.com

I.E.E.E., Boston Section
240 Bear Hill Rd., 202B
Waltham, MA 02451-1017
(781)890-5294
Fax: (781)890-5290

Business Planning and Consulting Services
20 Beechwood Ter.
Wellesley, MA 02482
(617)237-9151
Fax: (617)237-9151

Michigan

Walter Frederick Consulting
1719 South Blvd.
Ann Arbor, MI 48104
(313)662-4336
Fax: (313)769-7505

Fox Enterprises
6220 W Freeland Rd.
Freeland, MI 48623
(517)695-9170
Fax: (517)695-9174
E-mail: foxjw@concentric.net
Website: http://www.cris.com/~foxjw

G.G.W. and Associates
1213 Hampton
Jackson, MI 49203
(517)782-2255
Fax: (517)782-2255

Altamar Group Ltd.
6810 S Cedar, Ste. 2-B
Lansing, MI 48911
(517)694-0910
Free: 800-443-2627
Fax: (517)694-1377

Sheffieck Consultants Inc.
23610 Greening Dr.
Novi, MI 48375-3130
(248)347-3545
Fax: (248)347-3530
E-mail: cfsheff@concentric.net

Rehmann, Robson PC
5800 Gratiot
Saginaw, MI 48605
(517)799-9580
Fax: (517)799-0227
Website: http://www.rrpc.com

Francis & Co.
17200 W 10 Mile Rd., Ste. 207
Southfield, MI 48075
(248)559-7600
Fax: (248)559-5249

Private Ventures Inc.
16000 W 9 Mile Rd., Ste. 504
Southfield, MI 48075
(248)569-1977
Free: 800-448-7614
Fax: (248)569-1838
E-mail: pventuresi@aol.com

JGK Associates
14464 Kerner Dr.
Sterling Heights, MI 48313
(810)247-9055
Fax: (248)822-4977
E-mail: kozlowski@home.com

Minnesota

Health Fitness Corp.
3500 W 80th St., Ste. 130
Bloomington, MN 55431
(612)831-6830
Fax: (612)831-7264

Consatech Inc.
PO Box 1047
Burnsville, MN 55337
(612)953-1088
Fax: (612)435-2966

Robert F. Knotek
14960 Ironwood Ct.
Eden Prairie, MN 55346
(612)949-2875

DRI Consulting
7715 Stonewood Ct.
Edina, MN 55439
(612)941-9656
Fax: (612)941-2693
E-mail: dric@dric.com
Website: http://www.dric.com

Markin Consulting
12072 87th Pl. N
Maple Grove, MN 55369
(612)493-3568
Fax: (612)493-5744
E-mail: markin@markinconsulting.com
Website: http://www.markin
consulting.com

Minnesota Cooperation Office for Small Business & Job Creation Inc.
5001 W 80th St., Ste. 825
Minneapolis, MN 55437
(612)830-1230
Fax: (612)830-1232
E-mail: mncoop@msn.com
Website: http://www.mnco.org

Enterprise Consulting Inc.
PO Box 1111
Minnetonka, MN 55345
(612)949-5909
Fax: (612)906-3965

Amdahl International
724 1st Ave. SW
Rochester, MN 55902
(507)252-0402
Fax: (507)252-0402
E-mail: amdahl@best-service.com
Website: http://www.wp.com/amdahl_int

Power Systems Research
1365 Corporate Center Curve, 2nd Fl.
St. Paul, MN 55121
(612)905-8400
Free: (888)625-8612
Fax: (612)454-0760
E-mail: Barb@Powersys.com
Website: http://www.powersys.com

Missouri

Business Planning and Development Corp.
4030 Charlotte St.
Kansas City, MO 64110
(816)753-0495

E-mail: humph@bpdev.demon.co.uk
Website: http://www.bpdev.demon.co.uk

CFO Service
10336 Donoho
St. Louis, MO 63131
(314)750-2940
E-mail: jskae@cfoservice.com
Website: http://www.cfoservice.com

Nebraska

International Management Consulting Group Inc.
1309 Harlan Dr., Ste. 205
Bellevue, NE 68005
(402)291-4545
Free: 800-665-IMCG
Fax: (402)291-4343
E-mail: imcg@neonramp.com
Website: http://www.mgtcon
sulting.com

Heartland Management Consulting Group
1904 Barrington Pky.
Papillion, NE 68046
(402)339-2387
Fax: (402)339-1319

Nevada

The DuBois Group
865 Tahoe Blvd., Ste. 108
Incline Village, NV 89451
(775)832-0550
Free: 800-375-2935
Fax: (775)832-0556
E-mail: DuBoisGrp@aol.com

New Hampshire

Wolff Consultants
10 Buck Rd.
Hanover, NH 03755
(603)643-6015

BPT Consulting Associates Ltd.
12 Parmenter Rd., Ste. B-6
Londonderry, NH 03053
(603)437-8484
Free: (888)278-0030
Fax: (603)434-5388
E-mail: bptcons@tiac.net
Website: http://www.bptconsulting.com

New Jersey

Bedminster Group Inc.
1170 Rte. 22 E
Bridgewater, NJ 08807

(908)500-4155
Fax: (908)766-0780
E-mail: info@bedminstergroup.com
Website: http://www.bedminster
group.com
Fax: (202)806-1777
Terry Strong, Acting Regional Dir.

Delta Planning Inc.
PO Box 425
Denville, NJ 07834
(913)625-1742
Free: 800-672-0762
Fax: (973)625-3531
E-mail: DeltaP@worldnet.att.net
Website: http://deltaplanning.com

Kumar Associates Inc.
1004 Cumbermeade Rd.
Fort Lee, NJ 07024
(201)224-9480
Fax: (201)585-2343
E-mail: mail@kumarassociates.com
Website: http://kumarassociates.com

John Hall & Company Inc.
PO Box 187
Glen Ridge, NJ 07028
(973)680-4449
Fax: (973)680-4581
E-mail: jhcompany@aol.com

Market Focus
PO Box 402
Maplewood, NJ 07040
(973)378-2470
Fax: (973)378-2470
E-mail: mcss66@marketfocus.com

Vanguard Communications Corp.
100 American Rd.
Morris Plains, NJ 07950
(973)605-8000
Fax: (973)605-8329
Website: http://www.vanguard.net/

ConMar International Ltd.
1901 US Hwy. 130
North Brunswick, NJ 08902
(732)940-8347
Fax: (732)274-1199

KLW New Products
156 Cedar Dr.
Old Tappan, NJ 07675
(201)358-1300
Fax: (201)664-2594
E-mail: lrlarsen@usa.net
Website: http://www.klwnew
products.com

PA Consulting Group
315A Enterprise Dr.
Plainsboro, NJ 08536
(609)936-8300
Fax: (609)936-8811
E-mail: info@paconsulting.com
Website: http://www.pa-consulting.com

Aurora Marketing Management Inc.
66 Witherspoon St., Ste. 600
Princeton, NJ 08542
(908)904-1125
Fax: (908)359-1108
E-mail: aurora2@voicenet.com
Website: http://www.auroramarketing.net

Smart Business Supersite
88 Orchard Rd., CN-5219
Princeton, NJ 08543
(908)321-1924
Fax: (908)321-5156
E-mail: irv@smartbiz.com
Website: http://www.smartbiz.com

Tracelin Associates
1171 Main St., Ste. 6K
Rahway, NJ 07065
(732)381-3288

Schkeeper Inc.
130-6 Bodman Pl.
Red Bank, NJ 07701
(732)219-1965
Fax: (732)530-3703

Henry Branch Associates
2502 Harmon Cove Twr.
Secaucus, NJ 07094
(201)866-2008
Fax: (201)601-0101
E-mail: hbranch161@home.com

Robert Gibbons & Company Inc.
46 Knoll Rd.
Tenafly, NJ 07670-1050
(201)871-3933
Fax: (201)871-2173
E-mail: crisisbob@aol.com

PMC Management Consultants Inc.
6 Thistle Ln.
Three Bridges, NJ 08887-0332
(908)788-1014
Free: 800-PMC-0250
Fax: (908)806-7287
E-mail: int@pmc-management.com
Website: http://www.pmc-management.com

R.W. Bankart & Associates
20 Valley Ave., Ste. D-2

Westwood, NJ 07675-3607
(201)664-7672

New Mexico

Vondle & Associates Inc.
4926 Calle de Tierra, NE
Albuquerque, NM 87111
(505)292-8961
Fax: (505)296-2790
E-mail: vondle@aol.com

InfoNewMexico
2207 Black Hills Rd., NE
Rio Rancho, NM 87124
(505)891-2462
Fax: (505)896-8971

New York

Powers Research and Training Institute
PO Box 78
Bayville, NY 11709
(516)628-2250
Fax: (516)628-2252
E-mail: powercocch@compuserve.com
Website: http://www.nancypowers.com

Consortium House
296 Wittenberg Rd.
Bearsville, NY 12409
(845)679-8867
Fax: (845)679-9248
E-mail: eugenegs@aol.com
Website: http://www.chpub.com

Progressive Finance Corp.
3549 Tiemann Ave.
Bronx, NY 10469
(718)405-9029
Free: 800-225-8381
Fax: (718)405-1170

Wave Hill Associates Inc.
2621 Palisade Ave., Ste. 15-C
Bronx, NY 10463
(718)549-7368
Fax: (718)601-9670
E-mail: pepper@compuserve.com

Management Insight
96 Arlington Rd.
Buffalo, NY 14221
(716)631-3319
Fax: (716)631-0203
E-mail: michalski@foodservice insight.com
Website: http://www.foodservice insight.com

Samani International Enterprises, Marions Panyaught Consultancy
2028 Parsons
Flushing, NY 11357-3436
(917)287-8087
Fax: 800-873-8939
E-mail: vjp2@biostrategist.com
Website: http://www.biostrategist.com

Marketing Resources Group
71-58 Austin St.
Forest Hills, NY 11375
(718)261-8882

Mangabay Business Plans & Development Subsidiary of Innis Asset Allocation
125-10 Queens Blvd., Ste. 2202
Kew Gardens, NY 11415
(905)527-1947
Fax: 509-472-1935
E-mail: mangabay@mangabay.com
Website: http://www.mangabay.com
Lee Toh, Managing Partner

ComputerEase Co.
1301 Monmouth Ave.
Lakewood, NY 08701
(212)406-9464
Fax: (914)277-5317
E-mail: crawfordc@juno.com

Boice Dunham Group
30 W 13th St.
New York, NY 10011
(212)924-2200
Fax: (212)924-1108

Elizabeth Capen
27 E 95th St.
New York, NY 10128
(212)427-7654
Fax: (212)876-3190

Haver Analytics
60 E 42nd St., Ste. 2424
New York, NY 10017
(212)986-9300
Fax: (212)986-5857
E-mail: data@haver.com
Website: http://www.haver.com

The Jordan, Edmiston Group Inc.
150 E 52nd Ave., 18th Fl.
New York, NY 10022
(212)754-0710
Fax: (212)754-0337

KPMG International
345 Park Ave.
New York, NY 10154-0102
(212)758-9700

Fax: (212)758-9819
Website: http://www.kpmg.com

Mahoney Cohen Consulting Corp.
111 W 40th St., 12th Fl.
New York, NY 10018
(212)490-8000
Fax: (212)790-5913

Management Practice Inc.
342 Madison Ave.
New York, NY 10173-1230
(212)867-7948
Fax: (212)972-5188
Website: http://www.mpiweb.com

Moseley Associates Inc.
342 Madison Ave., Ste. 1414
New York, NY 10016
(212)213-6673
Fax: (212)687-1520

Practice Development Counsel
60 Sutton Pl. S
New York, NY 10022
(212)593-1549
Fax: (212)980-7940
E-mail: pwhaserot@pdcounsel.com
Website: http://www.pdcounsel.com

Unique Value International Inc.
575 Madison Ave., 10th Fl.
New York, NY 10022-1304
(212)605-0590
Fax: (212)605-0589

The Van Tulleken Co.
126 E 56th St.
New York, NY 10022
(212)355-1390
Fax: (212)755-3061
E-mail: newyork@vantulleken.com

Vencon Management Inc.
301 W 53rd St.
New York, NY 10019
(212)581-8787
Fax: (212)397-4126
Website: http://www.venconinc.com

Werner International Inc.
55 E 52nd, 29th Fl.
New York, NY 10055
(212)909-1260
Fax: (212)909-1273
E-mail: richard.downing@rgh.com
Website: http://www.wernertex.com

Zimmerman Business Consulting Inc.
44 E 92nd St., Ste. 5-B
New York, NY 10128

(212)860-3107
Fax: (212)860-7730
E-mail: ljzzbci@aol.com
Website: http://www.zbcinc.com

Overton Financial
7 Allen Rd.
Peekskill, NY 10566
(914)737-4649
Fax: (914)737-4696

Stromberg Consulting
2500 Westchester Ave.
Purchase, NY 10577
(914)251-1515
Fax: (914)251-1562
E-mail: strategy@stromberg_consulting.com
Website: http://www.stromberg_consulting.com

Innovation Management Consulting Inc.
209 Dewitt Rd.
Syracuse, NY 13214-2006
(315)425-5144
Fax: (315)445-8989
E-mail: missonneb@axess.net

M. Clifford Agress
891 Fulton St.
Valley Stream, NY 11580
(516)825-8955
Fax: (516)825-8955

Destiny Kinal Marketing Consultancy
105 Chemung St.
Waverly, NY 14892
(607)565-8317
Fax: (607)565-4083

Valutis Consulting Inc.
5350 Main St., Ste. 7
Williamsville, NY 14221-5338
(716)634-2553
Fax: (716)634-2554
E-mail: valutis@localnet.com
Website: http://www.valutisconsulting.com

North Carolina

Best Practices L.L.C.
6320 Quadrangle Dr., Ste. 200
Chapel Hill, NC 27514
(919)403-0251
Fax: (919)403-0144
E-mail: best@best:in/class
Website: http://www.best-in-class.com

Norelli & Co.
Bank of America Corporate Ctr.
100 N Tyron St., Ste. 5160

Charlotte, NC 28202-4000
(704)376-5484
Fax: (704)376-5485
E-mail: consult@norelli.com
Website: http://www.norelli.com

North Dakota

Center for Innovation
4300 Dartmouth Dr.
PO Box 8372
Grand Forks, ND 58202
(701)777-3132
Fax: (701)777-2339
E-mail: bruce@innovators.net
Website: http://www.innovators.net

Ohio

Transportation Technology Services
208 Harmon Rd.
Aurora, OH 44202
(330)562-3596

Empro Systems Inc.
4777 Red Bank Expy., Ste. 1
Cincinnati, OH 45227-1542
(513)271-2042
Fax: (513)271-2042

Alliance Management International Ltd.
1440 Windrow Ln.
Cleveland, OH 44147-3200
(440)838-1922
Fax: (440)838-0979
E-mail: bgruss@amiltd.com
Website: http://www.amiltd.com

Bozell Kamstra Public Relations
1301 E 9th St., Ste. 3400
Cleveland, OH 44114
(216)623-1511
Fax: (216)623-1501
E-mail: jfeniger@cleveland.bozellkamstra.com
Website: http://www.bozellkamstra.com

Cory Dillon Associates
111 Schreyer Pl. E
Columbus, OH 43214
(614)262-8211
Fax: (614)262-3806

Holcomb Gallagher Adams
300 Marconi, Ste. 303
Columbus, OH 43215
(614)221-3343
Fax: (614)221-3367
E-mail: riadams@acme.freenet.oh.us

Young & Associates
PO Box 711
Kent, OH 44240
(330)678-0524
Free: 800-525-9775
Fax: (330)678-6219
E-mail: online@younginc.com
Website: http://www.younginc.com

Robert A. Westman & Associates
8981 Inversary Dr. SE
Warren, OH 44484-2551
(330)856-4149
Fax: (330)856-2564

Oklahoma

Innovative Partners L.L.C.
4900 Richmond Sq., Ste. 100
Oklahoma City, OK 73118
(405)840-0033
Fax: (405)843-8359
E-mail: ipartners@juno.com

Oregon

INTERCON - The International Converting Institute
5200 Badger Rd.
Crooked River Ranch, OR 97760
(541)548-1447
Fax: (541)548-1618
E-mail: johnbowler@crookedriverranch.com

Talbott ARM
HC 60, Box 5620
Lakeview, OR 97630
(541)635-8587
Fax: (503)947-3482

Management Technology Associates Ltd.
2768 SW Sherwood Dr, Ste. 105
Portland, OR 97201-2251
(503)224-5220
Fax: (503)224-5334
E-mail: lcuster@mta-ltd.com
Website: http://www.mgmt-tech.com

Pennsylvania

Healthscope Inc.
400 Lancaster Ave.
Devon, PA 19333
(610)687-6199
Fax: (610)687-6376
E-mail: health@voicenet.com
Website: http://www.healthscope.net/

Elayne Howard & Associates Inc.
3501 Masons Mill Rd., Ste. 501

Huntingdon Valley, PA 19006-3509
(215)657-9550

GRA Inc.
115 West Ave., Ste. 201
Jenkintown, PA 19046
(215)884-7500
Fax: (215)884-1385
E-mail: gramail@gra-inc.com
Website: http://www.gra-inc.com

Mifflin County Industrial Development Corp.
Mifflin County Industrial Plz.
6395 SR 103 N
Bldg. 50
Lewistown, PA 17044
(717)242-0393
Fax: (717)242-1842
E-mail: mcide@acsworld.net

Autech Products
1289 Revere Rd.
Morrisville, PA 19067
(215)493-3759
Fax: (215)493-9791
E-mail: autech4@yahoo.com

Advantage Associates
434 Avon Dr.
Pittsburgh, PA 15228
(412)343-1558
Fax: (412)362-1684
E-mail: ecocba1@aol.com

Regis J. Sheehan & Associates
Pittsburgh, PA 15220
(412)279-1207

James W. Davidson Company Inc.
23 Forest View Rd.
Wallingford, PA 19086
(610)566-1462

Puerto Rico

Diego Chevere & Co.
Metro Parque 7, Ste. 204
Metro Office
Caparra Heights, PR 00920
(787)774-9595
Fax: (787)774-9566
E-mail: dcco@coqui.net

Manuel L. Porrata and Associates
898 Munoz Rivera Ave., Ste. 201
San Juan, PR 00927
(787)765-2140
Fax: (787)754-3285
E-mail: m_porrata@manuelporrata.com
Website: http://manualporrata.com

South Carolina

Aquafood Business Associates
PO Box 13267
Charleston, SC 29422
(843)795-9506
Fax: (843)795-9477
E-mail: rraba@aol.com

Profit Associates Inc.
PO Box 38026
Charleston, SC 29414
(803)763-5718
Fax: (803)763-5719
E-mail: bobrog@awod.com
Website: http://www.awod.com/gallery/business/proasc

Strategic Innovations International
12 Executive Ct.
Lake Wylie, SC 29710
(803)831-1225
Fax: (803)831-1177
E-mail: stratinnov@aol.com
Website: http://www.strategicinnovations.com

Minus Stage
Box 4436
Rock Hill, SC 29731
(803)328-0705
Fax: (803)329-9948

Tennessee

Daniel Petchers & Associates
8820 Fernwood CV
Germantown, TN 38138
(901)755-9896

Business Choices
1114 Forest Harbor, Ste. 300
Hendersonville, TN 37075-9646
(615)822-8692
Free: 800-737-8382
Fax: (615)822-8692
E-mail: bz-ch@juno.com

RCFA Healthcare Management Services L.L.C.
9648 Kingston Pke., Ste. 8
Knoxville, TN 37922
(865)531-0176
Free: 800-635-4040
Fax: (865)531-0722
E-mail: info@rcfa.com
Website: http://www.rcfa.com

Growth Consultants of America
3917 Trimble Rd.
Nashville, TN 37215

(615)383-0550
Fax: (615)269-8940
E-mail: 70244.451@compuserve.com

Texas

**Integrated Cost Management
Systems Inc.**
2261 Brookhollow Plz. Dr., Ste. 104
Arlington, TX 76006
(817)633-2873
Fax: (817)633-3781
E-mail: abm@icms.net
Website: http://www.icms.net

Lori Williams
1000 Leslie Ct.
Arlington, TX 76012
(817)459-3934
Fax: (817)459-3934

Business Resource Software Inc.
2013 Wells Branch Pky., Ste. 305
Austin, TX 78728
Free: 800-423-1228
Fax: (512)251-4401
E-mail: info@brs-inc.com
Website: http://www.brs-inc.com

Erisa Adminstrative Services Inc.
12325 Hymeadow Dr., Bldg. 4
Austin, TX 78750-1847
(512)250-9020
Fax: (512)250-9487
Website: http://www.cserisa.com

R. Miller Hicks & Co.
1011 W 11th St.
Austin, TX 78703
(512)477-7000
Fax: (512)477-9697
E-mail: millerhicks@rmhicks.com
Website: http://www.rmhicks.com

Pragmatic Tactics Inc.
3303 Westchester Ave.
College Station, TX 77845
(409)696-5294
Free: 800-570-5294
Fax: (409)696-4994
E-mail: ptactics@aol.com
Website: http://www.ptatics.com

Perot Systems
12404 Park Central Dr.
Dallas, TX 75251
(972)340-5000
Free: 800-688-4333
Fax: (972)455-4100
E-mail: corp.comm@ps.net
Website: http://www.perotsystems.com

ReGENERATION Partners
3838 Oak Lawn Ave.
Dallas, TX 75219
(214)559-3999
Free: 800-406-1112
E-mail: info@regeneration-partner.com
Website: http://www.regeneration-
partners.com

**High Technology Associates - Division
of Global Technologies Inc.**
1775 St. James Pl., Ste. 105
Houston, TX 77056
(713)963-9300
Fax: (713)963-8341
E-mail: hta@infohwy.com

MasterCOM
103 Thunder Rd.
Kerrville, TX 78028
(830)895-7990
Fax: (830)443-3428
E-mail: jmstubblefield@master
training.com
Website: http://www.mastertraining.com

PROTEC
4607 Linden Pl.
Pearland, TX 77584
(281)997-9872
Fax: (281)997-9895
E-mail: p.oman@ix.netcom.com

Alpha Quadrant Inc.
10618 Auldine
San Antonio, TX 78230
(210)344-3330
Fax: (210)344-8151
E-mail: mbussone@sbcglobal.net
Website:http://www.a-quadrant.com
Michele Bussone

Bastian Public Relations
614 San Dizier
San Antonio, TX 78232
(210)404-1839
E-mail: lisa@bastianpr.com
Website: http://www.bastianpr.com
Lisa Bastian CBC

**Business Strategy Development
Consultants**
PO Box 690365
San Antonio, TX 78269
(210)696-8000
Free: 800-927-BSDC
Fax: (210)696-8000

Tom Welch, CPC
6900 San Pedro Ave., Ste. 147
San Antonio, TX 78216-6207

(210)737-7022
Fax: (210)737-7022
E-mail: bplan@iamerica.net
Website: http://www.moneywords.com

Utah

Business Management Resource
PO Box 521125
Salt Lake City, UT 84152-1125
(801)272-4668
Fax: (801)277-3290
E-mail: pingfong@worldnet.att.net

Virginia

Tindell Associates
209 Oxford Ave.
Alexandria, VA 22301
(703)683-0109
Fax: 703-783-0219
E-mail: scott@tindell.net
Website: http://www.tindell.net
Scott Lockett, President

Elliott B. Jaffa
2530-B S Walter Reed Dr.
Arlington, VA 22206
(703)931-0040
E-mail: thetrainingdoctor@excite.com
Website: http://www.tregistry.com/
jaffa.htm

Koach Enterprises - USA
5529 N 18th St.
Arlington, VA 22205
(703)241-8361
Fax: (703)241-8623

Federal Market Development
5650 Chapel Run Ct.
Centreville, VA 20120-3601
(703)502-8930
Free: 800-821-5003
Fax: (703)502-8929

Huff, Stuart & Carlton
2107 Graves Mills Rd., Ste. C
Forest, VA 24551
(804)316-9356
Free: (888)316-9356
Fax: (804)316-9357
Website: http://www.wealthmgt.net

AMX International Inc.
1420 Spring Hill Rd. , Ste. 600
McLean, VA 22102-3006
(703)690-4100
Fax: (703)643-1279
E-mail: amxmail@amxi.com
Website: http://www.amxi.com

Charles Scott Pugh (Investor)
4101 Pittaway Dr.
Richmond, VA 23235-1022
(804)560-0979
Fax: (804)560-4670

John C. Randall and Associates Inc.
PO Box 15127
Richmond, VA 23227
(804)746-4450
Fax: (804)730-8933
E-mail: randalljcx@aol.com
Website: http://www.johncrandall.com

McLeod & Co.
410 1st St.
Roanoke, VA 24011
(540)342-6911
Fax: (540)344-6367
Website: http://www.mcleodco.com/

Salzinger & Company Inc.
8000 Towers Crescent Dr., Ste. 1350
Vienna, VA 22182
(703)442-5200
Fax: (703)442-5205
E-mail: info@salzinger.com
Website: http://www.salzinger.com

The Small Business Counselor
12423 Hedges Run Dr., Ste. 153
Woodbridge, VA 22192
(703)490-6755
Fax: (703)490-1356

Washington

Burlington Consultants
10900 NE 8th St., Ste. 900
Bellevue, WA 98004
(425)688-3060
Fax: (425)454-4383
E-mail: partners@burlington
consultants.com
Website: http://www.burlington
consultants.com

Perry L. Smith Consulting
800 Bellevue Way NE, Ste. 400
Bellevue, WA 98004-4208
(425)462-2072
Fax: (425)462-5638

St. Charles Consulting Group
1420 NW Gilman Blvd.
Issaquah, WA 98027
(425)557-8708
Fax: (425)557-8731
E-mail: info@stcharlesconsulting.com
Website: http://www.stcharlescon
sulting.com

Independent Automotive Training Services
PO Box 334
Kirkland, WA 98083
(425)822-5715
E-mail: ltunney@autosvccon.com
Website: http://www.autosvccon.com

Kahle Associate Inc.
6203 204th Dr. NE
Redmond, WA 98053
(425)836-8763
Fax: (425)868-3770
E-mail: randykahle@kahleassociates.com
Website: http://www.kahleassociates.com

Dan Collin
3419 Wallingord Ave N, No. 2
Seattle, WA 98103
(206)634-9469
E-mail: dc@dancollin.com
Website: http://members.home.net/
dcollin/

ECG Management Consultants Inc.
1111 3rd Ave., Ste. 2700
Seattle, WA 98101-3201
(206)689-2200
Fax: (206)689-2209
E-mail: ecg@ecgmc.com
Website: http://www.ecgmc.com

Northwest Trade Adjustment Assistance Center
900 4th Ave., Ste. 2430
Seattle, WA 98164-1001
(206)622-2730
Free: 800-667-8087
Fax: (206)622-1105
E-mail: matchingfunds@nwtaac.org
Website: http://www.taacenters.org

Business Planning Consultants
S 3510 Ridgeview Dr.
Spokane, WA 99206
(509)928-0332
Fax: (509)921-0842
E-mail: bpci@nextdim.com

West Virginia

**Stanley & Associates Inc./
BusinessandMarketingPlans.com**
1687 Robert C. Byrd Dr.
Beckley, WV 25801
(304)252-0324
Free: 888-752-6720
Fax: (304)252-0470
E-mail: cclay@charterinternet.com

Website: http://www.Businessand
MarketingPlans.com
Christopher Clay

Wisconsin

White & Associates Inc.
5349 Somerset Ln. S
Greenfield, WI 53221
(414)281-7373
Fax: (414)281-7006
E-mail: wnaconsult@aol.com

Small business administration regional offices

This section contains a listing of Small Business Administration offices arranged numerically by region. Service areas are provided. Contact the appropriate office for a referral to the nearest field office, or visit the Small Business Administration online at www.sba.gov.

Region 1

U.S. Small Business Administration
Region I Office
10 Causeway St., Ste. 812
Boston, MA 02222-1093
Phone: (617)565-8415
Fax: (617)565-8420
Serves Connecticut, Maine,
Massachusetts, New Hampshire, Rhode
Island, and Vermont.

Region 2

U.S. Small Business Administration
Region II Office
26 Federal Plaza, Ste. 3108
New York, NY 10278
Phone: (212)264-1450
Fax: (212)264-0038
Serves New Jersey, New York, Puerto
Rico, and the Virgin Islands.

Region 3

U.S. Small Business Administration
Region III Office
Robert N C Nix Sr. Federal Building
900 Market St., 5th Fl.
Philadelphia, PA 19107
(215)580-2807
Serves Delaware, the District of
Columbia, Maryland, Pennsylvania,
Virginia, and West Virginia.

Region 4

U.S. Small Business Administration
Region IV Office
233 Peachtree St. NE
Harris Tower 1800
Atlanta, GA 30303
Phone: (404)331-4999
Fax: (404)331-2354
Serves Alabama, Florida, Georgia, Kentucky, Mississippi, North Carolina, South Carolina, and Tennessee.

Region 5

U.S. Small Business Administration
Region V Office
500 W. Madison St.
Citicorp Center, Ste. 1240
Chicago, IL 60661-2511
Phone: (312)353-0357
Fax: (312)353-3426
Serves Illinois, Indiana, Michigan, Minnesota, Ohio, and Wisconsin.

Region 6

U.S. Small Business Administration
Region VI Office
4300 Amon Carter Blvd., Ste. 108
Fort Worth, TX 76155
Phone: (817)684-5581
Fax: (817)684-5588
Serves Arkansas, Louisiana, New Mexico, Oklahoma, and Texas.

Region 7

U.S. Small Business Administration
Region VII Office
323 W. 8th St., Ste. 307
Kansas City, MO 64105-1500
Phone: (816)374-6380
Fax: (816)374-6339
Serves Iowa, Kansas, Missouri, and Nebraska.

Region 8

U.S. Small Business Administration
Region VIII Office
721 19th St., Ste. 400
Denver, CO 80202
Phone: (303)844-0500
Fax: (303)844-0506
Serves Colorado, Montana, North Dakota, South Dakota, Utah, and Wyoming.

Region 9

U.S. Small Business Administration
Region IX Office
330 N Brand Blvd., Ste. 1270
Glendale, CA 91203-2304
Phone: (818)552-3434
Fax: (818)552-3440
Serves American Samoa, Arizona, California, Guam, Hawaii, Nevada, and the Trust Territory of the Pacific Islands.

Region 10

U.S. Small Business Administration
Region X Office
2401 Fourth Ave., Ste. 400
Seattle, WA 98121
Phone: (206)553-5676
Fax: (206)553-4155
Serves Alaska, Idaho, Oregon, and Washington.

Small business development centers

This section contains a listing of all Small Business Development Centers, organized alphabetically by state/U.S. territory, then by city, then by agency name.

Alabama

Alabama SBDC
UNIVERSITY OF ALABAMA
2800 Milan Court Suite 124
Birmingham, AL 35211-6908
Phone: 205-943-6750
Fax: 205-943-6752
E-Mail: wcampbell@provost.uab.edu
Website: http://www.asbdc.org
Mr. William Campbell Jr, State Director

Alaska

Alaska SBDC
UNIVERSITY OF ALASKA - ANCHORAGE
430 West Seventh Avenue, Suite 110
Anchorage, AK 99501
Phone: 907-274 -7232
Fax: 907-274-9524
E-Mail: anerw@uaa.alaska.edu
Website: http://www.aksbdc.org
Ms. Jean R. Wall, State Director

American Samoa

American Samoa SBDC
AMERICAN SAMOA COMMUNITY COLLEGE
P.O. Box 2609
Pago Pago, American Samoa 96799
Phone: 011-684-699-4830
Fax: 011-684-699-6132
E-Mail: htalex@att.net
Mr. Herbert Thweatt, Director

Arizona

Arizona SBDC
MARICOPA COUNTY COMMUNITY COLLEGE
2411 West 14th Street, Suite 132
Tempe, AZ 85281
Phone: 480-731-8720
Fax: 480-731-8729
E-Mail: mike.york@domail.maricopa.edu
Website: http://www.dist.maricopa.edu.sbdc
Mr. Michael York, State Director

Arkansas

Arkansas SBDC
UNIVERSITY OF ARKANSAS
2801 South University Avenue
Little Rock, AR 72204
Phone: 501-324-9043
Fax: 501-324-9049
E-Mail: jmroderick@ualr.edu
Website: http://asbdc.ualr.edu
Ms. Janet M. Roderick, State Director

California

California - San Francisco SBDC
Northern California SBDC Lead Center
HUMBOLDT STATE UNIVERSITY
Office of Economic Development
1 Harpst Street 2006A, Siemens Hall
Arcata, CA, 95521
Phone: 707-826-3922
Fax: 707-826-3206
E-Mail: gainer@humboldt.edu
Ms. Margaret A. Gainer, Regional Director

California - Sacramento SBDC
CALIFORNIA STATE UNIVERSITY - CHICO
Chico, CA 95929-0765
Phone: 530-898-4598
Fax: 530-898-4734

E-Mail: dripke@csuchico.edu
Website: http://gsbdc.csuchico.edu
Mr. Dan Ripke, Interim Regional Director

California - San Diego SBDC
SOUTHWESTERN COMMUNITY COLLEGE DISTRICT
900 Otey Lakes Road
Chula Vista, CA 91910
Phone: 619-482-6388
Fax: 619-482-6402
E-Mail: dtrujillo@swc.cc.ca.us
Website: http://www.sbditc.org
Ms. Debbie P. Trujillo, Regional Director

California - Fresno SBDC
UC Merced Lead Center
UNIVERSITY OF CALIFORNIA - MERCED
550 East Shaw, Suite 105A
Fresno, CA 93710
Phone: 559-241-6590
Fax: 559-241-7422
E-Mail: crosander@ucmerced.edu
Website: http://sbdc.ucmerced.edu
Mr. Chris Rosander, State Director

California - Santa Ana SBDC
Tri-County Lead SBDC
CALIFORNIA STATE UNIVERSITY - FULLERTON
800 North State College Boulevard, LH640
Fullerton, CA 92834
Phone: 714-278-2719
Fax: 714-278-7858
E-Mail: vpham@fullerton.edu
Website: http://www.leadsbdc.org
Ms. Vi Pham, Lead Center Director

California - Los Angeles Region SBDC
LONG BEACH COMMUNITY COLLEGE DISTRICT
3950 Paramount Boulevard, Ste 101
Lakewood, CA 90712
Phone: 562-938-5004
Fax: 562-938-5030
E-Mail: ssloan@lbcc.edu
Ms. Sheneui Sloan, Interim Lead Center Director

Colorado

Colorado SBDC
OFFICE OF ECONOMIC DEVELOPMENT
1625 Broadway, Suite 170
Denver, CO 80202
Phone: 303-892-3864
Fax: 303-892-3848
E-Mail: Kelly.Manning@state.co.us

Website: http://www.state.co.us/oed/sbdc
Ms. Kelly Manning, State Director

Connecticut

Connecticut SBDC
UNIVERSITY OF CONNECTICUT
1376 Storrs Road, Unit 4094
Storrs, CT 06269-1094
Phone: 860-870-6370
Fax: 860-870-6374
E-Mail: richard.cheney@uconn.edu
Website: http://www.sbdc.uconn.edu
Mr. Richard Cheney, Interim State Director

Delaware

Delaware SBDC
DELAWARE TECHNOLOGY PARK
1 Innovation Way, Suite 301
Newark, DE 19711
Phone: 302-831-2747
Fax: 302-831-1423
E-Mail: Clinton.tymes@mvs.udel.edu
Website: http://www.delawaresbdc.org
Mr. Clinton Tymes, State Director

District of Columbia

District of Columbia SBDC
HOWARD UNIVERSITY
2600 6th Street, NW Room 128
Washington, DC 20059
Phone: 202-806-1550
Fax: 202-806-1777
E-Mail: hturner@howard.edu
Website: http://www.dcsbdc.com/
Mr. Henry Turner, Executive Director

Florida

Florida SBDC
UNIVERSITY OF WEST FLORIDA
401 East Chase Street, Suite 100
Pensacola, FL 32502
Phone: 850-473-7800
Fax: 850-473-7813
E-Mail: jcartwri@uwf.edu
Website: http://www.floridasbdc.com
Mr. Jerry Cartwright, State Director

Georgia

Georgia SBDC
UNIVERSITY OF GEORGIA
1180 East Broad Street
Athens, GA 30602
Phone: 706-542-6762
Fax: 706-542-6776
E-mail: aadams@sbdc.uga.edu

Website: http://www.sbdc.uga.edu
Mr. Allan Adams, Interim State Director

Guam

Guam Small Business Development Center
UNIVERSITY OF GUAM
Pacific Islands SBDC
P.O. Box 5014 - U.O.G. Station
Mangilao, GU 96923
Phone: 671-735-2590
Fax: 671-734-2002
E-mail: casey@pacificsbdc.com
Website: http://www.uog.edu/sbdc
Mr. Casey Jeszenka, Director

Hawaii

Hawaii SBDC
UNIVERSITY OF HAWAII - HILO
308 Kamehameha Avenue, Suite 201
Hilo, HI 96720
Phone: 808-974-7515
Fax: 808-974-7683
E-Mail: darrylm@interpac.net
Website: http://www.hawaii-sbdc.org
Mr. Darryl Mleynek, State Director

Idaho

Idaho SBDC
BOISE STATE UNIVERSITY
1910 University Drive
Boise, ID 83725
Phone: 208-426-3799
Fax: 208-426-3877
E-mail: jhogge@boisestate.edu
Website: http://www.idahosbdc.org
Mr. Jim Hogge, State Director

Illinois

Illinois SBDC
DEPARTMENT OF COMMERCE AND ECONOMIC OPPORTUNITY
620 E. Adams, S-4
Springfield, IL 62701
Phone: 217-524-5700
Fax: 217-524-0171
E-mail: mpatrilli@ildceo.net
Website: http://www.ilsbdc.biz
Mr. Mark Petrilli, State Director

Indiana

Indiana SBDC
INDIANA ECONOMIC DEVELOPMENT CORPORATION
One North Capitol, Suite 900
Indianapolis, IN 46204

Phone: 317-234-8872
Fax: 317-232-8874
E-mail: dtrocha@isbdc.org
Website: http://www.isbdc.org
Ms. Debbie Bishop Trocha, State
Director

Iowa

Iowa SBDC
IOWA STATE UNIVERSITY
340 Gerdin Business Bldg.
Ames, IA 50011-1350
Phone: 515-294-2037
Fax: 515-294-6522
E-mail: jonryan@iastate.edu
Website: http://www.iabusnet.org
Mr. Jon Ryan, State Director

Kansas

Kansas SBDC
FORT HAYS STATE UNIVERSITY
214 SW Sixth Street, Suite 301
Topeka, KS 66603
Phone: 785-296-6514
Fax: 785-291-3261
E-mail: ksbdc.wkearns@fhsu.edu
Website: http://www.fhsu.edu/ksbdc
Mr. Wally Kearns, State Director

Kentucky

Kentucky SBDC
UNIVERSITY OF KENTUCKY
225 Gatton College of Business
Economics Building
Lexington, KY 40506-0034
Phone: 859-257-7668
Fax: 859-323-1907
E-mail: lrnaug0@pop.uky.edu
Website: http://www.ksbdc.org
Ms. Becky Naugle, State Director

Louisiana

Louisiana SBDC
**UNIVERSITY OF LOUISIANA -
MONROE**
College of Business Administration
700 University Avenue
Monroe, LA 71209
Phone: 318-342-5506
Fax: 318-342-5510
E-mail: wilkerson@ulm.edu
Website: http://www.lsbdc.org
Ms. Mary Lynn Wilkerson, State
Director

Maine

Maine SBDC
**UNIVERSITY OF SOUTHERN
MAINE**
96 Falmouth Street P.O. Box 9300
Portland, ME 04103
Phone: 207-780-4420
Fax: 207-780-4810
E-mail: jrmassaua@maine.edu
Website: http://www.mainesbdc.org
Mr. John Massaua, State Director

Maryland

Maryland SBDC
UNIVERSITY OF MARYLAND
7100 Baltimore Avenue, Suite 401
College Park, MD 20742
Phone: 301-403-8300
Fax: 301-403-8303
E-mail: rsprow@mdsbdc.umd.edu
Website: http://www.mdsbdc.umd.edu
Ms. Renee Sprow, State Director

Massachusetts

Massachusetts SBDC
UNIVERSITY OF MASSACHUSETTS
School of Management, Room 205
Amherst, MA 01003-4935
Phone: 413-545-6301
Fax: 413-545-1273
E-mail: gep@msbdc.umass.edu
Website: http://msbdc.som.umass.edu
Ms. Georgianna Parkin, State Director

Michigan

Michigan SBTDC
**GRAND VALLEY STATE
UNIVERSITY**
510 West Fulton Avenue
Grand Rapids, MI 49504
Phone: 616-331-7485
Fax: 616-331-7389
E-mail: lopuckic@gvsu.edu
Website: http://www.misbtdc.org
Ms. Carol Lopucki, State Director

Minnesota

Minnesota SBDC
**MINNESOTA SMALL BUSINESS
DEVELOPMENT CENTER**
1st National Bank Building
332 Minnesota Street, Suite E200
St. Paul, MN 55101-1351
Phone: 651-297-5773
Fax: 651-296-5287

E-mail: michael.myhre@state.mn.us
Website: http://www.mnsbdc.com
Mr. Michael Myhre, State Director

Mississippi

Mississippi SBDC
UNIVERSITY OF MISSISSIPPI
B-19 Jeanette Phillips Drive
P.O. Box 1848
University, MS 38677
Phone: 662-915-5001
Fax: 662-915-5650
E-mail: wgurley@olemiss.edu
Website: http://www.olemiss.edu/depts/
mssbdc
Mr. Doug Gurley, Jr., State Director

Missouri

Missouri SBDC
UNIVERSITY OF MISSOURI
1205 University Avenue, Suite 300
Columbia, MO 65211
Phone: 573-882-1348
Fax: 573-884-4297
E-mail: summersm@missouri.edu
Website: http://www.mo-sbdc.org/
index.shtml
Mr. Max Summers, State Director

Montana

Montana SBDC
DEPARTMENT OF COMMERCE
301 South Park Avenue, Room 114 /
P.O. Box 200505
Helena, MT 59620
Phone: 406-841-2746
Fax: 406-444-1872
E-mail: adesch@state.mt.us
Website: http://commerce.state.mt.us/
brd/BRD_SBDC.html
Ms. Ann Desch, State Director

Nebraska

Nebraska SBDC
**UNIVERSITY OF NEBRASKA -
OMAHA**
60th & Dodge Street, CBA Room 407
Omaha, NE 68182
Phone: 402-554-2521
Fax: 402-554-3473
E-mail: rbernier@unomaha.edu
Website: http://nbdc.unomaha.edu
Mr. Robert Bernier, State Director

Nevada

Nevada SBDC
UNIVERSITY OF NEVADA - RENO
Reno College of Business
Administration, Room 411
Reno, NV 89557-0100
Phone: 775-784-1717
Fax: 775-784-4337
E-mail: males@unr.edu
Website: http://www.nsbdc.org
Mr. Sam Males, State Director

New Hampshire

New Hampshire SBDC
UNIVERSITY OF NEW HAMPSHIRE
108 McConnell Hall
Durham, NH 03824-3593
Phone: 603-862-4879
Fax: 603-862-4876
E-mail: Mary.Collins@unh.edu
Website: http://www.nhsbdc.org
Ms. Mary Collins, State Director

New Jersey

New Jersey SBDC
RUTGERS UNIVERSITY
49 Bleeker Street
Newark, NJ 07102-1993
Phone: 973-353-5950
Fax: 973-353-1110
E-mail: bhopper@njsbdc.com
Website: http://www.njsbdc.com/home
Ms. Brenda Hopper, State Director

New Mexico

New Mexico SBDC
SANTA FE COMMUNITY COLLEGE
6401 Richards Avenue
Santa Fe, NM 87505
Phone: 505-428-1362
Fax: 505-471-9469
E-mail: rmiller@santa-fe.cc.nm.us
Website: http://www.nmsbdc.org
Mr. Roy Miller, State Director

New York

New York SBDC
STATE UNIVERSITY OF NEW YORK
SUNY Plaza, S-523
Albany, NY 12246
Phone: 518-443-5398
Fax: 518-443-5275
E-mail: j.king@nyssbdc.org
Website: http://www.nyssbdc.org
Mr. Jim King, State Director

North Carolina

North Carolina SBDTC
UNIVERSITY OF NORTH CAROLINA
5 West Hargett Street, Suite 600
Raleigh, NC 27601
Phone: 919-715-7272
Fax: 919-715-7777
E-mail: sdaugherty@sbtdc.org
Website: http://www.sbtdc.org
Mr. Scott Daugherty, State Director

North Dakota

North Dakota SBDC
UNIVERSITY OF NORTH DAKOTA
1600 E. Century Avenue, Suite 2
Bismarck, ND 58503
Phone: 701-328-5375
Fax: 701-328-5320
E-mail: christine.martin@und.nodak.edu
Website: http://www.ndsbdc.org
Ms. Christine Martin-Goldman, State
Director

Ohio

Ohio SBDC
**OHIO DEPARTMENT
OF DEVELOPMENT**
77 South High Street
Columbus, OH 43216
Phone: 614-466-5102
Fax: 614-466-0829
E-mail: mabraham@odod.state.oh.us
Website: http://www.ohiosbdc.org
Ms. Michele Abraham, State Director

Oklahoma

Oklahoma SBDC
**SOUTHEAST OKLAHOMA STATE
UNIVERSITY**
517 University, Box 2584, Station A
Durant, OK 74701
Phone: 580-745-7577
Fax: 580-745-7471
E-mail: gpennington@sosu.edu
Website: http://www.osbdc.org
Mr. Grady Pennington, State Director

Oregon

Oregon SBDC
LANE COMMUNITY COLLEGE
99 West Tenth Avenue, Suite 390
Eugene, OR 97401-3021
Phone: 541-463-5250
Fax: 541-345-6006
E-mail: carterb@lanecc.edu

Website: http://www.bizcenter.org
Mr. William Carter, State Director

Pennsylvania

Pennsylvania SBDC
UNIVERSITY OF PENNSYLVANIA
The Wharton School
3733 Spruce Street
Philadelphia, PA 19104-6374
Phone: 215-898-1219
Fax: 215-573-2135
E-mail: ghiggins@wharton.upenn.edu
Website: http://pasbdc.org
Mr. Gregory Higgins, State Director

Puerto Rico

Puerto Rico SBDC
**INTER-AMERICAN UNIVERSITY
OF PUERTO RICO**
416 Ponce de Leon Avenue, Union Plaza,
Seventh Floor
Hato Rey, PR 00918
Phone: 787-763-6811
Fax: 787-763-4629
E-mail: cmarti@prsbdc.org
Website: http://www.prsbdc.org
Ms. Carmen Marti, Executive Director

Rhode Island

Rhode Island SBDC
BRYANT UNIVERSITY
1150 Douglas Pike
Smithfield, RI 02917
Phone: 401-232-6923
Fax: 401-232-6933
E-mail: adawson@bryant.edu
Website: http://www.risbdc.org
Ms. Diane Fournaris, Interim State Director

South Carolina

South Carolina SBDC
UNIVERSITY OF SOUTH CAROLINA
College of Business Administration
1710 College Street
Columbia, SC 29208
Phone: 803-777-4907
Fax: 803-777-4403
E-mail: lenti@moore.sc.edu
Website: http://scsbdc.moore.sc.edu
Mr. John Lenti, State Director

South Dakota

South Dakota SBDC
UNIVERSITY OF SOUTH DAKOTA
414 East Clark Street, Patterson Hall
Vermillion, SD 57069

Phone: 605-677-6256
Fax: 605-677-5427
E-mail: jshemmin@usd.edu
Website: http://www.sdsbdc.org
Mr. John S. Hemmingstad, State
Director

Tennessee

Tennessee SBDC
TENNESSEE BOARD OF REGENTS
1415 Murfressboro Road, Suite 540
Nashville, TN 37217-2833
Phone: 615-898-2745
Fax: 615-893-7089
E-mail: pgeho@mail.tsbdc.org
Website: http://www.tsbdc.org
Mr. Patrick Geho, State Director

Texas

Texas-North SBDC
**DALLAS COUNTY COMMUNITY
COLLEGE**
1402 Corinth Street
Dallas, TX 75215
Phone: 214-860-5835
Fax: 214-860-5813
E-mail: emk9402@dcccd.edu
Website: http://www.ntsbdc.org
Ms. Liz Klimback, Region Director

Texas-Houston SBDC
UNIVERSITY OF HOUSTON
2302 Fannin, Suite 200
Houston, TX 77002
Phone: 713-752-8425
Fax: 713-756-1500
E-mail: fyoung@uh.edu
Website: http://sbdcnetwork.uh.edu
Mr. Mike Young, Executive Director

Texas-NW SBDC
TEXAS TECH UNIVERSITY
2579 South Loop 289, Suite 114
Lubbock, TX 79423
Phone: 806-745-3973
Fax: 806-745-6207
E-mail: c.bean@nwtsbdc.org
Website: http://www.nwtsbdc.org
Mr. Craig Bean, Executive Director

**Texas-South-West Texas Border
Region SBDC**
**UNIVERSITY OF TEXAS -
SAN ANTONIO**
501 West Durango Boulevard
San Antonio, TX 78207-4415
Phone: 210-458-2742
Fax: 210-458-2464

E-mail: albert.salgado@utsa.edu
Website: http://www.iedtexas.org
Mr. Alberto Salgado, Region Director

Utah

Utah SBDC
SALT LAKE COMMUNITY COLLEGE
9750 South 300 West
Sandy, UT 84070
Phone: 801-957-3493
Fax: 801-957-3488
E-mail: Greg.Panichello@slcc.edu
Website:http://www.slcc.edu/sbdc
Mr. Greg Panichello, State Director

Vermont

Vermont SBDC
VERMONT TECHNICAL COLLEGE
PO Box 188, 1 Main Street
Randolph Center, VT 05061-0188
Phone: 802-728-9101
Fax: 802-728-3026
E-mail: lquillen@vtc.edu
Website: http://www.vtsbdc.org
Ms. Lenae Quillen-Blume, State Director

Virgin Islands

Virgin Islands SBDC
**UNIVERSITY OF THE VIRGIN
ISLANDS**
8000 Nisky Center, Suite 720
St. Thomas, VI 00802-5804
Phone: 340-776-3206
Fax: 340-775-3756
E-mail: wbush@webmail.uvi.edu
Website: http://rps.uvi.edu/SBDC
Mr. Warren Bush, State Director

Virginia

Virginia SBDC
GEORGE MASON UNIVERSITY
4031 University Drive, Suite 200
Fairfax, VA 22030-3409
Phone: 703-277-7727
Fax: 703-352-8515
E-mail: jkeenan@gmu.edu
Website: http://www.virginiasbdc.org
Ms. Jody Keenan, Director

Washington

Washington SBDC
WASHINGTON STATE UNIVERSITY
534 E. Trent Avenue
P.O. Box 1495
Spokane, WA 99210-1495

Phone: 509-358-7765
Fax: 509-358-7764
E-mail: barogers@wsu.edu
Website: http://www.wsbdc.org
Mr. Brett Rogers, State Director

West Virginia

West Virginia SBDC
**WEST VIRGINIA DEVELOPMENT
OFFICE**
Capital Complex, Building 6, Room 652
Charleston, WV 25301
Phone: 304-558-2960
Fax: 304-558-0127
E-mail: csalyer@wvsbdc.org
Website: http://www.wvsbdc.org
Mr. Conley Salyor, State Director

Wisconsin

Wisconsin SBDC
UNIVERSITY OF WISCONSIN
432 North Lake Street, Room 423
Madison, WI 53706
Phone: 608-263-7794
Fax: 608-263-7830
E-mail: erica.kauten@uwex.edu
Website: http://www.wisconsinsbdc.org
Ms. Erica Kauten, State Director

Wyoming

Wyoming SBDC
UNIVERSITY OF WYOMING
P.O. Box 3922
Laramie, WY 82071-3922
Phone: 307-766-3505
Fax: 307-766-3406
E-mail: DDW@uwyo.edu
Website: http://www.uwyo.edu/sbdc
Ms. Debbie Popp, Acting State Director

Service corps of retired executives (score) offices

*This section contains a listing of all
SCORE offices organized alphabetically by
state/U.S. territory, then by city, then by
agency name.*

Alabama

SCORE Office (Northeast Alabama)
1330 Quintard Ave.
Anniston, AL 36202
(256)237-3536

SCORE Office (North Alabama)
901 South 15th St, Rm. 201
Birmingham, AL 35294-2060
(205)934-6868
Fax: (205)934-0538

SCORE Office (Baldwin County)
29750 Larry Dee Cawyer Dr.
Daphne, AL 36526
(334)928-5838

SCORE Office (Shoals)
612 S. COurt
Florence, AL 35630
(256)764-4661
Fax: (256)766-9017
E-mail: shoals@shoalschamber.com

SCORE Office (Mobile)
600 S Court St.
Mobile, AL 36104
(334)240-6868
Fax: (334)240-6869

SCORE Office (Alabama Capitol City)
600 S. Court St.
Montgomery, AL 36104
(334)240-6868
Fax: (334)240-6869

SCORE Office (East Alabama)
601 Ave. A
Opelika, AL 36801
(334)745-4861
E-mail: score636@hotmail.com
Website: http://www.angelfire.com/sc/
score636/

SCORE Office (Tuscaloosa)
2200 University Blvd.
Tuscaloosa, AL 35402
(205)758-7588

Alaska

SCORE Office (Anchorage)
510 L St., Ste. 310
Anchorage, AK 99501
(907)271-4022
Fax: (907)271-4545

Arizona

SCORE Office (Lake Havasu)
10 S. Acoma Blvd.
Lake Havasu City, AZ 86403
(520)453-5951
E-mail: SCORE@ctaz.com
Website: http://www.scorearizona.org/
lake_havasu/

SCORE Office (East Valley)
Federal Bldg., Rm. 104
26 N. MacDonald St.
Mesa, AZ 85201
(602)379-3100
Fax: (602)379-3143
E-mail: 402@aol.com
Website: http://www.scorearizona.
org/mesa/

SCORE Office (Phoenix)
2828 N. Central Ave., Ste. 800
Central & One Thomas
Phoenix, AZ 85004
(602)640-2329
Fax: (602)640-2360
E-mail: e-mail@SCORE-phoenix.org
Website: http://www.score-phoenix.org/

SCORE Office (Prescott Arizona)
1228 Willow Creek Rd., Ste. 2
Prescott, AZ 86301
(520)778-7438
Fax: (520)778-0812
E-mail: score@northlink.com
Website: http://www.scorearizona.org/
prescott/

SCORE Office (Tucson)
110 E. Pennington St.
Tucson, AZ 85702
(520)670-5008
Fax: (520)670-5011
E-mail: score@azstarnet.com
Website: http://www.scorearizona.org/
tucson/

SCORE Office (Yuma)
281 W. 24th St., Ste. 116
Yuma, AZ 85364
(520)314-0480
E-mail: score@C2i2.com
Website: http://www.scorearizona.org/
yuma

Arkansas

SCORE Office (South Central)
201 N. Jackson Ave.
El Dorado, AR 71730-5803
(870)863-6113
Fax: (870)863-6115

SCORE Office (Ozark)
Fayetteville, AR 72701
(501)442-7619

SCORE Office (Northwest Arkansas)
Glenn Haven Dr., No. 4
Ft. Smith, AR 72901
(501)783-3556

SCORE Office (Garland County)
Grand & Ouachita
PO Box 6012
Hot Springs Village, AR 71902
(501)321-1700

SCORE Office (Little Rock)
2120 Riverfront Dr., Rm. 100
Little Rock, AR 72202-1747
(501)324-5893
Fax: (501)324-5199

SCORE Office (Southeast Arkansas)
121 W. 6th
Pine Bluff, AR 71601
(870)535-7189
Fax: (870)535-1643

California

SCORE Office (Golden Empire)
1706 Chester Ave., No. 200
Bakersfield, CA 93301
(805)322-5881
Fax: (805)322-5663

SCORE Office (Greater Chico Area)
1324 Mangrove St., Ste. 114
Chico, CA 95926
(916)342-8932
Fax: (916)342-8932

SCORE Office (Concord)
2151-A Salvio St., Ste. B
Concord, CA 94520
(510)685-1181
Fax: (510)685-5623

SCORE Office (Covina)
935 W. Badillo St.
Covina, CA 91723
(818)967-4191
Fax: (818)966-9660

SCORE Office (Rancho Cucamonga)
8280 Utica, Ste. 160
Cucamonga, CA 91730
(909)987-1012
Fax: (909)987-5917

SCORE Office (Culver City)
PO Box 707
Culver City, CA 90232-0707
(310)287-3850
Fax: (310)287-1350

SCORE Office (Danville)
380 Diablo Rd., Ste. 103
Danville, CA 94526
(510)837-4400

SCORE Office (Downey)
11131 Brookshire Ave.
Downey, CA 90241
(310)923-2191
Fax: (310)864-0461

SCORE Office (El Cajon)
109 Rea Ave.
El Cajon, CA 92020
(619)444-1327
Fax: (619)440-6164

SCORE Office (El Centro)
1100 Main St.
El Centro, CA 92243
(619)352-3681
Fax: (619)352-3246

SCORE Office (Escondido)
720 N. Broadway
Escondido, CA 92025
(619)745-2125
Fax: (619)745-1183

SCORE Office (Fairfield)
1111 Webster St.
Fairfield, CA 94533
(707)425-4625
Fax: (707)425-0826

SCORE Office (Fontana)
17009 Valley Blvd., Ste. B
Fontana, CA 92335
(909)822-4433
Fax: (909)822-6238

SCORE Office (Foster City)
1125 E. Hillsdale Blvd.
Foster City, CA 94404
(415)573-7600
Fax: (415)573-5201

SCORE Office (Fremont)
2201 Walnut Ave., Ste. 110
Fremont, CA 94538
(510)795-2244
Fax: (510)795-2240

SCORE Office (Central California)
2719 N. Air Fresno Dr., Ste. 200
Fresno, CA 93727-1547
(559)487-5605
Fax: (559)487-5636

SCORE Office (Gardena)
1204 W. Gardena Blvd.
Gardena, CA 90247
(310)532-9905
Fax: (310)515-4893

SCORE Office (Lompoc)
330 N. Brand Blvd., Ste. 190
Glendale, CA 91203-2304

(818)552-3206
Fax: (818)552-3323

SCORE Office (Los Angeles)
330 N. Brand Blvd., Ste. 190
Glendale, CA 91203-2304
(818)552-3206
Fax: (818)552-3323

SCORE Office (Glendora)
131 E. Foothill Blvd.
Glendora, CA 91740
(818)963-4128
Fax: (818)914-4822

SCORE Office (Grover Beach)
177 S. 8th St.
Grover Beach, CA 93433
(805)489-9091
Fax: (805)489-9091

SCORE Office (Hawthorne)
12477 Hawthorne Blvd.
Hawthorne, CA 90250
(310)676-1163
Fax: (310)676-7661

SCORE Office (Hayward)
22300 Foothill Blvd., Ste. 303
Hayward, CA 94541
(510)537-2424

SCORE Office (Hemet)
1700 E. Florida Ave.
Hemet, CA 92544-4679
(909)652-4390
Fax: (909)929-8543

SCORE Office (Hesperia)
16367 Main St.
PO Box 403656
Hesperia, CA 92340
(619)244-2135

SCORE Office (Holloster)
321 San Felipe Rd., No. 11
Hollister, CA 95023

SCORE Office (Hollywood)
7018 Hollywood Blvd.
Hollywood, CA 90028
(213)469-8311
Fax: (213)469-2805

SCORE Office (Indio)
82503 Hwy. 111
PO Drawer TTT
Indio, CA 92202
(619)347-0676

SCORE Office (Inglewood)
330 Queen St.

Inglewood, CA 90301
(818)552-3206

SCORE Office (La Puente)
218 N. Grendanda St. D.
La Puente, CA 91744
(818)330-3216
Fax: (818)330-9524

SCORE Office (La Verne)
2078 Bonita Ave.
La Verne, CA 91750
(909)593-5265
Fax: (714)929-8475

SCORE Office (Lake Elsinore)
132 W. Graham Ave.
Lake Elsinore, CA 92530
(909)674-2577

SCORE Office (Lakeport)
PO Box 295
Lakeport, CA 95453
(707)263-5092

SCORE Office (Lakewood)
5445 E. Del Amo Blvd., Ste. 2
Lakewood, CA 90714
(213)920-7737

SCORE Office (Long Beach)
1 World Trade Center
Long Beach, CA 90831

SCORE Office (Los Alamitos)
901 W. Civic Center Dr., Ste. 160
Los Alamitos, CA 90720

SCORE Office (Los Altos)
321 University Ave.
Los Altos, CA 94022
(415)948-1455

SCORE Office (Manhattan Beach)
PO Box 3007
Manhattan Beach, CA 90266
(310)545-5313
Fax: (310)545-7203

SCORE Office (Merced)
1632 N. St.
Merced, CA 95340
(209)725-3800
Fax: (209)383-4959

SCORE Office (Milpitas)
75 S. Milpitas Blvd., Ste. 205
Milpitas, CA 95035
(408)262-2613
Fax: (408)262-2823

SCORE Office (Yosemite)
1012 11th St., Ste. 300
Modesto, CA 95354
(209)521-9333

SCORE Office (Montclair)
5220 Benito Ave.
Montclair, CA 91763

SCORE Office (Monterey Bay)
380 Alvarado St.
PO Box 1770
Monterey, CA 93940-1770
(408)649-1770

SCORE Office (Moreno Valley)
25480 Alessandro
Moreno Valley, CA 92553

SCORE Office (Morgan Hill)
25 W. 1st St.
PO Box 786
Morgan Hill, CA 95038
(408)779-9444
Fax: (408)778-1786

SCORE Office (Morro Bay)
880 Main St.
Morro Bay, CA 93442
(805)772-4467

SCORE Office (Mountain View)
580 Castro St.
Mountain View, CA 94041
(415)968-8378
Fax: (415)968-5668

SCORE Office (Napa)
1556 1st St.
Napa, CA 94559
(707)226-7455
Fax: (707)226-1171

SCORE Office (North Hollywood)
5019 Lankershim Blvd.
North Hollywood, CA 91601
(818)552-3206

SCORE Office (Northridge)
8801 Reseda Blvd.
Northridge, CA 91324
(818)349-5676

SCORE Office (Novato)
807 De Long Ave.
Novato, CA 94945
(415)897-1164
Fax: (415)898-9097

SCORE Office (East Bay)
519 17th St.
Oakland, CA 94612

(510)273-6611
Fax: (510)273-6015
E-mail: webmaster@eastbayscore.org
Website: http://www.eastbayscore.org

SCORE Office (Oceanside)
928 N. Coast Hwy.
Oceanside, CA 92054
(619)722-1534

SCORE Office (Ontario)
121 West B. St.
Ontario, CA 91762
Fax: (714)984-6439

SCORE Office (Oxnard)
PO Box 867
Oxnard, CA 93032
(805)385-8860
Fax: (805)487-1763

SCORE Office (Pacifica)
450 Dundee Way, Ste. 2
Pacifica, CA 94044
(415)355-4122

SCORE Office (Palm Desert)
72990 Hwy. 111
Palm Desert, CA 92260
(619)346-6111
Fax: (619)346-3463

SCORE Office (Palm Springs)
650 E. Tahquitz Canyon Way Ste. D
Palm Springs, CA 92262-6706
(760)320-6682
Fax: (760)323-9426

SCORE Office (Lakeside)
2150 Low Tree
Palmdale, CA 93551
(805)948-4518
Fax: (805)949-1212

SCORE Office (Palo Alto)
325 Forest Ave.
Palo Alto, CA 94301
(415)324-3121
Fax: (415)324-1215

SCORE Office (Pasadena)
117 E. Colorado Blvd., Ste. 100
Pasadena, CA 91105
(818)795-3355
Fax: (818)795-5663

SCORE Office (Paso Robles)
1225 Park St.
Paso Robles, CA 93446-2234
(805)238-0506
Fax: (805)238-0527

SCORE Office (Petaluma)
799 Baywood Dr., Ste. 3
Petaluma, CA 94954
(707)762-2785
Fax: (707)762-4721

SCORE Office (Pico Rivera)
9122 E. Washington Blvd.
Pico Rivera, CA 90660

SCORE Office (Pittsburg)
2700 E. Leland Rd.
Pittsburg, CA 94565
(510)439-2181
Fax: (510)427-1599

SCORE Office (Pleasanton)
777 Peters Ave.
Pleasanton, CA 94566
(510)846-9697

SCORE Office (Monterey Park)
485 N. Garey
Pomona, CA 91769

SCORE Office (Pomona)
485 N. Garey Ave.
Pomona, CA 91766
(909)622-1256

SCORE Office (Antelope Valley)
4511 West Ave. M-4
Quartz Hill, CA 93536
(805)272-0087
E-mail: avscore@ptw.com
Website: http://www.score.av.org/

SCORE Office (Shasta)
737 Auditorium Dr.
Redding, CA 96099
(916)225-2770

SCORE Office (Redwood City)
1675 Broadway
Redwood City, CA 94063
(415)364-1722
Fax: (415)364-1729

SCORE Office (Richmond)
3925 MacDonald Ave.
Richmond, CA 94805

SCORE Office (Ridgecrest)
PO Box 771
Ridgecrest, CA 93555
(619)375-8331
Fax: (619)375-0365

SCORE Office (Riverside)
3685 Main St., Ste. 350
Riverside, CA 92501
(909)683-7100

SCORE Office (Sacramento)
9845 Horn Rd., 260-B
Sacramento, CA 95827
(916)361-2322
Fax: (916)361-2164
E-mail: sacchapter@directcon.net

SCORE Office (Salinas)
PO Box 1170
Salinas, CA 93902
(408)424-7611
Fax: (408)424-8639

SCORE Office (Inland Empire)
777 E. Rialto Ave.
Purchasing
San Bernardino, CA 92415-0760
(909)386-8278

SCORE Office (San Carlos)
San Carlos Chamber of Commerce
PO Box 1086
San Carlos, CA 94070
(415)593-1068
Fax: (415)593-9108

SCORE Office (Encinitas)
550 W. C St., Ste. 550
San Diego, CA 92101-3540
(619)557-7272
Fax: (619)557-5894

SCORE Office (San Diego)
550 West C. St., Ste. 550
San Diego, CA 92101-3540
(619)557-7272
Fax: (619)557-5894
Website: http://www.score-sandiego.org

SCORE Office (Menlo Park)
1100 Merrill St.
San Francisco, CA 94105
(415)325-2818
Fax: (415)325-0920

SCORE Office (San Francisco)
455 Market St., 6th Fl.
San Francisco, CA 94105
(415)744-6827
Fax: (415)744-6750
E-mail: sfscore@sfscore.
Website: http://www.sfscore.com

SCORE Office (San Gabriel)
401 W. Las Tunas Dr.
San Gabriel, CA 91776
(818)576-2525
Fax: (818)289-2901

SCORE Office (San Jose)
Deanza College
208 S. 1st. St., Ste. 137
San Jose, CA 95113
(408)288-8479
Fax: (408)535-5541

SCORE Office (Silicon Valley)
84 W. Santa Clara St., Ste. 100
San Jose, CA 95113
(408)288-8479
Fax: (408)535-5541
E-mail: info@svscore.org
Website: http://www.svscore.org

SCORE Office (San Luis Obispo)
3566 S. Hiquera, No. 104
San Luis Obispo, CA 93401
(805)547-0779

SCORE Office (San Mateo)
1021 S. El Camino, 2nd Fl.
San Mateo, CA 94402
(415)341-5679

SCORE Office (San Pedro)
390 W. 7th St.
San Pedro, CA 90731
(310)832-7272

SCORE Office (Orange County)
200 W. Santa Anna Blvd., Ste. 700
Santa Ana, CA 92701
(714)550-7369
Fax: (714)550-0191
Website: http://www.score114.org

SCORE Office (Santa Barbara)
3227 State St.
Santa Barbara, CA 93130
(805)563-0084

SCORE Office (Central Coast)
509 W. Morrison Ave.
Santa Maria, CA 93454
(805)347-7755

SCORE Office (Santa Maria)
614 S. Broadway
Santa Maria, CA 93454-5111
(805)925-2403
Fax: (805)928-7559

SCORE Office (Santa Monica)
501 Colorado, Ste. 150
Santa Monica, CA 90401
(310)393-9825
Fax: (310)394-1868

SCORE Office (Santa Rosa)
777 Sonoma Ave., Rm. 115E
Santa Rosa, CA 95404

(707)571-8342
Fax: (707)541-0331
Website: http://www.pressdemo.com/
community/score/score.html

SCORE Office (Scotts Valley)
4 Camp Evers Ln.
Scotts Valley, CA 95066
(408)438-1010
Fax: (408)438-6544

SCORE Office (Simi Valley)
40 W. Cochran St., Ste. 100
Simi Valley, CA 93065
(805)526-3900
Fax: (805)526-6234

SCORE Office (Sonoma)
453 1st St. E
Sonoma, CA 95476
(707)996-1033

SCORE Office (Los Banos)
222 S. Shepard St.
Sonora, CA 95370
(209)532-4212

SCORE Office (Tuolumne County)
39 North Washington St.
Sonora, CA 95370
(209)588-0128
E-mail: score@mlode.com

SCORE Office (South San Francisco)
445 Market St., Ste. 6th Fl.
South San Francisco, CA 94105
(415)744-6827
Fax: (415)744-6812

SCORE Office (Stockton)
401 N. San Joaquin St., Rm. 215
Stockton, CA 95202
(209)946-6293

SCORE Office (Taft)
314 4th St.
Taft, CA 93268
(805)765-2165
Fax: (805)765-6639

SCORE Office (Conejo Valley)
625 W. Hillcrest Dr.
Thousand Oaks, CA 91360
(805)499-1993
Fax: (805)498-7264

SCORE Office (Torrance)
3400 Torrance Blvd., Ste. 100
Torrance, CA 90503
(310)540-5858
Fax: (310)540-7662

SCORE Office (Truckee)
PO Box 2757
Truckee, CA 96160
(916)587-2757
Fax: (916)587-2439

SCORE Office (Visalia)
113 S. M St,
Tulare, CA 93274
(209)627-0766
Fax: (209)627-8149

SCORE Office (Upland)
433 N. 2nd Ave.
Upland, CA 91786
(909)931-4108

SCORE Office (Vallejo)
2 Florida St.
Vallejo, CA 94590
(707)644-5551
Fax: (707)644-5590

SCORE Office (Van Nuys)
14540 Victory Blvd.
Van Nuys, CA 91411
(818)989-0300
Fax: (818)989-3836

SCORE Office (Ventura)
5700 Ralston St., Ste. 310
Ventura, CA 93001
(805)658-2688
Fax: (805)658-2252
E-mail: scoreven@jps.net
Website: http://www.jps.net/scoreven

SCORE Office (Vista)
201 E. Washington St.
Vista, CA 92084
(619)726-1122
Fax: (619)226-8654

SCORE Office (Watsonville)
PO Box 1748
Watsonville, CA 95077
(408)724-3849
Fax: (408)728-5300

SCORE Office (West Covina)
811 S. Sunset Ave.
West Covina, CA 91790
(818)338-8496
Fax: (818)960-0511

SCORE Office (Westlake)
30893 Thousand Oaks Blvd.
Westlake Village, CA 91362
(805)496-5630
Fax: (818)991-1754

Colorado

SCORE Office (Colorado Springs)
2 N. Cascade Ave., Ste. 110
Colorado Springs, CO 80903
(719)636-3074
Website: http://www.cscc.org/score02/
index.html

SCORE Office (Denver)
US Custom's House, 4th Fl.
721 19th St.
Denver, CO 80201-0660
(303)844-3985
Fax: (303)844-6490
E-mail: score62@csn.net
Website: http://www.sni.net/score62

SCORE Office (Tri-River)
1102 Grand Ave.
Glenwood Springs, CO 81601
(970)945-6589

SCORE Office (Grand Junction)
2591 B & 3/4 Rd.
Grand Junction, CO 81503
(970)243-5242

SCORE Office (Gunnison)
608 N. 11th
Gunnison, CO 81230
(303)641-4422

SCORE Office (Montrose)
1214 Peppertree Dr.
Montrose, CO 81401
(970)249-6080

SCORE Office (Pagosa Springs)
PO Box 4381
Pagosa Springs, CO 81157
(970)731-4890

SCORE Office (Rifle)
0854 W. Battlement Pky., Apt. C106
Parachute, CO 81635
(970)285-9390

SCORE Office (Pueblo)
302 N. Santa Fe
Pueblo, CO 81003
(719)542-1704
Fax: (719)542-1624
E-mail: mackey@iex.net
Website: http://www.pueblo.org/score

SCORE Office (Ridgway)
143 Poplar Pl.
Ridgway, CO 81432

SCORE Office (Silverton)
PO Box 480

Silverton, CO 81433
(303)387-5430

SCORE Office (Minturn)
PO Box 2066
Vail, CO 81658
(970)476-1224

Connecticut

SCORE Office (Greater Bridgeport)
230 Park Ave.
Bridgeport, CT 06601-0999
(203)576-4369
Fax: (203)576-4388

SCORE Office (Bristol)
10 Main St. 1st. Fl.
Bristol, CT 06010
(203)584-4718
Fax: (203)584-4722

SCORE office (Greater Danbury)
246 Federal Rd.
Unit LL2, Ste. 7
Brookfield, CT 06804
(203)775-1151

SCORE Office (Greater Danbury)
246 Federal Rd., Unit LL2, Ste. 7
Brookfield, CT 06804
(203)775-1151

SCORE Office (Eastern Connecticut)
Administration Bldg., Rm. 313
PO 625
61 Main St. (Chapter 579)
Groton, CT 06475
(203)388-9508

SCORE Office (Greater Hartford County)
330 Main St.
Hartford, CT 06106
(860)548-1749
Fax: (860)240-4659
Website: http://www.score56.org

SCORE Office (Manchester)
20 Hartford Rd.
Manchester, CT 06040
(203)646-2223
Fax: (203)646-5871

SCORE Office (New Britain)
185 Main St., Ste. 431
New Britain, CT 06051
(203)827-4492
Fax: (203)827-4480

SCORE Office (New Haven)
25 Science Pk., Bldg. 25, Rm. 366

New Haven, CT 06511
(203)865-7645

SCORE Office (Fairfield County)
24 Beldon Ave., 5th Fl.
Norwalk, CT 06850
(203)847-7348
Fax: (203)849-9308

SCORE Office (Old Saybrook)
146 Main St.
Old Saybrook, CT 06475
(860)388-9508

SCORE Office (Simsbury)
Box 244
Simsbury, CT 06070
(203)651-7307
Fax: (203)651-1933

SCORE Office (Torrington)
23 North Rd.
Torrington, CT 06791
(203)482-6586

Delaware

SCORE Office (Dover)
Treadway Towers
PO Box 576
Dover, DE 19903
(302)678-0892
Fax: (302)678-0189

SCORE Office (Lewes)
PO Box 1
Lewes, DE 19958
(302)645-8073
Fax: (302)645-8412

SCORE Office (Milford)
204 NE Front St.
Milford, DE 19963
(302)422-3301

SCORE Office (Wilmington)
824 Market St., Ste. 610
Wilmington, DE 19801
(302)573-6652
Fax: (302)573-6092
Website: http://www.scoredelaware.com

District of Columbia

SCORE Office (George Mason University)
409 3rd St. SW, 4th Fl.
Washington, DC 20024
800-634-0245

SCORE Office (Washington DC)
1110 Vermont Ave. NW, 9th Fl.

Washington, DC 20043
(202)606-4000
Fax: (202)606-4225
E-mail: dcscore@hotmail.com
Website: http://www.scoredc.org/

Florida

SCORE Office (Desota County Chamber of Commerce)
16 South Velucia Ave.
Arcadia, FL 34266
(941)494-4033

SCORE Office (Suncoast/Pinellas)
Airport Business Ctr.
4707 - 140th Ave. N, No. 311
Clearwater, FL 33755
(813)532-6800
Fax: (813)532-6800

SCORE Office (DeLand)
336 N. Woodland Blvd.
DeLand, FL 32720
(904)734-4331
Fax: (904)734-4333

SCORE Office (South Palm Beach)
1050 S. Federal Hwy., Ste. 132
Delray Beach, FL 33483
(561)278-7752
Fax: (561)278-0288

SCORE Office (Ft. Lauderdale)
Federal Bldg., Ste. 123
299 E. Broward Blvd.
Ft. Lauderdale, FL 33301
(954)356-7263
Fax: (954)356-7145

SCORE Office (Southwest Florida)
The Renaissance
8695 College Pky., Ste. 345 & 346
Ft. Myers, FL 33919
(941)489-2935
Fax: (941)489-1170

SCORE Office (Treasure Coast)
Professional Center, Ste. 2
3220 S. US, No. 1
Ft. Pierce, FL 34982
(561)489-0548

SCORE Office (Gainesville)
101 SE 2nd Pl., Ste. 104
Gainesville, FL 32601
(904)375-8278

SCORE Office (Hialeah Dade Chamber)
59 W. 5th St.
Hialeah, FL 33010

(305)887-1515
Fax: (305)887-2453

SCORE Office (Daytona Beach)
921 Nova Rd., Ste. A
Holly Hills, FL 32117
(904)255-6889
Fax: (904)255-0229
E-mail: score87@dbeach.com

SCORE Office (South Broward)
3475 Sheridian St., Ste. 203
Hollywood, FL 33021
(305)966-8415

SCORE Office (Citrus County)
5 Poplar Ct.
Homosassa, FL 34446
(352)382-1037

SCORE Office (Jacksonville)
7825 Baymeadows Way, Ste. 100-B
Jacksonville, FL 32256
(904)443-1911
Fax: (904)443-1980
E-mail: scorejax@juno.com
Website: http://www.scorejax.org/

SCORE Office (Jacksonville Satellite)
3 Independent Dr.
Jacksonville, FL 32256
(904)366-6600
Fax: (904)632-0617

SCORE Office (Central Florida)
5410 S. Florida Ave., No. 3
Lakeland, FL 33801
(941)687-5783
Fax: (941)687-6225

SCORE Office (Lakeland)
100 Lake Morton Dr.
Lakeland, FL 33801
(941)686-2168

SCORE Office (St. Petersburg)
800 W. Bay Dr., Ste. 505
Largo, FL 33712
(813)585-4571

SCORE Office (Leesburg)
9501 US Hwy. 441
Leesburg, FL 34788-8751
(352)365-3556
Fax: (352)365-3501

SCORE Office (Cocoa)
1600 Farno Rd., Unit 205
Melbourne, FL 32935
(407)254-2288

SCORE Office (Melbourne)
Melbourne Professional Complex
1600 Sarno, Ste. 205
Melbourne, FL 32935
(407)254-2288
Fax: (407)245-2288

SCORE Office (Merritt Island)
1600 Sarno Rd., Ste. 205
Melbourne, FL 32935
(407)254-2288
Fax: (407)254-2288

SCORE Office (Space Coast)
Melbourn Professional Complex
1600 Sarno, Ste. 205
Melbourne, FL 32935
(407)254-2288
Fax: (407)254-2288

SCORE Office (Dade)
49 NW 5th St.
Miami, FL 33128
(305)371-6889
Fax: (305)374-1882
E-mail: score@netrox.net
Website: http://www.netrox.net/~score/

SCORE Office (Naples of Collier)
International College
2654 Tamiami Trl. E
Naples, FL 34112
(941)417-1280
Fax: (941)417-1281
E-mail: score@naples.net
Website: http://www.naples.net/clubs/
score/index.htm

SCORE Office (Pasco County)
6014 US Hwy. 19, Ste. 302
New Port Richey, FL 34652
(813)842-4638

SCORE Office (Southeast Volusia)
115 Canal St.
New Smyrna Beach, FL 32168
(904)428-2449
Fax: (904)423-3512

SCORE Office (Ocala)
110 E. Silver Springs Blvd.
Ocala, FL 34470
(352)629-5959

Clay County SCORE Office
Clay County Chamber of Commerce
1734 Kingsdey Ave.
PO Box 1441
Orange Park, FL 32073
(904)264-2651
Fax: (904)269-0363

SCORE Office (Orlando)
80 N. Hughey Ave.
Rm. 445 Federal Bldg.
Orlando, FL 32801
(407)648-6476
Fax: (407)648-6425

SCORE Office (Emerald Coast)
19 W. Garden St., No. 325
Pensacola, FL 32501
(904)444-2060
Fax: (904)444-2070

SCORE Office (Charlotte County)
201 W. Marion Ave., Ste. 211
Punta Gorda, FL 33950
(941)575-1818
E-mail: score@gls3c.com
Website: http://www.charlotte-
florida.com/business/scorepg01.htm

SCORE Office (St. Augustine)
1 Riberia St.
St. Augustine, FL 32084
(904)829-5681
Fax: (904)829-6477

SCORE Office (Bradenton)
2801 Fruitville, Ste. 280
Sarasota, FL 34237
(813)955-1029

SCORE Office (Manasota)
2801 Fruitville Rd., Ste. 280
Sarasota, FL 34237
(941)955-1029
Fax: (941)955-5581
E-mail: score116@gte.net
Website: http://www.score-suncoast.org/

SCORE Office (Tallahassee)
200 W. Park Ave.
Tallahassee, FL 32302
(850)487-2665

SCORE Office (Hillsborough)
4732 Dale Mabry Hwy. N, Ste. 400
Tampa, FL 33614-6509
(813)870-0125

SCORE Office (Lake Sumter)
122 E. Main St.
Tavares, FL 32778-3810
(352)365-3556

SCORE Office (Titusville)
2000 S. Washington Ave.
Titusville, FL 32780
(407)267-3036
Fax: (407)264-0127

SCORE Office (Venice)
257 N. Tamiami Trl.
Venice, FL 34285
(941)488-2236
Fax: (941)484-5903

SCORE Office (Palm Beach)
500 Australian Ave. S, Ste. 100
West Palm Beach, FL 33401
(561)833-1672
Fax: (561)833-1712

SCORE Office (Wildwood)
103 N. Webster St.
Wildwood, FL 34785

Georgia

SCORE Office (Atlanta)
Harris Tower, Suite 1900
233 Peachtree Rd., NE
Atlanta, GA 30309
(404)347-2442
Fax: (404)347-1227

SCORE Office (Augusta)
3126 Oxford Rd.
Augusta, GA 30909
(706)869-9100

SCORE Office (Columbus)
School Bldg.
PO Box 40
Columbus, GA 31901
(706)327-3654

SCORE Office (Dalton-Whitfield)
305 S. Thorton Ave.
Dalton, GA 30720
(706)279-3383

SCORE Office (Gainesville)
PO Box 374
Gainesville, GA 30503
(770)532-6206
Fax: (770)535-8419

SCORE Office (Macon)
711 Grand Bldg.
Macon, GA 31201
(912)751-6160

SCORE Office (Brunswick)
4 Glen Ave.
St. Simons Island, GA 31520
(912)265-0620
Fax: (912)265-0629

SCORE Office (Savannah)
111 E. Liberty St., Ste. 103
Savannah, GA 31401
(912)652-4335

Fax: (912)652-4184
E-mail: info@scoresav.org
Website: http://www.coastalempire.com/
score/index.htm

Guam

SCORE Office (Guam)
Pacific News Bldg., Rm. 103
238 Archbishop Flores St.
Agana, GU 96910-5100
(671)472-7308

Hawaii

SCORE Office (Hawaii, Inc.)
1111 Bishop St., Ste. 204
PO Box 50207
Honolulu, HI 96813
(808)522-8132
Fax: (808)522-8135
E-mail: hnlscore@juno.com

SCORE Office (Kahului)
250 Alamaha, Unit N16A
Kahului, HI 96732
(808)871-7711

SCORE Office (Maui, Inc.)
590 E. Lipoa Pkwy., Ste. 227
Kihei, HI 96753
(808)875-2380

Idaho

SCORE Office (Treasure Valley)
1020 Main St., No. 290
Boise, ID 83702
(208)334-1696
Fax: (208)334-9353

SCORE Office (Eastern Idaho)
2300 N. Yellowstone, Ste. 119
Idaho Falls, ID 83401
(208)523-1022
Fax: (208)528-7127

Illinois

SCORE Office (Fox Valley)
40 W. Downer Pl.
PO Box 277
Aurora, IL 60506
(630)897-9214
Fax: (630)897-7002

SCORE Office (Greater Belvidere)
419 S. State St.
Belvidere, IL 61008
(815)544-4357
Fax: (815)547-7654

SCORE Office (Bensenville)
1050 Busse Hwy. Suite 100
Bensenville, IL 60106
(708)350-2944
Fax: (708)350-2979

SCORE Office (Central Illinois)
402 N. Hershey Rd.
Bloomington, IL 61704
(309)644-0549
Fax: (309)663-8270
E-mail: webmaster@central-illinois-
score.org
Website: http://www.central-illinois-
score.org/

SCORE Office (Southern Illinois)
150 E. Pleasant Hill Rd.
Box 1
Carbondale, IL 62901
(618)453-6654
Fax: (618)453-5040

SCORE Office (Chicago)
Northwest Atrium Ctr.
500 W. Madison St., No. 1250
Chicago, IL 60661
(312)353-7724
Fax: (312)886-5688
Website: http://www.mcs.net/~bic/

SCORE Office (Chicago–Oliver Harvey College)
Pullman Bldg.
1000 E. 11th St., 7th Fl.
Chicago, IL 60628
Fax: (312)468-8086

SCORE Office (Danville)
28 W. N. Street
Danville, IL 61832
(217)442-7232
Fax: (217)442-6228

SCORE Office (Decatur)
Milliken University
1184 W. Main St.
Decatur, IL 62522
(217)424-6297
Fax: (217)424-3993
E-mail: charding@mail.millikin.edu
Website: http://www.millikin.edu/
academics/Tabor/score.html

SCORE Office (Downers Grove)
925 Curtis
Downers Grove, IL 60515
(708)968-4050
Fax: (708)968-8368

SCORE Office (Elgin)
24 E. Chicago, 3rd Fl.
PO Box 648
Elgin, IL 60120
(847)741-5660
Fax: (847)741-5677

SCORE Office (Freeport Area)
26 S. Galena Ave.
Freeport, IL 61032
(815)233-1350
Fax: (815)235-4038

SCORE Office (Galesburg)
292 E. Simmons St.
PO Box 749
Galesburg, IL 61401
(309)343-1194
Fax: (309)343-1195

SCORE Office (Glen Ellyn)
500 Pennsylvania
Glen Ellyn, IL 60137
(708)469-0907
Fax: (708)469-0426

SCORE Office (Greater Alton)
Alden Hall
5800 Godfrey Rd.
Godfrey, IL 62035-2466
(618)467-2280
Fax: (618)466-8289
Website: http://www.altonweb.com/
score/

SCORE Office (Grayslake)
19351 W. Washington St.
Grayslake, IL 60030
(708)223-3633
Fax: (708)223-9371

SCORE Office (Harrisburg)
303 S. Commercial
Harrisburg, IL 62946-1528
(618)252-8528
Fax: (618)252-0210

SCORE Office (Joliet)
100 N. Chicago
Joliet, IL 60432
(815)727-5371
Fax: (815)727-5374

SCORE Office (Kankakee)
101 S. Schuyler Ave.
Kankakee, IL 60901
(815)933-0376
Fax: (815)933-0380

SCORE Office (Macomb)
216 Seal Hall, Rm. 214

Macomb, IL 61455
(309)298-1128
Fax: (309)298-2520

SCORE Office (Matteson)
210 Lincoln Mall
Matteson, IL 60443
(708)709-3750
Fax: (708)503-9322

SCORE Office (Mattoon)
1701 Wabash Ave.
Mattoon, IL 61938
(217)235-5661
Fax: (217)234-6544

SCORE Office (Quad Cities)
622 19th St.
Moline, IL 61265
(309)797-0082
Fax: (309)757-5435
E-mail: score@qconline.com
Website: http://www.qconline.com/
business/score/

SCORE Office (Naperville)
131 W. Jefferson Ave.
Naperville, IL 60540
(708)355-4141
Fax: (708)355-8355

SCORE Office (Northbrook)
2002 Walters Ave.
Northbrook, IL 60062
(847)498-5555
Fax: (847)498-5510

SCORE Office (Palos Hills)
10900 S. 88th Ave.
Palos Hills, IL 60465
(847)974-5468
Fax: (847)974-0078

SCORE Office (Peoria)
124 SW Adams, Ste. 300
Peoria, IL 61602
(309)676-0755
Fax: (309)676-7534

SCORE Office (Prospect Heights)
1375 Wolf Rd.
Prospect Heights, IL 60070
(847)537-8660
Fax: (847)537-7138

SCORE Office (Quincy Tri-State)
300 Civic Center Plz., Ste. 245
Quincy, IL 62301
(217)222-8093
Fax: (217)222-3033

SCORE Office (River Grove)
2000 5th Ave.
River Grove, IL 60171
(708)456-0300
Fax: (708)583-3121

SCORE Office (Northern Illinois)
515 N. Court St.
Rockford, IL 61103
(815)962-0122
Fax: (815)962-0122

SCORE Office (St. Charles)
103 N. 1st Ave.
St. Charles, IL 60174-1982
(847)584-8384
Fax: (847)584-6065

SCORE Office (Springfield)
511 W. Capitol Ave., Ste. 302
Springfield, IL 62704
(217)492-4416
Fax: (217)492-4867

SCORE Office (Sycamore)
112 Somunak St.
Sycamore, IL 60178
(815)895-3456
Fax: (815)895-0125

SCORE Office (University)
Hwy. 50 & Stuenkel Rd. Ste. C3305
University Park, IL 60466
(708)534-5000
Fax: (708)534-8457

Indiana

SCORE Office (Anderson)
205 W. 11th St.
Anderson, IN 46015
(317)642-0264

SCORE Office (Bloomington)
Star Center
216 W. Allen
Bloomington, IN 47403
(812)335-7334
E-mail: wtfische@indiana.edu
Website: http://www.brainfreezemedia.
com/score527/

SCORE Office (South East Indiana)
500 Franklin St.
Box 29
Columbus, IN 47201
(812)379-4457

SCORE Office (Corydon)
310 N. Elm St.
Corydon, IN 47112

(812)738-2137
Fax: (812)738-6438

SCORE Office (Crown Point)
Old Courthouse Sq. Ste. 206
PO Box 43
Crown Point, IN 46307
(219)663-1800

SCORE Office (Elkhart)
418 S. Main St.
Elkhart, IN 46515
(219)293-1531
Fax: (219)294-1859

SCORE Office (Evansville)
1100 W. Lloyd Expy., Ste. 105
Evansville, IN 47708
(812)426-6144

SCORE Office (Fort Wayne)
1300 S. Harrison St.
Ft. Wayne, IN 46802
(219)422-2601
Fax: (219)422-2601

SCORE Office (Gary)
973 W. 6th Ave., Rm. 326
Gary, IN 46402
(219)882-3918

SCORE Office (Hammond)
7034 Indianapolis Blvd.
Hammond, IN 46324
(219)931-1000
Fax: (219)845-9548

SCORE Office (Indianapolis)
429 N. Pennsylvania St., Ste. 100
Indianapolis, IN 46204-1873
(317)226-7264
Fax: (317)226-7259
E-mail: inscore@indy.net
Website: http://www.score-
indianapolis.org/

SCORE Office (Jasper)
PO Box 307
Jasper, IN 47547-0307
(812)482-6866

**SCORE Office (Kokomo/Howard
Counties)**
106 N. Washington St.
Kokomo, IN 46901
(765)457-5301
Fax: (765)452-4564

SCORE Office (Logansport)
300 E. Broadway, Ste. 103
Logansport, IN 46947
(219)753-6388

SCORE Office (Madison)
301 E. Main St.
Madison, IN 47250
(812)265-3135
Fax: (812)265-2923

SCORE Office (Marengo)
Rt. 1 Box 224D
Marengo, IN 47140
Fax: (812)365-2793

SCORE Office (Marion/Grant Counties)
215 S. Adams
Marion, IN 46952
(765)664-5107

SCORE Office (Merrillville)
255 W. 80th Pl.
Merrillville, IN 46410
(219)769-8180
Fax: (219)736-6223

SCORE Office (Michigan City)
200 E. Michigan Blvd.
Michigan City, IN 46360
(219)874-6221
Fax: (219)873-1204

SCORE Office (South Central Indiana)
4100 Charleston Rd.
New Albany, IN 47150-9538
(812)945-0066

SCORE Office (Rensselaer)
104 W. Washington
Rensselaer, IN 47978

SCORE Office (Salem)
210 N. Main St.
Salem, IN 47167
(812)883-4303
Fax: (812)883-1467

SCORE Office (South Bend)
300 N. Michigan St.
South Bend, IN 46601
(219)282-4350
E-mail: chair@southbend-score.org
Website: http://www.southbend-score.org/

SCORE Office (Valparaiso)
150 Lincolnway
Valparaiso, IN 46383
(219)462-1105
Fax: (219)469-5710

SCORE Office (Vincennes)
27 N. 3rd
PO Box 553
Vincennes, IN 47591
(812)882-6440
Fax: (812)882-6441

SCORE Office (Wabash)
PO Box 371
Wabash, IN 46992
(219)563-1168
Fax: (219)563-6920

Iowa

SCORE Office (Burlington)
Federal Bldg.
300 N. Main St.
Burlington, IA 52601
(319)752-2967

SCORE Office (Cedar Rapids)
2750 1st Ave. NE, Ste 350
Cedar Rapids, IA 52401-1806
(319)362-6405
Fax: (319)362-7861
E:mail: score@scorecr.org
Website: http://www.scorecr.org

SCORE Office (Illowa)
333 4th Ave. S
Clinton, IA 52732
(319)242-5702

SCORE Office (Council Bluffs)
7 N. 6th St.
Council Bluffs, IA 51502
(712)325-1000

SCORE Office (Northeast Iowa)
3404 285th St.
Cresco, IA 52136
(319)547-3377

SCORE Office (Des Moines)
Federal Bldg., Rm. 749
210 Walnut St.
Des Moines, IA 50309-2186
(515)284-4760

SCORE Office (Ft. Dodge)
Federal Bldg., Rm. 436
205 S. 8th St.
Ft. Dodge, IA 50501
(515)955-2622

SCORE Office (Independence)
110 1st. St. east
Independence, IA 50644
(319)334-7178
Fax: (319)334-7179

SCORE Office (Iowa City)
210 Federal Bldg.
PO Box 1853
Iowa City, IA 52240-1853
(319)338-1662

SCORE Office (Keokuk)
401 Main St.
Pierce Bldg., No. 1
Keokuk, IA 52632
(319)524-5055

SCORE Office (Central Iowa)
Fisher Community College
709 S. Center
Marshalltown, IA 50158
(515)753-6645

SCORE Office (River City)
15 West State St.
Mason City, IA 50401
(515)423-5724

SCORE Office (South Central)
SBDC, Indian Hills Community College
525 Grandview Ave.
Ottumwa, IA 52501
(515)683-5127
Fax: (515)683-5263

SCORE Office (Dubuque)
10250 Sundown Rd.
Peosta, IA 52068
(319)556-5110

SCORE Office (Southwest Iowa)
614 W. Sheridan
Shenandoah, IA 51601
(712)246-3260

SCORE Office (Sioux City)
Federal Bldg.
320 6th St.
Sioux City, IA 51101
(712)277-2324
Fax: (712)277-2325

SCORE Office (Iowa Lakes)
122 W. 5th St.
Spencer, IA 51301
(712)262-3059

SCORE Office (Vista)
119 W. 6th St.
Storm Lake, IA 50588
(712)732-3780

SCORE Office (Waterloo)
215 E. 4th
Waterloo, IA 50703
(319)233-8431

Kansas

SCORE Office (Southwest Kansas)
501 W. Spruce
Dodge City, KS 67801
(316)227-3119

SCORE Office (Emporia)
811 Homewood
Emporia, KS 66801
(316)342-1600

SCORE Office (Golden Belt)
1307 Williams
Great Bend, KS 67530
(316)792-2401

SCORE Office (Hays)
PO Box 400
Hays, KS 67601
(913)625-6595

SCORE Office (Hutchinson)
1 E. 9th St.
Hutchinson, KS 67501
(316)665-8468
Fax: (316)665-7619

SCORE Office (Southeast Kansas)
404 Westminster Pl.
PO Box 886
Independence, KS 67301
(316)331-4741

SCORE Office (McPherson)
306 N. Main
PO Box 616
McPherson, KS 67460
(316)241-3303

SCORE Office (Salina)
120 Ash St.
Salina, KS 67401
(785)243-4290
Fax: (785)243-1833

SCORE Office (Topeka)
1700 College
Topeka, KS 66621
(785)231-1010

SCORE Office (Wichita)
100 E. English, Ste. 510
Wichita, KS 67202
(316)269-6273
Fax: (316)269-6499

SCORE Office (Ark Valley)
205 E. 9th St.
Winfield, KS 67156
(316)221-1617

Kentucky

SCORE Office (Ashland)
PO Box 830
Ashland, KY 41105
(606)329-8011
Fax: (606)325-4607

SCORE Office (Bowling Green)
812 State St.
PO Box 51
Bowling Green, KY 42101
(502)781-3200
Fax: (502)843-0458

SCORE Office (Tri-Lakes)
508 Barbee Way
Danville, KY 40422-1548
(606)231-9902

SCORE Office (Glasgow)
301 W. Main St.
Glasgow, KY 42141
(502)651-3161
Fax: (502)651-3122

SCORE Office (Hazard)
B & I Technical Center
100 Airport Gardens Rd.
Hazard, KY 41701
(606)439-5856
Fax: (606)439-1808

SCORE Office (Lexington)
410 W. Vine St., Ste. 290, Civic C
Lexington, KY 40507
(606)231-9902
Fax: (606)253-3190
E-mail: scorelex@uky.campus.mci.net

SCORE Office (Louisville)
188 Federal Office Bldg.
600 Dr. Martin L. King Jr. Pl.
Louisville, KY 40202
(502)582-5976

SCORE Office (Madisonville)
257 N. Main
Madisonville, KY 42431
(502)825-1399
Fax: (502)825-1396

SCORE Office (Paducah)
Federal Office Bldg.
501 Broadway, Rm. B-36
Paducah, KY 42001
(502)442-5685

Louisiana

SCORE Office (Central Louisiana)
802 3rd St.
Alexandria, LA 71309
(318)442-6671

SCORE Office (Baton Rouge)
564 Laurel St.
PO Box 3217
Baton Rouge, LA 70801

(504)381-7130
Fax: (504)336-4306

SCORE Office (North Shore)
2 W. Thomas
Hammond, LA 70401
(504)345-4457
Fax: (504)345-4749

SCORE Office (Lafayette)
804 St. Mary Blvd.
Lafayette, LA 70505-1307
(318)233-2705
Fax: (318)234-8671
E-mail: score302@aol.com

SCORE Office (Lake Charles)
120 W. Pujo St.
Lake Charles, LA 70601
(318)433-3632

SCORE Office (New Orleans)
365 Canal St., Ste. 3100
New Orleans, LA 70130
(504)589-2356
Fax: (504)589-2339

SCORE Office (Shreveport)
400 Edwards St.
Shreveport, LA 71101
(318)677-2536
Fax: (318)677-2541

Maine

SCORE Office (Augusta)
40 Western Ave.
Augusta, ME 04330
(207)622-8509

SCORE Office (Bangor)
Peabody Hall, Rm. 229
One College Cir.
Bangor, ME 04401
(207)941-9707

SCORE Office (Central & Northern Arroostock)
111 High St.
Caribou, ME 04736
(207)492-8010
Fax: (207)492-8010

SCORE Office (Penquis)
South St.
Dover Foxcroft, ME 04426
(207)564-7021

SCORE Office (Maine Coastal)
Mill Mall
Box 1105
Ellsworth, ME 04605-1105

(207)667-5800
E-mail: score@arcadia.net

SCORE Office (Lewiston-Auburn)
BIC of Maine-Bates Mill Complex
35 Canal St.
Lewiston, ME 04240-7764
(207)782-3708
Fax: (207)783-7745

SCORE Office (Portland)
66 Pearl St., Rm. 210
Portland, ME 04101
(207)772-1147
Fax: (207)772-5581
E-mail: Score53@score.maine.org
Website: http://www.score.maine.org/
chapter53/

SCORE Office (Western Mountains)
255 River St.
PO Box 252
Rumford, ME 04257-0252
(207)369-9976

SCORE Office (Oxford Hills)
166 Main St.
South Paris, ME 04281
(207)743-0499

Maryland

SCORE Office (Southern Maryland)
2525 Riva Rd., Ste. 110
Annapolis, MD 21401
(410)266-9553
Fax: (410)573-0981
E-mail: score390@aol.com
Website: http://members.aol.com/
score390/index.htm

SCORE Office (Baltimore)
The City Crescent Bldg., 6th Fl.
10 S. Howard St.
Baltimore, MD 21201
(410)962-2233
Fax: (410)962-1805

SCORE Office (Bel Air)
108 S. Bond St.
Bel Air, MD 21014
(410)838-2020
Fax: (410)893-4715

SCORE Office (Bethesda)
7910 Woodmont Ave., Ste. 1204
Bethesda, MD 20814
(301)652-4900
Fax: (301)657-1973

SCORE Office (Bowie)
6670 Race Track Rd.
Bowie, MD 20715
(301)262-0920
Fax: (301)262-0921

SCORE Office (Dorchester County)
203 Sunburst Hwy.
Cambridge, MD 21613
(410)228-3575

SCORE Office (Upper Shore)
210 Marlboro Ave.
Easton, MD 21601
(410)822-4606
Fax: (410)822-7922

SCORE Office (Frederick County)
43A S. Market St.
Frederick, MD 21701
(301)662-8723
Fax: (301)846-4427

SCORE Office (Gaithersburg)
9 Park Ave.
Gaithersburg, MD 20877
(301)840-1400
Fax: (301)963-3918

SCORE Office (Glen Burnie)
103 Crain Hwy. SE
Glen Burnie, MD 21061
(410)766-8282
Fax: (410)766-9722

SCORE Office (Hagerstown)
111 W. Washington St.
Hagerstown, MD 21740
(301)739-2015
Fax: (301)739-1278

SCORE Office (Laurel)
7901 Sandy Spring Rd. Ste. 501
Laurel, MD 20707
(301)725-4000
Fax: (301)725-0776

SCORE Office (Salisbury)
300 E. Main St.
Salisbury, MD 21801
(410)749-0185
Fax: (410)860-9925

Massachusetts

SCORE Office (NE Massachusetts)
100 Cummings Ctr., Ste. 101 K
Beverly, MA 01923
(978)922-9441
Website: http://www1.shore.net/~score/

SCORE Office (Boston)
10 Causeway St., Rm. 265
Boston, MA 02222-1093
(617)565-5591
Fax: (617)565-5598
E-mail: boston-score-20@worldnet.att.net
Website: http://www.scoreboston.org/

SCORE office (Bristol/Plymouth County)
53 N. 6th St., Federal Bldg.
Bristol, MA 02740
(508)994-5093

SCORE Office (SE Massachusetts)
60 School St.
Brockton, MA 02401
(508)587-2673
Fax: (508)587-1340
Website: http://www.metrosouth
chamber.com/score.html

SCORE Office (North Adams)
820 N. State Rd.
Cheshire, MA 01225
(413)743-5100

SCORE Office (Clinton Satellite)
1 Green St.
Clinton, MA 01510
Fax: (508)368-7689

SCORE Office (Greenfield)
PO Box 898
Greenfield, MA 01302
(413)773-5463
Fax: (413)773-7008

SCORE Office (Haverhill)
87 Winter St.
Haverhill, MA 01830
(508)373-5663
Fax: (508)373-8060

SCORE Office (Hudson Satellite)
PO Box 578
Hudson, MA 01749
(508)568-0360
Fax: (508)568-0360

SCORE Office (Cape Cod)
Independence Pk., Ste. 5B
270 Communications Way
Hyannis, MA 02601
(508)775-4884
Fax: (508)790-2540

SCORE Office (Lawrence)
264 Essex St.
Lawrence, MA 01840
(508)686-0900
Fax: (508)794-9953

SCORE Office (Leominster Satellite)
110 Erdman Way
Leominster, MA 01453
(508)840-4300
Fax: (508)840-4896

SCORE Office (Bristol/Plymouth Counties)
53 N. 6th St., Federal Bldg.
New Bedford, MA 02740
(508)994-5093

SCORE Office (Newburyport)
29 State St.
Newburyport, MA 01950
(617)462-6680

SCORE Office (Pittsfield)
66 West St.
Pittsfield, MA 01201
(413)499-2485

SCORE Office (Haverhill-Salem)
32 Derby Sq.
Salem, MA 01970
(508)745-0330
Fax: (508)745-3855

SCORE Office (Springfield)
1350 Main St.
Federal Bldg.
Springfield, MA 01103
(413)785-0314

SCORE Office (Carver)
12 Taunton Green, Ste. 201
Taunton, MA 02780
(508)824-4068
Fax: (508)824-4069

SCORE Office (Worcester)
33 Waldo St.
Worcester, MA 01608
(508)753-2929
Fax: (508)754-8560

Michigan

SCORE Office (Allegan)
PO Box 338
Allegan, MI 49010
(616)673-2479

SCORE Office (Ann Arbor)
425 S. Main St., Ste. 103
Ann Arbor, MI 48104
(313)665-4433

SCORE Office (Battle Creek)
34 W. Jackson Ste. 4A
Battle Creek, MI 49017-3505

(616)962-4076
Fax: (616)962-6309

SCORE Office (Cadillac)
222 Lake St.
Cadillac, MI 49601
(616)775-9776
Fax: (616)768-4255

SCORE Office (Detroit)
477 Michigan Ave., Rm. 515
Detroit, MI 48226
(313)226-7947
Fax: (313)226-3448

SCORE Office (Flint)
708 Root Rd., Rm. 308
Flint, MI 48503
(810)233-6846

SCORE Office (Grand Rapids)
111 Pearl St. NW
Grand Rapids, MI 49503-2831
(616)771-0305
Fax: (616)771-0328
E-mail: scoreone@iserv.net
Website: http://www.iserv.net/
~scoreone/

SCORE Office (Holland)
480 State St.
Holland, MI 49423
(616)396-9472

SCORE Office (Jackson)
209 East Washington
PO Box 80
Jackson, MI 49204
(517)782-8221
Fax: (517)782-0061

SCORE Office (Kalamazoo)
345 W. Michigan Ave.
Kalamazoo, MI 49007
(616)381-5382
Fax: (616)384-0096
E-mail: score@nucleus.net

SCORE Office (Lansing)
117 E. Allegan
PO Box 14030
Lansing, MI 48901
(517)487-6340
Fax: (517)484-6910

SCORE Office (Livonia)
15401 Farmington Rd.
Livonia, MI 48154
(313)427-2122
Fax: (313)427-6055

SCORE Office (Madison Heights)
26345 John R
Madison Heights, MI 48071
(810)542-5010
Fax: (810)542-6821

SCORE Office (Monroe)
111 E. 1st
Monroe, MI 48161
(313)242-3366
Fax: (313)242-7253

SCORE Office (Mt. Clemens)
58 S/B Gratiot
Mt. Clemens, MI 48043
(810)463-1528
Fax: (810)463-6541

SCORE Office (Muskegon)
PO Box 1087
230 Terrace Plz.
Muskegon, MI 49443
(616)722-3751
Fax: (616)728-7251

SCORE Office (Petoskey)
401 E. Mitchell St.
Petoskey, MI 49770
(616)347-4150

SCORE Office (Pontiac)
Executive Office Bldg.
1200 N. Telegraph Rd.
Pontiac, MI 48341
(810)975-9555

SCORE Office (Pontiac)
PO Box 430025
Pontiac, MI 48343
(810)335-9600

SCORE Office (Port Huron)
920 Pinegrove Ave.
Port Huron, MI 48060
(810)985-7101

SCORE Office (Rochester)
71 Walnut Ste. 110
Rochester, MI 48307
(810)651-6700
Fax: (810)651-5270

SCORE Office (Saginaw)
901 S. Washington Ave.
Saginaw, MI 48601
(517)752-7161
Fax: (517)752-9055

SCORE Office (Upper Peninsula)
2581 I-75 Business Spur
Sault Ste. Marie, MI 49783
(906)632-3301

SCORE Office (Southfield)
21000 W. 10 Mile Rd.
Southfield, MI 48075
(810)204-3050
Fax: (810)204-3099

SCORE Office (Traverse City)
202 E. Grandview Pkwy.
PO Box 387
Traverse City, MI 49685
(616)947-5075
Fax: (616)946-2565

SCORE Office (Warren)
30500 Van Dyke, Ste. 118
Warren, MI 48093
(810)751-3939

Minnesota

SCORE Office (Aitkin)
Aitkin, MN 56431
(218)741-3906

SCORE Office (Albert Lea)
202 N. Broadway Ave.
Albert Lea, MN 56007
(507)373-7487

SCORE Office (Austin)
PO Box 864
Austin, MN 55912
(507)437-4561
Fax: (507)437-4869

SCORE Office (South Metro)
Ames Business Ctr.
2500 W. County Rd., No. 42
Burnsville, MN 55337
(612)898-5645
Fax: (612)435-6972
E-mail: southmetro@scoreminn.org
Website: http://www.scoreminn.org/
southmetro/

SCORE Office (Duluth)
1717 Minnesota Ave.
Duluth, MN 55802
(218)727-8286
Fax: (218)727-3113
E-mail: duluth@scoreminn.org
Website: http://www.scoreminn.org

SCORE Office (Fairmont)
PO Box 826
Fairmont, MN 56031
(507)235-5547
Fax: (507)235-8411

SCORE Office (Southwest Minnesota)
112 Riverfront St.

Box 999
Mankato, MN 56001
(507)345-4519
Fax: (507)345-4451
Website: http://www.scoreminn.org/

SCORE Office (Minneapolis)
North Plaza Bldg., Ste. 51
5217 Wayzata Blvd.
Minneapolis, MN 55416
(612)591-0539
Fax: (612)544-0436
Website: http://www.scoreminn.org/

SCORE Office (Owatonna)
PO Box 331
Owatonna, MN 55060
(507)451-7970
Fax: (507)451-7972

SCORE Office (Red Wing)
2000 W. Main St., Ste. 324
Red Wing, MN 55066
(612)388-4079

SCORE Office (Southeastern Minnesota)
220 S. Broadway, Ste. 100
Rochester, MN 55901
(507)288-1122
Fax: (507)282-8960
Website: http://www.scoreminn.org/

SCORE Office (Brainerd)
St. Cloud, MN 56301

SCORE Office (Central Area)
1527 Northway Dr.
St. Cloud, MN 56301
(320)240-1332
Fax: (320)255-9050
Website: http://www.scoreminn.org/

SCORE Office (St. Paul)
350 St. Peter St., No. 295
Lowry Professional Bldg.
St. Paul, MN 55102
(651)223-5010
Fax: (651)223-5048
Website: http://www.scoreminn.org/

SCORE Office (Winona)
Box 870
Winona, MN 55987
(507)452-2272
Fax: (507)454-8814

SCORE Office (Worthington)
1121 3rd Ave.
Worthington, MN 56187
(507)372-2919
Fax: (507)372-2827

Mississippi

SCORE Office (Delta)
915 Washington Ave.
PO Box 933
Greenville, MS 38701
(601)378-3141

SCORE Office (Gulfcoast)
1 Government Plaza
2909 13th St., Ste. 203
Gulfport, MS 39501
(228)863-0054

SCORE Office (Jackson)
1st Jackson Center, Ste. 400
101 W. Capitol St.
Jackson, MS 39201
(601)965-5533

SCORE Office (Meridian)
5220 16th Ave.
Meridian, MS 39305
(601)482-4412

Missouri

SCORE Office (Lake of the Ozark)
University Extension
113 Kansas St.
PO Box 1405
Camdenton, MO 65020
(573)346-2644
Fax: (573)346-2694
E-mail: score@cdoc.net
Website: http://sites.cdoc.net/score/

Chamber of Commerce (Cape Girardeau)
PO Box 98
Cape Girardeau, MO 63702-0098
(314)335-3312

SCORE Office (Mid-Missouri)
1705 Halstead Ct.
Columbia, MO 65203
(573)874-1132

SCORE Office (Ozark-Gateway)
1486 Glassy Rd.
Cuba, MO 65453-1640
(573)885-4954

SCORE Office (Kansas City)
323 W. 8th St., Ste. 104
Kansas City, MO 64105
(816)374-6675
Fax: (816)374-6692
E-mail: SCOREBIC@AOL.COM
Website: http://www.crn.org/score/

SCORE Office (Sedalia)
Lucas Place
323 W. 8th St., Ste.104
Kansas City, MO 64105
(816)374-6675

SCORE office (Tri-Lakes)
PO Box 1148
Kimberling, MO 65686
(417)739-3041

SCORE Office (Tri-Lakes)
HCRI Box 85
Lampe, MO 65681
(417)858-6798

SCORE Office (Mexico)
111 N. Washington St.
Mexico, MO 65265
(314)581-2765

SCORE Office (Southeast Missouri)
Rte. 1, Box 280
Neelyville, MO 63954
(573)989-3577

SCORE office (Poplar Bluff Area)
806 Emma St.
Poplar Bluff, MO 63901
(573)686-8892

SCORE Office (St. Joseph)
3003 Frederick Ave.
St. Joseph, MO 64506
(816)232-4461

SCORE Office (St. Louis)
815 Olive St., Rm. 242
St. Louis, MO 63101-1569
(314)539-6970
Fax: (314)539-3785
E-mail: info@stlscore.org
Website: http://www.stlscore.org/

SCORE Office (Lewis & Clark)
425 Spencer Rd.
St. Peters, MO 63376
(314)928-2900
Fax: (314)928-2900
E-mail: score01@mail.win.org

SCORE Office (Springfield)
620 S. Glenstone, Ste. 110
Springfield, MO 65802-3200
(417)864-7670
Fax: (417)864-4108

SCORE office (Southeast Kansas)
1206 W. First St.
Webb City, MO 64870
(417)673-3984

Montana

SCORE Office (Billings)
815 S. 27th St.
Billings, MT 59101
(406)245-4111

SCORE Office (Bozeman)
1205 E. Main St.
Bozeman, MT 59715
(406)586-5421

SCORE Office (Butte)
1000 George St.
Butte, MT 59701
(406)723-3177

SCORE Office (Great Falls)
710 First Ave. N
Great Falls, MT 59401
(406)761-4434
E-mail: scoregtf@in.tch.com

SCORE Office (Havre, Montana)
518 First St.
Havre, MT 59501
(406)265-4383

SCORE Office (Helena)
Federal Bldg.
301 S. Park
Helena, MT 59626-0054
(406)441-1081

SCORE Office (Kalispell)
2 Main St.
Kalispell, MT 59901
(406)756-5271
Fax: (406)752-6665

SCORE Office (Missoula)
723 Ronan
Missoula, MT 59806
(406)327-8806
E-mail: score@safeshop.com
Website: http://missoula.bigsky.net/
score/

Nebraska

SCORE Office (Columbus)
Columbus, NE 68601
(402)564-2769

SCORE Office (Fremont)
92 W. 5th St.
Fremont, NE 68025
(402)721-2641

SCORE Office (Hastings)
Hastings, NE 68901
(402)463-3447

SCORE Office (Lincoln)
8800 O St.
Lincoln, NE 68520
(402)437-2409

SCORE Office (Panhandle)
150549 CR 30
Minatare, NE 69356
(308)632-2133
Website: http://www.tandt.com/
SCORE

SCORE Office (Norfolk)
3209 S. 48th Ave.
Norfolk, NE 68106
(402)564-2769

SCORE Office (North Platte)
3301 W. 2nd St.
North Platte, NE 69101
(308)532-4466

SCORE Office (Omaha)
11145 Mill Valley Rd.
Omaha, NE 68154
(402)221-3606
Fax: (402)221-3680
E-mail: infoctr@ne.uswest.net
Website: http://www.tandt.com/score/

Nevada

SCORE Office (Incline Village)
969 Tahoe Blvd.
Incline Village, NV 89451
(702)831-7327
Fax: (702)832-1605

SCORE Office (Carson City)
301 E. Stewart
PO Box 7527
Las Vegas, NV 89125
(702)388-6104

SCORE Office (Las Vegas)
300 Las Vegas Blvd. S, Ste. 1100
Las Vegas, NV 89101
(702)388-6104

SCORE Office (Northern Nevada)
SBDC, College of Business
Administration
Univ. of Nevada
Reno, NV 89557-0100
(702)784-4436
Fax: (702)784-4337

New Hampshire

SCORE Office (North Country)
PO Box 34

Berlin, NH 03570
(603)752-1090

SCORE Office (Concord)
143 N. Main St., Rm. 202A
PO Box 1258
Concord, NH 03301
(603)225-1400
Fax: (603)225-1409

SCORE Office (Dover)
299 Central Ave.
Dover, NH 03820
(603)742-2218
Fax: (603)749-6317

SCORE Office (Monadnock)
34 Mechanic St.
Keene, NH 03431-3421
(603)352-0320

SCORE Office (Lakes Region)
67 Water St., Ste. 105
Laconia, NH 03246
(603)524-9168

SCORE Office (Upper Valley)
Citizens Bank Bldg., Rm. 310
20 W. Park St.
Lebanon, NH 03766
(603)448-3491
Fax: (603)448-1908
E-mail: billt@valley.net
Website: http://www.valley.net/~score/

SCORE Office (Merrimack Valley)
275 Chestnut St., Rm. 618
Manchester, NH 03103
(603)666-7561
Fax: (603)666-7925

SCORE Office (Mt. Washington Valley)
PO Box 1066
North Conway, NH 03818
(603)383-0800

SCORE Office (Seacoast)
195 Commerce Way, Unit-A
Portsmouth, NH 03801-3251
(603)433-0575

New Jersey

SCORE Office (Somerset)
Paritan Valley Community College,
Rte. 28
Branchburg, NJ 08807
(908)218-8874
E-mail: nj-score@grizbiz.com.
Website: http://www.nj-score.org/

SCORE Office (Chester)
5 Old Mill Rd.
Chester, NJ 07930
(908)879-7080

**SCORE Office
(Greater Princeton)**
4 A George Washington Dr.
Cranbury, NJ 08512
(609)520-1776

SCORE Office (Freehold)
36 W. Main St.
Freehold, NJ 07728
(908)462-3030
Fax: (908)462-2123

SCORE Office (North West)
Picantinny Innovation Ctr.
3159 Schrader Rd.
Hamburg, NJ 07419
(973)209-8525
Fax: (973)209-7252
E-mail: nj-score@grizbiz.com
Website: http://www.nj-score.org/

SCORE Office (Monmouth)
765 Newman Springs Rd.
Lincroft, NJ 07738
(908)224-2573
E-mail: nj-score@grizbiz.com
Website: http://www.nj-score.org/

SCORE Office (Manalapan)
125 Symmes Dr.
Manalapan, NJ 07726
(908)431-7220

SCORE Office (Jersey City)
2 Gateway Ctr., 4th Fl.
Newark, NJ 07102
(973)645-3982
Fax: (973)645-2375

SCORE Office (Newark)
2 Gateway Center, 15th Fl.
Newark, NJ 07102-5553
(973)645-3982
Fax: (973)645-2375
E-mail: nj-score@grizbiz.com
Website: http://www.nj-score.org

SCORE Office (Bergen County)
327 E. Ridgewood Ave.
Paramus, NJ 07652
(201)599-6090
E-mail: nj-score@grizbiz.com
Website: http://www.nj-score.org/

SCORE Office (Pennsauken)
4900 Rte. 70

Pennsauken, NJ 08109
(609)486-3421

SCORE Office (Southern New Jersey)
4900 Rte. 70
Pennsauken, NJ 08109
(609)486-3421
E-mail: nj-score@grizbiz.com
Website: http://www.nj-score.org/

SCORE Office (Greater Princeton)
216 Rockingham Row
Princeton Forrestal Village
Princeton, NJ 08540
(609)520-1776
Fax: (609)520-9107
E-mail: nj-score@grizbiz.com
Website: http://www.nj-score.org/

SCORE Office (Shrewsbury)
Hwy. 35
Shrewsbury, NJ 07702
(908)842-5995
Fax: (908)219-6140

SCORE Office (Ocean County)
33 Washington St.
Toms River, NJ 08754
(732)505-6033
E-mail: nj-score@grizbiz.com
Website: http://www.nj-score.org/

SCORE Office (Wall)
2700 Allaire Rd.
Wall, NJ 07719
(908)449-8877

SCORE Office (Wayne)
2055 Hamburg Tpke.
Wayne, NJ 07470
(201)831-7788
Fax: (201)831-9112

New Mexico

SCORE Office (Albuquerque)
525 Buena Vista, SE
Albuquerque, NM 87106
(505)272-7999
Fax: (505)272-7963

SCORE Office (Las Cruces)
Loretto Towne Center
505 S. Main St., Ste. 125
Las Cruces, NM 88001
(505)523-5627
Fax: (505)524-2101
E-mail: score.397@zianet.com

SCORE Office (Roswell)
Federal Bldg., Rm. 237

Roswell, NM 88201
(505)625-2112
Fax: (505)623-2545

SCORE Office (Santa Fe)
Montoya Federal Bldg.
120 Federal Place, Rm. 307
Santa Fe, NM 87501
(505)988-6302
Fax: (505)988-6300

New York

SCORE Office (Northeast)
1 Computer Dr. S
Albany, NY 12205
(518)446-1118
Fax: (518)446-1228

SCORE Office (Auburn)
30 South St.
PO Box 675
Auburn, NY 13021
(315)252-7291

SCORE Office (South Tier Binghamton)
Metro Center, 2nd Fl.
49 Court St.
PO Box 995
Binghamton, NY 13902
(607)772-8860

SCORE Office (Queens County City)
12055 Queens Blvd., Rm. 333
Borough Hall, NY 11424
(718)263-8961

SCORE Office (Buffalo)
Federal Bldg., Rm. 1311
111 W. Huron St.
Buffalo, NY 14202
(716)551-4301
Website: http://www2.pcom.net/score/buf45.html

SCORE Office (Canandaigua)
Chamber of Commerce Bldg.
113 S. Main St.
Canandaigua, NY 14424
(716)394-4400
Fax: (716)394-4546

SCORE Office (Chemung)
333 E. Water St., 4th Fl.
Elmira, NY 14901
(607)734-3358

SCORE Office (Geneva)
Chamber of Commerce Bldg.
PO Box 587

Geneva, NY 14456
(315)789-1776
Fax: (315)789-3993

SCORE Office (Glens Falls)
84 Broad St.
Glens Falls, NY 12801
(518)798-8463
Fax: (518)745-1433

SCORE Office (Orange County)
40 Matthews St.
Goshen, NY 10924
(914)294-8080
Fax: (914)294-6121

SCORE Office (Huntington Area)
151 W. Carver St.
Huntington, NY 11743
(516)423-6100

SCORE Office (Tompkins County)
904 E. Shore Dr.
Ithaca, NY 14850
(607)273-7080

SCORE Office (Long Island City)
120-55 Queens Blvd.
Jamaica, NY 11424
(718)263-8961
Fax: (718)263-9032

SCORE Office (Chatauqua)
101 W. 5th St.
Jamestown, NY 14701
(716)484-1103

SCORE Office (Westchester)
2 Caradon Ln.
Katonah, NY 10536
(914)948-3907
Fax: (914)948-4645
E-mail: score@w-w-w.com
Website: http://w-w-w.com/score/

SCORE Office (Queens County)
Queens Borough Hall
120-55 Queens Blvd. Rm. 333
Kew Gardens, NY 11424
(718)263-8961
Fax: (718)263-9032

SCORE Office (Brookhaven)
3233 Rte. 112
Medford, NY 11763
(516)451-6563
Fax: (516)451-6925

SCORE Office (Melville)
35 Pinelawn Rd., Rm. 207-W
Melville, NY 11747
(516)454-0771

SCORE Office (Nassau County)
400 County Seat Dr., No. 140
Mineola, NY 11501
(516)571-3303
E-mail: Counse1998@aol.com
Website: http://members.aol.com/Counse1998/Default.htm

SCORE Office (Mt. Vernon)
4 N. 7th Ave.
Mt. Vernon, NY 10550
(914)667-7500

SCORE Office (New York)
26 Federal Plz., Rm. 3100
New York, NY 10278
(212)264-4507
Fax: (212)264-4963
E-mail: score1000@erols.com
Website: http://users.erols.com/score-nyc/

SCORE Office (Newburgh)
47 Grand St.
Newburgh, NY 12550
(914)562-5100

SCORE Office (Owego)
188 Front St.
Owego, NY 13827
(607)687-2020

SCORE Office (Peekskill)
1 S. Division St.
Peekskill, NY 10566
(914)737-3600
Fax: (914)737-0541

SCORE Office (Penn Yan)
2375 Rte. 14A
Penn Yan, NY 14527
(315)536-3111

SCORE Office (Dutchess)
110 Main St.
Poughkeepsie, NY 12601
(914)454-1700

SCORE Office (Rochester)
601 Keating Federal Bldg., Rm. 410
100 State St.
Rochester, NY 14614
(716)263-6473
Fax: (716)263-3146
Website: http://www.ggw.org/score/

SCORE Office (Saranac Lake)
30 Main St.
Saranac Lake, NY 12983
(315)448-0415

SCORE Office (Suffolk)
286 Main St.
Setauket, NY 11733
(516)751-3886

SCORE Office (Staten Island)
130 Bay St.
Staten Island, NY 10301
(718)727-1221

SCORE Office (Ulster)
Clinton Bldg., Rm. 107
Stone Ridge, NY 12484
(914)687-5035
Fax: (914)687-5015
Website: http://www.scoreulster.org/

SCORE Office (Syracuse)
401 S. Salina, 5th Fl.
Syracuse, NY 13202
(315)471-9393

SCORE Office (Utica)
SUNY Institute of Technology, Route 12
Utica, NY 13504-3050
(315)792-7553

SCORE Office (Watertown)
518 Davidson St.
Watertown, NY 13601
(315)788-1200
Fax: (315)788-8251

North Carolina

SCORE office (Asheboro)
317 E. Dixie Dr.
Asheboro, NC 27203
(336)626-2626
Fax: (336)626-7077

SCORE Office (Asheville)
Federal Bldg., Rm. 259
151 Patton
Asheville, NC 28801-5770
(828)271-4786
Fax: (828)271-4009

SCORE Office (Chapel Hill)
104 S. Estes Dr.
PO Box 2897
Chapel Hill, NC 27514
(919)967-7075

SCORE Office (Coastal Plains)
PO Box 2897
Chapel Hill, NC 27515
(919)967-7075
Fax: (919)968-6874

SCORE Office (Charlotte)
200 N. College St., Ste. A-2015

Charlotte, NC 28202
(704)344-6576
Fax: (704)344-6769
E-mail: CharlotteSCORE47@AOL.com
Website: http://www.charweb.org/
business/score/

SCORE Office (Durham)
411 W. Chapel Hill St.
Durham, NC 27707
(919)541-2171

SCORE Office (Gastonia)
PO Box 2168
Gastonia, NC 28053
(704)864-2621
Fax: (704)854-8723

SCORE Office (Greensboro)
400 W. Market St., Ste. 103
Greensboro, NC 27401-2241
(910)333-5399

SCORE Office (Henderson)
PO Box 917
Henderson, NC 27536
(919)492-2061
Fax: (919)430-0460

SCORE Office (Hendersonville)
Federal Bldg., Rm. 108
W. 4th Ave. & Church St.
Hendersonville, NC 28792
(828)693-8702
E-mail: score@circle.net
Website: http://www.wncguide.com/
score/Welcome.html

SCORE Office (Unifour)
PO Box 1828
Hickory, NC 28603
(704)328-6111

SCORE Office (High Point)
1101 N. Main St.
High Point, NC 27262
(336)882-8625
Fax: (336)889-9499

SCORE Office (Outer Banks)
Collington Rd. and Mustain
Kill Devil Hills, NC 27948
(252)441-8144

SCORE Office (Down East)
312 S. Front St., Ste. 6
New Bern, NC 28560
(252)633-6688
Fax: (252)633-9608

SCORE Office (Kinston)
PO Box 95

New Bern, NC 28561
(919)633-6688

SCORE Office (Raleigh)
Century Post Office Bldg., Ste. 306
300 Federal St. Mall
Raleigh, NC 27601
(919)856-4739
E-mail: jendres@ibm.net
Website: http://www.intrex.net/score96/
score96.htm

SCORE Office (Sanford)
1801 Nash St.
Sanford, NC 27330
(919)774-6442
Fax: (919)776-8739

SCORE Office (Sandhills Area)
1480 Hwy. 15-501
PO Box 458
Southern Pines, NC 28387
(910)692-3926

SCORE Office (Wilmington)
Corps of Engineers Bldg.
96 Darlington Ave., Ste. 207
Wilmington, NC 28403
(910)815-4576
Fax: (910)815-4658

North Dakota

**SCORE Office
(Bismarck-Mandan)**
700 E. Main Ave., 2nd Fl.
PO Box 5509
Bismarck, ND 58506-5509
(701)250-4303

SCORE Office (Fargo)
657 2nd Ave., Rm. 225
Fargo, ND 58108-3083
(701)239-5677

SCORE Office (Upper Red River)
4275 Technology Dr., Rm. 156
Grand Forks, ND 58202-8372
(701)777-3051

SCORE Office (Minot)
100 1st St. SW
Minot, ND 58701-3846
(701)852-6883
Fax: (701)852-6905

Ohio

SCORE Office (Akron)
1 Cascade Plz., 7th Fl.
Akron, OH 44308

(330)379-3163
Fax: (330)379-3164

SCORE Office (Ashland)
Gill Center
47 W. Main St.
Ashland, OH 44805
(419)281-4584

SCORE Office (Canton)
116 Cleveland Ave. NW, Ste. 601
Canton, OH 44702-1720
(330)453-6047

SCORE Office (Chillicothe)
165 S. Paint St.
Chillicothe, OH 45601
(614)772-4530

SCORE Office (Cincinnati)
Ameritrust Bldg., Rm. 850
525 Vine St.
Cincinnati, OH 45202
(513)684-2812
Fax: (513)684-3251
Website: http://www.score.
chapter34.org/

SCORE Office (Cleveland)
Eaton Center, Ste. 620
1100 Superior Ave.
Cleveland, OH 44114-2507
(216)522-4194
Fax: (216)522-4844

SCORE Office (Columbus)
2 Nationwide Plz., Ste. 1400
Columbus, OH 43215-2542
(614)469-2357
Fax: (614)469-2391
E-mail: info@scorecolumbus.org
Website: http://www.scorecolumbus.org/

SCORE Office (Dayton)
Dayton Federal Bldg., Rm. 505
200 W. Second St.
Dayton, OH 45402-1430
(513)225-2887
Fax: (513)225-7667

SCORE Office (Defiance)
615 W. 3rd St.
PO Box 130
Defiance, OH 43512
(419)782-7946

SCORE Office (Findlay)
123 E. Main Cross St.
PO Box 923
Findlay, OH 45840
(419)422-3314

SCORE Office (Lima)
147 N. Main St.
Lima, OH 45801
(419)222-6045
Fax: (419)229-0266

SCORE Office (Mansfield)
55 N. Mulberry St.
Mansfield, OH 44902
(419)522-3211

SCORE Office (Marietta)
Thomas Hall
Marietta, OH 45750
(614)373-0268

SCORE Office (Medina)
County Administrative Bldg.
144 N. Broadway
Medina, OH 44256
(216)764-8650

SCORE Office (Licking County)
50 W. Locust St.
Newark, OH 43055
(614)345-7458

SCORE Office (Salem)
2491 State Rte. 45 S
Salem, OH 44460
(216)332-0361

SCORE Office (Tiffin)
62 S. Washington St.
Tiffin, OH 44883
(419)447-4141
Fax: (419)447-5141

SCORE Office (Toledo)
608 Madison Ave, Ste. 910
Toledo, OH 43624
(419)259-7598
Fax: (419)259-6460

SCORE Office (Heart of Ohio)
377 W. Liberty St.
Wooster, OH 44691
(330)262-5735
Fax: (330)262-5745

SCORE Office (Youngstown)
306 Williamson Hall
Youngstown, OH 44555
(330)746-2687

Oklahoma

SCORE Office (Anadarko)
PO Box 366
Anadarko, OK 73005
(405)247-6651

SCORE Office (Ardmore)
410 W. Main
Ardmore, OK 73401
(580)226-2620

SCORE Office (Northeast Oklahoma)
210 S. Main
Grove, OK 74344
(918)787-2796
Fax: (918)787-2796
E-mail: Score595@greencis.net

SCORE Office (Lawton)
4500 W. Lee Blvd., Bldg. 100, Ste. 107
Lawton, OK 73505
(580)353-8727
Fax: (580)250-5677

SCORE Office (Oklahoma City)
210 Park Ave., No. 1300
Oklahoma City, OK 73102
(405)231-5163
Fax: (405)231-4876
E-mail: score212@usa.net

SCORE Office (Stillwater)
439 S. Main
Stillwater, OK 74074
(405)372-5573
Fax: (405)372-4316

SCORE Office (Tulsa)
616 S. Boston, Ste. 406
Tulsa, OK 74119
(918)581-7462
Fax: (918)581-6908
Website: http://www.ionet.net/~tulscore/

Oregon

SCORE Office (Bend)
63085 N. Hwy. 97
Bend, OR 97701
(541)923-2849
Fax: (541)330-6900

SCORE Office (Willamette)
1401 Willamette St.
PO Box 1107
Eugene, OR 97401-4003
(541)465-6600
Fax: (541)484-4942

SCORE Office (Florence)
3149 Oak St.
Florence, OR 97439
(503)997-8444
Fax: (503)997-8448

SCORE Office (Southern Oregon)
33 N. Central Ave., Ste. 216

Medford, OR 97501
(541)776-4220
E-mail: pgr134f@prodigy.com

SCORE Office (Portland)
1515 SW 5th Ave., Ste. 1050
Portland, OR 97201
(503)326-3441
Fax: (503)326-2808
E-mail: gr134@prodigy.com

SCORE Office (Salem)
416 State St. (corner of Liberty)
Salem, OR 97301
(503)370-2896

Pennsylvania

SCORE Office (Altoona-Blair)
1212 12th Ave.
Altoona, PA 16601-3493
(814)943-8151

SCORE Office (Lehigh Valley)
Rauch Bldg. 37
Lehigh University
621 Taylor St.
Bethlehem, PA 18015
(610)758-4496
Fax: (610)758-5205

SCORE Office (Butler County)
100 N. Main St.
PO Box 1082
Butler, PA 16003
(412)283-2222
Fax: (412)283-0224

SCORE Office (Harrisburg)
4211 Trindle Rd.
Camp Hill, PA 17011
(717)761-4304
Fax: (717)761-4315

SCORE Office (Cumberland Valley)
75 S. 2nd St.
Chambersburg, PA 17201
(717)264-2935

SCORE Office (Monroe County-Stroudsburg)
556 Main St.
East Stroudsburg, PA 18301
(717)421-4433

SCORE Office (Erie)
120 W. 9th St.
Erie, PA 16501
(814)871-5650
Fax: (814)871-7530

SCORE Office (Bucks County)
409 Hood Blvd.
Fairless Hills, PA 19030
(215)943-8850
Fax: (215)943-7404

SCORE Office (Hanover)
146 Broadway
Hanover, PA 17331
(717)637-6130
Fax: (717)637-9127

SCORE Office (Harrisburg)
100 Chestnut, Ste. 309
Harrisburg, PA 17101
(717)782-3874

SCORE Office (East Montgomery County)
Baederwood Shopping Center
1653 The Fairways, Ste. 204
Jenkintown, PA 19046
(215)885-3027

SCORE Office (Kittanning)
2 Butler Rd.
Kittanning, PA 16201
(412)543-1305
Fax: (412)543-6206

SCORE Office (Lancaster)
118 W. Chestnut St.
Lancaster, PA 17603
(717)397-3092

SCORE Office (Westmoreland County)
300 Fraser Purchase Rd.
Latrobe, PA 15650-2690
(412)539-7505
Fax: (412)539-1850

SCORE Office (Lebanon)
252 N. 8th St.
PO Box 899
Lebanon, PA 17042-0899
(717)273-3727
Fax: (717)273-7940

SCORE Office (Lewistown)
3 W. Monument Sq., Ste. 204
Lewistown, PA 17044
(717)248-6713
Fax: (717)248-6714

SCORE Office (Delaware County)
602 E. Baltimore Pike
Media, PA 19063
(610)565-3677
Fax: (610)565-1606

SCORE Office (Milton Area)
112 S. Front St.
Milton, PA 17847

(717)742-7341
Fax: (717)792-2008

SCORE Office (Mon-Valley)
435 Donner Ave.
Monessen, PA 15062
(412)684-4277
Fax: (412)684-7688

SCORE Office (Monroeville)
William Penn Plaza
2790 Mosside Blvd., Ste. 295
Monroeville, PA 15146
(412)856-0622
Fax: (412)856-1030

SCORE Office (Airport Area)
986 Brodhead Rd.
Moon Township, PA 15108-2398
(412)264-6270
Fax: (412)264-1575

SCORE Office (Northeast)
8601 E. Roosevelt Blvd.
Philadelphia, PA 19152
(215)332-3400
Fax: (215)332-6050

SCORE Office (Philadelphia)
1315 Walnut St., Ste. 500
Philadelphia, PA 19107
(215)790-5050
Fax: (215)790-5057
E-mail: score46@bellatlantic.net
Website: http://www.pgweb.net/score46/

SCORE Office (Pittsburgh)
1000 Liberty Ave., Rm. 1122
Pittsburgh, PA 15222
(412)395-6560
Fax: (412)395-6562

SCORE Office (Tri-County)
801 N. Charlotte St.
Pottstown, PA 19464
(610)327-2673

SCORE Office (Reading)
601 Penn St.
Reading, PA 19601
(610)376-3497

SCORE Office (Scranton)
Oppenheim Bldg.
116 N. Washington Ave., Ste. 650
Scranton, PA 18503
(717)347-4611
Fax: (717)347-4611

SCORE Office (Central Pennsylvania)
200 Innovation Blvd., Ste. 242-B
State College, PA 16803

(814)234-9415
Fax: (814)238-9686
Website: http://countrystore.org/
business/score.htm

SCORE Office (Monroe-Stroudsburg)
556 Main St.
Stroudsburg, PA 18360
(717)421-4433

SCORE Office (Uniontown)
Federal Bldg.
Pittsburg St.
PO Box 2065 DTS
Uniontown, PA 15401
(412)437-4222
E-mail: uniontownscore@lcsys.net

SCORE Office (Warren County)
315 2nd Ave.
Warren, PA 16365
(814)723-9017

SCORE Office (Waynesboro)
323 E. Main St.
Waynesboro, PA 17268
(717)762-7123
Fax: (717)962-7124

SCORE Office (Chester County)
Government Service Center, Ste. 281
601 Westtown Rd.
West Chester, PA 19382-4538
(610)344-6910
Fax: (610)344-6919
E-mail: score@locke.ccil.org

SCORE Office (Wilkes-Barre)
7 N. Wilkes-Barre Blvd.
Wilkes Barre, PA 18702-5241
(717)826-6502
Fax: (717)826-6287

SCORE Office (North Central Pennsylvania)
240 W. 3rd St., Rm. 227
PO Box 725
Williamsport, PA 17703
(717)322-3720
Fax: (717)322-1607
E-mail: score234@mail.csrlink.net
Website: http://www.lycoming.org/
score/

SCORE Office (York)
Cyber Center
2101 Pennsylvania Ave.
York, PA 17404
(717)845-8830
Fax: (717)854-9333

Puerto Rico

SCORE Office (Puerto Rico & Virgin Islands)
PO Box 12383-96
San Juan, PR 00914-0383
(787)726-8040
Fax: (787)726-8135

Rhode Island

SCORE Office (Barrington)
281 County Rd.
Barrington, RI 02806
(401)247-1920
Fax: (401)247-3763

SCORE Office (Woonsocket)
640 Washington Hwy.
Lincoln, RI 02865
(401)334-1000
Fax: (401)334-1009

SCORE Office (Wickford)
8045 Post Rd.
North Kingstown, RI 02852
(401)295-5566
Fax: (401)295-8987

SCORE Office (J.G.E. Knight)
380 Westminster St.
Providence, RI 02903
(401)528-4571
Fax: (401)528-4539
Website: http://www.riscore.org

SCORE Office (Warwick)
3288 Post Rd.
Warwick, RI 02886
(401)732-1100
Fax: (401)732-1101

SCORE Office (Westerly)
74 Post Rd.
Westerly, RI 02891
(401)596-7761
800-732-7636
Fax: (401)596-2190

South Carolina

SCORE Office (Aiken)
PO Box 892
Aiken, SC 29802
(803)641-1111
800-542-4536
Fax: (803)641-4174

SCORE Office (Anderson)
Anderson Mall
3130 N. Main St.

Anderson, SC 29621
(864)224-0453

SCORE Office (Coastal)
284 King St.
Charleston, SC 29401
(803)727-4778
Fax: (803)853-2529

SCORE Office (Midlands)
Strom Thurmond Bldg., Rm. 358
1835 Assembly St., Rm 358
Columbia, SC 29201
(803)765-5131
Fax: (803)765-5962
Website: http://www.scoremid
lands.org/

SCORE Office (Piedmont)
Federal Bldg., Rm. B-02
300 E. Washington St.
Greenville, SC 29601
(864)271-3638

SCORE Office (Greenwood)
PO Drawer 1467
Greenwood, SC 29648
(864)223-8357

SCORE Office (Hilton Head Island)
52 Savannah Trail
Hilton Head, SC 29926
(803)785-7107
Fax: (803)785-7110

SCORE Office (Grand Strand)
937 Broadway
Myrtle Beach, SC 29577
(803)918-1079
Fax: (803)918-1083
E-mail: score381@aol.com

SCORE Office (Spartanburg)
PO Box 1636
Spartanburg, SC 29304
(864)594-5000
Fax: (864)594-5055

South Dakota

SCORE Office (West River)
Rushmore Plz. Civic Ctr.
444 Mount Rushmore Rd., No. 209
Rapid City, SD 57701
(605)394-5311
E-mail: score@gwtc.net

SCORE Office (Sioux Falls)
First Financial Center
110 S. Phillips Ave., Ste. 200
Sioux Falls, SD 57104-6727

(605)330-4231
Fax: (605)330-4231

Tennessee

SCORE Office (Chattanooga)
Federal Bldg., Rm. 26
900 Georgia Ave.
Chattanooga, TN 37402
(423)752-5190
Fax: (423)752-5335

SCORE Office (Cleveland)
PO Box 2275
Cleveland, TN 37320
(423)472-6587
Fax: (423)472-2019

SCORE Office (Upper Cumberland Center)
1225 S. Willow Ave.
Cookeville, TN 38501
(615)432-4111
Fax: (615)432-6010

SCORE Office (Unicoi County)
PO Box 713
Erwin, TN 37650
(423)743-3000
Fax: (423)743-0942

SCORE Office (Greeneville)
115 Academy St.
Greeneville, TN 37743
(423)638-4111
Fax: (423)638-5345

SCORE Office (Jackson)
194 Auditorium St.
Jackson, TN 38301
(901)423-2200

SCORE Office (Northeast Tennessee)
1st Tennessee Bank Bldg.
2710 S. Roan St., Ste. 584
Johnson City, TN 37601
(423)929-7686
Fax: (423)461-8052

SCORE Office (Kingsport)
151 E. Main St.
Kingsport, TN 37662
(423)392-8805

SCORE Office (Greater Knoxville)
Farragot Bldg., Ste. 224
530 S. Gay St.
Knoxville, TN 37902
(423)545-4203
E-mail: scoreknox@ntown.com
Website: http://www.scoreknox.org/

SCORE Office (Maryville)
201 S. Washington St.
Maryville, TN 37804-5728
(423)983-2241
800-525-6834
Fax: (423)984-1386

SCORE Office (Memphis)
Federal Bldg., Ste. 390
167 N. Main St.
Memphis, TN 38103
(901)544-3588

SCORE Office (Nashville)
50 Vantage Way, Ste. 201
Nashville, TN 37228-1500
(615)736-7621

Texas

SCORE Office (Abilene)
2106 Federal Post Office and Court Bldg.
Abilene, TX 79601
(915)677-1857

SCORE Office (Austin)
2501 S. Congress
Austin, TX 78701
(512)442-7235
Fax: (512)442-7528

SCORE Office (Golden Triangle)
450 Boyd St.
Beaumont, TX 77704
(409)838-6581
Fax: (409)833-6718

SCORE Office (Brownsville)
3505 Boca Chica Blvd., Ste. 305
Brownsville, TX 78521
(210)541-4508

SCORE Office (Brazos Valley)
3000 Briarcrest, Ste. 302
Bryan, TX 77802
(409)776-8876
E-mail: 102633.2612@compuserve.com

SCORE Office (Cleburne)
Watergarden Pl., 9th Fl., Ste. 400
Cleburne, TX 76031
(817)871-6002

SCORE Office (Corpus Christi)
651 Upper North Broadway, Ste. 654
Corpus Christi, TX 78477
(512)888-4322
Fax: (512)888-3418

SCORE Office (Dallas)
6260 E. Mockingbird
Dallas, TX 75214-2619

(214)828-2471
Fax: (214)821-8033

SCORE Office (El Paso)
10 Civic Center Plaza
El Paso, TX 79901
(915)534-0541
Fax: (915)534-0513

SCORE Office (Bedford)
100 E. 15th St., Ste. 400
Ft. Worth, TX 76102
(817)871-6002

SCORE Office (Ft. Worth)
100 E. 15th St., No. 24
Ft. Worth, TX 76102
(817)871-6002
Fax: (817)871-6031
E-mail: fwbac@onramp.net

SCORE Office (Garland)
2734 W. Kingsley Rd.
Garland, TX 75041
(214)271-9224

SCORE Office (Granbury Chamber of Commerce)
416 S. Morgan
Granbury, TX 76048
(817)573-1622
Fax: (817)573-0805

SCORE Office (Lower Rio Grande Valley)
222 E. Van Buren, Ste. 500
Harlingen, TX 78550
(956)427-8533
Fax: (956)427-8537

SCORE Office (Houston)
9301 Southwest Fwy., Ste. 550
Houston, TX 77074
(713)773-6565
Fax: (713)773-6550

SCORE Office (Irving)
3333 N. MacArthur Blvd., Ste. 100
Irving, TX 75062
(214)252-8484
Fax: (214)252-6710

SCORE Office (Lubbock)
1205 Texas Ave., Rm. 411D
Lubbock, TX 79401
(806)472-7462
Fax: (806)472-7487

SCORE Office (Midland)
Post Office Annex
200 E. Wall St., Rm. P121
Midland, TX 79701
(915)687-2649

SCORE Office (Orange)
1012 Green Ave.
Orange, TX 77630-5620
(409)883-3536
800-528-4906
Fax: (409)886-3247

SCORE Office (Plano)
1200 E. 15th St.
PO Drawer 940287
Plano, TX 75094-0287
(214)424-7547
Fax: (214)422-5182

SCORE Office (Port Arthur)
4749 Twin City Hwy., Ste. 300
Port Arthur, TX 77642
(409)963-1107
Fax: (409)963-3322

SCORE Office (Richardson)
411 Belle Grove
Richardson, TX 75080
(214)234-4141
800-777-8001
Fax: (214)680-9103

SCORE Office (San Antonio)
Federal Bldg., Rm. A527
727 E. Durango
San Antonio, TX 78206
(210)472-5931
Fax: (210)472-5935

SCORE Office (Texarkana State College)
819 State Line Ave.
Texarkana, TX 75501
(903)792-7191
Fax: (903)793-4304

SCORE Office (East Texas)
RTDC
1530 SSW Loop 323, Ste. 100
Tyler, TX 75701
(903)510-2975
Fax: (903)510-2978

SCORE Office (Waco)
401 Franklin Ave.
Waco, TX 76701
(817)754-8898
Fax: (817)756-0776
Website: http://www.brc-waco.com/

SCORE Office (Wichita Falls)
Hamilton Bldg.
900 8th St.
Wichita Falls, TX 76307
(940)723-2741
Fax: (940)723-8773

Utah

SCORE Office (Northern Utah)
160 N. Main
Logan, UT 84321
(435)746-2269

SCORE Office (Ogden)
1701 E. Windsor Dr.
Ogden, UT 84604
(801)629-8613
E-mail: score158@netscape.net

SCORE Office (Central Utah)
1071 E. Windsor Dr.
Provo, UT 84604
(801)373-8660

SCORE Office (Southern Utah)
225 South 700 East
St. George, UT 84770
(435)652-7751

SCORE Office (Salt Lake)
310 S Main St.
Salt Lake City, UT 84101
(801)746-2269
Fax: (801)746-2273

Vermont

SCORE Office (Champlain Valley)
Winston Prouty Federal Bldg.
11 Lincoln St., Rm. 106
Essex Junction, VT 05452
(802)951-6762

SCORE Office (Montpelier)
87 State St., Rm. 205
PO Box 605
Montpelier, VT 05601
(802)828-4422
Fax: (802)828-4485

SCORE Office (Marble Valley)
256 N. Main St.
Rutland, VT 05701-2413
(802)773-9147

SCORE Office (Northeast Kingdom)
20 Main St.
PO Box 904
St. Johnsbury, VT 05819
(802)748-5101

Virgin Islands

SCORE Office (St. Croix)
United Plaza Shopping Center
PO Box 4010, Christiansted
St. Croix, VI 00822
(809)778-5380

SCORE Office (St. Thomas-St. John)
Federal Bldg., Rm. 21
Veterans Dr.
St. Thomas, VI 00801
(809)774-8530

Virginia

SCORE Office (Arlington)
2009 N. 14th St., Ste. 111
Arlington, VA 22201
(703)525-2400

SCORE Office (Blacksburg)
141 Jackson St.
Blacksburg, VA 24060
(540)552-4061

SCORE Office (Bristol)
20 Volunteer Pkwy.
Bristol, VA 24203
(540)989-4850

SCORE Office (Central Virginia)
1001 E. Market St., Ste. 101
Charlottesville, VA 22902
(804)295-6712
Fax: (804)295-7066

SCORE Office (Alleghany Satellite)
241 W. Main St.
Covington, VA 24426
(540)962-2178
Fax: (540)962-2179

SCORE Office (Central Fairfax)
3975 University Dr., Ste. 350
Fairfax, VA 22030
(703)591-2450

SCORE Office (Falls Church)
PO Box 491
Falls Church, VA 22040
(703)532-1050
Fax: (703)237-7904

SCORE Office (Glenns)
Glenns Campus
Box 287
Glenns, VA 23149
(804)693-9650

SCORE Office (Peninsula)
6 Manhattan Sq.
PO Box 7269
Hampton, VA 23666
(757)766-2000
Fax: (757)865-0339
E-mail: score100@seva.net

SCORE Office (Tri-Cities)
108 N. Main St.

Hopewell, VA 23860
(804)458-5536

SCORE Office (Lynchburg)
Federal Bldg.
1100 Main St.
Lynchburg, VA 24504-1714
(804)846-3235

SCORE Office (Greater Prince William)
8963 Center St
Manassas, VA 20110
(703)368-4813
Fax: (703)368-4733

SCORE Office (Martinsvile)
115 Broad St.
Martinsville, VA 24112-0709
(540)632-6401
Fax: (540)632-5059

SCORE Office (Hampton Roads)
Federal Bldg., Rm. 737
200 Grandby St.
Norfolk, VA 23510
(757)441-3733
Fax: (757)441-3733
E-mail: scorehr60@juno.com

SCORE Office (Norfolk)
Federal Bldg., Rm. 737
200 Granby St.
Norfolk, VA 23510
(757)441-3733
Fax: (757)441-3733

SCORE Office (Virginia Beach)
Chamber of Commerce
200 Grandby St., Rm 737
Norfolk, VA 23510
(804)441-3733

SCORE Office (Radford)
1126 Norwood St.
Radford, VA 24141
(540)639-2202

SCORE Office (Richmond)
Federal Bldg.
400 N. 8th St., Ste. 1150
PO Box 10126
Richmond, VA 23240-0126
(804)771-2400
Fax: (804)771-8018
E-mail: scorechapter12@yahoo.com
Website: http://www.cvco.org/score/

SCORE Office (Roanoke)
Federal Bldg., Rm. 716
250 Franklin Rd.
Roanoke, VA 24011

(540)857-2834
Fax: (540)857-2043
E-mail: scorerva@juno.com
Website: http://hometown.aol.com/
scorerv/Index.html

SCORE Office (Fairfax)
8391 Old Courthouse Rd., Ste. 300
Vienna, VA 22182
(703)749-0400

SCORE Office (Greater Vienna)
513 Maple Ave. West
Vienna, VA 22180
(703)281-1333
Fax: (703)242-1482

SCORE Office (Shenandoah Valley)
301 W. Main St.
Waynesboro, VA 22980
(540)949-8203
Fax: (540)949-7740
E-mail: score427@intelos.net

SCORE Office (Williamsburg)
201 Penniman Rd.
Williamsburg, VA 23185
(757)229-6511
E-mail: wacc@williamsburgcc.com

SCORE Office (Northern Virginia)
1360 S. Pleasant Valley Rd.
Winchester, VA 22601
(540)662-4118

Washington

SCORE Office (Gray's Harbor)
506 Duffy St.
Aberdeen, WA 98520
(360)532-1924
Fax: (360)533-7945

SCORE Office (Bellingham)
101 E. Holly St.
Bellingham, WA 98225
(360)676-3307

SCORE Office (Everett)
2702 Hoyt Ave.
Everett, WA 98201-3556
(206)259-8000

SCORE Office (Gig Harbor)
3125 Judson St.
Gig Harbor, WA 98335
(206)851-6865

SCORE Office (Kennewick)
PO Box 6986
Kennewick, WA 99336
(509)736-0510

SCORE Office (Puyallup)
322 2nd St. SW
PO Box 1298
Puyallup, WA 98371
(206)845-6755
Fax: (206)848-6164

SCORE Office (Seattle)
1200 6th Ave., Ste. 1700
Seattle, WA 98101
(206)553-7320
Fax: (206)553-7044
E-mail: score55@aol.com
Website: http://www.scn.org/civic/score-
online/index55.html

SCORE Office (Spokane)
801 W. Riverside Ave., No. 240
Spokane, WA 99201
(509)353-2820
Fax: (509)353-2600
E-mail: score@dmi.net
Website: http://www.dmi.net/score/

SCORE Office (Clover Park)
PO Box 1933
Tacoma, WA 98401-1933
(206)627-2175

SCORE Office (Tacoma)
1101 Pacific Ave.
Tacoma, WA 98402
(253)274-1288
Fax: (253)274-1289

SCORE Office (Fort Vancouver)
1701 Broadway, S-1
Vancouver, WA 98663
(360)699-1079

SCORE Office (Walla Walla)
500 Tausick Way
Walla Walla, WA 99362
(509)527-4681

SCORE Office (Mid-Columbia)
1113 S. 14th Ave.
Yakima, WA 98907
(509)574-4944
Fax: (509)574-2943
Website: http://www.ellensburg.com/
~score/

West Virginia

SCORE Office (Charleston)
1116 Smith St.
Charleston, WV 25301
(304)347-5463
E-mail: score256@juno.com

SCORE Office (Virginia Street)
1116 Smith St., Ste. 302
Charleston, WV 25301
(304)347-5463

SCORE Office (Marion County)
PO Box 208
Fairmont, WV 26555-0208
(304)363-0486

SCORE Office (Upper Monongahela Valley)
1000 Technology Dr., Ste. 1111
Fairmont, WV 26555
(304)363-0486
E-mail: score537@hotmail.com

SCORE Office (Huntington)
1101 6th Ave., Ste. 220
Huntington, WV 25701-2309
(304)523-4092

SCORE Office (Wheeling)
1310 Market St.
Wheeling, WV 26003
(304)233-2575
Fax: (304)233-1320

Wisconsin

SCORE Office (Fox Cities)
227 S. Walnut St.
Appleton, WI 54913
(920)734-7101
Fax: (920)734-7161

SCORE Office (Beloit)
136 W. Grand Ave., Ste. 100
PO Box 717
Beloit, WI 53511
(608)365-8835
Fax: (608)365-9170

SCORE Office (Eau Claire)
Federal Bldg., Rm. B11
510 S. Barstow St.
Eau Claire, WI 54701
(715)834-1573
E-mail: score@ecol.net
Website: http://www.ecol.net/~score/

SCORE Office (Fond du Lac)
207 N. Main St.
Fond du Lac, WI 54935
(414)921-9500
Fax: (414)921-9559

SCORE Office (Green Bay)
835 Potts Ave.
Green Bay, WI 54304
(414)496-8930
Fax: (414)496-6009

SCORE Office (Janesville)
20 S. Main St., Ste. 11
PO Box 8008
Janesville, WI 53547
(608)757-3160
Fax: (608)757-3170

SCORE Office (La Crosse)
712 Main St.
La Crosse, WI 54602-0219
(608)784-4880

SCORE Office (Madison)
505 S. Rosa Rd.
Madison, WI 53719
(608)441-2820

SCORE Office (Manitowoc)
1515 Memorial Dr.
PO Box 903
Manitowoc, WI 54221-0903
(414)684-5575
Fax: (414)684-1915

SCORE Office (Milwaukee)
310 W. Wisconsin Ave., Ste. 425
Milwaukee, WI 53203
(414)297-3942
Fax: (414)297-1377

SCORE Office (Central Wisconsin)
1224 Lindbergh Ave.
Stevens Point, WI 54481
(715)344-7729

SCORE Office (Superior)
Superior Business Center Inc.
1423 N. 8th St.
Superior, WI 54880
(715)394-7388
Fax: (715)393-7414

SCORE Office (Waukesha)
223 Wisconsin Ave.
Waukesha, WI 53186-4926
(414)542-4249

SCORE Office (Wausau)
300 3rd St., Ste. 200
Wausau, WI 54402-6190
(715)845-6231

SCORE Office (Wisconsin Rapids)
2240 Kingston Rd.
Wisconsin Rapids, WI 54494
(715)423-1830

Wyoming

SCORE Office (Casper)
Federal Bldg., No. 2215
100 East B St.

Casper, WY 82602
(307)261-6529
Fax: (307)261-6530

Venture capital & financing companies

This section contains a listing of financing and loan companies in the United States and Canada. These listing are arranged alphabetically by country, then by state or province, then by city, then by organization name.

Canada

Alberta

Launchworks Inc.
1902J 11th St., S.E.
Calgary, AB, Canada T2G 3G2
(403)269-1119
Fax: (403)269-1141
Website: http://www.launchworks.com

Native Venture Capital Company, Inc.
21 Artist View Point, Box 7
Site 25, RR 12
Calgary, AB, Canada T3E 6W3
(903)208-5380

Miralta Capital Inc.
4445 Calgary Trail South
888 Terrace Plaza Alberta
Edmonton, AB, Canada T6H 5R7
(780)438-3535
Fax: (780)438-3129

Vencap Equities Alberta Ltd.
10180-101st St., Ste. 1980
Edmonton, AB, Canada T5J 3S4
(403)420-1171
Fax: (403)429-2541

British Columbia

Discovery Capital
5th Fl., 1199 West Hastings
Vancouver, BC, Canada V6E 3T5
(604)683-3000
Fax: (604)662-3457
E-mail: info@discoverycapital.com
Website: http://www.discoverycapital.com

Greenstone Venture Partners
1177 West Hastings St.
Ste. 400
Vancouver, BC, Canada V6E 2K3
(604)717-1977
Fax: (604)717-1976
Website: http://www.greenstonevc.com

Growthworks Capital
2600-1055 West Georgia St.
Box 11170 Royal Centre
Vancouver, BC, Canada V6E 3R5
(604)895-7259
Fax: (604)669-7605
Website: http://www.wofund.com

MDS Discovery Venture Management, Inc.
555 W. Eighth Ave., Ste. 305
Vancouver, BC, Canada V5Z 1C6
(604)872-8464
Fax: (604)872-2977
E-mail: info@mds-ventures.com

Ventures West Management Inc.
1285 W. Pender St., Ste. 280
Vancouver, BC, Canada V6E 4B1
(604)688-9495
Fax: (604)687-2145
Website: http://www.ventureswest.com

Nova Scotia

ACF Equity Atlantic Inc.
Purdy's Wharf Tower II
Ste. 2106
Halifax, NS, Canada B3J 3R7
(902)421-1965
Fax: (902)421-1808

Montgomerie, Huck & Co.
146 Bluenose Dr.
PO Box 538
Lunenburg, NS, Canada B0J 2C0
(902)634-7125
Fax: (902)634-7130

Ontario

IPS Industrial Promotion Services Ltd.
60 Columbia Way, Ste. 720
Markham, ON, Canada L3R 0C9
(905)475-9400
Fax: (905)475-5003

Betwin Investments Inc.
Box 23110
Sault Ste. Marie, ON, Canada P6A 6W6
(705)253-0744
Fax: (705)253-0744

Bailey & Company, Inc.
594 Spadina Ave.
Toronto, ON, Canada M5S 2H4
(416)921-6930
Fax: (416)925-4670

BCE Capital
200 Bay St.

South Tower, Ste. 3120
Toronto, ON, Canada M5J 2J2
(416)815-0078
Fax: (416)941-1073
Website: http://www.bcecapital.com

Castlehill Ventures
55 University Ave., Ste. 500
Toronto, ON, Canada M5J 2H7
(416)862-8574
Fax: (416)862-8875

CCFL Mezzanine Partners of Canada
70 University Ave.
Ste. 1450
Toronto, ON, Canada M5J 2M4
(416)977-1450
Fax: (416)977-6764
E-mail: info@ccfl.com
Website: http://www.ccfl.com

Celtic House International
100 Simcoe St., Ste. 100
Toronto, ON, Canada M5H 3G2
(416)542-2436
Fax: (416)542-2435
Website: http://www.celtic-house.com

Clairvest Group Inc.
22 St. Clair Ave. East
Ste. 1700
Toronto, ON, Canada M4T 2S3
(416)925-9270
Fax: (416)925-5753

Crosbie & Co., Inc.
One First Canadian Place
9th Fl.
PO Box 116
Toronto, ON, Canada M5X 1A4
(416)362-7726
Fax: (416)362-3447
E-mail: info@crosbieco.com
Website: http://www.crosbieco.com

Drug Royalty Corp.
Eight King St. East
Ste. 202
Toronto, ON, Canada M5C 1B5
(416)863-1865
Fax: (416)863-5161

Grieve, Horner, Brown & Asculai
8 King St. E, Ste. 1704
Toronto, ON, Canada M5C 1B5
(416)362-7668
Fax: (416)362-7660

Jefferson Partners
77 King St. West
Ste. 4010

PO Box 136
Toronto, ON, Canada M5K 1H1
(416)367-1533
Fax: (416)367-5827
Website: http://www.jefferson.com

J.L. Albright Venture Partners
Canada Trust Tower, 161 Bay St.
Ste. 4440
PO Box 215
Toronto, ON, Canada M5J 2S1
(416)367-2440
Fax: (416)367-4604
Website: http://www.jlaventures.com

McLean Watson Capital Inc.
One First Canadian Place
Ste. 1410
PO Box 129
Toronto, ON, Canada M5X 1A4
(416)363-2000
Fax: (416)363-2010
Website: http://www.mcleanwatson.com

Middlefield Capital Fund
One First Canadian Place
85th Fl.
PO Box 192
Toronto, ON, Canada M5X 1A6
(416)362-0714
Fax: (416)362-7925
Website: http://www.middlefield.com

Mosaic Venture Partners
24 Duncan St.
Ste. 300
Toronto, ON, Canada M5V 3M6
(416)597-8889
Fax: (416)597-2345

Onex Corp.
161 Bay St.
PO Box 700
Toronto, ON, Canada M5J 2S1
(416)362-7711
Fax: (416)362-5765

Penfund Partners Inc.
145 King St. West
Ste. 1920
Toronto, ON, Canada M5H 1J8
(416)865-0300
Fax: (416)364-6912
Website: http://www.penfund.com

Primaxis Technology Ventures Inc.
1 Richmond St. West, 8th Fl.
Toronto, ON, Canada M5H 3W4
(416)313-5210
Fax: (416)313-5218
Website: http://www.primaxis.com

Priveq Capital Funds
240 Duncan Mill Rd., Ste. 602
Toronto, ON, Canada M3B 3P1
(416)447-3330
Fax: (416)447-3331
E-mail: priveq@sympatico.ca

Roynat Ventures
40 King St. West, 26th Fl.
Toronto, ON, Canada M5H 1H1
(416)933-2667
Fax: (416)933-2783
Website: http://www.roynatcapital.com

Tera Capital Corp.
366 Adelaide St. East, Ste. 337
Toronto, ON, Canada M5A 3X9
(416)368-1024
Fax: (416)368-1427

Working Ventures Canadian Fund Inc.
250 Bloor St. East, Ste. 1600
Toronto, ON, Canada M4W 1E6
(416)934-7718
Fax: (416)929-0901
Website: http://www.workingventures.ca

Quebec

Altamira Capital Corp.
202 University
Niveau de Maisoneuve, Bur. 201
Montreal, QC, Canada H3A 2A5
(514)499-1656
Fax: (514)499-9570

Federal Business Development Bank
Venture Capital Division
Five Place Ville Marie, Ste. 600
Montreal, QC, Canada H3B 5E7
(514)283-1896
Fax: (514)283-5455

Hydro-Quebec Capitech Inc.
75 Boul, Rene Levesque Quest
Montreal, QC, Canada H2Z 1A4
(514)289-4783
Fax: (514)289-5420
Website: http://www.hqcapitech.com

Investissement Desjardins
2 complexe Desjardins
C.P. 760
Montreal, QC, Canada H5B 1B8
(514)281-7131
Fax: (514)281-7808
Website: http://www.desjardins.com/id

Marleau Lemire Inc.
One Place Ville-Marie, Ste. 3601
Montreal, QC, Canada H3B 3P2

(514)877-3800
Fax: (514)875-6415

Speirs Consultants Inc.
365 Stanstead
Montreal, QC, Canada H3R 1X5
(514)342-3858
Fax: (514)342-1977

Tecnocap Inc.
4028 Marlowe
Montreal, QC, Canada H4A 3M2
(514)483-6009
Fax: (514)483-6045
Website: http://www.technocap.com

Telsoft Ventures
1000, Rue de la Gauchetiere
Quest, 25eme Etage
Montreal, QC, Canada H3B 4W5
(514)397-8450
Fax: (514)397-8451

Saskatchewan

Saskatchewan Government Growth Fund
1801 Hamilton St., Ste. 1210
Canada Trust Tower
Regina, SK, Canada S4P 4B4
(306)787-2994
Fax: (306)787-2086

United states

Alabama

FHL Capital Corp.
600 20th Street North
Suite 350
Birmingham, AL 35203
(205)328-3098
Fax: (205)323-0001

Harbert Management Corp.
One Riverchase Pkwy. South
Birmingham, AL 35244
(205)987-5500
Fax: (205)987-5707
Website: http://www.harbert.net

Jefferson Capital Fund
PO Box 13129
Birmingham, AL 35213
(205)324-7709

Private Capital Corp.
100 Brookwood Pl., 4th Fl.
Birmingham, AL 35209
(205)879-2722
Fax: (205)879-5121

21st Century Health Ventures
One Health South Pkwy.
Birmingham, AL 35243
(256)268-6250
Fax: (256)970-8928

FJC Growth Capital Corp.
200 W. Side Sq., Ste. 340
Huntsville, AL 35801
(256)922-2918
Fax: (256)922-2909

Hickory Venture Capital Corp.
301 Washington St. NW
Suite 301
Huntsville, AL 35801
(256)539-1931
Fax: (256)539-5130
E-mail: hvcc@hvcc.com
Website: http://www.hvcc.com

Southeastern Technology Fund
7910 South Memorial Pkwy., Ste. F
Huntsville, AL 35802
(256)883-8711
Fax: (256)883-8558

Cordova Ventures
4121 Carmichael Rd., Ste. 301
Montgomery, AL 36106
(334)271-6011
Fax: (334)260-0120
Website: http://www.cordova
ventures.com

**Small Business Clinic of Alabama/AG
Bartholomew & Associates**
PO Box 231074
Montgomery, AL 36123-1074
(334)284-3640

Arizona

Miller Capital Corp.
4909 E. McDowell Rd.
Phoenix, AZ 85008
(602)225-0504
Fax: (602)225-9024
Website: http://www.themiller
group.com

The Columbine Venture Funds
9449 North 90th St., Ste. 200
Scottsdale, AZ 85258
(602)661-9222
Fax: (602)661-6262

Koch Ventures
17767 N. Perimeter Dr., Ste. 101
Scottsdale, AZ 85255
(480)419-3600

Fax: (480)419-3606
Website: http://www.kochventures.com

McKee & Co.
7702 E. Doubletree Ranch Rd.
Suite 230
Scottsdale, AZ 85258
(480)368-0333
Fax: (480)607-7446

Merita Capital Ltd.
7350 E. Stetson Dr., Ste. 108-A
Scottsdale, AZ 85251
(480)947-8700
Fax: (480)947-8766

Valley Ventures / Arizona Growth Partners L.P.
6720 N. Scottsdale Rd., Ste. 208
Scottsdale, AZ 85253
(480)661-6600
Fax: (480)661-6262

Estreetcapital.com
660 South Mill Ave., Ste. 315
Tempe, AZ 85281
(480)968-8400
Fax: (480)968-8480
Website: http://www.estreetcapital.com

Coronado Venture Fund
PO Box 65420
Tucson, AZ 85728-5420
(520)577-3764
Fax: (520)299-8491

Arkansas

Arkansas Capital Corp.
225 South Pulaski St.
Little Rock, AR 72201
(501)374-9247
Fax: (501)374-9425
Website: http://www.arcapital.com

California

Sundance Venture Partners, L.P.
100 Clocktower Place, Ste. 130
Carmel, CA 93923
(831)625-6500
Fax: (831)625-6590

Westar Capital (Costa Mesa)
949 South Coast Dr., Ste. 650
Costa Mesa, CA 92626
(714)481-5160
Fax: (714)481-5166
E-mail: mailbox@westarcapital.com
Website: http://www.westarcapital.com

Alpine Technology Ventures
20300 Stevens Creek Boulevard, Ste. 495
Cupertino, CA 95014
(408)725-1810
Fax: (408)725-1207
Website: http://www.alpineventures.com

Bay Partners
10600 N. De Anza Blvd.
Cupertino, CA 95014-2031
(408)725-2444
Fax: (408)446-4502
Website: http://www.baypartners.com

Novus Ventures
20111 Stevens Creek Blvd., Ste. 130
Cupertino, CA 95014
(408)252-3900
Fax: (408)252-1713
Website: http://www.novusventures.com

Triune Capital
19925 Stevens Creek Blvd., Ste. 200
Cupertino, CA 95014
(310)284-6800
Fax: (310)284-3290

Acorn Ventures
268 Bush St., Ste. 2829
Daly City, CA 94014
(650)994-7801
Fax: (650)994-3305
Website: http://www.acornventures.com

Digital Media Campus
2221 Park Place
El Segundo, CA 90245
(310)426-8000
Fax: (310)426-8010
E-mail: info@thecampus.com
Website: http://www.digital
mediacampus.com

BankAmerica Ventures / BA Venture Partners
950 Tower Ln., Ste. 700
Foster City, CA 94404
(650)378-6000
Fax: (650)378-6040
Website: http://
www.baventurepartners.com

Starting Point Partners
666 Portofino Lane
Foster City, CA 94404
(650)722-1035
Website: http://www.startingpoint
partners.com

Opportunity Capital Partners
2201 Walnut Ave., Ste. 210

Fremont, CA 94538
(510)795-7000
Fax: (510)494-5439
Website: http://www.ocpcapital.com

Imperial Ventures Inc.
9920 S. La Cienega Boulevar, 14th Fl.
Inglewood, CA 90301
(310)417-5409
Fax: (310)338-6115

Ventana Global (Irvine)
18881 Von Karman Ave., Ste. 1150
Irvine, CA 92612
(949)476-2204
Fax: (949)752-0223
Website: http://www.ventanaglobal.com

Integrated Consortium Inc.
50 Ridgecrest Rd.
Kentfield, CA 94904
(415)925-0386
Fax: (415)461-2726

Enterprise Partners
979 Ivanhoe Ave., Ste. 550
La Jolla, CA 92037
(858)454-8833
Fax: (858)454-2489
Website: http://www.epvc.com

Domain Associates
28202 Cabot Rd., Ste. 200
Laguna Niguel, CA 92677
(949)347-2446
Fax: (949)347-9720
Website: http://www.domainvc.com

Cascade Communications Ventures
60 E. Sir Francis Drake Blvd., Ste. 300
Larkspur, CA 94939
(415)925-6500
Fax: (415)925-6501

Allegis Capital
One First St., Ste. Two
Los Altos, CA 94022
(650)917-5900
Fax: (650)917-5901
Website: http://www.allegiscapital.com

Aspen Ventures
1000 Fremont Ave., Ste. 200
Los Altos, CA 94024
(650)917-5670
Fax: (650)917-5677
Website: http://www.aspenventures.com

AVI Capital L.P.
1 First St., Ste. 2
Los Altos, CA 94022

(650)949-9862
Fax: (650)949-8510
Website: http://www.avicapital.com

Bastion Capital Corp.
1999 Avenue of the Stars, Ste. 2960
Los Angeles, CA 90067
(310)788-5700
Fax: (310)277-7582
E-mail: ga@bastioncapital.com
Website: http://www.bastioncapital.com

Davis Group
PO Box 69953
Los Angeles, CA 90069-0953
(310)659-6327
Fax: (310)659-6337

Developers Equity Corp.
1880 Century Park East, Ste. 211
Los Angeles, CA 90067
(213)277-0300

Far East Capital Corp.
350 S. Grand Ave., Ste. 4100
Los Angeles, CA 90071
(213)687-1361
Fax: (213)617-7939
E-mail: free@fareastnationalbank.com

Kline Hawkes & Co.
11726 San Vicente Blvd., Ste. 300
Los Angeles, CA 90049
(310)442-4700
Fax: (310)442-4707
Website: http://www.klinehawkes.com

Lawrence Financial Group
701 Teakwood
PO Box 491773
Los Angeles, CA 90049
(310)471-4060
Fax: (310)472-3155

Riordan Lewis & Haden
300 S. Grand Ave., 29th Fl.
Los Angeles, CA 90071
(213)229-8500
Fax: (213)229-8597

Union Venture Corp.
445 S. Figueroa St., 9th Fl.
Los Angeles, CA 90071
(213)236-4092
Fax: (213)236-6329

Wedbush Capital Partners
1000 Wilshire Blvd.
Los Angeles, CA 90017
(213)688-4545
Fax: (213)688-6642
Website: http://www.wedbush.com

Advent International Corp.
2180 Sand Hill Rd., Ste. 420
Menlo Park, CA 94025
(650)233-7500
Fax: (650)233-7515
Website: http://www.adventinter
national.com

Altos Ventures
2882 Sand Hill Rd., Ste. 100
Menlo Park, CA 94025
(650)234-9771
Fax: (650)233-9821
Website: http://www.altosvc.com

Applied Technology
1010 El Camino Real, Ste. 300
Menlo Park, CA 94025
(415)326-8622
Fax: (415)326-8163

APV Technology Partners
535 Middlefield, Ste. 150
Menlo Park, CA 94025
(650)327-7871
Fax: (650)327-7631
Website: http://www.apvtp.com

August Capital Management
2480 Sand Hill Rd., Ste. 101
Menlo Park, CA 94025
(650)234-9900
Fax: (650)234-9910
Website: http://www.augustcap.com

Baccharis Capital Inc.
2420 Sand Hill Rd., Ste. 100
Menlo Park, CA 94025
(650)324-6844
Fax: (650)854-3025

Benchmark Capital
2480 Sand Hill Rd., Ste. 200
Menlo Park, CA 94025
(650)854-8180
Fax: (650)854-8183
E-mail: info@benchmark.com
Website: http://www.benchmark.com

Bessemer Venture Partners (Menlo Park)
535 Middlefield Rd., Ste. 245
Menlo Park, CA 94025
(650)853-7000
Fax: (650)853-7001
Website: http://www.bvp.com

The Cambria Group
1600 El Camino Real Rd., Ste. 155
Menlo Park, CA 94025
(650)329-8600

Fax: (650)329-8601
Website: http://www.cambriagroup.com

Canaan Partners
2884 Sand Hill Rd., Ste. 115
Menlo Park, CA 94025
(650)854-8092
Fax: (650)854-8127
Website: http://www.canaan.com

Capstone Ventures
3000 Sand Hill Rd., Bldg. One, Ste. 290
Menlo Park, CA 94025
(650)854-2523
Fax: (650)854-9010
Website: http://www.capstonevc.com

Comdisco Venture Group (Silicon Valley)
3000 Sand Hill Rd., Bldg. 1, Ste. 155
Menlo Park, CA 94025
(650)854-9484
Fax: (650)854-4026

Commtech International
535 Middlefield Rd., Ste. 200
Menlo Park, CA 94025
(650)328-0190
Fax: (650)328-6442

Compass Technology Partners
1550 El Camino Real, Ste. 275
Menlo Park, CA 94025-4111
(650)322-7595
Fax: (650)322-0588
Website: http://www.compass
techpartners.com

Convergence Partners
3000 Sand Hill Rd., Ste. 235
Menlo Park, CA 94025
(650)854-3010
Fax: (650)854-3015
Website: http://www.conver
gencepartners.com

The Dakota Group
PO Box 1025
Menlo Park, CA 94025
(650)853-0600
Fax: (650)851-4899
E-mail: info@dakota.com

Delphi Ventures
3000 Sand Hill Rd.
Bldg. One, Ste. 135
Menlo Park, CA 94025
(650)854-9650
Fax: (650)854-2961
Website: http://www.delphiventures.com

El Dorado Ventures

2884 Sand Hill Rd., Ste. 121
Menlo Park, CA 94025
(650)854-1200
Fax: (650)854-1202
Website: http://www.eldorado
ventures.com

Glynn Ventures

3000 Sand Hill Rd., Bldg. 4, Ste. 235
Menlo Park, CA 94025
(650)854-2215

Indosuez Ventures

2180 Sand Hill Rd., Ste. 450
Menlo Park, CA 94025
(650)854-0587
Fax: (650)323-5561
Website: http://www.indosuez
ventures.com

Institutional Venture Partners

3000 Sand Hill Rd., Bldg. 2, Ste. 290
Menlo Park, CA 94025
(650)854-0132
Fax: (650)854-5762
Website: http://www.ivp.com

Interwest Partners (Menlo Park)

3000 Sand Hill Rd., Bldg. 3, Ste. 255
Menlo Park, CA 94025-7112
(650)854-8585
Fax: (650)854-4706
Website: http://www.interwest.com

**Kleiner Perkins Caufield & Byers
(Menlo Park)**

2750 Sand Hill Rd.
Menlo Park, CA 94025
(650)233-2750
Fax: (650)233-0300
Website: http://www.kpcb.com

Magic Venture Capital LLC

1010 El Camino Real, Ste. 300
Menlo Park, CA 94025
(650)325-4149

Matrix Partners

2500 Sand Hill Rd., Ste. 113
Menlo Park, CA 94025
(650)854-3131
Fax: (650)854-3296
Website: http://www.matrixpartners.com

Mayfield Fund

2800 Sand Hill Rd.
Menlo Park, CA 94025
(650)854-5560
Fax: (650)854-5712
Website: http://www.mayfield.com

**McCown De Leeuw and Co. (Menlo
Park)**

3000 Sand Hill Rd., Bldg. 3, Ste. 290
Menlo Park, CA 94025-7111
(650)854-6000
Fax: (650)854-0853
Website: http://www.mdcpartners.com

Menlo Ventures

3000 Sand Hill Rd., Bldg. 4, Ste. 100
Menlo Park, CA 94025
(650)854-8540
Fax: (650)854-7059
Website: http://www.menloventures.com

Merrill Pickard Anderson & Eyre

2480 Sand Hill Rd., Ste. 200
Menlo Park, CA 94025
(650)854-8600
Fax: (650)854-0345

**New Enterprise Associates (Menlo
Park)**

2490 Sand Hill Rd.
Menlo Park, CA 94025
(650)854-9499
Fax: (650)854-9397
Website: http://www.nea.com

Onset Ventures

2400 Sand Hill Rd., Ste. 150
Menlo Park, CA 94025
(650)529-0700
Fax: (650)529-0777
Website: http://www.onset.com

Paragon Venture Partners

3000 Sand Hill Rd., Bldg. 1, Ste. 275
Menlo Park, CA 94025
(650)854-8000
Fax: (650)854-7260

**Pathfinder Venture Capital Funds
(Menlo Park)**

3000 Sand Hill Rd., Bldg. 3, Ste. 255
Menlo Park, CA 94025
(650)854-0650
Fax: (650)854-4706

Rocket Ventures

3000 Sandhill Rd., Bldg. 1, Ste. 170
Menlo Park, CA 94025
(650)561-9100
Fax: (650)561-9183
Website: http://www.rocketventures.com

Sequoia Capital

3000 Sand Hill Rd., Bldg. 4, Ste. 280
Menlo Park, CA 94025
(650)854-3927
Fax: (650)854-2977

E-mail: sequoia@sequioacap.com
Website: http://www.sequoiacap.com

Sierra Ventures

3000 Sand Hill Rd., Bldg. 4, Ste. 210
Menlo Park, CA 94025
(650)854-1000
Fax: (650)854-5593
Website: http://www.sierraventures.com

Sigma Partners

2884 Sand Hill Rd., Ste. 121
Menlo Park, CA 94025-7022
(650)853-1700
Fax: (650)853-1717
E-mail: info@sigmapartners.com
Website: http://www.sigmapartners.com

Sprout Group (Menlo Park)

3000 Sand Hill Rd.
Bldg. 3, Ste. 170
Menlo Park, CA 94025
(650)234-2700
Fax: (650)234-2779
Website: http://www.sproutgroup.com

TA Associates (Menlo Park)

70 Willow Rd., Ste. 100
Menlo Park, CA 94025
(650)328-1210
Fax: (650)326-4933
Website: http://www.ta.com

Thompson Clive & Partners Ltd.

3000 Sand Hill Rd., Bldg. 1, Ste. 185
Menlo Park, CA 94025-7102
(650)854-0314
Fax: (650)854-0670
E-mail: mail@tcvc.com
Website: http://www.tcvc.com

Trinity Ventures Ltd.

3000 Sand Hill Rd., Bldg. 1, Ste. 240
Menlo Park, CA 94025
(650)854-9500
Fax: (650)854-9501
Website: http://www.trinityventures.com

U.S. Venture Partners

2180 Sand Hill Rd., Ste. 300
Menlo Park, CA 94025
(650)854-9080
Fax: (650)854-3018
Website: http://www.usvp.com

USVP-Schlein Marketing Fund

2180 Sand Hill Rd., Ste. 300
Menlo Park, CA 94025
(415)854-9080
Fax: (415)854-3018
Website: http://www.usvp.com

Venrock Associates
2494 Sand Hill Rd., Ste. 200
Menlo Park, CA 94025
(650)561-9580
Fax: (650)561-9180
Website: http://www.venrock.com

Brad Peery Capital Inc.
145 Chapel Pkwy.
Mill Valley, CA 94941
(415)389-0625
Fax: (415)389-1336

Dot Edu Ventures
650 Castro St., Ste. 270
Mountain View, CA 94041
(650)575-5638
Fax: (650)325-5247
Website: http://www.dotedu
ventures.com

Forrest, Binkley & Brown
840 Newport Ctr. Dr., Ste. 480
Newport Beach, CA 92660
(949)729-3222
Fax: (949)729-3226
Website: http://www.fbbvc.com

Marwit Capital LLC
180 Newport Center Dr., Ste. 200
Newport Beach, CA 92660
(949)640-6234
Fax: (949)720-8077
Website: http://www.marwit.com

Kaiser Permanente / National Venture Development
1800 Harrison St., 22nd Fl.
Oakland, CA 94612
(510)267-4010
Fax: (510)267-4036
Website: http://www.kpventures.com

Nu Capital Access Group, Ltd.
7677 Oakport St., Ste. 105
Oakland, CA 94621
(510)635-7345
Fax: (510)635-7068

Inman and Bowman
4 Orinda Way, Bldg. D, Ste. 150
Orinda, CA 94563
(510)253-1611
Fax: (510)253-9037

Accel Partners (San Francisco)
428 University Ave.
Palo Alto, CA 94301
(650)614-4800
Fax: (650)614-4880
Website: http://www.accel.com

Advanced Technology Ventures
485 Ramona St., Ste. 200
Palo Alto, CA 94301
(650)321-8601
Fax: (650)321-0934
Website: http://www.atvcapital.com

Anila Fund
400 Channing Ave.
Palo Alto, CA 94301
(650)833-5790
Fax: (650)833-0590
Website: http://www.anila.com

Asset Management Company Venture Capital
2275 E. Bayshore, Ste. 150
Palo Alto, CA 94303
(650)494-7400
Fax: (650)856-1826
E-mail: postmaster@assetman.com
Website: http://www.assetman.com

BancBoston Capital / BancBoston Ventures
435 Tasso St., Ste. 250
Palo Alto, CA 94305
(650)470-4100
Fax: (650)853-1425
Website: http://www.bancboston
capital.com

Charter Ventures
525 University Ave., Ste. 1400
Palo Alto, CA 94301
(650)325-6953
Fax: (650)325-4762
Website: http://www.charterventures.com

Communications Ventures
505 Hamilton Avenue, Ste. 305
Palo Alto, CA 94301
(650)325-9600
Fax: (650)325-9608
Website: http://www.comven.com

HMS Group
2468 Embarcadero Way
Palo Alto, CA 94303-3313
(650)856-9862
Fax: (650)856-9864

Jafco America Ventures, Inc.
505 Hamilton Ste. 310
Palto Alto, CA 94301
(650)463-8800
Fax: (650)463-8801
Website: http://www.jafco.com

New Vista Capital
540 Cowper St., Ste. 200

Palo Alto, CA 94301
(650)329-9333
Fax: (650)328-9434
E-mail: fgreene@nvcap.com
Website: http://www.nvcap.com

Norwest Equity Partners (Palo Alto)
245 Lytton Ave., Ste. 250
Palo Alto, CA 94301-1426
(650)321-8000
Fax: (650)321-8010
Website: http://www.norwestvp.com

Oak Investment Partners
525 University Ave., Ste. 1300
Palo Alto, CA 94301
(650)614-3700
Fax: (650)328-6345
Website: http://www.oakinv.com

Patricof & Co. Ventures, Inc. (Palo Alto)
2100 Geng Rd., Ste. 150
Palo Alto, CA 94303
(650)494-9944
Fax: (650)494-6751
Website: http://www.patricof.com

RWI Group
835 Page Mill Rd.
Palo Alto, CA 94304
(650)251-1800
Fax: (650)213-8660
Website: http://www.rwigroup.com

Summit Partners (Palo Alto)
499 Hamilton Ave., Ste. 200
Palo Alto, CA 94301
(650)321-1166
Fax: (650)321-1188
Website: http://www.summit
partners.com

Sutter Hill Ventures
755 Page Mill Rd., Ste. A-200
Palo Alto, CA 94304
(650)493-5600
Fax: (650)858-1854
E-mail: shv@shv.com

Vanguard Venture Partners
525 University Ave., Ste. 600
Palo Alto, CA 94301
(650)321-2900
Fax: (650)321-2902
Website: http://www.vanguard
ventures.com

Venture Growth Associates
2479 East Bayshore St., Ste. 710
Palo Alto, CA 94303

(650)855-9100
Fax: (650)855-9104

Worldview Technology Partners
435 Tasso St., Ste. 120
Palo Alto, CA 94301
(650)322-3800
Fax: (650)322-3880
Website: http://www.worldview.com

Draper, Fisher, Jurvetson / Draper Associates
400 Seaport Ct., Ste.250
Redwood City, CA 94063
(415)599-9000
Fax: (415)599-9726
Website: http://www.dfj.com

Gabriel Venture Partners
350 Marine Pkwy., Ste. 200
Redwood Shores, CA 94065
(650)551-5000
Fax: (650)551-5001
Website: http://www.gabrielvp.com

Hallador Venture Partners, L.L.C.
740 University Ave., Ste. 110
Sacramento, CA 95825-6710
(916)920-0191
Fax: (916)920-5188
E-mail: chris@hallador.com

Emerald Venture Group
12396 World Trade Dr., Ste. 116
San Diego, CA 92128
(858)451-1001
Fax: (858)451-1003
Website: http://www.emerald
venture.com

Forward Ventures
9255 Towne Centre Dr.
San Diego, CA 92121
(858)677-6077
Fax: (858)452-8799
E-mail: info@forwardventure.com
Website: http://www.forward
venture.com

Idanta Partners Ltd.
4660 La Jolla Village Dr., Ste. 850
San Diego, CA 92122
(619)452-9690
Fax: (619)452-2013
Website: http://www.idanta.com

Kingsbury Associates
3655 Nobel Dr., Ste. 490
San Diego, CA 92122
(858)677-0600
Fax: (858)677-0800

Kyocera International Inc.
Corporate Development
8611 Balboa Ave.
San Diego, CA 92123
(858)576-2600
Fax: (858)492-1456

Sorrento Associates, Inc.
4370 LaJolla Village Dr., Ste. 1040
San Diego, CA 92122
(619)452-3100
Fax: (619)452-7607
Website: http://www.sorrento
ventures.com

Western States Investment Group
9191 Towne Ctr. Dr., Ste. 310
San Diego, CA 92122
(619)678-0800
Fax: (619)678-0900

Aberdare Ventures
One Embarcadero Center, Ste. 4000
San Francisco, CA 94111
(415)392-7442
Fax: (415)392-4264
Website: http://www.aberdare.com

Acacia Venture Partners
101 California St., Ste. 3160
San Francisco, CA 94111
(415)433-4200
Fax: (415)433-4250
Website: http://www.acaciavp.com

Access Venture Partners
319 Laidley St.
San Francisco, CA 94131
(415)586-0132
Fax: (415)392-6310
Website: http://www.access
venturepartners.com

Alta Partners
One Embarcadero Center, Ste. 4050
San Francisco, CA 94111
(415)362-4022
Fax: (415)362-6178
E-mail: alta@altapartners.com
Website: http://www.altapartners.com

Bangert Dawes Reade Davis & Thom
220 Montgomery St., Ste. 424
San Francisco, CA 94104
(415)954-9900
Fax: (415)954-9901
E-mail: bdrdt@pacbell.net

Berkeley International Capital Corp.
650 California St., Ste. 2800
San Francisco, CA 94108-2609

(415)249-0450
Fax: (415)392-3929
Website: http://www.berkeleyvc.com

Blueprint Ventures LLC
456 Montgomery St., 22nd Fl.
San Francisco, CA 94104
(415)901-4000
Fax: (415)901-4035
Website: http://www.blue
printventures.com

Blumberg Capital Ventures
580 Howard St., Ste. 401
San Francisco, CA 94105
(415)905-5007
Fax: (415)357-5027
Website: http://www.blumberg-
capital.com

Burr, Egan, Deleage, and Co. (San Francisco)
1 Embarcadero Center, Ste. 4050
San Francisco, CA 94111
(415)362-4022
Fax: (415)362-6178

Burrill & Company
120 Montgomery St., Ste. 1370
San Francisco, CA 94104
(415)743-3160
Fax: (415)743-3161
Website: http://www.burrillandco.com

CMEA Ventures
235 Montgomery St., Ste. 920
San Francisco, CA 94401
(415)352-1520
Fax: (415)352-1524
Website: http://www.cmeaventures.com

Crocker Capital
1 Post St., Ste. 2500
San Francisco, CA 94101
(415)956-5250
Fax: (415)959-5710

Dominion Ventures, Inc.
44 Montgomery St., Ste. 4200
San Francisco, CA 94104
(415)362-4890
Fax: (415)394-9245

Dorset Capital
Pier 1
Bay 2
San Francisco, CA 94111
(415)398-7101
Fax: (415)398-7141
Website: http://www.dorsetcapital.com

Gatx Capital
Four Embarcadero Center, Ste. 2200
San Francisco, CA 94904
(415)955-3200
Fax: (415)955-3449

IMinds
135 Main St., Ste. 1350
San Francisco, CA 94105
(415)547-0000
Fax: (415)227-0300
Website: http://www.iminds.com

LF International Inc.
360 Post St., Ste. 705
San Francisco, CA 94108
(415)399-0110
Fax: (415)399-9222
Website: http://www.lfvc.com

Newbury Ventures
535 Pacific Ave., 2nd Fl.
San Francisco, CA 94133
(415)296-7408
Fax: (415)296-7416
Website: http://www.newburyven.com

Quest Ventures (San Francisco)
333 Bush St., Ste. 1750
San Francisco, CA 94104
(415)782-1414
Fax: (415)782-1415

Robertson-Stephens Co.
555 California St., Ste. 2600
San Francisco, CA 94104
(415)781-9700
Fax: (415)781-2556
Website: http://www.omegaad
ventures.com

Rosewood Capital, L.P.
One Maritime Plaza, Ste. 1330
San Francisco, CA 94111-3503
(415)362-5526
Fax: (415)362-1192
Website: http://www.rosewoodvc.com

Ticonderoga Capital Inc.
555 California St., No. 4950
San Francisco, CA 94104
(415)296-7900
Fax: (415)296-8956

21st Century Internet Venture Partners
Two South Park
2nd Floor
San Francisco, CA 94107
(415)512-1221
Fax: (415)512-2650
Website: http://www.21vc.com

VK Ventures
600 California St., Ste.1700
San Francisco, CA 94111
(415)391-5600
Fax: (415)397-2744

Walden Group of Venture Capital Funds
750 Battery St., Seventh Floor
San Francisco, CA 94111
(415)391-7225
Fax: (415)391-7262

Acer Technology Ventures
2641 Orchard Pkwy.
San Jose, CA 95134
(408)433-4945
Fax: (408)433-5230

Authosis
226 Airport Pkwy., Ste. 405
San Jose, CA 95110
(650)814-3603
Website: http://www.authosis.com

Western Technology Investment
2010 N. First St., Ste. 310
San Jose, CA 95131
(408)436-8577
Fax: (408)436-8625
E-mail: mktg@westerntech.com

Drysdale Enterprises
177 Bovet Rd., Ste. 600
San Mateo, CA 94402
(650)341-6336
Fax: (650)341-1329
E-mail: drysdale@aol.com

Greylock
2929 Campus Dr., Ste. 400
San Mateo, CA 94401
(650)493-5525
Fax: (650)493-5575
Website: http://www.greylock.com

Technology Funding
2000 Alameda de las Pulgas, Ste. 250
San Mateo, CA 94403
(415)345-2200
Fax: (415)345-1797

2M Invest Inc.
1875 S. Grant St.
Suite 750
San Mateo, CA 94402
(650)655-3765
Fax: (650)372-9107
E-mail: 2minfo@2minvest.com
Website: http://www.2minvest.com

Phoenix Growth Capital Corp.
2401 Kerner Blvd.
San Rafael, CA 94901
(415)485-4569
Fax: (415)485-4663

NextGen Partners LLC
1705 East Valley Rd.
Santa Barbara, CA 93108
(805)969-8540
Fax: (805)969-8542
Website: http://www.nextgen
partners.com

Denali Venture Capital
1925 Woodland Ave.
Santa Clara, CA 95050
(408)690-4838
Fax: (408)247-6979
E-mail: wael@denaliventurecapital.com
Website: http://www.denali
venturecapital.com

Dotcom Ventures LP
3945 Freedom Circle, Ste. 740
Santa Clara, CA 95045
(408)919-9855
Fax: (408)919-9857
Website: http://www.dotcom
venturesatl.com

Silicon Valley Bank
3003 Tasman
Santa Clara, CA 95054
(408)654-7400
Fax: (408)727-8728

Al Shugart International
920 41st Ave.
Santa Cruz, CA 95062
(831)479-7852
Fax: (831)479-7852
Website: http://www.alshugart.com

Leonard Mautner Associates
1434 Sixth St.
Santa Monica, CA 90401
(213)393-9788
Fax: (310)459-9918

Palomar Ventures
100 Wilshire Blvd., Ste. 450
Santa Monica, CA 90401
(310)260-6050
Fax: (310)656-4150
Website: http://www.palomar
ventures.com

Medicus Venture Partners
12930 Saratoga Ave., Ste. D8
Saratoga, CA 95070

(408)447-8600
Fax: (408)447-8599
Website: http://www.medicusvc.com

Redleaf Venture Management
14395 Saratoga Ave., Ste. 130
Saratoga, CA 95070
(408)868-0800
Fax: (408)868-0810
E-mail: nancy@redleaf.com
Website: http://www.redleaf.com

Artemis Ventures
207 Second St., Ste. E
3rd Fl.
Sausalito, CA 94965
(415)289-2500
Fax: (415)289-1789
Website: http://www.artemisventures.com

Deucalion Venture Partners
19501 Brooklime
Sonoma, CA 95476
(707)938-4974
Fax: (707)938-8921

Windward Ventures
PO Box 7688
Thousand Oaks, CA 91359-7688
(805)497-3332
Fax: (805)497-9331

National Investment Management, Inc.
2601 Airport Dr., Ste.210
Torrance, CA 90505
(310)784-7600
Fax: (310)784-7605

Southern California Ventures
406 Amapola Ave. Ste. 125
Torrance, CA 90501
(310)787-4381
Fax: (310)787-4382

Sandton Financial Group
21550 Oxnard St., Ste. 300
Woodland Hills, CA 91367
(818)702-9283

Woodside Fund
850 Woodside Dr.
Woodside, CA 94062
(650)368-5545
Fax: (650)368-2416
Website: http://www.woodsidefund.com

Colorado

Colorado Venture Management
Ste. 300
Boulder, CO 80301

(303)440-4055
Fax: (303)440-4636

Dean & Associates
4362 Apple Way
Boulder, CO 80301
Fax: (303)473-9900

Roser Ventures LLC
1105 Spruce St.
Boulder, CO 80302
(303)443-6436
Fax: (303)443-1885
Website: http://www.roserventures.com

Sequel Venture Partners
4430 Arapahoe Ave., Ste. 220
Boulder, CO 80303
(303)546-0400
Fax: (303)546-9728
E-mail: tom@sequelvc.com
Website: http://www.sequelvc.com

New Venture Resources
445C E. Cheyenne Mtn. Blvd.
Colorado Springs, CO 80906-4570
(719)598-9272
Fax: (719)598-9272

The Centennial Funds
1428 15th St.
Denver, CO 80202-1318
(303)405-7500
Fax: (303)405-7575
Website: http://www.centennial.com

Rocky Mountain Capital Partners
1125 17th St., Ste. 2260
Denver, CO 80202
(303)291-5200
Fax: (303)291-5327

Sandlot Capital LLC
600 South Cherry St., Ste. 525
Denver, CO 80246
(303)893-3400
Fax: (303)893-3403
Website: http://www.sandlotcapital.com

Wolf Ventures
50 South Steele St., Ste. 777
Denver, CO 80209
(303)321-4800
Fax: (303)321-4848
E-mail: businessplan@wolf
ventures.com
Website: http://www.wolfventures.com

The Columbine Venture Funds
5460 S. Quebec St., Ste. 270
Englewood, CO 80111

(303)694-3222
Fax: (303)694-9007

Investment Securities of Colorado, Inc.
4605 Denice Dr.
Englewood, CO 80111
(303)796-9192

Kinship Partners
6300 S. Syracuse Way, Ste. 484
Englewood, CO 80111
(303)694-0268
Fax: (303)694-1707
E-mail: block@vailsys.com

Boranco Management, L.L.C.
1528 Hillside Dr.
Fort Collins, CO 80524-1969
(970)221-2297
Fax: (970)221-4787

Aweida Ventures
890 West Cherry St., Ste. 220
Louisville, CO 80027
(303)664-9520
Fax: (303)664-9530
Website: http://www.aweida.com

Access Venture Partners
8787 Turnpike Dr., Ste. 260
Westminster, CO 80030
(303)426-8899
Fax: (303)426-8828

Medmax Ventures LP
1 Northwestern Dr., Ste. 203
Bloomfield, CT 06002
(860)286-2960
Fax: (860)286-9960

James B. Kobak & Co.
Four Mansfield Place
Darien, CT 06820
(203)656-3471
Fax: (203)655-2905

Orien Ventures
1 Post Rd.
Fairfield, CT 06430
(203)259-9933
Fax: (203)259-5288

ABP Acquisition Corporation
115 Maple Ave.
Greenwich, CT 06830
(203)625-8287
Fax: (203)447-6187

Catterton Partners
9 Greenwich Office Park
Greenwich, CT 06830
(203)629-4901

Fax: (203)629-4903
Website: http://www.cpequity.com

Consumer Venture Partners
3 Pickwick Plz.
Greenwich, CT 06830
(203)629-8800
Fax: (203)629-2019

Insurance Venture Partners
31 Brookside Dr., Ste. 211
Greenwich, CT 06830
(203)861-0030
Fax: (203)861-2745

The NTC Group
Three Pickwick Plaza
Ste. 200
Greenwich, CT 06830
(203)862-2800
Fax: (203)622-6538

**Regulus International Capital Co.,
Inc.**
140 Greenwich Ave.
Greenwich, CT 06830
(203)625-9700
Fax: (203)625-9706

Axiom Venture Partners
City Place II
185 Asylum St., 17th Fl.
Hartford, CT 06103
(860)548-7799
Fax: (860)548-7797
Website: http://www.axiomventures.com

Conning Capital Partners
City Place II
185 Asylum St.
Hartford, CT 06103-4105
(860)520-1289
Fax: (860)520-1299
E-mail: pe@conning.com
Website: http://www.conning.com

First New England Capital L.P.
100 Pearl St.
Hartford, CT 06103
(860)293-3333
Fax: (860)293-3338
E-mail: info@firstnewenglandcapital.com
Website: http://www.firstnewengland
capital.com

Northeast Ventures
One State St., Ste. 1720
Hartford, CT 06103
(860)547-1414
Fax: (860)246-8755

Windward Holdings
38 Sylvan Rd.
Madison, CT 06443
(203)245-6870
Fax: (203)245-6865

Advanced Materials Partners, Inc.
45 Pine St.
PO Box 1022
New Canaan, CT 06840
(203)966-6415
Fax: (203)966-8448
E-mail: wkb@amplink.com

RFE Investment Partners
36 Grove St.
New Canaan, CT 06840
(203)966-2800
Fax: (203)966-3109
Website: http://www.rfeip.com

Connecticut Innovations, Inc.
999 West St.
Rocky Hill, CT 06067
(860)563-5851
Fax: (860)563-4877
E-mail: pamela.hartley@ctin
novations.com
Website: http://www.ctinnovations.com

Canaan Partners
105 Rowayton Ave.
Rowayton, CT 06853
(203)855-0400
Fax: (203)854-9117
Website: http://www.canaan.com

Landmark Partners, Inc.
10 Mill Pond Ln.
Simsbury, CT 06070
(860)651-9760
Fax: (860)651-8890
Website: http://
www.landmarkpartners.com

Sweeney & Company
PO Box 567
Southport, CT 06490
(203)255-0220
Fax: (203)255-0220
E-mail: sweeney@connix.com

Baxter Associates, Inc.
PO Box 1333
Stamford, CT 06904
(203)323-3143
Fax: (203)348-0622

Beacon Partners Inc.
6 Landmark Sq., 4th Fl.
Stamford, CT 06901-2792

(203)359-5776
Fax: (203)359-5876

Collinson, Howe, and Lennox, LLC
1055 Washington Blvd., 5th Fl.
Stamford, CT 06901
(203)324-7700
Fax: (203)324-3636
E-mail: info@chlmedical.com
Website: http://www.chlmedical.com

Prime Capital Management Co.
550 West Ave.
Stamford, CT 06902
(203)964-0642
Fax: (203)964-0862

Saugatuck Capital Co.
1 Canterbury Green
Stamford, CT 06901
(203)348-6669
Fax: (203)324-6995
Website: http://www.sauga
tuckcapital.com

Soundview Financial Group Inc.
22 Gatehouse Rd.
Stamford, CT 06902
(203)462-7200
Fax: (203)462-7350
Website: http://www.sndv.com

TSG Ventures, L.L.C.
177 Broad St., 12th Fl.
Stamford, CT 06901
(203)406-1500
Fax: (203)406-1590

Whitney & Company
177 Broad St.
Stamford, CT 06901
(203)973-1400
Fax: (203)973-1422
Website: http://www.jhwhitney.com

**Cullinane & Donnelly Venture
Partners L.P.**
970 Farmington Ave.
West Hartford, CT 06107
(860)521-7811

**The Crestview Investment and
Financial Group**
431 Post Rd. E, Ste. 1
Westport, CT 06880-4403
(203)222-0333
Fax: (203)222-0000

**Marketcorp Venture Associates, L.P.
(MCV)**
274 Riverside Ave.
Westport, CT 06880

(203)222-3030
Fax: (203)222-3033

Oak Investment Partners (Westport)
1 Gorham Island
Westport, CT 06880
(203)226-8346
Fax: (203)227-0372
Website: http://www.oakinv.com

Oxford Bioscience Partners
315 Post Rd. W
Westport, CT 06880-5200
(203)341-3300
Fax: (203)341-3309
Website: http://www.oxbio.com

Prince Ventures (Westport)
25 Ford Rd.
Westport, CT 06880
(203)227-8332
Fax: (203)226-5302

LTI Venture Leasing Corp.
221 Danbury Rd.
Wilton, CT 06897
(203)563-1100
Fax: (203)563-1111
Website: http://www.ltileasing.com

Delaware

Blue Rock Capital
5803 Kennett Pike, Ste. A
Wilmington, DE 19807
(302)426-0981
Fax: (302)426-0982
Website: http://www.bluerockcapital.com

District of Columbia

Allied Capital Corp.
1919 Pennsylvania Ave. NW
Washington, DC 20006-3434
(202)331-2444
Fax: (202)659-2053
Website: http://www.alliedcapital.com

Atlantic Coastal Ventures, L.P.
3101 South St. NW
Washington, DC 20007
(202)293-1166
Fax: (202)293-1181
Website: http://www.atlanticcv.com

Columbia Capital Group, Inc.
1660 L St. NW, Ste. 308
Washington, DC 20036
(202)775-8815
Fax: (202)223-0544

Core Capital Partners
901 15th St., NW
9th Fl.
Washington, DC 20005
(202)589-0090
Fax: (202)589-0091
Website: http://www.core-capital.com

Next Point Partners
701 Pennsylvania Ave. NW, Ste. 900
Washington, DC 20004
(202)661-8703
Fax: (202)434-7400
E-mail: mf@nextpoint.vc
Website: http://www.nextpointvc.com

Telecommunications Development Fund
2020 K. St. NW
Ste. 375
Washington, DC 20006
(202)293-8840
Fax: (202)293-8850
Website: http://www.tdfund.com

Wachtel & Co., Inc.
1101 4th St. NW
Washington, DC 20005-5680
(202)898-1144

Winslow Partners LLC
1300 Connecticut Ave. NW
Washington, DC 20036-1703
(202)530-5000
Fax: (202)530-5010
E-mail: winslow@winslowpartners.com

Women's Growth Capital Fund
1054 31st St., NW
Ste. 110
Washington, DC 20007
(202)342-1431
Fax: (202)341-1203
Website: http://www.wgcf.com

Sigma Capital Corp.
22668 Caravelle Circle
Boca Raton, FL 33433
(561)368-9783

North American Business Development Co., L.L.C.
111 East Las Olas Blvd.
Ft. Lauderdale, FL 33301
(305)463-0681
Fax: (305)527-0904
Website: http://www.northamericanfund.com

Chartwell Capital Management Co. Inc.
1 Independent Dr., Ste. 3120

Jacksonville, FL 32202
(904)355-3519
Fax: (904)353-5833
E-mail: info@chartwellcap.com

CEO Advisors
1061 Maitland Center Commons
Ste. 209
Maitland, FL 32751
(407)660-9327
Fax: (407)660-2109

Henry & Co.
8201 Peters Rd., Ste. 1000
Plantation, FL 33324
(954)797-7400

Avery Business Development Services
2506 St. Michel Ct.
Ponte Vedra, FL 32082
(904)285-6033

New South Ventures
5053 Ocean Blvd.
Sarasota, FL 34242
(941)358-6000
Fax: (941)358-6078
Website: http://www.newsouthventures.com

Venture Capital Management Corp.
PO Box 2626
Satellite Beach, FL 32937
(407)777-1969

Florida Capital Venture Ltd.
325 Florida Bank Plaza
100 W. Kennedy Blvd.
Tampa, FL 33602
(813)229-2294
Fax: (813)229-2028

Quantum Capital Partners
339 South Plant Ave.
Tampa, FL 33606
(813)250-1999
Fax: (813)250-1998
Website: http://www.quantumcapitalpartners.com

South Atlantic Venture Fund
614 W. Bay St.
Tampa, FL 33606-2704
(813)253-2500
Fax: (813)253-2360
E-mail: venture@southatlantic.com
Website: http://www.southatlantic.com

LM Capital Corp.
120 S. Olive, Ste. 400
West Palm Beach, FL 33401

(561)833-9700
Fax: (561)655-6587
Website: http://www.lmcapital
securities.com

Georgia

Venture First Associates
4811 Thornwood Dr.
Acworth, GA 30102
(770)928-3733
Fax: (770)928-6455

Alliance Technology Ventures
8995 Westside Pkwy., Ste. 200
Alpharetta, GA 30004
(678)336-2000
Fax: (678)336-2001
E-mail: info@atv.com
Website: http://www.atv.com

Cordova Ventures
2500 North Winds Pkwy., Ste. 475
Alpharetta, GA 30004
(678)942-0300
Fax: (678)942-0301
Website: http://www.cordovaventures.
com

Advanced Technology Development Fund
1000 Abernathy, Ste. 1420
Atlanta, GA 30328-5614
(404)668-2333
Fax: (404)668-2333

CGW Southeast Partners
12 Piedmont Center, Ste. 210
Atlanta, GA 30305
(404)816-3255
Fax: (404)816-3258
Website: http://www.cgwlp.com

Cyberstarts
1900 Emery St., NW
3rd Fl.
Atlanta, GA 30318
(404)267-5000
Fax: (404)267-5200
Website: http://www.cyberstarts.com

EGL Holdings, Inc.
10 Piedmont Center, Ste. 412
Atlanta, GA 30305
(404)949-8300
Fax: (404)949-8311

Equity South
1790 The Lenox Bldg.
3399 Peachtree Rd. NE
Atlanta, GA 30326

(404)237-6222
Fax: (404)261-1578

Five Paces
3400 Peachtree Rd., Ste. 200
Atlanta, GA 30326
(404)439-8300
Fax: (404)439-8301
Website: http://www.fivepaces.com

Frontline Capital, Inc.
3475 Lenox Rd., Ste. 400
Atlanta, GA 30326
(404)240-7280
Fax: (404)240-7281

Fuqua Ventures LLC
1201 W. Peachtree St. NW, Ste. 5000
Atlanta, GA 30309
(404)815-4500
Fax: (404)815-4528
Website: http://www.fuquaventures.com

Noro-Moseley Partners
4200 Northside Pkwy., Bldg. 9
Atlanta, GA 30327
(404)233-1966
Fax: (404)239-9280
Website: http://www.noro-moseley.com

Renaissance Capital Corp.
34 Peachtree St. NW, Ste. 2230
Atlanta, GA 30303
(404)658-9061
Fax: (404)658-9064

River Capital, Inc.
Two Midtown Plaza
1360 Peachtree St. NE, Ste. 1430
Atlanta, GA 30309
(404)873-2166
Fax: (404)873-2158

State Street Bank & Trust Co.
3414 Peachtree Rd. NE, Ste. 1010
Atlanta, GA 30326
(404)364-9500
Fax: (404)261-4469

UPS Strategic Enterprise Fund
55 Glenlake Pkwy. NE
Atlanta, GA 30328
(404)828-8814
Fax: (404)828-8088
E-mail: jcacyce@ups.com
Website: http://www.ups.com/sef/
sef_home

Wachovia
191 Peachtree St. NE, 26th Fl.
Atlanta, GA 30303

(404)332-1000
Fax: (404)332-1392
Website: http://www.wachovia.com/wca

Brainworks Ventures
4243 Dunwoody Club Dr.
Chamblee, GA 30341
(770)239-7447

First Growth Capital Inc.
Best Western Plaza, Ste. 105
PO Box 815
Forsyth, GA 31029
(912)781-7131

Financial Capital Resources, Inc.
21 Eastbrook Bend, Ste. 116
Peachtree City, GA 30269
(404)487-6650

Hawaii

HMS Hawaii Management Partners
Davies Pacific Center
841 Bishop St., Ste. 860
Honolulu, HI 96813
(808)545-3755
Fax: (808)531-2611

Idaho

Sun Valley Ventures
160 Second St.
Ketchum, ID 83340
(208)726-5005
Fax: (208)726-5094

Illinois

Open Prairie Ventures
115 N. Neil St., Ste. 209
Champaign, IL 61820
(217)351-7000
Fax: (217)351-7051
E-mail: inquire@openprairie.com
Website: http://www.openprairie.com

ABN AMRO Private Equity
208 S. La Salle St., 10th Fl.
Chicago, IL 60604
(312)855-7079
Fax: (312)553-6648
Website: http://www.abnequity.com

Alpha Capital Partners, Ltd.
122 S. Michigan Ave., Ste. 1700
Chicago, IL 60603
(312)322-9800
Fax: (312)322-9808
E-mail: acp@alphacapital.com

Ameritech Development Corp.
30 S. Wacker Dr., 37th Fl.
Chicago, IL 60606
(312)750-5083
Fax: (312)609-0244

Apex Investment Partners
225 W. Washington, Ste. 1450
Chicago, IL 60606
(312)857-2800
Fax: (312)857-1800
E-mail: apex@apexvc.com
Website: http://www.apexvc.com

Arch Venture Partners
8725 W. Higgins Rd., Ste. 290
Chicago, IL 60631
(773)380-6600
Fax: (773)380-6606
Website: http://www.archventure.com

The Bank Funds
208 South LaSalle St., Ste. 1680
Chicago, IL 60604
(312)855-6020
Fax: (312)855-8910

Batterson Venture Partners
303 W. Madison St., Ste. 1110
Chicago, IL 60606-3309
(312)269-0300
Fax: (312)269-0021
Website: http://www.battersonvp.com

William Blair Capital Partners, L.L.C.
222 W. Adams St., Ste. 1300
Chicago, IL 60606
(312)364-8250
Fax: (312)236-1042
E-mail: privateequity@wmblair.com
Website: http://www.wmblair.com

Bluestar Ventures
208 South LaSalle St., Ste. 1020
Chicago, IL 60604
(312)384-5000
Fax: (312)384-5005
Website: http://www.bluestarventures.com

The Capital Strategy Management Co.
233 S. Wacker Dr.
Box 06334
Chicago, IL 60606
(312)444-1170

DN Partners
77 West Wacker Dr., Ste. 4550
Chicago, IL 60601
(312)332-7960
Fax: (312)332-7979

Dresner Capital Inc.
29 South LaSalle St., Ste. 310
Chicago, IL 60603
(312)726-3600
Fax: (312)726-7448

Eblast Ventures LLC
11 South LaSalle St., 5th Fl.
Chicago, IL 60603
(312)372-2600
Fax: (312)372-5621
Website: http://www.eblastventures.com

Essex Woodlands Health Ventures, L.P.
190 S. LaSalle St., Ste. 2800
Chicago, IL 60603
(312)444-6040
Fax: (312)444-6034
Website: http://www.essexwood
lands.com

First Analysis Venture Capital
233 S. Wacker Dr., Ste. 9500
Chicago, IL 60606
(312)258-1400
Fax: (312)258-0334
Website: http://www.firstanalysis.com

Frontenac Co.
135 S. LaSalle St., Ste.3800
Chicago, IL 60603
(312)368-0044
Fax: (312)368-9520
Website: http://www.frontenac.com

GTCR Golder Rauner, LLC
6100 Sears Tower
Chicago, IL 60606
(312)382-2200
Fax: (312)382-2201
Website: http://www.gtcr.com

High Street Capital LLC
311 South Wacker Dr., Ste. 4550
Chicago, IL 60606
(312)697-4990
Fax: (312)697-4994
Website: http://www.highstr.com

IEG Venture Management, Inc.
70 West Madison
Chicago, IL 60602
(312)644-0890
Fax: (312)454-0369
Website: http://www.iegventure.com

JK&B Capital
180 North Stetson, Ste. 4500
Chicago, IL 60601
(312)946-1200
Fax: (312)946-1103

E-mail: gspencer@jkbcapital.com
Website: http://www.jkbcapital.com

Kettle Partners L.P.
350 W. Hubbard, Ste. 350
Chicago, IL 60610
(312)329-9300
Fax: (312)527-4519
Website: http://www.kettlevc.com

Lake Shore Capital Partners
20 N. Wacker Dr., Ste. 2807
Chicago, IL 60606
(312)803-3536
Fax: (312)803-3534

LaSalle Capital Group Inc.
70 W. Madison St., Ste. 5710
Chicago, IL 60602
(312)236-7041
Fax: (312)236-0720

Linc Capital, Inc.
303 E. Wacker Pkwy., Ste. 1000
Chicago, IL 60601
(312)946-2670
Fax: (312)938-4290
E-mail: bdemars@linccap.com

Madison Dearborn Partners, Inc.
3 First National Plz., Ste. 3800
Chicago, IL 60602
(312)895-1000
Fax: (312)895-1001
E-mail: invest@mdcp.com
Website: http://www.mdcp.com

Mesirow Private Equity Investments Inc.
350 N. Clark St.
Chicago, IL 60610
(312)595-6950
Fax: (312)595-6211
Website: http://www.meisrow
financial.com

Mosaix Ventures LLC
1822 North Mohawk
Chicago, IL 60614
(312)274-0988
Fax: (312)274-0989
Website: http://www.mosaix
ventures.com

Nesbitt Burns
111 West Monroe St.
Chicago, IL 60603
(312)416-3855
Fax: (312)765-8000
Website: http://www.harrisbank.com

Polestar Capital, Inc.
180 N. Michigan Ave., Ste. 1905
Chicago, IL 60601
(312)984-9090
Fax: (312)984-9877
E-mail: wl@polestarvc.com
Website: http://www.polestarvc.com

Prince Ventures (Chicago)
10 S. Wacker Dr., Ste. 2575
Chicago, IL 60606-7407
(312)454-1408
Fax: (312)454-9125

Prism Capital
444 N. Michigan Ave.
Chicago, IL 60611
(312)464-7900
Fax: (312)464-7915
Website: http://www.prismfund.com

Third Coast Capital
900 N. Franklin St., Ste. 700
Chicago, IL 60610
(312)337-3303
Fax: (312)337-2567
E-mail: manic@earthlink.com
Website: http://www.third
coastcapital.com

Thoma Cressey Equity Partners
4460 Sears Tower, 92nd Fl.
233 S. Wacker Dr.
Chicago, IL 60606
(312)777-4444
Fax: (312)777-4445
Website: http://www.thomacressey.com

Tribune Ventures
435 N. Michigan Ave., Ste. 600
Chicago, IL 60611
(312)527-8797
Fax: (312)222-5993
Website: http://www.tribuneventures.com

Wind Point Partners (Chicago)
676 N. Michigan Ave., Ste. 330
Chicago, IL 60611
(312)649-4000
Website: http://www.wppartners.com

Marquette Venture Partners
520 Lake Cook Rd., Ste. 450
Deerfield, IL 60015
(847)940-1700
Fax: (847)940-1724
Website: http://www.marquette
ventures.com

Duchossois Investments Limited, LLC
845 Larch Ave.
Elmhurst, IL 60126

(630)530-6105
Fax: (630)993-8644
Website: http://www.duchtec.com

Evanston Business Investment Corp.
1840 Oak Ave.
Evanston, IL 60201
(847)866-1840
Fax: (847)866-1808
E-mail: t-parkinson@nwu.com
Website: http://www.ebic.com

Inroads Capital Partners L.P.
1603 Orrington Ave., Ste. 2050
Evanston, IL 60201-3841
(847)864-2000
Fax: (847)864-9692

The Cerulean Fund/WGC Enterprises
1701 E. Lake Ave., Ste. 170
Glenview, IL 60025
(847)657-8002
Fax: (847)657-8168

Ventana Financial Resources, Inc.
249 Market Sq.
Lake Forest, IL 60045
(847)234-3434

Beecken, Petty & Co.
901 Warrenville Rd., Ste. 205
Lisle, IL 60532
(630)435-0300
Fax: (630)435-0370
E-mail: hep@bpcompany.com
Website: http://www.bpcompany.com

Allstate Private Equity
3075 Sanders Rd., Ste. G5D
Northbrook, IL 60062-7127
(847)402-8247
Fax: (847)402-0880

KB Partners
1101 Skokie Blvd., Ste. 260
Northbrook, IL 60062-2856
(847)714-0444
Fax: (847)714-0445
E-mail: keith@kbpartners.com
Website: http://www.kbpartners.com

Transcap Associates Inc.
900 Skokie Blvd., Ste. 210
Northbrook, IL 60062
(847)753-9600
Fax: (847)753-9090

**Graystone Venture Partners, L.L.C. /
Portage Venture Partners**
One Northfield Plaza, Ste. 530
Northfield, IL 60093

(847)446-9460
Fax: (847)446-9470
Website: http://www.portage
ventures.com

Motorola Inc.
1303 E. Algonquin Rd.
Schaumburg, IL 60196-1065
(847)576-4929
Fax: (847)538-2250
Website: http://www.mot.com/mne

Indiana

Irwin Ventures LLC
500 Washington St.
Columbus, IN 47202
(812)373-1434
Fax: (812)376-1709
Website: http://www.irwinventures.com

Cambridge Venture Partners
4181 East 96th St., Ste. 200
Indianapolis, IN 46240
(317)814-6192
Fax: (317)944-9815

CID Equity Partners
One American Square, Ste. 2850
Box 82074
Indianapolis, IN 46282
(317)269-2350
Fax: (317)269-2355
Website: http://www.cidequity.com

Gazelle Techventures
6325 Digital Way, Ste. 460
Indianapolis, IN 46278
(317)275-6800
Fax: (317)275-1101
Website: http://www.gazellevc.com

Monument Advisors Inc.
Bank One Center/Circle
111 Monument Circle, Ste. 600
Indianapolis, IN 46204-5172
(317)656-5065
Fax: (317)656-5060
Website: http://www.monumentadv.com

MWV Capital Partners
201 N. Illinois St., Ste. 300
Indianapolis, IN 46204
(317)237-2323
Fax: (317)237-2325
Website: http://www.mwvcapital.com

First Source Capital Corp.
100 North Michigan St.
PO Box 1602
South Bend, IN 46601

(219)235-2180
Fax: (219)235-2227

Iowa

Allsop Venture Partners
118 Third Ave. SE, Ste. 837
Cedar Rapids, IA 52401
(319)368-6675
Fax: (319)363-9515

InvestAmerica Investment Advisors, Inc.
101 2nd St. SE, Ste. 800
Cedar Rapids, IA 52401
(319)363-8249
Fax: (319)363-9683

Pappajohn Capital Resources
2116 Financial Center
Des Moines, IA 50309
(515)244-5746
Fax: (515)244-2346
Website: http://www.pappajohn.com

Berthel Fisher & Company Planning Inc.
701 Tama St.
PO Box 609
Marion, IA 52302
(319)497-5700
Fax: (319)497-4244

Kansas

Enterprise Merchant Bank
7400 West 110th St., Ste. 560
Overland Park, KS 66210
(913)327-8500
Fax: (913)327-8505

Kansas Venture Capital, Inc. (Overland Park)
6700 Antioch Plz., Ste. 460
Overland Park, KS 66204
(913)262-7117
Fax: (913)262-3509
E-mail: jdalton@kvci.com

Child Health Investment Corp.
6803 W. 64th St., Ste. 208
Shawnee Mission, KS 66202
(913)262-1436
Fax: (913)262-1575
Website: http://www.chca.com

Kansas Technology Enterprise Corp.
214 SW 6th, 1st Fl.
Topeka, KS 66603-3719
(785)296-5272
Fax: (785)296-1160

E-mail: ktec@ktec.com
Website: http://www.ktec.com

Kentucky

Kentucky Highlands Investment Corp.
362 Old Whitley Rd.
London, KY 40741
(606)864-5175
Fax: (606)864-5194
Website: http://www.khic.org

Chrysalis Ventures, L.L.C.
1850 National City Tower
Louisville, KY 40202
(502)583-7644
Fax: (502)583-7648
E-mail: bobsany@chrysalisventures.com
Website: http://www.chrysalis
ventures.com

Humana Venture Capital
500 West Main St.
Louisville, KY 40202
(502)580-3922
Fax: (502)580-2051
E-mail: gemont@humana.com
George Emont, Director

Summit Capital Group, Inc.
6510 Glenridge Park Pl., Ste. 8
Louisville, KY 40222
(502)332-2700

Louisiana

Bank One Equity Investors, Inc.
451 Florida St.
Baton Rouge, LA 70801
(504)332-4421
Fax: (504)332-7377

Advantage Capital Partners
LLE Tower
909 Poydras St., Ste. 2230
New Orleans, LA 70112
(504)522-4850
Fax: (504)522-4950
Website: http://www.advantagecap.com

Maine

CEI Ventures / Coastal Ventures LP
2 Portland Fish Pier, Ste. 201
Portland, ME 04101
(207)772-5356
Fax: (207)772-5503
Website: http://www.ceiventures.com

Commwealth Bioventures, Inc.
4 Milk St.
Portland, ME 04101

(207)780-0904
Fax: (207)780-0913

Maryland

Annapolis Ventures LLC
151 West St., Ste. 302
Annapolis, MD 21401
(443)482-9555
Fax: (443)482-9565
Website: http://www.annapolis
ventures.com

Delmag Ventures
220 Wardour Dr.
Annapolis, MD 21401
(410)267-8196
Fax: (410)267-8017
Website: http://www.delmag
ventures.com

Abell Venture Fund
111 S. Calvert St., Ste. 2300
Baltimore, MD 21202
(410)547-1300
Fax: (410)539-6579
Website: http://www.abell.org

ABS Ventures (Baltimore)
1 South St., Ste. 2150
Baltimore, MD 21202
(410)895-3895
Fax: (410)895-3899
Website: http://www.absventures.com

Anthem Capital, L.P.
16 S. Calvert St., Ste. 800
Baltimore, MD 21202-1305
(410)625-1510
Fax: (410)625-1735
Website: http://www.anthemcapital.com

Catalyst Ventures
1119 St. Paul St.
Baltimore, MD 21202
(410)244-0123
Fax: (410)752-7721

Maryland Venture Capital Trust
217 E. Redwood St., Ste. 2200
Baltimore, MD 21202
(410)767-6361
Fax: (410)333-6931

New Enterprise Associates (Baltimore)
1119 St. Paul St.
Baltimore, MD 21202
(410)244-0115
Fax: (410)752-7721
Website: http://www.nea.com

T. Rowe Price Threshold Partnerships
100 E. Pratt St., 8th Fl.
Baltimore, MD 21202
(410)345-2000
Fax: (410)345-2800

Spring Capital Partners
16 W. Madison St.
Baltimore, MD 21201
(410)685-8000
Fax: (410)727-1436
E-mail: mailbox@springcap.com

Arete Corporation
3 Bethesda Metro Ctr., Ste. 770
Bethesda, MD 20814
(301)657-6268
Fax: (301)657-6254
Website: http://www.arete-microgen.com

Embryon Capital
7903 Sleaford Place
Bethesda, MD 20814
(301)656-6837
Fax: (301)656-8056

Potomac Ventures
7920 Norfolk Ave., Ste. 1100
Bethesda, MD 20814
(301)215-9240
Website: http://www.potomacventures.com

Toucan Capital Corp.
3 Bethesda Metro Center, Ste. 700
Bethesda, MD 20814
(301)961-1970
Fax: (301)961-1969
Website: http://www.toucancapital.com

Kinetic Ventures LLC
2 Wisconsin Cir., Ste. 620
Chevy Chase, MD 20815
(301)652-8066
Fax: (301)652-8310
Website: http://www.kineticventures.com

Boulder Ventures Ltd.
4750 Owings Mills Blvd.
Owings Mills, MD 21117
(410)998-3114
Fax: (410)356-5492
Website: http://www.boulderventures.com

Grotech Capital Group
9690 Deereco Rd., Ste. 800
Timonium, MD 21093
(410)560-2000
Fax: (410)560-1910
Website: http://www.grotech.com

Massachusetts

Adams, Harkness & Hill, Inc.
60 State St.
Boston, MA 02109
(617)371-3900

Advent International
75 State St., 29th Fl.
Boston, MA 02109
(617)951-9400
Fax: (617)951-0566
Website: http://www.adventinternational.com

American Research and Development
30 Federal St.
Boston, MA 02110-2508
(617)423-7500
Fax: (617)423-9655

Ascent Venture Partners
255 State St., 5th Fl.
Boston, MA 02109
(617)270-9400
Fax: (617)270-9401
E-mail: info@ascentvp.com
Website: http://www.ascentvp.com

Atlas Venture
222 Berkeley St.
Boston, MA 02116
(617)488-2200
Fax: (617)859-9292
Website: http://www.atlasventure.com

Axxon Capital
28 State St., 37th Fl.
Boston, MA 02109
(617)722-0980
Fax: (617)557-6014
Website: http://www.axxoncapital.com

BancBoston Capital/BancBoston Ventures
175 Federal St., 10th Fl.
Boston, MA 02110
(617)434-2509
Fax: (617)434-6175
Website: http://www.bancbostoncapital.com

Boston Capital Ventures
Old City Hall
45 School St.
Boston, MA 02108
(617)227-6550
Fax: (617)227-3847
E-mail: info@bcv.com
Website: http://www.bcv.com

Boston Financial & Equity Corp.
20 Overland St.
PO Box 15071
Boston, MA 02215
(617)267-2900
Fax: (617)437-7601
E-mail: debbie@bfec.com

Boston Millennia Partners
30 Rowes Wharf
Boston, MA 02110
(617)428-5150
Fax: (617)428-5160
Website: http://www.millenniapartners.com

Bristol Investment Trust
842A Beacon St.
Boston, MA 02215-3199
(617)566-5212
Fax: (617)267-0932

Brook Venture Management LLC
50 Federal St., 5th Fl.
Boston, MA 02110
(617)451-8989
Fax: (617)451-2369
Website: http://www.brookventure.com

Burr, Egan, Deleage, and Co. (Boston)
200 Clarendon St., Ste. 3800
Boston, MA 02116
(617)262-7770
Fax: (617)262-9779

Cambridge/Samsung Partners
One Exeter Plaza
Ninth Fl.
Boston, MA 02116
(617)262-4440
Fax: (617)262-5562

Chestnut Street Partners, Inc.
75 State St., Ste. 2500
Boston, MA 02109
(617)345-7220
Fax: (617)345-7201
E-mail: chestnut@chestnutp.com

Claflin Capital Management, Inc.
10 Liberty Sq., Ste. 300
Boston, MA 02109
(617)426-6505
Fax: (617)482-0016
Website: http://www.claflincapital.com

Copley Venture Partners
99 Summer St., Ste. 1720
Boston, MA 02110
(617)737-1253
Fax: (617)439-0699

Corning Capital / Corning Technology Ventures
121 High Street, Ste. 400
Boston, MA 02110
(617)338-2656
Fax: (617)261-3864
Website: http://www.corningventures.com

Downer & Co.
211 Congress St.
Boston, MA 02110
(617)482-6200
Fax: (617)482-6201
E-mail: cdowner@downer.com
Website: http://www.downer.com

Fidelity Ventures
82 Devonshire St.
Boston, MA 02109
(617)563-6370
Fax: (617)476-9023
Website: http://www.fidelityventures.com

Greylock Management Corp. (Boston)
1 Federal St.
Boston, MA 02110-2065
(617)423-5525
Fax: (617)482-0059

Gryphon Ventures
222 Berkeley St., Ste.1600
Boston, MA 02116
(617)267-9191
Fax: (617)267-4293
E-mail: all@gryphoninc.com

Halpern, Denny & Co.
500 Boylston St.
Boston, MA 02116
(617)536-6602
Fax: (617)536-8535

Harbourvest Partners, LLC
1 Financial Center, 44th Fl.
Boston, MA 02111
(617)348-3707
Fax: (617)350-0305
Website: http://www.hvpllc.com

Highland Capital Partners
2 International Pl.
Boston, MA 02110
(617)981-1500
Fax: (617)531-1550
E-mail: info@hcp.com
Website: http://www.hcp.com

Lee Munder Venture Partners
John Hancock Tower T-53
200 Clarendon St.
Boston, MA 02103

(617)380-5600
Fax: (617)380-5601
Website: http://www.leemunder.com

M/C Venture Partners
75 State St., Ste. 2500
Boston, MA 02109
(617)345-7200
Fax: (617)345-7201
Website: http://www.mcventure
partners.com

Massachusetts Capital Resources Co.
420 Boylston St.
Boston, MA 02116
(617)536-3900
Fax: (617)536-7930

Massachusetts Technology Development Corp. (MTDC)
148 State St.
Boston, MA 02109
(617)723-4920
Fax: (617)723-5983
E-mail: jhodgman@mtdc.com
Website: http://www.mtdc.com

New England Partners
One Boston Place, Ste. 2100
Boston, MA 02108
(617)624-8400
Fax: (617)624-8999
Website: http://www.nepartners.com

North Hill Ventures
Ten Post Office Square
11th Fl.
Boston, MA 02109
(617)788-2112
Fax: (617)788-2152
Website: http://www.northhill
ventures.com

OneLiberty Ventures
150 Cambridge Park Dr.
Boston, MA 02140
(617)492-7280
Fax: (617)492-7290
Website: http://www.oneliberty.com

Schroder Ventures
Life Sciences
60 State St., Ste. 3650
Boston, MA 02109
(617)367-8100
Fax: (617)367-1590
Website: http://www.shroderventures.com

Shawmut Capital Partners
75 Federal St., 18th Fl.
Boston, MA 02110

(617)368-4900
Fax: (617)368-4910
Website: http://www.shawmutcapital.com

Solstice Capital LLC
15 Broad St., 3rd Fl.
Boston, MA 02109
(617)523-7733
Fax: (617)523-5827
E-mail: solticecapital@solcap.com

Spectrum Equity Investors
One International Pl., 29th Fl.
Boston, MA 02110
(617)464-4600
Fax: (617)464-4601
Website: http://www.spectrumequity.com

Spray Venture Partners
One Walnut St.
Boston, MA 02108
(617)305-4140
Fax: (617)305-4144
Website: http://www.sprayventure.com

The Still River Fund
100 Federal St., 29th Fl.
Boston, MA 02110
(617)348-2327
Fax: (617)348-2371
Website: http://www.stillriverfund.com

Summit Partners
600 Atlantic Ave., Ste. 2800
Boston, MA 02210-2227
(617)824-1000
Fax: (617)824-1159
Website: http://www.summitpartners.com

TA Associates, Inc. (Boston)
High Street Tower
125 High St., Ste. 2500
Boston, MA 02110
(617)574-6700
Fax: (617)574-6728
Website: http://www.ta.com

TVM Techno Venture Management
101 Arch St., Ste. 1950
Boston, MA 02110
(617)345-9320
Fax: (617)345-9377
E-mail: info@tvmvc.com
Website: http://www.tvmvc.com

UNC Ventures
64 Burough St.
Boston, MA 02130-4017
(617)482-7070
Fax: (617)522-2176

Venture Investment Management Company (VIMAC)
177 Milk St.
Boston, MA 02190-3410
(617)292-3300
Fax: (617)292-7979
E-mail: bzeisig@vimac.com
Website: http://www.vimac.com

MDT Advisers, Inc.
125 Cambridge Park Dr.
Cambridge, MA 02140-2314
(617)234-2200
Fax: (617)234-2210
Website: http://www.mdtai.com

TTC Ventures
One Main St., 6th Fl.
Cambridge, MA 02142
(617)528-3137
Fax: (617)577-1715
E-mail: info@ttcventures.com

Zero Stage Capital Co. Inc.
101 Main St., 17th Fl.
Cambridge, MA 02142
(617)876-5355
Fax: (617)876-1248
Website: http://www.zerostage.com

Atlantic Capital
164 Cushing Hwy.
Cohasset, MA 02025
(617)383-9449
Fax: (617)383-6040
E-mail: info@atlanticcap.com
Website: http://www.atlanticcap.com

Seacoast Capital Partners
55 Ferncroft Rd.
Danvers, MA 01923
(978)750-1300
Fax: (978)750-1301
E-mail: gdeli@seacoastcapital.com
Website: http://www.seacoast
capital.com

Sage Management Group
44 South Street
PO Box 2026
East Dennis, MA 02641
(508)385-7172
Fax: (508)385-7272
E-mail: sagemgt@capecod.net

Applied Technology
1 Cranberry Hill
Lexington, MA 02421-7397
(617)862-8622
Fax: (617)862-8367

Royalty Capital Management
5 Downing Rd.
Lexington, MA 02421-6918
(781)861-8490

Argo Global Capital
210 Broadway, Ste. 101
Lynnfield, MA 01940
(781)592-5250
Fax: (781)592-5230
Website: http://www.gsmcapital.com

Industry Ventures
6 Bayne Lane
Newburyport, MA 01950
(978)499-7606
Fax: (978)499-0686
Website: http://
www.industryventures.com

Softbank Capital Partners
10 Langley Rd., Ste. 202
Newton Center, MA 02459
(617)928-9300
Fax: (617)928-9305
E-mail: clax@bvc.com

Advanced Technology Ventures (Boston)
281 Winter St., Ste. 350
Waltham, MA 02451
(781)290-0707
Fax: (781)684-0045
E-mail: info@atvcapital.com
Website: http://www.atvcapital.com

Castile Ventures
890 Winter St., Ste. 140
Waltham, MA 02451
(781)890-0060
Fax: (781)890-0065
Website: http://www.castileventures.com

Charles River Ventures
1000 Winter St., Ste. 3300
Waltham, MA 02451
(781)487-7060
Fax: (781)487-7065
Website: http://www.crv.com

Comdisco Venture Group (Waltham)
Totton Pond Office Center
400-1 Totten Pond Rd.
Waltham, MA 02451
(617)672-0250
Fax: (617)398-8099

Marconi Ventures
890 Winter St., Ste. 310
Waltham, MA 02451
(781)839-7177

Fax: (781)522-7477
Website: http://www.marconi.com

Matrix Partners
Bay Colony Corporate Center
1000 Winter St., Ste.4500
Waltham, MA 02451
(781)890-2244
Fax: (781)890-2288
Website: http://www.matrix
partners.com

North Bridge Venture Partners
950 Winter St. Ste. 4600
Waltham, MA 02451
(781)290-0004
Fax: (781)290-0999
E-mail: eta@nbvp.com

Polaris Venture Partners
Bay Colony Corporate Ctr.
1000 Winter St., Ste. 3500
Waltham, MA 02451
(781)290-0770
Fax: (781)290-0880
E-mail: partners@polarisventures.com
Website: http://www.polar
isventures.com

Seaflower Ventures
Bay Colony Corporate Ctr.
1000 Winter St. Ste. 1000
Waltham, MA 02451
(781)466-9552
Fax: (781)466-9553
E-mail: moot@seaflower.com
Website: http://www.seaflower.com

Ampersand Ventures
55 William St., Ste. 240
Wellesley, MA 02481
(617)239-0700
Fax: (617)239-0824
E-mail: info@ampersandventures.com
Website: http://www.ampersand
ventures.com

Battery Ventures (Boston)
20 William St., Ste. 200
Wellesley, MA 02481
(781)577-1000
Fax: (781)577-1001
Website: http://www.battery.com

Commonwealth Capital Ventures, L.P.
20 William St., Ste.225
Wellesley, MA 02481
(781)237-7373
Fax: (781)235-8627
Website: http://www.ccvlp.com

Fowler, Anthony & Company
20 Walnut St.
Wellesley, MA 02481
(781)237-4201
Fax: (781)237-7718

Gemini Investors
20 William St.
Wellesley, MA 02481
(781)237-7001
Fax: (781)237-7233

Grove Street Advisors Inc.
20 William St., Ste. 230
Wellesley, MA 02481
(781)263-6100
Fax: (781)263-6101
Website: http://www.groves
treetadvisors.com

Mees Pierson Investeringsmaat B.V.
20 William St., Ste. 210
Wellesley, MA 02482
(781)239-7600
Fax: (781)239-0377

Norwest Equity Partners
40 William St., Ste. 305
Wellesley, MA 02481-3902
(781)237-5870
Fax: (781)237-6270
Website: http://www.norwestvp.com

Bessemer Venture Partners (Wellesley Hills)
83 Walnut St.
Wellesley Hills, MA 02481
(781)237-6050
Fax: (781)235-7576
E-mail: travis@bvpny.com
Website: http://www.bvp.com

Venture Capital Fund of New England
20 Walnut St., Ste. 120
Wellesley Hills, MA 02481-2175
(781)239-8262
Fax: (781)239-8263

Prism Venture Partners
100 Lowder Brook Dr., Ste. 2500
Westwood, MA 02090
(781)302-4000
Fax: (781)302-4040
E-mail: dwbaum@prismventure.com

Palmer Partners LP
200 Unicorn Park Dr.
Woburn, MA 01801
(781)933-5445
Fax: (781)933-0698

Michigan

Arbor Partners, L.L.C.
130 South First St.
Ann Arbor, MI 48104
(734)668-9000
Fax: (734)669-4195
Website: http://www.arborpartners.com

EDF Ventures
425 N. Main St.
Ann Arbor, MI 48104
(734)663-3213
Fax: (734)663-7358
E-mail: edf@edfvc.com
Website: http://www.edfvc.com

White Pines Management, L.L.C.
2401 Plymouth Rd., Ste. B
Ann Arbor, MI 48105
(734)747-9401
Fax: (734)747-9704
E-mail: ibund@whitepines.com
Website: http://www.whitepines.com

Wellmax, Inc.
3541 Bendway Blvd., Ste. 100
Bloomfield Hills, MI 48301
(248)646-3554
Fax: (248)646-6220

Venture Funding, Ltd.
Fisher Bldg.
3011 West Grand Blvd., Ste. 321
Detroit, MI 48202
(313)871-3606
Fax: (313)873-4935

Investcare Partners L.P. / GMA Capital LLC
32330 W. Twelve Mile Rd.
Farmington Hills, MI 48334
(248)489-9000
Fax: (248)489-8819
E-mail: gma@gmacapital.com
Website: http://www.gmacapital.com

Liberty Bidco Investment Corp.
30833 Northwestern Highway, Ste. 211
Farmington Hills, MI 48334
(248)626-6070
Fax: (248)626-6072

Seaflower Ventures
5170 Nicholson Rd.
PO Box 474
Fowlerville, MI 48836
(517)223-3335
Fax: (517)223-3337
E-mail: gibbons@seaflower.com
Website: http://www.seaflower.com

Ralph Wilson Equity Fund LLC
15400 E. Jefferson Ave.
Gross Pointe Park, MI 48230
(313)821-9122
Fax: (313)821-9101
Website: http://www.Ralph
WilsonEquityFund.com
J. Skip Simms, President

Minnesota

Development Corp. of Austin
1900 Eighth Ave., NW
Austin, MN 55912
(507)433-0346
Fax: (507)433-0361
E-mail: dca@smig.net
Website: http://www.spamtownusa.com

Northeast Ventures Corp.
802 Alworth Bldg.
Duluth, MN 55802
(218)722-9915
Fax: (218)722-9871

Medical Innovation Partners, Inc.
6450 City West Pkwy.
Eden Prairie, MN 55344-3245
(612)828-9616
Fax: (612)828-9596

St. Paul Venture Capital, Inc.
10400 Vicking Dr., Ste. 550
Eden Prairie, MN 55344
(612)995-7474
Fax: (612)995-7475
Website: http://www.stpaulvc.com

Cherry Tree Investments, Inc.
7601 France Ave. S, Ste. 150
Edina, MN 55435
(612)893-9012
Fax: (612)893-9036
Website: http://www.cherrytree.com

Shared Ventures, Inc.
6550 York Ave. S
Edina, MN 55435
(612)925-3411

Sherpa Partners LLC
5050 Lincoln Dr., Ste. 490
Edina, MN 55436
(952)942-1070
Fax: (952)942-1071
Website: http://www.sherpapartners.com

Affinity Capital Management
901 Marquette Ave., Ste. 1810
Minneapolis, MN 55402
(612)252-9900

Fax: (612)252-9911
Website: http://www.affinitycapital.com

Artesian Capital
1700 Foshay Tower
821 Marquette Ave.
Minneapolis, MN 55402
(612)334-5600
Fax: (612)334-5601
E-mail: artesian@artesian.com

Coral Ventures
60 S. 6th St., Ste. 3510
Minneapolis, MN 55402
(612)335-8666
Fax: (612)335-8668
Website: http://www.coralventures.com

Crescendo Venture Management, L.L.C.
800 LaSalle Ave., Ste. 2250
Minneapolis, MN 55402
(612)607-2800
Fax: (612)607-2801
Website: http://www.crescendo
ventures.com

Gideon Hixon Venture
1900 Foshay Tower
821 Marquette Ave.
Minneapolis, MN 55402
(612)904-2314
Fax: (612)204-0913

Norwest Equity Partners
3600 IDS Center
80 S. 8th St.
Minneapolis, MN 55402
(612)215-1600
Fax: (612)215-1601
Website: http://www.norwestvp.com

Oak Investment Partners (Minneapolis)
4550 Norwest Center
90 S. 7th St.
Minneapolis, MN 55402
(612)339-9322
Fax: (612)337-8017
Website: http://www.oakinv.com

Pathfinder Venture Capital Funds (Minneapolis)
7300 Metro Blvd., Ste. 585
Minneapolis, MN 55439
(612)835-1121
Fax: (612)835-8389
E-mail: jahrens620@aol.com

U.S. Bancorp Piper Jaffray Ventures, Inc.
800 Nicollet Mall, Ste. 800
Minneapolis, MN 55402

(612)303-5686
Fax: (612)303-1350
Website: http://www.paperjaffrey
ventures.com

The Food Fund, Ltd. Partnership
5720 Smatana Dr., Ste. 300
Minnetonka, MN 55343
(612)939-3950
Fax: (612)939-8106

Mayo Medical Ventures
200 First St. SW
Rochester, MN 55905
(507)266-4586
Fax: (507)284-5410
Website: http://www.mayo.edu

Missouri

Bankers Capital Corp.
3100 Gillham Rd.
Kansas City, MO 64109
(816)531-1600
Fax: (816)531-1334

Capital for Business, Inc. (Kansas City)
1000 Walnut St., 18th Fl.
Kansas City, MO 64106
(816)234-2357
Fax: (816)234-2952
Website: http://
www.capitalforbusiness.com

De Vries & Co. Inc.
800 West 47th St.
Kansas City, MO 64112
(816)756-0055
Fax: (816)756-0061

InvestAmerica Venture Group Inc. (Kansas City)
Commerce Tower
911 Main St., Ste. 2424
Kansas City, MO 64105
(816)842-0114
Fax: (816)471-7339

Kansas City Equity Partners
233 W. 47th St.
Kansas City, MO 64112
(816)960-1771
Fax: (816)960-1777
Website: http://www.kcep.com

Bome Investors, Inc.
8000 Maryland Ave., Ste. 1190
St. Louis, MO 63105
(314)721-5707
Fax: (314)721-5135

Website: http://www.gateway
ventures.com

Capital for Business, Inc. (St. Louis)
11 S. Meramac St., Ste. 1430
St. Louis, MO 63105
(314)746-7427
Fax: (314)746-8739
Website: http://www.capitalfor
business.com

Crown Capital Corp.
540 Maryville Centre Dr., Ste. 120
Saint Louis, MO 63141
(314)576-1201
Fax: (314)576-1525
Website: http://www.crown-
cap.com

Gateway Associates L.P.
8000 Maryland Ave., Ste. 1190
St. Louis, MO 63105
(314)721-5707
Fax: (314)721-5135

Harbison Corp.
8112 Maryland Ave., Ste. 250
Saint Louis, MO 63105
(314)727-8200
Fax: (314)727-0249

Heartland Capital Fund, Ltd.
PO Box 642117
Omaha, NE 68154
(402)778-5124
Fax: (402)445-2370
Website: http://www.heartland
capitalfund.com

Odin Capital Group
1625 Farnam St., Ste. 700
Omaha, NE 68102
(402)346-6200
Fax: (402)342-9311
Website: http://www.odincapital.com

Nevada

Edge Capital Investment Co. LLC
1350 E. Flamingo Rd., Ste. 3000
Las Vegas, NV 89119
(702)438-3343
E-mail: info@edgecapital.net
Website: http://www.edgecapital.net

The Benefit Capital Companies Inc.
PO Box 542
Logandale, NV 89021
(702)398-3222
Fax: (702)398-3700

Millennium Three Venture Group LLC
6880 South McCarran Blvd., Ste. A-11
Reno, NV 89509
(775)954-2020
Fax: (775)954-2023
Website: http://www.m3vg.com

New Jersey

Alan I. Goldman & Associates
497 Ridgewood Ave.
Glen Ridge, NJ 07028
(973)857-5680
Fax: (973)509-8856

CS Capital Partners LLC
328 Second St., Ste. 200
Lakewood, NJ 08701
(732)901-1111
Fax: (212)202-5071
Website: http://www.cs-capital.com

Edison Venture Fund
1009 Lenox Dr., Ste. 4
Lawrenceville, NJ 08648
(609)896-1900
Fax: (609)896-0066
E-mail: info@edisonventure.com
Website: http://www.edisonventure.com

Tappan Zee Capital Corp. (New Jersey)
201 Lower Notch Rd.
PO Box 416
Little Falls, NJ 07424
(973)256-8280
Fax: (973)256-2841

The CIT Group/Venture Capital, Inc.
650 CIT Dr.
Livingston, NJ 07039
(973)740-5429
Fax: (973)740-5555
Website: http://www.cit.com

Capital Express, L.L.C.
1100 Valleybrook Ave.
Lyndhurst, NJ 07071
(201)438-8228
Fax: (201)438-5131
E-mail: niles@capitalexpress.com
Website: http://www.capitalexpress.com

Westford Technology Ventures, L.P.
17 Academy St.
Newark, NJ 07102
(973)624-2131
Fax: (973)624-2008

Accel Partners
1 Palmer Sq.
Princeton, NJ 08542

(609)683-4500
Fax: (609)683-4880
Website: http://www.accel.com

Cardinal Partners
221 Nassau St.
Princeton, NJ 08542
(609)924-6452
Fax: (609)683-0174
Website: http://www.cardinal
healthpartners.com

Domain Associates L.L.C.
One Palmer Sq., Ste. 515
Princeton, NJ 08542
(609)683-5656
Fax: (609)683-9789
Website: http://www.domainvc.com

Johnston Associates, Inc.
181 Cherry Valley Rd.
Princeton, NJ 08540
(609)924-3131
Fax: (609)683-7524
E-mail: jaincorp@aol.com

Kemper Ventures
Princeton Forrestal Village
155 Village Blvd.
Princeton, NJ 08540
(609)936-3035
Fax: (609)936-3051

Penny Lane Parnters
One Palmer Sq., Ste. 309
Princeton, NJ 08542
(609)497-4646
Fax: (609)497-0611

Early Stage Enterprises L.P.
995 Route 518
Skillman, NJ 08558
(609)921-8896
Fax: (609)921-8703
Website: http://www.esevc.com

MBW Management Inc.
1 Springfield Ave.
Summit, NJ 07901
(908)273-4060
Fax: (908)273-4430

BCI Advisors, Inc.
Glenpointe Center W.
Teaneck, NJ 07666
(201)836-3900
Fax: (201)836-6368
E-mail: info@bciadvisors.com
Website: http://www.bci
partners.com

Demuth, Folger & Wetherill / DFW Capital Partners
Glenpointe Center E., 5th Fl.
300 Frank W. Burr Blvd.
Teaneck, NJ 07666
(201)836-2233
Fax: (201)836-5666
Website: http://www.dfwcapital.com

First Princeton Capital Corp.
189 Berdan Ave., No. 131
Wayne, NJ 07470-3233
(973)278-3233
Fax: (973)278-4290
Website: http://www.lytellcatt.net

Edelson Technology Partners
300 Tice Blvd.
Woodcliff Lake, NJ 07675
(201)930-9898
Fax: (201)930-8899
Website: http://www.edelsontech.com

New Mexico

Bruce F. Glaspell & Associates
10400 Academy Rd. NE, Ste. 313
Albuquerque, NM 87111
(505)292-4505
Fax: (505)292-4258

High Desert Ventures, Inc.
6101 Imparata St. NE, Ste. 1721
Albuquerque, NM 87111
(505)797-3330
Fax: (505)338-5147

New Business Capital Fund, Ltd.
5805 Torreon NE
Albuquerque, NM 87109
(505)822-8445

SBC Ventures
10400 Academy Rd. NE, Ste. 313
Albuquerque, NM 87111
(505)292-4505
Fax: (505)292-4528

Technology Ventures Corp.
1155 University Blvd. SE
Albuquerque, NM 87106
(505)246-2882
Fax: (505)246-2891

New York

New York State Science & Technology Foundation
Small Business Technology Investment Fund
99 Washington Ave., Ste. 1731
Albany, NY 12210

(518)473-9741
Fax: (518)473-6876

Rand Capital Corp.
2200 Rand Bldg.
Buffalo, NY 14203
(716)853-0802
Fax: (716)854-8480
Website: http://www.randcapital.com

Seed Capital Partners
620 Main St.
Buffalo, NY 14202
(716)845-7520
Fax: (716)845-7539
Website: http://www.seedcp.com

Coleman Venture Group
5909 Northern Blvd.
PO Box 224
East Norwich, NY 11732
(516)626-3642
Fax: (516)626-9722

Vega Capital Corp.
45 Knollwood Rd.
Elmsford, NY 10523
(914)345-9500
Fax: (914)345-9505

Herbert Young Securities, Inc.
98 Cuttermill Rd.
Great Neck, NY 11021
(516)487-8300
Fax: (516)487-8319

Sterling/Carl Marks Capital, Inc.
175 Great Neck Rd., Ste. 408
Great Neck, NY 11021
(516)482-7374
Fax: (516)487-0781
E-mail: stercrlmar@aol.com
Website: http://www.serling
carlmarks.com

Impex Venture Management Co.
PO Box 1570
Green Island, NY 12183
(518)271-8008
Fax: (518)271-9101

Corporate Venture Partners L.P.
200 Sunset Park
Ithaca, NY 14850
(607)257-6323
Fax: (607)257-6128

Arthur P. Gould & Co.
One Wilshire Dr.
Lake Success, NY 11020
(516)773-3000
Fax: (516)773-3289

Dauphin Capital Partners
108 Forest Ave.
Locust Valley, NY 11560
(516)759-3339
Fax: (516)759-3322
Website: http://www.dauphincapital.com

550 Digital Media Ventures
555 Madison Ave., 10th Fl.
New York, NY 10022
Website: http://www.550dmv.com

Aberlyn Capital Management Co., Inc.
500 Fifth Ave.
New York, NY 10110
(212)391-7750
Fax: (212)391-7762

Adler & Company
342 Madison Ave., Ste. 807
New York, NY 10173
(212)599-2535
Fax: (212)599-2526

Alimansky Capital Group, Inc.
605 Madison Ave., Ste. 300
New York, NY 10022-1901
(212)832-7300
Fax: (212)832-7338

Allegra Partners
515 Madison Ave., 29th Fl.
New York, NY 10022
(212)826-9080
Fax: (212)759-2561

The Argentum Group
The Chyrsler Bldg.
405 Lexington Ave.
New York, NY 10174
(212)949-6262
Fax: (212)949-8294
Website: http://www.argentum
group.com

Axavision Inc.
14 Wall St., 26th Fl.
New York, NY 10005
(212)619-4000
Fax: (212)619-7202

Bedford Capital Corp.
18 East 48th St., Ste. 1800
New York, NY 10017
(212)688-5700
Fax: (212)754-4699
E-mail: info@bedfordnyc.com
Website: http://www.bedfordnyc.com

Bloom & Co.
950 Third Ave.

New York, NY 10022
(212)838-1858
Fax: (212)838-1843

Bristol Capital Management
300 Park Ave., 17th Fl.
New York, NY 10022
(212)572-6306
Fax: (212)705-4292

**Citicorp Venture Capital Ltd.
(New York City)**
399 Park Ave., 14th Fl.
Zone 4
New York, NY 10043
(212)559-1127
Fax: (212)888-2940

CM Equity Partners
135 E. 57th St.
New York, NY 10022
(212)909-8428
Fax: (212)980-2630

Cohen & Co., L.L.C.
800 Third Ave.
New York, NY 10022
(212)317-2250
Fax: (212)317-2255
E-mail: nlcohen@aol.com

Cornerstone Equity Investors, L.L.C.
717 5th Ave., Ste. 1100
New York, NY 10022
(212)753-0901
Fax: (212)826-6798
Website: http://www.cornerstone-
equity.com

CW Group, Inc.
1041 3rd Ave., 2nd fl.
New York, NY 10021
(212)308-5266
Fax: (212)644-0354
Website: http://www.cwventures.com

DH Blair Investment Banking Corp.
44 Wall St., 2nd Fl.
New York, NY 10005
(212)495-5000
Fax: (212)269-1438

Dresdner Kleinwort Capital
75 Wall St.
New York, NY 10005
(212)429-3131
Fax: (212)429-3139
Website: http://www.dresdnerkb.com

East River Ventures, L.P.
645 Madison Ave., 22nd Fl.

New York, NY 10022
(212)644-2322
Fax: (212)644-5498

Easton Hunt Capital Partners
641 Lexington Ave., 21st Fl.
New York, NY 10017
(212)702-0950
Fax: (212)702-0952
Website: http://www.eastoncapital.com

Elk Associates Funding Corp.
747 3rd Ave., Ste. 4C
New York, NY 10017
(212)355-2449
Fax: (212)759-3338

EOS Partners, L.P.
320 Park Ave., 22nd Fl.
New York, NY 10022
(212)832-5800
Fax: (212)832-5815
E-mail: mfirst@eospartners.com
Website: http://www.eospartners.com

Euclid Partners
45 Rockefeller Plaza, Ste. 3240
New York, NY 10111
(212)218-6880
Fax: (212)218-6877
E-mail: graham@euclidpartners.com
Website: http://www.euclidpartners.com

Evergreen Capital Partners, Inc.
150 East 58th St.
New York, NY 10155
(212)813-0758
Fax: (212)813-0754

Exeter Capital L.P.
10 E. 53rd St.
New York, NY 10022
(212)872-1172
Fax: (212)872-1198
E-mail: exeter@usa.net

Financial Technology Research Corp.
518 Broadway
Penthouse
New York, NY 10012
(212)625-9100
Fax: (212)431-0300
E-mail: fintek@financier.com

4C Ventures
237 Park Ave., Ste. 801
New York, NY 10017
(212)692-3680
Fax: (212)692-3685
Website: http://www.4cventures.com

Fusient Ventures
99 Park Ave., 20th Fl.
New York, NY 10016
(212)972-8999
Fax: (212)972-9876
E-mail: info@fusient.com
Website: http://www.fusient.com

Generation Capital Partners
551 Fifth Ave., Ste. 3100
New York, NY 10176
(212)450-8507
Fax: (212)450-8550
Website: http://www.genpartners.com

Golub Associates, Inc.
555 Madison Ave.
New York, NY 10022
(212)750-6060
Fax: (212)750-5505

Hambro America Biosciences Inc.
650 Madison Ave., 21st Floor
New York, NY 10022
(212)223-7400
Fax: (212)223-0305

Hanover Capital Corp.
505 Park Ave., 15th Fl.
New York, NY 10022
(212)755-1222
Fax: (212)935-1787

Harvest Partners, Inc.
280 Park Ave, 33rd Fl.
New York, NY 10017
(212)559-6300
Fax: (212)812-0100
Website: http://www.harvpart.com

Holding Capital Group, Inc.
10 E. 53rd St., 30th Fl.
New York, NY 10022
(212)486-6670
Fax: (212)486-0843

Hudson Venture Partners
660 Madison Ave., 14th Fl.
New York, NY 10021-8405
(212)644-9797
Fax: (212)644-7430
Website: http://www.hudsonptr.com

IBJS Capital Corp.
1 State St., 9th Fl.
New York, NY 10004
(212)858-2018
Fax: (212)858-2768

InterEquity Capital Partners, L.P.
220 5th Ave.
New York, NY 10001

(212)779-2022
Fax: (212)779-2103
Website: http://www.interequity-
capital.com

The Jordan Edmiston Group Inc.
150 East 52nd St., 18th Fl.
New York, NY 10022
(212)754-0710
Fax: (212)754-0337

Josephberg, Grosz and Co., Inc.
633 3rd Ave., 13th Fl.
New York, NY 10017
(212)974-9926
Fax: (212)397-5832

J.P. Morgan Capital Corp.
60 Wall St.
New York, NY 10260-0060
(212)648-9000
Fax: (212)648-5002
Website: http://www.jpmorgan.com

The Lambda Funds
380 Lexington Ave., 54th Fl.
New York, NY 10168
(212)682-3454
Fax: (212)682-9231

Lepercq Capital Management Inc.
1675 Broadway
New York, NY 10019
(212)698-0795
Fax: (212)262-0155

Loeb Partners Corp.
61 Broadway, Ste. 2400
New York, NY 10006
(212)483-7000
Fax: (212)574-2001

Madison Investment Partners
660 Madison Ave.
New York, NY 10021
(212)223-2600
Fax: (212)223-8208

MC Capital Inc.
520 Madison Ave., 16th Fl.
New York, NY 10022
(212)644-0841
Fax: (212)644-2926

**McCown, De Leeuw and Co.
(New York)**
65 E. 55th St., 36th Fl.
New York, NY 10022
(212)355-5500
Fax: (212)355-6283
Website: http://www.mdcpartners.com

Morgan Stanley Venture Partners
1221 Avenue of the Americas, 33rd Fl.
New York, NY 10020
(212)762-7900
Fax: (212)762-8424
E-mail: msventures@ms.com
Website: http://www.msvp.com

Nazem and Co.
645 Madison Ave., 12th Fl.
New York, NY 10022
(212)371-7900
Fax: (212)371-2150

Needham Capital Management, L.L.C.
445 Park Ave.
New York, NY 10022
(212)371-8300
Fax: (212)705-0299
Website: http://www.needhamco.com

Norwood Venture Corp.
1430 Broadway, Ste. 1607
New York, NY 10018
(212)869-5075
Fax: (212)869-5331
E-mail: nvc@mail.idt.net
Website: http://www.norven.com

Noveltek Venture Corp.
521 Fifth Ave., Ste. 1700
New York, NY 10175
(212)286-1963

Paribas Principal, Inc.
787 7th Ave.
New York, NY 10019
(212)841-2005
Fax: (212)841-3558

Patricof & Co. Ventures, Inc.
(New York)
445 Park Ave.
New York, NY 10022
(212)753-6300
Fax: (212)319-6155
Website: http://www.patricof.com

The Platinum Group, Inc.
350 Fifth Ave, Ste. 7113
New York, NY 10118
(212)736-4300
Fax: (212)736-6086
Website: http://www.platinumgroup.com

Pomona Capital
780 Third Ave., 28th Fl.
New York, NY 10017
(212)593-3639
Fax: (212)593-3987
Website: http://www.pomonacapital.com

Prospect Street Ventures
10 East 40th St., 44th Fl.
New York, NY 10016
(212)448-0702
Fax: (212)448-9652
E-mail: wkohler@prospectstreet.com
Website: http://www.prospectstreet.com

Regent Capital Management
505 Park Ave., Ste. 1700
New York, NY 10022
(212)735-9900
Fax: (212)735-9908

Rothschild Ventures, Inc.
1251 Avenue of the Americas, 51st Fl.
New York, NY 10020
(212)403-3500
Fax: (212)403-3652
Website: http://www.nmrothschild.com

Sandler Capital Management
767 Fifth Ave., 45th Fl.
New York, NY 10153
(212)754-8100
Fax: (212)826-0280

Siguler Guff & Company
630 Fifth Ave., 16th Fl.
New York, NY 10111
(212)332-5100
Fax: (212)332-5120

Spencer Trask Ventures Inc.
535 Madison Ave.
New York, NY 10022
(212)355-5565
Fax: (212)751-3362
Website: http://www.spencertrask.com

Sprout Group (New York City)
277 Park Ave.
New York, NY 10172
(212)892-3600
Fax: (212)892-3444
E-mail: info@sproutgroup.com
Website: http://www.sproutgroup.com

US Trust Private Equity
114 W.47th St.
New York, NY 10036
(212)852-3949
Fax: (212)852-3759
Website: http://www.ustrust.com/
privateequity

Vencon Management Inc.
301 West 53rd St., Ste. 10F
New York, NY 10019
(212)581-8787
Fax: (212)397-4126
Website: http://www.venconinc.com

Venrock Associates
30 Rockefeller Plaza, Ste. 5508
New York, NY 10112
(212)649-5600
Fax: (212)649-5788
Website: http://www.venrock.com

Venture Capital Fund of America, Inc.
509 Madison Ave., Ste. 812
New York, NY 10022
(212)838-5577
Fax: (212)838-7614
E-mail: mail@vcfa.com
Website: http://www.vcfa.com

Venture Opportunities Corp.
150 E. 58th St.
New York, NY 10155
(212)832-3737
Fax: (212)980-6603

Warburg Pincus Ventures, Inc.
466 Lexington Ave., 11th Fl.
New York, NY 10017
(212)878-9309
Fax: (212)878-9200
Website: http://www.warburgpincus.com

Wasserstein, Perella & Co. Inc.
31 W. 52nd St., 27th Fl.
New York, NY 10019
(212)702-5691
Fax: (212)969-7879

Welsh, Carson, Anderson, & Stowe
320 Park Ave., Ste. 2500
New York, NY 10022-6815
(212)893-9500
Fax: (212)893-9575

Whitney and Co. (New York)
630 Fifth Ave. Ste. 3225
New York, NY 10111
(212)332-2400
Fax: (212)332-2422
Website: http://www.jhwitney.com

Winthrop Ventures
74 Trinity Place, Ste. 600
New York, NY 10006
(212)422-0100

The Pittsford Group
8 Lodge Pole Rd.
Pittsford, NY 14534
(716)223-3523

Genesee Funding
70 Linden Oaks, 3rd Fl.
Rochester, NY 14625
(716)383-5550
Fax: (716)383-5305

Gabelli Multimedia Partners
One Corporate Center
Rye, NY 10580
(914)921-5395
Fax: (914)921-5031

Stamford Financial
108 Main St.
Stamford, NY 12167
(607)652-3311
Fax: (607)652-6301
Website: http://www.stamford
financial.com

Northwood Ventures LLC
485 Underhill Blvd., Ste. 205
Syosset, NY 11791
(516)364-5544
Fax: (516)364-0879
E-mail: northwood@northwood.com
Website: http://www.north
woodventures.com

Exponential Business Development Co.
216 Walton St.
Syracuse, NY 13202-1227
(315)474-4500
Fax: (315)474-4682
E-mail: dirksonn@aol.com
Website: http://www.exponential-ny.com

Onondaga Venture Capital Fund Inc.
714 State Tower Bldg.
Syracuse, NY 13202
(315)478-0157
Fax: (315)478-0158

Bessemer Venture Partners (Westbury)
1400 Old Country Rd., Ste. 109
Westbury, NY 11590
(516)997-2300
Fax: (516)997-2371
E-mail: bob@bvpny.com
Website: http://www.bvp.com

Ovation Capital Partners
120 Bloomingdale Rd., 4th Fl.
White Plains, NY 10605
(914)258-0011
Fax: (914)684-0848
Website: http://www.ovation
capital.com

North Carolina

Carolinas Capital Investment Corp.
1408 Biltmore Dr.
Charlotte, NC 28207
(704)375-3888
Fax: (704)375-6226

First Union Capital Partners
1st Union Center, 12th Fl.
301 S. College St.
Charlotte, NC 28288-0732
(704)383-0000
Fax: (704)374-6711
Website: http://www.fucp.com

Frontier Capital LLC
525 North Tryon St., Ste. 1700
Charlotte, NC 28202
(704)414-2880
Fax: (704)414-2881
Website: http://www.frontierfunds.com

Kitty Hawk Capital
2700 Coltsgate Rd., Ste. 202
Charlotte, NC 28211
(704)362-3909
Fax: (704)362-2774
Website: http://www.kittyhawk
capital.com

Piedmont Venture Partners
One Morrocroft Centre
6805 Morisson Blvd., Ste. 380
Charlotte, NC 28211
(704)731-5200
Fax: (704)365-9733
Website: http://www.piedmontvp.com

Ruddick Investment Co.
1800 Two First Union Center
Charlotte, NC 28282
(704)372-5404
Fax: (704)372-6409

The Shelton Companies Inc.
3600 One First Union Center
301 S. College St.
Charlotte, NC 28202
(704)348-2200
Fax: (704)348-2260

Wakefield Group
1110 E. Morehead St.
PO Box 36329
Charlotte, NC 28236
(704)372-0355
Fax: (704)372-8216
Website: http://www.wakefiel
dgroup.com

Aurora Funds, Inc.
2525 Meridian Pkwy., Ste. 220
Durham, NC 27713
(919)484-0400
Fax: (919)484-0444
Website: http://www.aurora
funds.com

Intersouth Partners
3211 Shannon Rd., Ste. 610
Durham, NC 27707
(919)493-6640
Fax: (919)493-6649
E-mail: info@intersouth.com
Website: http://www.intersouth.com

Geneva Merchant Banking Partners
PO Box 21962
Greensboro, NC 27420
(336)275-7002
Fax: (336)275-9155
Website: http://www.geneva
merchantbank.com

The North Carolina Enterprise Fund, L.P.
3600 Glenwood Ave., Ste. 107
Raleigh, NC 27612
(919)781-2691
Fax: (919)783-9195
Website: http://www.ncef.com

Ohio

Senmend Medical Ventures
4445 Lake Forest Dr., Ste. 600
Cincinnati, OH 45242
(513)563-3264
Fax: (513)563-3261

The Walnut Group
312 Walnut St., Ste. 1151
Cincinnati, OH 45202
(513)651-3300
Fax: (513)929-4441
Website: http://www.thewal
nutgroup.com

Brantley Venture Partners
20600 Chagrin Blvd., Ste. 1150
Cleveland, OH 44122
(216)283-4800
Fax: (216)283-5324

Clarion Capital Corp.
1801 E. 9th St., Ste. 1120
Cleveland, OH 44114
(216)687-1096
Fax: (216)694-3545

Crystal Internet Venture Fund, L.P.
1120 Chester Ave., Ste. 418
Cleveland, OH 44114
(216)263-5515
Fax: (216)263-5518
E-mail: jf@crystalventure.com
Website: http://www.crystal
venture.com

Key Equity Capital Corp.
127 Public Sq., 28th Fl.
Cleveland, OH 44114
(216)689-3000
Fax: (216)689-3204
Website: http://www.keybank.com

Morgenthaler Ventures
Terminal Tower
50 Public Square, Ste. 2700
Cleveland, OH 44113
(216)416-7500
Fax: (216)416-7501
Website: http://www.morgenthaler.com

National City Equity Partners Inc.
1965 E. 6th St.
Cleveland, OH 44114
(216)575-2491
Fax: (216)575-9965
E-mail: nccap@aol.com
Website: http://www.nccapital.com

Primus Venture Partners, Inc.
5900 LanderBrook Dr., Ste. 2000
Cleveland, OH 44124-4020
(440)684-7300
Fax: (440)684-7342
E-mail: info@primusventure.com
Website: http://www.primusventure.com

Banc One Capital Partners (Columbus)
150 East Gay St., 24th Fl.
Columbus, OH 43215
(614)217-1100
Fax: (614)217-1217

Battelle Venture Partners
505 King Ave.
Columbus, OH 43201
(614)424-7005
Fax: (614)424-4874

Ohio Partners
62 E. Board St., 3rd Fl.
Columbus, OH 43215
(614)621-1210
Fax: (614)621-1240

Capital Technology Group, L.L.C.
400 Metro Place North, Ste. 300
Dublin, OH 43017
(614)792-6066
Fax: (614)792-6036
E-mail: info@capitaltech.com
Website: http://www.capitaltech.com

Northwest Ohio Venture Fund
4159 Holland-Sylvania R., Ste. 202
Toledo, OH 43623
(419)824-8144

Fax: (419)882-2035
E-mail: bwalsh@novf.com

Oklahoma

Moore & Associates
1000 W. Wilshire Blvd., Ste. 370
Oklahoma City, OK 73116
(405)842-3660
Fax: (405)842-3763

Chisholm Private Capital Partners
100 West 5th St., Ste. 805
Tulsa, OK 74103
(918)584-0440
Fax: (918)584-0441
Website: http://www.chisholmvc.com

Davis, Tuttle Venture Partners (Tulsa)
320 S. Boston, Ste. 1000
Tulsa, OK 74103-3703
(918)584-7272
Fax: (918)582-3404
Website: http://www.davistuttle.com

RBC Ventures
2627 E. 21st St.
Tulsa, OK 74114
(918)744-5607
Fax: (918)743-8630

Oregon

Utah Ventures II LP
10700 SW Beaverton-Hillsdale Hwy.,
Ste. 548
Beaverton, OR 97005
(503)574-4125
E-mail: adishlip@uven.com
Website: http://www.uven.com

Orien Ventures
14523 SW Westlake Dr.
Lake Oswego, OR 97035
(503)699-1680
Fax: (503)699-1681

OVP Venture Partners (Lake Oswego)
340 Oswego Pointe Dr., Ste. 200
Lake Oswego, OR 97034
(503)697-8766
Fax: (503)697-8863
E-mail: info@ovp.com
Website: http://www.ovp.com

Oregon Resource and Technology Development Fund
4370 NE Halsey St., Ste. 233
Portland, OR 97213-1566
(503)282-4462
Fax: (503)282-2976

Shaw Venture Partners
400 SW 6th Ave., Ste. 1100
Portland, OR 97204-1636
(503)228-4884
Fax: (503)227-2471
Website: http://www.shawventures.com

Pennsylvania

Mid-Atlantic Venture Funds
125 Goodman Dr.
Bethlehem, PA 18015
(610)865-6550
Fax: (610)865-6427
Website: http://www.mavf.com

Newspring Ventures
100 W. Elm St., Ste. 101
Conshohocken, PA 19428
(610)567-2380
Fax: (610)567-2388
Website: http://www.news
printventures.com

Patricof & Co. Ventures, Inc.
455 S. Gulph Rd., Ste. 410
King of Prussia, PA 19406
(610)265-0286
Fax: (610)265-4959
Website: http://www.patricof.com

Loyalhanna Venture Fund
527 Cedar Way, Ste. 104
Oakmont, PA 15139
(412)820-7035
Fax: (412)820-7036

Innovest Group Inc.
2000 Market St., Ste. 1400
Philadelphia, PA 19103
(215)564-3960
Fax: (215)569-3272

Keystone Venture Capital Management Co.
1601 Market St., Ste. 2500
Philadelphia, PA 19103
(215)241-1200
Fax: (215)241-1211
Website: http://www.keystonevc.com

Liberty Venture Partners
2005 Market St., Ste. 200
Philadelphia, PA 19103
(215)282-4484
Fax: (215)282-4485
E-mail: info@libertyvp.com
Website: http://www.libertyvp.com

Penn Janney Fund, Inc.
1801 Market St., 11th Fl.
Philadelphia, PA 19103

(215)665-4447

Fax: (215)557-0820

Philadelphia Ventures, Inc.

The Bellevue

200 S. Broad St.

Philadelphia, PA 19102

(215)732-4445

Fax: (215)732-4644

Birchmere Ventures Inc.

2000 Technology Dr.

Pittsburgh, PA 15219-3109

(412)803-8000

Fax: (412)687-8139

Website: http://www.birchmerevc.com

CEO Venture Fund

2000 Technology Dr., Ste. 160

Pittsburgh, PA 15219-3109

(412)687-3451

Fax: (412)687-8139

E-mail: ceofund@aol.com

Website: http://www.ceoventure

fund.com

Innovation Works Inc.

2000 Technology Dr., Ste. 250

Pittsburgh, PA 15219

(412)681-1520

Fax: (412)681-2625

Website: http://www.innovation

works.org

Keystone Minority Capital Fund L.P.

1801 Centre Ave., Ste. 201

Williams Sq.

Pittsburgh, PA 15219

(412)338-2230

Fax: (412)338-2224

Mellon Ventures, Inc.

One Mellon Bank Ctr., Rm. 3500

Pittsburgh, PA 15258

(412)236-3594

Fax: (412)236-3593

Website: http://www.mellon

ventures.com

Pennsylvania Growth Fund

5850 Ellsworth Ave., Ste. 303

Pittsburgh, PA 15232

(412)661-1000

Fax: (412)361-0676

Point Venture Partners

The Century Bldg.

130 Seventh St., 7th Fl.

Pittsburgh, PA 15222

(412)261-1966

Fax: (412)261-1718

Cross Atlantic Capital Partners

5 Radnor Corporate Center, Ste. 555

Radnor, PA 19087

(610)995-2650

Fax: (610)971-2062

Website: http://www.xacp.com

Meridian Venture Partners (Radnor)

The Radnor Court Bldg., Ste. 140

259 Radnor-Chester Rd.

Radnor, PA 19087

(610)254-2999

Fax: (610)254-2996

E-mail: mvpart@ix.netcom.com

TDH

919 Conestoga Rd., Bldg. 1, Ste. 301

Rosemont, PA 19010

(610)526-9970

Fax: (610)526-9971

Adams Capital Management

500 Blackburn Ave.

Sewickley, PA 15143

(412)749-9454

Fax: (412)749-9459

Website: http://www.acm.com

S.R. One, Ltd.

Four Tower Bridge

200 Barr Harbor Dr., Ste. 250

W. Conshohocken, PA 19428

(610)567-1000

Fax: (610)567-1039

Greater Philadelphia Venture Capital Corp.

351 East Conestoga Rd.

Wayne, PA 19087

(610)688-6829

Fax: (610)254-8958

PA Early Stage

435 Devon Park Dr., Bldg. 500, Ste. 510

Wayne, PA 19087

(610)293-4075

Fax: (610)254-4240

Website: http://www.paearlystage.com

The Sandhurst Venture Fund, L.P.

351 E. Constoga Rd.

Wayne, PA 19087

(610)254-8900

Fax: (610)254-8958

TL Ventures

700 Bldg.

435 Devon Park Dr.

Wayne, PA 19087-1990

(610)975-3765

Fax: (610)254-4210

Website: http://www.tlventures.com

Rockhill Ventures, Inc.

100 Front St., Ste. 1350

West Conshohocken, PA 19428

(610)940-0300

Fax: (610)940-0301

Puerto Rico

Advent-Morro Equity Partners

Banco Popular Bldg.

206 Tetuan St., Ste. 903

San Juan, PR 00902

(787)725-5285

Fax: (787)721-1735

North America Investment Corp.

Mercantil Plaza, Ste. 813

PO Box 191831

San Juan, PR 00919

(787)754-6178

Fax: (787)754-6181

Rhode Island

Manchester Humphreys, Inc.

40 Westminster St., Ste. 900

Providence, RI 02903

(401)454-0400

Fax: (401)454-0403

Navis Partners

50 Kennedy Plaza, 12th Fl.

Providence, RI 02903

(401)278-6770

Fax: (401)278-6387

Website: http://www.navis

partners.com

South Carolina

Capital Insights, L.L.C.

PO Box 27162

Greenville, SC 29616-2162

(864)242-6832

Fax: (864)242-6755

E-mail: jwarner@capitalinsights.com

Website: http://www.capitalin

sights.com

Transamerica Mezzanine Financing

7 N. Laurens St., Ste. 603

Greenville, SC 29601

(864)232-6198

Fax: (864)241-4444

Tennessee

Valley Capital Corp.

Krystal Bldg.

100 W. Martin Luther King Blvd.,

Ste. 212

Chattanooga, TN 37402
(423)265-1557
Fax: (423)265-1588

Coleman Swenson Booth Inc.
237 2nd Ave. S
Franklin, TN 37064-2649
(615)791-9462
Fax: (615)791-9636
Website: http://
www.colemanswenson.com

Capital Services & Resources, Inc.
5159 Wheelis Dr., Ste. 106
Memphis, TN 38117
(901)761-2156
Fax: (907)767-0060

Paradigm Capital Partners LLC
6410 Poplar Ave., Ste. 395
Memphis, TN 38119
(901)682-6060
Fax: (901)328-3061

SSM Ventures
845 Crossover Ln., Ste. 140
Memphis, TN 38117
(901)767-1131
Fax: (901)767-1135
Website: http://www.ssm
ventures.com

Capital Across America L.P.
501 Union St., Ste. 201
Nashville, TN 37219
(615)254-1414
Fax: (615)254-1856
Website: http://
www.capitalacrossamerica.com

Equitas L.P.
2000 Glen Echo Rd., Ste. 101
PO Box 158838
Nashville, TN 37215-8838
(615)383-8673
Fax: (615)383-8693

Massey Burch Capital Corp.
One Burton Hills Blvd., Ste. 350
Nashville, TN 37215
(615)665-3221
Fax: (615)665-3240
E-mail: tcalton@masseyburch.com
Website: http://www.masseyburch.com

Nelson Capital Corp.
3401 West End Ave., Ste. 300
Nashville, TN 37203
(615)292-8787
Fax: (615)385-3150

Texas

Phillips-Smith Specialty Retail Group
5080 Spectrum Dr., Ste. 805 W
Addison, TX 75001
(972)387-0725
Fax: (972)458-2560
E-mail: pssrg@aol.com
Website: http://www.phillips-smith.com

Austin Ventures, L.P.
701 Brazos St., Ste. 1400
Austin, TX 78701
(512)485-1900
Fax: (512)476-3952
E-mail: info@ausven.com
Website: http://www.austinventures.com

The Capital Network
3925 West Braker Lane, Ste. 406
Austin, TX 78759-5321
(512)305-0826
Fax: (512)305-0836

Techxas Ventures LLC
5000 Plaza on the Lake
Austin, TX 78746
(512)343-0118
Fax: (512)343-1879
E-mail: bruce@techxas.com
Website: http://www.techxas.com

Alliance Financial of Houston
218 Heather Ln.
Conroe, TX 77385-9013
(936)447-3300
Fax: (936)447-4222

Amerimark Capital Corp.
1111 W. Mockingbird, Ste. 1111
Dallas, TX 75247
(214)638-7878
Fax: (214)638-7612
E-mail: amerimark@amcapital.com
Website: http://www.amcapital.com

AMT Venture Partners / AMT Capital Ltd.
5220 Spring Valley Rd., Ste. 600
Dallas, TX 75240
(214)905-9757
Fax: (214)905-9761
Website: http://www.amtcapital.com

Arkoma Venture Partners
5950 Berkshire Lane, Ste. 1400
Dallas, TX 75225
(214)739-3515
Fax: (214)739-3572
E-mail: joelf@arkomavp.com

Capital Southwest Corp.
12900 Preston Rd., Ste. 700
Dallas, TX 75230
(972)233-8242
Fax: (972)233-7362
Website: http://
www.capitalsouthwest.com

Dali, Hook Partners
One Lincoln Center, Ste. 1550
5400 LBJ Freeway
Dallas, TX 75240
(972)991-5457
Fax: (972)991-5458
E-mail: dhook@hookpartners.com
Website: http://www.hookpartners.com

HO2 Partners
Two Galleria Tower
13455 Noel Rd., Ste. 1670
Dallas, TX 75240
(972)702-1144
Fax: (972)702-8234
Website: http://www.ho2.com

Interwest Partners (Dallas)
2 Galleria Tower
13455 Noel Rd., Ste. 1670
Dallas, TX 75240
(972)392-7279
Fax: (972)490-6348
Website: http://www.interwest.com

Kahala Investments, Inc.
8214 Westchester Dr., Ste. 715
Dallas, TX 75225
(214)987-0077
Fax: (214)987-2332

MESBIC Ventures Holding Co.
2435 North Central Expressway, Ste. 200
Dallas, TX 75080
(972)991-1597
Fax: (972)991-4770
Website: http://www.mvhc.com

North Texas MESBIC, Inc.
9500 Forest Lane, Ste. 430
Dallas, TX 75243
(214)221-3565
Fax: (214)221-3566

Richard Jaffe & Company, Inc,
7318 Royal Cir.
Dallas, TX 75230
(214)265-9397
Fax: (214)739-1845

Sevin Rosen Management Co.
13455 Noel Rd., Ste. 1670
Dallas, TX 75240

(972)702-1100
Fax: (972)702-1103
E-mail: info@srfunds.com
Website: http://www.srfunds.com

Stratford Capital Partners, L.P.
300 Crescent Ct., Ste. 500
Dallas, TX 75201
(214)740-7377
Fax: (214)720-7393
E-mail: stratcap@hmtf.com

Sunwestern Investment Group
12221 Merit Dr., Ste. 935
Dallas, TX 75251
(972)239-5650
Fax: (972)701-0024

Wingate Partners
750 N. St. Paul St., Ste. 1200
Dallas, TX 75201
(214)720-1313
Fax: (214)871-8799

Buena Venture Associates
201 Main St., 32nd Fl.
Fort Worth, TX 76102
(817)339-7400
Fax: (817)390-8408
Website: http://www.buenaventure.com

The Catalyst Group
3 Riverway, Ste. 770
Houston, TX 77056
(713)623-8133
Fax: (713)623-0473
E-mail: herman@thecatalystgroup.net
Website: http://www.thecatalyst
group.net

Cureton & Co., Inc.
1100 Louisiana, Ste. 3250
Houston, TX 77002
(713)658-9806
Fax: (713)658-0476

Davis, Tuttle Venture Partners (Dallas)
8 Greenway Plaza, Ste. 1020
Houston, TX 77046
(713)993-0440
Fax: (713)621-2297
Website: http://www.davistuttle.com

Houston Partners
401 Louisiana, 8th Fl.
Houston, TX 77002
(713)222-8600
Fax: (713)222-8932

Southwest Venture Group
10878 Westheimer, Ste. 178

Houston, TX 77042
(713)827-8947
(713)461-1470

AM Fund
4600 Post Oak Place, Ste. 100
Houston, TX 77027
(713)627-9111
Fax: (713)627-9119

Ventex Management, Inc.
3417 Milam St.
Houston, TX 77002-9531
(713)659-7870
Fax: (713)659-7855

MBA Venture Group
1004 Olde Town Rd., Ste. 102
Irving, TX 75061
(972)986-6703

First Capital Group Management Co.
750 East Mulberry St., Ste. 305
PO Box 15616
San Antonio, TX 78212
(210)736-4233
Fax: (210)736-5449

The Southwest Venture Partnerships
16414 San Pedro, Ste. 345
San Antonio, TX 78232
(210)402-1200
Fax: (210)402-1221
E-mail: swvp@aol.com

Medtech International Inc.
1742 Carriageway
Sugarland, TX 77478
(713)980-8474
Fax: (713)980-6343

Utah

First Security Business Investment Corp.
15 East 100 South, Ste. 100
Salt Lake City, UT 84111
(801)246-5737
Fax: (801)246-5740

Utah Ventures II, L.P.
423 Wakara Way, Ste. 206
Salt Lake City, UT 84108
(801)583-5922
Fax: (801)583-4105
Website: http://www.uven.com

Wasatch Venture Corp.
1 S. Main St., Ste. 1400
Salt Lake City, UT 84133
(801)524-8939

Fax: (801)524-8941
E-mail: mail@wasatchvc.com

Vermont

North Atlantic Capital Corp.
76 Saint Paul St., Ste. 600
Burlington, VT 05401
(802)658-7820
Fax: (802)658-5757
Website: http://www.north
atlanticcapital.com

Green Mountain Advisors Inc.
PO Box 1230
Quechee, VT 05059
(802)296-7800
Fax: (802)296-6012
Website: http://www.gmtcap.com

Virginia

Oxford Financial Services Corp.
Alexandria, VA 22314
(703)519-4900
Fax: (703)519-4910
E-mail: oxford133@aol.com

Continental SBIC
4141 N. Henderson Rd.
Arlington, VA 22203
(703)527-5200
Fax: (703)527-3700

Novak Biddle Venture Partners
1750 Tysons Blvd., Ste. 1190
McLean, VA 22102
(703)847-3770
Fax: (703)847-3771
E-mail: roger@novakbiddle.com
Website: http://www.novakbiddle.com

Spacevest
11911 Freedom Dr., Ste. 500
Reston, VA 20190
(703)904-9800
Fax: (703)904-0571
E-mail: spacevest@spacevest.com
Website: http://www.spacevest.com

Virginia Capital
1801 Libbie Ave., Ste. 201
Richmond, VA 23226
(804)648-4802
Fax: (804)648-4809
E-mail: webmaster@vacapital.com
Website: http://www.vacapital.com

Calvert Social Venture Partners
402 Maple Ave. W
Vienna, VA 22180

(703)255-4930
Fax: (703)255-4931
E-mail: calven2000@aol.com

Fairfax Partners
8000 Towers Crescent Dr., Ste. 940
Vienna, VA 22182
(703)847-9486
Fax: (703)847-0911

Global Internet Ventures
8150 Leesburg Pike, Ste. 1210
Vienna, VA 22182
(703)442-3300
Fax: (703)442-3388
Website: http://www.givinc.com

Walnut Capital Corp. (Vienna)
8000 Towers Crescent Dr., Ste. 1070
Vienna, VA 22182
(703)448-3771
Fax: (703)448-7751

Washington

Encompass Ventures
777 108th Ave. NE, Ste. 2300
Bellevue, WA 98004
(425)486-3900
Fax: (425)486-3901
E-mail: info@evpartners.com
Website: http://www.encom
passventures.com

Fluke Venture Partners
11400 SE Sixth St., Ste. 230
Bellevue, WA 98004
(425)453-4590
Fax: (425)453-4675
E-mail: gabelein@flukeventures.com
Website: http://www.flukeventures.com

Pacific Northwest Partners SBIC, L.P.
15352 SE 53rd St.
Bellevue, WA 98006
(425)455-9967
Fax: (425)455-9404

Materia Venture Associates, L.P.
3435 Carillon Pointe
Kirkland, WA 98033-7354
(425)822-4100
Fax: (425)827-4086

OVP Venture Partners (Kirkland)
2420 Carillon Pt.
Kirkland, WA 98033
(425)889-9192
Fax: (425)889-0152
E-mail: info@ovp.com
Website: http://www.ovp.com

Digital Partners
999 3rd Ave., Ste. 1610
Seattle, WA 98104
(206)405-3607
Fax: (206)405-3617
Website: http://www.digitalpartners.com

Frazier & Company
601 Union St., Ste. 3300
Seattle, WA 98101
(206)621-7200
Fax: (206)621-1848
E-mail: jon@frazierco.com

Kirlan Venture Capital, Inc.
221 First Ave. W, Ste. 108
Seattle, WA 98119-4223
(206)281-8610
Fax: (206)285-3451
Website: http://www.kirlanventure.com

Phoenix Partners
1000 2nd Ave., Ste. 3600
Seattle, WA 98104
(206)624-8968
Fax: (206)624-1907

Voyager Capital
800 5th St., Ste. 4100
Seattle, WA 98103
(206)470-1180
Fax: (206)470-1185
E-mail: info@voyagercap.com
Website: http://www.voyagercap.com

Northwest Venture Associates
221 N. Wall St., Ste. 628
Spokane, WA 99201
(509)747-0728
Fax: (509)747-0758
Website: http://www.nwva.com

Wisconsin

Venture Investors Management, L.L.C.
University Research Park
505 S. Rosa Rd.
Madison, WI 53719
(608)441-2700
Fax: (608)441-2727
E-mail: roger@ventureinvestors.com
Website: http://www.venture
investers.com

Capital Investments, Inc.
1009 West Glen Oaks Lane, Ste. 103
Mequon, WI 53092
(414)241-0303
Fax: (414)241-8451
Website: http://
www.capitalinvestmentsinc.com

Future Value Venture, Inc.
2745 N. Martin Luther King
Dr., Ste. 204
Milwaukee, WI 53212-2300
(414)264-2252
Fax: (414)264-2253
E-mail: fvventures@aol.com
William Beckett, President

Lubar and Co., Inc.
700 N. Water St., Ste. 1200
Milwaukee, WI 53202
(414)291-9000
Fax: (414)291-9061

GCI
20875 Crossroads Cir., Ste. 100
Waukesha, WI 53186
(262)798-5080
Fax: (262)798-5087

Glossary of Small Business Terms

Absolute liability
Liability that is incurred due to product defects or negligent actions. Manufacturers or retail establishments are held responsible, even though the defect or action may not have been intentional or negligent.

ACE
See Active Corps of Executives

Accident and health benefits
Benefits offered to employees and their families in order to offset the costs associated with accidental death, accidental injury, or sickness.

Account statement
A record of transactions, including payments, new debt, and deposits, incurred during a defined period of time.

Accounting system
System capturing the costs of all employees and/or machinery included in business expenses.

Accounts payable
See Trade credit

Accounts receivable
Unpaid accounts which arise from unsettled claims and transactions from the sale of a company's products or services to its customers.

Active Corps of Executives (ACE)
A group of volunteers for a management assistance program of the U.S. Small Business Administration; volunteers provide one-on-one counseling and teach workshops and seminars for small firms.

ADA
See Americans with Disabilities Act

Adaptation
The process whereby an invention is modified to meet the needs of users.

Adaptive engineering
The process whereby an invention is modified to meet the manufacturing and commercial requirements of a targeted market.

Adverse selection
The tendency for higher-risk individuals to purchase health care and more comprehensive plans, resulting in increased costs.

Advertising
A marketing tool used to capture public attention and influence purchasing decisions for a product or service. Utilizes various forms of media to generate consumer response, such as flyers, magazines, newspapers, radio, and television.

Age discrimination
The denial of the rights and privileges of employment based solely on the age of an individual.

Agency costs
Costs incurred to insure that the lender or investor maintains control over assets while allowing the borrower or entrepreneur to use them. Monitoring and information costs are the two major types of agency costs.

Agribusiness
The production and sale of commodities and products from the commercial farming industry.

America Online
An online service which is accessible by computer modem. The service features Internet access, bulletin boards, online periodicals, electronic mail, and other services for subscribers.

Americans with Disabilities Act (ADA)
Law designed to ensure equal access and opportunity to handicapped persons.

Annual report
Yearly financial report prepared by a business that adheres to the requirements set forth by the Securities and Exchange Commission (SEC).

Antitrust immunity
Exemption from prosecution under antitrust laws. In the transportation industry, firms with antitrust immunity are permitted under certain conditions to set schedules and sometimes prices for the public benefit.

Applied research
Scientific study targeted for use in a product or process.

Asians
A minority category used by the U.S. Bureau of the Census to represent a diverse group that includes Aleuts, Eskimos, American Indians, Asian Indians, Chinese, Japanese, Koreans, Vietnamese, Filipinos, Hawaiians, and other Pacific Islanders.

Assets
Anything of value owned by a company.

Audit
The verification of accounting records and business procedures conducted by an outside accounting service.

Average cost
Total production costs divided by the quantity produced.

Balance Sheet
A financial statement listing the total assets and liabilities of a company at a given time.

Bankruptcy
The condition in which a business cannot meet its debt obligations and petitions a federal district court either for reorganization of its debts (Chapter 11) or for liquidation of its assets (Chapter 7).

Basic research
Theoretical scientific exploration not targeted to application.

Basket clause
A provision specifying the amount of public pension funds that may be placed in investments not included on a state's legal list (see separate citation).

BBS
See Bulletin Board Service

BDC
See Business development corporation

Benefit
Various services, such as health care, flextime, day care, insurance, and vacation, offered to employees as part of a hiring package. Typically subsidized in whole or in part by the business.

BIDCO
See Business and industrial development company

Billing cycle
A system designed to evenly distribute customer billing throughout the month, preventing clerical backlogs.

Birth
See Business birth

Blue chip security
A low-risk, low-yield security representing an interest in a very stable company.

Blue sky laws
A general term that denotes various states' laws regulating securities.

Bond
A written instrument executed by a bidder or contractor (the principal) and a second party (the surety or sureties) to assure fulfillment of the principal's obligations to a third party (the obligee or government) identified in the bond. If the principal's obligations are not met, the bond assures payment to the extent stipulated of any loss sustained by the obligee.

Bonding requirements
Terms contained in a bond (see separate citation).

Bonus
An amount of money paid to an employee as a reward for achieving certain business goals or objectives.

Brainstorming
A group session where employees contribute their ideas for solving a problem or meeting a company objective without fear of retribution or ridicule.

Brand name
The part of a brand, trademark, or service mark that can be spoken. It can be a word, letter, or group of words or letters.

Bridge financing
A short-term loan made in expectation of intermediateterm or long-term financing. Can be used when a company plans to go public in the near future.

Broker
One who matches resources available for innovation with those who need them.

Budget
An estimate of the spending necessary to complete a project or offer a service in comparison to cash-on-hand and expected earnings for the coming year, with an emphasis on cost control.

Bulletin Board Service (BBS)
An online service enabling users to communicate with each other about specific topics.

Business and industrial development company (BIDCO)
A private, for-profit financing corporation chartered by the state to provide both equity and long-term debt capital to small business owners (see separate citations for equity and debt capital).

Business birth
The formation of a new establishment or enterprise. The appearance of a new establishment or enterprise in the Small Business Data Base (see separate citation).

Business conditions
Outside factors that can affect the financial performance of a business.

Business contractions
The number of establishments that have decreased in employment during a specified time.

Business cycle
A period of economic recession and recovery. These cycles vary in duration.

Business death
The voluntary or involuntary closure of a firm or establishment. The disappearance of an establishment or enterprise from the Small Business Data Base (see separate citation).

Business development corporation (BDC)
A business financing agency, usually composed of the financial institutions in an area or state, organized to assist in financing businesses unable to obtain assistance through normal channels; the risk is spread among various members of the business development corporation, and interest rates may vary somewhat from those charged by member institutions. A venture capital firm in which shares of ownership are publicly held and to which the Investment Act of 1940 applies.

Business dissolution
For enumeration purposes, the absence of a business that was present in the prior time period from any current record.

Business entry
See Business birth

Business ethics
Moral values and principles espoused by members of the business community as a guide to fair and honest business practices.

Business exit
See Business death

Business expansions
The number of establishments that added employees during a specified time.

Business failure
Closure of a business causing a loss to at least one creditor.

Business format franchising
The purchase of the name, trademark, and an ongoing business plan of the parent corporation or franchisor by the franchisee.

Business license
A legal authorization issued by municipal and state governments and required for business operations.

Business name
Enterprises must register their business names with local governments usually on a "doing business as" (DBA) form. (This name is sometimes referred to as a "fictional name.") The procedure is part of the business licensing process and prevents any other business from using that same name for a similar business in the same locality.

Business norms
See Financial ratios

Business permit
See Business license

Business plan
A document that spells out a company's expected course of action for a specified period, usually including a detailed listing and analysis of risks and uncertainties. For the small business, it should examine the proposed products, the market, the industry, the management policies, the marketing policies, production needs, and financial needs. Frequently, it is used as a prospectus for potential investors and lenders.

Business proposal
See Business plan

Business service firm
An establishment primarily engaged in rendering services to other business organizations on a fee or contract basis.

Business start
For enumeration purposes, a business with a name or similar designation that did not exist in a prior time period.

Cafeteria plan
See Flexible benefit plan

Capacity
Level of a firm's, industry's, or nation's output corresponding to full practical utilization of available resources.

Capital
Assets less liabilities, representing the ownership interest in a business. A stock of accumulated goods, especially at a specified time and in contrast to income received during a specified time period. Accumulated goods devoted to production. Accumulated possessions calculated to bring income.

Capital expenditure
Expenses incurred by a business for improvements that will depreciate over time.

Capital gain
The monetary difference between the purchase price and the selling price of capital. Capital gains are taxed at a rate of 28% by the federal government.

Capital intensity
The relative importance of capital in the production process, usually expressed as the ratio of capital to labor but also sometimes as the ratio of capital to output.

Capital resource
The equipment, facilities and labor used to create products and services.

Caribbean Basin Initiative
An interdisciplinary program to support commerce among the businesses in the nations of the Caribbean Basin and the United States. Agencies involved include: the Agency for International Development, the U.S. Small Business Administration, the International Trade Administration of the U.S. Department of Commerce, and various private sector groups.

Catastrophic care
Medical and other services for acute and long-term illnesses that cost more than insurance coverage limits or that cost the amount most families may be expected to pay with their own resources.

CDC
See Certified development corporation

CD-ROM
Compact disc with read-only memory used to store large amounts of digitized data.

Certified development corporation (CDC)
A local area or statewide corporation or authority (for profit or nonprofit) that packages U.S. Small Business Administration (SBA), bank, state, and/or private money into financial assistance for existing business capital improvements. The SBA holds the second lien on its maximum share of 40 percent involvement. Each state has at least one certified development corporation. This program is called the SBA 504 Program.

Certified lenders
Banks that participate in the SBA guaranteed loan program (see separate citation). Such banks must have a good track record with the U.S. Small Business Administration (SBA) and must agree to certain conditions set forth by the agency. In return, the SBA agrees to process any guaranteed loan application within three business days.

Champion
An advocate for the development of an innovation.

Channel of distribution
The means used to transport merchandise from the manufacturer to the consumer.

Chapter 7 of the 1978 Bankruptcy Act
Provides for a court-appointed trustee who is responsible for liquidating a company's assets in order to settle outstanding debts.

Chapter 11 of the 1978 Bankruptcy Act
Allows the business owners to retain control of the company while working with their creditors to reorganize their finances and establish better business practices to prevent liquidation of assets.

Closely held corporation
A corporation in which the shares are held by a few persons, usually officers, employees, or others close to the management; these shares are rarely offered to the public.

Code of Federal Regulations
Codification of general and permanent rules of the federal government published in the Federal Register.

Code sharing
See Computer code sharing

Coinsurance
Upon meeting the deductible payment, health insurance participants may be required to make additional health care cost-sharing payments. Coinsurance is a payment of a fixed percentage of the cost of each service; copayment is usually a fixed amount to be paid with each service.

Collateral
Securities, evidence of deposit, or other property pledged by a borrower to secure repayment of a loan.

Collective ratemaking
The establishment of uniform charges for services by a group of businesses in the same industry.

Commercial insurance plan
See Underwriting

Commercial loans
Short-term renewable loans used to finance specific capital needs of a business.

Commercialization
The final stage of the innovation process, including production and distribution.

Common stock
The most frequently used instrument for purchasing ownership in private or public companies. Common stock generally carries the right to vote on certain corporate actions and may pay dividends, although it rarely does in venture investments. In liquidation, common stockholders are the last to share in the proceeds from the sale of a corporation's assets; bondholders and preferred shareholders have priority. Common stock is often used in firstround start-up financing.

Community development corporation
A corporation established to develop economic programs for a community and, in most cases, to provide financial support for such development.

Competitor
A business whose product or service is marketed for the same purpose/use and to the same consumer group as the product or service of another.

Computer code sharing
An arrangement whereby flights of a regional airline are identified by the two-letter code of a major carrier in the computer reservation system to help direct passengers to new regional carriers.

Consignment
A merchandising agreement, usually referring to secondhand shops, where the dealer pays the owner of an item a percentage of the profit when the item is sold.

Consortium
A coalition of organizations such as banks and corporations for ventures requiring large capital resources.

Consultant
An individual that is paid by a business to provide advice and expertise in a particular area.

Consumer price index
A measure of the fluctuation in prices between two points in time.

Consumer research
Research conducted by a business to obtain information about existing or potential consumer markets.

Continuation coverage
Health coverage offered for a specified period of time to employees who leave their jobs and to their widows, divorced spouses, or dependents.

Contractions
See Business contractions

Convertible preferred stock
A class of stock that pays a reasonable dividend and is convertible into common stock (see separate citation). Generally the convertible feature may only be exercised after being held for a stated period of time. This arrangement is usually considered second-round financing when a company needs equity to maintain its cash flow.

Convertible securities
A feature of certain bonds, debentures, or preferred stocks that allows them to be exchanged by the owner for another class of securities at a future date and in accordance with any other terms of the issue.

Copayment
See Coinsurance

Copyright
A legal form of protection available to creators and authors to safeguard their works from unlawful use or claim of ownership by others. Copyrights may be acquired for works of art, sculpture, music, and published or unpublished manuscripts. All copyrights should be registered at the Copyright Office of the Library of Congress.

Corporate financial ratios
The relationship between key figures found in a company's financial statement expressed as a numeric value. Used to evaluate risk and company performance. Also known as Financial averages, Operating ratios, and Business ratios.

Corporation
A legal entity, chartered by a state or the federal government, recognized as a separate entity having its own rights, privileges, and liabilities distinct from those of its members.

Cost containment
Actions taken by employers and insurers to curtail rising health care costs; for example, increasing

employee cost sharing (see separate citation), requiring second opinions, or preadmission screening.

Cost sharing
The requirement that health care consumers contribute to their own medical care costs through deductibles and coinsurance (see separate citations). Cost sharing does not include the amounts paid in premiums. It is used to control utilization of services; for example, requiring a fixed amount to be paid with each health care service.

Cottage industry
Businesses based in the home in which the family members are the labor force and family-owned equipment is used to process the goods.

Credit Rating
A letter or number calculated by an organization (such as Dun & Bradstreet) to represent the ability and disposition of a business to meet its financial obligations.

Customer service
Various techniques used to ensure the satisfaction of a customer.

Cyclical peak
The upper turning point in a business cycle.

Cyclical trough
The lower turning point in a business cycle.

DBA
See Business name

Death
See Business death

Debenture
A certificate given as acknowledgment of a debt (see separate citation) secured by the general credit of the issuing corporation. A bond, usually without security, issued by a corporation and sometimes convertible to common stock.

Debt
Something owed by one person to another. Financing in which a company receives capital that must be repaid; no ownership is transferred.

Debt capital
Business financing that normally requires periodic interest payments and repayment of the principal within a specified time.

Debt financing
See Debt capital

Debt securities
Loans such as bonds and notes that provide a specified rate of return for a specified period of time.

Deductible
A set amount that an individual must pay before any benefits are received.

Demand shock absorbers
A term used to describe the role that some small firms play by expanding their output levels to accommodate a transient surge in demand.

Demographics
Statistics on various markets, including age, income, and education, used to target specific products or services to appropriate consumer groups.

Demonstration
Showing that a product or process has been modified sufficiently to meet the needs of users.

Deregulation
The lifting of government restrictions; for example, the lifting of government restrictions on the entry of new businesses, the expansion of services, and the setting of prices in particular industries.

Desktop Publishing
Using personal computers and specialized software to produce camera-ready copy for publications.

Disaster loans
Various types of physical and economic assistance available to individuals and businesses through the U.S. Small Business Administration (SBA). This is the only SBA loan program available for residential purposes.

Discrimination
The denial of the rights and privileges of employment based on factors such as age, race, religion, or gender.

Diseconomies of scale
The condition in which the costs of production increase faster than the volume of production.

Dissolution
See Business dissolution

Distribution
Delivering a product or process to the user.

Distributor
One who delivers merchandise to the user.

Diversified company
A company whose products and services are used by several different markets.

Doing business as (DBA)
See Business name

Dow Jones
An information services company that publishes the Wall Street Journal and other sources of financial information.

Dow Jones Industrial Average
An indicator of stock market performance.

Earned income
A tax term that refers to wages and salaries earned by the recipient, as opposed to monies earned through interest and dividends.

Economic efficiency
The use of productive resources to the fullest practical extent in the provision of the set of goods and services that is most preferred by purchasers in the economy.

Economic indicators
Statistics used to express the state of the economy. These include the length of the average work week, the rate of unemployment, and stock prices.

Economically disadvantaged
See Socially and economically disadvantaged

Economies of scale
See Scale economies

EEOC
See Equal Employment Opportunity Commission

8(a) Program
A program authorized by the Small Business Act that directs federal contracts to small businesses owned and

operated by socially and economically disadvantaged individuals.

Electronic mail (e-mail)
The electronic transmission of mail via phone lines.

E-mail
See Electronic mail

Employee leasing
A contract by which employers arrange to have their workers hired by a leasing company and then leased back to them for a management fee. The leasing company typically assumes the administrative burden of payroll and provides a benefit package to the workers.

Employee tenure
The length of time an employee works for a particular employer.

Employer identification number
The business equivalent of a social security number. Assigned by the U.S. Internal Revenue Service.

Enterprise
An aggregation of all establishments owned by a parent company. An enterprise may consist of a single, independent establishment or include subsidiaries and other branches under the same ownership and control.

Enterprise zone
A designated area, usually found in inner cities and other areas with significant unemployment, where businesses receive tax credits and other incentives to entice them to establish operations there.

Entrepreneur
A person who takes the risk of organizing and operating a new business venture.

Entry
See Business entry

Equal Employment Opportunity Commission (EEOC)
A federal agency that ensures nondiscrimination in the hiring and firing practices of a business.

Equal opportunity employer
An employer who adheres to the standards set by the Equal Employment Opportunity Commission (see separate citation).

Equity
The ownership interest. Financing in which partial or total ownership of a company is surrendered in exchange for capital. An investor's financial return comes from dividend payments and from growth in the net worth of the business.

Equity capital
See Equity; Equity midrisk venture capital

Equity financing
See Equity; Equity midrisk venture capital

Equity midrisk venture capital
An unsecured investment in a company. Usually a purchase of ownership interest in a company that occurs in the later stages of a company's development.

Equity partnership
A limited partnership arrangement for providing start-up and seed capital to businesses.

Equity securities
See Equity

Equity-type
Debt financing subordinated to conventional debt.

Establishment
A single-location business unit that may be independent (a single-establishment enterprise) or owned by a parent enterprise.

Establishment and Enterprise Microdata File
See U.S. Establishment and Enterprise Microdata File

Establishment birth
See Business birth

Establishment Longitudinal Microdata File
See U.S. Establishment Longitudinal Microdata File

Ethics
See Business ethics

Evaluation
Determining the potential success of translating an invention into a product or process.

Exit
See Business exit

Experience rating
See Underwriting

Export
A product sold outside of the country.

Export license
A general or specific license granted by the U.S. Department of Commerce required of anyone wishing to export goods. Some restricted articles need approval from the U.S. Departments of State, Defense, or Energy.

Failure
See Business failure

Fair share agreement
An agreement reached between a franchisor and a minority business organization to extend business ownership to minorities by either reducing the amount of capital required or by setting aside certain marketing areas for minority business owners.

Feasibility study
A study to determine the likelihood that a proposed product or development will fulfill the objectives of a particular investor.

Federal Trade Commission (FTC)
Federal agency that promotes free enterprise and competition within the U.S.

Federal Trade Mark Act of 1946
See Lanham Act

Fictional name
See Business name

Fiduciary
An individual or group that hold assets in trust for a beneficiary.

Financial analysis
The techniques used to determine money needs in a business. Techniques include ratio analysis, calculation of return on investment, guides for measuring profitability, and break-even analysis to determine ultimate success.

Financial intermediary
A financial institution that acts as the intermediary between borrowers and lenders. Banks, savings and loan associations, finance companies, and venture capital companies are major financial intermediaries in the United States.

Financial ratios
See Corporate financial ratios; Industry financial ratios

Financial statement
A written record of business finances, including balance sheets and profit and loss statements.

Financing
See First-stage financing; Second-stage financing; Thirdstage financing

First-stage financing
Financing provided to companies that have expended their initial capital, and require funds to start full-scale manufacturing and sales. Also known as First-round financing.

Fiscal year
Any twelve-month period used by businesses for accounting purposes.

504 Program
See Certified development corporation

Flexible benefit plan
A plan that offers a choice among cash and/or qualified benefits such as group term life insurance, accident and health insurance, group legal services, dependent care assistance, and vacations.

FOB
See Free on board

Format franchising
See Business format franchising; Franchising

401(k) plan
A financial plan where employees contribute a percentage of their earnings to a fund that is invested in stocks, bonds, or money markets for the purpose of saving money for retirement.

Four Ps
Marketing terms referring to Product, Price, Place, and Promotion.

Franchising
A form of licensing by which the owner-the franchisor- distributes or markets a product, method, or service through affiliated dealers called franchisees. The product, method, or service being marketed is identified by a brand name, and the franchisor

maintains control over the marketing methods employed. The franchisee is often given exclusive access to a defined geographic area.

Free on board (FOB)
A pricing term indicating that the quoted price includes the cost of loading goods into transport vessels at a specified place.

Frictional unemployment
See Unemployment

FTC
See Federal Trade Commission

Fulfillment
The systems necessary for accurate delivery of an ordered item, including subscriptions and direct marketing.

Full-time workers
Generally, those who work a regular schedule of more than 35 hours per week.

Garment registration number
A number that must appear on every garment sold in the U.S. to indicate the manufacturer of the garment, which may or may not be the same as the label under which the garment is sold. The U.S. Federal Trade Commission assigns and regulates garment registration numbers.

Gatekeeper
A key contact point for entry into a network.

GDP
See Gross domestic product

General obligation bond
A municipal bond secured by the taxing power of the municipality. The Tax Reform Act of 1986 limits the purposes for which such bonds may be issued and establishes volume limits on the extent of their issuance.

GNP
See Gross national product

Good Housekeeping Seal
Seal appearing on products that signifies the fulfillment of the standards set by the Good Housekeeping Institute to protect consumer interests.

Goods sector
All businesses producing tangible goods, including agriculture, mining, construction, and manufacturing businesses.

GPO
See Gross product originating

Gross domestic product (GDP)
The part of the nation's gross national product (see separate citation) generated by private business using resources from within the country.

Gross national product (GNP)
The most comprehensive single measure of aggregate economic output. Represents the market value of the total output of goods and services produced by a nation's economy.

Gross product originating (GPO)
A measure of business output estimated from the income or production side using employee compensation, profit income, net interest, capital consumption, and indirect business taxes.

HAL
See Handicapped assistance loan program

Handicapped assistance loan program (HAL)
Low-interest direct loan program through the U.S. Small Business Administration (SBA) for handicapped persons. The SBA requires that these persons demonstrate that their disability is such that it is impossible for them to secure employment, thus making it necessary to go into their own business to make a living.

Health maintenance organization (HMO)
Organization of physicians and other health care professionals that provides health services to subscribers and their dependents on a prepaid basis.

Health provider
An individual or institution that gives medical care. Under Medicare, an institutional provider is a hospital, skilled nursing facility, home health agency, or provider of certain physical therapy services.

Hispanic
A person of Cuban, Mexican, Puerto Rican, Latin American (Central or South American), European Spanish, or other Spanish-speaking origin or ancestry.

HMO
See Health maintenance organization

Home-based business
A business with an operating address that is also a residential address (usually the residential address of the proprietor).

Hub-and-spoke system
A system in which flights of an airline from many different cities (the spokes) converge at a single airport (the hub). After allowing passengers sufficient time to make connections, planes then depart for different cities.

Human Resources Management
A business program designed to oversee recruiting, pay, benefits, and other issues related to the company's work force, including planning to determine the optimal use of labor to increase production, thereby increasing profit.

Idea
An original concept for a new product or process.

Import
Products produced outside the country in which they are consumed.

Income
Money or its equivalent, earned or accrued, resulting from the sale of goods and services.

Income statement
A financial statement that lists the profits and losses of a company at a given time.

Incorporation
The filing of a certificate of incorporation with a state's secretary of state, thereby limiting the business owner's liability.

Incubator
A facility designed to encourage entrepreneurship and minimize obstacles to new business formation and growth, particularly for high-technology firms, by housing a number of fledgling enterprises that share an array of services, such as meeting areas, secretarial services, accounting, research library, on-site financial and management counseling, and word processing facilities.

Independent contractor
An individual considered self-employed (see separate citation) and responsible for paying Social Security taxes and income taxes on earnings.

Indirect health coverage
Health insurance obtained through another individual's health care plan; for example, a spouse's employersponsored plan.

Industrial development authority
The financial arm of a state or other political subdivision established for the purpose of financing economic development in an area, usually through loans to nonprofit organizations, which in turn provide facilities for manufacturing and other industrial operations.

Industry financial ratios
Corporate financial ratios averaged for a specified industry. These are used for comparison purposes and reveal industry trends and identify differences between the performance of a specific company and the performance of its industry. Also known as Industrial averages, Industry ratios, Financial averages, and Business or Industrial norms.

Inflation
Increases in volume of currency and credit, generally resulting in a sharp and continuing rise in price levels.

Informal capital
Financing from informal, unorganized sources; includes informal debt capital such as trade credit or loans from friends and relatives and equity capital from informal investors.

Initial public offering (IPO)
A corporation's first offering of stock to the public.

Innovation
The introduction of a new idea into the marketplace in the form of a new product or service or an improvement in organization or process.

Intellectual property
Any idea or work that can be considered proprietary in nature and is thus protected from infringement by others.

Internal capital
Debt or equity financing obtained from the owner or through retained business earnings.

Internet
A government-designed computer network that contains large amounts of information and is accessible through various vendors for a fee.

Intrapreneurship
The state of employing entrepreneurial principles to nonentrepreneurial situations.

Invention
The tangible form of a technological idea, which could include a laboratory prototype, drawings, formulas, etc.

IPO
See Initial public offering

Job description
The duties and responsibilities required in a particular position.

Job tenure
A period of time during which an individual is continuously employed in the same job.

Joint marketing agreements
Agreements between regional and major airlines, often involving the coordination of flight schedules, fares, and baggage transfer. These agreements help regional carriers operate at lower cost.

Joint venture
Venture in which two or more people combine efforts in a particular business enterprise, usually a single transaction or a limited activity, and agree to share the profits and losses jointly or in proportion to their contributions.

Keogh plan
Designed for self-employed persons and unincorporated businesses as a tax-deferred pension account.

Labor force
Civilians considered eligible for employment who are also willing and able to work.

Labor force participation rate
The civilian labor force as a percentage of the civilian population.

Labor intensity
The relative importance of labor in the production process, usually measured as the capital-labor ratio; i.e., the ratio of units of capital (typically, dollars of tangible assets) to the number of employees. The higher the capital-labor ratio exhibited by a firm or industry, the lower the capital intensity of that firm or industry is said to be.

Labor surplus area
An area in which there exists a high unemployment rate. In procurement (see separate citation), extra points are given to firms in counties that are designated a labor surplus area; this information is requested on procurement bid sheets.

Labor union
An organization of similarly-skilled workers who collectively bargain with management over the conditions of employment.

Laboratory prototype
See Prototype

LAN
See Local Area Network

Lanham Act
Refers to the Federal Trade Mark Act of 1946. Protects registered trademarks, trade names, and other service marks used in commerce.

Large business-dominated industry
Industry in which a minimum of 60 percent of employment or sales is in firms with more than 500 workers.

LBO
See Leveraged buy-out

Leader pricing
A reduction in the price of a good or service in order to generate more sales of that good or service.

Legal list
A list of securities selected by a state in which certain institutions and fiduciaries (such as pension funds, insurance companies, and banks) may invest. Securities not on the list are not eligible for investment. Legal lists typically restrict investments to high quality securities meeting certain specifications. Generally, investment is

limited to U.S. securities and investment-grade blue chip securities (see separate citation).

Leveraged buy-out (LBO)
The purchase of a business or a division of a corporation through a highly leveraged financing package.

Liability
An obligation or duty to perform a service or an act. Also defined as money owed.

License
A legal agreement granting to another the right to use a technological innovation.

Limited partnerships
See Venture capital limited partnerships

Liquidity
The ability to convert a security into cash promptly.

Loans
See Commercial loans; Disaster loans; SBA direct loans; SBA guaranteed loans; SBA special lending institution categories Local Area Network (LAN) Computer networks contained within a single building or small area; used to facilitate the sharing of information.

Local development corporation
An organization, usually made up of local citizens of a community, designed to improve the economy of the area by inducing business and industry to locate and expand there. A local development corporation establishes a capability to finance local growth.

Long-haul rates
Rates charged by a transporter in which the distance traveled is more than 800 miles.

Long-term debt
An obligation that matures in a period that exceeds five years.

Low-grade bond
A corporate bond that is rated below investment grade by the major rating agencies (Standard and Poor's, Moody's).

Macro-efficiency
Efficiency as it pertains to the operation of markets and market systems.

Managed care
A cost-effective health care program initiated by employers whereby low-cost health care is made available to the employees in return for exclusive patronage to program doctors.

Management Assistance Programs
See SBA Management Assistance Programs

Management and technical assistance
A term used by many programs to mean business (as opposed to technological) assistance.

Mandated benefits
Specific treatments, providers, or individuals required by law to be included in commercial health plans.

Market evaluation
The use of market information to determine the sales potential of a specific product or process.

Market failure
The situation in which the workings of a competitive market do not produce the best results from the point of view of the entire society.

Market information
Data of any type that can be used for market evaluation, which could include demographic data, technology forecasting, regulatory changes, etc.

Market research
A systematic collection, analysis, and reporting of data about the market and its preferences, opinions, trends, and plans; used for corporate decision-making.

Market share
In a particular market, the percentage of sales of a specific product.

Marketing
Promotion of goods or services through various media.

Master Establishment List (MEL)
A list of firms in the United States developed by the U.S. Small Business Administration; firms can be selected by industry, region, state, standard metropolitan statistical area (see separate citation), county, and zip code.

Maturity
The date upon which the principal or stated value of a bond or other indebtedness becomes due and payable.

Medicaid (Title XIX)
A federally aided, state-operated and administered program that provides medical benefits for certain low income persons in need of health and medical care who are eligible for one of the government's welfare cash payment programs, including the aged, the blind, the disabled, and members of families with dependent children where one parent is absent, incapacitated, or unemployed.

Medicare (Title XVIII)
A nationwide health insurance program for disabled and aged persons. Health insurance is available to insured persons without regard to income. Monies from payroll taxes cover hospital insurance and monies from general revenues and beneficiary premiums pay for supplementary medical insurance.

MEL
See Master Establishment List

MESBIC
See Minority enterprise small business investment corporation

MET
See Multiple employer trust

Metropolitan statistical area (MSA)
A means used by the government to define large population centers that may transverse different governmental jurisdictions. For example, the Washington, D.C. MSA includes the District of Columbia and contiguous parts of Maryland and Virginia because all of these geopolitical areas comprise one population and economic operating unit.

Mezzanine financing
See Third-stage financing

Micro-efficiency
Efficiency as it pertains to the operation of individual firms.

Microdata
Information on the characteristics of an individual business firm.

Mid-term debt
An obligation that matures within one to five years.

Midrisk venture capital
See Equity midrisk venture capital

Minimum premium plan
A combination approach to funding an insurance plan aimed primarily at premium tax savings. The employer self-funds a fixed percentage of estimated monthly claims and the insurance company insures the excess.

Minimum wage
The lowest hourly wage allowed by the federal government.

Minority Business Development Agency
Contracts with private firms throughout the nation to sponsor Minority Business Development Centers which provide minority firms with advice and technical assistance on a fee basis.

Minority Enterprise Small Business Investment Corporation (MESBIC)
A federally funded private venture capital firm licensed by the U.S. Small Business Administration to provide capital to minority-owned businesses (see separate citation).

Minority-owned business
Businesses owned by those who are socially or economically disadvantaged (see separate citation).

Mom and Pop business
A small store or enterprise having limited capital, principally employing family members.

Moonlighter
A wage-and-salary worker with a side business.

MSA
See Metropolitan statistical area

Multi-employer plan
A health plan to which more than one employer is required to contribute and that may be maintained through a collective bargaining agreement and required to meet standards prescribed by the U.S. Department of Labor.

Multi-level marketing
A system of selling in which you sign up other people to assist you and they, in turn, recruit others to help them. Some entrepreneurs have built successful

companies on this concept because the main focus of their activities is their product and product sales.

Multimedia
The use of several types of media to promote a product or service. Also, refers to the use of several different types of media (sight, sound, pictures, text) in a CD-ROM (see separate citation) product.

Multiple employer trust (MET)
A self-funded benefit plan generally geared toward small employers sharing a common interest.

NAFTA
See North American Free Trade Agreement

NASDAQ
See National Association of Securities Dealers Automated Quotations

National Association of Securities Dealers Automated Quotations
Provides price quotes on over-the-counter securities as well as securities listed on the New York Stock Exchange.

National income
Aggregate earnings of labor and property arising from the production of goods and services in a nation's economy.

Net assets
See Net worth

Net income
The amount remaining from earnings and profits after all expenses and costs have been met or deducted. Also known as Net earnings.

Net profit
Money earned after production and overhead expenses (see separate citations) have been deducted.

Net worth
The difference between a company's total assets and its total liabilities.

Network
A chain of interconnected individuals or organizations sharing information and/or services.

New York Stock Exchange (NYSE)
The oldest stock exchange in the U.S. Allows for trading in stocks, bonds, warrants, options, and rights that meet listing requirements.

Niche
A career or business for which a person is well-suited. Also, a product which fulfills one need of a particular market segment, often with little or no competition.

Nodes
One workstation in a network, either local area or wide area (see separate citations).

Nonbank bank
A bank that either accepts deposits or makes loans, but not both. Used to create many new branch banks.

Noncompetitive awards
A method of contracting whereby the federal government negotiates with only one contractor to supply a product or service.

Nonmember bank
A state-regulated bank that does not belong to the federal bank system.

Nonprofit
An organization that has no shareholders, does not distribute profits, and is without federal and state tax liabilities.

Norms
See Financial ratios

North American Free Trade Agreement (NAFTA)
Passed in 1993, NAFTA eliminates trade barriers among businesses in the U.S., Canada, and Mexico.

NYSE
See New York Stock Exchange

Occupational Safety & Health Administration (OSHA)
Federal agency that regulates health and safety standards within the workplace.

Optimal firm size
The business size at which the production cost per unit of output (average cost) is, in the long run, at its minimum.

Organizational chart
A hierarchical chart tracking the chain of command within an organization.

OSHA
See Occupational Safety & Health Administration

Overhead
Expenses, such as employee benefits and building utilities, incurred by a business that are unrelated to the actual product or service sold.

Owner's capital
Debt or equity funds provided by the owner(s) of a business; sources of owner's capital are personal savings, sales of assets, or loans from financial institutions.

P & L
See Profit and loss statement

Part-time workers
Normally, those who work less than 35 hours per week. The Tax Reform Act indicated that part-time workers who work less than 17.5 hours per week may be excluded from health plans for purposes of complying with federal nondiscrimination rules.

Part-year workers
Those who work less than 50 weeks per year.

Partnership
Two or more parties who enter into a legal relationship to conduct business for profit. Defined by the U.S. Internal Revenue Code as joint ventures, syndicates, groups, pools, and other associations of two or more persons organized for profit that are not specifically classified in the IRS code as corporations or proprietorships.

Patent
A grant made by the government assuring an inventor the sole right to make, use, and sell an invention for a period of 17 years.

PC
See Professional corporation

Peak
See Cyclical peak

Pension
A series of payments made monthly, semiannually, annually, or at other specified intervals during the lifetime of the pensioner for distribution upon retirement. The term is sometimes used to denote the portion of the retirement allowance financed by the employer's contributions.

Pension fund
A fund established to provide for the payment of pension benefits; the collective contributions made by all of the parties to the pension plan.

Performance appraisal
An established set of objective criteria, based on job description and requirements, that is used to evaluate the performance of an employee in a specific job.

Permit
See Business license

Plan
See Business plan

Pooling
An arrangement for employers to achieve efficiencies and lower health costs by joining together to purchase group health insurance or self-insurance.

PPO
See Preferred provider organization

Preferred lenders program
See SBA special lending institution categories

Preferred provider organization (PPO)
A contractual arrangement with a health care services organization that agrees to discount its health care rates in return for faster payment and/or a patient base.

Premiums
The amount of money paid to an insurer for health insurance under a policy. The premium is generally paid periodically (e.g., monthly), and often is split between the employer and the employee. Unlike deductibles and coinsurance or copayments, premiums are paid for coverage whether or not benefits are actually used.

Prime-age workers
Employees 25 to 54 years of age.

Prime contract
A contract awarded directly by the U.S. Federal Government.

Private company
See Closely held corporation

Private placement
A method of raising capital by offering for sale an investment or business to a small group of investors (generally avoiding registration with the Securities and Exchange Commission or state securities registration agencies). Also known as Private financing or Private offering.

Pro forma
The use of hypothetical figures in financial statements to represent future expenditures, debts, and other potential financial expenses.

Proactive
Taking the initiative to solve problems and anticipate future events before they happen, instead of reacting to an already existing problem or waiting for a difficult situation to occur.

Procurement
A contract from an agency of the federal government for goods or services from a small business.

Prodigy
An online service which is accessible by computer modem. The service features Internet access, bulletin boards, online periodicals, electronic mail, and other services for subscribers.

Product development
The stage of the innovation process where research is translated into a product or process through evaluation, adaptation, and demonstration.

Product franchising
An arrangement for a franchisee to use the name and to produce the product line of the franchisor or parent corporation.

Production
The manufacture of a product.

Production prototype
See Prototype

Productivity
A measurement of the number of goods produced during a specific amount of time.

Professional corporation (PC)
Organized by members of a profession such as medicine, dentistry, or law for the purpose of conducting their professional activities as a corporation. Liability of a member or shareholder is limited in the same manner as in a business corporation.

Profit and loss statement (P & L)
The summary of the incomes (total revenues) and costs of a company's operation during a specific period of time. Also known as Income and expense statement.

Proposal
See Business plan

Proprietorship
The most common legal form of business ownership; about 85 percent of all small businesses are proprietorships. The liability of the owner is unlimited in this form of ownership.

Prospective payment system
A cost-containment measure included in the Social Security Amendments of 1983 whereby Medicare payments to hospitals are based on established prices, rather than on cost reimbursement.

Prototype
A model that demonstrates the validity of the concept of an invention (laboratory prototype); a model that meets the needs of the manufacturing process and the user (production prototype).

Prudent investor rule or standard
A legal doctrine that requires fiduciaries to make investments using the prudence, diligence, and intelligence that would be used by a prudent person in making similar investments. Because fiduciaries make investments on behalf of third-party beneficiaries, the standard results in very conservative investments. Until recently, most state regulations required the fiduciary to apply this standard to each investment. Newer, more progressive regulations permit fiduciaries to apply this standard to the portfolio taken as a whole, thereby allowing a fiduciary to balance a portfolio with higher-yield, higher-risk investments. In states with more progressive regulations, practically every type of security is eligible for inclusion in the portfolio of investments made by a fiduciary, provided

that the portfolio investments, in their totality, are those of a prudent person.

Public equity markets
Organized markets for trading in equity shares such as common stocks, preferred stocks, and warrants. Includes markets for both regularly traded and nonregularly traded securities.

Public offering
General solicitation for participation in an investment opportunity. Interstate public offerings are supervised by the U.S. Securities and Exchange Commission (see separate citation).

Quality control
The process by which a product is checked and tested to ensure consistent standards of high quality.

Rate of return
The yield obtained on a security or other investment based on its purchase price or its current market price. The total rate of return is current income plus or minus capital appreciation or depreciation.

Real property
Includes the land and all that is contained on it.

Realignment
See Resource realignment

Recession
Contraction of economic activity occurring between the peak and trough (see separate citations) of a business cycle.

Regulated market
A market in which the government controls the forces of supply and demand, such as who may enter and what price may be charged.

Regulation D
A vehicle by which small businesses make small offerings and private placements of securities with limited disclosure requirements. It was designed to ease the burdens imposed on small businesses utilizing this method of capital formation.

Regulatory Flexibility Act
An act requiring federal agencies to evaluate the impact of their regulations on small businesses before the regulations are issued and to consider less burdensome alternatives.

Research
The initial stage of the innovation process, which includes idea generation and invention.

Research and development financing
A tax-advantaged partnership set up to finance product development for start-ups as well as more mature companies.

Resource mobility
The ease with which labor and capital move from firm to firm or from industry to industry.

Resource realignment
The adjustment of productive resources to interindustry changes in demand.

Resources
The sources of support or help in the innovation process, including sources of financing, technical evaluation, market evaluation, management and business assistance, etc.

Retained business earnings
Business profits that are retained by the business rather than being distributed to the shareholders as dividends.

Revolving credit
An agreement with a lending institution for an amount of money, which cannot exceed a set maximum, over a specified period of time. Each time the borrower repays a portion of the loan, the amount of the repayment may be borrowed yet again.

Risk capital
See Venture capital

Risk management
The act of identifying potential sources of financial loss and taking action to minimize their negative impact.

Routing
The sequence of steps necessary to complete a product during production.

S corporations
See Sub chapter S corporations

SBA
See Small Business Administration

SBA direct loans
Loans made directly by the U.S. Small Business Administration (SBA); monies come from funds appropriated specifically for this purpose. In general, SBA direct loans carry interest rates slightly lower than those in the private financial markets and are available only to applicants unable to secure private financing or an SBA guaranteed loan.

SBA 504 Program
See Certified development corporation

SBA guaranteed loans
Loans made by lending institutions in which the U.S. Small Business Administration (SBA) will pay a prior agreed-upon percentage of the outstanding principal in the event the borrower of the loan defaults. The terms of the loan and the interest rate are negotiated between theborrower and the lending institution, within set parameters.

SBA loans
See Disaster loans; SBA direct loans; SBA guaranteed loans; SBA special lending institution categories

SBA Management Assistance Programs
Classes, workshops, counseling, and publications offered by the U.S. Small Business Administration.

SBA special lending institution categories
U.S. Small Business Administration (SBA) loan program in which the SBA promises certified banks a 72-hour turnaround period in giving its approval for a loan, and in which preferred lenders in a pilot program are allowed to write SBA loans without seeking prior SBA approval.

SBDB
See Small Business Data Base

SBDC
See Small business development centers

SBI
See Small business institutes program

SBIC
See Small business investment corporation

SBIR Program
See Small Business Innovation Development Act of 1982

Scale economies
The decline of the production cost per unit of output (average cost) as the volume of output increases.

Scale efficiency
The reduction in unit cost available to a firm when producing at a higher output volume.

SCORE
See Service Corps of Retired Executives

SEC
See Securities and Exchange Commission

SECA
See Self-Employment Contributions Act

Second-stage financing
Working capital for the initial expansion of a company that is producing, shipping, and has growing accounts receivable and inventories. Also known as Second-round financing.

Secondary market
A market established for the purchase and sale of outstanding securities following their initial distribution.

Secondary worker
Any worker in a family other than the person who is the primary source of income for the family.

Secondhand capital
Previously used and subsequently resold capital equipment (e.g., buildings and machinery).

Securities and Exchange Commission (SEC)
Federal agency charged with regulating the trade of securities to prevent unethical practices in the investor market.

Securitized debt
A marketing technique that converts long-term loans to marketable securities.

Seed capital
Venture financing provided in the early stages of the innovation process, usually during product development.

Glossary

Self-employed person
One who works for a profit or fees in his or her own business, profession, or trade, or who operates a farm.

Self-Employment Contributions Act (SECA)
Federal law that governs the self-employment tax (see separate citation).

Self-employment income
Income covered by Social Security if a business earns a net income of at least $400.00 during the year. Taxes are paid on earnings that exceed $400.00.

Self-employment retirement plan
See Keogh plan

Self-employment tax
Required tax imposed on self-employed individuals for the provision of Social Security and Medicare. The tax must be paid quarterly with estimated income tax statements.

Self-funding
A health benefit plan in which a firm uses its own funds to pay claims, rather than transferring the financial risks of paying claims to an outside insurer in exchange for premium payments.

Service Corps of Retired Executives (SCORE)
Volunteers for the SBA Management Assistance Program who provide one-on-one counseling and teach workshops and seminars for small firms.

Service firm
See Business service firm

Service sector
Broadly defined, all U.S. industries that produce intangibles, including the five major industry divisions of transportation, communications, and utilities; wholesale trade; retail trade; finance, insurance, and real estate; and services.

Set asides
See Small business set asides

Short-haul service
A type of transportation service in which the transporter supplies service between cities where the maximum distance is no more than 200 miles.

Short-term debt
An obligation that matures in one year.

SIC codes
See Standard Industrial Classification codes

Single-establishment enterprise
See Establishment

Small business
An enterprise that is independently owned and operated, is not dominant in its field, and employs fewer than 500 people. For SBA purposes, the U.S. Small Business Administration (SBA) considers various other factors (such as gross annual sales) in determining size of a business.

Small Business Administration (SBA)
An independent federal agency that provides assistance with loans, management, and advocating interests before other federal agencies.

Small Business Data Base
A collection of microdata (see separate citation) files on individual firms developed and maintained by the U.S. Small Business Administration.

Small business development centers (SBDC)
Centers that provide support services to small businesses, such as individual counseling, SBA advice, seminars and conferences, and other learning center activities. Most services are free of charge, or available at minimal cost.

Small business development corporation
See Certified development corporation

Small business-dominated industry
Industry in which a minimum of 60 percent of employment or sales is in firms with fewer than 500 employees.

Small Business Innovation Development Act of 1982
Federal statute requiring federal agencies with large extramural research and development budgets to allocate a certain percentage of these funds to small research and development firms. The program, called the Small Business Innovation Research (SBIR) Program, is designed to stimulate technological innovation and make greater use of small businesses in meeting national innovation needs.

Small business institutes (SBI) program
Cooperative arrangements made by U.S. Small Business Administration district offices and local colleges and

universities to provide small business firms with graduate students to counsel them without charge.

Small business investment corporation (SBIC)

A privately owned company licensed and funded through the U.S. Small Business Administration and private sector sources to provide equity or debt capital to small businesses.

Small business set asides

Procurement (see separate citation) opportunities required by law to be on all contracts under $10,000 or a certain percentage of an agency's total procurement expenditure.

Smaller firms

For U.S. Department of Commerce purposes, those firms not included in the Fortune 1000.

SMSA

See Metropolitan statistical area

Socially and economically disadvantaged

Individuals who have been subjected to racial or ethnic prejudice or cultural bias without regard to their qualities as individuals, and whose abilities to compete are impaired because of diminished opportunities to obtain capital and credit.

Sole proprietorship

An unincorporated, one-owner business, farm, or professional practice.

Special lending institution categories

See SBA special lending institution categories

Standard Industrial Classification (SIC) codes

Four-digit codes established by the U.S. Federal Government to categorize businesses by type of economic activity; the first two digits correspond to major groups such as construction and manufacturing, while the last two digits correspond to subgroups such as home construction or highway construction.

Standard metropolitan statistical area (SMSA)

See Metropolitan statistical area

Start-up

A new business, at the earliest stages of development and financing.

Start-up costs

Costs incurred before a business can commence operations.

Start-up financing

Financing provided to companies that have either completed product development and initial marketing or have been in business for less than one year but have not yet sold their product commercially.

Stock

A certificate of equity ownership in a business.

Stop-loss coverage

Insurance for a self-insured plan that reimburses the company for any losses it might incur in its health claims beyond a specified amount.

Strategic planning

Projected growth and development of a business to establish a guiding direction for the future. Also used to determine which market segments to explore for optimal sales of products or services.

Structural unemployment

See Unemployment

Sub chapter S corporations

Corporations that are considered noncorporate for tax purposes but legally remain corporations.

Subcontract

A contract between a prime contractor and a subcontractor, or between subcontractors, to furnish supplies or services for performance of a prime contract (see separate citation) or a subcontract.

Surety bonds

Bonds providing reimbursement to an individual, company, or the government if a firm fails to complete a contract. The U.S. Small Business Administration guarantees surety bonds in a program much like the SBA guaranteed loan program (see separate citation).

Swing loan

See Bridge financing

Target market

The clients or customers sought for a business' product or service.

Targeted Jobs Tax Credit
Federal legislation enacted in 1978 that provides a tax credit to an employer who hires structurally unemployed individuals.

Tax number
A number assigned to a business by a state revenue department that enables the business to buy goods without paying sales tax.

Taxable bonds
An interest-bearing certificate of public or private indebtedness. Bonds are issued by public agencies to finance economic development.

Technical assistance
See Management and technical assistance

Technical evaluation
Assessment of technological feasibility.

Technology
The method in which a firm combines and utilizes labor and capital resources to produce goods or services; the application of science for commercial or industrial purposes.

Technology transfer
The movement of information about a technology or intellectual property from one party to another for use.

Tenure
See Employee tenure

Term
The length of time for which a loan is made.

Terms of a note
The conditions or limits of a note; includes the interest rate per annum, the due date, and transferability and convertibility features, if any.

Third-party administrator
An outside company responsible for handling claims and performing administrative tasks associated with health insurance plan maintenance.

Third-stage financing
Financing provided for the major expansion of a company whose sales volume is increasing and that is breaking even or profitable. These funds are used for further plant expansion, marketing, working capital,

or development of an improved product. Also known as Third-round or Mezzanine financing.

Time deposit
A bank deposit that cannot be withdrawn before a specified future time.

Time management
Skills and scheduling techniques used to maximize productivity.

Trade credit
Credit extended by suppliers of raw materials or finished products. In an accounting statement, trade credit is referred to as "accounts payable."

Trade name
The name under which a company conducts business, or by which its business, goods, or services are identified. It may or may not be registered as a trademark.

Trade periodical
A publication with a specific focus on one or more aspects of business and industry.

Trade secret
Competitive advantage gained by a business through the use of a unique manufacturing process or formula.

Trade show
An exhibition of goods or services used in a particular industry. Typically held in exhibition centers where exhibitors rent space to display their merchandise.

Trademark
A graphic symbol, device, or slogan that identifies a business. A business has property rights to its trademark from the inception of its use, but it is still prudent to register all trademarks with the Trademark Office of the U.S. Department of Commerce.

Translation
See Product development

Treasury bills
Investment tender issued by the Federal Reserve Bank in amounts of $10,000 that mature in 91 to 182 days.

Treasury bonds
Long-term notes with maturity dates of not less than seven and not more than twenty-five years.

Treasury notes
Short-term notes maturing in less than seven years.

Trend
A statistical measurement used to track changes that occur over time.

Trough
See Cyclical trough

UCC
See Uniform Commercial Code

UL
See Underwriters Laboratories

Underwriters Laboratories (UL)
One of several private firms that tests products and processes to determine their safety. Although various firms can provide this kind of testing service, many local and insurance codes specify UL certification.

Underwriting
A process by which an insurer determines whether or not and on what basis it will accept an application for insurance. In an experience-rated plan, premiums are based on a firm's or group's past claims; factors other than prior claims are used for community-rated or manually rated plans.

Unfair competition
Refers to business practices, usually unethical, such as using unlicensed products, pirating merchandise, or misleading the public through false advertising, which give the offending business an unequitable advantage over others.

Unfunded accrued liability
The excess of total liabilities, both present and prospective, over present and prospective assets.

Unemployment
The joblessness of individuals who are willing to work, who are legally and physically able to work, and who are seeking work. Unemployment may represent the temporary joblessness of a worker between jobs (frictional unemployment) or the joblessness of a worker whose skills are not suitable for jobs available in the labor market (structural unemployment).

Uniform Commercial Code (UCC)
A code of laws governing commercial transactions across the U.S., except Louisiana. Their purpose is to bring uniformity to financial transactions.

Uniform product code (UPC symbol)
A computer-readable label comprised of ten digits and stripes that encodes what a product is and how much it costs. The first five digits are assigned by the Uniform Product Code Council, and the last five digits by the individual manufacturer.

Unit cost
See Average cost

UPC symbol
See Uniform product code

U.S. Establishment and Enterprise Microdata (USEEM) File
A cross-sectional database containing information on employment, sales, and location for individual enterprises and establishments with employees that have a Dun & Bradstreet credit rating.

U.S. Establishment Longitudinal Microdata (USELM) File
A database containing longitudinally linked sample microdata on establishments drawn from the U.S. Establishment and Enterprise Microdata file (see separate citation).

U.S. Small Business Administration 504 Program
See Certified development corporation

USEEM
See U.S. Establishment and Enterprise Microdata File

USELM
See U.S. Establishment Longitudinal Microdata File

VCN
See Venture capital network

Venture capital
Money used to support new or unusual business ventures that exhibit above-average growth rates, significant potential for market expansion, and are in need of additional financing to sustain growth or further research and development; equity or equity-type financing traditionally provided at the

Glossary

commercialization stage, increasingly available prior to commercialization.

Venture capital company

A company organized to provide seed capital to a business in its formation stage, or in its first or second stage of expansion. Funding is obtained through public or private pension funds, commercial banks and bank holding companies, small business investment corporations licensed by the U.S. Small Business Administration, private venture capital firms, insurance companies, investment management companies, bank trust departments, industrial companies seeking to diversify their investment, and investment bankers acting as intermediaries for other investors or directly investing on their own behalf.

Venture capital limited partnerships

Designed for business development, these partnerships are an institutional mechanism for providing capital for young, technology-oriented businesses. The investors' money is pooled and invested in money market assets until venture investments have been selected. The general partners are experienced investment managers who select and invest the equity and debt securities of firms with high growth potential and the ability to go public in the near future.

Venture capital network (VCN)

A computer database that matches investors with entrepreneurs.

WAN

See Wide Area Network

Wide Area Network (WAN)

Computer networks linking systems throughout a state or around the world in order to facilitate the sharing of information.

Withholding

Federal, state, social security, and unemployment taxes withheld by the employer from employees' wages; employers are liable for these taxes and the corporate umbrella and bankruptcy will not exonerate an employer from paying back payroll withholding. Employers should escrow these funds in a separate account and disperse them quarterly to withholding authorities.

Workers' compensation

A state-mandated form of insurance covering workers injured in job-related accidents. In some states, the state is the insurer; in other states, insurance must be acquired from commercial insurance firms. Insurance rates are based on a number of factors, including salaries, firm history, and risk of occupation.

Working capital

Refers to a firm's short-term investment of current assets, including cash, short-term securities, accounts receivable, and inventories.

Yield

The rate of income returned on an investment, expressed as a percentage. Income yield is obtained by dividing the current dollar income by the current market price of the security. Net yield or yield to maturity is the current income yield minus any premium above par or plus any discount from par in purchase price, with the adjustment spread over the period from the date of purchase to the date of maturity.

Index

Listings in this index are arranged alphabetically by business plan type, then alphabetically by business plan name. Users are provided with the volume number in which the plan appears.

Index

Index